WATERGATE

THE HIDDEN HISTORY

WATERGATE
THE HIDDEN HISTORY

★★★★★

NIXON, THE MAFIA, AND THE CIA

★★★★★

LAMAR WALDRON

COUNTERPOINT
BERKELEY

Library of Congress Cataloging-in-Publication Data is available

ISBN: 978-1-58243-813-9

Cover Design by John Yates

Counterpoint
1919 Fifth Street
Berkeley, CA 94710
www.counterpointpress.com

Distributed by Publishers Group West

10 9 8 7 6 5 4 3 2 1

This book is dedicated to the following authors, journalists, and investigators. In the 1970s, they uncovered crucial evidence about Watergate and related matters—and decades later, they're still waiting for some of the most important files to be declassified.

William Turner
Anthony Summers
Peter Dale Scott
Dick Russell
Peter Noyes
Dan Moldea
Gaeton Fonzi

Contents

PART I

PART II

PART III

PART I

CHAPTER 1

"I ordered that they use any means necessary, including illegal means . . ."
President Richard Nixon to Chief of Staff Alexander Haig, 5-23-73

Almost forty years after the Watergate arrests on June 17, 1972, three myths about it are still pervasive. First, that the scandal only concerned "a third-rate burglary" of the headquarters of the Democratic National Committee (DNC), at the Watergate complex in Washington, D.C. Second, that the "cover-up was worse than the crime." And finally, that two reporters—Bob Woodward and Carl Bernstein of *The Washington Post*—"brought down" President Richard M. Nixon.

Not one of these is true.

The three myths of Watergate have been demonstrably false for decades. President Nixon had his spokesman minimize the scandal's importance by calling it "a third-rate burglary," and Nixon was initially successful: Watergate was not a factor in—or even widely reported during—the fall 1972 Presidential campaign between President Nixon and Democratic candidate George McGovern. Richard Nixon was reelected in a landslide.

What's wrong with the "third-rate burglary" claim? To begin with, even the singular term "burglary" is misleading, since Congressional and Justice Department investigations showed that four burglaries were actually attempted at the Watergate. Additionally, in the weeks before the final Watergate break-in, Nixon's Watergate operatives committed several other burglaries. Their targets ranged from Democratic offices (including those of McGovern, Gary Hart, and Sargent Shriver) to journalists to the Chilean embassy in Washington.

Was the "the cover-up" worse than "the crime?" No—that's another completely inaccurate myth, since Nixon's own words prove that there wasn't just one "crime." From February 1971 to July 1973, Nixon secretly recorded his conversations at the Oval Office, and his other offices away from the White House. Only a handful of his closest aides knew about the taping system, and Nixon never intended for the tapes to become public. On those tapes, many released only in recent years, Nixon discussed many dozens of serious felonies, ranging from illegal political espionage (surveillance, bugging, wiretaps, beatings) to massive corporate bribes and illegal slush funds. In the early 1970s, evidence of Nixon's clear culpability for those crimes was known only to a few dozen officials and investigators at the Justice Department and in Congress. With that proof now more widely available, it clearly shows the pervasive criminal culture of Nixon's White House.

Finally, it's true that *The Washington Post* played a leading role in reporting the crimes that led Nixon to resign rather than face impeachment. However, for decades Bob Woodward, Carl Bernstein, and *The Post* have been trying to point out that their reporting was not what "brought down" Nixon. Instead, it was the huge range of proven felonies that Richard Nixon and his men committed that resulted in Nixon's resignation, and the convictions of more than thirty of his officials and associates.

Yet these three basic myths have kept the public and most journalists from looking at the tremendous amount of important new information about Nixon and Watergate that has emerged in recent years.

While Richard Nixon's culpability for the Watergate break-ins has long been established, most recently by PBS in 2003, what's truly remarkable is that after almost forty years, conventional accounts of the scandal still don't address Nixon's motive. Why was President Nixon willing to risk his reelection with so many repeated burglaries at the Watergate, and at other Washington offices, in just a few weeks? What motivated Nixon to jeopardize his Presidency by ordering the wide range of criminal operations that resulted in Watergate? What was Nixon so desperate to get at the Watergate, and how does it explain the deeper context surrounding his crimes?

For the first time, the groundbreaking investigative research in *Watergate: The Hidden History* pulls together documented answers to all of these questions. It adds crucial missing pieces to the Watergate story, information that President Nixon wanted but couldn't get—and that wasn't available to the Senate Watergate Committee, or to Woodward and Bernstein. This new information not only reveals Nixon's motivation for Watergate, but also answers the two most important remaining questions: What were the Watergate burglars after? And why was Nixon willing to risk his Presidency to get it?

Many people think the Watergate burglars broke in just to bug the DNC, yet why were the burglars caught with enough film to take photos of over fourteen hundred pages of documents? Why were all of the Watergate burglars current or former CIA agents? And why were most of those agents Cuban exiles, veterans of the CIA's anti-Castro operations of the early 1960s?

Watergate: The Hidden History explains why by reexamining the historical record, including new material only available in recent years. This includes thousands of recently declassified CIA and FBI files, newly released Nixon tapes, and exclusive interviews with those involved in the events surrounding Watergate. This book also builds on decades of investigations by noted journalists and historians, as well as long-overlooked investigative articles from publications such as *Time* magazine, the *Los Angeles Times*, and *The New York Times*.

This book provides dramatic new revelations by focusing on three key areas overlooked by previous Watergate books:

- Richard Nixon's long ties to the Mafia, especially to associates of Miami-based godfather Santo Trafficante.
- Two top secret CIA anti-Castro operations linked to Nixon, both involving key Watergate participants.
- The secret Cuban Dossier that Nixon was after at the Watergate, an explosive file that could link the Mafia to his secret CIA anti-Castro operations. This Dossier of CIA attempts to kill Castro—attempts that began when Nixon was Vice President and continued while Nixon was President—is published here, for the first time in any book.[1]

Richard Nixon's use of the Mafia and CIA anti-Castro personnel in both 1960 and 1972 is the most important missing piece of the Watergate story. In 1960, Vice President Nixon had helped to forge perhaps the darkest connection in American politics, bringing together the CIA and the Mafia in plots to assassinate Fidel Castro. Remarkably, for his 1972 campaign, President Nixon brought several of the same players together again.[2]

In September 1960, Vice President Richard Nixon faced a close race in his run for the Presidency against Senator John F. Kennedy. Nixon had been President Eisenhower's point man for Cuba, and he used that role to pressure the CIA to work with the Mafia to assassinate Cuban leader Fidel Castro before the election. The mobsters chosen included godfather Santo Trafficante and his associate, Mafia don Johnny Rosselli. At the same time, Nixon received a $500,000 bribe from Santo Trafficante and his closest Mafia partner, Louisiana/Texas godfather Carlos Marcello, to stop the federal prosecution of their ally, Teamsters President Jimmy Hoffa.[3]

Richard Nixon lost the 1960 election by a narrow margin, but those CIA-Mafia plots would continue to haunt him for the rest of his political career. Nixon was finally elected President in 1968, narrowly winning the popular vote over Vice President Hubert Humphrey. As the 1972 election approached, Nixon faced what he feared would be another close election, either against Humphrey or possible nominees such as Senators Ted Kennedy, Edmund Muskie, Henry "Scoop" Jackson, or (Nixon's preferred choice) George McGovern.

In 1972, three veterans of Nixon's 1960 CIA-Mafia plots to kill Fidel Castro were part of Nixon's Watergate burglary team: E. Howard Hunt, Bernard Barker, and Frank Fiorini (a.k.a. Frank Sturgis). All three were former CIA agents who had also worked with Trafficante or Rosselli. Watergate burglars Barker and Fiorini—plus Nixon's hush-money paymaster, Cuban exile Manuel Artime (Hunt's best friend)—were still working for Trafficante during the time of Watergate. Also in the months before Watergate, President Nixon had the CIA continuing operations against Cuba, including a CIA plot to assassinate Fidel Castro. At the same time that Nixon's CIA was targeting Castro, Nixon's men had arranged another huge bribe involving Trafficante and Marcello, just prior to the start of the 1972 campaign. That $1 million Mafia bribe, verified by the FBI and *Time* magazine, was part of a deal to release Jimmy Hoffa from prison, which occurred less than five months before the first Watergate break-in.[4]

This book carefully documents how Nixon's ties to the CIA-Mafia plots to kill Fidel Castro became inexorably linked to the Mafia's two massive Hoffa bribes to Nixon. While CIA assassination plots with the Mafia may seem like old news now, it's important to remember they were only first revealed to the American public in 1975, after Nixon's 1974 resignation. In 1972, Nixon—and his CIA Director, Richard Helms—would have gone to any lengths to keep voters from finding out about his Castro assassination plots. Those plots were entwined with Nixon's huge Mafia bribes for Hoffa, and the exposure of those massive payoffs during the 1972 campaign would have dominated the headlines and shattered Nixon's chances of winning reelection. Richard Nixon was worried that the Democrats (and the Chilean embassy) had one specific Dossier that, if released, could unravel everything. That Dossier—the previously mentioned compilation of CIA attempts to assassinate Castro, which spanned Nixon's terms as Vice President and President—was the main target of the Watergate burglars, as one of them admitted after his arrest.[5]

Why aren't the ties between Nixon's Watergate crimes, the Mafia, and the CIA more widely known? Primarily because the conventional view of Watergate was—and still is—largely shaped by *All The President's Men*, the book by *Washington Post* reporters Bob Woodward and Carl Bernstein. Many people know the story of Watergate and *All the President's Men* from the acclaimed 1976 film of the same name. The movie was a faithful, though simplified, story of the book—but like the book itself, the film told only part of the Watergate story.

It's often overlooked that Woodward and Bernstein's book was completed in February 1974, six months before Nixon resigned on August 6, 1974. The book was also finished months before the White House released twelve hundred pages of carefully selected, heavily sanitized tape transcripts (remembered for their repeated use of "expletive deleted," to hide Nixon's frequent profanity). *All the President's Men* had been in bookstores for more than a month when—on July 24, 1974—the Supreme Court finally ordered Nixon to release crucial tapes about his leading role in the criminal cover-up of Watergate, including the "smoking gun" tape. The CIA-Mafia anti-Castro plots under Nixon wouldn't start to become officially known until the following year, in Senate hearings led by Senator Frank Church, so that crucial connection is also missing from *All the President's Men*.

As critics have pointed out, much of Woodward and Bernstein's book is about the two reporters and their delving into areas only tangentially related to Watergate. The result is that more people's view of Watergate was shaped by their book—and by lines invented for the film, such as "follow the money"—than by the numerous crimes that Nixon committed.[6]

Instead of focusing on two intrepid reporters gradually working their way up the food chain of aides, getting closer and closer to Nixon, *Watergate: The Hidden History* starts at the top. By focusing on

Nixon, it adds deeper historical context while simplifying (and often eliminating) the welter of low-level aides and connections detailed in *All the President's Men*, people who were simply carrying out Nixon's orders.

In addition, *Watergate: The Hidden History* explores little-known connections of Woodward and *The Washington Post* that could have impacted how they reported the story and decided what to cover—and not to cover. For example, it's not well known that just two years before Watergate, Navy Lieutenant Bob Woodward, as he would later write, "had a Top Secret security clearances" at the Pentagon and was regularly "dispatched" to take briefing material to "the West Wing of the White House."[7]

Several authors claim that Lieutenant Bob Woodward briefed White House aide General Alexander Haig at that time. Woodward has denied that. But Lieutenant Woodward's superior at the time—Chief of Naval Operations Admiral Thomas Moorer—as well as Nixon's Defense Secretary, Melvin Laird, have both stated in taped interviews (available online) that Lieutenant Woodward did indeed brief Haig at the White House. Alexander Haig was then an aide to Nixon's National Security Advisor, Henry Kissinger, and Haig later became Richard Nixon's final Chief of Staff. In that final role, Haig also reportedly became a source for journalist Bob Woodward for his second book, *The Final Days*.[8]

The importance of Alexander Haig in the full story of Watergate and Nixon's resignation—and thus any tie to Woodward—cannot be overstated. Today, Haig is largely remembered for his "I'm in charge" comment after the shooting of President Ronald Reagan, when Haig was Reagan's Secretary of State. But it's well documented that Haig essentially became America's "shadow President" in the final months of President Nixon's administration, as Nixon was consumed by the prospect of impeachment or resignation. Haig had become Nixon's Chief of Staff eleven months after the Watergate scandal broke, and he played the most important role in getting President Nixon to resign. But Haig did so only after ordering a secret military investigation by "the Army's Criminal Investigation Command" that confirmed "Nixon connections with huge cash contributions from . . . organized crime," as reported by *The Washington Star*.[9]

Only in 2009 was it revealed that Haig played a key role in getting Nixon to agree not to demand a trial in return for a pardon from new

President Gerald Ford. In fact, until a 2009 *Washington Post* report, most people didn't realize that Nixon had actually wanted a Watergate trial after his resignation, since—as shown later—Nixon was confident that national security concerns would result in his acquittal and vindication. This book documents many new revelations about Alexander Haig, including his rise to prominence in 1963, under President John F. Kennedy. In the summer and fall of that year, then Lieutenant Colonel Haig was part of John and Robert Kennedy's top secret plan to bring democracy to Cuba. For decades, knowledge of that operation was completely withheld from the press, the public, and Congress, and full information about it has emerged only in recent years. Significantly, the Kennedys' secret 1963 operation included not only high-ranking CIA official Richard Helms, but also three CIA agents arrested for the final Watergate burglary: E. Howard Hunt, Bernard Barker, and, allegedly, James McCord.[10]

All the President's Men is notable for its relative lack of information about the CIA's ties to Watergate. It's striking that Nixon's CIA Director, Richard Helms, figures very prominently in the Watergate story, yet Woodward and Bernstein's book mentions him exactly once, near the end. It is an odd omission since all of the Watergate burglars—and planner E. Howard Hunt, who observed the burglary from across the street—had worked for the CIA as agents or high-ranking officers. Nixon himself mentioned the CIA's connection to Watergate in a speech that led to a Congressional investigation. Additionally, *New York Times* reporter Tad Szulc published intriguing information during Watergate linking former CIA agents Hunt, Barker, and McCord to the same top secret CIA anti-Castro operation in the 1960s. But *All the President's Men* ignored those revelations.[11]

Perhaps Woodward's CIA omissions can be explained in part by a high-level internal CIA memo from March 1, 1973. In it, a CIA official writes that CIA asset (and future U.S. Senator) Robert Bennett "was feeding stories to Bob Woodward who [in return] was protecting Bennett, and Mullen and Company."[12] Bennett's firm has been described as a "CIA front" that provided cover employment for Hunt, and "cover arrangements" for other Agency operations. In another Agency report, Bennett's CIA case officer said that within weeks of the final Watergate break-in, Bennett was leaking information to dissuade *The Washington Post* and another newspaper from focusing on Agency involvement in the matter.[13]

All the President's Men doesn't mention the Mafia at all and refers to Jimmy Hoffa only once, in passing. Yet there were indications of Mafia links to Watergate reported by other news media, links that Woodward, Bernstein, and *The Post* avoided. From reading *All the President's Men*, you'd never know that Nixon had pardoned Hoffa just over four months before the first Watergate break-in, or about Nixon's meetings with Hoffa's mob-linked successor, or the reported bribe for Hoffa's release (with special conditions demanded by the Mafia).[14] Woodward and Bernstein's second book, *The Final Days*, failed to note ex-President Nixon's personal meeting with Mafia figures Tony Provenzano ("a convicted Mafia killer") and Allen Dorfman ("soon to be murdered gangland style") even though *The New York Times* found the Nixon-mobster meeting worthy of coverage.[15]

Few historians, let alone journalists, realize that a notorious Mafia don, Johnny Rosselli, was interviewed by three investigators for the Senate Watergate Committee on February 20, 1974. Rosselli was questioned about Nixon's 1960 CIA-Mafia anti-Castro plots, and the Committee investigators made it clear that the Watergate burglaries occurred because Nixon worried the DNC had "a document . . . showing Nixon was involved with . . . the CIA and the assassination of Castro and Rosselli." In 1960, after Nixon had pressured the CIA to assassinate Fidel Castro, Rosselli had brought his close associate Santo Trafficante into the CIA-Mafia plots because Trafficante had owned casinos in Cuba before the Revolution and still had contacts there. Thus, Rosselli's Watergate interview went to the very heart of why the Watergate burglars were after the secret Cuban Dossier. Rosselli testified at a time when Woodward and Bernstein had just finished *All the President's Men*, but there is also no mention of Rosselli or his testimony in their next book, *The Final Days*. However, to be fair, no newspaper or TV network mentioned Rosselli's Watergate interview, then or even two years later, when Rosselli's name exploded in front-page news across the country. Those headlines—about Rosselli's spectacularly gruesome Mafia murder, following his final meeting with Trafficante—triggered a massive new Congressional investigation (though not about Watergate).[16]

Instead of focusing on the CIA and Mafia material left out of *All the President's Men*, most of the press and public tried for over three decades to figure out the identity of "Deep Throat," who was finally exposed in 2005 as former FBI official Mark Felt. But a *Washington Post* editor during Watergate, Barry Sussman, has pointed out that Felt actually provided little important information. He wrote that "Deep Throat barely figured in the *Post's* Watergate coverage . . . Deep Throat confined his help to telling Woodward whether information we had was correct . . . I can't recall any story we got because of him."[17]

In many ways, Deep Throat was an excellent dramatic device for Bob Woodward, one that focused attention on Woodward and drew it away from aspects of Watergate that he wasn't the first to uncover—or that he or *The Post* may not have wanted to cover, like the CIA and the Mafia. Also, it's important to point out that ever since Felt was identified as Deep Throat, no Watergate book has looked at information he must have known, but apparently failed to tell Woodward. For example, this book documents for the first time that Felt and the FBI were well aware of the longtime Mafia ties of two of the Watergate burglars, former CIA agents Bernard Barker and Frank Fiorini (who went by the name of Frank Sturgis during Watergate).[18]

One other very significant omission from *All the President's Men* is any mention of Joseph A. Califano Jr., the close friend and mentor of Alexander Haig. In 1969, Califano had recommended Haig for his first position in the Nixon White House. They remained in frequent contact and were so close that when Nixon first offered to make Haig his Chief of Staff, Haig immediately called Califano for advice. Yet at the time of Watergate, and Haig's call, Califano was also *The Washington Post's* attorney. As such, Califano was frequently consulted on Watergate stories and represented *The Post* in court when Nixon's associates tried to uncover *The Post's* sources. But Califano had other key roles in Watergate as well, some first revealed in his 2004 autobiography.[19]

In an amazing coincidence, in addition to being Haig's good friend and the attorney for *The Washington Post*, Joseph Califano was also the attorney for the Democratic National Committee (DNC), headquartered at the Watergate office complex. In that role, Califano was called within hours of the arrest of the Watergate burglars. Califano then phoned *The Washington Post* and suggested it cover the story. Even at that early stage, Califano accurately wondered, "What if this goes all the way to the White House?" Three days later, Califano announced a DNC lawsuit against the Republicans, which—along with *The Post's* reporting—was the only thing that kept the Watergate story barely alive for months, until it finally led to the creation of the Senate Watergate Committee in early 1973 (which Califano also advised).[20]

Joseph Califano's many roles started to become known only in 1991, in a few pages of a non-Watergate book by *Newsweek* editor Evan Thomas, and in a few paragraphs of Haig's 1992 autobiography. But far more facts about Califano and Haig and their work together started to emerge years later, in Califano's 2004 autobiography and in this author's *Ultimate Sacrifice* (2005) and *Legacy of Secrecy* (2008, both with Thom Hartmann).

As Califano and Haig have written, Califano worked with, and sometimes supervised, Haig in 1963, when they helped with John and Robert Kennedy's previously mentioned secret plan to bring democracy to Cuba. In the aftermath of that operation, both men worked with Alexander Butterfield, the Nixon aide who first revealed Richard Nixon's taping system to the world. Butterfield was physically the closest aide to President Nixon, being the first to see him in the morning and the last to see him at night. After Alexander Butterfield first revealed Nixon's taping system to Congressional investigators—but before it became public, in the widely watched televised hearings—Butterfield called his friend Joseph Califano for advice.[21]

As this book shows, Califano, Haig, and Butterfield all played crucial roles in exposing not just Watergate, but the other crimes of Richard Nixon that led to his resignation. Califano wrote in his 2004 autobiography (largely ignored in Watergate coverage, even today) that he "viewed my activities during Watergate . . . as part of a citizen's crusade to protect democracy and eventually to bring down Nixon . . . "[22]

However, there were some former RFK associates who helped to keep information about Nixon and his criminal associates from being exposed, both during the Watergate investigation and for decades afterward. Still others, like Haig, helped to uncover some of Nixon's crimes while hiding others.

As alluded to earlier, *The Washington Post* reported only in 2009 that Alexander Haig and Robert F. Kennedy's former chief Mafia prosecutor —Herbert J. Miller—worked to "broker the pardon of President Richard M. Nixon," thus avoiding the Watergate trial Nixon had originally wanted. But *The Post* also pointed out that Miller, after becoming Nixon's attorney, had "prevented the release of Nixon's White House tapes after the Watergate scandal" for more than two decades. In fact, Herbert J. Miller, who had been close to Robert Kennedy until RFK's murder and remained close to the Kennedy family, oversaw the lawsuits and agreements that still keep some Nixon tapes secret today.[23]

This book finally explains why some former RFK aides and associates like Miller, Haig, and others would help Nixon keep certain information from coming out. For example, after Nixon's resignation but before his pardon, Haig tried to have a truck convoy take Nixon's papers out of the White House, away from new President Ford and the Watergate Special Prosecutor. Other RFK aides who played key roles were the first Chief Counsel of the Senate Watergate Committee (Carmine Bellino) and E. Howard Hunt's first attorney (William Bittman), both veterans of Robert Kennedy's war on organized crime.[24]

There is one other individual linked to Robert Kennedy who played a crucial role, perhaps *the* crucial role, in exposing the Watergate cover-up: James McCord, the former CIA official and Watergate burglar. McCord's March 1973 letter to Judge John Sirica blew the lid off Nixon's cover-up, at a time when all of the Watergate burglars (along with planners Hunt and G. Gordon Liddy) had pleaded guilty and claimed there was no White House involvement. When Judge Sirica read James McCord's dramatic letter in open court, on the day all the defendants were to be sentenced, the Watergate story finally became front-page news across the country, and the sudden notoriety gave the Senate Watergate Committee its first big break.[25]

James McCord's link to Robert F. Kennedy also involved the top secret plan of RFK and JFK to put Cuba on the road to democracy by the end of 1963. The CIA had only a supporting role in the plan, code-naming part of their operation AMWORLD. But it included CIA security official James McCord, according to *Vanity Fair*, former FBI agent William Turner, and key RFK aide Enrique "Harry" Ruiz-Williams ("Harry Williams"). The same sources also stated that CIA officer E. Howard Hunt and CIA agent Bernard Barker were part of the Kennedys' covert 1963 Cuba plan.[26]

Though dedicated to the CIA, James McCord was a devoutly religious man, according to all sources. Kennedy aides only spoke well of McCord to this author and others such as William Turner. Yet in 1963, McCord had to work on AMWORLD with Hunt, whose assistant Bernard Barker was also working at the same time for godfather Santo Trafficante. By 1972, McCord had to collaborate directly with Barker and another Trafficante man, Frank Fiorini/Sturgis, as Watergate burglars. Working with such men greatly troubled McCord, as indicated by his own obscure autobiography.[27]

It's extremely interesting and important that McCord, Haig, Califano, and Butterfield—the four men who played perhaps the most important roles in exposing the Watergate scandal and getting Nixon to resign—had all worked on the same 1963 effort by JFK and RFK to bring democracy to Cuba. Then, nine years later, their paths crossed again during Watergate.

Nixon's Crimes, the Mafia, and the CIA

Many of Nixon's White House tapes were kept secret for decades, and almost one thousand hours still remain secret today. Hundreds of hours of important tapes weren't released until after Nixon's death in 1994. Most—but not all—of the important tapes about his crimes released in the mid-1990s were compiled in a 1997 book by noted historian Stanley Kutler, *Abuse of Power*. It's hard to read more than a few pages of those tape transcripts without encountering Nixon, in his own words, talking about planning, committing, or covering up one or more crimes. Yet the new Nixon tapes received little attention from most of the news media, and today many news outlets talk about Nixon and Watergate as if those tapes had never been released.

The new Nixon tapes—including those not included in Kutler's book, and others released since 1997—clearly show that Nixon was the man in charge, with an astonishing grasp of overall political strategy and street-level criminal action.

On June 17, 1971, a year before Watergate, an angry President Nixon talked about files that might be at the Brookings Institute (a centrist Washington think tank): "Goddamnit, get in and get those files. Blow the safe and get it." Nixon later told an aide, "Talk to [E. Howard] Hunt. I want the break-in. Hell, they do that. You're to break into the place, rifle the files, and bring them in . . . just go in and take it." Nixon's orders evolved into a plot to firebomb the Brookings Institute to cover the theft of the files, before it was finally canceled. However, Nixon talks on the tapes about a wide range of crimes actually carried out against opponents, ranging from illegal IRS audits to having "thugs" attack his critics. The members of Nixon's political crimes squad with Hunt are commonly called the "Plumbers," because they were supposedly formed to plug Daniel Ellsberg's leak of the Pentagon Papers. But the Nixon tapes and other files show that Nixon's illegal operations had begun well before Ellsberg's leak was known.[28]

Since Richard Nixon knew he was being recorded, he didn't talk overtly about some of his well-documented crimes, yet amazing admissions sometimes slipped through. One tape initially withheld for "national security" and only released in 1999 was the one on which Nixon admitted to the break-in of the Chilean embassy in Washington, D.C., just twelve days before the first Watergate break-in. Regarding Hunt and his men, Nixon says on tape: "the Chilean embassy—that thing was a part of the burglars' plan, as a . . . CIA cover." Puzzlingly, the explosive news in that tape became only a minor story in a few papers, including *The New York Times*.[29]

Many journalists and historians still have a conventional view of Watergate that not only excludes important revelations in the hundreds of hours of new Nixon tapes and millions of pages of fresh files released since the 1990s, but also ignores material that was reported or declassified back in the 1970s. In part, that's because reporters in the 1970s hustled to cover the scandals as they broke, piecing them together from fragmentary public evidence and leaks. They saw and reported the events as separate Nixon scandals, but there were so many they often hadn't finished writing about one before a new one surfaced. Those scandals included Watergate, ITT, huge corporate slush funds, illegal domestic surveillance, covert operations to topple democracy in Chile, Nixon's $2 million dollar bribe from the dairy industry, and many more.

Today, however, we can show how—and why—those scandals were related. For example, part of the March 23, 1971, $2 million dairy industry bribe to Nixon, which Nixon talked about on tape, funded some of the criminal operations of Nixon's "Plumbers."[30] That's why Nixon's various crimes make more sense when viewed as a single, large criminal operation, rooted in decades of similar behavior by Nixon.

The true extent of Nixon's crimes has been so vastly underreported that today it's difficult to find, in books or on the Internet, even a complete list of the dozens prosecuted in the wake of Watergate. Nixon's criminal acts that involved the Mafia or that can be linked to the CIA are missing from most books, but they are documented in this one, starting in this chapter. The following are just a few examples.

Nixon's own tapes, along with news reports largely overlooked for decades, clearly show Nixon's willingness to solicit money from a variety of illegal sources: huge corporations, reclusive billionaire Howard Hughes, U.S.-backed dictators, and the Mafia. Having faced a close election in 1968 (despite outspending his opponent two to one) and fearing a tight contest in 1972, Nixon felt he needed to raise as much money as possible, even from organized crime.[31]

Though Nixon's mob ties are rarely even acknowledged today, in the 1970s some major news organizations documented them. Less than a year after Watergate, the *Los Angeles Times* ran a lead editorial entitled "Nixon, the Teamsters, the Mafia." *Time* magazine reported that in 1973, the Nixon "White House had received a $1 million underworld bribe." After that bribe, when an aide told President Nixon the Watergate burglars required "a million dollars" in fresh hush money, Nixon responded: "We could get that . . . a million dollars. You could get it in cash. I know where it could be gotten."[32]

When the aide worried that laundering the money was "the type of thing Mafia people can do," Nixon knowingly replied: "Maybe it takes a gang to do that."[33]

The Mafia got something in return for their money: a Justice Department official complained that Nixon "pardoned organized crime figures after millions were spent by the government putting them away." Over eight hundred organized crime indictments had to be voided because Nixon's first Attorney General, John Mitchell, used "improper procedures" to get court approvals for wiretaps.[34] Mitchell was later convicted and sent to prison for Watergate crimes.

Nixon's second Attorney General, Richard Kleindienst, was also convicted for an illegal operation that eventually resulted in the arrest of mob boss Santo Trafficante. Another Nixon official, a man who screened "potential appointees to the Justice Department," was later arrested in the same "drug-money-laundering" scheme as a brother of Louisiana/Texas godfather Carlos Marcello, Trafficante's closest Mafia ally.[35] Veteran *Time* reporter Robert Sam Anson pointed out that under President Nixon, CIA Director Richard Helms intervened to stop the deportation of Mafia don Johnny Rosselli, Trafficante's partner in the 1960 CIA-Mafia plots.[36]

Nixon aide Charles Colson told journalist Dick Russell that he'd heard the Mafia "got their hooks into Nixon early, and of course, that ties into the overlap of the CIA and the mob."[37] Southern California Mafia boss Mickey Cohen admitted in his autobiography that he donated $5,000 to Nixon for his first Congressional race in 1946, and raised another "$75,000 from Las Vegas gamblers" for Nixon's 1950 U.S. Senate run.[38]

Mafia money continued to flow to Richard Nixon during the rest of his political career with the help of Nixon's closest confidants, Murray Chotiner and Charles G. "Bebe" Rebozo. Chotiner, Nixon's longtime political fixer, guided the seamy side of Nixon's ascent to power from 1946 until Watergate, when Chotiner "had a private office in the White House," according to mob expert David E. Scheim. While working for Nixon in the 1950s, Scheim notes that attorney Chotiner and his brother "defended Syndicate figures in a total of 221 prosecutions" in Southern California.[39] Chotiner oversaw much of the Mafia's long effort—first chronicled by *Life* magazine—that eventually led to Nixon's 1971 release of Jimmy Hoffa.[40]

Bebe Rebozo, Nixon's trusted best friend for decades, had deep mob ties that made him an ideal Mafia conduit to Nixon. President Nixon's daily logs show many long, private talks with just the two of them, often on a yacht or a secluded beach, or at Rebozo's home next to Nixon's in the Presidential compound at Key Biscayne, Florida.[41]

Charles Colson heard the Mafia "owned Bebe Rebozo." *The New York Times* reported in 1974 that Rebozo's Miami bank "was a suspected conduit for mob dollars skimmed from" a casino in the Bahamas that *Life* magazine said "was controlled by '[Meyer] Lansky & Co.'"[42] Investigative journalist Anthony Summers documented long ties between Rebozo and Meyer Lansky, whose lieutenant said Rebozo "was the one who picked up the money for Nixon."[43] When *Newsday* documented Rebozo's Mafia ties, President Nixon retaliated by cutting off the access of *Newsday*'s White House reporter, making sure that "FBI and Secret Service agents ran surveillance on *Newsday* reporters," and ordering "tax probes of [*Newsday*'s] publisher and senior editors."[44]

Newsday also ran a Pulitzer Prize–winning series about the exploding heroin problem under Nixon, highlighting the poor performance of his agencies against Santo Trafficante and his "French Connection" heroin associates. President Nixon was closely involved in business with Rebozo, while Rebozo at the same time did business with drug traffickers and Trafficante associates like Bernard Barker—a concern Nixon talked about on White House tapes.[45]

The CIA's role in Watergate has also been hugely underreported since the 1970s, for several reasons. Not only were all five Watergate burglars, plus their supervisor E. Howard Hunt, current or former CIA agents, but Hunt and James McCord had recently been important, high-ranking CIA officials. Even worse for Nixon's CIA Director, Richard Helms, E. Howard Hunt was his trusted, longtime, personal protégé until the moment of Hunt's arrest.[46]

If all of that information had surfaced soon after Watergate, Richard Helms would have been forced to resign in disgrace and no doubt would have become a target of investigation himself. For Helms, that was unthinkable. He had been with the CIA since its creation twenty-five years earlier, and had risen through its ranks by being "the man who kept the secrets"—not just those of the Agency, but any that could link him to controversy or failure. For example, before Helms became Director he had continued the CIA-Mafia plots to kill Castro in 1962 and 1963, without telling President Kennedy or then–CIA Director John McCone. When Helms's unauthorized plotting resulted in a tragic intelligence failure, Helms not only managed to keep his actions hidden from his superiors, he even continued his unauthorized mob-linked Castro assassination attempts until 1965. Helms had kept information about those operations away from President Nixon and couldn't allow it to come out after the Watergate arrests.[47]

That is why Helms made sure the true nature of the CIA employment of some of the Watergate burglars was obscured or hidden from investigators and the press. Hunt and McCord were consistently depicted in news accounts and testimony as minor, somewhat bumbling retired CIA agents, barely known to Helms—a fiction that persists to this day in most Watergate accounts.

Richard Helms began his close relationship with E. Howard Hunt in the 1950s, when Hunt was involved in overthrowing Latin American governments for the CIA. Hunt then became heavily involved in the CIA's anti-Castro efforts in the 1960s, from the CIA-Mafia plots to the Bay of Pigs. In 1963, Helms trusted Hunt to handle the most sensitive parts of John and Robert Kennedy's top secret plan to bring democracy to Cuba. By the mid-1960s, Hunt would later admit that Helms used him as a key liaison with U.S. press and publishers. (The massive CIA effort to manipulate the U.S. and world press was not exposed until 1975, by the same Congressional hearings that uncovered the 1960 CIA-Mafia plots.)[48]

With Helms as his mentor, E. Howard Hunt rose high in the CIA. By 1969, during Nixon's first term, a CIA-approved account says Hunt was the CIA's Chief of Covert Operations for Western Europe. With its Iron Curtain and Berlin Wall, Western Europe was ground zero for the Cold War, thus a crucially important post. It also gave Hunt even more press contacts, with foreign bureau chiefs of major U.S. news organizations.[49]

In 1970, when Nixon's CIA Director Helms needed access to FBI intelligence that he could get only through White House channels, Hunt suddenly "retired" from the CIA. The "official story" says Hunt was hired by the White House—at the suggestion of Charles Colson—on July 7, 1971, and that Nixon didn't know Hunt prior to that. Neither is true. Hunt and his assistant Bernard Barker both admit that four months earlier, in April 1971, Hunt recruited Barker and others to do covert work for the White House. President Nixon himself mentioned Hunt as a clandestine operative in a June 1971 tape. Nixon had far more ties to Hunt than anyone realized during the Watergate investigations, beginning in the 1950s and continuing after the 1960 CIA-Mafia plots, as detailed in later chapters.[50]

Once Hunt was a White House operative, he continued his close ties to Helms and was in a position to provide a steady stream of important information to his mentor. CIA Director Helms was so fond of Hunt that he gave visitors to his office copies of the hack spy novels Hunt wrote. More important, it's now documented that in the weeks leading up to Watergate, Helms was involved with pitching a TV series based on Hunt's novels to Hollywood producers. That should end speculation that has persisted for years, that the failure of the last Watergate break-in was a CIA operation deliberately designed to bring down Nixon.[51]

President Nixon and Richard Helms would have both been frantic when Hunt's name first surfaced in the June 20, 1972 *Washington Post*, three days after the Watergate break-in. That same day, *Post* and DNC attorney Joseph Califano announced a DNC lawsuit against the Republicans that could have uncovered Hunt's deeper ties to Nixon and Helms. It's no coincidence that this is also the date of the infamous "18-minute gap" in Nixon's White House tape.[52]

It's easy to see why E. Howard Hunt's high-level ties to the CIA didn't surface soon after Watergate. None of the publishers or journalists Hunt had dealt with for the CIA had any incentive to acknowledge their past involvement with Hunt. It was easier for them—and the rest of the press—not to question the "official" CIA story of Hunt as a minor, bumbling CIA agent barely known to Helms. The reluctance of editors and journalists to reveal their past contacts with Hunt was augmented by the considerable skills of Richard Helms at manipulating journalists.[53]

The Watergate burglars that Hunt used for Nixon's operation had far more extensive links to the CIA than were reported at the time. The recently retired James McCord had been Richard Helms's "Assistant Director for security for the entire Central Intelligence Agency [just] a year before the break-in," according to journalist Edward J. Epstein. Eugenio Martinez, a supposedly "retired" veteran of CIA anti-Castro operations, was still an active agent on the CIA payroll when he was arrested at the Watergate. The remaining Watergate burglars—Barker, Frank Fiorini/Sturgis, and Virgilio Gonzalez—were all former CIA agents, though the Agency denied Fiorini's CIA status for years, even though it was confirmed by two CIA Directors.[54]

The extensive CIA ties of Hunt and the Watergate burglary team caused Helms and the Agency to keep much crucial information away from the press, the Special Prosecutor, and a series of Congressional investigations. Even after Helms was no longer CIA Director, the withholding continued, for decades. Thanks to the 1992 JFK Act and the eventual release of four million pages of files, many about the CIA and anti-Castro operations, this book finally delivers key information that the CIA and Richard Helms withheld from the Senate Watergate Committee.

The huge array of new information available today finally provides the crucial missing chapters to the story of Nixon and Watergate. However, it's important to point out exactly what this book is—and isn't. It exposes the hidden history of Nixon and Watergate, including the important events that led to the scandal, like the 1960 CIA-Mafia plots to kill Castro that began at the behest of then–Vice President Nixon. This book is not a complete history of all the details and people involved in Watergate. Instead, it focuses on important aspects that have not received wide exposure in other books. This includes Nixon's ties to organized crime, and the unauthorized operations of Richard Helms that led to Watergate.

While telling those stories and others, the book also reveals a striking assortment of current political and media figures who began their rise to prominence with roles in the story of Nixon and Watergate, including Hillary Clinton, Diane Sawyer, Karl Rove, Dick Cheney, Donald Rumsfeld, George H.W. Bush, Roger Ailes, Pat Buchanan,

G. Gordon Liddy, and many more. Their later actions sometimes involved repeating what they'd done—or the lessons they'd learned—during the Nixon era, so this book notes their often-overlooked roles.

It's ironic that it has taken until 2012 for enough information to become available to finally tell the full story of Watergate, since this is not only the fortieth anniversary of Watergate, but it's also a Presidential election year, like 1972. That makes Watergate more relevant today than ever, since fully exposing Nixon's political crimes is one way to ensure that no candidate can commit the same types of malfeasance again. In addition, as explained in the book's final chapter, Watergate also paved the way for several later scandals and tragedies.

While much of the book focuses on Richard Nixon, other chapters are devoted to people and events important for the hidden history of Watergate. Most prominent among those is longtime CIA official Richard Helms, who in some ways played the second-most-important role in the Watergate scandal. Nixon and Helms shared the same basic motivation: fear that exposure of their past actions could cost them their powerful positions, along with a willingness to go to extraordinary lengths to keep that from happening. Other important people and events detailed in the book include three key Mafia bosses, several of Helms's fellow CIA officials, various covert U.S. operations to topple or eliminate Fidel Castro, and the people who tried to expose—or cover up—the crimes of Watergate.

Watergate: The Hidden History is not a complete biography of Nixon's entire life, but it covers the important and frequently overlooked aspects of his political and personal life that led him to the crimes of Watergate. Because this book is about the hidden history of the crimes of Watergate, it highlights Nixon's illegal actions and unsavory ties far more than his accomplishments. The latter have been covered in hundreds of books and documentaries, while the former are rarely detailed. It also shows the often-ignored traits of Nixon that help to explain Watergate, from his ability to be charming and engaging to his skill at manipulating much of the news media. (For example, even after the Watergate arrests, 753 daily newspapers endorsed Nixon in 1972, ten times the number who endorsed his opponent, McGovern.)[55]

The facts ultimately show that Nixon was a tragic figure, a politically brilliant man who could have done much for the country. But like a figure in Greek tragedy, he was deeply flawed, consumed by a drive for power, status, and money that he (apparently) believed he could obtain only through decades of Mafia and corporate corruption, along with access to covert intelligence, legal or otherwise. That insecurity led to his continuing those illegal aspects of his political life even when, as his 1972 landslide victory shows, he may no longer have needed them.

But Nixon had been involved with criminals and criminal activity for so long—from the very start of his political career—that by 1972, he seemingly didn't know how to run a political race without them. And the historical record shows that in many ways, what Nixon did as President (and what he did to become President) simply repeated on a larger scale what he'd done for years, during two terms as Vice President, as a U.S. Senator, and in his election to Congress in 1946. That was the year that Nixon first began amassing power and money using the Mafia, illegal corporate slush funds, and crimes to get elected.

Once Nixon was in office, he used his access to covert intelligence to get publicity and power, by becoming a "master leaker" to the press, as he admitted on his own tapes. Those four corrupt practices he began using in the 1940s—the Mafia, illegal corporate slush funds, campaign crimes, and U.S. intelligence agencies—would set a pattern for the rest of Nixon's life. They would lead inexorably, perhaps inevitably, to Watergate.[56]

CHAPTER 2

Richard Nixon Runs for Congress

Richard Nixon launched his political career in 1946, a year after the end of World War II, in a race that would set the tone for his later campaigns. That year marked a turning point not just for Nixon, but also for the country, ushering in a decade of Red Scares and fearmongering. For the Republican Party in 1946, Richard Nixon was the right man at a pivotal time. The Republicans had been out of power in Congress and the White House since the 1932 elections that first swept Franklin D. Roosevelt into office. Their efforts to regain power presented enormous challenges for the Republicans, perhaps best summarized by three Congressional investigations in the 1930s—the Pecora Commission, the Nye Committee, and the "Business Plot" hearings—that were highly publicized at the time, but are little known today.

The Depression had ended only five years earlier, and Republican leaders had to find some reason for average working Americans to vote for their "Grand Old Party." The "Republican Depression" of the 1930s, as President Truman still called it, was a phrase that Franklin Roosevelt had used to great advantage in his four victorious Presidential elections. Democratic candidates would no doubt use the term yet again in the 1946 Congressional races.

In 1934 and 1935, Senate hearings into the causes of the Depression had made headlines for weeks, and their findings still resonated a decade later. The hearings—named the Pecora Commission, after Chief Counsel Ferdinand Pecora—documented the excesses of Wall Street and many of America's biggest corporations. The Pecora Commission demonstrated how eight years of Republican White House and Congressional control led to the 1929 stock market crash, followed by four more years of Republican control that did even more damage to the U.S. economy. By 1946 the Republican Party's ongoing public relations effort to rebrand the "Republican Depression" as the "Great Depression" was gaining traction, but the financial crash wasn't the only lingering painful memory its candidates would have to overcome.[1]

Even as America struggled to recover from World War II, many World War I veterans were still bitter over their suffering during the Depression.* Senate hearings by the Nye Committee from 1934 to 1936 had exposed not only rampant profiteering during World War I by many of America's largest corporations, but also showed how the companies had helped to spark the war by heavily arming both sides. Some of those same firms had then helped to mount a major public relations and propaganda campaign to get America into the First World War.[2]

As if that weren't enough, hearings by the forerunner to the House Un-American Activities Committee found that some of those same U.S. corporate titans had tried to stage a coup against President Franklin Roosevelt in 1934. Sometimes called the "Business Plot," the scheme was led by Irénée du Pont, whose family controlled not just the corporation that bears their name but also General Motors. The group tried to recruit then-famous retired Marine General Smedley Butler to lead a coup against Roosevelt. General MacArthur had also signaled his support for the coup. The patriotic Butler tipped off Roosevelt, who then leaked the coup to the press as something not to be taken seriously. Congressional hearings about the "Business Plot" in the House by the McCormack-Dickstein Committee made headlines in 1934, though its full final report—confirming Butler's charges—was not released until four years later.[3]

The Pecora, Nye, and "Business Plot" hearings are rarely mentioned today, and missing from most history textbooks, partly because of public relations experts working for Irénée du Pont and the corporations involved. However, in the 1930s they were huge news, and they continued to have an effect on American popular fiction for years afterward, helping to keep the issues alive for voters in the 1940s.[4] If the Republicans were going to prevail in 1946, they had to find candidates and issues who would overcome the stigma left by—and avoid any obvious connections to—those three hearings. Richard Nixon was the type of candidate who could offer the GOP a clean slate in that regard.

* In 1932 the last Republican administration had General Douglas MacArthur forcibly remove World War I veterans and their families peacefully camped in Washington, D.C.

Equally important for Republican leaders was that their victory in 1946 could prevent another round of Congressional hearings that had the potential to keep the GOP out of power even longer. That was of great concern because several of America's largest corporations had aided the rise of Adolph Hitler and the Nazis, even continuing their aid to Germany after World War II began.

During the 1930s some American tycoons and public figures such as Henry Ford and aviator Charles Lindbergh openly admired Hitler and embraced anti-Semitism. For other American companies, including some Wall Street banks, dealing with the Nazis was simply a matter of money. Ford, IBM, DuPont, Standard Oil (of New Jersey, later to become Exxon), and other companies conducted regular and profitable business with Nazi Germany. Some, such as Standard Oil and Ford, continued to do business with the Nazis after World War II began in 1939—and, incredibly, even after America entered the war in 1941.[5]

Allen Dulles was a distinguished Wall Street banker who had dealt with the Nazis, even as he seemed opposed to their policies. In Dulles's case, some of his dealings involved his undercover work for the Office of Strategic Services (OSS), the World War II forerunner of the CIA. Both Allen Dulles and his brother, John Foster Dulles, were very interested in Republican politics and world affairs. Yet for either to have any political future, Allen Dulles's dealings with Nazis couldn't be exposed, certainly not amid growing calls for a Congressional investigation into the ties between Wall Street and recently vanquished Nazi Germany.[6]

According to Justice Department investigator John Loftus, the U.S. Navy was reviewing captured Nazi documents in the fall of 1945, some of which dealt with Allen Dulles. Among those reviewing the Nazi-Dulles files was a thirty-two-year-old Lieutenant Commander who was soon to leave the Navy. Loftus documented that "Allen Dulles told [the Navy man] to keep quiet about what he had seen and, in return, arranged to finance the young man's first Congressional campaign," the following year.[7]

That Navy Lieutenant Commander was Richard Nixon.[8]

Richard Milhous Nixon was one of the fresh crop of Republican candidates for the 1946 Congressional elections. Like the others, he—and his family—had no obvious connection to the big corporate and banking scandals that had been, or could soon be, investigated by

Congress. But more than the other new candidates, Nixon was exactly the right man, at the right time, with the skills and temperament to make good use of his opportunity.

Born in 1913, Richard Nixon grew up in the small Quaker-founded towns of Whittier and Yorba Linda, east of Los Angeles. Absent from both were the obvious signs of "vice" common in many American towns, from bars and gambling to burlesque and brothels. Nixon grew up in surroundings that presented a pleasant if somewhat bland facade on the surface, something that would come to characterize the political image he would try to project to the public.

The Milhous family, on his mother's side, was well off, but not wealthy, in a time when the middle class was far smaller than it would be by the 1950s. Nixon's parents struggled in the early years to raise him and his four brothers, but by the time Richard Nixon was a teenager, the family led a comfortable life. His staunchly Republican parents had a house and a small grocery store. In the Depression that followed the stock-market crash of 1929, the Nixons' relative prosperity left them much better off than most others in town.

Richard Nixon—intelligent, hardworking, and studious—excelled in school and appeared to have a bright future. By the time he entered high school, a scholarship to an excellent college seemed within reach. Nixon's social skills had also begun to catch up to his studies, which promised to make high school a golden time for him, even as the country's economy continued to decline during the final years of Republican President Herbert Hoover's administration.

When Nixon won a scholarship to Harvard University, thanks to his outstanding debating skills, it should have signaled the start of the promising high school senior's eventual ascent into the Eastern establishment. But three years earlier, his brother Harold had contracted tuberculosis. Only two years before Harold Nixon became sick, Nixon's younger brother had died, possibly from tubercular meningitis. Despite that—and even though Whittier had a county tuberculosis hospital that Nixon described as "one of the best in the country"—Nixon's steadfastly Republican father refused to send Harold there, considering the use of a county-funded hospital as "charity." So, the family had to drain their finances to pay for his brother Harold's treatment, in Arizona. To help his family with household expenses, Richard had to take a series of part-time jobs.[9]

The scholarship that Harvard University offered Richard Nixon was for tuition only and didn't include room and board, textbooks, or other necessities. His family's financial straits forced Nixon to make a choice that would alter the course of his life and leave a lingering bitterness. Unable to afford the additional expenses, Nixon had to decline the prize of a scholarship to Harvard.

Even worse, one of his summer part-time jobs was as a janitor at a country club in Arizona, the state where his mother was overseeing his brother's tuberculosis treatment. Instead of looking forward to being a prestigious Harvard graduate, who could realistically aspire to join a country club, he instead had to serve club members as a lowly janitor. It must have been a crushing blow to the teenage Nixon, and his bitterness against the Eastern elites and Harvard in particular—so evident in his later White House tapes—could have originated at this time.[10]

Nixon hated his janitorial job at the country club, but he found another unlikely vocation that he both liked and excelled at: being a carnival barker. He was the tout who stood beside a midway "Wheel of Fortune" attraction, using fast talk and exorbitant promises to persuade small-town Americans to part with their money during hard times. The task was even more challenging because Nixon had to take their money in a way that not only didn't leave his customers angry, but hopefully left them anxious to be "fleeced" again. Nixon was very successful at this, and his attraction made the most money for the carnival's owner. In addition, Nixon probably gained his first sustained exposure to small-time vice, gambling, and drinking during his time with the carnival.[11]

Even during the Depression, Richard Nixon was still better off than most of his high school classmates, since his maternal grandparents had endowed a comfortable scholarship for family members at Whittier College. After his high school graduation, while the other graduates scrambled for scarce and difficult jobs, Nixon spent four years as a popular and academically excellent student at Whittier College. As in high school, the few criticisms of Nixon by his peers were that he was very ambitious and seemed more concerned with putting up a sociable front than revealing his true feelings. At Whittier College, in addition to excelling at debating, Nixon also distinguished himself as an actor, winning accolades from his drama coach and rave reviews that hailed his performances as "outstanding" and "exceptional."[12]

Wanting to be a lawyer, but being unable to afford—or obtain a scholarship to—the elite Eastern law schools, Nixon was glad to receive instead a scholarship to the new Duke University Law School in North Carolina. Again the scholarship covered only tuition, and his father could afford to send him just $30 a month to help with expenses. That still wasn't enough. Fortunately, one of President Franklin Roosevelt's New Deal programs funded a part-time job at Duke that gave Nixon just enough money to get by.[13]

Unlike his enjoyable years at Whittier, Nixon's time at Duke was spartan and devoted to study, for two reasons. First, he had little time and no money for socializing or even for nice clothes. Indeed, some of his convincing talk in political campaigns of growing up "poor" stemmed not so much from his childhood but from his financially pinched existence at Duke, where for a time he lived in an unheated cabin. More important, he knew that his only chance at getting a job with a prestigious law firm after attending a new law school such as Duke would be to graduate at or near the top of his class. Competition was so intense that Nixon was involved in a break-in at Duke when he desperately wanted to check his grades.[14]

Nixon graduated third in his class in 1937, which was good enough to land him an interview with a powerful New York City law firm. The firm called him back for a second interview, but Nixon didn't go, either because of his reluctance to move to New York or because he realized he would never truly advance at the firm without an Ivy League degree. He applied to join the FBI, but the Bureau rejected his application. Nixon returned home to Whittier, and became an attorney of no particular legal distinction. He did, however, become the president of four civic and alumni clubs. Nixon also soon became the president of the Young Republicans, and he liked to give speeches to civic groups slamming President Franklin Roosevelt.[15]

Nixon still lived with his parents, and there—and in public—he projected a "clean" image of not drinking alcohol. That was important in Whittier, a dry town where businesses were still not allowed to serve or sell alcohol, despite the end of Prohibition three years earlier. Nixon's teetotaler image became especially important when he became the Assistant City Attorney, responsible for enforcing the city's "no alcohol" laws. However, in private, associates said Nixon "cheerfully broke the laws with his friends."[16]

In 1938, while auditioning for a community theater play, Nixon met Thelma Catherine "Pat" Ryan, an intelligent and vivacious school teacher who'd had bit parts in a couple of films. After a two-year courtship, Richard Nixon married Pat—as she liked to be called—in 1940. Nixon would later claim to have been a virgin until his marriage at age twenty-seven. Not for the last time, Nixon's ambition outstripped his bank account, and Pat had to dip into her small savings to help pay for her own engagement ring, their honeymoon, and a new car.[17]

Despite Richard Nixon's limited financial means, "within weeks of meeting Nixon, Pat had told friends that he was going to be President someday," according to Nixon biographer Anthony Summers. In self-serving speeches and written accounts, Nixon would always later downplay his early political aspirations. Even before marrying Pat, Nixon had wanted to enter politics by running for the California State Assembly, but to his disappointment Whittier's leading banker and Republican power broker told Nixon he simply wasn't ready.[18]

Early in 1942, just one month after the Japanese bombed Pearl Harbor, Nixon and Pat moved to Washington, D.C., where Nixon had secured a job with the Office of Price Administration, a new Roosevelt agency tasked with protecting consumers "from price gouging and wartime profiteers." Though the job gave him a deferment, Nixon decided in June 1942 to join the U.S. Navy. He spent most of his service in the Pacific theater. Though Nixon didn't see combat, while he was stationed in the Solomon Islands his base was bombed "twenty-eight nights out of thirty," though he remained unscathed.[19]

His Navy time in the Pacific improved both Nixon's social skills and his finances. Nixon rose to the rank of Lieutenant Commander, and was well liked by his men and fellow officers. He was later described as being a type of "Mr. Roberts" character, evoking the likeable and affable Navy officer played by Henry Fonda in the 1955 film of the same name. For those who know Nixon only from his embattled Watergate persona, this side of Nixon is a revelation, and one that helps to explain much of his political success.

Also as a harbinger of his later political life, some of Nixon's letters reveal that he looked down on the enlisted men, seeing them as a social class below him, as "men he never would have . . . mingled with by choice." Yet, at the same time, he projected an image that won their respect and got them to do what he wanted—a skill he wound hone as a politician. However, even in the Navy, he lacked access to the elite social class to which he aspired, a status that would have allowed him to "hobnob with the rich and powerful as an Admiral's aide."[20]

Richard Nixon's time in the Navy was also critical for his political and financial future, thanks to his amazing skill at playing poker. During his U.S. Navy service, Nixon won $10,000 at poker (almost $120,000 in today's dollars), an incredible sum. He claimed to have learned the secret of poker from a fellow Navy officer, but it's possible he learned the fine points of the game during his stint with the carnival. There are no indications he cheated and, remarkably, though he once won as much as $1,500 on one hand, he remained on good terms with those he played with. Given Nixon's later clean-cut image, it's ironic that his huge poker winnings gave him the financial cushion he needed to help start his storied political career.[21]

Nixon's final months in the Navy were spent on the East Coast, where he received a letter from Whittier's leading banker asking if he'd like to be considered as a possible Republican candidate to run for the Congressional seat of a longtime Democratic incumbent.[22] Nixon was definitely interested and—consistent with the earlier account of Allen Dulles funding Nixon—soon there would be reports that "a representative of a large New York financial house" was involved in Nixon's campaign, and one of his contributors would later become a "legal advisor" for Dulles. With a good start on the funding for his campaign, Nixon and Pat returned to Whittier to begin a new chapter in his life.[23]

In late 1945 and early 1946, Nixon began lining up more support for his Congressional run, beginning a pattern of legal and ethical compromises that would define almost all of his future campaigns. As an apparently clean-living, married veteran with no messy past ties to bankers or Wall Street, Nixon offered an appealing choice for the Republican "Committee of 100," the small business group in Southern California's Twelfth District that selected Nixon to run. However, Anthony Summers found ample evidence that Nixon's "campaign was a creature of big Eastern financial interests . . . the Bank of America, the big private utilities, the major oil companies." He points out that Nixon's Democratic opponent "had exposed a shady deal that gave Standard Oil . . . massive profits" and that a noted political operative "for Standard Oil . . . had sat in on the selection meeting that picked Nixon as a candidate." Representatives of at least two other major oil companies—Richfield and Signal—contributed to Nixon's war chest, and helped his campaign. Supposedly, Nixon's campaign would cost $32,000, but some historians find that "improbably low," since one backer alone had "contributed $10,000." Nixon's Democratic opponent would spend only $1,900.[24]

Richard Nixon also received financial support in 1946 from America's biggest corporate titan and richest man, billionaire Howard Hughes, as verified by Hughes's top aide at the time, Noah Dietrich. That began an important financial connection between Nixon and Hughes that would continue to grow throughout Nixon's political life, and it would be a factor in the events that triggered Watergate.[25]

Thus, Nixon became one of the first postwar politicians to perfect the technique of claiming support from small businesses and working to help them, while actually taking most of his money from—and supporting legislation for—powerful corporate interests. However, Nixon could make his "small business" claims to working people in a credible way that a distinguished banker or longtime Republican politician couldn't.

With more than enough funds to finance an expensive campaign to overwhelm his opponent, Nixon also looked out for his own financial interests, beginning yet another pattern that would grow during his life in politics. Just campaigning would be a full-time job for almost a whole year, and if he won, Nixon told the Republican power brokers that he couldn't be expected to live on a Congressman's salary. He needed substantial money for his personal use, even though his old law firm created a position for him that would pay Nixon a salary while he campaigned full-time.[26]

To get Richard Nixon the money he wanted, his supporters created the first Nixon slush fund in 1946. "I was a bagman for Nixon," stated former corporate executive William Ackerman, whose company's chairman "was a director of Standard Oil," while another board member owned Crocker Bank. According to a journal Ackerman kept in 1946, at "a meeting of seventy-five executives . . . north of Los Angeles" the men were told that Nixon "says he can't live on a Congressman's salary. Needs a lot more than that to match what he knows he could make in private law practice [and needs] cash to make up the difference. We're going to help." Their goal was to "get at least five thousand" for Nixon (over $45,000 in today's dollars). And they did—but that was the amount Nixon got from only one company. The big business group raising money for Nixon, "the California Club," was getting money from other companies as well. Thus was born Nixon's taste for corporate slush funds, an appetite that would continue to grow and result in several scandals over the years.[27]

The 1946 election offered the thirty-three-year-old Nixon his best, and perhaps only, chance to live the type of life he aspired to. His public pronouncements aside, Nixon certainly didn't see himself as working class, yet he clearly wasn't on track for a prestigious legal career that might help him one day become a millionaire or join an elite country club. Politics offered him access to the wealthy and powerful, and he was determined to make the most of this opportunity. If he lost his first race, he had little chance of finding so much money or backing again.

From that perspective, it's not surprising that Nixon's 1946 campaign would be one of the dirtiest in memory, setting a new standard in smear techniques that are still used today. Much of Nixon's overall political strategy in 1946—and later—appears to have come from the writings of Wall Street public relations expert Edward Bernays, who had worked for former Presidents Calvin Coolidge and Woodrow Wilson. Bernays literally wrote the book on propaganda (in 1928), a work that also influenced Joseph Stalin and Hitler's propaganda minister, Joseph Goebbels. (Bernays himself would later play a role in Nixon's first foreign covert intelligence operation.) In 1946, Nixon would make up for his lack of political experience by combining Bernays's proven propaganda techniques with his own debating and acting skills to make himself a formidable candidate.*[28]

Richard Nixon's major advantages in his 1946 race would be his status as a war veteran, a campaign war chest three times the size of an ordinary California Congressional candidate's, and the support of every major newspaper in the district. In addition, almost half the voters in his district were registered Republicans. However, he would need all those advantages and more, since his opponent—five-time incumbent Jerry Voorhis, a Yale graduate—had a distinguished record in Congress. Voted by Washington newsmen as "first in integrity among the 435 [House] members, the House itself had voted [Voorhis]

*Bernays helped to inflame anti-German frenzy in the United States before the country entered World War I, then sold his expertise to Wall Street, major American corporations, and President Calvin Coolidge. Much of Bernays's 1928 book *Propaganda* reads like a primer for Nixon's strategy, in which people are "governed [and have] our minds melded, our tastes formed, [and our] ideas suggested" by a small elite of those with "natural leadership" ability backed by the wealthy and large corporations.

its hardest working member." He also had a solid record of opposing both Communism and pro-Nazi, pro-fascist groups, and Congress had unanimously passed "the Voorhis Act, which [required] the registration with the Department of Justice [of] any political organization that is controlled by a foreign power" or that engages in "subversion of our government." Voorhis was very much a Roosevelt New Deal liberal at a time when the Democratic Party encompassed the full political spectrum, from extremely liberal to extremely conservative Southern Democrats.[29]

Just weeks after Nixon was anointed the Republican challenger, his backers added a crucial component to his team: Los Angeles attorney Murray Chotiner. He was brought in as a "public relations consultant," but the law practice Chotiner shared with his brother would mainly be distinguished by its defense of 221 of Mickey Cohen's bookies in just a four-year period. Murray Chotiner would quietly arrange for Mickey Cohen and the Mafia to contribute to Nixon's campaign, beginning another pattern Nixon would continue the rest of his political life.[30]

As Los Angeles mobster Mickey Cohen later admitted in a sworn affidavit, he "gave Nixon a check for five thousand dollars." Though the money came from Cohen, he later made it clear it had been authorized by East Coast mob figures Meyer Lansky and Frank Costello, then America's most powerful Mafia leaders. Mickey Cohen controlled bookmaking for organized crime in the Los Angeles area. Organized crime in Los Angeles was more diffuse than in the East, where a single crime family—often part of the traditional Sicilian Mafia—usually controlled the rackets in a city or even an entire state. In Los Angeles, Cohen was the top lieutenant of the faction led by Benjamin "Bugsy" Siegel, who represented Meyer Lansky and other East Coast mobsters. The other major mob faction in Los Angeles was run by Jack Dragna along with Johnny Rosselli, who represented the Chicago Mafia. In 1946, Johnny Rosselli was in federal prison for his role in a scandal in which the Mafia extorted funds from the major movie studios to ensure low wages for a key union.[31]

Given the political realities of the time, it's possible that Richard Nixon saw taking money from Cohen and his men as nothing unusual. As reflected in the tough, gritty film noir movies then emerging from Hollywood, most American cities and states struggled with—and some were controlled by—organized crime. It wasn't just metropolises like Chicago or New York City. From Dallas to Miami to tiny Phenix City, Alabama—proclaimed "the most corrupt city in America"—organized crime was a major and growing problem. In 1946, some large U.S. corporations still used organized crime to help break strikes and take control of unions. And in many states, wealthy patrons frequented illegal Mafia casinos, some more lavish than country clubs.[32]

In addition, Richard Nixon's background had given him little or no experience with the dark, violent side of organized crime. The brutal murder of Bugsy Siegel in Beverly Hills was over a year away. In 1946, Siegel was still socializing with movie stars and studio chiefs, as had Johnny Rosselli before going to prison. Richard Nixon probably saw Mickey Cohen's bookmaking operation as a relatively victimless crime, and Nixon later described Chotiner's work for Cohen's operation as routine legal work. The bottom line was that Nixon was a political novice facing a relatively popular incumbent, and he apparently felt he needed all the money he could get, regardless of its source.[33]

In Murray Chotiner—the tough, mobbed-up lawyer and public relations expert—Nixon had found a legal and political soul mate for life. Chotiner's basic political philosophy was simple: "Hit 'em, hit 'em, and hit 'em again." In 1946, Nixon and Chotiner developed a more refined three-step attack strategy that would become the template for Nixon, and many other Republicans, for the next decade and into the twenty-first century. According to Jerry Voorhis, their first step was to discredit their opponent "in every possible way." Next, the goal was to associate "one's opponent in the public mind with an unpopular idea, concept or—better yet—organization." Finally, Nixon and Chotiner's plan was to "attack, attack, attack, [and] never defend."[34]

Richard Nixon and Chotiner set about smearing Voorhis and the Democrats carefully, in ways that kept Voorhis on the defensive and made it hard to disprove one set of claims before another variation—or new claims—appeared. Many were simply blatant lies. Richard Nixon first denounced "the foreign ideologies of the New Deal Administration." Then he claimed that Voorhis "had the support of radical groups [and] his voting record in Congress is more Socialistic and Communistic than Democratic." Among the forty-six votes in Congress Nixon stressed were "Communistic" were a vote for an "anti-racketeering bill that included labor leaders," a "wartime loan to Britain, abolition of the poll tax" that prevented blacks from voting in the South, and the "establishment of the school lunch program." In most cases, Voorhis had voted with the majority of House members. But Nixon kept the focus on the total number of votes (which he greatly exaggerated), not the individual votes themselves. Callers were hired to ask voters by phone if they knew "that Jerry Voorhis is a Communist?"[35] Years later, Nixon would privately admit, "Of course I know Jerry Voorhis wasn't a Communist . . . there was scarcely ever a man with higher ideals . . . [but] I had to win . . . the important thing is to win."[36]

With that single goal in mind, Richard Nixon resorted to tactics reminiscent of some he would still be using into the 1970s. He had hecklers follow Voorhis from speech to speech to boo him, and he planted others in audiences to ask Nixon-sympathetic questions. Banks warned local businesses they could lose their credit lines if they supported Voorhis. Nixon refused to condemn or disown a flyer deriding Voorhis as representing "subversive Jews and Communists [trying to] destroy Christian America and our form of government." Those are just a small sample of the dirty tactics used by Nixon and Chotiner against Voorhis in 1946.[37]

Nixon was able to exploit the fact that in the 1920s Voorhis had briefly been a member of the Socialist Party, getting conservative voters in his district to equate it erroneously with the Communist Party. From the 1920s to the early 1940s, the Socialist Party in America was a very small but real factor in America politics on a national and statewide level. Because the Socialist Party was dedicated to democracy and freedom, their frequent adversary was the Communist Party, which was well-funded but so tiny as to never be a factor in U.S. state or national politics.[38]

With their advantage in funding, Nixon and Chotiner spared no expense in making sure their message got across. According to a reporter for one of the district's leading newspapers, Nixon actually paid for "front-page space" weekly, "not for ads, but for planted news stories and pictures" designed to make Nixon look good. The largest newspaper in the region, the *Los Angeles Times*, limited the ad space it would sell Voorhis, but not Nixon, and its political editor "wrote some of Nixon's speeches."[39]

Richard Nixon won the election by fifteen thousand votes. His victory was just part of a Republican takeover of both houses of Congress, the first time they controlled either since the 1932 elections.

Nixon and Chotiner would keep refining their attack strategy and use it in most of his future races. The campaign tactics Nixon used were adapted by others, and would eventually be used in more recent Presidential and Congressional races by political strategists ranging from Newt Gingrich to Karl Rove.

However, to win in 1946 Nixon had also used corporate slush funds, Mafia money, and what some call "dirty tricks." Nixon would soon add the political use of covert intelligence, and all of those activities would become part of the fabric of his political life.[40]

CHAPTER 3

Nixon: Congress, the Senate, and the Race for Vice President

Soon after arriving in Washington in early 1947, Richard Nixon became friends with Wisconsin's Republican freshman Senator, Joseph McCarthy, who—in a few years—would take the type of Red-baiting Nixon had done to Voorhis to new heights, on a national scale. In 1947 Nixon also met new Massachusetts Congressman John F. Kennedy. They were cordial acquaintances but never friends, and JFK—along with his legacy—would haunt the last decade and a half of Nixon's political life. Kennedy represented almost everything that Nixon resented: the handsome young war hero was a Harvard graduate, and his father, Joseph Kennedy, was one of America's wealthiest men. Joseph Kennedy had made a fortune in the stock market (getting out before the collapse), in motion pictures, in real estate (he owned the enormous Chicago Merchandise Mart, one of the world's largest buildings), and in legal—and rumored illegal—liquor distribution. Joseph Kennedy had been one of the few corporate titans to support Franklin D. Roosevelt when he first ran for President. Roosevelt rewarded him by first making the expert stock trader the head of FDR's new Securities and Exchange Commission, and later his Ambassador to England from 1938 to 1940. In many ways, the elder Kennedy was far more conservative than Roosevelt, but young JFK had managed to distance himself from his father's opinions and carve out his own, more liberal image. The Irish Catholic Joseph Kennedy liked Senator Joe McCarthy, who had a similar background, which is why a young Robert F. Kennedy would eventually work briefly on McCarthy's staff.[1]

Richard Nixon's first important Congressional assignment was on the House Un-American Activities Committee (HUAC), chaired by conservative Republican J. Parnell Thomas. Just over ten years earlier, the forerunner of HUAC had investigated the "Business Plot" to overthrow Roosevelt. But in the different climate of 1947, corporate crimes would no longer be a target for investigation, even though HUAC would have been a logical committee to investigate corporations such as Ford and Standard Oil that helped the Nazi war machine. Alternatively, HUAC could have investigated racist groups like the Ku Klux Klan, or lynchings, or the anti-Semitism that still barred Jewish families from some American hotels, apartments, and neighborhoods—but the Republican leadership chose not to. Instead, HUAC would use a strategy that Nixon had found effective and focus on Communists, especially those likely to generate publicity for HUAC and its members.

While Nixon was just a freshman member of Congress, and his Republican elders in the party and on HUAC were in control, he was extremely ambitious and a fast learner. His recent campaign had shown he was quick to take advantage of any real or manufactured weakness of an opponent and ruthless in achieving his goals, and he would demonstrate both with his rapid progress as a member of HUAC.

In making the exaggerated threat of domestic Communism their main focus, HUAC and Nixon weren't just trying to localize the justifiable anxiety Americans felt over the Soviet occupation of Eastern Europe. HUAC and Nixon were also recycling the Red Scare tactic of 1919 and 1920, which had helped Republicans keep control of both houses of Congress and the White House throughout the 1920s and until 1932. Those pushing the 1919–1920 Red Scare had used the opportunity to smear Jewish people and labor unions, leading to public statements like those in Henry Ford's overtly anti-Semitic newspaper, *The Dearborn Independent*, and the book of articles reprinted from it, *The International Jew: The World's Foremost Problem*. The resulting dramatic decrease in union membership and power had stymied wage growth and had been a major cause of the "Republican Depression," once—for example—the average Ford worker could no longer afford to buy even the inexpensive car he was making.

Thanks to Franklin Roosevelt, unions had made a tremendous comeback, so in 1947 HUAC looked for easier targets, though still with an anti-Semitic tinge. The Committee focused on Hollywood, where most of the major studio heads—and some of their talent, such as stars, directors, and screenwriters—were Jewish. During the 1930s, especially in the earliest years of the Depression, some of their talent had been members of the Communist Party or had associated with Communists. In fact, a very small number still were (the few highly paid actors and screenwriters who were still party members were called "swimming pool" Communists). In the 1930s the American Socialist Party and the far smaller Communist Party were the only national parties to endorse ending anti-Semitism and giving blacks equal rights. (Due to conservative opposition, even Roosevelt was unable to get an anti-lynching law or effective civil rights law passed during his administration.) However, many Hollywood Communists had become disenchanted with the Communist Party in 1932–1933 after the Hearst newspapers first reported the widespread famine in the Ukraine, and more left after 1939, when Soviet leader Josef Stalin briefly aligned himself with Hitler, before the Nazis invaded the Soviet Union.

When the Soviet Union had been the ally of the United States during World War II, Hollywood had produced three films as part of the war effort that were sympathetic to Russia (*Song of Russia*, *Mission to Moscow*, and *The North Star*). In the jittery postwar atmosphere, studio heads and others involved in those films—and any films deemed to have a liberal slant—would be called to account, along with the few Communist Party members left in the film community.

In October 1947, Richard Nixon was present for the first round of HUAC hearings focusing on Hollywood, which generated sensational publicity. After Jack Warner boasted that his Warner Brothers studio had produced forty-three anti-Nazi films, Nixon pressed Warner for how many anti-Communist movies his studio had made or was making. Warner tried to talk about the "thirty-nine pro-American short subjects" his studio had made, but Nixon then "lectured Warner on his . . . duty to produce films that exposed Communist methods." Historian Stephen Ambrose pointed out that "always unspoken in Nixon's remarks, but always there, was the implication that the Jewish studio owners and the Communist movie writers were involved in a conspiracy."[2]

Nixon remained absent from the remaining hearings until the important vote in November of 1947 on whether to charge ten directors and screenwriters (known as the "Hollywood Ten") for contempt of Congress. As the House of Representatives prepared to vote, the first member to address the House on the matter was Mississippi's

John Rankin, described as "a notorious anti-Semite." Rankin "pointed out that HUAC had discovered that Danny Kaye's real name was David Kaminsky, that Edward G. Robinson's was Emanuel Goldenberg, that Melvyn Douglas's was Melvyn Hesselberg" and implied that only Jewish people "were critical of HUAC." Such attitudes might have been one reason Nixon hadn't been more involved in the hearings, for while he privately made anti-Semitic remarks, to do so in public would not be good for his image.[3]

Richard Nixon was the next speaker, and he pushed for the contempt charges, pointing out the witnesses couldn't take the Fifth Amendment in the hearings, because "it is not a crime to be a member of the Communist Party." (What Nixon didn't mention in his speech was that several months earlier, he had fought *against* making the U.S. Communist Party illegal, apparently preferring to keep the supposedly deadly U.S. organization legal for political reasons.) After Nixon's speech, the committee voted to press the contempt charges, the Hollywood Ten were sent to prison, and the Hollywood blacklist officially began. Ironically, HUAC Chairman J. Parnell Thomas would soon go to the same prison as some of the Hollywood Ten, after being convicted of making his own staff pay him kickbacks.[4]

Nixon's ensuing Red Scare tactics would contribute mightily to the atmosphere that caused the Hollywood blacklist to grow and flourish into the next decade and beyond. The best-remembered film playing in 1947 was the much-loved classic *It's a Wonderful Life*, and one of that film's screenwriters, the uncredited Michael Wilson, would be one of the 324 people officially blacklisted. His credits for later films like *The Bridge on the River Kwai* and *Lawrence of Arabia* would only be added decades later. Even the director of *It's a Wonderful Life*, Frank Capra, would find himself "graylisted" in the coming years, along with performers like Charlie Chaplin, who was eventually forced to leave America. A disproportionate number of those blacklisted or graylisted would be Jewish.*[5]

Nixon became the star of HUAC's next major round of hearings, in 1948, thanks to FBI Director J. Edgar Hoover. Initially, Hoover was

*Those graylisted were often subject to illegal surveillance, rejected security clearances, travel restrictions, or studios were pressured to drop their projects. Actors graylisted to some degree included John Garfield (whose death may have been hastened by his graylisting), Gene Kelly, Vincent Price, and Boris Karloff. Like all of the preceding, many of those graylisted or blacklisted had never been Communist Party members. One could be targeted just for being a film union activist or a "premature anti-Fascist" (opposed to Hitler before the United States entered the war).

wary of Nixon, saying "this fellow Nixon blows hot and cold." However, the different factions in U.S. intelligence had been fighting a turf war that Hoover's FBI lost, and as a result he would find it useful to leak information to Nixon, at first indirectly. That started what became a close relationship between the two men, one that would last until Hoover's death three weeks before the first Watergate break-in.[6]

During World War II and its immediate aftermath, the FBI had handled U.S. intelligence needs in Latin America, while the OSS handled the war-related efforts in Asia and Europe, in cooperation with the intelligence offices of the Army and Navy. But with civil war raging in China, the Soviet "Iron Curtain" dividing Europe, and some major Nazi leaders still unaccounted for, the United States needed a more coordinated effort.

J. Edgar Hoover tried to secure the leading role for the FBI, offering to expand his Latin American agent network. But OSS figures like Allen Dulles wanted an enlarged peacetime version of the OSS. The Joint Chiefs wanted military intelligence to play a leading role. Though Hoover cooperated with the other agencies—for example, helping Army Intelligence with the Soviet cables secretly intercepted under the operation code-named VENONA—he doggedly lobbied Congress and Truman to essentially make him the nation's supreme intelligence and law enforcement czar.

Hoover lost, both with President Truman and in Congress. Truman created the Central Intelligence Group by executive order in January 1946. Only Congress could create a new federal agency, and it did so on September 18, 1947, creating the Central Intelligence Agency. Military intelligence was placated by the requirement that the No. 1 or No. 2 CIA official had to be a military officer. A resentful Hoover, forced to dismantle his Latin American intelligence network, was able to insert language into the CIA's charter limiting the information the FBI had to share with the new CIA. The CIA was also forbidden to mount operations against Americans inside the United States, meaning the FBI essentially retained responsibility for domestic intelligence. Both of those limitations—and constant turf wars between the CIA, the FBI, and military intelligence—would cause problems with intelligence sharing and coordination that would plague Presidents from Truman to JFK to Nixon to George Bush (contributing to intelligence failures uncovered by the 9/11 Commission). Some intelligence coordination problems between the FBI and CIA still persist today.

By the time of the battles that created the CIA, J. Edgar Hoover and the FBI had spent two years trying to get evidence to back up the claims of Elizabeth Bentley, the self-confessed courier of a Communist spy ring in America. If Hoover's FBI agents had been able to find evidence supporting her sensational claims, the resulting publicity could have turned the tide in Hoover's quest to become America's intelligence czar. It would have been a brilliant coup for Hoover, since Bentley had named as Soviet spies more than a hundred people, including Truman officials like Harry Dexter White, the Assistant Treasury Secretary who was taking a leading role in trying to hold accountable German and American industrialists who'd backed Hitler. But Bentley had only hearsay to support her list of names and lacked any evidence. For two years an FBI agent named William Harvey had headed the effort to find such evidence, without success. (Harvey would soon leave the FBI to join the new CIA, where he would become known as one of its best agents.)[7]

In 1948, J. Edgar Hoover didn't have enough evidence to arrest any of the alleged spies named by Bentley. In addition, his rare Congressional loss over the CIA issue showed that he needed more allies in Congress. However, there was a way to meet both of Hoover's needs. It would be too risky, and too obviously political, to go after former Truman officials like Harry Dexter White, then with the International Monetary Fund. But one of the men Bentley had identified as a spy still had name value, and he had been the target of so much suspicion that he had been eased out of government.

Alger Hiss was, in the words of Richard Nixon, a former "assistant to the Assistant Secretary of State and [had served] as one of President Roosevelt's advisers at the Yalta Conference with Stalin and Churchill . . . [he was] one of the primary architects of the United Nations" and was then-President of the Carnegie Endowment. Claims about Hiss possibly being a Soviet spy, though backed by no real evidence, had been raised in 1939, 1942, and twice in 1945. Starting in 1943, those allegations had been passed along first to President Roosevelt and then President Truman, and may be why Hiss was eased out of his government post. Possible references to Hiss would show up in the highly secret VENONA cables intercepted from the Soviets, but that operation was so restricted that even President Truman hadn't been told about it, so they couldn't be used in court or in Congress. (Then, too, some VENONA references seemed to exclude Hiss or were open to interpretation.)

Still, Hoover was well aware of the enormous publicity the HUAC

Hollywood hearings had generated, resulting in prison sentences for directors and writers who'd never really committed a crime. If information about Hiss could be leaked somehow to an ambitious Congressman on HUAC, it might be possible to use Congressional hearings to do the same to some of those named by Bentley. For Hoover, it would help if the HUAC Congressman was an expert at twisting or exaggerating facts to smear opponents. Richard Nixon was the perfect man to help Hoover achieve his goals.

Richard Nixon always tried to make it appear as if he'd simply stumbled on the Alger Hiss case with no help or prodding from Hoover or the FBI. The evidence available now shows a different story. According to Anthony Summers, "within a month of taking office, Nixon" had met "Father John Cronin, a Catholic priest" the FBI used "as a conduit for deliberate leaks." Cronin had written a report that "named Hiss as the most influential Communist in the State Department." Cronin "recalled having shown Nixon that report and having discussed Hiss with him." As Cronin later said, "Nixon was playing with a stacked deck in the Hiss case."[8]

The public record at the time—and the version Nixon stressed in accounts for the rest of his life—showed that Bentley's testimony to HUAC aroused little excitement. But when *Time* magazine editor and former Communist Party member Whittaker Chambers was brought in, to attempt to corroborate Bentley's testimony, Nixon—the most junior member of the Committee—began to assert himself. When Nixon questioned Chambers, he was careful to draw him out about Hiss. Nixon managed to elicit testimony that generated provocative headlines about Hiss in the press. Alger Hiss took the bait and asked to testify to clear himself, and the resulting publicity would permanently vault Nixon into the public spotlight for the rest of his life.

For Nixon, the Hiss matter became "personal" as well as political when Hiss stated in his testimony, "I am a graduate of Harvard Law School—and I believe yours is Whittier?" Nixon's chief investigator, Robert Stripling, said Hiss's remark "absolutely ripped Nixon apart" and "from that moment on [Nixon] could not stand Hiss." Stripling said that Nixon "was no more concerned about whether Hiss was [a Communist] than a billy goat," but it became "a personal thing" and he recalled an "outraged" Nixon in private pounding on a desk as he called Hiss "a son of a bitch."[9]

In public, Nixon was always calm and deliberate, while using the

Hiss hearings and the resulting investigation for maximum political gain. Nixon often used carefully worded statements and questions to imply the Truman administration had taken no action against Hiss and others because it was so riddled with Communists that it was practically Communist itself. In reality, two years of intense investigation by Hoover's FBI hadn't turned up enough evidence to indict, let alone convict, Hiss or any of the other alleged spies accused by Bentley.

But J. Edgar Hoover knew that inflammatory information in the right hands could accomplish in the press what the FBI couldn't do in court. As Nixon's investigation of Hiss heated up, Father Cronin explained that information on Hiss was given to him "by my friends of the FBI . . . who would tell me what they had turned up . . . I told Dick." Soon, Nixon was getting his information directly from the FBI and "was on the phone late at night with one of Hoover's top aides, Louis Nichols, and meeting in his hotel room with former FBI agents." One former FBI agent, Lou Russell, even went to work for HUAC as Nixon's investigator on the case, making the flow of FBI information to Nixon even easier. (Lou Russell would later play a key role for Nixon in Watergate.)[10]

Using Hoover's information, Richard Nixon essentially convicted Hiss in the press, a fact confirmed by Nixon himself more than two decades later, in his White House tapes. Nixon brought up the Hiss case dozens of times to his aides, often when he was discussing some crime of his own. On the July 1, 1971, tape, Nixon declared, "We won the Hiss case in the papers. We did. I had to leak stuff all over the place . . . It was won in the papers . . . I leaked everything . . . I leaked out the testimony. I had Hiss convicted before he ever got to the grand jury." On that same tape, Nixon ordered an illegal break-in at the Brookings Institute think tank, saying he wanted the "Institute's safe cleaned out." As part of Nixon's later September 11, 1972, rant about Hiss, almost three months after the Watergate arrests, Nixon made his famous remark that "the cover-up is what hurts you."[11]

Hiss was later convicted of perjury for supposedly lying both about whether or not he knew Chambers and about spying for the Soviets; he spent the rest of his life trying to clear himself. Was he guilty? Even the release of the Hiss grand jury testimony, many of the VENONA cables, and other information emerging after the fall of the Soviet Union haven't provided a definitive answer. Experts on both sides can point to evidence of Hiss's guilt or innocence. In a way, that vindicates Hoover's decision to use Nixon to essentially convict Hiss in the press, since there wasn't enough solid evidence for the FBI simply to arrest Hiss as a spy. As for Nixon's HUAC files on Hiss, which might answer lingering questions about Hiss's and Nixon's actions, those remain sealed until the year 2026.

HUAC held more hearings in the wake of the Hiss affair. The committee produced no evidence against former Truman official Harry Dexter White, but he died of a heart attack three days after his HUAC testimony. In the furor of the new Red Scare, the Truman administration's efforts to deal with the German and American companies that had supported Hitler's war machine sputtered to a halt. Instead, Truman had to protect himself and the Democrats politically by trying to make sure no Communists were on the federal payroll. In 1947, by executive order, Truman created the Federal Employees Loyalty Program, which resulted in FBI background checks for all two million federal employees. Approximately three hundred would lose their jobs as "security risks," though some were fired only because of the slightest rumor of socialism, past Communism, or homosexuality. Nixon and the Republicans then seized on those terminations as proof the government was full of Communists.

Because of the tremendous press coverage of the Hiss case, Nixon was now a national figure, hitting the campaign trail for Congressional Republicans and their Presidential ticket of Thomas Dewey and Earl Warren. Truman faced opposition in the general election by two factions of his own Democratic Party. Democrats on the far left used the Progressive Party to nominate Henry Wallace for President, while conservative Southern "Dixiecrats" on the far right nominated South Carolina's Strom Thurmond. As a result, the Dewey/Warren ticket looked unbeatable.

Nixon took advantage of the Democratic criticism of Truman and ensured his own Congressional reelection by using a novel strategy that allowed him to win both the Democratic and Republican primaries. Since all the major newspapers in his district supported him, they stopped identifying Nixon as a Republican in their many favorable stories about him during the campaign. Nixon's campaign then had a postcard mailed to "thousands of Democrats" in his district, which began "dear fellow Democrat" and asked the recipient to "re-elect Congressman Nixon," without any mention that Nixon was a

Republican. The strategy worked, Nixon won both the Republican and Democratic primaries, and so was reelected with no opposition.[12]

Nationally, Republicans and Dewey were not so fortunate. Though up to the last minute the polls had shown Dewey winning, Truman used a strategy adopted from Franklin Roosevelt. By 1948, most news organizations used the Republican-preferred term of the "Great Depression" when referring to the severe downturn that had been over for less than a decade. To get his message out, Truman devised a "whistle-stop" campaign across America, in which his train would pull into towns large and small. Speaking from a train car, Truman reminded voters of the "Republican Depression" and condemned the anti-consumer and anti-labor legislation the Republicans had pushed through Congress, sometimes over his veto. Truman's strategy worked, much to the surprise of pundits, pollsters, and Richard Nixon. He was not only reelected, but the Democrats took back both houses of Congress.

After Nixon experienced in 1949 what it was like to be in Congress but out of the majority party, he set his sights on becoming a U.S. Senator in 1950. In the Senate, Nixon could influence decisions and build his reputation whether his party was in the majority or not. World events, and his friend Joe McCarthy (and the help of J. Edgar Hoover), would make his a goal a possibility. Nixon's wealthy backers, and a new standard of smears in Nixon's first Senate campaign, would make it a reality.

The average American's fears of Communist expansion began to spike in the fall of 1949, when Mao Zedong's Communist revolution chased the corrupt dictatorship of Chiang Kai-shek to the island of Taiwan. In September of that year, "Truman announced that the Russians had exploded an atomic bomb." Four months later, in January 1950, former Los Alamos scientist Klaus Fuchs was arrested in England for passing atomic secrets to the Russians. Several months later, authorities broke another Soviet atomic spy ring, which soon led to the arrests of Julius and Ethel Rosenberg. Also in 1950, Communist North Korea, backed by China and the Soviet Union, crossed the dividing line of the thirty-eighth parallel to attack South Korea.[13]

In a February 1950 speech to a small "Women's Club in Wheeling, West Virginia," Richard Nixon's good friend Senator Joe McCarthy ignited a political firestorm by "claiming the State Department was riddled with Communists." However, some journalists have pointed out that several parts of McCarthy's speech "were lifted virtually verbatim from a speech on Hiss made in the House two weeks earlier by Richard Nixon." McCarthy's charges against the Truman administration grew and constantly changed, and he was soon being fed information by Hoover's FBI. When joined with the still-unfolding Hiss saga, McCarthy's charges—along with Nixon's interpretation of world events (like denouncing how Truman and traitors in the State Department "lost" China to the "Reds")—gave Nixon the weapons he needed in his fight to become a California Senator.[14]

Not all Republicans endorsed the "fear, ignorance, bigotry, and smear" tactics used by Nixon and McCarthy. Maine Republican Senator Margaret Chase Smith denounced them, using that exact phrase—which abbreviates to the word "fibs," essentially calling them liars. But she was one of the few liberal or moderate Republicans who tried to be a voice of reason, and after she lost committee assignments, almost no other Republicans dared to oppose the McCarthy/Nixon Red Scare tidal wave for years.[15]

Nixon and his close aide Murray Chotiner raised at least $1.6 million for his 1950 Senate campaign, though a precise count is impossible, since all of the expense records were destroyed after the election. His main backers were once more the large corporations, including "power brokers in the oil business [since] Nixon was pushing for the oil policy that" would make them more money, and this included Texas "oil tycoons . . . Clint Murchison and Sid Richardson." Other contributors included "big industry, real estate, and banking," as well as billionaire Howard Hughes. Mickey Cohen, whose position in organized crime in Southern California had outlived his mentor Bugsy Siegel, admitted that Chotiner asked him to raise money for Nixon. Cohen raised $75,000 ($660,000 in today's dollars) in one night at "the Banquet Room in the Hollywood Knickerbocker Hotel." Cohen's contributors were mainly his bookies and a group of Mafia leaders, including Los Angeles mob boss Jack Dragna (Johnny Rosselli's ally) and a representative of Meyer Lansky. According to Mickey Cohen, Nixon actually gave a brief "thank-you" speech to his group of mobsters, though Cohen said "the guy that really" did most of "of the speaking was Murray Chotiner," whose firm represented so many of his bookies.[16]

Richard Nixon topped his previous campaign excesses in his

Senate race against his Democratic opponent, Congresswoman Helen Gahagan Douglas. Representative Douglas was known for wanting to "rein in big business, [especially] the oil industry," and she was the wife of Jewish actor Melvyn Douglas. In Congress, Representative Douglas had opposed Nixon on the Hollywood Ten contempt charges even before her husband had been the target of an anti-Semitic smear by one of Nixon's fellow HUAC members. Now, Nixon continued the anti-Semitic attacks, though carefully. When he would call her "Helen Hesselberg"—using her husband's birth surname, which neither she nor her husband ever used—Nixon would quickly "correct himself, as though it had been an unintentional slip." Nixon used a massive anonymous phone call campaign to raise "Douglas's Jewish connection" and ask voters, "Did you know Helen Douglas is a Communist?" In reality, Douglas was "outspokenly anti-Communist," but Nixon and his supporters would dub her the "Pink Lady" and hammer the smear against her repeatedly, in a "half-million . . . leaflets printed on pink paper."[17]

Nixon used a variety of "dirty tricks" in the campaign, including some that foreshadowed his later tactics as President. As documented by Summers, Nixon made sure that Douglas faced "flying squads of pickets . . . heckling her at every stop." Once Nixon's operatives drenched Douglas with water during a college appearance, and other times they "pelted [her] with red ink and even stones." That left Douglas no choice but to start "traveling with bodyguards," draining her already meager campaign funds. It was a prudent decision, since her "San Diego organizer was forced off the road" in one attack.[18]

Representative Douglas couldn't even afford "to pay printers for brochures" to replace the many "thousands" that Nixon's operatives "dumped." But Nixon's people filled the void by distributing "phony Douglas [flyers] purporting to have been issued by 'the Communist League of Negro Women.'" As for Nixon's own involvement in the questionable tactics, Murray Chotiner would later say that Nixon was like "a general who demanded absolute precision and carefully planned coordination in every move." Another campaign aide, Tom Dixon, confirmed that "Nixon knew everything that was going on."[19]

Nixon had learned much about dealing with the press from the Hiss hearings, and he secured the support of three-fourths of the state's major newspapers. Their help went beyond just endorsing Nixon. For example, the *Los Angeles Times* didn't "run a single picture of Douglas during the campaign," those controlled by "William Randolph Hearst [featured] pro-Nixon articles," and the *Los Angeles Daily News* had been the first to call Douglas the "Pink Lady."

Unlike his crusade against Hiss, Nixon's attacks on Douglas weren't personal for him. Though Nixon would in public make crude remarks like "she was pink down to her underpants" and in private insinuate that "she had slept with President Truman," his own feelings about Douglas were quite different. Late in the campaign, after drinks with a columnist, Nixon admitted that "he hated having to end Helen Douglas's career because he admired her so much." But the thirty-seven-year-old Nixon desperately wanted to be a Senator, because he said "the House offered too slow a road to leadership and I went for broke."[20]

Richard Nixon's 1950 smears against Douglas were even more effective than the ones he used four years earlier against Voorhis, and Nixon won his Senate seat decisively. On the other hand, his tactics also won him the nickname "Tricky Dick" that would remain for the rest of his life. Nixon's backers were no doubt especially happy with their investment once it was clear that Republicans had regained control of the Senate. Though the House remained nominally in Democratic hands, the presence of so many conservative Southern Democrats meant that Republicans could align with them to block any truly progressive legislation.[21]

Just as Nixon had wanted a "slush fund" from his backers to supplement his Congressional salary, he apparently needed even more money now that he was going to be a U.S. Senator. Since his campaign spent $1.6 million to make him a Senator, Nixon may have felt entitled to some small portion of that, especially since he had consistently delivered both the votes and the publicity his well-funded backers wanted. The ambitious Nixon finally had some degree of power, giving him access to the wealthy and powerful on a national scale. Yet he was essentially just serving his backers, and not making enough to live anything like a lavish lifestyle.

So, "within a week of Nixon's election to the Senate," a special "Trust Fund"—more like a slush fund—was set up to help give Nixon the life he wanted and to help with his political future. Murray Chotiner later "admitted that the fund had been his idea," to get "the money Nixon needed to advance his career." The known contributors were, in the later words of *The New York Times*, a "Who's Who of wealthy and influential southern California business figures." They included major "millionaires . . . from the world of real estate . . . oil magnates, and manufacturers."[22]

One contributor later said that he donated funds after being told that "the Nixons needed a larger home and were 'so poor they haven't got a maid.'" Nixon soon bought a $41,000 home, with a down payment of $21,000, and was able to hire both "an interior decorator to furnish it in style" and his first "full-time maid." In a candid moment, Nixon later essentially admitted that the Fund provided a significant part of "the down payment."[23]

In return, all of the contributors generally benefited from Nixon's anti-consumer, anti-union, pro-big-business approach—but some of them quickly received very specific help from Senator Nixon. For example, early in Nixon's Senate term he "introduced a bill designed to allow precisely the sort of oil exploration" two oilmen contributors wanted; he voted to keep out imported dairy products as requested by a dairy industry figure; and Nixon spoke out against public housing to help a group of "real estate brokers." With such quick results, the initial Trust Fund proved so successful that two additional slush funds were created, both more secretive than the first.[24]

As 1950 drew to a close, the Red Scare stoked by Nixon and his friend McCarthy continued to inflame the country, even as President Truman and thousands of American troops were fighting a very real Communist menace in Korea. When General MacArthur had American troops in Korea push north—well past the thirty-eighth parallel, almost to the Yalu River (North Korea's border with China)—he minimized to Truman any significant risk that the Chinese would enter the war. When hundreds of thousands of Chinese troops poured across the frozen Yalu to attack the U.S. forces, the Americans took heavy casualties and fell into full retreat. MacArthur's misjudgment and his actions, bordering on insubordination, meant that the Korean War would not be the quick or easy fight against Communist aggression that some had originally envisioned.

Domestically, the Communist Party USA, already tiny at the start of new Red Scare, continued to shrink. However, mindful of Nixon's earlier admonition to Jack Warner, Hollywood studio heads made plans to hype fears of widespread domestic subversion in typical American towns with a slate of films like *I Was a Communist for the FBI*. To twenty-first-century audiences and historians the exaggerated domestic threat presented in those films seems almost laughable, but the fears and anxiety they produced fed the political careers of Nixon and his friend Joe McCarthy.

However, in 1950 Democrats were trying to focus attention on a very real domestic menace: organized crime. There had been some Mafia prosecutions under Truman by the Justice Department, even though J. Edgar Hoover maintained that the Mafia didn't exist. In response to the growing problem, Democratic Tennessee Senator Estes Kefauver chaired the first nationwide hearings looking into organized crime, especially the Mafia. Because Kefauver went after high-profile, colorful witnesses like America's top Mafia chief Frank Costello, the hearings quickly captured the attention of the emerging medium of television. Soon, Americans were watching televised coverage that exposed the true extent of the Mafia for the first time. As the Kefauver hearings revealed, organized crime was a truly national problem, involving not just illegal gambling and loan sharking, but public corruption, murders, and beatings. There was also a growing narcotics problem in the United States, due to the growing power of the French Connection heroin network, organized in America by the Trafficante Mafia family in Tampa. That pipeline had started to boom after the new CIA had used heroin mobsters in Marseilles, France, to battle striking workers in the French port.[25]

One of Kefauver's witnesses was Los Angeles Mafia don Johnny Rosselli, now out of prison—due to a bribe. Now the national spotlight damaged Rosselli's attempts to reestablish his previous glamorous Hollywood lifestyle. Once, Rosselli had hobnobbed with studio heads and had helped them control a key union. Now, court records show that while on parole Rosselli was only able to help produce—being paid, but getting no screen credit—three independent, low-budget film noir B-movies: *Canon City*, *T-Men*, and *He Walked by Night*.*[26]

Even so, Johnny Rosselli was still a Mafia force in Los Angeles, close to entertainers ranging from actor Peter Lawford to singing stars Dean Martin and Frank Sinatra. By the early 1950s, studios considered Sinatra a has-been, with one of his films so bad it was held back from release for three years. As documented by Rosselli's biographers, the

* *He Walked by Night* involved a crazed ex-serviceman, a killer who hides his rifle by wrapping it in a blanket, and then uses a pistol to shoot a patrolman on a lonely street—plot points Rosselli would later use in real life. After the Kefauver hearings, Rosselli could only get backing for another B-movie, the Red Scare film *Invasion USA*.

Mafia don helped reignite Sinatra's career by getting his old friend Harry Cohn of Columbia Pictures to give Sinatra a serious dramatic role in the prestigious film *From Here to Eternity*. Sinatra received an Academy Award for Best Supporting Actor and soon enjoyed a revitalized career as a movie star, recording artist, and Las Vegas headliner.[27]

Rosselli also began spending more time in Las Vegas, representing the interests of the Chicago Mafia as he did in Los Angeles. But Las Vegas in the early 1950s was not yet the glamorous "Rat Pack" paradise it would become by the early 1960s for Rosselli's friends Sinatra, Martin, and Lawford. Prior to the emergence of Las Vegas as America's exclusive casino mecca, Havana, Cuba, would become the main center for well-heeled Americans who wanted to gamble in the 1950s.

In 1952, Senator Richard Nixon wrote to the State Department on behalf of a California constituent who felt he had been swindled out of $4,200 in a Havana casino. At least, that was the simple story reported by most American newspapers. The *St. Louis Post-Dispatch* was the only newspaper to really investigate the matter, and they documented that Nixon was much more deeply involved. More recent research into the affair shows that Nixon's intervention inadvertently increased the American Mafia's control of gambling in Cuba.[28]

According to five witnesses interviewed in 1952 by the *St. Louis Post-Dispatch*, Richard Nixon—and his new best friend, Bebe Rebozo—had been with the California man (a Nixon campaign aide) when he lost money at the Cuban casino. Nixon himself confirmed as much to the *St. Louis Post-Dispatch* reporter, who said Nixon's main concern was making it clear that Nixon and his friends didn't have women with them at the casino. Nixon had been going to Cuba since 1940 and had liked Havana, so why didn't he just admit he'd been at the casino during the incident? The most obvious explanation is that going to a shady mob-run casino in Havana wouldn't fit with the clean-cut, all-American public image that Senator Nixon had so carefully cultivated.[29]

Two important developments came out of Nixon's 1952 Cuba incident. First, Nixon played an indirect role in causing the Mafia to upgrade their Havana gambling holdings. Nixon was good at getting the type of publicity he wanted in the 1950s, and other newspapers didn't report or follow up on the *St. Louis Post-Dispatch*'s stories about Nixon's presence in the Cuban casino, focusing instead on the image of Havana casinos as shady operations. That was a problem for both the Mafia and Cuban dictator Fulgencio Batista, who had recently overthrown Cuban President Carlos Prio (who'd had small-time Mafia ties). To improve both the management and the image of Havana's casinos, and to attract a steady stream of wealthy U.S. patrons, Batista arranged for Meyer Lansky and his Mafia allies—such as Tampa godfather Santo Trafficante—to control the casinos in Cuba. The Mafia would build or refurbish hotels and casinos, run relatively honest games, and give a portion of their profits to Batista. Nixon's intervention in the 1952 Cuba affair thus inadvertently gave the Mafia complete control of Cuban gambling. That led to even more corruption in Batista's regime, which became increasingly brutal in its efforts to retain power, triggering a cycle of events that would eventually lead to revolution for the island nation.[30]

The second important development was that the incident showed Nixon that his friend Bebe Rebozo could be trusted not to talk, something that drew the two men even closer together. As former Nixon aide William Safire later said, "Bebe is never going to blab." Born Charles Gregory Rebozo in Tampa, Florida, of Cuban immigrant parents, Bebe was the same age as Nixon. The men had met the previous year on an outing aboard Rebozo's yacht. It took a second meeting before Rebozo warmed up to Nixon, but the two quickly became close friends.[31]

Rebozo was divorced, polished, and on the surface, a successful Miami businessman. He was a real estate speculator who also owned "a self-service laundry chain [and] two finance companies, at a time when Florida law permitted the charging of exorbitant interest." However, *Newsday* and Anthony Summers compiled extensive information showing that "organized crime figures were a presence in Rebozo's real estate and banking ventures." In fact, "a former FBI agent who specialized in organized crime in" Miami said that Rebozo was a "non-member associate of organized crime figures." A former OSS official said that "Rebozo was involved in [Meyer] Lansky's gambling [near] Miami [and] the Miami Police said [Rebozo] was very close to Meyer."[32]

"The really close friendship between Nixon and Rebozo began in Cuba," according to an IRS investigator. The investigator said that in one instance, at Meyer Lansky's Hotel Nacional "in the early fifties . . .

Nixon was gambling pretty heavily [and] lost thousands of dollars . . . and Bebe picked up the marker on it." The former OSS official discovered that "when Nixon stayed at the Hotel Nacional, which Lansky owned, they comped the whole deal." The Lansky lieutenant who signed for Nixon's comp, Vincent "Jimmy Blue Eyes" Alo, confirmed that Nixon knew Lansky, saying "he met him in Havana, in the old days."[33]

After their 1952 Cuban trip, the friendship of Richard Nixon and Bebe Rebozo would continue to grow with each passing year, with Nixon often spending much time with Rebozo alone on his yacht. The men would either talk or Nixon would sit by himself, plotting his political strategy on a legal pad.[34]

Richard Nixon had more power and influence in the Senate than he'd had in his last Congressional term, but his party was still out of the majority—and Nixon was extremely ambitious. Not one to shy away from a challenge, the freshman Senator set his sights on the Vice Presidential slot of the 1952 Republican ticket. Nixon's goal was not the long shot it might seem, since his Red Scare and do-anything-to-win reputation would be a good contrast with the moderate at the top of the ticket.

In 1952 the Republicans were able to convince General Dwight Eisenhower—revered for World War II's D-Day and recently the Allied Commander in Europe—to run for President as a Republican. Eisenhower seemed an excellent choice, since he had a squeaky clean public image. In fact, Eisenhower had a hidden history of his own—two scandals in his past, both concerning D-Day—but neither would be exposed for decades, so they weren't factors in the election.*[35]

Eisenhower was far more moderate than most of the official Republican positions in 1952, and some questioned why he would even run as a Republican (he was courted by some Democrats, since many of his views were more in sync with their party). Still, "Ike" was welcomed as the Republican standard-bearer because he gave the party a good chance of winning. GOP power brokers knew that by adding Nixon to the ticket as Vice President, they could maintain their conservative

*They were Eisenhower's affair with his aide Kate Sommersby prior to the D-Day invasion, and the covered-up, failed practice landing for D-Day off the English coast code-named Operation Tiger. On April 28, 1944, that disaster resulted in the deaths of 946 American servicemen, including 308 killed by friendly fire. More details about each can be found in the endnote for the above paragraph.

base of voters and major funders, while using Eisenhower to appeal to independents and some Democrats. Plus, Nixon had shown he was willing to use incendiary campaign rhetoric that Eisenhower would never use.

Eisenhower remained above much of the political fray in 1952, leaving Richard Nixon to smear the Democratic challengers, liberal Illinois Senator Adlai Stevenson for President and conservative Senator John Sparkman of Alabama for Vice President. Stephen Ambrose wrote that Nixon was true to form, claiming that liberals like Stevenson "were plotting . . . to turn the United States over to Moscow's rule." Nixon said in one newspaper interview that "there's one difference between the Reds and Pinks. The Pinks"—referring to Stevenson—"want to socialize America. The Reds want to socialize the world and make Moscow the world capital." Nixon said a vote to make Stevenson President would be the "ultimate national suicide" and derided him as "a weakling" tied to "mobsters, gangsters, and remnants of the old Capone gang." Stevenson was not in fact tied to the Mafia (as were Nixon and Rebozo), and he tried to take the high road in the campaign, to little success.[36]

Everything was going well for Nixon in the 1952 campaign—until accusations about one of his slush funds brought him to the brink of disaster, staved off only by what came to be known as his "Checkers Speech." On September 18, 1952, the front page of the *New York Post* blared "SECRET NIXON FUND," and the story revealed that a "secret rich men's trust fund keeps Nixon in style far beyond his salary." The article had only very general details about just one of Nixon's three slush funds, the "Trust Fund" noted earlier. Even so, it ignited a firestorm of controversy, and Nixon faced his first real crisis in any campaign.[37]

Initial attempts to explain the $18,000 slush fund claimed it was "to compensate for Nixon's 'personal lack of funds'" and was used only for things like "office expenses . . . Christmas cards . . . radio and television broadcasts, airfares, and hotel costs." But that didn't quiet the growing storm, especially as new details continued to emerge. Eisenhower didn't rush to Nixon's aid and in fact kept his distance from Nixon, both in public and in his private discussions with Republican power brokers like Thomas Dewey. Eisenhower appeared ready to jettison Nixon as his running mate and was simply looking for a good way to do it.[38]

In reading recent, objective accounts of the incident, it's interesting how much political hardball Nixon played with Eisenhower and his advisors. Still, it's now clear that Nixon really had no choice. He might have been able to explain the Trust Fund, but the problem was that more secret funds existed, and they dated back to the start of his political life. Simply saying he was going to step off the ticket to avoid hurting Eisenhower wasn't an option. Nixon had made too many enemies, and stepping aside now could provoke his enemies to start digging into his past, which might uncover his longtime use of illegal money. That could force him to resign from the Senate or potentially send him to prison, like his original HUAC Chairman.[39]

Nixon and his trusted aide Murray Chotiner focused on the idea of Nixon giving a speech to the American people, one that drew on an unlikely source: Franklin Roosevelt. During World War II, Roosevelt had faced frequent criticism from Republicans in Congress, including an incident involving his dog, Fala. In response, Roosevelt had delivered a successful speech evoking Fala, and scolding Republicans for sinking so low as to drag his family's dog into politics. Nixon would use his own dog, Checkers—and other homilies—to divert attention from the slush fund that had been uncovered.[40]

Richard Nixon's prime-time televised speech was the first big political event most Americans had seen on television, though many still only heard it on the radio. Nixon used all of his debating and acting skills, together with everything he'd learned about politics. The "Checkers Speech" was a smashing success for Nixon. Eisenhower finally embraced his Vice President publicly, and they were victorious in November, with the Republicans regaining control of the Senate and the House.

In just over five years, Richard Nixon had incredibly propelled himself from Congressman to Senator to Vice President of the United States. He was more than living up to all the potential he'd shown in high school and college and law school, vindicating his wife Pat's early faith in him. Yet he'd achieved those goals by running three of the dirtiest campaigns in recent memory and by taking money—legally and illegally—from corporate titans and the Mafia. He had also learned how to benefit from intelligence leaked to him by the FBI and how to effectively leak to the press. Even when one of his slush funds had been uncovered, Nixon had escaped relatively unscathed, and that would help to set a pattern for his Vice Presidency.

CHAPTER 4

Vice President Richard Nixon: The First Five Years

Richard Nixon assumed the Vice Presidency in 1953, and the next five years proved crucial for his own political development and that of the country. Nixon's business and political dealings became more complex and sophisticated during that time, sometimes crossing the line into criminal conduct. In addition, several of the crises and conflicts that America would still be struggling with decades later actually began during Nixon's terms as Vice President. Strikingly, during his first five years in office, Nixon began dealing with several men who would later play key roles in Watergate.

As Vice President, Nixon occasionally presided over the U.S. Senate, which had three new members who would play important roles in his future. Freshman Senator John F. Kennedy would not be a major force in politics for the first few years of his term, but before its end he would emerge as the Democrats' fastest-rising star and a challenge to Nixon. On the Republican side, Arizona's new Senator Barry Goldwater would take several more years to parlay an unlikely combination of far-right conservatism and a love of Las Vegas partying into becoming yet another Nixon challenger. Also important for the new Vice President, Connecticut's freshman Republican Senator Prescott Bush began a political dynasty that would usually support Nixon.

The Red Scare hysteria Nixon had helped start, fed by his recent campaign and stoked by his friend Senator Joseph McCarthy, peaked in 1953 and early 1954. A popular TV program, *I Led Three Lives*—based on a real deep-cover FBI asset, pretending to be a Communist—showed how seemingly average Americans were really Soviet agents.

Communist and Russian villains populated the movies, even as the Hollywood blacklist took a grim toll of death, suicide, and career destruction for those blacklisted or graylisted.*

Now that Nixon had no need to live up to his excessive campaign rhetoric—and no doubt also to placate the much more moderate President Eisenhower—the new Vice President largely left fanning the flames of the Red Scare to Senator McCarthy. As had been the case from the start of McCarthy's smears, his information continued to come primarily from FBI Director J. Edgar Hoover. For reasons still unexplained, Hoover had allowed a longtime Soviet spy at the U.S. nuclear laboratories at Los Alamos—Theodore Hall—to leave the country without being arrested or even exposed. Why Hall wasn't prosecuted like the Rosenbergs or outed to a member of Congress like Hiss was remains unclear. Perhaps Hoover saw no political advantage to be gained in going after Hall.[1]

Instead, J. Edgar Hoover tried to use Senator McCarthy to settle old scores from the intelligence war Hoover had lost to Allen Dulles and Army Intelligence. Hoover began leaking information to McCarthy smearing both the CIA and the Army. Soon after Nixon and Eisenhower took office, Allen Dulles became the first civilian CIA Director. This was a significant development in the history of the CIA, since the previous four CIA Directors had been military men, Generals or Admirals. At the same time, Allen's brother, John Foster Dulles, was appointed Secretary of State. Vice President Nixon was now a central figure among several spheres of power: still cordial with his old patron Allen Dulles, increasingly close to Hoover, and good friends with McCarthy. Nixon had the perfect position to mediate with McCarthy and keep the CIA out of the spotlight.[2]

However, that still left the Army feeling heat from McCarthy at a time when much of the country—including the mainstream news media—seemed afraid of the Senator, despite his increasingly wild charges and erratic behavior. (Edward R. Murrow was one of the only major journalists willing to take on McCarthy, as later depicted in the

*Some of those blacklisted or graylisted, like TV star Philip Loeb, committed suicide. Many blacklisted directors, screenwriters, and actors never worked again, and others (such as Zero Mostel and Lee Grant) didn't work in U.S. films again until the late 1960s or early 1970s, when Nixon was President. Shortly before John Wayne's death, the conservative actor (who won an Oscar for *True Grit*, scripted by a formerly blacklisted writer) admitted the Hollywood blacklist had simply been a way to "get the liberals."

film *Good Night, and Good Luck.*) Even President Eisenhower refused to directly rein in or take on McCarthy, apparently for fear of offending his supporters. On the other hand, Nixon, with more political experience and savvy than the President, did start to distance himself from his old friend.

Perhaps Nixon knew that J. Edgar Hoover was playing a dangerous game by feeding information to McCarthy, since many historians have observed that by then McCarthy's alcoholism was taking an increasing toll. McCarthy also had another, more severe problem, one that wasn't reported for years: an addiction to morphine, as eventually revealed by Harry Anslinger, the Commissioner of the Bureau of Narcotics for the Eisenhower-Nixon administration.[3]

In 1954, Senator McCarthy imploded in front of a national television audience during hearings designed to smear the Army. McCarthy was investigating supposed Army retribution against the close friend of McCarthy's aide, the notorious right-wing attorney Roy Cohn. The televised stinging chastisement of McCarthy by Army General Counsel Joseph Welch marked the beginning of the end for the Red-baiting Senator. After the Republicans lost both houses of Congress in the November 1954 election, McCarthy was overwhelmingly "condemned" in a vote by the Senate, though Republican Senators were evenly split. When three years later McCarthy died from alcohol-related hepatitis, Nixon and his wife Pat, along with Roy Cohn, were the only notables who attended the funeral of the man who had once terrorized an entire nation.[4]

However, Nixon had distanced himself only from McCarthy, not the Red Scare in general, which remained a major force for the rest of the 1950s. Writers such as Dashiell Hammett and Arthur Miller, artists like Rockwell Kent, and performers including Pete Seeger and Paul Robeson fell prey to varying degrees of prosecution and persecution, blacklisting and graylisting.* Across America, the climate of suspicion and fear affected thousands of average Americans as well.

Richard Nixon boasted that during his first year in office, 2,400 federal employees were fired essentially for being security risks—though that could include private matters like being gay or simply being accused of being gay. Fear of Communism meant that pri-

* Black singer and actor Paul Robeson was blacklisted not just from Hollywood, but from any public performance, yet he was not allowed to leave the United States—even though he'd committed no crime.

vate and public organizations imposed "loyalty oaths" on their employees. The Red Scare caused thousands of ordinary Americans to be fired or forced to resign from military-related industries, universities, public school systems, and state and local governments. Their dismissal could be for something as minor as having once supported a liberal cause or being a member of an organization that supported the same cause (like opposition to lynching) as a group named by conservatives as a "Communist-front organization." Private industry, especially companies with government contracts, also tried to purge its ranks of such potential "subversives." A thriving industry of private investigations developed, often employing former FBI agents who worked for those companies to identify suspected "Reds," but who could also help to "clear" someone caught up in the Red Scare hysteria.

For a brief time in 1954, three such investigators shared offices in Washington, D.C. One was Carmine Bellino, later the first General Counsel of the Senate Watergate Committee. Bellino was close to Joe Kennedy and would soon abandon investigating alleged Communists to work as a Senate investigator for Robert Kennedy. Another of the three investigators was Guy Banister, the hard-drinking former FBI Special Agent in Charge for Chicago. He would soon go to New Orleans, where he would work on a sensitive CIA operation involving Cuba for the Eisenhower-Nixon administration.

The last of the three was Robert Maheu, a former FBI agent who was doing increasing amounts of work for reclusive billionaire Howard Hughes. In 1954, Maheu also performed jobs for the CIA and for Richard Nixon. Maheu's activities for Nixon would foreshadow both the Watergate scandal and Maheu's role in key events leading to the scandal.

Vice President Nixon took a special interest in foreign affairs, one of the few subjects on which Eisenhower consulted him. Minutes from a 1954 National Security Council meeting show that Nixon heard Greek shipping tycoon Aristotle Onassis was close to securing a deal for exclusive rights to transport Saudi Arabian oil. Eisenhower ordered an operation "to break" Onassis, and Nixon became Ike's point man for the anti-Onassis operation.[5]

In 1954, investigator Robert Maheu met with Richard Nixon, and was contracted for the Onassis operation. Nixon said it was a matter of "national security," so he would deny any role "if anything should go wrong." Working out of Republican offices in New York City, Robert Maheu and his operatives broke into Onassis's main office and tapped the telephones. They also planted false anti-Onassis smears in the press, filed multiple frivolous lawsuits, and lied to the King of Saudi Arabia about Onassis. Foreshadowing another foreign affairs operation Maheu would take on for Richard Nixon, the Vice President told Maheu, "if it turns out we have to kill the bastard, just don't do it on American soil." The Nixon-Maheu operation successfully led the Saudi King to terminate the contract with Onassis. Nixon had learned that a national security justification could be used to cover and justify what would otherwise be criminal behavior—a tactic he would continue to use in the future.

President Eisenhower didn't fully trust Nixon and wasn't close to him, but foreign affairs was the one area where Eisenhower allowed Nixon to have even a small role. Nixon would have an impact—often negative—in foreign relations in the 1950s, and his actions would also affect succeeding decades.[6]

In July 1953, President Eisenhower had approved an armistice to end the Korean War (still in place today), a solution opposed by Nixon, who wanted a much broader, all-out war to continue. Nixon visited the U.S.-backed dictator of South Korea, but he didn't push for real democracy there, and the dictator—and his successors—would hold sway until after Nixon's Presidency.

In 1953, Nixon made his first trip to Vietnam, a country that would occupy much of his attention after he became President. It was then nominally under French control, though the French faced escalating attacks by anti-colonial Communist rebels. Nixon was soon pressing Eisenhower to send U.S. combat forces to aid the French. Eisenhower rejected his pleas, and like Korea, Vietnam would be partitioned, with a Communist-controlled north and a French- and U.S.-backed government (essentially a corrupt dictatorship) in the south. Nixon pressed for the United States to send military "advisors" to help South Vietnam's dictator stay in power, and this time he succeeded. Those "advisors" Nixon wanted were soon the first U.S. casualties in Vietnam, and their role and number (and casualties) would continue to grow until March 1965, when President Lyndon B. Johnson would send the first U.S. combat troops to Vietnam.[7]

Nixon's and Eisenhower's large corporate contributors often

seemed to prefer predictable U.S.-backed dictatorships (as long as their leaders professed to be anti-Communist) to unpredictable elected democracies. With the approval of Eisenhower and Nixon, CIA Director Allen Dulles and Secretary of State John Foster Dulles helped stage a CIA-backed coup against the elected government of Iran, triggering a chain of dictatorship and revolution that still affects the country today. Just a few months after the CIA's coup, Nixon visited the new U.S.-backed dictator of Iran, Mohammad Reza Pahlavi, later proclaimed as the "Shah of Iran." The trip marked the beginning of a close relationship between Nixon and the Shah that would eventually result in the Shah's funneling "more than one million dollars" in illegal campaign contributions to Nixon.[8]

In 1954, America's United Fruit Company became increasingly concerned about the progressive democratic government of President Jacobo Árbenz in Guatemala. United Fruit hired the father of American propaganda, Edward Bernays, to mount a massive PR campaign that convinced Eisenhower and Nixon to approve a CIA plan—optimistically code-named PB/SUCCESS—to overthrow Árbenz. The American news media would portray the operation as a nearly bloodless coup, primarily accomplished by propaganda and what today would be called psyops (psychological operations).

CIA officer E. Howard Hunt played a major role in the CIA's Guatemala coup. The son of an "influential Republican leader" and "lobbyist," Hunt graduated from Brown University. During World War II he joined the Navy, then used his father's business friendship with William Donovan to join Donovan's wartime intelligence agency, the OSS. A promising writer, Hunt published five novels by 1950 and won a Guggenheim Fellowship. But he was also extremely conservative, and joined the CIA in 1949 to fight the "Red" menace. When he happened to meet Congressman Nixon in a restaurant, Hunt praised his pursuit of Hiss and the two men wound up talking over dinner for an hour. Hunt was assigned to the Mexico City CIA station in the early 1950s, where he supervised a young agent named William F. Buckley, who became his lifelong friend.* While in Mexico City, Hunt oversaw his first surreptitious break-in, of the Guatemalan embassy—something he would still be doing during the Watergate era—which helped lead to Hunt's work on the CIA's Guatemala coup in 1954.[9]

*Buckley later gained fame as the publisher of the *National Review* and host of the PBS show *Firing Line*.

While working on the coup plan, the thirty-six-year-old Hunt began a long friendship with CIA agent David Atlee Phillips, four years his junior. Phillips's CIA career would often overlap Hunt's at key times. A native of Forth Worth, Phillips had joined the CIA when he was a journalist in Chile (where he would later help President Nixon stage a coup). Phillips also had talent as a writer, but instead of novels he focused on public relations copy.[10]

The gist of the CIA's Guatemala plan was to use publicity and psyops to make it appear that the CIA-backed dictator-in-waiting, Castillo Armas, commanded a much larger force than he really did. The propaganda also falsely claimed heavy popular support for Armas and his rebel forces, and fed the press exaggerated accounts of his progress. The plan worked, and President Árbenz fled the country.

That was the way the CIA's 1954 Guatemala coup has generally been presented, as a mostly nonviolent operation that used smoke and mirrors to achieve regime change. However, the plan involved much more. We now know that the CIA also targeted for assassination Guatemalan nationals like Árbenz supporters and pro-democracy activists. The CIA still maintains that none of those assassinations were carried out and that casualties during the coup were minimal. However, as of 2011, the CIA has refused to release the names of their assassination targets, making it impossible to learn if any of those people were killed (or went missing) during or soon after the coup. The assassination aspect of the coup is important in terms of the future CIA assignments of Hunt and Phillips, since both would later be involved in Nixon-linked plots to assassinate Fidel Castro.

In addition, the United States had a far stronger hand in the coup than just the PR and propaganda produced by Hunt and Phillips. At one point during the operation, CIA Director Dulles told President Eisenhower that unless he approved U.S. air support, the coup's "chances were about zero." In response, Ike "authorized two fighters to be sent into the battle." The U.S. Navy also dispatched "five amphibious assault ships [and an] aircraft carrier" to the region to pressure Guatemala's elected President and his government.[11]

The 1954 Guatemala coup was successful for the Eisenhower-Nixon administration, especially for the CIA. It also gave a boost to the Agency careers of E. Howard Hunt and David Atlee Phillips. Richard Nixon was present at the White House's post-coup briefing delivered by Phillips and CIA Director Allen Dulles, and Nixon would later personally congratulate Hunt.

The Guatemalan people weren't so lucky. The 1954 U.S.-backed coup led to a civil war that lasted forty years and cost two hundred thousand civilian lives. Árbenz and his family escaped with their lives, as did a young supporter of Árbenz, an Argentine doctor named Ernesto "Che" Guevara. For Guevara, the coup would mark a turning point, and he would soon take a more active role in opposing another U.S.-backed dictator.[12]

As for Richard Nixon, he soon made an official trip to the region, including a stop in Guatemala to praise the new U.S.-backed dictator, Castillo Armas. He also visited, and was well received by, several other U.S.-backed dictators in Latin America, including Cuba's General Batista, Nicaragua's Anastasio Somoza, and the Dominican Republic's Rafael Trujillo, all known for their brutal reputations.[13]

In 1955, President Eisenhower suffered a moderately severe heart attack that sidelined him for almost three months, leaving Vice President Nixon in a unique position. At times, he was almost an acting President, while at other times, his ambition and political gamesmanship got the better of him. It left a recovering Eisenhower doubting not just whether his Vice President would ever be Presidential material, but whether he could even tolerate having Nixon on the ticket for the 1956 election. Eisenhower's concerns alarmed Nixon and got the attention of other prominent Republicans, who realized just how close Nixon had come—and could come again—to running the country as President.

Harold Stassen, an advisor to Eisenhower and a former Minnesota Governor, began a "Dump Nixon for '56" movement. An anxious Richard Nixon turned once again to investigator Robert Maheu, now primarily working for reclusive billionaire Howard Hughes, who had been donating money to Nixon since his first race for Congress. Maheu mounted a covert political operation for Nixon that torpedoed the "Dump Nixon" movement.

Soon afterward, Hughes made a very unusual $205,000 "loan" to Nixon's brother's failing restaurant business, which quickly went bankrupt. The word "loan" is in quotations, because Nixon's brother wasn't even required to repay the money, making it look much more like a contribution—or a payoff. Some investigators think the money was really intended for Richard Nixon, since he was soon able to buy a lavish "sixteen-room Tudor-style" mansion, a beautifully landscaped estate in Washington, D.C., even though he hadn't sold his previous home.[14]

What did Hughes get for his $205,000 "loan" that involved Richard Nixon? Two months after the "loan," the IRS suddenly reversed their opposition to granting "tax-exempt status" to a Hughes company. Even though the company gave "84 percent of its vast income . . . to Hughes" and was described as nothing but "a tax dodge," it was now deemed a nonprofit charity. In addition, "the month of the Hughes loan, the Civil Aeronautics Board gave TWA"—Hughes's airline—special loan provisions and then granted them "new domestic and international routes and long-delayed fare increases." A major contributor to Nixon also became TWA's new president. To all appearances, Hughes made a good investment with his $205,000 "loan."[15]

Nixon would be one of the few public figures to meet with Hughes after the billionaire slipped into seclusion. The 1956 "loan" was part of a stream of often-illegal Hughes money that flowed to Nixon as long as he was in politics. The "loan" wouldn't cause problems for Nixon until 1960, the same year Robert Maheu would take on his most critical task for Vice President Nixon.[16]

No sooner had the "Dump Nixon" movement been quashed by Hughes and Maheu than a new issue surfaced, not only threatening to keep Richard Nixon off the 1956 ticket, but also to expose his Mafia backing. Nixon's closest political advisor—and link to the Mafia—Murray Chotiner had come under legal scrutiny. With the Democrats back in control of both houses of Congress, a Senate subcommittee launched hearings on Chotiner's involvement in a military procurement scandal. The subcommittee's Chief Counsel, Robert F. Kennedy, and Congressional investigator Carmine Bellino soon uncovered Chotiner's links to mobsters and Nixon in the shady deals. The crisis escalated quickly. On April 25, 1956, the Senate subcommittee subpoenaed Chotiner for the following day. Chotiner, the Vice President's closest aide, didn't show up, essentially risking contempt of Congress.[17]

"Dick Nixon's Secret Link to the Underworld" was the next day's headline for the article about Chotiner in the *New York World-Telegram*. America's most trusted investigative newspaper columnist, Drew Pearson, said in his radio broadcast that mobster Mickey Cohen had "collected money from the underworld" for Chotiner to give to Nixon.[18]

Chotiner and Nixon tried to defuse the crisis. Both realized that not just Nixon's place on the 1956 ticket was at stake—the investigation could also end his political career. Chotiner lied to *The Washington Post*, denying the charges of Pearson and the *New York World-Telegram*. One of the increasingly few papers that didn't support the Eisenhower-Nixon administration, *The Post* was a canny choice, giving Chotiner's denial more credibility.[19]

Murray Chotiner then directly refused to answer the Senate subcommittee's questions about the scandal. While such refusal to testify had sent the Hollywood Ten to prison eight years earlier, Chotiner escaped any consequences, in part because he raised the issue of attorney-client privilege.[20]

Very concerned about the charges, Eisenhower was ready to use them as an excuse to finally get Nixon off the ticket. However, Nixon simply lied to Eisenhower about Chotiner, claiming he was "merely an employee" of Nixon's. He admitted that Chotiner was "involved with people who are bad people," but apparently tried to claim that was simply a function of being an attorney.[21]

Nixon and Chotiner tried to hide the true extent of their close relationship. Yet up until a month before the scandal broke, Chotiner had signed letters "on behalf of the Vice President" and "left phone messages asking to be called back through the White House" switchboard.[22]

However, the newspaper, Drew Pearson, and the Senate subcommittee had acted before having ironclad proof against Chotiner that could either convict him in the press or be used in court. With Chotiner's denials to the press and his refusal to give clear answers to Congress, there was no way he could be charged, so the investigation of Chotiner ground to a halt. Aside from his basic distrust of Nixon, Eisenhower could be blind about matters involving subordinates, as shown when his longtime Chief of Staff was forced to resign two years later because of accepting lavish gifts.* As a result, Eisenhower finally agreed to keep Nixon as his running mate for the 1956 election.[23] After that situation faded into the background, the 1956 campaign went well for Eisenhower and Nixon. The generally anti-union Nixon actually got the backing of the leader of a major union, Teamsters President David Beck, who would soon be charged with corruption. Nixon's skills with the press continued to improve, and he was even able to secure the endorsement of *The New York Times* for the ticket.[24]

* While Eisenhower's and Truman's administrations had corruption scandals, they involved subordinates and the Presidents weren't seen as benefiting from what their subordinates did without their knowledge. Nixon—with his extensive use of illegal money and slush funds—was quite a different matter.

Nixon and Eisenhower also benefited from the tense Cold War situation in the mid-1950s, epitomized by Soviet leader Nikita Khrushchev's widely publicized taunt to the United States that "we will bury you." When just before the election the people of Hungary revolted against Soviet rule, their rebellion helped to send the Republican ticket—with the former General and with America's top Cold Warrior—to a resounding victory over Democratic challenger Adlai Stevenson. However, once the election was over, Nixon and other administration hawks such as Allen and John Foster Dulles ignored pleas for help from the Hungarian rebels, and the Soviets put down the revolt with brutal force.[25]

The 1950s became the most profitable decade for American organized crime, both in the United States and for its expanding operations in Latin America and other parts of the world. The Mafia flourished under the Eisenhower-Nixon administration partly because J. Edgar Hoover still denied that such an organization even existed. America was an odd dichotomy in that era, one that typified Nixon himself. On the surface, the decade was a time of prim conformity, when TV shows depicted fathers wearing ties at the family dinner table while dutiful wives cooked while wearing pearls. Yet beneath those illusions—and the less glamorous daily life of most Americans—popular culture grew incredibly sleazy. Lurid covers on paperbacks and magazines crowded the newsstands, depicting a world of vice and corruption that for many represented reality.

Organized crime had briefly become national news again in 1954, when mobsters in the small town of Phenix City, Alabama—across the river from the huge U.S. Army base of Fort Benning—assassinated the Attorney General-elect of Alabama. Tampa godfather Santo Trafficante was one of those who controlled Phenix City in partnership with other mob bosses, since he had long since learned the benefits of extending his reach through such arrangements. In the Eisenhower-Nixon administration's only major move against organized crime, the President arranged for the National Guard to put Phenix City under "Martial Rule," to end the reign of mobsters who had preyed for years on Fort Benning's soldiers. However, the assassins—who fled to Trafficante's base of Florida and to Mississippi—were never convicted.

Though in that one tiny town the authorities broke the mob's grip, the Mafia went largely unchallenged in the rest of America. Trafficante's other operations—including his share of the French Connection heroin network, which involved partnerships with Mafia leaders in New York, New Orleans, Canada, and France—continued to grow. Along with many other forms of vice, heroin trafficking and addiction became a growing problem in America's larger cities.

Nixon began his second term in 1957, a year that saw the American Mafia reach new heights of power in America and Latin America. The man who helped rekindle Frank Sinatra's career—Mafia don Johnny Rosselli—had his fingers in an increasing array of criminal operations in the United States and overseas. Senator Barry Goldwater had become friends with Willie Bioff, whose testimony had sent Rosselli to prison in the 1940s. Bioff even helped to get Goldwater elected. However, Bioff's friendship with the Senator didn't keep Rosselli and the Mafia from assassinating him just two years after Goldwater took office. Johnny Rosselli, an obvious suspect in the murder, wasn't even interviewed by the police or FBI, and no one was prosecuted for the hit. The same would be true when another notable friend of Senator Goldwater was later murdered by the Mafia in Las Vegas; such was the near impunity of the Mafia in 1950s under the Eisenhower-Nixon administration.

In Guatemala, dictator Castillo Armas continued to receive American government and corporate support after Nixon's visit. Johnny Rosselli, representing both American business and the Mafia, frequently traveled to Guatemala and became a major behind-the-scenes presence there. In July 1957, some of his criminal associates were pressuring Armas over casino gambling. When Armas resisted, he was assassinated. A patsy on hand took the blame, palace guard Romeo Vásquez, who was quickly killed by security forces. Planted Communist literature ensured that the U.S. government and American news media reported that Armas had been assassinated by a fanatical, lone, Communist assassin—even though many Guatemalans saw the murder as linked to organized crime. Shortly after Armas's assassination, General José Miguel Ramón Ydígoras Fuentes took power, and the Eisenhower-Nixon administration quickly backed the new dictator.[26]

Johnny Rosselli was conveniently out of Guatemala at the time of President Armas's assassination. The mobster was spending an increasing amount of time in Havana, helping to oversee one of Santo Trafficante's casinos in Cuba's booming gambling industry. It seemed that the more posh hotels and casinos that Trafficante and Meyer Lansky built in Havana, the more repressive and brutal dictator Batista became toward his own people. Even so, the corrupt Batista retained the official support of the United States and the personal support of Nixon.

New York Mafia chief Albert Anastasia wanted Santo Trafficante to cede him more of the Havana action, and he also resented Trafficante's share of the New York side of the French Connection heroin network. On October 24, 1957, Trafficante met Anastasia in his Manhattan hotel suite. Foreshadowing the ruthlessness that would soon make Trafficante attractive to the CIA, the next day Anastasia was assassinated in a New York barbershop, a brazen daylight killing that inspired a similar scene in the film *The Godfather*. Trafficante quickly checked out of his hotel and left New York, and authorities failed to interview him about the crime. Though the Anastasia hit was front-page news across the country, the administration and Hoover took no serious action.[27]

Santo Trafficante—and the other godfathers—were so confident of safety that they returned to New York the following month for a major conclave of Mafia leaders from across the nation. In the wake of Anastasia's murder, the bosses planned to sort out Mafia concerns related to New York and Havana. On November 14, 1957, almost a hundred of them met at a secluded country estate near the small town of Apalachin, New York, just across the border from Pennsylvania. Most of the major Mafia chiefs were present, though Carlos Marcello was represented by his Dallas underbosses Joe Civello and Joe Campisi. Jewish organized crime leaders like Meyer Lansky didn't attend.[28]

While Hoover's FBI and the Eisenhower-Nixon administration dragged their feet in any action against organized crime, local officers in Apalachin noticed the odd gathering. They raided the country estate and arrested fifty-eight of the mob leaders who weren't able to flee, including Santo Trafficante. Since the FBI and Justice Department hadn't been building cases against them, most of the mob leaders were quickly released, but the story once again propelled the Mafia onto America's front pages. It must have left many in America wondering if any official in Washington was willing to take on the Mafia.

Although his efforts were not yet front-page news like the Apalachin arrests or the Anastasia hit, one elected official had begun a crusade against the Mafia several months earlier: Senator John F. Kennedy, aided by his Chief Counsel and younger brother Robert F. Kennedy, had started focusing on the Mafia and its allies. Their investigation and the results it would spawn would eventually have enormous consequences for themselves, for the Mafia, and for Richard Nixon.[29]

. . .

Richard Nixon's friendship with Bebe Rebozo, and their mutual affinity for Cuba, continued to grow. An FBI memo, only declassified in 2000, reported a claim that "Rebozo fronted for the Italian money" in Cuban businesses—some involving Nixon—while General Fulgencio Batista ruled the country. Anthony Summers found that "according to a law enforcement source and an FBI informant, the two men [Nixon and Rebozo] jointly invested in interests in pre-Castro Cuba." As Vice President, in addition to personal trips to Cuba with Rebozo, Nixon also made official state visits, full of pomp and ceremony.[30]

During Nixon's official visits to Cuba in 1955 and 1957, he lavished praise and U.S. support on the increasingly repressive Batista, who was prospering from his share of the Havana casino revenue from Meyer Lansky and Santo Trafficante. Batista even presented Nixon with a medal. After Nixon's 1955 visit, Batista was so confident of U.S. backing for his regime that he released several prisoners who several years earlier had tried to stage a tiny rebellion at a military barracks. Among those released were two who would soon be plotting a new Cuban revolution: Fidel Castro and his brother Raul.[31]

Nixon again visited Batista in Cuba in 1957 and wrote in a memo that the brutal, corrupt dictator "is concerned with social development [and] will give stability to Cuba."[32] Another event in 1957 would lead Nixon to attempt to apply his well-received Cuban diplomacy to the rest of Latin America.

On November 25, 1957, President Eisenhower suffered a mild stroke. This once again put Nixon in an unusual position, one that he fumbled. Nixon initially received praise for his performance during the first few days after Ike's stroke. But then Nixon met privately with Secretary of State John Foster Dulles and they discussed whether Nixon should take power by declaring Eisenhower "incompetent." However, the day after Nixon's conversation with Dulles, Eisenhower was able to preside over Cabinet and National Security Council meetings. President Eisenhower saw the Nixon/Dulles meeting as yet another attempt by Nixon to grab power too quickly, and Ike was described as "put out at . . . Nixon."[33]

Richard Nixon was already looking ahead to the next Presidential election, when it would be his turn to run for the highest office in the land. Unfortunately for him, Eisenhower made it clear that he wasn't giving Nixon any kind of early support or endorsement. Nixon clearly resented Ike's stance, which meant that if Nixon were going to establish himself as the early favorite in the race, he would have to do it on his own.[34]

After Eisenhower's recovery, Nixon spent the first two weeks of 1958 at the home of his best friend, Bebe Rebozo, in Key Biscayne, Florida (near Miami). Spending such time alone with Rebozo, away from Pat Nixon and their two daughters, was a pattern that would become increasingly common for Nixon over the next three decades. With Rebozo, Nixon could truly relax, socialize, and plot strategy.

Nixon decided to burnish his credentials as a statesman and foreign policy expert by making a tour of Latin America, especially South America. After all, Nixon's earlier visits to U.S.-backed dictators in Cuba, Guatemala, Nicaragua, and the Dominican Republic had gone well. By making the trip a major "goodwill tour" with a large entourage—including Pat—Nixon hoped to generate much positive press for himself. As historians point out, there was no real official purpose for Nixon's Latin American tour.[35]

Some of the stops went well, but others became disasters. While Nixon was always well-received by officials, who relished the rare chance to host a U.S. Vice President, the public perception of Nixon—and the United States—was often negative. In 1958, the United States, and Nixon in particular, seemed to support every Latin American dictator, and the South American press had often reported events like the coup in Guatemala far differently than the American press had done. Many in Latin America seethed with resentment at U.S. policy toward the region.

Angry demonstrators often confronted Nixon. In Lima, Peru, he tried to talk to some of them, only to be forced to leave the area. Worse, in Caracas, Venezuela, he was spat upon and attacked by angry mobs, and he and Pat were caught up in an ugly riot. They escaped without injury, but much of the U.S.—and world—press coverage was disastrous, chastising Nixon for making the trip without realizing how he and the United States were perceived in the region.[36]

One of the relatively good stops on Nixon's tour was Montevideo, the capital of Uruguay. It was an important city in the region because it had a pro-U.S. administration yet more Communist embassies than any other country in South America. As such, its CIA Station Chief, E. Howard Hunt, considered it a plum assignment. Hunt even had the President of Uruguay ask Eisenhower if Hunt could remain CIA Station Chief, even though the U.S. Ambassador wanted him replaced.

Hunt was not successful, and the Ambassador would cause problems for him later in his CIA career.[37]

While heading the CIA station in Uruguay, E. Howard Hunt admits he oversaw the "technical penetrations of a number of embassies and . . . residences." In other words, the same types of break-in and bugging operations Hunt would do for President Nixon years later.[38]

In Uruguay, E. Howard Hunt met with Vice President Nixon, who remembered him from their private dinner several years earlier. Hunt explained his leading role in the Guatemalan coup, which Nixon viewed as a great success. *New York Times* journalist Tad Szulc would later write that around this time Hunt was involved in planning a coup against the seemingly pro-U.S. President of Uruguay. Could those plans have been a topic of conversation between the two men? Nixon was accompanied on his South American trip by his new National Security Advisor General Robert Cushman, who would later become President Nixon's first Deputy CIA Director. Also with Nixon in Uruguay, officially acting as translator, was Colonel Vernon Walters, who would later serve as President Nixon's second Deputy CIA Director and play important roles in Watergate. The meeting between Hunt and Vice President Nixon apparently went well, because Hunt would soon be working with General Cushman on a new covert operation pushed by Nixon.[39]

As Hunt would later write, "shortly after the Nixon tour left, I received a cable from Washington," where the CIA "needed [him] for an important new project that was similar to the" coup in Guatemala. Hunt's CIA superior told him they were reassembling some of the same team because "this operation . . . must be handled even more carefully . . . it's extremely sensitive. Eisenhower insists on complete deniability." His superior told him the target was "Castro—we're taking down Fidel Castro."[40]

CHAPTER 5

Nixon, the Mafia, and the CIA vs. Fidel Castro

In the late 1950s, Cuba became an increasingly important issue for the United States and especially for Richard Nixon, who believed it could help him become the next President. As Cuba began to move away from being a repressive dictatorship, the CIA became more involved in the island nation. Cuba was still a major center for the Mafia's legal gambling casinos, but in the United States the mob and its ally Jimmy Hoffa were finally coming under government pressure—not from the Eisenhower-Nixon administration, but from John and Robert Kennedy. The efforts of the two Kennedys to expose the crimes of Hoffa and the Mafia would become entwined with the issue of Cuba, setting the stage for the epic election battle between Nixon and the Kennedy brothers. Joining Nixon's covert Cuban operations during the heated election would be CIA officer E. Howard Hunt and other figures whose actions would later generate the Watergate scandal.

In 1957, Richard Nixon and the world began hearing about Cuban rebel leader Fidel Castro and his band of revolutionaries, as they waged a growing guerilla war against corrupt Cuban dictator Fulgencio Batista. Well-educated Fidel, his brother Raul, and their street-savvy friend Juan Almeida had been among those released from Batista's prison after Nixon's visit. The three traveled to Mexico, where they obtained enough financial support from Cuba's last elected President, Carlos Prio, to stage a small invasion of Cuba. Fidel's tiny group was joined by a likeminded Argentine physician, Che Guevara, who'd witnessed the 1954 U.S. coup in Guatemala. Soon, the Castros, Almeida, and Guevara had trained a force of eighty-one to return to Cuba.

Using a yacht, the *Granma*, Fidel Castro and his men landed in

Cuba on December 2, 1956—only to face disaster. The small band was almost wiped out by Batista's forces. Che Guevara was one of the wounded, though he was saved by Juan Almeida. A Christ-like legend was born that only Fidel and twelve disciples survived, fleeing into the Sierra Maestra mountains. The actual total was twenty-two, still an absurdly low number to face Batista's feared military, secret police, and death squads.

Fidel was a publicity-savvy, charismatic figure who attracted both fighters and support from an ever-widening array of Cubans tired of Batista's corruption and repression. Raul Castro aided Fidel while remaining out the spotlight, while Che Guevara soon became a compelling symbolic figure who would define "the Revolution" to the world. Juan Almeida proved adept at running what was being called the Revolutionary Army. As weeks turned into months, other revolutionary leaders and groups joined the fray, and by the early months of 1958 what had been one small group had swelled into a broad coalition that presented a serious challenge to the U.S.-backed Batista dictatorship. The standard of living—and education, and medical care—for the average Cuban was low. Many Cubans felt betrayed by Batista, because U.S. corporations owned much of the arable land, along with many of Cuba's larger businesses. All of that led increasing numbers of Cubans to provide covert or overt support to the rebels.

Civil war in Cuba would endanger the hordes of America tourists who flocked to Havana's Mafia casinos, so in March 1958, the Eisenhower-Nixon administration placed an arms embargo on Cuba. However, the arms ban lacked any real enforcement mechanism. Since Cuba was only ninety miles from the United States, with frequent commercial and private flights, arms smuggling into Cuba quickly became a booming business.

Allen Dulles and the CIA could see the growing support among Cubans for the Revolution, and they actually began providing some support to Castro. It was both a way to gain intelligence on the revolutionaries and an insurance policy in case the rebels prevailed. The CIA's support included giving tacit approval for arms smuggling to Fidel, sending actual CIA officers to assist him, and using CIA assets to both help and monitor the revolutionaries.[1]

One of those CIA assets—who later became a CIA contract agent—was Frank Fiorini, a thirty-five-year-old soldier of fortune, hungry for publicity. Powerfully built, Fiorini was a Marine veteran of World

War II who'd seen fierce combat on Guadalcanal and Okinawa. After the war, he joined the U.S. Army, where he did intelligence work. In the mid-1950s, bored as a Virginia bar owner and manager, he left the United States to join the Cuban Revolution, feeding his dual desire for espionage and adventure. In Cuba, Fiorini developed his love of publicity, and there he also began dealing with high-level U.S. mobsters like Santo Trafficante. That began a relationship with the Mafia that would last from his time in Cuba until he was arrested as a Watergate burglar, under the name Frank Sturgis.[2]

Meyer Lansky, the most powerful U.S. crime boss in Cuba, was still closely aligned with Batista against Fidel. On the other hand, Santo Trafficante was one of several Mafia chiefs who—like the CIA—was hedging his bets by helping Fidel at the same time he continued his payoffs to Batista. Mob associates providing support and running guns into Cuba included the new Teamsters President, Jimmy Hoffa.

Hoffa initially supplied arms to both Batista and Fidel, "making the most money possible," according to one of Hoffa's top lieutenants. But as the tide turned increasingly toward Fidel, Hoffa started favoring the revolutionaries and "for a long time he continued to give money for arms for Castro and they got on a very solid basis." Another Hoffa aide said, "I was right there on several occasions when they were loading the guns and ammunition on the barges [and] Hoffa was directing the whole thing."[3]

On New Year's Day 1959, the Revolution finally triumphed: Batista fled Cuba after Che took Santa Clara while Fidel captured Santiago de Cuba. In addition to Raul and Revolutionary Army Commander Juan Almeida, many other rebel leaders had also proven crucial in the fighting, including psychiatrist Manuel Artime, Spaniard Eloy Menoyo, and student leader Rolando Cubela. There were now many revolutionary groups, and factions, including a small group of old-guard Cuban Communists. Though Fidel was not in Havana when Batista fled, he knew how to maximize his publicity. Fidel quickly began traveling in an open jeep across Cuba toward Havana, while his motorcade drew accolades from ever-growing thongs.

Fidel was not the first President or Prime Minister of the new Cuban government, but he worked hard behind the scenes to become the real power while publicly becoming the face of a new Cuba. Initially, the revolutionaries closed all the mob's casinos. However, many people don't realize that in February of 1959, the Mafia's casinos were quickly reopened. Frank Fiorini, whom Fidel had come to trust in the Sierra Maestra, was placed in charge of overseeing the gambling establishments. Now, instead of the Mafia giving Batista a sizable cut from their take, the new Revolutionary government got a huge share. It badly needed the funds, since Batista had taken most of the Cuban treasury when he fled. In his role overseeing the casinos for Fidel, Fiorini began dealing with a *Who's Who* of America mob leaders, including Santo Trafficante. Fiorini's biographers write that he "was never 'a made man,' but he was well connected to the underworld," for years to come.[4]

Media coverage in the United States about romantic revolutionaries soon took on a disapproving tone as the new rulers exacted revenge against Batista's men and supporters. The well-heeled, well-dressed Americans who'd frequented Havana's casinos and hotels before Batista's fall came in dwindling numbers, since they were alarmed by the jeeps and the fatigues-clad young revolutionaries now common in the streets.

To boost Cuba's image in the United States and the rest of the world, Fidel—accompanied by Almeida and Fiorini—visited the United States in April 1959. Raul and Che remained in Cuba, where they continued to consolidate power inside Cuba's governing coalition, while trials of Batista supporters continued. Fidel had been invited to America not by the U.S. government, but by the Association of Newspaper Editors. Colleges deluged Fidel with speaking invitations, and he gave talks at Columbia, Princeton, and Harvard. The Cuban leader appeared on NBC's *Meet the Press*, addressed a meeting of the newspaper editors, and met with the Senate Foreign Relations Committee.

President Eisenhower made sure he was not in Washington when the controversial Fidel arrived, so the task of meeting him fell to Richard Nixon, which made Nixon Eisenhower's "point man" on Cuba for the remainder of his term. Nixon and Fidel met for three hours, and Nixon apparently spent much of the time lecturing Fidel, without offering any U.S. assistance to the cash-strapped country. In public, Richard Nixon put his arm around Fidel, and said on TV "we're going to work with this man." But Nixon wrote a memo to Eisenhower saying that Fidel was "either incredibly naive about Communism or under Communist discipline." In private, to close associates, Nixon was more blunt, saying Fidel was a Communist and a "lunatic." Nixon's assessment at that time must be considered in light of the numerous liberals and moderates Nixon had denounced as Communists over the years.[5]

CIA personnel also met with Fidel, giving him a two-hour talk about the dangers of Communism. Afterward, "the CIA's senior expert on Communism in Latin America" proclaimed Fidel was "not only not a Communist, but he is a strong anti-Communist fighter." There was some truth to that, since the old-line Communists in Cuba would be a thorn in Fidel's side for several more years. Although Fidel's brother Raul considered himself a Communist, Almeida did not. Historians still debate when Fidel became a Communist, but a Russian diplomat would later say "that Castro had made no approaches to Moscow until the year after his meeting with Nixon."[6]

As for Fidel, "he thought Nixon wanted economic catastrophe to hit Cuba, so that the people would overthrow" Fidel, and that "Nixon just wanted to see him toppled." Fidel's meeting with Nixon had produced no offers of American financial aid for his impoverished country, and none were forthcoming after he returned to Cuba. As a result, Fidel and the Cuban government soon "seized American businesses in Cuba . . . representing a billion-dollar investment."[7]

By June 1959, just two months after the Vice President met Fidel, Nixon started working covertly to remove Castro from the scene. Richard Nixon would become more of a driving force for U.S. policy toward Castro than Eisenhower or the CIA. Nixon and his associates would use increasingly dangerous methods to remove Castro, which soon grew to include assassination attempts. Those efforts to eliminate Fidel included both Jimmy Hoffa and the Mafia, who had become the targets of a Senate investigation spearheaded by John and Robert Kennedy.[8]

The crime hearings involving Senator John F. Kennedy and younger brother Robert F. Kennedy were grabbing headlines in June 1959. Those hearings had actually begun in January 1957. They were officially called the Senate Select Committee's "Investigation of Improper Activities in the Labor or Management Field," and they were chaired by Senator John McClellan. Other Senators on the committee included Arizona's Barry Goldwater and North Carolina's Sam Ervin (later Chairman of the Senate Watergate Committee). McClellan insisted the ailing Senator Joe McCarthy also serve, though he attended few meetings and was soon replaced. Later joining the committee was

Senator Frank Church, who in the mid-1970s would head the famous Church Committee hearings into the CIA's plots with the Mafia to kill Fidel Castro. Though the Senate investigation was often called the McClellan Committee, Chief Counsel Robert Kennedy was the driving force behind the hearings. However, his brother received the lion's share of the publicity, and the hearings catapulted JFK to national prominence.[9]

Robert Kennedy had been frustrated by his previous experience with two earlier Congressional committees and was determined to do things differently now that he was essentially in charge. With brother John on the committee, Robert had a high degree of control that he'd lacked in his previous two Congressional committees. RFK had resigned from the original McCarthy committee after six months because no real investigations were being conducted. Then Robert had been frustrated by the premature actions and stonewalling he'd encountered with the committee that uncovered the mob ties of Murray Chotiner. This time RFK's committee would conduct more thorough investigations and not act until it had all the evidence. Robert had forensic accountant Carmine Bellino on his team and added experienced investigator Walter Sheridan and JFK's future Press Secretary, Pierre Salinger.

The Kennedys' initial target in early 1957 was Teamsters President David Beck, who'd been convicted not long after the Teamsters had endorsed Nixon and Eisenhower in the last Presidential race. It didn't take long for Robert and his investigators to zero in on the man soon to be Beck's successor, Jimmy Hoffa. Robert found that twice before, in 1953 and 1954, earlier Congressional committees had been prepared to move against Hoffa, due to his numerous mob connections. Both times the Republican-controlled committees had backed off. Now that the Democrats were in control, Robert Kennedy was determined not to let that happen again.[10]

When RFK first targeted Hoffa, a public relations man for the Teamsters had invited Robert Kennedy to a private dinner with Jimmy Hoffa, saying Hoffa had changed. Kennedy accepted the invitation. But shortly before he met Hoffa, Robert was approached by an attorney from New York who showed Kennedy money that he'd been given by Hoffa. Jimmy Hoffa's goal was to get the attorney to join Robert's staff, while actually becoming an informant for Hoffa—all for $2,000 a month in bribes. Robert took the information to McClellan, who got Hoover and the FBI involved. Robert immediately began feeding certain information to the New York attorney to pass along to Hoffa. And Robert kept his dinner date with Hoffa.[11]

At dinner, Hoffa tried to project a tough image, telling Robert Kennedy, "I do to others what they do to me, only worse." Robert responded, "Maybe I should have worn my bulletproof vest." Hoffa hinted that he knew something about the upcoming hearings, but Robert didn't reveal anything that would show he knew about the bribed attorney.[12]

The FBI soon arrested Hoffa for attempting to infiltrate the Senate Committee, and he faced trial later that year, in July 1957. Hoffa's noted attorney, Edward Bennett Williams, was a friend of Robert Kennedy (and would later be involved in Watergate). The evidence against Hoffa was overwhelming, so Williams resorted to highly unusual tactics. Williams stacked the jury with mostly black jurors and brought in two black attorneys—whom he usually didn't use—to help him. He also bought the appearance of black boxing legend Joe Louis for two days, having him embrace Hoffa in the courtroom. Williams placed a full-page ad of himself and one of his black attorneys in a leading black newspaper, then had copies delivered to the black jurors. He even hired the law partner of the Judge's brother to assist in the trial.[13]

Hoffa was acquitted.

On August 20, 1957, Robert Kennedy and Jimmy Hoffa confronted each other again, this time with Robert grilling Hoffa for the McClellan Committee. Hoffa was not yet a truly national figure, and was still five months way from becoming President of the Teamsters. But Hoffa's confrontation with John—and especially Robert—Kennedy would set a poisonous pattern that would impact all of their lives, until their own murders.

Hoffa's predecessor, Beck, had simply evoked his Fifth Amendment rights numerous times when called before the committee. But Hoffa was afraid to do that because it might cause the Teamster's court-required Board of Monitors to stop him from running for the presidency. Then, too, Robert Kennedy had perfected a technique of conveying information—to Senators, the press, and the public—via his questions, so it would look bad if Hoffa didn't at least try to answer him.

Jimmy Hoffa tried to respond with tortuously long, involved, and overly complicated answers, even when only a "yes" or "no" was required. Hoffa tried to show some civility to the Senators, but soon abandoned that for Counsel Robert Kennedy.[14]

In his questioning, Robert Kennedy began to reveal the sprawling web of organized crime that had aided Hoffa's rise in the Teamsters. Hoffa's crimes and Mafia ties have been the subject of many books, with the best being *The Hoffa Wars*, by Dan Moldea, whose mentor was the committee's Walter Sheridan. Many of Hoffa's crimes and criminal associates used extreme forms of violence. For example, a close mobster associate who'd helped Hoffa take over the New York Teamsters had thrown acid in the face of a labor reporter, blinding him. That mobster's brother was part of Trafficante's heroin network, and his uncle—James Plumeri—was a mob boss who would soon help Hoffa and the CIA plot Fidel Castro's assassination.[15] Robert Kennedy was beginning a crusade against Hoffa that would soon expand to include the Mafia, and it would greatly affect the rest of his life. To Robert, the crusade was needed because Hoffa's obvious crimes and criminal ties should have made him a target for prosecution many times over by the Eisenhower-Nixon administration.[16]

Robert heard a federal narcotics agent explain how "Jimmy Hoffa had protected Detroit's major drug traffickers," how a "Teamsters official [had] laundered drug profits through a union welfare fund," and how heroin kingpin Santo "Trafficante had an office at a Teamsters local in Miami." Hoffa's supporters pointed out that he could be a tough negotiator with trucking firms, basically saying that the ends—helping Teamsters—justified Hoffa's illicit means. But Robert Kennedy documented that Hoffa sometimes made "sweetheart" deals with firms at the expense of his members, all while funneling Teamster funds to himself and his cronies.[17]

On the other hand, Jimmy Hoffa saw the efforts of John and Robert Kennedy as a personal attack. Robert wrote that during the hearings, he saw Hoffa "glaring at me . . . with a deep, strange, penetrating expression of intense hatred . . . the look of a man obsessed," adding that "from time to time, he directed the same shriveling look at my brother." Because of the hearings, Robert said that Hoffa "marked . . . my brother for political extinction." That would lead to Hoffa's support of Richard Nixon, and to Hoffa's close ties with some of America's most dangerous godfathers.[18]

Following leads from their Hoffa investigation, the Kennedy brothers soon had the committee focusing on organized crime. Robert

Kennedy preferred the term "the Syndicate," which could include not just the traditional Mafia, but non-Sicilians involved in organized crime, like Meyer Lansky and Mickey Cohen. After the lurid headlines about the Anastasia barbershop hit, and the accounts of all the Mafia leaders arrested and released at Apalachin, America was eager for someone to take on the Mafia. The hearings began to generate much positive press coverage across the nation—on TV, radio, and newspapers—for Senator Kennedy, laying the groundwork for his Presidential run against Nixon. Additionally, if voters ever heard rumors about his father's supposed mob ties, going after the Mafia was a good way for JFK to distance himself from such talk.

By 1959 the crime hearings had forced top Mafia chiefs to testify for the first time since the Kefauver hearings, nine years earlier. The committee sought to question Tampa godfather Santo Trafficante about the Anastasia murder, but he fled to Cuba to avoid testifying. In his place, they had the Miami Crime Commission Chief testify about Trafficante's heroin network and the Trafficante organization's "twenty-one gang killings" in twenty years, "none of which . . . were ever solved." To show he wasn't afraid, Trafficante had ordered another mob hit the previous day, and Robert had to announce in the hearing that he had been informed "there was another one yesterday." Like the others, it would never be solved.[19]

The Kennedys were able to force Chicago Mafia leader Sam Giancana to appear before their Committee. Giancana, Rosselli's boss, was not a godfather, but was still powerful and essentially ran the Chicago outfit for a couple of older Mafia chieftains. Robert's detailed questions forced Giancana to plead the Fifth more than three dozen times. Robert's questions were designed to get Giancana's criminal background into the record and included asking him if he tried to "dispose of" opponents "by having them stuffed in a truck? Is that what you do, Mr. Giancana?" When Giancana laughed at one question, Robert tried to goad him, saying, "I thought only little girls laughed, Mr. Giancana." Giancana didn't take the bait, but Robert was still able to lay out Giancana's crimes for all the country to see by having his investigator, Pierre Salinger, testify about them.[20]

Also forced to appear before the committee was Louisiana/Texas godfather Carlos Marcello, who was becoming one of the most powerful Mafia leaders in the country. Like Giancana, Marcello pleaded the Fifth, but Robert used other witnesses to establish Marcello's extensive network of crime, corruption, and violence. Putting Carlos Marcello's crimes in the headlines for voters to see could make it harder for public officials to accept graft from godfathers like Marcello.

During the hearings, Robert revealed that Carlos Marcello wasn't even a U.S. citizen, which had kept Marcello from simply fleeing to Cuba like his closest mob ally, Santo Trafficante. Carlos Marcello had been under a deportation order since 1953, and Senator Sam Ervin grilled Marcello about that. Ervin demanded to know how Marcello had avoided deportation for so long, especially since he had two felony convictions. Marcello finally answered, "I wouldn't know," but some of those watching must have wondered if someone in the administration had been paid off. While no direct proof of that has ever emerged, the following year—despite the headlines generated by Marcello's committee appearance—Richard Nixon would accept a $500,000 cash "donation" from Marcello.[21]

In the summer of 1959, the Kennedys' crime hearings shared front-page headlines with those about Cuba's Fidel Castro, and the two became linked in ways that almost no one realized at the time. Robert and his investigators had been looking into an extremely complicated deal involving Hoffa and his mob associates selling surplus planes to Cuba, financed by Teamsters money and involving stolen securities. Hoffa had learned that Robert's forensic accountant, Carmine Bellino, could unravel any ordinary criminal transactions, which was one reason for the complexity of the deal. However, the Committee made only limited progress in its hearings, for two other reasons. First, they were unable to locate a key member of the deal, a low-level gunrunner using the alias of "Jack La Rue."[22]

The second reason emerged in 1959, when Robert and his aides met with one mob boss to demand his testimony, and were shocked by the mobster's response. As first reported sixteen years later by Pulitzer Prize–winning journalist Sy Hersh in *The New York Times*, the mob boss told RFK: "You can't touch me. I've got immunity." Robert demanded to know "who gave you immunity?" The Mafia boss replied, "The CIA. I'm working for them, but I can't talk about it. Top Secret." Robert must have been stunned, but when he looked into it, he found that "sure enough, the CIA had made a deal with" the mob boss. Sy Hersh was unable uncover the name of that Mafia chief working for the CIA, since it was so many years after the fact.[23]

What we now know, as documented by Teamsters expert Dan

Moldea, is that Hoffa's complex transaction was actually a cover for the first 1959 attempt to assassinate Fidel Castro, an operation that involved both the CIA and the Mafia. Moldea explained that because of Hoffa's credibility with Fidel and his men, Hoffa became the first intermediary—a "cutout"—between the CIA and the Mafia in their efforts to eliminate Fidel. A cutout was needed to preserve deniability for the CIA officials trying to kill Fidel, as well as for whatever executive branch official who had approved the operation.[24]

For the CIA, dealing with Jimmy Hoffa—whom many saw as a legitimate labor leader—was preferable to dealing directly with the Mafia, though they were certainly aware (from the newspapers if not their own agents) that Hoffa was close to several key mob leaders. Hoffa had also been involved in CIA-sanctioned arms smuggling to Cuba, so CIA officials must have felt they could trust the Teamsters leader. Finally, using Hoffa as a cutout gave the CIA an extra level of protection. As for Hoffa, he could use whatever legal leverage that helping the CIA could give him.[25] The main Mafia chiefs named by *Time* and other publications as having worked on the Hoffa-brokered Castro assassination plots in 1959 were James Plumeri, Russell Bufalino, and Salvatore Granello.[26]

Earlier plots—in the winter and spring of 1959—to assassinate Fidel had been hatched (by Frank Fiorini, among others), motivated in part by a million-dollar contract offered by Meyer Lansky. The CIA first stalled, then monitored those attempts, none of which had succeeded. According to a close associate of Meyer Lansky, the CIA had initially turned down Lansky's offer of help and the use of his million-dollar bounty on Castro. Lansky then tried a different approach: "contacting Vice President Richard Nixon," first via Florida Senator George Smathers (who had first introduced Nixon to Bebe Rebozo), and then through a former Nixon aide. In June of 1959, some high U.S. official—likely Nixon—made the decision to have the CIA actively work to get rid of Fidel Castro.[27]

Richard Nixon himself would twice write, years before any of the CIA-Mafia assassination plots were exposed, that June 1959 was a turning point for him regarding U.S. action to remove Castro. Nixon wrote that his secret anti-Castro "program had been in operation" starting around June 1959. He also said that using "the CIA" to overthrow Castro "was a policy I had been advocating" within the administration at that time. Historians noted that since the time of

Eisenhower's stroke, Nixon had acted more like a "deputy President," and there is no evidence that Eisenhower himself ever authorized any attempts to assassinate Fidel Castro.

As one of Hoffa's lieutenants later explained, "Hoffa wanted to continue gunrunning after Castro took control of Cuba [and] wanted to utilize Teamster money . . . $300,000," plus "a few army surplus planes . . . to aid friends involved with gunrunning." He said this was "Hoffa's way of trying to help organized crime figures." The Hoffa lieutenant added that "Richard Nixon was becoming involved with Hoffa's people and the Cuba connection around this time."[28]

The evidence suggests—but is not definitive—that Nixon might well have been the highest-ranking U.S. official to authorize these 1959 CIA-Mafia plots. The situation would be less uncertain the following year, when evidence more clearly shows that Nixon was the driving force behind the 1960 CIA-Mafia plots that would help lead to Watergate.[29]

Godfather Santo Trafficante was not directly involved in the 1959 CIA-Mafia plots, as he would be the following year, because on June 9, 1959, Fidel had put Trafficante in comfortable detention in Havana, along with several of his mob associates. Historians still debate the reasons for Trafficante's detention. There are some indications that Trafficante wanted to be detained in Cuba to ensure he wouldn't have to return to the United States to testify about the Anastasia killing to the Kennedys or to New York City authorities. Trafficante's confinement was comfortable, and he was even allowed to attend his daughter's lavish wedding at the Habana Hilton. Once released, Trafficante stayed in Havana for almost three months before returning to the United States.[30]

Other historians cite Trafficante's later testimony, and some of his associates, who say that his detention wasn't voluntary and that he feared for his life at times. It's been documented that Trafficante's closest mob ally, Carlos Marcello, sent Jack Ruby to Havana to carry messages to Trafficante. Much evidence shows that Ruby had been active in Cuban gun smuggling, was on the fringe of Hoffa's arms deal, and may have been the elusive "Jack La Rue" sought by Robert Kennedy. While Santo Trafficante wasn't part of the 1959 CIA-Mafia plots, he did know Hoffa and all of the mobsters linked to the 1959 CIA-Mafia plots to kill Fidel. Given the timing of Trafficante's detention, it's possible that Fidel's men felt that Trafficante was involved in those plots, or knew who was. Ultimately, Mafia money was paid to Cuban officials for Trafficante's release and he returned to the United States once the Kennedy crime hearings had finished.[31]

The 1959 CIA-Mafia plots to kill Fidel weren't succeeding, for at least two reasons. First, Hoffa was using Mafia leaders based mostly in the northeastern United States, who didn't control many men in Cuba. Second, the 1959 plots were not nearly as closely supervised by high-ranking CIA officials as they would be the following year. While that helped to insulate the CIA from blame, it also hindered the plots' effectiveness. Frank Fiorini had flown a B-25 out of Cuba on June 30, 1959, before he could be arrested for plotting against Fidel. Others were not so lucky and were killed or arrested. After that, a plan to have a group of anti-Fidel fighters land from the Dominican Republic once Fidel was assassinated collapsed. One CIA official who later admitted supervising some of the 1959 CIA plotting to overthrow Fidel was David Atlee Phillips, E. Howard Hunt's good friend and colleague from the Guatemala coup. But Phillips was running a Havana PR firm as a cover, and could hardly give the plots the full-time attention that might have made them more successful.[32]

While the CIA continued the Hoffa-brokered plots, the Agency also began a separate coup attempt against Fidel. Several Cubans who would become important in the life and career of E. Howard Hunt, and later in Watergate, were leaders in the CIA's fall 1959 coup plan. Among the coup plotters was Manuel Artime, an extremely conservative Cuban psychiatrist who had worked with Fidel in the Sierra Maestra. Manuel Artime would become Hunt's lifelong best friend, a leader of the Bay of Pigs, a key player in future CIA attempts to assassinate Fidel, and a hush-money paymaster for the Watergate burglars. By the mid-1960s, Artime would also become involved in drug trafficking with Santo Trafficante.

Another coup planner for the CIA was Antonio "Tony" Varona, a former head of the Cuban Senate and Vice President in the Cuban government of Carlos Prio that Batista had overthrown. Tony Varona, like Prio, was not only a skilled politician but was also known for being corrupt. Varona, like his mentor Prio, had been involved with Santo Trafficante, a relationship the CIA would take advantage of the following year.[33]

Liberal activist Manolo Ray was also part of the coup plot. Ray would have a turbulent relationship with Manuel Artime and

E. Howard Hunt in the coming years. However, probably to preserve its deniability, the CIA did not closely oversee the fall 1959 plan, and the coup attempt fell apart. Manolo Ray, Tony Varona, and Manuel Artime all had to flee Cuba to the United States. Others involved were captured or killed.

Helping Artime and Varona escape Cuba (or "exfiltrate," as the CIA called it) was Bernard Barker, a future aide to E. Howard Hunt and a future Watergate burglar. Barker had been born in Cuba to an American father, and he had attended school in the United States. Originally having dual American-Cuban citizenship, Barker enlisted in the U.S. Army Air Corps right after Pearl Harbor. He was part of a bomber crew that was shot down over Germany, and he spent sixteen months in a prisoner-of-war camp. By the late 1940s, Barker was living in Cuba and "became associated in gangster activities," according to an FBI report.

Barker's activities in the 1950s are difficult to pin down, since many accounts are contradictory and key files about Barker continue to be withheld by the FBI and CIA (and important files that have been released are often censored). Barker and Hunt say that Barker worked for the CIA for several years in the 1950s, though Barker's released CIA file says he began working for the Agency only in the spring of 1959, when he was forty-one. The name of the person who first recruited Barker into the CIA remains classified, though files say that CIA officer was involved in the Agency's 1954 Guatemala coup. Bernard Barker's U.S. citizenship was revoked in the mid-1950s; Barker claimed it was because of his service in Batista's secret police—but his own testimony, and other information, indicates his involvement in criminal or suspicious activity was the reason. Barker married a Cuban woman from a wealthy family, and in addition to helping manage her large farm, he served as a corrupt housing inspector in Cuba. Barker also continued his "gangster activities," as the FBI called them, and by the end of the 1950s he was involved with Santo Trafficante's organization, while also working for the CIA. Barker's relationship with Trafficante would outlast his CIA career, and Barker would eventually be fired from the Agency because, as a CIA Director testified, Barker was "involved in certain gambling and criminal elements."

After helping Artime and Varona flee Cuba, Barker himself fled to the United States in January 1960. A CIA memo about his escape describes Barker as "5′ 8″, 160 pounds, brown thinning hair and eyes, round face, stocky build," and able to speak "American English without [an] accent." Within months, Barker would meet and be assigned to assist CIA officer E. Howard Hunt in a new phase of the CIA-Mafia plots to assassinate Fidel, beginning a partnership that would last through Watergate.[34]

CHAPTER 6

Nixon, Hunt, and the CIA-Mafia Plots to Kill Fidel

On December 11, 1959, CIA Western Hemisphere Chief J.C. King laid the groundwork for ramping up the Agency's attempts to assassinate Fidel Castro. In his memo that day to CIA Director Allen Dulles, King put in writing what to that point had probably only been handled verbally: the need for the "elimination" of Fidel Castro to "greatly accelerate the fall of the present government" in Cuba. Dulles gave his handwritten approval. Richard Bissell, the CIA's Chief of Clandestine Services—officially called the Deputy Director for Plans—also approved.[1]

Now based in Washington, D.C., E. Howard Hunt wrote that his "new boss [was] Richard Bissell." Bissell's assistant briefed Hunt: This "operation" would be like the Guatemala coup, only it needed to "be handled even more carefully [since President] Eisenhower insists on complete deniability." Hunt was told the CIA was "taking down Fidel Castro."[2]

Regarding the CIA's high-level talks about assassinating Fidel, Hoffa expert Dan Moldea wrote that "President Eisenhower and Vice President Nixon were informed of these discussions." Moldea adds that "perhaps because he 'knew' Cuba, Nixon was delegated to be the White House's liaison to the CIA on the matter."[3]

In early 1960, Richard Nixon was consumed with his campaign for the Presidency, first winning the Republican nomination, then facing a Democratic challenger in November. Even without a ringing endorsement from his own President, Nixon faced an easy path to the nomination. Nixon had worked hard in the 1958 Congressional elections, and though the Republicans had fared poorly, many who had won—such as Michigan Congressman Gerald Ford—owed Nixon their support. Nixon also sought the backing of rising Republican stars like actor Ronald Reagan, who toured the country delivering a conservative message sponsored by General Electric. Richard Nixon's only real challenger for his party's nomination—the moderate-to-liberal New York Governor Nelson Rockefeller—was reluctant to campaign openly, so he never really stood a chance.[4]

On the Democratic side in 1960, those vying for the nomination included Senator John F. Kennedy, Texas Senator Lyndon B. Johnson, and Minnesota Senator Hubert Humphrey (whom Nixon would face in 1968). In January 1960, Nixon predicted that JFK would be the nominee, an opinion not widely shared by Republicans, since Senator Kennedy was relatively young and many thought some voters wouldn't choose a Catholic for President.*[5]

Richard Nixon knew that foreign policy would be the key to the November election. He told a group of Republican leaders that if they let the Democrats "campaign only on domestic issues, they'll beat us—our only hope is to keep it on foreign policy." With Cuba, Nixon had an issue that could boost his campaign more than any other foreign policy issue. As 1960 progressed, Fidel Castro would make increasing overtures to the Soviet Union, while nationalizing more American businesses. Most upper-class, and some middle-class, Cubans were leaving the turbulent island for the United States.[6]

What if Fidel Castro were eliminated before the election, and the U.S. government had to send troops into Cuba to protect Americans, keep order, and prevent a Soviet takeover? Surely the nation would turn to the experienced Nixon over a less-experienced challenger like JFK. As part of Nixon's 1960 campaign, he touted the fact that he had attended 217 National Security Council (NSC) meetings "and had presided over" twenty-six of them, in addition to attending "163 Cabinet meetings [and] presiding over nineteen" of them, as well as meeting forty-seven heads of state. Even without Eisenhower's full support, Nixon tried to portray himself to the public as the "deputy President" that he—and some of his associates—felt he was.[7]

To take advantage of his foreign policy experience, Nixon made

* In the 1920s and 1930s, when the Ku Klux Klan was a nearly mainstream organization in much of the country, it targeted Catholics along with blacks and Jewish people. That started to change by the late 1930s, when Catholics like anti-Semitic radio commentator Father Coughlin became conservative leaders, but anti-Catholic sentiment still lingered in some parts of the country.

Cuba an important part of his 1960 campaign and developed a three-track strategy to use it to his advantage. First, for public consumption, Nixon made tough but statesman-like pronouncements about the Cuban government. Second, Nixon was part of a covert Cuban strategy that was known and approved by President Eisenhower and the rest of the National Security Council. Not just content to oppose Fidel on economic and diplomatic fronts, Ike and the NSC also explored ways to undermine Castro, and hopefully topple him from power, by backing Cuban exiles. Nixon became a major part of that effort. But it was as a prominent part of that process that Nixon became the driving force in an even more secret third track for Cuba, one that probably no one else on the NSC knew about, except for Allen Dulles. Nixon was essentially Eisenhower's point man for Cuba and, in the words of E. Howard Hunt, "the White House action officer for our covert project." It's now clear the primary goal of the "covert project" that Nixon ran for the White House was the physical elimination of Fidel—his assassination.

Historians still debate whether President Eisenhower authorized or even knew about the CIA's attempts to assassinate Fidel Castro during his term. If Ike did know, even in a vague or general sense, he would have been content to let Nixon take the risk—and garner the potential reward—for pushing that effort, since it gave Eisenhower an added level of "deniability."[8]

Richard Nixon's highly secret third track for Cuba initially involved continuing the original 1959 CIA-Mafia plots into 1960, even as the CIA looked for more direct ways to assassinate Fidel. Multiple Eisenhower aides testified to Senate investigators that Ike never authorized any attempt on Castro's life, and no documentary evidence ever surfaced proving otherwise. Hunt's boss Bissell testified that he never told Eisenhower about any assassination plots. However, historian Michael Beschloss pointed out that years later, "during Congressional hearings in the 1970s, CIA officials insisted under oath that the plotting against Castro" involving the Mafia "was approved by someone at a high political level of the Eisenhower administration." Beschloss, writing in 1991, found considerable evidence that "Vice President Nixon flashed the green light for a CIA-Mafia attempt against Castro," though he says the evidence available to him wasn't conclusive. Since that time, much more information has emerged, and Nixon's key role in the matter seems certain. According to a Senate committee, "authorization outside the CIA for a Castro assassination could . . .

only have come from President Eisenhower [or] *from someone speaking for him.*" (Emphasis added.) All the evidence shows that person could only have been Richard Nixon.[9]

In early January 1960, just three weeks after CIA Director Allen Dulles had officially approved the memo calling for the "elimination" of Fidel, Richard Nixon discussed the situation over dinner with an extraordinary man close to both Nixon and Dulles. William Pawley was described as a "wealthy, high-ranking former diplomat" who had made fortunes in real estate and airlines. Pawley had also "owned the Havana bus system and gas company" under Batista. William Pawley told an associate that to "get Castro" he'd "pay anything, almost anything" and his key contact "in that endeavor was Richard Nixon."[10]

On January 4, 1960, Nixon told his secretary, Rose Mary Woods (who would still be his secretary during Watergate), to "call Pawley" about the "problem we are having just south of Miami," a reference to Castro. She was to tell Pawley that Nixon "has been in the middle of some very intense discussions on the Cuba situation with people in government outside of State, and with people outside of government. Within the next week to ten days [Nixon] will know more about what he thinks our position should be . . . and he will contact you then."[11]

Five days later, "on January 9, Nixon invited Pawley to his home for lunch," according to historian Beschloss. Three days after that, Nixon met with a former close aide who was partners with private investigator and CIA operative Robert Maheu. Nixon had used Maheu twice before on sensitive matters, including the possible assassination of Aristotle Onassis in 1954. However, by 1960 Maheu was spending much of his time on the West Coast and working almost exclusively for billionaire Howard Hughes, aside from occasional work for the CIA. After meeting with Maheu's partner on January 12, 1960, Nixon wrote to Pawley about the Cuba matter, saying "we had a very satisfactory conversation with the President on Monday morning. Your name was well and favorably mentioned . . . I have not yet heard from our West Coast inquiries, but will be in touch with you just as soon as I get some news." Robert Maheu was apparently too busy at that time, so it would be seven months until Maheu could replace Jimmy Hoffa to become the new cutout in the CIA-Mafia plot to kill Fidel Castro.[12]

Even as Nixon and the CIA explored new avenues for eliminating Fidel with Pawley and others in the early months of 1960, the original Hoffa-brokered CIA-Mafia plots continued. In January 1960, Nixon's national security aide General Cushman talked in a meeting about the "need to get some goon squads into Cuba." He wasn't just talking about having people beaten up; "goon" is defined in the dictionary as someone "hired to . . . eliminate opponents."[13]

Also in January 1960, the gangster manager of Havana's lavish Tropicana casino—Lewis McWillie—asked Jack Ruby to legally buy four Colt Cobra revolvers in Dallas and bring them to Havana. Jack Ruby was then the manager of two small Dallas nightclubs, including one he fronted for Carlos Marcello's organization. Ruby also knew Jimmy Hoffa and some of Hoffa's associates, and—as previously explained—several months earlier had been on the fringe of 1959 CIA-Mafia plots brokered by Hoffa. For a short time in 1959, Ruby had even become an FBI informant to provide cover for his Cuban trips. The Colt revolvers McWillie wanted in January 1960 could easily be obtained by a gangster in Havana, because of all the recent gunrunning into Cuba. Likewise, Ruby—a career, low-level criminal—could have easily obtained such weapons illegally in Dallas. But apparently those employing McWillie needed these pistols to be easily traced back to a legal purchase in Dallas so that it was clear they weren't linked to organized crime or any illegal—or CIA—gunrunning operation.[14]

For some reason, Jack Ruby balked at McWillie's request to go to Cuba, even though he admittedly "idolized" McWillie, and Ruby had visited Cuba several times the previous summer. After Ruby's reluctance to go to Cuba, the Tropicana's McWillie asked Ruby to ship the four pistols to him, in Havana. Records and testimony are murky about what happened next, and whether or not some of the guns were shipped to Cuba. What is known is that Ruby definitely purchased at least one Colt Cobra.[15]

The overall evidence indicates that the whole episode was part of the continuing CIA-Mafia plots brokered by Hoffa. Gangster Lewis McWillie had been part of Ruby's Cuban venture with a Hoffa associate the previous year, and government files show that McWillie had solid Mafia connections to Meyer Lansky, who was still offering his one-million-dollar bounty on Fidel Castro. When Ruby bought the pistol for McWillie, evidence indicated that Ruby was accompanied by an ex-boxer (Ruby would later be linked by phone records to ex-boxer Barney Baker, described by Robert Kennedy as one of Jimmy Hoffa's "roving emissaries of violence.") Some journalists have asked if Jack Ruby was "supplying the pistols to [Lewis] McWillie so they could be [used in an assassination] plot against Castro," as part of the CIA-Mafia plots. In fact, a Cuban government Dossier of CIA assassination attempts prepared in the 1970s—a document that would be at the heart of the Watergate scandal—describes a "plot" to assassinate Fidel just months after McWillie's request for the pistols. This assassination attempt involved at least one Cuban "gangster," and the Cuban Dossier says their weapons were provided "by the CIA." The gangster and his associate were arrested, their weapons confiscated, and all were photographed. One of the pistols looks like the type of Colt Cobra requested by McWillie, though the Dossier's photo is not of sufficient quality to be conclusive.[16]

The one Colt Cobra definitely purchased by Jack Ruby in January 1960 would find greater infamy over three years later. It was the same pistol Ruby used to shoot accused assassin Lee Oswald on live television, on November 24, 1963.[17]

March of 1960 brought a new stage in official U.S. operations against Fidel. There was a flurry of meetings about Cuba in mid-March, in both the NSC and a smaller subcommittee, the Special Group. Nixon was present at most meetings, and no doubt listened with interest to official statements of those such as Admiral Arleigh Burke of the Joint Chiefs of Staff, who told the NSC "that any plan for the removal of Cuban leaders should be a package deal, since many of the leaders around Castro were even worse." In one of the meetings, the group discussed in detail what would happen if "Fidel and Raul Castro and Che Guevara should disappear simultaneously."[18]

In the March 10, 1960, NSC meeting, CIA Director Allen Dulles presented Eisenhower and Nixon with a formal "Program of Covert Action Against the Castro Regime." Dulles "suggested" that his program might topple Castro "before the November election." Eisenhower approved the program, though exactly what he approved remains a huge point of controversy. In later years, claims were made that Eisenhower had approved what would become known the following year as the Bay of Pigs disaster, a U.S.-sponsored Cuban exile invasion of Cuba. Eisenhower denied that, and no "invasion" is mentioned in the plan, which talks about creating "a paramilitary force outside of Cuba for future guerilla action."[19]

However, the number of Cuban exile trainees would initially be only in the dozens, perhaps 150 by September, and barely four hundred by the time of the election—hardly enough to stage an invasion against Fidel and Commander Almeida's 32.000-plus Cuban Army soldiers. Eisenhower and his aides later indicated they thought the plan called for guerilla fighters who could drop into Cuba for sabotage and tactical raids to cause primarily economic damage. Indeed, in the months before and after this meeting, various little raids and small air attacks struck at targets in Cuba, sorties launched from the United States. CIA-backed Cuban exiles and CIA contract agents like Frank Fiorini conducted many, if not most, of these small-scale raids. Less than a week before the NSC meeting, a French ship loaded with Belgian arms blew up while docked in Havana. The explosion killed "100 workers and soldiers," though attacks with such high casualty figures were rare.[20]

Some have claimed that in March 1960 Eisenhower had officially approved, in a deniable, roundabout way, the CIA-Mafia plots to assassinate Fidel. Certain comments at the meetings could be interpreted as possibly referring to assassination, in a general sense. But those present who later testified to a Senate committee in 1975 said that wasn't the case, insisting that they were discussing an effort with Cuban exiles to overthrow Cuba's government. As previously mentioned, Eisenhower's aides denied he even knew about the CIA-Mafia plots, let alone approved them.[21]

The facts seem to support Eisenhower and his aides, because what became known as the Bay of Pigs would only become a large Cuban exile invasion force after Nixon lost the election. While Eisenhower had no contact with those who admitted plotting assassinations against Castro (aside from his official meetings with Allen Dulles, with whom he was not especially close), Nixon had many such contacts, in 1960 and in later years. In addition, because of the election, Nixon stood to gain far more from the removal of Fidel than did Eisenhower, even if an assassination plunged Cuba into chaos, requiring U.S. military intervention.

Dulles's March 1960 plan presented to Eisenhower and Nixon also included a Cuban "government in exile, a propaganda offensive, [and more] covert action" to sabotage economic targets in Cuba. Those parts clearly echoed the CIA's successful 1954 Guatemala coup, and the CIA was going to use several veterans of that operation on this one, including E. Howard Hunt.[22]

Hunt had been one of "a dozen veterans of the 1954 Guatemala coup" to meet in Washington with the CIA's Western Hemisphere Chief, just weeks after the Chief had written the memo about the "elimination" of Fidel. Hunt apparently got the message, and in April 1960 he wrote his own memo arguing that "first and foremost, all efforts should be made to assassinate Castro before or coincident with the invasion."[23]

The "invasion" being planned at that time was not a large-scale amphibious landing, of almost two thousand men, as would happen a year later, at the infamous Bay of Pigs. The planning for that type of operation would not even begin for another seven months. As far as Eisenhower and most of the National Security Council knew, the "invasion" they approved in the spring of 1960 would consist of a few hundred exile guerilla fighters, with some landing in boats and almost half that many parachuting into Cuba. The landing would include a select group of Cuban exile leaders, who would then proclaim a new Cuban government, which would be quickly recognized by the United States and other U.S.-backed foreign governments in Latin America. Supposedly, Cuban dissidents would rise up and join the U.S.-backed Cuban exiles and their leaders.[24]

E. Howard Hunt's official role would be to choose those leaders and persuade them to work together, deciding who would have which post—and what power—before they got to Cuba. The initial plan was to recruit moderate leaders who might actually stand a chance to win the support of most Cubans. However, Hunt was extremely conservative, and it's no surprise he chose extreme right-wing leaders like Manuel Artime, the corrupt Tony Varona, and two others.

The only way such a tiny "invasion" plan could stand any remote chance of succeeding against Cuba's huge army—and two hundred thousand militia members—would be if Fidel (and likely Raul and Che) were assassinated first. Fidel's assassination would also create a pretext to justify U.S. military intervention in Cuba. Hunt's role in what would become the 1960 CIA-Mafia assassination plots is borne out by a memo obtained by the CIA in the 1970s, in which Hunt told a publisher that he had "recommended *and planned* assassination/Castro operation." Emphasis was added because in his own published accounts, Hunt only admits that he "recommended" Castro's "assassination," not that he also "planned" it.[25]

Richard Nixon was eager to help Hunt and sent his aide General

Cushman to meet with him. Hunt wrote that "Cushman had urged me to inform him of any project difficulties the Vice President might be able to resolve. For Nixon was, Cushman told me, determined that the effort should not fail."[26] Cushman told Hunt that Nixon was the "chief architect . . . the honcho" of the U.S. effort to topple Fidel. That was confirmed years later, when President Nixon told a White House aide that he had been "deeply involved" in the Cuban operation. Nixon himself would write in his first memoir that "the covert training of Cuban exiles by the CIA was due in substantial part, at least, to my efforts. This had been adopted as a policy as a result of my direct support."[27]

E. Howard Hunt "confirmed that his proposal that Castro be killed had been discussed at his June [1960] meeting with Nixon's aide General Cushman." Anthony Summers points out "that Cushman would have passed the information on to Nixon; it was after all his responsibility to do so." Given Hunt's positive previous meetings with Nixon, and Hunt's key role in the successful Guatemala coup, it's logical that Nixon would have viewed Hunt—and his proposal—positively. Additionally, Nixon would have known that the United States had been trying without success to assassinate Fidel, as Hunt wanted, since the previous year. If Hunt wasn't involved in helping to plan Fidel's assassination before his meeting with Nixon's aide, he almost certainly was after it.[28]

Hunt, like Nixon, publicly denied knowing about, let alone working on, the CIA-Mafia plots to kill Fidel. Yet Hunt's mentor—and Nixon's future CIA Director—Richard Helms disagrees. Much later, Helms testified that the CIA-Mafia plots to kill Fidel "were known 'to almost everybody in high positions in government.'" At the time Helms testified about that, he was exaggerating slightly, blurring the line between the general effort to overthrow Fidel and the much more secret CIA-Mafia plots to assassinate him. But evidence shows Hunt knew about the CIA-Mafia plots—and that no high U.S. official outside the CIA, except for Richard Nixon, knew about the CIA-Mafia plots at that time.[29]

E. Howard Hunt had first met Richard Helms in 1956 and, according to Hunt, they became friendly and soon developed a mentor/protégé relationship. Hunt greatly admired Helms, who was described by a former CIA agent and journalist as "an Ivy Leaguer, a cautious career

[CIA] officer . . . cool, elegant, suave, socially adept, and quiet." Richard Helms was known as "the man who kept the secrets." However, Helms could also be arrogant, keeping secrets that could harm his career from his own CIA Directors as well as from Presidents from Kennedy to Nixon. Helms's excuse would be that as high-ranking CIA officials, "we all had the feeling that we were hired out to keep those things out of the Oval Office." In later years, Helms would blatantly lie to the press and to Congress, leading to his being indicted for lying to Congress.[30]

Helms was part of the Eastern establishment, and not known to be far-right like Hunt, yet somehow the two clicked. In many ways, Helms was what Hunt aspired to be. Both men had been in the CIA's forerunner, the OSS, during World War II. In 1960, Helms was a rising star in the CIA, the Chief of Operations for Clandestine Services—just below Richard Bissell—so Hunt had chosen a promising mentor.[31]

However, Richard Helms did something unusual in 1960 that would greatly accelerate his career the following year, after the Cuba plan had grown and evolved into the debacle at the Bay of Pigs: Helms chose to stay out of the Cuban operation, at least officially. It's odd that his protégé Hunt remained such a key part of the Cuban operation, though perhaps that allowed Helms a deniable degree of influence over the plan, without risking his own career.[32]

Even though Richard Helms officially kept his hands off the Cuban operation until January 1962, he would be responsible for much of the controversy about it, through the time of Watergate and in the decades that followed. On at least two occasions, in 1967 and again in early 1973, Richard Helms destroyed information about the CIA's Cuban operations. That included much information specifically about the CIA-Mafia plots to assassinate Fidel and also related information about his protégé Hunt, as detailed in later chapters of this book.

A report Richard Helms ordered the CIA's Inspector General (IG) to prepare in 1967 about the CIA-Mafia plots has long been considered by journalists and most historians as the definitive account. Helms, then CIA Director, was asked to produce the report by President Lyndon Johnson, in response to the first press reports about the CIA-Mafia plots by Jack Anderson in March 1967. However, more recent file releases have shown Helms's 1967 IG Report about the CIA-Mafia plots—which Helms would later refuse to give to President Nixon—to be grossly incomplete and often misleading. The Inspector

General and his staff did not even interview Helms (who ran the plots from 1962 to 1966) or Allen Dulles for the report. It admits the plots started in 1959, but provides no details until August 1960—and those are incomplete or misleading. The report is also filled with what are now known as weasel words, such as "imperfect history," "no official records were kept," "few written records," "cryptic references," "skeletal notes," and "memories fogged by time." Essentially, the IG Report ordered by Helms was designed as much to conceal information—from others within the CIA (including Helms's successors) and Presidents—as to reveal. Thus, in the remainder of this book's account of the CIA-Mafia plots we won't dwell on the points journalists have covered over and over for decades, but will focus on important matters that have emerged only in recent years.[33]

With that in mind, it should be pointed out that much of E. Howard Hunt's CIA file about his Cuban operations from 1959 to 1966 remains classified or has been destroyed. That's remarkable, considering that Hunt has been investigated by at least four Congressional committees and by the Watergate Special Prosecutors. None of those groups had access to key Cuba files that Hunt himself has written about, ranging from his April 1960 memo calling for Fidel's assassination to the vast majority of Hunt's 1960 Cuban operations file to his work on 1961's Bay of Pigs and his later Cuban operations. Thus, even determining exactly when Hunt began working on Cuban matters is difficult, since so much has not been declassified and his own accounts are often misleading or self-serving. For example, one of Hunt's main CIA cover identities, "Don Eduardo"—a name that he used from 1960 until the Watergate era—shows up in memos linked to Jimmy Hoffa and the 1959 CIA-Mafia plots to kill Fidel.[34]

By the early summer of 1960, it is documented that Hunt was focusing on the portion of his assignment that involved molding his chosen group of Cuban exile leaders into a government-in-exile that could quickly take control in Cuba (with U.S. help) after Fidel was assassinated. His efforts initially took place in Mexico so the United States could deny that it was forging the coalition. Hunt began to grow very close to the politically like-minded Manuel Artime, forging a lifelong friendship and covert intelligence partnership. Hunt had less admiration for former Cuban Senator Tony Varona and the other older leaders, but the coalition needed mature men since Artime was only twenty-eight. By 1960, Hunt's friend David Atlee Phillips had left

Cuba, and he assumed control of the propaganda arm of the Cuban operation. Meanwhile, the first young Cuban exile "freedom fighters" were being recruited, though their actual training would be handled by another CIA officer who was often at odds with Hunt. The young Cubans were going to be based in Guatemala, though there would be numerous delays in constructing their airfields and facilities.

With the 1960 political conventions rapidly approaching, matters were not proceeding fast enough for Richard Nixon. As he told "a press aide . . . the toppling of Castro would be 'a real trump card'" for the election. Just a month after Dulles's presentation to the NSC, Nixon told his aide General Cushman that the CIA agents "ought to get off their tails and do something."[35] Later, Nixon pressed Cushman again, asking, "How the hell are they coming? How are the boys doing at the [CIA]?" Nixon wanted to know "what in the world are they doing that takes months?" He couldn't understand what was taking so long, since Nixon saw the operation as mainly "rifle training." In a way, he was right, since the main goal was assassination.[36]

The CIA's official historian, with access to files still not released to the public, phrased things more politely, writing that "the Vice President had a great interest in the Agency's progress in organizing the ouster of Castro" and "that Nixon [and his aide General] Cushman attended dozens of meetings" about it.[37] The minutes and notes from almost all of Nixon's "dozens of meetings" with the CIA have still not been declassified.

What Nixon saw as needless CIA delays were needed to preserve the deniability of the operation, should it fail—and even if it succeeded, the Agency didn't want it traced back to U.S. officials. That became especially important after Cuba and the Soviet Union established diplomatic relations in May 1960. Two months later, Soviet leader Nikita Khrushchev threatened to use Soviet missiles against America if the U.S. military attacked Cuba. Khrushchev repeated that threat three months later, just before the U.S. Presidential election. That is why the CIA needed it to appear to the world that the Eisenhower-Nixon administration was simply reacting to the unexpected death of Fidel Castro after his assassination by "gangsters" or disgruntled exiles.[38]

Richard Nixon continued his contacts regarding Cuba with William Pawley, who was also friends with Allen Dulles. A memo records that in the spring of 1960, Pawley "discussed with" a CIA officer for

Cuban operations "the killing of . . . 'somebody' inside Cuba."[39] By July 13, a "message, sent to Allen Dulles, reports an offer by a Cuban contact of Pawley's to collaborate in Castro's assassination." On July 18, "Pawley wrote to Nixon [saying,] 'I'm in touch with Dulles' people almost daily and things are shaping up reasonably well. The matter is a very delicate problem and every care should be taken to handle it so as not to affect our Nation adversely, nor our political campaign.'"[40]

Two days later, CIA headquarters sent a cable to the Havana CIA station referring to the assassination of Fidel and Raul Castro and Che, saying that the "possible removal top three leaders is receiving serious consideration at HQS." The CIA cable promised an Air Cubana pilot "a ten-thousand-dollar reward should he succeed in killing Raul" in a way that made it look like an accident. Headquarters quickly realized they were breaking procedure and security by cabling so openly about murdering a foreign official, so they quickly sent another cable saying to disregard the assassination message. This incident demonstrates why the preferred method for communicating about assassinations was through deniable intermediaries or cutouts, and not directly by official CIA cables. The CIA was clearly having trouble trying to assassinate Fidel or Raul on its own, especially in a deniable way, which is why the CIA continued to search for ways to utilize the Mafia in that regard. E. Howard Hunt's role coordinating the CIA's exile government with the Agency's exile training program also put him in the perfect position to also coordinate those two efforts with the CIA's attempts to have the Mafia assassinate Fidel, which would soon be elevated to a new level.[41]

In the summer of 1960, Nixon saw his prediction of John F. Kennedy as the Democratic nominee come true, though many were surprised that JFK chose Texas Senator Lyndon B. Johnson as his running mate. Feelings had been especially hard between LBJ and Robert Kennedy, JFK's campaign manager. However, the more liberal JFK knew that LBJ would be important in helping him carry the Southern states, especially LBJ's own Texas.

E. Howard Hunt's newly formed Cuban exile leadership group announced its formation in Mexico on June 22, and in July Artime, Varona, and the others met with John F. Kennedy, the new Democratic nominee. JFK couldn't have realized it then, but Varona and Artime would play key parts in his life and Presidency.[42]

Richard Nixon easily became his party's nominee, and the only suspense was whom he would choose as his Vice Presidential running mate. One of five finalists was Michigan Congressman Jerry Ford, though he lost out to Henry Cabot Lodge, the U.N. Ambassador. Lodge had been the candidate that JFK had beaten in 1952 to become a Massachusetts Senator. By selecting Lodge as his running mate, Nixon was sticking to his strategy of making the race about foreign policy. Nixon probably also felt that the longtime U.N. Ambassador would be helpful in dealing with world leaders in the aftermath of the big transition in Cuba that Nixon was planning.[43]

September 1960 had been the original target date for toppling Fidel. But after the CIA delays that made the Vice President anxious, Nixon "wanted it to occur in October, before the election," his campaign press aide later admitted. Now that Nixon was the nominee, he needed to see that the CIA-Mafia plots were ramped up, to ensure they produced the results he needed in time.[44]

CHAPTER 7

August–October 1960: Nixon and the CIA-Mafia Plots to Kill Castro

August and September of 1960 could well be the most crucial months in Richard Nixon's storied political career. Nixon's actions during these two months, along with those of the CIA and the Mafia, laid the groundwork for the Watergate break-ins that eventually cost Nixon his political life. By the end of September 1960, ten key Watergate figures had been drawn into the web surrounding the CIA-Mafia plots to assassinate Fidel before the election.

Those figures included Watergate planner E. Howard Hunt, Watergate burglars Bernard Barker and Frank Fiorini (a.k.a. Frank Sturgis), Nixon's Watergate hush-money paymaster Manuel Artime, Santo Trafficante, Johnny Rosselli, Jimmy Hoffa, and Nixon's associate Robert Maheu. Important Watergate figures aware of, but not part of, the secret CIA-Mafia plots at this time included Richard Helms and Maheu's primary employer, Howard Hughes. Richard Nixon's best friend Bebe Rebozo would soon join the mix.

In August of 1960, just a week after Nixon secured the nomination, developments began on what would become a new—and much more important—phase of the CIA-Mafia plots to kill Fidel. Tony Varona, already an associate of godfather Santo Trafficante, had a meeting with exiled Mafia kingpin Meyer Lansky, who was still offering a huge sum for Fidel's murder. Nixon's aide General Cushman received a letter dated August 1, 1960, from a Nixon associate's secretary that introduced a figure later described as a "Washington mob liaison man for [Meyer] Lansky and [Santo] Trafficante." And the CIA officer soon to take charge of the CIA-Mafia plots was "in touch with William Pawley."[1]

A transition had begun: Jimmy Hoffa would no longer be the CIA's cutout to ineffective Mafia bosses from the northeastern United States. Hoffa's attention to the matter in recent months was essentially nil, because he was consumed by other events. As result of John and Robert Kennedy's crime hearings—and Robert's best-selling book about them, *The Enemy Within*—Hoffa faced increasing scrutiny and potential prosecutions. For example, in August 1960, "a Florida grand jury was ready to indict Hoffa for misusing union funds." So Hoffa was out as the CIA's Mafia liaison, though Nixon would soon find a way to reward him for his help, since he still needed Hoffa's influence for the upcoming election.[2]

Also in August 1960, the CIA's Security Director, Sheffield Edwards, said that "he was advised by some higher official that it was in the national interest that Mr. Castro be—liquidated." In response, Edwards called Richard Bissell and asked for a private meeting. The question has never been answered as to which "higher official" told Edwards to liquidate "Mr. Castro." It wasn't Bissell, since Edwards approached him about the matter. Bissell was the CIA's Deputy Director for Plans, essentially the CIA's highest covert operations officer, since the CIA's Director (Allen Dulles) and Assistant Director (General Charles Cabell) focused mainly on high-level administrative, bureaucratic, and Congressional functions for the huge organization. But it wasn't Dulles or Cabell who asked Edwards to meet with Bissell, since both Dulles and Cabell wouldn't be briefed about this new phase of the CIA-Mafia plots until September.[3]

That leaves only a "higher official" outside the CIA to have sparked this new phase in the CIA-Mafia plots. Richard Nixon had been the most ardent advocate of Castro's removal. As the election drew closer, Nixon was almost certainly the "higher official" who pressed the sensitive matter at one of the "dozens of meetings" the CIA admits that Nixon and his aide attended about the CIA's Castro operation.

When CIA Security Director Sheffield Edwards met with Hunt's boss Bissell, they "weighed ways to 'eliminate' or 'assassinate' Castro." Edwards "proposed that the assassins be hand-picked by the American underworld, specifically" Mafia leaders who'd had to leave Cuba after Castro took power. This was an odd proposal for Edwards to make on his own, since he had no previous documented experience with the Mafia. Though as Security Director—essentially responsible for maintaining the security of CIA secrets—he probably would have heard at least informally about the failed 1959 CIA-Mafia plots. Again, it seems likely that Edwards was essentially relaying the suggestion of someone else, since his men were in touch with Nixon associates like William Pawley.[4]

Richard Bissell liked Edward's proposal, since using the Mafia to recruit hit men would give the CIA "the ultimate cover [since] there was very little chance that anything the syndicate would try to do would be traced back" to the CIA or the Eisenhower-Nixon administration. That point is important, because what the CIA really needed was someone to take the blame for Fidel's murder. The CIA had contacts and agents who could do or arrange hits, but what they wanted was someone the public could logically blame—besides the CIA—for Fidel's assassination.

Bissell, who almost certainly knew about the failed 1959 and early 1960 plots, approved this new Mafia proposal and put Edwards in charge. This time, the new CIA-Mafia plots would be much more closely managed by the CIA than the previous effort.[5]

Sheffield Edwards turned to his Operational Support Chief, James O'Connell, to handle the details. There is some evidence that O'Connell, a former FBI agent, may have been involved in the World War II effort involving Mafia chief "Lucky" Luciano's assistance to Naval Intelligence. For the CIA's new cutout to the Mafia, O'Connell first looked at another former FBI man, Guy Banister, the ex–FBI Chief of Chicago, now working as a private investigator in New Orleans. Banister also did intelligence work, for the FBI, Naval Intelligence, and—according to Hunter Leake, Deputy CIA Chief in New Orleans—the CIA. The port of New Orleans did much trade with Latin America, and Banister had excellent contacts throughout the region.[6]

However, CIA files show that the security check on Banister begun in August 1960, to clear him for a sensitive operation, was soon stopped. Instead, Banister would work on a different Cuban operation for the CIA, one that wouldn't reach fruition until much later in the year. In his place, the CIA turned to Banister's former office mate from a few years earlier: private investigator Robert Maheu.[7]

Maheu later admitted that Richard Nixon was behind the ramped-up CIA-Mafia plots to assassinate Fidel Castro, and that Nixon had chosen Maheu to be the CIA's new cutout to the Mafia. Eight years later, Maheu told his friend Pierre Salinger "that the CIA had been in touch with Nixon, who had asked them to go forward with this project . . . It was Nixon who had him do a deal with the Mafia in Florida to kill Castro."[8]

It was logical that Nixon would want Maheu on the project, since he'd worked with him on two previous covert operations, one of which could have led to an assassination. Both operations had been successful. Nixon's wealthy friend William Pawley was good for making connections, but was far too prominent to serve as an effective intermediary, and he lacked hands-on espionage skills. In addition, until recently Nixon's most trusted former aide had been a partner of Maheu's. Also, Howard Hughes, Maheu's main client, was closer to Nixon than he was to any politician. Though Hughes had vanished from public view, a Nixon memo confirms that the reclusive billionaire had actually met with Nixon personally the previous year.[9]

In August 1960, the ramped-up Cuban operation of Vice President Richard Nixon and the CIA progressed rapidly. No one informed President Eisenhower about the new phase of the CIA-Mafia plots because the President was not in favor of assassinating Fidel. The secretary of Eisenhower's National Security Council later said that he had "discussed the possible assassination of Castro" with the President. But he said Eisenhower "rejected the idea—but on purely pragmatic grounds [, saying,] 'Why should anyone assassinate the head of Cuba, Castro? Because we'd only get his brother instead, who's worse.'"[10]

However, an enthusiastic Nixon apparently told Eisenhower enough about the non-assassination aspects of the overall Cuban operation. In Eisenhower's August 18, 1960, Cabinet meeting, he approved a $13 million budget for the CIA's new Cuban operation. In the final months of the administration, that was a huge sum for a covert operation, especially with the small number of Cuban exile "troops" being trained, which had grown from dozens to just over a hundred at that time. However, Nixon anticipated a tight race with Senator John F. Kennedy, and felt that foreign policy was the only key that could ensure his triumph.

The following week, Nixon—growing more confident the Cuba plan would work—gave an almost too-revealing campaign speech in Detroit. Nixon proudly proclaimed his "determination [to stop] a foreign-controlled Communist dictatorship in Cuba. The United States has the power—and Mr. Castro knows this—to throw him out of office any day that we would choose." Nixon soon sensed he had gone too far, given the secret nature of the Cuba plan and Soviet leader

Khrushchev's missile threat the month before. That same day, Nixon "clarified" his statement for reporters, saying it was true that "if the United States wanted to use its full military and economic power, it could topple Mr. Castro." But Nixon disingenuously added that in bringing up the matter in his earlier speech, "My point was that is simply out of the question."[11]

Meanwhile, the CIA has admitted it began working with Nixon's associate Robert Maheu to have him reach out to a new mob leader to handle the assassination of Fidel. Maheu said that his CIA case officer, James O'Connell, had specifically requested Johnny Rosselli for the job. O'Connell—and his superior, CIA Security Director Sheffield Edwards—had met Rosselli at a small party given by Maheu earlier that summer. According to Maheu, at the party, "Sheff Edwards had cornered Rosselli for a little chat" and "soon after" the party, "Edwards and the CIA checked out Rosselli to determine just how far [up] his connections ran" in the Mafia. The CIA "learned that Johnny Rosselli had access to the highest levels of the Mafia." The CIA then contacted Maheu after—as noted previously—"the CIA had been in touch with Nixon," who gave the go-ahead and had Maheu "do a deal with the Mafia . . . to kill Castro." O'Connell could have approached Rosselli himself, but the point was to have Maheu do it, so that—the CIA hoped—Rosselli wouldn't realize he was actually working for the CIA.[12]

The CIA probably regarded Rosselli as a logical choice to help arrange Fidel's assassination in Cuba. Rosselli had managed a Havana casino for godfather Santo Trafficante, and the CIA no doubt hoped he still had some contacts there. The CIA probably knew that Rosselli had been very active in Guatemala just prior to the assassination of that country's President in 1957. In 1960, Rosselli's main mob role was as the Chicago Mafia's point man in Hollywood and Las Vegas. Rosselli was such a powerful force in Las Vegas that the CIA probably knew that less than two years earlier, Rosselli had approved the high-profile 1958 murders of Gus Greenbaum and his wife by two hit men from Miami, a murder that was never solved. The high-profile Greenbaum was the unofficial mayor of the Las Vegas strip and a good friend of Senator Barry Goldwater.

Johnny Rosselli was also a good choice for the CIA given the ongoing Presidential campaign and the possibility that JFK might be elected President. Rosselli had a low-enough profile that he hadn't been called to testify before JFK's Senate crime hearings, and he wasn't named in Robert Kennedy's book *The Enemy Within*. Yet Rosselli was close to powerful mob leaders the Kennedys had targeted, men like Sam Giancana and Santo Trafficante. In addition, Johnny Rosselli was known to be a longtime, close associate of Frank Sinatra, who was a very high-profile supporter of JFK's campaign.

This new phase of the CIA-Mafia plots, with Rosselli and Maheu, is extremely well documented by the CIA Inspector General's Report cited earlier and from Senate and House investigations in the 1970s. However, more recently declassified files show that important parts of this phase of the CIA-Mafia plots were withheld from those investigations and even from Nixon after he became President.

Robert Maheu would later admit that he told Howard Hughes about the CIA-Mafia plots, saying his secret work for the U.S. government "included plans to dispose of Mr. Castro." The secret of Nixon's involvement held by Maheu, Hughes, and Rosselli—and others they told or might have told—would help to trigger the Watergate scandal. Rosselli and Maheu would have to submit to interviews by investigators for the Senate Watergate Committee. Ultimately, Richard Nixon's choice of Robert Maheu as the CIA's new intermediary to Johnny Rosselli and the Mafia would have consequences that would haunt Nixon for the rest of his political life.[13]

In early September 1960, private investigator Robert Maheu met his old friend Johnny Rosselli at the Brown Derby restaurant in Beverly Hills, according to the Senate testimony of both men. Maheu was supposed to tell Rosselli he represented wealthy "businesses interests of Wall Street" who were willing to pay "$150,000" to get rid of Fidel Castro. When Rosselli proved reluctant, Maheu abandoned the cover story and instead told Rosselli the truth: that "high government officials" in Washington wanted him to hire Cubans to assassinate Fidel Castro. Maheu stressed that the operation had to be completely deniable, both for the government and for Maheu. Rosselli later claimed that he decided to help assassinate Fidel not for the money, but out of patriotism. However, as historians have pointed out, Rosselli was actually hoping for something else: official protection from any criminal prosecution the government might take against him, especially since—like Carlos Marcello—he wasn't a U.S. citizen. Rosselli agreed to meet with Maheu's backers to hear more. It's also important to point out that while most of the documentation revolves around the assassination of Fidel, Maheu said he was told by his CIA case officer O'Connell that Fidel's "brother Raul and Che Guevara" also should be "assassinated."[14]

Rosselli couldn't have proceeded with the deal without the approval of his boss, Sam Giancana. Unlike Trafficante and Marcello, Giancana wasn't a godfather. Ultimate Chicago Mafia power rested with Giancana's mentor, sixty-three-year-old Paul "The Waiter" Ricca, and consigliere Tony "Big Tuna" Accardo. They had final say on all major decisions, but the fifty-two-year-old Sam Giancana ran the Chicago Mafia on a daily basis. Starting as a driver for Prohibition gangster Al Capone, Giancana had risen high in the Chicago mob's hierarchy by combining a flair for brutality and murder with a surface charm that many women found irresistible. Sam Giancana was ruthless—as Robert Kennedy had shown in his questioning of Giancana and other witnesses—but also smart. As Giancana allegedly said to his brother about the possibility of a JFK Presidency, "You don't know what the hell Jack'll do once he's elected. With Nixon, you know where you stand." Giancana would have quickly approved Rosselli's participation in the CIA-Mafia plots for any leverage over the government the scheme could generate. As an added bonus, if Fidel were assassinated, that would only increase Giancana's stature among Mafia leaders.[15]

On September 14, 1960, Johnny Rosselli and Robert Maheu met with the CIA's Operational Support Chief, James O'Connell, at New York City's Plaza Hotel, as the CIA admits and Senate testimony confirms. The three had met socially at Maheu's home months before. James O'Connell says he stuck to the "Wall Street" cover story and wanted Rosselli to do the same when he went to Miami to start making plans for Fidel's assassination. James O'Connell told Rosselli he wanted a "gangland style killing." Much evidence indicates that the CIA really wanted the Mafia involved so the United States could blame Fidel's assassination on the mob. After the anti-U.S. demonstrations and riots that plagued Nixon's 1958 Latin American tour, the CIA realized that the Agency would be blamed for Fidel's death unless they could arrange another obvious suspect. However, the savvy Rosselli realized what the CIA was up to and knew the Mafia could not operate its casinos in Cuba if the Cuban people blamed the mob for Fidel's murder. He knew his boss, Giancana, would feel the same way, as would godfather Santo Trafficante, who really had the connections in Cuba to have Fidel assassinated. Accordingly, Rosselli would soon insist on a quieter form of assassination. O'Connell pressed Rosselli to introduce him to his Mafia superior, "Sam [Giancana] who either had or could arrange contacts with syndicate elements in Cuba who might want the job" of assassinating Fidel. Rosselli agreed, and the trio planned to meet again soon in Miami, Florida. It's ironic that at the time the three were in New York, the city's newspapers were filled with articles about the impending visit of Fidel Castro to the U.N.[16]

CIA officials believed the O'Connell-Rosselli-Maheu meeting had gone well, and the Agency began making plans to coordinate this new phase of the CIA-Mafia plots with its ongoing Cuban exile operation involving E. Howard Hunt. On September 20, 1960—six days after the CIA's New York meeting with Rosselli and four days before Rosselli's next CIA meeting in Miami—the Agency assigned two new cover identities to Hunt. They were "Eduardo," the primary code name under which Hunt would become known to many exiles, and "Mr. Edwards," an alias Hunt would use until Watergate. Despite all the Congressional investigations of Hunt in the 1970s—from the Senate Watergate Committee to the Church Committee to the House Select Committee on Assassinations—his CIA records under those cover identities were never provided to Congressional investigators, not even when they were specifically requested. That strongly indicates Hunt was involved in extremely sensitive—or potentially embarrassing or criminal—activities while working under those cover identities for the CIA.[17]

CIA agents and officers often have several cover identities, sometimes specific to a particular project. That's because different projects can have different supervisors and chains of command. For example, because of Congressional investigations, we know that Hunt's good friend and CIA associate David Atlee Phillips sometimes operated under three different cover identities and chains of command in the same time period. Each cover identity can have its own files, background, cover employment, ID, and specific "pocket litter"—unassuming material, such as notes, transportation tickets, or photographs, that back up an agent's cover. As shown in later chapters, regarding Hunt's "Eduardo" identity, sometimes one cover identity for a sensitive operation could be used by two different CIA officers. Part of the reason for such secrecy—even within the CIA—was the constant worry by some high-ranking Agency officials that the CIA itself had been penetrated by one or more high-level Soviet "moles." Thus, even if one operation or cover identity were compromised, the same agent's other operations and cover identities might be kept secure from the Soviets. However, that also made it possible for the CIA to give Congressional investigators some files on a target like Hunt, while withholding others.

Strong evidence indicates that E. Howard Hunt had a role in the CIA-Mafia plots by this time, if not earlier. As documented earlier, Hunt himself admitted that he had a "planned assassination [of] Castro operation." Hunt's boss, Richard Bissell, was personally running the CIA-Mafia plots at this time. Hunt's new "Eduardo" alias had previously shown up in the 1959 CIA-Mafia assassination plots brokered by Jimmy Hoffa. The focus of this new phase of the CIA-Mafia plots was going to be Miami, where Hunt's Cuban activities were then based. Since Hunt was responsible for forming the exile leadership and getting them quickly into Cuba to rule (with U.S. help) right after Fidel's murder, it's only logical that he would be involved in the CIA-Mafia plots to some degree. Two of Hunt's main exile leaders were Tony Varona and Manuel Artime, whom he met on a regular basis and who were involved in the CIA-Mafia plots. The CIA admitted Varona's involvement in 1975 Senate hearings. It was only in 2005 that this author first published a declassified CIA file withheld from Congress that revealed "Artime [was] supported by CIA. He was also used by the Mafia in the Castro operation." Artime also became Hunt's lifelong best friend and a hush-money paymaster for Hunt and Nixon during Watergate.[18]

A CIA-approved book by former CIA agent Bayard Stockton even confirms that Hunt and Rosselli worked together at times. According to Stockton, Johnny Rosselli went to the Dominican Republic within months of his meeting with Maheu and O'Connell, "accompanied by Howard Hunt of the CIA." Senate investigators confirmed that at the time of the Hunt-Rosselli visit, the CIA was providing "pistols" and "carbines" for the assassination of the Dominican leader.[19]

On September 21, the day after Hunt received his new cover identities and three days before CIA Support Chief O'Connell was to meet with Rosselli in Miami, the CIA assigned Hunt a new assistant: CIA agent Bernard Barker, a longtime mob associate (and future Watergate burglar). Rosselli had worked for Trafficante, and Trafficante was also Barker's Mafia boss. A Kennedy aide confirmed to this author that after Barker fled to the United States from Cuba, "Barker was connected to [Santo Trafficante]," as this book details later. "Bernard Barker [was] closely associated with organized crime, and specifically with . . . Santo Trafficante," wrote noted historian John H. Davis. Barker's ties to Trafficante were confirmed by two Congressional investigators, Michael Ewing and attorney Bud Fensterwald (who also represented Barker's fellow Watergate burglar, former CIA officer James McCord).[20]

Not surprisingly, within a week of Barker's becoming Hunt's assistant, the CIA admits that Trafficante officially joined the CIA-Mafia plots. As documented earlier, FBI and CIA files confirm Barker's mob ties, and it is interesting that Barker would be fired from the CIA in 1966, just after the CIA-Mafia plots finally ended. However, the CIA needed a mob associate like Barker in 1960, and it made sense for the Agency to make Barker Hunt's assistant, since Hunt had no previous experience with the Mafia and had spent much of his CIA career overseas. Then too, as a Cuban exile, Barker knew both the target country and the exile community.[21]

Bernard Barker would later tell NBC News that "Mr. Hunt personally always had the theory that the physical elimination of Fidel Castro was the proper way for the liberation of Cuba." Barker's criminal background gave him another skill the CIA found useful for Hunt. Former FBI agent William Turner wrote that Barker's job "as Hunt's right-hand man was to deliver CIA cash laundered through foreign banks to the [Cuban] exile groups." Pulitzer Prize–winning journalist Haynes Johnson put it more bluntly when he said, "Barker was [a] bagman in Miami [who] dispersed money to Cubans from CIA funds." According to one report, "Hunt carried as much as $115,000 in his briefcase." When Hunt tried to rent "a lavish house with indoor swimming pool, facing Biscayne Bay" to use as a base for himself and Barker, "the deal fell through because Hunt could not disabuse the owner of the notion that he was a major racketeer."[22]

As noted earlier, Barker—born in Cuba of U.S. parents—had lost his American citizenship because of his unsavory activities with the Cuban police in the 1950s. Barker had also helped two of Hunt's primary Cuban exile leaders—Manuel Artime and Tony Varona—escape from Cuba. Like Barker, both Varona and Artime were involved in illegal activities with Santo Trafficante. Barker was in regular contact with Varona and Artime while both were involved in the CIA-Mafia plots, and Artime became good friends with Barker.[23]

The preponderance of the evidence shows that E. Howard Hunt and his new assistant Bernard Barker were almost certainly involved with the Nixon-driven CIA-Mafia plots with Johnny Rosselli. That would also explain why the identities of all of Barker's CIA supervisors—for his entire official CIA career, from 1959 to 1966—were withheld from Congressional investigators, even though Barker was subject to the same intense Congressional scrutiny as Hunt. It's known that Hunt was Barker's supervisor, at least for his most sensitive activities, from September 1960 through the end of 1963, because both men have admitted it. Yet that basic fact is missing from all the operational files released about Barker (and Hunt) so far made public. Only in recent years has it been revealed that Bernard Barker had several cover identities, and at least one secret CIA cryptonym (code name), "AMCLATTER-1."*[24]

Bebe Rebozo, Richard Nixon's best friend, was another important figure distributing CIA money to Hunt's Cuban exiles: "According to CIA sources, Barker and Rebozo met . . . when both were funneling money to the CIA-financed" Cuban exiles, according to an investigative report in *Rolling Stone*. Rebozo's money role with CIA exiles was also documented by *Newsday*. At the same time Rebozo was "funneling money" for the CIA, Miami Police Intelligence said that "Rebozo was running a numbers racket out of one of his coin laundry businesses [while] fronting for a mobster." Historian Richard D. Mahoney wrote that "Rebozo is a well-known fixture in various mob families." The Rebozo-Barker relationship would grow in the coming years, and would be a source of worry for Nixon during Watergate.[25]

On September 24, 1960, Johnny Rosselli met with investigator Robert Maheu and CIA officer James O'Connell at a Miami hotel. Rosselli began using the cover names of "John Rawlston" and "J.A. Rollins" for his hotel registration and other business. Their discussions "to work out the details" about the Mafia's search for Cubans to assas-

*Hunt's CIA colleague David Atlee Phillips used the cover identity "Lawrence F. Barker" for Cuban operations, and kept using it even after Bernard Barker began working on Cuban operations for Hunt. Having two "Barkers" in Cuban operations seems confusing, unless Phillips had been one of Barker's supervisors—perhaps when both men were in Cuba.

sinate Fidel Castro went well, and in the coming weeks, CIA man O'Connell would spend much time in Miami.[26]

Following his meeting with Rosselli in Miami, O'Connell reported to his supervisor, CIA Security Director Sheffield Edwards, that he was making progress. Edwards and Richard Bissell, Hunt's supervisor, together decided to brief CIA Director Allen Dulles about the CIA-Mafia plots. They met with Dulles and CIA Deputy Director General Charles Cabell in late September and managed to get their points across, though without—as they later claimed—using any "bad words" like "assassination." That was done to keep things deniable for Dulles and Cabell, though Bissell later testified that he was sure that "Dulles knew exactly what he had approved." After the meeting, Bissell gave Sheffield Edwards $150,000 to use with the Mafia. The new CIA-Mafia plots were about to take a large step up the Mafia food chain.[27]

Godfather Santo Trafficante and Chicago mobster Sam Giancana officially joined the CIA-Mafia plotting "during the week of September 25, 1960," according to CIA files. Trafficante and Giancana met with their associate Johnny Rosselli and Robert Maheu at Miami Beach's stylish Fontainebleau, the city's most glamorous hotel. CIA officer James O'Connell would soon also meet Trafficante and Giancana as the assassination plots progressed. According to some CIA reports, Maheu and the CIA didn't initially know the true identities of Trafficante and Giancana and learned them only weeks later from a newspaper article. However, Congressional investigators found no evidence to support the article claim, and other CIA reports make it clear that the whole point of using Rosselli was to approach Mafia leaders like Giancana and especially Trafficante, since he was the one "who had . . . syndicate elements in Cuba who might handle the job."[28]

Santo Trafficante was important for the plots because a CIA report says the Agency knew that "gambling casinos were still operating in Cuba, and Trafficante was making regular trips between Miami and Havana on syndicate business." In addition, Trafficante was the most important Mafia chief in Miami. While Miami was technically an "open city," like Las Vegas, where any mob family could operate, Trafficante was quickly becoming the dominant Mafia force there. The city was not only a fashionable and glamorous resort destination but also home to increasing numbers of Cuban exiles, who became a profit source for Trafficante because of his hold on their popular *bolita* gambling racket.[29]

Though still based in Tampa, Santo Trafficante spent increasing amounts of time in Miami, where he shared an office with one of Jimmy Hoffa's Teamsters locals. Rosselli later took one of the CIA's assassination planners to Trafficante's lavish office. In addition, Trafficante had known almost all of those involved in the 1959 phase of the CIA-Mafia plots, and thus knew what hadn't worked. While Trafficante's Cuban ties, fluent Spanish, and heavy presence in Miami made him a logical choice for the CIA-Mafia plots, mob protocol required that Rosselli bring Sam Giancana into the scheme. Both Trafficante and Giancana no doubt wanted to be part of the operation for whatever leverage over the U.S. government the plots could give them.[30]

At the Fontainebleau meeting in Miami, CIA reports say that experienced killer Sam Giancana ruled out "a typical gangland-style killing in which Castro would be gunned down." Giancana also excluded any "use of firearms," since the hit men's "chance of survival and escape would be negligible." Instead, Rosselli suggested killing Fidel in a way that was "nice and clean, without getting into any kind of out-and-out ambushing." According to the CIA, "Giancana stated a preference for a lethal pill that could be put into Castro's food or drink."[31]

By October 18, 1960, the CIA had gone along with Rosselli and Giancana's suggestion, as verified by a memo sent that day by FBI Director J. Edgar Hoover to the CIA's Richard Bissell. Hoover says that:

> During recent conversations with several friends, Giancana stated that Fidel Castro was to be done away with very shortly . . . that Castro's assassination would occur in November [and] that he had already met with the assassin-to-be on three occasions. . . . Giancana [said] the "assassin" had arranged with a girl, not further described, to drop a "pill" in some drink or food of Castro's.[32]

Vice President Richard Nixon and his aide General Cushman had ties to the origin of the CIA-Mafia plot to poison Fidel that was outlined in Hoover's memo. A CIA memo dated only four months earlier confirms that Nixon aide Cushman had been told about a young American woman who had returned to the United States after working in Castro's Havana office. She had told the CIA about a coworker in Havana, Marita Lorenz, who'd had an affair with Fidel before coming to the United States. Twenty-year-old Marita Lorenz had been photographed with the thirty-three-year-old Fidel, and one American magazine had run an article about her romance with Fidel. Sensing an opportunity, CIA files show the Agency began monitoring Marita Lorenz.[33]

Richard Nixon had been talking with his friend, the wealthy former diplomat William Pawley, about the problem of Fidel Castro since January 1960. Those contacts continued into the summer, when Marita Lorenz was approached by "a close Pawley associate," a former FBI agent now helping the CIA. Pawley's ex-FBI friend then introduced Marita Lorenz to Frank Fiorini. Pawley's associate and Fiorini began pressuring Lorenz to become part of a plot to "eliminate" Fidel. Fiorini "told Lorenz that her mission was a CIA-backed operation." After her talks with Fiorini, Lorenz says, "she met a CIA officer known to anti-Castro fighters as Eduardo," and after Watergate, she identified the man as E. Howard Hunt.[34]

Fiorini (known as "Frank Sturgis" when he was a Watergate burglar) was a logical choice for this part of the CIA-Mafia plot to kill Fidel, because he was later confirmed to be a CIA contract agent. Fiorini also worked for Santo Trafficante and he knew Sam Giancana, the two most powerful mob chiefs in the CIA-Mafia plots. CIA files show that Fiorini was very close to Hunt's new assistant, Bernard Barker, who—like Fiorini—also worked for Santo Trafficante. For decades, Fiorini and Hunt both denied they had ever met until their work together for Richard Nixon in 1972—something that strains credibility, given Fiorini's dozens of documented meetings with Hunt's assistant Barker in the early 1960s. However, near the end of his life, Hunt finally admitted he had known Fiorini in the early 1960s.[35]

In October 1960, after many weeks of Fiorini's coaxing, Marita Lorenz finally agree to return to Havana to kill her former lover, Fidel. She was given "two . . . odorless and tasteless . . . poison capsules" to "slip into one of Castro's drinks." To prevent discovery when she arrived at the Havana airport, she "hid the [poison] capsules in a jar of cold cream." Fidel had agreed to meet her in a suite at the former Habana Hilton (now the Habana Libre). After reuniting with Fidel, Lorenz tried to retrieve the capsules when she was alone in the suite's bathroom. Lorenz says "she dug the capsules out of the cold cream only to find them glutinous and greasy, in no state to slip unnoticed into Castro's coffee." Panicked, she "flushed them down the drain."[36]

After Lorenz flew back to Miami the next day, she faced Fiorini's "rage and scorn" for failing in her mission to kill Fidel. Fiorini later said he thought Lorenz had just lost her nerve or changed her mind about killing Fidel. However, Fiorini was apparently rewarded for at least mounting the poison pill operation. Like Barker, Fiorini had lost his U.S. citizenship because of his earlier work for the Cuban government. Despite Fiorini's Mafia activities and numerous violations of U.S. neutrality laws, the U.S. government would restore Fiorini's citizenship just months after the fall 1960 attempt to poison Fidel.* [37]

CIA memos and reports confirm that poisons were being developed to use against Castro in the summer of 1960, providing further confirmation of the fall 1960 CIA-Mafia plot to poison Fidel. Richard Bissell had approved ordering the CIA's "Technical Services Division [to] investigate techniques of assassination" for Fidel, including poison. The memos show that Marita Lorenz's pills dissolved too soon because the first batch CIA Technical Services prepared had just the opposite problem: The pills "didn't dissolve" in a glass of water, but "just sank to the bottom of the glass." Unfortunately in making a pill that dissolved, the CIA made them too fragile to withstand Lorenz's cold cream.[38]

The Agency also admits that "botulinum toxin" was used on a "box of Castro's favorite cigars," and the poison was "so potent that a person would die after putting one in his mouth." The poison-tainted "cigars were ready on October 7, 1960," but apparently the Agency dropped that idea to focus on pills instead. The same week that Trafficante and Giancana joined the CIA-Mafia plots, the CIA admits it also had an Agency scientist take a special poison to Africa on September 26, 1960, to try to assassinate the charismatic leader of the Congo, Patrice Lumumba. The CIA gave the ominous code name ZR/RIFLE to its overall effort to assassinate foreign leaders Fidel and Lumumba.[39]

. . .

*Marita Lorenz remained bitter at Fiorini and "Eduardo," and after Watergate, she embellished and invented 1963 activities for Fiorini and Hunt to put them in a bad light. Despite her later embellishments, her 1960 activities with Castro are remarkably well documented. Even a 1977 internal CIA report that attempted to discredit the accounts of Lorenz and Fiorini had to ignore proven facts like Fiorini's status as a CIA contract agent, which was confirmed by two CIA Directors.

In addition to their assassination plots, the CIA mounted other covert actions against Cuba, most involving Cuban exiles conducting sabotage and espionage on the island. For example, on October 4, 1960, twenty-one CIA-backed guerillas were arrested—and their leader, a U.S. citizen, killed—when they disembarked in Cuba's Oriente Province. The CIA's most skilled "boatman" for sneaking CIA-backed exiles into Cuba was CIA agent Eugenio Martinez, who made hundreds of clandestine runs during his career. Martinez would later join his friend Bernard Barker as one of the Watergate burglars.[40]

Other CIA efforts against Fidel ranged from the serious to the ridiculous. As an example of the former, on September 8, 1960, three CIA agents were captured in Cuba as part of a plot to bug the office of the Communist Chinese News Agency. For the latter, the CIA admits that in 1960, it looked at using an LSD-like chemical on Fidel so that he would appear mentally ill. At Richard Helms's suggestion, the Agency also tried to develop a chemical to damage Fidel's image by causing his trademark beard to fall out.[41]

By the last half of October, time was running short for the Mafia and the CIA to assassinate Fidel before Richard Nixon's deadline of election day. Johnny Rosselli, Santo Trafficante, and Sam Giancana turned to Chicago mobster Richard Cain for their next attempt to murder Fidel. Cain—whose real name was Ricardo Scalzetti—was an experienced "made" member of the Chicago Mafia and a former Chicago police detective. The thirty-six-year-old Cain was a veteran investigator who specialized in wiretaps and bugging, which meant he was good at surreptitious entries and exits. Richard Cain worked hard to appear to be a good cop while he was actually helping the Chicago Mafia, often acting as Giancana's "bagman," even as he carried out his official police duties.[42]

Richard Cain "knew his way around Cuba" and "was fluent in Spanish," which made the mobster a good potential assassin. After botulin tablets had been delivered to "Giancana and Rosselli," Richard "Cain filed a passport application in Chicago, stating . . . he was leaving from Miami on October 15, 1960." To help cover his lethal mission—and provide a degree of protection for himself—Cain arranged on his own to file general reports about Cuba with the head of the CIA's Chicago office. But his Chicago CIA contact knew nothing about Cain's assassination mission, since the Agency's plots with the

Mafia were known to fewer than ten CIA officials, officers, and agents (and to none of the CIA agents stationed in Cuba, not even the CIA's Havana Station Chief).* [43]

Overtly, Richard Cain claimed to be going to Cuba for *Life* magazine, and he traveled with a Cuban woman so they could appear to be an innocent couple. They took several "trips into Cuba, to try and hatch a plan" to get to Castro. Keeping in mind the CIA's two previously mentioned female sources who had actually worked in Fidel Castro's office, it's not surprising that Cain focused his attention on that office rather than on any of Fidel's several residences. As Cain later revealed to two of his family members, he finally "made it into Castro's office."[44]

But once Richard Cain was actually inside Castro's office with the CIA's lethal pills, Cain "was unable to locate a suitable way to plant the botulin tablets to ensure they would be ingested by Castro." Though not mentioned in his brief account to his family members, there's a chance Cain also carried one or more of "Castro's favorite cigars" treated with the CIA poison, since the CIA admits they were ready eight days before Cain left for Cuba.[45]

Cain's female Cuban companion had waited for him while he went into Castro's office. When he returned they tried to leave the area, but "while exiting the grounds [she] was captured and [Cain] only narrowly escaped himself." Cain quickly "left the island," while his former companion was "quickly tried and executed," leaving Cain "shaken by the experience." Cain met with his boss Sam Giancana at the Rivera Hotel, to deliver the bad news. No doubt the CIA was disappointed when they got the news, but they were impressed that Cain had managed to get inside Fidel's office. The CIA "asked the FBI to conduct a background investigation of Cain," and the FBI interviewed him in Miami on November 2, 1960 (about his general background, not the Castro assassination attempt). The CIA would use Cain in several roles for the next four years, as verified by numerous declassified files, including one involving a top secret Cuban operation that also involved E. Howard Hunt and Tony Varona. As for the fall 1960 CIA-Mafia plots, Giancana talked to Cain about "trying to recruit a Cuban for the job" of assassinating Fidel. But CIA files show that

*Among the CIA personnel who knew about the CIA-Mafia plots at this time were Allen Dulles, Charles Cabell, Richard Bissell, Sheffield Edwards, James O'Connell, E. Howard Hunt, Bernard Barker, and contract agent Frank Fiorini.

would be done by Santo Trafficante, who had far more Cuban contacts than Cain or Giancana.[46]

Since Robert Maheu said "it was Nixon who had him do a deal with the Mafia in Florida to kill Castro," it's supremely ironic that so many future Watergate figures would come out of—or be touched by—those CIA-Mafia plots: Hunt, Barker, Fiorini/Sturgis, Artime, Trafficante, Rosselli, Hoffa, Rebozo, Maheu, Helms, and Hughes. As for Richard Nixon, at the same time this new phase of the plots was unfolding in September and October of 1960, he was in the fight of his political life with John F. Kennedy. Yet if the CIA-Mafia plots succeeded, and Cuba was in turmoil after Fidel's murder, Nixon could hope that most voters would stick with a sitting Vice President with eight years of proven foreign affairs experience over the younger and comparatively inexperienced Senator Kennedy.

CHAPTER 8

September–November 1960: Nixon's First Mafia Bribe for Hoffa, and the Election

From September 1960 to the November election, the final months of Richard Nixon's campaign played out against the backdrop of Fidel Castro's Cuba. However, the public pronouncements of Nixon and JFK about Castro were only part of the story. The hidden history of the CIA's plot with the Mafia to assassinate Fidel often puts the candidates' public statements in a different light. It also casts more light on Watergate, since the CIA's newly ramped-up plot with Santo Trafficante and Johnny Rosselli was just one of two related developments in September 1960 that would trigger that 1972 scandal. The other hugely important development was a $500,000 bribe to Richard Nixon from Trafficante and other mob leaders, on behalf of Jimmy Hoffa.[1]

In September of 1960, even as Richard Nixon looked ahead to his first debate with JFK, Nixon held only a slim lead in the polls. He needed both cash to run his campaign and any labor support he could find, since organized labor overwhelmingly supported JFK. In the weeks before his first debate, Nixon cut a deal to get both, using some of the same people who were in the CIA-Mafia plots to kill Fidel.[2]

Teamster President Jimmy Hoffa was under increasing legal pressure because of the publicity John and Robert Kennedy had generated from their crime hearings. As Hoffa expert Dan Moldea discovered, "the CIA feared that further involving Hoffa, who was under growing government surveillance, could endanger the entire project" of assassinating Fidel before the election. After Maheu and Rosselli began working on the plots for the CIA, the Agency no longer needed Hoffa.

Yet Nixon couldn't afford to alienate the leader of the only major labor union that might support him.[3]

Richard Nixon, or his associates, found a solution that would take Hoffa out of the CIA-Mafia plots and secure Nixon the union support—and money—that his campaign needed. Easing Hoffa out as CIA-Mafia liaison wasn't a difficult transition, since Hoffa knew most of the new participants. In fact, Hoffa had employed the new intermediary, Robert Maheu, several years earlier to sweep his office for bugging devices. Maheu had been introduced to Hoffa by Washington attorney Edward Bennett Williams, who also represented Sam Giancana and Bernard Barker. And Hoffa shared Florida attorney Frank Ragano with Santo Trafficante.[4]

By September 1960, Richard Nixon and Jimmy Hoffa had been courting each other for months. Earlier that year, Nixon had a close friend, former California Congressman Allan Oakley Hunter, meet with Hoffa. After the meeting Allan Hunter reported back to Nixon, saying Hoffa had complained that due to publicity from the Kennedy hearings, Attorney General William Rogers was now "harassing him [with] a large number of investigators." Hoffa also raised the matter of the "Grand Jury" looking into his "Florida land case" regarding the Sun Valley development and Hoffa "asked that the judge be removed." Some considered Jimmy Hoffa's Sun Valley scandal "an open-and-shut" case that was sure to result in his conviction, even though Hoffa was being represented by the capable Ragano.[5]

The first meeting between Nixon's emissary Allan Hunter and Jimmy Hoffa had been followed by another in late July, "at the Republican National Convention." Nixon wasn't seeking a personal endorsement from the controversial Hoffa, who was about to be indicted. But Hoffa explained to Allan Hunter that he would help Nixon by "generating endorsements from local Teamster officials" and by harshly criticizing JFK. Hoffa could also promise Nixon an endorsement from the Teamsters union itself.[6]

By early September, Nixon had clearly struck a deal with Hoffa, because on September 7, 1960, the Teamsters' "general executive board gave" Nixon "the union's official support," while calling JFK "a very real danger to our nation." At the same time, Hoffa began to "hammer away at [JFK in the press] for the duration of the campaign."[7]

Jimmy Hoffa's Mafia friends were an important part of his deal with Richard Nixon. Prior to September 26, 1960, Hoffa went to

Louisiana "to meet Carlos Marcello." Louisiana-based Hoffa aide Grady Edward Partin, who later "turned government informant," was with Hoffa at the meeting. The informant Partin said, "Marcello had a suitcase filled with $500,000 cash which was going to Nixon." That was only half of a promised total payment to Nixon of $1 million (over $6 million in today's dollars), with "the other half coming from the mob boys in New Jersey and Florida." The Florida mobster contributing was Santo Trafficante, who was at the time joining the CIA-Mafia plots. Among the "mob boys" in New Jersey was Mafia capo Tony Provenzano, Vice President of a New Jersey Teamster local who was close to one of the mob figures in the original Hoffa-brokered plots between the CIA and the Mafia. In a boast to a family member, Sam Giancana claimed that he was also part of the group "giving the Nixon campaign a million bucks."[8]

The September 1960 Mafia-Hoffa-Nixon bribe has been extensively documented. The man who witnessed Jimmy Hoffa accepting $500,000 from Carlos Marcello for Richard Nixon was Louisiana Teamster official Grady Partin. Two years later, Partin became a trusted informant for the Justice Department, and that's when he first told Justice about the bribe for Nixon. Partin would remain an undercover informant against Hoffa for another year and a half, and his testimony against Hoffa would eventually send the Teamster President to prison. Partin passed a government polygraph test about the bribe, and the Justice Department found independent "information confirming the Marcello donation" to Hoffa for Nixon. Though the 1960 Mafia-Hoffa-Nixon bribe would also be independently verified by Senate investigator Michael Ewing, the public would not learn about Nixon's bribe until 1978, long after the Watergate investigations were over. Partin was able to date the timing of the bribe to shortly before September 26, 1960—the date of the first JFK-Nixon televised debate—because Partin recalled the bribe was paid before its broadcast.[9]

The Mafia-Hoffa bribe to Richard Nixon produced immediate results. "Almost coincident with the Marcello donation [to Nixon], the Eisenhower-Nixon Justice Department abruptly stopped the indictment process in the [Sun Valley] corruption case Hoffa had raised" with Nixon's emissary, Allan Hunter. If Nixon won the election, Hoffa expected to be home free. Amazingly, at the same time Nixon received the Hoffa bribe—and just weeks after the Teamsters endorsed Nixon—a Nixon aide told a reporter "you may be assured, that neither the Vice President nor the Republican Party will ever ally themselves with men like Mr. Hoffa."[10]

Richard Nixon's huge bribe orchestrated by Carlos Marcello had another important goal in addition to persuading Nixon to help Hoffa and trying to prevent John F. Kennedy from becoming President. According to Grady Partin, Marcello said he "hoped . . . to extract a pledge that a Nixon administration would not deport him." The specter of deportation was a special concern for Marcello ever since Robert Kennedy had focused so much attention on Marcello's lack of citizenship during the crime hearings.[11]

The importance to Watergate of the September 1960 Mafia-Hoffa-Nixon bribe, together with Nixon's ramped-up CIA-Mafia plots that began the same month, cannot be overstated. Those two events have never before been connected, even though the CIA's intensified plotting with the Mafia involved Santo Trafficante, who was also part of the huge Nixon bribe. While some information about those events has been public knowledge for years, this book marks the first time that all of Nixon's connections to the 1960 CIA-Mafia plots have been pulled together to document that he was the driving force behind them.

The CIA-Mafia plots with Rosselli and Trafficante have rarely been acknowledged in Watergate history, even though Rosselli was asked about them by investigators from the Senate Watergate Committee, and two of the Watergate burglars—Barker and Fiorini—were working for Trafficante at the time. Nixon's 1960 Mafia-Hoffa bribe has not been linked to Watergate before, even though Nixon would receive a second Mafia-Hoffa bribe as part of a deal finalized just six months before the Watergate break-ins began. That was in late 1971, when Marcello, Trafficante, and Provenzano were part of the second huge bribe to Richard Nixon—by then President Nixon—to secure Hoffa's release from prison, with special conditions set by the Mafia. At that same time, there would be yet another CIA plot to assassinate Fidel Castro, run by E. Howard Hunt's former partner and involving a Mafia associate. Trying to keep secret those 1971 activities, along with Nixon's original 1960 CIA-Mafia plots and Hoffa bribe, would lead to the involvement of E. Howard Hunt and three of Trafficante's men in the Watergate affair.[12]

Nixon's second Mafia-Hoffa bribe, in the Watergate era, was verified by *Time* magazine and FBI reports as being for $1 million. That amount would be discussed by Nixon on a White House tape as possible hush money for E. Howard Hunt, Bernard Barker, and the other Watergate burglars. Incredibly, a year after Nixon's resignation—and just two months after Hoffa's 1975 murder—Nixon would make his first public appearance at a high-profile golf outing with Tony Provenzano, while Provenzano was the top suspect in Hoffa's disappearance. (Provenzano would later be convicted of another murder.)[13]

Despite its importance, the original 1960 Mafia-Hoffa-Nixon bribe didn't become part of the story of Watergate because—as explained earlier—the general public did not learn about it until 1978, even though a small group of Justice Department investigators had known of it since 1962. By 1978, six years after Watergate, all the official accounts of that scandal had been written and public interest had moved on to new stories they didn't realize were related to Watergate, like the sensational murders of Hoffa, Rosselli, and Giancana (all three slayings would have links to Santo Trafficante).

As Richard Nixon prepared for his first debate with JFK, set for September 26, 1960, he still anticipated Fidel's removal before the election. Nixon's Press Secretary said later he "expected the overthrow of Castro perhaps still in October," but "if it had to be November, he would have been grateful if it were to be November 1 rather than closer to the election on the eighth." Nixon needed the boost, given the little support he had gotten from President Eisenhower. When newsmen asked Ike "to name a Nixon idea that he had adopted, Eisenhower responded with: 'If you give me a week I might think of one.'" In fact Eisenhower had adopted many of Nixon's ideas about Cuba, but with a few hundred Cuban exiles in covert training the President couldn't reveal that to the press.[14]

Nixon, hanging on to his very slim lead in the polls, campaigned furiously before the first debate, and—as has often been recounted—refused his usual TV makeup. That left the exhausted Nixon looking tired and worn. A majority of the record TV audience of seventy million thought the energetic, healthy-looking John F. Kennedy won the debate, while a far smaller radio audience gave Nixon the edge. The Republican candidate for Vice President, Henry Cabot Lodge, acidly said of Nixon, "That son of a bitch has just cost us the election." Winning the TV battle pulled JFK slightly ahead of Nixon in the polls. Four debates had been scheduled, but the next three drew much smaller audiences than the first, and the race would remain extremely close.[15]

. . .

As September of 1960 progressed, Richard Nixon—and the CIA—must have worried that some part of their covert Cuban operation might leak to the press and public. That was especially true for the Cuban exile "invasion" training, which, while small, was still far larger than the closely held CIA-Mafia plot to assassinate Fidel.

That very month, *The Miami Herald* investigated the shooting of "an American youth" near a Cuban-exile training camp near Homestead, Florida. Charges against the Cuban exiles had been dropped due to "a confidential request from federal authorities." *The Herald*'s Washington reporter used "sources at the FBI, the State Department, and the White House" to assemble a detailed article, reporting "the CIA had organized not only the Homestead camp, but a much wider recruiting effort" for exiles "to be spirited into Cuba for guerrilla warfare against Cuba." The article even mentioned the pressure on Eisenhower from "the Justice and State Departments . . . to move all such CIA training operations out of the country."[16]

CIA Director Allen Dulles met personally with *The Herald*'s reporter and bureau chief, persuading them not to run the article because it would harm "the national interest." This began a pattern of suppressing important news related to covert U.S. operations against Cuba that continued for decades.[17]

Dulles and Nixon could keep the lid on the press in America, but not in other parts of the world. Speaking to the U.N. on October 7, 1960, Cuban's Foreign Minister denounced "the CIA . . . for training exiles and mercenaries in Guatemala for an attack on Cuba." Those comments were even more accurate than the suppressed *Herald* story, showing the difficulty of keeping secret the recruitment and training of even a few hundred exiles. Still, no American newspaper, news service, or TV network appears to have reported the story, no doubt to the relief of Nixon and Dulles.[18]

Richard Nixon met with President Eisenhower on October 17, urging, "we ought to take some action with respect to Cuba at an early date," and insisting that he "wanted to be tied into the President's action in Cuba." The President gave his support to both points. The next day, Nixon's campaign speech to the American Legion denounced Fidel, calling him "an intolerable cancer" and promising that the current administration planned to "very promptly take the strongest possible economic measures." The following day, the Eisenhower-Nixon administration proclaimed "an embargo on all trade with Cuba except for . . . medicine and food." They also recalled the U.S. Ambassador to Cuba, though the American embassy remained open since it was needed as the CIA base for the impending Cuban exile operation.[19]

That same day, Fidel Castro declared that the United States planned "a large-scale invasion within the next few days." JFK felt the need to respond to Nixon and Fidel on the Cuba issue, so he had two aides—Richard Goodwin and Pierre Salinger—write a strong statement released the next day, on October 20. JFK's position paper on Cuba called the trade embargo "a dramatic but almost empty gesture," and accurately predicted it would force Cuba to increase trade with the Soviet Union. Senator Kennedy also urged more U.S. support "to strengthen the non-Batista democratic anti-Castro forces in exile and in Cuba itself, who offer eventual hope of overthrowing Castro," indicating they appeared to be getting little help from the U.S. government.[20]

JFK's statement was important because it became a major point of contention between Nixon and JFK in the campaign. The fourth debate occurred on October 21, 1960, the day after JFK's Cuba statement. Surprisingly, in the debate, Nixon mounted an eloquent case *against* a U.S.-backed "invasion of Cuba." Citing the charters of the U.N. and the Organization of American States (OAS), Nixon called JFK's Cuba statement "the most dangerous, irresponsible recommendations that he's made during the course of this campaign."[21]

Furious with JFK over his Cuba statement, Richard Nixon wrote later that as Vice President he had to publicly oppose a Cuban invasion—one that he knew was being planned—to preserve the secrecy of the operation. Nixon blamed JFK for having issued his statement before the debate, claiming that "Kennedy had been briefed by Dulles on the invasion plans," that JFK "had full knowledge of the facts" and had revealed too much. However, Nixon was being disingenuous when he wrote those comments a year and a half after the debate and a year after the disaster at the Bay of Pigs.[22]

Dulles had briefed JFK in July, when the exile training was in its infancy. Even by the time of the last debate in late October, the exile force numbered only four-hundred-plus men, and there was no plan at all for the type of large-scale, amphibious landing that would happen the following year at the Bay of Pigs. A small force of four hundred—or even two or three times that number—could never hope to stage a major landing and prevail against Fidel's army of over 32,000, backed by Cuba's two hundred thousand militia members. In October 1960, the four hundred exiles were being trained so that some could parachute into Cuba, while the rest landed in small boats, hopefully undetected. What JFK didn't know, but Dulles and Nixon did, was that the exiles were intended only to help E. Howard Hunt's Cuban exile leaders take power after the assassination of Fidel. As Richard Bissell later said, assassination was always part of the CIA's Cuban operation, which intended "that Castro would be dead before the landing." It was the assassination that was the key, not the landing. Bissell even admitted that Castro's assassination wouldn't just make the CIA's exile landing "much easier," but could even render it "unnecessary."[23]

Regarding the CIA-Mafia plots, as documented earlier, CIA Director Allen Dulles was only (lightly) briefed by Bissell about them in September 1960, so there is no way Dulles could have told JFK about the plots in July. Rumors of an exile invasion of some type ran rampant in Guatemala, the site of their training camp, and in Miami, where most of the exiles had been recruited and their families still resided. So, JFK and his aides needed no special information from Dulles to know that some type of exile action was brewing.[24]

As for Nixon's statements against U.S. help for the Cuban exiles in the fourth debate, Nixon biographer Stephen Ambrose pointed out that Nixon had no reason to say anything in public about the matter. As Vice President, he could have said in the debate (or to JFK, before the debate) that the subject of what the United States was or wasn't doing about helping the Cuban exiles "was inappropriate for a political campaign." Perhaps Nixon simply said the opposite of the truth, as so many writers have pointed out he did on numerous occasions about serious matters. Judging by Nixon's past campaign history, he probably felt comfortable using his aide Murray Chotiner's old trick: When confronted with an unpleasant reality, "deny, deny, deny."[25]

But within days after the debate, Nixon, or his aides, realized that the Vice President's comments had made him appear less forceful than Kennedy about Cuba. Three days after the debate, Nixon raised the specter of his administration's 1954 Guatemala coup, claiming that after the Árbenz government was quarantined, "the Guatemalan people themselves eventually rose up and they threw him out." Given the many CIA Guatemala coup veterans, such as E. Howard Hunt, were working at that moment on his covert Cuban operation, Nixon's comment was far more accurate than the public realized. Trying to recoup, Nixon even challenged JFK to a fifth debate, solely about "What should the U.S. government do about Cuba?" but JFK declined.[26]

On October 26, 1960—even as the CIA's plots with the Mafia had dispatched mobster Richard Cain on a new mission to slip CIA-provided poison into Castro's office—Nixon made an even bolder statement about Cuba. Nixon declared (emphasis added):

> We have quarantined Mr. Castro so that the Cuban people will see what kind of man he is, and in their own good time—and it will be a good time, and *sooner . . . than you think—that they will get rid of him*, in their own way.[27]

Richard Nixon's statement seems almost recklessly accurate, but the election was less than two weeks away, and Nixon was no doubt anxious to seize any advantage with the Cuban issue. In contrast, JFK moderated his statements about Cuba. In addition to declining the proposed fifth debate, solely about Cuba, JFK made public promises to honor all U.N. and OAS agreements, and said he actually favored only U.S. propaganda directed at Cuba so "the forces of freedom in Cuba know that we believe that freedom will again rise in their country."[28]

With over four hundred Cuban exile trainees in or heading to the CIA's training camps in Guatemala, that aspect of the operations Nixon had pushed for became more widely known. On October 30, 1960—nine days before the election—a Guatemalan newspaper "published a story disclosing that the CIA had built a heavily guarded $1-million base" near a town it named, "to train Cuban counterrevolutionaries for landing in Cuba." But it would be almost three weeks—after the election—until even a small U.S. publication mentioned the account.[29]

In late October of 1960, the Mafia chiefs began using their work for the CIA to pressure the U.S. government. This type of Mafia blackmail of the government—in return for the help the Mafia was providing and for keeping the CIA's assassination plots secret—would continue for years, into Nixon's Presidency. Sam Giancana loved the limelight and celebrities, and his girlfriend Phyllis McGuire was a member of America's top recording act at the time. Often busy in October working on the CIA-Mafia plots in Miami, Giancana worried that McGuire might be getting too close to Las Vegas comic Dan Rowan.* The suspicious Giancana asked Maheu to have the CIA tap the comedian's hotel telephone (some accounts say it was a "bug" to pick up all conversations in Rowan's hotel room). The Agency admits that CIA officer James O'Connell was agreeable, but his superior refused to allow the CIA to install the tap, although the Agency would pay to have a private detective do it.[30]

However, the private detective was arrested on October 31, 1960, after a hotel maid found the wiretap equipment in the detective's room. Though Johnny Rosselli quickly paid the man's bail, the FBI became involved in the case, setting off a year-and-a-half-long chain of events that would culminate in May 1962 with important repercussions for John and Robert Kennedy, CIA official Richard Helms, and the Mafia. The episode shows that a major motivation for mob leaders like Giancana, Rosselli, and Trafficante to help the CIA was to extract special treatment.[31]

Two men who would become household names during the Watergate era worked on Richard Nixon's 1960 campaign that fall. H.R. "Bob" Haldeman† was a veteran advertising executive with the J. Walter Thompson Agency in Los Angeles, handling accounts ranging from 7-Up and Sani-Flush to Walt Disney Productions. His ad agency gave him paid leave to work with Nixon's campaigns, because most of their corporate clients supported Nixon. For the crew-cut Haldeman, Nixon wasn't just another client; Haldeman was a true believer in what Nixon stood for and would work diligently on all of his future campaigns, eventually becoming President Nixon's Chief of Staff. By the time of Watergate, H.R. Haldeman would know that Nixon was "deeply involved" in the covert Cuban operations that grew into the Bay of Pigs and lasted until 1963, and that "Nixon knew more about the genesis of the Cuban invasion than almost anyone."[32] However, Haldeman would apparently not know the full story. That was reserved for Haldeman's friend, John Ehrlichman, the advance man for the 1960 campaign.[33]

*Later famous as costar of TV's *Rowan and Martin's Laugh-In*.
†His full name was Harry Robbins Haldeman.

John Ehrlichman, a young Seattle lawyer, would also serve Nixon loyally, from the 1960 campaign to the Nixon White House, where he became a top aide. At a critical time when President Nixon would try to retrieve all the information on his Cuban operation (and its aftermath) from his CIA Director, Richard Helms, Nixon would tell a confused Haldeman, "Ehrlichman will know what I mean."[34]

But in the fall of 1960, Haldeman and Ehrlichman both focused on Nixon's campaign, which was far different from Nixon's past (or future) campaigns. Haldeman was an excellent ad man, but since Nixon's public record was so well known, the candidate was difficult to package and sell in 1960. Haldeman would have far more success reinventing and selling Nixon's image eight years later, after Nixon had been out of the national spotlight.

Nixon muted his traditionally inflammatory campaign rhetoric in 1960 for several reasons. First, because of the Congressional investigation covered in Chapter 4, Murray Chotiner didn't play as large a role as in previous campaigns. Chotiner was still an advisor, but couldn't actually run Nixon's campaign as he had in the past. Second, unlike many previous opponents, JFK—whose father was one of the wealthiest men in America—had the resources to fight back against any smears. Third, Nixon wanted to appear Presidential, so the gutter politics of 1946, 1950, and 1952 hardly seemed appropriate in 1960. Nixon's usual Red-baiting was no longer as in vogue as it had been in the McCarthy era, and even the Hollywood blacklist started to crumble in 1960, with Kirk Douglas's credited use of blacklisted screenwriter Dalton Trumbo for *Spartacus*. Nixon still managed to issue personal attacks—like making an issue of JFK's religion, as a Roman Catholic—but that was done indirectly by associates and friends, to limit any blowback against Nixon.[35]

In the 1960 race, Richard Nixon committed far fewer campaign crimes (which Nixon's men later termed "dirty tricks") than he would in the Watergate era. Before Nixon had secured the Republican nomination, Nixon managed to position John Ehrlichman as a driver for his rival, New York's Nelson Rockefeller, to spy on him. That wasn't a crime, but a secret effort to obtain JFK's personal medical records was. JFK's healthy appearance on TV belied several medical problems, including his chronic back problems that required both painkillers and a back brace. More serious was JFK's Addison's disease, which also required medication.[36]

William Casey, a prominent New York Republican who later became CIA Director for Ronald Reagan, headed the effort of "Nixon people" to steal JFK's medical records. Burglars "broke into the offices of both of Kennedy's New York doctors," looking for medical information on JFK that could be used in the campaign. Neither burglary was ever solved.[37]

Richard Nixon also planned to use JFK's sexual liaisons against him, until FBI Director J. Edgar Hoover and Republican Senator Barry Goldwater talked him out of it. Hoover knew if JFK won, keeping that information for himself would ensure that JFK could never force him to resign, while Goldwater himself enjoyed the company of entertainers and showgirls in Las Vegas.[38]

It's well documented that both John and Robert Kennedy were tough campaigners, and often played political hardball in the 1960 campaign. Thirteen years later, Nixon had the head of the Republican National Committee accuse John and Robert Kennedy of using Carmine Bellino to bug Nixon aides and supporters during the 1960 contest. However, that claim was made when Bellino was named Chief Investigator for the Senate Watergate Committee, and no evidence was found to substantiate the accusation.[39]

However, it was with some help from the Kennedys that a major story about a past Nixon crime started to break, on October 25, 1960. Two people tried to give Kennedy associates the story of Howard Hughes's highly suspicious $205,000 ($1.2 million today) "loan" to Nixon's brother's failing business in 1956—money that some historians and journalists think was really for Richard Nixon. The Kennedys made sure the information went to a newspaper sympathetic to them, the *St. Louis Post-Dispatch*. However, the story involved not just Richard Nixon, but also America's wealthiest man, Howard Hughes, who immediately devoted his considerable resources to suppress it.[40]

Howard Hughes ordered his investigator Robert Maheu to leave Miami, where Maheu was still working on the CIA-Mafia plots to kill Fidel before the election, and fly immediately to Los Angeles. Maheu tried to find some way to squelch the account of the Hughes-Nixon loan. After reviewing Hughes's copies of the files, Maheu decided to use a sympathy angle with the *St. Louis Post-Dispatch* reporter, claiming (falsely) that if the paper printed the story, Nixon's mother would lose all her assets. As a formality, she had pledged her assets as security for the loan, since the son the funds were ostensibly for—Donald, not Richard—was almost bankrupt when Hughes gave him the "loan." The trick worked, and the editors of the *Post-Dispatch* decided not to print the story, and other editors followed their lead—until Nixon personally got involved.[41]

Not content to let the story die, Richard Nixon tried to assert control by giving a phony version of the whole loan scenario—which completely omitted both Hughes and Nixon himself—to a friendly reporter he'd used before. When that false story appeared, popular muckraking columnist Drew Pearson and his aide Jack Anderson published the true account on October 25 and October 27. After Richard Nixon denied Pearson's story, on November 1, 1960—a week before the election—"his brother Donald" contradicted Richard's phony account, when he "admitted Hughes was the source of the money." In addition, "the accountant in the case . . . said the major decisions on the arrangement for the loan had been made by Richard Nixon."[42]

However, the story quickly died without blowing up into a major scandal, probably due to additional pressure from the powerful Hughes and because many newspapers supported Nixon. Drew Pearson—and Jack Anderson, who'd already written about "Cuban freedom fighter" Frank Fiorini—would become increasingly painful thorns in Nixon's side. Years later, Nixon told H.R. Haldeman and Bebe Rebozo that the Hughes-Nixon loan "furor had been a major factor in his defeat." In fact, though, polls showed only a slight uptick for JFK after the story broke, and by election day the outcome was still too close to call. However, ironically, in a way Nixon was right: Dealing with the loan scandal had pulled Robert Maheu away from the CIA-Mafia plots at their most crucial time. It appears that October 30 was the last day Robert Maheu worked on the assassination scheme before the election, with the rest of his time devoted to keeping the Hughes-Nixon loan story from gaining traction.[43]

The CIA's plotting with Trafficante's man Frank Fiorini and Marita Lorenz, as well as with Giancana's operative Richard Cain, had failed. After Maheu was out of the picture, there is no evidence that any further attempt was planned or made before the election on November 8. The CIA had a related covert Cuban scheme in the planning stages—a fake attack on the U.S. naval base at Guantánamo Bay, designed to force Eisenhower to use the U.S. military against Cuba—but that was still over a month away. The few CIA officers and officials who knew about the CIA's plots with the Mafia had a longer-term view of the situation than Nixon, one that went well beyond the election.

For this reason, on November 4, 1960—four days before the election—the CIA admits that it formally changed "the course of the project by greatly expanding the size of the Cuban" exile force, changing its training from the guerilla actions Eisenhower had originally approved to more "conventional military lines." The timing is remarkable, coming less than a week after Robert Maheu temporarily left Miami (and the plots), and after Richard Cain's failed attempt to assassinate Fidel. However, the CIA held off issuing orders for the new expansion until after the election, when they would know whether or not Nixon would be the new President. The CIA-Mafia plots would stay in place regardless of the outcome, but if JFK won, the 471-man exile force would be tremendously expanded—something that would lead to tragedy the following year.[44]

The story of how Richard Nixon lost one of the closest elections in U.S. history to John F. Kennedy has been well recounted. Extremely bitter at the time, Nixon claimed privately that the contest had been stolen from him, focusing mainly on voter irregularities in Illinois and Texas, though also in other states (six were decided by less than 1 percent). Nixon refused to officially concede until the afternoon after election day, even though the vote totals clearly favored JFK.

Before looking at conventional views about Nixon's 1960 loss, it's important to relate more recent information about an incident now known to have cost Nixon more votes than the Hughes-Nixon loan scandal or any election irregularities by the Democrats. As documented in 2000 by historian and *Newsweek* editor Evan Thomas, Nixon lost the election because "in a half-dozen states in the East and Midwest carried by Kennedy by very narrow margins on election day, black turnout made the difference."

On October 25, 1960, rising civil rights leader Dr. Martin Luther King had been sentenced by a Georgia judge to four months hard labor for what was essentially a traffic violation. Dr. King had been sent in chains to Reidsville, a rural Georgia prison not long removed from the notorious "chain gang" era, where black prisoners faced harsher treatment than white inmates. Dr. King's wife, Coretta Scott King, feared her husband wouldn't survive his prison sentence.[45]

Richard Nixon "had good relations with Dr. King, better than

Kennedy," according to historian Stephen Ambrose. "Dr. King had voted for the Republicans in 1956," and his influential "father had endorsed Nixon." Some Democratic leaders in the South were avowed racist conservatives, which had helped Nixon and Eisenhower—representing the party of Lincoln—take 40 percent of the black vote in the 1956 election.[46]

Nixon was well aware of Dr. King's highly publicized arrest and sentencing, and it was a golden opportunity for him to maintain or even increase his share of black voters in the close 1960 race. All he had to do was issue a statement of concern about the matter. But much of the country harbored racist views in 1960, not just the Democratic South, and Nixon didn't want to alienate his conservative base of voters and major financial supporters. Nixon privately expressed sympathy for Dr. King, and he tried to persuade Eisenhower to issue a statement, but Ike refused.[47]

Nixon had not been a racist in his small Quaker hometown. He had helped the only black student at Whittier College and had "raised his voice against" the racism he saw at Duke University Law School. Nixon's bigoted statements on his White House tapes were still years in the future. Whatever Nixon's private feelings, his public actions seem to have been dictated by his desire to win at any cost. Even if Nixon didn't want to risk alienating his base by issuing a public statement, he still could have called Mrs. King to express his personal support. But Nixon made no call and issued no statement about the matter.[48]

With no help coming from Nixon or the administration, Mrs. King desperately reached out to John and Robert Kennedy, who had fought hard for a pro-civil-rights platform at the Democratic Convention. She called a Kennedy aide, pleading for her husband: "They are going to kill him . . . I know they are going to kill him." Though John F. Kennedy risked alienating his Democratic base in the South, he called Mrs. King, expressing his concern and support. JFK then called Georgia's Democratic Governor to pressure him on the issue, and had Robert Kennedy—his campaign manager—call the judge in King's case.[49]

The following day, newspapers announced that Dr. King had been released from prison after Robert Kennedy's call to the judge. Word of JFK's personal call to Mrs. King spread like wildfire in the civil rights movement. Dr. King's father, a respected civil rights leader, announced that he was switching his endorsement to JFK, and a seismic shift began in American politics that persists to this day. The story was front-page news in America's many black newspapers, and the Kennedy campaign got the word out to black churches. The toll on "'no comment' Nixon"—as he was soon being called in black communities—proved decisive in such a close election.[50]

A close analysis of voting totals confirms the conclusion of Evan Thomas: Nixon's refusal to make any public or private statement cost him the Presidency. Nixon lost half of his black support from 1956, receiving only about 20 percent of the black vote in November 1960. Decisive were the black vote totals in New Jersey and Missouri, where Nixon lost the total vote by less than 1 percent, and in Illinois, which Nixon lost by less than .2 percent. The black vote could also have been a deciding factor in Texas, which Nixon lost by 2 percent.*[51]

Richard Nixon would have won the Presidency by carrying just the additional states of Illinois, New Jersey, and Missouri, even if Texas stayed in the Democratic column. Despite all the work and attention Nixon had paid to Cuba and his efforts to have the CIA and the Mafia eliminate Fidel Castro, Nixon's last-minute failure in the area of civil rights cost him the election. That would be a lesson he would learn all too well for his next Presidential run.[52]

At the time of his loss, Nixon was looking to blame anyone but himself, since he felt he'd been cheated out of a victory. A myth has grown up that Nixon and the Republicans were stoic about the election and did not challenge the results, but as with so much else about Nixon, that spin is simply not true.[53]

Just as Richard Nixon tried to get Eisenhower to issue a statement about Dr. King—in order to reap some benefit without taking a public stand himself—Nixon met with the head of the Republican National Committee (RNC) soon after the election. Nixon didn't want to look like a sore loser to the press and public, so it was the RNC Chairman

*Richard Nixon lost Missouri by .52 percent, but the state had a black population around 10 percent, so he could have easily won that state by maintaining his previous black support. Nixon lost New Jersey by .8 percent, but its black population was close to 13 percent. The same was true even for states with wider margins like Texas, which Nixon lost by 2 percent, or 46,000 votes, amid allegations of fraud by Democrats loyal to JFK's Vice Presidential running mate, Texas Senator Lyndon Johnson. Texas had a black population of about 10 percent, meaning that if Nixon had maintained his previous level of black support, he might have won a narrow victory. The result was clearer in Illinois, which Nixon lost by a tiny .2 percent, but which had a black population of almost 15 percent; if Nixon had lost only 10 percent of the black vote—instead of the 20 percent he lost because of the Dr. King matter—he would have easily won Illinois.

who officially challenged the election results in eleven states. The challenges remained in the courts until the summer of 1961. No fraud was ever found, and the only initial election result changed was in Hawaii, where Kennedy—not original winner Nixon—won after a recount.[54]

Nixon focused on JFK's vote totals in Chicago, which helped JFK carry Illinois, since the vast majority of the state outside of Chicago usually voted Republican. Sam Giancana later boasted he had helped JFK in certain precincts where journalists found irregularities. However, Giancana's efforts with the CIA to assassinate Fidel before the election have been well documented, and a successful strike against Castro could have aided only Nixon. As revealed earlier, Giancana also boasted that he'd been part of the Mafia-Hoffa-Nixon bribe. In addition, both John and Robert Kennedy had clearly targeted Giancana when they forced him to appear before their Senate crime hearings, with Robert repeatedly taunting him. It is not surprising that Giancana would later try to claim credit for JFK's victory to his family and friends, but his boast ignores the powerful presence of Chicago's powerful Mayor Richard Daley. Historian Michael Beschloss said that "Daley's citywide control counted for more than the mob-run wards, which were solidly Democratic in any case." A published statistical analysis by political scientist Edmund Kallina shows "clearly that the Illinois Presidential vote was not stolen for Kennedy by the mob or anybody else."[55]

Even in Illinois after the election, the Republican-dominated State Board of Elections unanimously rejected any challenge to the results, perhaps because there were also reports of irregularities downstate, in Republican-controlled areas. Even the RNC abandoned its Illinois vote challenges after only a month, but in other states Republican challenges lasted well into the following year.[56]

JFK had been dogged by rumors of Mafia help in the West Virginia primary, and those, along with the Illinois results and a stream of stories by Giancana family members and supporters in recent decades, have led to the false impression that JFK actively courted Sam Giancana. There are unsubstantiated reports that JFK's father, Joseph Kennedy, sought Mafia assistance to help his son in the election, though hard evidence is lacking and it's difficult to see why one of America's richest men would need $50,000 from the Mafia to help JFK. On the other hand, Mafia leaders do like to gain every advantage, and it's no surprise that months before the election Frank Sinatra—indebted to

Johnny Rosselli since the early 1950s—had introduced JFK to one of Rosselli's sometime female companions, Judith Campbell. She was JFK's "type" and they began a well-documented affair. However, Campbell's later claims that she carried messages between JFK and Sam Giancana, including notes about assassinating Castro, have all been disproved. Then too, even before taking office, JFK reiterated his pledge to go after the Mafia, and as President he began the biggest war on organized crime that America had ever seen.[57]

Richard Nixon's defeat in the election affected several aspects of the Watergate story. His bitterness over the loss, and his actions while still in office, would help lead to tragic results regarding Cuba the following year. If Nixon had won, he might have been able to cover up the CIA's plots with the Mafia—and his role in them—forever, especially given his close relationship to CIA Director Dulles. It's remarkable that the 1960 CIA-Mafia plots were finally exposed in 1975 only because of Watergate, which is ironic because the Watergate break-ins were mainly about protecting the secrecy of the CIA-Mafia plots and the related Mafia-Hoffa-Nixon bribes.

PART II

CHAPTER 9

November 1960–Early April 1961: The CIA Hides Its Mafia Plots from JFK

Though a bitter Richard Nixon had lost the election, he remained Vice President for the next two and a half months, when U.S. actions against Cuba entered an unusual twilight period. Nixon had pushed for the CIA-Mafia plots in conjunction with a tiny invasion, to help install a U.S.-backed regime, but he would soon be out of power. However, perhaps things could be done while Nixon was still in office to eliminate Fidel, to help position himself for his political future.

Judging from the available evidence, Vice President Nixon probably knew more about the CIA's Cuban operations than did even President Eisenhower. It's possible that Eisenhower, a savvy military man and capable politician, could have planned it that way. Ike might have made Nixon his White House "action officer" for Cuba to get the job done while protecting both Eisenhower's reputation while he was President and his legacy after he left office. On the other hand, after the election the CIA began a well-documented pattern of deception with John F. Kennedy, both before he was President and after he assumed office. That yields the distinct possibility that the CIA and Nixon had done the same thing with Eisenhower.

Two days after Nixon's defeat, the CIA sent new orders to their bases in Miami and Guatemala, "greatly expanding the size of the Cuban" exile invasion force. The whole invasion concept changed radically. Up to that time, approximately 101 exiles were being trained to parachute into Cuba, with 370 exile troops to be brought in by boat. In many ways the pre-election exile training was just a supporting operation to provide cover for the CIA's scheme with the Mafia to assassinate Fidel. But after the election, the number of troops to be brought in by boat became far more important than the number parachuting in. The CIA's new concept was to mount a significant amphibious landing of exiles by "greatly expanding" the 370-man boat force. It would swell over the coming months to four times its original strength.*[1]

The all but open secret of CIA exile training in Guatemala was slated to finally be reported in the American press, in an editorial in *The Nation* magazine titled "Are We Training Cuban Guerillas?" The editorial stemmed from a Stanford professor's visit to Guatemala, where he found the U.S. training of exiles to be "common knowledge." That caused *The Nation* to ask for "public pressure [on] the Administration to abandon this dangerous . . . project." The editorial urged that "all US news media with correspondents in Guatemala" should investigate the operation. The editorial was schedule to run in the magazine's November 19 issue; the day before its release CIA Director Allen Dulles and Richard Bissell went to Palm Beach to brief President-elect Kennedy on their new plan for Cuba.[2]

At the November 18, 1960, meeting Dulles and Bissell explained to JFK their greatly expanded plan, using "large maps and charts." Kennedy listened intently, "surprised . . . by the [huge] scale of the plans." JFK told Dulles he wanted time "to consider the matter," but Dulles pressed him, saying, "there isn't much time" since "Soviet military aid was now flowing into Cuba" and "the longer an invasion was postponed, the more difficult it would be."[3]

At this point, for the first time top CIA officials Dulles and Bissell were presenting, and pitching, a major amphibious exile invasion of Cuba—the operation that would become known as the Bay of Pigs invasion (though that wasn't the landing site at this time). As verified by a 1975 Senate investigation, Dulles and Bissell did not tell JFK about the CIA's plots with the Mafia to assassinate Fidel. That had been the main point of the Cuban plan that Dulles, Bissell, and Nixon had been pursuing for a year and a half. Nor did the CIA officials inform JFK that the large-scale amphibious exile invasion plans they were showing him had not yet been approved by Eisenhower, or that the CIA had finalized them just over a week earlier. Agency officials would

* Many journalists assumed the number of exiles being trained by November 1960 was much greater. One reason was that in order to make their numbers appear larger, the exiles were numbered as they joined starting at No. 2,500. Thus, the very first exile recruited was No. 2,501, the second was No. 2,502, etc.

continue deceiving JFK about the Cuban operation until, and well after, the ill-fated invasion.[4]

Remarkably, CIA Director Dulles and Bissell didn't bother briefing President Eisenhower on the new, expanded invasion operation until two days *after* they'd talked to President-elect Kennedy. That was more than a week after CIA headquarters had already issued the orders to Miami and Guatemala to make the huge change. These facts raise the question: Who authorized Dulles and Bissell to greatly expand the operation in the first place? It wasn't Eisenhower, so the only other official who could have done so was the President's White House "action officer" for Cuba, Richard Nixon.

In later years, Nixon seemed publicly proud of the fact that he'd pressed for action against Fidel in the last half of 1959 and throughout all of 1960, despite the failure of the Bay of Pigs invasion—a debacle that Nixon blamed on JFK, not the plan itself. Of course, Nixon's later public accounts also left out the CIA-Mafia plots to assassinate Fidel, a secret Nixon continued to hide for years to come, even at the cost of his Presidency. In hindsight, the original Cuba plan had to be greatly expanded in early November 1960 for it to have any chance of gaining JFK's approval. The original tiny force of several hundred stood zero chance of succeeding or even of being approved by JFK, since he didn't know about its most important component: Fidel's assassination by the mob. In light of the new President's strong stance against organized crime, Dulles couldn't tell JFK about the Agency's plots with the Mafia, especially since one of its main participants, Sam Giancana, had been grilled before JFK's crime committee.[5]

We can only speculate about Richard Nixon's motivation if he did authorize the huge expansion. He might have felt he was doing what Eisenhower wanted him to do as his point man for Cuba. It's also possible Nixon thought Fidel could be toppled before he left office, especially since the CIA continued to plot his downfall with the Mafia. If Fidel were disposed of before Nixon's term expired, Nixon would at least leave office on a high note, which would be good for his political future. In addition, if enough of the RNC's election challenges were successful, Nixon might still have harbored a slim hope of becoming President in January. At any rate, just weeks after Eisenhower and JFK were briefed, another effort to topple Fidel was made, though it involved nothing that had been revealed to the President or the President-elect.

. . .

Cuba claims that in December 1960, the United States planned to stage a fake attack on the U.S. naval base at Guantánamo Bay to justify U.S. military action against Cuba, something that might appear far-fetched. However, CIA personnel would later testify that the United States was planning just such an operation within weeks of that time period. In addition, the CIA actually tried to stage the same type of U.S. operation directed at the Guantánamo Naval Base several months later. Finally, the U.S. Joint Chiefs of Staff later proposed and endorsed just such a plan in official documents, code-named Operation Northwoods. ABC News reported the Joint Chiefs' startling Northwoods operation as a proposal "to kill innocent people and commit acts of terrorism in US cities to create public support for a war against Cuba." Their proposal included "blowing up a US ship and even orchestrating violent terrorism in US cities . . . to trick the American public . . . into supporting a war to oust . . . Fidel Castro." One of the plans in the declassified Northwoods files suggested, "We could blow up a US ship in Guantanamo Bay and blame Cuba." With that kind of documented thinking among the Joint Chiefs, it is possible the Cuban accounts are correct, and that the CIA—and possibly Nixon—planned to goad Eisenhower to use U.S. military force against Cuba, by using a fake attack on the Guantánamo Bay Naval Base.[6]

Cuban reports claim that on "December 3, 1960, Cuban State Security arrested more than 40" participants in the plan to stage the phony attack on Guantanamo. "At their trial . . . the alleged CIA agent and Anti-Communist League of the Caribbean Head of Action and Sabotage . . . testified and publicly unmasked the CIA's participation" in planning the phony attack.[7]

Guy Banister was "instrumental in the Anti-Communist League of the Caribbean," according to former FBI agent William Turner. In December 1960, Banister—ex-FBI Chief of Chicago and former office mate of Robert Maheu—was a well-connected private investigator in New Orleans, and a newspaper there reported that he "was a key liaison man for US government-sponsored anti-Communist activities in Latin America." As documented earlier, Banister had been looked at by the CIA's Office of Security before it decided to go with Robert Maheu as the liaison for the CIA-Mafia plots. Banister might instead have been assigned to help with the fake attack on the Guantánamo Bay Naval Base.[8]

Such a deception would need the cooperation of some U.S. Navy officials to have any chance of succeeding. Three months before the December 1960 arrests, an Office of Naval Intelligence (ONI) memo confirms that Banister had written an ONI contact about a plan "to overthrow the Castro government." It's also well documented by U.S. government files that within weeks of the arrests in Cuba, the CIA began work on an unusual, secret Cuban exile base outside of New Orleans. There, Cuban exiles would be trained for a landing on the far eastern shore of Cuba, near the U.S. base at Guantánamo Bay (far from the main exile invasion site, on the other side of Cuba). According to some accounts, those Cuban exiles would actually be part of a plan to stage a fake attack on the Guantánamo Bay Naval Base (more elaborate than the failed December 1960 attempt). That Louisiana training camp would be linked to E. Howard Hunt's CIA associate David Atlee Phillips, and Guy Banister would help to equip Cuban exile front groups in the area. By early the following year, the rabidly anti-Communist Banister would start accepting funding for his anti-Castro activities from the New Orleans Mafia family of Carlos Marcello. Soon after, Banister would begin doing work for Marcello; joining him would be David Ferrie, an Eastern Airlines pilot involved with Marcello and anti-Castro activities.[9]

After the December 1960 arrests of the men involved in the fake Guantánamo Bay attack, the CIA began to run out of funds for the Cuban operation. Just between November 3 and December 16 the Agency had burned through over $2 million, but it soon obtained "an additional $28,200,000" in funding "from the Bureau of the Budget" (over $170,000,000 in today's dollars). That was more than twice the original amount Eisenhower had authorized back in August. To secure such a large amount so quickly could indicate the CIA received help from Vice President Nixon, the main White House proponent of the covert Cuban operation.[10]

By December 1960, the CIA and the Mafia had resumed their plotting, only with Santo Trafficante taking more of a leading role. The CIA's Inspector General's report says that "Trafficante . . . was in touch with a disaffected Cuban official [named] Juan Orta, who was then Office Chief and Director General of [Castro's office]." The CIA quoted Trafficante as saying that Orta "was a sort that would . . . surreptitiously poison Castro" because "Orta had once been in a position to receive kickbacks from the gambling interests, had since lost that source of income, and needed the money." The CIA had been in contact with Juan Orta since earlier in 1960. The office Orta oversaw was the same one where Marita Lorenz had worked and to which Richard Cain had been able to gain entry. As already noted, the CIA really just needed Trafficante and the Mafia to take the blame if the plot to kill Fidel succeeded.[11]

The CIA also began developing another asset who knew both Juan Orta and Santo Trafficante. "CIA cables confirm that a poisoning plot was underway in late 1960," and a cable from December 1960 "referred to the possibility of giving a [poison] 'H capsule' to Rolando Cubela, the former [student group] leader who was now a disaffected associate of Castro." Historian David Kaiser of the Naval War College points out that Orta's plot with the Mafia appears to have been related to the CIA's contact with Cubela, since a CIA cable suggests "that the two men may have been working together." Rolando Cubela would not become a well-documented major player for the CIA until 1963, though the CIA would continue to note several mob ties to his operation. In fact the CIA admits that Cubela was first brought to the attention of the CIA by a Trafficante associate code-named AMWHIP-1.[12]

Finally, the CIA seems not to have given up on simply having an assassin shoot Fidel. "In late 1960, the Agency sent a sniper rifle to Havana via diplomatic pouch," according to the later Congressional testimony of "CIA General Counsel Laurence Houston" uncovered by historian Kaiser.[13]

In late 1960 Vice President Richard Nixon had to deal with a serious loose end from his defeat at the hands of JFK: Jimmy Hoffa, who had delivered Nixon's $500,000 bribe from Carlos Marcello. After Nixon lost the election, Attorney General William Rogers suddenly "reconsidered the [stalled] grand jury date against Hoffa and indicted him for the Sun Valley" real estate scam. Like Nixon, Attorney General Rogers would be leaving office soon, and he "did not want to leave behind him what might appear to be a fixed case for Jimmy Hoffa." Hoffa was furious at the news, and "union insiders say that Hoffa felt Nixon had double-crossed him." With a Kennedy administration soon to take office, Hoffa was facing his worst nightmare.[14]

Trying to begin damage control, Nixon appealed to his friend Rogers, but to no avail. Nixon then had his original emissary to Hoffa, ex-Congressman Hunter, write to the Teamsters President, saying he knew "for a fact that your side of the case was put before the Vice President and that he discussed the case with the Attorney General." He added, "the Vice President has been sympathetic toward you," but since "Nixon lost the election" he no longer had "any decisive degree of influence" and could not "order the Attorney General to do anything."[15]

Near the end of 1960, Nixon took a "brief vacation" in Florida with his best friend Bebe Rebozo and Attorney General William Rogers. Whatever their strategy, the Hoffa indictment stood, perhaps because soon after their vacation journalist Drew Pearson and his aide Jack Anderson broke the story in *The Washington Post* and other papers "that Nixon had intervened with Rogers on Hoffa's behalf." Once the story appeared, Rogers couldn't drop Hoffa's indictment in the Sun Valley case without appearing guilty of obstruction of justice. Hoffa had apparently intended the still-secret $500,000 bribe not just to stall, but to stop the Sun Valley charges, so that he wouldn't have to face a trial. The Sun Valley indictment now began a series of charges and trials against Hoffa that lasted until he finally went to prison.[16]

Nixon continued trying to quell Hoffa's anger in the following year, when the matter was finally settled in a surprising way. But the Mafia-Hoffa-Nixon bribe produced ramifications that would play a major part in Watergate and its aftermath. More than a decade later, Jimmy Hoffa once more believed he had been double-crossed by Nixon after yet another Mafia bribe was paid, this time to release Hoffa from prison. After Watergate, an angry Hoffa retaliated against Nixon by exposing Johnny Rosselli's role in the CIA-Mafia plots, setting off a chain of events that would lead Santo Trafficante to order Rosselli's grisly murder and hasten Hoffa's own demise.[17]

On January 3, 1961, the Eisenhower-Nixon administration abruptly announced the closing of the U.S. embassy in Havana and broke diplomatic ties with the Cuban government. Some high-level CIA personnel stationed in Havana—based, as many were, at the U.S. embassy—were caught by surprise. That indicated the administration's decision had been made with little or no advance input from the CIA.[18]

The day before the announcement, at a meeting of the U.N. Security

Council in New York, Cuba's Foreign Minister "formally charges that the United States is preparing an invasion." He then "denounces the US Embassy in Havana for espionage" and asked that the U.S. embassy staff in Havana "be reduced to 11 persons," the same as Cuba's embassy in Washington. The Security Council rejected Cuba's charges without a vote, and the United States usually simply ignored or denied Cuba's claims and requests. The abrupt closing of the U.S. embassy seemed a huge overreaction, fraught with severe consequences.[19]

The U.S. embassy was critical to any chance the CIA's amphibious invasion plan—as outlined to JFK and Eisenhower—had of succeeding. Though no U.S. Ambassador had been stationed in Cuba for months, the embassy had still functioned, giving cover to many CIA operatives. Now, just as the CIA's Cuban new invasion plan started to unfold, the United States was without a crucial listening post to gauge the reactions of the Cuban people and of other diplomats in Cuba. The Havana CIA personnel didn't know about the Agency's assassination plots with the Mafia, but they could have provided a stream of information to Washington demonstrating the fallacy of the invasion plan as outlined. They could have pointed out that Fidel remained popular, the Cuban Army remained loyal to him and to its Commander, Juan Almeida, and that any anti-Castro guerilla networks in Cuba were few, scattered, and very small.

It seems odd that Eisenhower would close the embassy and break relations when JFK was just over two weeks away from taking office. President Eisenhower knew the escalating invasion plans also involved extensive use of Cuban guerillas and dissidents. Ike must have realized that closing the embassy would severely hamstring if not doom those plans for JFK. It prevented the new President from having his own diplomatic staff in place at the embassy, which could provide him with independent analysis of the Cuban situation and let JFK know the Cuban populace was still overwhelmingly pro-Fidel. Now JFK and his new team would have to judge everything from Washington and be completely dependent on the CIA (and reports from Miami and a few stay-behind agents in Cuba) for their information.

Given the emphasis and attention Richard Nixon admits he'd given Cuba over the past eighteen months, one has to wonder if Nixon played a role in closing the embassy at such a critical time. He was still bitter over what he felt was JFK's theft of an election victory that was rightfully his, and as Eisenhower's "action officer" for Cuba, Nixon should have been influential in the decision. Less than two weeks later—only four days before JFK was to take office—the Eisenhower-Nixon administration struck again, this time ordering the State Department to implement travel restrictions for U.S. citizens traveling to Cuba. Often overlooked is the fact that two of the major legacies of the U.S. cold war against Cuba that remain today—the travel restrictions and the lack of diplomatic relations—went into effect the last month Vice President Nixon was in office.

By early January 1960 Nixon must have known that the greatly expanded CIA invasion plan had no chance of succeeding before he left office. The CIA-Mafia plots weren't close to producing results, and at this stage they focused only on using the CIA's poison pills (passed from Rosselli and Trafficante to Juan Orta). However, another CIA attempt to assassinate Fidel—not connected to the Mafia—looked as if it might produce results while Nixon remained Vice President.

A Cuban exile being trained by the CIA, Felix Rodriguez, had volunteered to join a team that would go into Cuba to assassinate Fidel. He wrote that "early in January" his superior "told me my idea had been accepted by the people in charge." For such a sensitive mission at such a critical time, that approval could have only come from a high-ranking CIA official like Richard Bissell or Director Allen Dulles. It strains credibility to think that either man would have authorized a U.S.-trained team to try to assassinate Fidel without the approval of someone in the executive branch. As had been the case in the previous year, there is no evidence that Eisenhower knew about, let alone approved, any of the plots to assassinate Fidel—which leaves his "action officer" for Cuba, Richard Nixon, as the most likely suspect.[20]

Felix Rodriguez says he was flown to Miami with another exile trainee, where a third exile—"a radio operator"—joined them. Rodriguez was given "a beautiful German bolt-action rifle with a powerful telescopic sight . . . in a custom-made padded carrying case [with] twenty rounds" of ammo. CIA assets in Cuba "had obtained a building in Havana facing a location that Castro frequented at the time, and they'd managed to presight the rifle."[21]

This new plot to assassinate Fidel was fast-tracked, and twice the Agency attempted to move the three-man assassination team into Cuba. They were on their third attempt when their mission was "canceled." When Rodriguez "got back to Florida, they took away the rifle and the ammunition, and said that they'd changed their minds about the mission." That was just before the inauguration of a new President and Vice President, so some official had wisely canceled the assassination attempt. Felix Rodriguez—who says he didn't realize he was working for the Agency at the time—went on to become a legendary CIA agent who helped to capture Che Guevara.[22]

One foreign leader was assassinated in the final days when Nixon and Eisenhower were still in office, and the story sheds some light on the attempts against Fidel. The CIA admits it had begun in September 1960 trying to assassinate Patrice Lumumba, the former Premier of the newly liberated Congo. As covered earlier, that month a CIA doctor delivered to the Congo a poison similar to that planned for use against Fidel. However, unlike the attempts to kill Fidel, this effort left a fairly clear paper trail, which later led the Senate Church Committee to conclude that Eisenhower had possibly authorized the assassination plotting against Lumumba. The National Security Council and a Special Group of its members discussed the topic without once using the term "assassination." There is also a documented trail of CIA cables showing the CIA considered using poison, two European assassins—code-named QJWIN and WIROGUE—and other methods to kill Lumumba.[23]

Four months after the CIA began trying to assassinate Patrice Lumumba, he was finally killed on January 17, 1961, three days before Eisenhower and Nixon left office. The Church Committee concluded the CIA was not directly involved, though it cited many pages of cables that show the CIA played a major supporting role in his murder. Lumumba's assassination is especially relevant for the story of the United States and Cuba because it was overseen by renowned CIA officer William Harvey, as part of his ZR/RIFLE assassination project (euphemistically called an "executive action"). Before joining the CIA, William Harvey had been part of the FBI project that helped to uncover the Alger Hiss case, as covered in Chapter 2. A few weeks after Lumumba's death, CIA files say that William Harvey began work on the Castro assassination project. Harvey's role in the Cuban operation in 1961 isn't clear from the records, perhaps because his surviving notes say that files for the project should be "forged and backdated"—meaning that what survives today may not tell the whole story. From the files that do exist, it appears that Robert Maheu and CIA officer James O'Connell still ran the operation with Rosselli in 1961. However, those records also reveal that William Harvey became the Castro project's driving force the following year, when he began a close friendship with Johnny Rosselli that would have tragic consequences for both men.[24]

In January 1961 the CIA's invasion plan took off at a rapid rate, thanks to the recruiting skills of CIA officer E. Howard Hunt and the Agency money distributed by his aide Bernard Barker. Bebe Rebozo was also distributing CIA money to the exiles in Miami, and his contacts with Barker eventually led the two to business arrangements that would eventually cause problems for Richard Nixon.

The CIA's force swelled so rapidly that the supposedly clandestine plan quickly became an open secret throughout the United States, as it already was in Miami and Latin America. When E. Howard Hunt took exile leader Tony Varona to Guatemala to visit the camps, Hunt photographed the training. Back in the United States, Hunt met with his supervisor, Richard Bissell, and other CIA officials, and said the photos ought to be published "to stimulate recruiting" of more exiles. The other officials were shocked at the thought of breaking security by publicizing a covert operation, but to their surprise, Bissell approved Hunt's idea. Tony Varona was stunned when he saw photos of the supposedly secret training camps in Miami newspapers.[25]

On January 10, 1961, *The New York Times* finally gave the covert training national coverage in the United States. Its headline blared "U.S. Helps Train an Anti-Castro Force at Secret Guatemalan Air-Ground Base," and the article explained that that United States "is assisting this effort not only in personnel but in material and the construction of ground and air facilities." A map outlined the secret facilities. The *Times* article was accurate, unlike a series in New York's *Daily News* about "Castro's Black Future," that claimed "over 35,000 saboteurs [were] ready to strike from within [and] 6,000 Cuban patriots [were] poised to swarm ashore." The claims of the *Daily News* read like the press material being dreamed up by David Atlee Phillips and E. Howard Hunt, modeled on the wild claims they had used for the 1954 Guatemala coup. In reality, only around six hundred exiles were being trained at that time.[26]

One can only imagine what Richard Nixon thought when he saw coverage of the Cuban operation in the press. Yet the actions of Hunt, Phillips, and Bissell in publicizing the supposedly secret invasion make sense in a way. They knew that all the expanded training was really just a sort of cover, and the real way Fidel was going to be eliminated was by assassination. Also, as mentioned earlier, the CIA had another plan to force JFK to commit U.S. military forces to help overthrow Fidel: having U.S.-backed Cuban exiles dressed as Castro's soldiers attack the U.S. base at Guantánamo Bay. If done coincidently with Fidel's assassination and the invasion, this operation could ensure that U.S. troops occupied Cuba. And even if Fidel were not assassinated, this new Guantánamo Bay provocation—a much more elaborate version of what had been planned for the previous month—would force JFK to act militarily.[27]

Richard Nixon saw one last dart to throw at the incoming Kennedy administration when JFK announced he was making his brother Robert the new Attorney General. Nixon saw "a golden opportunity to embarrass [Robert] Kennedy," according to Stephen Ambrose. Robert had to be confirmed by the Senate Judiciary Committee, and Nixon saw those hearings "as an opportunity to put on the record the entire Kennedy financial empire." Robert's father, Joseph Kennedy, was one of America's richest men, with massive holdings that stretched from Chicago's largest building to Texas oil fields. He had also set up a series of trusts for all of his children, including JFK and Robert. Starting in the late 1950s, the sometimes-controversial Joseph Kennedy—who was far more conservative than JFK—had stayed out of the limelight. With Nixon's experience using Congressional hearings to generate press coverage, he saw Robert's confirmation as a way to drag Joseph Kennedy and his huge financial holdings (and baggage) into the light. The resulting press coverage could distract and damage JFK's incoming administration, especially if Robert withdrew from consideration to avoid such a spectacle. Robert's failure to be confirmed would have helped Nixon smooth over Hoffa's anger that the $500,000 Carlos Marcello bribe hadn't quashed the Sun Valley charges, as undoubtedly Marcello and Hoffa would be RFK's top priorities as Attorney General.[28]

Nixon spoke to the leading Republican Senator on the Judiciary Committee, Illinois Senator Everett Dirksen, about using the hearing to embarrass RFK and the Kennedy family. In his talk with Nixon, Senator Dirksen was "vague but hopeful." But when the time came, "not one Republican asked an embarrassing question," causing Nixon to express "'amazement' at the 'lousy job'" done by Dirksen and the other Republican Senators.[29]

• • •

Three days before JFK was to take the oath of office, President Eisenhower gave his famous Farewell Address warning about the dangers of the "military-industrial complex." Ironically, it would be Richard Nixon who would take that alliance to new heights when he finally became President eight years later. The day before JFK's inauguration, President Eisenhower told JFK "the CIA's Cuban project was going well" and that it would be JFK's "responsibility to do 'whatever is necessary' to make it succeed." Of course, Eisenhower didn't know about the project's most crucial ingredient, the plot to have the Mafia kill Fidel before the invasion. Nor did Ike know about the Castro assassination plot with Cuban exile Felix Rodriguez—which ended around the time JFK took office—or that the CIA had plans underway to force the new President's hand with a fake Cuban attack on the Guantánamo Bay Naval Base.[30]

On January 20, 1961, Richard Nixon had to watch John F. Kennedy take the oath of office and give the kind of soaring, inspiring speech that Nixon, for all of his political skill, could never quite match. Combined with the fact that Fidel Castro remained in power, despite all of Nixon's efforts to get rid of him, the day must have been a crushing disappointment for the former Vice President. The forty-eight-year-old Nixon found himself out of public office for the first time in fourteen years.

On January 28, 1961, CIA Director Allen Dulles briefed President Kennedy and his new National Security Council about the situation in Cuba. Dulles told the men that "popular opposition to [Castro's] regime [was] growing rapidly"—something JFK would have known wasn't true if he'd had his own diplomatic staff in Havana's now-closed U.S. embassy. The CIA focused on "securing a beachhead" near the Cuban city of Trinidad, "while B-26s took control of the air and destroyed Cuban transport and communications." (The landing site would soon be changed to the more secluded and infamous Bay of Pigs.) As in 1954 in Guatemala, "Castro would be overwhelmed with rumors of numerous landings; dissidents would be encouraged to take up arms." What Dulles didn't tell JFK and his officials was that any real chance of success depended on the Mafia murdering Fidel just before the invasion.[31]

CIA Director Allen Dulles later admitted in his own notes that "he had not alerted Kennedy to certain issues that might 'harden' him against the project, such as the falsity of the notion that the exiles could melt into the mountains." While Dulles kept raising the CIA's successful 1954 Guatemala coup to JFK and others as an example, he left out a vital aspect of that operation. As explained in Chapter 3, when that coup "seemed near collapse, Eisenhower had saved it by openly sending US airplanes to the [CIA-backed] rebels. Allen Dulles expected the same reaction from Kennedy on Cuba." But Dulles likely hoped events wouldn't even come to that. Recall that his top CIA official running the plan, Hunt's boss Richard Bissell, later admitted that Castro's "assassination" wouldn't just make the invasion "much easier," but could render the questionable invasion operation "unnecessary."[32]

The heads of U.S. government agencies heard only the rosiest of scenarios about the invasion, and JFK's newly inherited Joint Chiefs of Staff soon joined the CIA in feeling "quite enthusiastic about the invasion." On February 8, 1960, President Kennedy's National Security Advisor McGeorge Bundy told him that both groups thought even in a worst-case scenario, "the invaders would be able to get into the mountains and at the best, they think they might get a full-fledged civil war in which we could then back the anti-Castro forces openly." But at the height of the Cold War, with Europe—and Berlin—divided by a heavily guarded Iron Curtain, JFK feared that any obvious U.S. support or military involvement could cause Russian leader Nikita Khrushchev to move against West Berlin.[33]

Ironically, many of the Cuban exiles, from leaders like Tony Varona to the mostly young trainee fighters, soon heard a different scenario from E. Howard Hunt and others in the CIA. They were essentially told that once they landed in Cuba and secured a beachhead, they could announce their new government—and JFK would immediately recognize it and then use U.S. military force to back them up. That made the exiles involved in the invasion "enthusiastic," but the "U.S. military force" part simply wasn't true. Essentially, the CIA was telling JFK, the Cabinet, the Joint Chiefs, and the exiles whatever it took to sell them on the project, without giving them the most important parts of the story.[34]

Incredibly, the CIA had two little-known chances in early 1961 that might have actually allowed it to pull off a successful invasion even without Fidel's assassination. A CIA memo from February 20, 1961, said that "Commander Juan Almeida, who is Chief of Fidel's army, actually is very much disgusted with the communistic situation in Cuba and is about to defect." On March 7, 1961, another CIA memo stated that "Major Juan Almeida, Chief of Staff of the Cuban Army, has been approaching certain Latin Ambassadors in Havana to determine whether he would be accepted" for political asylum. Both reports about Almeida's dissatisfaction with Castro went to CIA headquarters in Washington.[35]

This was a golden opportunity for the CIA. Commander Almeida was extremely popular in Cuba, and far more powerful than Che Guevara, who wasn't even Cuban. In a population that was 70 percent of African heritage, Almeida was the highest-ranking black Cuban official. He was essentially the third-most-powerful man in the country, after Fidel and his brother, Raul Castro.

Yet CIA officials Allen Dulles and Richard Bissell were so confident that either the Mafia would assassinate Fidel or that they could get JFK to use U.S. military force that the Agency made no approach to Commander Almeida. President Kennedy was not even told what the CIA had heard about Almeida. Those CIA memos were also never revealed during the investigations, later that year, into the failure of the invasion, not even to the Agency's own Inspector General. In fact, the files about Almeida's offers were so sensitive that they weren't declassified for decades, and remained unpublished until 2005 (after this author was the first to find them in the National Archives).

Even as high CIA officials ignored Commander Almeida's growing disaffection with Fidel, JFK expressed his dissatisfaction with the CIA's proposed landing site near the city of Trinidad. What if the exiles couldn't land because they were spotted at sea near the busy city? What if there were civilian casualties, or house-to-house fighting broke out? Given what the CIA was telling him, JFK, a combat veteran from his PT boat days, thought a more secluded landing spot made more sense. That way, at least the exiles would be able to make their initial landing. Accordingly, the CIA chose a new landing spot on Cuba's southwest coast, in an area called the Bay of Pigs.

In a tragic irony of history, when Fidel divided command of Cuba into thirds for defense against the upcoming invasion, Commander Almeida was given control of the portion of Cuba that included the Bay of Pigs.

. . .

One more likely reason high CIA officials failed to pursue Commander Almeida involved the Agency's plans to stage its fake attack on the U.S. naval base at Guantánamo Bay, something that would force JFK to use U.S. military force against Fidel. The Cuban exile troops for that operation were being trained separately from the main group in Guatemala. A CIA memo "routed to David Atlee Philips" says they were instead based eight miles from New Orleans at the "Belle Chasse training camp," located "at the US Naval Ammunition Depot." After being trained at the secluded 3,500-acre camp adjoining the Mississippi River, the exiles would sail into Cuba on their own ship, the *Santa Ana*. They weren't being told ahead of time the true nature of their mission. Like JFK, they believed they were going to stage a "diversionary landing" on the far eastern shore of Cuba to distract Fidel from the main force at the Bay of Pigs. Not until they neared shore would their CIA commanders break out Castro's Cuban military uniforms and explain they were to attack the U.S. naval base at Guantánamo Bay. E. Howard Hunt's associate David Atlee Phillips was handling propaganda for the whole Cuban operation and could ensure that the United States and the world quickly heard about Castro's supposed attack on Guantánamo Bay. That would force JFK to use U.S. military force against Cuba.[36]

It's possible the "Guantánamo provocation," as it's sometimes called, was originally planned as a real diversionary landing. However, the idea of a small diversionary landing makes little sense, because it would either be so small as to be unnoticed or—if the Cuban military did become aware of it—the force would be quickly obliterated. That had to be obvious to Bissell and other CIA officials, so the operation morphed into a fake attack on the U.S. base at Guantánamo Bay. The CIA-Mafia plots had also hit a snag, which might have caused the CIA to proceed with plans for their Guantánamo provocation.

In early 1961, the CIA-Mafia plots still involved the same core group as when Richard Nixon was Vice President: Nixon's old associate Robert Maheu as intermediary, Johnny Rosselli, Rosselli's boss Sam Giancana, and Florida-based godfather Santo Trafficante. They were in touch with Juan Orta, the manager of Fidel's office in Havana, which had already been linked to two earlier attempts to assassinate Fidel. But on January 26, 1961, less than a week after JFK became President, Orta lost his position in Fidel's office. That removed the best chance for the Mafia and the CIA to get their special poison to Fidel. Juan Orta grew increasingly worried that Cuban State Security knew he'd been trying to help the United States, and two and a half months later, just before the Bay of Pigs invasion, Orta would seek asylum in the Venezuelan embassy in Havana.[37]

However, it's often overlooked that the CIA admits the Mafia found a replacement for Orta—someone apparently in a similar position—"who made several attempts without success" to assassinate Fidel. Though that replacement has never been identified, CIA reports confirm that Trafficante's contact for that unnamed individual was Tony Varona, the exile leader whom E. Howard Hunt had been dealing with for almost a year as part of the CIA's exile government. CIA files reveal that the Agency had been in touch with Varona since at least 1959, and Hunt and Barker dealt with him several times a week, so there was really no need to use Trafficante to get to Varona. Once again, the real reason the CIA needed Trafficante wasn't to handle Varona, but to have someone to take the blame for Fidel's death or if something went wrong. Varona was happy to take the CIA's money from Trafficante and Rosselli, and the CIA admits it gave Johnny Rosselli "$50,000" to turn over to Varona for the expenses involved in assassinating Fidel. That was in addition to the Agency money that E. Howard Hunt was funneling to Varona and Hunt's other exile leaders.[38]

While the CIA has laid out a chronology of its plots with the Mafia in 1961 (and in fact from 1960 through 1966)—including the roles of Varona, Trafficante, Maheu, Giancana, and Rosselli—CIA records and recollections often conflict. The official CIA account is full of disclaimers about missing files and foggy memories, and it shows odd gaps in the timeline and logic. Much of that may be because of the involvement of Hunt and Barker in the CIA-Mafia plots, since their own records from early 1961 are largely missing or still classified. Because of the frequent meetings between Hunt, Barker, and Varona—involving Varona's role in the new exile government—the CIA would have been highly inefficient not to include Hunt and Barker in their plots with Trafficante and Varona. An added value for the CIA was Barker's longtime links to organized crime, documented by the FBI and CIA. As detailed later, a Kennedy aide says he later learned that by this time Barker was tied to Trafficante. (Recall that Barker was assigned as Hunt's assistant within days of Trafficante's joining the plots, and Barker would be fired from the Agency once its Mafia plots were over.) The corrupt Tony Varona had been involved with Trafficante for some time, and a January 1961 FBI report links Varona to efforts "by U.S. racketeers to finance anti-Castro activities in hopes of securing the gambling, prostitution, and dope monopolies in Cuba [when] Castro was overthrown."[39]

At the same time the CIA admits it was busy plotting Fidel's assassination with Trafficante and the other Mafia chiefs, new Attorney General Robert F. Kennedy launched his massive war on organized crime, leaving him little time to advise his brother about the Cuban operation. Though as Attorney General Robert was technically J. Edgar Hoover's superior, in practical terms that wasn't the case. The FBI agent assigned as the liaison between RFK and Hoover, Courtney Evans, explained to this author in an exclusive interview the complicated relationship between the two powerful figures. Richard Nixon had gotten along well with Hoover for the past thirteen years because he always deferred to the FBI Director. RFK, on the other hand, initially tried to assert his authority over Hoover, to the aging Director's resentment. The result was a difficult relationship, in which Hoover would appear to try to do what RFK wanted, while dragging his feet and making only painfully slow progress (or none at all) in areas important to RFK and JFK, like organized crime and civil rights.[40]

The FBI had begun making some moves against organized crime after the glare of publicity from the Kennedys' crime hearings, but it was much too little for RFK. The Attorney General began hiring his own Justice Department prosecutors to go after the Mafia and its allies such as Jimmy Hoffa. The largest group, the Organized Crime Division, was headed by Washington attorney Herbert J. "Jack" Miller. Ironically, Miller later became Nixon's lawyer from 1974 until Nixon's death—and beyond, as he continued to fight to keep many of Nixon's Watergate-era tapes and records secret until Miller himself died in 2009. At the same time Jack Miller represented Nixon (and his estate), Miller was also a leading attorney for the Kennedy family.[41]

Courtney Evans explained that, somewhat separate from his Organized Crime Division, RFK also formed what came to be known as the "Get Hoffa Squad," devoted to prosecuting mob ally Jimmy Hoffa. Walter Sheridan, who would become a lifelong friend of RFK, headed that unit. The following year, Sheridan discovered the $500,000 Mafia bribe to Nixon in 1960 to stall Hoffa's indictment (covered in

Chapter 8), though it would remain secret from the press and public until 1978, even while Sheridan played a key role in the events surrounding Watergate.[42]

With Richard Nixon no longer in power, agencies like the Immigration and Naturalization Service (INS) moved quickly in matters related to godfather Carlos Marcello that they hadn't pressed very hard during the Eisenhower-Nixon administration. RFK insisted on more aggressive action against Marcello, who wasn't a citizen (Marcello was born in Tunisia) and had only falsified birth records from Guatemala. Attorney General Kennedy decided to use Marcello's own forgeries against him and had the INS arrange Marcello's deportation to Guatemala.

On April 4, 1961, when Carlos Marcello went to the local INS office for what he thought was a routine visit, he was detained and then flown to Guatemala without a hearing. RFK publicly took full responsibility "for the expulsion of" Marcello, and the following week had the IRS file "tax liens in excess of $835,000 against" Marcello and his wife.[43]

Just seven months earlier, Marcello had given a half-million dollars to the man he thought would be the next President, and now the enraged godfather found himself in Guatemala, the same small country where the CIA was training Cuban exiles for the upcoming Bay of Pigs invasion. The U.S.-backed dictator of Guatemala, already under pressure from his country's press and populace for allowing the U.S.-supported Cuban exile training, faced new scrutiny for allowing a notorious American godfather to reside in the country. He had Marcello and his American attorney detained and escorted to the border with El Salvador. From there Marcello was taken "20 miles into Honduras [and] unceremoniously dumped . . . on a forested hilltop with no signs of civilization in sight." Soon, the man who had been America's most powerful godfather was scrambling through the jungle-lined back roads of Honduras in his expensive Gucci shoes while swearing eternal vengeance against John and Robert Kennedy for his ordeal and humiliation.[44]

President Kennedy continued to hear only good reports from the CIA during late March and early April of 1961, even as the Agency suffered setbacks in its plans for the Cuban invasion and Fidel's assassination. According to the Cuban government Dossier that later became the main target of the Watergate burglars, just weeks before the Bay of Pigs invasion CIA-backed Cuban exile leader Sorí Marin and four others slipped into Cuba to prepare Cuban support for the invasion and to help assassinate Fidel. But Cuban forces soon arrested Marin and his small band of CIA-backed exiles, along with their many weapons, which included Thompson submachine guns (the famous "Tommy guns" from the 1930s gangster era). Cubans helping Marin and his men were also taken into custody. This began a huge wave of dissident arrests in Cuba in the weeks leading up to the Bay of Pigs invasion. Almost everyone who was suspected of being against Fidel would be detained, depriving the CIA of the few, small dissident networks the Agency had counted on to rise up against the Cuban government after Fidel had been assassinated and the invasion had begun.[45]

As Richard Nixon was building a new life outside of public office, the Cuban operation he'd helped to spawn—both the invasion and the highly secret assassination plots between the CIA and the Mafia—began to spiral out of control. Those operations would change and greatly impact the lives of many later involved with Watergate, including E. Howard Hunt, Bernard Barker, Frank Fiorini, Eugenio Martinez, and Richard Helms. More importantly, the events related to Cuba that Nixon had set in motion would come to dominate the Presidency of John F. Kennedy until his tragic death. Richard Nixon couldn't imagine how the past year's events involving Cuba and the Mafia would come back to haunt him after he finally achieved the pinnacle of power. As a result, Nixon would spend much of his own Presidency obsessed with the hidden history of what he called "the Bay of Pigs thing."

CHAPTER 10

April 1960: The Real Reasons "the Bay of Pigs Thing" Failed

President John F. Kennedy trusted Allen Dulles and the CIA to plan and oversee the Bay of Pigs operation, now only weeks away. JFK exerted influence only occasionally, such as making sure the CIA's new exile government included at least one liberal leader who would appeal to a broader range of Cubans. For almost a year, E. Howard Hunt had been working to form a viable government-in-exile, but he appeared to have made little progress in persuading the fractious exile leaders to work together on a post-Fidel government. The original exile government, the Frente, was a six-man group that included Tony Varona and Manuel Artime, now Hunt's good friend.

Hunt was drawn to Artime's extremely conservative politics, but a fellow exile who worked with Artime told this author that Artime was so far to the right he was practically "a Nazi." Hunt apparently thought the young, energetic Artime would be the perfect U.S.-backed dictator for Cuba after the invasion and assassination of Fidel. Bay of Pigs historian Peter Wyden confirms that one of the primary reasons for the lack of progress in forming a viable government-in-exile was that Hunt "kept stirring up dissension among the competing revolutionary groups by pushing his friend Manuel Artime, the flamboyant psychiatrist turned politician."[1]

In addition to Artime, the original Frente government-in-exile group had included long-established—and sometimes corrupt—politicians like Varona, all more or less conservatives. President Kennedy wanted at least one progressive leader, so he ordered the inclusion of liberal exile Manolo Ray, who'd helped with the fall 1959 coup attempt against Fidel before fleeing Cuba. However, Hunt considered a liberal like Manolo Ray to be a Communist, little better than Fidel.

Hunt resisted and resented JFK's attempt to broaden the political appeal of the post-coup government.

In the lead-up to the Bay of Pigs, as with Watergate, it's sometimes hard to tell where E. Howard Hunt's official CIA duties ended and where his personal actions began. Thanks to a 1961 letter written by Arthur Schlesinger Jr. to fellow Presidential aide Richard Goodwin, we have some insight into a dark operation that may have been planned before the invasion. The letter was written after the Bay of Pigs, but it refers to a CIA-backed group, "Operation 40," that was part of the invasion. Schlesinger revealed that "liberal Cuban exiles believe that the real purpose of Operation 40" after the invasion was to "kill Communists—and, after eliminating hardcore Fidelistas, to go on to eliminate first the followers of Ray, then the followers of Varona and finally to set up a right-wing dictatorship presumably under Artime."[2]

The use of Operation 40 to install Artime as the new dictator of Cuba after Fidel's assassination and the invasion might seem far-fetched if not for Schlesinger's letter. More information emerged about Operation 40 from Frank Fiorini, the contract CIA agent and Trafficante operative. In 1975, Fiorini testified to Rockefeller Commission investigators that he'd been part of Operation 40, which he described as "a CIA top secret operation." Fiorini added that "Bernard Barker had asked him in 1961 if he would be willing to take on an assassination of some unknown person" for the CIA. To a journalist, Fiorini admitted that Operation 40 did have an "assassination section, which I was part of." CIA files about Operation 40 have never been released, and inaccurate information about it fills the Internet.[3]

Fiorini and Barker were in frequent contact during this time, which continued for several years and is reflected in CIA files. Unlike Barker, a regular CIA agent drawing a monthly salary and undergoing annual performance reviews, Fiorini was only a "contract agent" working on specific projects or for specific time periods. The daring pilot and "freedom fighter" loved attention and had even been the subject of a flattering article by Jack Anderson. However, the publicity Fiorini craved was not good for his CIA activities, and Trafficante didn't trust him with truly important operations. The Bay of Pigs era marked the peak of Fiorini's prominence, and afterward he would slowly drift downward, becoming just a lowly bagman for Trafficante while continually trying to mount ever-smaller operations against Fidel. Fiorini wouldn't regain the limelight until his arrest at the Watergate under the name Frank Sturgis. He would be bailed out of jail for that arrest by Jack Anderson, by that time America's most famous journalist.

Though Frank Fiorini and Bernard Barker stayed in weekly, sometimes daily, contact throughout the early 1960s, Fiorini seemed to greatly resent his fellow CIA and Trafficante associate. Barker has described his work as E. Howard Hunt's aide during that time in glowing terms, but Fiorini later derided Barker. In the exile community, Barker's nickname was "Macho," but Fiorini thought that calling Barker by that name was ridiculous since Fiorini said that "a man who is macho is supposed to be some kind of virile hard-charger. Calling Barker 'Macho' is like calling Liberace 'Slugger.'" His reference to the popular closeted gay entertainer of the time might have been Fiorini's way of calling attention to the fact that the four-times-married Barker was alleged to be—according to a former Kennedy aide who worked with Barker—a hebephile who preyed on young teenage boys. Fiorini later said that during the run-up to the Bay of Pigs, when Barker "is around Hunt . . . Barker is like a valet. Servile . . . It's disgusting. 'Yes sir, Mr. Hunt, let me refresh your drink, sir.'" Fiorini added that Barker behaved that way not just with Hunt, but with "anybody that's over him," a possible reference to their mutual boss, godfather Santo Trafficante.[4]

The months leading up to the Bay of Pigs were also Bernard Barker's high point in the Cuban exile community of Miami. As aide to the powerful CIA officer E. Howard Hunt (known to most exiles only as "Eduardo"), Barker distributed or helped Hunt distribute many thousands of dollars to exile recruits and operatives. Barker's experience laundering the CIA's money through foreign banks made him valuable to the CIA and to Trafficante. His skill later proved useful for Richard Nixon during Watergate, when Barker laundered $114,000 in illegal campaign contributions for Nixon, including some that funded the Watergate break-ins.[5]

As the date for the Bay of Pigs invasion approached, Santo Trafficante continued to work with Tony Varona and Johnny Rosselli on the CIA-Mafia plots to assassinate Fidel. Two months before the invasion, the CIA had delivered poison pills and poisoned cigars matching Fidel's favorite brand, using the same botulism toxin tried before the 1960 election. The problem now was how to deliver the poison to Fidel. As mentioned earlier, Juan Orta, Fidel's former office manager, no longer had access to Fidel, but apparently an unidentified associate acceptable to Varona and Trafficante did. Varona's job was to get the pills to his contact in Cuba, and the fatal dose would be delivered when Varona gave the signal, just before the invasion. While the invasion itself was an increasingly open secret in Cuba and in Miami, the exact timing of its start was seemingly the only thing the CIA was able to keep secret, probably because President Kennedy would have to give final approval.[6]

Thanks to E. Howard Hunt, the timing of Varona's signal to deliver the poison to Fidel became problematic. To deal with the problems of forging the Frente into an effective post-Fidel government, Hunt had helped form a new, broader group, the Cuban Revolutionary Council (the CRC). Hunt's new CRC would soon have offices in cities outside of Miami, including New Orleans, where Marcello associates including Guy Banister and David Ferrie worked with the local CRC office. However, President Kennedy was still demanding a prominent role for liberal Manolo Ray in the Cuban exile government slated to take control after the invasion. After some shuffling among the groups, Manolo Ray was finally added to the government-in-exile.[7]

In response, E. Howard Hunt suddenly quit his leading role in the Cuban operation just weeks before the invasion was scheduled to launch. According to journalist Tad Szulc, a friend of JFK and an expert on Cuba, Hunt quit over Manolo Ray's inclusion. (Two years later, Tad Szulc would actually work with JFK and the CIA on a secret operation to overthrow Fidel.) Some accounts say that Richard Bissell took Hunt off the Cuba project due to lack of progress, but Tad Szulc's account seems accurate, given the coincident timing of Hunt's departure and Ray's inclusion in the potential new Cuban government.[8]

As Hunt's own account of the Bay of Pigs—and many others—have stated, Hunt had been one of the major architects of the Cuban invasion since its first stages, a year earlier. The loss of a critical player like Hunt only weeks before the invasion was bound to have an impact on the project, and it did, especially on the CIA's plots with Johnny Rosselli and Santo Trafficante. Now, the Cuba project's biggest booster, Richard Nixon, and one of its main planners, E. Howard Hunt, would both be on the sidelines as the Bay of Pigs unfolded.[9]

E. Howard Hunt originally had three roles for the Bay of Pigs: acting as a political officer; overseeing the recruitment of exile fighters in the

Miami area; and coordinating with Varona and Artime regarding their roles in the CIA-Mafia plots. When Hunt was replaced as political officer for the Bay of Pigs operation by Jim Noel, the CIA's last Station Chief in Havana, the CIA essentially replaced Hunt for only one of his three roles. Noel knew nothing about the CIA's deal to have the Mafia assassinate Fidel, and saw his role in the invasion as just dealing with Ray, Varona, Artime, and the rest of the exile leadership. Tony Varona had been working only with Johnny Rosselli, Santo Trafficante, and likely Hunt (and his assistant Barker) on the secret assassination plot, and he had no reason to tell Noel about the murder scheme, since that operation had a separate chain of command. The same was true of Manuel Artime, who may have dealt only with Hunt and Barker about assassination plotting, and had no desire for his rival Manolo Ray to find out about the Agency's relationship with the Mafia.[10]

For much of the preceding year, E. Howard Hunt had spent most of his time in Miami and traveling to places like Mexico City and Guatemala as part of his work. But he was now recalled to Washington, where Hunt was permanently reassigned. By the end of March 1961, Hunt's official duties for the Cuban operation were limited to assisting his friend David Atlee Phillips with propaganda for the impending invasion.[11]

According to a long-secret CIA report on the Bay of Pigs, Hunt had actually done quite well recruiting exiles for the invasion. In early February of 1960, 644 recruits were in training; by March 10 the number rose to 973, and by the first week of April—just after Hunt's departure—1,390 were being trained. With the invasion tentatively set for the second week of April, the CIA probably felt no more recruiting was necessary, especially since some new volunteers were still being processed.[12]

Missing from most books and articles about the Bay of Pigs is the surprising fact that over half of the exile invaders were recruited after March 10 for an invasion just over four weeks away. This clearly allowed almost no time for any effective training at the CIA's base in Guatemala. However, it does make sense from the perspective of high-ranking CIA officials like Richard Bissell, who knew the huge amphibious invasion scenario—developed only in early November 1960—was essentially just a cover to sell the project to JFK. The real plan had been developed under Nixon: Fidel would be assassinated, allowing the U.S.-backed exile leaders to take over Cuba. If the assassination attempt failed, Bissell's backup plan was the fake attack on the U.S. naval base at Guantánamo Bay, designed to force JFK to use American military might against Cuba. Most likely, Bissell felt no need to tell Hunt's replacement, Jim Noel, about the CIA's use of the Mafia, since Bissell's main chain of command for that was still through Jim O'Connell and Sheffield Edwards, the CIA's Security Director. Besides, Noel was also busy organizing personnel for the new CIA station in Havana, which he had been told would reopen as soon as the invasion succeeded.[13]

However, before E. Howard Hunt left Miami, he and Barker had one last meeting with a group of potential recruits, revealed here for the first time. One of the potential exile recruits at the secret meeting said the group of young men in Miami was excited both about joining the upcoming fight against Fidel and meeting the legendary CIA official known to them then only as "Eduardo." They all knew his assistant "Macho," and some knew his real name was Bernard Barker. Many of their friends had already signed on for the fight, and the newcomers were eager to join them. The group was stunned when Hunt told them they shouldn't enlist in the exile Brigade. Hunt explained that President Kennedy didn't seem to have the same stomach for the invasion that the previous administration had, and Hunt believed JFK might not give the operation the backing it needed. Because the operation might fail, Hunt advised them to return to their homes and hope for the best. Hunt also told them not to tell anyone what he had said.[14]

The young exiles were left in shock at what they'd just heard, but Hunt was actually being surprisingly honest with them. Hunt probably realized that with he and Barker no longer officially working with Varona and Artime, it would be hard to coordinate the timing of the CIA-Mafia plots with the invasion and the move of the exile leaders into Cuba. Any failure would leave only the backup plan of the fake attack on the Guantánamo Bay Naval Base, in which his friend David Atlee Phillips had some involvement (likely so he could quickly spread news about it in the United States). The exiles in that operation hadn't even been told what they were really going to be used for. In addition, Hunt knew that the massive dissident uprising his boss Bissell had promised JFK and the Joint Chiefs was largely a fiction (as Hunt himself would later write). Once in Washington and away from the action in Miami, Hunt was "out of the loop" on the important parts of the whole project and had to be content with writing press releases for David Atlee Phillips to issue in the name of the exile leadership.[15]

Bernard Barker remained in Miami after Hunt returned to Washington. But without Hunt, Barker was just a lowly CIA agent who had to file routine weekly reports to earn his monthly salary (which was around $400 a month, after taxes, during his CIA career). Barker remained a low-level associate of Santo Trafficante's organization, but after Hunt's reassignment to Washington, Barker wasn't officially dealing with the busy Varona for the CIA. Still, Hunt told Barker that Bissell had promised that as soon as the exile leaders landed in Cuba, Hunt would be flown in to join him. That could create new opportunities for Barker—if the CIA's plan succeeded.

Even as the new invasion date of April 17, 1961, loomed, the early days of April did not bode well for the CIA leaders planning the Bay of Pigs. On April 1, Soviet leader Nikita Khrushchev told an American journalist that the United States was preparing an exile invasion of Cuba. Six days later, on April 6, *The New York Times* featured a major article "about the imminent invasion" of Cuba. In response to pressure from the Kennedy administration, *The Times* reduced the size of the originally planned headline by three-fourths and removed a reference to "the role of the CIA," calling them only "experts." *The Times* declared the invasion preparations "an open secret in Miami" and said "boats 'run a virtual shuttle between the Florida coast and Cuba carrying instructions, weapons and explosives.'"[16]

Unfortunately, the part about that virtual shuttle is the least accurate part of the article and is based more on the stories spread by Phillips and Hunt than on reality. The CIA had promised JFK a substantial uprising of dissident fighters to help the invasion, but those networks were never large to begin with. The arrests of dissidents and suspected dissidents—which had continued to expand after the arrest of exile Sorí Marin—decimated the few networks in Cuba that did exist. Thousands of Cuban dissidents had reportedly been detained or jailed by the second week of April.

President Kennedy had remained consistent in meetings with the CIA, the Joint Chiefs, and his Cabinet, saying that U.S. military forces would not take an active role in the upcoming Cuban invasion. On April 12, just five days before the scheduled invasion, JFK made that point forcefully in a press conference. In doing so, he was sending a message not only to the world, but also to the CIA, the U.S. military, and especially the exile leaders. He wanted no misunderstanding on that crucial point. Even in private, top CIA officials raised no objection to JFK's order of "no US military force."[17]

The overt events of the Bay of Pigs invasion are widely available, but our focus here is on the hidden history of that tragedy. Interestingly, of all the civilian exile leadership, only Manuel Artime actually became part of the invasion force, potentially giving him a huge advantage over the other exile leaders such as Manolo Ray and Tony Varona. Artime was No. 3 in the exile Brigade, which was commanded by Pepe San Ramon. At the same time two ships carrying most of the exile invaders, including Artime, left Guatemala for the Bay of Pigs, another ship named the *Santa Ana* left Louisiana, heading toward the U.S. base at Guantánamo Bay, on the opposite side of Cuba.[18]

Cuba itself stood at high alert, with anyone considered a dissident either in custody or being watched by Cuban State Security. As cited earlier, Cuba had been divided into thirds, with Raul Castro responsible for the eastern third (including Guantánamo Bay), Fidel covering the middle third (with Havana), and Army Commander Juan Almeida, who the CIA knew was "disgusted" with Fidel, responsible for the western third, with the Bay of Pigs.

Near the coast of Cuba, Mafia bosses Russell Bufalino and James Plumeri, both part of the original Hoffa-brokered 1959 deal between the CIA and the Mafia, were on "a syndicate-owned boat with a CIA man aboard, ready to land" after the invasion and Fidel's assassination. This was apparently their reward for helping the CIA with the first phase of the plots. The Mafia bosses and the CIA agent were accompanied on the boat by two mob associates of Frank Fiorini.[19]

The current phase of the CIA-Mafia plots to kill Fidel was at a critical stage in the days leading up to the invasion. The CIA admits that their poison pills and cigars had been delivered to Rosselli and Trafficante, and they had in turn given them to Tony Varona. A fearful Juan Orta, Castro's former office manager, had gained asylum in the Venezuelan embassy, but another plotter the CIA has never named had been lined up to deliver the poison to Fidel. According to FBI veteran William Turner, the plotter was awaiting the "go" signal to administer the poison to Fidel, a signal that Tony Varona planned to send once he'd been told the invaders were almost ready to land.[20]

Over the years much has been made about President Kennedy's canceling one of two rounds of air strikes that were supposed to wipe out the Cuban Air Force before the Brigade landed. Less well known is the fact that Bissell had a hand in the matter as well. Originally, plans called for a sixteen-plane air strike to wipe out Fidel's air force prior to the invasion. The CIA's cover story was to be that "defecting" Cuban pilots were carrying out the air strikes, though they would really be done by U.S.-trained exile and Alabama Air National Guard pilots. Then, after the landing had secured an airstrip at the Bay of Pigs, there would be another round of air strikes, supposedly flown from that location, but really originating from the CIA's secret exile air base in Central America.[21]

However, after the CIA's initial "defecting pilot" story was widely exposed as an American hoax, President Kennedy worried that the sixteen-plane strike would be too obviously a U.S. operation. JFK ordered Richard Bissell to scale it back, leaving the final number of planes up to Bissell. Richard Bissell cut it all the way back to six planes; the air strike was too small and left Fidel with several planes. General Charles Cabell, the CIA's Deputy Director, had the authority to order the second round of air strikes before the invasion, but—for reasons never clearly explained—decided to check first with Dean Rusk, JFK's Secretary of State. Rusk worried that if the air strikes occurred before the invaders had established their airstrip in Cuba, the world would know the whole thing was a U.S. operation, so he advised JFK to cancel the second round. JFK did so, "unless there were 'overriding considerations,'" like the survival of the mission. General Cabell and Richard Bissell met with Rusk, who talked to JFK again, who once more agreed with the cautious Rusk. However, JFK offered to talk to General Cabell to see if the air strikes were really essential. With Bissell beside him, Cabell declined to speak to JFK, to press the matter.[22]

It's important to point out that even if President Kennedy hadn't canceled the final round of air strikes, the CIA's 1,443 exile invaders would have been quickly surrounded on their tiny beachhead by thousands of Cuban Army troops who could have shelled them at will. Fidel's initial response force would have been soon joined by tens of thousands more troops and Cuban militia members. It's possible that General Cabell, with military experience going back to D-Day, didn't press for the air strikes with JFK because he realized they couldn't make a real difference in light of those odds. In addition, JFK was still expecting the massive uprising the CIA had promised, the only reason he had gone along with the Agency's plan in the first place.[23]

Richard Bissell and Allen Dulles still might have pulled off their "invasion" if not for two problems they hadn't foreseen. With Hunt no longer in Miami or in daily contact with Tony Varona, Bissell didn't realize that Varona had been designated to give the "go" signal to poison Fidel. That was a level of detail that Bissell had left to Security Director Sheffield Edwards, and that Edwards had left to Jim O'Connell. However, neither Edwards nor O'Connell was involved in the invasion operation, aside from the assassination plot. Amazingly, because the CIA-Mafia plots were such a tightly held secret, known only to a small number of CIA officials, a fateful decision was made. On the invasion side of the operation, at a level below Bissell's, some CIA official had decided to detain all six of the CIA's exile leaders—including Tony Varona—at a remote part of the former Naval Air Station in Opa-locka, Florida, just before the scheduled beginning of the invasion. Various reasons were given later for the detention, from needing to have the exile leaders ready to fly into Cuba to worries that one or more of them might try to beat the others into Cuba.[24]

The remote, primitive building on the Base where the exile leaders were detained didn't even have a phone. "Armed US soldiers barred the doors," according to historian Peter Wyden. Manolo Ray and the others were angry at being detained, but Varona was furious. Later described as "the most volatile" about the situation, he accused the two CIA handlers there "of 'treason.'" Three exile leaders had sons in the invasion Brigade, including Varona. But unlike the others, only Varona knew that without his "go" signal to the assassin to poison Fidel, the invaders were most likely doomed. The two CIA men holding Varona knew nothing about the Agency's plan with the Mafia, and there was no way for Varona to reach Hunt, Barker, Trafficante, or Rosselli, or anyone who did. And Manuel Artime, the only other exile leader who knew about the plots, was on a ship getting ready to land on the beach at the Bay of Pigs.[25]

Richard Bissell and Allen Dulles still had one ace in the hole: the phony attack on the U.S. naval base at Guantánamo Bay. Former FBI agent William Turner wrote that the existence of that plan was later confirmed when "former CIA officer James B. Wilcott testified before" the House Select Committee on Assassinations. Nine-year CIA veteran Wilcott "said the Guantanamo deception was widely discussed by Agency personnel at the time. It was conceived, he said, after it became clear that there would be no popular uprising." James Wilcott testified that the Guantánamo provocation involved "the creation of an incident that would call for an all-out attack by the US military. Kennedy was not to know of this."[26]

The Cuban exiles aboard the *Santa Ana* thought they were to stage a "diversionary landing" on the far eastern side of Cuba to distract Cuban forces from the real landing site on the other side of the island. But as they neared Guantánamo Bay, their CIA handlers opened crates with Cuban military uniforms and weapons. They were told they were supposed to attack the U.S. base in order to draw the U.S. military into an attack on Cuba.[27]

The exiles, and their commander, Nino Diaz, refused to don the hated Cuban military uniforms. They were ready to sacrifice their lives in a real attack, but not this. For three nights a standoff persisted on the ship between the CIA men and the exiles, but in the end, Nino Diaz and his men refused to go along with the deception.[28]

As the main invasion force began to land at the Bay of Pigs, E. Howard Hunt and David Atlee Phillips swung into action, using the same type of PR strategy that had worked so well for them during the CIA's Guatemala coup seven years earlier. Hunt had a press release issued (in the name of one of the exile leaders who he didn't realize was being detained in Florida), saying, "Before dawn, Cuban patriots in the cities and in the hills began the battle to liberate our homeland from the despotic rule of Fidel Castro." David Atlee Phillips had a special CIA radio station, Radio Swan, broadcast calls to action to Cuba: "Take up strategic positions that control roads and railroads! Make prisoners or shoot those who refuse to obey your orders." Those were followed by odd messages that sounded like code intended for a vast underground movement, with phrases such as "the fish will rise soon. The sky is blue. The fish is red." But these were simply nonsense phrases made up by Phillips and Hunt. There was no vast underground network, only scattered and uncoordinated scattered acts of sabotage by the few dozen dissidents and exile saboteurs that remained at large.[29]

The exile invasion was essentially doomed from the start, but many of the exiles fought valiantly against overwhelming odds. Once Fidel realized the Bay of Pigs was the invasion site, he assumed control over the Cuban military response, which had initially been overseen by Commander Almeida. In the words of E. Howard Hunt, of the 1,443 exiles who landed, "1,189 were captured, 114 were killed, and some 150 were able to escape."[30]

As the scale of the disaster unfolded, both the CIA and the Joint Chiefs pressured JFK to intervene militarily, but he remained true to his public (and private) pledge and refused to give in. To ensure the safety of the exile POWs, JFK issued word that if Cuban exile prisoners were executed or slaughtered, only then would the U.S. military retaliate against Cuba.

One unplanned, well-documented incident almost resulted in Fidel's death just after the Bay of Pigs battle ended, and it would later have major ramifications. One of the most notable exile heroes of the battle was Enrique Ruiz-Williams, who liked to be called "Harry Williams." He was a mining engineer who, at almost forty, was much older than most of the young exile fighters. Author Nestor T. Carbonell wrote that Williams had been "blown into the air by an enemy shell . . . and hit by more than seventy pieces of shrapnel," leaving both feet "smashed and . . . a hole near his heart and a large one in his neck." Soon Williams joined other injured exiles as a prisoner in a primitive Cuban field hospital. According to Pulitzer Prize–winning journalist Haynes Johnson, Fidel unexpectedly entered the makeshift hospital, filled with wounded exiles. The seriously injured "Williams . . . recognized him at once. He groped under a thin mattress and tried to reach a .45 pistol he had concealed there earlier in the afternoon." Williams told this author the pistol had originally been hidden in his bloody, badly mangled boot. Williams managed to point the pistol at Fidel and pull the trigger—only to hear not a shot, but just a "click."[31]

Fidel's men immediately grabbed the pistol and Williams as the other injured exiles looked on. They were sorry now they had removed the bullets from Williams's gun for fear that he might use it to end his own severe pain. Haynes Johnson wrote that Fidel told his guards not to hurt Williams, and instead asked him, "'What are you trying to do, kill me?' and Williams replied, 'That's what I came here for.' [But] Castro was not angry [and] gave orders to put" Williams and the others in a real hospital.[32]

Williams told this author that soon after, in a prison hospital, he had a very private visit from an old friend he knew before the Revolution: Commander Almeida. Ostensibly, Almeida wanted to hear the story of Harry trying to shoot Fidel, which Fidel himself had delighted in telling other high Cuban officials. But the real reason for Almeida's visit was to see how Williams was and to let him know that he no longer trusted Fidel. Commander Almeida was convinced that Fidel was becoming too powerful and was pushing aside those who had helped him win the Revolution. From his prison hospital bed, Williams tried to talk Almeida into taking some type of action against Fidel. But Commander Almeida replied that Fidel was more powerful than ever after the Bay of Pigs victory over the United States, and the time just wasn't right. It would be two years before Almeida was ready to take dramatic action against Fidel for JFK, in an operation that would eventually have significant implications for Watergate.[33]

Arthur Schlesinger Jr. and another JFK aide finally tracked down the exile leaders being detained by the CIA in Opa-locka, Florida, and brought them to the White House. JFK personally accepted responsibility for the invasion's failure, explaining that overt U.S. military intervention would have led to a Soviet attack on West Berlin, which was completely surrounded by Soviet-controlled East Germany. JFK also went on television to deliver a dramatic mea culpa, accepting public responsibility for the disaster. In private, he railed against the CIA for leading him into the fiasco.[34]

As the invasion disaster was still unfolding on April 19, 1961, Allen Dulles had gone to visit Richard Nixon at his home. Nixon was still living in Washington, D.C., even though he was starting to practice law in Los Angeles. When Nixon offered Dulles a drink, the CIA Director replied, "I really need one. This is the worst day of my life." Dulles told Nixon "everything is lost" and "the Cuban invasion is a total failure." Nixon later said that Dulles blamed the failure on the canceled air strikes, but that Dulles admitted "I should have told him that we must not fail . . . but I didn't. It was the greatest mistake of my life."[35]

We have only Nixon's account of his meeting with Dulles, which omits any reference to the CIA-Mafia plots. It's hard to imagine that subject didn't come up, considering all of the attention the two had given the matter the previous year and the fact that Dulles knew the plots were still ongoing. If anything, the two might have at least talked about how the plotting between the Agency and the Mafia could be kept secret from any investigation that was sure to follow in the wake of the disaster. Keeping those plots secret became an obsession for Nixon, even after he was President, when he would repeatedly stress to his top aides the importance of finding out what files the CIA had on the "the Bay of Pigs thing."[36]

The day after Allen Dulles's visit, President Kennedy summoned Richard Nixon to the White House. It must have given Nixon great satisfaction knowing that the Harvard-educated wealthy man he'd lost to just five months earlier now felt forced to seek his counsel.

When the two former opponents met in the Oval Office, JFK echoed Dulles when he said he wanted to talk about "the worst experience of my life." JFK asked the former Vice President for advice about what he should do. In Nixon's responses, we find a pretty clear scenario of what the CIA had hoped JFK would do, and what Nixon himself had planned if Fidel had been killed while he was Vice President. Nixon said that if he were President, "I would find a proper legal cover and I would go in." He even pointed out to JFK the possible "legal cover" of "defending our base at Guantanamo," which seems odd given that there was no attack on that base. It's important to point out that at the time of Dulles's meeting with Nixon, and Nixon's meeting with JFK, the CIA ship with the exiles who were supposed to attack was still in position near Guantánamo Bay.[37]

Nixon stressed to JFK that "the most important thing at this point is that we do whatever is necessary to get Castro." When Nixon later wrote that he "'never' thought 'it would be allowed to fail,'" he was basically saying that when he'd had some authority, he did "whatever is necessary" to get rid of Castro, and had likely always envisioned the U.S. military going into Cuba after Fidel's assassination.[38]

As for the Soviets attacking Berlin, Nixon granted to President Kennedy that Khrushchev might "probe and prod" with small attacks, but he thought that the Soviet leader would "back down" if the United States fought back. Nixon then doubled down, saying that the United States shouldn't attack just Cuba using troops and "American air power," but do the same to Laos, a country neighboring Vietnam. Basically, Nixon suggested a strategy that could trigger major wars with the Soviets over Berlin and Cuba, and with—in the words of JFK—"millions of Chinese" if the United States attacked Laos.[39]

But Nixon still wasn't finished. He told JFK that he promised to "publicly support you to the hilt if you make such a decision in regard to either Laos or Cuba." He stressed that, saying, "I am one who will never make that a political issue," regardless of the outcome—but only if JFK followed his advice. Historian Stephen Ambrose points out it was "actually . . . a threat," with Nixon saying "if Kennedy adopted his policies, he would not criticize Kennedy," with the implication being that he would criticize JFK if the President didn't follow his aggressive advice.[40]

JFK thanked Nixon for his advice but indicated he wouldn't be following it. And true to his implied threat, in a matter of weeks Nixon began publicly attacking JFK over Cuba.

Less than three weeks after his Oval Office meeting with JFK, Richard Nixon launched a nationwide speaking tour, giving speeches to executive and business groups that he knew would be sympathetic to him. He began his typical speech on this tour by stating that it "would be the 'easy choice'" not to talk about "Cuba and Kennedy." But Nixon added that "no matter what the cost to himself . . . he was determined to speak out because 'our existence is threatened and in recent weeks the threat has manifestly increased.'" He repeatedly used the word "failure" in relation to JFK, and asserted that "we must be willing to commit enough power to obtain our objective."[41]

In his speeches, Nixon sometimes added that the United States should be "prepared to risk the possibility of war on a small scale if it is to avoid the eventual certainty of war on a large scale," evoking his advice to JFK about Cuba, Berlin, and Laos. Nixon sometimes added lines to his speeches about "open intervention" in Cuba or "a naval blockade" of Cuba. "Republican leaders and contributors flocked to him," according to Stephen Ambrose. And even though Nixon "insisted he was not a candidate for the 1964 Republican nomination, no one believed him." Nixon had thought Cuba would help him win the 1960 election, and now he seemed determined to use it to help him win the next one.[42]

CHAPTER 11

Spring 1961–Fall 1962: Bay of Pigs Aftermath to the Cuban Missile Crisis

Two major investigations into the Bay of Pigs failure were underway by May 1961. Both were highly secret, at the time and in the years that followed, and neither uncovered the CIA-Mafia plots. JFK ordered the largest investigation, supervised by retired General Maxwell Taylor, the former Army Chief and President of New York's Lincoln Center. Attorney General Robert Kennedy regretted that he hadn't been able to give his brother adequate advice before the invasion, so he tried to learn all he could by taking a major role in what became known as the Taylor Commission. In doing so, Robert—and JFK—developed a strong bond of trust with Maxwell Taylor (RFK later named a son after him), and Robert gradually took on the role of JFK's "point man" for Cuba policy.[1]

However, reading the Taylor Commission's report shows that witnesses and documents told the investigators nothing about the CIA's plots with the Mafia to assassinate Fidel or informed them that the invasion's "diversionary landing" had actually been a cover for a fake attack on the U.S. naval base at Guantánamo Bay. Buried among the thousands of pages of files reviewed and hundreds of hours of testimony heard, only one line from Sheffield Edwards "vaguely described the use of Giancana as relating to 'clandestine efforts against the Castro Government.'" However, the much later Senate Church Committee investigation stressed that Edwards's vague testimony to the Taylor Commission made "no mention of assassination." In his separate role as Attorney General, Robert Kennedy received a memo from J. Edgar Hoover about the Las Vegas wiretapping incident from October 1960 involving Giancana, but it also made no mention of the assassination plots. Even if Robert made the connection between the mention of Giancana in the Bay of Pigs investigation and Hoover's memo, he would probably have assumed that whatever Giancana had done for the CIA had transpired six months before the invasion. In any event, the Taylor Commission's report remained classified for decades.[2]

Even the CIA's own internal investigation, conducted by Inspector General Lyman Kirkpatrick, wasn't told about the Agency's use of the Mafia to try to kill Fidel. As covered earlier, fewer than ten people in the CIA had been aware of the plots, and even fewer knew significant details about them. Those in the know maintained secrecy partially because the plots were illegal and partly because the assassination plans might not have been authorized by Eisenhower and certainly hadn't been authorized by JFK. But there was also the matter of security, which is likely why the CIA's Office of Security had taken charge of the plotting in August 1960. In the early 1960s—and until Nixon's Presidency—there was a widespread fear within the CIA that the Agency might have been penetrated by one or more high-level Soviet moles, a particular concern for CIA Counterintelligence Chief James Angleton. Given the high stakes of the Cold War in the 1960s, it was not an unreasonable worry.

However, protecting secrets like the CIA-Mafia plots from the Soviets also made it easy to conceal them not just from Presidents like Eisenhower and JFK, but also from others within the CIA itself, such as the Agency's Inspector General. As Kirkpatrick's investigation played out, CIA official Richard Helms could watch from the sidelines, pleased that he'd removed himself from any ties (or at least any obvious ties) to the invasion plan and the plots. Even so, Helms would learn how the careful compartmentalization of an operation like the CIA's use of the Mafia could work in the future to hide the plots from his own superiors.

Even though President Kennedy didn't find out about either the CIA's attempts to assassinate Fidel using the mob or the fake Guantánamo attack plans, the failure of the Bay of Pigs invasion sealed the fates of CIA Director Dulles and Deputy Director for Plans Bissell. JFK made it clear they would have to go after a respectable period of time. Dulles likely decided not to tell JFK about the CIA's plots with the Mafia or the Guantánamo provocation because that would have resulted in even more CIA firings. Richard Nixon certainly had no motivation to reveal to his rival JFK the Agency's use of the Mafia that had begun on his watch, a secret Nixon would protect for the rest of his life. Finally, one more reason—or rationale—helps explain the

CIA's decision to hide its utilization of the Mafia from JFK, General Taylor, and Inspector General Kirkpatrick: The assassination operations were continuing, and not just against Fidel Castro.

Even as Richard Nixon slammed JFK over Cuba during his May speaking tour, he was keeping a hand in foreign affairs—and covert plots—via his friends Bebe Rebozo and former Ambassador William Pawley. One of the most brutal dictators in the Caribbean was the Dominican Republic's Rafael Trujillo. During Nixon's term as Vice President, the United States. had launched efforts to remove Trujillo, and those continued under JFK, according to National Security Council (NSC) and State Department cables.[3]

However, an important distinction that the CIA and Nixon never grasped was that while President Kennedy hadn't ordered plans for Trujillo's assassination, JFK was in favor of—and approved—helping dissidents inside the Dominican Republic take action to remove their dictator. In other words, if Dominicans were willing to risk their lives to free their country, then the U.S. government was willing to help. JFK remained consistent about that policy, regarding not just the Dominican Republic, but later Cuba as well.

CIA cables from the spring of 1961 show the Agency providing arms to the Dominican dissidents, and in one case Richard Bissell "approved shipping the weapons via diplomatic pouch." Bissell went even further, and around the time E. Howard Hunt resigned from his role as political officer for the Bay of Pigs, he went on a mission to the Dominican Republic. Mafia don Johnny Rosselli, who at this point was very heavily involved in the CIA-Mafia plots to kill Fidel, accompanied Hunt. The fact that Hunt and Rosselli had been sent to the Dominican Republic in March 1961 was withheld from the Taylor Commission, the Church Committee, and all of the committees that investigated Hunt, including the Senate Watergate Committee. However, it was finally confirmed in 2006 in a CIA-approved book, *Flawed Patriot*, written by former CIA agent Bayard Stockton, who became a longtime *Newsweek* bureau chief after leaving the Agency. Stockton revealed that "in March 1961 [Johnny] Rosselli went to the Dominican Republic, accompanied by Howard Hunt of the CIA." Stockton's CIA-reviewed disclosure also reveals that E. Howard Hunt not only knew Johnny Rosselli, but also actively worked on assassination plotting with him.[4]

Richard Bissell may have utilized Hunt and Rosselli on the JFK-approved effort to aid Dominican dissidents in order to help cover his own unauthorized use of the pair on the plots to assassinate Fidel. Or, it might have simply been expedient to have two experienced assassination planners already working on one plot assist with another.

Declassified CIA cables show that by May 1961 the efforts to help the Dominican dissidents eliminate Trujillo continued. Mindful of the recent debacle in Cuba, JFK was determined "to disassociate the United States from any obvious intervention in the Dominican Republic and even more so from any political assassination that might occur." Then, too, as JFK stated bluntly at a May 5, 1961, NSC meeting, "The United States should not initiate the overthrow of Trujillo before knowing what kind of government would succeed him."[5]

With President Kennedy against the CIA's preferred method of using people like Rosselli and Hunt to arrange Trujillo's assassination, two of Richard Nixon's associates entered the picture. William Pawley admitted to veteran FBI agent William Turner that "a short time before the Dominican dictator was assassinated in a CIA-backed plot," he received a "CIA request" to meet with Trujillo and ask him to step down. For reasons never explained, "accompanying Pawley on his visit to Trujillo was . . . Bebe Rebozo." The CIA must have been aware of, and likely approved, Rebozo's participation. Pawley was still close to Nixon, and it's possible that having Bebe Rebozo accompany him was a way for the former Vice President to keep his hand in the situation. If the mission succeeded, it would be his two friends who engineered Trujillo's removal. If not, Nixon still had an inside track for information about the situation.[6]

The dictator Trujillo refused the request of Pawley and Rebozo, who returned to the United States. Still, the Pawley-Rebozo mission, coming so soon after the mission of Rosselli and Hunt, confirms that Nixon's associates remained on the fringe of the plots between the CIA and the Mafia. A wealthy businessman like Rebozo, on the surface respectable and not an obvious mobster, was useful to both the CIA and the Mafia. That was especially important now that Attorney General Robert Kennedy was intensifying his war on the Mafia and its leaders such as Marcello, Trafficante, and Giancana.*

*Rebozo had dated and had a sexual encounter with Giancana's adult daughter on June 28, 1958, after she'd met Rebozo and Nixon in a posh Miami restaurant. Rebozo might not have realized who she was, since she says she used an alias.

On May 30, 1961, Trujillo died in a spectacular gangland-style slaying in his car. The hit was carried out the same way that the CIA had originally wanted the Mafia to kill Fidel. The Church Committee would conclude in 1975 that the CIA's involvement in the actual assassination was limited to the fact that "CIA-supplied weapons may have been used." However, the earlier-noted information about Johnny Rosselli and E. Howard Hunt's mission to the Dominican Republic, and other CIA information about the two, had been withheld from that Committee. Years later, after Watergate, Frank Fiorini—tired of the CIA's spin that Hunt was a minor, bumbling CIA figure—said in a published interview that "Howard [Hunt] was in charge of other CIA operations involving 'disposal' [assassination] and . . . some of them worked."[7]

Richard Nixon had one final role to play in the Trujillo saga. After his speaking tour, he resumed his legal career with a Los Angeles law firm while he began looking for a house there for his family. In one of his first cases for the firm, Nixon "handled attempts to recover Trujillo's fortune for the dictator's family."[8]

President Kennedy still had to struggle with the aftermath of the Bay of Pigs, making a major effort to win the release of almost twelve hundred exile prisoners. According to two Kennedy aides interviewed by this author, JFK felt terrible about their plight on a personal level, feeling that he'd let them—and their families—down in the most awful way.[9]

Fidel "demanded a $62 million ransom" for the prisoners. Nixon's allies on the right loudly demanded that no ransom be paid, lest it be used to spread Communism throughout Latin America. John and Robert Kennedy searched hard for a solution that would be politically palatable for conservatives in both parties. Finally, they came up with a plan called "Tractors for Freedom," a committee fronted by a group of distinguished Americans that included Eleanor Roosevelt. The idea was "to ransom the prisoners with agricultural equipment."[10]

But Richard Nixon joined other conservatives in roundly condemning the effort. Nixon "issued a statement asking the President to withdraw his approval of the Committee" and declaring that "human lives are not something to be bartered." Nixon seemed unbothered by the fact that he had pressed so hard for the Cuban operation that led to the exiles' captivity. Because of the attacks by Nixon, Arizona Senator

Barry Goldwater, and other conservatives, the Kennedys had to end the attempt, abandoning the Bay of Pigs prisoners to their plight.[11]

While Nixon lived well and the Bay of Pigs prisoners languished, CIA officials Bissell and Dulles appear to have continued cooperating with the Mafia in plans to assassinate Fidel. Though the testimony of some CIA officials indicates the plots took a breather during the remainder of 1961, the CIA's Operational Support Chief James O'Connell told a later internal CIA investigation that "something [was] going on" with the CIA-Mafia plots "between April 1961 and April 1962." The Cuban government's Dossier of CIA attempts to kill Fidel—that would later trigger the Watergate burglaries—details several assassination plans during the remainder of 1961. Its accounts are confirmed by Congressional testimony and Cuban news reports.[12]

However, CIA files regarding the exact roles of the Agency and the Mafia in those attempts are still missing. A much later internal CIA report tried to put a good face on the missing files from this time, by saying "it is possible that CIA simply found itself involved in providing additional resources for independent operations that the syndicate already had under way [and the] CIA . . . in addition to its material contributions—was also supplying an aura of official sanction."[13]

A more likely explanation is that Allen Dulles and Richard Bissell were desperately trying to keep their jobs by assassinating Fidel. Accounts of the Bay of Pigs always state that, though both men were officially allowed to resign, Dulles and Bissell were essentially fired after the invasion's failure. But Dulles remained in office for seven months after the disaster, and Bissell for over nine months. If something happened to Fidel in the interim, it would at least end their careers on a victorious note and possibly vindicate their Cuba actions enough to allow one or both to remain in their positions.[14]

The Cuban Dossier details a plan to assassinate Fidel Castro in June 1961, using bazookas fired from a jeep. Three men, and their weapons, were captured and photographed. On July 26, there was a planned attempt to kill Fidel in Revolution Square. The Cuban Dossier's description of this attempt even includes the names of the CIA officers whom one of the assassins met with on his undercover trip to the United States. But the four plotters were all arrested, and Cuban State Security captured their large cache of weapons and equipment.[15]

Since July 26 was a major holiday in Cuba, it was one of the relatively few times when the movements of Fidel and other top officials could be predicted. It's not surprising that another CIA assassination plot was also being planned "during the second fortnight of July, 1961," according to the Cuban Dossier. It goes on to say that the Cuban assassination plotters were receiving instructions from Cuban exile "Tony Varona . . . and CIA agents" stationed at the U.S. naval base at Guantánamo Bay. This attempt could have been part of the CIA's plots with the Mafia, since the Agency admits that Varona had been working with Trafficante and Rosselli on the Agency's behalf just four months earlier, and he was working with them again several months later. This attempt was more advanced than the three previous plots mentioned, since twelve men were arrested and they had a great deal of weaponry and supporting equipment that almost certainly came from the CIA.[16]

On September 30, 1961, the last casino in Havana closed, though several nightclubs (some linked to French members of Trafficante's heroin network) remained open. The closing of the casinos reduced the Mafia's pool of former Cuban employees who could provide assistance to those trying to assassinate Fidel. Knowing that, the CIA had been trying to develop its own small groups of Cuban dissidents into a team that could kill the Cuban leader.[17]

One of the most violent of those Cuban groups was Alpha 66, headed by a former Cuban banking accountant named Antonio Veciana. It was only in 2007 that E. Howard Hunt admitted, and a CIA review confirmed, that his good friend and associate David Atlee Phillips "helped to support Alpha 66" for the CIA. During the Congressional investigations of the 1970s, the CIA and Phillips always denied his role with Alpha 66, and those files were never provided to Congress. Perhaps due to the murders in the 1970s of several people involved in the CIA's attempts to assassinate Fidel (Veciana himself was shot on one occasion), Antonio Veciana was reluctant to publicly name Phillips as his CIA case officer who used the cover identity of "Maurice Bishop." However, in private conversations with Congressional investigator Gaeton Fonzi, Veciana gave strong indications that Phillips was Bishop. In a 1993 interview with Veciana arranged by this author, Veciana strongly implied that Phillips had been his case officer, saying he'd based the name Alpha 66 on the Phillips 66 gas station signs.[18]

On October 4, 1961, Antonio Veciana was helping to plan another "attempt on [Fidel] Castro's life" using bazookas. This was not part of the CIA's plots with the Mafia. David Atlee Phillips, using his "Bishop" alias, pushed the bazooka plan in his role as Veciana's case officer. "Veciana . . . recruited the action men and organized the operation, including renting the apartment from which the shot was to be fired," according to a Congressional report. However, Phillips "urged [Veciana] to leave [Cuba] because, he said, Castro's agents were becoming suspicious of Veciana's activities." Veciana "escaped from Cuba by boat" to the United States, where he continued to work against Fidel for Phillips. One reason the CIA withheld files about Phillips's work with Veciana and Alpha 66 from Congress stems from the Agency's later Castro assassination plots, including one in 1963 and another in 1971, when Nixon was President.[19]

On November 19, 1961, President Kennedy finally replaced CIA Director Allen Dulles with John McCone, the former head of the Atomic Energy Commission. Replacing General Cabell was the new No. 2 man at the CIA, Lieutenant General Marshall A. Carter of the U.S. Army. JFK was trying to exert some control over the Agency by putting people in charge who weren't career CIA officers. Richard Bissell remained as the Deputy Director for Plans, but he knew his time was almost up. Just four days before Dulles left office, Bissell appointed CIA officer William Harvey to run the Castro assassination operation. Agency files confirm that Harvey was still running the CIA's overall "Executive Action" assassination program, code-named ZR/RIFLE. That program continued to employ assets like a European assassin recruiter—linked to narcotics trafficking—code-named QJWIN.*[20]

Two things would greatly affect John McCone's tenure as head of the CIA. First, McCone had little use for J. Edgar Hoover. There was "personal hostility between Hoover and McCone," wrote historian Mark Riebling, and "McCone . . . never even tried to make friends with . . . Hoover." By 1961, the CIA and FBI had gradually developed

*Released files about QJWIN are still censored, though William Harvey's notes identify him as Jose Micahel Mankel. However, other notes indicate Mankel was only QJWIN-1, and assassins he recruited could also be called QJWIN. Other names identified by historians as QJWIN include Moses Maschkivitzan, Jean Voignier, and Michel Mancuso. The CIA files of the European criminal assassins QJWIN tried to recruit are all heavily censored, especially those with last names beginning with "M." Santo Trafficante's French Connection heroin associate Michel Victor Mertz has more than a dozen parallels with QJWIN.

some intelligence sharing and had even cooperated on some operations, such as one earlier in 1961 when David Atlee Phillips had targeted a small pro-Castro group called the Fair Play for Cuba Committee. However, CIA-FBI cooperation would begin to deteriorate under McCone, a trend that ultimately led to a complete break in 1970, helping to precipitate Watergate.[21]

Also haunting McCone's time as CIA Director was the fact that he wasn't told when he began about the CIA-Mafia plots to kill Fidel, either that they had occurred or that they were continuing. In December 1961, within weeks of assuming office, "McCone took Cuba from Bissell and gave it to [Richard] Helms," according to historian Thomas Powers. McCone also decided to make Richard Helms his new Deputy Director for Plans, though Helms did not officially assume that position until February 1, 1962, when Bissell "retired." Unlike Bissell, Richard Helms had no taint from the Bay of Pigs fiasco—but like Bissell, Helms wouldn't tell McCone about his use of the Mafia, even when Helms began to expand the plots. To a later Senate committee, John McCone "testified that he was not briefed about the assassination plots by Dulles, Bissell, Helms, or anyone else," something Helms confirmed in his own testimony. Also kept in the dark about the plots' continuation were President Kennedy and Robert Kennedy, beginning a pattern of deceptive arrogance for Helms that would continue into the early 1970s, when Helms was CIA Director and Richard Nixon was President.[22]

Richard Helms was a pivotal figure in U.S. intelligence matters from the time of his promotion until Nixon fired him after Watergate (a scandal in which Helms played a major part). Helms oversaw U.S. covert operations against Cuba for a decade, and he shares responsibility for the fact that U.S.-Cuba relations remain essentially unchanged today. In early 1962, Helms was forty-eight years old and had been with the CIA for fifteen years. Historian Evan Thomas concisely described Helms as having "spent a year at a posh Swiss boarding school, Le Rosey [whose alumni included the Shah of Iran]; graduated from Williams, and played tennis . . . at the Chevy Chase Club." Helms was "well-bred" in an Eastern establishment way, though not independently wealthy like some of his CIA compatriots, a circumstance that would influence his actions in later years. Before his intelligence work, Helms had been a journalist for United Press International (UPI) and had scored an interview with Adolph Hitler in September

1936. Helms went on to serve in the OSS during World War II, worked for the postwar precursor of the CIA (the Central Intelligence Group), and was part of the CIA from its start in 1947. In short, he was a career intelligence official to his core and, thanks to avoiding the Bay of Pigs fiasco, was on a career track that could realistically see him rise to the Agency's No. 1 or 2 position.[23]

Helms had a reputation for being efficient, organized, and "the man who kept the secrets," the title of his biography by Thomas Powers. Tall, suave, and imposing, he was also sometimes described as arrogant. He was known for having a cool demeanor. But two of the very few documented times Helms lost his temper in meetings or in public occurred after Watergate, once concerning the Bay of Pigs and another over the CIA's use of the Mafia.

By 1962, Richard Helms was well connected in Washington and traveled in prominent social circles. According to one account, a year earlier Helms had helped to broker the acquisition of *Newsweek* by *The Washington Post* because of his friendship with Ben Bradlee, then *Newsweek*'s Washington bureau chief. The CIA had been helpful to *The Post* since the Alger Hiss case, when the Agency showed *The Post*'s owner, Phil Graham, sensitive information about the case. The CIA–*Washington Post* relationship continued to develop in the 1950s, when the CIA paid "for *Post* reporters' trips" to other countries, since *The Post* at that time couldn't "afford foreign correspondents." (In the 1950s and 1960s, *The Post* wasn't even Washington's largest newspaper, let alone a national force.) Richard Helms was one of several high CIA officials who were quite friendly with Graham and *The Post*, and journalist Carl Bernstein would later quote "a former deputy director of the Agency as saying, 'It was widely known within the Agency that Phil Graham was somebody you could get help from.'" After Phil Graham's death, Helms remained on good terms with *The Post* under the stewardship of his widow, Katherine Graham.[24]

According to CIA accounts, in early 1962 Helms supposedly first learned about the CIA-Mafia plots. However, that isn't definitive, since Helms himself oversaw the preparation of those accounts, and the admitted destruction of files after one of them was written occurred at his direction. The fact that Helms's protégé E. Howard Hunt had been involved in aspects of the Agency's plots with the Mafia since at least September 1960 suggests that Helms could have learned about them much earlier. Also, if Helms hadn't known about the plots prior to early 1962—and didn't think they were a good idea when he officially found out about them—he logically would have shut them down. Instead, and without telling either his CIA Director, Assistant Director, or the CIA's new "Executive Director," Lyman Kirkpatrick (the former Inspector General, in a newly created position), Helms not only continued the CIA's use of the Mafia, but reorganized and ramped up the operation yet again. Since the top three CIA positions were mainly bureaucratic and not operational, as the new Deputy Director for Plans, Helms could essentially conduct tightly compartmentalized covert operations with no real oversight from any superior.[25]

President Kennedy and his brother, Attorney General Robert Kennedy, constantly pressured the CIA to do more about Cuba. By early 1962 the CIA was part of a new, Kennedy-approved anti-Castro effort called "Operation Mongoose," which is well known today though its one-year existence remained largely secret for more than a decade. Apparently not willing to trust a CIA official to oversee the operation, the Kennedys instead picked General Edward Lansdale, fresh from the Vietnam conflict. Operation Mongoose was in some ways a joint CIA-U.S. military effort, though by far the lion's share of the operation fell under CIA control. By early 1962, "the CIA station in Miami [had] quickly expanded into the world's largest [with] six hundred case officers and as many as three thousand contract agents," according to Thomas Powers. This huge domestic expansion of the CIA had ramifications far beyond Cuban operations because it helped to lay the groundwork for the domestic intelligence abuses of the late 1960s that expanded once Nixon became President.[26]

Operation Mongoose called for a variety of sabotage raids and for establishing guerilla networks within Cuba, all to "create an opposition to Castro inside Cuba, followed by insurgency and a general uprising." It was all supposed to culminate in a triumphant dissident march on Havana in October 1962 that would lead to Castro's fall. In hindsight, parts of the plan appear to be based on things the CIA had told President Kennedy about the Bay of Pigs plan ("insurgency and a general uprising") that simply weren't true. According to all official records and most informal accounts, Fidel's assassination was not officially part of Operation Mongoose. Based on the President's remarks to friends (Senator Smathers, journalist Tad Szulc), it appears that JFK was pressed by the CIA to approve Fidel's assassination. Szulc's notes of his meeting with JFK say he was "under terrific pressure from advisors . . . intelligence people . . . to okay a Castro murder. [JFK] said he was resisting the pressure." That may explain why Richard Helms simply decided on his own to continue with the CIA-Mafia plots without telling either JFK or Helms's new CIA superiors.[27]

CIA records and Senate investigators reveal that in early April 1962 Helms ordered William Harvey to meet with Johnny Rosselli to begin transferring supervision of the operation from James O'Connell to Harvey. On April 8, 1962, Rosselli and Robert Maheu met with Harvey and O'Connell in New York City. That meeting began a friendship between Harvey and Rosselli that eventually became more important to Harvey than his own CIA career, then at its peak. Though Harvey was described as "America's James Bond" to the Kennedys, he was overweight, anything but suave, and a very heavy drinker—the complete opposite of the smooth and polished Rosselli. Johnny Rosselli was also an expert manipulator and deal maker who exploited his relationship with Harvey for all it was worth.[28]

The surviving records state that Richard Helms and William Harvey wanted to continue working only with Rosselli and Tony Varona on the CIA-Mafia plots, and thus officially eased Robert Maheu, Sam Giancana, and Santo Trafficante out of the plotting. However, that simply wasn't possible for the two mob bosses in terms of the hierarchy of the Mafia. Rosselli owed all of his mob power to Giancana, and though Miami was still technically an open city for the Mafia, realistically Rosselli could not operate extensively there without the approval of godfather Santo Trafficante. As Miami continued to attract Cuban exiles, Trafficante's ability to profit from them only increased his power, and he often spent more time in Miami than in his home city of Tampa. So, regardless of Helms's desire, evidence indicates that Trafficante and Giancana maintained a hand in the CIA-Mafia plots, as did Carlos Marcello (who was no longer in Central America, having been secretly flown back to Louisiana by his pilot, David Ferrie).[29]

By late April, William "Harvey delivered four poison pills to Rosselli in Miami. In May, Rosselli reported that the pills were inside Cuba," according to declassified records summarized by Thomas Powers. The plots were now a high priority for Harvey and Helms, a hidden but crucial part of the CIA's portion of Operation Mongoose, in the same way the assassination component had been the only real chance of success for the Bay of Pigs operation.[30]

By the first of May 1962, President Kennedy and Attorney General Robert Kennedy still knew nothing about the CIA-Mafia meetings or the poison pills—but that was about to change. The previous month three related issues had surfaced concerning Sam Giancana. First, FBI Director J. Edgar Hoover had met with JFK to inform him the Bureau had learned that a woman JFK was calling—Judith Campbell—was also calling Sam Giancana. (While in later years Campbell exaggerated her activities with JFK, claiming she carried messages between Giancana and JFK—which didn't happen—most historians and Congressional investigators acknowledge that she did have a sexual relationship with JFK.) The President thanked Hoover and ended his relationship with Campbell, who was also close to Johnny Rosselli. Second, around this same time the relationship between Sam Giancana and Frank Sinatra became so close that JFK had to terminate his friendship with Sinatra as well. For Rosselli and the Mafia, JFK's ending his relationships with two of Rosselli's close friends was a critical blow. Campbell and Sinatra had potentially represented ways that John or Robert Kennedy might have been pressured—or blackmailed—to back off from their massive assault on the Mafia. In fact, RFK's pressure had finally forced the FBI to establish wiretaps on the Mafia, and the Bureau had recorded one Mafioso talking about Sinatra's fruitless attempt to persuade JFK to ease up on the mob.[31]

Finally, the Las Vegas wiretapping case involving the CIA, Robert Maheu, and Sam Giancana that dated from October 1960 had reached a crucial stage. The CIA asked the FBI not to proceed against Maheu because he'd been working for the CIA at the time. The FBI could have simply dropped the matter, but because of the poor relationship between Hoover and new CIA Director John McCone, Hoover took a more formal approach. Essentially, Hoover said the decision not to prosecute officially rested with the Justice Department, so the Attorney General would have to be told.

Richard Helms faced having to reveal the CIA-Mafia plots to Robert Kennedy. However, Helms had just reactivated the plots, and he must have believed they stood a good chance of working. Helms then made a fateful decision: He decided to tell RFK only about the past plots, not the continuing ones. Helms sent CIA General Counsel Lawrence Houston and Security Director Sheffield Edwards to brief Attorney General Kennedy. Houston didn't know the plots were continuing, but Sheffield Edwards, who had originated the Rosselli-Trafficante-

Giancana plots in August 1960 and was basically Jim O'Connell's supervisor, did know the plots were still active.[32]

Robert Kennedy was angry when heard the CIA had been plotting murder with Giancana and Rosselli, and that to protect the secrecy of these plans the CIA didn't want the wiretap charges against Maheu pursued. With lawyerly understatement, Lawrence Houston later testified, "If you have seen Mr. Kennedy's eyes get steely and his jaw set and his voice get low and precise, you get a definite feeling of unhappiness." A frustrated Robert Kennedy said that because of the CIA, "It would be very difficult to initiate any prosecution against Giancana, as Giancana would immediately bring out the fact the US Government had approached him to arrange for the assassination of Castro."[33]

That was a huge matter for Robert Kennedy, since the Chicago Mafia had been a particular target of his war against organized crime, along with Trafficante's empire in Florida and Marcello's organization in Louisiana. The scope of the Kennedy brothers' war on the Mafia was indeed massive when compared to the relatively minor efforts of the Eisenhower-Nixon administration. Robert Kennedy had hired ten times the number of Mafia prosecutors, and by 1962 those prosecutors were spending nine times as much time presenting cases to grand juries as under the previous administration. Though RFK's relationship with J. Edgar Hoover was strained, he'd at least been able to get JFK to pressure the Director to start mounting FBI operations against the Mafia.[34]

As Robert Kennedy faced the two CIA men in his office on May 7, 1962, he demanded that they check with him first if the CIA ever decided to work with the Mafia again. That message was passed along to Richard Helms, who promptly ignored it and continued to have William Harvey work with Johnny Rosselli and exile leader Tony Varona. The CIA admits that in June 1962 Rosselli told Harvey that Varona had sent a three-man assassination team into Cuba.[35]

During 1962, Richard Helms and the CIA made no attempt to reach out to Commander Almeida in Cuba, who still headed the Cuban Army, even though the Agency knew of Almeida's dissatisfaction with Castro. In addition, the CIA's representatives on the various subcommittees of the National Security Council that handled Cuba—which sometimes included Helms, and other times William Harvey—never put Almeida's name forward as a top Cuban official who might take action against Fidel for the United States. It was as if Helms preferred to simply go along with Operation Mongoose while actually counting on his unauthorized assassination plot to really do the job, essentially repeating the same mistake high CIA officials had made with the Bay of Pigs.

As for Helms's protégé E. Howard Hunt, his role in Cuban activities in 1962—or in any official CIA activities—is vague at best. His released CIA file for that year is very thin, including only censored, very general summaries characterizing his work as good though not identifying what that work was. Officially, Hunt was assigned to the Domestic Operations Division, whose very name seems to go against the CIA's charter of not staging operations in the United States (a mandate already stretched by the CIA's huge Miami station). Unofficially, it's been reported that Hunt helped Allen Dulles write his memoirs, essentially acting as his ghostwriter. Before Richard Bissell had been fired, he'd been Hunt's "boss," and now that Richard Helms had replaced Bissell, he was Hunt's new boss.[36]

As for Bernard Barker, his released CIA 1962 files show no contact with Hunt (the same as his clearly incomplete 1961 files), and depict him as simply a routine CIA agent, passing along regular reports from CIA contract agent Frank Fiorini, who was still trying to mount anti-Castro operations on his own. Their released CIA files for 1962 (and 1963) don't list their work with the Mafia, though their later files do.[37]

The U.S. military side of Operation Mongoose had begun in the spring of 1962, when the Joint Chiefs presented JFK with a series of shocking proposals for action against Cuba. Code-named Operation Northwoods, it consisted of provocations the U.S. government could stage to justify a U.S. military invasion of Cuba. As documented in Chapter 8, one of the Northwoods proposals was for a fake attack on an American ship at the U.S. naval base at Guantánamo Bay, similar to what the CIA had actually planned during the Bay of Pigs. Northwoods actually offered two options for false Guantánamo attacks, another being to "pay someone in the Castro government to attack US forces at the Guantánamo Naval Base." Neither President Kennedy nor the CIA's Inspector General and JFK's new CIA Director had ever learned about the Guantánamo provocation for the Bay of Pigs. The inclusion of a similar item in the Joint Chief's Northwoods proposal in 1962 suggests that the head of the Joint Chiefs in the spring of 1962—General Lyman L. Lemnitzer, who'd had that same position in 1961—had been a witting participant in the CIA's original Guantánamo provocation for the Bay of Pigs. From a practical point of view this makes sense, so the fake CIA attack could be coordinated with the U.S. military at a high level.[38]

According to ABC News, the Joint Chiefs' Northwoods proposal also featured such outrageous provocations as "sinking boats of Cuban refugees on the high seas, hijacking planes, blowing up a U.S. ship, and even orchestrating violent terrorism in U.S. cities"—all to be blamed on Fidel Castro. In hindsight, all of the other options, except for the fake Guantánamo attack, seem so far-out and so likely to produce unacceptable civilian fatalities that they could have been simply window dressing to make a Guantánamo provocation seem almost sensible and safe by comparison.[39]

The Northwoods proposals shocked President Kennedy, and he rejected them all. The proposals apparently showed JFK that some of the Joint Chiefs—especially its Chairman, General Lemnitzer—were very much out of touch with JFK's view of the world. Within months, JFK replaced Lemnitzer with General Maxwell Taylor, who had headed JFK's Bay of Pigs inquiry.

But first, the U.S. military stepped up its actions against Cuba in the summer of 1962 by more conventional means. Since Operation Mongoose called for installing "a new Cuban government" by "October 20, 1962," two weeks after an "open revolt" had started, the U.S. military began preparing for just such an event. Thirty years later, Pulitzer Prize–winning journalist Sy Hersh reported that in August 1962 "hundreds of thousands of American soldiers and sailors took part in military exercises in the Caribbean under the watchful eye of Cuban intelligence." He reported that "65,000 men participated in [a simulated] attack on an island like Cuba," while "7,500 marines conducted a mock invasion of an island near Puerto Rico named 'Ortsac'—Castro spelled backwards."[40]

Those exercises were intended to have a negative psychological effect on Fidel and his government and a positive effect on the supposedly growing Cuban underground resistance movement. Richard Helms knew that underground resistance was largely a fiction, so he continued the CIA-Mafia plots. As covered previously, the CIA admits that on June 21, "Rosselli reported to Harvey [that Tony] Varona had dispatched a team of three men to Cuba" and "if an opportunity to kill Castro presented itself, they or the person they recruited were to make the attempt—perhaps using the pills." Though William Harvey was now handling the Mafia plots for Helms, in the summer of 1962 the October deadline for Mongoose was drawing ever closer, so CIA Security Director Sheffield Edwards also met with "Rosselli [in] the summer of 1962."[41]

Fidel Castro was well aware of the massive U.S. military exercises meant to scare him and of the increasing number of exile "hit-and-run" and sabotage raids that were part of Operation Mongoose. At least partly in response to that pressure, Fidel was receptive when Soviet leader Nikita Khrushchev asked him to allow the Soviets to install nuclear missiles in Cuba for the island's defense.

The Cuban Missile Crisis, which most Americans think began in mid-October, has its own hidden history, in many ways the culmination of three years of U.S. covert action against Cuba. The first U.S. official to sound the alarm about Soviet missiles in Cuba was CIA Director John McCone on August 10, 1962, even though his more experienced subordinates believed he lacked evidence. At first, no one knew if the Soviet missiles had nuclear warheads, but by September 19 evidence started accumulating that they did. On September 27, the U.S. military began preparing contingency invasion plans using the original Mongoose target date of October 20. JFK was told on October 16 that "hard photographic evidence" from a U-2 spy plane flight confirmed that Soviet medium-range nuclear ballistic missiles were being installed in Cuba. He made plans to reveal the crisis to the nation six days later, after having daily consultations with a full range of top military and civilian advisors.[42]

On October 22, 1962, at 7 PM (Eastern), President John F. Kennedy went on national television to tell the American people the country was on the brink of nuclear war. Families across America were riveted to their television screens as President Kennedy described the missiles and the blockade of Cuba he was instituting in order to be sure that no more "offensive military equipment" reached the island. Essentially, JFK drew a blockade line around Cuba, one that several Soviet ships were fast approaching. If the ships refused to submit to inspection, the United States was prepared to stop them by force. The Red Scare hysteria of the 1950s had been replaced by a red-hot Cold War, suddenly brought into millions of U.S. living rooms. After JFK's seventeen-minute speech, most Americans were left stunned. Individuals could do little except hold civil defense drills for possible nuclear attacks, which quickly became common in schools across the country.[43]

While strategizing with advisors and conducting overt and covert negotiations with the Soviets, the Kennedys had CIA Director McCone order an immediate halt to U.S. covert missions into Cuba. They didn't want some small CIA raid to trigger World War III.

William Harvey, who had constantly clashed with both Robert Kennedy and Mongoose chief General Lansdale, had other ideas. Thomas Powers writes that "on October 21 [1962] the day before President Kennedy announced a blockade of Cuba in a televised speech, a CIA team headed by future Watergate burglar Eugenio Martinez landed two agents on the northern coast of Cuba. At least one other team made a similar landing the same night." Harvey told a subcommittee of the National Security Council that "several agents had already landed [and] there was no way to communicate with them, and thus no way to recall them." The *New York Daily News* later found "intelligence sources" who confirmed that one of Harvey's teams was actually "an execution squad [sent] to ambush Castro near Santiago de Cuba as he drove to a memorial service . . . snipers hid among trees and bushes lining the road . . . machine guns and rifles sprayed the second jeep [of a five-jeep motorcade] with bullets, killing the driver and his passenger, who turned out to be Castro's lookalike bodyguard, Captain Alfredo Gamonal. [Harvey's] assassins escaped." Robert Kennedy was furious when he found out and wanted CIA Director McCone to immediately fire Harvey, "but Helms talked" both men out of it.[44]

Since both the CIA's actions and the Kennedys' negotiations to end the Cuban Missile Crisis continued out of public view, most Americans could only watch and wait as they monitored the news. Reporters said that Soviet ships were drawing ever closer to the American warships at the blockade line. It's probably fortunate that at the time Americans didn't know that Soviet leader Nikita Khrushchev had ordered "the captains of Soviet ships . . . to ignore [the blockade line] and hold course for the Cuban ports."[45]

CHAPTER 12

Late 1962: "You Won't Have Nixon to Kick Around Anymore"

It's intriguing to speculate how Nixon might have handled a situation like the Cuban Missile Crisis had he been President, but in the fall of 1962 Nixon had his hands full trying to become California's next Governor. Nixon entered the race after polls had shown him beating Democratic incumbent Edmund "Pat" Brown and many supporters had encouraged Nixon to run. However, Pat Brown was a tough, shrewd politician and a formidable opponent. The father of current California Governor Jerry Brown, Pat Brown wasn't as liberal as his son and drew support from the same independent voters Nixon traditionally targeted.

Before jumping into the race, Nixon had been doing remarkably well financially for the first time in his life. In May 1961, when he began his previously noted speaking tour, Nixon had also started earning $40,000 a year for writing a nationally syndicated newspaper column. He had also joined "a top Los Angeles law firm," with a six-figure salary and "a large percentage of any business he brought [in]." According to Anthony Summers, in his first year at the firm, Nixon made $350,000 ($2.1 million in today's dollars). Later in 1961, Nixon would almost double his law firm earnings by signing a contract for "an estimated advance of $345,000" for a book, *Six Crises.*[1]

With his new wealth, Nixon built a lavish house for his family "near the exclusive Bel Air section of Los Angeles, overlooking Beverly Hills." In the summer of 1961, "the *Los Angeles Times* reported . . . that the generous seller was none other than Teamster boss Jimmy Hoffa," according to historian Stephen Ambrose. By this time, Nixon—or his wealthy and powerful supporters—must have smoothed over Hoffa's anger from the previous fall. The newspaper also found that Nixon "had been given a 'celebrity discount' [and] it was also rumored that subcontractors were asked to 'donate' some of their work." Summers pointed out that the lot alone listed for $104,250, but Nixon officially paid just over a third of that, only $35,000. The owner of the posh development had bought it "with financing from the Teamsters Union pension fund," which is how Hoffa became involved in the deal.[2]

After the article came out, Nixon quickly called an editor at the *Los Angeles Times* not to deny the story, but to say, "I don't see what's wrong" with "what I did."[3] When finished, Nixon's house was described as having "a panoramic view of the city [and] a library, guest and servants quarters, a swimming pool," and seven bathrooms. Nixon even had a butler, and his family now lived close to movie legends like Groucho Marx and top TV stars.[4]

For an ex–Vice President who claimed to have left Washington "with $38,000 in my savings account and a four-year-old Oldsmobile," it seemed a remarkable turnaround. In addition, Nixon owned other assets he didn't like to talk about. Just as Nixon and Bebe Rebozo had "jointly invested in interests in pre-Castro Cuba," Rebozo's banking colleague said that Nixon and Rebozo "shared in the ownership of a Coral Gables motel, with Rebozo fronting for Nixon on the ownership documents." Rebozo would help Nixon "invest" some of his new earnings, drawing the two closer together both financially and personally. As Richard Nixon's Vice Presidential Press Secretary once said, Nixon "liked to live well," but as for money itself, "where it came from . . . didn't concern him."[5]

Even though Nixon was making what to most people would have been a small fortune, he felt extremely restless. He hated being out of politics and off the public—and world—stage. But running for U.S. Senator would have been a step backward, and the Presidential race was still two years away. So, Nixon entered the next major race that seemed a good stepping-stone to the Presidency: the contest to become California's Governor.[6]

By the spring of 1962 Nixon was riding high with the release of his best-selling book *Six Crises,* described as "Nixon's personal account of his political career, from the Hiss case to his defeat at Kennedy's hands." Nixon's book was a masterful spin job that made him look like an accomplished statesman. Although Nixon initially claimed to have written it himself, most of it was later found to have been ghostwritten by others.*[7]

*One of Nixon's assistants admitted in 1998 that he had written five of the book's six chapters, with Nixon going back through his work to add "Nixon expressions."

Richard Nixon also settled old scores in the book. As covered earlier, this is where he claimed that JFK had been briefed about preparations for the Bay of Pigs invasion before the 1960 election, then endangered national security by calling for U.S. action against Cuba. In contrast, Nixon made it seem as if he'd lost the election by protecting national security and appearing "soft" on Cuba. The Kennedy White House quickly issued a statement denying that JFK had been fully briefed. Even Nixon-sympathetic biographers like Stephen Ambrose have documented that Nixon's charges were untrue. In hindsight, Nixon's whole approach for the book, with its emphasis on foreign affairs, was more suitable for a race for President than one for Governor.[8]

In fact, Nixon had a hard time adjusting his national sights to the more local issues important in a Governor's race: He emphasized "the perils of domestic communism" and "the strength of his international experience," instead of focusing on specific California concerns. Nixon also resented having to campaign in California's smaller towns. When the turnout was low at one rally, Nixon complained to one reporter, "That's what you have to expect from these fucking local yokels." On another occasion, when Nixon was "advised to drop in to talk with representatives of a local newspaper, he responded, 'I wouldn't give them the sweat off my balls,'" according to Summers. In response, an editor said of Nixon that "kind of thing turns people off," and soon "word got around that Nixon disdained the 'little people'" of California.[9]

Slick, TV-driven, pre-packaged, sound-bite campaigns were still years away in 1962, but Nixon gathered his trusted aides—and added some new ones—to find ways to effectively challenge Pat Brown. Los Angeles–based advertising executive H.R. Haldeman took another leave from his major corporate accounts to become Nixon's campaign manager. John Ehrlichman took the job of being Nixon's advance man, and Maurice Stans assumed the role of Nixon's finance chairman, while Herb Kalmbach was in charge of campaigning in Southern California. All of those men would later plead guilty or go to jail after Watergate, so it's no surprise that Nixon and his men came up with a secret campaign strategy that didn't just stretch the law, but broke it. Also helping Nixon in California was Murray Chotiner, once again.[10]

This time, Nixon would not be able to count on Chotiner's Mafia friends—or on any major mob figures—to help with the election. An early patron of Nixon's, Los Angeles mobster Mickey Cohen, had made the mistake of becoming too well known to the public. It was the same mistake that Sam Giancana was making by associating so publicly with stars like Frank Sinatra and singer Phyllis McGuire. Godfathers like Carlos Marcello and Santo Trafficante knew that staying out of the limelight was a key to staying out of prison. However, Mickey Cohen had enjoyed becoming first an L.A. celebrity and then a national figure, appearing on Mike Wallace's TV talk show and showcasing flashy girlfriends like stripper Candy Barr. Cohen lived a high-profile, lavish lifestyle supposedly supported only by income from a small west Los Angeles clothing store. With the new Kennedy focus on organized crime, Cohen had already been prosecuted by the IRS for avoiding taxes on $400,000.[11]

By May 1962, Cohen faced a long sentence in Alcatraz. It's not known if Cohen asked Nixon for help, but Nixon wasn't in a position to have helped even if he'd wanted to. Robert Kennedy flew to Alcatraz to meet with Cohen personally to ask him to become an informant against the Mafia, but Cohen refused.[12]

Richard Nixon would also have to be careful about taking money from another longtime supporter, Howard Hughes. The matter of the "Hughes-Nixon loan" from 1956 surfaced again in the California campaign. Even though "Kennedy Justice Department officials had investigated but discarded the possibility of bringing prosecutions" over the matter, it still hounded Nixon at rallies and sometimes in the press.[13]

Some campaign tricks typical of Nixon were used in 1962. These included retouching a photo of Governor Pat Brown bowing to a young Asian girl—removing the girl, and adding to the photo an image of Khrushchev, a caption saying "Premier Khrushchev, we who admire you, we who respect you, welcome you to California." But the usual tricks weren't working. By October, Nixon, Haldeman, Chotiner, and other advisors came up with new scheme. They planned to start a phony "Democrats for Nixon" organization that would demonize a liberal group, the California Democratic Council. Nixon's group would be called the "Committee for the Preservation of the Democratic Party in California"—but as a court later found, it was "fully financed and under the control of the Nixon campaign." The court also judged that Nixon was personally involved in the whole operation, even going over the copy for the fake literature with Haldeman, while California GOP Chairman Caspar Weinberger approved the operation.[14]

Nixon planned to have his staff mail nine hundred thousand

postcards to Democrats in conservative precincts asking them to "throw off the shackles of this left-wing minority, now so powerful." The postcard's suggested solution was to not vote for "their candidates" and instead look at voting for "acceptable Republicans." A slanted, misleading poll questionnaire was also included. Half a million of the postcards had actually been mailed before a young Republican volunteer, substituting for her mother, inadvertently called Democratic Party headquarters about the remaining four hundred thousand cards. Democratic Party officials immediately asked for a court injunction on October 22, 1962. The injunction was granted, and a lawsuit filed against Nixon and the Republicans. Nixon's gambit had gone beyond just being a "dirty trick" and was clearly illegal, if not criminal. However, Nixon's direct role in the matter would take time to uncover, and in the meantime, the tactic generated little negative publicity for his campaign.[15]

Robert Kennedy held two pieces of information that could have seriously damaged Richard Nixon's chances, but RFK didn't use either in the campaign. First, while Mickey Cohen hadn't been willing to help RFK's Justice Department to spring himself from Alcatraz, in October 1962 the mobster did give a statement detailing his contributions to Nixon. A Pat Brown official obtained Cohen's affidavit, apparently with the authorization of Robert Kennedy. However, nothing appeared in the press about Cohen's donations to Nixon.[16]

Second, RFK's "Get Hoffa Squad" had just secured an informant who was working closely with Jimmy Hoffa, Louisiana Teamster official Grady Partin. As mentioned in Chapter 8, Partin told the head of RFK's "Get Hoffa Squad," Walter Sheridan, about the $500,000 bribe that Carlos Marcello had given to Jimmy Hoffa for Richard Nixon. Partin passed a government lie detector test about Nixon's Hoffa-Mafia bribe and his other revelations.[17]

But the Democrats used none of that information in the campaign. Grady Partin was still undercover, and for another year and a half Hoffa wouldn't suspect Partin was secretly helping the Justice Department. RFK didn't want to jeopardize or politicize his war against the Mafia, which was finally starting to produce the results he and JFK wanted.

The Cuban Missile Crisis had been a constant distraction for the Nixon and Brown campaigns since the story first became public on October

22, 1962. That was the same day the Democrats filed their injunction against the Republicans, which is probably one reason news of Nixon's phony Democratic mailing received little attention. On November 2, the Crisis tension eased somewhat after President Kennedy addressed the nation briefly at 5:30 PM, telling the country "that Soviet missiles bases in Cuba are being dismantled." The nation and the world breathed a collective sigh of relief at the news. However, complex secret negotiations were still going on and JFK announced no permanent resolution to the Crisis, since Soviet bombers remained in Cuba. As a result, many Americans remained on edge and distracted by the events in Cuba.[18]

Four days later, on November 6, 1962, Richard Nixon lost the election to Governor Pat Brown "by 297,000 out of 6 million votes cast." A switch of 149,000 votes would have thrown the victory to Nixon, which makes it interesting to contemplate what would have happened if the remaining 400,000 fake Democratic postcards had been mailed to the state's conservative Democrats. Nixon, however, blamed his loss on the Cuban Missile Crisis, still unfolding at the time of the election.[19]

Richard Nixon took the loss personally and hard. The next day, when an aide told him "the press was waiting to see him, Nixon . . . said 'screw them' [and] 'to hell with those bastards.'" Apparently, H.R. Haldeman had wanted Nixon to tell off the press, whom Haldeman blamed for their defeat. Nixon's press aide, on the other hand, hadn't thought the media coverage had been "unfair to Nixon that year," and Stephen Ambrose later pointed out that "a majority of the big papers in California had endorsed Nixon." Still, when an "angry" Nixon finally appeared before the group of reporters, he launched into a disjointed, "rambling speech." Three times, Nixon said "one last thing," as if to end his appearance, but his final pronouncement, said with "a fearsome scowl," was what everyone would remember:

> One last thing. I leave you gentlemen now and you will now write it. You will interpret it. That's your right. But as I leave you I want you to know—just think how much you're going to be missing. You won't have Nixon to kick around any more because, gentlemen, this is my last press conference . . .[20]

Many of the reporters present—and others when the news quickly spread nationally—thought they had witnessed the end of Nixon's political career. *The Washington Star*, then the capital's leading newspaper, called his appearance "exit snarling." Five days later, ABC News ran a prime-time special, *The Political Obituary of Richard Nixon*, its guests a *Who's Who* of important personalities in Nixon's life: Jerry Voorhis, Alger Hiss, Gerald Ford, and, in a rare public appearance, Murray Chotiner. The inclusion of Hiss caused Nixon's supporters to flood ABC with eighty thousand letters and cables criticizing the show. Nixon reveled in the outpouring of support, but that wasn't what changed his mind about staying in politics—he'd already made the decision to continue within hours of his "kick around anymore" speech.[21]

For decades, November 20, 1962, was seen as the end of the Cuban Missile Crisis for a triumphant President Kennedy. On that date, JFK gave a televised speech announcing the lifting of the U.S. naval blockade of Cuba. He told Americans that Soviet "Chairman Khrushchev [had] agreed to remove from Cuba all weapons systems capable of offensive use," which included not just the nuclear missiles, but all of the Soviet IL-28 bombers. JFK explained that Khrushchev had also agreed "to permit appropriate United Nations observation and supervision," and "that once these adequate arrangements for [U.N.] verification had been established [the U.S.] would . . . give assurances against an invasion of Cuba."[22]

JFK had lost the first round with Cuba and Communism at the Bay of Pigs, but now the world believed he had won the second round, when the Soviets backed down and agreed to remove their missiles from Cuba. However, numerous files declassified and published in 1992, and confirmed by this author's interview with JFK's Secretary of State Dean Rusk, prove that the Missile Crisis never truly ended while JFK was President. It was this lack of resolution that set off a chain of events that soon had dramatic consequences.[23]

The enormous press coverage accompanying the Cuban Missile Crisis initially reported that the Soviets had simply backed down over JFK's blockade of Cuba. Later, the media learned that JFK's agreement with Soviet leader Khrushchev to end the Crisis involved the removal of U.S. Jupiter missiles based in Turkey. The other key provision in the JFK-Khrushchev deal, the requirement of U.N. inspections to make sure all the missiles had been removed, was only briefly reported at the time. It quickly vanished from the headlines, even though JFK had pointed out in his November 20 televised speech that "the Cuban Government has not yet permitted the United Nations to verify where all offensive weapons have been removed."[24]

As Dean Rusk, JFK's Secretary of State, explained to this author, and files confirm, Fidel Castro had not been party to the deal between JFK and Khrushchev, so an angry Fidel refused to allow the U.N. weapons inspectors into Cuba. But America's "no invasion pledge" would take effect only after those U.N. inspections had been completed. America and the world had been on edge until the tense nuclear standoff seemed to end, and JFK didn't want to prolong the stress by continuing to make a public issue of the U.N. inspections. In the following weeks and months, JFK and his officials worked behind the scenes trying to find a solution to the impasse. Khrushchev was fully aware that the U.S. "no invasion pledge" was not yet in effect, but JFK and his officials placated Khrushchev by saying they were working with the U.N. to help resolve the matter. On November 21, 1962, the day after his televised speech, JFK wrote to Khrushchev, saying that "there need be no fear of any invasion of Cuba while matters take their present favorable course" of trying to arrange for the U.N. weapons inspections. (Ironically, as detailed later, in 1970 it would be President Richard Nixon who would finally make the U.S. "no invasion pledge" official.)[25]

However, the talks between JFK's officials, the U.N., and Cuba reached an irresolvable stalemate. The same day President Kennedy wrote to Khrushchev, JFK "told a National Security Council meeting . . . that the U.S. objective 'is to reserve our right to invade Cuba in the event of civil war, if there were guerrilla activities in other Latin American countries or if offensive weapons were reintroduced in Cuba,'" according to a 1997 Associated Press article. However, word of Castro's refusal to allow U.N. inspections and JFK's determination not to give a "no invasion pledge" without them was kept out of the mainstream press at the time. Still, it would not take long for JFK's conservative critics and rivals to start raising the possibility that Soviet missiles remained hidden in Cuba. First, however, John and Robert Kennedy had to deal with another, more pressing Cuban problem, even as the United States, the United Nations, and Cuba continued negotiations.[26]

The problem was that 1,113 prisoners from the failed Bay of Pigs invasion remained in Cuba. Seven months earlier, Castro had released sixty injured exile prisoners, to try to jumpstart U.S. efforts to ransom the remaining prisoners. Before their release, Cuban authorities had told the men they had to return to prison in Cuba by the end of 1962 if ransom hadn't been paid to release the rest of the prisoners. Worse, they were told that one Bay of Pigs prisoner would be shot for each released prisoner who didn't return.[27]

One of those sixty released prisoners was Enrique "Harry" Ruiz-Williams. Known as Harry Williams, he was the badly wounded exile who had almost shot Fidel and who was friendly with the Commander of Cuba's Army, Juan Almeida. At forty, Williams was older than most of the other exile fighters. He had been a mining engineer raising a family in Cuba before the Revolution. Now Williams took a leading role in trying to win the release of his imprisoned comrades, whose number included Manuel Artime. The Kennedys were sympathetic, and Harry developed a working relationship with Robert Kennedy while trying to find some way to free the prisoners. At the height of the Cuban Missile Crisis, when it looked as if the United States would have to take military action against Cuba, Williams had agreed to guide U.S. troops on a mission to try to rescue the Bay of Pigs prisoners once the U.S. attack began. Williams knew that Fidel had placed high explosives in the old mining tunnels below the prison on the Isle of Pines to deter any rescue attempt, but he still agreed to go.[28]

Robert Kennedy had been impressed by Williams's willingness to guide what would have been a suicide mission and was glad his new friend hadn't had to go. But Robert was shocked when Williams started making preparations to return to Cuba, since most of the released prisoners were unwilling to return. Both Kennedys had felt great sympathy for the prisoners' plight, but now freeing them became a personal matter for Robert Kennedy. As documented by journalist Haynes Johnson, a friend of the Kennedys, Robert Kennedy moved heaven and earth in December 1962 to try to win the prisoners' release. It was difficult because earlier Republican and conservative criticism had made it clear the United States could neither simply pay the Cuban government nor provide any goods as ransom that could be used militarily by Fidel.[29]

Rusk and other Kennedy officials this author interviewed detailed just how tough the negotiations were and how close they came to falling apart. Finally, Robert Kennedy himself, with the aid of New York attorney James Donovan, put together a deal by which U.S. drug manufacturers would "donate" to Cuba "$53 million in medicine and baby food." In return, the Kennedy administration gave the American manufacturers tax incentives that allowed them to turn a profit on the arrangement. Even after the deal was struck, a half-dozen roadblocks threatened to derail the release at the last minute.[30]

There was a tremendous sense of relief when the first planeload of prisoners arrived in Miami on Christmas Eve 1962. Harry Williams was on hand to greet them, as was E. Howard Hunt, who welcomed home his good friend Manuel Artime. Later, Williams, Artime, and the other Brigade leaders attended a private reception at JFK's Palm Beach mansion, where President Kennedy explained that Soviet threats to invade Berlin had kept him from doing more for them at the Bay of Pigs. JFK told the men a huge ceremony was planned for December 29, 1962, at Miami's Orange Bowl stadium, where JFK and popular First Lady Jacqueline Kennedy would personally welcome all the prisoners.[31]

At the Orange Bowl, an elated President Kennedy addressed the prisoners, thousands of their family members, and throngs of other exiles. Caught up in the moment, JFK went beyond his prepared remarks, when—after being presented with the flag of the Brigade—JFK promised that "I can assure you that this flag will be returned to this brigade in a free Havana!" Thousands of exiles erupted with shouts of joy at his pledge, while JFK's surprised aides wondered how he could ever make that a reality.[32]

Six weeks after JFK delivered his impromptu public pledge to the cheering exiles, he made a surprising and ominous private remark to *Newsweek*'s Washington bureau chief, Ben Bradlee, speaking to him not as a journalist but as a trusted friend.* The two had known each other since 1958, and Bradlee was fascinated by the fact that JFK could be "urbane, debonair, suave [and] witty," while also being a "tough Irishman."[33]

JFK displayed both sides of his personality six weeks after his Orange Bowl speech, when he hosted "a private dinner party" at

*Both Ben Bradlee and his wife, Tony, were friends with JFK. Tony's sister, Mary Pinchot Meyer, had a rumored relationship with JFK; she was an artist who had divorced CIA official Cord Meyer two years before she began seeing JFK.

the White House. As usual, JFK was witty and urbane with his dinner guests, who included Ben Bradlee. But in a private moment with Bradlee, JFK became serious and frank. JFK bluntly "confided" to a stunned Bradlee "that Hoffa's Teamsters had planned to send an assassin to Washington to kill his brother," Robert. JFK explained the shooting was "to be carried out by an assassin equipped with 'a gun fitted with a silencer.'" Bradlee was so shocked that he jotted notes about JFK's disclosure the following day, though he didn't reveal the story for thirteen years.[34]

President Kennedy had received the information from RFK, who had heard it from Justice Department informant Grady Partin, the same man who told RFK and his "Get Hoffa Squad" about the Mafia's $500,000 Hoffa bribe for Nixon. Partin had originally approached officials about becoming an informant in September 1962, after hearing Jimmy Hoffa discuss plans to assassinate Attorney General Kennedy. In October 1962, Robert Kennedy had first learned about Hoffa's plan to assassinate him. Partin had passed "a meticulous FBI polygraph examination" and was providing to RFK's Justice Department a stream of information about Hoffa's crimes, including jury tampering in a recent case.

Hoffa trusted Partin, a Louisiana Teamster official, so Hoffa told him about two different plans he was considering to end RFK's war against him and the Mafia. One plan "involved firebombing Hickory Hill, Robert Kennedy's Virginia estate," hoping that RFK would either be killed by the blast or "would be incinerated, since 'the place will burn after it blows up.'" Jimmy Hoffa's other plan to murder Robert Kennedy was to have him "shot to death from a distance away" by a "gunman . . . without any traceable connection to Hoffa and the Teamsters [and using] a high-powered rifle with a telescopic sight." Hoffa thought the best place to do it would be "somewhere in the South [while] Kennedy" was in a "convertible." Jimmy Hoffa declared to Partin that "somebody needs to bump that son of a bitch [RFK] off." Partin said that Hoffa also badly "hated [President] Kennedy . . . he'd fly off [when JFK's] name was even mentioned."[35]

However, by the late fall of 1962, Hoffa was no longer telling Partin about his plans to assassinate RFK. Godfathers Carlos Marcello and Santo Trafficante, both associates of Jimmy Hoffa, had apparently persuaded him that the problem of Robert Kennedy required a different solution, one that didn't involve murdering the Attorney

General, despite Marcello's visceral hatred of RFK and JFK. In October 1962, another FBI informant—Edward Becker—heard Carlos Marcello explain that solution, at Marcello's secluded three-thousand-acre Churchill Farms property outside of New Orleans.[36]

Carlos Marcello felt comfortable talking to Becker, a former public relations man for two Las Vegas casinos, because Becker was in business with Marcello's favorite nephew, who was also at the meeting. The only other man with them, in the middle of the vast property, was Marcello's trusted longtime driver, Jack Liberto. After swearing in rage when Robert Kennedy's name was mentioned in passing, Marcello said, "Don't worry about that Bobby son-of-a-bitch. He's going to be taken care of." When Becker said that if Marcello went after RFK, he'd "get into a hell of a lot of trouble," Marcello explained how he would avoid any retaliation from JFK.[37]

Marcello used the analogy of dealing with a mad dog, with JFK being the dog's head and Attorney General Robert Kennedy being the tail. Marcello explained to Becker that "if you want to kill a dog, you don't cut off the tail"—if you do, the head will turn around and bite you. Instead, Marcello declared, if you want to kill the tail (RFK), you "cut off the head" of the dog (JFK), and the tail dies.[38]

Many people knew that Robert Kennedy and Vice President Johnson hated each other, and one of them was Marcello, who had his own Washington lobbyist and "owned" U.S. Senators, members of Congress, Governors, and Judges. If President Kennedy were dead, RFK's status as the second-most-powerful man in America—with far more power than a typical Attorney General—would end. Months after indicating to Becker that JFK would be killed to end RFK's war on the Mafia and Hoffa, Marcello said essentially the same thing to another trusted associate. In his New Orleans patois, Marcello explained that "you hit [RFK] and his brother calls out the National Guard. No, you gotta hit de top man and what happen with de next top man? He don't like de brother. Sure as I stand here somethin' awful is gonna happen to dat man [JFK]." Ed Becker says he reported Marcello's threat to kill JFK to his FBI contact.[39]

Around the same time, another FBI informant, Jose Aleman, told the Bureau about a similar threat to JFK that he heard from Santo Trafficante, the close ally of Marcello and Hoffa. Aleman was a formerly wealthy Cuban exile from a distinguished family, who now needed money. In October 1962, Aleman was dealing with Trafficante while also informing to the FBI, something Aleman would do for the next two years. Aleman had once been forced by the FBI to testify against a Trafficante associate, but Santo Trafficante had told him not to worry about that. Trafficante trusted Jose Aleman because Aleman's family had just helped Hoffa get control of a Miami bank, which Hoffa and Trafficante could use for money laundering.[40]

When Hoffa's name came up during a long conversation, Santo Trafficante told Aleman that JFK "will get what is coming to him . . . [President] Kennedy's not going to make it to the election [in 1964]. He is going to be hit." Like Becker, Aleman repeated his story not only to the FBI at the time but also, much later, to investigators for the House Select Committee on Assassinations (HSCA). To the HSCA in the late 1970s, Aleman stressed "that Trafficante 'made it clear [that] he was not guessing about the killing, rather he . . . knew Kennedy was going to be killed." The head of that Congressional investigation, G. Robert Blakey—a former Mafia prosecutor for Robert Kennedy—told this author that he found both Becker's and Aleman's accounts credible and believed them.[41]

It's important to point out that Becker and Aleman were informants only for the FBI, unlike Grady Partin, who was an informant for both the FBI and for Robert Kennedy's Justice Department. When interviewed by this author, Courtney Evans, the FBI's liaison with RFK, confirmed that J. Edgar Hoover never gave him any information about the Marcello or Trafficante threats to pass along to RFK. Thus RFK and JFK knew nothing about the threats Becker and Aleman had heard from the godfathers. Today it's unimaginable that such threats against a President would not be given to the Chief Executive or the Secret Service, but Hoover was a powerful force unto himself in the early 1960s, with no effective oversight. However, it should be noted that the FBI received reports of several other Mafia chiefs raging against both Kennedy brothers in 1962 and 1963, so it's possible Hoover and the Bureau failed to view the two threats as seriously as, in hindsight, they should have.[42]

After JFK's murder, both Carlos Marcello and Santo Trafficante made additional credible confessions to organizing the hit on JFK. "Credible" here means the confessions were made late in life, only to very trusted associates, and were supported by other evidence.

Carlos Marcello's JFK confession was discovered in declassified, uncensored FBI files at the National Archives in 2006 by this author, who first published them in 2009. The documents were vetted and featured on CNN and in a special produced by NBC News. The FBI files and their contents were verified by the FBI agents who wrote the original reports, and by the Bureau's informant, who was Marcello's trusted cell mate. (Those files are slated to be the subject of a major Warner Bros. film starring Leonardo DiCaprio and Robert De Niro in 2013.)[43]

The FBI files show that on December 15, 1985, Carlos Marcello made a startling confession to his cell mate at Texarkana Federal Prison, Jack Van Laningham. When talking about JFK, Marcello said, "Yeah, I had the son of a bitch killed. I'm glad I did. I'm sorry I couldn't have done it myself." Marcello later revealed more details. The files confirm that Marcello was very close to Van Laningham, who was working as an FBI informant at the time for the Bureau's undercover operation code-named CAMTEX. That operation included making Marcello the target of extensive court-authorized bugging of his cell, resulting in "hundreds of hours" of secret FBI audiotape of the godfather talking about his many crimes. That included Marcello's discussing other aspects of JFK's assassination, including his "meeting with Oswald" and the fact that Jack Ruby worked for Marcello. It's important to point out that Robert Kennedy himself, after his own secret investigations, told his trusted associate Richard Goodwin that Carlos Marcello was behind his brother's murder.*[44]

In 1987, approximately four days before his death, Santo Trafficante made his JFK confession to Frank Ragano, the attorney Trafficante had shared with Hoffa. To Ragano, the elderly and ailing Trafficante lamented, "We shouldn't have killed John. We should have killed Bobby" Kennedy instead. Ragano himself admitted having a small role in JFK's assassination, though a December 1963 FBI memo gives Ragano a larger financial role in the murder than the attorney ever acknowledged. In addition, one of Trafficante's confirmed operatives, John Martino, made his own, more detailed JFK confession to a journalist in 1975, shortly before his death, as documented by the House Select Committee on Assassinations and by *Vanity Fair*.[45]

The HSCA compiled a mountain of evidence documenting the

*For a detailed account of Marcello's confession and CAMTEX, including confirmation from FBI agents and numerous quotes from CAMTEX files from the National Archives, see the 2009 trade paperback edition of *Legacy of Secrecy*.

involvement of Trafficante and Marcello in JFK's assassination. Its investigation in the late 1970s had access to far more information—and lasted much longer—than that of the 1964 Warren Commission, which wasn't given critical information the HSCA had access to, such as the CIA-Mafia plots or the threats reported by Becker and Aleman. Even though authorities questioned more than a dozen of Marcello's associates and family members about JFK's murder soon after the crime—and one was even arrested—Carlos Marcello's name does not appear in the Warren Report.[46]

In contrast, the HSCA officially concluded "that Trafficante, like Marcello, had the motive, means, and opportunity to assassinate President Kennedy." It's important to note that the HSCA had enough information to reach that conclusion in 1979, long before Marcello's CAMTEX confession to the FBI was discovered in 2006 and Ragano's information about Trafficante became available in 1992.[47]

Thanks to 4.5 million pages of JFK assassination files released in the 1990s, it's now clear that the CIA and FBI withheld much crucial information from the HSCA, especially about the CIA's Cuban operations and Johnny Rosselli. That is why the HSCA couldn't include Rosselli in its conclusion along with Trafficante and Marcello. During the entire time of the HSCA investigation, Rosselli was the subject of an open homicide investigation, and his murder had actually sparked the HSCA's creation. Johnny Rosselli had been the victim of a gruesome dismemberment slaying in Florida twelve days after his last meeting with Santo Trafficante. A year before Rosselli's murder, Sam Giancana and Jimmy Hoffa had also been killed in crimes also linked to Trafficante. All three slayings occurred in a thirteen-month span, from June 19, 1975, to July 1976, with the murders of Giancana and Hoffa less than six weeks apart. Rosselli, Giancana, and Hoffa had all been targeted for testimony by the Senate committee that first revealed the CIA's plots with the Mafia, though only Rosselli lived to testify.

Rosselli confessed his part in JFK's assassination to his attorney, Tom Wadden, as revealed by one of RFK's Mafia prosecutors, William Hundley. Rosselli's confession of his "role in plotting to kill the President" was made to his attorney shortly before Rosselli's grisly murder, following his final meal in Miami with Santo Trafficante. A topic of conversation between the two Mafiosi was no doubt Rosselli's increasingly problematic testimony to Congressional investigating committees. First Rosselli was interviewed by three investigators for the Senate Watergate Committee, which then led to his testifying to the

Senate Church Committee about the CIA-Mafia plots and JFK's assassination. Shortly before his murder, Rosselli also essentially confessed to journalist Jack Anderson, to whom he'd leaked information for explosive stories about the CIA's plots with the Mafia to kill Castro.[48]

As numerous investigations and books—including two by RFK's Mafia prosecutors and two by this author—have documented, Marcello, Trafficante, and Rosselli felt they had to kill JFK in order to end RFK's unrelenting and ever-escalating war against the Mafia, which targeted their mob families in particular. Carlos Marcello had returned to the country illegally, and it was only a matter of time until he faced more federal charges and prison, followed by yet another deportation. Eight months before Santo Trafficante's threat, federal charges had been filed against him, charging that he owed the IRS $46,000. Trafficante's three brothers had also been indicted. Trafficante worried not about the money, but about the dreaded IRS, which had successfully used tax-evasion charges against mobsters since the days of Al Capone, most recently sending Mickey Cohen to prison. Johnny Rosselli's boss—Sam Giancana—was finally under pressure from the FBI. The Bureau would soon place Giancana under "lockstep" surveillance, meaning agents were often only a few yards away whenever he was in public. Rosselli's power flowed from Giancana, so something had to be done. Now that JFK had ended his ties to Rosselli associates such as Frank Sinatra, Judy Campbell, and the late Marilyn Monroe, the Mafia chiefs had no way to blackmail or pressure JFK to make RFK back off. The mobsters could no longer flee to Cuba, as they had before the Revolution. To the Mafia chiefs, assassination seemed to be the only solution.[49]

Marcello, Trafficante, and Rosselli had remained powerful for so long by being careful and cautious, and they would have wanted a way to stifle a truly thorough investigation after JFK's assassination. Because all three were CIA assets for the highly secret plots to assassinate Fidel Castro, they were in a unique position to manipulate national security concerns to help hide their involvement in JFK's murder. With the tense nuclear standoff of the Cuban Missile Crisis still a vivid memory, and with the United States still at odds with Cuba, it was clear that if they could link their planned murder of JFK to Cuba and Fidel it would trigger the national security concerns the three mob leaders needed to hide their crime. The fact that the CIA-Mafia plots were continuing into 1963 would help to make that possible.

• • •

Santo Trafficante and Johnny Rosselli had been trying to assassinate Fidel Castro since 1960, with Marcello joining the effort later, and by early 1963 the same three mob bosses were plotting to murder President Kennedy. For Richard Nixon, who helped to originate the CIA-Mafia plots, this created an indirect but dark connection that would haunt him throughout Watergate, until his resignation and pardon by Gerald Ford. It's important to emphasize that Richard Nixon had no way of knowing that the mobsters involved in the CIA-Mafia plots would become involved in JFK's assassination, and that Nixon had no role in JFK's death. But Nixon would gradually gain some sense of what had happened—or might have happened—at least from the information that Rosselli would leak to Nixon's nemesis Jack Anderson for articles published in 1967 and 1971, and possibly from his associates close to the Mafia and the CIA.[50]

Richard Nixon would eventually realize that, through his associates from the era of the Bay of Pigs and the CIA-Mafia plots, he had unknowingly come uncomfortably close to those involved in JFK's murder. That's true whether Nixon learned that the Mafia had killed JFK, or even if he believed (like President Lyndon Johnson) that Fidel Castro had killed JFK in response to the CIA-Mafia plots. In the Watergate era, Nixon aide H.R. Haldeman would say—regarding Nixon's obsession with "the Bay of Pigs thing"—that "in all those references to the 'Bay of Pigs,' he [Nixon] was actually referring to the Kennedy assassination." Haldeman wrote that Nixon's reason for linking the Bay of Pigs to JFK's assassination was that Nixon realized it was "a CIA operation that may have triggered the Kennedy tragedy."[51]

After Richard Nixon became President, he would go to great lengths to prevent the public from finding out that the CIA plotted with the Mafia to kill Fidel Castro. His pressure had helped to spawn that alliance, which had somehow been involved in JFK's assassination. Richard Nixon's worries about possible exposure would later be heightened because of events in the spring of 1963 involving Nixon and his close associate William Pawley.

CHAPTER 13

January–June 1963: Nixon, JFK, and Cuban Operations

The Kennedy administration's plans for Cuba during the first five months of 1963 were unfocused as the President and Attorney General sought an approach that could yield results without provoking another conflict like the Cuban Missile Crisis or the Bay of Pigs. The Kennedy brothers' plans for Cuba were driven to some degree by Richard Nixon and other critics on the right, who constantly pressed for stronger action against the island nation. It would take until late May for the Kennedys to finally develop a focused plan, one that would dominate their Cuban strategy for the rest of JFK's Presidency. John and Robert Kennedy thought they were gaining firmer control of U.S. operations against Cuba. Yet without telling JFK, RFK, or CIA Director John McCone, Richard Helms was secretly continuing the CIA-Mafia plots with Johnny Rosselli, which had originally begun under Nixon.

By January 1963, Richard Nixon was recovering from his disastrous November 1962 press conference, and had set his sights again on the White House. Nixon had told reporters that he planned to spend time with his family. Instead, Nixon had taken a three-week vacation on Paradise Island in the Bahamas with his best friend, Bebe Rebozo, leaving his family behind. Nixon emerged from the trip to find that his national base had rallied to him after his criticism of the press. Encouraged by the support, Nixon decided that a Presidential run was feasible. Nixon blamed his California election loss on the Cuban Missile Crisis and his 1960 loss to JFK on Kennedy's supposed misuse of a Cuba briefing. Therefore, in the words of Stephen Ambrose, a 1964 "victory over Kennedy would be a sweet vindication, especially if he could use Cuba to do it."[1]

Before going after JFK over Cuba, Nixon had to make arrangements for his more immediate future. After his rejection by the voters of California, Nixon wanted to leave the state, preferably moving to Washington or New York City, either of which he could use as a base for another Presidential bid. Nixon turned down positions ranging from Major League Baseball Commissioner to Chairman of the Board of Chrysler. Instead, he wanted "a job that would give him a big salary, free time, and plenty of overseas travel," so he could burnish his foreign policy credentials. Nixon decided to move to New York and find a large Wall Street firm to join. Two corporate CEO friends from Pepsi and Warner-Lambert helped Nixon locate a firm willing to pay his required $250,000 salary: Mudge, Stern, Baldwin, and Todd, soon to add Nixon as a full partner. Nixon sold his California house for a hefty profit and bought a ten-room Fifth Avenue apartment overlooking Central Park, in the same building where New York Governor Nelson Rockefeller—his potential rival for the 1964 nomination—had an apartment.[2]

Nixon's anger at John and Robert Kennedy increased in February 1963, when RFK had the Justice Department look into the 1956 Hughes-Nixon "loan," which had resurfaced as an issue in the recent Governor's race. Apparently in conjunction with that, the IRS "began an extensive audit of Nixon's tax returns." Thinking the Kennedys were being vindictive, Nixon later may have used that audit to rationalize his own extensive political use of the IRS to attack opponents after he became President. However, it's possible that Robert Kennedy was also having the IRS look into Nixon's $500,000 Mafia-Hoffa bribe, something that Nixon couldn't know that RFK had uncovered.[3]

In late February, Nixon filmed an episode of *The Jack Paar Show*, then America's most popular late-night television show. The show aired in mid-March, with Nixon declaring he was going to be as active as possible in "public affairs" and would be a "constructive critic" of President Kennedy. He then "called for a blockade of Cuba until the last Soviet soldier left the island."[4]

To current and potential financial supporters, Nixon began a series of private letters attacking JFK over Cuba. He followed that up with a public offensive on April 20, 1963, in a speech "to the American Society of Newspaper Editors in Washington." After starting with a vague apology for his California press conference, Nixon launched into his first attack on JFK, saying, "In Cuba, we have goofed an invasion, paid tribute to Castro for the prisoners, then given the Soviets squatter's rights in our backyard."[5]

Richard Nixon then declared to the editors that "Cuba is western Russia, and the rest of Latin America is in deadly peril." He called JFK's policy "creeping surrender," and said that at the Bay of Pigs the Kennedy administration "proceeded to pull defeat out of the jaws of victory." He then surprised the editors by calling for "whatever is necessary to force the removal of the Soviet beachhead." In the question-and-answer session after the speech, Nixon explained his remark, saying "he was not calling for 'an invasion immediately with maximum power.'" His addition of the qualifiers "immediately" and "maximum" did little to temper his inference. It was as if Nixon were campaigning again, and "several of his listeners [said] that he sounded for all the world like a man still seeking the presidency."[6]

Nixon would make similar remarks about Cuba in speeches and interviews into the summer and fall of 1963. Because he hoped to use Cuba as a major issue to help him win the Republican nomination, it's not hard to see why Nixon and his friend Pawley would soon prove receptive to a story about Russian missile technicians wanting to leave Cuba for the United States. Yet harsh though his words were, Nixon's criticisms of JFK were almost mild compared to the stronger attacks coming from extreme conservatives in both parties. Nixon's potential rivals for the Republican nomination were Goldwater on the far right, Rockefeller on the moderate left, and Michigan Governor George Romney on the moderate right. Nixon tried to position himself near Romney in the middle, though with a foreign policy experience advantage that none of his rivals could match. Ironically, if Nixon had not chosen to run for Governor of California, he would have been the clear front-runner. Now Nixon needed an issue like Cuba to differentiate himself from the pack.

The attacks by Nixon and other critics meant that John and Robert Kennedy couldn't ignore Fidel and Cuba, as many Americans and much of the press were doing now that the Cuban Missile Crisis had faded from the headlines. Cuba was clearly going to be a major issue in the 1964 campaign, so the Kennedys would have to take some action or find some solution by the end of the year.

Operation Mongoose officially ended before 1963 began, and General Edward Lansdale was gone from Cuban matters. Remnants of the operation continued, with the CIA supporting dozens of exile groups to varying degrees and still running up to "three thousand contract agents" out of its huge Miami station, code-named JMWAVE.[7]

Replacing the volatile William Harvey, at least officially, was Desmond FitzGerald, a patrician figure from a family more wealthy and blue-blooded than that of Richard Helms. FitzGerald was brought over from Far Eastern operations, had no previous experience in Cuban affairs, and his private comments reveal him to be somewhat racist. On the other hand, FitzGerald was friendly with John and Robert Kennedy, which was probably one reason Helms chose him to run Cuban operations. FitzGerald's group, called the Special Affairs Staff, wasn't part of the CIA's overall Western Hemisphere Division, and he reported directly to Helms.[8]

Richard Helms later testified that John and Robert Kennedy had not been told about the continuation of the CIA-Mafia plots into 1963, nor were they aware that William Harvey was still working with Johnny Rosselli. The first six months of 1963 appear to have been a transition period, with Harvey continuing to manage Rosselli while Desmond FitzGerald got up to speed on the huge array of CIA anti-Castro operations.[9]

Under Deputy Director for Plans Richard Helms, a crucial dichotomy was developing. In addition to the CIA's Cuban operations known to the Kennedys, the National Security Council, and CIA Director John McCone, there was a small but critical group of operations known only to CIA officials like Helms and FitzGerald (and Harvey). This dichotomy would play a major role in how the CIA's anti-Castro operations unfolded in 1963.[10]

The Kennedys wanted to provide some level of support for the released Bay of Pigs prisoners, especially Brigade leaders like Manuel Artime, and for that they looked to the U.S. military and the CIA. E. Howard Hunt resumed close contact with his friend Manuel Artime. Bernard Barker began dealing with both men again, even though released files depicted Barker only as a low-level CIA agent making weekly reports of information from anti-Castro figures like Frank Fiorini. However, a January 6, 1963, CIA report shows that the contacts between Hunt, Artime, and Barker aroused concern within official CIA channels, perhaps because Hunt was too close to Artime personally to be his official case officer. Another CIA official, Henry Hecksher, later to play a major role in Chile for President Nixon, was assigned that role. Extensive contacts between Hunt, Artime, and Barker continued in 1963, though most of these are missing from records released so far.[11]

A likely explanation for those missing 1963 Hunt-Artime-Barker records is provided by a handful of CIA memos withheld from later Congressional investigators. When they were finally declassified in the late 1990s and early 2000s and first published by this author, they showed that not only was Artime involved in the CIA-Mafia plots to kill Fidel, but that the CIA looked at utilizing Artime's Mafia ties as a cover for supplying weapons to him. Like Hunt, Barker, and David Atlee Phillips, Artime played multiple roles for the CIA in 1963, some of which weren't reflected in the main, official files that could easily be seen by Richard Helms's superiors.

Hunt's official CIA role in 1963 was as the Chief of Covert Action for the new Domestic Operations Division, an oxymoronic title, since the CIA's charter supposedly barred it from domestic operations. Aside from his work with U.S. publishers, little is known about Hunt's 1963 and 1964 activities, aside from brief, very general, and censored CIA performance evaluations, which are full of praise for Hunt and his supervision of seven Agency employees. Hunt's work with publishers—described in his evaluation as "expertise in the field of propaganda and publication"—came to light only in 1975 because of a post-Watergate Senate investigation. But much crucial information about the CIA's 1963 Cuban operations was withheld from that investigation. Based on what is known, it's probable that, like Artime, both Hunt and Barker retained a role in the CIA-Mafia plots in 1963.[12]

By early 1963, another original member of the CIA-Mafia plots from 1960, Frank Fiorini, was still involved in anti-Castro activities, though his days of prominence were over. He was only on the fringe of official CIA activities, and it's not clear if he continued to be a CIA contract agent into 1963. Constantly seeking funding for his small anti-Castro raids and schemes, Fiorini drifted into working for the Mafia, though he was strictly a small-time mob figure, described by one anti-Castro associate as being "a bagman for Trafficante." His love of publicity limited his usefulness for both the CIA and Trafficante, though later that year the godfather would find a way to use it to his advantage.

The Kennedys knew only that Artime and the other Bay of Pigs leaders were getting support from the CIA and the U.S. Army, but not toward any specific goal. Robert Kennedy began sporadic personal contact with Artime, though the two men's dealings would not become the kind of friendship RFK had with Harry Williams. Artime's requests and demands carried a whiff of "blackmail" as he exploited the Kennedys' guilt over his time in prison after the Bay of Pigs.[13]

One promising idea that emerged for the Kennedys was to find some Cuban official who might be willing to organize a coup to overthrow Fidel. In January 1963, the Kennedys even had the CIA work with *New York Times* journalist Tad Szulc on an operation code-named AMTRUNK, designed to "overthrow the Cuban government by means of a conspiracy among high-level military and civilian leaders of the [Cuban] government." CIA memos confirm that "the proposal for this operation was presented to CIA by Tad Szulc via . . . the State Department." Szulc met with CIA officials, including David Morales, the CIA's Operations Chief at the Miami Station, and the attempt lasted for many months. Although its operatives eventually made a few contacts in Fidel's government, none were high enough to stand a realistic chance of overthrowing Fidel. Along those same lines, John and Robert Kennedy had the CIA work with the relatively new Defense Intelligence Agency (DIA) to draw up a list of potential Cuban officials and officers who might help to stage a coup. The DIA was headed by General Joseph Carroll, who had played a key role the previous year in discovering the Soviet missiles in Cuba. However, inter-service rivalry limited the effectiveness of the DIA in 1963, and some branches, like Naval Intelligence, chafed at having to subordinate their own operations to the new agency.[14]

On January 22, 1963, JFK ordered the U.S. military to update "their plans for an invasion of Cuba" in case the Soviets decided to move on West Berlin. These updates usually took a month or a month and a half. On February 25, after rumors surfaced of a "failed uprising inside Cuba," JFK "told the Joint Chiefs of Staff that he wanted to introduce troops immediately if a revolt showed any chance of success." The rumors proved to be false, leaving U.S. officials with no palatable, realistic way of overthrowing Fidel.[15]

Even before the Bay of Pigs prisoners were released, Richard Nixon's friend William Pawley had become involved again in Cuban matters with Johnny Rosselli. Historian Richard D. Mahoney, who had special access to Kennedy papers at the John F. Kennedy Presidential

Library, wrote that "former Eisenhower Ambassador (and Flying Tiger cofounder) William D. Pawley [had] approached [Robert] Kennedy [about wanting] to raise money to pay the ransom of the imprisoned Bay of Pigs fighters through the sale of Cuban government bonds." Robert "Kennedy looked at it" before turning Pawley down. Perhaps one reason RFK didn't pursue Pawley's suggestion was that "one of the major subscribers [to Pawley's scheme] was Johnny Rosselli."[16]

In late February or early March of 1963, an FBI memo reports that Pawley met with Richard Nixon and Bebe Rebozo, just as Pawley was beginning a new Cuban operation with Johnny Rosselli. This time, Pawley would be working closely with Rosselli and Trafficante's operative John Martino, an electronics expert who had been released from a Cuban prison only five months earlier. John Martino was extremely bitter over his imprisonment and what he felt were inadequate efforts by the Kennedy administration to win his release. (Martino later made a credible confession to helping Trafficante kill JFK, as mentioned in Chapter 11.) The CIA admits that in 1963, Martino was a CIA asset, as was Rosselli.[17]

A pilot who had first met Johnny Rosselli in the late 1950s told the FBI that:

> In March 1963, he flew into Tampa, Florida, where he met Rosselli [and then] flew Rosselli and John V. Martino from Tampa to Rivera Beach, Florida . . . he learned that one Ambassador Pawley . . . was trying to arrange a raid to remove [Soviet] missile technicians from Cuba. He was under the impression that Pawley was organizing the raid through Rosselli [and] Martino . . . after the raid he flew Rosselli to Bimini Island where he was to meet with Pawley, Martino, and others . . . three weeks before this meeting, Pawley met at Bimini with Bebe Rebozo and Richard Nixon.[18]

Supposedly, three dissident Soviet missile technicians in Cuba were willing to defect and prove to the world that Soviet nuclear missiles remained on the island. David Kaiser, historian and professor at the Naval War College, wrote that Nixon's friend "Pawley immediately recognized that this information would utterly discredit the Kennedy administration," thus helping Nixon's political future. It would also "revive plans to invade Cuba," something Pawley and Nixon had worked on together in 1960. William Pawley's goal was to "spring the defectors on the public in testimony before the [Senate Internal Security] Committee." That Committee, a Senate version of HUAC, was chaired by Mississippi Senator James Eastland, who detested JFK's support of civil rights.[19]

Richard Nixon and Bebe Rebozo's meeting with Pawley, as the operation was beginning, was probably Nixon's attempt to secure inside information that could help in his quest for the White House. The question of whether all the Soviet missiles had been removed from Cuba was already a hot topic in Republican circles and would be a major issue in the 1964 Presidential campaign. If Nixon had the inside story on Soviet missiles still in Cuba, he would have an edge over his Republican rivals.[20]

"On April 18, [1963, Pawley] came to the office of JMWAVE's [Ted] Shackley in Miami to ask for assistance" from the CIA, according to declassified files studied by historian Kaiser. Shackley was reluctant, so Pawley simply called "General Marshall Carter, Deputy Director of" the CIA, who approved Pawley's plan, which the Agency gave the code name of Operation TILT. CIA personnel were assigned to assist the operation, including Eugenio Martinez, the future Watergate burglar. The CIA's premier "boat man," Martinez had most recently been the "chief pilot" for Mongoose infiltration missions, and he would become the "navigator and coastal guide for" Operation TILT.[21]

However, Kaiser found that "Rosselli and Trafficante were using Martino and Pawley as cut-outs to enlist the help of the CIA" for the operation. William Pawley had access to the CIA's second-highest official and received quick approval for the scheme because Pawley had worked with the CIA on Cuban matters since 1960. Declassified files show that Pawley "retained the [CIA] cryptonym (code name) QDDALE as late as 1963."[22]

William Pawley wanted maximum publicity for his operation, so he also approached *Life* magazine, America's most widely read pictorial magazine. *Life* "promised [to give] each of the three Soviet defectors $2,500 in return for their stories."[23]

The narrative that Pawley pitched to *Life* and the CIA was compelling, if far-fetched, and was based on what Pawley had been told by Martino and Rosselli. The stated purpose of the plan was to send a ten-man Cuban exile team into Cuba to bring back three Soviet technicians, who were supposedly ready to defect and reveal that Soviet nuclear missiles were hidden in caves in Cuba. The scenario sounded plausible to CIA officials and *Life* because thousands of Soviet technicians and troops remained in Cuba. Fidel had never allowed the U.N. weapons inspections, so there was no way to prove with absolute certainty that some missiles weren't hidden in caves or underground, beyond the view of American U-2 spy plane flights.[24]

The ten-man exile team Pawley's operation planned to send into Cuba was originally going to include Loran Hall, a U.S. mercenary who had earlier spent time in detention with Santo Trafficante, in Cuba. Kaiser writes that John "Martino . . . asked Hall if he might be interested in something bigger than a raid, backed by 'people' from Chicago and Miami." Hall was then taken to a meeting in Miami in April 1963, first with "Trafficante [then with] Giancana and Rosselli." Trafficante's man Martino explained "that the assassination of Castro was the real object of the raid." Hall, smelling something fishy, wisely stayed out of the operation.[25]

Eventually, a team of ten armed Cuban exiles headed off toward Cuba as Pawley watched from his yacht. Also on hand were a photographer from *Life* magazine, two CIA agents, and John Martino. The experienced Eugenio Martinez did not accompany the exiles. The team never returned from Cuba to rendezvous with Pawley. Cuban government officials say the ten never landed in Cuba. Kaiser explained that William Pawley had really been "a pawn in an elaborate scheme hatched by John Martino," Trafficante, and Rosselli. Nixon's wealthy friend Pawley had taken the bait when the mobsters had dangled it.[26]

There were no Soviet technicians ready to defect—the entire story had been a ruse by Rosselli and Trafficante, spread by Martino to Pawley and his associates. Kaiser points out that "ample evidence, however, shows that the raid was actually just another mob plot against Castro's life, having nothing to do with Soviet technicians." It was really an "attempt to land about ten men with the mission of assassinating Fidel [that was] sold to the Agency under a false cover." But it was also much more than just another Castro assassination attempt.[27]

William Pawley's Operation TILT was in fact one of three Castro assassination attempts planned in the spring of 1963 as part of the CIA's plots with the Mafia—only the mob was going to use them for their own ends. Even as Pawley's operation was beginning, two more plots to kill Fidel were underway.

The pilot who told the FBI about the Nixon-Pawley-Rebozo

meeting also told the Bureau that in March 1963 "he was instructed to pick up $15,000.00 at Miami, which was to be used for the purchase of guns from the New Orleans, Louisiana, area . . . his instructions were to deliver the money to Rosselli." The rest of the memo was not released by the FBI, perhaps because the money and the guns were part of the CIA-Mafia plots to kill Fidel.[28]

Most 1963 CIA files about Johnny Rosselli and CIA officer William Harvey have never been declassified. But historian Mahoney reviewed the few available CIA files about the pair from 1963, writing that "on February 18, 1963, Harvey and Rosselli had drinks together in Los Angeles [and left] the bounty on Castro of $150,000 where it was." The "bounty" was the $150,000 the CIA was willing to pay exiles or others who tried to kill Fidel. Mahoney found "there is evidence that Harvey's collaboration with Rosselli continued [because] in April [1963] Harvey submitted an expense sheet to CIA administrators covering the period April 13 to 21," which included "a hotel receipt" for Johnny Rosselli and a boat chartered "at Islamorada, Florida," in the Keys. Chartering a boat was an odd thing for Harvey to do unless it was for a highly covert mission, since, as Mahoney points out, there was "a veritable navy of CIA craft in the vicinity."[29]

Even as Operation TILT was slowly developing, the CIA made an attempt to kill Fidel Castro on March 13, 1963, according to the Cuban Dossier of Fidel assassination attempts mentioned previously. That Cuban Dossier, which will figure so prominently in Watergate, says the March attempt involved "a plan to assassinate [Castro] from a house near the University of Havana shooting with a mortar" and other weapons. "Bazookas, mortars, and machine guns were" captured and photographed, along with an assassination team of five men, including one named as a CIA agent. According to the Cuban Dossier, "the instructions" for the attempted assassination "were given by the CIA through Guantanamo Naval Base."[30]

Historian Kaiser documented that Johnny "Rosselli identified the team as his own" twice in later years. Rosselli and his attorney would later spread provocative stories to journalists Jack Anderson and Drew Pearson—stories that reached President Johnson and other high-ranking U.S. officials—claiming "that the team had been tortured and captured and had confessed that they were on an official mission for the US government; and that this led to Castro's decision to arrange the assassination of Kennedy." Rosselli's most detailed leak to Jack Anderson about this attempt was published in January 1971; it specified the Castro attempt occurred in "March 1963 [and] actually named Rosselli, [Robert] Maheu, [Jim] O'Connell, and [William] Harvey" as being part of the operation. As detailed later, that 1971 story about Rosselli's March 1963 CIA-Mafia assassination attempt set off alarm bells in the Nixon White House and helped lead to the Watergate break-ins the following year.[31]

According to the Cuban Dossier and a 1975 article by *The Miami Herald*, an even larger CIA attempt to kill Fidel occurred "at the Latin American Stadium on April 7, 1963." It involved "sixteen men armed with pistols and fragmentation grenades." At least three of the men were captured and once again photographed, along with a large array of weapons that included sniper rifles, machine guns, assault rifles, and pistols. Based on Rosselli's later remarks, that attempt was also part of the CIA-Mafia plots. It was only after the failure of that attempt that William Pawley—no doubt at the urging of Rosselli and Trafficante associate John Martino—approached the CIA to sponsor what became Operation TILT, which was yet another CIA-Mafia attempt to kill Fidel.[32]

As documented by historian Richard Mahoney, Operation TILT was actually an early attempt to lay the groundwork for the Mafia's plot to assassinate JFK. Mahoney wrote that it "fit nicely with Rosselli's later claim that President Kennedy was assassinated by an anti-Castro sniper team sent in to murder Castro, captured by the Cubans, tortured, and redeployed in Dallas." All three of the spring 1963 CIA-Mafia plots against Fidel, including Operation TILT and the arms from New Orleans, were early manifestations of the plans to assassinate JFK by Johnny Rosselli, Santo Trafficante, and Carlos Marcello, whose confessions were covered in the previous chapter. The mob bosses' goal was to take advantage of their work with the CIA to stifle any truly thorough investigation of JFK's murder, while pinning the blame for JFK's assassination on Fidel Castro. They needed to draw the CIA—and hopefully the Kennedys—into supporting an operation that would later force the Agency and Attorney General Robert Kennedy into a cover-up. Because Pawley was heavily involved, and Nixon had been at an early meeting, their scheme would even have compromised Nixon.[33]

Linking JFK's assassination to any of the three exile teams or their equipment would also ensure a widespread U.S. government cover-up for national security reasons, to prevent World War III by hiding the existence of Operation TILT and the years of CIA-Mafia plots to kill Fidel. When the story that JFK was killed by Castro in retaliation for a U.S. attempt to kill Fidel was floated by Martino and Rosselli after JFK's death, officials ranging from CIA Director McCone to President Lyndon Johnson actually thought it could be true.[34]

Certainly by the time Operation TILT finally ended in early June 1963, and possibly even earlier, Trafficante and Rosselli no longer saw killing Fidel as their top priority. As mentioned previously, pressure on the mob chiefs from JFK and RFK had been intense in the fall of 1962, when Marcello and Trafficante began their careful planning—but it was even worse by the spring of 1963. Carlos Marcello faced federal charges later in the year, and these would be personally prosecuted by RFK's men. Trafficante's operations were under increasing assault, and their ally Jimmy Hoffa faced three trials for various crimes. Rosselli's boss Sam Giancana was severely impacted by the FBI's "lockstep" surveillance. Killing Fidel Castro while JFK and RFK were still in power would do the mob bosses little good, so murdering JFK was much more important—and time-sensitive—for the Mafia chiefs.*[35]

However, there was a major problem with Rosselli and Trafficante's plan in the spring of 1963: Neither John nor Robert Kennedy supported Operation TILT, and they also didn't know about the CIA-Mafia plots in March and April 1963. RFK would have no incentive to protect them if they appeared linked to his brother's murder. However, by the time Operation TILT ended on June 9, 1963, a new U.S. operation against Cuba had evolved—one the Kennedys fully supported—that the three Mafia leaders would attempt to compromise.

As part of the Kennedy administration's diffuse—and ineffective—Cuban strategy, small-scale U.S.-backed sabotage forays into Cuba continued through the spring of 1963, along with minor raids on Cuban ships authorized by the National Security Council and its several Cuba subcommittees. On their own, these actions seemed incapable of doing any real damage to Fidel, so Richard Helms apparently wanted to force JFK's hand into more forceful action.[36]

Six days after the failure of one of the CIA-Mafia attempts to assas-

*It's important to note that Pawley, Nixon, and CIA agent Eugenio Martinez had nothing to do with the JFK assassination aspect of Operation TILT and had simply been taken in by the Mafia's phony "missile technicians" cover story.

sinate Fidel, on March 15, 1963, *The Wall Street Journal* ran an article headlined "Castro's Assassination becomes the major US hope for de-communizing Cuba." It explained that "some officials maintain rising public discontent is bound to bring a successful assassination attempt sooner or later" with the hope that "original revolutionaries still in key posts would make a strong bid for power against old-line Communists." Unlike *The New York Times* and favored journalists like Tad Szulc, the conservative *Wall Street Journal* wasn't a media outlet to which the Kennedys disseminated information they wanted the public to see. Instead, the leak smacks of the type of PR psyops that Hunt and David Atlee Phillips had employed for the Guatemala coup and the Bay of Pigs. Whether it was meant as a sort of cover for the recent failed Castro assassination attempt or as an outreach to disaffected Cuban officials is hard to say. But Phillips's next action was unmistakably provocative.[37]

On March 18, 1963, Antonio Veciana's Alpha 66—the Cuban exile group handled by David Atlee Phillips—"announced that it had [attacked] a Russian ship and a Russian training area" in Cuba. Veciana milked the operation for maximum publicity, Phillips's specialty. Outraged at the unauthorized and dangerous attack on a Russian ship, JFK had the U.S. State Department immediately condemn the raid. It's highly unlikely that Phillips would have had Veciana undertake the attack, which could have led to a new confrontation between the United States and the Soviets, without Helms's approval. While the Kennedys wanted Alpha 66 and Veciana to receive no CIA assistance, Helms—without informing JFK or RFK—had Phillips continued to supervise Veciana and his group.[38]

Richard Helms approved an even more outrageous provocation in 1963, one that endangered the lives of three CIA agents as well as JFK's personal emissary, who was then trying to negotiate their release. The three agents, arrested in the previously noted September 1960 attempt to bug Havana's Chinese News Agency office, were among the last twenty-seven U.S. citizens still held in Cuban prisons. From January through April 1963, JFK had prominent New York attorney James Donovan working to secure their release. Donovan had helped Robert Kennedy negotiate the release of the Bay of Pigs prisoners, and his rapport with the Cuban government soon translated to a working relationship with Fidel, which included accompanying the Cuban leader on skin-diving trips.

The CIA developed two plans to assassinate Fidel while he was skin diving with Donovan, something the Agency admitted both in internal reports and Congressional testimony. While Desmond FitzGerald settled into his new post of running CIA Cuban operations, he oversaw a plan to devise "an exotic seashell" to attract Fidel's attention "in an area where Castro commonly went skin diving." However, the shell would actually be "rigged to explode underwater," killing Castro and anyone who might be with him. CIA Technical Services—the same group that created the poison pills for the Mafia to use against Fidel—"explored" the idea, but found too many problems, so the scheme was "discarded as impractical."[39]

The "second plan involved having James Donovan . . . present Castro with a contaminated diving suit" as a gift. CIA Technical Services actually "bought a diving suit, dusted the inside with a [deadly] fungus . . . and contaminated the breathing apparatus with [tuberculosis bacteria]." The only reason "the plan was abandoned [was] because Donovan gave Castro a different diving suit on his own initiative" and "Helms testified that the [poisoned] diving suit never left the [CIA]."[40]

The lethal plans approved by Helms and FitzGerald were never revealed to Donovan, CIA Director McCone, JFK, or RFK. Donovan was already in some danger, since the CIA's March 1963 and April 1963 assassination operations (about which Donovan knew nothing) were being planned while Donovan was in Cuba, negotiating with Fidel. Ironically, Castro actually talked with Donovan about the CIA's attempts to kill him while the men were on a skin-diving excursion. In a very general, vague way, Fidel also brought up to Donovan the possibility of some type of rapprochement between Cuba and the United States. Castro's idea was relayed to President Kennedy, but it wasn't specific enough to really pursue at that point. As for Donovan, his negotiations were successful, and the twenty-seven U.S. citizens, including the three CIA agents, were released in April 1963.[41]

In the spring of 1963, Kennedy administration policy about Cuba remained muddled, with some officials wanting attacks on Cuban (not Russian) ships to continue, while RFK argued that the raids had to stop. JFK asked "the CIA to give the Cuban exiles guidance" about the raids, while having "the FBI crack down on unauthorized groups and raids." Within a month, exile raids on Cuban ships resumed. In a private meeting with JFK on April 15, 1963, CIA Director McCone advised him to either "establish relations with Castro" or "to overthrow him." Surprisingly, JFK "suggested that both options might simultaneously be pursued"—a dual strategy that would become a reality by the fall. McCone followed up his meeting with a memo saying that "a military coup in Cuba [was] the United States' only hope" to resolve the Cuba situation. Two days before McCone's memo, Defense Secretary Robert McNamara told a National Security Council subcommittee "that Castro must be overthrown, preferably by provoking an internal revolt that would allow the United States [military] to intervene." Unfortunately, efforts by AMTRUNK and the CIA-DIA Task Force to find possible Cuban officials who could reasonably lead a coup weren't producing results.[42]

By this time, President Kennedy had delegated Cuba to RFK because he didn't have time to give it the attention it needed, but Robert Kennedy was frustrated by the constant bickering and requests for money being made by Cuban exile groups receiving CIA support. In addition, the extensive attention RFK gave to Cuban matters was on top of an already full plate of activities he had to oversee as Attorney General, issues ranging from civil rights matters to the war on organized crime. However, the success of Donovan in winning the Americans' release, on the heels of the privately negotiated Bay of Pigs prisoners' release, convinced RFK that private back channels could be much more effective than using traditional, cumbersome government bureaucracies.

Robert Kennedy turned to his exile friend Harry Williams, telling him he didn't want any more Cuban exile leaders coming to RFK for money. Instead, he wanted them to go through Williams, who would then identify for RFK the select few he thought were serious and deserved U.S. backing. By using Williams, RFK also established his own channel into the exile community, so he wouldn't be completely dependent on the CIA. RFK turned to Williams because they had grown increasingly close since the Bay of Pigs prisoner release. A frequent visitor at RFK's Hickory Hill estate, Williams even stayed at RFK's New York apartment on visits to Manhattan. The fact that Williams was close to—and trusted by—RFK has been confirmed in accounts by Pulitzer Prize–winning journalist Haynes Johnson, *Newsweek* editor Evan Thomas, and historian Richard Mahoney.[43]

Word soon spread in the exile community that Williams was essentially the gatekeeper for RFK and JFK when it came to their support for the exiles. RFK ordered the CIA to provide Williams with any assistance he wanted and to begin cutting support for all the other exile groups. Even organizations such as the Cuban Revolutionary Council, founded by E. Howard Hunt in the Bay of Pigs era, were slated to have their financial support ended. Exile Tony Varona, then running the Council, was to receive a final lump-sum payment before being cut off. The politically savvy Varona quickly moved to align himself with Williams, as did Manuel Artime, for whom JFK and RFK were trying to help find a base far from the United States, in Central America.[44]

RFK and Williams attempted to operate quietly, away from the glare of publicity, so both were surprised when an Associated Press article about their efforts appeared on May 10, 1963, in *The New York Times* and other newspapers:

> A new all-out drive to unify Cuban refugees into a single, powerful organization to topple the Fidel Castro regime was disclosed today by exile sources. The plan calls for formation of a junta in exile to mount a three-pronged thrust consisting of sabotage, infiltration, and ultimate invasion. The exile sources said the plan had been discussed with Cuban leaders by US Central Intelligence agents. Seeking to put together the junta was Enrique [Harry] Ruiz Williams, a Bay of Pigs invasion veteran and friend of US Attorney General Robert F. Kennedy . . . [Tony] Varona, former Premier and now coordinator of the revamped Cuban Revolutionary Council, said he had told Mr. Ruiz Williams he would cooperate in plans to unify the exiles.[45]

RFK and Harry Williams were furious when they saw the article, which was probably leaked by Tony Varona. A similar article appeared nine days later in the *Miami News*, headlined "Bobby's friend another hope" and reporting "a close friend of Attorney General Robert Kennedy, Williams has made numerous trips to Washington, New York, and Puerto Rico, talking to exile leaders." Williams confronted the reporter, denied that he was working for RFK, and stopped the unwanted press coverage. However, the first article had immediately caught the attention of Williams's old friend in Cuba, Commander Juan Almeida, still head of the Cuban Army.[46]

Commander Almeida quickly reached out to Williams, telling him that Fidel was becoming nothing more than a dictator, betraying the very Revolution they had all fought so hard for. So Almeida offered to stage a coup against Fidel—if JFK would back him. Williams immediately took Almeida's offer to Robert Kennedy. RFK's official phone logs at the National Archives verify some of the timing. They show that on May 13, 1963, at 5:50 PM, RFK took a call from President Kennedy. The very next call RFK accepted, at 6:05 PM, was from Harry Williams. RFK told Williams that JFK had accepted Almeida's offer to stage a coup to overthrow Fidel, and that the U.S. government would give Almeida its full backing for the attempt.[47]

Thus began the JFK-Almeida coup plan, one of the most secret covert U.S. operations since D-Day, which would help to define the remainder of JFK's Presidency. The coup plan would be a significant factor in Watergate, and even today, it still haunts U.S.-Cuba relations. It was verified to the author by Williams and other aides to John and Robert Kennedy, including Secretary of State Dean Rusk (who also gave an "on the record" confirmation to *Vanity Fair*). Though the vast majority of files about the coup plan are still classified, a surprising number have slipped through. They include a 1963 CIA report to the Agency's Director, using information from Bernard Barker about an "operation including Juan Almeida" designed to "overthrow" Fidel, who would be replaced by a new Cuban government to "be recognized immediately" by JFK's administration. Another CIA dispatch discusses a plan for "an internal uprising" in Cuba by "Cuban military figures, who are conspiring against Fidel Castro. Among the key figures in the plot are Juan Almeida." Hundreds of pages of files about the U.S. military side of the operation have been declassified, some of which are quoted below.[48]

JFK's plan was vastly different from anything that Richard Nixon or anyone at the CIA had conceived. As it developed in weeks and months that followed, its goal was to replace Fidel's dictatorship initially with a coalition government that would include not just Almeida and Williams, but conservatives like Varona and Artime and liberals like Manolo Ray and Eloy Menoyo. Their administration would be only temporary, until free elections could be held under the supervision of the Organization of American States (OAS). In aiding the coup, John and Robert Kennedy saw themselves as assisting "Cubans helping other Cubans," something they regarded as far different from an assassination plan.[49]

The mid-May 1963 agreement between JFK, RFK, and Commander

Almeida—with Harry Williams acting as intermediary—resulted in a flurry of official paperwork that continued for the next six months. For example, on May 29, 1963—two weeks after Almeida contacted the Kennedys—Joint Chiefs of Staff Chairman General Maxwell Taylor wrote a memo saying it was "a matter of priority" to examine the possibility "of an invasion of Cuba at a time controlled by the United States in order to overthrow the Castro government," including "a proposed date for D-Day."[50]

In the five months of Cuba planning in 1963 before Almeida's offer, Army Secretary Cyrus Vance and General Taylor had approved three drafts of a hypothetical "Plan for a Coup in Cuba." After Almeida's offer was relayed to the Kennedys, the planning took on a sense of urgency, and in just the next four months ten drafts were completed, some of them growing to more than eighty pages. All were approved by the CIA and State Department. Since at that point no one at State knew about Almeida (Dean Rusk would be told about him only later), these drafts give only a general, but surprisingly accurate, overview of the coup plan. None of those files were declassified for over three decades, until the mid-1990s.[51]

According to the plans, the Cuban leader of the coup must "have some power base in the Cuban army," and the United States would also "seek the cooperation of selected Cuban exile leaders." The point of the plan was to stage a seemingly internal "palace coup in Cuba [that would] neutralize the top echelon of Cuban leadership." The plan stresses that "it is important [that] the revolt appear genuine and not open to the charge of being a facade for a forcible US overthrow of Castro [since] a well-planned and successful 'rescue' of a revolt could be made politically acceptable" to U.S. allies and the Soviets. After Castro's death, President Kennedy would "warn [the] Soviets not to intervene." The leaders of the coup "would have announced via radio and other means the . . . establishment of a Provisional Government. They would have appealed to the US for recognition and support, particularly for air cover and a naval blockade, ostensibly to make certain that the Soviets do not intervene but actually, by prearrangement, to immobilize the Cuban Air Force and Navy." That was important, since "twelve to thirteen thousand Soviet military personnel of all kinds remain [in Cuba]." After "completion of such initial air attacks as may be necessary, provision will be made for the rapid, incremental introduction of balanced forces, to include full-scale invasion if . . . necessary." The "US military forces employed against Cuba should be accompanied by US military–trained free Cubans." Finally, since the Kennedys' ultimate goal was a free and democratic Cuba, the plans say, "The OAS [Organization of American States] will send representatives to the island to assist the Provisional Government in preparing for and conducting of free elections."* [52]

While a small group of military, State, and CIA officials worked on those plans—some knowing about Almeida but most not—Robert Kennedy directed additional planning. JFK had delegated overall responsibility for the coup operation to Robert, and two June 1963 memos outline their goals. "The ultimate objective [was for] dissident elements in the military . . . of the Cuban regime to bring about the eventual liquidation of [Fidel] Castro [and] the elimination of the Soviet presence from Cuba." The handful of exile leaders, chosen by Harry Williams and approved by RFK, who were willing to help do that would receive major funding from the Kennedy administration to base their operations "outside the territory of the United States." Those exiles had to be dedicated "to the idea that the overthrow of [Castro] must be accomplished by Cubans inside and outside Cuba working in concert." In addition, "an experienced [CIA] liaison officer would be assigned to each group to provide general advice, funds, and material support." Although the groups would be called "autonomous," RFK made it clear they were really working for the United States, but "if ever charged with complicity, the US Government would publicly deny any participation in the groups' activities."[53]

Commander Almeida would handle what was euphemistically called the "elimination" of Fidel and Raul.† Almeida was extremely popular in Cuba, not just as a hero of the Revolution and the founder and leader of the Cuban Army, but because he was the highest-ranking black official in a country that was an estimated 70 percent African descent. Still, even he couldn't shoulder the blame for "eliminating" the popular Fidel. As Williams explained, and declassified

*This is only a tiny, representative sample from the many hundreds of pages of files about the "Plan for a Coup in Cuba" that are covered in much more depth in the trade paperback editions of *Ultimate Sacrifice* and *Legacy of Secrecy*. The files are available from the National Archives and a few are online on its website, nara.gov.

†For an extensive treatment of the coup plan and Che Guevara—and the CIA report that stated on November 30, 1963, "Che Guevara was alleged to be under house arrest for plotting to overthrow Castro"—see the author's trade paperback editions of *Ultimate Sacrifice* and *Legacy of Secrecy*.

memos indicate, the person who would "take the fall" for killing Fidel would likely be a Russian or Russian sympathizer. If Almeida went on Cuban radio and TV to announce that such a person had assassinated their beloved Fidel, that news would instantly neutralize the thousands of Soviet troops, technicians, and officials still in Cuba. As one declassified memo says, the coup leader "would have declared that Soviet nationals will not be harmed if they remain in their compounds while awaiting repatriation to the Soviet Union."[54]

Almeida's announcement of Fidel's death would be followed by his asking for U.S. military assistance, to help prevent a Soviet takeover. The declassified coup plan explains that the leader of the coup "would have appealed to the US for . . . air cover and a naval blockade, ostensibly to make certain that the Soviets do not intervene." The Kennedys soon had a special multi-racial group of Cuban exile Bay of Pigs veterans training at Fort Benning, Georgia, to be the first (and hopefully only) U.S. troops needed to help Commander Almeida stabilize the situation. However, files show that once the coup began, JFK and Joint Chiefs Chairman General Maxwell Taylor were prepared to use the full force of the U.S. military, including air power.[55]

It's very important to emphasize—for history and for Watergate—that JFK's role with Almeida in the coup was *never* supposed to be revealed. The Cuban people were always meant to think that Almeida was simply reacting to a tragic situation caused by the Soviets, and U.S. citizens were supposed to believe that JFK simply reacted well to an unexpected situation in Cuba. JFK and RFK hoped that their new ally Almeida would remain prominent in Cuban politics for years if not decades, so the fact that he'd been secretly working for JFK could never be disclosed.[56]

This need for such long-term concealment is one reason the JFK-Almeida coup plan was wrapped in several layers of secrecy, a covering so tight that it protected any of it from being declassified until the 1990s. Almeida's role was not officially released until 2006. Another reason for such intense secrecy was that the Kennedys and the few CIA and high-ranking military personnel who knew about Almeida were also concerned that the plan not leak before it was ready, as had happened with the Bay of Pigs invasion. Secrecy was important even within an organization like the CIA or the DIA, both of which were concerned about possible high-level Soviet moles. In January 1963, it was finally confirmed that high-ranking British Intelligence official Kim Philby had for many years spied for the Soviets. If a similar mole in a U.S. intelligence agency were to tell the Soviets about the coup plan, it might mean the deaths of Almeida and his allies, but even more seriously it could trigger a new confrontation with the Soviets that could go nuclear, causing—in the words of an earlier memo—"World War III."[57]

The JFK-Almeida coup plan was supposed to achieve the ultimate goal of the Bay of Pigs invasion without any of the problems that plagued that debacle. But how could extensive, high-level planning be done by U.S. officials without the plan becoming an open secret? The answer was explained to this author by JFK's Secretary of State Dean Rusk and later confirmed by hundreds of pages of declassified files. Top Kennedy officials such as Rusk, who had large staffs and who met often with the press, knew the United States had been looking for Cuban officials who could stage a coup. Therefore, Rusk and most other high-ranking officials were told only that the United States needed to do extensive pre- and post-coup planning "just in case" an official were found so the United States could act quickly to take advantage of the situation. This allowed comprehensive planning to be done with input and "buy-in" from necessary officials and departments, but without most of them knowing the Kennedys were already working with the third-most-powerful official in Cuba, after the Castro brothers. Dean Rusk himself told this author—and later confirmed to *Vanity Fair*—that he believed the planning was "just in case" until right after JFK's assassination. That was when Rusk and a few other officials finally learned the coup plans hadn't been a mere contingency, but were for an operation with Almeida that was active and imminent when JFK was killed.[58]

Before JFK's death, only about a dozen U.S. officials knew, to varying degrees, about Commander Almeida's secret alliance with JFK. Aside from John and Robert Kennedy, those who knew included Joint Chiefs Chairman Maxwell Taylor and Defense Intelligence Agency Chief Joseph Carroll, but not the other Joint Chiefs such as Air Force General Curtis LeMay, a far-right hawk. There is no indication that Defense Secretary Robert McNamara—who, like Rusk, was a very high-profile public figure in 1963—was told, and he declined to comment when contacted by this author. JFK "designated" Army Secretary Cyrus Vance "as the executive agent for the entire federal government in dealing with Cuba [including] responsibility for coordinating a secret war against Cuba," according to Vance's aide, Alexander Haig. Vance was given that responsibility because he was not a high-profile public figure like McNamara and Rusk. RFK often dealt directly with Vance about the coup plan, bypassing traditional bureaucratic channels. In addition to those on the military side, CIA officials John McCone, Richard Helms, and Desmond FitzGerald knew about Commander Almeida's role in the coup plan.[59]

Lyndon Johnson was not informed about the coup plan while he was Vice President, and neither was FBI Director J. Edgar Hoover, though Hoover's extensive intelligence network no doubt allowed him to piece together at least part of the story. Even most Kennedy aides weren't told about Almeida and the coup plan, as later confirmed by Dave Powers, JFK's closest aide and friend in the White House. Harry Williams and a Kennedy aide who knew about and worked on the coup plan indicated that JFK's brother, Senator Ted Kennedy, wasn't told about Almeida at the time, to spare the political career of at least one Kennedy brother in case the coup plan failed and the roles of JFK and RFK became known.*[60]

The summer of 1963, at the height of the Cold War, was a complex time for President Kennedy and U.S. foreign policy. Amid the top secret planning for the coup in Cuba, JFK made a speech at American University on June 14, 1963, calling for "a partial nuclear test ban treaty" with the Soviets. He followed that up less than two weeks later with his historic speech to 150,000 people in West Berlin, with his famous line "*Ich bin ein Berliner*." (A couple of weeks later, Richard Nixon made his own Berlin appearance, to a considerably smaller crowd of "a dozen reporters.") With so much on his plate, including a raft of important domestic issues, JFK relied on his brother Robert to deal with the hands-on oversight of the coup plan.[61]

RFK oversaw the entire Cuban coup operation, and the U.S. military had a leading role, while the CIA had only a supporting role, primarily in three critical areas. As detailed in a declassified memo finalized just days after Commander Almeida reached out to JFK and RFK, one of the "supporting operations" was "the introduction by CIA as soon as practicable of assets in Cuba for the development of intelligence . . . and the development of a suitable cover plan." With no American embassy, the CIA needed more assets in Cuba, especially those who could move freely among the Cuban people and lower

*This Kennedy aide spoke only on the condition that his identity remain confidential until after his death.

officials. Related to that was the CIA's second supporting role, that of making sure one or more of those U.S. assets could "take the fall" for the assassination of Castro if Almeida had any problems in that area. Though as the Commander of the Cuban Army Almeida had access to many Russians and Russian sympathizers, that aspect of the plan was so crucial for neutralizing the thousands of Soviets in Cuba that it's not surprising that Williams was told the CIA intended to have a backup plan for someone to "take the fall." The third CIA responsibility was aiding the chosen Cuban exile leaders, who would eventually include Harry Williams, Tony Varona, Manuel Artime, Eloy Menoyo, and Manolo Ray. (The leadership of the Cuban-American troops at Fort Benning was handled by Cyrus Vance and his assistants, including Alexander Haig.)[62]

As RFK and Williams developed the most secret aspects of the coup plan with Almeida, it called for Williams to go into Cuba to meet with Almeida shortly before the coup. After Fidel's death, the chosen exile leaders would quickly join them in Cuba, coming not from the United States but from U.S.-financed bases in other countries. Williams explained that RFK was JFK's right arm for Cuba, and RFK called Williams his right hand. Williams saw the five exile leaders as his five fingers, and—holding his hand open—he demonstrated how, at Fidel's death, the leaders would rush into Cuba, like a hand closing, making a fist. The CIA had to help support all that and, as one declassified memo put it, the "CIA would, as appropriate and with Presidential approval, deal with the potential leaders of a coup in Cuba."[63]

As essentially the highest-ranking operations official in the CIA, Deputy Director for Plans Richard Helms had overall responsibility for the CIA's supporting role in the coup plan. In later years, Helms seemed to express resentment toward the pressure RFK exerted on him, telling the Discovery Channel, "There isn't any doubt as to who was running that effort. It was Bobby Kennedy on behalf of his brother." Helms complained to another interviewer that "you haven't lived until you've had Bobby Kennedy rampant on your back [over Cuba]."[64]

It's no surprise that Richard Helms picked his experienced protégé, E. Howard Hunt, to be the main CIA official assisting the most important of RFK's exiles. It would be a fateful decision for both men.

CHAPTER 14

Summer and Early Fall 1963: Nixon, Hunt, and JFK's Cuban Coup Plan

In the summer and fall of 1963, E. Howard Hunt and his aide Bernard Barker were involved in two of the most sensitive aspects of the JFK-Almeida coup plan, which had to remain secret through Watergate and for decades beyond. Hunt's and Barker's involvement in the coup plan has been confirmed by multiple sources, including *Vanity Fair*, veteran FBI agent William Turner, the Kennedy aide cited previously, and Harry Williams in several taped interviews with this author. The primary responsibilities of Hunt and Barker were to assist Harry Williams with delicate matters involving Commander Almeida and his family.[1]

Williams said there were "dozens [of meetings] from May to November [1963]" with E. Howard Hunt and a CIA security official assigned to the operation. For security reasons, Bernard Barker arranged the meetings, most of them held away from Miami. "Barker was Hunt's assistant, very close to Hunt," Williams explained.[2]

While Barker never acknowledged being officially privy to the JFK-Almeida coup plan, one of his routine CIA reports from November 14, 1963, mentions an "operation including Juan Almeida [to] overthrow [Fidel]." Years later, Barker told journalist (and former LBJ aide) Bill Moyers that "I would have followed Howard Hunt to hell and back." In another TV program, Barker said that "at the time [of] the Kennedy assassination . . . President Kennedy's government had reached its 'peak' in its efforts to overthrow Castro," something not reflected in any history books or government reports at the time Barker made his comments.[3]

Hunt and Barker were involved in the payment of $50,000 to Almeida, the initial installment of an agreed-upon total sum of

$500,000 (over $3 million today). The money had been authorized by Robert Kennedy, in the event the coup was unsuccessful and Almeida had to flee Cuba, or, if he were killed, the money would provide for his wife and two children. Considering that Barker's job before the Bay of Pigs "was to deliver CIA cash laundered through foreign banks," he might have had a larger role than usual in assisting Hunt with Almeida's secret payment. In fact, the CIA memo written by Barker mentioned earlier reveals another CIA payment of $200,000 to a top Cuban journalist, who other CIA files confirm was working with Williams and the Kennedys on the coup plan.[4]

In addition to handling the payment to Commander Almeida, Hunt and Barker were also part of a covert operation in which Almeida's wife and two children left Cuba on a seemingly innocent pretext prior to the date set for the coup. The plan was for Almeida's family to wait out the coup in another country, while they were under secret CIA surveillance. RFK had also authorized Williams and the CIA to assure Almeida that if anything happened to him and his family couldn't return to Cuba, his family would be taken care of. In addition to providing for their safety, having the family in another country under the watchful eye of the CIA could ensure that Almeida didn't double-cross the CIA and the Kennedys.[5]

In the summer and fall of 1963, even Barker's routine CIA reports show him submitting a stream of information linked either to the mob or the coup plan. For example, Barker filed reports about a meeting between Artime and Varona to discuss unity, noting Artime's meeting with Frank Fiorini in Dallas to buy an airplane, Menoyo's "Plan Omega" operation for overthrowing Fidel, and the plans of Manolo Ray. Barker also reported on one part of the CIA-Mafia plots to kill Fidel, involving the efforts of Sam Benton, a private detective working for Carlos Marcello, to recruit an American mercenary. The mercenary backed out when he learned that an associate of Johnny Rosselli was involved in the plot.[6]

Bernard Barker was also connected to a phony Cuban exile group financed by Rosselli and the Mafia, Paulino Sierra's JGCE (Junta of the Government of Cuba in Exile). Sierra wanted it to become one of Williams's special exile groups. However, a journalist raised suspicions about Sierra's Mafia funding, and this author's interview with Sierra's daughter confirmed Sierra's ties to the mob. But Williams and the Kennedys were determined to keep the Mafia out of the coup plan, so files show that Sierra was shunted off to the State Department and not given U.S. backing.[7]

Harry Williams explained that "Hunt had a lot of confidence in Barker and presented him as very much a man of action," but that in reality "Barker did dirty work for Hunt." He went on to say that Barker "was dishonest" and "I think the CIA knew" about Barker's criminal behavior. Williams felt that Barker was "a crook [and he] was one of my [biggest] problems" while working on the coup plan. He was even more of a problem than Williams realized at the time.[8]

During 1963, Harry Williams didn't know that "Barker was connected to [Santo Trafficante]," as he later learned. Williams was not privy to FBI and CIA files (released decades later) tying Barker to the mob, nor did he realize that his associates Tony Varona and Manuel Artime also had ties to Trafficante. The links between Trafficante, Barker, Varona, and Artime will help to explain several attempts by the Mafia to compromise Williams and the coup plan in the summer and fall of 1963.[9]

Planning for the coup proceeded in June 1963 with Robert Kennedy's various committees submitting plans involving the chosen exile leaders who comprised Harry Williams's "five fingers": Manuel Artime, Tony Varona, Eloy Menoyo, Manolo Ray, and the exile leadership of the Cubans training at Fort Benning. All except the last received CIA support, but by far the lion's share of Agency funding went to Manuel Artime, who was called the CIA's "Golden Boy" because of his special treatment. Artime was the best friend of E. Howard Hunt, and the two shared an extremely conservative political outlook. In addition, Hunt was the protégé of Richard Helms, all of which helps to explain Artime's favored status.[10]

Like Varona, Menoyo, and Ray, Manuel Artime was to be based outside the United States in order to help maintain the cover story that the exiles weren't backed by the U.S. government. However, Artime received so much CIA money that Congressional investigators later documented that by "October 1963," Artime had "four bases, two in Costa Rica and two in Nicaragua," with "two large ships, eight small vessels, two speed boats, three planes, and more than 200 tons of weapons and armaments and about $250,000 in electronic equipment." With such high-profile resources, it's not hard to see why Artime and his group drew occasional attention from reporters, and why the Cuban government denounced his operation before the U.N.[11]

Artime's well-financed and well-equipped exile force would be responsible for most of the hit-and-run sabotage raids into Cuba during the summer and fall of 1963. Those raids didn't do much significant damage, but they were important for another reason. When the day for the coup was at hand, it couldn't appear as if Artime or the other exile leaders were suddenly stepping up operations or doing anything unusual. Hence, as long as occasional small attacks struck at Cuba and infiltration boats landed at secluded Cuban locations, it wouldn't arouse undue Cuban suspicion when one of those infiltration runs brought Artime—and the other exile leaders—into Cuba as the coup commenced.[12]

Only about a dozen U.S. officials and Kennedy aides knew about Commander Almeida, but more CIA personnel would have to know about the Agency's support for Artime, so the CIA created an operation code-named AMWORLD for Artime's part of the JFK-Almeida coup plan. By creating AMWORLD, planning could go forward for the coup without revealing the identity of Almeida to more CIA officials and their staffs. AMWORLD was still extremely secret, and that code name had never appeared in any book, article, or Congressional report until this author first published it in 2005. While only a few dozen officials within the CIA knew about AMWORLD, some officials outside the Agency knew about Artime's operation, but not about the AMWORLD code name or Almeida.[13]

Robert Kennedy's official phone logs show he took a call from Richard Helms on June 25, 1963, at 10:15 AM, followed by a call from Harry Williams at 10:25 AM. Three days later, the partially coded five-page CIA memo creating AMWORLD was sent only to "Chiefs of Certain Stations and Bases," primarily those in Latin America. (The memo was written by J.C. King, the CIA official who had written the first CIA memo about assassinating Fidel.) AMWORLD was so secret that at the CIA's huge Miami CIA station, it even had its own secure "separate communications" center and base-within-a-base, code-named "LORK." That gave David Morales, the Miami station's Chief of Operations, a role in AMWORLD.[14]

The CIA admits that on June 20, 1963, Johnny Rosselli went to CIA officer William Harvey's home in the Virginia suburbs of Washington,

D.C., to meet with him. The Agency had to admit the meeting occurred because the FBI was monitoring Rosselli and told Harvey they knew about the meeting. In internal documents and to Congress, the CIA claimed this was the final meeting between Rosselli and Harvey, marking the end of the CIA-Mafia plots. However, much evidence shows that was far from true. Rosselli and Harvey would continue meeting, and would remain friends, into 1964 and beyond. Johnny Rosselli would be seen regularly at the Miami JMWAVE CIA station and at an exile training camp for sharpshooters into the fall of 1963, under the name "Col. Rosselli."[15]

However, after the FBI learned of the June meeting between Rosselli and Harvey, the CIA assigned Rosselli to a new contact: David Morales, the Miami Operations Chief. A gruff, forceful man of Southwestern Native American descent, Morales had headed covert operations for the CIA in Havana before the U.S. embassy closed, where he had supervised David Atlee Phillips. Morales also had a role in the Bay of Pigs operation and was extremely bitter at its tragic outcome, which he blamed exclusively on President Kennedy.

David Morales was bluntly described by the No. 2 official at the Miami CIA station this way: "If the US government . . . needed someone or something neutralized, Dave would do it, including things that were repugnant to a lot of people." Former U.S. diplomat Wayne Smith, who worked with Morales at the U.S. embassy in Havana, said that "if [Morales] were in the mob, he'd be called a hit man."[16]

Morales was a hard-drinking operative like William Harvey and, like Harvey, he was quickly seduced by Johnny Rosselli and the two became close friends—though for Rosselli, Morales was just another CIA agent he could use for his own ends. Morales would remain friends with Rosselli into at least the following year, even accompanying the Mafia don on a trip to Las Vegas.

While CIA officials such as Richard Helms withheld crucial information from JFK and his own CIA Director, one agent would distinguish himself in a positive sense: James McCord. Nine months after his arrest at the Watergate complex, McCord would play what was in many ways the most crucial role in exposing the crimes of Richard Nixon. Like Hunt and Barker, McCord was also said to be involved in the JFK-Almeida coup plan in 1963, though his attitude about the operation, like his background, was quite different from theirs.[17]

The thirty-nine-year-old McCord "grew up in Texas" and appears to have held a conservative religious outlook for most of his life. According to his official CIA biography and other accounts, including his own, McCord did intelligence work for the military during and immediately after World War II. He attained the rank of Lieutenant Colonel before joining the FBI, where he held a position from 1948 to 1951 and is said to have worked with Robert Maheu in the Bureau. McCord joined the CIA in 1951 and for most of his career there worked in its Security Office. He began dealing with especially sensitive matters for the CIA early on: McCord was apparently the first CIA agent assigned to investigate the controversial death of CIA scientist Frank Olsen in 1953.[18]

James McCord also assisted early attempts to free the three CIA agents caught in Havana trying to bug the Chinese News Agency office. An internal CIA memo quoted McCord as reporting that he "was [the] case officer for three agents . . . whose task was to gain entry to prisons in Cuba . . . where three Agency staffers were being held." The memo shows "McCord being credited with being 'an actual case officer for Cuban agents—for 24 months,' from 1960 to 1962."* In February 1961, CIA files show that McCord was involved with David Atlee Phillips in an operation, which also included the FBI, that was directed at the Fair Play for Cuba Committee, a small pro-Castro organization. In May 1962, McCord was made "Chief of the Security Staff in (deleted) European area." Most of McCord's CIA work and files for 1963 have never been declassified. One of the few CIA memos about McCord released from that year shows that in October 1963, he sought and received special clearance for an especially sensitive operation that has never been identified. Another confirms that his wife was flown from Europe back to Texas in March 1963.[19]

According to published accounts by *Vanity Fair* and former FBI agent William Turner, and interviews with Harry Williams, McCord was one of the two main CIA officials—along with Hunt—assigned to assist Williams with the JFK-Almeida coup plan. McCord himself declined any comment when contacted by this author and by *Vanity Fair*. Harry Williams said that it appeared to him that Hunt was higher in rank than McCord at that time. Williams also said that both

*The CIA apparently withheld that information from the Senate Watergate Committee, since the Agency had told the Committee that McCord had not been involved in Cuban activities in the 1960s.

men told him to use only the name "Eduardo" with them, and that, with one exception in Washington, he never met with both men at the same time.*[20]

James McCord appears to have played a security role for the JFK-Almeida coup plan, which included learning if Harry Williams, like so many other exile leaders, could be bribed. In the summer of 1963, McCord drove an "old car" to meet Williams, something McCord often did to look inconspicuous. While driving, McCord suddenly told Williams, "There is a lot of money to be made" in this operation. Williams, surprised, looked at McCord and asked, "How?" McCord explained, "There is a lot of money in the budget for this thing, and some people have . . . "[21]

Harry Williams didn't realize that the total budget for just the AMWORLD portion of the JFK-Almeida coup plan was at least $7 million and some CIA agents estimated it was many times that amount. Williams worried that McCord "was trying to buy me," so he said, "Look, when I want to make money I [will] go back to my profession [as a mining engineer]. I am not here to make money. I am not interested." McCord seemed to accept his answer and dropped the subject. The CIA knew that unlike the other exile leaders, Williams had no exile organization of his own to support and that he didn't take money for himself from the U.S. government. He was in the operation strictly for patriotic reasons, and in some ways, so was McCord. As CIA Counterintelligence Chief James Angleton once said, "McCord never did anything when he was not wrapped in a flag."[22]

Perhaps that's why Williams says he got along very well with McCord, whose attitude was quite different from Hunt's. Williams said that McCord was very professional and seemed to genuinely want to help him with the operation, unlike Hunt, who clearly resented having to take orders from a Cuban exile. [23]

On one occasion, Harry Williams said that McCord asked to meet him at a Miami restaurant. Once there, McCord excused himself. While waiting for him, Williams noticed Santo Trafficante sitting in the restaurant's bar. Trafficante got Williams's attention, saying he wanted to talk. Williams knew Trafficante's reputation "as a Mafia

*James McCord has never admitted to working on Cuban operations in 1963, and testified that he never met E. Howard Hunt until 1972.

guy" and was surprised that he looked "like a gentleman." Their conversation lasted only a few minutes, as Trafficante explained he "wanted to see" Williams, in order "to give me money." Trafficante said the amount Williams could get "would be big." The godfather added, "Look, I am a businessman . . . I want to go back to Cuba and I want to recover what I" had there. He told Williams, if "you win, I want my casinos back." Harry politely declined and quickly excused himself. When James McCord returned, he didn't mention Trafficante at all.[24]

When viewed as a CIA Security operation to test Harry, the restaurant incident with Trafficante makes sense. It's possible McCord was simply testing Harry to see if he could be bribed. It could be that Richard Helms ordered the meeting in order to link RFK's friend Williams to Helms's unauthorized continuation of the CIA-Mafia plots. It's also possible that Bernard Barker, who often arranged Williams's meetings with the CIA, had taken advantage of a scheduled meeting with McCord and tipped Trafficante that Williams would be there, in which case McCord could have been unaware of Trafficante's presence in the restaurant. In any event, Harry Williams told Robert Kennedy about the odd meeting. Due to RFK's prodding, the FBI had finally begun keeping tabs on Trafficante at times, and two weeks after the meeting an FBI agent tried to question Williams about his brief encounter with the godfather. Harry Williams brushed off the FBI agent, saying it's "none of your business," and the agent "just laughed."[25]

A FBI report confirms that in June 1963 Trafficante was working in Miami in coordination with corrupt former Cuban President Carlos Prio to supply arms and money to Cuban exiles. Harry Williams's own FBI file for 1963, a massive one given his many meetings with exile leaders the FBI kept files on, has never been released and was never given to any Congressional investigation. The same is true for Williams's CIA file; it would be interesting to see show the CIA depicted the restaurant meeting with Trafficante.[26]

Harry Williams maintained his positive view of James McCord even after the Trafficante restaurant incident. McCord had no known ties to the CIA-Mafia plots or organized crime, unlike the top official in the Office of Security, Sheffield Edwards, who had originally brought Rosselli and Trafficante into the CIA-Mafia plots. According to some accounts, McCord reached a high position in the CIA's Security Office before "retiring" from the CIA in 1970 to start working for Nixon and the Republicans, leading to his arrest at the Watergate complex. Nine months later, James McCord would play one of the most important roles in exposing Richard Nixon's role in the Watergate cover-up.

Lieutenant Colonel Alexander M. Haig—who, as President Nixon's last Chief of Staff, would engineer his resignation—was also heavily involved in the JFK-Almeida coup plan. Since the CIA had only a supporting role in the plan, the main responsibility for the coup and subsequent "invited invasion" (if needed) fell on parts of the U.S. military. Alexander Haig often wrote or coordinated many of the drafts of the "Plan for a Coup in Cuba" generated in the summer and fall of 1963.

Today, Haig is mainly remembered as Ronald Reagan's Secretary of State who famously declared "I am in control" after Reagan's 1981 shooting. Others recall Haig's role as a shadow President in the last months of Nixon's Presidency, as recounted in the book *The Final Days* by Bob Woodward and Carl Bernstein. Often seen as simply a militaristic Cold War hawk, Haig was much more: a man with ambition and political savvy reminiscent in many ways of Richard Nixon, only without the criminal behavior. The same sharp political sense that helped Haig to rise in the U.S. military would allow him to do the same in Nixon's White House.

Alexander Haig, like McCord, was thirty-nine years old in 1963. It was not unusual that a successful military man like Haig was a West Point graduate (class of '47), but many would be surprised to know that the also earned an MBA from Columbia in 1955 and a Masters in International Relations from Georgetown University in 1961. Haig served in the Korean War, both administratively, with the imperious General Douglas MacArthur (which no doubt helped him deal later with Nixon), and in combat, where he earned two Silver Stars and a Bronze Star. By 1962 he was working in the Pentagon, and in 1963 he became the "military assistant" for Army Secretary Cyrus Vance, a civilian. Haig wrote in his autobiography that JFK named "Vance . . . as the executive agent for the entire federal government in dealing with Cuba [including] responsibility for coordinating a secret war against Cuba." Soon after, Haig also became the aide to Vance's "special assistant [Joseph] Califano." But Alexander Haig was much more than an aide to an assistant, and Haig continued to deal directly with Vance, and most importantly, with Robert Kennedy.[27]

When it came to the Cuban operations, Haig told an interviewer that "Bobby Kennedy was running it—hour by hour." Haig declared that for Cuban operations, "Bobby Kennedy was the President. He was the President! Let me repeat, as a reasonably close observer, HE WAS THE PRESIDENT!" Haig made it clear that Cyrus Vance—and himself, and Califano—were really just carrying out the Cuban operations of Robert Kennedy. That's why, Haig explained, Vance was able to tell "the State Department, the CIA, and the National Security Council" what to do about Cuba, because he was always acting for RFK. Haig also admits that he was "intimately involved" in those operations. He pointed out that even though three subcommittees of the National Security Council handled Cuba (the Standing Group, the Special Group, and the ICE), Robert Kennedy's name appeared on none of their organizational charts, yet RFK was the one calling the shots. RFK essentially used the fragmented committees, sometimes bypassing Secretary of State Rusk and Secretary of Defense Robert McNamara, to control the flow of information about Cuban operations. Unlike Rusk, Alexander Haig (and Cyrus Vance) did know about Commander Almeida in the summer and fall of 1963 prior to JFK's assassination, which is one reason Haig was given important tasks for the JFK-Almeida coup plan.[28]

"Haig was very pragmatic" about his work on the coup plan, according to Harry Williams. Another Haig associate in the coup plan said that "Haig really wanted to free Cuba" from Fidel, and he always gave "straightforward opinions and counsel." In contrast, Haig's associate said that Vance's aide, attorney Joseph Califano, "was just going through the motions." Califano has not acknowledged knowing about Commander Almeida, but in his 2004 autobiography, he wrote extensively about his work on Cuba in 1963 with Vance and Haig. Califano wrote that in 1963, "Presidential demands for a covert program to [eliminate] the Soviet military presence in Cuba . . . intensified. Helping develop this covert program and direct the Defense Department's role in it occupied much of my time in 1963." Califano goes on to say, "I felt I was working directly for the Attorney General and through him, for the President." (Years later, Califano would be a key Watergate figure, writing that as the attorney for the Democratic National Committee and for *The Washington Post*, he helped "to bring down Nixon.")[29]

Much of Haig's work in 1963 involved helping Cuban exile Bay of

Pigs veterans, the best of whom were being trained at Fort Benning, Georgia, just across the river from Phenix City, Alabama, the former mob vice center. Those exile troops would be a critical part of the coup plan, since they would be the first U.S. forces into Cuba after Commander Almeida had eliminated Fidel Castro. As a career military officer, unlike Vance and Califano, Lieutenant Colonel Haig was well positioned to coordinate the many drafts of the "Plan for a Coup in Cuba" with the updated, massive, detailed invasion plans that might be needed for Cuba. Those invasion plans, code-named SYNCLINE OPALS 312 and 316, were being prepared by the Joint Chiefs. Haig would also liaise effectively with General Carroll's Defense Intelligence Agency, which was important since General Carroll was the only other member of the Joint Chiefs, besides Chairman Maxwell Taylor, who knew about Commander Almeida.[30]

Haig and Califano were soon joined in Vance's office by Alexander Butterfield, whose revelation of Richard Nixon's White House tapes would be a critical turning point in the Watergate investigation, after James McCord had revealed Nixon's role in Watergate. Due to the intense secrecy and compartmentalization surrounding the JFK-Almeida coup plan, Haig, Califano, and Butterfield didn't work directly with McCord in 1963, but it's amazing that the four men who played the biggest roles in exposing Watergate and ending Richard Nixon's Presidency were working on different parts of essentially the same operation (and its aftermath) in 1963 and early 1964.[31]

Wiretaps and surveillance would play a critical role in Watergate, but surprising types of both were going on in 1963. Joseph Califano wrote in his autobiography that on "June 11, 1963, Cy Vance and I were sitting in the Army war room at the Pentagon, with sophisticated communications . . . capabilities." So that Califano and Vance would "know everything the White House and Justice Department were doing, we secretly ran all their communication lines though the Army war room. Sitting there, Vance and I were able to listen to any conversations the President or Attorney General had" regarding a civil rights matter they were dealing with at the time. "Because we assumed Robert Kennedy would have objected to our eavesdropping, we never let him know." Califano's admission is remarkable—especially since Nixon himself would be the target of surveillance by the Joint Chiefs before Watergate, something that had been going on since JFK's Presidency.[32]

Congressional investigations in the mid-1970s exposed a tremendous amount of domestic spying directed at U.S. citizens by the CIA, FBI, and U.S. military, which had gone on since the 1950s. However, government officials could also be targets. The CIA monitored important exile leaders like Manuel Artime and Harry Williams very closely. When they stayed at a CIA safe house or the Ebbitt Hotel in Washington (where the CIA housed exile leaders), their phone conversations were often monitored and recorded. Since Artime, and especially Williams, were both in frequent contact with Robert Kennedy, the CIA was in effect spying on the Attorney General.[33]

The CIA also kept tabs on the U.S. military, as revealed by a November 1963 CIA memo about General Carroll, the Defense Intelligence Agency Director. Possibly for security reasons, General Carroll spoke to an exile about the upcoming coup and complained about the CIA's role in the operation while the two sat in a car. General Carroll didn't realize his complaints were going to a CIA informant, who promptly reported them to the Agency.[34]

Unfortunately, the CIA and other agencies were sometimes more concerned with collecting and protecting information both from other agencies and from others within the CIA than with using it effectively. In August 1963, the CIA received information that exile leader Tony Varona had received $200,000 from associates of Johnny Rosselli. A few weeks later, another CIA memo from a completely different source shows that Varona secretly agreed to bring into the coup plan another Trafficante associate, Rolando Masferrer, a former death-squad leader under Batista. Varona ominously told Masferrer he could join the coup plan after certain "obstacles" were removed.[35]

Robert Kennedy and Harry Williams were never told about Varona's payoff from the Mafia or his dealings with Rolando Masferrer. Because Varona had been part of the CIA-Mafia plots for three years—and the plots were continuing—CIA officials like Richard Helms and Desmond FitzGerald might not have viewed the Mafia's payment to Varona as anything to be worried about.

However, Harry Williams and Robert Kennedy did have cause to be concerned about Rolando Masferrer and his associates. Since Williams couldn't be bribed by Trafficante at the Miami restaurant, Masferrer confronted him at RFK's New York apartment. Masferrer was accompanied by two "torpedoes"—who looked like mob enforcers—but that attempt at intimidation also proved fruitless. Trafficante's next attempt went much farther. When Williams went to Guatemala to meet Artime the next day, two thugs shot at him while he was dining in a fashionable Guatemala City restaurant. Wary after his confrontation with Masferrer, Williams was carrying a pistol and he shot one of the assailants, then fled through the restaurant's kitchen. Williams called RFK, who had him return to the United States the next day without meeting Artime. At the airport, Williams thought it odd the shooting wasn't reported in any of the Guatemala City newspapers. (An FBI memo mentions in passing that Williams returned from Guatemala on July 16, 1963.) As covered in a later chapter, *The New York Times* would report an almost identical shooting in Guatemala City around the time of the last Watergate break-in, which also had links to Manuel Artime.[36]

Trafficante's ties to Barker, Varona, and Artime gave the godfather a direct pipeline into the JFK-Almeida coup plan, despite the best efforts of Williams, RFK, and JFK to keep the Mafia out of their operation. Whatever Barker knew, Trafficante knew. As the story of the coup plan unfolds, it's important to recognize how critical Barker's dual role would be, as he worked for the CIA while selling out the coup plan to Trafficante.[37]

Williams discovered only later that Bernard "Barker . . . had something to do with the assassination of the President . . . He's involved, I'm sure!" Williams would also affirm that, in hindsight, there's "no question" that Trafficante "was involved" as well and had helped to finance JFK's assassination (something later confirmed by FBI files). However, it would take Williams several years to put all those pieces together, and he didn't realize any of that in 1963.[38]

The summer of 1963 brought new reminders that the Mafia could use the threat of exposing the CIA-Mafia plots in the press or in court to effectively blackmail the U.S. government, something that would continue for more than a decade. The same month that Varona received $200,000 from Rosselli's associates in Chicago, the CIA's plots with the Mafia finally affected Robert Kennedy's war on the Mafia. The FBI's lockstep surveillance of Giancana had so hindered his ability to run his operations that he'd actually taken the unusual step of filing a federal lawsuit to stop it. RFK had "pushed to get Giancana at any cost," according to Mafia prosecutor William Hundley, who represented the Justice Department at the Chicago hearing on Giancana's lawsuit. The FBI and Justice Department still lacked enough evidence to successfully prosecute the well-insulated Mafia boss, which is why the FBI had resorted to lockstep surveillance to simply disrupt his operations. Once Giancana took the stand, RFK—back in Washington—faced a dilemma. If RFK had Hundley interrogate Giancana, he would risk Giancana's disclosing his work for the government on the CIA-Mafia plots as a way to curry favor with the judge. RFK had been told the plots had ended back in May 1962, but the Attorney General knew that his own operation to topple Fidel was at a critical stage. RFK therefore instructed Hundley not to cross-examine Giancana in court, and the mobster won his lawsuit, the judge ordering the FBI to stay farther away from him in public.[39]

When an appeals court reversed Giancana's victory, the mob boss apparently pushed the issue of the CIA-Mafia plots again. The *Chicago Sun-Times* ran an article saying that "Sam Giancana had done work for the CIA," helping the Agency with intelligence related to Cuba in 1960. The story didn't mention assassination, but it did reveal the October 1960 bugging incident with Giancana and singer Phyllis McGuire that had involved the CIA. Accounts vary as to whether Sam Giancana or RFK's Justice Department was the source for the article, though Giancana could have initially given the CIA information to the reporter, who then checked with the Justice Department. In any event, Attorney General Kennedy soon sent a Justice Department prosecutor to Los Angeles to meet with the local IRS, FBI, and U.S. Attorney to explore bringing charges against Giancana's friend Frank Sinatra. The singer and Giancana were involved in various business deals, but nothing came of RFK's effort. However, the Attorney General was working on a plan to drive the Mafia out of Las Vegas, threatening to eliminate a major source of revenue for Giancana and the Chicago Mafia. Then, too, RFK had godfather Carlos Marcello set to go to trial in New Orleans on November 2. Across the country, RFK's other Mafia prosecutors—and an FBI that was finally starting to go after the Mafia in some cities—were stepping up the pressure. Marcello wasn't wiretapped by the FBI, but some other mobsters were, and the FBI heard their anguish. A Philadelphia mobster complained, "With Kennedy, a guy should take a knife . . . and stab and kill that fucker, I mean it." The mob chief of Buffalo went even farther, saying of the Kennedys, "They should kill the whole family."[40]

The Giancana-CIA article in the *Chicago Sun-Times* had gotten the attention of CIA Director John McCone, which led to another fateful decision for Richard Helms. Instead of giving McCone the full story of the CIA-Mafia plots to kill Fidel, Helms instead told his Director the plots had lasted only from 1960 to May 1962 and had ended. Helms didn't tell the Director that he'd continued the plots into 1963 without any authorization, and they were not only continuing, but on the verge of expansion.

Richard Helms probably felt that since he'd continued the CIA-Mafia plots without telling McCone or RFK, he couldn't suddenly reveal his deceit to them without losing his position. The CIA-Mafia plots were a deep secret even within the CIA, with only a handful of trusted officials like Desmond FitzGerald, E. Howard Hunt, and David Morales still working on them. Helms might have felt confident the secret would never leak. In addition, many accounts of Helms make him appear to be quite arrogant, and he may have simply thought that he and the CIA could do a better job than RFK, Vance, General Carroll, and the others. It's likely he chafed at having only a supporting role in the JFK-Almeida coup plan, and by contrast the CIA-Mafia plots were something that he could control (at least he thought he could).

The most generous view of the actions of Richard Helms in deceiving McCone and RFK would be that Helms saw the CIA-Mafia plots as a kind of backup plan in case something happened to Almeida before he launched the coup. After all, the government was spending thousands of hours and millions of dollars planning the coup, its aftermath, and a possible invasion. If Commander Almeida should lose his position or be injured, imprisoned, or killed—or decide to flee prior to the coup—Helms might have seen the CIA-Mafia plots as a way of saving the operation. Even if Almeida were able to initiate the coup, Helms might have thought it would still be helpful to have Mafia or exile sharpshooters to help finish the job, just in case anything went wrong.

As part of that thinking, an old element of the CIA-Mafia plots took on new prominence in the summer of 1963. Rolando Cubela had headed a student group, the Directo Revolucionario (DR), that helped win the Revolution. Though Cubela, a physician, had no real power within the Cuban government, he received a generous travel budget as the former head of the DR, and he frequently traveled to Europe and Communist-bloc countries. That enabled him to contact the CIA. The Agency first began its relationship with Cubela back in December

1960, after the Mafia's initial attempts to poison Fidel had failed. Cubela already knew CIA-Mafia plot members Santo Trafficante and Juan Orta, and he had been brought to the CIA's attention by a Trafficante associate code-named AMWHIP-1. A December 19, 1960, CIA memo refers to "a contact giving an 'H capsule' [of poison] to Rolando Cubela" to use against Fidel. It's possible that Cubela was working closely with Juan Orta on the CIA-Mafia plots in late 1960 and early 1961, since both men wanted to leave Cuba at the same time.[41]

But Cubela remained in Cuba, though he continued his extensive world travels. The CIA resumed contact with Cubela in the early summer of 1962, when the CIA-Mafia plots were again sending assassination teams into Cuba. The Cuban Missile Crisis intervened, and the CIA contacted Cubela again in June 1963 just as Johnny Rosselli's supervision was being switched from William Harvey to David Morales. According to Cuban reports, Morales himself actually met with Cubela in Paris in September 1963, and the CIA admits that a series of meetings between Cubela and CIA personnel followed. Cubela says the CIA kept pressuring him to assassinate Fidel, while the CIA claims assassination was Cubela's idea.[42]

Cubela wasn't part of the JFK-Almeida coup plan, and, as Dean Rusk confirmed to this author and CIA files clearly show, Cubela didn't have any real power or following inside Cuba that would have allowed him to stage a coup on his own. For decades, it was thought that Cubela's contacts with the CIA were known only inside the Agency, where he was identified as a potential assassin code-named AMLASH. However, Rusk and another committee member told this author that Cubela was discussed in some of RFK's Cuba subcommittees of the National Security Council, though not as a possible assassin. Richard Helms and Desmond FitzGerald told some of the subcommittee members about Cubela only as someone who might help them find a higher-ranking, more powerful official that could stage a coup. To an official like Rusk, who didn't yet know about Almeida, that sounded reasonable. Years later, when Rusk found out that the CIA was actually using Cubela as a potential assassin, he was livid at Richard Helms's deceit, with an anger that the usually calm statesman demonstrated in his interview with this author.[43]

Only a mid-level official at best, Rolando Cubela had even less of a role in Cuban affairs as fall 1963 progressed. CIA files establish that Cubela lost his ceremonial military title after he "resigned from the

Army after difficulties with Raul Castro," and an October 18, 1963, CIA memo confirms "that Cubela has no official position in the government." Yet Richard Helms and Desmond FitzGerald increased CIA pressure on Cubela to assassinate Fidel, with FitzGerald even flying to Paris to meet personally with Cubela that same month. Though FitzGerald claimed to be the personal emissary of Robert Kennedy, Helms later admitted that RFK was never told about the meeting or the assassination aspect of the CIA's dealings with Cubela.[44]

The CIA admits it tried to persuade Cubela to poison Fidel, but CIA files also show that the Miami CIA station, where David Morales ran operations, was prepared to provide rifles to him. Cubela owned a house next to Fidel's at Varadero Beach, the resort that Fidel drove to on many weekends in an open jeep, in a sort of re-creation of his triumphant drive across Cuba after the Revolution. AMWORLD files indicate the CIA at one point planned to assassinate Fidel using snipers to shoot him in his jeep as Fidel drove to his Varadero Beach home next to Cubela's beach house. Clearly, having Fidel's neighbor Cubela as part of that plot would be very advantageous. Someone in the CIA, likely David Morales, arranged for Cubela to be in a meeting with his case officer in Paris on November 22, 1963, when JFK was scheduled to be in Dallas.[45]

E. Howard Hunt and Manuel Artime both later became involved with Cubela. It's likely that Hunt had some involvement in the Cubela operation—and the rest of the CIA-Mafia plots—in 1963, in order to coordinate them with the JFK-Almeida coup plan he was working on.

By the fall of 1963, the CIA-Mafia plots also involved Charles Nicoletti, an experienced hit man from Rosselli's Chicago Mafia, and the previously mentioned Sam Benton, a private detective for Carlos Marcello. Johnny Rosselli continued to work with CIA official David Morales near Miami, where an Army Rangers Captain saw Rosselli working with Cuban exile sharpshooters. Also in October 1963, Rosselli met twice in Miami with Jack Ruby, a former gunrunner to Cuba who had been caught stealing from the Dallas club he fronted for Carlos Marcello's organization. Richard Helms had kept European assassin recruiter QJWIN, whose job was to recruit CIA assassins from the underworld, on the CIA payroll, though the surviving files show him doing nothing to earn his money. However, one of Santo Trafficante's most ruthless French Connection heroin network partners, experienced assassin and French intelligence asset Michel Victor Mertz, had several interesting connections to QJWIN, and Mertz traveled in the United States, including trips to Dallas. Still another attempt to assassinate Fidel in Cuba occurred on September 28, 1963, one that the Cuban government's Dossier says involved a "CIA agent . . . who was a French citizen living in Cuba." The plot involved using "dynamite . . . under the presidential palace," and it's interesting that Mertz had once been involved in an explosives plot against French President Charles de Gaulle.[46]

While covert plans simmered far from public view, Richard Nixon was gradually increasing his public profile in hopes of becoming the Republican nominee in 1964. Pawley's effort with Operation TILT had been a flop as far as Nixon's political fortunes were concerned, but Nixon still seemed to want to make Cuba a focus of his effort to win the nomination.

"Nixon calls Cuba situation important issue in US '64 Presidential election" ran the headline in the September 24, 1963, edition of *The New York Times*. Nixon continued to complain about JFK's handling of the Cuba issue, even as the Kennedys hoped to keep Cuba out of the headlines in the lead-up to the coup. On the other hand, Nixon and the Republicans weren't about to let Cuba stay on the back burner. Their escalating comments in the summer and fall of 1963 showed JFK that he could expect to face even more criticism and heat over Cuba once the race began in earnest in January 1964.[47]

Nixon's attacks on JFK regarding Cuba would have to keep up with his Republican rivals, and his challenger from the far right, Barry Goldwater, was especially vocal, claiming that JFK was "doing everything in his power" to prevent the Cuban exile flag "from ever flying over Cuba again." Nixon's other main rival, Nelson Rockefeller, also attacked JFK in the press over Cuba, as did the chairman of the Republican Party. The latter's views generated headlines claiming, "Kennedy Ducking Cuba Problem," which appeared in *The Miami Herald* and the *Los Angeles Times*. In the articles, the RNC chairman claimed "the Kennedy administration had 'swept Cuban affairs under the rug' since the Missile Crisis."[48]

Richard Nixon's strategy of emphasizing Cuba to help win the nomination played to his strength of having far more foreign policy experience than any of his rivals. He needed an issue where he could present himself as the experienced statesman, since he'd decided not to take on Goldwater and Rockefeller directly, especially in the early primaries next year. Goldwater had an energized far-right base, while the moderate Rockefeller had his well-oiled New York political machine, and Nixon could match neither organization. Still, Nixon sensed that the supporters of the moderate Rockefeller and the ultra-conservative Goldwater were so far apart that neither would clinch enough delegates to win the nomination on the first ballot. Moreover, the two disparate sides were unlikely to support a nominee who came from the other side of the political spectrum. At a deadlocked convention, Nixon hoped the delegates would turn to an experienced elder statesman—himself. Nixon's strategy was viable because in the early 1960s, primaries weren't as important as they are today, leaving party bosses and Republican officials to play a decisive role in choosing the nominee at the convention. The only other major Republican touted as a compromise candidate was Michigan Governor George Romney. But Romney lacked Nixon's foreign policy experience, a crucial factor if Nixon could use the press to keep the political focus on Cuba.[49]

As he'd done earlier in the year with Pawley, Nixon was also trying to secure inside information about Cuba in the fall of 1963. Though the Kennedys tried hard to keep their Cuba plans out of the press, one major article in Miami slipped through in the summer, leaked by Manuel Artime. Headlined "Backstage with Bobby," it outlined RFK's support for Artime's exile camps in Central America. The article created a stir in RFK's various Cuba subcommittees of the NSC, but their main response was simply to clamp down on future leaks. Still, Nixon would have been aware that the Kennedys had something in the works about Cuba.[50]

Corrupt Cuban ex-President Carlos Prio, also an associate of Santo Trafficante and Tony Varona, had been kept out of the coup plan by RFK (who had access to Justice Department files about Trafficante). But the wealthy and determined Prio tried to use his money to ingratiate himself with Manuel Artime, his old friend Varona, and other exile leaders. CIA files show that Prio was able to learn some details of the coup plan, which he and his lieutenants gave the telling nickname of "Plan Judas." Fidel had often told the partially true story of how he and twelve disciples—including Juan Almeida, Raul Castro, and Che Guevara—had gone into the mountains of Cuba to start the

Revolution. CIA files make it clear that Prio knew one of those twelve was going to betray Fidel by helping the United States.[51]

Both Nixon and "Plan Judas" are mentioned in a fall 1963 CIA cable about Carlos Prio that was kept classified for the next thirty years and wasn't discovered at the National Archives until after Nixon's death. In the cable, Prio discusses several aspects of the coup plan before mentioning two exiles who were part of Prio's operation "and have become associated [with] Richard Nixon in accordance with [the] Republican Party plan [to] bring up the Cuban case before elections." Thus Richard Nixon had some access to inside information about the Kennedys' impending plan to overthrow Fidel. A review of all of the released CIA files about Prio (some remain classified) shows that Prio had a good general understanding of the coup plan, though he sometimes had details wrong. Prio was also determined that he should run Cuba after the coup, not Artime or any of RFK's other chosen exile leaders.[52]

Richard Nixon and Bebe Rebozo had several associates in common with Carlos Prio, who would later play a small role in the Watergate operations. Shortly before the first Watergate break-in, and after a visit from E. Howard Hunt and Bernard Barker, Carlos Prio would become "head of Cuban-Americans for Nixon-Agnew." Following up on an earlier approach used by Hunt and his Watergate operatives against Daniel Ellsberg, Prio would also direct "a goon squad that roughed up anti-war demonstrators."[53]

With his inside track for information about JFK and Cuba, Richard Nixon seemed well positioned to keep focusing on Cuba. As for dealing with his Republican rivals, Nixon and his aides hatched an ingenious plan: Richard Nixon was going to write—or rather, have researched and ghostwritten for him—a book about the 1964 election. Nixon's book would be modeled on the best-selling book about JFK by Theodore H. White, *The Making of a President 1960*. That would allow Nixon to learn the inner workings of the operations of his Republican rivals, all for a seemingly innocent purpose. The other candidates would want to make sure the book portrayed them positively, and in public Nixon always downplayed any chance that he would seek the nomination in 1964. By the time of the 1964 Republican Convention, Nixon hoped to garner enough inside information to help him in his quest to become a compromise nominee. It should be pointed out that Nixon really did plan on producing the book; it wasn't just a political trick. Nixon was set to sign the contract with the publisher in New York City on November 22—after he returned from Dallas, where he was slated to attend "a board meeting of the Pepsi-Cola Company, one of [Nixon's law] firm's clients."[54]

President Kennedy, RFK, and other key officials in the Kennedy administration were concerned about Cuba and the 1964 election. JFK's special U.N. advisor, William Attwood, said they needed to "remove the Cuban issue from the 1964 campaign." Talks with other Kennedy aides show that John and Robert Kennedy shared that opinion, and it was one factor in scheduling the JFK-Almeida coup plan for December 1, 1963. That way, the Cuba situation would be resolved—one way or the other—before the official start of the campaign in January 1964. The December 1 date was early enough so that U.S. troops wouldn't be fighting in Cuba during the Christmas holidays, and U.S. air support for the coup would be over before the Pearl Harbor anniversary on December 7. In addition, CIA files confirm that after December 1, Cuban officials planned to institute a draft that would dilute the loyalty of Commander Almeida's army and also allow Cuban intelligence and other rival factions in the Cuban government to infiltrate his ranks.[55]

William Attwood didn't know about the JFK-Almeida coup plan at that time, but he would lead a last-ditch attempt by JFK and RFK to find a peaceful alternative to what one memo called "a bloody coup." In an outreach well documented in many books, articles, and documentaries, Attwood became JFK's intermediary for secret peace negotiations with Fidel Castro. Lisa Howard, the pioneering newscaster who was the Diane Sawyer of her day, had been initially involved. Attwood's secret peace feelers began in September 1963, but they were complicated. JFK couldn't go through traditional diplomatic channels for fear that Nixon and the Republicans, as well as conservatives within his own party, would find out about them and raise a storm of protest in the press and in Congress. Fidel Castro also had to be careful. As Fidel's representative told Attwood, Fidel didn't want Che Guevara to find out about the secret talks, because "there was a rift between Castro and the Guevara [and] Almeida group on the question of Cuba's future course."[56]

To preserve deniability in case the secret talks were exposed, JFK had to work through William Attwood, who in turn talked to Fidel's doctor, who then dealt with Fidel. The parties were wary of each other, and the negotiations slow. In one memo, Attwood commented that "he is not hopeful" about the negotiations. As the December 1 date for the coup with Almeida drew ever closer, JFK began yet another secret channel to Fidel. In late October 1963, JFK asked journalist Jean Daniel to talk privately to Fidel on JFK's behalf. But Fidel kept Daniel cooling his heels in Havana for weeks. Daniel wouldn't get to see Fidel to deliver JFK's personal message until November 21, the day before JFK's trip to Dallas. Fidel was intrigued enough by Daniel's message from JFK that he invited the journalist to a follow-up lunch on November 22 at Castro's Varadero Beach villa. However, Daniel was just a journalist and could not securely communicate directly with JFK or Bobby about his talks with Castro, so the Kennedys had no way to know that Daniel was finally talking with the Cuban leader.[57]

While historians had long known about JFK's outreach to Fidel through Attwood and Daniel, it was never clear why JFK had gone to such lengths at that particular time for negotiations that—if prematurely exposed—could have harmed his chance for reelection. Additionally, it was risky having two separate, secret channels at the same time, but JFK and RFK seem to have been determined to try every possible avenue to avoid the "bloody coup" if only they could find a politically viable peaceful way to coexist with Fidel. Neither channel appeared to be producing solid results fast enough, but a last-minute breakthrough was still possible, even as the date for the coup approached.

JFK's Secretary of State, Dean Rusk, explained to this author how, in hindsight, he thought the Kennedys had done the right thing in pursuing both peace negotiations and the coup plan at the same time. Rusk later talked to *Vanity Fair* about the Kennedys' pursuit of peace negotiations with Fidel while they were also planning a violent coup to eliminate him: "There's no particular contradiction there . . . It was just an either/or situation. That went on frequently." However, Rusk said that by doing so, JFK and Bobby "were playing with fire."[58]

When Attwood's peace feelers with Fidel came up in one of the NSC subcommittees, Richard Helms was wary. Helms told RFK and Cyrus Vance the outreach to Fidel was a "problem" and said he was leery about Attwood—or anyone higher up in the U.S. government—"making any contacts" with Fidel's representative. JFK and RFK didn't agree with Helms, so the Attwood initiative continued.[59]

That left John and Robert Kennedy with basically one overall goal for Cuba in late 1963: to resolve the situation so that the United States could coexist in peace with the Cuban people. That could be with a peacefully negotiated settlement if possible, but if not, they would try to bring it about by supporting Commander Almeida and the Cuban exile leaders with their coup, designed to lead eventually to free elections and democracy in Cuba.

CHAPTER 15

September–November 1963: Nixon and JFK Go to Dallas

In the fall of 1963, President Kennedy resisted any temptation to respond directly to Richard Nixon and other Republican critics who claimed JFK wasn't taking strong action against Fidel Castro. That approach helped John and Robert Kennedy maintain a press blackout over anything that might expose their plan for Commander Almeida to stage a coup against Fidel. Only one article had slipped through, apparently leaked by Manuel Artime, and it focused on the Kennedys' broader effort to back certain Cuban exile leaders, but it hadn't gained national attention or even hinted at Almeida's involvement.[1]

However, the Kennedys recognized that Fidel could discover the JFK-Almeida coup plan through his spies if not from the press and might retaliate against the United States in some way. Accordingly, in September 1963, Robert Kennedy instructed some of those working on the "Plan for a Coup in Cuba" to develop additional plans for just such a contingency, and that process continued into October and November 1963.[2]

The resulting Cuba Contingency Plans considered several possible scenarios in which Fidel might try to retaliate. As Army Secretary Cyrus Vance had said in a related memo about the coup, the administration vitally needed certain types of "information . . . to enable the President to make" viable decisions so they could avoid any situation where the President "would lack essential, evaluated information . . . but would at the same time be under heavy pressure to respond quickly." A Kennedy aide familiar with the plans explained to this author that Robert Kennedy didn't want President Kennedy to come under pressure from the public, the press, or Congress to take hasty action against Cuba if—for example—initial reports indicated Cuban involvement in the death of a U.S. ambassador in Latin America. After all, a hasty U.S. military attack against Cuba could provoke devastating retaliation from Russia. Also, imagine the disaster if the United States started bombing Havana if later evidence emerged that the U.S. official had not been killed by Fidel's agents.[3]

The Cuba Contingency Plans that have been released were written by Alexander Haig and were based on information discussed and approved by one of RFK's National Security Council subcommittees that included Joseph Califano and CIA representatives such as Desmond FitzGerald. However, some of those working on the Cuba Contingency Plans, like Rusk's representatives from the State Department, didn't know about Commander Almeida and the impending coup—they only knew the United States was looking for someone who might be able to stage a coup. Thus, some of those making the Cuba Contingency Plans realized how imminent and deadly serious their work was, while others on the subcommittee viewed it with far less urgency.[4]

The possible "assassination of American officials" was a major focus of the Cuba Contingency planning done by Alexander Haig and the others, along with less serious forms of possible Castro retaliation, such as sabotage. Of the many files from the Cuba Contingency planning, only a few have been declassified. Those show that the subcommittee believed the "assassination of American officials" to be "likely" in the fall of 1963. However, the subcommittee wrote that assassination attempts against U.S. officials were "unlikely in the US." If Fidel found out about U.S. plans and decided to retaliate, the members of the subcommittee believed he would risk assassinating an American official only outside the United States—for example, in a Latin American country.[5]

This Cuba Contingency planning for dealing with the "assassination of American officials" was still under way in November 1963. A Kennedy aide familiar with the plans explained some of the conditions necessary for JFK to make an informed, reasoned response to the apparent assassination of a U.S. official in Latin America. U.S. officials would need to control and limit initial publicity, to keep the news media from generating an outcry for an immediate military response against Cuba. To protect Almeida, any possible links between the assassination and the coup plan would have to be hidden from the press and law enforcement. As soon as possible, U.S. investigating agencies would need to take control of the investigation from local authorities, including gaining possession of important evidence. The autopsy would have to be conducted at a secure U.S. military facility to ensure that information couldn't be leaked to the press. All of that would give JFK the time and information needed to make an appropriate response.[6]

However, Alexander Haig and the others doing the planning—even those who knew about Commander Almeida and the impending coup—were missing crucial information. They hadn't been told that the Secret Service had uncovered a plot to assassinate JFK during his planned motorcade in Chicago on November 2. That operation appeared to have a possible, though hazy, link to Cuba. Apparently those making the Cuba Contingency Plans—who weren't told about the Chicago attempt—never considered that President Kennedy could be one of the "American officials" targeted for retaliatory assassination. Because of that, the Secret Service played no role in the Contingency planning. In addition, high-ranking U.S. officials apparently decided that sharing any information about the Chicago attempt with the entire subcommittee—and potentially its supervisors, aides, and secretaries—might compromise the security of the entire coup plan.

To help maintain the secrecy of their Cuban operations, John and Robert Kennedy kept everything about the November 2, 1963, plot to kill JFK in Chicago out of the press at the time. According to former Secret Service Agent Abraham Bolden, who was assigned to their Chicago office at the time of JFK's motorcade, his office learned of a plot by four men—possibly Cubans or Cuban exiles—to assassinate the President. At least two of the gunmen remained at large, forcing JFK to cancel his motorcade at the very last minute, even as Chicagoans lined the motorcade route. As JFK's Press Secretary, Pierre Salinger, explained to this author, he had to issue two different phony excuses for the cancellation in less than an hour.[7]

In Chicago, the Secret Service had also been monitoring ex-Marine Thomas Vallee, who was arrested shortly before Pierre Salinger announced the cancellation of JFK's trip. When taken into custody, Vallee—who had recently gotten a job at a warehouse overlooking JFK's motorcade route—had an M1 rifle and three thousand rounds of ammunition in his car. The former Marine had recently moved back to Chicago after spending time at a Cuban exile training camp, where he had trained the exiles for a mission involving "the assassination of Castro."[8]

On orders from the White House, a press blackout prevented any news reports from mentioning the plot to kill JFK in Chicago, Vallee's arrest, or the real reason for JFK's cancellation. Ex-Agent Bolden later testified, and told the author, that everything about the Chicago plot was handled differently from more routine threats to the President, though the Chicago agents were never told why. Because the CIA and the Secret Service rarely shared information, the Chicago agents didn't realize the significance of Cubans in the threat or that the CIA had their own reports of a possible Cuban agent in Chicago. The phony reports of the Cuban agent, who'd supposedly traveled to Chicago before JFK's motorcade, would be traced only decades later to informants working for CIA officer David Morales.[9]

In addition, Pierre Salinger—a crime investigator for JFK against Carlos Marcello in the late 1950s—helped this author uncover information about Marcello's man Jack Ruby receiving a payoff of approximately $7,000 from a Hoffa associate in Chicago shortly before the attempt to kill JFK there. However, no authorities at the time knew about Jack Ruby's payoff in his old hometown of Chicago. Marcello himself had gone on trial in New Orleans the day before the Chicago attempt on federal charges prosecuted by RFK's Justice Department.*[10]

In hindsight, it's amazing that RFK's subcommittee of the NSC—tasked with making Cuba Contingency Plans for how the U.S. government should react if an American official was assassinated by Fidel—was not told about the Chicago plot. While individual members of the subcommittee may have learned about the plot through their own contacts, that information was apparently not shared with the full subcommittee, judging from their November 12, 1963, notes. However, as a Kennedy aide familiar with the Cuba Contingency Plans explained to this author, the thinking behind the plans could still be used—by the Kennedys and other high-ranking officials—even as the planning continued.[11]

Vietnam also played a role in helping to keep the Chicago plot out of the press. The final fake excuse that Pierre Salinger gave the press and public for JFK's sudden Chicago cancellation was his need to stay in Washington to deal with the fallout from the assassination of U.S.-

*Documentation for Ruby's Chicago payoff—and the entire Chicago plot—can be found in the books *Legacy of Secrecy* (2009) and *Ultimate Sacrifice* (2006).

backed South Vietnamese dictator Ngo Dinh Diem. As Salinger later explained, that was just a pretext, since after Diem's death became public—but before JFK's cancellation—Salinger had announced that Diem's murder would not affect JFK's Chicago trip. Salinger had told the press that "a special communications facility would be rush constructed [in Chicago] to keep the President" up to date on events in Vietnam. In fact, Salinger had emphasized to reporters that "Kennedy would not cancel the trip" because of the events in Vietnam. Just forty-five minutes later, Salinger announced JFK's cancellation, first claiming JFK had a cold, then later using the excuse of Diem's murder.[12]

JFK had authorized a Vietnamese military coup to overthrow the corrupt Diem, but had ordered that it be "bloodless" and that Diem and his brother would be flown to exile in Taiwan. A famous White House photo of an anguished JFK is said to have captured his reaction to the news that Diem and his brother had been murdered on their way to the airport. This messy, confused situation only added to JFK's growing frustration with the issue of Vietnam. The previous month, JFK had issued a statement saying he planned by the end of the year to withdraw 116,000 U.S. "advisors" in Vietnam. The number of U.S. "advisors" had steadily increased in the last years of the Eisenhower-Nixon administration and the early years of JFK's. Just over a hundred of those U.S. "advisors" had died by November 1963. While historians still debate what JFK would have done about Vietnam in 1964, the political reality was that he couldn't withdraw too many advisors too quickly, or he would risk a backlash in the 1964 election. Years later, during the Watergate era, Richard Nixon—beset by a greatly expanded Vietnam War—would have E. Howard Hunt attempt to fake cables to make it appear as if JFK had directly ordered Diem's assassination.[13]

Work on the JFK-Almeida coup plan continued to progress in mid-November 1963. By this time, Robert Kennedy and Harry Williams—with the assistance of E. Howard Hunt and Bernard Barker—had paid Commander Almeida his initial $50,000 payment to stage the coup. The CIA had also helped provide a pretext (possibly medical) for Almeida's wife and two children to leave Cuba for another country friendly to both Cuba and the United States. The CIA maintained surreptitious surveillance of the three, careful to avoid alarming any of Fidel's intelligence agents who might also be watching them. (It's not known what role, if any, James McCord might have played in the operation involving Almeida's family.)[14]

As the coup date of December 1, 1963, approached, Almeida began asking for a direct assurance from President Kennedy that he would fully back his effort once it had begun. On November 18, JFK was set to ride in the longest domestic motorcade of his career in Tampa, Florida, where he was to give four speeches before going on to Miami to speak to the Inter-American Press Association. In order to give Almeida the assurance he needed, JFK had special lines inserted in the middle of his Miami speech. Most of this address was written by JFK aide Richard Goodwin, with input from Arthur Schlesinger Jr. and others. However, journalist Sy Hersh learned that Desmond FitzGerald's assistant, Seymour Bolton, said that he "had 'carried a paragraph [to the White House] to be inserted into Kennedy's November 18 speech.'" In addition, Senate investigators found a declassified CIA memo confirming that in "Kennedy's speech of November 18, 1963 . . . the CIA intended President Kennedy's speech to serve as a signal to dissident elements in Cuba that the US would support a coup," and the memo specifically says those "dissident elements" were "in the Cuban Armed Forces."[15]

Before JFK could even begin his Florida trip, two related assassination threats surfaced, one in Miami and one in Tampa. The one in Miami involved Miami police undercover recordings of a South Georgia white supremacist, Joseph Milteer, saying there was a plan "to assassinate the President with a high-powered rifle from a tall building" and that authorities "will pick up somebody within hours afterwards . . . just to throw the public off." The FBI launched an investigation of Milteer, though J. Edgar Hoover didn't share important information—like JFK's impending trip to Tampa, or that Milteer's remarks were on tape—with the Georgia FBI agents assigned to the case. Unknown to both the agents and Hoover, three months earlier Milteer had met in New Orleans with associates of Carlos Marcello, including fellow white supremacist Guy Banister, the former FBI Chief of Chicago who had become Marcello's private detective. Banister also did occasional work related to Cuba for the CIA, according to the CIA's No. 2 official in New Orleans, Hunter Leake.[16]

The second threat against JFK was uncovered in Tampa, Florida. As detailed to the author by then–Tampa Police Chief J.P. Mullins—and verified by newspaper files and other authorities—the threat involved "two men" and the "use [of] a gun." One suspect was described in a Secret Service memo as being "white, male, 20, slender build," but police could locate neither of the two suspects. Chief Mullins advised the Secret Service to have JFK cancel his trip, since his protection couldn't be assured for multiple reasons. For example, Tampa's tallest building was a hotel overlooking JFK's motorcade route that would be packed with visitors and all of its windows could open, meaning that any of them could harbor a shooter. However, JFK made the trip anyway, perhaps because Jackie wasn't traveling with him and because of how it would look to Commander Almeida if JFK canceled his own motorcade while he was trying to get Almeida to go ahead with a dangerous coup. Then, too, after suddenly canceling his Chicago motorcade barely two weeks earlier, if JFK canceled again, it would look suspicious and generate unwanted press scrutiny.[17]

Security precautions were even tighter than usual for JFK's Tampa trip on November 18, 1963, and according to Chief Mullins, JFK showed the strain when he was away from cameras, but not in front of the public. As in Chicago, the White House ordered a complete press blackout about the Tampa threat. What President Kennedy and Chief Mullins didn't realize was that Santo Trafficante had called off the attempt to kill JFK in Tampa. As explained by another high-ranking Florida law enforcement official, Trafficante's main man on the Tampa police force—Sergeant Jack de la Llana, had warned the godfather that authorities had uncovered the threat to kill JFK.*[18]

Remarkably, as with Chicago, there is no evidence that the NSC subcommittee with Alexander Haig, making Contingency Plans in the event of a possible assassination of an American official, was ever informed about the attempt to kill JFK in Tampa. That can't be stated conclusively, since only three memos out of dozens from their meetings from September to November 1963 have ever been released. As with the Chicago plot, individual members of the subcommittee might have been aware of the Tampa attempt, through their own agencies. It's also important to point out that those like Haig on the subcommittee drafting the Contingency Plans were not themselves high-ranking officials, such as Cyrus Vance, Robert Kennedy, or Richard Helms. However, those high officials—some of whom, like RFK

*Extensive documentation for the Tampa attempt can be found in *Legacy of Secrecy* (2009) and *Ultimate Sacrifice* (2006).

and Helms, were definitely aware of the Tampa attempt—were seeing the committee's work and would be guided by some of that planning in the days to come.

As for President Kennedy, after his tense Tampa motorcade he continued on to Miami and delivered his speech to the Inter-American Press Association, including the few lines written to reassure Almeida. Those carefully crafted sentences were also designed so they would not upset JFK's back-channel negotiations with Fidel through William Attwood. In his speech, JFK proclaimed that:

> What now divides Cuba from my country . . . is that fact that a small band of conspirators has stripped the Cuban people of their freedom and handed over the independence and sovereignty of the Cuban nation to forces beyond the hemisphere. They have made Cuba a victim of foreign imperialism . . . This, and this alone, divides us. As long as this is true, nothing is possible. Without it, everything is possible. Once this barrier is removed, we will be ready and anxious to work with the Cuban people . . .[19]

Commander Almeida was satisfied with JFK's remarks in Miami and communicated that to Harry Williams. Declassified files show that in the days following Almeida's response to JFK's speech, Robert Kennedy had his final meetings in Washington with Manuel Artime and Harry Williams before the coup. Everything was almost set: The Cuban-American troops at Fort Benning were trained and ready; Artime and Varona were prepared for their roles in the post-coup government; and exile leaders Manolo Ray and Eloy Menoyo had met with Williams about the coup, though they weren't told as much as Artime and Varona. Robert Kennedy arranged for Harry Williams to have a crucial meeting with CIA officials on November 22, 1963, as later confirmed by *The Washington Post*. Among those at the meeting would be Lyman Kirkpatrick, the CIA's No. 3 official, because he had prepared the scathing critique of the Agency's performance in the Bay of Pigs. If he and the other CIA officials saw no problem, Williams would immediately go from that meeting to Miami. On November 23 or 24, he would leave Miami for the U.S. base at Guantánamo. After a day or two at the base, Williams would slip into Cuba to meet face-to-face with Almeida before the coup, which was still slated for December 1, 1963. Once Williams was inside Castro's Cuba, it would be difficult—if not impossible—for JFK to call off the coup plan.[20]

JFK and RFK were already planning for post-coup news coverage by aiding NBC News' preparation of a Bay of Pigs special to run soon after the coup. They were also helping Haynes Johnson with a book of the same name, giving the Kennedys' view of the Bay of Pigs invasion. One of Haynes' coauthors was Manuel Artime, and a CIA memo confirms that Artime was feeding information about the book project to his official CIA case officer for AMWORLD, Henry Heckshер, who in turn was passing Artime's concerns along to Desmond FitzGerald. In addition, Artime increasingly resented Harry Williams's leading role in the coup, feeling that he should be in charge instead.[21]

Richard Helms, who had argued against the Attwood-Fidel secret peace feelers, saw President Kennedy for the last time on November 19 at the White House after JFK returned from his Florida trip. Helms showed JFK captured weapons, part of a three-ton cache that Fidel had supposedly sent to rebels in Venezuela. JFK seemed impressed, and Helms's visit appears to have been designed to help ensure the coup plan went forward, in lieu of any peace negotiations. Helms didn't tell JFK or RFK that on November 22, 1963, one of his CIA agents would be meeting in Paris with Rolando Cubela—the mid-level Cuban official linked to the Mafia—and giving him a weapon to assassinate Fidel. Then again, Helms didn't know the significance of the timing of that meeting, whose date had been set not by Cubela, but by a CIA official in Miami, most likely David Morales.[22]

Declassified memos indicate that Cabinet officials such as Dean Rusk, who didn't know about Almeida, would discuss Cuba on Monday, November 25, 1963, after returning from a conference in Hawaii about Vietnam. That is probably when Rusk and the other officials would have been told that someone high enough in Fidel's government to stage the coup had been found and the operation was set for December 1, 1963, using the "Plans for a Coup in Cuba" they and their staffs had been working on intensively for the past five months.[23]

In the fall of 1963, Richard Helms oversaw a huge array of programs for the CIA that had varying levels of secrecy and authorization. Helms supervised worldwide CIA operations as the Agency's Deputy Director for Plans, essentially its highest operational official. That included the entire official CIA effort against Cuba, which was known to the National Security Council and all high-ranking CIA officials. However, the NSC knew about U.S. support for Manuel Artime, Manolo Ray, Tony Varona, and Eloy Menoyo only as being exile leaders backed by the United States, not as part of the real coup plan with Commander Almeida. In addition, Helms coordinated the CIA's role in the highly secret JFK-Almeida coup plan, which was known to Helms's CIA superiors but to only a few on the NSC. Finally, Helms was supervising his own unauthorized plots to assassinate Fidel, primarily the CIA-Mafia plots, which ranged from those with Johnny Rosselli to Rolando Cubela to QJWIN. Helms had also authorized David Atlee Phillips's work with Antonio Veciana and Alpha 66 to assassinate Fidel. It important to stress that none of those assassination plots were known to Richard Helms's CIA superiors, by JFK or RFK, or by the NSC. Richard Helms's need to hide those unauthorized schemes was the primary reason that he would have to destroy or withhold so much information in 1963, 1964, 1967, and again during Richard Nixon's Presidency.

In September, October, and November of 1963, Richard Helms and the Agency continued their critical supporting roles for the JFK-Almeida coup plan. As noted earlier, a declassified memo identified one of the Agency's "supporting operations" as "the introduction by CIA as soon as practicable of assets in Cuba for the development of intelligence." It was crucial that the CIA move more U.S. intelligence assets into Cuba before the coup, especially assets who had openly arrived in Cuba. Unlike the CIA agents slipped into Cuba secretly on speedboats, these assets could move about the island with much more freedom, assisting with parts of the coup plan and talking to the Cuban people (and lower-level officials) to gauge support for Almeida after Fidel's death. Getting those "open" assets into Cuba was an especially secret and delicate task because of Agency worries about Soviet moles in the CIA and the difficulty of getting Americans into Cuba without arousing the suspicion of Cuban authorities.[24]

The preferred route for these CIA assets was through Mexico City, which had regular flights to Havana. David Atlee Phillips headed covert operations at the Agency's Mexico City station, though that was just one of at least three roles—and two chains of command—he had for the CIA. In addition to assisting the Alpha 66 group, Phillips also helped with AMWORLD, with a chain of command bypassing the Mexico City Chief of Station (Win Scott), and going straight to Desmond FitzGerald and Richard Helms. Phillips's dual chains of command sometimes resulted in two sets of cables about the same CIA asset being sent from Mexico City to Washington: one for broader

Agency consumption that made the asset look like nothing special, and another—going only to FitzGerald and Helms—that indicated a much more serious role for the asset.[25]

Most Agency files about the many assets the CIA tried to get into Cuba via Mexico City in the fall of 1963 are still classified, but those about four young men were later released to Congressional investigators. Most of the four had documented or likely ties to David Atlee Phillips or Manuel Artime, or both. In one case, a Congressional investigator documented that Phillips personally met with the CIA asset in Texas, several weeks before the asset's trip to Mexico City for his attempt to get into Cuba. Before leaving the United States for Mexico City, that CIA asset, and at least one other, had tried to burnish their public "pro-Castro" image to encourage the Cuban embassy to allow them into Cuba—even though other information shows the assets were anti-Castro.[26]

The known time periods targeted by the CIA to move those assets into Cuba were late September 1963 and again in the last week of November, just before the coup. All four of the known young men who tried to get into Cuba before the coup were in their early twenties. In one documented instance, three of the young men visited the Cuban embassy in Mexico City in one twenty-four-hour period in late September, causing the embassy to confuse the identities of two of them (which might have been the CIA's intent). It was as if the CIA were making several attempts at the same time in hopes that one or more might get through. Most of the assets known today did not get past the cautious Cuban embassy, but one of the November assets did make it into Cuba (and remained there for years, perhaps decades).[27]

Some of the known assets appear to have been more important than others, and those had a Soviet tie that could be exploited if their role in the coup plan to eliminate Fidel became known. That was consistent with CIA policy on the elimination of Fidel going back to William Harvey's original notes for assassination operations, which said that "planning should include provision for blaming Soviets."[28]

Both Robert F. Kennedy and Richard Helms tried to use compartmentalization to protect the security of their operations, but each had a fatal flaw. RFK had one group in the Justice Department handling his Mafia prosecutions and another group there prosecuting Jimmy Hoffa (the "Get Hoffa Squad"). As members of both groups have told his author, they were completely separate from the handful of aides who assisted Robert Kennedy with the JFK-Almeida coup plan. In hindsight, as Kennedy aides told this author, RFK's compartmentalization might have prevented his organized crime experts from realizing how mob bosses had infiltrated the coup plan—an infiltration made possible because of how Richard Helms organized his CIA operations.[29]

Richard Helms's compartmentalization was fatally flawed in a different way, because he used some of the same officials working on the coup plan—such as Desmond FitzGerald, E. Howard Hunt, Bernard Barker, and David Morales—to also work on the CIA-Mafia plots to assassinate Fidel. Helms might have been simply using the fewest number of people possible to work on his most secret operations. In addition, some exile leaders, like Tony Varona and Manuel Artime, were involved with both the coup plan and Helms's use of the Mafia to try to kill Fidel. Helms probably also realized that the same tight compartmentalization that could keep the JFK-Almeida coup plan secret from even a high-level Soviet mole in the CIA could also keep his unauthorized CIA-Mafia plots away from his Agency superiors, like CIA Director John McCone.

It's important to keep in mind that all the Cuban operations of Richard Helms were just a fraction of his overall responsibilities for the CIA. The United States was locked in a huge, global Cold War at the time, its front extending from Europe's Iron Curtain to Southeast Asia, and the CIA had to deal with additional hot spots in the Middle East, Africa, South America, Central America, South Korea, and more. Helms had to delegate most of the oversight for Cuban operations to Desmond FitzGerald, who had been in his post only since January 1963. As with any large organization, those at the top can't possibly oversee or know about everything happening at the lower levels. In the same way that Richard Helms hid operations from his own CIA Director, Miami Operations Chief David Morales and CIA agent Bernard Barker could easily hide some of their actions from Helms.

Unfortunately for Richard Helms, that's exactly what happened. Helms's whole approach gave David Morales a critical role he could exploit. Because of Morales's relatively high position at the crucial Miami CIA station, because he was working on the CIA-Mafia plots with Rosselli, and because Morales had an official role in part of the JFK-Almeida coup plan, Morales was a key player ideally situated to help Rosselli. Like Rosselli, Morales would eventually confess late in life to having some role in the murder of JFK. Morales made his confession to his attorney and to a lifelong friend after a tirade about how JFK was responsible for the failure of the Bay of Pigs, leaving Morales "to watch all the men he had recruited and trained get wiped out because of Kennedy." Morales then told his friends that "we took care of that son of a bitch" JFK. Congressional investigator Gaeton Fonzi, who worked for both the Senate Church Committee and the House Select Committee on Assassinations (HSCA), uncovered Morales's JFK confession and found it credible. Morales died after being targeted for testimony by the HSCA, before he could testify.[30]

In the fall of 1963, at the same time David Morales was involved with Johnny Rosselli, he worked closely with David Atlee Philips in Miami and Mexico City. Morales had supervised Phillips in Havana and still outranked him, so he was also in a position to direct or influence Phillips's actions with Alpha 66 or in AMWORLD, such as overseeing the CIA assets trying to get into Cuba.[31]

Like David Morales, Bernard Barker also represented a critical intersection between the CIA and the Mafia. However, Barker had worked far longer with organized crime than he had with the Agency. Because Barker was E. Howard Hunt's assistant, he worked on or had access to the most sensitive parts of the top secret JFK-Almeida coup plan: the payments to Almeida and others, helping with Almeida's family, the timing for the coup, which exile leaders were participating, and more. As cited in the previous chapter, Harry Williams said Bernard Barker was "involved" in JFK's assassination along with Barker's boss Trafficante, an assessment buttressed by additional evidence implicating both men.

Just as David Morales's hatred of JFK over of the Bay of Pigs fiasco motivated him to help with JFK's murder, it was also a factor for Bernard Barker. As Harry Williams confirmed, "Barker was very much against JFK," since Barker blamed only JFK for the failure of the Bay of Pigs invasion. That debacle had stopped the climb of Barker's budding CIA career, ensuring that he remained only a low-level agent. Barker had another incentive to end JFK's Presidency, one that he probably also shared with Morales. JFK's use of William Attwood to reach out to Fidel Castro was extremely secret at the time, but Barker managed to find out about it. When Barker and an associate were interviewed about the matter on television after Watergate, they said, "We knew that thing was not going to work." Barker probably found out about the Attwood negotiations from E. Howard Hunt, since

Hunt's superior Richard Helms knew about Attwood. If a lowly CIA agent like Barker knew about JFK's secret peace initiative, then the much higher-ranking David Morales almost certainly did—and neither man wanted to see any type of negotiated peace with Castro.[32]

By the fall of 1963, Santo Trafficante and Carlos Marcello had been methodically working on their plan to assassinate President Kennedy for almost a year, according to Congressional investigators. Historians Richard Mahoney and David Kaiser both documented that Johnny Rosselli had joined their plot to kill JFK early in 1963. The three mob bosses used their ongoing work on the CIA-Mafia plots as a cover, to hide their JFK assassination planning. All three could sometimes meet, safe from any FBI, police, or Justice Department surveillance, at the Safety Harbor Spa outside Tampa, Florida. Usually it was safer for just two of them to meet at a time, and there are many FBI memos about meetings between Marcello and Trafficante in Tampa or near New Orleans. Marcello was never bugged or wiretapped by the FBI in 1963 (despite pressure from RFK), and only one phone of Trafficante's was wiretapped, though he rarely used regular phones for business, preferring to use only random pay phones. Unlike Marcello and Trafficante, Johnny Rosselli was subject to FBI surveillance and wiretaps, though apparently not when he was in Miami on CIA business, since no Miami surveillance records for Rosselli from the summer and fall of 1963 have been released.[33]

The three Mafia chiefs had developed one basic plan that could be used to kill JFK in any of three cities: Chicago, Tampa, or Dallas. The mob bosses had initially planned to assassinate JFK during his motorcade in Chicago (home to Rosselli's mob family) on November 2. The backup plan for Chicago was Tampa, Trafficante's territory, during JFK's November 18, 1963, motorcade. The backup for Tampa would be Dallas, on November 22, 1963, in Marcello's territory. In each city, the Mafia bosses had one or more key people involved in law enforcement, like Richard Cain, the No. 2 man in the Chicago/Cook County Sheriff's Office.*[34]

The Mafia lords also had people working for them who could

* In Tampa, Trafficante's key man on the police force was Sergeant Jack de la Llana of the Intelligence Unit, while the family of Dallas Police Lieutenant Vernon S. Smart said he "worked for the mob" and met weekly with Marcello's Dallas underboss Joe Campisi. While there is no evidence Smart was knowingly involved in the plot to murder JFK, he was in a position to be helpful to Marcello.

feed information—and disinformation, blaming JFK's assassination on Castro—into various intelligence and law enforcement agencies. These included CIA asset Richard Cain; CIA assets working for Marcello, such as David Ferrie and Guy Banister (who also worked with the FBI and Naval Intelligence); CIA agent Bernard Barker, who also worked for Trafficante; and Rosselli's new good friend, CIA official David Morales. All of those involved had their own reasons for wanting JFK to die, in addition to the money they were being paid. Just over a dozen people were knowingly involved in the Mafia's plot to assassinate JFK, about the same number of U.S. officials and aides who knew about Commander Almeida.[35] The Mafia leaders' plot was based in part on what was planned for Fidel in the JFK-Almeida coup plan. Thanks to Morales and Barker, the mob bosses knew how Fidel was supposed be to killed on December 1 at Varadero Beach in Cuba to start the coup: in an open car, in public, by snipers. By using that same basic scenario to kill JFK, they could immediately raise national security alarms among high-ranking U.S. officials who knew about the coup plan. In addition, someone apparently linked to Cuba would be set up ahead of time to "take the fall" for JFK's assassination. Other evidence that David Morales would plant in CIA files ahead of time—and that John Martino and associates of Barker and Artime would spread after JFK's murder—would make it appear that Fidel was behind JFK's murder. The public shooting and the Cuban-linked patsy would prompt an immediate outcry for a U.S. invasion of Cuba in retaliation, an invasion that associates of the godfathers like David Morales knew was ready. [36]

It would probably appear to high-ranking officials in Washington that someone involved in the coup plan was a double agent who had sold out the operation to Fidel, who then retaliated by killing JFK. Even if the United States didn't invade Cuba, national security concerns would prevent U.S. officials from conducting any truly thorough or public investigation for fear of exposing the JFK-Almeida coup plan and triggering another nuclear confrontation with the Soviets over Cuba. Just to make sure those concerns were aroused, information linking JFK's assassination and the coup plan appears to have been planted ahead of time. Even the bullet that would be found in Oswald's gun was linked to the coup plan, using information planted earlier in FBI files. If JFK were murdered under such potentially explosive circumstances, high officials like Richard Helms and J. Edgar Hoover would also have to cover up much crucial information of their own, like Helms's unauthorized CIA-Mafia plots and Hoover's intelligence failures.

The three mob chiefs were essentially going to use the intense secrecy surrounding the JFK-Almeida coup plan to stifle any real investigation of their crime. The mob had already bribed Tony Varona, and a CIA memo withheld from Congressional investigators confirms that Manuel Artime and AMWORLD had also become mobbed up. The memo states that the CIA looked at using the "Mafia" as a way "to cover CIA support . . . to AMWORLD bases" since there were already "rumors of Mafia support of AMWORLD."[37]

According to a CIA memo by John McCone, the date for the JFK-Almeida coup plan had been set for December 1, 1963, ten days after Dallas—something Trafficante or Rosselli could have easily learned from Barker or Morales. The Mafia had nothing to gain by letting the coup go forward while JFK was still alive, since they had been banned from reopening their casinos after the coup. The Mafia had everything to gain—protecting their empires and freedom from RFK's Justice Department—by assassinating JFK before that date, and linking JFK's murder to the top secret coup plan to compromise any investigation. That's why JFK had to be killed while the coup was still secret, which explains why the mob chiefs made three attempts in just three weeks as the coup date drew ever closer.[38]

Though killing JFK was a huge risk, the Mafia bosses had both the motivation and the means to carry out such an operation. Their power, families, and freedom were at stake, and Marcello and Rosselli both faced possible deportation unless the Kennedys' war on the Mafia was stopped. The money at stake was enormous and shows the mob bosses' ability to manage huge, and often ruthless, organizations. Santo Trafficante effectively managed a large portion of the French Connection heroin network that went through numerous Mafia territories in a dozen states and at least four foreign countries. Carlos Marcello's empire alone was reported to have generated as much annual income as the largest American company, over $1 billion ($6 billion in today's dollars). Johnny Rosselli would soon best America's wealthiest businessman, Howard Hughes, in several multimillion-dollar Las Vegas casino deals. In addition, their mob families had a history of literally getting away with murder, from the 1963 hit of a Chicago public official to the 1954 assassination of the Alabama Attorney General-elect in Phenix City.[39]

. . .

Unaware of what the three mob leaders were planning in the fall of 1963, John and Robert Kennedy also dealt with a potential scandal that had important ramifications for both men, as well as for J. Edgar Hoover and future President Lyndon Johnson. J. Edgar Hoover was nearing the mandatory federal retirement age of seventy, and it was no secret that Robert Kennedy wanted to replace the hugely powerful Hoover as FBI Director. JFK had avoided giving Hoover a firm commitment to sign an executive order, which was the only way Hoover could avoid mandatory retirement. Both JFK and RFK looked forward to Hoover's forced retirement early in JFK's next term. However, in October 1963 Hoover first almost exposed—but then agreed to cover up—JFK's liaison with an East German beauty, Ellen Rometsch. Anthony Summers first documented the meetings that resulted in JFK's agreement to keep Hoover on as FBI Director past normal retirement age and into JFK's next term.[40]

Lyndon Johnson's former aide Bobby Baker had first introduced JFK to Rometsch. The press was starting to devote attention to Baker's and Johnson's financial activities in the fall of 1963, using some information initially leaked by RFK. But because what became known as "the Bobby Baker scandal" touched JFK and involved members of both parties, investigations into it would soon be shut down. They had to be, otherwise Nixon and the other potential Republican nominees would have had a field day with the information. Some insiders and observers—including Richard Nixon—have said that JFK was going to drop LBJ from the ticket in 1964, but JFK could hardly dump LBJ because of a scandal in which the President was also involved. In addition, it would have made little sense for JFK to tie himself to LBJ so closely in numerous public events in Texas in November 1963 if he really planned to shed his Vice President a few months later. Given the unpopularity of JFK's civil rights stance in much of the South, the whole point of JFK's Texas trip was to increase his chances of carrying the huge state again in 1964, something that would be impossible if JFK dropped LBJ from the ticket.[41]

On November 21, 1963, Richard Nixon was in Dallas to attend a board meeting of the Pepsi-Cola Company, one of his law firm's clients. To get Nixon his very well-paid position with the New York law firm, Pepsi's CEO Donald Kendall, a major Nixon supporter, had agreed to give the firm most of Pepsi's legal business. Nixon was still something of celebrity, especially in the business world, as was the wife of Pepsi's CEO, actress Joan Crawford. Both Dallas newspapers would report the next day that Nixon and Crawford were the highlights at the fashionable Empire Room nightclub at Dallas's Statler Hilton hotel until late into the night.*[42]

On the morning of November 22, 1963, Harry Williams began his RFK-arranged meeting with CIA officials in Washington, D.C, at an Agency safe house. Writing about that meeting twenty years later in *The Washington Post*, Pulitzer Prize–winning journalist Haynes Johnson said that Williams's work for the Kennedys about "the problem of Cuba . . . had reached an important point." As a result, on that day Williams "participated in the most crucial of a series of secret meetings with top-level CIA and government people." Haynes confirmed in his article that Williams was the Cuban exile leader closest to JFK's administration. As reported by *Vanity Fair* and former FBI agent William Turner, those at the meeting included Harry Williams, E. Howard Hunt, James McCord, and CIA Executive Director Lyman Kirkpatrick.† Richard Helms and Desmond FitzGerald have also been reported as having attended at least a brief part of the meeting. Kirkpatrick, anxious to make sure the coup with Almeida didn't become another Bay of Pigs disaster for the United States and the Agency, asked probing questions, but no problems surfaced and the plan looked ready to go forward.[43]

While the CIA men met with Williams in Washington early on November 22, 1960, JFK was in Fort Worth, where he and Jackie had spent the previous night. That night and that morning JFK seemed preoccupied with assassination, no doubt due to his recent experience in Tampa and having to cancel his Chicago motorcade at the last minute. JFK told Jackie and aide Lawrence O'Donnell, "If somebody

*Conspiracy theories that Nixon and J. Edgar Hoover attended a meeting that night at the home of a Texas multimillionaire, where the assassination of JFK was discussed, have been thoroughly discredited.

†James McCord testified that he never met E. Howard Hunt until 1972. In his 2007 book, *American Spy*, E. Howard Hunt—dogged by false accusations that he was photographed in Dealey Plaza—published a 1976 letter written by James McCord. In the letter, McCord states that "I know that Hunt was not in Dallas" on November 22, 1963. Since Hunt testified he did not go to his CIA office that day, how did McCord "know that Hunt was not in Dallas"?

wants to shoot me from a window with a rifle, nobody can stop it, so why worry about it?" JFK added, "Last night would have been a hell of a night to assassinate a president. I mean it—the rain and the night and we were all getting jostled," as JFK acted out the shooting scenario for Jackie. The couple planned to depart soon for the airport, where they would make the short flight to Dallas's Love Field. From there, the couple would take a motorcade through downtown Dallas, then to the Dallas Trade Mart, where JFK would give a speech. So far, the Texas crowds—in Houston the day before, and in Fort Worth—had been large and warm, and the trip seemed to be going well.[44]

As JFK greeted morning crowds in Fort Worth before flying to Love Field in Dallas, Richard Nixon was already at Love Field, preparing to catch "American Airlines Flight 82" to return to New York City. Later that day, Nixon planned to sign the contract for this 1964 campaign book, which would give him an inside view of the campaigns of his rivals Goldwater and Rockefeller, and let him position himself as the compromise candidate. Nixon already had an inside line on JFK's plans for Cuba, thanks to corrupt former Cuban President Carlos Prio, so he seemed well positioned politically for the following year.[45]

Since he hoped to run against JFK in 1964, Richard Nixon would have been pleased to see the front page of *The Dallas Morning News* before he left Love Field on November 22, 1963. One of the main articles featured "the prediction of former Vice President Nixon that LBJ would be dropped from the ticket in 1964." Since JFK was featuring LBJ prominently on the trip, which would conclude with JFK's visit to LBJ's ranch, Nixon's comment was a good way to rain on JFK's parade. The article also reported Nixon's boast that "I am going to work as hard as I can to get the Kennedys out" in 1964. It's ironic that JFK had planned a similar dig at his possible 1964 rival that evening, in the speech he planned to give in Austin, Texas. JFK's speech included the line "I can testify from my trips to Mexico, Colombia, Venezuela, and Costa Rica that American officials are no longer booed and spat upon south of the border"—a reference to Nixon's earlier treatment in Latin America.[46]

Two and a half hours after Richard Nixon's flight left for New York, Air Force One landed at Love Field. JFK and Jackie saw excited crowds as they disembarked, and then they began their motorcade toward downtown Dallas.

CHAPTER 16

November 22, 1963: Dallas, Washington, New York, Tampa, New Orleans

Richard Nixon learned that President Kennedy had been shot soon after his flight landed in New York City. It's commonly said that all Americans remember where they were when they first heard the tragic news from Dallas, but Nixon appears to be an exception, making it hard to pin down exactly how and when he first heard the news. He gave the most generally accepted account four years later:

> I was in a taxicab when I got the news . . . [The shooting] must have happened just as my plane was landing. My cab was stopped for a light in Queens, and a guy ran over and said, "Have you got a radio? The President's been wounded." I thought, "Oh my god, it must have been one of the [right-wing] nuts."[1]

However, in a later *Esquire* article, Nixon said his taxi "missed a turn somewhere and we were off the highway [when] a woman came out of her house screaming and crying . . . when she saw my face she turned even paler. She told me that John Kennedy had just been shot in Dallas." Another journalist pointed out that Nixon "might have even learned of the shooting before his cab ride." That's because a November 22, 1963, UPI wire photo showing a "glum-looking Nixon [sitting] in what appears to be an airline terminal" was captioned "Shocked Richard Nixon, the former vice president who lost the presidential election to President Kennedy in 1960, is shown Friday after he arrived at Idlewild Airport in New York following a flight from Dallas, Tex., where he had been on a business trip." Oddly, three months later

Nixon denied to the FBI that he had even been in Dallas on November 22, 1963, telling the Bureau he was only there "two days prior to the assassination."[2]

Regardless of how Nixon first learned of JFK's shooting, later accounts added that when Nixon arrived at his posh New York apartment building, "a weeping doorman told him Kennedy was dead." When a writing aide joined Nixon in his apartment "minutes later," Nixon was "very shaken" and indicated, "I didn't have anything to do with creating this"—the climate of hate—since Nixon "was very concerned then that Kennedy had been assassinated by a right-winger and that somehow Nixon would be accused of unleashing political hatred."[3]

Fifteen minutes after gunfire erupted in Dealey Plaza, Robert Kennedy received a call from J. Edgar Hoover informing him that his brother had been shot. RFK was eating lunch by the pool behind his Hickory Hill mansion with his wife, Ethel, and New York's U.S. Attorney, Robert Morgenthau, when he got the news. In a flat tone, Hoover told RFK that he thought it was serious and that he'd call back when he found out more. According to author William Manchester, after RFK hung up he turned toward his guests: His "jaw sagged . . . it seemed that every muscle was contorted with horror. 'Jack's been shot,' he said, gagging, and clapped his hand over his face."[4]

RFK made a flurry of calls: to Parkland Hospital in Dallas and to officials such as Secretary of Defense McNamara (who was getting his information from General Carroll's DIA) and CIA Director John McCone, who was only five minutes away at the Agency's headquarters in Langley, Virginia.[5]

John McCone heard about the shooting from his assistant as he was dining in a small private room beside his office with five CIA officials, including Richard Helms and CIA Executive Director Lyman Kirkpatrick. Helms's own account of that day in his autobiography is self-serving and at best incomplete. He perpetuates the myth that there was nationwide TV coverage of JFK's Dallas trip, writing that "one of McCone's aides who had been following the President's trip to Texas on live TV in a nearby office brought the news of the shooting in Dallas." It's important to stress that there was no live TV coverage of JFK's motorcade in Dallas, let alone in the rest of the country, which is why so many facts about the shooting are still in dispute. Helms's version avoids potentially troubling questions of how and when CIA headquarters was first informed of JFK's shooting.[6]

Helms's usually cool outward demeanor probably didn't reveal his shock upon hearing the news, though it must have affected him even more than the others present. The stunning report had additional resonance for Helms even aside from the JFK-Almeida coup plan, which was known to at least McCone and Kirkpatrick. But of all those present, only Helms knew about the host of unauthorized Castro assassination operations he was running, including at least one proceeding that day. Only Helms—and Desmond FitzGerald—knew that, in the words of a later CIA Inspector General's report, "at the very moment President Kennedy was shot, a CIA officer was meeting with a Cuban agent [Rolando Cubela] in Paris and giving him an assassination device for use against Castro." As more details arrived from Dallas, Helms decided to withhold information about the Paris meeting—and the rest of the ongoing CIA-Mafia plots—from CIA Director McCone and the others in the room.[7]

McCone's lunch meeting had included a discussion of Cuba, reviewing the morning briefing that he, Kirkpatrick, and Richard Helms had given the President's Foreign Intelligence Advisory Board (PFIAB) at the White House. Those PFIAB notes include McCone saying, "The CIA has had a very active operation against Cuba," though an entire paragraph apparently about Cuba is still censored. Though it's unlikely McCone would have revealed a closely held secret like the JFK-Almeida coup plan to an advisory board, the presence of Helms and Kirkpatrick at the meeting means it's possible they might have at least laid the groundwork for what could happen with Cuba in ten days. It's not known if McCone's CIA lunch meeting included discussion of the coup, though the secure setting and the high-level CIA attendees make that a possibility.[8]

When CIA Director McCone first heard JFK had been shot, he checked with the Agency Crisis Watch Committee, whose files about that day have never been made public or given to Congressional investigators. McCone then called Robert Kennedy, who asked McCone to come to his Hickory Hill estate, and McCone complied.[9]

Richard Helms allowed McCone to leave without telling him about any of the unauthorized Cuban operations Helms was still running, most of them basically expansions of the original CIA-Mafia plots. They included the Cubela/AMLASH operation, which even the

CIA's Inspector General would later confirm had an amazing number of links to Santo Trafficante and others involved in the CIA-Mafia plots. Trafficante's longtime bodyguard, Herminio Diaz, had been of interest to Helms's Miami Chief of Station, Ted Shackley, since September 1963, and Diaz was working on a Castro assassination plot set for early December. Johnny Rosselli, supervised by CIA officer David Morales, was continuing his own exile sharpshooter training. Helms had also authorized continuing payments to European assassin recruiter QJWIN (CIA files show his regular monthly salary was paid on November 22, 1963). The only Cuban operation Helms was hiding that wasn't part of the CIA-Mafia plots was his unsanctioned authorization of David Atlee Phillips to continue working on a Castro assassination plot with the JFK-banned Antonio Veciana and Alpha 66.[10]

When Helms made the decision to withhold so much that day from his CIA Director, the die was cast regarding what Helms could reveal—or allow the CIA to reveal—not just for the coming weeks, but for decades. That would apply not just to new President Lyndon Johnson, but also to Richard Nixon after he became President. Helms must have felt tremendous pressure as he realized his career would be finished if his unauthorized schemes came to light.

In retrospect, it's easy to see why Helms had thought he could get away with running his own unauthorized Castro assassination operation without telling JFK, McCone, or RFK. With the impending date for the coup rapidly approaching, everything would come to a head in less than two weeks anyway, and if the Kennedys' coup plan failed, Helms might even be rewarded for having backup plans already in place. However, after JFK's shooting, Helms's efforts suddenly looked extremely problematic and very suspicious.

After McCone had left for RFK's estate, Richard Helms received the news that JFK was dead. When Helms heard that JFK had been shot in an open car, by one or more snipers, his anxiety must have intensified. That's because the way in which JFK was shot mirrored later AMWORLD memos and a passage in David Atlee Phillips's autobiographical novel outline about the CIA's plan to shoot Fidel at Varadero Beach. Phillips later wrote that JFK was shot using "precisely the plan we had devised against Castro [which involved using] a sniper's rifle from an upper floor window of a building on the route where Castro often drove in an open jeep."[11]

Now, just ten days before Almeida's scheduled coup, Helms had to wonder if some aspect of his plans had been turned on JFK. Did Castro somehow retaliate against JFK for the coup plan or for one of Helms's unauthorized operations? Or had someone involved in Helms's own plots turned his sights on JFK instead of Fidel?

When Lee Harvey Oswald surfaced as the prime suspect in JFK's slaying, what had been a horrible situation for Helms turned even worse. John Whitten was Helms's Covert Operations Chief for all of Mexico and Central America. In a detailed report that he wrote soon after JFK's death, one kept classified for thirty years, Whitten said that after "word of the shooting of President Kennedy reached the [CIA] offices . . . when the name of Lee Oswald was heard, the effect was electric." JFK's murder was now tied to someone with CIA connections.[12]

Clearly, a massive intelligence failure had occurred and as essentially the head of CIA operations, Helms was responsible. To Helms, it would have appeared that someone linked to, or even part of, his unauthorized operations had murdered the President. That meant he had to conceal those operations from the public, the press, Congress, McCone, and even the new President, or else the CIA itself would come under suspicion. On a more personal level, the ambitious Helms, who later served as CIA Director under two Presidents, would not only be washed up professionally if any link between his operations and JFK's murder came out, but he could even become a target of suspicion himself. The same would apply to the people working on Helms's unauthorized operations, like FitzGerald, Morales, Phillips, and Hunt, who would have to keep quiet as well if they wanted to continue their careers and avoid suspicion or even prosecution.

The reason "the effect was electric" in CIA offices handling covert operations for Helms "when the name of Lee Oswald was heard" has only become clear in recent years, due to the 4.5 million pages of JFK assassination files released in the 1990s. Once Oswald's background is stripped of the Red Scare attitudes of the early 1960s, the long-known basic facts of his life are remarkably revealing. It was still the height of the Cold War in 1963, and it had been just a year since the tense nuclear standoff of the Cuban Missile Crisis. That atmosphere determined not only how the media and the public perceived the initial reports about Oswald, but also what agencies such as the CIA, DIA, and FBI would release to the public, to investigators, and even to each other.

Early reports focused on the fact that the ex-Marine Lee Harvey Oswald was a former defector to the Soviet Union, which at the time was enough to convict Oswald in the minds of many. However, while the Warren Commission would soon paint Oswald as a confirmed Communist from the time he was a teenager, it's a simple fact that Oswald joined the U.S. Marines in the Nixon-McCarthy 1950s, when teenaged Communists weren't flocking to—or being welcomed by—the Marines. Not only did Oswald enlist, but he'd been so eager that he tried to join a year before he was even old enough. Once in the Marines, Oswald spoke Russian and spouted such love of Russia that his fellow Marines called him "Oswaldskovich," yet not once was he ever disciplined or written up for openly embracing America's Cold War enemy. Instead, the supposedly budding Communist was assigned to a sensitive U-2 spy plane base in Japan. And once Oswald returned from his unusual "defection" to Russia with his new Russian wife, the highly publicized defector promptly got a job at a map firm in Dallas that helped to prepare secret government briefing maps from U-2 spy plane photos. Even more amazing, the well-publicized, recently returned ex–Russian defector Oswald got the job at the height of the Cuban Missile Crisis![13]

The pre-assassination actions of both Oswald and the U.S. government can be understood by looking objectively at his background. Oswald's father died two months before he was born, and his family was poor. Oswald looked up to his two older brothers, both of whom joined the military, one serving in an intelligence service that tried to uncover Communists. The only other father figure in Oswald's life was his uncle Dutz Murret, a bookie for Carlos Marcello. Lee Oswald had an above-average IQ of 118, but learning disabilities and a poor home situation limited his academic achievement. He originally wanted to join the Air Force but couldn't because of a hearing impairment. However, a stint in the New Orleans Civil Air Patrol—where he met David Ferrie, later to become Carlos Marcello's pilot—helped persuade Oswald to join the U.S. Marines. Oswald served at the "Marine Air Control Squadron" at the Atsugi Air Force Base in Japan, which handled U-2 spy plane flights over the Soviet Union. Oswald's fellow Marines there and at other bases said Oswald was involved in intelligence work. While in the Marines, Oswald supposedly taught himself Russian, a notoriously difficult language. When the Marines gave Oswald a Russian language proficiency test on February 25, 1959, he didn't do well, but by the following summer he was fluent in Russian.

His rapid progress could be explained by a long-secret Warren Commission staff memo, which revealed that Oswald "studied at the Monterey School of the Army," now the Defense Language Institute. Author Dick Russell discovered that when Oswald "defected" to Russia, he was one of five young men to do so in a four-month span in 1959, with two more defecting in 1960. Six of these seven returned to the United States, some with Russian wives, like Oswald.[14]

In hindsight, Lee Oswald clearly was trying to be like—or better than—his idol from what all accounts was his favorite TV show, *I Led Three Lives*. That show was based on the best-selling nonfiction book by Herbert Philbrick, who in real life had seemed to be a regular American who had joined the Communist Party—all while actually working for the U.S. government. Philbrick eventually emerged from years of deep undercover work to fame and fortune, which included his best-selling book, a speaking tour, and the TV show. Notes that Oswald wrote in 1963 for a speech he planned to give after his own "big reveal" were found by the FBI after his death. In them, Oswald declares that he has "many personal reasons to know—and therefore hate and mistrust—Communism," a stark contrast to the way Oswald was depicted after JFK's murder. In addition, Naval Intelligence kept Oswald under "tight" surveillance from the time he returned to the United States, hoping to learn how the KGB might try to recruit Oswald or his wife. To remain an attractive prospect for the KGB, Oswald had to maintain the pretense of being a Marxist, and during the Cuban Missile Crisis his job at the U-2 map firm was no doubt intended to make him an irresistible target for Russian agents. However, the KGB didn't bite.[15]

Oswald appears to have come under the influence of David Ferrie again in early 1963, along with Ferrie's sometime employer, New Orleans private detective Guy Banister, the former FBI Chief of Chicago. Both men were working for Carlos Marcello and were also involved with U.S. intelligence. According to New Orleans CIA agent Hunter Leake, both Ferrie and Banister did anti-Castro work for the CIA—and Oswald helped them. Once back in the United States, Oswald avoided real American Communists and pro-Castro activists like the plague. But in early 1963, Oswald joined by mail the Fair Play for Cuba Committee, the tiny group targeted by David Atlee Phillips in 1961 and by the FBI and the CIA in 1963. Guy Banister was a white supremacist involved in many far-right causes, and in

April 1963, Oswald also had some role in a publicity stunt: a shooting involving Banister's fellow far-right reactionary, former General Edwin Walker.[16]

By the summer of 1963, evidence shows that Lee Oswald was preparing for another intelligence assignment. He had moved his family to New Orleans, where—according to seven credible witnesses—Oswald worked for Banister and with Ferrie. According to Banister's secretary, Ferrie took Oswald to an exile training camp near New Orleans, later found to be part of Manuel Artime's AMWORLD operation. Oswald also obtained a huge burst of TV, radio, and newspaper publicity for his one-man Fair Play for Cuba chapter in New Orleans, including a half-hour radio interview, a half-hour radio debate, and a filmed TV interview. It strains credibility that a lone individual like Oswald, not part of any real Communist or left-wing group in New Orleans, could garner that much publicity on his own in a conservative city like New Orleans. However, CIA publicity expert David Atlee Phillips had worked with Guy Banister the previous year and was easily capable of engineering Oswald's amazing run of pro-Castro publicity. Oswald would soon take an exceptionally well-written résumé of his pro-Castro activities to the Cuban and Russian embassies in Mexico City in an attempt to get into Cuba.[17]

But first Oswald had an unusual meeting in Dallas with David Atlee Phillips and Alpha 66 exile leader Antonio Veciana in the first week of September 1963. The meeting was in broad daylight, in what Veciana described as "downtown . . . in the newest building in Dallas . . . in the lobby of an office building [in a very] public place." Phillips was from nearby Fort Worth and still had friends and former classmates in the area, any one of whom could have happened to see Phillips with the soon-to-be-notorious Oswald (which likely indicates that Phillips wasn't knowingly involved in JFK's assassination, as several authors have claimed). Congressional investigator Gaeton Fonzi found Veciana's account of the meeting credible, and even E. Howard Hunt alluded to the meeting several times in his last autobiography. When asked by this author's representatives, Veciana said the topic of conversation was what "we can do to kill Castro." Amazingly, eight years later, when Helms had become CIA Director under President Nixon, Veciana was still working with David Atlee Phillips on yet another Castro assassination attempt.[18]

At the time of the 1963 Phillips-Oswald-Veciana meeting, Veciana's group Alpha 66 had been banned from the Kennedys' coup plan and was not supposed to receive any U.S. support. However, Veciana's best friend Eloy Menoyo—whose exile group was called the SNFE (Second National Front of the Escambray)—was being wooed by Harry Williams for the JFK-Almeida coup plan. Having Oswald meet Veciana may have been a way to link Oswald to the coup plan, as Ferrie had done when he took Oswald to Manuel Artime's small training camp near New Orleans. In 1963, David Morales—who, as noted earlier, admitted he helped assassinate JFK—still outranked David Atlee Phillips and could easily have proposed the meeting to Phillips. To Phillips, Oswald might have seemed simply a good potential U.S. intelligence asset to get into Cuba before the coup.[19]

Soon after meeting with Phillips and Veciana in Dallas, Oswald made an unusual visit to the Cuban and Russian embassies in Mexico City. David Atlee Phillips was the Chief of Cuban Operations at the CIA's Mexico City station, but for at least one sensitive operation declassified files now show that Phillips had a separate chain of command that bypassed the local CIA Station Chief and went straight to CIA headquarters in Washington, to Desmond FitzGerald and Richard Helms. Phillips's special assignment also involved trips to Miami, where David Morales was based, and Morales sometimes traveled to Mexico City.[20]

Whole books and a lengthy Congressional report have been written about the unusual aspects of Oswald's trip to Mexico City, but for our purposes only a few things are key. First is that Oswald visited the Cuban embassy on the same day as two other young men who both had potential links to Manuel Artime, as did Oswald. (One of the two young men would later try to implicate Fidel and the Cubans in JFK's murder.) As explained previously, the CIA was attempting to slip multiple assets into Cuba in the hopes that some might get through. In addition, Oswald's image was captured by the CIA's photo surveillance operation in Mexico City, which was under the control of David Atlee Phillips. However, only unrelated photos of someone else (who looked nothing like Oswald) would be given to the Warren Commission and eventually made public. The Mexico City CIA Station Chief had copies of the real Oswald photos and the HSCA found other evidence that actual photos of Oswald in Mexico City had definitely existed. Finally, someone didn't want Oswald to actually get to Cuba, because five phony calls claiming to be from him were made to the Russian and Cuban embassies. We know these calls, monitored for the CIA, weren't really from Oswald because the person (or persons) making them spoke broken Russian (in which Oswald was fluent) and excellent Spanish (a language Oswald didn't speak). The Mafia had other plans for Oswald, and it had the connections to ensure that his trip to Cuba didn't happen. A Mexican police agency involved with Trafficante's heroin network monitored the Cuban and Russian embassy calls for the CIA, while mobster (and active CIA asset) Richard Cain had formerly bugged a Communist embassy in Mexico City.[21]

At the time of Oswald's visit, a flurry of odd cables flowed between the Mexico City CIA station and CIA headquarters in Washington, along two different paths. The accurate path went to Desmond FitzGerald and Richard Helms. *Washington Post* reporter Jefferson Morley interviewed a former CIA official who said that "CIA records suggested that members of [FitzGerald's staff] seemed to be carefully guarding information about Oswald in the weeks before Kennedy was killed." The person managing both the accurate and inaccurate information about Oswald was Helms's assistant. After JFK's murder, and for almost three decades later, Helms maintained that before the assassination the CIA hadn't even noticed Oswald's embassy visits. Declassified files now show that claim to be completely false, as documented by retired Major John Newman, a noted historian and twenty-year veteran of military intelligence.[22]

The actions of Oswald and the CIA are consistent with Oswald being one of several U.S. intelligence assets the CIA was trying to get into Cuba openly. In fact, a Warren Commission memo, left out of its final Report, showed exactly how Oswald could have been planning to get to Mexico City, and on to Cuba, on November 22, 1963. As an American with a pro-Castro persona, Oswald could have openly walked the streets of Havana or Varadero Beach, talking to Cubans and low-level officials, unlike the CIA's exile agents smuggled into Cuba by boat. Additionally, Oswald's time in Russia would have made it possible to blame any problem he had in Cuba on the Russians, something CIA notes by William Harvey indicated was always essential for an assassination mission. After analyzing many recently declassified files, Naval War College professor and historian David Kaiser concluded in 2008 that "in all probability, Oswald's attempt to reach Cuba via Mexico City . . . was designed to give him an opportunity to assassinate Castro." This author differs slightly, concluding that Oswald was part of an operation against Fidel when he was in Mexico City, and after his failure to get into Cuba, Oswald had been told—probably by Banister and Ferrie—that he still was part of such an operation. The very attributes that made Oswald valuable to the CIA also made him useful to the Mafia in another way.[23]

During Oswald's work with Guy Banister and David Ferrie in the summer of 1963, he had been linked to three of the "five fingers" exile leaders for the JFK-Almeida coup plan. As mentioned earlier, Oswald visited Artime's small training camp outside New Orleans and met with Veciana, the partner of Kennedy-backed exile leader Eloy Menoyo. In addition, Oswald had been linked to exile leader Manolo Ray via an odd visit by Oswald in September 1963 to Sylvia Odio, a female member of Ray's group. Congressional investigator Gaeton Fonzi extensively documented this meeting. (That provocative visit appears to have been engineered with the assistance of two of Trafficante's men: John Martino, who'd met Odio's sister in Dallas, and Rolando Masferrer, whose brother lived in Odio's apartment complex.)[24]

By connecting Oswald to several parts of the JFK-Almeida coup plan, Marcello's men Banister and Ferrie helped ensure that the CIA and other agencies would have to cover up much information to protect the sensitive coup plan. An FBI memo confirms that Ferrie himself knew about "Attorney General Robert Kennedy [and] plans for a Cuban second invasion." Guy Banister knew as well, since a close associate of his wrote about parts of the highly secret plan in August 1963, describing "Kennedy Administration planning" for Cuba in which Castro "would be the fall guy in a complete reorganization for the regime [to make it] free of Soviet influence." Banister's friend even knew that JFK's "new government" for Cuba would include "such men as . . . Manolo Ray." However, authorities would soon seek David Ferrie himself for having a role in JFK's murder, an accusation that would also be made against Guy Banister.[25]

Lee Oswald wasn't the only young man involved with the Fair Play for Cuba Committee trying to get into Cuba in the fall of 1963. Another was Gilberto Policarpo Lopez, a Cuban exile who had recently moved to Tampa. Lopez had at least eighteen parallels to Oswald in 1963, ranging from leaving his wife around the same time Oswald left his wife to getting into fist fights over his supposed pro-Castro sympathies (while at other times appearing anti-Castro). Tampa law enforcement officials also believed Lopez to be an asset or informant for some U.S. government agency, though they weren't sure which one. Just as Oswald got a job near JFK's motorcade route through Dallas, Lopez was working near the route of JFK's motorcade in Tampa four days before his trip to Dallas. The day before JFK's Tampa motorcade, someone attempted to link Lopez to Oswald. And on November 22, 1963, Lopez was in Texas trying to get to Mexico City, and then on to Cuba—though unlike Oswald, Lopez was successful.[26]

Oswald also had several provocative parallels to Thomas Vallee, the ex-Marine arrested in Chicago with a rifle and ammo the same day JFK had to cancel his Chicago motorcade because of an assassination plot. At the same time Oswald got a job in a warehouse overlooking JFK's Dallas motorcade route, Thomas Valle got a job in a warehouse overlooking JFK's Chicago motorcade route. Just before that, after Oswald returned to Texas from Mexico City, he moved into a YMCA at the same time Vallee moved into a YMCA in Chicago. Around the same time Oswald was visiting Artime's Cuban exile training camp near New Orleans and talking to exile leader Veciana about assassinating Castro, Vallee was at a Cuban exile training camp in Long Island, helping train men for a Castro assassination mission. Like Oswald, Vallee told some associates that he was working for U.S. intelligence.[27]

Richard Helms would not have to bear all the responsibility for covering up information about Oswald, as he would for his own Castro assassination plots. Lee Oswald was a "former" Marine, and thus the ultimate responsibility of Marine and Naval Intelligence and General Carroll's DIA. Moreover, the testimony of CIA official John Whitten about Oswald's name being "electric" within the covert operations offices of the Agency indicates Oswald's intelligence role was widely enough known that John McCone, the CIA Director, would also have had a role in the matter.

CIA Director McCone later told author William Manchester his thoughts on the afternoon of JFK's murder: "You wonder who could be responsible . . . was this an international plot?" In the CIA's copy of the original transcript of McCone's interview, the CIA Director admitted "this was a question that plagued us day and night for a long time." McCone said that after Oswald surfaced as the prime suspect, "we went to work in depth on this thing to determine whether Oswald had any association [with] or was receiving direction from any external [source]. And there were days there where we didn't know." In the weeks after Dallas, McCone received many disturbing reports linking the Soviets or Fidel Castro to JFK's murder, all of which turned out not to be true. There's no evidence that McCone considered the possibility that false information had been deliberately fed to the Agency.[28]

McCone didn't know that Helms was withholding a wealth of critical data from him, and when McCone met with Robert Kennedy at Hickory Hill, he was talking to someone else who'd been denied the same crucial information. Not long after McCone's arrival, RFK received a call telling him his brother was dead. McCone described RFK as "being just aghast, as though he had received unbelievable news," though RFK quickly regained his composure and remained stoic.[29]

McCone said that he met with Robert Kennedy for almost two hours on November 22, 1963. As Robert later told his top Hoffa investigator, Walter Sheridan, "At the time, I asked McCone . . . if they [the CIA] had killed my brother, and I asked him in a way that he couldn't lie to me, and [McCone said] they hadn't." Despite this reassurance, McCone (and RFK) didn't know that Helms was continuing the CIA-Mafia plots, or that CIA agents like Morales and Barker were also working with mob bosses like Rosselli and Trafficante. McCone also told RFK at some point that he "thought there were two people involved in the shooting."[30]

Timing makes it almost impossible for Oswald's name to have triggered RFK's question to McCone (Hoover wouldn't call RFK with Oswald's name until thirty-one minutes after McCone left his meeting with RFK). More likely, Robert asked McCone because both men knew that Almeida's coup, which could have involved Fidel Castro being assassinated in an open car, was only ten days away. However, RFK's suspicions on the afternoon of November 22 were not directed at Castro, but instead at the CIA, the Mafia, and the possibility that someone involved with the JFK-Almeida coup plan had used some part of that operation to kill JFK instead of Castro.[31]

RFK and McCone would have discussed what to do about the coup, and what to tell incoming President Lyndon Johnson, who had been completely excluded from its planning. Starting the next day, McCone met with LBJ every day, sometimes several times a day, for the next few weeks. On November 22—and for the years that followed—both

RFK and McCone wanted to preserve Commander Almeida's life and his position, since the odds were overwhelmingly against the United States ever finding another Cuban official with Almeida's power and prestige willing to risk his life to overthrow Fidel.[32]

Avoiding the exposure of Almeida also meant continuing to cover up other information, like the Chicago and Tampa assassination attempts. On the afternoon of November 22, that was pretty much Robert Kennedy's call to make, and something he might have discussed with McCone. Revealing those attempts, so similar to what happened in Dallas, would have led to questions about why they had been kept secret, inviting investigations that could have exposed the coup plan. The Chicago and Tampa attempts were kept secret on November 22 for the same reasons they had been kept secret in the first place, and that lid of secrecy would be slammed even tighter the following day when word about Tampa leaked in one small article.

From the afternoon of November 22 forward, RFK would remain trapped by his desire to learn what had happened to his brother without revealing the coup plan and exposing Almeida or his family to harm—a task eventually assumed by some of his close associates. RFK made at least two phone calls that day that showed where his suspicions lay. Even before McCone arrived at RFK's estate, the Attorney General had called CIA headquarters. RFK spoke to a high-level CIA official at headquarters about the shooting of JFK and demanded to know: "Did your outfit have anything to do with this horror?"* [33]

Robert Kennedy made another call that afternoon, to "Julius Draznin in Chicago, an expert on union corruption for the National Labor Relations Board." Author David Talbot says that RFK "asked Draznin to look into whether there was any Mafia involvement in the killing of his brother." Draznin turned in his report five days later, three days after Ruby had shot Oswald in the basement of Dallas Police headquarters before live television cameras. Draznin's report "detailed Ruby's labor racketeering activities [and] wide syndicate contacts." RFK later said that "when he saw Ruby's phone records, 'The list was almost a duplicate of the people I called before the [Senate] Rackets Committee.'"[34]

. . .

*This account comes from George Bailey and Seymour Freidin, the *New York Herald Tribune*'s foreign-affairs editor, later revealed by Jack Anderson to have been a paid CIA informant in the 1960s. Author David Talbot believes Freidin got his information about RFK's call directly from one of his CIA contacts.

Before word came that JFK had been shot, Harry Williams's important meeting in Washington with CIA officials about the coup plan had taken a long lunch break. Williams ate separately from the CIA officials, some of whom returned to have lunch with John McCone at CIA headquarters. Before Williams returned to the CIA safe house to resume the meeting in the afternoon, he learned from new reports of the shooting in Dallas.[35]

As his meeting with the CIA men resumed, word came that JFK was dead. Only two CIA officials were present for the afternoon session, E. Howard Hunt and a very "high official" of the Agency, who a Kennedy aide later said was CIA Executive Director Lyman Kirkpatrick. In the morning session, Williams said he felt that "we were really advancing," but in the afternoon the atmosphere was totally different. Williams said Kirkpatrick was very "upset" and seemed suspicious of Williams. The gathering soon broke up, since the planned coup was clearly on hold in the wake of the tragedy in Dallas. Kirkpatrick went back to CIA headquarters to meet with Helms and John McCone at 5 PM.[36]

Harry Williams headed back to his room at Washington's Ebbitt Hotel, where earlier he had arranged to meet journalist Haynes Johnson. Along with Manuel Artime, Williams had been working with Haynes on the RFK-approved Bay of Pigs book. Before Haynes arrived at the Ebbitt Hotel, Williams had placed a call to RFK. Robert Kennedy called Williams back shortly after Haynes arrived. A *Vanity Fair* investigation put RFK's call at or just before 4 PM (Eastern), fifteen minutes before the first network news reports of Oswald's arrest. It could not have happened even a minute later, because at 4:01 PM, RFK received a phone call from J. Edgar Hoover first alerting him to Oswald's capture.[37]

After RFK had spoken on the phone to Harry Williams for a few moments, Williams mentioned that Haynes Johnson was with him. RFK asked to speak to Haynes, who writes that "Robert Kennedy was utterly in control of his emotions when he came on the line, and sounded almost studiedly brisk as he said: 'One of your guys did it.'"[38]

It's important to stress that both Haynes Johnson and Williams agree that RFK said "one of your guys did it"—killed JFK—to Haynes, not to Williams. Haynes confirmed that to this author in 1992 and again in May 2007. Williams said RFK never voiced any suspicion like that to him on that day or any other, and they remained friends until RFK's murder. A close Kennedy aide who knew RFK, Haynes, and Williams backed up Williams's account.[39]

Haynes wrote that he assumed at the time that RFK had received an early FBI or Secret Service report that "had identified Lee Harvey Oswald as being involved with the anti-Castro group." However, the tight timing makes it uncertain if RFK had even heard Oswald's name by the time he spoke to Haynes. Even J. Edgar Hoover didn't learn Oswald's name until 3:50 PM (Eastern). That means it's probable that RFK's reaction and comment to Haynes was due not to Oswald's name, but to whatever feeling or clue that had caused him to question McCone a short time earlier, most likely the fact that JFK was shot by one or more snipers while riding in an open car, like the plan for Castro in a later AMWORLD memo. In any event, the evidence indicates that the link RFK had in mind was Artime or someone in his AMWORLD organization. That would explain why RFK would make the "your guys" comment to Haynes and not Williams, since there had been recent friction between Williams and Artime. Haynes later wrote that within a year or so after JFK's death he heard that Artime was involved in the drug trade in Miami.[40]

At 4:01 PM on November 22, 1963—only an hour after Oswald's arrival at Dallas police headquarters, and just ten minutes after J. Edgar Hoover learned Oswald's name—Hoover was able to tell Robert Kennedy that he "thought we had the man who killed the President," and that Oswald was "not a communist." Hoover probably knew that because the FBI had assisted Naval Intelligence with its tight surveillance on Oswald, especially in landlocked cities like Dallas, where Naval Intelligence had few assets. This information almost slipped out right after the assassination, when James Hosty, the Dallas FBI agent assigned to Oswald, allegedly told Dallas police "officer Jack Revill on November 22 . . . that Oswald . . . had been under observation. When Revill protested that the information had not been shared with the Dallas police, he was reminded of the FBI policy forbidding the sharing of information pertaining to espionage."[41]

In New York City, Richard Nixon placed a call to FBI Director J. Edgar Hoover at 4:18 PM, wanting to know the inside story. Nixon asked, "What happened? Was it one of the right-wing nuts?" Hoover told him, "No, it was a Communist." An aide with Richard Nixon said that "Nixon was somewhat relieved by the news." It's interesting that Hoover told Nixon that Oswald "was a Communist," when just minutes earlier, he'd told RFK Oswald was "not a communist."[42]

After talking to Hoover, Richard Nixon and his aide prepared brief remarks that Nixon delivered to a television news crew, saying that "the greatest tribute we can pay to his memory is in our everyday lives to do everything we can to reduce the forces of hatred which drive men to do such terrible deeds." Nixon also wrote a cordial sympathy note to Jackie, saying that "fate made Jack and me political opponents" but "we were personal friends from the time we came to the Congress together in 1947."[43]

The circumstances of President Kennedy's assassination have been the subject of endless debate, generating many hundreds of books, thousands of articles, and dozens of documentaries (including two produced by NBC News based on the work of this author). The subject of JFK's murder has been extraordinarily controversial, in large part because so much crucial information was withheld from the public, the press, and investigators at the time and for decades that followed on grounds of national security. However, thanks to seven government investigations since the Warren Commission, today we know much more than in 1963, 1972, or at any time prior to the release of 4.5 million pages of JFK assassination files in the mid-to-late 1990s (some of which weren't processed or published until 2009).

The remainder of this chapter, and the next, focuses on parts of the JFK assassination story that are important for understanding Watergate. They concentrate on the actions of key Watergate figures—from Richard Helms to Bernard Barker—so that their motivations are clear, both in 1963 and in 1972 (and beyond). However, there isn't space in this book, or any normal-sized book, to provide all of the documentation for that story, including relevant quotes from the thousands of records at the National Archives. That was done in this author's two books with Thom Hartmann dealing with JFK's murder and the JFK-Almeida coup plan—*Ultimate Sacrifice* (2006) and *Legacy of Secrecy* (2009)—each over nine hundred pages, with a combined total of almost four thousand endnotes documenting sources. That information, and more, is used to briefly tell the basic story in the following two chapters. For those wanting more information or extensive documentation, additional resources are listed in this endnote.[44]

. . .

On November 22, 1963, the circumstances of JFK's shooting in Dealey Plaza were still unclear as details and testimony continued to emerge. Much evidence clearly shows that JFK had been hit once in the throat from the front, leaving a small entrance wound; once in the back, almost six inches below his collar; plus his horrible, fatal head wound. Texas Governor John Connally was struck by one bullet, but it was physically impossible for his wounds to have been caused by any of the bullets that struck JFK. In addition, at least one bullet missed JFK's limousine, hitting a curb on the other side of the Plaza and knocking up concrete that struck a bystander. That meant at least five shots were fired; later acoustic analysis by the House Select Committee on Assassinations found evidence for at least four and as many as seven shots. Most "ear witnesses" in the plaza gave estimates ranging from two to five shots, many depending on whether they were standing nearer to the "grassy knoll" (to the front right of JFK's limousine) or the Texas School Book Depository (to the right rear of JFK's motorcade).[45]

This book cannot cover all of the details about the shooting, but several facts are important for the story of Watergate.* It's well documented that many people—including three Secret Service agents in the motorcade, Dallas Police Chief Jesse Curry, and Sheriff Bill Decker—thought the shots came from the picket fence on the grassy knoll (behind the fence was a parking lot for the Dallas Sheriff's Office, and behind that, a railroad yard). Dallas Patrolman Bobby Hargis parked his motorcycle and headed up the grassy knoll. Dallas Deputy Sheriff Harold Elkins said he "immediately ran to the area [of the knoll] between the railroads and the Texas School Book Depository." Dallas Deputy Harry Weatherford "heard a loud report, which . . . sounded as if it came from the railroad yard." After hearing two more shots, he began "running towards the railroad yards where the sound seemed to come from."[46]

Dallas Deputy Seymour Weitzman ran to the knoll after hearing the shots. He was one of several law enforcement personnel who saw someone behind the picket fence claiming to be a Secret Service agent, even though no real Secret Service agents were stationed there, or anywhere on the ground in Dealey Plaza. Dallas Police Officer Joe Smith ran to the knoll after hearing a woman scream, "They're shooting

*Heavily documented, lengthy minute-by-minute and hour-by-hour accounts can be found in this author's *Legacy of Secrecy* and *Ultimate Sacrifice.*

the President from the bushes!" Once Officer Smith was behind the fence, he noticed "the lingering smell of gunpowder." Smith noticed a man near one of the cars, and, as he later testified to the Warren Commission, Smith pulled his pistol on him. The man then "showed me that he was a Secret Service agent." Smith later explained that the credentials "satisfied me and the deputy sheriff" who had joined him. The Deputy, Seymour Weitzman, confirmed in his Warren Commission testimony that he had met the fake Secret Service agent. Officer Smith later explained his regret at allowing the phony agent to leave, because—instead of looking like a typically clean-cut, suit-and-tie Secret Service agent—this man "had on a sports shirt and sports pants. But he had dirty fingernails and hands that looked like an auto mechanic's hands."[47]

Years later, in April 1975, journalist Michael Canfield talked to retired Deputy Seymour Weitzman, who'd "had a nervous breakdown" soon after the arrest of the Watergate burglars. Canfield interviewed Weitzman in Dallas at "a home for aged war veterans." Canfield asked that Weitzman's doctor be present during the interview, but Canfield said that "Weitzman's memory seemed clear and sharp." Weitzman described the man who claimed to be a Secret Service agent, saying the man "produced credentials and told him everything was under control." Deputy Weitzman said the man was of "medium height, [with] dark hair and wearing a light windbreaker." Canfield then "showed him a photo of Sturgis [Fiorini] and [Bernard] Barker" because there had been speculation that Fiorini and E. Howard Hunt had been photographed in Dealey Plaza after JFK's murder.* Instead of reacting to Fiorini's photo, Weitzman "immediately stated, 'Yes, that's him,' pointing to Bernard Barker." Just to be sure, "Canfield asked, 'Was this the man who produced the Secret Service credentials?' Weitzman responded, 'Yes, that's the same man.'" Weitzman even said he'd be willing "to make a tape recorded statement for official investigators." The next day he recorded a statement for Canfield, by phone, in which he reaffirmed the Barker identification. However, skeptics could say that Weitzman's age and emotional illness make his identification questionable.[48]

* Claims that Hunt and Fiorini were two of the "three tramps" photographed in Dealey Plaza were investigated by the Rockefeller Commission and the House Select Committee on Assassinations, and found to be groundless. The identities of the actual tramps were later released by the Dallas Police. This author went to Dealey Plaza, where he confirmed the conclusions of the two government committees.

More recently, another Dealey Plaza witness also identified a photo of Bernard Barker as being the "Secret Service agent" he encountered on the grassy knoll at the time of the shooting. Three witnesses—Jean Hill, soldier Gordon Arnold, and Malcolm Summers—also saw what they thought were Secret Service agents on the knoll. Malcolm Summers, who gave a statement to authorities on the day of the assassination, explained in 1988 to "the PBS program *Nova* [that] he encountered a man with a gun on the knoll." Over ten years later, when researchers showed him a photo of Bernard Barker, Malcolm Summers identified Barker as the armed man he encountered on the knoll moments after JFK had been assassinated. (Fake Secret Service agents were also seen away from the grassy knoll—Dallas Police Sergeant D.V. Harkness talked to two men behind the Texas School Book Depository who claimed to be Secret Service agents.)[49]

What about Bernard Barker's own statements about his whereabouts on November 22, 1963? Michael Canfield was party to a lawsuit involving E. Howard Hunt in which he and his coauthor obtained a sworn deposition from Barker. When their attorney asked Barker where he was on November 22, 1963, Barker initially remarked, "This is a question that came up during the Watergate Hearing." A review of Barker's Watergate testimony reveals no such questioning, but Barker could have been asked by an investigator privately, perhaps after Johnny Rosselli's secret testimony helped to bring the JFK assassination into the Watergate investigation.[50]

In Barker's deposition, he said that "I was working for the Agency, they know exactly everywhere I was, I reported to them daily." Barker was soon forced to clarify that he "didn't report necessarily every day, but just about every day I would get a call or assignment." That's not supported by the released files on Barker, but they also don't reflect his work as Hunt's assistant. Much of Barker's reporting consisted of calling in, which he could easily do from another city. In addition, the CIA would know about Barker's travel only if he told them or asked for reimbursement.[51]

Barker claimed to be at home watching television at the time of the assassination, though he said no one but his family and friends could vouch for him that day. The attorney questioning Barker then "asked what soap opera he was watching at the time," and Barker replied that "he could not remember." The attorney then asked if Barker "heard of the assassination via a news flash." But Barker responded, "No," saying, "I think I saw the parade, how the whole thing happened."[52]

If Barker "saw . . . how the whole thing happened," he didn't see it on live TV, or even on the news later that night, because the motorcade wasn't broadcast live, even in Dallas. The Zapruder film so well known today wasn't shown on TV at all until almost twelve years after JFK's murder, and at the time of Barker's deposition, the film had been shown on TV only a handful of times. In addition, the rarely televised film was not the bright, colorful, and sharp restored version we're now used to, but a grainy, dark copy of the somewhat fuzzy eight-millimeter film that looked nothing like the high-quality videotape or sixteen-millimeter news footage shown on TV at the time.[53]

We find interesting—but not conclusive—the identifications of Barker in Dealey Plaza by Deputy Weitzman and Malcolm Summers, as well as Barker's deposition. If Barker was in Dallas on November 22, it would not have been as a shooter; Carlos Marcello told FBI informant Jack Van Laningham he had imported professionals for that. But someone like Barker would have been very useful in keeping bystanders and law enforcement away from the area behind the fence on the knoll.[54]

Richard Helms had more suspicions about the possible involvement of CIA personnel in JFK's death than he ever acknowledged to the Warren Commission or to any of the Congressional investigations. In a rarely noted television interview in 1992, Helms admitted that "we checked [to] be sure that nobody [with the CIA] had been in Dallas on that particular day [of JFK's assassination]." Helms said they not only checked "at the time" but later, "when the Warren Commission was sitting." Those investigations have never been released, so there's no way to know if Helms suspected Barker or other agents.[55] Harry Williams never knew any of the preceding information about Weitzman, Summers, Helms, or Barker's deposition, but he told this author in 1992 that he "wouldn't be surprised if Barker was in Dallas when JFK was shot."[56]

Of the three Mafia bosses who later made credible confessions to JFK's murder, the actions of Carlos Marcello and Santo Trafficante that day are well documented. Almost no confirmed information about Johnny Rosselli's whereabouts has emerged, since sketchy, unconfirmed reports placing Rosselli in Dallas lack supporting evidence or credibility.[57]

On the early afternoon of November 22, 1963, in a packed federal courtroom in New Orleans, Carlos Marcello was listening to the judge charging his jury. One hour after the shooting in Dallas, the judge got a note from the bailiff and then announced to the stunned courtroom that JFK had been shot and might be dead. The judge declared an immediate recess, and Carlos Marcello and his pilot, David Ferrie—who'd been sitting with him—left the courtroom.

Court resumed an hour and a half later, at 3 PM (Central), though RFK's Justice Department prosecutor for the case, John Diuguid, told this author he recalls that David Ferrie was no longer with Marcello. The jury reached a "not guilty" verdict in less than fifteen minutes. In addition to threatening the government's main witness during the trial, Marcello had bribed a key juror, who later boasted that "he had also convinced several of his fellow jurors to vote not guilty." With no conviction, there would be no deportation for Marcello, so the godfather, his family, and his supporters all headed out for a big celebration.[58]

However, Marcello had to miss his own party because of several problems. First, Oswald was still alive. In addition, David Ferrie's library card had reportedly been found on Oswald when he was arrested and accusations about the assassination were made to authorities by one of Guy Banister's employees. Those problems for the godfather would be resolved when Marcello's nightclub manager Jack Ruby murdered Oswald two days later. Ferrie would be arrested the day after Oswald's murder, but Guy Banister's clout as a former FBI Chief of Chicago—and his intelligence work for the CIA—would help to resolve Ferrie's arrest the following day.[59]

On the afternoon of November 22, 1963, Frank Ragano—the attorney Santo Trafficante shared with Jimmy Hoffa—received a call from the elated Teamsters President, who said, "Did you hear the good news? They killed the son-of-a-bitch bastard."[60]

In Tampa that evening, Ragano joined the usually reclusive Santo Trafficante at the International Inn, where JFK had given a speech just four days earlier. The hotel's posh restaurant had fewer than a dozen customers besides Trafficante, Ragano, and Ragano's girlfriend. Trafficante had not yet heard from Marcello about the problems with Ferrie and Banister, and with so few people around, the normally cautious Trafficante was far more publicly effusive than usual. Ragano says that Trafficante hugged and kissed him on the cheeks as the Tampa godfather gloated about JFK, saying, "The son of a bitch is dead."

According to Ragano, Trafficante's face was "wreathed in joy" as he boasted, "We'll make big money out of this and maybe go back to Cuba."[61]

Ragano wrote that he and an ebullient Trafficante raised their glasses in a toast "as Santo said merrily, 'For a hundred years of health and to John Kennedy's death.'" Ragano's girlfriend was horrified and "she rushed out of the restaurant" in tears, while Ragano continued celebrating with Trafficante.[62]

As night fell in Washington, D.C., on November 22, 1963, Robert Kennedy went to Bethesda Naval Medical Center along with Jackie and a caravan that included the hearse with JFK's body. During the twenty-minute ride, RFK heard Jackie's account of the shooting. At Bethesda, the man really calling the shots was Robert Kennedy, from the family suite on the hospital's seventeenth floor. Robert was part of a group that included Jackie as well as JFK aides Dave Powers and Kenneth O'Donnell. RFK was no doubt shocked when he heard what Powers and O'Donnell had seen from their vantage point in the motorcade, in the limo directly behind JFK's. As Powers told this author's investigator—and as Powers and O'Donnell both confirmed to former House Speaker Tip O'Neill—they clearly saw shots from the front, from the grassy knoll. Powers and O'Donnell had known and worked with RFK for years; the Attorney General would have trusted their observations. In addition, White House physician Admiral George Burkley—the only doctor at Bethesda who had also seen JFK at Parkland—later stated that he believed JFK had been killed by more than one gunman. All of this presented a dilemma for RFK: If Oswald had been shooting from the rear, as Hoover and the news were now reporting, who had been shooting from the front?[63]

Entire books have been written about JFK's autopsy, which several government commissions studied over the course of thirty-five years, yet substantial controversies remain. The location and size of wounds on some autopsy X-rays and photos don't match what others show, or what some at Parkland or Bethesda observed. Even worse, crucial evidence is missing, ranging from photos and tissue samples to JFK's brain. At the root of these controversies is the fact that Robert Kennedy controlled the autopsy.[64]

Only a few basic facts about the autopsy are not in dispute. All agree that the Bethesda doctors didn't realize JFK had been shot in the throat, since a tracheotomy incision obscured that wound. The Bethesda doctors did find JFK's small back wound, so they initially assumed he had been shot once in the back and once in the head, and that Connally had been hit by a separate shot. Not until the next day, Saturday, did lead autopsy physician Dr. James Humes learn about the throat wound, and he burned his first draft of the autopsy report on Sunday, November 24. Beyond those key points, much has been disputed over the years and remains controversial, ranging from what the autopsy doctors did or didn't do (and why) to what type of casket JFK arrived in.*[65]

Accounting for much of the controversy were the national security implications of the autopsy, a nightmare scenario beyond what had originally been contemplated for the Cuba Contingency Plans that Alexander Haig and others had been working on. Oswald was still alive, so the official results would be part of a public trial—so there are many indications a hasty "national security" autopsy was performed before the "official" autopsy.[66]

What is well documented is what happened after the autopsy: JFK's body and funeral arrangements were put in the hands of Cyrus Vance's two trusted aides, Alexander Haig and Joseph Califano. Haig has written that he "was assigned the duty of helping with the preparations for the President's funeral [and] handling details concerning the burial site." Califano wrote that after JFK's murder, he went to the Pentagon and met Vance, who put him in charge of arranging JFK's burial at Arlington National Cemetery and meeting RFK there the next day.[67]

Califano and Haig have always been careful to distance themselves from the most sensitive parts of Vance's work on RFK's plans to eliminate Castro, and neither ever admitted to knowing about the JFK-Almeida coup plan. Harry Williams confirmed that Al Haig did know about Commander Almeida. However, declassified files confirm that Califano and Haig worked on the Cuba Contingency Plans for dealing with the possible "assassination of American officials." Vance's use of Califano and Haig makes sense even if Califano had not yet been told about the JFK-Almeida coup plan, since Vance knew he could count on both men if any national security problems arose.[68]

*For book-length accounts of JFK's autopsy, see *In the Eye of History,* by William Matson Law, and *Best Evidence,* by David Lifton. This author detailed much of the most compelling evidence in *Legacy of Secrecy* and *Ultimate Sacrifice*.

In fact, when a problem did occur, Haig showed how information could be destroyed for reasons of national security. In his autobiography, Haig wrote that "very soon after JFK's death, an intelligence report crossed my desk. In circumstantial detail, it stated that Oswald had been seen in Havana in the company of Cuban intelligence officers several days before the events in Dallas . . . the detail—locale, precise notations of time, and more—was very persuasive. I was aware that it would not have reached so high a level if others had not judged it plausible . . . I walked it over to my superiors . . . 'Al,' said one of them, 'you will forget, as from this moment, that you ever read this piece of paper, or that it ever existed.' The report was destroyed." Haig didn't realize that many similar reports were later shown to be false, and most were connected to associates of David Morales, Johnny Rosselli, Santo Trafficante, Manuel Artime, and David Atlee Phillips.[69]

Alexander Haig, Richard Helms, and the CIA weren't the only ones in Washington who needed to hide information from the press, public, and investigators to protect national security—and their own reputations. A confidential Naval Intelligence source, who helped to compile reports of the "tight surveillance" of Oswald since his return to the United States from Russia, said that "on the day of the assassination," he and a coworker "were called back to their office in Washington." On orders from their commander, they "destroyed and sanitized lots of the Oswald file." Confirmation for such document destruction comes from FBI memos describing the Bureau's own interviews with Marines who had served with Oswald. However, the FBI agents discovered that some of them had earlier been interviewed by Naval Intelligence—but those reports were all missing, leading an FBI agent to say in a memo, "Perhaps they have been destroyed."[70]

The Naval Intelligence file the source handled in the fall of 1963 concerned only the close surveillance of Oswald. According to the source, "A note on the top of the file jacket said to contact the CIA if Oswald was arrested or got into any trouble. There was a name and some sort of code given for someone at the CIA." The one person at the CIA who is alleged to have been in contact with Oswald is David Atlee Phillips.

Naval Intelligence and its close counterpart, Marine Intelligence (G-2), were components of the Defense Intelligence Agency (DIA) headed by General Joseph Carroll, who knew about the JFK-Almeida coup plan. A journalist told former Senate investigator Bernard Fensterwald that "Oswald had connections to an 'intelligence service . . . called the Defense Intelligence Agency . . . The General [who] supposedly made the arrangements [was] General Joe Carroll, founder of the DIA . . . The Army was going nuts over Oswald's part in the assassination.'" Army Intelligence would destroy its entire Oswald file in 1973, after Watergate.[71]

To show how sensitive Oswald's military file was, on the day of JFK's death Naval Intelligence considered withholding information in it from General Carroll. When Carroll asked to see Oswald's Naval Intelligence file, a memo says they were "cautious about passing [the] file to DIA." It took an order from Joint Chiefs Chairman General Maxwell Taylor—who, like Carroll, knew about the coup plan—to allow General Carroll to see the file, but even he was not permitted to keep a copy. It's hard to say if Naval Intelligence was initially reluctant to share the file for national security reasons or because by that time it was already incomplete.[72]

As for General Maxwell Taylor, his concerns on November 22 were more global. The DEFCON alert status indicates the degree of U.S. defense readiness, and declassified files show that the level was raised to DEFCON 4, from 5, an hour and twenty minutes after JFK was shot. One command even raised it to DEFCON 3. FBI agent James Hosty said that just after Oswald's arrest, "fully armed warplanes were sent screaming toward Cuba." Peter Dale Scott wrote that a "cable [had been issued] from US Army Intelligence in Texas, dated November 22, 1963, telling the US Strike Command (falsely) that Oswald had defected to Cuba in 1959 and was 'a card-carrying member of the Communist Party.'" Clearly, someone had been feeding erroneous intelligence into the system, stories similar to the false tales that John Martino would soon spread to the public. Luckily, cooler heads prevailed, and "just before [the U.S. planes] entered Cuban airspace, they were hastily called back." But it would be almost two days before the DEFCON alert status returned to normal. Even then, the specter of a nuclear crisis with the Soviets over Cuba would keep coming up for weeks after JFK's assassination.[73]

Even as JFK's autopsy continued at Bethesda, the lines were buzzing between the White House and Dallas in an effort to rein in public comments and legal action that could launch an outcry for action against Cuba or the Soviet Union. Earlier that evening, Dallas Assistant

District Attorney Bill Alexander had talked about filing charges against Oswald for murdering JFK "as part of an international communist conspiracy." Reports like that quickly reached Washington, alarming President Lyndon Johnson, now at the White House. Given the constant stream of TV news coverage on all three networks, much of it from Dallas, LBJ knew that one inflammatory statement on live TV by an official in Texas could generate demands for retaliation that could be hard for a new President to resist.[74]

On the night of November 22, an LBJ aide placed urgent calls to Texas Attorney General Waggoner Carr, U.S. Attorney Harold Sanders, Dallas District Attorney Henry Wade, and Dallas Police Chief Jesse Curry. Author Larry Hancock says the message was the same in each case: "Avoid any official statements, charges, or discussion relating to conspiracy" that involved Russia, Cuba, or international Communism. District Attorney Wade later said that "President Johnson's aide called me three times from the White House that Friday night. He said that President Johnson felt any word of a conspiracy—some plot by foreign nations to kill President Kennedy—would shake our nation to its foundation." Hancock documented that "the FBI also moved quickly to bring pressure on Chief Curry to retract statements . . . that Oswald was known to be a Communist and potentially dangerous."[75]

CHAPTER 17

Late November and Early December 1963: National Security Cover-Ups

By November 23, speculation in the press about foreign involvement in JFK's murder—or any shooter besides the accused Oswald—was being cut off in favor of a "lone assassin" scenario. In hindsight, it strains credibility to think that all the relevant information about the shooting and an unusual former defector like Oswald could be uncovered less than twenty-four hours after the assassination.

Even J. Edgar Hoover, in a phone call recorded at 10:01 AM on November 23, admitted to President Lyndon Johnson that "the case, as it stands now, isn't strong enough to be able to get a conviction." However, investigations touching on covert matters would have to be conducted in secret so as not to alarm the public or force LBJ to retaliate against Cuba or the Soviet Union. Journalists didn't have to be made aware of the JFK-Almeida coup plan—or the Cuba Contingency Plans to protect it—to get them to withhold information from the public. They could simply be told that certain information was too sensitive, could compromise U.S. operations, or that it could force another confrontation with the Soviets just a year after the Cuban Missile Crisis.[1]

When some information linking Oswald to David Ferrie started to surface the weekend of JFK's murder, an FBI agent warned an NBC cameraman "that I should never discuss what we discovered for the good of the country." That same phrase, "for the good of the country," would be used to stop Dave Powers and Kenneth O'Donnell from revealing they had seen shots from the grassy knoll, and it was probably used to silence others as well. Longtime television journalist

Peter Noyes confirmed to this author that he was told by several "members of NBC News who covered the events in Dallas [that] they were convinced their superiors wanted certain evidence suppressed at the request of someone in Washington."[2]

The intense, enormous media coverage of JFK's assassination was unlike anything the country would see again until the 9/11 disaster. For almost four days, all three networks devoted most of their programming time to the tragedy. This extensive coverage also helped launch or ignite the careers of several journalists who were prominent in Watergate and even today. Walter Cronkite went from being just another network news anchor before his coverage of the assassination to becoming America's most trusted newsman, a role he would later use to help keep the Watergate story alive. Texan Dan Rather's career-making scoop was being the first journalist to view and report on the Zapruder film, though so firmly entrenched by the weekend was the "official" story of the lone-assassin-shooting-from-behind that Rather claimed the home movie showed JFK's "head went forward with considerable violence" after he was shot. The public wouldn't get the see the film for themselves—and learn that JFK was pitched backward, not forward—for another twelve years. Before that, Rather would go on to play a very major role covering Richard Nixon before and during Watergate.[3]

Other later prominent newsmen covering—and at times involved in—the story include future PBS broadcasters Jim Lehrer and Robert MacNeil (as Oswald calmly left the Texas School Book Depository, MacNeil asked him were he could find a phone), Bob Schieffer (who gave Oswald's mother a ride to Dallas), and Peter Jennings. While covering the assassination helped their careers, it sometimes impeded any questioning of the "official" version of the lone assassin. As Rather later indicated, if there was a conspiracy behind JFK's death, why didn't the reporters in Dallas find it? However, in later comments Rather and Schieffer both made it clear that the biggest concern for reporters in Dallas at the time was trying to scoop the competition and get something sensational out quickly, hardly conducive to a careful investigation but very conducive to putting out leaks from authorities designed to calm the public.[4]

Only a few U.S. newspaper articles slipped through that didn't adhere to the official "lone assassin" story, and those were quickly suppressed.

One was the November 23, 1963, newspaper article about the Tampa assassination attempt that appeared only in the back pages of *The Tampa Tribune*. It was based on information from local officials such as Tampa Police Chief J.P. Mullins and a White House Secret Service memo. The November 8 memo quoted in the article said a "subject made statement of a plan to assassinate the President . . . stated he will use a gun . . . Subject is described as: white, male, 20, slender build." That description matches Lee Oswald much better than the first alert issued in Dallas, which described a suspect much older and heavier than Oswald. A sheriff based near Tampa confirmed in the article that officers had been "warned about 'a young man' who had threatened to kill the President during his Tampa trip."[5]

In the article, Chief Mullins mentioned a second Tampa suspect who was still at large and wondered "if the . . . two may have followed the Presidential caravan to Dallas." Unknown to Mullins at that time, Gilberto Policarpo Lopez—the young Cuban exile mentioned earlier, who was linked to the Fair Play for Cuba Committee and had other recent parallels to Oswald—had indeed left Tampa and headed to Texas. Once Lopez was in Texas, Congressional investigators found that he "crossed the border into Mexico," then went to Mexico City and into Cuba, just as Oswald had tried to do in late September. Lopez used the same border crossing as Oswald, and apparently like Oswald on the return leg of his Mexico trip "crossed [the border] in a privately owned automobile owned by another person." Someone had to have helped both young men, since neither owned a car or had a driver's license.[6]

The Tampa article's description was also similar to Gilberto Lopez, so if JFK had been killed in Tampa, authorities would have already been primed to look for a suspect like Lopez or Oswald. (Oswald's whereabouts the day before the Tampa attempt have never been determined, though one unconfirmed report places him in Tampa with associates of Lopez.) While a later newspaper report placed Lopez in Dallas on the day of the assassination, there is no credible evidence that he was knowingly involved either in JFK's death or the Tampa attempt. Given the many parallels between Lopez and Oswald, it's likely that someone they trusted in intelligence or law enforcement, who was actually working for one of the three Mafia chiefs, influenced or manipulated both men. The same is probably true for ex-Marine Vallee in Chicago.[7]

Neither the *Tampa Tribune* article nor any mention of the Tampa attempt were ever brought to the attention of the Warren Commission or the later investigating committees like the House Select Committee on Assassinations. This author and Thom Hartmann discovered it only after reviewing thousands of pages of newspaper microfilm in Tampa and Miami, painstakingly reading through each edition. When this author contacted former Tampa Police Chief Mullins in 1996, Mullins confirmed everything in the article and provided additional information and law enforcement contacts involved in the Tampa matter. In the thirty-three years since the article appeared, no other reporters—or historians or government investigators—had ever asked the long-retired Chief Mullins about it.[8]

The *Tampa Tribune* article was only a small filler item on an inside page, but since all word of the Tampa threat had been kept out of the press, it quickly got the attention of *The Miami Herald* and the Associated Press. It's not hard to imagine the reactions of RFK, Hoover, LBJ, the Secret Service, and McCone when they learned the Tampa threat had started to leak. If the public found out that JFK had been targeted during his Tampa motorcade four days earlier, they might not be willing to swallow the official account of a lone, unaided assassin in Dallas. Worse, if the Tampa attempt emerged, then the Chicago threat just over two weeks earlier might also come out, raising the suspicion that JFK had been stalked by Cubans or other agents of the "international communist conspiracy," the very thing LBJ had his aides order Texas officials to avoid.[9]

Chief Mullins was never told why he had been ordered to cut off all mention of the Tampa threat to the press, even after JFK's death. But in those days, as today, the Tampa police cooperated with the local FBI, Secret Service, and CIA offices. Mullins did as he was told, so when the Associated Press and *The Miami Herald* attempted to follow up on the revelations in the *Tampa Tribune* article, they hit a wall of secrecy. *The Herald* reported the next day that "the FBI, Secret Service, and local officers declined to discuss the matter," with the Secret Service only saying "no comment." As for the Secret Service memo quoted in the original *Tampa Tribune* article, it was never released or given to Congressional investigators.[10]

In Washington on November 23, 1963, Richard Helms had to take control of all the CIA's material on Oswald, both for national security reasons and probably to protect his own career. Historian Michael Kurtz has written that Hunter Leake, the Deputy Chief of the New Orleans CIA office at the time, told him "that on the day after the assassination, he was ordered to collect all of the CIA's files on Oswald from the New Orleans office and transport them to the Agency's headquarters in Langley, Virginia."[11] Kurtz writes that

> [along with] other employees of the New Orleans office, Leake gathered all of the Oswald files. They proved so voluminous that Leake had to rent a trailer to transport them to Langley. Stopping only to eat, use the restroom, and fill up with gas, Leake drove the truck pulling the rental trailer filled with the New Orleans office's files on Oswald to CIA headquarters. Leake later learned that many of these files were . . . "deep sixed." Leake explained that . . . the CIA dreaded the release of any information that would connect Oswald with it. Leake speculated that his friend Richard Helms, the Agency's Deputy Director for Plans, was probably the person who ordered the destruction of the files because Helms had a paranoid obsession with protecting the "company."[12]

Leake's description of the Oswald files as "voluminous" makes sense, given the information from our independent source about the "tight surveillance" of Oswald, something not known to Kurtz at the time of his interview with Leake. (Professor Kurtz asked Helms about Leake's story, but Helms declined to confirm or deny Leake's account.) Buttressing Leake's credibility is the fact that no routine reports from the CIA's New Orleans office have ever surfaced about former defector Oswald's several well-publicized pro-Castro activities in New Orleans during August 1963, despite the CIA's interest in both former defectors and the Fair Play for Cuba Committee. Also, Leake's statement to Kurtz that "Oswald indeed performed chores for the CIA during his five months in New Orleans during the spring and summer of 1963" fits with other information about Oswald's work for Guy Banister, such as Oswald's visit with David Ferrie to Manuel Artime's small Louisiana training camp that was part of AMWORLD. There is also the remarkable amount of media coverage Oswald generated before his meeting with CIA media expert David Atlee Phillips, at the same time Phillips was working on AMWORLD. The last part suggests that Oswald had some role in an authorized CIA operation like AMWORLD; otherwise, Helms couldn't have hoped to keep the efforts of Leake and "other employees of the New Orleans office" secret from CIA Director McCone.[13]

In addition, Victor Marchetti, a former executive assistant to the CIA's Deputy Director who worked with Richard Helms, said "Helms stated that David Ferrie was a CIA agent and that he was still an agent at the time of the assassination." Marchetti was also told that "Ferrie had been a contract agent to the Agency in the early sixties and had been involved in some of the Cuban activities." When Ferrie's name surfaced that weekend in law-enforcement and official circles in relation to JFK's assassination, Helms was no doubt frantic. Ferrie wasn't linked to JFK's murder in the press that weekend, but four years later when he finally was, Agency veteran Marchetti observed "consternation on the part of then CIA Director Richard Helms and other senior officials when Ferrie's name was first publicly linked with the assassination."[14]

It's important to remember that while Helms was engaged in his cover-ups, several authorized and unauthorized anti-Castro operations were still active and viable, meaning that Helms had to conceal information while still preserving those operations and his options. He had to decide what to hide, and from whom, and what to reveal. Some of the decisions Helms made that day would become CIA dogma for decades, even as evidence was declassified showing that the claims of Helms and the CIA couldn't possibly be true.

Richard Helms apparently authorized Desmond FitzGerald, his head of Cuban operations, to tell John McCone's executive assistant only that a CIA case officer had been meeting with Rolando Cubela in Paris when JFK was shot, and that FitzGerald himself had met with Cubela the previous month. FitzGerald didn't tell him anything about the assassination aspects of the Cubela operation, since McCone hadn't been informed about that portion of the plan (which was part of the CIA-Mafia plots Helms was also hiding from McCone). That meant McCone's assistant wasn't told about the poison pen the case officer tried to give Cubela or about his promise to deliver high-powered rifles with scopes for Cubela to use in assassinating Castro. As a result, McCone and his assistant probably saw little to be concerned about.[15]

McCone's assistant was struck by how emotional Desmond

FitzGerald was as FitzGerald was telling him about Cubela. He told *Newsweek* editor Evan Thomas that "Des was normally imperturbable, but he was very disturbed . . . shaking his head and wringing his hands." He couldn't understand why FitzGerald appeared to be "distraught and overreacting," but he didn't realize how much crucial information FitzGerald was withholding from him and McCone. It's also revealing that Helms had FitzGerald tell McCone's assistant about the Cubela meeting, instead of Helms telling McCone directly. Helms apparently wanted to preserve Cubela as his own, unauthorized backup (or replacement) for the Almeida coup plan, so two days later he ordered FitzGerald to have Cubela's case officer remove a reference to the poison pen from a memo about Cubela's Paris meeting.[16]

The resulting Cubela memo seen by McCone obscures the subject of the scoped rifles by saying only that Cubela needed to be sent a seventy-five-pound cache of explosives that also included "weapons and ammo." It sounds like material for one of the small sabotage operations the CIA was still occasionally running, and there is no mention of assassination. This longer, more narrative memo for McCone doesn't specifically mention the rifles with scopes, as does the much shorter, bare-bones operational memo McCone didn't see.[17]

On November 23, 1963, President Johnson, CIA Director McCone, and other top officials started receiving ominous information from Mexico City implicating Fidel Castro and the Soviet KGB in JFK's assassination. Johnson heard these troubling reports even as he was first learning from McCone the outlines of the CIA's authorized Cuban operations, like the coup plan with Almeida. CIA officers in Mexico City, in particular David Atlee Phillips, were sending the first of what would become a steady stream of reports incriminating Oswald, essentially claiming he was working for Cuba or Russia. However, all of these reports would later be discredited, and most originated with or were promoted by associates of David Morales, Manuel Artime, Santo Trafficante, and Johnny Rosselli.

Even though the allegations were false, they sounded alarms not only during the weekend of November 23 and in the weeks that followed, but also through much of 1964 and 1965, into the 1970s, and even later. The same long-discredited claims were raised again as recently as 2005 in a controversial German television documentary.[18]

The first of these false allegations concerned Silvia Duran, whom retired Major John Newman—a historian and twenty-year veteran of military intelligence—describes as "the secretary working in the Cuban consulate at the time of Oswald's visit to Mexico City." On November 23, David Atlee Phillips sent a mildly incriminating memo about Duran, which was soon followed by ever more incredible accusations that eventually included Duran supposedly entertaining Oswald at a "twist" party, having a torrid affair with Oswald, and working with Oswald on a plot to kill JFK. The exact origin of all the accusations against Duran is still murky, but when added to other wild allegations that would start flowing on November 23, the stories were meant to emphasize Oswald's guilt while also pressuring President Johnson to order a retaliatory invasion of Cuba.[19]

The CIA's Mexico City station asked "Mexican authorities" to have Silvia Duran, a Mexican citizen, "arrested as soon as possible [and] held incommunicado," while insisting "her arrest is kept absolutely secret." Caught off guard by Duran's arrest, Richard Helms had the Mexico City station called to "tell them not to [arrest Duran]," but the Agency's Mexico City Station Chief, Win Scott, replied it was already "too late to call off the arrest."[20]

Sylvia Duran's interrogation by the Mexican authorities on November 23, 1963, was brutal, and she later told a trusted CIA informant that she was "beaten until she admitted that she had an affair with Oswald." In a phone call bugged by the CIA a few days after later, Cuba's Ambassador to Mexico told Cuban President Osvaldo Dorticos that Duran "has black and blue marks on her arms, which she said she got during the interrogation process." Even though Duran confessed to the story she'd been given about her supposed affair with Oswald only after being beaten, Win Scott later reported it to Washington as fact.[21]

Duran later told Congressional investigators that her Mexican interrogators told her she "was a very important person for . . . the Cuban Government and that I was the link for the International Communists—the Cuban Communists, the Mexican Communists, and the American Communists, and that we were going to kill Kennedy." The Mexican national police (the Federal Security Directorate, or DFS) were using information about Duran that someone at the Mexico City CIA station had told them.

Duran was released that weekend, but four days later—and three days after Oswald's death—the CIA asked Mexican authorities to arrest Duran yet again and once more interrogate her "vigorously and exhaustively." This time, Helms was on board, as was the FBI, because incriminating (though eventually discredited) stories about Oswald had emerged from Mexico City tying Oswald to the Soviets.

The CIA informed the FBI on November 23 about information that "indicated [Oswald] had been in contact with Valery Kostikov, Soviet Embassy, Mexico City, and that Kostikov had been tentatively identified as being with the department in KGB which handles sabotage and assassinations." However, in the following days, this claim also started falling apart. By November 27, the CIA was able to confirm to the FBI only that Kostikov "is an official for the KGB," but dropped the allegation about his being part of the KGB's assassination department. It turned out that Kostikov just happened to be one of three officials at the embassy when Oswald visited there and had actually helped to calm down the agitated Oswald.[22]

However, starting on November 23, 1963, and continuing for years, LBJ, Hoover, McCone, and James Angleton, the CIA's Counterintelligence Chief, would all take the allegations about Kostikov and Duran very seriously. In addition, disinformation involving a young Nicaraguan named Gilberto Alvarado began flowing through David Atlee Phillips to CIA headquarters on November 26, 1963. At the American embassy in Mexico City on that day, Alvarado claimed that two months earlier he had seen Oswald receive $6,500 at the Cuban embassy "for the purpose of killing someone." Alvarado's accusations created a huge stir among high-ranking officials in Washington for more than a week, convincing U.S. Ambassador to Mexico Thomas Mann that Fidel Castro was behind JFK's murder.[23]

Alvarado soon admitted he was lying—only to then claim that he wasn't lying. After failing a lie detector test, Alvarado finally admitted that he was really a Nicaraguan intelligence agent. Anthony Summers writes that Alvarado "explains his presence at the Cuban Embassy" around the same time as Oswald by saying "he had been sent to Mexico to try to get to Cuba on an infiltration mission." Alvarado was one of three young men mentioned earlier who, along with Oswald, tried to get into Cuba by visiting the Cuban embassy in the same twenty-four-hour period. It's worth noting that Manuel Artime had an AMWORLD training camp in Nicaragua, and was close to both the country's strongman Luis Somoza and to Nicaraguan intelligence. The Alvarado investigation was dropped, and even the CIA concluded that "Alvarado's allegation was indeed fabricated."[24]

David Atlee Phillips was a central figure in these and several other false allegations that sprang up in the following days. Was he acting on his own to prod an invasion he knew had been prepared, or was he passing along information he was being given by others, like David Morales? Phillips was the CIA agent most compromised by connections to Oswald, which included personally meeting him in Dallas, the surveillance of Oswald in Mexico City, Phillips's work against the Fair Play for Cuba Committee, and his probable responsibility for Oswald's incredible spate of pro-Castro publicity in New Orleans. Even if the disinformation Phillips sent up the chain of command did not come from others, it could have been his attempt to pin JFK's murder on Castro and the Cubans to divert attention from his own intelligence failures and to force the United States to invade Cuba. Others, like Congressional investigator Gaeton Fonzi, view Phillips's actions in a far more sinister light.[25]

Informants working for David Morales under the code name AMOT were soon providing wild claims that were sent to CIA headquarters about the phony Cuban agent—Miguel Casas Saez—who was supposedly near Chicago at the time of the plot against JFK there. The reports alleged that Saez was in Dallas for JFK's murder, then returned to Cuba with money and new clothes. Unlike the Alvarado, Duran, and Kostikov stories, the Saez allegations circulated only within secure CIA channels that went to FitzGerald, Helms, and other high-ranking officials. The third- and fourth-hand allegations soon fell apart, but not before they—and the unusual travels of Gilberto Lopez from Tampa to Texas to Mexico City to Cuba—convinced CIA Counterintelligence Chief James Angleton that Fidel Castro was behind JFK's murder. On the other hand, Richard Helms, who knew more about the CIA's Cuban operations than Angleton, stated that he didn't believe Castro killed JFK. Helms was so confident that Castro hadn't penetrated his assassination operation that he would continue to utilize Cuban official Rolando Cubela in his operation for more than two more years.[26]

According to a CIA memo, a French criminal linked to both Santo Trafficante and Carlos Marcello—Michel Victor Mertz—was deported from Dallas on November 23, 1963. Mertz had recently been in Texas and Louisiana, using the name of an old adversary, Jean Souetre, while the real Souetre was in Spain. Mertz's alias was sure to generate cover-ups by the CIA and FBI, since the real Souetre was wanted by French authorities for his role in an infamous 1962 attempt to assassinate

Charles de Gaulle that left the French President's car riddled with bullets. While the real Jean Souetre was a fugitive in Europe in May 1963, a CIA official (later said to be E. Howard Hunt) had filed a report about his meeting with Souetre, though Helms decided in July 1963 to reject Souetre's overtures. In the days before JFK's trip to Dallas, former Senate investigator Bud Fensterwald discovered that "the FBI had traced [the man they thought was] Souetre to Dallas a day before the assassination and then lost him." As Souetre told this author, via French journalist Stephane Risset—and other information confirms—the man in Dallas was actually Michel Victor Mertz, using Souetre's name.[27]

Only one page of Mertz's CIA file has been released, and the following memo is just part of a much longer document that is still being withheld. Responding to FBI and French requests for information, the memo states that "Michel Mertz . . . had been expelled from the US at Fort Worth or Dallas 48 hours after the assassination of President Kennedy," adding that the Frenchman "was in Fort Worth on the morning of November 22 [as was JFK] and in Dallas in the afternoon." It also provides the Jean Souetre alias, as well as that of a twenty-three-year-old aspiring French chef who was visiting Dallas, although official records confirm the chef was not deported and left Dallas legitimately.[28] This CIA memo was copied to Robert Kennedy's FBI liaison, Courtney Evans. However, the memo wasn't sent until more than three months after JFK's assassination, meaning that RFK probably wasn't aware of Mertz's presence in Dallas until then.

The assassination of Lee Oswald on live television by Jack Ruby on November 24, 1963, would have a huge impact on government efforts to protect national security. As documented in Chapter 5, the Colt Cobra pistol Ruby used to shoot Oswald was purchased in early 1960, when Ruby was on the fringe of the earliest phase of the CIA-Mafia plots to kill Fidel, soon after Ruby's odd stint as an FBI informant. The Executive Director of the House Select Committee on Assassinations—G. Robert Blakey, in 1963 a Mafia prosecutor for Robert Kennedy—later said "the murder of Oswald by Jack Ruby had all the earmarks of an organized crime hit." The Committee concluded that Ruby's act wasn't "spontaneous" as the mobster claimed, and that Ruby probably had help getting into the basement of the Dallas police station where the shooting occurred. Blakey said the policeman who aided

Ruby was Sergeant Patrick Dean, who boasted "of his longtime relationship" with the underboss who ran organized crime in Dallas for Carlos Marcello. It's interesting that after Ruby's arrest, police said he seemed "extremely agitated and nervous" until he was told Oswald was dead, when "Ruby calmed down." One officer said it seemed as "if Oswald had not died, he, Jack Ruby, would have been killed." Ruby's excuse for being near the police station that day was to wire money to one of his dancers, Karen Carlin. Later that day, a "highly agitated" Carlin told a Secret Service agent that "Oswald, Jack Ruby, and others individuals unknown to her were involved in a plot to assassinate Kennedy, and that she would be killed if she gave any information to authorities."[29]

Since there would now be no public trial of Lee Oswald, the efforts of various agencies and officials to protect national security, Almeida, and their own reputations began to shift focus. More unusual activities concerning JFK's autopsy happened that day, like the burning of the first draft of JFK's autopsy report. Naval Intelligence's goals also changed radically. On the afternoon of November 24, the organization transitioned from shredding files about its "tight surveillance" of Oswald to conducting its own, secret internal investigation of JFK's assassination. Also involved were personnel from Marine Intelligence, and the operation was probably known to the head of the Defense Intelligence Agency, General Joseph Carroll. Our Naval Intelligence source participated in this secret investigation, aspects of which were later independently confirmed by the House Select Committee on Assassinations.[30]

Our source "became part of a 6-week Naval Intelligence investigation into JFK's assassination." He said "their mission was 'Did [Oswald] do it?' not 'Who did it?'" As part of their investigation, Naval Intelligence personnel went to Dallas, but "they were forbidden to have anything to do with the autopsy." He said, "The result of the Naval Intelligence investigation was that [it] concluded Oswald was not the shooter, due to his skills, the gun, etc., [and that] Oswald was incapable of masterminding the assassination or of doing the actual shooting." The report's summary was "6–7 pages, with hundreds of supporting documents." Our source had "some knowledge that the CIA also conducted [its] own investigation," a fact that wasn't widely known when this author talked to the source in 1991.[31]

It's significant that Naval Intelligence had the same men involved with Oswald's "tight surveillance" conduct this secret investigation.

On one hand, this kept Navy brass from having to let more Navy personnel know about the extensive surveillance Oswald had been under. On the other, the men were essentially investigating their own organization and their own work and were hardly in a position to be objective if leads pointed to problems with some of those who had been providing Naval Intelligence information about Oswald (such as Guy Banister).[32]

Our source "signed a disclosure agreement" after the investigation, and even after almost thirty years he would convey information to us only through a trusted intermediary. The House Select Committee on Assassinations uncovered evidence of what appears to be a related Marine Intelligence investigation that reached similar conclusions. However, the U.S. military stonewalled the Committee about critical information until the Committee's mandate expired. When this author interviewed another source, the son of a U.S. Navy Admiral, he independently claimed to have seen a copy of the Naval Intelligence report while he was stationed at a large U.S. Navy base in the Pacific in the early 1970s. His account of the report's conclusions matched very closely to those of our Naval Intelligence source.[33]

Early results from the Naval Intelligence investigation, or the fact that Naval Intelligence was keeping such close tabs on Oswald, might account for an unusual "top secret, eyes only" memo about Oswald. Less than two weeks after Oswald's death, even as LBJ and McCone worried that Oswald might have been acting for Cuba or the Soviets, "Gordon Chase of the National Security Council staff" indicated that the "President's Special Assistant for National Security Affairs," McGeorge Bundy (who had held the same position under JFK), could provide "assurances re: Oswald" not being an agent for Castro. Only an official in an agency with access to the surveillance on Oswald, like Naval Intelligence or the CIA, could have given Bundy the information necessary to make such a definitive statement.[34]

On November 25, 1963, Richard Nixon was one of hundreds of dignitaries attending the funeral of John F. Kennedy. Nixon kept a fairly low public profile in the funeral's immediate aftermath while mapping out his political future. Meanwhile, a right-wing publication soon promoted Oswald's involvement in an alleged assassination attempt against far-right General Edwin Walker in Dallas, helping to clinch the case against the now-dead Oswald. Added to that was a later claim that Oswald had once planned to assassinate Richard Nixon. At that time, Oswald's Russian wife, Marina, was under tremendous pressure from authorities and made a series of often-changing statements. The Nixon claim has since been debunked, and the Walker claim ignores critical evidence, such as the FBI report that Jack Ruby was a regular visitor to Walker before the alleged attempt and that Walker had ties to white supremacists involved in JFK's assassination, such as Joseph Milteer.[35]

Richard Nixon and Richard Helms would have worried about the disinformation implicating Castro in JFK's assassination that began surfacing in small media outlets in the days following Oswald's murder because the stories sometimes included shockingly accurate details about U.S. efforts to eliminate Fidel. Spread by associates of Marcello, Trafficante, and Rosselli, the accounts continued to trickle out to the press and officials over the coming year and beyond. Appearing in small-market newspapers and radio broadcasts, the stories blamed Castro, hinted at the JFK-Almeida coup plan, and were just detailed enough to draw the attention of U.S. officials, but not enough to become major news stories. Still, the stories helped to force top officials into a continuing cover-up about JFK's assassination in order to prevent a public outcry to invade Cuba and to avoid exposing Almeida. The stories began two days after Oswald's murder, when David Ferrie was essentially cleared of involvement in JFK's death. With those loose ends out of the way, the more national security pressure the Mafia bosses could keep on officials to stifle the investigation the better, and the more Oswald looked like a Communist working for Fidel Castro, the more Jack Ruby looked like a patriot (and not a mobster). The most public spokesman for spreading these stories was Santo Trafficante's operative John Martino, who had worked closely with Nixon's friend William Pawley just five months earlier.

On November 26, 1963, Martino began implicating Castro in JFK's murder and hinting at the JFK-Almeida coup plan in radio, newspaper, and magazine appearances. Martino was touring the country as a prominent member of the far-right John Birch Society Speakers Bureau, ostensibly to promote his book *I Was Castro's Prisoner*. It's unlikely that David Atlee Phillips or others in the CIA were behind Martino's publicity efforts, because Martino's book actually mentioned the name of Phillips's associate, David Morales, a fact that the CIA wanted to keep secret.[36]

Martino's phony stories started out mildly, claiming that Oswald had gone to Cuba in the fall of 1963 and had passed out pro-Castro literature in Miami and New Orleans. Those tales brought Martino a visit from the FBI on November 29, but he refused to identify his sources. As press reports about the JFK investigation continued, Martino ramped up his rhetoric.[37]

An article under Martino's name appeared in the December 21, 1963, issue of the right-wing journal *Human Events,* in which Martino took credit for revealing that "the Kennedy Administration planned to eliminate Fidel Castro . . . through a putsch, [and] the plan involved a more or less token invasion from Central America to be synchronized with the coup. A left-wing coalition government was to be set up, [and] the plan involved [the] US [military] occupation of Cuba." At the time, that was more than many high-ranking U.S. officials in the Johnson administration knew about the coup plan.[38]

Martino knew about the involvement of Manolo Ray's JURE exile group and wrote in the article that "Oswald made . . . approaches to JURE, another organization of Cuban freedom fighters, but was rejected." As previously noted, three months earlier Martino and Masferrer had been linked to the attempt to smear Ray's group by tying it to Oswald via Dallas JURE member Silvia Odio. When Martino's article was published, only the FBI and a handful of Odio's closest family and friends knew about Oswald's visit to her in Dallas and nothing about it had appeared in the press.[39]

In Martino's first major article, he only hinted that Oswald was working for Fidel Castro when he killed JFK. The following month, Martino revealed new details about the coup plan and implicated Fidel more directly, in a January 30, 1964, *Memphis Press-Scimitar* article headlined "Oswald Was Paid Gunman for Castro, Visitor Says." It quotes John Martino as saying, "Lee Harvey Oswald was paid by Castro to assassinate President Kennedy," and claiming that the murder was in retaliation for JFK's "plan to get rid of Castro." Martino described JFK's top secret coup plan with remarkable precision, saying: "There was to be another invasion and uprising in Cuba . . . and the Organization of American States . . . was to go into Cuba [and help] control the country until an election could be set up." Martino even knew that "since the death of Kennedy, the work on an invasion has virtually stopped."[40]

We can only imagine the consternation Martino's increasingly provocative articles caused among high-ranking officials in Washington. They attracted the attention of J. Edgar Hoover, since FBI agents interviewed Martino yet again on February 15, 1964. In an era when Presidents and Congress treated Hoover and his FBI with deference, Martino basically thumbed his nose at the agents, declaring that "President Kennedy was engaged in a plot to overthrow the Castro regime by preparing another invasion attempt against Cuba." The frustrated FBI agents wrote that "Martino refused to divulge the sources of his information or how they might know what plans President Kennedy might have had."[41]

Frank Fiorini, the future Watergate burglar under the name Frank Sturgis, was one of the other Trafficante associates also leaking information to the press implicating Fidel Castro in JFK's murder. However, none of these other leaks hinted at the JFK-Almeida coup plan, and Martino's stories were unique in that regard, probably because (by his own admission) he had actually been part of the assassination plot. Fiorini's information implicating Fidel and the Cubans appeared in a Florida newspaper on November 26, 1963. In the article, Fiorini "claimed Oswald had been in touch with Cuban intelligence officials . . . and had been in touch with Castro agents in Miami." The FBI immediately interviewed Fiorini, who maintained he'd been misquoted. Later, Fiorini admitted he'd received his information from John Martino.[42]

Despite over three decades of speculation and investigations, no credible evidence or testimony has surfaced showing that Frank Fiorini played a role in JFK's assassination. Speculation that Fiorini was one of the "three tramps" arrested in Dealey Plaza has been disproven, as was an allegation that Fiorini, Oswald, and others drove from Miami to Dallas in the days before JFK's murder. (Numerous witnesses saw Oswald at work during that time.) A recent alleged confession recorded by E. Howard Hunt places Fiorini in a position of trust within the CIA that he never had. Then, too, Fiorini was such a publicity seeker (resulting in his friendship with top columnist Jack Anderson) that no one as careful as Trafficante would have used him in any significant way in the JFK hit. However, Fiorini was a trusted mob asset who could be used to spread disinformation about Oswald and Castro to divert attention from the Mafia.[43]

Others who spread stories tying Fidel Castro to JFK's assassination included Rolando Masferrer and drug-linked associates of Manuel

Artime. The fact that Trafficante's and Rosselli's associates planted so many phony stories implicating Castro raises the question of whether they were also feeding disinformation to David Atlee Phillips. Because of their work together on AMWORLD (and earlier), David Morales knew what type of material Phillips would be receptive to, and that Phillips had a direct pipeline to Desmond FitzGerald, who could immediately bring information to Richard Helms's attention. Using Phillips as a pipeline for disinformation would allow it to reach very high levels in a credible way, very quickly.[44]

Other efforts to link Oswald and Ruby to Fidel were less sophisticated, though they sometimes echoed the information in the memo that so alarmed Alexander Haig and his superior. These additional efforts range from the fake "Pedro Charles" letter mailed to Oswald from Havana on November 28, 1963, to stories linking Ruby to Cuban plots. It's amazing how many dozens, sometimes hundreds, of pages of follow-up FBI and CIA memos were generated because of one or two obviously false letters or stories. It's likely that even more phony information implicating Fidel, with hundreds of pages of official follow-up memos, remains unreleased.[45]

All of the information that appeared in the press would continue to trouble Helms, CIA Director McCone, and other high-ranking U.S. officials, even though so far it had appeared only in small markets and didn't get national attention. There was always the possibility that some national reporter looking for a scoop might give one of the stories wide exposure. Plus, the small but steady flow from Mexico City of false information implicating Fidel continued to worry McCone, who shared some of it with President Johnson. The sum effect was to strengthen their resolve to keep any sinister Cuban (or Russian) connections to Oswald and JFK's assassination from reaching the public by keeping a tight lid on any investigations.

For Commander Almeida in Cuba, the days after JFK's assassination must have been fraught with tension, especially when Harry Williams told him that Robert Kennedy had put the coup plan on hold. Some Cuban officials worried about an American attack because of Oswald's very public pro-Cuba stance, but Almeida had more reason for concern than most because he knew the United States was already prepared to invade. Even worse, within days of JFK's death, at least one rumor of a coup surfaced in Cuban government circles. The fact that two of Artime's Miami exile associates had recently reported such rumors to their CIA contacts meant that Fidel's Miami agents might also have heard such rumblings. It's also possible that Fidel's agents had detected the coup preparations of one of Almeida's allies in the Cuban government.

Almeida decided to leave Cuba, but in a way that would not arouse suspicion. On Thursday, November 28, 1963, a CIA memo was sent from the Miami station to McCone, reporting the "departure [of] 2 Britannias [airliners], probably for Algeria, with 170 Cubans aboard headed by Juan Almeida."[46]

Commander Almeida's information, or his instincts, was correct because just two days later, on Saturday, November 30, a CIA memo revealed that "a Western diplomat . . . had learned [from someone in the Cuban government] that Che Guevara was alleged to be under house arrest for plotting to overthrow Castro." This wasn't just some rumor off the street because the CIA said the "source" of the information about Che's involvement "in an anti-Castro plot" was a "trained observer of proven reliability who is a member of the Western diplomatic community in Cuba." The timing of Che's arrest, just one day before the originally scheduled coup date, raises the possibility that Fidel had learned something about the coup and had arrested one of those he thought was responsible.[47]

While it's possible Che planned to be an ally of Almeida for the coup, Fidel might have focused suspicion on Che for another reason. Three decades later, historian Jorge Castaneda first documented that Che had been making secret plans to leave Cuba in late December 1963, intending to return to his home country, Argentina, for an extended period of time. Che told only three of his most trusted subordinates about his plan, but not even they were told why Che was leaving Cuba. Had Castro found out about Che's plans to leave Cuba, put them together with reports of a possible coup, and decided to arrest Che?[48]

Che's problems with Fidel, the Russians, and Cuba's Communist Party were well known by the fall of 1963. Even William Attwood, JFK's special envoy for the secret peace talks, wrote that Fidel's intermediary in Cuba told him that "[Che] Guevara . . . regarded Castro as dangerously unreliable, and would get rid of Castro if [Che] could carry on without [Castro] and retain his popular support." With Castro's intermediary revealing such concerns about Che to Attwood, it's not surprising that Fidel would have arrested Che if word of a coup and assassination plot surfaced.[49]

Che's house arrest probably lasted for only a short time, perhaps just a day or two. December 2 is one of Cuba's biggest holidays, the anniversary of the founding of the Cuban Army, whose first battle saw Almeida save his friend Che's life. As Commander of Cuba's Army, Almeida was also considered its founder, so the Cuban public would definitely notice if he didn't appear for the celebration. Apparently things had calmed down enough for Almeida to return from Algeria to be part of the celebration, something Almeida would not have done if he feared that he was returning home to the same fate as Che.[50]

The day after the big December 2, 1963, celebration, a CIA report says Almeida "expressed [his] despair" to a subordinate. Whatever his private worries, Almeida put on a good public face, and on December 6, 1963, the Cuban radio-news service mentioned Almeida's presence at a ceremony to install a new communications minister.[51]

It's often overlooked that President Lyndon Johnson and J. Edgar Hoover didn't want the entity that became known as the Warren Commission. Associates of Robert Kennedy, who didn't trust LBJ or Hoover to do a thorough investigation, actually pressed for its formation. LBJ had to exert tremendous pressure on Chief Justice Earl Warren to chair the Committee, since it represented a huge conflict of interest in case another conspirator surfaced or Jack Ruby's case reached the Supreme Court. However, Warren agreed after LBJ raised the specter of World War III if speculation about Soviet or Cuban involvement in JFK's murder continued.[52]

Michigan Congressman Gerald Ford was one of the seven members of the Warren Commission, and unlike Warren, Ford quickly and eagerly agreed to serve. His history as a canny and ambitious politician is at odds with the clumsy, amiable image portrayed by comedians and the media. Most of the members of the Warren Commission had demanding jobs that limited the time they could spend on the investigation, but Ford made it a point to be the most active member, viewing his appointment as a break for his career, one of the few ways in which a young, conservative Republican could gain notice in a Congress under firm Democratic control.

Ford wasted no time in using his new position to curry favor with the person who had replaced Robert Kennedy as America's second-most-powerful man, J. Edgar Hoover. Just a week after the Warren Commission's first meeting, Ford went to one of Hoover's top aides, who wrote that Ford told him "he would keep me thoroughly advised as to the activities of the Commission. He stated this would have to be on a confidential basis." Five days later, Ford started delivering on his promise and was soon telling his FBI contact that "two members of the Commission [were] still were not convinced that the President had been shot from the sixth floor window of the Texas Book Depository." Hoover's Assistant Director, William Sullivan, later said that Gerald Ford "was our man on the Commission . . . it was to him that we looked to protect our interest and keep us fully advised of any development that we did not like . . . and this he did." While Ford's general role as an FBI informant has been known for years, almost all of his reports were kept classified until August 2008, when several were released.[53]

Gerald Ford had another distinction among Warren Commission members. The Commission as a whole was never officially told about the CIA-Mafia plots (including Cubela) or the JFK-Almeida coup plan, but *Vanity Fair* found that "according to Earl Warren's son and grandson . . . the Chief Justice did know about the plots." The other Warren Commission member who indicated, years later, that he had been told something about the efforts to eliminate Castro was Ford. In fact, it would be President Ford's inadvertent slip about U.S. assassination plots against Fidel in 1974 that would finally trigger the widespread public exposure of the plots and a Congressional investigation into them in 1975.[54]

According to historian Michael Kurtz, "Richard Helms personally persuaded Lyndon Johnson to appoint former CIA Director Allen Dulles to the Warren Commission." That meant that only one member, Allen Dulles, knew a great deal about U.S. efforts to assassinate Fidel using the Mafia while two—Ford and Warren—knew a little, but the rest knew nothing. They were Georgia Senator Richard Russell, Kentucky Senator John Cooper, Louisiana Congressman Hale Boggs, and disarmament official John J. McCloy.[55]

The fact that Chief Justice Warren and Congressman Ford were the only members of the Warren Commission to know anything about the CIA-Mafia plots to kill Fidel might explain why they would be the only members who went to Dallas to interview Jack Ruby. They even denied the request of the Commission's expert on Ruby to accompany them. When Ruby begged Warren and Ford to take him to Washington for questioning away from Dallas, they refused.

The Warren Commission's real purpose was to end speculation about foreign involvement in JFK's murder. After the Commission was appointed, but before they had begun gathering evidence, their final conclusion was preordained when J. Edgar Hoover leaked the FBI's own report and conclusions to the press on December 8, 1963. Hoover used his extensive media connections to make sure the FBI's conclusions—that Oswald acted alone, Ruby acted alone, the two had no connection, and there was no conspiracy in JFK's death—became front-page news. Warren Commission member Hale Boggs fumed that the Bureau had completed its investigation, "tried the case, and reached a verdict" in barely two weeks. Since the Warren Commission would depend on the Bureau for most of their investigative material, the Commission basically had to adopt the FBI's conclusions as its own.[56]

CHAPTER 18

December 1963–Mid-1966: Nixon in New York, Helms Is Promoted, Hunt Prospers, Barker Is Fired

During December 1963, in the wake of President Kennedy's murder, Richard Nixon was still sorting out his political future. Nixon had begun the process the day after JFK was shot, in a hastily called meeting with his major New York supporters. When Nixon first heard JFK had died, he said privately that his murder would mean "a 'bloodbath' in the Democratic Party, as President Johnson struggled with [RFK] for control" of the organization, possibly leading "to an Adlai Stevenson nomination for 1964." He based this early speculation on the fact that at the time, no one saw LBJ as a significant national political force. In addition, the antipathy between LBJ and RFK was well known in political circles. By the day after the assassination, Nixon's sharp political instincts had kicked in, and at the meeting with his New York supporters he voiced a new view, accurately predicting that LBJ "would have it under control" and "the country would unite behind him." As for his own chances, Nixon wanted "to keep his options open," and so decided not to sign the contract with Doubleday for the campaign book originally designed to give him an inside look at the operations of his potential opponents.[1]

By late December, Nixon had made no indication to the public he planned to seek the nomination in 1964. However, in private Nixon was pulling together a much larger meeting to plot his political future, to be held the following month at New York's Waldorf-Astoria. Attending would be advertising and marketing expert H.R. "Bob" Haldeman and fourteen other strategists, supporters, and politicians from across the country.[2]

However, some factors in Nixon's decision couldn't be debated in such a large strategy meeting, like the one that surfaced on December 21, 1963: John Martino's aforementioned article in *Human Events* about Oswald and Castro. If Nixon and his friend William Pawley hadn't heard any of the rumblings from Martino's earlier efforts to publicize the claim that "Castro killed JFK because of US efforts against him," they certainly knew after Martino's article appeared in the influential conservative journal. Pawley had worked very closely with Martino the previous spring, and Nixon had been involved at the start of their operation, so Martino's allegations surely would have raised troubling questions for the two: Was the Pawley-Martino-Rosselli operation involved in—or had it led to—JFK's assassination? Would Martino in some future article reveal his operation's ties to Pawley, or Pawley's to Nixon?[3]

Nixon had another reason to worry: Martino's article was basically about JFK's coup plan, the operation Nixon had a pipeline into via ex–Cuban President Carlos Prio, another Trafficante associate. The article indicated that Fidel Castro had killed JFK in retaliation for that operation, implying that Fidel had somehow learned about the coup plan, as had Nixon. Even though Martino continued to issue even more incendiary "Castro had JFK killed" allegations in small markets, off the national stage, the issue didn't seem like it would go away and was almost certainly a factor in the following months as Nixon debated his political plans. There's also a good probability that by December 1963, Nixon had heard from friends such as J. Edgar Hoover about some of the "Castro killed JFK" disinformation that had trickled up through official channels. Nixon's concerns about what information might come out about his role in anti-Cuban operations would continue to varying degrees for the rest of his political career, culminating in the Watergate scandal.[4]

In the meantime, Nixon could do little except bide his time regarding a Presidential run. He passed the New York bar in December 1963, clearing the way for him to become a full partner in the law firm he'd joined. Much—perhaps half—of Nixon's time in the next months was spent on political, not legal, activities. As Nixon prepared to turn fifty-one the following month, his future held much potential but was also plagued by uncertainty over the Cuban issue.[5]

High-ranking CIA official Richard Helms no doubt joined Nixon in his concerns about Martino's public disclosures, mirroring the joint worries the two would share over the next decade about sensitive

Cuban operations. In addition, Helms had to contend with the troubling disinformation that kept bubbling up through CIA channels from Mexico City. While these falsehoods were eventually discredited and rarely left government circles, Helms would have been anxious about Martino's public disclosures of the highly secret coup plan, as well as Martino's close involvement with the Agency in Operation TILT.[6]

Helms had the CIA conduct its own internal investigation into Oswald and JFK's assassination, a little-known fact first uncovered years later by Congressional investigators. Helms initially appointed an AMWORLD veteran, CIA officer John Whitten, to head the Agency's secret investigation, but as soon as Whitten asked Helms for "files on Oswald's Cuba-related activities," he was taken off the JFK investigation and reassigned. In Congressional testimony long after the fact, Whitten said that Helms hadn't told him anything about the CIA-Mafia plots to kill Fidel, and he was "appalled" when he heard about them twelve years later. It's also clear now that Whitten wasn't allowed to see the files on Oswald that CIA agent Hunter Leake had delivered from the CIA's New Orleans office to Helms.[7]

After Whitten was removed from the investigation, Helms replaced him with CIA Counterintelligence Chief James Angleton, under whom the internal CIA investigation seems to have been designed more to hide information than to uncover it. Angleton heard all of the claims from Mexico City that Oswald had killed JFK on Fidel Castro's orders and had access to other incendiary reports, like those concerning shadowy Cuban agent Miguel Cases Saez (who seemed to have stalked JFK—if the shaky reports of David Morales's informants were believed). Angleton also followed with interest the trail of young Cuban exile Gilberto Policarpo Lopez from Tampa to Texas to Mexico City. Not surprisingly, the paranoid Angleton concluded that Fidel had killed JFK and that both Saez and Lopez were involved, according to intelligence journalist Joseph Trento. Fifteen years later, when Congressional investigators got to see many of the files about Saez and Lopez, they exposed the flaws in Angleton's conclusion. Based on this author's review of all the relevant files and an exclusive interview with Lopez's wife, Lopez had no knowing involvement in JFK's murder and "Saez" may not even have even existed.[8]

Also in December 1963, one CIA memo says that President Johnson received a secret Agency report about Oswald and JFK's assassination. Though it's not known what that report contained, Angleton's conclusions probably fed Johnson's belief that Fidel had orchestrated JFK's assassination. In addition, Helms made Angleton his key contact with the Warren Commission, both for providing it information and for withholding material Helms didn't want the Commission to see. Hence, the Warren Commission saw nothing about the JFK-Almeida coup plan, AMWORLD, the surveillance of Oswald, any of his intelligence activities, or anything else that might have triggered a real investigation or cost Helms his job.[9]

Moreover, Helms and the CIA didn't mislead just the Warren Commission, but other agencies as well. Numerous historians have fully documented how Helms blatantly lied to the Commission on several points. But on the same day that Helms himself testified to the Warren Commission, the FBI asked the CIA about reports that Manuel Artime's camps in Guatemala were "under the direct control of the US, that there were three military camps . . . originally organized for an invasion of Cuba." In response, Helms simply had the CIA lie to the FBI, claiming the reports about Artime and his camps were false.[10]

Amid his still-intense grief in December 1963, Robert Kennedy made a major decision that would further strain his already rocky relationship with President Lyndon Johnson: He decided to try to persuade the new President to continue the coup plan with Almeida. Harry Williams had received a communication from Almeida indicating that he was still willing to lead the coup. Williams was ready as well, and RFK believed that a free and democratic Cuba would be the best memorial to his slain brother.[11]

The first approach to President Johnson hinted at the problems to come. Williams tried to use his contact in Cyrus Vance's office—Joseph Califano—to arrange a meeting with LBJ. At that time, Califano was becoming a key aide to Johnson. Williams said that Califano told him that upon hearing Williams's name, LBJ had evoked the Kennedys' responsibility for the Bay of Pigs disaster, and then declared, "I don't want to see any god-damn Cuban, especially that son of a bitch Williams." Apparently, LBJ had heard enough about the coup plan from McCone to wonder if JFK's death was retaliation from Castro. Then, too, LBJ knew that Williams was a personal friend of RFK, whom he still didn't trust.[12]

In the early weeks of January 1964, RFK and Williams tried one last time to persuade LBJ to continue with Almeida's coup plan. Since LBJ wouldn't see Williams, there was only one course left to try: RFK would have to swallow his pride, put his own feelings aside, and plead his case personally to President Johnson. Their relationship had been terrible since 1960, and had worsened since JFK's death, because Robert Kennedy felt that Johnson had moved into the White House and asserted control too quickly. However, LBJ had tried to reach out to RFK at times, so perhaps RFK felt that talking to LBJ directly was worth a try. Also, RFK apparently intended to tell LBJ some details about the coup plan only if the new President agreed to continue it. LBJ could become RFK's political rival in the future, so it made little sense for Robert to describe every aspect of his most sensitive plan to President Johnson before he knew if LBJ was going to keep it going.[13]

Robert Kennedy's meeting with LBJ about the coup plan did not go well. Only the two of them were present, and RFK later told Williams that President Johnson listened sympathetically but made it clear that he would not continue with the plan. LBJ's decision also included ending the Cuban exile troop training program at Fort Benning, since those exiles' real purpose had been to be among the first U.S. troops into Cuba after the coup. However, LBJ did agree to continue funding RFK's favored Cuban exile groups in case they proved useful in the future. This was LBJ's way of preserving his options and asserting control: Formerly, Cuban operations had essentially been run by Robert Kennedy through Army Secretary Cyrus Vance and Richard Helms. Now the CIA would take primary responsibility, with McCone reporting to LBJ. Probably at RFK's urging, LBJ agreed to meet with the leader of the Fort Benning Cuban-American troops the following day to break the news to him personally.[14]

The leader of the Cuban-American troops at Fort Benning was Second Lieutenant Erneido Oliva, later a Major General in the National Guard and a protégé of Alexander Haig. Oliva had been second in command at the Bay of Pigs and was one of the men who presented JFK with the flag of the Brigade at the Orange Bowl ceremony. An Afro-Cuban, Oliva had been praised in a speech by JFK, who had planned to give Oliva a major role in the new Cuban provisional government after Almeida's coup. Oliva later wrote this account of his mid-January 1964 meeting with LBJ and RFK:

> President Johnson . . . said that he really wanted to help Cubans recover their homeland from communism, but . . . the moment

was not appropriate for any anti-Castro activity. He added that he was sorry to terminate the Special Presidential Program established by President Kennedy the previous year, but each Cuban officer would be given the opportunity to "stay in the service or find a new job."[15]

After one last plea from Oliva, a resolute LBJ referred him and Robert Kennedy to the Secretary of Defense:

> At the Pentagon, Oliva and Kennedy were welcomed by Secretary of Defense Robert McNamara, Secretary of the Army Cyrus Vance, Army General Counsel Joseph Califano, and Lieutenant Colonel Alexander M. Haig Jr. . . . Thus, with a short sixteen-minute meeting at the White House and twenty at the Pentagon . . . President Kennedy's plans for removing Castro from power were ended. . . .[16]

Oliva's mentor Alexander Haig, and Joseph Califano, believed the information—since discredited—suggesting that Fidel Castro was behind JFK's death. As documented by several journalists, President Johnson shared this belief, and that's one reason LBJ choose not to continue with the risky coup plan.[17]

Following RFK's meeting with LBJ and Oliva about Cuba, Cyrus Vance had his men begin the process of shutting down the special training for the Cuban exile troops. Joining Califano and Haig in that endeavor was Alexander Butterfield, a career military officer and veteran of World War II. Butterfield would later become one of President Nixon's key aides (physically, though not personally, close to the Nixon), eventually revealing the existence of Nixon's White House tapes to the Senate Watergate Committee.[18]

As for the pre-assassination operations of Vance, Califano, and Haig, Joseph Califano later wrote that:

> No one on the Warren Commission . . . talked to me or (so far as I know) anyone else involved in the covert attacks on Castro and Cuba about those attacks. The Commission was not informed of any of the efforts of Desmond FitzGerald, the CIA and Robert Kennedy to eliminate Castro and stage a coup.[19]

Given all of the recent events, the sensitive status of the Cold War, and LBJ's concerns, it's remarkable that by early December 1963, various parts of the CIA-Mafia plots to kill Fidel were apparently back in operation. A December 6, 1963, attempt to assassinate Fidel Castro involving Herminio Diaz was first documented in 2006 by author Larry Hancock. More CIA files have since been discovered that report the "wide rumor of [an] assassination attempt against Fidel Castro after his TV appearance Dec. 6, resulting in [the] killing of [a] man next to him. Castro [was] uninjured. Would-be killer at large." Hancock quotes a CIA cable to LBJ's national security advisor, McGeorge Bundy, describing "an assassination attempt on Fidel Castro after his TV appearance on 12/6," as reported by the wife of a Havana diplomat. CIA headquarters, likely FitzGerald or one of his men, added a comment linking that attempt to "continuing rumors of a plot to assassinate Castro which is connected with Herminio Diaz."[20]

The CIA comment about Diaz is important, since FBI files show that Diaz was a narcotics trafficker for Santo Trafficante. CIA records released so far about Diaz are clearly incomplete, raising the possibility that Diaz was involved in CIA activities that Helms kept secret. In the 1990s, a former Cuban official claimed that Herminio Diaz had been involved in JFK's assassination; if true, Diaz's work on the Castro assassination plots might have been a cover for his role in JFK's murder. It's unclear from the declassified files if the December 6 attempt was at the behest of Richard Helms or Desmond FitzGerald, or simply the Mafia bosses such as Trafficante pressing ahead, trying to tie themselves and their men more closely to the CIA for protection. The best indication that Helms and FitzGerald were involved with the attempt is the fact that immediately afterward, Helms authorized continuing another aspect of the CIA-Mafia plots.[21]

On the day after Diaz's attempt to kill Fidel, Helms approved a December 7, 1963, memo sending low-level Cuban official Rolando Cubela a weapons cache of shotguns, pistols, grenades, "C-4 [explosives]," and "rifles with scopes." The material, especially appropriate for an assassination attempt, was slated to be delivered in January 1964 under David Morales's supervision. Helms kept other aspects of the CIA-Mafia plots going as well, retaining European assassin recruiter QJWIN on the CIA payroll in December and for several months thereafter until reports about Trafficante's associate Michel Victor Mertz surfaced in Europe and to the CIA, at which point QJWIN was fired.[22]

Though LBJ kept most of the key exile leaders RFK had supported on the government payroll for a time, Richard Helms mysteriously dumped exile leader Tony Varona in January 1964 for reasons not clear in his declassified CIA file. Congressional investigators found that Varona left Miami in early 1964 and moved to New York, suddenly giving up his full-time work for the exile cause. Just months after that, a CIA memo cited a *New York Times* article about Varona that said he was earning money by selling cars in New Jersey at night.

Was Helms worried that Varona had somehow been part of the assassination of JFK? Perhaps he realized in hindsight that Varona looked suspicious, since he had taken $200,000 from Rosselli's Chicago Mafia and then dealt with Trafficante associate Rolando Masferrer. Also, Varona had been heavily involved in the CIA-Mafia plots and the JFK-Almeida coup plan. Legally, if Helms thought Varona, or any other CIA asset, was involved in JFK's murder, he didn't have to tell any other agency. Author Peter Dale Scott found that an "agreement was in force from the mid-1950s to the mid-1970s, exempting the CIA from a statutory requirement to report [to the Justice Department] any criminal activity by any of its employees or assets."

Johnny Rosselli's role in the CIA-Mafia plots had apparently ended, though not Rosselli's close friendship with Miami CIA official David Morales. They remained good friends, and in 1964 Morales made at least one trip to visit Rosselli in Las Vegas. Rosselli continued to split his time between Las Vegas and Los Angeles, where he moved into a large, lavish apartment on Beverly Glen, near Beverly Hills. Prospering in the immediate years after the JFK assassination, Rosselli even joined the prestigious L.A. Friars Club. The career criminal was soon bilking stars of the era, including Milton Berle and Phil Silvers, in an elaborate poker scam involving hidden mirrors.[23]

Although Richard Helms lied and obfuscated to the Warren Commission about Oswald, the coup plan, and his unauthorized operations, he did pass on to the Commission troubling information that kept its members worried about a potentially devastating confrontation with the Soviets. A KGB officer named Yuri Nosenko had recently defected to America, and he claimed he had read the KGB file on Lee Oswald, which showed the Russians had no interest in Oswald. One of the CIA officers who helped Nosenko get from Europe to America was James McCord, the future Watergate burglar. Once Nosenko was in the United States, a CIA memo confirms that "Howard Hunt [was] told about the doubts regarding AEFOXTROT [Nosenko's] bona fides" on April 9, 1964.[24]

By February 1964, the still-depressed Robert Kennedy was changing his mind about Castro and Cuba. In an exchange with Desmond FitzGerald, RFK proposed seeking an accommodation with Fidel instead of trying to overthrow him. RFK was still concerned about Almeida's safety and that of Almeida's family, still outside of Cuba on a seemingly innocent pretext. (That was one reason RFK and his associates gave no information about the coup plan to the Warren Commission.) According to Harry Williams, RFK made sure Almeida's family was covertly sent "$3,000 that the family used. And then [in addition to that money] Bobby send them a pension. You know, they received a check every month. Out of the budget." As for who in the CIA continued making those covert payments and monitoring the CIA's surveillance of Almeida's family, those files have not been released, but the most logical candidate would be E. Howard Hunt and his aide Bernard Barker.

Robert Kennedy also began his own secret investigation of JFK's murder, using Walter Sheridan, one of his key Hoffa investigators. Harry Williams, who remained friends with RFK, was not part of that secret investigation, but he kept searching for more information among the Cuban exile community in Miami, which kept leading him back to Bernard Barker and Santo Trafficante. However, he found nothing concrete enough for prosecution or to turn over to authorities.

By January 1964, Richard Nixon was the marquee name in his law firm, rechristened "Nixon, Mudge, Rose, Guthrie, and Alexander," but politics remained his real interest, and Stephen Ambrose wrote that Nixon "was still the favorite of more Republicans than anyone else and a mid-January poll had him running better against Johnson than any other man." Yet at Nixon's January 1964 strategy meeting with Haldeman and others at the Waldorf, the former Vice President had to face harsh political realities.[25]

Because Nixon lacked the necessary time, organization, and money for a full-time campaign, he and his men decided his only course remained to hope for "a deadlock between Goldwater and Rockefeller," the leading candidates. Toward that end, Nixon decided not to attack either man, but to "concentrate on Johnson." He also instructed aides do small things to fan the flames, like having one send a *Newsweek* columnist a "list of men nominated for the Presidency who had previously lost an election." He also gave a flurry of speeches criticizing the Kennedy-Johnson administration and announced that "he was 'neither encouraging nor discouraging' a write-in vote in the New Hampshire" primary. Without spending a cent, Nixon placed a respectable fourth in that state, which was won by his former running mate from 1960, Henry Cabot Lodge, who'd spent $100,000 on his own write-in campaign.[26]

Nixon took a late March trip overseas, ostensibly for business (and paid for by Pepsi), but also designed to generate publicity for himself as well. Still burnishing his statesmanship credentials for a possible Presidential run, the former Vice President met with heads of state when he visited Lebanon, Pakistan, India, Malaysia, Thailand, Hong Kong, the Philippines, and Taiwan. When he stopped in South Vietnam, Nixon generated much press coverage from the ever-growing number of journalists reporting the war as he called for "immediate escalation" of the conflict, which still didn't officially involve U.S. combat troops. That endeared Nixon to Goldwater's hawkish supporters.[27]

By carefully exploiting write-in campaigns, not antagonizing Goldwater or Rockefeller, and judiciously using the press, by "the second half of May, Nixon could see himself as not just a possible, but rather the likely GOP candidate," according to Stephen Ambrose. Nixon also continued to criticize the late President Kennedy's Cuba policy, castigating him for the Bay of Pigs debacle and claiming the Cuban Missile Crisis was a failure for the United States. While that helped Nixon with Republicans, especially Goldwater's more conservative supporters, it would have hurt him in the general election, since regard for JFK remained extremely high.[28]

However, Nixon's chances of facing LBJ evaporated in June 1964, when Barry Goldwater unexpectedly won the California primary, giving Goldwater enough votes to clinch the nomination and ending any chance Nixon had of becoming the 1964 Republican nominee. Still desperately hoping for a deadlocked convention, Nixon tried to get Michigan Governor George Romney or Pennsylvania Governor William Scranton to jump into the race, knowing that many moderate Rockefeller delegates would support them. Both men eventually declined.[29]

However, before getting Romney's final decision, Nixon made a rare public slip that sounded as if he were attacking Goldwater, telling reporters that "Goldwater's views" needed to be "challenged and repudiated." Goldwater responded to reporters that Nixon must not "know my views very well" even though "I got most of them from him,"[30] and he was partially right. While publicly embracing the most extreme of Nixon's views, but lacking Nixon's moderating political sense, Goldwater actively courted the large and influential John Birch Society, whose literature was filled with racist attacks on Martin Luther King Jr. Nixon would have been satisfied to have the votes of Birchers, but would not have offered them public support to avoid offending moderates. Goldwater attracted the support of groups even farther to the right than the Birchers, with his slogan "Extremism in the defense of Liberty is no vice"—a dangerous mantra when civil rights killings were still occurring the South. In addition, the Birchers had even denounced Eisenhower as "a dedicated conscious agent of the communist conspiracy"—not that Goldwater himself held such views. Many who knew Goldwater found him to be quite personable, and, as mentioned earlier, he enjoyed Las Vegas gambling and showgirls. Ironically, he was married to a wealthy Jewish woman, and some of the far-right groups he courted made no secret of their anti-Semitic beliefs.[31]

Goldwater's defeat was almost assured when his supporters at the Republican National Convention refused to pass a Rockefeller-supported plank condemning not just the John Birch Society, but also the murderous Ku Klux Klan. Nixon introduced the victorious Goldwater at the Convention, where party elders were already predicting a Republican defeat and looking to Nixon "to pick up the pieces" before the 1968 race. Still, Nixon campaigned diligently for Goldwater and the Republicans in 1964, and Goldwater would later say that Nixon "worked harder than any one person for the ticket."[32]

By the spring of 1964, Robert Kennedy's Justice Department and the head of his "Get Hoffa Squad," Walter Sheridan, had finally succeeded in convicting Jimmy Hoffa for the first time. Hoffa had originally invited Louisiana Teamsters official Grady Partin to his trial for jury tampering in Chattanooga, and he was shocked when Partin was finally revealed as a Justice Department informant who became a key witness in the trial. Partin's information about Hoffa's $500,000 bribe from the Mafia for Richard Nixon didn't come out in testimony, because it wasn't part of the current charges. Hoffa soon filed the first of what would be three appeals, remaining free—and Teamsters President—while his appeal worked its way through the courts. To avoid complicating Hoffa's conviction or giving him more grounds for appeal, Robert Kennedy decided to keep the Nixon-Hoffa-Mafia bribe a secret known by only a few others inside the Justice Department. It was also probably known to FBI Director J. Edgar Hoover, though it's not clear when he might have told his friend Richard Nixon that it had been discovered.[33]

With Hoffa's conviction, Robert Kennedy—who had slowly recovered from the tragedy of his brother's murder—resigned as Attorney General to begin a successful run for the Senate from New York. RFK left plans in place for the Justice Department to prosecute Carlos Marcello for jury tampering (stemming from his November 22, 1963, acquittal), though Marcello would eventually be acquitted.[34]

On August 2, 1964, the Gulf of Tonkin incident began to unfold, which would soon lead to a dramatic escalation of the Vietnam War, though LBJ wouldn't send actual combat troops until four months after the November 1964 election. After Nixon later became President, he liked to say "that he had inherited a war not of his making," but even Stephen Ambrose, usually supportive of Nixon, points out that Nixon "was being too modest. From the time of the Gulf of Tonkin Resolution onward, Nixon spurred Johnson to ever greater involvement in Vietnam."[35]

In June 1965, LBJ officially authorized "commanders in Vietnam to commit US ground forces to combat," while also sending "21,000 additional US troops—followed by 50,000 the following month, for a total of 125,000." Ambrose notes that Nixon soon became the "number one critic of Johnson's war . . . no matter how rapidly Johnson stepped up the bombing campaign" and "no matter how many troops the President sent to Vietnam, it was not enough to satisfy Nixon." At the same time, Nixon would oppose Representative Gerald Ford's suggestion "that the US declare war on North Vietnam," leading Ambrose to point out Nixon's hypocrisy in calling "for victory with one breath" while refusing "to even consider declaring war with the next." However, it should be pointed out that many—perhaps most—in Congress shared Nixon's stance. On the other hand, Nixon's law firm also "had as a client the Government of South Vietnam," which was increasingly corrupt.[36]

. . .

In the winter, spring, and summer of 1964, the Warren Commission pressed ahead, with Gerald Ford—later to become President after Nixon's resignation—playing a key role on the Committee, both burnishing his political credentials and currying favor with J. Edgar Hoover. At one point the Warren Commission hit an impasse over the "single bullet theory," which required that for one assassin shooting from one location, a single, almost pristine bullet had to have struck JFK in the back, somehow exited his throat, then dived down and inflicted all of Governor Connally's injuries. It's well documented from all accounts that JFK's back wound had been almost six inches below his collar, and made by a bullet traveling at a steep downward angle—yet for the "single bullet theory" to work, that bullet had to change course in JFK's body to travel upward to exit his throat before changing direction again in midair, to then dive down and hit Connally. It was clearly a physical impossibility.[37]

Gerald Ford came up with a solution: He raised the troublesome "back" wound to become a less problematic "back of the neck" wound. As reported by the Associated Press in 1997, Ford had changed the line "A bullet had entered his back" so that the published Warren Commission Report eventually read "a bullet had entered the back of his neck." The "single bullet theory" still strained credibility, but with some additional distortion, it allowed a theoretical bullet to enter JFK's neck and go downward to exit his throat, before supposedly causing all of Governor Connally's wounds. Ford's solution still ignored the fact that JFK's throat wound was an entrance wound from the front, and the fact that the bullet that had supposedly shattered Connally's bones was almost pristine. Those facts—along with Ford's tinkering—led some critics to later rename the "single bullet theory" the "magic bullet theory."[38]

The flaws of the Warren Commission's investigation have been well documented in numerous books, including those by noted historians like Dr. David Kaiser, Major John Newman, Dr. Michael Kurtz, and Dr. Gerald McKnight. The Warren Commission began with a preordained conclusion (lone assassin, no conspiracy) and largely depended on what J. Edgar Hoover and the FBI would give it from their investigation, plus what little of value that Richard Helms authorized James Angleton to share. In addition, more recent disclosures about AMWORLD, the JFK-Almeida coup plan, and the confessions of Carlos Marcello and Santo Trafficante show that the scope of information withheld from the Warren Commission was even greater than could be documented just a few years ago.[39]

Yet the Warren Commission fulfilled its real goal: to reassure the public that there was no foreign involvement in JFK's assassination. That's also why members of the Commission didn't pursue lines of investigation that could have uncovered information that might have pointed toward Cuban or Russian involvement. Hence the Warren Report makes no mention of the CIA-Mafia plots even though three of the Commission members knew about them, Jack Ruby wasn't taken away from Dallas and to Washington for questioning as he begged, and the commission failed to investigate the published articles of John Martino, even though staff members were aware of them (and Martino's FBI interviews).[40]

Eventually, Gerald Ford boasted that just before the Warren Commission Report was published, he played a final, pivotal role. It's well documented that four members of the Commission—Richard Russell, John McCloy, Hale Boggs, and John Cooper—harbored doubts about the Commission's conclusion. For example, *Vanity Fair* documented that Russell told an associate he was "not completely satisfied in my own mind that he [Oswald] did plan and commit this act altogether on his own." Most of the suspicions of those four Commission members leaned toward Cuban or Soviet involvement. So that all of the members could present a united front to the public, Ford indicated that he was responsible for a key phrase in the Warren Report. It said their investigation "found no evidence" of a conspiracy, rather than stating flatly there was no conspiracy. Ford himself had expressed his own doubts, but it tells a lot about his personality and political ambition that he knew the importance for the country and his career of staying on message in public, regardless of the facts.[41]

Ford's political instincts were right, and the Warren Report was widely praised and accepted by the press and public when it was released in September 1964. Ford was part of a well-coordinated public relations effort that insured the Report was well received, writing for *Life* magazine before its release that the Commission's "monumental record . . . will stand like a Gibraltar of factual literature through the ages to come." Praise flowed from officials and the media, including *The New York Times*, which published a best-selling paperback edition of the report. While the overseas press was more skeptical, in the United States, media accolades were almost unanimous.[42]

Richard Helms was no doubt relieved at the Warren Report's broad acceptance in the United States. He had successfully kept the Warren Commission, President Johnson, and his own CIA Director from discovering his unauthorized continuation of the CIA-Mafia plots, all under the guise of protecting AMWORLD and the remnants of the JFK-Almeida coup plan. The latter no longer included JFK, Almeida, RFK, or Harry Williams, but did include ongoing CIA support for Manuel Artime, Manolo Ray, and Eloy Menoyo. In addition, Helms continued parts of the CIA-Mafia plots, including CIA contact with the mob-linked Cuban official Rolando Cubela, all of which Helms planned to merge with Artime's operation.[43]

Like Helms, Richard Nixon would have also been relieved that the JFK investigation had officially ended. John Martino's name was nowhere in the Warren Report, nor were the CIA-Mafia plots to kill Fidel that Nixon had spawned. As for the 1964 election, Nixon had been right about Goldwater's chances. President Johnson won by a landslide, with a popular vote of "61% and 486 electoral votes to Goldwater's 39% and 52 electoral votes." But at least Nixon had not been on a losing ticket, and he was content for the time being "earning more than $250,000 a year" (almost $1.5 million today) at his law firm.[44]

President Johnson scaled back, but didn't end, the CIA's 1964 Cuban operations, so E. Howard Hunt continued working on them for Richard Helms. Hunt likely maintained a role in providing CIA support for (and surveillance of) Commander Almeida's family, still outside of Cuba. Almeida remained unexposed and high in the Cuban government, but was no longer actively involved in the coup plan, so the CIA's main focus shifted to the Mafia-linked Rolando Cubela. The CIA's goal was to persuade Cubela and Hunt's close friend Artime to work together, and Spain was one of the countries where the men could meet. According to journalist Tad Szulc, after JFK's death Helms had tried to appoint Hunt as the CIA's Deputy Chief of Station in Madrid, but the U.S. ambassador at that time was the same one Hunt had clashed with in Uruguay in 1959, and he vetoed Hunt's appointment. That meant Hunt's role with Artime in Spain would have to be under very deep cover. That began a pattern—of a fake resignation from the CIA, while continuing to work for the Agency—that Hunt would repeat during Watergate.[45]

While Hunt was in Spain, Bernard Barker remained a CIA agent in Miami. Since Barker was still friends with Artime (who split his time between Miami and his camps in Central America), he was in an ideal position to help coordinate between Hunt and Artime. Just as Barker the previous year had arranged meetings between Hunt and Harry Williams, Barker probably had a similar role in facilitating the arrangements between Hunt and Artime.[46]

Well-documented meetings between Artime and Cubela were set up in Europe, and plans were made to assassinate Fidel. However, because Almeida was not involved in the operation at all, the men's first priority was to look for other high-ranking officials who could become part of their plot. Cubela drew up and shared with Artime lists of high Cuban officers and officials who might be willing to help assassinate Fidel, or who might alternatively support Cubela and Artime after Fidel was dead. However, even approaching those officers and officials was fraught with danger, and no real attempts were made. In addition, troubling reports from Trafficante associates began filtering in to Helms and the CIA, showing that Cubela's operation was growing insecure. For example, CIA reports show that after Artime's last meeting with Cubela on February 12, 1965, the following month, a Trafficante associate from Cuba talked about the Cubela plot to a CIA "station officer." However, aside from the mob-linked security breaches surrounding the Cubela operation, Fidel Castro's intelligence agents had actually penetrated Artime's group a year earlier, something that would have prevented Fidel's assassination even if Artime and Cubela had gone forward with their plans.[47]

Richard Helms was no doubt livid when he saw a January 25, 1965, article in *The Nation* that gave an all-too-accurate description of Artime's operation. Written by *The Miami Herald*'s Al Burt, the story reported that Artime's operation in Central America hoped "a coup could be engendered inside Cuba [and] that Castro might be assassinated." Burt even pointed out that JFK's November 18, 1963, Miami speech was "obviously intended for Cubans inside Cuba" who were part of Artime's operation (which had been true at the time JFK made his speech). Burt documented official U.S. support for Artime by detailing secret monetary transactions, including one for "$167,784 in a plain white envelope . . . issued on November 19, 1963" for Artime to buy "two World War II torpedo boats" which could have been used to move Artime into Cuba after the coup.[48]

That publicity, various problems with Artime, and the insecurity of Cubela's operation because associates of Santo Trafficante knew about it proved too much for Helms, and he began the gradual process of shutting down Artime's operation. Helms probably hoped that as long as Almeida was still in place and unexposed, the Cuban Commander might be willing to help the United States at some point in the future.

As the process of closing down AMWORLD and Artime's operation continued in 1965, E. Howard Hunt, Manuel Artime, and Bernard Barker had an unexpected encounter with Harry Williams. Williams still occasionally saw or spoke with Robert Kennedy, but he stayed away from anti-Castro activities even though many exiles still revered him. In 1965, Williams dropped by an exile's house in Miami on an impromptu social visit and was welcomed by his host, who assumed Williams was there to attend a small meeting just underway.[49]

Williams was surprised to see several of his associates from 1963, including Hunt, Artime, and Barker (who Williams had since learned was working for Santo Trafficante). The men were getting ready to sell off the arms and equipment from Artime's huge AMWORLD program, which was being shut down. Williams advised them not to sell the armaments, arguing they should be kept secure in case the situation in Cuba changed. Hunt, Barker, and the others replied that they were selling the arms and planned to keep all the money for themselves. They offered to cut Williams in for a share, but he declined. Williams said the attitude of the men—except for his friend—turned menacing and he felt glad to make it out of the door alive.[50]

Richard Helms or Desmond FitzGerald may have ordered Hunt to help liquidate the AMWORLD supplies, though it's unclear whether Helms knew that his protégé Hunt was pocketing some of the money. Helms might have been in a hurry to dismantle the AMWORLD operation, because on April 28, 1965, President Johnson replaced John McCone as CIA Director with Vice Admiral William Raborn. Even though Johnson promoted Helms to Deputy CIA Director, the less Helms had to tell Raborn about Cuban operations, especially those with a troubled past history, the better. (Desmond FitzGerald took Helms's old position as Deputy Director for Plans.)

CIA files declassified so far put the total amount spent on AMWORLD at just over $7 million (over $35 million today), though one former CIA official told *Newsweek* editor Evan Thomas the total was $50 million. Even if much of the material was sold or fenced for pennies on the dollar, that still meant a substantial sum for Hunt, Artime, Barker, and the others. By the following year, Hunt and his family would appear to be living well beyond the means of an ordinary CIA officer.* [51]

With a new CIA Director onboard, Deputy Director Richard Helms might have felt that it was better for Hunt to dispose of the material quietly, rather than doing it openly in a way that might reveal the CIA's massive support for Artime. Williams indicated the arms and equipment were sold off with the assistance of Bernard Barker's connections to Trafficante. If the Mafia was involved in the transaction, that might not have concerned Helms, since memos reveal that a year earlier the CIA had considered using the Mafia as a cover for providing supplies to Artime. In addition, Artime had been part of the CIA-Mafia plots, so he already had a connection to the mob. Even if Helms knew that Artime and some of his associates were keeping the money, Helms might have seen it as an appropriate reward both for Artime's years of service to the CIA (including a year and a half in Cuban prisons after the Bay of Pigs) and as a way to keep Artime from publicly protesting the U.S. shutdown of his operation. Essentially, it was hush money, ensuring that Artime didn't expose Helms's unauthorized operations to Congress or the press (which Artime had shown with the *Nation* article he was capable of doing). Ironically, in 1972 and 1973 Artime would be one of Nixon's hush-fund paymasters after Watergate, funneling money to Hunt and Barker (and the other Watergate burglars) to keep quiet.[52]

On February 28, 1966, Rolando Cubela (AMLASH) was arrested in Cuba, due in part to information from Fidel's agent in Artime's camp. Eloy Menoyo, who had been arrested after sneaking into Cuba in 1965 and who confessed after beatings, was already serving what amounted to a life sentence. Menoyo was not part of Cubela's trial, possibly indicating that Fidel didn't realize Menoyo and Artime had worked together prior to Menoyo's capture.[53]

Fidel Castro made sure Cubela's trial was a highly publicized spectacle, but Che Guevara was conspicuously absent, even though

*Hunt tried to ascribe his lavish lifestyle to money from his paperback spy novels, but they never sold nearly that well.

he was apparently back in Cuba. Commander Almeida was present for Cubela's trial, and the CIA worried that the man who was by far its highest-ranking asset in Cuba might be exposed. Five days after Cubela's arrest was announced, a cable sent from the CIA Director's office said that CIA headquarters was "most interested [in] ascertaining Almeida's current status [in] view [of] AMLASH and other arrests." It asked for a friend of Almeida "to write . . . to Almeida in hopes of eliciting [an] interesting response."[54]

Almeida's name didn't come out in the trial, much to CIA officials' relief, as expressed in an April 14, 1966, memo saying there had been "no indication whatsoever that Rolando Cubela revealed anything more than his 'weakness, playboy attitude,' in plotting with a man like Manuel Artime to assassinate Fidel Castro. Under private interrogation to date there is no known possibility that Rolando Cubela has revealed the names of the real military leaders with whom he really was in contact. . . . None of these major individuals, whose names are known to us, have been arrested or detained." Because of Cubela's public contrition, he was spared execution and sentenced to thirty years.[55]

Richard Helms knew that as long as Almeida remained in place and unexposed, he had a possible asset to use in the future—if he could keep his job by concealing his unauthorized assassination schemes with Cubela from other U.S. officials. *The New York Times* reported on March 6, 1966, that Cubela planned "to shoot Premier Castro with a high-powered telescopic rifle and later share [power] with Mr. Artime." Former FBI agent William Turner wrote that when LBJ's Secretary of State, Dean Rusk, read about Cubela's arrest "in the *New York Times*, [he] demanded to know what the CIA's role might have been." The CIA's Richard "Helms sent him a soothing memo stating that contact with Cubela had been confined to 'the express purpose' of intelligence gathering. 'The Agency was not involved with Cubela in a plot to assassinate Fidel Castro,' Helms wrote [to Rusk], 'nor did it ever encourage him to attempt such an act.'"[56]

Helms's statement was clearly false, as Rusk himself finally learned almost ten years later, when Senate hearings finally exposed Helms's Cubela assassination operation and the rest of the CIA-Mafia plots. When this author spoke to Dean Rusk about this incident, his anger about Helms's deception was still quite evident. It was the only time in the interview when the consummate diplomat showed a flash of real emotion. Rusk felt the CIA had gone far beyond the scope of what the Johnson administration wanted, and then lied to him about it. His anger at Richard Helms also extended to information Helms gave him in 1964, during the Warren Commission, which Rusk learned later was also false.[57]

The information Richard Helms hid from Rusk, President Johnson, and his own CIA Directors about his unauthorized CIA-Mafia Castro plots kept Helms from being fired, but it was Helms's astute political skills and his ability to manage information that allowed his CIA career to flourish. Dissatisfied with Vice Admiral Raborn's performance as CIA Director, President Johnson began grooming Helms to replace him.

Richard Helms officially became CIA Director on June 30, 1966, putting him in an even better position to ensure that his unauthorized activities under JFK and LBJ were not exposed. Helms wasted no time in "firing" Bernard Barker the following month because—as Helms later testified—Barker "was involved in certain gambling and criminal elements." With Cubela's arrest, the CIA-Mafia plots—that Nixon had spawned so many years before—had officially ended, meaning that Helms no longer needed Barker and his mob ties. In fact, the heyday of all anti-Castro Cuban operations was over, though some smaller-scale efforts would continue. The CIA's main focus in 1966 was Vietnam and Southeast Asia, giving Helms an opportunity to send several of his operatives as far away as possible.[58]

Six veterans of AMWORLD and the anti-Castro operations were shipped off to Laos in 1966, where the United States had been waging a secret war for years. These included Artime's deputy Rafael "Chi Chi" Quintero, former Miami CIA Chief Ted Shackley, and (after an assignment in South America) David Morales. Some writers have portrayed their transfer to Laos as a reward, giving them a choice assignment in an intelligence hotspot where their covert war expertise could flourish. However, living for long stretches in that country's relatively primitive conditions was a long way from the poolside talks and ocean breezes Morales and Shackley had enjoyed in Miami. In addition, Helms knew that their anti-Castro operations had been a failure at best, and at worst, somehow involved in JFK's assassination.[59]

As for Manuel Artime, though he was trained as a physician, he became a prosperous businessman, no doubt helped by the money and contacts he had gained from selling off the AMWORLD supplies.

Artime traveled frequently to Central America to pursue business ventures with the notoriously corrupt Somoza family who ruled Nicaragua. Artime also maintained his involvement in the narcotics trade, even as he continued to receive a regular salary from the CIA into 1966.[60]

By the winter of 1966, Richard Nixon had his sights set firmly on the 1968 Presidential nomination. Whatever he might have heard from friends like Bebe Rebozo, William Pawley, or J. Edgar Hoover about the end of the CIA's Cuban operations would have eased Nixon's worries about any possible exposure of his links to them. Nixon seems to have distanced himself from Pawley after John Martino's articles, but he grew closer to Rebozo, a much more profitable relationship for the former Vice President. Throughout Nixon's moves over the past five years—from Washington to Los Angeles to New York—visits with Rebozo had been a reassuring constant for Nixon as he prospered financially and plotted strategy for his next political battle.

Unlike his election losses of 1960 and 1962, Nixon now had plenty of time to carefully lay the groundwork for his next race, something he'd been doing since Goldwater's defeat. In the past two years, Richard Nixon had addressed "more than four hundred GOP groups in forty states, raising money for local candidates." Stephen Ambrose added that "No one else worked like that for the party, and no one else, save only Ike, drew people as Nixon did." After seeing how courting the John Birch Society and other extremist groups had cost Goldwater moderate votes, Nixon called for "a formal renunciation of the Birchers." Nixon's efforts would pay huge dividends in the coming years as he worked to secure the Republican nomination and the Presidency.[61]

Richard Nixon's future looked bright on all fronts: politically, personally, and financially. He couldn't know that the threads of his covert Cuban operations would start to unravel in the coming year, setting him on the road to Watergate. Nixon didn't realize that his ties to the Mafia—especially the CIA-Mafia plots to kill Fidel that he had helped to create—would eventually drive him from the office he was working so hard to attain.[62]

PART III

CHAPTER 19

1966: Nixon & Rebozo, Helms & Hunt

From mid-1966 until the late 1970s, the lives and careers of Richard Nixon and Richard Helms would become inexorably linked. The two men shared crucial secrets about the CIA-Mafia plots spawned under Vice President Nixon in 1960, which had touched Nixon's associates again in 1963 after Helms continued the plots without authorization from JFK or CIA Director McCone. Nixon and Helms's common concern of ensuring that those secrets never became public would keep drawing them together, at times as allies and on other occasions as adversaries. Yet even as Helms tried to keep a tight lid on information about the Agency's plotting with mobsters like Johnny Rosselli and Santo Trafficante—to avoid losing his new position at the pinnacle of the CIA—Nixon's associates became ever more involved with Trafficante's organization. Those two trajectories would eventually merge, with unexpected results, resulting in the Watergate scandal, the firing of Helms, and Nixon's resignation from the Presidency he'd sought for so long.

The extensive assistance Richard Nixon rendered to Republican candidates in the 1966 races was designed to firm up his support for the 1968 Presidential nomination. Though after Goldwater's 1964 debacle Nixon was already viewed as the front-runner, the former Vice President had been through too much to take anything for granted. Still, Nixon was well positioned to campaign for the 1966 contenders, since the lucrative position at his New York law firm gave him all the time off he needed for his political activities.[1]

From outward appearances, Nixon and his family seemed very comfortable living in their lavish Manhattan apartment. Nixon was a member of two "fashionable country clubs" and three "exclusive Manhattan clubs," gaining a degree of social acceptance he'd lacked even as Vice President. In some ways, Nixon was now part of the "elite he habitually scorned" in his later public speeches. Yet, he still wasn't a member of the truly wealthy, old money circles of the GOP. Instead, Nixon still had to serve them through his legal work, which included helping families who enjoyed a high net worth avoid paying U.S. income taxes. Ironically, this would help to create in Nixon a surprising resentment of those establishment families and of the traditional Republican hierarchy, as would become evident in his recorded comments just a few years later. The work also fueled his ambition to become President, at almost any cost, with the same degree of fervor he'd demonstrated in his first race back in 1946. However, in public at least, Nixon carefully distanced himself from any talk of seeking the Republican nomination.[2]

One place Nixon always felt entirely comfortable was with his longtime best friend, Bebe Rebozo, and they grew even closer while Nixon was out of political office. Their personal and financial relationship is much more clearly understood now than when Nixon was alive. Rebozo was not a sycophant like Bernard Barker, but the polished, suave, and successful businessman gladly did anything that Nixon wanted—or needed—him to do. In hindsight, it's quite clear that one of Rebozo's key roles was to help Richard Nixon make money, raise money, and hide money.[3]

As the 1960s progressed, Richard Nixon set his sights on much more lucrative schemes and investments than the ones he and Rebozo had shared earlier, like the Coral Gables motel Rebozo fronted for Nixon. A less legitimate investment was one noted in a Miami Police Intelligence report that involved "Rebozo . . . running a numbers racket out of one of his coin laundry businesses . . . 'fronting in this operation for ex-Vice President Nixon.'"[4]

In 1964, Rebozo had founded "his own financial institution, the Key Biscayne Bank," And according to Anthony Summers, Nixon took center stage at the groundbreaking and "held Savings Account No. 1." However, Key Biscayne was no regular bank and ranked next to last among all Florida banks in the number of loans it made. Instead, investigators discovered that "Rebozo's bank was primarily a place that held money or assisted in the movement of money."[5]

Some of the money in Rebozo's small bank belonged to the Mafia. According to senior Congressional investigator William Gallinaro, "Bebe Rebozo was a friendly banker when it came to the mob." Former

Miami FBI agent Charles Stanley categorized Rebozo as an individual "determined to have significant, witting association with 'made members' of La Cosa Nostra [the Mafia]." According to Alvin Kotz, convicted for dealing in stolen securities (stock certificates), "Bebe and Bebe's bank were an outlet for these things [stolen securities]. It was a well-known thing in organized crime circles." That was confirmed by Vincent Teresa, a "high-ranking Mafioso . . . turned government informant [who] told the Watergate Special Prosecution Force that he had used Rebozo's bank to cash . . . stolen stock."[6]

Richard Nixon also became involved in Rebozo's extensive real estate speculations, even though Summers documented that "organized crime figures were a presence in Rebozo's real estate and banking ventures." One example was a development called Fisher's Island, near Miami Beach, where in the 1960s Nixon invested $185,891, before doubling his money when he sold his shares for $371,782 (about $1.8 million today). Nixon got his Fisher's Island investment funds "from Rebozo's bank and an additional hundred thousand dollars from" a Miami bank linked to Meyer Lansky.[7]

Nixon would soon use his windfall to buy "palatial residences [in] Key Biscayne, and San Clemente in Southern California," both with the aid of Bebe Rebozo. The properties cost far more than Nixon could afford, even with the profits Nixon earned courtesy of Rebozo and his quarter-million-dollar salary from the law firm. But Rebozo made it possible by coordinating complex "sales, mortgages, and resales, [which] left Nixon technically owning" just his homes and their immediate property, while still having full use "of the entire property," which was four times larger than what Nixon officially owned.[8]

CIA expert "boatman" Eugenio Martinez—still on the CIA payroll, and later a Watergate burglar—"was vice president of a real estate firm [that] brokered the purchase of Nixon's house on Key Biscayne." While "Rebozo had extensive dealings" with Martinez's firm, it's important to stress that Martinez did not have mob connections like those of Rebozo and Martinez's friend, Bernard Barker.[9]

Nixon would also buy two lots in a development near Key Biscayne "for half the price of two lots close by," and Rebozo got a similar deal. But "both Nixon and Rebozo delayed recording their purchases of two of the [lots] until several years later" so they could clear one lot of "previous mortgages held by an associate of Lansky and Teamsters leader Jimmy Hoffa." Mob connections like that crop up constantly in the dealings Nixon had with Rebozo. For example, one of Rebozo's other investors in Fisher's Island "was a convicted sugar bootlegger. Rebozo was a co-owner of another island, close by Fisher's, with a gambler [who] fronted for a Meyer Lansky associate [and whose] phone records . . . revealed calls to associates of mob bosses Carlos Marcello and Santo Trafficante."[10]

Another mob associate involved with Nixon's friend Rebozo was Bernard Barker. Summers documented that both "Bernard Barker and Eugenio Martinez were officers of real estate firms that acted in property deals for Nixon and Rebozo." That fact helps to explain why, soon after the arrest of Barker and Martinez during the final Watergate burglary, Nixon said on the White House tapes that he should use Rebozo to raise hush money for "the boys," referring to Watergate burglars with a familiarity missing from most conventional Watergate accounts.[11]

Two quite different views of Bernard Barker emerge from late 1966 to 1969, one from his released CIA file and the other from the public record. According to his CIA file, in July of 1966 Barker received a small CIA termination payment of $1,500 and moved to Chicago. Barker's CIA file portrays him as someone who could hope to get at best a low-level technical job after the Agency let him go, but in reality Barker did exceedingly well after his CIA employment, and he soon owned a thriving real estate business with a dozen employees. Of course, Barker's released CIA file contains no hint of all the money Barker made from his share of the AMWORLD arms sell-off with E. Howard Hunt and Manuel Artime. Barker's declassified CIA file also contains very little information about his ties to the Mafia. In fact, through the 1960s and into the 1970s, Barker was linked to Trafficante's organization even more closely than Rebozo was tied to Meyer Lansky's. Both mob bosses thrived as the 1960s progressed, with Trafficante spending more time in Miami and Lansky increasing his holdings and influence in the Bahamas, which had replaced Cuba as the Caribbean's gambling mecca—something that would soon involve Nixon.[12]

In the early months of 1966, Trafficante's associate Johnny Rosselli was living in a posh apartment building near Beverly Hills, described by his biographers as having "some of the most beautiful and luxurious apartments in the nation." The FBI kept the sixty-one-year-old Rosselli under tighter surveillance than in 1963 and noted that a "very attractive blonde woman [was] staying at Rosselli's apartment" and "cooking his meals."[13]

But on the morning of May 12, 1966, Rosselli's world came crashing down when two FBI agents confronted him during his stroll near Rodeo Drive. Using information from a two-year investigation, the agents called the Mafia don by his birth name, one he hadn't used since his youth in Boston: Filippo Sacco. Hearing that name from federal officials no doubt sent a chill through Rosselli, since he'd been born in Italy and had always been in the United States illegally.[14]

Johnny Rosselli's morning confrontation with the FBI in Beverly Hills began a ten-year effort by Rosselli to avoid deportation. It also set off a deadly chain reaction that wouldn't end until the Mafia don was gruesomely murdered—on Trafficante's orders—even as Rosselli was in the midst of testifying to Congress about the CIA-Mafia plots to kill Fidel Castro. In the intervening years, Rosselli's efforts would cause huge problems for CIA Director Richard Helms, and, once Richard Nixon was President, ultimately trigger events that led to Watergate.

CIA Director Richard Helms quickly heard about Rosselli's dilemma, because the Mafia don wasted no time in contacting his old CIA associates Sheffield Edwards and William Harvey. Though Edwards had retired and was no longer Chief of the CIA's seven-hundred-person Security Division, he still had high-level contacts at the Agency. William Harvey was still an officer, though he was no longer the star he'd been from the 1950s until late 1962. Harvey and Rosselli had kept in touch and remained friends, and both Harvey and Edwards made sure that CIA Director Helms got Rosselli's message: He wanted the Agency to get the FBI off his back, to keep him out of prison, and to make sure he wasn't deported.[15]

However, even as Rosselli's plea reached Helms, the CIA Director had to take action to deal with Sam Giancana, Rosselli's boss. Giancana had been in jail almost a year for refusing to testify about the Mafia to a grand jury, after being granted immunity. The grand jury's term was almost up, but the government could empanel a new one and keep Giancana in prison for another year.

Powerful Washington attorney Edward Bennett Williams—later to play a pivotal role in exposing Watergate—represented Giancana, negotiating a deal that allowed Giancana to go free in return for leaving the country and not divulging the CIA-Mafia Castro assassination plots. Giving up the mantle of Chicago mob boss that had been slipping from his grasp for the past year, Giancana went to Mexico, where he was joined by his longtime associate, mobster Richard Cain, who had also been part of the Agency's October 1960 attempt to assassinate Fidel.[16]

Congressional investigators confirmed that the CIA played a role in Giancana's release. Richard Helms apparently believed he had no choice but to help the mobster if he wanted to hide the CIA-Mafia plots and Giancana's role in them. But Giancana was only one of three such problems Helms had to deal with. Next up was Robert Maheu, the longtime CIA asset who was now working almost exclusively for billionaire Howard Hughes.[17]

It must have been frustrating for Helms, just settling in as CIA Director, to have to deal with reminders of his unauthorized CIA-Mafia operation. Helms had to come to the aid of Robert Maheu because of events set in motion by Teamsters President Jimmy Hoffa. By the summer of 1966, Hoffa had been convicted in trials in Chicago and Memphis, and only a flurry of appeals was delaying the start of his long prison sentences. FBI and Justice Department informant Edward Partin had been a key part of the prosecution's cases against Hoffa, but the Teamsters leader thought that Robert Kennedy had also used illegal wiretaps to gain evidence against him. At that time, U.S. law didn't allow wiretap evidence to be used in court, and only phone records were admissible. Hoffa therefore encouraged his ally, Missouri Senator Edward Long, to hold hearings on the legality of Justice Department phone taps, particularly those authorized by Robert Kennedy when he was Attorney General.[18]

One of the witnesses called by Senator Long's committee was Robert Maheu. The key role Maheu played in the CIA-Mafia plots under then–Vice President Nixon had led to Maheu's involvement in the October 1960 Las Vegas bugging incident for Sam Giancana, when the CIA had paid to bug the hotel room of comedian Dan Rowan, whom Giancana suspected was seeing his girlfriend. In the summer of 1966, Senator Long and some members of Congress knew only about the bugging incident, and nothing about the Castro assassination plots. Maheu didn't want to testify, fearing it would damage his relationship with Howard Hughes. According to Rosselli's biographers, Maheu "contacted the CIA general counsel" about the matter. Helms obviously didn't want Congress to find out about the Agency's plots with the Mafia—or the CIA's own illegal extensive domestic surveillance—so the CIA's General Counsel "persuaded Long to drop his demand that Maheu testify."*[19]

Richard Helms had been forced to deal with the issue of the CIA-Mafia plots twice in only a month, and on June 24, 1966, a "summary of the operation [was] prepared by the [CIA's] Office of Security." The fewer people who knew anything about the plots, either inside the CIA or out, the smaller the chance the plans would leak, unraveling the cover-up Helms had managed so carefully on his climb to the CIA's highest post. It's possible Helm's and the CIA's interventions in the Giancana and Maheu matters led to Helms's firing of Bernard Barker around this same time, giving Helms one less Mafia-linked loose end to deal with.[20]

In Johnny Rosselli's case, unlike those of Giancana and Maheu, Richard Helms was reluctant to play the same card a third time, so Helms made no move to intervene with the FBI to help Rosselli. As a result, a June 1966 FBI memo said that Rosselli "looked sick and worried and recently has not had his usual dapper appearance." But Rosselli was a master "strategist"—the title he used on his business card—and he still had a hand to play. Because Maheu retained his powerful position with Howard Hughes, Rosselli would use his relationship with Maheu to get to Hughes. In addition, Rosselli began plotting a careful strategy, which wouldn't take effect until early the following year, with his trusted friend, longtime Hoffa attorney Edward Morgan, who was well connected in Washington power circles. If Helms didn't want to help Rosselli as he'd helped Maheu and Giancana, then Rosselli would find a way to force the CIA to act.[21]

The summer of 1966 brought the first wave of American books critical of the Warren Report, and Richard Helms's reaction would have far-reaching implications. Previously, only a smattering of books about the assassination—most of which initially appeared overseas—had criticized the Warren Report. The first significant critical book to originate in America was *The Unanswered Questions about President Kennedy's Assassination*, by veteran reporter Sylvan Fox, who soon joined *The*

*The following year, Senator Long was investigated by the Senate Ethics Committee, and he eventually had to step down because of his ties to Hoffa.

New York Times. It set a pattern of using the Warren Commission's own Report and twenty-six volumes of supporting evidence to pick apart the Commission's "lone nut, magic bullet" conclusion. By the summer and fall of 1966, Fox's tome was joined by a host of well-documented pro-conspiracy books, including attorney Mark Lane's best-selling *Rush to Judgment*, Sylvia Meagher's *Accessories after the Fact*, Josiah Thompson's *Six Seconds in Dallas*, and Edward Jay Epstein's *Inquest*.

Senator Robert Kennedy's friend, former JFK aide Richard Goodwin, was very impressed with *Inquest*, which focused on problems with the medical evidence and the "magic bullet." Goodwin wrote a glowing review of *Inquest* for the July 23, 1966, *Washington Post*, declaring that an "independent group should look at [Epstein's] charges and determine whether the Commission investigation was so flawed that another inquiry is necessary."[22]

Goodwin's comments were the subject of an article in the next day's *New York Times*, which called him "the first member of the President's inner circle to suggest publicly that an official re-examination be made of the Warren Report." The following day, Goodwin was at Robert Kennedy's New York apartment, trying to talk to him about *Inquest* and the need for a new investigation. However, Robert could only reply, "I'm sorry, Dick, I just can't focus on it." Goodwin persisted, telling RFK, "We should find our own investigator—someone with absolute loyalty and discretion." Robert suggested, "You might try Carmine Bellino. He's the best in the country."[23]

Later that night, Robert Kennedy returned to the subject of the assassination. He said, "About that other thing"—JFK's murder—"I never thought it was the Cubans. If anyone was involved it was organized crime. But there's nothing I can do about it. Not now." Richard Goodwin would not write about RFK's comments for twenty-two years. Four years after he did, Goodwin told Robert's biographer Jack Newfield in 1992 that RFK had specifically pointed to "that mob guy in New Orleans" as being responsible for JFK's assassination. Goodwin confirmed to this author that RFK definitely meant Carlos Marcello.[24]

Not for decades would it be clear that Robert Kennedy wasn't guessing when he pointed to Marcello. After recovering from the months-long shock of his brother's murder, and while still Attorney General, Robert Kennedy had begun investigating the crime with the aid of Walter Sheridan, the head of his "Get Hoffa Squad." Sheridan's widow later admitted that her husband had helped Robert look into JFK's murder and that they "continued working on the case even after Bobby left the Justice Department. The two of them would sometimes go back to the Justice Department to look over evidence together."[25]

Marcello's biographer, John Davis, independently confirmed that Walter Sheridan had "conducted an informal investigation and concluded . . . Marcello might well have been involved." According to Sheridan's son, this search left Sheridan "convinced that President Kennedy had been killed by a conspiracy." However, after helping to secure Hoffa's convictions, Sheridan left the Justice Department in 1965 to work for NBC News as a producer and investigator.[26]

For Robert Kennedy, the whole matter of his brother's murder was extremely problematic. On one hand, RFK told Arthur Schlesinger on October 30, 1966, that he "wondered how long he could continue to avoid comment on the [Warren] Report," given the spate of books pointing out its flaws. Schlesinger wrote that while Robert "believes that it was a poor job and will not endorse it [in public] he is unwilling to criticize it and thereby reopen the whole tragic business."[27]

One reason was that Robert Kennedy knew his ally in the JFK-Almeida coup plan, Commander Juan Almeida, was still alive and still held power in Cuba. Any thorough or public investigation could put Almeida, and any hope of a U.S.-friendly government in Cuba, in jeopardy. From time to time, reports continued to surface from Mexico City pointing to Fidel's involvement in JFK's death, and though RFK didn't believe them (and the accounts were later discredited), they helped to reinforce the beliefs of some high-ranking U.S. officials that Fidel had murdered JFK in response to U.S. efforts against him.

RFK's concerns had caused him to take action with respect to evidence in the case. The previous year, on April 26, 1965, "the Secret Service transferred the autopsy photographs and x-rays, and certain vital documents and biological materials, to the custody of the Kennedy family at the request of Robert F. Kennedy," according to a government investigator. RFK also obtained crucial physical evidence, such as JFK's brain and tissue samples. On February 18, 1966, RFK had the bronze coffin that transported JFK's body from Dallas to Washington "taken from the basement of the National Archives" then "loaded with sandbags and riddled with holes . . . and dumped from an Air Force C-130 into the Atlantic Ocean," as later reported by CNN. On October 31, 1966, the day after RFK's remarks about the Warren

Report to Schlesinger, RFK ordered the lawyer for the Kennedy estate—Jack Miller, who'd formerly headed RFK's organized crime effort—to transfer some of the autopsy evidence to the official custody of the National Archives. However, RFK didn't include some of the most crucial evidence, like the steel container that apparently held JFK's brain and tissue samples taken from around the wounds. Also missing from the transfer were some of the autopsy photos, including those of JFK's open chest and others that official photographers had taken at the Bethesda autopsy.[28]

CIA Director Richard Helms would have also been worried about the rising tide of books and articles concerning the Warren Report's conclusion and what they might uncover. Helms knew he'd withheld a vast amount of information from the Warren Commission, and was no doubt concerned about what any new investigation might uncover. Helms had to keep his unauthorized 1963 Castro assassination plots with the Mafia from being exposed, since he had to have at least suspected they had somehow been linked to JFK's assassination. Helms's national security cover for his efforts would be protecting Commander Almeida, his family (still outside of Cuba receiving CIA support), and the CIA's ongoing operations against Cuba.

However, with Deputy Director for Plans Desmond FitzGerald in declining health and David Atlee Phillips serving as CIA Station Chief in the Dominican Republic, Helms turned to someone else who had every incentive to prevent the intelligence failures from 1963 from coming to light: E. Howard Hunt. In the summer of 1966, Richard Helms ordered Hunt to return to the United States from Spain to resume his important CIA role of dealing with U.S. publishers and the press. The emerging skepticism of the U.S. press and public regarding the Warren Report was a double-edged sword for E. Howard Hunt. It increased his value to Helms but raised the possibility that a journalist might come across Harry Williams or someone else who could implicate Hunt's associates in the events surrounding JFK's assassination. For the next six years, Helms made sure that Hunt was in a good position to ensure that Helms's unauthorized Castro assassination attempts—primarily the CIA-Mafia plots, which included Rosselli, Trafficante, Cubela, and QJWIN—didn't become known to the press, public, or Congress. That would have destroyed both of their careers. During Cubela's public trial in Havana, Cubela had named Artime and the CIA's Madrid Station Chief as part of the plot, but neither he nor any other witness had mentioned either Hunt's real name or his code name, "Eduardo." Escaping notice, Hunt remained valuable to Helms and returned to the United States, apparently expecting great things and a very bright future. Hunt later called his 1966 return to the U.S. "the beginning of the period that would make [him] a household name."[29]

Hunt bought an estate twenty minutes from CIA headquarters that he described as a "sprawling horse ranch." *New York Times* reporter Tad Szulc noted that its cost was "reported to have been $200,000," more than a million dollars in today's money. Szulc points out that "even with income from books and his CIA salary . . . Hunt could not have afforded that much." What Szulc couldn't know was that Hunt had profited from selling Artime's AMWORLD multimillion-dollar trove of CIA-supplied arms and supplies. Hunt's lavish life-style apparently didn't arouse the interest of the usually extremely observant CIA Counterintelligence Chief James Angleton, possibly because Hunt enjoyed CIA Director Helms's patronage and support.[30]

E. Howard Hunt probably also played a role in the CIA's continuing support for Commander Almeida's family outside Cuba. A CIA memo from the summer of 1966 made it clear that "military leaders like Juan Almeida [still had] the respect and admiration of the troops," even though Almeida was "supporting the regime more out of loyalty than [out] of conviction [and] without becoming influenced by Communist ideology." As long as Almeida remained unexposed and subject to use in the future, Helms could rationalize (and potentially justify on national security grounds) anything that would keep secret the full range of operations the CIA had used in its attempts to eliminate Castro.[31]

However, only a relative handful of CIA officials knew of Hunt's role with Almeida's family, and since it wasn't a full-time job, Hunt needed a more traditional position once he returned to the United States to "officially" rejoin the CIA. (Hunt's phony resignation before going to Spain had been just a matter of paperwork, to provide cover.) Helms's position as CIA Director allowed him to give Hunt a prestigious title and assignments, and Hunt's official position would soon be "chief of covert action for Western Europe," a key battleground in the Cold War.[32]

But before Hunt transitioned into that role, Congressional investigators found that Helms put Hunt "in charge of contacts with U.S. publishers in the late 1960s," a position Hunt admits he'd also held before his phony resignation and sojourn to Spain. While much information was withheld from those investigators, they were able to discover a few examples of Hunt's handiwork, such as when Hunt arranged a CIA-authored review of a CIA-authored "book which appeared in the *New York Times*." CIA operations targeting citizens inside the United States are forbidden by its charter, and a 1948 law appears to forbid federal agencies from spreading propaganda inside the U.S. However, as one of Desmond FitzGerald's men later told *Newsweek* editor Evan Thomas, when it came to targeting the U.S. news media, "we were not the least inhibited by the fact that the CIA had no internal security role in the US."[33]

It's important to note that Hunt's CIA role as a liaison with publishers—and his upcoming assignment as "chief of covert action for Western Europe"—would bring him into contact with many news bureau chiefs for U.S. newspapers and TV networks. A former *New York Times* bureau chief explained to this author that given Hunt's key positions, he'd be surprised if there weren't numerous people at *The Times* and other news outlets who dealt with Hunt as part of their normal journalistic activities. However, none of those journalists, editors, or bureau chiefs ever revealed their contacts with Hunt after he was arrested because of Watergate.[34]

Hunt justified his CIA work with the media by saying the CIA "had a very real public relations problem within the US." With few exceptions, the CIA had seemed to get most of what it wanted from the American news media until late 1966. In addition to the flood of books and articles questioning the Warren Commission, that year also marked the start of a gradual shift in the mainstream media away from unwavering support for the war in Vietnam. At the same time, the illegal activities of the CIA, FBI, and other federal agencies were starting to be exposed in progressive publications like *Ramparts* magazine.[35]

The CIA continued a range of intelligence gathering and some covert action against Fidel Castro, and Hunt had the background and contacts to know whether any press or publishing plans might affect those operations. Hunt could also try to present a more positive view of the CIA in print, just as the Agency's image was starting to come under attack. According to Senate investigators, approximately 250 books written in English "were produced, subsidized, or sponsored by the CIA before the end of 1967." The investigators found that some of the books "were written by witting Agency assets" with access to "actual case materials," and at times "the publisher was unaware" of the CIA's involvement.[36]

E. Howard Hunt actually wrote a few of those books, and two of his writing projects in particular are important in that regard. The first was Hunt's nonfiction book about the Bay of Pigs invasion, titled *Give Us This Day*, which he began writing in 1966. Hunt claims he wrote the detailed, emotional account simply for his own pleasure, with no plans to have it published. However, Hunt's manuscript reads like a CIA response to the 1964 Kennedy-sympathetic book *The Bay of Pigs*, written by Haynes Johnson with the support of Robert Kennedy. At a time when so much information about the CIA's role in the Bay of Pigs invasion was still secret, it's hard to believe that Hunt would have devoted the time and energy needed to write such a book unless he had at least informal approval from his patron, Richard Helms. Though Hunt's book about the fiasco would not be published until 1973, Hunt's CIA file reveals that he had submitted it to a publisher by mid-1968. That raises the possibility that Hunt had completed the book so that it, or an advance excerpt, could have been used against Robert Kennedy if he ran for President in 1968 and tried to blame the CIA for the Bay of Pigs fiasco.[37]

Hunt's other writing project in 1966 was a series of paperback fiction books designed to cast the CIA in a good light. Neither the tawdry glitz of James Bond nor the bleaker depictions of espionage in books and movies like John le Carré's *The Spy Who Came in from the Cold* were especially flattering to the Agency, so Richard Helms championed Hunt's idea for a series of CIA-approved spy novels. Helms kept copies of the paperbacks in his drawer to give to visitors, and nine of the novels would appear until 1972 under the pseudonym David St. John, the name of Hunt's infant son. These books would surface in an important way for Hunt and Helms just weeks before Watergate.[38]

Godfathers Santo Trafficante and Carlos Marcello, both veterans of the CIA-Mafia plots, would have watched Johnny Rosselli's problems with concern. Even though none of the growing number of critical books and mainstream articles about JFK's assassination had named any of them, two investigations would soon come close.

Carlos Marcello had successfully avoided prosecution at his trial the previous year for bribing a juror and threatening a witness at his November 1963 trial. After JFK's murder, the FBI had finally begun keeping track of Marcello's movements, though J. Edgar Hoover still refused to use wiretaps or bugging against the godfather. The FBI noted several meetings between Marcello and Trafficante in the summer of 1966, first in Tampa—where "Marcello and Trafficante sat alone in the backyard [of] Trafficante's home" for hours—and two weeks later, when "Santo Trafficante . . . visited Carlos Marcello at his Churchill Farms Estate." Cautious even there, the FBI learned that "several lengthy private conversations occurred [while] Marcello and Trafficante walked out into the middle of the fields behind the main house and sat for many hours." They were most likely discussing two topics: Rosselli's problem and how to keep their ally Jimmy Hoffa out of prison.[39]

Hoffa was probably the topic in New York City, when the godfathers kicked off a surprisingly public series of three meetings with other mob bosses in three days, starting on September 21, 1966. At the next day's meeting at La Stella restaurant, eleven other Mafia chiefs—including Carlo Gambino and Joey Gallo—joined them, and all were promptly arrested for consorting with mobsters. Each was released on $100,000 bail, and the charges were later dropped. Just to show they weren't intimidated, Marcello, Trafficante, his attorney Frank Ragano (who also worked for Hoffa), and four others returned to La Stella to celebrate, where they were photographed by the *New York Daily News*. Soon after the three meetings, a group of Mafia leaders reportedly authorized Marcello to spend up to $2 million to keep Jimmy Hoffa out of prison.[40]

However, when Marcello returned to New Orleans on October 1, 1966, he was in for a shock. The local FBI office was slowly overcoming Hoover's lax attitude about Marcello that had prevailed for years. Perhaps hoping to force Hoover to take action against Marcello, an FBI agent staged a public confrontation with the godfather at the airport. Accounts vary as to the reasons for what happened next, but the physical act was well documented by witnesses and a photographer: Marcello took a swing at the FBI agent and hit him. The resulting arrest and charges would dog Marcello for years, eventually sending him to a short stay in federal prison.[41]

Marcello—and Trafficante—faced another blow on October 5, 1966, when the Texas Court of Appeals ordered a new trial for Jack Ruby.

Two months later, the same court would order a change of venue to Wichita Falls, Texas, away from Dallas and its mob-affiliated sheriff. Ruby would no longer be in a cell that reportedly overlooked Dealey Plaza, a constant reminder of what happened to those who crossed Marcello and Trafficante.[42]

On October 12, 1966, Santo Trafficante went to Las Vegas, probably to meet with Johnny Rosselli about the story Rosselli was preparing to leak to pressure Richard Helms and the CIA to intervene for him with the FBI. As a trial balloon for bigger things to come, Rosselli used his old friend, Hoffa attorney Edward Morgan, to leak an early version of the story to another mutual friend, Hank Greenspun, the colorful publisher of the *Las Vegas Sun* newspaper. Rosselli's story—and the resulting article—hinted at the CIA's attempts to assassinate Fidel in 1963 and implied the assassins had been captured and "turned around," then used to kill JFK instead. Echoing the small-media-market strategy that John Martino had used to spread his "Castro killed JFK" stories in 1963 and 1964, the small *Sun* article attracted no national attention—except in Washington, where files show that both the CIA and FBI took notice.[43]

While Johnny Rosselli waited to see how the CIA would react to his leak, he also began a new relationship with Richard Nixon's long-time patron, the now very reclusive billionaire Howard Hughes. Rosselli worked with—and probably took advantage of—his old friend, Hughes aide Robert Maheu. Hughes moved into the Desert Inn, where Rosselli lived when he was in Las Vegas, on November 27, 1966, taking up two whole floors. When Howard Hughes didn't want to move out, Rosselli arranged for Hughes to buy the hotel/casino from its mob owner, Moe Dalitz. Since Hughes had no experience running casinos, Rosselli also arranged for Dalitz and his mob crew to manage the hotel for the reclusive billionaire. Rosselli received a $50,000 finder's fee, Maheu was put on a $100,000 retainer, and Dalitz continued to skim profits for the Mafia. Also helping to arrange the deal for Rosselli were attorney Ed Morgan and journalist Jack Anderson, junior partner of America's leading news columnist, Drew Pearson. All three would soon figure prominently in Rosselli's plans to pressure the CIA. Two more hotel/casino deals between Hughes and the crafty Rosselli soon followed. Rosselli now had a new sort-of patron in Hughes, at least until the billionaire uncovered the Mafia skimming.[44]

. . .

By November 1966, *The New York Times*—which had published the paperback edition of the Warren Report—had joined the new investigations into JFK's murder. Also launching investigations were the *New York Observer* and two of America's leading magazines, *Life* and *The Saturday Evening Post*, but it was *The Times*'s investigation that would inadvertently trigger another inquiry that would impact Rosselli, Marcello, Trafficante, and Helms. The *Times* Houston bureau quickly focused on ties between the JFK assassination and David Ferrie, even noting that Ferrie's employer at the time of JFK's murder was Carlos Marcello. But before publishing anything, the *Times* Houston bureau wrote to the New Orleans Police Department, asking thirty-two detailed questions, primarily about Ferrie, his ties to Oswald, why he'd been arrested, and what Ferrie said while detained. One of *The Times'* questions was about Carlos Marcello. The New Orleans Police passed the explosive questions to District Attorney Jim Garrison. Though the FBI and Secret Service had actually been behind Ferrie's release soon after JFK's murder, their lack of comment to a New Orleans newspaper left the impression that District Attorney Garrison had been responsible for Ferrie's release.[45]

On December 15, 1966, Jim Garrison quietly brought David Ferrie in for questioning, kicking off what would soon become a widely publicized and controversial investigation. Garrison's detractors and defenders continue to debate his ties—or lack of ties—to Carlos Marcello, and why his investigation became so compromised. In terms of Watergate, the issue is important primarily because of the effects it would have on Richard Helms and the CIA, as well as on Rosselli, Marcello, and Trafficante. The Garrison investigation—at first followed mainly by law enforcement and intelligence agencies, and later by the world press—would unfold in the months to come, influencing what information the CIA would withhold and what the mob bosses would leak.[46]

Though Johnny Rosselli had seen no positive results from his cautious leak to Hank Greenspun about the CIA-Mafia plots, the resulting article and his talks with his former CIA contacts Sheffield Edwards and William Harvey were beginning to affect Richard Helms. They were also complicating the already difficult relationship between Helms's CIA and Hoover's FBI, furthering a strain that would finally rupture during Nixon's Presidency. A declassified memo from December

21, 1966, to Helms from the CIA's Security Director (Howard Osborne, who had replaced Edwards) summarized the problem: The FBI had wanted to "subpoena . . . Edwards to appear before a Grand Jury to testify as to his last contact with Johnny [Rosselli]."[47]

Helms probably realized that J. Edgar Hoover wanted to find out more about the CIA-Mafia plots in order to use the information as leverage against the CIA in its ongoing bureaucratic struggle for funding and power. Hoover knew about only a few parts of the CIA-Mafia plots and would have relished getting Rosselli or the CIA in a position where he could learn the full story, something Helms had to prevent if he hoped to protect his own position and reputation.

The CIA strongly objected to Hoover's request for Edward's testimony about Rosselli, since that "would link this Agency and Rosselli and . . . lead to further and more embarrassing inquires." The FBI also wanted Edwards to pressure Rosselli to cooperate with the FBI, using "the implied threat of deportation" if Rosselli refused. The FBI was told that this tactic "would be strongly resisted" by the CIA because the whole matter with Rosselli was "extraordinarily sensitive."[48]

Richard Helms gave his signed endorsement to the CIA's refusal to help the FBI, while the CIA's General Counsel pointed out that the issue had also come up regarding Maheu in Senator Edward Long's hearings and in Giancana's prosecution. While it must have looked to Helms as if this Rosselli problem would keep recurring, he didn't realize how soon it would threaten to become public, or that his Security Office would still be dealing with the Rosselli problem for years to come.[49]

Johnny Rosselli probably didn't realize that Helms had gone to bat for him, because those communications traveled only between high-ranking officials of the FBI and CIA. Rosselli's troubles, Marcello's arrest, Ruby's new trial, and Ferrie's questioning—all amid the growing tide of JFK investigations by the news media—had no doubt alarmed Sam Giancana. In December 1966, Giancana fled even father away, going from Mexico to Argentina. [50]

On December 29, 1966, Johnny Rosselli was arrested in Las Vegas on a minor charge—a misdemeanor for not registering as a convicted felon—and he was bailed out almost immediately by his friend, publisher Hank Greenspun. It's possible Rosselli's arrest was a kind of retaliation, instigated by Hoover and the FBI in response to Helms's refusal to assist the Bureau with Rosselli. The earlier leak to Greenspun about the CIA's Castro plots hadn't helped Rosselli, so the Mafia don made plans to increase the pressure considerably, with the help of his friends attorney Ed Morgan and journalist Jack Anderson.[51]

Rosselli—as well as Marcello and Trafficante—finally felt some relief on January 3, 1967, when their former associate, Jack Ruby, died at Parkland Hospital in Dallas. Three days after the court had ordered a change of venue to Wichita Falls, Texas, Ruby had been diagnosed with lung cancer, even though a recent physical exam had given him a clean bill of health. Now no new information could emerge from a trial of Ruby.[52]

Richard Nixon's work for Republican Congressional candidates had paid huge dividends in November 1966, both for the GOP and for Nixon's future political prospects. Nixon helped the Republicans win forty-seven seats in the House, plus "3 Senate seats [and] 8 governorships," including the California victory of Nixon's friend Ronald Reagan. House candidates that Nixon campaigned for had won 70 percent of their races, as opposed to only 45 percent for those without Nixon's help. With his position as Presidential front-runner secured, Nixon announced that he was taking "a holiday from politics for at least six months." What Nixon meant was that he would maintain a lower public profile for a time, while privately building up his financial and political support.[53]

CHAPTER 20

January–March 1967: Jack Anderson, Rosselli, and Helms

In early January 1967, the public didn't yet know about Jim Garrison's investigation, though high-ranking officials like Richard Helms and J. Edgar Hoover were aware of it. Also in the know were some in the media, including the publishers of *Life* magazine, who had cut a deal with Garrison. To handle any publicity Garrison might generate, and to deal with the growing swell of JFK investigations by journalists, on January 4, 1967, Richard Helms and the CIA began a major new effort to counter critics of the Warren Commission. On that day, the CIA issued a fifty-three-page memo detailing the Agency's plan to attack critics of the Warren Report's "lone assassin" theory.[1]

While E. Howard Hunt didn't write the memo, his position of being "in charge of contacts with US publishers" for the CIA means he would have been responsible for helping to implement many of its recommendations. In this light, later CIA memos revealing the Agency's obsessive monitoring of books and articles about the Garrison investigation (including those with even the briefest mention of Hunt associates such as Manuel Artime, Tony Varona, and Harry Williams) take on a new significance.[2]

One of Richard Helms's goals with the lengthy memo wasn't just to support the Warren Commission's conclusion, but also to convince CIA personnel—from Station Chiefs to CIA officers—that attacks on the Warren Commission were an attack on the CIA itself. The overt result would be to rally key CIA personnel to defend the Warren Commission and attack critics of its "lone nut" conclusion, no matter how well documented the critics' books, articles, or arguments were. The covert result, known only to Helms and a few others, would be to make Helms's private worries the concerns of the CIA as an organization.

Helms hoped that the CIA's efforts would prevent the exposure of his unauthorized Castro plots with the Mafia—and any tie they might have had to JFK's murder—without Helms having to reveal those plots to additional CIA personnel.[3]

In the second week of January 1967, Johnny Rosselli got in touch with Santo Trafficante to secure his approval for the story he was about to leak. Rosselli intended to increase the pressure on Richard Helms and the CIA, hoping to receive the same help the Agency had given to other veterans of the CIA-Mafia plots, like Maheu and Giancana.[4]

Johnny Rosselli had decided to leak the CIA-Mafia plots and his "turned-around assassins" cover story to America's best-known investigative journalist, Drew Pearson, the muckraking reporter who penned the "Washington Merry-Go-Round" column, read by fifty million people in six hundred newspapers. Pearson, a longtime foe of Richard Nixon, was known to be close to President Johnson and other powerful Washington figures, including Chief Justice Earl Warren. By revealing the Castro assassination plots and the "turned-around assassins" story to Pearson, Rosselli would show those in power that he wasn't bluffing: He wanted CIA help with his legal problems, or else more stories—with more unsavory details—could be leaked. In addition, if Pearson printed the story, it would present the Mafia not as potential suspects in JFK's murder, but as patriots who had tried to help the U.S. government, only to be caught up in a Robert Kennedy plot against Fidel that Castro turned to his own advantage. With this one crucial leak, Rosselli could help himself and deflect any suspicion that might arise about him, Trafficante, or Marcello in JFK's assassination.[5]

To help spread the story, Rosselli used Edward Morgan, known as an attorney for Jimmy Hoffa, though he wasn't handling Hoffa's current appeal. A former FBI agent, Morgan was highly respected in Washington and could use attorney-client privilege to shield his contact with Rosselli. Drew Pearson's junior partner, journalist Jack Anderson, was involved with Ed Morgan in yet another business venture involving Howard Hughes, so Rosselli was essentially working with the same trusted associates he'd used in the Hughes–Desert Inn deal.[6]

On January 13, 1967, Jack Anderson arranged for Drew Pearson to meet attorney Morgan and hear "a client of his who was on the fringe of the underworld" reveal how "Bobby Kennedy had organized a group who went to Cuba to kill Castro; that all were killed or imprisoned . . . that subsequently Castro decided to utilize the same procedure to kill President Kennedy." Pearson found the story amazing but credible, since Morgan was a distinguished attorney who had helped direct the Congressional investigation of Pearl Harbor. Pearson wanted to take the story directly to President Johnson, and Morgan agreed.[7]

At the White House on January 16, 1967, Pearson told LBJ the story in a one-hour meeting. Pearson wrote in his diary: "I told the president about Ed Morgan's law client . . . Lyndon listened carefully and made no comment. There wasn't much he could say." At first, LBJ didn't take the account very seriously, since he knew little or nothing about the CIA-Mafia plots and had only a partial understanding of Robert Kennedy's and the CIA's extensive 1963 operations against Fidel. Pearson told LBJ he didn't plan to write the story until November. LBJ suggested that Pearson take the story to Chief Justice Earl Warren, who'd headed the Warren Commission, and accordingly Pearson outlined the tale to a "decidedly skeptical" Warren on January 19, 1967. However, Warren might not have wanted to let Pearson know that he had heard something about the CIA-Mafia plots when he headed the Warren Commission. Pearson asked Warren to meet with Morgan to hear more for himself, but Warren declined, saying he would refer the matter to the Secret Service.[8]

Though Warren appeared skeptical to Morgan, the Chief Justice took the matter seriously enough to meet with the head of the U.S. Secret Service, James Rowley. In Earl Warren's private chambers at the U.S. Supreme Court on January 31, 1967, Warren told Rowley the story of Morgan's underworld client. After the meeting, Rowley attempted to have his agents interview Morgan, who didn't keep the appointment. The attorney knew that spreading a story privately to LBJ or Earl Warren was one thing, but making statements to federal agents was quite another.[9]

Santo Trafficante was arrested when he flew into Miami on February 3, 1967, after spending two days plotting strategy in New Orleans with Carlos Marcello. According to Frank Ragano, Trafficante was arrested for vagrancy when he stepped off the plane at the Miami airport, even though he was "wearing an $800 silk Brioni suit and . . . had $1,000 in cash in his pockets and was on his way to his home in Miami." Within hours, Ragano paid Trafficante's bail, chalking up the arrest to harassment by the Dade County sheriff's office. However, the timing of Trafficante's arrest is interesting, since it suggests that some officials were starting to suspect that Trafficante and Marcello had had a role in JFK's death. The following month, Ragano would write a letter to J. Edgar Hoover, saying that "some of the allegations involving Trafficante have been ridiculous." Author Dick Russell describes the rest of the letter as trying "to deflect any suspicion of Trafficante's involvement in the [JFK] assassination." It isn't clear whose "suspicion" that was, since the press would not publicly link Trafficante to JFK's assassination until well into the next decade.[10]

Events in New Orleans would make President Lyndon Johnson more receptive to the story about the CIA-Mafia plots that Johnny Rosselli was trying to leak. FBI reports confirm that around February 12, 1967, Carlos Marcello and Santo Trafficante met for three days in New Orleans. Five days later, on February 17, 1967, the world learned about Jim Garrison's investigation when the front page of the New Orleans States-Item blared, "DA Here Launches Full JFK Death 'Plot' Probe." It signaled the start of a barrage of Garrison publicity that would dominate media coverage of the JFK assassination for the next two years. On February 18, the newspaper revealed that David Ferrie was a prime target of District Attorney Garrison's investigation. However, the article made no mention of Carlos Marcello, nor did any other news article about the matter while the Garrison investigation was in progress. That lack of coverage seems odd, since Ferrie was working for Marcello at the time of JFK's murder and had been sitting with the godfather in court at the moment JFK was shot.[11]

The news about Ferrie caused President Johnson to take Pearson's story from Rosselli far more seriously. The day after Ferrie was named, LBJ called the acting Attorney General, Ramsey Clark, to discuss the Pearson-Rosselli story. LBJ told the Attorney General the story was about "a man brought into the CIA with a number of others and instructed by the CIA and the Attorney General [Bobby Kennedy] to assassinate Castro."[12]

At CIA headquarters in Langley, Virginia, the public identification of Ferrie caused considerable anxiety for the Agency. As noted earlier, Victor Marchetti, the former executive assistant to the CIA's Deputy Director, told Anthony Summers "he observed consternation on the part of then CIA Director Richard Helms and other senior officials when Ferrie's name was first publicly linked with the assassination in 1967 . . . and was told 'Ferrie had been a contract agent to the Agency in the early sixties and had been involved in some of the Cuban activities.'" To Marchetti, "Helms stated that David Ferrie was a CIA agent and that he was still an agent at the time of [JFK's] assassination."[13]

Richard Helms's concerns make sense in light of the CIA activities of Ferrie and Guy Banister confirmed by New Orleans CIA official Hunter Leake to Dr. Michael Kurtz, Louisiana state historian. Helms's worries help to explain why declassified memos show the CIA maintained an intense interest in all of the news coming out of Garrison's investigation, for years to come. Just two months after Ferrie was first named, the CIA generated a file card for internal use, saying that as far as Lee Harvey Oswald was concerned, inside the CIA

> there had been no secret as far as anyone was concerned in regard to the fact that [Guy] Banister [and] David William Ferrie and [Oswald] may have known or been acquainted with one another.[14]

At 11:40 AM February 22, 1967, David Ferrie's dead body was found at his home. The unusual circumstances surrounding Ferrie's death created a new firestorm of publicity across the country. Initially, the New Orleans coroner determined that Ferrie's death must have occurred the previous evening. However, he had to change his finding after *Washington Post* reporter George Lardner revealed that he had interviewed Ferrie from midnight to 4 AM. Garrison hinted at suicide and even murder, but the coroner determined the cause of death to be a brain aneurysm that caused a fatal cerebral hemorrhage. Essentially, David Ferrie had died of natural causes from a burst blood vessel. He had a history of high blood pressure and was no doubt under tremendous stress, knowing what would happen to him if Carlos Marcello thought Ferrie might betray him. Robert Kennedy was aware of Ferrie's connection to Marcello, since RFK's Mafia prosecutors had encountered Ferrie, so Robert called the New Orleans coroner at his home to hear the details for himself. President Johnson was briefed about Ferrie's death by Attorney General Ramsey Clark.*[15]

. . .

*The same day Ferrie's body was found, police in Florida found the body of his friend, Eladio del Valle, an operative of Santo Trafficante said by Cuban authorities to have been involved in JFK's murder. Garrison's investigators had been in Florida, trying to

Robert Kennedy soon helped launch two private investigations into his brother's murder, and he was in personal contact with two more. Ed Guthman—RFK's former press aide at the Justice Department, now a top editor at the *Los Angeles Times*—conducted one investigation and kept RFK informed. William Attwood, formerly JFK's special Cuban envoy, planned another investigation, since he was now the editor-in-chief of *Look* magazine, *Life*'s chief rival. Attwood discussed his plans with RFK, who "told Attwood that he agreed his brother had been the victim of a conspiracy. 'But I can't do anything until we get control of the White House.'" However, Attwood suffered a heart attack, which stalled his JFK investigation. (Attwood would later helm a Pulitzer Prize–winning investigation into the French Connection heroin network of Santo Trafficante and would investigate Nixon's financial ties to Bebe Rebozo.)[16]

In addition to monitoring Guthman's and Attwood's efforts, Robert Kennedy launched two investigations of his own. One of the trusted people RFK turned to was journalist and attorney Frank Mankiewicz, who was Robert's press aide. RFK told Mankiewicz, "I want you to look into [JFK's murder and] read everything you can, so if it gets to a point where I can do something about this, you can tell me what I need to know." Mankiewicz said he "came to the conclusion that there was some sort of conspiracy, probably involving the mob, anti-Castro Cuban exiles, and maybe rogue CIA agents." But when he tried to tell RFK, "it was like he just couldn't focus on it. He'd get this look of pain, or more like numbness, on his face. It just tore him apart."[17]

Robert Kennedy's confidant, Walter Sheridan, who had joined NBC News after leaving the Justice Department, went to New Orleans to dig into the matter. According to author David Talbot, Sheridan "began feeding [RFK] information about [NBC's] investigation." Sheridan was assisted in New Orleans by a former fellow Hoffa prosecutor, Frank Grimsley, who shared Sheridan's feeling that Marcello was behind JFK's murder. However, when Sheridan tried to tell Robert what he'd found, RFK stopped him and said he "didn't want to know."

However, thinking that Garrison was a fraud, Sheridan would help to torpedo the District Attorney's investigation with an NBC News

---

question del Valle. The *St. Petersburg Times* reported that "police said del Valle's body was found crumpled, beaten, and shot on the floor of his red Cadillac convertible . . . at the time, the death was portrayed as being mob-related."

special. A similar CBS special with Walter Cronkite also helped discredit Garrison to the public and the mainstream press.[18]

Another problem for Garrison was that Santo Trafficante and Carlos Marcello had links to several men who had infiltrated his investigation, and who diverted it toward dead ends. Because of that, Garrison's suspicions about Marcello and JFK's murder were never made public, and are only known from FBI informant reports. Instead, a low-level attorney who worked for Marcello helped to send the investigation toward the distinguished Clay Shaw, who'd formerly headed New Orleans's International Trade Mart. Files show that Shaw had been a low-level CIA asset, but no credible evidence linked him to any knowing participation in JFK's murder, and he was eventually acquitted.[19]

In March 1967, Jimmy Hoffa was enjoying his last taste of freedom as he prepared to begin serving his thirteen-year prison sentence. With only days to go, Carlos Marcello and his men tried to bribe Grady Partin, the Teamsters official and Justice Department informant whose testimony had been crucial to Hoffa's conviction. If Partin changed his testimony, Hoffa could get a new trial. An aide to Louisiana's Governor set up a meeting between Partin and a close associate of Marcello, who told Partin that if he changed sides and helped Hoffa, "the sky's the limit. It's worth at least a million bucks." During their talk, Marcello's associate called Allen Dorfman, a high-ranking Teamsters official who was Hoffa's key financial link with the Mafia. Marcello's man explained to Partin that while Dorfman was running the bribe attempt, Marcello was actually "holding the money." Marcello's associate then boasted to Partin of the political power wielded by Marcello and Dorfman, saying that they "had helped Senator Russell Long (of Louisiana) get elected whip" in the U.S. Senate by paying for the votes of seven U.S. Senators. But none of this swayed Partin, who refused to change his testimony. Since Hoffa's three appeals were exhausted, the Teamsters President would soon begin serving time at Lewisburg Federal Prison. Even so, Marcello's attempts to "spring Hoffa" would continue and eventually would involve Richard Nixon. It's also important to note that the 1960 Mafia-Hoffa-Nixon bribe was still known only to its participants and to key Justice Department and FBI personnel, though an increasing number of Robert Kennedy's original Hoffa and Mafia prosecutors were leaving government service to join private law firms.[20]

. . .

On March 2, 1967, New York Senator Robert Kennedy—whose relationship with President Johnson was already poor—gave a major speech in the Senate in which he publicly broke with LBJ over the hugely expanded war in Vietnam. During JFK's entire Presidency, the U.S. casualties from the war had been just over a hundred. In LBJ's first year in office, there had been 143 U.S. deaths. Now the U.S. casualties rate was "nearly 1,000 a month and rising," with no end in sight. U.S. personnel in Vietnam now numbered over four hundred thousand, with U.S. Generals demanding more. Historian Stephen Ambrose pointed out that "in 1967, [President] Johnson implemented the policy changes Nixon had been demanding for two years," by escalating the war and bombing North Vietnam.[21]

In his speech, Robert Kennedy announced his support for a suspension of the bombing of North Vietnam as part of an effort to bring that country into peace talks. His public break with LBJ accelerated speculation that Robert Kennedy might run for President in 1968, but events unfolding that same day involving Johnny Rosselli would have a major impact on Robert's plans.[22]

On March 2 and 3, 1967, three explosive news stories would break about Johnny Rosselli's claim that Castro killed JFK in retaliation for Robert Kennedy's secret efforts to assassinate Fidel Castro. These three related articles would have a tremendous impact on Richard Helms, President Lyndon Johnson, Robert Kennedy, and later Presidents Richard Nixon and Gerald Ford. Rosselli's initial leak to Jack Anderson and Drew Pearson—about RFK's supposedly ordering CIA assassins to kill Fidel—had produced no tangible results. Though the leak had traveled to President Johnson, Chief Justice Earl Warren, Secret Service Chief James Rowley, and J. Edgar Hoover, Rosselli had nothing to show for it. So Rosselli had part of the same story leaked to Jim Garrison and to a reporter with New York's WINS radio.[23]

The version given to WINS radio was similar to Rosselli's leak to Anderson and to a discredited tale briefly promoted in 1964 by associates of Santo Trafficante and exile leader Manuel Artime. Those similarities have become clear only recently, since WINS didn't broadcast all the information it had. The station gave the non-broadcast portion to Texas Governor John Connally, who relayed it to President Lyndon Johnson in a phone call recorded on LBJ's White House taping system.[24]

On March 2, 1967, at 9:55 PM, John Connally called his old friend LBJ from New York. Connally told LBJ there had been a "long story on [WINS] tonight . . . from a man who saw the files in Garrison's office . . . that there were four assassins in the US sent here by Castro or Castro's people." Since the two Texans had been in JFK's Dallas motorcade, they shared a personal interest in the WINS story.[25]

The reporters' confidential information, which Connally said was "not going on the air," was that "six months after the Missile Crisis was over, the CIA was instructed to assassinate Castro." That time frame matches the one Rosselli gave to Pearson and Anderson, and it coincides with the start of the JFK-Almeida coup plan. Highlighting the anti-RFK spin of Rosselli's tale, Connally said that JFK's "brother ordered the CIA to send a team into Cuba to assassinate Castro [and] some of [the CIA team] were captured and tortured, and Castro and his people . . . heard the whole story [and] one of Castro's lieutenants, as a reprisal measure, sent four teams into the US to assassinate President Kennedy."[26]

President Johnson told Connally a similar tale, explaining he'd gotten "that story [from] one of Hoffa's lawyers [Ed Morgan, who] went to one of our mutual friends and asked him to come and relay that to us . . . just about like you have related it. A week or two passed, and then [Drew] Pearson came to me [and] told me [that Hoffa's lawyer] had told him the same thing."

LBJ said he had been "reconstructing the requests that were made of me [about Cuban operations] right after I became president." LBJ told Connally he was going to discuss this new information further with Attorney General Clark so that he and J. Edgar Hoover could "watch [the story] very carefully." LBJ told Connally that "some of these same sources" trying to prevent "this jail thing" for Hoffa "have [also] been feeding stuff to Garrison as they did here." Historian Michael Beschloss says that LBJ was worried that the story was being spread by "Hoffa's allies to keep the Teamster leader out of prison," by hoping "Johnson might be willing to intervene at the last minute at the price of tamping down public revelations about the CIA-Mafia conspiracy against Castro."[27]

There is one important difference between the story Rosselli leaked to Anderson and Pearson, and the ones leaked to WINS and Garrison: the Mafia. Apparently, word about the Mafia's role with the CIA had been given only to Anderson and Pearson. As LBJ and Connally ended their call on the evening of March 2, 1967, Jack Anderson was getting ready to go on television to reveal Rosselli's story. He had already submitted an explosive column about the story, set to run the following day in more than six hundred newspapers. Aside from not wanting to be scooped by WINS, Anderson might have come under additional pressure from attorney Ed Morgan to run the story, since Hoffa was only days away from having to report to prison.

Anderson ran Rosselli's story when his boss, Drew Pearson, was not just out of town, but out of the country, on a tour of five South American countries with his friend Chief Justice Earl Warren. Pearson said in his diaries that he would not have run the Rosselli story.[28]

Decades later, Anderson would finally admit that by spreading Rosselli's story, he "may have been a card [Rosselli] was playing." As a Congressional report later concluded, "Rosselli manipulated the facts of the plots into the retaliation theory in efforts to force the CIA to intervene favorably into his legal affairs." However, in March 1967, Anderson believed what he was hearing from the Mafia don, especially when CIA officer William Harvey—in the last, sad days of his once notable career—confirmed Rosselli's account. Harvey was still a CIA official at the time, though Anderson didn't realize that Harvey might have been acting more for himself and his friend Rosselli than for the CIA.[29]

Anderson was convinced he had a real scoop, because by March 2, 1967, he claimed to have "two memos from the CIA's most sensitive files, which summarize the whole operation." A later internal CIA Inspector General's report appears to confirm that Anderson and Pearson had at least one sensitive government memo about assassinating Castro.[30]

Much has been written about Jack Anderson's March 3, 1967, column, but almost nothing has appeared about his first revelation of the story, on Washington's WDCA-TV at 10:55 PM on March 2. Anderson's disclosure on the TV show *Exposé* was discovered only recently because it was the subject of a newly declassified CIA memo showing the Agency had monitored the explosive broadcast.[31]

Jack Anderson's Washington TV broadcast on March 2 is important because *The Washington Post* decided not to carry his March 3 column with Rosselli's story, perhaps because the column reflected badly on Robert Kennedy, who had good relations with *The Post*. The editor of *The Post* was now JFK's good friend Ben Bradlee, and Robert himself had written *Post* owner Katherine Graham the previous day about his

Vietnam speech. However, *The Post* did carry the next Anderson column about the subject, so it's also possible that Anderson's televised preview of his column caught the attention of Richard Helms or one of his men, who then asked *The Post* not to run the initial column. Helms and the CIA also maintained good relations with Bradlee, Graham, and *The Post*.[32]

In contrast to his boss Drew Pearson, one of America's most famous journalists, Jack Anderson was relatively unknown. But Anderson knew the Rosselli story contained enough bombshells to make a name for himself, and it did. As recorded in the CIA summary of the broadcast, Anderson said that JFK

> was angered at the failure of the Bay of Pigs invasion and blamed [the] CIA. He quoted Kennedy as desiring to break up the Agency. [JFK] assigned his brother, the Attorney General, to watch over [the] CIA. Anderson implies Robert Kennedy controlled the Agency. The Attorney General, seeking revenge on Castro for the Bay of Pigs, planned through [the] CIA the assassination of Castro or considered it. Castro learned of the CIA plot to kill him, or obtained information which led him to believe such a plot existed. Castro arranged the assassination of the President in retaliation.[33]

Anderson submitted the next day's column with a special byline: "Today's column is by Jack Anderson," to ensure he got credit for the scoop. In this story, and the next, Anderson was careful to avoid any mention of Johnny Rosselli by name, though the Mafia don knew that his intended targets at the CIA would know who was behind the story. A few newspapers, like the *New York Post*, joined *The Washington Post* in not carrying column, but most of Anderson's six-hundred-plus newspapers weren't so cautious. Rosselli's leaked information was soon being read by millions of people from coast to coast. Anderson's column opened by saying, "President Johnson is sitting on a political H-Bomb—an unconfirmed report that Sen. Robert Kennedy may have approved an assassination plot which then possibly backfired against his late brother."[34]

Anderson's column quickly made it clear that this wasn't idle rumor or wild speculation: "Top officials, queried by this column, agreed that a plot to assassinate Cuban dictator Fidel Castro was 'considered' at the highest levels of the Central Intelligence Agency at the time Bobby was riding herd on the agency. The officials disagreed, however, over whether the plan was approved and implemented." However, Anderson made it clear that he also knew about the CIA-Mafia plots, writing, "One version claims that underworld figures actually were recruited to carry out the plot. Another rumor has it that three hired assassins were caught in Havana . . . The rumor persists, whispered by people in a position to know, that Castro did become aware of an American plot upon his life and decided to retaliate against President Kennedy." Anderson points out that "some insiders are convinced that Castro learned enough at least to believe the CIA was seeking to kill him. With characteristic fury, he is reported to have cooked up a counterplot against President Kennedy."[35]

This Anderson-Rosselli implication that Castro had orchestrated JFK's murder would continue to reverberate within official circles in Washington into the Watergate era and even today. Blaming Castro for JFK's death would be "whispered by people in a position to know," among them Alexander Haig, who went on to become President Richard Nixon's Chief of Staff and Ronald Reagan's Secretary of State.[36]

The Anderson column revealed more information that would have worried Richard Helms, Robert Kennedy, and other officials:

> After the Bay of Pigs fiasco . . . the President's real watchdog was his brother, Bobby, who ended up calling the shots at the CIA . . . During this period, the CIA hatched a plot to knock off Castro. It would have been impossible for this to reach the high levels it did, say insiders, without being taken up with the younger Kennedy. Indeed, one source insists that Bobby, eager to avenge the Bay of Pigs fiasco, played a key role in the planning.[37]

Of course, Anderson's source was conflating the CIA-Mafia plots to assassinate Fidel with the JFK-Almeida coup plan. While Rosselli's main goal was to reach CIA Director Richard Helms, Anderson's column left Robert Kennedy in a state of shock. Arthur Schlesinger Jr., who didn't know about the JFK-Almeida coup plan, observed RFK shortly after the column and wrote that "an indefinable sense of depression hung over him, as if he felt cornered by circumstance and did not know how to break out." It's important to keep in mind that in 1967, it was still inconceivable to the average American that the U.S. government would try to murder foreign officials. (It would be another eight years before the American press widely reported such plots.)[38]

Ironically, Richard Helms, who had withheld so much from John and Robert Kennedy, was one of the few people RFK could turn to for help and information in the aftermath of Anderson's column. Perhaps hoping Helms could help him find out who was talking to Anderson, Robert arranged to meet Helms for lunch the following day. Helms was also no doubt shocked by Anderson's column and TV broadcast, and he would have feared that the CIA-Mafia plots he'd hidden for so long could be completely exposed at any moment.

On March 4, 1967, when Helms met RFK for lunch, both men were probably glad that the major newspapers and TV networks had not yet followed up on Anderson's sensational column. That lack of coverage could have been due to pressure on the media from Helms and the CIA, who could have obstructed any reporter who asked the Agency about Anderson's revelations. It's also possible Anderson's news was drowned out by news from New Orleans about Garrison's investigation. At their meeting, Helms and RFK likely discussed a range of topics, including what Helms had told—or was going to tell—LBJ about the CIA-Mafia plots and the 1963 coup plan with Almeida. RFK would have also wanted to know about the current status of Almeida and the CIA's ongoing support for Almeida's family, which was still outside of Cuba.[39]

As for what Helms would tell LBJ about the CIA-Mafia plots, it appears that LBJ had learned very little about them at that point. However, Anderson's column would soon change that. If LBJ asked, Helms would at least have to give the President the same information LBJ could learn from J. Edgar Hoover. That would explain why, on the day of RFK's lunch meeting with Helms, RFK had his secretary call Hoover's office and ask for a copy of the FBI's May 7, 1962, memo about the CIA-Mafia plots.[40]

Once Helms returned to CIA headquarters after his meeting with RFK, he no doubt discussed the situation with Desmond FitzGerald, the CIA's Deputy Director for Plans. They both had much to lose if their unauthorized continuation of the CIA-Mafia plots in 1963 became known to LBJ or was exposed in the press. Their careers were on the line, to say nothing of the possibility of being dragged into Garrison's investigation.

The Helms-RFK lunch is the only clearly documented meeting between the two men in the aftermath of Anderson's first column. However, it is likely that the two men communicated further, especially after Anderson's next column about the matter and after LBJ requested that Helms give him a full report about the 1963 CIA-Mafia plots. Their subsequent communication about the matter could have been handled through Desmond FitzGerald, whom RFK still saw socially. FitzGerald knew the secrets as well as Helms, including those Helms continued to withhold from RFK.

Any actions Helms undertook in the next two weeks regarding the matter are not documented but can be inferred from declassified files about related matters. In 2007, the CIA admitted that in the 1960s it had tapped the phones of Washington columnists Robert Allen and Paul Scott, suspected of "publishing news articles based on, and frequently quoting, classified [CIA] materials." A CIA memo says those phone taps were "particularly productive in identifying contacts of the newsmen . . . and many of their sources of information." Also disclosed in 2007 was that a few months before Watergate, Richard Helms himself had the CIA conduct covert surveillance of Jack Anderson and his assistants. The CIA admits the surveillance Helms ordered was "to determine Anderson's sources [of] highly classified Agency information appearing in his syndicated columns."[41]

Helms would have wanted to know who was leaking the CIA-Mafia plot information to Jack Anderson, and what other relevant information Anderson possessed that had not yet been published. As detailed shortly, the CIA was able to discover that Anderson and also Drew Pearson had additional sensitive information about the CIA-Mafia plots they had not yet printed. It's also important to keep in mind that Helms's concerns about Anderson's column were occurring while the Garrison investigation in New Orleans was still unfolding.

While Pearson was still traveling in South America with Chief Justice Earl Warren, Jack Anderson submitted his follow-up column on March 6, to run on March 7, the same day Jimmy Hoffa was scheduled to report to prison. Unknown to Anderson, on March 6 his first column was finally starting to have the impact Rosselli sought. On that date, LBJ's Attorney General, Ramsey Clark, received a detailed FBI report provocatively titled "Central Intelligence Agency's Intentions to Send Hoodlums to Cuba to Assassinate Castro."[42]

That memo soon came to LBJ's attention, and in it the FBI detailed much of what its top officials knew about the CIA-Mafia plots involving Johnny Rosselli, Sam Giancana, and Robert Maheu. However, the FBI memo included nothing about the origin of the plots under then–Vice President Richard Nixon. The FBI reported that Robert Kennedy had been made aware of the use of the mobsters "to obtain intelligence . . . in Cuba" in May 1961, and that RFK had learned of the operation's assassination aspects in May 1962, at which time he had "issued orders that [the] CIA should never again take such steps without first checking with [him]." The FBI also noted that William Harvey had met with Rosselli in June 1963, when Harvey claimed he finally shut down the operation. The FBI memo didn't mention the Bureau's surveillance of Rosselli in Miami in the fall of 1963, when he was working on the CIA-Mafia plots while meeting with David Morales and Jack Ruby—indicating those sensitive files were already being held separately from the FBI's main Rosselli files.[43]

The FBI said that Rosselli had "used his prior connections with [the] CIA to his best advantage." According to the FBI, the CIA's Director of Security "admitted to us that Rosselli has [the] CIA in an unusually vulnerable position and that [Rosselli] would have no qualms about embarrassing [the] CIA if it served his own interests." The CIA had taken the rare step of admitting to the FBI that Rosselli had the Agency over a barrel.[44]

Though LBJ had been skeptical of the Anderson/Pearson story, Hoover's report confirmed that the CIA had indeed plotted extensively with Rosselli and the Mafia to kill Castro. This knowledge caused LBJ to take the whole matter far more seriously, and he would soon demand a full report from Richard Helms and order the FBI to interview William Morgan.[45]

The Washington Post ran Anderson's new revelations on March 7, 1967, even though he had tacked them onto the end of a much longer story about Congressional corruption, where they would have been easy to cut. The column's subhead, "Castro Counterplot," signaled the start of four short paragraphs updating the March 3, 1967, story. Anderson wrote that the publicity surrounding Garrison's investigation "has focused attention in Washington on a reported CIA plan in 1963 to assassinate Cuba's Fidel Castro, which, according to some sources, may have resulted in a counterplot by Castro to assassinate President Kennedy." He then added that "Sen. Russell Long (D-La.) has told us that Lee Harvey Oswald . . . trained with Castro revolutionaries in Minsk during his Soviet stay," and that "Long swore [the] information . . . is reliable." Anderson's column in *The Post* concluded by saying his "sources agree that a plot against Castro definitely was taken up inside the CIA at the time. Sen. Robert Kennedy, D-N.Y., was riding herd on the agency for his brother. The report is that Castro got wind of the plot and threatened to find someone to assassinate President Kennedy." The main difference between this story and Anderson's first article was the elimination of any reference to the "underworld," meaning the Mafia.[46]

Neither LBJ, Richard Helms, nor RFK (or Richard Nixon) would have wanted to see the story pursued. The same was true for J. Edgar Hoover, who could have easily leaked his report on the CIA-Mafia plots to the press—but didn't, probably so he could have something to hold over the heads of the CIA and RFK. No other mainstream journalist printed any type of follow-up to Anderson's story, or even noted what Anderson had reported.

For Richard Helms, Anderson's second story was apparently the last straw as far as William Harvey's career was concerned. According to later CIA Director William Colby, Harvey had been recalled from Rome "in February of 1967 [and] reassigned to CIA headquarters." That was apparently when Harvey began talking to Jack Anderson, supporting Rosselli's story. "One of the CIA's most senior officers" told intelligence journalist David Martin that not long after Harvey returned to CIA headquarters, Harvey was asked to resign after CIA personnel "began finding gin bottles in his desk drawer." However, the CIA had previously used a noted mental-health facility near Towson, Maryland, for its officials who needed help. If Helms had wanted to retain the legendary Harvey, he could have sent him to that facility for a few weeks or months; one CIA official had even stayed in treatment there for two years. Since the CIA didn't even attempt to treat Harvey's alcoholism, the request for Harvey's resignation was probably punitive.[47]

For pension purposes, Harvey's official retirement date was set at the end of the year, but CIA files show that he was effectively out of the Agency long before that. These CIA files also reveal that Harvey even considered joining Ed Morgan's law firm, and one account says he did become affiliated with the firm. According to still other Agency documents, by 1967, Harvey's loyalty lay more with Johnny Rosselli than with the CIA. Harvey would later tell the CIA's Director of

Security that "'Johnny' [Rosselli] was his friend," and "that he would not turn his back on his friends." Just weeks after Anderson's second article, Harvey would suggest to the CIA's Security Director that "it would be a simple matter for the Director [Helms] to see Mr. [J. Edgar] Hoover personally and determine . . . what actual case the Justice Department had against Johnny [Rosselli]."[48]

Robert Kennedy was also in a vulnerable position, and on March 14, 1967, he literally buried crucial medical evidence. JFK had originally been laid to rest next to the bodies of his infant son and daughter, in a relatively plain grave distinguished only by an eternal flame. In the summer of 1966 (during the first wave of JFK conspiracy books), work had begun on a more elaborate site twenty feet away, though some have wondered why it couldn't have been constructed around the original grave.[49]

RFK still possessed important medical evidence—including JFK's brain, tissue samples, and possibly X-rays and photographs from JFK's autopsy—that are not at the National Archives. In addition to whatever they might have revealed, RFK had wanted to ensure that JFK's autopsy material never became a public spectacle. After Garrison's investigation became public and a grand jury was impaneled in New Orleans to investigate, RFK's concerns must have increased. They would have grown even more when Clay Shaw was arrested on March 1, 1967, because that meant a trial could be held in the near future. Declassified U.S. military memos show that activity for JFK's re-interment accelerated greatly that very day.[50]

As one author noted, once a New Orleans grand jury started considering the possibility of "exhuming [JFK's] body for a proper autopsy," plans were finalized in Washington to move the body on the night of March 14, 1967. That evening, author Gus Russo wrote that "300 military personnel arrived and closed Arlington National Cemetery to the public, clearing it of all unauthorized persons. An Army road block shut down Arlington Memorial Bridge [and] troops ringed the area."[51]

At the time of JFK's original autopsy, his personal physician, Admiral Burkley, had told two of the autopsy doctors that JFK's "brain, as well as tissue samples" would be given to "Bobby Kennedy for subsequent burial." Frank Mankiewicz told a Congressional investigator that JFK's "brain is in the grave . . . Bobby . . . buried it when the body was transferred." JFK's secretary, Evelyn Lincoln, reportedly said to a friend that JFK's brain was "where it belongs." On the morning of March 15, 1967, LBJ joined RFK, Jackie, and a few other family members and associates at the site for a private memorial service.[52]

Three days after seeing LBJ at the ceremony, Robert Kennedy surprised his close associates by proclaiming that he was supporting LBJ in the next year's Presidential election. Newspapers quoted RFK as saying that LBJ "has been an outstanding president and I look forward to campaigning for him in 1968."[53]

Johnny Rosselli asked Ed Morgan to talk to Drew Pearson in mid-March, after Pearson had returned from South America. Morgan told Pearson he had seen Rosselli in Las Vegas, and he claimed that Rosselli had been "most indignant" about the stories Jack Anderson had written. Pearson wrote in his diary that Morgan told him Rosselli "will not cooperate in advancing the story any further." However, Morgan's comment wasn't accurate, because Rosselli would later leak more information to Anderson, indicating that Rosselli had actually liked Anderson's columns.[54]

Drew Pearson also wrote in his diary that he originally thought Anderson's columns were "a poor story . . . and violated a confidence." On March 13, 1967, Pearson and Earl Warren met with LBJ at the White House. Before meeting with Pearson, LBJ met privately for forty minutes with only Warren and LBJ's liaison to the FBI. A few days later, Pearson agreed to fund an almost two-week investigative trip to New Orleans for Jack Anderson, so he could meet with Jim Garrison. It's interesting to note that according to a CIA Inspector General's Report, "Jim Garrison, Edward Morgan, and Rosselli were all in Las Vegas at the same time . . . Garrison was in touch with Rosselli; so was Morgan."[55]

Four days after meeting with Pearson and Warren, LBJ had one of his aides tell FBI official Clyde Tolson that the FBI should "try to interview" Rosselli's attorney, Ed Morgan. Tolson protested, but LBJ insisted, so the FBI complied.[56]

The FBI's interview with Ed Morgan on March 21, 1967, provides an almost unfiltered version of Rosselli's tale, and is as close as we can get to hearing it from Rosselli himself. Some of its points were not in Anderson's articles, but were heard by officials like President Johnson and had an impact on their later beliefs and actions. It's clear from reading Morgan's story, as taken down by the FBI agents, that one of Rosselli's goals was to conflate the CIA-Mafia plots with the JFK-

Almeida coup plan. One indication that Rosselli achieved this goal is the fact that Morgan's FBI interview, together with memos about LBJ's reaction to Rosselli's story, are in a massive and highly sensitive 318-page FBI file at the National Archives that contains most of the FBI's released information about Commander Almeida.[57]

After Morgan's FBI interview began, the attorney said his goal in talking to the agents was to get "complete immunity" for his clients from "some competent authority." Morgan told the FBI his clients had been

> called upon by a Governmental agency to assist in a project which was said to have the highest Governmental approval. The project had as its purpose the assassination of Fidel Castro . . . Elaborate plans involving many people were made. These plans included the infiltration of the Cuban government and the placing of informants in key posts within Cuba.[58]

Rosselli knew that having Morgan mention the "infiltration of the Cuban government" would set off alarm bells with the high-ranking U.S. officials who knew about Almeida. In addition, the "informants . . . within Cuba" was meant to explain how Morgan's clients learned about Fidel's retaliatory hit teams. The rest of Morgan's story was a clearer version of the account related in Anderson's columns.

Ed Morgan also slammed the CIA, saying that "it was inconceivable to him that an agency of the Government . . . has not [made] this most important data available to the Warren Commission." Morgan conveyed the information Rosselli wanted him to, while refusing to give up the mobster's name to the FBI. The Bureau wasted no time in getting a summary of Morgan's interview to President Johnson and Attorney General Clark, where it would set off a chain of events that would echo into the next decade—and trigger yet another round of cover-ups by Richard Helms.[59]

CHAPTER 21

Spring–Fall 1967: Another Helms Cover-Up and Nixon Decides to Run

President Lyndon Johnson received the results of the FBI's interview with Ed Morgan, Johnny Rosselli's attorney, on March 22, 1967. That evening, LBJ demanded a full explanation from CIA Director Richard Helms, but he didn't get one. Instead, Helms would provide an incomplete and often misleading account to the President who had appointed him. The very limited report Helms would allow the CIA's Inspector General to generate about the CIA-Mafia plots to kill Fidel Castro would become the object of Presidential fascination and Congressional investigations, and large parts of it would remain beyond the public's reach for decades. Not until the 1990s did the almost uncensored 1967 Inspector General's Report finally become available, and it took longer still for files to be declassified that showed just how much crucial information Helms had withheld from LBJ.[1]

According to a memo from a high-ranking FBI official who had talked to LBJ aide Marvin Watson, President Johnson "was now convinced that there was a plot in connection with the assassination [of JFK]. Watson stated the President felt that [the] CIA had had something to do with this plot." Perhaps Helms either sensed LBJ's suspicion or was told about it, resulting in Helms's decision to withhold crucial information from the President.[2]

LBJ's worry that the "CIA had something to do with" JFK's assassination did not last long and would apparently be dispelled by the incomplete report Helms made sure the Agency generated. But President Johnson still harbored those doubts on the evening of March 22, when he met with Richard Helms at the White House. According to Helms's biographer, Thomas Powers, LBJ "asked [Helms] directly, formally, and explicitly, in a tone and manner which did not [foresee] evasion," for a full report about the matters in the Anderson articles. LBJ made it clear that he expected "an honest answer." For good measure, LBJ also told Helms to address any CIA involvement in the assassinations of Vietnam's leader Diem in 1963 and Dominican dictator Trujillo in 1961. (Helms wouldn't be forthcoming to LBJ about Trujillo's murder either, since his protégé E. Howard Hunt had been involved in the lead-up to that affair, along with Johnny Rosselli.)[3]

LBJ's formal request was one of two overriding factors dictating the form of Helms's resulting report. First, LBJ's request would have to be referred to the CIA's Inspector General, Jack Earman, who had given Helms a hard time in the summer of 1963 about the CIA's MKULTRA mind-control program. Second, it is not clear how much LBJ told Helms about the information he had received from the FBI about the CIA-Mafia plots. While the CIA appears to have received copies of the FBI memos that went to LBJ and the Attorney General, Helms didn't know what additional information J. Edgar Hoover might have shared privately with his friend LBJ. Helms was aware of earlier memos the CIA had provided to the FBI about the plots, after the FBI discovered parts of the plots in 1961 and 1962.

Richard Helms's report would have to account for everything he knew the FBI had, plus any additional information the Bureau might have uncovered without telling the CIA. At the same time, Helms would have to avoid telling LBJ about the most sensitive parts of his unauthorized Castro assassination plots with the Mafia, especially any of those activities from 1963 that might have been linked in some way to JFK's assassination.

Helms protected himself and some of his associates by withholding important information from the CIA Inspector General's investigation, and thus from LBJ and any later President who might ask to see the Report. From Helms's perspective, he had no other choice if he wanted to keep his job—and he had several ways to control, restrict, and direct the Inspector General's investigation. First, it was up to Helms to verbally convey LBJ's request to the Inspector General. By choosing his words carefully, Helms could shade his request so that it generated a lengthy report that addressed some of LBJ's concerns but avoided sensitive subjects that could cost Helms his career.

Like a savvy politician talking to a journalist, Helms relied on the strategy of not answering the question that was asked, but instead answering the question he wished had been asked. Peter Dale Scott has pointed out that the final Inspector General's report (henceforth called the IG Report) devoted scant attention to what LBJ had wanted investigated, which was primarily the story in Jack Anderson's columns on March 3 and March 7. Scott points out that the IG Report itself admits that Anderson's March 7 column "refers to a reported CIA plan in 1963 to assassinate . . . Castro," but Scott also found that less than 10 percent of the IG Report refers "to a 1963 plot at all, and that one is not the one Anderson was writing about." In fact, "less than a dozen lines" in the 134-plus-page IG Report "are devoted to" the main point of Anderson's columns, the "political H-bomb" about the alleged "counterplot by Castro to assassinate President Kennedy." He observes that the IG Report "wholly fails to investigate . . . the central theses [of the Anderson articles:] that Robert Kennedy authorized a CIA plot which then 'possibly backfired' against Kennedy."[4]

Richard Helms apparently directed the IG to focus on finding out who had leaked the information to journalists Anderson and Pearson, and what could be done about it. Helms also worded the request, and controlled access to information, so that the investigation focused only on the plots from the summer of 1960 through 1962, which were made to look as if they had essentially ended by early 1963—well before JFK's assassination. That approach was safer for Helms than focusing on operations Robert Kennedy had authorized in 1963, or on the unauthorized CIA-Mafia plots Helms ran into in the late fall of 1963. Though the IG investigation did extensively cover the CIA-Mafia plots while Nixon was Vice President, it neglected to mention his role—or any executive branch involvement—at all.

No doubt LBJ hoped Helms would turn up information he could use to stop Robert Kennedy from entering the race for President, but the IG Report is devoid of information that reflects badly on RFK. In fact, there isn't much about RFK in the IG Report at all, since Helms knew the young Senator could become President at some point in the future. One of the two CIA staffers assigned to actually write the IG Report, a man who was definitely not a Kennedy partisan, said he "simply never heard [Robert] Kennedy cited as a mastermind [of operations to eliminate Castro] by any of the CIA officials he interviewed." Then again, Helms himself, who had much contact with RFK about Cuban matters in 1963, was never interviewed for the IG Report.[5]

In protecting RFK, Helms was also protecting himself. Thus, the entire coup plan with Almeida is missing from the IG Report, as are the 1963 portions of AMWORLD (the code name appears nowhere in the IG Report) and the CIA's extensive support for Manuel Artime and Manolo Ray in the last six months of JFK's Presidency. Omitting all of that information made it easy for Helms to hide the fact that Artime had been working on the CIA-Mafia plots at the same time that he was working on AMWORLD and the Almeida coup plan.

Richard Nixon had made a remarkable political comeback by 1967, and Helms knew he had an excellent chance of running for President in 1968. Hence, the IG Report does not mention Vice President Nixon's 1959 push for the CIA to find ways to eliminate Fidel. Also missing is any indication of Nixon's leading role regarding Cuba policy under President Eisenhower and any explanation of why the CIA-Mafia plots were ramped up so extensively three months before the 1960 election, when Rosselli, Trafficante, and Giancana were all recruited. Ironically, throughout Richard Nixon's Presidency, Nixon would press Helms and the CIA for information they had about those and related events, not realizing he had nothing to worry about from Helms's whitewashed IG Report.

Even after Helms assigned the report to the CIA's Inspector General on March 23, 1967, as Director he still had many ways to control and limit its content. In consultation with Desmond FitzGerald, Helms could withhold certain information and witnesses while making others more easily available. This tactic would ensure that the two IG investigators covered easily documentable high points, especially those the FBI already knew about, while steering them away from information that could expose the extent of Helms's unauthorized plans or the Mafia's infiltration of Almeida's coup plan.[6]

Even though CIA officer E. Howard Hunt had been very active in the coup plan with Almeida and with members of the CIA-Mafia plots such as Tony Varona, one of the two IG investigators would later testify to Congress that "at the time of our investigation in 1967, Howard Hunt's name did not come up." Also, some CIA personnel who should have been interviewed were conveniently out of the country during the IG investigation, including several in Southeast Asia. Among those were David Morales, Ted Shackley, AMWORLD case officers like Henry Hecksher, and CIA employees who had worked closely with Artime, such as Rafael "Chi Chi" Quintero. Even though the IG Report mentions Artime's contacts with Rolando Cubela in late

1964 and 1965, Artime was not interviewed for the IG Report, despite that fact that he was still living in Miami. As a result, the investigators failed to learn about Artime's massive $7 million AMWORLD effort, his Mafia ties, or his role in the CIA-Mafia plots with Rosselli and Trafficante. That was important because the 1967 IG Report points out several Mafia and Trafficante ties to the Cubela operation, but treats that matter as completely separate from the rest of the CIA-Mafia plots. The Inspector General didn't interview Manolo Ray, and his contacts with Cubela—first documented by this author in 2006—are missing from the IG Report, even though recently declassified CIA files and Ray himself have now confirmed those contacts. Especially glaring is that fact that investigators didn't talk to Tony Varona, even though he and his contact with the Mafia were mentioned many times in the IG Report. The IG Report also contains no mention of the CIA memo describing how Varona received $200,000 from the Mafia in the summer of 1963.[7]

Helms would basically use the IG investigation to learn which sensitive files the investigators could find on their own, how those files meshed with what the FBI had, and how people who weren't involved in the original operations might interpret those files. Helms would also use the IG Report's preparation as an excuse to systematically destroy some of the sensitive material the investigators uncovered.

Essentially, Helms attempted what would later be termed a "limited hangout": allowing some negative material about the CIA to be disclosed to LBJ, but nothing that could get Helms fired. It's important to keep in mind that the Rosselli matter and Jack Anderson's investigation, as well as covert operations against Cuba, were still ongoing at the time of Helms's IG investigation. It was a fluid situation that limited what Helms could safely allow the Inspector General to see or investigate.

Drew Pearson spoke to President Johnson on April 5, 1967. LBJ had seen the results of Morgan's FBI interview and had talked with Helms, so he admitted to Pearson that "we think there's something to . . . Morgan's information. There were some attempts to assassinate Castro through the Cosa Nostra [the Mafia], and they point to your friends in the Justice Department." Pearson corrected him, saying, "You mean one friend"—a reference to former Attorney General Robert Kennedy.[8]

According to Senate investigators, Jack Anderson told former CIA

Director John McCone he was "preparing [yet another] column on Castro assassination attempts, implicating President Kennedy and Robert Kennedy." McCone then talked "with Anderson at Robert Kennedy's request," after which "McCone dictated [an] April 14, 1967, memorandum" to Helms that probably mirrored what McCone had told Anderson. In it, McCone admitted only that in early August 1962, he recalled having heard in Operation Mongoose meetings "a suggestion being made to liquidate top people in the Castro regime, including Castro." McCone said he "took immediate exception to this suggestion." Ironically, at that very moment Helms was allowing the IG Report to include some of the critical information about the CIA-Mafia plots he had withheld from RFK and McCone when he was CIA Director, apparently hoping that neither man would ever see the report.[9]

For reasons that are still unclear, Jack Anderson suddenly dropped his plans for a third article. By then Anderson certainly knew he had a good story, based on LBJ's confirmation to Pearson and McCone's admission that the subject of assassinating Castro had surfaced during an official meeting in 1962. The CIA was somehow able to learn that Anderson and Pearson had additional "information, as yet unpublished, to the effect that there was a meeting at the State Department at which assassination of Castro was discussed and that a team actually landed in Cuba with pills to be used in an assassination attempt." The CIA's IG Report would confirm that "there is basis in fact for each of those . . . reports," but didn't indicate how the CIA knew what information the journalists possessed. As noted earlier, based on Helms's behavior in other cases, it's possible that Anderson and Pearson were being wiretapped or bugged or both.[10]

It's also possible that President Johnson, after telling Pearson that Anderson's story had a factual basis, had asked or even pressured Pearson not to pursue the story. Jack Anderson would not resume writing about the leaks from Johnny Rosselli for almost four years, when his articles were again connected with the legal problems of Rosselli and Hoffa and helped lead to the Watergate scandal.

By April 24, 1967, the Inspector General was starting to deliver his report to Helms in installments, while Helms continued to track the related matters of Cuban operations and the Jim Garrison investigation. A short time later, District Attorney Garrison subpoenaed Helms to appear before the grand jury in New Orleans. Helms felt obliged only to tell Georgia Senator (and former Warren Commission member) Richard Russell about Garrison's subpoena—which Helms then ignored.[11]

Commander Almeida remained prominent in Cuba, helping to fill the vacuum created by Che Guevara's mysterious absence. UPI reported that on May 1, 1967, "Havana radio announced that Cuba's acting Armed Forces Minister, Major Juan Almeida, will preside over May Day ceremonies today, instead of Premier Fidel Castro . . . Almeida recently was designated acting Armed Forces Minister in place of Major Raul Castro, the Premier's brother. The reason for that move never was explained." At the huge ceremony, Almeida revealed only that Che Guevara had been "serving the revolution somewhere in Latin America." He didn't say that Che was in Bolivia on another doomed mission, even more poorly supplied and supported than Che's first exile to Africa.[12]

That Almeida was trusted with heading Cuba's big May Day celebration in Fidel's absence was a very positive development for Richard Helms. It indicated that Almeida still wielded enough power in Cuba to be valuable to the United States in the future, allowing Helms to rationalize withholding from the Inspector General information about Almeida's secret work for JFK and the CIA's ongoing covert support for Almeida's wife and children outside Cuba. It also allowed Helms to withhold from both the Inspector General's Report and President Johnson all information concerning the Mafia's infiltration of the Almeida coup plan and Rosselli's role in the CIA-Mafia plots in the fall of 1963.

The story that emerged from the IG Report succeeded in separating the CIA-Mafia plots from JFK's assassination by claiming the plots had ended by early 1963. Only brief passages in the IG Report mentioned Helms's unauthorized operations, but nothing tied them to JFK's assassination.[13]

The overall thrust of the IG Report was damage control, with an ancillary goal of discovering who was leaking information and how to stop the leaks. Ironically, the same concern would result from the next round of Rosselli revelations to Jack Anderson, and would set in motion the actions of E. Howard Hunt and the Watergate "Plumbers," so named because one of their roles was to find and stop leaks. Hunt's men would even consider killing Jack Anderson, and while the 1967

IG Report does have a section entitled "Should we try to silence those who are talking or might later talk?", the options considered in the IG Report weren't lethal.[14]

Having dealt with several Presidents, Helms understood how they operated: LBJ was not going to read the 134-plus-page IG Report himself, and likely not even a several-page summary. The matter was so explosive that LBJ would probably not even have a trusted staff member read it for him. Helms therefore prepared a few pages of notes, so that he could give LBJ a verbal summary of the IG Report. He went to the White House to brief LBJ orally about the Inspector General's Report on May 10, 1967, taking only his notes and not even a copy of the Report. Helms apparently hoped that LBJ would be content to trust Helms to keep the whole situation under wraps—and that was exactly what happened.

Helms neglected to tell LBJ of details in the IG Report such as the poison pen the CIA tried to give to Rolando Cubela on the day JFK was killed. Eight years later, when Senator Frank Church asked Richard Helms about that, Helms testified, "I just can't recall having done so." Helms tried to claim to Church and the other Senators that the Cubela operation hadn't been an assassination plot, but by then the Senators had seen the IG Report and knew Helms was lying. Congressional investigators also found that Helms hadn't bothered to prepare any notes for his meeting with LBJ covering the continuation of the CIA-Mafia plots with Rosselli into 1963. In his testimony to Congress, Helms was at a loss to explain why, but he clearly never intended to detail for LBJ the CIA activities that were most relevant to Anderson's columns and JFK's assassination.[15]

When Helms briefed President Johnson on May 10, 1967, the only other person present was LBJ's Press Secretary, probably in case the material ever surfaced in the news. By the end of the session, LBJ was apparently content to let the matter rest with Helms as long as it stayed out of the press. By feeding LBJ's suspicions of Castro, Helms's presentation also appears to have succeeded in removing the CIA from LBJ's list of suspects in JFK's assassination. In later years, LBJ would admit privately to a journalist that "we were running a damn Murder Incorporated in the Caribbean" and "Kennedy was trying to get Castro, but Castro got to him first." Leaving LBJ with that impression would also help Helms justify his ongoing anti-Castro operations, which were proving increasingly problematic.[16]

After his meeting with LBJ, Helms held on to the IG Report for twelve days before returning it to the CIA's Inspector General. Helms probably kept the report for as long as he did because he wanted to make sure nothing new about the CIA-Mafia plots surfaced from the investigations of Jack Anderson or Jim Garrison. On the following day, May 23, 1967, Senate investigators later found that "all notes and other derived source material of the IG Report are destroyed." Thomas Powers writes that the destruction of material included "every scrap" of the Inspector General's investigation: "every transcript of an interview, every memo, every note made by the investigators."[17]

Richard Helms apparently ordered it all destroyed so that even his successor (or future Presidents) could at best access only the whitewashed report, not the actual documents and interviews that could lead to matters that Helms wanted to remain hidden. The process of having the report done had given Helms the opportunity to corral, and in some cases destroy, files that could have ended his career or ruined his reputation after he left the Agency.

Helms made sure the IG Report went "into a safe, his briefing notes neatly attached to the front, and it stayed there, untouched and unread, until . . . 1973," after Richard Nixon had sacked Helms in the wake of Watergate. Once Nixon became President, he spent years fruitlessly trying to get a copy of material like the IG Report and other files about the Castro assassination plots from Helms—but a stubborn Helms refused to give it to him.[18]

By mid-May 1967, Helms had succeeded in fending off LBJ's interest in the 1963 CIA plots involving the Mafia, and someone had persuaded Jack Anderson to stop writing articles about the matter. But what about the original catalyst for the affair, Johnny Rosselli?

Rosselli had finally accomplished what he—along with Marcello and Trafficante—had wanted for almost a year. Page 132 of the IG Report relates a May 3, 1967, discussion between the CIA and the FBI's liaison to the Agency. The FBI liaison said Rosselli had the "CIA 'over a barrel' because of 'that operation.' [The FBI liaison] said that he doubted that the FBI would be able to do anything about either Rosselli or Giancana because of 'their previous activities with [the CIA].'"[19]

Rosselli's triumph would be ironic in two ways. First, shortly before his own murder nine years later, Rosselli would admit to his attorney the true version of the story: that Trafficante's men who had been involved in plots to kill Fidel had actually killed JFK instead, knowledge that led to Rosselli's own murder. Second, in 1967 the sixty-three-year-old Rosselli would be able to savor his successful pressure on the CIA that stalled his deportation for scarcely two months.

In the summer of 1967, the longtime career criminal Rosselli couldn't resist continuing a card-cheating scam at the prestigious Los Angeles Friars Club, a scheme that had bilked some of the club's wealthy members out of $400,000. On July 20, 1967, the FBI raided the Friars Club and found the electronic equipment Rosselli and his men used in their scam. The government then used a grand jury to pressure Rosselli. Because of the high-profile nature of the case, a new Criminal Division Chief at the U.S. Attorney's office in Los Angeles also used it to press the immigration case against Rosselli. According to Rosselli's biographers, "on October 21, 1967, Rosselli was indicted on six counts for failure to register as an alien."[20]

Though Rosselli was "released on $5,000 bond," he would be indicted in December 1967 for the Friars Club charges along with five codefendants. Rosselli's first reaction was to hire notorious hit man Jimmy "The Weasel" Fratianno to kill the main witness in the Friars Club case. However, that approach failed when the man vanished into the Federal Witness Protection Program, leaving Rosselli with few options. One of Johnny Rosselli's codefendants hired prominent Los Angeles attorney Grant Cooper as his attorney of record. Cooper would soon mysteriously come into possession of illegal copies of the grand jury's testimony against Rosselli and the others.[21]

Rosselli turned to his old friend William Harvey for help, calling him on the day of his indictment and asking Harvey to represent him, but Harvey—in the process of leaving the CIA after Helms had fired him—declined. However, Harvey still wanted to help his friend, so he tried to pressure the CIA's FBI liaison, Sam Papich, over lunch on November 6, 1967. Harvey became "incensed" when Papich suggested that he end his relationship with Rosselli. Instead, Harvey warned that if he cut off Rosselli, "the Agency could get itself in serious trouble"—which sounds like Harvey was threatening that he or Rosselli might reveal more about Helms's unauthorized operations to someone like Jack Anderson. The JFK assassination anniversary was just over two weeks away, and that could have been an opportune time for Anderson to run his third article. The journalist still had unused material from the spring, and November had been the month when Anderson's boss, Drew Pearson, had originally planned to run the first article.[22]

According to declassified files, William Harvey and Johnny Rosselli met on November 26, 27, and 28, and finding some way to pressure the FBI again was no doubt their main topic of discussion. But no additional Jack Anderson article about the matter appeared that month, and there wouldn't be one for almost four years. FBI official Sam Papich no doubt conveyed William Harvey's request to J. Edgar Hoover, but the Bureau refused to back off on Rosselli as it had in the spring.[23]

Richard Nixon was surely aware of Jack Anderson's 1967 articles about the CIA-Mafia plots and Robert Kennedy's 1963 Cuban operation. Unlike four years later, when Watergate files document the worried reaction of Nixon's White House to even more explicit Anderson articles about the plots, we only have a few indications of Nixon's reactions in 1967.

Nixon would have worried about Anderson's 1967 articles on three counts, all of which have been covered in earlier chapters. First, as confirmed by Robert Maheu, Nixon had originated the CIA's plotting with Johnny Rosselli. Second, in 1963 Nixon had been on the fringe of one of the CIA-Mafia plot attempts, while William Pawley, his friend at the time, had been heavily involved with Johnny Rosselli. Finally, as a CIA memo confirms, by the fall of 1963 Nixon had a pipeline into Robert Kennedy's plan to stage a coup against Fidel, via two associates of corrupt ex–Cuban President Carlos Prio.[24]

Around March 4—the day after the first Jack Anderson article about the CIA-Mafia plots was published—the CIA turned down Nixon's request for a briefing, the first time the ex–Vice President had been so denied. Nixon had sought the CIA briefing as a routine matter before taking an overseas trip on March 5, and given Nixon's status as a former Vice President, the briefing likely would have come from Richard Helms or one of his deputies. Had he been able to meet with a CIA representative, Nixon would almost certainly have asked about Anderson's explosive CIA disclosures—which is probably why Nixon was denied any briefing.[25]

Especially after the second article appeared, Nixon would have been concerned about what else Jack Anderson might disclose, particularly since Drew Pearson and Jack Anderson had been his adversaries for years. But Nixon was out of government circles, and, unlike Robert Kennedy, he lacked direct access to men like Richard Helms and John McCone. Worse, from his point of view, because of Nixon's unceasing attacks on President Johnson, he had no way of knowing what LBJ was doing about the matter.

The highest personal connection Nixon still had in the administration was J. Edgar Hoover, who could have informed Nixon of what his agents learned from questioning Rosselli's attorney, Ed Morgan. The same would have been true when William Harvey pressured Sam Papich, the FBI's liaison to the CIA, in November 1967; Nixon could have learned about that—and Hoover's decision not to give in to Rosselli's demands—as well. If so, that could explain some unusual timing in Nixon's account of his decision to run for the Presidency.

In his last autobiography, Nixon said that he made his decision about "whether to run for the presidency" when he had "flown alone to Florida" during Christmas of 1967. There, Nixon "made his decision to enter the race in the company of two men, the evangelist Billy Graham and [Bebe] Rebozo." However, it's well documented that Nixon had already made his decision almost a year earlier, when he held his first major strategy meetings at the Waldorf-Astoria, "on January 7 and 8, 1967." According to Stephen Ambrose, Nixon met at the Waldorf to plot strategy with seven advisors, including one of his key speechwriters, William Safire. Why the discrepancy of almost a year? And why—in December of 1967—would Nixon, the overwhelming favorite, who'd been clearly campaigning for the office he longed for throughout 1967, have any decision to make about "whether to run for the presidency"?[26]

Perhaps after Nixon had made his Presidential decision in January 1967, he became worried about what else Jack Anderson or Drew Pearson might disclose that could harm his campaign. Then as the months progressed, it became clear that Anderson wasn't going to publish a third article, and that no other mainstream journalist in America was going to follow up on Anderson's dramatic revelations. The last blip on the radar would have been William Harvey's pressure on the FBI liaison on November 4, 1967, and Harvey's implicit threat to reveal more information from Rosselli. When the anniversary of JFK's assassination came and went with no new article from Anderson, Nixon would have been relieved. His Christmas 1967 meeting with Rebozo and Graham could have been when Nixon decided it was safe to go forward. Rebozo would have been perhaps the only person that Nixon could have discussed the matter with, due to their trusted friendship and because Rebozo had met with Nixon and Pawley in early 1963, when Pawley was beginning his work with Johnny Rosselli.[27]

Rosselli's associates—Carlos Marcello, Santo Trafficante, and Jimmy Hoffa—had varying experiences in the wake of the 1967 Jack Anderson articles. Trafficante and Marcello would have been concerned by Rosselli's new troubles, but both godfathers would have been glad the Garrison investigation was off course and scorned by the mainstream media, thanks in part to the work of some of their own operatives. Marcello still faced a trial for his swing at an FBI agent, though his powerful legal team kept securing postponements. As for Jimmy Hoffa, the efforts of his attorney Ed Morgan with Rosselli hadn't affected the Teamsters chief's incarceration at all. Even worse for Hoffa, the press still constantly speculated on the possibility that Robert Kennedy might challenge LBJ for the Presidency. A win by RFK, while Hoffa remained incarcerated, would be Hoffa's worst nightmare.

According to FBI files, on May 30, 1967, an inmate overheard Hoffa say "that he had a contract out on Senator Robert F. Kennedy." The inmate's account contained credible details, and "stated that on or about Memorial Day, 1967, he was in the dining hall at the Lewisburg Federal Penitentiary and at the table next to him was James Hoffa, who was talking to the two . . . individuals [both Americans] of Italian descent." One of the unnamed individuals fit the description of fifty-seven-year-old Mafia underboss Carmine Galante, Hoffa's closest mob confidant in prison. Galante had been prosecuted when Bobby was Attorney General and was serving twenty years for running part of the French Connection heroin network. Galante was also aligned with Carlos Marcello and Santo Trafficante.[28]

The Lewisburg inmate told the FBI that he'd overheard Hoffa tell the two Italian-Americans, "I have a contract out on Kennedy and if he ever gets in the primaries or ever gets elected, the contract will be fulfilled within six months." Another, more heavily censored FBI report might confirm the inmate's story: Marcello biographer John Davis writes that one year later, just weeks before Robert Kennedy's murder, "an inmate informant in . . . Lewisburg told the FBI that he had overheard Jimmy Hoffa and New York Mafia boss Carmine Galante, an ally of Carlos Marcello's, discussing a 'mob contract to kill

Bob Kennedy.'" Names and other information in FBI memos about this 1968 threat are still censored, so how this information relates to the May 1967 Lewisburg report can't be determined. In any event, the FBI apparently didn't get around to asking Hoffa about his May 1967 threat against Robert Kennedy for more than a year—not until six weeks after RFK's assassination.[29]

While Richard Helms had emerged from the 1967 Anderson-Rosselli article situation with his position and reputation intact, his Cuban operations were in a transitional stage. The heyday of the big Miami CIA station and its thousands of contract agents was long past, and the new paradigm for covert Cuban operations was for the Agency to back a far smaller group of violent Cuban exiles in a more deniable way. On July 23, 1967, Desmond FitzGerald—the CIA's Deputy Director for Plans, and Helms's close ally—died of a heart attack. It was a sharp loss for Helms, since FitzGerald had been the highest-ranking CIA official who had collaborated with Helms on the unauthorized CIA-Mafia Castro assassination plots. Helms appointed his trusted former deputy Thomas Karamessines to take FitzGerald's position, heading worldwide covert operations.[30]

To run Cuban operations, Helms needed someone with experience that he could trust. Just as Helms had turned to E. Howard Hunt almost a year earlier, Helms now called on another trusted associate, David Atlee Phillips. Like Hunt, Phillips had the advantage of not only being experienced, but also already knowing about (and having worked on) the CIA's most sensitive Cuban operation: AMWORLD and the coup plan with Almeida, the remnants of which involved the ongoing secret monitoring and support of Almeida's wife and children outside of Cuba.

David Atlee Phillips left his post in the Dominican Republic to become the CIA's new Chief of Cuban Operations. Even while Phillips had been the Agency's Chief of Station of the Dominican Republic, he had apparently continued to supervise Cuban exile leader Antonio Veciana. Their type of "deniable" relationship was exactly what Helms was looking to use on a broader scale, since the CIA's more loosely controlled Cuban exile agents and assets sometimes went too far with their violent activity, including bombings in the United States and Canada.[31]

It's interesting that even after Helms had struggled to contain the fallout from Jack Anderson's first articles on the CIA-Mafia plots, Helms and key CIA officials continued to tolerate—and possibly to encourage—contact between the CIA's exiles and organized crime. For example, CIA files document that in the summer of 1967, exile Luis Posada was dealing explosives with Frank "Lefty" Rosenthal, a Miami mob figure (Rosenthal was the basis for the character portrayed by Robert De Niro in the film *Casino*).[32]

According to a CIA report to the FBI on June 27, 1967, Rosenthal was "tied in with organized crime figures in [the] Miami area and also involved with 7 recent bombings in Miami." Rosenthal got "in touch with Posada" by going through mob figure Norman Rothman. Rothman's ties to Cuba went back to the early 1950s and to the incident noted earlier when Nixon's associate stopped payment on a check to a Cuban casino. Rothman, who worked for Trafficante in Havana, had also been on the fringe of the 1959 CIA-Mafia plots to kill Fidel and had run guns to Cuba with Jack Ruby and Cuban ex–President Carlos Prio. The reason the CIA tolerated agents such as Posada having such mob contacts was the same in 1967 as it had been from 1959 to 1963: It helped to hide the CIA's own involvement in anti-Castro operations.[33]

But Helms and his subordinates had learned to be more cautious, so a CIA memo says that Luis "Posada [was] terminated 7/11/67 because . . . JMWAVE does not have current need." However, other CIA files place Posada's termination from full-time CIA employment in 1968, and another CIA memo says the Agency retained "Posada [until] 2-13-76." In any event, an Agency memo admits that the CIA rehired Posada almost immediately after his termination, only this time "as an independent contractor from 1968–75." This method of having someone apparently leave the CIA—only to continue working for the Agency—would soon be repeated with E. Howard Hunt and other Watergate figures. Likewise, the confusing dates on the CIA files for Luis Posada anticipates in a small way the missing and sometimes contradictory files for Hunt and the other Agency veterans who later worked on Nixon's covert White House operations.[34]

Many former Cuban exile CIA agents and assets weren't retained (or were perhaps used only on a job-to-job basis), and according to intelligence journalist Joseph Trento, the Federal Bureau of Narcotics (FBN) would find "itself arresting scores of former CIA employees. These Cuban 'freedom fighters' were using their CIA training for a life of crime [and justifying] their actions by claiming that they were using the ill-gotten funds to continue the effort against Castro, an effort that the CIA had abandoned. Many of these men were working directly for Santo Trafficante" in the drug trade.[35]

Tom Tripodi was a Federal Bureau of Narcotics agent assigned to the Miami CIA station's security office. Tripodi was Chief of Special Operations, which he wrote was "responsible for extralegal domestic covert activities." He said that "some of the guys who later would be bagged in the Watergate affair worked for me. I understand that when I left the Agency, most of the functions of [Special Operations] were transferred to a unit supervised by E. Howard Hunt."[36]

Frank Fiorini's official CIA status in 1967 and 1968 is unclear, though his treatment indicates he could have still been an occasional contract agent for the Agency. As indicated earlier, even though two CIA Directors—one of them Helms—admitted Fiorini had been a CIA contract agent, those contract files have never been released. However, Fiorini was frequently engaged in activities for Santo Trafficante.[37]

By 1968, Frank Fiorini was involved in a smuggling operation on the Texas-Mexico border. According to the Justice Department, Fiorini's scheme "was really a conspiracy to smuggle stolen automobiles out of the United States" into Mexico, an activity which Fiorini claimed was all leading up to "a commando raid on Castro's Cuba." One of Fiorini's men in the car-smuggling operation had also helped Fiorini spread John Martino's phony stories after JFK's assassination.[38]

Fiorini's scheme went on for quite some time and involved more than a hundred cars, after which Fiorini and some of his men were captured in British Honduras while supposedly en route to Cuba. However, according to *The Miami Herald*, Fiorini called "somebody in Washington," and subsequently "a Fort Lauderdale lawyer says he got a call 'from a man at the State Department'" about representing Fiorini and the others. Fiorini and his crew were all released with no charges against them at the time. The lawyer said, "I gather it had the tacit approval of somebody in the government, or they would have been in trouble." Fiorini was not prosecuted for the 1968 charges until five years later, after he was arrested for Watergate.[39]

Fiorini's car smuggling scheme was just part of a large, ongoing operation involving Mafia associates of Marcello and Trafficante, the corrupt Mexican Federal Police (the DFS), and the heroin network they shared. As author Peter Dale Scott noted, Sam Giancana and Richard Cain were living in Mexico at the time, and their mob was "simultaneously involved in smuggling stolen cars . . . in an international ring which appeared to overlap with narcotics operations." The ring would last into the 1970s and 1980s, until "thirteen DFS officials were indicted in California," though the "DFS Director . . . was initially protected from indictment by the CIA."* It's ironic that within a few years, Fiorini would be working for the Nixon White House, supposedly on "anti-drug" activities, along with his friend Bernard Barker.[40]

On October 8, 1967, CIA and Bolivian forces captured Che Guevara, giving Richard Helms and new Cuban Operations Chief David Atlee Phillips a major boost to their reputations. On hand for Che's capture and interrogation was CIA veteran Felix Rodriguez, the Cuban exile who had undertaken a Castro assassination mission in the last days of Richard Nixon's Vice Presidency and was later involved in AMWORLD. Felix Rodriguez wrote a firsthand account of his involvement in Che's death, and he was one of what some reports say were several CIA agents present for Che's execution. Rodriguez said the cover name for his "CIA colleague" there was "Eduardo."[41]

While Rodriguez has said the CIA wanted Che to be kept alive, E. Howard Hunt later stated, "We wanted deniability. We made it possible for him to be killed . . . it was just important that it was done." Congressional investigator Gaeton Fonzi writes that David Morales claimed he was "involved in the capture of Che Guevara in Bolivia." He noted that Morales, formerly Phillips's superior back in pre-Castro Havana, had by 1967 become "David Atlee Phillips's most valuable action man," as Phillips now outranked his former boss. Author Larry Hancock confirmed that "Morales's Army cover documents do show him as being assigned to Bolivia [in 1967]." David Morales later confided to his attorney and close friend that he "had the Bolivian police arrest [Che and] told them to shoot him."[42]

While Che's capture was a publicity coup for CIA Director Helms, he had little time to savor it, since in the fall of 1967 he had his hands full with the aftermath of Israel's Six-Day War in the Middle East, Cold War fronts from South America to Europe, and especially Vietnam. Helms was also overseeing the CIA's own rapidly expanding illegal domestic surveillance operation, which would soon be named Operation CHAOS.[43]

* The DFS was the Mexican police agency that had tortured Cuban embassy employee Sylvia Duran for the CIA, and also monitored phone calls to the Cuban and Soviet embassies in Mexico City for the Agency.

As writer Verne Lyon pointed out, CHAOS grew out of the CIA's early Cuban operations with exiles in the United States. It became so large that the CIA created "a new super-secret branch called the Domestic Operations Division (DOD), the very title of which mocked the explicit intent of Congress to prohibit CIA operations inside the US." As mentioned previously, E. Howard Hunt was one of those assigned to this new branch, whose responsibilities included "burglarizing foreign diplomatic sites at the request of the National Security Agency (NSA)," something Hunt would do just before the Watergate break-ins. Lyon writes that "by August 1967, the illegal collection of domestic intelligence had become so large and widespread that [Helms] was forced to create a Special Operations Group [that] provided data on the US peace movement . . . on a regular basis."[44]

The FBI and military intelligence were also large parts of the growing domestic surveillance network. Journalist James Dickerson wrote that "by 1967 the U.S. Army" effort to "gather information about the political activity of American citizens [had grown to] 1,500 plainclothes agents . . . assigned to over 350 secret record centers." They assembled "information on individuals attending protest rallies, business executives who contributed money to political causes, and politicians who voted for unpopular legislation." According to Hancock and Wexler, the rationale was that "army surveillance [was] designed to provide early warning of demonstrations, rallies, and other gatherings which could lead to civil disturbances requiring the deployment of Federal troops." As documented previously, President Kennedy had sometimes been a target of Army surveillance, and within a few years the U.S. military would be caught spying on President Richard Nixon.[45]

Oddly enough, the turf wars that had raged between the CIA, the FBI, and military intelligence were reduced somewhat by the cooperation necessary for their often illegal domestic spying. According to Lyons, the CIA also expanded its cooperation "with local police and their intelligence units . . . and began in earnest to pull off burglaries, illegal entries, use of explosives, criminal frame-ups, shared interrogations, and disinformation." While federal agencies still protected their turf, they also had to share information and sometimes coordinate surveillance, all below the radar of the American public and most of Congress and the press.[46]

. . .

In 1967 the war in Vietnam grew increasingly problematic for the country and President Johnson, with seemingly no end in sight. One reason was that U.S. Commander General William Westmoreland had been underestimating the strength of the Viet Cong forces in South Vietnam by half, "for political reasons." As explained by twenty-seven-year CIA veteran Ray McGovern, an analyst at the time, "in early 1967, CIA analysts . . . demonstrated that there were more than twice as many Vietnamese Communist forces as the US military listed on its books." But Richard Helms gave in to pressure from the U.S. military, and "in November 1967 Helms signed and gave to President Johnson a formal National Intelligence Estimate enshrining the Army's count of between 188,000 and 208,000 for enemy strength. My CIA analyst colleagues were aghast; their best estimate was 500,000."[47]

Defense Secretary Robert McNamara had begun to have doubts about the war, so in "June 1967 [he] commissioned a task force to write a history of the U.S. decision making during the Vietnam Conflict using primary source documents. McNamara appointed [a] task force, which ultimately employed 36 staff members and took eighteen months to complete." According to the National Archives, the resulting report was a "47 volume document given the title *United States-Vietnam Relations 1945-1967*. The entire report was classified at the Top Secret level" and only about fifteen copies of the report were printed. Several years later when a copy was leaked by one of its authors, Daniel Ellsberg, the report became famous as the Pentagon Papers, and both it and Ellsberg would play important roles in the events that grew into the Watergate scandal.[48]

CHAPTER 22

1968: Tragedy for America, Triumph for Nixon

The year 1968 was pivotal and tumultuous for the country on every front. Major upheavals and unexpected tragedies rocked America, tearing and dividing it along political, generational, racial, and cultural lines. Jarring change was the only constant, whipsawing the country from one emotional extreme to the other, and out of all that turmoil Richard Nixon finally emerged victorious as the country's newly elected President. In doing so, Nixon built on his past patterns of behavior to set a new template for the crimes that would eventually help to drive him from office.

On January 30, 1968, President Lyndon Johnson and CIA Director Richard Helms, along with Richard Nixon and the rest of the country, were stunned by reports that Saigon was under heavy mortar attack during the Buddhist holiday period known as Tet. The Viet Cong's Tet Offensive had begun, and the U.S. embassy and diplomatic compound in Saigon soon became a battleground. According to historian Taylor Branch, at least "seventy thousand guerrillas launched similar attacks of coordinated surprise" throughout most of Vietnam's provinces. The attacks dragged on for weeks, "killing nearly four thousand American and six thousand South Vietnamese soldiers, plus an estimated 58,000 Communist soldiers and 14,000 civilians."[1]

As Robert Kennedy said, "Tet changed everything." By 1968, U.S. officials and the press had been assuring the American public for years that U.S. forces had nearly prevailed, the end of the war was in sight, and troops would soon start coming home. But in the grimmest possible way, the Tet Offensive shattered the rosy image LBJ and his Generals had tried to depict. One infamous incident and image from

Tet galvanized the transition of American feeling about the war: a starkly disturbing photograph, taken near a Buddhist temple, showing the South Vietnamese national police chief firing a pistol point-blank into the head of a Vietnamese suspect. After that, Branch wrote, U.S. polls "recorded the most decisive single drop in American support for the Vietnam War." Senator Eugene McCarthy, running as a peace candidate to challenge President Johnson, saw his support increase to 40 percent in New Hampshire, the site of the first primary race, giving him a realistic chance to beat LBJ.[2]

Walter Cronkite had become America's most admired newscaster in the wake of JFK's assassination, and on February 27, 1968, broadcasting from Vietnam, he pronounced the war a "quagmire." On March 6, Cronkite took the then-unprecedented step of announcing his opposition to the war during his broadcast, using terms like "futile" and "immoral." His statement was a courageous act at the time, as other news anchors remained neutral or, like ABC's Howard K. Smith, encouraged an expansion of the war. Cronkite's willingness to use his status and stake his reputation to report unpopular or underreported news would come to distinguish him, and his newscasts would play an important role in Watergate.[3]

In March 1968, the political landscape began to shift dramatically when LBJ mustered less than half the vote in the New Hampshire primary. Though he still won, with 49 percent to Eugene McCarthy's 42 percent, LBJ was shocked, as was much of America. On March 16, 1968, Robert Kennedy made a dramatic entry into the race for President, staging his announcement in the same Senate hearing room where he had grilled Jimmy Hoffa and Carlos Marcello nine years earlier.[4]

Unbeknownst to the country, the press, and most of his advisors, President Johnson began to consider withdrawing from the race. On March 26, 1968, LBJ received an extraordinarily blunt and bleak assessment of Vietnam from a senior team of advisors that included former JFK officials such as Cyrus Vance and Maxwell Taylor. Most of the advisors argued that the United States "must begin the steps to disengage" from Vietnam.[5]

Few in the meeting knew of Richard Helms's decision to cut estimates of enemy strength in half, but indirectly, the faked numbers were a major factor in the decision of Vance and the others to push for withdrawal. Helms had agreed to military estimates asserting that there were around two hundred thousand Communist combatants before Tet, yet the U.S. military also claimed that eighty thousand of the enemy had been killed and another two hundred and forty thousand wounded. The figures simply didn't add up—in the words of Arthur Goldberg, LBJ's U.N. Ambassador, "Who the hell is there left for us to be fighting?" Yet the U.S. commander in Vietnam, General Westmoreland, was requesting two hundred thousand more American troops.[6]

On March 31, 1968, the nation was hit with another bombshell when President Johnson announced at the end of his prime-time televised speech about Vietnam that he was withdrawing from the Presidential race. Robert Kennedy asked to meet with LBJ, and the President agreed to see RFK and his aide, Ted Sorensen, on April 3. The meeting between RFK and LBJ, facilitated by LBJ's aide Joseph Califano, was as friendly as it was unlikely. After mutual compliments, LBJ reveled that North Vietnam had just agreed to start the process leading to peace talks and he was using RFK's old Cuban operations subordinate Cyrus Vance as one of two U.S. negotiators.[7]

Richard Nixon now faced an uncertain opponent in November 1968. Thanks to his work in the 1966 elections, Nixon had the Republican nomination all but wrapped up, so his focus was increasingly on which Democrat he would face in the fall. Vice President Hubert Humphrey also decided to seek the Democratic nomination, joining Robert Kennedy and Eugene McCarthy in the race. Complicating matters for Nixon even more, no matter who emerged as the Democratic nominee, he would still have to deal with the looming political presence of former Alabama Governor George Wallace. Though Wallace would run a third-party campaign for the American Independent Party, polls showed that he would probably receive 20 percent of the vote. Originally a moderate on racial issues in 1940s and 1950s, Wallace had even received the endorsement of the NAACP for the 1958 Democratic primary for Governor. After losing to a candidate endorsed by the Ku Klux Klan, Wallace made racism his trademark, and it raised him to state and national prominence.[8]

More stunning news rocked the nation on April 4, 1968, when Dr. Martin Luther King was assassinated in Memphis. Robert Kennedy announced the devastating news at a campaign rally in Indianapolis, Indiana, giving a brief and poignant speech that helped to spare that city the massive riots that plagued dozens of other cities. Two months later, authorities in England captured the suspect in the case, an escaped convict and low-level drug runner named James Earl Ray.* Ray confessed at his trial but spent the rest of his life trying to recant his confession. A decade later, the House Select Committee on Assassinations conducted a two-year investigation and "concluded that there was a likelihood of conspiracy in the assassination of Dr. King" and that "the expectation of financial gain was Ray's primary motivation."[9]

Richard Nixon discussed with his close advisors the question of his attending King's funeral. Speechwriter William Safire urged him to go, but Nixon's law partner John Mitchell was against the idea. As noted by Ambrose, because "some of his aides convinced him that his refusal to come to King's aid [in 1960] had cost him the election, [Nixon] decided to pay his respects." On April 7, two days before Dr. King's funeral, Richard Nixon went to Atlanta to meet privately with Dr. King's widow, Coretta Scott King, and her family. Ambrose writes that on April 9 Nixon "returned for the funeral" but "he did not march in the procession," which included his rivals Robert Kennedy, Vice President Humphrey, and Eugene McCarthy. Possibly worried that his absence would send the wrong message, Nixon visited Mrs. King again the following day, with a photographer recording the scene.[10]

Even as King was laid to rest, many areas were only beginning to recover from the massive rioting that had devastated cities in the wake of Dr. King's murder. Nixon's conservative campaign aide Pat Buchanan brought the response of one Governor to Nixon's attention. After riots began in Baltimore, Maryland, Governor Spiro Agnew "had called the black leadership of the city to a conference . . . one hundred came, ministers and lawyers and politicians . . . expecting the governor to ask their help in working together to save the inner city." Ambrose wrote that

> To their astonishment, Agnew [instead] blamed them for the riots. They . . . listened aghast as the governor called them . . . "Hanoi-visiting . . . caterwauling, riot-inciting, burn-America-down type of leaders" . . . Eighty of the black leaders walked out [of the Agnew meeting].

*Before and after King's assassination, Ray traveled from Missouri to Canada to Alabama, and then Mexico, to Los Angeles and New Orleans, back to L.A., back to New Orleans, then to Atlanta and then Memphis for King's assassination, back to Atlanta, then to Canada, England, and Portugal, and then back to England.

Nixon told Buchanan, "That guy Agnew is really an impressive fellow. He's got guts. He's got a good attitude." After meeting Agnew only once, well before the Republican convention, Nixon decided to make the Governor his running mate. Nixon was so impressed with Agnew that he didn't even "ask Agnew any questions about his finances, or whether he had any skeletons in his closet." Anthony Summers notes that "Nixon would admit years later that he had opted for Agnew knowing that his running mate was corrupt."[11]

It may seem hard to reconcile Nixon's visits to King's family with his admiration for Agnew's race baiting, but both were part of a "Southern Strategy" Nixon was developing to deal with the charged racial dynamics of the time. Only in the previous year had LBJ appointed Thurgood Marshall as the first black U.S. Supreme Court Justice. The day before Marshall's appointment, the U.S. Supreme Court had finally struck down laws in sixteen states barring interracial marriage—even though polls showed that three-fourths of the American public at the time was against it. The Justices had reversed a Virginia Supreme Court decision that had upheld the ban so that "a mongrel breed of citizens" would not result in "the obliteration of racial pride" for the white race. With such attitudes not uncommon among even well-educated leaders—and not just in the South—it shouldn't be surprising that in the summer of 1967 there had been race riots in "Harlem, Toledo, Grand Rapids, Newark," and other cities. Stephen Ambrose points out that the "worst were in Detroit, where 38 were killed and thousands were arrested, where LBJ sent in forty-five hundred paratroopers."[12]

Those searing images in the media served to inflame further racial tensions in many American cities, some undergoing desegregation in schools and housing for the first time. For the latter, "block-busting" by real estate firms and banks—targeting certain neighborhoods for rapid integration, often using scare tactics, while more affluent areas were kept all white—intensified racial anxiety among voters. A variety of political and business groups, ranging from the Ku Klux Klan (then in decline) to the White Citizens Councils (respectable in many cities) to the John Birch Society, and even to more "mainstream" groups, exploited those anxieties for financial and political gain.

Nixon had actually begun planning his Southern Strategy in 1966, when he campaigned for Congressional candidates "in all eleven of the former Confederate states." Nixon's Southern campaign director, Howard "Bo" Callaway, epitomized what Nixon's press aide called "the new spirit of Republicanism in the South." That spirit deemphasized the racist rhetoric of George Wallace in favor of presenting a more business-like public image, while offering subtle reassurance that the candidates weren't overly pro–civil rights. As Ambrose pointed out, "Nixon . . . knew that no Republican could win without solid support from independents and conservative Democrats, but also that no Republican could win without the enthusiastic support of the Old Guard." The Southern Strategy could deliver all three groups. Nixon's selection of the racially divisive Agnew for his running mate sent a clear signal to white voters in the South and to conservatives in other parts of the country. At the same time, Agnew was not so openly racist as to turn off many independent voters or the more socially moderate of the GOP's Old Guard. To them, Nixon could depict—or voters could rationalize—Agnew's stance as being not racist, but simply as supportive of "law and order." Nixon's Southern Strategy had far more mainstream appeal than Wallace's racist bluster and would become Nixon's blueprint for 1968 and the future, eventually dominating the Republican Party—and helping the GOP eventually dominate the South. Nixon's Southern Strategy wasn't just about the South—it was a template Nixon would use across the country. Nixon showed this in 1966, when he raised money for Ronald Reagan, even as Reagan courted California's John Birch Society, a group Nixon had condemned.[13]

Oddly, a survey at the time showed that a quarter of Wallace's supporters had an unexpected second choice for President: Robert Kennedy. Those voters did not support Wallace primarily because of racism, but also because he was an outsider who claimed to stand for law and order while vowing to change things in Washington to help average working Americans (as long as they were white). Wallace even added increases for Social Security to his platform to reassure and attract older voters. Those themes—without the overt racism—also became part of Nixon's campaign.[14]

Still, Nixon knew he would have to face two opponents in the fall, and that would drive him to seek money and advantages by extreme, and sometimes illegal, measures. Nixon realized that even though Wallace couldn't win, he might get enough votes in the Electoral College to force the election into the Democratic-controlled House of Representatives, where Nixon would almost certainly lose.

. . .

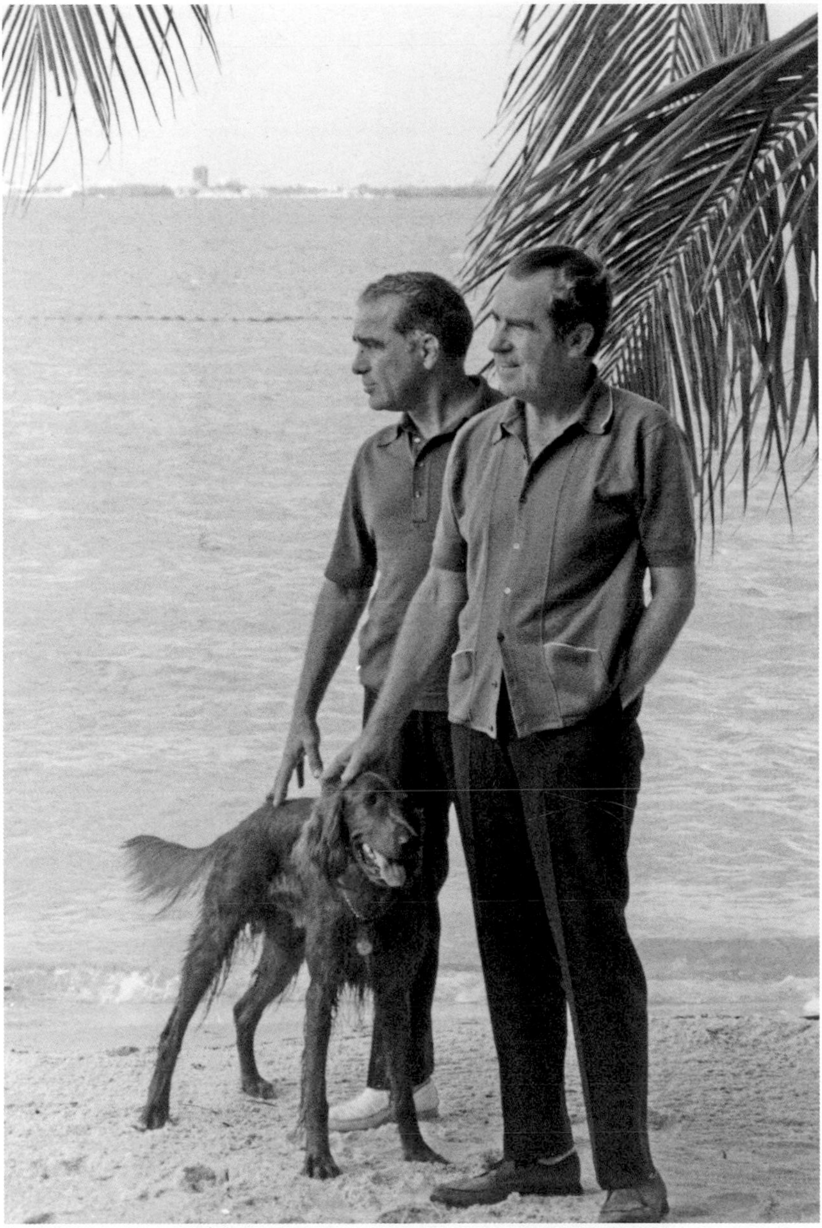

Corbis

President **Richard Nixon** *(right)* at Key Biscayne, Florida, with **Charles G. "Bebe" Rebozo**, his best friend and close business partner of more than four decades. Rebozo was described as "non-member associate of organized crime figures," who was "very close to Meyer [Lansky]." Rebozo—and in one case Nixon—also had business ties to Watergate burglars Bernard Barker and Eugenio Martinez.

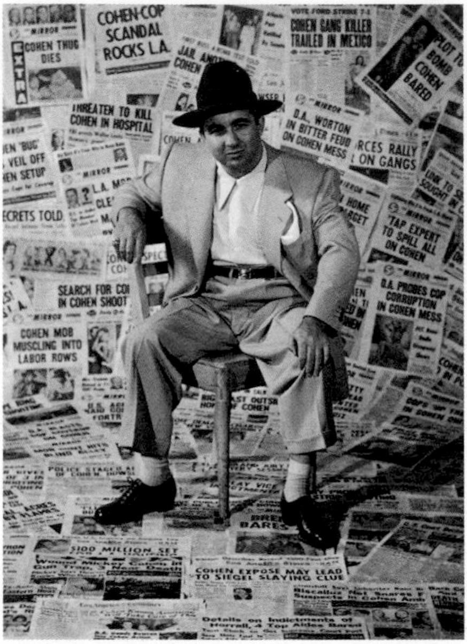

Ed Clark

(Above) Los Angeles mob figure **Mickey Cohen** and his allies supported Nixon in his successful race for Congress in 1946 and again when Nixon won his Senate seat in 1950.

(Below) **Murray Chotiner**—attorney, fixer, and strategist—was Nixon's primary link to the mob from 1946 until Chotiner had an office in Nixon's White House. Chotiner and his brother "defended Syndicate figures in a total of 221 prosecutions," many of whom worked for Mickey Cohen.

Getty, John Swope

Library of Congress

Library of Congress

(*Above, left*) From his first race, Nixon received both legal and illegal money from large corporations and business tycoons, including **Howard Hughes**. Hughes aide **Robert Maheu** (*above, right*), who worked on covert assignments for Vice President Richard Nixon and the CIA, said that in 1960 "the CIA had been in touch with Nixon . . . It was Nixon who had him do a deal with the Mafia in Florida to kill Castro." At the behest of Nixon and the CIA, Maheu hired Mafia don **Johnny Rosselli** (*below, left*) to assassinate Cuban leader **Fidel Castro** (*below, right*) before the Nov. 1960 presidential election.

HSCA

Library of Congress

National Archives

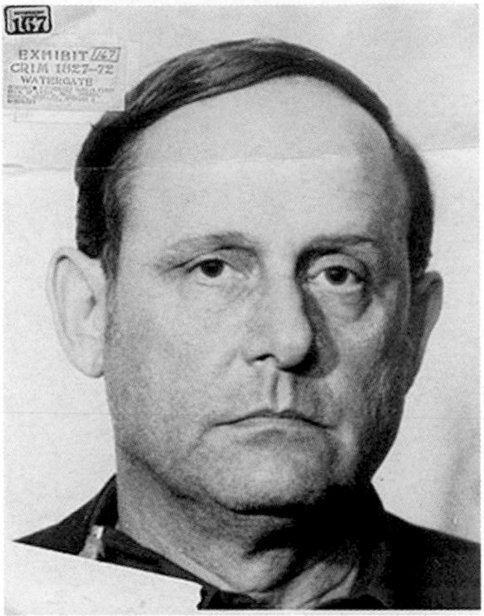

National Archives

In September 1960, Rosselli brought other mob figures into the CIA-Mafia Castro plots, including his boss Sam Giancana and Florida-based godfather **Santo Trafficante** *(above, left)*, who still had men in Cuba. CIA files confirm that two of Trafficante's men working on the plots were also CIA agents: future Watergate burglars **Bernard Barker** *(above, right)* and **Frank Fiorini**, AKA **Frank Sturgis** *(below, left)*. **E. Howard Hunt** *(below, right)*, their Watergate supervisor, also worked on the CIA-Mafia plots to kill Castro, from 1960 to 1965. Hunt had documented meetings with Nixon's national security advisor in 1960 and with Rosselli in 1961.

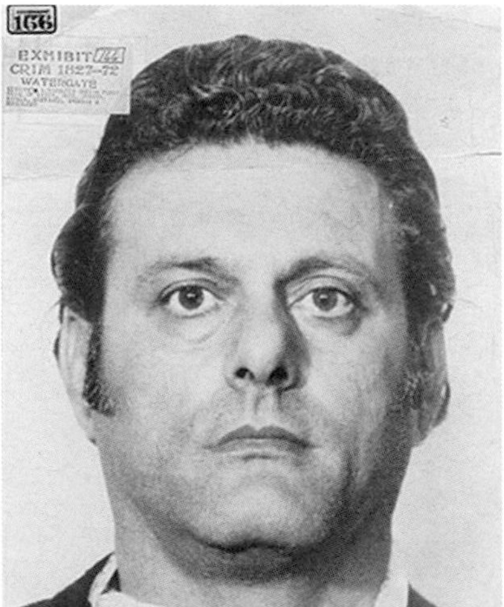

National Archives

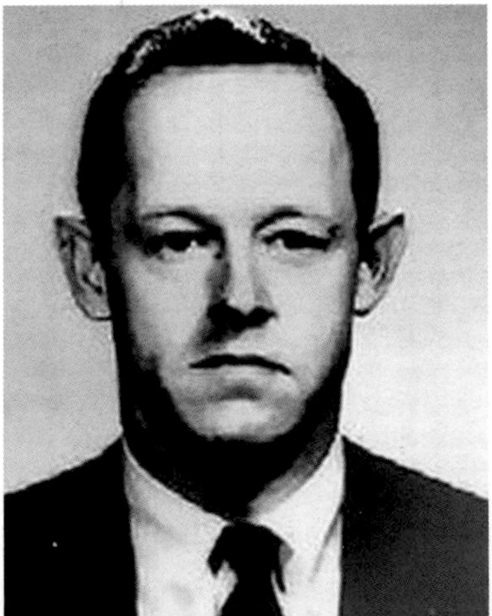

HSCA

Associated Press

In September 1960, Teamsters President **Jimmy Hoffa** *(left)* carried a $500,000 bribe from Louisiana godfather **Carlos Marcello** *(below)* to Nixon's campaign, in return for stalling a federal indictment against Hoffa. Santo Trafficante also contributed to the bribe, which solidified the Teamsters' support for Nixon.

National Archives

Despite having the CIA use the Mafia to try to kill Castro, and the $500,000 Mafia-Hoffa bribe, **Richard Nixon** *(above)* lost the extremely close 1960 election to **John F. Kennedy** *(below, right)*. Under the Eisenhower-Nixon administration, FBI Director **J. Edgar Hoover** *(below, center)* had been reluctant to go after the Mafia, but President Kennedy and new Attorney General **Robert Kennedy** *(below, left)* mounted a major war against the mob.

National Archives

National Archives

The 1960 CIA-Mafia plots grew into the Bay of Pigs operation, which ended in disaster for JFK. CIA official **Richard Helms**, who avoided the debacle, was promoted in 1962 to run covert operations for the CIA. Helms continued the CIA-Mafia plots with Rosselli into 1963, without telling JFK, RFK or his own CIA Director. Helms later become CIA Director for both Lyndon Johnson and Richard Nixon, and played a key role in Watergate regarding the CIA-Mafia plots.

RFK *(below, second from right)* engineered the release of the Bay of Pigs prisoners with the help of his friend **Harry Williams (Enrique "Harry" Ruiz-Williams**; *below, far right*). RFK began working with Williams and exile leader **Manuel Artime** *(below, far left)* on a new plan to bring democracy to Cuba by staging a coup. Artime was Hunt's best friend, and the CIA assigned agents Hunt, Barker, and allegedly James McCord, to assist Williams.

Associated Press

AP Photo/Ismael Francisco/Prensa Latina

Secretly working with John and Robert Kennedy to stage a "palace coup" on December 1, 1963, was **Juan Almeida** *(above, left)*, the Commander of the Cuban Army, and essentially Cuba's third most powerful official after Fidel and **Raul Castro** *(above, right in a 2008 photo)*. Almeida would remain in place and unexposed for decades, contributing to the secrecy surrounding Watergate.

JFK's Secretary of State **Dean Rusk** *(below)* confirmed to the author and *Vanity Fair* that plans for the coup were active at the time of JFK's assassination, even as JFK also tried to find a peaceful solution to the Cuban issue. The CIA had only a supporting role in the coup plan, and the Mafia was barred from the plan or from reopening their casinos after the coup. Army Secretary Cyrus Vance had a leading role in the plan; working for Vance on many drafts of the coup plan were Alexander Haig and Joseph Califano. They were later joined by Alexander Butterfield, and he—along with Haig and Califano—would all play crucial roles in Watergate.

Library of Congress

Library of Congress

Nixon only narrowly won a popular vote victory the 1968 election, despite outspending his Democratic opponent **Hubert Humphrey** *(above)* two-to-one and helping to stall Vietnam peace talks just before the election. Nixon fended off independent candidate George Wallace by using his "Southern Strategy," which later became a template for the Republican Party.

President Nixon in the Oval Office in 1970 with **Elvis Presley** *(below, center)* and White House aide **Egil Krogh** *(below, right)*. Also in 1970, E. Howard Hunt "retired" from the CIA and the following year Krogh oversaw for Nixon one of the first missions of Hunt's new White House "Plumbers" Unit.

National Archives

National Archives

National Archives

Nixon's Chief of Staff, **H. R. Haldeman** *(above, left)* and Nixon's political aide **John Ehrlichman** were both perplexed by Nixon's obsession with getting the CIA's files on "the Bay of Pigs thing," not realizing Nixon was worried about the exposure of his role in the CIA-Mafia plots. CIA Director Richard Helms refused to give the files to Nixon.

Nixon aide **Charles Colson** *(below, left)* was one of three aides—along with Krogh and Jeb Magruder--who played a role in overseeing Hunt's White House activities. White House Counsel **John Dean** *(below, right)* had little contact with Nixon before the Watergate arrests, but played a major role after that.

National Archives

National Archives

National Archives

While Jimmy Hoffa was in prison, **Frank Fitzsimmons** *(above, left)* ran the union, and many mob bosses preferred the easy-going Fitzsimmons. To arrange Hoffa's December 1971 release with special conditions barring Hoffa from the Teamsters, a new Mafia bribe was paid to Nixon, this time for $1 million, according to investigations by the FBI and *Time* magazine. Involved in the bribe—just as in 1960—were mob bosses Carlos Marcello and Santo Trafficante.

E. Howard Hunt's friend, **David Atlee Phillips** *(right)*, headed Latin American operations for the CIA in 1971. Nixon was especially concerned about Cuba and the new socialist president in Chile, so Phillips masterminded a new attempt to kill Fidel Castro, in Chile in December 1971.

Fonzi/HSCA

National Archives

In early 1972, Senator **Edmund Muskie** *(left)* was the front-runner for the Democratic presidential nomination. But he was targeted by five of Nixon's "dirty tricks" teams, including three supervised by E. Howard Hunt.

After Muskie dropped out of the race, Senator **George McGovern** *(below)* became the new Democratic front-runner. But even winning the California primary in early June didn't secure the nomination for McGovern, due to delegate challenges and because Hubert Humphrey, Henry "Scoop" Jackson, and Terry Sanford all retained delegates. Three years after Watergate, McGovern would first reveal to the public a secret Cuban Dossier of CIA attempt to kill Castro, not realizing that an earlier version was what the burglars were after at the Watergate. (See Appendix)

Library of Coongress

Associated Press

When the Pentagon Papers, leaked by **Daniel Ellsberg** *(above, center)*, were published in June 1971, E. Howard Hunt had already been working for the White House and recruiting "Plumbers" like Barker and Fiorini (Sturgis) for two months. Hunt organized the burglary of Ellsberg's psychiatrist for Nixon in September 1971, using some of the same people he would use for Watergate.

Library of Congress

Richard Nixon admitted on a White House tape released in 1999 that he knew about the burglary of the Chilean embassy in Washington, on May 13, 1972. Hunt, Barker, Fiorini/Sturgis, and his other Plumbers were looking for the same thing at the embassy that they would be looking for at the Watergate, less than two weeks later.

Library of Congress

The offices of the Democratic National Committee were on the sixth floor of the Watergate complex of offices, apartments, and a hotel. Hunt and his crew made four attempts to burglarize the DNC office, two of them successful. According to Watergate Committee investigators and one of the burglars, their main goal was to find information that might link Nixon to the CIA-Mafia plots, specifically the secret Cuban Dossier of CIA attempts to kill Fidel. (See Appendix).

National Archives

National Archives

G. Gordon Liddy *(above, left)* supposedly supervised the Plumbers, but **E. Howard Hunt** *(above, right)* was really in control. Hunt recruited all the men, who—like himself—were all former or current CIA agents. Liddy later admitted he didn't know why the Watergate operation changed from a small bugging operation to a larger mission to photograph 1,400 pages of documents.

The Watergate burglars were all veterans of the CIA's anti-Castro operations of the early 1960s, and two—Barker and Fiorini/Sturgis—had worked on the CIA-Mafia plots in 1960 with Hunt. While Hunt and Liddy waited in the Watergate Hotel, their five men burglarized the DNC offices: *(below, left to right)* **Virgilio Gonzalez**, **Barker**, **Fiorini/Sturgis**, **Eugenio Martinez**; pictured separately is James McCord.

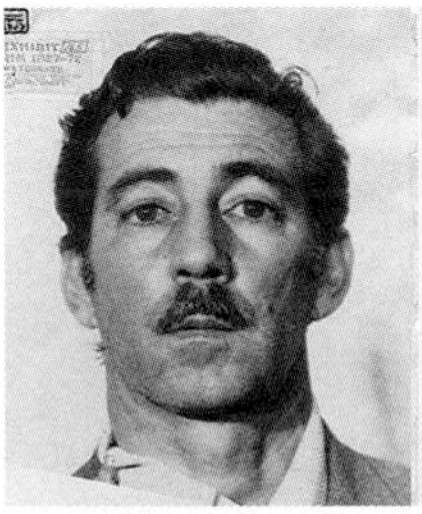

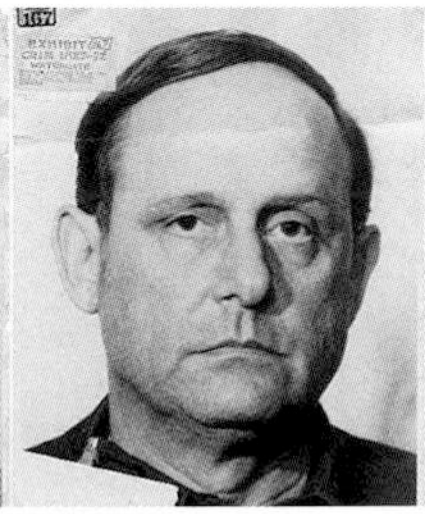

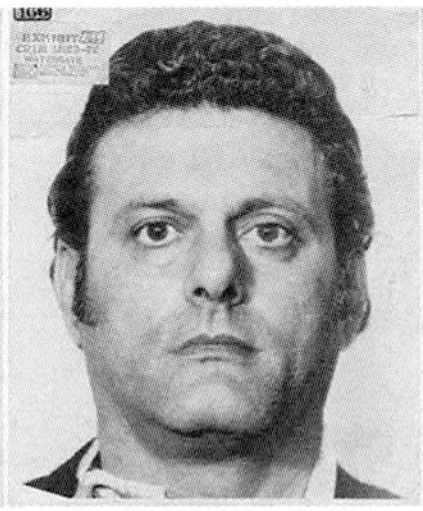

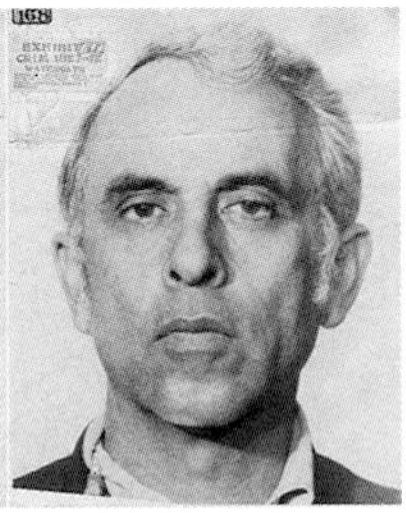

National Archives

© Bettmann/CORBIS

James McCord *(left)*, a former CIA security official, would play a crucial role in exposing the Watergate cover-up and Nixon's role, nine months after the final Watergate break-in.

Joseph Califano *(above, left)* was the attorney for the DNC, based at the Watergate, and for *The Washington Post*. Informed before dawn of the early-morning burglary, Califano got *The Post* to cover the story, and he filed a lawsuit against Nixon's campaign. Nixon aide **Alexander Butterfield** *(above, right)* had been recommended for his position by Califano, whom he'd worked for as Cyrus Vance's anti-Castro operation wound down. Butterfield's revelation of Nixon's taping system would jolt the Senate Watergate Hearings, turning them into a national obsession.

Alexander Haig *(above, far right)* became Nixon's new Chief of Staff in the spring of 1973, after Haig consulted with Califano, his friend and mentor from 1963. Haig had originally been an aide to **Henry Kissinger** *(above, far left)*, a position for which he'd been recommended by Califano. Haig played a pivotal role in finally getting Nixon to resign, more than two years after the Watergate arrests.

Source Unknown

Five months after Nixon's resignation, the Senate began investigating the CIA-Mafia plots to kill Castro. Richard Helms was forced to testify, and faded mob boss **Sam Giancana** *(left)* was scheduled to appear, until he was murdered in his Chicago home, on June 19, 1975.

Associated Press

© Bettmann/CORBIS

The Senate Committee investigating the CIA-Mafia plots was also interested in talking to **Jimmy Hoffa** *(above, left)*, but he was murdered on July 30, 1975, less than six weeks after Giancana. The following year, **Johnny Rosselli** *(above, right)* was murdered after being told that he would have to testify yet again to the Senate Committee about the CIA-Mafia plots. All three slayings were linked to Santo Trafficante. Rosselli's little-known interview by Watergate Committee investigators on February 20, 1974 helped to confirm that the target of the Watergate burglars was the secret Cuban Dossier of CIA attempts to kill Castro, whose disclosure could have cost Nixon the 1972 election.

As the country attempted to recover from the turmoil of the first months of 1968, Carlos Marcello, Johnny Rosselli, and Jimmy Hoffa each faced a different set of challenges. Thanks to a change of venue, Marcello finally stood trial in Laredo, Texas, on May 20, 1968, on the charge of hitting an FBI agent in New Orleans in 1966. John H. Davis writes that "amid widespread rumors of tampering, the trial ended in a hung jury." Robert Kennedy could perhaps take solace that the Justice Department's new Organized Crime Strike Force was determined to retry Marcello on the same charges.[15]

In March of 1968, Johnny Rosselli had met with William Harvey, now out of the CIA. After their meeting, Agency files show that Harvey told his contact at the CIA "he has a very strong feeling that if either of the two trials that now threaten Johnny result in deportation, he will blow the whistle on the Agency" regarding the CIA-Mafia plots to kill Castro. Because of Rosselli's weakened position and the locally high-profile nature of the Friars Club case, Rosselli was no longer trying to get both cases against him dropped. Rosselli's new demand to the CIA was much more realistic: to simply protect him from being deported if he were convicted.[16]

It's known that CIA Director Richard Helms was told about Rosselli's new demand, as well as his earlier ones, because the CIA's Security Chief who met with William Harvey wrote that he "told [Harvey] on numerous occasions . . . that I have passed his views on this to the Director." Helms knew what would happen to his career if Rosselli decided to "blow the whistle on" Helms's unauthorized operations, especially those from 1963. The reaction of Helms to Rosselli's new demand can be gauged by the results, since Rosselli's biographers discovered that a high FBI official wrote that in 1968, "certain efforts are being made to hamper the government's investigation into Rosselli." The authors also found that the U.S. Attorney in Los Angeles said "unnamed people in the circles in Washington [are] saying that John was a patriotic citizen who deserved some form of consideration." Though Rosselli would be convicted in both trials, including his May 23, 1968, conviction proving that he was an illegal alien, the mob boss would never be deported, thanks to his role in the CIA-Mafia plots to kill Fidel.[17]

Rosselli's other trial, for the Friars Club charges, would drag on through 1968 and into 1969. Those charges also involved Rosselli's four codefendants. Rosselli's attorney was working closely on the defense team's strategy with distinguished Los Angeles lawyer Grant Cooper. One of Rosselli's codefendants, Cooper's client, had also worked with Rosselli on an aborted hit scheme to silence the key witness in the case.[18]

While Marcello and Rosselli dealt with their legal issues, Jimmy Hoffa remained in Lewisburg Federal Prison. Evan Thomas documented that in the spring of 1968, after Robert Kennedy announced his run for the Presidency:

> A Teamster leader came to Senator Edward Kennedy proposing that the Teamsters would give RFK $1 million and help him at the polls—if RFK would . . . shorten Jimmy Hoffa's prison sentence . . . RFK told brother Ted, "Well, you tell so and so that if I get to be president, then Jimmy Hoffa will never get out of jail and there will be a lot more of them in jail."[19]

Following RFK's negative response, in May 1968 a heavily censored FBI memo (noted earlier) revealed that Jimmy Hoffa was overheard for a second time talking to mob boss Carmine Galante (an ally of Marcello and Trafficante) about a "mob contract to kill Bob Kennedy." As with Hoffa's previous May 1967 threat to RFK, the FBI apparently didn't question Hoffa about his May 1968 RFK threat at this time.[20]

In the spring of 1968, Robert Kennedy met with his old friend Harry Williams, who had sought out RFK to discuss something important. It wasn't to encourage RFK's Presidential run, in the hope that a victory would reinvigorate action to topple Castro—Williams had left those dreams far behind. Instead, Williams had a different message for RFK. Having seen the coverage of the huge crowds Kennedy was drawing, Williams told him, "You got thousands of people around you [but] if some son of a bitch comes out . . . and just starts shooting . . . " Harry didn't have any specific information, but said that "with all these Mafia people [still around], they [are] going to try to kill you." Williams wasn't the only one to warn RFK. At a small Hollywood gathering with actors Warren Beatty and Shirley MacLaine, novelist Romain Gary essentially told RFK the same thing. Robert Kennedy's simple reply to Gary was "That's the chance I have to take."[21]

In the vitriolic atmosphere of the time—which mirrors much of the political tenor today—blunt assessments also came from those on the right, including Richard Nixon. Upon hearing that RFK had entered the race, Nixon initially said "we can beat the little S.O.B." But aide John Ehrlichman said Nixon paused and "shook his head for a long moment, then said: 'We've just seen some very terrible forces unleashed. Something bad is going to come of this.'" According to historian Thurston Clarke, "the right-wing columnist Westbrook Pegler . . . welcomed the possibility that, as he put it, 'some white patriot of the Southern tier will spatter [Kennedy's] spoonful of brains in public premises before the snow flies.'" Forty years later, Sarah Palin shocked many when she quoted another piece by Pegler in her acceptance speech for the 2008 Republican Vice Presidential nomination.[22]

Because of his stance on civil rights and migrant workers, as well as his fights against Hoffa and organized crime, Robert Kennedy had amassed many enemies. Among the remaining primaries, California was the biggest prize, and RFK campaigned hard there before its June 4, 1968, primary.

At 12:15 AM on June 5, 1968, Robert Kennedy left the Ambassador Hotel ballroom in Los Angeles after speaking about his victory in the California primary, only to be shot in a crowded pantry. In a scene reminiscent of Ruby's shooting of Oswald, Sirhan Bishara Sirhan had emptied a revolver at RFK and others on the scene. Sirhan was later reported to have appeared dazed, which isn't surprising since the diminutive aspiring jockey "drank four Tom Collins" cocktails a short time before the shooting.[23]

Still alive, Robert Kennedy was rushed by ambulance from the Ambassador Hotel, first to Central Receiving Hospital to be stabilized, then to the nearby Good Samaritan Hospital, which had a much larger trauma unit. There, six surgeons worked feverishly on RFK's most serious injury, trying to remove the bullet from his brain.[24]

Robert F. Kennedy clung to life though June 5, 1968, but his injuries were too severe. He was pronounced dead at 1:44 PM on June 6. RFK's Press Secretary, Frank Mankiewicz, made the tragic announcement to a waiting world.[25]

On June 6, 1968, as the body of Robert F. Kennedy was being flown from Los Angeles to New York City, Senator Edward Kennedy talked to NBC TV newsman Sander Vanocur during the grim flight. William Turner wrote that, to Vanocur, "Edward Kennedy had remonstrated bitterly about the 'faceless men' who had been charged with the slayings of his brothers and Martin Luther King . . . Always faceless men with no apparent motive. 'There has to be more to it,' Ted Kennedy had told Vanocur," who broadcast the Senator's comment on NBC after they landed.[26]

In Washington, D.C., something had made President Lyndon Johnson think of the Mafia as soon as he heard RFK had been shot in Los Angeles. On his White House notepad, LBJ scribbled, "[La] Cosa Nostra," "Ed Morgan," and "Send in to get Castro planning." LBJ must have believed something connected RFK's shooting with the stories about Johnny Rosselli and the CIA-Mafia plots that Jack Anderson had written a year earlier.[27]

Sirhan Sirhan, charged with RFK's murder, was a twenty-four-year-old former horse trainer and aspiring jockey who had lived mostly with his mother on a pleasant suburban street in Pasadena, California. Organized-crime expert David E. Scheim documented that the first racetrack where Sirhan worked was "a Syndicate meeting place," and another "was frequented by some of the nation's most infamous racketeers." That milieu was ripe for organized crime, which ran the illegal bookie network that extended gamblers credit for large bets. Scheim noted "Sirhan's compulsive racetrack gambling and his heavy losses, particularly in the months before the assassination." Hoffa expert Dan Moldea quoted the LAPD as saying that Sirhan "bet most of his salary on the horses, [and] a school acquaintance . . . described Sirhan as a heavy bettor, betting as much as sixty to eighty dollars on one race." Moldea points out that Sirhan "was making only $75 a week," and FBI reports said "he made bets with a Pasadena bookmaker [that led to gambling] debts he accumulated."[28]

On May 18, 1968, Sirhan had written in his notebook the date and then "RFK must die" and "Robert F. Kennedy must be assassinated before 5 June '68." On the same page, Sirhan wrote more statements about assassinating RFK, followed by "Please pay to the order of." There are repeated references in the notebook to money, especially to the amount of $100,000, which was written several times.[29]

In addition to the drug conviction of his former boss, whom Sirhan still saw at the races, Larry Hancock documented from LAPD files that in the spring of 1968, Sirhan had lived with a brother who "had served 9 months in jail [and] was still on probation from a conviction relating to the possession and sale of narcotics." Another of Sirhan's brothers, Saidallah, had been arrested for attempted murder in 1963.[30]

The Mafia was in a position to have influenced Sirhan's actions not just before but even after RFK's murder. No more than four days after RFK died, perhaps even before he passed away, Sirhan picked Los Angeles attorney Grant Cooper to represent him—at the same time that Cooper was busy as part of the defense team for Johnny Rosselli's Friars Club trial. Cooper "was in direct and extensive contact with Rosselli's lawyer" throughout much of 1968.[31]

Grant Cooper's representation of Sirhan would have a huge impact on Sirhan's trial, resulting in his receiving a death sentence and ensuring that future appeals were fruitless. Sirhan himself would later tell Dan Moldea that "Cooper sold me out" and that

> Grant Cooper conned me to say that I killed Robert Kennedy [acting alone and not as part of any conspiracy]. I went along with him because he had my life in his hands. I was duped into believing he had my best interests in mind. It was a futile defense. Cooper sold me out . . . I remember Cooper once told me, "You're getting the best, and you're not paying anything. Just shut up."[32]

Because Cooper would be busy with the Friars Club trial for months, he brought in Mafia attorney Russell Parsons to help on Sirhan's case, meaning that both of Sirhan's attorneys were linked to the mob. Moldea notes that "Parsons was well known for serving as counsel to southern California mobster Mickey Cohen and members of his gang." As David Scheim pointed out, Russell Parsons "had once been investigated himself by . . . Robert Kennedy." Parsons had originally worked for the Los Angeles District Attorney, but in 1940 he had switched sides to represent the Mafia after being shot at one night through the wind wing (side window vent) of his car. In a well-documented but rarely noted incident, on July 3, 1968—just weeks after RFK's assassination—Sirhan's brother Saidallah was the victim of a similar nighttime shooting, through the wind wing of his vehicle.[33]

Today, it's possible for anyone to search and review online many of the thousands of pages of LAPD files about RFK's assassination.* Those files reveal key leads that weren't pursued, or investigations that were aborted prematurely, many of them involving organized

*The best resource is the nonprofit Mary Ferrell Foundation at maryferrell.org

crime. Moldea quoted a key LAPD supervisor as saying that he "never supervised any phase of [looking into] a conspiracy allegation [in RFK's murder] involving the mob."[34]

After RFK's assassination, the FBI finally talked to Jimmy Hoffa about his two threats against Robert Kennedy. When FBI agents interviewed Hoffa at Lewisburg Federal Prison, Hoffa did not directly deny making the remarks, possibly because he knew that lying to a federal officer was a crime. Hoffa even refused to "sign the waiver" saying that he had been informed of his rights. According to FBI files, Hoffa was asked if "he had made the statement that he had a contract out on Senator Robert F. Kennedy, and if he, Kennedy, ever got in the primaries or ever got elected, the contract would be fulfilled within six months." In response, "Hoffa stated he would not answer such a 'stupid' allegation. He stated, 'You know as well as I do how many nuts there are in this place who would say anything.' Hoffa said, 'You have my statement,' and refused to comment further regarding this allegation or the assassination of Senator Kennedy."[35]

With the assassinations of Dr. Martin Luther King and Robert Kennedy, the riots that followed Dr. King's murder, and the increasingly large demonstrations across the country protesting a deadly and seemingly futile war, in 1968 America seemed to be falling apart. That was especially true of the Democratic Party after the disaster of its convention in Chicago, accompanied by a televised police riot. Vice President Hubert Humphrey emerged as the party's nominee, but many McCarthy and RFK supporters were angry and frustrated at his choice, and they picketed or heckled Humphrey's appearances. By almost all accounts Humphrey was an honest and decent man, but he loyally supported President Johnson and his war, angering many Democrats.[36]

For Richard Nixon, the disarray of the Democrats presented both an opportunity and a challenge. After the Democratic National Convention, Nixon had "a twelve-point lead (Nixon 43 percent, Humphrey 31 percent, Wallace 19 percent)." Old tactics like hiring people to heckle and demonstrate against Humphrey weren't needed because disgruntled Democrats and liberals were already doing that. Still, the seasoned Nixon knew his boost was temporary, and the more Humphrey got his message across—and the more time independents had to think about what a Nixon Presidency might mean—the gap would begin to close. The polls continued to narrow until, just before the election, Humphrey held a slight lead, though the race was essentially a dead heat.[37]

In addition, if LBJ's secret negotiations—using Cyrus Vance—to end the war produced any breakthrough before the election, Nixon knew that could be a game changer. If Hubert Humphrey no longer had to support an increasingly unpopular war and could benefit from the announcement of a cease-fire or a peace plan, that alone could give Humphrey the election. That made Nixon work not just as hard, but even harder than he had on any past election.

The strategy Nixon used in the summer and fall of 1968 was more nuanced and evolved than his old Red Scare tactics of "fear, ignorance, bigotry, and smear," though it included some of those elements. There was plenty of fear in the country already, but Nixon would be careful to stoke it in subtle ways for his own ends. He would sometimes mix fear with soft-pedaled bigotry in his Southern Strategy. Smears were not especially egregious for Nixon in 1968, though some would consider his remarks about Humphrey over the top. As for ignorance, Nixon and his advisors spent much of their time devising and using the first effective television strategy to wage a truly national media campaign for the first time. (It was summed up the following year in Joe McGinniss's *The Selling of the President.*)

Ambrose called Richard Nixon's 1968 approach "the politics of resentment and outrage," as Nixon seemed to be willing to say anything to appeal to those who were dissatisfied. However, Nixon refused to debate Humphrey, so he could stick with platitudes and not be pinned down to specifics. Nixon also restricted his access to the press, barring journalists he believed would not be favorable to him. As Ambrose and McGinness explained, "by refusing to face the press . . . Nixon was presenting a false picture of himself, a package designed to create an image of Nixon that was the opposite of the reality. Nixon was selling a product, not discussing the issues."[38]

For Nixon in 1968, advertising expert H.R. Haldeman finally had a candidate that he and others could package and sell like Sani-Flush, 7Up, and the other products he handled for the J. Walter Thompson Agency. To his media team Nixon added "chief television advisor" Roger Ailes, who would later go on to create Fox News, essentially an around-the-clock distillation of much that Nixon had espoused. Ailes also reportedly created "seemingly spontaneous Nixon interview programs" and bypassed objective "journalists who might pose tough questions [by] creating fake 'town hall' events that enabled the candidate to field softball queries from voters handpicked by the campaign."[39]

Nixon's television campaign—at that point the most expensive in history—is best summed up by an ad run on America's most popular TV show, late in the campaign, and thus too late for the Democrats to strike back, even if they'd had the money. Nixon's commercial showed "battle scenes in Vietnam, black rioters in a burning American city, and a frail starving child, interspersed with scenes of Humphrey laughing and smiling and promoting the politics of joy."[40]

To run his enormous advertising and media campaign, and to be prepared to deal with any peace breakthrough on Vietnam, Richard Nixon needed an equally enormous amount of campaign funds. As in past years, Nixon would take them from a variety of sources, including some that were illegal, only now he was doing it on a much larger scale. Nixon's illegal fund-raising in 1968 set the tone not just for that election, but also for his Presidency and the scandals—not just Watergate—surrounding the 1972 election.

Howard Hughes was again a major funder for Nixon in the 1968 election—and amazingly, Hughes's contribution involved Bebe Rebozo, Johnny Rosselli's friend Robert Maheu, and even attorney Ed Morgan, who'd helped Rosselli spread his story to journalist Jack Anderson the previous year. Regarding Hughes's 1968 contribution for Nixon, Pulitzer Prize-winning journalist J. Anthony Lukas wrote that Rebozo had a Nixon associate first raise "the matter with Edward P. Morgan, a Washington attorney" in the "summer of 1968." Senate Watergate Committee records cited by author Peter Dale Scott show that money started flowing to Hughes's top aide, "Robert Maheu, for possible payment to Nixon, beginning July 30, 1968."[41]

The involvement of Hughes, Maheu, and other Rosselli associates echoes the 1960 election, when Hughes supported Nixon even as Maheu and Rosselli were deeply involved in Nixon's CIA-Mafia plots to kill Fidel. It may seem surprising that Nixon would keep exploiting those same ties, especially given the 1967 Anderson-Rosselli articles. But Nixon had been getting money from Hughes for twenty-two years and dealing with Maheu for fourteen years, and Nixon's later actions indicate he simply took those relationships for granted. However, those ties—and Rebozo's involvement—would later come back to haunt Nixon.

Congressional investigators documented that Hughes gave Nixon at least $100,000, though some suspect the amount was far greater. Hughes also made clear exactly what he wanted in return: "to recoup the huge losses he had suffered from disastrously budgeted helicopter production, he wanted the Vietnam War to continue. He also sought an end to atomic testing in the Nevada desert." Hughes didn't get the latter, but he did persuade Nixon—after his election—to approve his purchase of an airline with foreign routes, Air West. In addition, Maheu and his friend Rosselli may have gained another benefit because of Hughes's 1968 contribution to Nixon. Though Rosselli would soon be convicted and sentenced, once Nixon became President, Rosselli would remain free for almost two and a half years before finally beginning his prison sentence. Maheu was running Hughes's organization in 1968 and had no desire to see information become public that might disrupt his relationship with Hughes, such as his work for Nixon on the 1960 CIA-Mafia plots or Maheu's casino deals for Hughes brokered by Johnny Rosselli.[42]

Howard Hughes apparently wanted to hedge his bets in the unpredictable year 1968, so he also donated $50,000 to Hubert Humphrey's campaign. In addition, Humphrey's campaign manager Lawrence O'Brien was elected Chairman of the Democratic National Committee (DNC), and he would soon begin doing public relations and lobbying work for Hughes. O'Brien would still be heading the DNC in 1972, and it was his offices at the Watergate that Nixon's men would burglarize. But in 1968 the connection—and the possible flow of information damaging to Nixon—between O'Brien and Hughes and Maheu was not yet the major concern it would become a few years later.[43]

Richard Nixon officially raised and spent a record $36.5 million dollars for his 1968 campaign, twice as much as Humphrey. Much of Nixon's campaign fund came from major corporate donors and a wide variety of tycoons, the traditional financial base of the GOP. Though Nixon publicly pledged to find a way to end U.S. involvement in Vietnam, he appears to have been privately supported by most of the "military-industrial complex" that Eisenhower had warned the country about in his farewell address. While Humphrey publicly supported LBJ—who had also benefited from a cozy relationship with some of America's largest military contractors—it was clear to many that if elected, Humphrey really would move quickly to end the war.[44]

While Nixon usually left the actual handling of contributions to others, "W. W. Keeler, the president of Phillips Petroleum . . . admitted that in 1968 he delivered a package containing fifty thousand dollars 'personally to Nixon at his New York City apartment.'" Most illegal contributions to Nixon were never uncovered, and Summers points out that Keeler's admission surfaced only because of a later stockholder lawsuit, after Phillips gave Nixon "twice that sum in the 1972 election." Other contributions that eventually became known included those from San Diego banker "Arnholt Smith [who] personally donated $250,000 in 1968" and generated additional contributions totaling $1,000,000. *The New York Times* later noted that "Mr. Smith and his enterprises [had] a long history of dealings with organized crime." Smith's associate, "an alleged Syndicate figure" named "John Alessio, gave $26,000" to Nixon. Both "Smith and Alessio would later go to prison for tax evasion, but only after secret efforts by the Nixon White House to intervene on their behalf." The owners of one of America's largest grocery chains "contributed seventy-five thousand dollars [in an envelope] to Rebozo's home." Even J. Paul Getty, one of the few Americans said to be richer than Howard Hughes, donated to Nixon's campaign, with Rebozo as "the go-between." This tide of illegal money for Nixon would continue to rise until, and even after, Watergate.[45]

Richard Nixon also used his foreign affairs experience and relationships with world leaders to extract illegal campaign contributions from several dictators. It is now known that Nixon received contributions from the U.S.-backed junta running Greece, from dictator Ferdinand Marcos in the Philippines, from Nationalist China's strongman Chiang Kai-shek, and from the U.S.-installed Shah of Iran. Since those contributions were illegal, it's not known if they were laundered so they could be included in Nixon's official expenditures or if they—together with Nixon's other illegal contributions—represent an even greater group of undocumented campaign expenditures.[46]

Nixon's law partner John Mitchell was the "power at the center" of Nixon's 1968 campaign, and would become Nixon's first Attorney General after the election (and the first U.S. Attorney General to go to prison). Anthony Summers explained that "the real heart" of Nixon's campaign wasn't its official headquarters, "an old bank building in Washington," but "the candidate's New York law office." In hindsight, it's easy to see why, since attorney-client privilege would shield some of Nixon's illegal campaign activities.[47]

John Mitchell's outspoken wife Martha would later become a

controversial figure before, during, and after Watergate, when she began speaking to reporters about the crimes she was aware of. At the time, many in the press ridiculed her, but later much of what she said was shown to be true. Watergate reporter Don Fulsom documented that Martha Mitchell told a UPI reporter that "Nixon is involved with the Mafia. The Mafia was involved in his election" in 1968.[48]

Only a few mainstream reporters pursued Nixon's ties to the mob during Watergate, but none were looking into them at the time of the 1968 election. (In fairness to Nixon, it should be pointed out that was also true for the mob ties of other politicians, which is probably why Nixon felt secure in having mob associate Bebe Rebozo for his best friend.) Murray Chotiner, Nixon's original liaison to the Mafia, again played a key role in the 1968 campaign, though he remained out of the limelight. Along with Rebozo, Chotiner would remain a key link between Nixon and organized crime and the Teamsters during the campaign and into his Presidency.[49]

Jimmy Hoffa was still in prison and anxious to get out. Remarkably, Hoffa "remained president of the union, coordinating contract negotiations and investing the huge pension fund from his cell." Historian Ambrose also notes a "rumor . . . that the Teamsters had contributed $100,000 to Nixon's 1968 campaign, with the understanding that this would secure Hoffa's pardon." The rumor appeared to be true, since Nixon's campaign aide John Ehrlichman—later a White House official—would begin "pressing" Nixon for Hoffa's pardon "shortly after Nixon became President." Chotiner would continue to play a role in the Hoffa pardon efforts with associates of Carlos Marcello (who still controlled the Mafia's $2,000,000 "Spring Hoffa Fund"), until the deal—and Hoffa's release—was eventually completed at a far higher price.[50]

Richard Nixon was apparently able to mix mob and mob-linked money and his campaign because his own personal finances—and those of his best friend Bebe Rebozo—were similarly mixed. Even during Nixon's 1968 campaign, Rebozo continued his dealings with organized crime; Rebozo's finances are important because they were so entwined with Nixon's, and Rebozo, as explained earlier, often fronted for Nixon's investments. In 1968, Rebozo had a large shopping center in Miami built by a construction company run by "Big Al" Polizzi, who had recently been "named by the Bureau of Narcotics [as] 'one of the most influential members of the underworld in the United States.'" At that time, Rebozo had been involved with Polizzi for at least three years. One of Rebozo's tenants in his mob-constructed shopping center was former AMWORLD exile leader Manuel Artime, who was involved in the drug network of godfather Santo Trafficante.[51]

The question of Bebe Rebozo's stolen stock (mentioned earlier) finally became the subject of intense law enforcement investigation in 1968, even as his friend Nixon campaigned for the highest office in the land. Rebozo and his bank were found to possess "IBM stocks . . . that had been stolen from a New York brokerage firm," and the scheme once more involved men working for Meyer Lansky. The stocks were worth $195,000, and Summers notes that "even after [Rebozo] had been visited by FBI agents" and questioned about the stolen stock, Rebozo wrote "a warm note to" the man from whom he'd received them, saying "Everything thus far has worked out well for both of us." An insurance investigator wrote a report stating that Rebozo's stolen stock was "a shady deal, and I suspect that Mr. Rebozo is aware of this."[52]

A staff member with the Senate Subcommittee on Investigations later talked about Rebozo and his bank: "We were going after him. He was keeping stock in there that was fraudulent, stolen [until] somebody tipped him off to watch himself. And the next thing we know he sold the stolen stock. That's a crime in itself, and he should have been arrested and gone to prison for that." The investigation of Rebozo would drag on until after the election, and in the end Rebozo didn't go to prison or even face trial. An eventual civil suit about the matter would be "terminated after one day" by a judge who was an appointee of President Richard Nixon. As documented previously, the stock case wasn't a onetime matter for Rebozo; a mob associate said the fact that Rebozo and his bank were "an outlet for" stolen stock "was a well known thing in organized crime circles."[53]

Nixon and Rebozo had also developed close ties to a casino owner in the Bahamas, an association that would also result in personal money for Nixon as well as funds for his 1968 campaign. Six years later, *The New York Times* would report that Rebozo's Miami bank "was a suspected conduit for mob dollars skimmed from" a casino in the Bahamas that *Life* magazine stated "was controlled by '[Meyer] Lansky & Co.'" Mob kingpin Meyer Lansky was using Paradise Island in the Bahamas to replace the casinos he'd lost in Cuba.[54]

It appears that Rebozo helped with financial matters regarding the Paradise Island casino while Nixon focused on campaigning. The casino's owner viewed Nixon with favor because an FBI agent stated that "'both Rebozo and Nixon were in on the negotiations' for the Paradise Island casino license." The owner gave $100,000 to Nixon's 1968 campaign, with "at least as much, and perhaps more" coming from the owner's friends. What was described as "an opulent new hotel and casino" on Paradise Island was connected to Nassau by "an elegant bridge." To cross the bridge cost each of the casino's wealthy patrons $2, and the tolls alone generated "$1 million to $1.5 million a year." Summers points out that investigators found that the bridge's "ownership . . . involved a shadowy Swiss Bank."

Huntington Hartford, who originally built the casino (which he sold to Nixon's associate), said "he had 'reason to believe' that" one of the owners of the bridge was "a close friend of President Nixon," and Hartford also "claimed knowledge of massive deposits Nixon had made in a Swiss bank." The "founder of Butler's Bank in Nassau" went farther, saying that "one of the banks that owned the bridge . . . was acting as nominee for Nixon, Rebozo, and a third party." John Mitchell finally admitted in 1987 that "he knew of offshore holdings by Nixon" that involved "whatever he received from his interest in the Paradise Island Bridge," confirming that "Nixon had the bridge." The amount controlled by the Swiss Bank was 20 percent, meaning that Nixon and Rebozo—and perhaps one other person—were splitting an annual take of at least $200,000 (worth a million in today's dollars), thanks to the mob-"controlled" casino.[55]

In 1968, Rebozo was also aiding Richard Nixon's campaign with the help of Bernard Barker, the former CIA agent. Barker had become extremely well connected and wealthy, thanks to the money from the AMWORLD arms sell-off, his real-estate business, and his continued association with Santo Trafficante. As noted, the relationship between Barker and Rebozo had begun years earlier, but it really began to blossom when Nixon sought the Presidency. It's not widely known that during the 1968 campaign, Barker and Rebozo's main business partner, Edgardo Buttari Sr., ran a group in Miami called "Cubans for Nixon-Agnew."* Rebozo was fifty-five and Barker just five years

* All references to "Buttari" or "Edgardo Buttari" refer only to Edgardo Buttari Sr., not to his son, who had no involvement in any of the questionable matters discussed.

younger, so they were part of the same generation. Though Rebozo was born in Tampa, his parents were Cuban, but Rebozo tried to keep an arm's-length distance between himself and the often fractious world of exile politics. That's where his business partner Buttari and Bernard Barker came in handy. And what was helpful for Rebozo was also helpful for Richard Nixon. Barker, Rebozo, Nixon, Buttari, and some of Barker's close associates became tied together in a series of complex, interlocking real estate deals and companies that were carefully organized to avoid legal or press scrutiny and protect Nixon's reputation. In addition, Barker's good friend Manuel Artime also became involved in supporting Nixon's candidacy in the hopes that Nixon would revive the anti-Castro operations he'd run as Vice President.[56]

Aside from John Mitchell and Roger Ailes, the trusted core of Richard Nixon's campaign staff in 1968 was made up largely of veterans from past campaigns. They included John Ehrlichman, H.R. Haldeman, Maurice Stans, and Herb Kalmbach, all of whom would later be prosecuted—along with Mitchell—after Watergate. Nixon's main speechwriters included William Safire (for more moderate speeches) and Pat Buchanan, who provided fiery conservative rhetoric.

On August 8, 1968, Richard Nixon officially accepted the Republican nomination for the Presidency, which for months had been a foregone conclusion. Ambrose reports that there were "gasps" from the packed convention when Nixon announced Agnew as his running mate. The delegates were expecting either a rising star like Texas Congressman George H.W. Bush or a seasoned veteran like Representative Gerald Ford. Still, the crowd seemed otherwise happy with Nixon and his well-written speech about "the American Dream." In it, Nixon reiterated his promise from his standard campaign speech: "ending the war in Vietnam" would be "his first order of business" as President. [57]

Following his nomination, Nixon stopped en route to California for a meeting in Texas with President Johnson, Secretary of State Dean Rusk, and CIA Director Richard Helms. This marks one of the first documented meetings between Nixon and Helms, who in the coming years would prove so important to each other's future. The discussion was primarily to bring the new nominee up to date on foreign affairs, including the situation in Vietnam.[58]

Now that he was the nominee, Nixon expanded his attacks on

Humphrey, using some of the same "fear and smear" techniques he'd been honing for years, though leaving Agnew to make the most outrageous remarks on his behalf. Nixon also made use of a "spy in the Humphrey camp," identified as "Hearst journalist Seymour Freidin . . . a veteran CIA informant." Freidin received "thousands of Republican dollars to phone reports on the Democrats to a secretary in Murray Chotiner's office. Chotiner edited the messages, then wired them to Nixon's plane." As the bitter memories of the Chicago convention started to fade and Humphrey was subject to fewer real demonstrations, Nixon began using techniques that dated back to his first race, in 1946. Nixon had "busloads of pro-Nixon hecklers [who] followed Humphrey from rally to rally, trying to drown out his speeches." Joining Nixon's team around this time was Lucianne Goldberg, later to become infamous during the Monica Lewinsky scandal in Bill Clinton's Presidency.[59]

Nixon tried to ensure that he faced no hecklers by having ticket-only rallies, from which anyone who didn't look clean-cut was "turned away" or diverted to exits. When even after these precautions Nixon was faced with hecklers, he first "ordered John Ehrlichman to have the Secret Service detail rough them up." When the Secret Service refused, "Nixon told [Ehrlichman] to create a flying goon squad to rough up the hecklers." Ehrlichman did so, usually paying "cash to off-duty police." This use of goon squads would later become more organized and part of the Watergate operation.[60]

Through September and October Nixon maintained his lead in the polls, yet despite his massive ad campaign, his lead was shrinking as Humphrey began a gradual ascent. Right after Nixon's nomination, his lead in the polls had been sixteen points. By October 20, that lead had dwindled to only five points according to one poll, and the trend was obvious. Nixon's critical worry was what might happen to the numbers if President Johnson announced a peace breakthrough in Vietnam.[61]

Many in Washington circles knew that President Johnson had Cyrus Vance and Ambassador Averell Harriman holding preliminary talks with the North Vietnamese in Paris, but their progress was not reported to the press on a regular basis. However, only select members of the administration knew they were close to finding a way to bring South Vietnam into the process, to begin real peace talks between the three countries. As documented by Stephen Ambrose,

> In mid-September 1960 . . . Henry Kissinger approached John Mitchell, offering his assistance. Kissinger claimed that he was privy to the innermost circles of the Johnson Administration, and . . . was eager to pass on information to the Nixon camp, if his role could be kept confidential . . . Nixon agreed to open communication with Kissinger. Two weeks later, Kissinger called Mitchell [saying] he was just back from Paris, where he had learned that something big was about to happen . . . at the end of September, Kissinger reported that "there is a better than even chance that Johnson will order a bombing halt [in North Vietnam] at approximately mid-October."[62]

Kissinger was right, and on October 16, President Johnson "placed a conference call to all three candidates [saying] there had been a breakthrough" in the peace talks. "Hanoi had agreed to allow the government of [South] Vietnam . . . to participate in the peace talks if Johnson stopped the bombing." LBJ also wanted North Vietnam to cease attacks on South Vietnamese cities as part of the deal. Still, Johnson was very close to the breakthrough he desperately wanted for his legacy, so he could start ending the war before he left office. Ambrose points out that if LBJ could accomplish what he wanted in the next two weeks "then Humphrey, already closing fast, would be a sure winner."[63]

Nixon's only hope would be "if the [South Vietnamese government] refused to sit down with the communists." So, "Nixon made contact with [South Vietnamese] President Thieu in an effort to scuttle the peace prospects." Nixon used "Anna Chennault, the Chinese widow of . . . General Claire Chennault," the founder of World War II's famous Flying Tigers and former partner of William Pawley, Nixon's friend in covert Cuban operations. Anna Chennault ran the Flying Tigers airline and had known Nixon since the mid-1950s. She was "co-chair of the Republican Women for Nixon," where she raised $250,000 for him. Chennault lived in Washington at the new Watergate apartment/hotel/office complex. She was also "close to [South Vietnam's] President Thieu and his aides."[64]

Communication for the secret deal usually flowed from Chennault to John Mitchell to Nixon, but Nixon had personally told South Vietnam's Ambassador that he would "see that Vietnam gets better treatment from me than under the Democrats." Nixon had also told the Ambassador that "Chennault was to be 'the only contact between myself and your government.'" Later, Nixon had John Mitchell call Chennault to say that he was "speaking on behalf of Mr. Nixon" and that it was "very important that our Vietnamese friends understand our Republican position and I hope you have made that clear to them." He wanted "Mrs. Chennault [to] persuade [South Vietnamese President] Thieu to refuse to go to the peace table."[65]

After the contact on behalf of Nixon, South Vietnamese President Thieu balked at proceeding with the peace arrangements, even though North Vietnam had agreed to LBJ's additional conditions. President Johnson had his men push hard to bring Thieu along, but to no avail. With progress stalled, LBJ made a bold move and publicly announced a bombing halt on October 31, hoping it would force President Thieu's hand. That step, five days before the election, raised hopes throughout the country. Two days later, Humphrey had surged to a three-point lead in the Harris Poll, while Nixon led by only 2 percent in the Gallup Poll, both figures within the margin of error.[66]

Nixon, knowing he had a deal with President Thieu, refrained from making much comment about the matter. Thieu had assumed office after a series of coups, and was widely considered corrupt, along with the other top officers running South Vietnam. Nixon's assurance was apparently more important to the ruling clique than LBJ's pressure. Chennault was asked by Nixon to send another message, picked up by an FBI wiretap, in which Chennault told South Vietnam's ambassador "Her boss"—meaning Nixon—said to tell him "Hold on, we are gonna win." Accordingly, Thieu called LBJ's bluff, and on November 2, 1960, announced that his government would not participate in the peace talks. Ambrose notes that Nixon "moved quickly," having his staff privately tell reporters that Nixon "had been 'surprised' by Thieu's refusal to go to Paris" and that LBJ had "acted hastily in order to help Humphrey." Nixon's charge soon spread through the media, though when asked about it on NBC's *Meet the Press* Nixon disingenuously stated, "No, I don't make that charge." Nixon then went even further, offering to go himself "to Paris or to go to Saigon" to help move the peace process along.[67]

President Johnson knew what Nixon had done, since Anna Chennault's phone had been tapped by the FBI. After Nixon's outrageous comments on *Meet the Press*, an angry LBJ called Nixon and "demanded to know what Mrs. Chennault was up to." Nixon claimed to LBJ that "she was acting on her own."[68]

The other important part of the story is that the actions of Nixon,

Chennault, and Thieu in stopping the peace talks were "widely known among the reporters covering the campaign." However, they lacked hard evidence and looked to LBJ or Humphrey to break the story. Unfortunately for his campaign, Humphrey declined to issue what would have been a "bombshell" story that could have helped him win the election. As a result, the story wasn't reported at the time, though it emerged briefly in a newspaper article a month and a half later. The lack of press coverage may explain why Nixon thought he could get away with more crimes once he became President, even after the arrests at the Watergate. While Nixon's actions in the matter have been extensively documented since that time, the incident remains missing from most mainstream profiles and documentaries about the Vietnam War and about Nixon.[69]

Richard Nixon might have simply seen LBJ's peace attempt not as a sincere effort, but as a cynical last-minute ploy to help Humphrey; if so, that's likely because Nixon himself had attempted a foreign policy "October Surprise"—using Cuba—during the 1960 election. It also appears that during the 1968 election, Nixon didn't realize the gravity of what he'd done and viewed Thieu and the peace process as something that could be turned on an off like a faucet. Nixon's actions came just past the halfway point for U.S. casualties in Vietnam, meaning that Nixon might have been responsible for a bloody toll to ensure that he won an election.

Just days after the election, in response to a request from LBJ, Nixon had John Mitchell call Anna Chennault "to ask her to tell Thieu that he should go to Paris" for the peace talks, a request with which Chennault refused to comply. The question still lingers: Did Nixon torpedo peace talks that could have led to a cease-fire and an end to the war? On one hand, it's possible that Thieu would have found some other rationale or excuse not to participate in the peace talks. On the other, Nixon's actions have been called illegal by some, with a few going so far as to term them treasonous.[70]

On election night, November 5, 1968, fifty-five-year-old Richard Nixon finally won the prize he'd sought for so long. The final results showed him receiving "31,770,237 votes (43.4 percent)" to Humphrey's "31,270,533 votes (42.7 percent)," echoing the close vote between JFK and Nixon in the 1960 race. But the Electoral College vote was not nearly so close, with Nixon getting "301 votes to Humphrey's

191 and Wallace's 46." Still, because of Wallace, Nixon had won a majority in the Electoral College by only thirty-one votes—so while Nixon's actions in stopping the Paris Peace Talks might have been illegal, they may well have given him enough electoral votes to keep the election from being decided in the Democratic-controlled House of Representatives. In a way, Nixon's victory brought a measure of definitive closure to an otherwise turbulent year for the country.[71]

That fact that Nixon only narrowly won a popular-vote margin, after outspending Humphrey two-to-one and after undertaking his probably illegal actions with Chennault, had a decisive impact on Nixon and how he would conduct his Presidency. Nixon began the concept of the "perpetual campaign," determined to raise an even greater volume of money for the next election in 1972. That effort would include illegal foreign donations, more Mafia money, more illegal corporate contributions, and far more crimes. As LBJ's National Security Assistant Walt Rostow would later say, "the Republican operation in 1968 relates to the Watergate affair of 1972 . . . as the same men faced the election of 1972, there were memories of how close an election could get," so they were willing to go to almost any lengths to ensure they would win.[72]

CHAPTER 23

1969, Nixon's First Year in Office: Leaks, Electronic Surveillance, and "Dirty Tricks"

Richard Nixon had finally achieved his long-sought dream of the Presidency, and he would move the country forward in some ways (helping to create the Environmental Protection Agency and opening relations with China) while holding it back in others (not completely enforcing civil rights laws or fully prosecuting the Mafia). But having what Nixon saw as absolute power seemed to magnify his worst traits, as he gave increasingly free rein to his battles against those he saw as his enemies.

Nixon had been elected President with the help of organized crime, with illegal campaign contributions from U.S. companies and foreign governments, and by scuttling LBJ's pre-election Vietnam peace agreement. Those actions foreshadowed events in Nixon's first term, in which he would greatly expand his use of illegal funds from all of those sources, even as he remained haunted by the Vietnam war.

Richard Nixon's accomplishments during his first term as President have been widely acknowledged. This book cites only his most notable achievements, especially as they apply to Watergate. The remaining chapters of this book focus primarily on Nixon's most important crimes, especially those involving Watergate and the Mafia. It also documents the actions of others involved in those crimes, especially those that have rarely been covered.

In mid-January 1969, Richard Nixon spent time in Florida with his close friend Bebe Rebozo, while he worked on his inaugural address. They would share much time together while Nixon was in office, and by one calculation, "Rebozo was at his side one day in ten for the duration of [his] presidency." His time with Rebozo away from Washington would give Nixon not only a welcome respite from the pressures of the Oval Office, but also time for the men to expand their already close financial relationship.[1]

Nixon was sworn in by Chief Justice Earl Warren on January 20, 1969, in a solemn ceremony. Years later, E. Howard Hunt's friend William Buckley revealed that following Watergate, Warren would call Nixon "despicable . . . a cheat, a liar, and a crook [who] abused the American people." While Nixon's first patron, former CIA Director Allen Dulles, lived to see Nixon become President, he died eight days after Nixon's inauguration. It would be an even bigger personal loss for Nixon when Dwight Eisenhower passed away just over two months after Nixon took office.[2]

President Nixon's White House staff included familiar names from his recent campaign, and they were soon augmented by others who became infamous because of Watergate. John Mitchell, Nixon's law partner and campaign manager, became his first Attorney General. H.R. Haldeman was his new Chief of Staff, a position Nixon called "the gatekeeper of the Oval Office." John Ehrlichman was appointed White House Counsel for Domestic Affairs. They were joined by Rose Mary Woods, Nixon's White House secretary. Maurice Stans became Nixon's Secretary of Commerce. Woods was the only one of this group who wouldn't be convicted after Watergate.[3]

John Mitchell, Rose Mary Woods, and Maurice Stans all moved into the new Watergate complex, a posh five-year-old development that included a hotel, apartments, and offices. In the latter was the office of the Democratic National Committee. Real estate agents for the complex touted "the tight security throughout the buildings featuring TV-monitored elevators and private guards patrolling the halls at night." However, as would be revealed during Watergate, the complex had some security issues, since just weeks after Nixon's inauguration Rose Mary Wood's apartment "was robbed of some $7,000 worth of jewelry" while she was out of town.[4]

Joining the Cabinet as Nixon's Secretary of State was William Rogers, Eisenhower's Attorney General in 1960 when Rogers had temporarily stalled charges against Jimmy Hoffa after the Mafia bribed Nixon. For his new Secretary of Defense, Nixon turned to Wisconsin Representative Melvin Laird, described as "an expert on defense appropriations." George Schultz, later caught up in the Iran-Contra scandal under President Ronald Reagan, was tapped as Nixon's Secretary of Labor.[5]

Nixon's first Cabinet was once described as having "no blacks, no women, no Jews, no Democrats." Though President Nixon would make a surprising number of anti-Semitic remarks in private, he turned to the Jewish Henry Kissinger to fill the important role of National Security Advisor. Under Nixon, that position would be more influential on foreign policy than the Secretary of State, and Kissinger would work closely with Nixon on all global matters. However, Nixon saw himself as being the prime arbiter of U.S. foreign affairs, and it would be—at times—perhaps his greatest role as President.[6]

Though Nixon was supported by many in the media, he felt a growing adversarial relationship with the three television networks, *The New York Times*, and columnists like Drew Pearson. Nixon focused much of his energy on driving the news cycles and trying to manipulate the press, and was usually successful during his first term. Nixon and his staff had developed a list of ten thousand journalists, broadcasters, editors, and publishers—often referred to as simply "the 10,000"—who were supportive of Nixon and could be counted on to put out his statements, views, and spin.[7]

In a move that would make things more difficult for Nixon after his scandals started to surface, Nixon bypassed longtime press advisor Herb Klein and instead named as his Press Secretary Ron Ziegler, a veteran of the J. Walter Thompson ad agency who was not yet thirty. Roger Ailes continued to be a key Nixon media advisor. For speeches, Nixon continued to rely on William Safire and Pat Buchanan. By the summer, Nixon wanted even more focus on spinning and manipulating the press, so three full-time public relations staffers were added. The most notorious after Watergate would be Charles "Chuck" Colson, said to have "turned down a Harvard scholarship because he thought the faculty there 'too radical.'" Joining him was Jeb Stuart Magruder from California, who would later reveal Nixon's authorization of the Watergate break-ins. Also from California "was Franklin 'Lynn' Nofziger [the] former press secretary for [Governor] Ronald Reagan." The following year, Ziegler would add to the press staff a young Diane Sawyer, who would later help Nixon write his memoirs before becoming an network news anchor.[8]

Other notable Nixon officials and staff included Donald Rumsfeld, initially Nixon's director for the Office of Economic Opportunity, soon to become one of the President's White House counsels. Dick Cheney would become Rumsfeld's assistant, though the two wouldn't become powerful until the next administration. A more influential White House counsel named John Dean, who would play crucial roles after the Watergate arrests, would be added to Nixon's staff in his second year. They were all part of a growing group described as "clean-up, upright-seeming young men," who all seemed loyal and perfectly in sync with Nixon's conservative views.[9]

In 1969, Alexander Haig and Alexander Butterfield joined Nixon's White House staff. Both were veterans of John and Robert Kennedy's Cuban campaign, as was Joseph Califano, who helped Haig and Butterfield get their White House positions. Haig and Califano had worked extensively on the Kennedys' 1963 efforts, while Butterfield had joined their operation as it was winding down, when they were resettling Cuban exiles originally trained by the U.S. Army. After completing those efforts for Lyndon Johnson's administration, Haig and Butterfield had resumed their regular military careers. Joseph Califano became a close aide to President Johnson and remained with LBJ until he left office. In 1969, Califano joined a Washington law firm, where one of his most important clients was the Democratic National Committee (DNC), headed by Larry O'Brien (who was also working for billionaire Howard Hughes). Haig, Butterfield, and Califano would all play pivotal roles in the Watergate saga.[10]

Nixon aide Charles Colson said Joseph Califano recommended Butterfield's hiring as a Nixon aide. At the time, Butterfield was "the senior American military officer in Australia," where his duties included being the military's "CIA liaison there." Butterfield had written Haldeman about a possible position, since the two had known each other at UCLA in the late 1940s. Haldeman, apparently impressed by Califano's recommendation to Colson, offered Butterfield an important position as "a sort of personal assistant to the President." Butterfield resigned from the Air Force to take the position, even though Haldeman says he told Butterfield that wasn't necessary.[11]

Alexander Butterfield's role was different from Chief of Staff Haldeman's, in that Butterfield's role was administrative and not political, so it didn't involve the wide range of criminal activities that Haldeman was soon pursuing with Nixon. In his role, Butterfield had "nearly daily contact with the President," and as Haldeman began to work more closely with Nixon on illegal activities, Butterfield took on more of Haldeman's original administrative duties. Within a year, Butterfield said "his office adjoined the Oval Office. I was in and out more times than anyone. I was the first guy to see the president every morning and the last guy to see him at night." Butterfield was also "in charge of Nixon's papers and the files"—and would eventually oversee the White House taping system, after it was installed two years into Butterfield's tenure.[12]

When Butterfield had worked with Alexander Haig in early 1964 on closing down the U.S. military side of the anti-Castro operation, Butterfield said he and Haig "were very, very close." Butterfield's old friend joined him at the White House in early 1969. Colonel Alexander Haig had gone to Vietnam in 1966, where he'd been awarded the Distinguished Service Cross after his helicopter was shot down during a fierce battle. Haig's combination of combat experience and his degrees from West Point, Columbia, and Georgetown made him a prime candidate when Henry Kissinger began looking for a military aide. As with Butterfield, Joseph Califano also played a role in helping his old friend and protégé Haig get a position in the Nixon White House. Another NSC staff member wrote that "Joe Califano . . . never tired of telling reporters how ardently and in what bipartisan spirit he had recommended his old aide when Kissinger came asking for counsel" about whom to choose.[13]

Also like Butterfield, Colonel Haig would flourish at the White House, soon rising to the rank of General and within a year becoming Nixon's Deputy Assistant for National Security. Haig was a relative rarity—in a White House full of hawks on the war in Vietnam, Haig was one of the few who had actual combat experience. Haig, Califano, and Butterfield would remain friends, even though two were Nixon White House officials and Califano was an ardent Democrat who represented the DNC. When problems started to surface for Nixon, both Haig and Butterfield would turn to Califano for advice.[14]

For important positions in his administration, Nixon still valued old and trusted friends. Now that Nixon was President, he felt comfortable giving a more prominent role to his longtime campaign specialist and mob connection, Murray Chotiner. Initially, Chotiner wanted to be named Chairman of the Republican National Committee, but Nixon knew Chotiner had too much baggage for such a highly public position, and that Chotiner functioned best in the shadows, out of the limelight. Instead, Nixon brought Chotiner into the White House in stages, first naming him "general counsel in the obscure Office of the Special Representative for Trade Negotiations," even though "a routine FBI background check . . . suggested Chotiner had links with organized crime." When that brought no press attention, Anthony Summers notes that "a year later" Chotiner was quietly "named special counsel to the president."[15]

While working for Richard Nixon, Chotiner would have a hand in numerous crimes for the President: helping with secret funds from Howard Hughes; "overseeing the extortion of millions . . . from the heads of the dairy industry"; giving the IRS "lists of political enemies"; handling "secret payouts to Congressional candidates"; and helping to arrange a new bribe from the Mafia to release Jimmy Hoffa from prison. Chotiner's criminal activities with Nixon aren't more widely known because he left the White House before Watergate, though he continued to work for Nixon.[16]

Another of Nixon's trusted friends in his administration was FBI Director J. Edgar Hoover, one of only two top civilian officials to keep their posts from the Johnson administration. Though Nixon would come to resent Hoover at times as the President tried to expand his own domestic intelligence network, Nixon knew that he could never force the seventy-four-year-old Bureau chief to retire, event though he was long past the mandatory federal retirement age. Hoover was much better as a friend, since he had far too much information that Nixon never wanted to become public. Hoover began sharing information he knew Nixon would want right after the election, telling him about the FBI's wiretap on Anna Chennault's phone that had recorded her work for Nixon. The FBI Director also warned Nixon that LBJ had set up taping systems in the Oval Office and through the White House switchboard. Nixon ordered Haldeman to "get that Goddamn bugging crap out of the White House in a hurry."[17]

The other LBJ official that Nixon retained was CIA Director Richard Helms, even though Nixon may have only first met Helms shortly after winning the election. Given the high value Nixon placed on intelligence information, it may seem odd that he would retain a CIA Director from a Democratic administration, especially one he barely knew. Yet like Hoover, Richard Helms also had access to information that Nixon would never want made public. That included Nixon's pressure on the CIA to ramp up the 1960 CIA-Mafia plots by adding

Nixon's associate Robert Maheu, Johnny Rosselli, and Santo Trafficante, an operation that had eventually developed into "the Bay of Pigs thing."[18]

President Nixon tried to assert control over Helms, and he succeeded at times. In an early Cabinet meeting, Nixon corrected Helms on a matter about a small country in Africa, showing the CIA Director that he wouldn't blindly swallow whatever Helms said, and that he knew more about some matters than Helms. However, Helms clearly wanted to curry favor with the new President, and Helms's biographer Thomas Powers wrote that the CIA Director was soon providing "Nixon with information and quiet support that trod hard on the heels of the Agency's charter." Among the first of Helms's illegal activities for Nixon was his February 18, 1969, "delivery to Henry Kissinger of a special CIA study on US student protest movements." Helms acknowledged in his cover letter that such domestic spying was "an area not within the charter of this Agency . . . Should anyone learn of its existence it would prove most embarrassing for all concerned." With that, Helms began moving the CIA even more into the field of domestic spying, though "the CIA's Office of Security" had already been "monitoring radical organizations" for at least a year and a half at that point, and its Domestic Operations Division had been active for several years.[19]

Helms's domestic espionage for President Nixon was a double-edged sword, helping him keep his position, but also giving Nixon something to possibly hold over the CIA Director. However, there was no way Nixon could effectively use the domestic spying issue against Helms, because the CIA Director was spying with the knowledge of—and sometimes for—the President. In many ways that gave Helms more leverage over the President than Nixon had over Helms.

According to Nixon's Chief of Staff H.R. Haldeman, President Nixon began trying in early 1969 to get "all the facts and documents the CIA had on the Bay of Pigs." It was the start of a long crusade for Richard Nixon, one that Nixon would never fully achieve, leaving him unsure what CIA documentation might exist about his role in the CIA-Mafia plots and other events that resulted in the Bay of Pigs fiasco. Helms's successor would call Nixon's quest for those files an "obsession." Nixon's only excuse for his "obsession" in his memoirs was that he needed the information for political reasons, to use against the Democrats. That explanation doesn't ring true, because by 1969,

John and Robert Kennedy were both dead, and Edward Kennedy had no connection to the Bay of Pigs. In addition, Nixon would try repeatedly to get the information on the Bay of Pigs from Helms with a zeal that didn't match his quest of other potentially embarrassing information he could use against possible Democratic opponents.[20]

A far more likely explanation, especially given Nixon's future actions about the matter, is that the politically savvy Nixon realized that President Johnson would have demanded information from Richard Helms about the 1967 Jack Anderson articles. Nixon probably couldn't have known specifically about the highly secret 1967 Inspector General's Report Helms had prepared, but Nixon knew Helms would have had to give LBJ some type of information about Anderson's bombshell revelations that covered the CIA-Mafia plotting, their 1963 attempt to kill Castro, and Robert Kennedy's efforts against Fidel. As discussed earlier, Nixon was very vulnerable on several points, since he helped to originate the CIA-Mafia plots, had met with this friend William Pawley as Pawley was starting to work with Johnny Rosselli in 1963, and had a pipeline into some information about John and Robert Kennedy's 1963 effort to stage a coup against Fidel.

Nixon used the general term "Bay of Pigs" to keep from having to reveal his closely guarded secrets to his aides. Nixon's many meetings with the CIA in 1960 about Cuba did eventually grow into the 1961 Bay of Pigs invasion, after the initial round of CIA-Mafia plots had failed. In private, even the CIA made the connection between the plots and the Bay of Pigs, with one CIA official earlier telling J. Edgar Hoover that the CIA-Mafia plots were "the most sensitive information relating to the abortive Cuban invasion in April 1961." Also, as previously documented, Haldeman later speculated that Nixon also saw some tie between the Bay of Pigs and JFK's assassination, an astute observation given the confessed roles of Johnny Rosselli and Santo Trafficante in both. Any political dirt the files might reveal about the Kennedys would be gravy, but what Nixon really needed to know was what CIA files about the matter said about him—and what Helms might have told, shown, or given to President Johnson that could conceivably be used in the next election against Nixon.[21]

In the early months of Nixon's Presidency, John Ehrlichman relayed to Helms the President's order demanding all of the Bay of Pigs material. Amazingly, the CIA Director turned him down and refused to turn over the material. After six months of waiting, Nixon commanded that Helms come to the Oval Office, so he could personally "give him a direct order to turn over" the material. However, after Nixon and Helms had "a long secret conversation" in private, Nixon shocked Ehrlichman by telling him he was to "now forget all about that CIA document [and to] cease and desist from trying to obtain it." After hearing that from Nixon, a puzzled and confused Ehrlichman "burst into [Haldeman's] office," complaining to him about Nixon's sudden and unexplained reversal.[22]

Helms's refusal to comply with the President's order raises the possibility that Helms was subtly blackmailing Nixon, in order to keep his post in the new administration. Perhaps Helms told Nixon that as long as he was CIA Director, he would make sure that material in CIA files embarrassing to the President—which Helms could have described only vaguely—would be kept secret. As Senator Howard Baker would say after the Watergate investigation, "Nixon and Helms have so much on each other, neither of them can breathe."[23]

Nixon drew upon another trusted associate to help him deal with Helms and the CIA. In 1960, Nixon's National Security Advisor General Robert Cushman had worked with the CIA and E. Howard Hunt on the effort to get rid of Fidel Castro. So, on May 7, 1969, Nixon appointed General Cushman to become the Deputy Director of the CIA. Soon after taking office, Nixon—like LBJ when he assumed office—was told about ongoing US covert operations against Fidel Castro. Helms would have briefed Nixon about Commander Almieda's past work for the US and the continuing CIA support for his family outside of Cuba.

It has been newly documented, from a Senate Watergate Committee memo (see Appendix), that early in 1969, Nixon's new "Assistant Atrtorney General . . . requested the [Justice Department's] file" on Johnny Rosselli and the CIA-Mafia plots. He no doubt reviewed that file with Attorney General Mitchell, who would have then told President Nixon about its contents.

Because Nixon was trying to get the Bay of Pigs information as soon as he took office, it's likely he also asked Attorney General John Mitchell for any information damaging to himself that might be in Justice Department files. Nixon would use Mitchell and the Justice Department for political purposes, so it stands to reason he would want to know about any files that could harm him politically. The Justice Department had a long history of prosecuting Jimmy Hoffa and Carlos Marcello—and thus had voluminous files about each—while Nixon knew he was vulnerable because of his September 1960 $500,000 bribe for Hoffa from Marcello and other mobsters. When Nixon was elected—and for another ten years—the press and public had no access to information about Nixon's 1960 Mafia-Hoffa bribe, which was witnessed by FBI and Justice Department informant Grady Partin. It's also possible that once Nixon became President, J. Edgar Hoover told him that the Justice Department had information about the 1960 bribe, since the FBI had administered Partin's polygraph test.

In early 1969, as documented by Stephen Ambrose, John Ehrlichman began pressing Nixon about a pardon for Jimmy Hoffa, apparently in response to a campaign contribution from the Teamsters, which Hoffa still ran from prison. However, Charles Colson and others convinced Nixon to wait until after the 1971 union election, so that Hoffa couldn't challenge Teamsters Vice President Frank Fitzsimmons, who planned to run for the union's presidency. Since Hoffa's role was limited by being in prison, Fitzsimmons was taking over more and more of the day-to-day operation of the union. Nixon's campaign—and several Mafia leaders—were increasingly comfortable with the easygoing Fitzsimmons, who could be much more agreeable to deal with than the volatile Hoffa.[24]

On May 9, 1969, *The New York Times* first reported that Nixon had expanded the Vietnam War by secretly bombing the adjacent country of Cambodia, ostensibly to destroy enemy supply lines and bases. Nixon was furious and assumed that one or more of this new staff members must have leaked the story to *The Times*. In actuality, the *Times* "story was based on an on-site report from a British correspondent in Cambodia, not on a leak."[25]

It says a lot about Nixon, and his ability to manipulate much of the press, that he would not only repeatedly bomb a sovereign country and think he could keep it out of the press, but that when an article appeared, he assumed it couldn't be because of reporting and must be because of a leak. As covered earlier during the Alger Hiss case, Nixon considered himself a master leaker to the press, something he continued to do as President. Even though President Nixon had aides feed "the 10,000" favorable journalists a steady stream of information and spin, he and his staff carefully cultivated a more select group with exclusive leaks helpful to Nixon.[26]

Nixon's anger at *The Times*, and his paranoia about leaks, was in many ways a reflection of his own inability to completely control the news about his administration, and his own extensive use of leaks. His response was overwhelming, and really began the illegal domestic surveillance that would become a major part of Watergate and his related criminal campaign operations. In many ways, Nixon's Presidential obsession with leaks and his use of illegal political espionage began with this May 1969 *Times* report and not with the Pentagon Papers in 1971, as many think.

As reported by Ambrose, Henry "Kissinger supplied the names" of those to be wiretapped, and Attorney General John Mitchell signed the authorizations. Among those wiretapped were aides to Kissinger, including former Harvard professor Morton Halperin (his phone stayed tapped for almost two years). Taps were also "placed on the phones of the closest aides of the Secretary of State and the Secretary of Defense." Nixon wanted his own brother Donald tapped, but "the FBI and CIA both refused to spy on the president's brother." Also tapped were the phones of speechwriter William Safire, and one of Nixon's own aides. Nixon also had the phones tapped of "four newspapermen." There were a total of seventeen wiretaps. Three years later, all would be ruled illegal by the Supreme Court. Nixon and Mitchell had used a very broad interpretation of the law to justify their surveillance, one that essentially said that if the President did it, then it must be legal. This doctrine would be stretched and stretched in the ensuing years, ultimately leading to the crimes that forced Nixon's resignation.[27]

In 1969, "Nixon also ordered [spying] he knew to be illegal." Hoover refused to tap the phone of "columnist Joseph Kraft," who wasn't suspected of leaking and whose only offense was writing "a critical piece on Nixon." In response, Nixon had Haldeman find someone else to do the job, in this case private investigator John Caulfield, a former member of the New York Police Department's Special Services Bureau. That began a series of illegal political acts that Caulfield and his partner committed for Nixon.* They targeted "Democratic Senators and Congressmen" with "extensive surveillance and smear operations." That would include "round-the-clock surveillance of Senator [Edward] Kennedy," whom Nixon saw as his likely rival in the 1972 Presidential race. As uncovered by the Senate Watergate Committee,

*His partner was Anthony Ulasewicz.

those efforts included their own investigation of the Chappaquiddick incident, and a "secret program to sexually 'entrap' the various women who had been" at the Chappaquiddick party, so they could be "blackmailed."[28]

In addition, Nixon had John Caulfield and his partner collect "extensive amounts of alleged 'dirt' on various 'enemies' of the Nixon Administration." The Watergate Committee eventually "published a fifty-item list of various Caulfield . . . 'investigations' for the Nixon circle, the vulgarity of which had astonished even some hard-nosed Senate investigators." Caulfield and his partner would continue to work on such projects into 1973, and though they were separate from what would become known as E. Howard Hunt's White House "Plumbers" political espionage unit, they set the pattern for what the Plumbers would do on a much larger scale.[29]

Bebe Rebozo was in a unique position that made him different from others working on Nixon's illegal operations, such as Murray Chotiner and John Caulfield. Rebozo's political crimes involved money, and they occurred at the same he was handling much of Richard Nixon's personal business and financial matters. After the election, Anthony Summers found their "friendship grew so close that Rebozo effectively had the run of the White House and his own phone number there. He flew on Air Force One . . . cruised on the presidential yacht with Nixon," and relaxed with Nixon "at Camp David."[30]

Rebozo even lived in Nixon's Florida White House compound at Key Biscayne, occupying a house next to Nixon's, which was only appropriate since Rebozo had arranged Nixon's complex purchase of the property. At the same time, Rebozo was involved in various questionable or illegal business transactions, including land deals with men tied to mobsters and imprisoned Teamsters President Jimmy Hoffa. According to recent report by *The New York Times*, before Nixon was elected, his net worth was $800,000 (almost $5 million today) while Rebozo's was only $673,000. However, only "a few years later," *The Times* would point out that Rebozo had increased his net worth sixfold, to $4 million dollars (over $16 million today).[31]

Given their complex business deals for Key Biscayne and San Clemente (Nixon's fourteen-room Western White House), and their close personal relationship—was well as Rebozo's huge increase in wealth during Nixon's Presidency—it's clear in hindsight that Rebozo's role was to make money for both of them while Nixon was President, to be shared with Nixon after he left office. As detailed later, there is evidence that happened, including Rebozo essentially just giving Nixon $2 million a few years after he left office.[32]

When illegal money was raised after Nixon became President, Nixon apparently felt entitled to some of that money for his personal use, as had been the case back in 1946 and the 1950s. In 1969 and into the early 1970s, Rebozo helped to provide that money, from some of the same sources who'd given for Nixon's campaign. Commerce Secretary Maurice Stans later admitted that "Rebozo . . . told me, 'I've set up a trust fund for Richard Nixon's family." Stans went on to say that "the fund, which he believed was started in 1968, never became public knowledge and he himself never learned of its [full] extent."[33]

Information later emerged indicating that Nixon and Rebozo had Swiss bank accounts where they could hide millions. That was confirmed by Robert Morgenthau, the U.S. Attorney for New York City in the late 1960s. Morgenthau "had information on a visit Nixon had made to . . . an expert in helping people set up Swiss bank accounts," and Morgenthau was certain about one Swiss bank in particular that Nixon used. In the late 1960s, Morgenthau was helping "the House Banking and Currency Committee to formulate a new law that would have made it much harder for U.S. citizens . . . to operate secret accounts abroad." However, "Nixon removed Morgenthau from office—over the protests of senior Republicans as well as Democrats."[34]

In one lengthy deposition, a longtime Nixon associate described Rebozo as "a politically savvy fund-raiser who operated—[especially] with respect to contributions from Howard Hughes—with Nixon's knowledge and authority." Rebozo was the key go-between for the $100,000 Howard Hughes contribution described in the previous chapter. Robert Maheu was responsible for delivering the money from Hughes to Rebozo, which came in at least two $50,000 installments. The first time, Maheu used a mutual friend of Rebozo and Nixon to deliver "ten batches of hundred-dollar bills . . . the source of the cash was a Hughes casino." It's incredibly ironic—or appropriate—that Nixon was getting illegal money from a casino whose purchase by Hughes had been brokered by Johnny Rosselli. Rebozo met with Nixon immediately after getting the illegal contribution. As for Rosselli, Rebozo's FBI file—released after his death—says that Rosselli would later testify about the "$100,000 transaction among

Bebe Rebozo, Howard Hughes, and Robert Maheu" to "a Senate committee investigating campaign practices of former President Richard M. Nixon."[35]

The second installment of $50,000 from Hughes was personally delivered to Rebozo by Robert Maheu, in a "chauffeured limousine . . . followed by gin martinis . . . and a lavish dinner." In addition to the Hughes airline purchase approval noted earlier, Hughes also got approval from Attorney General John Mitchell to buy another Las Vegas casino. Mitchell approved, even though Hughes's purchase "involved an anti-trust issue and Mitchell gave his consent against senior staff advice." Senate investigators would later conclude that "there is evidence suggesting there may have been more than two deliveries" of Hughes money "to Rebozo," and the amounts could have been far in excess of $100,000. For example, Anthony Summers noted an uncorroborated account from a "former Hughes employee" who said "a million-dollar delivery to Rebozo did take place, in 1969."[36]

As for what the $100,000 was used for, phone calls between Maheu's first intermediary and Rebozo were accompanied by a diary notation saying "house project." Summers notes the money was delivered when Nixon was in the midst of buying and improving his Key Biscayne property and that "Senate investigators [suspect the money] had been used to pay for such items as architects fees, remodeling, a swimming pool, and . . . an 'Arnold Palmer Putting Green.'"[37]

Professor Mark Feldman, in his recent book about Nixon and Jack Anderson, wrote that

> Senate investigators later determined that Rebozo had paid at least $50,000 of the President's private expenses with cash collected from Hughes and other wealthy patrons: $45,000 in improvements on Nixon's two vacation homes . . . another $5,000 for platinum earrings studded with eighteen pear-shaped diamonds . . . for the First Lady . . . In addition, Rebozo confided that he also passed out wads of Hughes's hundred-dollar bills as gifts to the President's brothers.[38]

Nixon's aides "referred to the president's slush fund as the 'tin box.'" According to H.R. Haldeman, "there was much more money in Bebe's 'tin box' than the Hughes $100,000." He said it was "only part of a much larger cash kitty kept in [Rebozo's] safety deposit box. Rebozo, in effect, maintained a private fund for Nixon to use as he wished."[39]

Nixon wasn't just using the illegal money from Hughes and other "wealthy patrons" to save the government money, by paying for some of his home remodeling costs himself. Nixon could have expensive tastes, especially when he wasn't footing the bill. As documented by Summers, "the government [had to] spend more than ten million dollars—more than forty-four million dollars at today's values—to install special features not only at Nixon's out-of-town homes but also at houses he frequented . . . in the Bahamas." It's often overlooked that "Nixon had nine offices for his personal use: the Oval Office, a hideaway in the [Old] Executive Office Building, a room in his private quarters, two at Camp David, one at the Key Biscayne house, another at [a patron's] Caribbean house, and two at San Clemente . . . A former Budget Bureau official would calculate that, by four years into the presidency, Nixon's household expenses had added up to a hundred million dollars."[40]

In addition to the illegal money Bebe Rebozo pursued for Nixon, *Newsday* and former FBI agent William Turner would later uncover several unusual land deals in the 1960s and early 1970s involving Nixon, Bebe Rebozo, and Miami's Keyes Realty. As mentioned in Chapter 19, both "Bernard Barker and Eugenio Martinez were officers of real estate firms that acted in property deals for Nixon and Rebozo." Former CIA agent Barker was now described as "a prosperous real estate man," whose firm had "ten salesmen" and a dozen employees in all. Barker, Rebozo, Nixon, and Barker's good friend Eugenio Martinez were involved in a complex series of land and real estate deals. Martinez—still a CIA agent and soon to be a Watergate burglar—was a vice president of Keyes Realty, which Nixon used "to broker the deal establishing the Florida White House on Key Biscayne." Barker's own real estate firm was "located in the Keyes building" and shared an important executive with Keyes. Barker's firm would later be "the corporate cover for the burglars in the Watergate break-in." Since Barker had run through much of the money from the sale of Artime's AMWORLD arms starting up his business, "Barker was financed in many of his real estate ventures by Bebe Rebozo." Barker and Rebozo were in business together at the same time that "Rebozo [was also] the silent partner to Richard Nixon" in various shady deals, as documented by Turner. At that same time, Barker was still doing work for godfather Santo Trafficante.[41]

As noted in the previous chapter, Barker worked with Rebozo's business partner—Edgardo Buttari Sr.—to help get Nixon elected. Meanwhile, Barker's good friend Manuel Artime was laying the groundwork for another chance to make money by going after Fidel Castro. An FBI memo states that just before Nixon's election, "Artime claimed he had arranged an interview with . . . Richard M. Nixon, in order to establish the basis for a new plan [to overthrow Fidel Castro] which Artime hoped to put into effect." The FBI says that Artime got the interview with Nixon "through the assistance of [Buttari] who is acquainted with Mr. Charles G. 'Bebe' Rebozo [the] personal friend of President Nixon."[42]

Artime wanted Nixon to fund a new version of AMWORLD, telling the FBI's confidential informant that "he hoped to set up a training camp for Cuban exiles in Nicaragua." Artime said he had also "gone to Haiti . . . for the purpose of establishing a staging area for his future operations." The FBI memo said that according to information from Artime, "Mr. Rebozo would be the 'head man' for the next plan concerning Cuba." Though Rebozo wasn't a Cuban exile like Artime and Barker, he had a well-documented hatred of Fidel Castro.[43]

The FBI said that accompanying Artime on his 1968 and 1969 trips and participating in his efforts was a close friend of his, a Bay of Pigs veteran *The Nation* later described as being "an important Miami contact for the 'French connection' heroin ring," which Santo Trafficante controlled in Florida. According to the FBI, Artime's heroin-connected friend owned real estate with Barker's associate, Edgardo Buttari Sr. Artime himself had been involved in drug trafficking with Trafficante's organization for at least five years at this point.[44]

Artime's Cuban plans caught the eye of the FBI, which asked the CIA if he was again working for them. The Miami CIA office initially replied that it did have an "operational interest" in Artime. However, CIA headquarters told a different story. On January 6, 1969, a high FBI official received a memo about Artime, saying that "Mrs. Jane Roman, Central Intelligence Agency (CIA) advised . . . that CIA does not have any operational interest in the subject [or] plan to utilize Artime. [But the] CIA is interested in his activities and would appreciate receiving any information coming to our attention concerning [Artime]."[45]

Despite the CIA's lack of support, Artime's efforts appeared to be paying off, according to the FBI memo, because "on January 22, 1969 Artime . . . received word from [Buttari] a close friend of Mr. Rebozo, that in February of 1969, Artime would get the 'okay' signal." Artime explained to the FBI informant that "Buttari . . . was helping Artime so much in his contacts with Mr. Rebozo." Artime was so confident of success that he offered the exile FBI informant the position of Chief of Intelligence for this new operation, and Artime asked him to provide "10 additional names" of "prospective recruits."[46]

Bebe Rebozo's FBI file calls Bernard "Barker [a] long-time operator for the CIA." After Nixon took office, Barker took advantage of other Cuban exiles to help his own standing with Rebozo and Nixon. Barker continued to work closely with Buttari, whom the FBI says "was later called to Washington by the Nixon Administration to act as a consultant . . . when Nixon announced the blockade of Haiphong Harbor [in North Vietnam] Buttari and Barker planned to take some action to support the Nixon administration. Barker called different exile groups around the United States and raised some money under the pretext it was for an operation against Cuba. The money was actually designated for pro-Nixon demonstrations to be held in Miami and other places."[47]

In 1969, Nixon was still interested in taking action against Fidel Castro and Cuba. Ambrose points out that as soon as Nixon became President "he promptly ordered the CIA to step up covert action against Castro," which LBJ had been having "wound down." That included "pinprick raids, sabotage, recruiting, [and] organizing resistance cells." The U.S. sanctions in place at that time—and still today—banning travel to Cuba, as well as the lack of formal diplomatic ties, both date from Nixon's last days in office as Vice President. Eight years later, in 1969, Summers noted that President Nixon tried to get legislation passed "to prevent Americans from helping the Cuban economy." The following year, in response to "the apparent construction of a Soviet naval base in Cuba . . . Nixon demanded an immediate CIA briefing on '*any* kind of action which will irritate Castro." (Emphasis in original.) A year after Nixon's demand, the CIA would take two extraordinary actions against Cuba. First, the Agency gave "African swine flu virus to anti-Castro operatives who then smuggled it into Cuba." When there was "an outbreak of the disease [it resulted in] the slaughter of half a million pigs to avert an epidemic." A year after Nixon's demand for "*any* kind of action," there would also be a new assassination attempt against Fidel Castro, involving familiar names from the early 1960s such as CIA officer David Atlee Phillips and exile leader Antonio Veciana.[48]

Nixon's first year as President had many echoes of the past, from his concern over Cuba to his involvement with illicit money and business dealings with Bebe Rebozo. That year, 1969, also saw the seeds of Nixon's illegal activities that would grow in the coming years, such as his concerns with leaks that led to electronic surveillance and the use of White House operatives for "dirty tricks" and political espionage. All of these would help to set the stage for the events that would culminate in the Watergate scandal.

CHAPTER 24

1970: Nixon's Covert Actions Involving Vietnam, Cuba, and Chile

Richard Nixon's actions regarding the war in Vietnam during 1970 and into 1971 would be driven in part by a flurry of events at the end of the preceding year. Also in 1970, a surprising tie between the Vietnam War and the American Mafia started to emerge, one that would have unexpected implications for Nixon and others involved in Watergate.

On September 4, 1969, North Vietnamese leader Ho Chi Minh had died, further complicating any possibility of negotiating an end to the conflict. President Nixon tried to seize the opportunity by announcing he was going to withdraw another sixty thousand troops from South Vietnam. When his former opponent Hubert Humphrey praised the President's actions, Nixon ordered his White House PR staff to send Humphrey one hundred phony telegrams, congratulating him on his stance. Nixon also wanted a like number to "barrage" key Senators who opposed his attempt to gradually wind down the war.[1]

In announcing further withdrawals, Nixon was also trying to stem an increasing tide of protests against the war and his Presidency. Nixon seemed perplexed by the growing nature of the demonstrations, feeling that he shouldn't be held accountable for what he viewed as the Democrats' war that he simply inherited. However, Nixon's view is disingenuous, since even historians sympathetic to Nixon like Stephen Ambrose point out Nixon's long support of the Vietnam War, from its start in the 1950s when he was Vice President to the mid-1960s, when LBJ could never commit enough forces to satisfy Nixon and the other hawks. Nixon's perspective also ignores his actions to stall the peace talks before the 1968 election and his failure to act quickly to end the conflict, as he'd promised during the campaign.[2]

Nixon had won his narrow Presidential victory because of support from some independents and moderates, who believed his campaign promise that he would end the war honorably, soon after he took office. Nixon didn't seem to realize that some of the protestors simply resented the fact that he hadn't fulfilled his campaign pledge. Huge protests were held at the White House and across the country on October 15, 1969, and while they included some young radicals—who got most of the press attention—many of the protestors were average Americans, a growing number of whom were frustrated with Nixon and the war. Though Nixon had starting making some troop withdrawals—and the weekly death toll had dropped from three hundred, to two hundred, and then below one hundred—for many it still seemed a high cost for a war with no end in sight.[3]

College-age males were a driving force in organizing the mass protests, primarily because of the draft they faced. To undercut the protest leaders, Nixon had announced a draft lottery, which put the focus primarily on nineteen-year-olds, instead of the much broader age range of draft-eligible males in place since the conflict had escalated.[4]

Even larger protests were planned for mid-November 1969, so Nixon went on a public relations offensive. As historians have pointed out, it seemed that "PR not policy was his concern." Nixon relied on tried-and-true methods he'd used before. First, he prepared an impassioned speech calculated to stir support for him and his policies, even as he really offered nothing new or concrete. Second, using the classic techniques of PR specialists like Edward Bernays, Nixon planned ahead of time how to spin the public's reaction—or what appeared to be the public's reaction—to his speech.

After Nixon delivered his carefully prepared prime-time speech on November 3, 1969, he had Charles Colson deliver "supposedly spontaneous support from thousands of veterans across the nation." This gave a false impression of Nixon's support to the press and Congress, while also helping to undercut press coverage of groups like Vietnam Veterans Against the War. In addition to Nixon's usual PR efforts with "the 10,000" sympathetic journalists and editors, Nixon also had Jeb Magruder and other aides unleash

> a supposedly spontaneous telegram barrage of support to the White House. The President piled them up on his desk and called in photographers. "The great silent majority," he said, "has spoken."[5]

After his speech and the carefully manipulated reaction—the combination of which generated much genuine support—Nixon's poll numbers shot up to a 68 percent approval rating. But Nixon had little time to celebrate because of a massive antiwar demonstration in Washington, D.C., that began on November 14. While the huge demonstration was still going on, in South Vietnam U.S. troops wiped out a small village named My Lai. While the My Lai massacre wouldn't be reported by the press for some time, it underscored the increasing problems that Nixon faced the longer weary U.S. troops remained in the country. On December 15, 1969, Nixon announced that more U.S. troops would be leaving the country, even as the fighting continued.[6]

In January 1970, Nixon had Alexander Haig go to South Vietnam on a fact-finding mission, where Haig found growing morale problems among the South Vietnamese troops. The rampant corruption of South Vietnamese leaders, from President Thieu on down, was probably a significant factor. There was no real democracy in South Vietnam, and that country's troops—as well as U.S. forces—were likely growing increasingly tired of fighting for what was essentially a corrupt dictatorship by Thieu and his military leaders.[7]

With no possibility of a military victory or meaningful peace talks, Nixon went on the attack. In February 1970, he expanded the U.S. ground war in Vietnam into neighboring Laos, triggering more concern in a Congress that had already been growing restive. Throughout much of Nixon's first year, conservative and moderate members of Congress had been generally supportive of Nixon and the war. The huge military contracts that had begun when LBJ was President had largely been continued or even expanded. According to figures compiled later by CIA officer—and Watergate burglar—James McCord, four U.S. companies supplying the U.S. military had annual contracts of over a billion dollars, while six more had nearly that much. Especially targeted by protesters was the Texas military contractor Brown and Root—called "Burn and Loot" by demonstrators—which would later become part of the company known as Halliburton. But by 1970, rumors of cost overruns and mismanagement were growing rampant, and not just in the small progressive press, but among some in Congress.[8]

Nixon's invasion of Laos marked a tipping point in the U.S. Senate, and in April 1970 the "Senate Foreign Relations Committee voted unanimously to repeal the [1964] Gulf of Tonkin Resolution." That resolution had originally authorized the expanded war, but President Nixon not only ignored their repeal but also expanded the war yet again. Nixon also began a major effort to win more Senate seats for Republicans in the fall 1970 Congressional elections.[9]

In May 1970, Nixon sent large numbers of U.S. ground forces into Cambodia, which he had started bombing the previous year. That led to more demonstrations, and outrage among some in Congress. A combative Nixon thought it was a positive sign politically that only 39 percent of the American public disapproved of his expanding the war into Cambodia.[10]

By 1970, heroin use was exploding in the United States, and much of the problem was rooted in Southeast Asia, the source of much of the heroin in America, which was also increasingly finding its way to U.S. troops in South Vietnam. The surging use of heroin in the United States and Vietnam was well documented at the time by mainstream newspaper articles that included a Pulitzer Prize–winning series in *Newsday*, along with U.S. military and Congressional studies. While godfather Santo Trafficante's leading role in heroin trafficking was mentioned prominently by *Newsday*, it's often overlooked that the trail of illicit drug profits reached into surprising places.[11]

Unhampered by prosecution or prison, Santo Trafficante's empire had continued to grow during the 1960s and into 1970. In the ten years since he'd started working on the CIA-Mafia plots—while Nixon was Vice President—Trafficante had expanded into more legitimate and semi-legitimate businesses. His operatives now included seemingly respectable businessmen like Manuel Artime and Bernard Barker, who were both involved with Bebe Rebozo. Like a modern, international business executive, the fifty-five-year-old Trafficante had greatly expanded the reach of his heroin network. Decades later, noted intelligence journalist Joseph Trento documented that after the Mafia chief made a 1968 trip to South Vietnam, Hong Kong, and Singapore, Trafficante

> decided to have his Hong Kong-based deputy . . . take control of every big Saigon nightspot catering to US servicemen. By 1970, [Trafficante's] Saigon-produced heroin was being sold directly to American GI's at bargain prices at each of these nightspots.[12]

Though largely forgotten today, the "Service Club Scandal" was major news at the time, because Trento points out that "by 1970, Congress estimated that a full fifteen percent of the US troops in Vietnam were hooked on heroin." While more recent analysis has shown those Congressional figures to be somewhat inflated, the actual numbers were still shockingly high.[13]

There is a surprising amount of evidence—including an investigation by the U.S. Army's Criminal Investigation Command—that some of Trafficante's drug profits found their way to associates of Richard Nixon. The U.S. Army investigation, ordered by Alexander Haig, found "strong indications of a history of Nixon connections with money from organized crime." Teamsters expert Dan Moldea found that[14]

> a former Nixon aide, not privy to the Haig investigation, says that one of his associates in the White House mentioned to him . . . Nixon's possible "organized crime involvement." That conversation involved "a massive payoff" from those in [the] "Army Service Club scandals in Vietnam," during 1969 or 1970. The aide says that the Service Club rip-offs "involved the Mafia and millions of dollars," and that the main focus of the interest by "someone high up" in the White House was on whether "the top Mafia guy" who ran "all these things in Southeast Asia" had made payoffs to Nixon. The crime figure, he says was "the one who was apparently known as the so-called mastermind or architect of the Southeast Asian drug trade . . . who was very powerful and very well known as a mob leader."[15]

Moldea pointed out that "according to government narcotics experts, the central figure in the Indochina–Golden Triangle narcotics traffic was Santo Trafficante."[16]

The information from the Nixon aide Moldea interviewed about the President's tie to the Service Club Scandal in 1970 provides important corroborating information for Alexander Haig's Army investigation into Nixon's "organized crime" money. Haig's investigation didn't become part of the conventional story of Watergate because it wasn't revealed until more than two years after Nixon's resignation, in a December 5, 1976 article in *The Washington Star* (by then no longer the Capitol's largest newspaper).[17]

Haig's investigation began when he became suspicious of two of Nixon's operatives, wondering if they "had been to the Far East and carried back any money for Nixon." Haig "also wanted to know whether Nixon had ever been mixed up with organized crime." The head of the Army's Criminal Investigation Command—Colonel Henry H. Tufts—assigned Special Investigator Russell L. Bintliff to look into the matter for Haig. He "concluded that [the two Nixon operatives] had gone to Vietnam" for Nixon, and found the earlier noted "strong indications" of Nixon's "connections with money from organized crime." As detailed later, Haig ordered his investigation after the Watergate scandal helped him become Nixon's Chief of Staff, but it's noted here because—as the Nixon aide quoted above said—the payments began by 1970 with the Service Club scandal.[18]

The Washington Star's article about Haig's investigation was found credible by Nixon aide John Dean, who cited it in his book, *Lost Honor*. Dean wrote that "to my knowledge, Al Haig . . . never commented on his actions in calling for this investigation." Moldea looked into the article's source and information, and also deemed them credible, both in his landmark book on Jimmy Hoffa and to this author.

The money for Nixon could have been coming from South Vietnamese leaders, or from Trafficante's men in the region, or both. According to the newspaper article, both Haig and investigator Bintliff were aware of Nixon possibly receiving "huge cash contributions from countries in the Far East," specifically "unverified reports that South Vietnamese President Nguyen Van Thieu and Air Marshal Nguyen Cao Ky, former President of South Vietnam, had sent several millions of dollars to the United States for Nixon's political campaign activities." According to Congressional testimony and Alfred McCoy's well-documented *Politics Of Heroin in Southeast Asia*, both Thieu and Ky "were specifically involved" in the heroin network linked to Santo Trafficante. As noted earlier, Nixon had dealt with the junta that included Thieu and Ky since 1964, when his law firm handled legal work for the South Vietnamese government.[19]

The ties of Richard Nixon's friend Rebozo to Trafficante associates like Barker, Artime, and the "Miami contact for the 'French connection' heroin ring" mentioned previously would have made it easy for Rebozo to arrange such payoffs to Nixon from Trafficante. When Nixon was at his Florida White House, Rebozo frequently visited because he lived next door, and the men often went out on Rebozo's yacht or the Presidential yacht, far from prying eyes or ears. Trafficante had casino interests in the Bahamas, as did several Nixon associates the President and Rebozo saw when they visited the Bahamas.[20]

Nixon's highly promoted official reaction to the drug crisis was to order the Bureau of Narcotics and Dangerous Drugs (BNDD) to crack down on U.S. heroin trafficking. However, the ties between Nixon and Trafficante associates might explain why Trento found that "the BNDD could not get the Nixon administration to go after Trafficante directly." Unofficially, as part of the buildup to Watergate, Nixon would soon build his own small White House anti-drug squad, one that included Trafficante associates like Frank Fiorini, Manuel Artime, and Bernard Barker.

With his supplies in Southeast Asia secure, by 1970 the U.S. distribution side of Trafficante's heroin network was undergoing a major shift. Cuban exiles began playing an increasing role in the network, as France finally began to arrest some of their most notorious traffickers, like Michel Victor Mertz. Trafficante's Cuban exiles filled the void left by the French arrests to such an extent that *Newsday* reported the BNDD had discovered that 8 percent of the fifteen hundred Bay of Pigs veterans had "been investigated or arrested for drug dealing." That total didn't include prominent exiles like former Bay of Pigs leader Manuel Artime, who would never be arrested for his drug trafficking activities, and who would soon be working for the Nixon White House.

In 1970, Alexander Haig was continuing his climb to prominence within the Nixon administration. While he still worked with Nixon's powerful National Security Advisor Henry Kissinger, he was now also Nixon's Deputy Assistant for National Security Affairs. As such, the ambitious Haig took on increasingly important roles and missions for President Nixon and his National Security Council. One of his fellow NSC staff members later wrote that in March 1970, "Haig became the sole liaison between the White House and the Joint Chiefs on the Cambodian bombing."[21]

The Chairman of the Joints Chiefs in 1970 was Admiral Thomas Moorer, and he developed a close working relationship with Haig. Al Haig later said he had "daily contact with" Admiral Moorer, who was based at the Pentagon. In addition to meetings and phone calls between the two, young officers from the Pentagon regularly came to the White House to bring material and/or brief Haig and the other NSC staffers and members about matters involving Admiral Moorer and the Joint Chiefs.[22]

Two important figures in the Watergate scandal first enter the story at this point: Bob Woodward—not yet a reporter—and the man who would become his most famous source, Mark Felt, better known as "Deep Throat." As Woodward himself has written, in 1969 he was "a full lieutenant in the United States Navy, assigned to the Pentagon as a watch officer, overseeing world wide Teletype communications for then Admiral Thomas H. Moorer, who later became the chairman of the Joint Chiefs of Staff." Woodward added that he "had a Top Secret security clearance" at the time.[23]

Bob Woodward wrote that he "acted at times as a courier, taking packages of messages or other documents . . . to the White House." He gives the example of one instance, "in the first half of 1970," when he "was dispatched with a package to the lower level of the West Wing of the White House." Wearing his formal "dress-blue Navy uniform," Woodward sat for a while in a "waiting area near the Situation Room and the offices of some National Security Council staff."[24]

Soon, a "distinguished-looking" man who appeared "25 to 30 years older" than Woodward took the seat beside him. Woodward introduced himself, and the man said his name was "Mark Felt." Woodward—ambitious like Haig, but with far fewer achievements at that point—said he tried to impress Felt by telling him he "was bringing documents from Admiral Moorer's office." Because of Woodward's pressing, the two men gradually began a conversation, and Woodward learned that Felt was "an assistant director of the FBI."[25]

Woodward said he was seeking some direction in his life, so he talked to Felt about his future. The 1965 Yale graduate had taken some graduate courses at Georgetown University, which Felt had also attended, giving them a tenuous bond. Otherwise, the first conversation appears to have been mostly that of an older, wiser man giving career advice to a young man uncertain about what to do with his life. But the conversation ended cordially, and Woodward would continue to develop this high-level government connection over the next two years.[26]

In August 1970, after leaving the Navy, Bob Woodward would briefly work at *The Washington Post* for only two weeks, before being sent to a suburban newspaper to get more "seasoning." He would return to *The Post* just nine months before he started to cover the biggest story of his life, with Assistant FBI Director Mark Felt as his most famous confidential source.[27]

Woodward's admissions raise an obvious question that could be relevant for Watergate: Did Bob Woodward meet Alexander Haig on any of his visits to the National Security Council offices for Admiral Moorer? Woodward denies ever meeting or briefing Al Haig at that time, but there is also evidence to the contrary.[28]

Admiral Moorer said in a taped interview that he was aware that Woodward had briefed Alexander Haig at the White House. Moorer explained that the briefings were part of his close work with Haig, saying that he "was on the telephone with Haig 8 or 9 times a day about whatever's going on." The Admiral explained the frequent contact was because "Haig was simply the channel . . . it went from Haig to the President." President Nixon's Secretary of Defense, Melvin Laird, also stated in a taped interview that "I was aware that Haig was being briefed by Woodward, yeah." Laird's recollection was confirmed by his "aide at the time, Jerry Friedheim, who agreed that Woodward 'was one of several briefers.'" In addition, one of Haig's fellow NSC staff members—Roger Morris, who later wrote the first biography of Haig—"saw Woodward enter Haig's room" at the White House.* [29]

The different views between Woodward and the others may simply be a matter of semantics. What all admit is that Bob Woodward was handling official business for Joint Chiefs Chairman Moorer at the Nixon White House before Watergate. For many readers of *All the President's Men*, or those who know Woodward from either his portrayal by Robert Redford in the famous film or from Woodward's numerous TV appearances, that revelation is surprising enough.

By the spring of 1970, former FBI official Deke DeLoach said that "President Nixon was insatiable in his desire for intelligence. He would constantly ask the FBI for more and more intelligence to prove that the riots in our country were being caused by insurgent groups in foreign countries. And they weren't." The FBI, CIA, and U.S. military did ever-increasing amounts of domestic surveillance, primarily of anti-war and pro-civil-rights groups, but also at times of those Nixon perceived as his enemies.[30]

*The audio files of Moorer and Laird talking about Woodward briefing Haig can be heard at watergate.com.

It all came to a head on June 5, 1970, when Nixon met with J. Edgar Hoover, Richard Helms, and the heads of the National Security Agency and the Defense Intelligence Agency. As the DIA Chief later said, "Nixon chewed our butts." Pulitzer Prize–winning journalist Tim Weiner recently wrote that Nixon said "'revolutionary terrorism' was now the gravest threat" because in May of 1970,

> Campuses across the country had exploded after Nixon invaded Cambodia . . . National Guardsmen had shot and killed four students at Kent State . . . More than a hundred bombings, arson attacks, and shootings had followed . . . The Weathermen and the Panthers . . . had shown that they could hit draft boards, police stations, and banks at will.[31]

Nixon ordered Helms, Hoover, and the rest to come up with "a plan which will enable us to curtail the illegal activities of those who are determined to destroy our society." Working with a White House aide, Tom Huston, one of Hoover's Assistant Directors—William Sullivan—had already developed such a plan. Called the "Huston Plan," it "would all but abolish the restraints on intelligence collection." Even more, it would centralize control of domestic intelligence in the White House, giving Nixon complete control of an apparatus then spread through several agencies.[32]

President Nixon heartily embraced the plan and approved it. It would let Nixon and his staff take control of the U.S. government's large, mostly illegal domestic surveillance operation, with a view toward using it against Nixon's enemies. The plan would also help to keep damaging intelligence about the crimes of Nixon and his allies under their control. Nixon didn't want other federal agencies, or U.S. military intelligence, to find out about his illegal campaign contributions, not just from Howard Hughes, but also from foreign governments (South Vietnam, the U.S.-backed junta running Greece), large corporations, and mob-linked sources.[33]

On July 23, 1970, the Huston Plan was formally approved. But J. Edgar Hoover was livid about the plan, since he would be legally responsible for the Plan's abuses but not in full control of its operations. Nixon is said to have canceled the Plan a few days later, because of Hoover's complaints.[34]

Nixon's attempted power-grab had several important ramifications. First, White House Counsel John Dean was put in "charge of salvaging [parts of] the plan." As a result, Weiner writes that "electronic surveillances and surreptitious entries increased." Sometimes they were authorized by Sullivan, "sometimes at the command of Attorney General Mitchell, and sometimes on orders from the president himself." Thus began the expansion of White House domestic surveillance operations.[35]

As a result of the whole process, the already strained relationship between Hoover's FBI and Helms's CIA was finally broken. The aging-but-powerful FBI Director completely cut off intelligence sharing with the Agency. This left Helms in a dilemma on several fronts. He was being pressured by Nixon for more domestic intelligence, but Helms no longer had direct access to the Bureau, which helped to collect it. Helms was also being asked to do more and more risky operations—some outside the scope of the CIA's charter—whose exposure could end his career. In addition, he was at a huge disadvantage now with President Nixon, who had access to far-reaching FBI sources of information that Helms couldn't get.[36]

Ultimately, Richard Helms came up with a solution, one that would involve putting "retired" CIA officers in a position where they could access FBI information the Bureau was still supplying to the Nixon White House. Helms could also have the same CIA personnel undertake Nixon's risky political espionage activities, once they were no longer—or appeared to be no longer—employed by the CIA. This approach would have huge implications for Watergate.

Helms took advantage of a recent situation involving his trusted protégé E. Howard Hunt to put the CIA on the road to gaining access to intelligence the White House had, but that Helms couldn't get from the Bureau. It would also help to make Helms privy to the Nixon White House's increasing intelligence operations of its own, and later, even put some of those White House operations under Hunt's control.

After several years of lavish living, E. Howard Hunt had undergone financial problems because of injuries one of his children suffered in a car accident. Apparently having gone through most of the money from his share of the AMWORLD arms sell-off, Hunt needed more income than his CIA position could provide. In 1965, Hunt had apparently "retired" from the CIA for his covert assignment to Spain during the last of the CIA-Mafia plots with Rolando Cubela and Manuel Artime. However, a much later internal CIA investigation—after Watergate and the firing of Richard Helms—found that during

Hunt's first so-called retirement in 1965, "the statement disseminated for consumption within the Agency was that Mr. Hunt was retiring," but a former CIA official told investigators that "this was not generally believed." Indeed, Hunt's first retirement was just a sham, and he later officially rejoined the Agency in 1966.[37]

On April 24, 1970, Hunt would once more appear to retire from the CIA. Only 51, Hunt immediately joined the Mullen Company, a public relations company which had long assisted the CIA. According to a handwritten note on Hunt's CIA retirement memo, Richard Helms's Deputy Director for Plans told Hunt to "'stay in touch'—that the firm does provide cover" for CIA operatives.[38]

Peter Dale Scott summed up Hunt's CIA status after his official April 1970 retirement date by saying "we now have the CIA's first post-Watergate memo on Howard Hunt, showing that in 1970 he had not retired from the CIA, but instead had been released on covert assignment to the Mullen Agency." Declassified CIA memos, some possibly withheld from Watergate investigators, confirm that even after his retirement Hunt continued to do work for the CIA. Four weeks after Hunt's "retirement," two CIA officials said a Covert Security Approval "under project QKENCHANT was requested concerning Mr. Hunt." Five months later, the "Corporate Cover Branch" of the CIA granted the "Covert Security Approval" allowing Hunt to be used for CIA operations.[39]

The bottom line is that after his "retirement," Hunt was available to handle domestic operations in a more deniable way for Helms. Much of the time, the CIA assisted Hunt as if he were still an Agency employee, supplying fake identities, a disguise, technical equipment, and photo processing. For example, when Hunt asked the CIA "for an individual having skills in the area of locks and surreptitious entry [for a break-in involving] the Howard Hughes organization in Las Vegas," the CIA promptly referred a former Agency employee to Hunt.[40]

Hunt could be useful not only in handling domestic operations Helms didn't want the CIA officially involved in, but also in dealing with Cuban matters, especially now that he was outside the official CIA chain of command that included Nixon's man General Cushman. The Mullen Company had previously handled "the public relations effort of a covert Agency activity known as the Free Cuba Committee."[41]

The Mullen company's Robert Bennett was friendly with the White House, and that would give Hunt an opportunity to access some White House intelligence. An Agency memo confirms Hunt's statement that when he "retired" from the CIA, the original plan was for Hunt to eventually head the Mullen Company. From that position, Hunt would have been able to perform and direct work for both the CIA and the Nixon White House. However, when Robert Bennett purchased the Mullen firm, those plans changed, and Hunt would soon set his sights on joining the White House itself.[42]

Hunt wasn't the only longtime CIA veteran involved in 1960s Cuban operations to retire around this time. Shortly after the Huston Plan debacle, CIA officer James McCord retired from the Agency in August 1970. According to journalist Edward Jay Epstein, when he retired "McCord had been employed in the highly sensitive position of assistant director for security for the entire Central Intelligence Agency." McCord has indicated in testimony and his own writing that his resignation from the CIA was genuine. A future Watergate burglar, McCord established his own security firm. A year later, he would become Security Director for Richard Nixon's infamous Committee to Re-elect the President, known by some as CREEP.[43]

There was an odd postscript to the 1970 retirements of McCord and especially E. Howard Hunt, since Hunt had played such an important role for the CIA in helping Nixon (and JFK and LBJ) try to topple Fidel Castro. As documented earlier, President Kennedy's offer of a "no invasion pledge" for Cuba had never gone into effect after the Cuban Missile Crisis, because Fidel had never allowed the U.N. inspections for weapons of mass destruction that might remain in Cuba. As noted earlier, President Nixon had reinvigorated anti-Cuban operations, but they were on a far smaller scale than those of JFK. Still, Nixon-backed exile attacks on Cuba in March, April, and May of 1970 so worried Cuba that Castro had the Soviet Ambassador ask the United States to reaffirm JFK's pledge not to invade Cuba. In a surprising development, Nixon actually agreed. Thus, that "no invasion" pledge by a U.S. President still stands today, though in contrast to conventional history, it was actually made by Nixon in 1970, not by JFK in 1962.[44]

In 1970, Richard Nixon was far more worried about Chile than Cuba, because Chile appeared close to electing its first socialist President, Salvador Allende. Nixon was adamant that the U.S. government should not let that happen, and he directed the CIA to bear the brunt of that effort. To help prevent Allende's election, Richard Helms promoted David Atlee Phillips from heading Cuban operations to run all Latin American operations, including the CIA's Chile Task Force. Initially, the Nixon-CIA effort consisted of supplying "Allende's opponents with some millions of dollars" and covert election support ranging from propaganda to "dirty tricks," some of which echoed Nixon's past and future tactics. When Allende was elected on September 4, 1970, with just 36.3 percent of the vote, Nixon seized on that to claim he couldn't legitimately rule the country. (An odd rationale, since Nixon had only gotten 43 percent of the vote when he became the U.S. President.)[45]

Allende's victory still had to be confirmed by Chile's Congress, six weeks later. So, on September 15, 1970, with Richard Helms, Henry Kissinger, and Attorney General John Mitchell, an angry President Nixon

> told Helms that he wanted the CIA to make a major effort to prevent Allende's accession to power, including bribes to congressmen in Chile . . . If Helms needed $10 million, Nixon would approve it. More, if necessary. The President . . . wanted Helms to "make the [Chilean] economy scream." He ordered Helms to undertake the project as a "full-time job," using the "best men we have," but keeping the [American] embassy in the dark.[46]

However, the U.S. efforts were in vain, and Allende was sworn in on November 3, 1970. Nixon then ordered Helms and the CIA to begin an all-out campaign to overthrow Allende, which was similar in some ways to the anti-Castro operations of the early 1960s. The general effort was even code-named "Project Camelot," echoing the JFK-era operations. General Alexander Haig was involved, along with Nixon's National Security Advisor, Henry Kissinger. However, most of the burden fell on the Agency. One U.S. effort to topple Allende would be like a twisted version of the JFK-Almeida coup plan, involving some of the same people (Haig, Helms, Phillips, etc.). JFK had wanted to overthrow a dictator and establish a democracy, while in contrast Nixon wanted a coup to replace Chile's democracy with a dictator. However, Chile's most admired General, René Schneider, refused to be part of the coup plan and was killed by CIA-supported officers, leaving Allende in office. Working with Helms and Phillips on the coup was Artime's former case officer, Henry Heckshher, now the CIA Chief for Chile. CIA officer David Morales was soon deployed in Chile, to deadly effect.[47]

JFK's former CIA Director John McCone was on the board of ITT, a U.S. company that pushed for Allende's ouster, even as it donated heavily to President Nixon. (ITT had offered Helms and the CIA $1 million to block Allende's election.) The entire U.S. and CIA role in trying to topple Allende was supposed to be kept completely secret from Congress, the press, and the public. The following year, Nixon's Chile and Cuban operations would briefly merge, when David Atlee Phillips would oversee an assassination attempt against Fidel Castro in Chile.[48]

President Nixon also had the midterm elections to worry about in the fall of 1970. As part of his major effort to gain more Republican seats in the Democratic-controlled Senate, Nixon had convinced freshman Congressman George H.W. Bush of Texas to run for the Senate instead of defending his seat in Congress. To help his Senate candidates, Nixon had Herbert Kalmbach and other aides set up an illegal $3.9 million campaign slush fund called "Operation Town House," since "the money was disbursed out of a back room at a townhouse . . . near DuPont Circle in Washington." According to veteran AP and *Newsweek* reporter Robert Parry, after Watergate "Bush acknowledged that his [1970] campaign received the $106,000 from the Town House Project." Kalmbach "served six months in jail" for the illegal operation, but Parry wrote that even though Bush "was the principal beneficiary of the illegal operation, Bush wasn't charged in the criminal case." Bush lost the Senate election, and even with the help of Nixon's illegal campaign slush fund, Nixon's big push yielded only a two-seat gain in the Senate, while Republicans lost nine seats in the House. However, an appreciative Nixon made George H.W. Bush his U.N. Ambassador.[49]

In late 1970, Richard Nixon first faced off against one of his main antagonists during Watergate, the folksy-but-blunt North Carolina Senator Sam Ervin. Their battleground was the President's growing use of domestic surveillance. Ervin had become interested in the U.S. Army's domestic espionage activities in 1970 because of revelations by a whistleblower, former Army Intelligence officer Christopher H. Pyle. The officer revealed that "the U.S. Army Intelligence Command for the Continental United States ('CONUS intelligence') included more than one thousand undercover agents operating in a nationwide system with more than three hundred offices." The Army maintained a huge "data bank" that had "descriptions of lawful political activities of civilians wholly unassociated with the military." A magazine article resulted from Pyle's disclosures to Ervin, but the U.S. Army and Nixon administration rebuffed Senator Ervin's requests to learn more.[50]

According to the best account of what became known as "the Army Spy Scandal," the Army's "General Counsel . . . froze all responses to congressional inquiries. Agents received orders to gather only 'essential elements of information,' and not to discuss the CONUS operation with any civilian." Nixon's White House similarly stalled Ervin's investigation. A notation in H.R. Haldeman's diary for December 17, 1970 says, "the whole episode poses a major problem for us in the area of repression," then adds that "last June . . . the files [were] destroyed."

The frustrated Senator Ervin resorted to an old Nixon tactic and decided to hold hearings to expose the Army's domestic surveillance. Nixon again stymied Ervin, this time by sending

> . . . Assistant Attorney General William H. Rehnquist (later Chief Justice of the Supreme Court) to testify before Ervin's subcommittee . . . Rehnquist admitted that isolated examples of an abuse of government power had occurred [but] as had all other administration witnesses, he refused to divulge any more information about either the Army's previous domestic spying or the Justice Department's newest domestic security programs.[51]

An angry Senator Sam Ervin eventually had to close his hearings, since the Nixon White House was so uncooperative. The aging, portly Ervin was the type of conservative Southern Democrat that usually supported Richard Nixon—but not now. Less than two years later, Sam Ervin would confront Nixon's stonewalling again as Chairman of the Senate Watergate Committee, with far different results.[52]

In the final months of 1970, the top management of Howard Hughes's organization underwent a major shake-up, one that would soon critically impact Richard Nixon and Johnny Rosselli. Robert Maheu—Rosselli's friend and Nixon's long time associate, who had worked with both on the 1960 CIA-Mafia plots—had been running Howard Hughes's empire for the reclusive billionaire. In recent years, Hughes had been living at the Desert Inn casino and hotel, whose sale had been brokered by Rosselli. But the mobsters who originally owned that casino, and others bought by Hughes, had continued to skim sizable profits for themselves, since Maheu had retained them to manage the casinos. After two Mormon business associates of Hughes discovered the skimming, the billionaire secretly left the Desert Inn and flew to the Bahamas, where Hughes made a new home. Hughes also fired Robert Maheu, replacing him with Hughes's Mormon business associates.

As a result of the shake-up, Hughes stopped using the services of Larry O'Brien, who was still the Chairman of the Democratic National Committee, based at the Watergate. O'Brien had been earning more than $10,000 a month from Hughes for lobbying and public relations work. Nixon aide Charles Colson heard about the split, and in December 1970 wrote a memo to Nixon, saying that "Howard Hughes was dropping Larry O'Brien from his payroll (as his PR man in Washington) and replacing him with Bob Bennett . . . son of Republican Senator Wallace Bennett of Utah. Colson ended his memo, 'Bennett is a good friend of ours and has volunteered to do anything we want at any time with the Hughes people.'" Instead of Maheu, Nixon's new connection to Howard Hughes and the men running his empire would be Robert Bennett, whose PR firm, the Mullen Company, now employed E. Howard Hunt.[53]

A few weeks later, Nixon toyed with the idea of going after DNC Chairman Larry O'Brien, telling H.R. Haldeman, "We're going to nail O'Brien on this, one way or the other." John Dean was assigned to look into the matter. Robert Bennett was receptive to helping Nixon "expose O'Brien, but it had to be done in such a way as not to embarrass Hughes." After hearing that, Nixon had second thoughts, realizing there was no way to expose O'Brien without also dragging Hughes—and Bebe Rebozo, who'd gotten at least $100,00 from Hughes—into the matter. After ordering his aides to "keep Bob Bennett and Bebe out of this at all costs," Nixon dropped the whole O'Brien matter. A far bigger concern for Nixon had arisen, one involving Johnny Rosselli that the President needed to keep from being fully exposed.[54]

CHAPTER 25

January–July 1971: The Road to Watergate

On January 11, 1971, in a move that would have a major impact on Nixon's Presidency, Johnny Rosselli resumed contact with columnist Jack Anderson. The Mafia don faced both having to report to federal prison in only six weeks and being deported by INS after serving his sentence. Rosselli was desperate and was willing to do almost anything that might help him avoid that fate.[1]

Rosselli not only faced five years in prison for his Friars Club scheme and immigration violations, but his partner in the Friars Club scam had turned state's evidence and was giving information to the government. Two months earlier, Rosselli had tried having his new attorney, Tom Wadden, once again press the CIA to intervene for their former asset. Rosselli's case had gotten too much attention for him to avoid prison, but Rosselli wanted to at least avoid deportation. Toward that end, Rosselli had meetings with William Harvey, CIA official Jim O'Connell, and his old friend Robert Maheu. But a CIA memo says that "on November 18, 1970 . . . Mr. Helms flatly refused to intercede with INS on Rosselli's behalf."[2]

Johnny Rosselli's former allies in the CIA-Mafia plots—Carlos Marcello, Santo Trafficante, and Sam Giancana—weren't in a position to render much assistance to Rosselli. Fifty-nine-year-old Carlos Marcello was in prison, serving his sentence for striking the New Orleans FBI agent. Marcello had used his considerable political clout to shorten his sentence and ensure that he served it in a comfortable facility. Marcello had backed Nixon for years, and one of Marcello's "fixers"—who treaded the thin line between politics and crime—was close to Nixon's longtime aide Murray Chotiner. According to Marcello's biographer John H. Davis, the godfather "and his lawyers pulled every string at their command to get Carlos's two year sentence reduced . . . to six months and made arrangements for him to spend that time at the Medical Center for Federal Prisoners in Springfield, Missouri," one of the least secure and most comfortable federal facilities.[3]

As Rosselli had done prior to his previous leaks to Anderson in 1967, the Mafia don almost certainly got Santo Trafficante's approval before making his bold new move with Anderson in January 1971. To do otherwise could be fatal, as Rosselli would learn five years later. But Trafficante was apparently too busy running his ever-growing heroin network to provide Rosselli with any other assistance. Rosselli's original boss, Sam Giancana, was out of the picture, since he was still in Mexico and no longer ran the Chicago mob.

Another avenue of help no longer available to Rosselli was Robert Maheu and Howard Hughes. Rosselli had remained out of prison as long as Hughes lived in the United States, and Rosselli's friend Maheu ran the billionaire's empire, but now Hughes was in the Bahamas and Maheu had been fired. Maheu could no longer use Hughes's influence to render assistance to Rosselli—but he could help the Mafia don with their mutual associate, columnist Jack Anderson.

In January 1971, Johnny Rosselli was running out of time and options, so this time he made sure that Jack Anderson knew far more than he'd been told back in 1967. That was Rosselli's way of pressuring the CIA and Richard Helms—and the Nixon administration—to take some type of action to at least avoid his deportation. Rosselli had a willing collaborator in Jack Anderson. They shared some of the same associates (Robert Maheu, attorney Ed Morgan, publisher Hank Greenspun), and Anderson himself was desperate for big stories. His mentor and employer Drew Pearson had died a year and half earlier, leaving Anderson to carry on the column. While Pearson had been America's most popular columnist, and knew high officials like LBJ and Chief Justice Earl Warren, the forty-six-year-old Anderson was struggling to build his reputation. Anderson also shared his deceased mentor's dislike of Richard Nixon. However, Anderson was an odd mix, a devout Mormon who didn't drink, yet was willing to make ethical compromises for a big story or money.[4]

On January 18, Anderson ran the first of two new articles about the CIA-Mafia plots, asking again, "Could the plot against Castro have backfired against President Kennedy?" The new articles discussed "six [CIA] attempts against Cuba's Fidel Castro," including those involving CIA-trained "Cuban assassination teams equipped with high-powered rifles." Anderson said the Castro assassination plot he was writing about "began as part of the Bay of Pigs operation . . . to eliminate the Cuban dictator before the motley invaders landed." Anderson's linking of the Bay of Pigs operation to the CIA-Mafia plots would hit Nixon especially hard and would eventually light a new fire under his effort to get all the information the CIA had about "the Bay of Pigs thing."[5]

Anderson for the first time named some of the participants in the CIA-Mafia plots: Johnny Rosselli, William Harvey, James O'Connell, and Robert Maheu. However, Anderson's column didn't mention Santo Trafficante, Sam Giancana, or CIA officer David Morales. Richard Helms realized that Rosselli still had those bombshells—and others—to drop, if he chose. Even worse for Helms, Anderson had spoken to former CIA Director John McCone, who "vigorously denied that the CIA had ever participated in any plot on Castro's life. Asked whether the attempts could have been made without his knowledge, [McCone] replied: 'It could not have happened.'" But Helms knew the CIA-Mafia plots had happened and just how much he'd kept hidden from McCone, JFK, and LBJ.[6]

In the articles, Anderson wrote that the CIA-Mafia plots continued until March 1963. Helms would have known that Rosselli had included some details from a real incident: the March 13, 1963, attempt to assassinate Fidel near the University of Havana, using mortars, bazookas, and machine guns. As mentioned earlier, JFK's personal emissary, James Donovan, had been in Cuba around that time, trying to negotiate the release of twenty-one prisoners, including three CIA agents. Like all the attempts, that March 1963 Castro assassination attempt had been totally unauthorized by, and unknown to, the Kennedys and McCone. That plot wouldn't become public until 1975, when the press finally got a look at the Cuban government Dossier that detailed the attempt, the same Dossier that was the main target of the Watergate break-ins. Helms and the CIA must have gotten some inquires from the press about Anderson's columns, which appeared in hundreds of newspapers. If so, they were effectively quashed, and just as in 1967, Anderson's new 1971 revelations weren't followed up, or even reported, by any of the nation's press or television networks.

Jack Anderson's early 1971 columns about Rosselli also alarmed the Nixon White House. The day Anderson's second column ran, Nixon's

Attorney General, John Mitchell, called Robert Maheu, who was being pressured by a grand jury at the time. Maheu immediately flew to Washington and told Mitchell what he knew about the CIA-Mafia plots. Robert Maheu later told Anthony Summers that Mitchell was "shaking" when he finished. Mitchell was a tough, gruff, no-nonsense New York power lawyer and World War II veteran. However, it's not hard to imagine Mitchell "shaking" if Maheu gave Mitchell the same accurate account that Maheu had recently confided to his friend Pierre Salinger, whom Maheu had told[7]

> that the CIA [in 1960] had been in touch with Nixon, who had asked them to go forward with this project . . . It was Nixon who had him do a deal with the Mafia in Florida to kill Castro.[8]

Attorney General Mitchell, Nixon's former campaign manager, would have known what it would mean to Nixon's chances in the next election if that information ever became public. Mitchell let Maheu avoid the grand jury in return for keeping the plots secret. In addition, Mitchell then had his Assistant Attorney General look for any Justice Department files about the CIA-Mafia plots.[9]

The Anderson-Rosselli articles also "triggered a spate of memos inside the Nixon White House," according to Peter Dale Scott. A February 1, 1971, memo to John Dean about "Jack Anderson's column" and "Maheu's covert activities . . . with [the] CIA" warned President Nixon that "Maheu's controversial activities . . . might well shake loose Republican skeletons from the closet." Nixon's young aides, like Counsel John Dean and Chief of Staff H.R. Haldeman, didn't know about the CIA-Mafia plots, but they were worried about Maheu's involvement with Howard Hughes. Their worries ranged from all the money Nixon had received from Hughes—especially the $100,000 given to Rebozo—to Maheu's ongoing friendship with Larry O'Brien, chairman of the DNC.[10]

But Richard Nixon's concerns about the Jack Anderson columns were even more serious than those of his aides, and they went beyond Nixon's work on the plots in 1960. As related by Anderson, Rosselli dated one of the CIA-Mafia attempts to kill Fidel in March 1963. That was when Nixon's friend William Pawley was getting involved with Rosselli in the Soviet missile technician scam (detailed in Chapter 12) that was part of the CIA-Mafia attempts. Rosselli's work for the CIA had continued through the time of JFK's assassination, essentially linking all of the plotting against Castro to JFK's November 1963 murder.

Also in November 1963, Nixon had become involved with two partners of former Cuban President Carlos Prio, who had infiltrated part of the JFK-Almeida coup plan.* Nixon could ill afford to have it come out that his associates had infiltrated a plot that somehow backfired on JFK, or that the CIA was plotting assassinations with the Mafia while he was Vice President. Nixon had enough direct and indirect ties to Trafficante and Rosselli that—as H.R. Haldeman later wrote—Nixon accurately suspected the CIA-Mafia plots that spawned the Bay of Pigs invasion were somehow tied to JFK's murder.[11]

A Senate Watergate Committee memo, quoted here for the first time, said the Justice Department's "sensitive 'Castro file'" about Rosselli and the CIA-Mafia plots was shown "to Attorney General Mitchell, in January 1971." Given "the political implications of the information . . . Attorney General Mitchell discussed the contents of the sensitive [Rosselli] file with President Nixon." Their "concerns" would later spur the Watergate break-ins.[12]

President Nixon took two lines of attack to deal with his worries over the Anderson-Rosselli revelations. First, to deal with the overall problem, Nixon aides John Dean and H.R. Haldeman turned to the Mullen Company, the Washington public relations firm recently taken over by Robert Bennett. The company often worked for the CIA, including providing cover for CIA employees, and it also counted Howard Hughes as a client. In a January 26, 1971, memo, Nixon aide Chuck Colson stressed again that Robert Bennett was "a trusted and good friend of the Administration." Bennett had also assumed the role of giving the Nixon campaign legal contributions from Howard Hughes, and Bennett's employee at the Mullen Company, E. Howard Hunt, had his own ties to Nixon and the CIA-Mafia plots with Rosselli.[13]

Second, Nixon would begin pressing CIA Director Richard Helms for more information about the "Bay of Pigs thing," meaning the CIA-Mafia plots (and any tie they might have had to JFK's assassination). Nixon wouldn't get the reports he wanted from Helms—but he would get E. Howard Hunt.[14]

As for Johnny Rosselli, Jack Anderson's columns produced no

*As described earlier, a fall 1963 CIA memo said that two of Prio's partners "have become associated [with] Richard Nixon in accordance with [a] Republican Party plan [to] bring up the Cuban case before [1964] elections."

immediate benefit, but—as Helms and/or Nixon had time to consider their alternatives—Rosselli would soon see some positive results. On February 25, 1971, Rosselli entered the federal prison system. Less than three weeks later, Carlos Marcello was released from his brief stay in prison. Like Rosselli, Marcello was an illegal alien, and the godfather should have been deported decades earlier. However, when Marcello was released from prison, he wasn't deported, and instead returned home to his Louisiana mansion to resume hands-on control of his billion-dollar crime empire. Perhaps Marcello's knowledge of his $500,000 bribe to Nixon in 1960 accounted for the Nixon administration's seeming lack of interest in having Marcello deported. Marcello had been able to run his empire from prison and, thanks to Springfield's excellent medical staff, emerged from prison much healthier and more fit, ready for his most prosperous decade.*[15]

After Rosselli entered prison, Senate investigators later documented that "the CIA approached the Immigration and Naturalization Service, Department of Justice, to 'forestall public disclosure of Rosselli's past operational activity with the CIA' that might occur if deportation proceedings were brought." As a result of that approach, which had to have been authorized by Richard Helms, the CIA admitted that it had a "meeting with INS regarding the status of the deportation proceedings [in] March 1971," just after Rosselli entered prison. The INS deportation efforts were halted at that time, sparing Helms—and Nixon—further revelations about the CIA-Mafia plots.[16]

For reasons never explained, Rosselli's prison sentence mysteriously got shorter. Rosselli's attorney's plea to the original judge in July 1971, to reduce Rosselli's sentence because of his service to the CIA, was rejected in open court by the judge. Yet three months later, for no apparent reason and with no additional hearing, the judge suddenly took one year off Rosselli's sentence. That way, Rosselli would wind up serving barely half of his original sentence. It's not known whether that intervention was due to Helms or Attorney General Mitchell or someone else. Now that he had a shorter sentence and no current deportation proceedings, Rosselli stopped leaking information to Jack Anderson—at least for a while.[17]

. . .

*When Marcello returned to prison in the 1980s, FBI officials bugged his prison cell (with court authorization), recording the godfather talking about dozens of his crimes, including the murder of JFK. There is no evidence Hoover attempted to similarly monitor Marcello at Springfield in 1970–71.

President Nixon had his famous audio taping system installed, beginning in February 1971, following in the footsteps of previous chief executives like JFK and LBJ. Nixon, however, far outdid his predecessors; his system was much more elaborate and went beyond the Oval Office. Nixon also had microphones installed at his little-known office in the Old Executive Office Building, where several of his crimes were planned. All of the microphones were voice-activated, and more were installed in White House's Lincoln Sitting Room, at Camp David, and in the Cabinet Room. Certain of Nixon's phones were set to be recorded as well.

Nixon never intended for these recordings to be heard by the public or most of his staff. They were intended only for Nixon, primarily to use in preparing his memoirs and to have a record of key discussions should questions arise about what was said. In many ways, they give us a fascinating historical record and a look into Nixon's Presidency. However, since Nixon always knew when and where he was being recorded, other parts of his Presidency remain hidden—especially those parts he knew he would never want to include in his memoirs or have a record of. Nixon was careful not to talk about his actions involving the Mafia and the sources of some his large illegal contributions, so those had to be documented later by government investigators and journalists.

Still, it is amazing just how many crimes Nixon did discuss on tape, from the system's beginning in 1971 until taping stopped on July 12, 1973. Nixon talked on the tapes about planning crimes and about crimes already committed, including bribery, obstruction of justice, and illegal retaliation against perceived enemies, including break-ins. Even bombings were discussed.

When Nixon and his staff demanded a campaign contribution of $2 million from the dairy industry, some of the conversations—and Nixon's Oval Office meeting with members of the group—were actually recorded. In return, Nixon and his administration agreed to make sure higher government price supports were approved, which—according to some estimates—resulted in the U.S. government spending more than ten times that amount. Some of that $2 million dollars would be spent on Nixon's criminal campaign activities by the Watergate crew. In addition, the milk bribe was just part of a flood of illegal corporate cash that flowed into Nixon's campaign coffers in 1971 and 1972, often from some of America's most prominent companies.[18]

Only seventy hours of tapes—out of thousands of hours—were

released in the 1970s. More began to be released in the 1990s, and they reveal Nixon to be both racist and sexist. While Nixon's personal views on race had been quite tolerant into the 1950s, he does not appear to have changed with the times. Nixon also made numerous anti-Semitic remarks.[19]

Nixon's extensive taping system was known by only few in the White House: Nixon, Chief of Staff H. R. Haldeman, Alexander Butterfield, and the four Secret Service agents who managed the equipment. The taping system was basically under the control of Alexander Butterfield while he was in the White House—and it would be Butterfield's dramatic revelation of the tapes that would doom any chance Nixon had of riding out the Watergate scandal.

Understanding why, when, and how E. Howard Hunt first got his job in Richard Nixon's White House is critical to the hidden history of Watergate, and the documented story is often at odds with conventional accounts of the scandal. For example, many articles about Watergate say it all began after *The New York Times* first published the leaked Pentagon Papers on June 13, 1971. As the story goes, Nixon was furious, so his aides created a group to plug leaks, called the "Plumbers." Because Charles Colson was acquainted with E. Howard Hunt, the retired CIA agent Hunt was hired to work with the Plumbers on July 7, 1971. And the rest—including the Watergate break-ins the following year—is history. Except a close examination of the documentation shows that's not exactly what happened.[20]

Why did Hunt want a job in the Nixon White House? As discussed earlier, his plan to eventually own the Mullen Company hadn't worked out, after Robert Bennett purchased the firm. However, given Hunt's oft-stated financial needs and concerns, and the fact that he'd left the CIA for the more lucrative business world, it does seem odd that he would seek a political position that could end with next year's election. Hunt's PR and writing skills—and the patronage of his mentor, CIA Director Helms—surely could have landed him a lucrative and stable career in any number of CIA proprietary firms or companies that sometimes helped the Agency.

However, it's not difficult to imagine Richard Helms's stunned reaction to Jack Anderson's two recent articles about the CIA-Mafia plots, the Bay of Pigs invasion, and the Kennedys' 1963 anti-Castro operations—all of which had involved Helms's protégé, Hunt. Some of their concerns would have also matched those of President Nixon. Getting Hunt into Nixon's White House would be good for both Helms and Hunt. Keeping the CIA-Mafia plots from being further exposed would help all three men ensure their roles in them were never revealed. As discussed earlier, if Helms got Hunt into the White House in an intelligence role, that would give Helms—and the CIA—access to FBI and White House intelligence that Helms had no other way to obtain. Finally, the more Hunt could do in Nixon's domestic spying as part of the President's staff, the fewer risky political missions the CIA and Helms would have to undertake for Nixon.

Getting Hunt into the Nixon White House was the perfect solution to several problems, but the approach would have to be made carefully, to avoid arousing the suspicions of Nixon or his aides that CIA veteran Hunt was some type of CIA "plant." In hindsight, it's obvious to many that's exactly what Hunt was. Pulitzer Prize–winning *New York Times* journalist J. Anthony Lukas wrote that "there are those who believe that Hunt had never really resigned from the CIA and was still acting more or less on behalf of the Agency" when he went to work for the Nixon White House. Included among those with that opinion would be Charles Colson, who—after Watergate—realized that "all the time Hunt was on the White House payroll . . . Hunt's secretary was on the CIA payroll." That led Colson to ask, "Was Hunt, supposedly a retired CIA agent, actually an active agent while in the White House?" Even Richard Nixon harbored similar suspicions after Watergate, asking Haldeman, "[Did you know] that Helms ordered Bennett to hire Howard Hunt? Did you know that Hunt was on the payroll of the Bennett firm at the same time that he was on the White House payroll?" The House Intelligence Committee would later find a CIA report admitting "a practice of detailing CIA employees to the White House [including] in 'intimate components of the Office of the President.'"[21]

But those views would only come out in the mid-1970s, after the Watergate scandal exploded. In 1971, after the Anderson-Rosselli articles, Hunt carefully maneuvered himself into position. Nixon aide Charles Colson told H.R. Haldeman that "early in 1971, Hunt and Bennett began visiting me from time to time to offer their services on a volunteer basis to help the White House in outside efforts or in political matters." Hunt and Colson had met "in the late 1960s" at Washington's alumni club for Brown University, where Colson was president and Hunt vice president. E. Howard Hunt "cultivated Colson carefully," according to J. Anthony Lukas.[22]

Hunt's efforts paid off, because in April 1971 he resumed contact with his former assistant, Cuban exile and former CIA agent Bernard Barker. Hunt has told and written many times how he reconnected with Barker in Miami for the tenth anniversary of the Bay of Pigs in April 1971, telling him things were getting started again about Cuba, with a new operational group to be backed by the Nixon White House. Hunt offered Barker a role in his new White House group, and Barker quickly accepted.[23]

The problem with the conventional story of Watergate is that it says Hunt was not offered a position by the White House until July 7, almost three months *after* Hunt reconnected with Barker in April 1971. Yet Hunt's account was confirmed by both Barker and Eugenio Martinez, who was also recruited by Hunt at the same time in Miami. In addition, April 1971 is almost two months before Richard Nixon and his staff first heard about the Pentagon Papers or their publication—the conventional story's rationale for the White House hiring Hunt in the first place. As for how Hunt came to be working for the White House in April 1971, previous chapters have documented that Nixon had met Hunt at least twice before, and Hunt had dealt with Nixon's aide General Cushman—if not Nixon himself—during the 1960 era of the CIA-Mafia plots with Johnny Rosselli. By 1971, Cushman was Nixon's Deputy CIA Director, while Hunt was looking for a way out of the CIA-proprietary PR firm the Mullen Company, and a way to get into the White House. Since the weight of the evidence demonstrates that Hunt was still working for Helms and the Agency after his retirement (under deep cover, as he had in Spain in 1965), the mission Hunt was recruiting Barker for in April could be viewed as a CIA mission as well as one for the Nixon White House.[24]

It's logical that Hunt would turn to Barker, regardless of whatever doubts Helms might have had about Barker because of his Mafia ties. Barker had made Hunt wealthy for a time, and Hunt trusted him. For Helms, Barker could also be useful because of the business ties he and his associates—like Eugenio Martinez—had to Bebe Rebozo and Richard Nixon. That meant if an operation involving Barker (or Hunt) ever backfired, Nixon would need to cover it up to protect himself, which would also protect the CIA—which is exactly what happened after Watergate. As for Barker, he had much incentive to make sure sensitive information didn't become widely known about the full extent of the CIA's plotting with the Mafia. The same was true for Barker's boss in organized crime, Santo Trafficante, who probably welcomed the chance for one of his men to be close to both CIA and White House operations, just as Barker had worked on Kennedy and CIA operations back in 1963.[25]

The original plan E. Howard Hunt explained to Barker in April 1971 was much larger than what eventually developed, even though the full extent of Watergate and related operations has never really been established. Hunt originally told Barker that his new operation "would reactivate 120 CIA veterans." The total never came close to that, but most people don't realize that at least a dozen rarely noted Cuban exiles (including Artime and Prio) were involved with Hunt, in addition to those eventually arrested at the Watergate. There are some indications that the total was much higher. In any event, as Barker said in a later interview, "I recruited the men and started the training."[26]

Barker worked for Hunt for free (aside from expense reimbursement), even though Hunt and fellow "Plumber" G. Gordon Liddy were reportedly paid more than a thousand dollars for each break-in (eventually much more), and Hunt was paid $100 a day in his role as a White House "consultant." Barker claimed he worked for Hunt and the White House out of patriotism and because he hoped the operation would eventually topple Castro. While those likely were factors, the normally tightfisted Barker's largesse is probably more attributable to the fact he was also doing it for Trafficante.[27]

It's logical that Barker would soon recruit for Hunt another Trafficante man, Frank Fiorini, by then using the name "Frank Sturgis." (For consistency, this book will continue to refer to him as "Frank Fiorini," unless quoting from a source that uses "Sturgis.") FBI reports say that "Fiorini has the reputation among Cuban exile activists of being a most untrustworthy, discredited, unsavory gangster type" and "of being a mercenary with Mafia type connections." Also aiding Hunt and Barker would be Hunt's good friend, Manuel Artime, who was still involved with Trafficante's drug network.[28]

Most of the others recruited by Barker for Hunt would be Cuban exiles with connections to the CIA but not the Mafia, and in several months they would be joined by former FBI agent G. Gordon Liddy. In a much later deposition, Liddy testified that when he joined the group, "Mr. Hunt, to impress upon me the high caliber of these individuals, stated that they had accounted among them for a substantial number of deaths [and] he indicated that these . . . Cuban individuals were connected in some way with organized crime."[29]

For the next year and a half, in the months leading to the Watergate arrests, godfather Santo Trafficante would have Barker do essentially the same thing Barker had done for him during the JFK-Almeida coup plan. Barker would work on the most secret operations of the President and the CIA (specifically those of Richard Helms), while also advancing Trafficante's interests and protecting the godfather. As in 1963, while Barker would have wanted to help Hunt or Nixon when possible, Barker's main loyalty would have been to Trafficante, simply as a matter of self-preservation.

As with the JFK-Almeida coup plan, Barker didn't have a highly placed role in the Plumbers operations leading to Watergate (though he was more highly placed than he had been in 1963), but Barker was once again in the right place at the right time to serve Trafficante's needs. As a result of his long experience in "gangster activities" and his seven years with the CIA, apparently Barker was able to juggle his many roles with few problems: being a successful businessman and working for Hunt, while also still dealing with Trafficante.[30]

J. Anthony Lukas analyzed Barker's carefully compartmentalized life, providing insight into how Barker could commit the crimes he did. Lukas said that

> In Miami, Barker led the life of a prosperous real estate man. But he had another life which he kept quite separate. Later, [Barker] wrote about his two lives: "If I am asked my name on a mission, I give my operating name. That is not a lie; it is a cover. I am not Barker then. I am another person. It is a different dimension. I, Barker, would never go into a building in the dark of night, but . . . this other guy with a false name . . . could very well do this."[31]

Overtly, Hunt was using Cuban exiles in what became the Plumbers unit because—as later explained by a Cuban exile to a Congressional committee—"When Bay of Pigs operatives like Hunt moved [on] to Watergate, they sent for their old Cubanos. They work a little like a Mafia [and] when they want to issue . . . what looks like an anti-Communist contract, they contact us. We're reliable, intelligent, professional. And we're learning to keep our mouths shut [because] we fear the [CIA] . . . the [CIA] can drop a word and change your life." Of course, another reason Hunt used primarily Cuban exile CIA agents like Barker would have been to protect Agency secrets about Cuban operations that Hunt and Helms wanted to stay hidden.[32]

Bernard Barker's business partner Eugenio Martinez also became one of the Watergate burglars, but he was different from Barker in several important ways. As noted earlier, Martinez was not tied to the Mafia as was Barker. But more importantly, when Martinez was recruited by Hunt and Barker in April 1971—and through the time Martinez was arrested at the Watergate—the Agency admits that Martinez was an active-duty CIA agent. He drew a small salary and met regularly with his CIA case officer. While the CIA's former premier "boatman" was no longer covertly ferrying agents into—and out of—Cuba, Martinez was still a valued and respected member of Miami's Cuban exile community. The use of an active CIA agent like Martinez is one more indication that Hunt's operation for the White House also served the needs of Richard Helms and the CIA.[33]

Eugenio Martinez has written about going with his "lifelong friend, Bernard Barker," to meet E. Howard Hunt—the famous "Eduardo" from the Bay of Pigs—on April 16, 1971. Appropriately, that was the tenth anniversary of the invasion, and they met at the Miami monument dedicated to the exiles who fought in the invasion. Over lunch at a Cuban restaurant, Hunt

> told us that he had retired from the CIA in 1971 . . . I knew just what he was saying. I was also officially retired from the Company. Two years before, my case officer had gathered all the men in my Company unit and handed us envelopes with retirement announcements inside. But mine was a blank paper. Afterward he explained to me that I would stop making my boat missions to Cuba but I would continue my work with the Company . . . I was quite certain that day that [Hunt] knew [I was still employed by the CIA]. We talked about the liberation of Cuba, and he assured us that "the whole thing is not over."

Finally, Martinez was unlike Barker in another important way: He didn't share the far-right, ultra-conservative viewpoint of Hunt, Barker, and their friend Manuel Artime. Years later, when journalist Haynes Johnson wrote in *The Washington Post* about a post-Watergate Bill Moyers special covering the "Secret War" between the United States and Cuba, Haynes said,

> Bernard Barker and [Eugenio] Martinez could not be more different. Barker comes over sneering, posturing, with an air of ugly venality as he defends the various illegal acts in which he participated. When [journalist] George Crile remarks that it sounds like declaring war on the democratic system itself, with an analogy to the Nazis, Barker reacts venomously and angrily: "In other words we can't organize anything to defend ourselves. Huh? Because we are afraid that some people may call us Nazis." [In contrast,] Martinez speaks with disturbing eloquence, expressing in a rush of emotion so many doubts and so many contradictions and so many dilemmas.

As 1971 progressed, President Richard Nixon struggled with the domestic reaction to the increasingly unpopular war in Vietnam. On May 3, 1971, there was another large antiwar demonstration in Washington, but this time it turned violent, with "policemen swinging their nightsticks indiscriminately." Author James Rosen said that "more than seven thousand citizens were dragged off the streets . . . the largest number of mass arrests in American history." And it wasn't just demonstrators who wanted the United States out of Vietnam. By May of that year, 61 percent of all those surveyed in a Gallup Poll said "the Vietnam War was a mistake," a record high for any U.S. war. The American public was about to see evidence of that mistake, thanks to Daniel Ellsberg and what came to be called the Pentagon Papers.[34]

Daniel Ellsberg has been a progressive icon for four decades, but he didn't start out that way. Ellsberg had a Ph.D. in economics from Harvard and had been a First Lieutenant in the Marines. In 1964, he'd gone to work at the Pentagon, where on his first day he helped to first report the Gulf of Tonkin incident to Defense Secretary McNamara. In 1965 and 1966, Ellsberg was sent to Vietnam to work with General Edward Lansdale, the former head of JFK's Operation Mongoose.[35]

In Vietnam, Daniel Ellsberg's biographer writes that Ellsberg "was a fierce defender of [the war] and seemingly a genuine war lover." While in Vietnam in 1966, Ellsberg became quite friendly with writer Francis FitzGerald, the daughter of Desmond FitzGerald, then the CIA's Deputy Director for Plans under Richard Helms. Daniel Ellsberg's associates in Vietnam say that Ellsberg "was going out with [Frances] FitzGerald" and that Ellsberg "squired her around Saigon all the time when she was there." Though Ellsberg was a hawk, FitzGerald said he "was one of the few people in the government . . . who you could really have a serious talk with about the war."[36]

After returning to the United States in 1967, Ellsberg did Pentagon-related work for the RAND think tank. Ellsberg was also one of thirty-six people who worked for eighteen months on Defense Secretary Robert McNamara's forty-seven-volume, seven-thousand-page study of U.S. decision making during the Vietnam conflict. The results were highly classified, and only about fifteen copies were made.

In 1969, Ellsberg was still working for RAND when he had a change of heart after hearing a draft resister speak at a conference. Ellsberg then made an unauthorized copy of the massive classified Vietnam study he'd helped to prepare, and in 1970 he tried without success to leak it to several Senators. He then shared it with *New York Times* reporter Neil Sheehan. *The Times* decided to print the documents—the Pentagon Papers—in several installments.

Richard Nixon wasn't especially concerned when *The Times* published the first installment of the Pentagon Papers as a major front-page story on Sunday, June 13, 1971. Nixon "skipped over the *Times* story" and focused instead on "coverage of his daughter Tricia's wedding." It was Alexander Haig who told Nixon about "this Goddamn *New York Times* expose of the most highly classified documents of the war." Nixon still didn't seem overly concerned, since—as Henry Kissinger later pointed out—"none of the Pentagon Papers dealt with the Nixon administration."[37]

Kissinger shared Haig's concern, but President Nixon was in no rush to take action. Nixon mused that "if the statue of limitations is a year" on leaking classified files, they would wait until the statue was almost up and then "charge them . . . subpoena all the bastards and bring the case." Haig said "immediate action would only escalate the crisis," and Nixon agreed.[38]

Over the course of the next few days, Nixon's attitude started to change, as *The Times* continued to run more of the Pentagon Papers. After the second day's story—headlined "A Consensus to Bomb Developed Before '64 Election, Study Says"—it was Al Haig who told Nixon that Daniel Ellsberg had leaked the story. Attorney General Mitchell wanted to send a "cease and desist" order to *The Times,* but Nixon said, "Hell, I wouldn't prosecute the *Times*. My view is to prosecute the Goddamn pricks that gave [the Pentagon Papers] to them." That was the day when Henry Kissinger finally got Nixon to take on the matter as a major cause, to stop *The Times* from publishing more of the Pentagon Papers. Henry Kissinger changed Nixon's mind by giving what Haldeman called one of Kissinger's "most passionate tirades [that was] beyond belief." Nixon was likely receptive to Kissinger's performance, because even though the Pentagon Papers had nothing to do with Nixon, they showed all too well how Presidents could say one thing in public and do exactly the opposite in private.[39]

Nixon had Mitchell send the cease-and-desist order, but *The Times* made Mitchell's telegram its lead story the next day, along with another installment of the Pentagon Papers, headlined "Study Tells How Johnson Secretly Opened Way to Ground Combat." Nixon then went on the attack. Amid anti-Semitic rants against *The Times* and Ellsberg, the President had Mitchell get a court injunction against *The Times* to stop the publication of more stories. Ellsberg and an associate were also sought, so they could be charged with violating the Espionage Act. And in an ironic twist, Nixon would reference his tactics of leaking against Alger Hiss more than two decades earlier, when he told Mitchell to "try him [Ellsberg] in the press. Everything, John, there is on the investigation—get it out, leak it out. We want to destroy him in the press." Nixon told Haldeman that "We won the Hiss case in the papers [and now] we're destroying these people in the papers."[40]

The court injunction halting the series by *The Times* was a chilling "freedom of the press" ruling. Other newspapers rallied to the cause of *The Times* and the Pentagon Papers, including *The Washington Post* and its editor Ben Bradlee. After he had one of his reporters get a set of the Pentagon Papers, Bradlee wanted to publish them despite the court injunction against *The Times*. He also wanted the circulation boost, since *The Post* was not yet a national paper and still wasn't even the largest newspaper in Washington (that was *The Washington Star*). But the attorneys at the New York law firm used by *The Post* warned Bradlee to wait until after *The Times*'s appeal against the injunction had been decided.[41]

By 1971, thirty-nine-year-old Joseph Califano and his new law partner, Edward Bennett Williams, badly wanted *The Post* as a client for their small firm in Washington. Williams had formerly represented clients such as Jimmy Hoffa and Sam Giancana, in cases discussed earlier, and had first introduced Johnny Rosselli to Robert Maheu. But in recent years Williams had dropped those mob-linked clients (though he still represented the Teamsters) while trying to build a more reputable image and clientele. Adding Joseph Califano to his firm was part of that effort, as was Williams's ownership of the Washington Redskins football team; adding a prestigious client like *The Post* would be a major coup for his firm. When Ben Bradlee called Edward Bennett Williams for his advice about whether to publish the Pentagon Papers, Williams said *The Post* should go ahead and publish them. *Washington Post* owner Katherine Graham agreed, and *The Post* published the Pentagon Papers for two days—starting on June 18, 1971—before Nixon and Mitchell were granted another injunction that forced them to stop.[42]

Ben Bradlee wanted Williams to argue *The Post*'s appeal, but Williams and Califano were tied up with other cases. Still, Williams's advice—and the resulting attention *The Post* gained from its publication of the Pentagon Papers—left a very favorable impression on Ben Bradlee and Katherine Graham. By the end of the year, Joseph Califano and Edward Bennett Williams would become the law firm for *The Washington Post,* adding the newspaper to a client list that already included Larry O'Brien's Democratic National Committee, headquartered at the Watergate. A year after *The Post*'s publication of the Pentagon Papers, Joseph Califano would be the key figure who first got *The Post*—and the DNC—to go after the story of Watergate.[43]

On June 30, 1971, the U.S. Supreme Court lifted the Nixon administration's injunction against *The Times* and *The Post*, allowing publication of the Pentagon Papers to resume. During this time, Nixon became consumed with paranoia about leaks, ordering H.R. Haldeman to "confront personally every single Cabinet officer and agency head, brutally chew them out and threaten them with extinction if they don't stop all leaks in the future." Yet at the same time, Nixon told Haldeman and other aides that he wanted to "develop a new program, a program for leaking out information" that would benefit Nixon.[44]

Four days after the first publication of the Pentagon Papers, Nixon decided to try to obtain an LBJ administration file about the October 1968 bombing halt in Vietnam to leak to the press in order to embarrass former LBJ officials who were critical of Nixon's conduct of the war. President Nixon thought the file was at the Brookings Institute, a centrist Washington think tank—and Nixon was shockingly blunt on the White House tapes about what he wanted done.[45]

"Goddamnit, get in and get those files. Blow the safe and get it!"

Nixon ordered Haldeman and Kissinger on June 17, 1971, in the Oval Office. Nixon reiterated his orders on June 30, this time to a group of five officials that included Haldeman, Attorney General John Mitchell, and Defense Secretary Melvin Laird. Only this time, Nixon suggested E. Howard Hunt for the operation.[46]

> *President Nixon:* "Brookings, I want them just to break in and take it out. Do you understand?
>
> *Haldeman:* "Yeah. But you have to have somebody to do it."
>
> *President Nixon:* That's what I'm talking about. Don't discuss it here. You talk to [E. Howard] Hunt. I want the break-in. Hell, they do that. You're to break into the place, rifle the files, and bring them in . . . just go in and take it . . . I mean *clean it up*![47] [Emphasis added.]

As discussed earlier, the conventional story says that Hunt would not even be interviewed for a White House job for another week, yet Nixon was already familiar with Hunt, who had previously recruited Barker and Martinez in April. The President was even familiar with Hunt's special skills (Hunt had burglarized embassies for the CIA since the 1950s, when he first met Nixon). It's also important to point out that Nixon said "don't discuss it here," because they were being recorded and because Nixon's order was completely illegal.

Richard Nixon expected Hunt to be ready for quick action, because the next day, July 1, Nixon asked, "Did they get the Brookings Institute raided last night? No. Get it done. I want it done. I want the Brookings Institute's safe *cleaned out* and have it cleaned out in a way that it makes somebody else [responsible.]" (Emphasis in original.)[48]

Soon after Nixon's orders, John Dean would later write that "Jack Caulfield arrived in my office to tell me that Chuck Colson had ordered him to 'fire-bomb' the Brookings Institute, and then to send burglars in to retrieve government papers related to what the President wanted." Not aware "that Nixon himself had ordered the break in," Dean "flew to San Clemente" and protested to Nixon. The Brookings Institute wasn't firebombed or burglarized, but Nixon's willingness to order political break-ins using Hunt and others would soon surface again.[49]

. . .

On June 24, 1971, Nixon decided to leak information from government files to harm the Democrats, proclaiming to Haldeman and Press Secretary Ron Ziegler: "We're going to expose them . . . and the Democratic Party will [be] gone without a trace if we do this correctly." Nixon said, "What you really need is . . . an Ellsberg who's on our side" to do the leaking. The President worried that after the Ellsberg leaks, "people are . . . probably burning stuff and hiding stuff as fast as they can." Nixon knew where he wanted to start, saying "I want to go back to the Cuban Missile Crisis and I want to go to the Bay of Pigs." Nixon mentioned those subjects again on July 1, and once more on July 2, when he said "we do really need . . . somebody that understands the Cuban Missile Crisis and understands the Bay of Pigs." Nixon's concern about the Bay of Pigs material is understandable, given the Anderson-Rosselli articles earlier in the year and Ellsberg's example of how classified material can leak with no prior warning—and Nixon's concerns about the Cuban operation would only grow in the coming months.[50]

On July 1, 1971, Nixon aide Charles Colson called his acquaintance E. Howard Hunt to ask if he might be interested in helping to "mount a major public case against Ellsberg and [his] co-conspirators." Using Colson's own words, Hunt agreed that they should "go down the line to nail the guy cold."[51]

Also on July 1, in a meeting with Nixon, Haldeman, and Ehrlichman, Charles Colson began to tell the President about "one guy on the outside that has this capacity and ideological bent who might be able to do all of this." Nixon asked "who's that?", and when Colson started to explain, there is a "national security" deletion on the tape. (That deletion was made in 1996, when this particular tape was first released.) After the censored portion, the tape continues with Colson telling Nixon about the man, saying, "He's hard as nails. He's a brilliant writer. He's written forty books . . . "

President Nixon: What's his name?
Colson: His name is Howard Hunt . . . He just got out of the CIA. Fifty. Kind of a tiger.[52]

Nixon didn't tell Colson he was already familiar with Hunt, or that the President himself had mentioned Hunt for the Brookings job the previous day. (Colson wasn't in that meeting.) Instead, Nixon says that Hunt "can do it," since even at fifty, "he may still have the energy."[53]

The next day, July 2, 1971, Nixon and Haldeman in a private meeting discussed Helm's recommendation of Hunt. Haldeman told the President that "[Richard] Helms describes this guy [Hunt] as ruthless, quiet and careful, low profile. He gets things done. He will work well with all of us." It's remarkable to compare Helms's description of Hunt here to the way Hunt would be depicted by CIA sources to Congress and the press a year later, after Watergate: as a bumbling, low-level publicity-seeker. Helms's 1971 description and recommendation is much closer to Hunt's glowing CIA performance evaluations than to Hunt's post-Watergate image.*[54]

After Colson had talked to Hunt on the phone, he sent John Ehrlichman a memo pointing out that Hunt "was the mastermind on the Bay of Pigs. He told me long ago that if the truth were ever known, Kennedy would be destroyed." There's no evidence to back up Hunt's claim about JFK. However, the CIA-Mafia plotting was still so secret in 1971 that Hunt may have erroneously assumed that Allen Dulles or Richard Bissell—the architects of the Bay of Pigs—had told JFK about the plots prior to the invasion. (It would be four more years before Bissell would testify to the Senate Church Committee that he had not told JFK about them.)[55]

On July 7, 1971—seven days after Nixon first mentioned Hunt on tape, and six days after Colson made what he thought was the first recommendation of Hunt to Nixon—"Colson took Hunt" to the White House to first meet John Ehrlichman. Though Ehrlichman "didn't think the former agent was the man to head up the operation [he] agreed to hire him as a White House 'consultant' . . . effective the day before at $100 a day." A CIA memo says that July 19, 1971, was when Hunt "joined the White House staff as a Consultant to President Nixon." However, Charles Colson later said that Hunt was hired for his White House position on July 1, 1971. Such confusion over basic matters like the date Hunt was hired foreshadow the larger controversies about Hunt to come.[56]

Even though Hunt was given "a small office on the third floor of the Executive Office Building," he also kept his supposedly full-time,

* In that same meeting, Nixon brought up the name of Washington attorney Ed Morgan to work on the anti-Ellsberg project, possibly indicating that Nixon didn't realize that Morgan was good friends with Johnny Rosselli.

salaried position at the Mullen Company. In actuality, Hunt was mostly just paid by the CIA front company and seems to have done only a couple of projects for Mullen (one a public service announcement involving Nixon's daughter, Julie Nixon Eisenhower). However, the Mullen Company allowed Hunt to spend most of his time on White House projects, since Hunt was doing what Helms wanted, and it was Helms who had "ordered" Bennett and the Mullen Company to hire Hunt in the first place.[57]

Colson originally wanted Hunt hired "to head up the Pentagon Papers investigation," but Lukas documented that "Hunt says he worked under Colson's direction for the next year on a wide variety of matters, most of which had nothing to do with the Pentagon Papers." One of his first assignments for the White House was trying to dig up dirt on Senator Edward Kennedy, whom Nixon still viewed as a possible contender for the Democratic Presidential nomination, even after the tragic incident at Chappaquiddick.[58]

While Nixon wanted a range of information to use against the Democrats—from World War II to Korea to the Berlin crisis—he singled out the Bay of Pigs for special treatment. On July 27, 1971, Nixon told H.R. Haldeman he wanted "to get for me personally, particularly the documents concerning the Bay of Pigs." Nixon's desire for those files would grow even larger by the fall.[59]

Having already stalled Nixon's demand for the Bay of Pigs files in 1969, Richard Helms had most likely realized that E. Howard Hunt—the self-described "mastermind on the Bay of Pigs"—would have been irresistible for Nixon and his staff. If Nixon couldn't have the files, he now had working for him the next best thing. Nixon's staff knew he was interested in anything that might smear the Kennedy legacy, so Nixon didn't have to explain to them his other reasons for wanting material on "the Bay of Pigs thing" or the earlier contacts he'd had with Hunt. Nixon didn't seem to know about the close relationship between Hunt and Helms, and that Hunt's loyalty was apparently more to the CIA Director than to the President. However, Helms had to tread a fine line between making it look like Hunt could be valuable to Nixon and not arousing suspicion that he was simply a CIA plant. Hence, Hunt had overt contact with the Agency that was "arranged" through Nixon's aides, while Hunt had his own, less obvious channels of communication to Helms and the Agency.

On July 7, the day Hunt was hired, Helms's Deputy CIA Director—

General Cushman—was called by White House aide John Ehrlichman. He told Cushman that "Howard Hunt has been asked by the President to do some special-consultant work on security problems. He may be contacting you sometime in the future for some assistance. I wanted you to know that he was in fact doing some things for the President. He is a longtime acquaintance with the people here. You should consider he has pretty much carte blanche."[60]

Ehrlichman's comment that Hunt was "a longtime acquaintance with the people here" is at odds with the conventional story, since the only acknowledged contact Hunt had was a couple of years casual acquaintance with Charles Colson. Of course, Hunt had known Nixon on a professional level far longer, something Nixon might have confided to Ehrlichman in a rare moment of candor. As described in earlier chapters, Cushman had first met Hunt with Nixon in Uruguay in the late 1950s and had worked with Hunt on the efforts to eliminate Fidel Castro for Nixon in 1960, when Cushman was Vice President Nixon's "military aide." Lukas wrote that Cushman and Hunt had once "shared an office during the spring of 1950" at the CIA, but he also points out that Cushman's main loyalty was to Nixon, not to Helms.[61]

At CIA headquarters on July 22, Hunt met with General Cushman. Hunt asked for "flash alias identification . . . and some degree of physical disguise." The next day, CIA Technical Services gave Hunt "a red wig, thick glasses, and a speech-alteration device . . . as well as a Social Security card, a driver's license, and several association cards and other 'pocket litter' in the name of Edward Joseph Warren." From his CIA days, Hunt still "retained the alias Edward J. Hamilton; in his work for Nixon, Hunt would often call himself simply 'Mr. Edward.' A couple of weeks later, CIA Technical Services gave Hunt a stereo tape recorder and high-quality microphones; the CIA staffer later said "he had been told by his superiors to provide 'all possible assistance' to the man called 'Mr. Edward.'"[62]

E. Howard Hunt became part of what was officially called the "White House Special Investigations Unit," which is often referred to as the "Plumbers." While it's often said their main job was to stop leaks, all of the files and testimony show it was more of a political crimes unit. Charles Colson was in charge of the overall program, though he later claimed that was just for budgetary reasons. Even though Hunt would be the Unit's consistent, driving force for many of their most serious operations, the official head of the Plumbers was White House staffer Egil Krogh. Previously, Krogh had been a White House liaison to the FBI and the Bureau of Narcotics and Dangerous Drugs (BNDD); his most noted achievement was engineering Elvis Presley's visit to the Oval Office the previous year.[63]

Joining the Plumbers on July 19, 1971, was G. Gordon Liddy, a former FBI agent. Lukas wrote that Liddy "had been forced out of the Treasury Department only weeks before," after he'd "vigorously lobbied against the [Nixon] administration's gun-control legislation," which Liddy had denounced in "a rousing speech" at a National Rifle Association's convention. If anyone was farther to the right than E. Howard Hunt, it was Liddy, but the two quickly became friendly on a professional and social level.[64]

G. Gordon Liddy "reported to his superiors in writing on August 2, 1971 . . . that the FBI was not aggressively investigating Ellsberg, and that the FBI was no longer conducting 'clandestine operations.'" J. Edgar Hoover had downgraded the investigation because he realized "the Ellsberg case did not involve espionage" and was simply "a political battle between the Administration and the press—a battle in which he would only get hurt," according to Lukas. In some ways worse for Nixon was that the Bureau "was no longer conducting 'clandestine operations'"—which referred to much of the domestic spying the FBI had been engaged in for decades, including "black bag" break-ins of domestic political groups. The FBI might do that sort of thing for real criminal investigations or foreign agents in the United States, but no longer for overtly political reasons. Tasks like that would now fall to the Plumbers.[65]

Nixon's Plumbers unit was a criminal operation from the start, not some legitimate operation that went sour or simply had a few bad apples. It was basically a political crimes unit, which is why Colson, Krogh, Hunt, Liddy, and most of the other Plumbers would later go to prison. Yet Nixon's Plumbers were also extremely useful for the CIA and the job security of its Director, Richard Helms.

Hunt's new White House position was a hugely important—and some might say carefully orchestrated—development for Helms on several fronts. With the FBI no longer conducting "clandestine operations" for the President, pressure for Helms to conduct those could have increased. In the coming election year, that could have included more nakedly political operations, not just the antiwar domestic spying the CIA had primarily been doing for Nixon. As the stymied hearings by Senator Sam Ervin had shown, it was increasingly risky for U.S. agencies to be heavily involved in domestic surveillance. Now, instead of the CIA, Hunt could handle or direct such tasks from the White House. In addition, Hunt was soon reading FBI files in his new White House position, files that Helms himself could no longer get directly from the Bureau.

The first six months of 1971 had been critical in creating the dynamic that would lead to the Watergate scandal. The unexpected Anderson-Rosselli stories at the start of the year had helped to accelerate Helms's efforts to deal with Richard Nixon, leading to his protégé Hunt doing work for the White House by April. Due to the Pentagon Papers, by July, Hunt actually had an official position inside the White House, one that put the Nixon administration on the road to Watergate.

CHAPTER 26

Summer and Fall 1971: Nixon, Hunt, Barker, and the First Burglary

E. Howard Hunt had been doing clandestine work for the Nixon White House since April 1971, but his first major operation with the Plumbers was the September 1971 break-in at the Beverly Hills office of Daniel Ellsberg's psychiatrist, Dr. Lewis Fielding. While that burglary is a minor part of most Watergate accounts, it is extremely important, because it laid the groundwork for the far better-known events that followed. John Ehrlichman called the Ellsberg-Fielding "break-in the 'seminal Watergate episode,'" while Egil Krogh—who ostensibly supervised the Plumbers for Nixon—"considered it far more important than the Watergate break-in." Indeed, many of the sentences served by Watergate figures such as Ehrlichman, Colson, Liddy, and Krogh involved this 1971 break-in. Like the Watergate burglaries the following year, the Ellsberg-Fielding burglary has its own hidden history, woven together here with the conventional account for the first time.[1]

Overlooked in many accounts is the fact that the idea to burglarize the office of Ellsberg's psychiatrist originated with E. Howard Hunt, who planned and pressed for the operation. However, the break-in was authorized by President Nixon, at least in a general sense and—according to John Ehrlichman—very specifically. Nixon had said the Plumbers' "first priority" was "to find out all it could about Mr. Ellsberg's associates and his motives." To achieve Nixon's goal, Hunt wrote a memo titled "Neutralization of Ellsberg." It outlined a thorough operation, involving the collection of not just "all press material on Ellsberg," but also interviewing his first wife, talking to the owner of a restaurant in Saigon that Ellsberg had frequented (and even the owner's mistress), and collecting data on Ellsberg from "the CIA,

FBI, military counterintelligence agencies, and [the] RAND" think tank where Ellsberg had worked. Hunt also recommended the CIA perform "a covert psychological assessment/evaluation on Ellsberg." Finally, Hunt said in his memo that somehow, "Ellsberg's files from his psychiatric analyst" should be obtained.[2]

Hunt had learned about Daniel Ellsberg's psychiatrist in California from Ellsberg's FBI files. Thanks to his White House position, Hunt now had access to Bureau files, something that even CIA Director Richard Helms could not obtain. Hunt saw that FBI agents had tried to interview Dr. Fielding on July 20, 1971, but the psychiatrist had turned them away, and six days later the psychiatrist refused a phone call from the Bureau.[3]

Richard Helms had authorized the psychological "personality assessment" Hunt requested, and it was delivered on August 11. But the CIA's assessment didn't contain any revelations that could be used to smear Ellsberg or undermine his credibility. Nixon's main goal was the keep the Ellsberg story in the press, feeling that the story harmed the Democrats, so something more was needed.[4]

In the Plumbers' office in Room 13 of the Old Executive Office Building (EOB), across from the White House, G. Gordon Liddy and Egil Krogh listened to Hunt present his plan for the burglary of Dr. Fielding's practice. The Plumbers' office was on the ground floor, near the access tunnel that connected the EOB to the White House. Hunt's private office for his White House work was on the EOB's third floor (in Room 338), well away from the main Plumbers' office. As noted earlier, President Nixon also had what's often called a "hideaway" office at the EOB.[5]

Nixon's aide John Ehrlichman gave his written approval for the break-in when he responded to an August 11, 1971, memo about the plan. In an August 12, 1971, meeting between President Nixon and Charles Colson—just after Colson had told Nixon how much Hunt admired him—Nixon told Colson, "I briefed Ehrlichman on [the Ellsberg operation] today, on the investigative side. Krogh is working on that, too." John Ehrlichman testified that "Nixon was [so] frustrated by the apparent indifference" of Hoover to the Ellsberg investigation that Nixon "phoned Hoover to say he was 'having to resort to sending two people out there,'" meaning he was sending Liddy and Hunt to Los Angeles.[6]

Nixon's tapes and documents present compelling evidence that

Nixon ordered and approved the Ellsberg-Fielding burglary. However, it is not conclusive, and some say Nixon only approved a general operation against Ellsberg and not a specific burglary. When the Ellsberg-Fielding break-in later surfaced while Nixon was mired in the Watergate scandal, the President was understandably reluctant to take responsibility for it. When Egil Krogh visited Nixon "less than a week" after the President's resignation in 1974, Nixon seemed unsure if he'd approved the burglary in advance (asking, "Did I know about that in advance?"), but admitted to Krogh, "If you had come to me I would have approved it." Two years after Nixon's resignation, Nixon told Haldeman, "maybe I did order that break-in." Later, two of Nixon's post-resignation aides told Ehrlichman that "Nixon now admits what he formerly denied; [that] he knew of the [Ellsberg] break-in before it occurred, and he encouraged it."[7]

Ehrlichman wanted Hunt to make sure the operation couldn't be traced back to the White House, and Egil Krogh "wanted surrogates used" in case anything went wrong. Hunt turned to his old CIA assistant Bernard Barker and to CIA Agent Eugenio Martinez, both of whom he'd recruited for White House operations back in April. With Hunt's approval, they added their Cuban exile associate Felipe De Diego to the team.[8]

Felipe De Diego, forty-three at the time, was later described by Martinez as "a real-estate partner of ours. He is an old Company man and a Bay of Pigs veteran whom we knew we could trust." De Diego was an experienced intelligence operative who Lukas says "once took part in a successful raid to capture Castro government documents, and later served for four years as an officer in U.S. Army Intelligence." That meant Hunt had selected three CIA agents—two former and one current—to help him with the Ellsberg burglary. De Diego isn't well known today because he wasn't arrested with Barker and Martinez during the fourth Watergate burglary attempt, even though he was originally part of the first Watergate burglary team.[9]

In his notes, John Ehrlichman called the Ellsberg-Fielding burglary "Hunt/Liddy Special Project No. 1." Preliminary expenses had been covered using "government vouchers" that could be traced, which wasn't acceptable as the illegal project progressed. So, in less than a week's time, White House aides received bribes totaling $10,000 from executives with the dairy industry, a small part of the $2 million deal Nixon had made earlier.[10]

On August 25, 1971, Hunt "got a Tessina camera concealed in a tobacco pouch from . . . his contact in the CIA's Technical Services Division." Hunt also helped G. Gordon Liddy get his own elaborate disguise and fake identification from the Agency. That same day, both men left for Los Angeles to case the three-story building where Dr. Fielding had his office on the second floor. The next day, they first cased the outside of the building, then—that evening—actually entered the office building. When they encountered a cleaning woman, Hunt used the situation to his advantage. Speaking excellent Spanish, Hunt told her that he and Liddy were doctors and needed "to leave a message for Dr. Fielding." So she let Liddy inside the psychiatrist's office and he "photographed its interior while Hunt [was] chatting with the cleaning lady." They returned to Washington the next day and gave the camera to the CIA to develop the photos.[11]

The reasons for what happened next remain unclear, though the result is well documented. General Cushman, the CIA's Deputy Director, called Ehrlichman on August 27 to "say that the CIA would no longer provide assistance to Howard Hunt" because of his "excessive" demands. Some say it was because of the photos, but Cushman denied that. It's also possible that Cushman was angry because Hunt had requested that his former CIA secretary from Paris be assigned to him, a request the CIA denied. Regardless of the reason, Cushman's call seemed to be of no concern to Ehrlichman. Nixon's aide told Cushman he'd talk to Hunt about it, but he never did. And even though Cushman wrote to CIA Director Helms about his cutting off Hunt, it's well documented that "CIA assistance continued well into 1972." Some authors see Cushman's call and memo to Helms as simply "papering the record" to cover the Agency for the help they were giving Hunt. That may have been especially true for Cushman, who realized that Hunt was getting the Agency into risky, illegal activity. But Hunt still clearly had the support of Helms—for whom the Ellsberg mission was important, for reasons explained shortly—so the mission, and the CIA assistance to Hunt, continued.[12]

Based on the results from Hunt and Liddy's mission to Los Angeles, approval was given by Krogh and Ehrlichman for the burglary to proceed. Even after Cushman's memo had supposedly ended CIA assistance to Hunt, the team was well supplied and still included active CIA agent Eugenio Martinez. Their equipment included a Minox spy camera, a small tripod, a "copying stand, flash unit, waist-level finder, and darkroom equipment." They also had a Polaroid camera, four walkie-talkies, a glass cutter, a crowbar, and other break-in supplies. Some accounts say the psychiatrist's office was to be photographed first (with the Polaroid) so it could be left the way it was, with the burglary hopefully remaining undetected, which is what Ehrlichman thought was supposed to happen. However, the crowbar, glass cutter, and lack of a locksmith on the team seems to indicate that the break-in would be obvious.[13]

The break-in occurred on the night of September 3, 1972, at the start of a Labor Day weekend. E. Howard Hunt assigned himself the task of watching Dr. Fielding's apartment, to make sure the doctor didn't return to the office unexpectedly. At the office building, G. Gordon Liddy waited outside, while Barker, Martinez, and De Diego went into the building after dark. Most accounts claim that Barker didn't tell Martinez and De Diego they were looking for material on a "traitor" named "Ellsberg" until just before the burglary began.* When they tried to use the glass cutter, it didn't work, so Martinez had to break a window on the ground floor. Once they found that they needed to pry open the psychiatrist's file cabinets, the three Cuban exiles say they abandoned the "clean" operation and tried to make it look like a desperate drug burglary, leaving the office "in disarray." They left some vitamin pills scattered on the floor and took Polaroid photos of the disheveled office.[14]

Hunt was conveniently away from the break-in while it was going on, supposedly keeping an eye on Dr. Fielding's apartment and car. Later, Hunt claimed that the doctor had somehow slipped out, and Hunt had to race back to Fielding's office, hoping the psychiatrist hadn't gone there. Once Hunt arrived, the burglary crew was just exiting the building.[15]

Almost all accounts agree on what happened next, but not why. Back at their hotel, Martinez wrote that Hunt congratulated them all, saying, "Well done." Hunt then opened a bottle of champagne and told them, "This is a celebration. You deserve it." Martinez says he was perplexed by Hunt's cheerful reaction, since he—and Barker (and Hunt and Liddy)—say that no Ellsberg file had been found in Dr. Fielding's office. Hunt's reaction made Martinez think that "maybe

*Martinez says he did not even recognize the name "Ellsberg," even though Ellsberg had been the subject of numerous headlines and television news stories over the previous nine weeks.

these people already had the papers of Ellsberg . . . It seemed that these people already had what we were looking for because no one invites you to have champagne and is happy when you fail."[16]

However, Felipe De Diego—the only member of the burglary team that didn't go to jail for the operation—testified to a House Committee that "the Ellsberg file was in fact located and photographed . . . with the Minox" spy camera. Ellsberg's psychiatrist provides some confirmation for De Diego's account. Dr. Fielding said that "his notes on the Ellsberg case were indeed in his office at the time [and] the burglars had obviously found them [since] the notes were lying on the floor when he arrived at his office on the morning after the burglary."[17]

After they returned to Washington, Hunt tried to get authorization to burglarize Dr. Fielding's apartment. But "when John Ehrlichman saw the" Polaroid pictures of the destruction, "he was 'appalled' by . . . what was supposed to have been a 'covert' operation," and he denied Hunt's request. In Miami, Eugenio Martinez reported his actions to his CIA case officer, who made no comment. And in Beverly Hills, after the burglary was discovered, police soon arrested a drug addict who Hunt says "conveniently confessed to our crime in return for a suspended sentence."[18]

Based on conventional history, it appears to have made little sense for Nixon and his White House aides to have approved the Ellsberg-Fielding burglary. It was a very risky operation, and any material they obtained couldn't be used—in the press, as Nixon wanted, or in prosecuting Ellsberg—without revealing the break-in as its source. Likewise, the operation seems to have been a tremendous gamble for CIA Director Richard Helms, given his close ties to Hunt and the high level of CIA assistance for the operation. It seems odd that Helms would jeopardize his access to White House operations and information, now that his trusted protégé Hunt could get FBI reports the CIA could no longer acquire through official channels.

The explanation for the actions of Helms and Nixon—and why Hunt and the others likely denied finding the Ellsberg file—can be found in the previously noted clippings and reports about Ellsberg, compiled by Hunt earlier. More than two years after the Ellsberg-Fielding break-in, a CIA statement was uncovered by the House Judiciary Committee showing that E. Howard Hunt "was regularly and secretly sending packages to the CIA from the White House." The man who made the statement was "a CIA liaison to the National Security Council [NSC]" named Rob Roy Ratliff. In his sworn statement, Ratliff said, "I was aware that Hunt had frequently transmitted sealed envelopes via our [NSC] office to the Agency." In a later interview with journalist Jim Hougan, Ratliff confirmed that "Hunt's packages were routinely received and hand-carried to the CIA." Ratliff said Hunt's secret channel to the CIA had started at "the beginning of Hunt's consultancy at the White House." Ratliff never opened any of the packages, but his predecessor—handling Hunt's secret packages at the time of the Ellsberg operation—"had opened one." According to the sworn statement, he told Ratliff that Hunt's package "appeared to contain 'gossip' information about an unknown person—he assumed that it had something to do with a psychological study of that person."[19]

Jim Hougan dug deeper into Ratliff's sworn statement, which had been partially censored. Hougan found "a source with access to Ratliff's uncensored statement," who said that "CIA Director Helms" was one of only two "recipients" that Hunt's secret packages had been sent to. This is the secure pipeline Hunt could have used to send information about Ellsberg to Richard Helms, and this provides further support for those who believe that Hunt continued to work for Helms and the Agency while he was also working for the Nixon White House.[20]

In addition to his mentor Helms, Hunt was still friends with David Atlee Phillips, who now headed CIA operations not just for Cuba, but for all of Latin America, including the CIA's Chile Task Force. Phillips would have overseen the CIA's ongoing support for Commander Juan Almeida's wife and family outside of Cuba. Commander Almeida—whose work for JFK remained secret, and who was still very high in the Cuban government—would soon be a factor in Phillips's plans to assassinate Fidel Castro in Chile, in December 1971.

In many ways, David Atlee Phillips's sensitive CIA operations that were ongoing (Almeida) and upcoming (the Castro assassination attempt set for Chile) were continuations of those that Desmond FitzGerald had begun running in 1963. It's no coincidence that all of the men involved in the Fielding break-in had worked on Desmond FitzGerald's anti-Castro operations for the Agency in 1963, except for Liddy. Even the two highest-ranking officials who approved the Fielding break-in, President Nixon and Richard Helms, had ties to FitzGerald: Richard Helms had supervised his friend FitzGerald in 1963, and Nixon had come up against a couple of FitzGerald's anti-Castro plots that year. Desmond FitzGerald also had a surprising connection to the burglary of Ellsberg's psychiatrist.

The crucial connection that worried Hunt, Helms, and probably Nixon was Ellsberg's close friendship with Desmond FitzGerald's daughter, Frances FitzGerald. Jim Hougan documented that "at the time of the [Ellsberg-Fielding] break-in, the CIA's Office of Security was profoundly worried about Daniel Ellsberg [and] what seems to have been their panic—stemmed from the fact that [Frances] FitzGerald was the daughter of the late Desmond FitzGerald."[21]

Hougan located "a former staff member of the [Senate Watergate] Committee" who showed him

> documents—FBI reports, newspaper clips, and memoranda from various government agencies—that the Plumbers had provided to the CIA . . . These documents all concerned Daniel Ellsberg, and they had been provided to the Agency as background material for its psychological study . . . I was struck by . . . the marginal notations, circled phrases and exclamation points that crowded the pages whenever Ellsberg's relationship to a writer named Frances FitzGerald was mentioned . . . the notes had been written by analysts assigned to the CIA's . . . Office of Security.[22]

That was the material supplied by E. Howard Hunt, who had recommended the psychological study and who was the CIA's only source for the "FBI reports" on Ellsberg. Hougan found that "the CIA saw [Frances FitzGerald's] friendship with Ellsberg as a threat and worried that it might lead to the exposure of operations that the CIA hoped would remain state secrets." The CIA's worry was "that the Pentagon Papers leak might be succeeded by a second leak, and that this second leak would hit the CIA directly." Coming just seven months after the Jack Anderson-Rosselli articles, which threatened to fully expose the CIA-Mafia plots, the concerns of Helms and the CIA were understandable.[23]

Ellsberg's biographer found an associate who "told [Ellsberg's commander in Vietnam, Edward] Lansdale that it was his understanding that [Frances] FitzGerald was writing 'dutiful and favorable reports' on Ellsberg to her father," Desmond FitzGerald. Frances FitzGerald later wrote a Pulitzer Prize–winning book about her Vietnam experience, *Fire in the Lake*.* Frances FitzGerald and Daniel Ellsberg

*Frances FitzGerald gained additional fame as a writer for publications such as *The Atlantic Monthly*, *The Village Voice*, and *The New York Times*.

were good friends in Vietnam in 1966. That was the same year the end of the CIA-Mafia plots of Desmond FitzGerald and Richard Helms was reported in U.S. newspapers—though not identified as such—with the public trial in Cuba of accused assassin Rolando Cubela. That matter could easily have been a topic of conversation between Ellsberg and Frances FitzGerald, or between Frances and her father. Desmond FitzGerald himself had personally met with Cubela in Paris about Fidel's assassination, just three years before Cubela went on trial in Cuba.[24]

Richard Helms would have been especially worried that Desmond FitzGerald—who knew all of Helms's most closely guarded secrets, from the CIA-Mafia plots to the JFK-Almeida coup plan—might have confided or hinted at some of those activities to his talented and worldly daughter. And she, in turn, might have said something to her friend Daniel Ellsberg, who was involved in sensitive government work when she knew him in Vietnam.[25]

The CIA's documented concern over the Ellsberg-FitzGerald connection did, however, give Helms a national security justification for the Ellsberg-Fielding break-in, and not just to make sure his unauthorized operations hadn't been exposed. The Almeida portion of Desmond FitzGerald's 1963 operations was still ongoing (with the family) and could be a factor again in David Atlee Phillips's plans for Castro and Chile in December 1971. Helms clearly wanted the break-in to occur, otherwise he could have told his protégé Hunt not to do it, or he could have had Eugenio Martinez's case officer order Martinez not to go.

The FitzGerald connection to Ellsberg also gave President Nixon a "national security" justification for the break-in, and for his whole anti-Ellsberg operation. While Nixon wouldn't have known the full extent of Desmond FitzGerald and Helms's 1963 anti-Castro operations, Nixon knew he'd come up against a couple of them that year, as documented in Chapters 13 and 14. That helps to explain why—when the Ellsberg-Fielding break-in started to become "public in early 1973," historian Stanley Kutler pointed out that the Nixon "White House insisted repeatedly that the break-in was required by considerations of 'national security.'" Nixon said in a speech soon after the break-in's exposure that the "matter was 'of vital importance to the national security.'" Nixon's new Attorney General at the time, Elliot Richardson, was told that "President [Nixon] did not want Richardson to intrude into the 'national-security' area." The Watergate Special

Prosecutor at the time "demanded that the White House produce proof" of their national security justification for the Ellsberg-Fielding break-in, but Nixon provided none.[26]

The Ellsberg-Fielding break-in set the stage in many ways for the Watergate break-ins the following year. Both were authorized by President Nixon as part of broader operations, both had the support of Richard Helms, and both involved Hunt, Barker, Martinez, and Liddy (and initially for Watergate, De Diego). Both operations had national security justifications, to protect ongoing CIA Cuban operations, but both were also designed to help prevent the release of information about CIA Cuban operations from the early 1960s that could have damaged Nixon and Helms. Nixon's national security justification/excuse also explains why, when more men were added to the Watergate operation, they were all former CIA agents who had also worked on Cuban operations. Years later, Plumbers supervisor Egil Krogh wrote that the Ellsberg-Fielding break-in "was the seminal event in the chain of events that led to Nixon's resignation" and that "the burglary set a precedent" that Hunt and Liddy "could rely on when planning and executing the Watergate break-in of 1972."[27]

If Felipe De Diego was right, then Helms, Hunt, and the CIA got what they wanted—Ellsberg's file—and found no evidence that Ellsberg had heard information about Desmond FitzGerald's secret Cuban operations from his daughter. For Nixon, it was soon back to business as usual. On September 8, 1971, Nixon and Ehrlichman were discussing Ellsberg, and Ehrlichman told the President, "we had one little operation. It's been aborted out in Los Angeles which, I think, is better that you don't know about." They then went into a discussion that kept coming back to "the CIA and the Bay of Pigs." Based on a review of all the evidence, and Nixon's later statements, it seems possible that Nixon had access to more information about the Ellsberg-Fielding break-in than he got from Ehrlichman, either from Richard Helms or from E. Howard Hunt (since both Hunt and Nixon had offices at the Old Executive Office Building).[28]

Richard Nixon wanted to keep the Ellsberg issue alive and in the press, thinking it would help him going into next year's Presidential election. Hunt worked with the CIA on more psychological profile material about Ellsberg on October 12, October 27, and November 12. Pulitzer Prize–winning reporter J. Anthony Lukas documented another Ellsberg-related burglary that might have been the work of the Plumbers. He wrote that "early in November [1971], the penthouse office of . . . a Manhattan psychiatrist [who] had had once treated" Ellsberg's second wife, Patricia, "was broken into, searched, and left in considerable disarray," just like Dr. Fielding's office. "The thieves apparently rifled an unlocked cabinet containing a file on Mrs. Ellsberg." In addition, "the doctor recalls that the day after" the Pentagon Papers were first published, "two FBI agents had come to his office seeking information," but "like Dr. Fielding, [he] refused to talk to the FBI."[29]

On December 30, 1971, Nixon's Justice Department would expand "the government indictment against Ellsberg . . . to 12 criminal charges, including conspiracy and the violation of espionage statues." Ironically, because Nixon was still having those charges pursued so aggressively ten months after the Watergate break-ins, the spring 1973 revelation to the public of the Ellsberg-Fielding burglary by the Plumbers would play a major role in convincing the public that Nixon had also been involved in Watergate.

By October 1, 1971, James McCord—the future Watergate burglar—was working part-time for the Committee to Re-elect the President (CREEP).* McCord had retired from the CIA the previous year, four months after Hunt's more suspicious retirement, as mentioned in Chapter 24. McCord had established his own security firm and was now CREEP's Director of Security. It is interesting that a former high-ranking CIA Office of Security official like McCord joined CREEP just six weeks after the CIA's Office of Security had been so concerned about a possible connection between Daniel Ellsberg and the late Desmond FitzGerald.[30]

Even as the Ellsberg saga played out during the fall of 1971, President Nixon kept coming back to issues involving the early 1960s, Cuba, and JFK. In the September 8, 1971, conversation quoted earlier between Nixon and Ehrlichman about Ellsberg, both men kept discussing the Bay of Pigs and Richard Helms. Ehrlichman told Nixon

> We're running into a little problem. I've got to talk to Helms about getting some documents which the CIA have on the Bay of Pigs . . . which they would rather not leak out. It's a challenge.[31]

*Some accounts put McCord's start in September 1971

Nixon agreed, saying that "it's going to be hard" to get those files from Helms. "They are very sensitive about that. Helms is definitely the one . . . [unintelligible] now for CIA and the Bay of Pigs." It's interesting that even the President agreed that "it's going to be hard," indicating that Helms was apparently in a strong position to resist even the Chief Executive.[32]

Against others, Nixon didn't hesitate to use—or threaten to use—the powers of his office, telling Ehrlichman moments later that "we have the power" and then asking if they were using it against his potential rivals in next year's election: " Are we using it to investigate contributors to Hubert Humphrey, contributors to [Maine Senator Edmund] Muskie, the Jews . . . Teddy [Kennedy]?" After talking about the White House's ongoing surveillance of Senator Edward Kennedy, the President also brought up using the IRS against his perceived enemies."[33]

But the Bay of Pigs was back in the conversation ten days later, when Nixon, Ehrlichman, Chief of Staff H.R. Haldeman, and Attorney General John Mitchell discussed how to use the Pentagon Papers and other matters against the Democrats. In this September 18, 1971, conversation, Ehrlichman brought up "the whole Bay of Pigs business." Nixon, mindful of the Anderson-Rosselli articles earlier that year and possibly of Ellsberg's tie to Desmond FitzGerald's daughter, said, "The matter . . . is going to arise without question as time goes on—the Cuban thing." Nixon gave Ehrlichman an order: "Tell Helms . . . I want this . . . in order to protect ourselves in the clinches." Weeks later, Ehrlichman wrote in his notes about Helms and the Bay of Pigs, "Purpose of presidential request for documents: must be fully advised in order to know what to duck." Anthony Summers asked, "Why did Nixon believe 'the Cuban thing' was bound to come up?" Given that Nixon was trying to dig up dirt on his rivals, he likely assumed they were doing the same—and given the Jack Anderson articles and the Ellsberg-FitzGerald matter, there was no way to tell what might surface. Summers also wondered, "What was there that [Nixon] needed to protect himself from?" The answers include: Nixon's many meetings at the CIA in 1960 which spawned the CIA-Mafia plots that led to the Bay of Pigs; his friend Pawley's involvement with Johnny Rosselli in 1963; and Nixon's own pipeline into JFK's Cuban coup plan in November 1963.[34]

Nixon had "demanded the Bay of Pigs documents . . . four times in as many weeks," and in the September 18 meeting, Nixon increased his efforts. In John Ehrlichman's notes, he wrote, "Bay of Pigs—[Nixon] order to CIA; [Nixon] is to have the *full* file or else; Nothing w/held." (Emphasis in original.) Ehrlichman's notes from the meeting also contain this telling phrase, saying that Nixon "was involved in Bay of Pigs . . . deeply involved." Of course, there was no Bay of Pigs invasion planned while Nixon was Vice President, or any large amphibious invasion plan before he lost the election—but there were the CIA-Mafia plots Nixon had pressed for, with Robert Maheu, Johnny Rosselli, and Santo Trafficante. Ehrlichman and Haldeman always denied they knew the exact secret about the Bay of Pigs that Nixon was worried about, but Haldeman did learn that "Nixon knew more about the genesis of the Cuban invasion than almost anyone."[35]

Once more, however, Nixon's attempt to get the crucial files about "the Bay of Pigs thing" was stymied by Richard Helms. Nixon himself wrote in his memoirs that "Helms refused to give Ehrlichman the Agency's internal reports . . . At one point, he told Ehrlichman on the phone that even he did not have a copy of one of the key Bay of Pigs reports." We know now Helms's statement was not true and Nixon suspected as much back in 1971. As Nixon described it,

> Helms finally brought me several of the items after I had requested them from him personally. I promised him I would not use them to hurt him, his predecessor, or the CIA. "I have one President at a time," he responded. "I work only for you." When Ehrlichman read the materials Helms had delivered, however, he found that several of the reports, including the one of the Bay of Pigs, were still incomplete.[36]

Nixon summed it up well, saying that even to the President, "the CIA was closed like a safe, and we could find no one who would give us the combination to open it." Hiring E. Howard Hunt was probably one way Nixon hoped to protect himself even without the files he'd been denied since taking office in 1969. (Given Nixon's longtime concern over "the Bay of Pigs thing," it's hard to imagine that he didn't privately discuss the Bay of Pigs with Hunt, away from his other aides and taping system.) It's important to point out that Helms gave Nixon "three thin files," but nothing about the 1967 Inspector General's Report about the CIA-Mafia plots. Nixon didn't know about that report specifically, but—based on the Jack Anderson articles from 1967 and 1971—he probably suspected that something like it had to exist. For the time being, Nixon would have to be satisfied with Helms's meager response. But matters concerning Jack Anderson would bring Nixon and his CIA Director closer together the following year, before their problems over "the Bay of Pigs thing" would explode again soon after Watergate.[37]

As for Richard Helms, he didn't want to give in to Nixon and lose what was clearly important leverage over the President. Also, Helms was still mounting operations against Fidel, including a major one planned for later that year, and would not want that disrupted. In addition, Nixon might try to leak something to the press from the Cuba files, to strike at Senator Ted Kennedy by smearing John F. Kennedy, without realizing what other secrets of Helms he might expose. In Nixon's memoirs, published in 1978, Nixon makes it sound like Helms was worried that Hunt might leak material to the press from the CIA files, but Hunt was only pursuing that type of information for Nixon, as is now clear from the Nixon tapes released in the mid-1990s.[38]

In September 1971, Richard Nixon was also continuing an effort to blame JFK for the assassination of Vietnamese leader Diem in November 1963, showing that Helms's press concerns were justified. On September 16, Nixon told a press conference "that the way we got into Vietnam was through . . . complicity in the murder of Diem." On September 18, 1971, John Ehrlichman told Nixon "the assassination [of President Diem]" could "really open up the contents of the Pentagon Papers," calling it "one of the really juicy things that [could] get a controversy going." E. Howard Hunt had been working on the JFK-Diem assignment since at least July 8, having interviewed the General that had commanded U.S. forces at the time of Diem's murder and "an old friend [of Hunt's,] Col. Lucien Conein, who had been the CIA's liaison man with the Vietnamese plotters."[39]

Nixon pressed Helms for the CIA's material about Diem's murder, though not as hard as for the Bay of Pigs material. Once again, Nixon only got some of the material he wanted and nothing he could use to smear JFK. But the President's men had more luck with the State Department, run by Nixon's longtime associate William Rogers. E. Howard Hunt was allowed to look at 240 State Department cables, but none was the "smoking gun" Nixon wanted. J. Anthony Lukas wrote that "according to Hunt, Colson asked, 'Do you think you could improve on them?'", though Colson denies ordering Hunt to do so. Still, Hunt cut apart copies of real cables with a razor blade and pasted together two fake cables implicating JFK in Diem's assassination. A writer for *Life* magazine was sent to see Hunt and the faked cables. The writer was cautiously interested, but *Life* folded before his story could run. However, Hunt was successful in leaking the story to Lucien Conein, who talked about the cables as if they were real in a two-part NBC News special, *White Paper: Vietnam Hindsight*, broadcast on December 22 and 23, 1971.[40]

To get an idea of Nixon's clout with the press, and his determination to get the fake story out, Conein's interview had been filmed before he saw the phony cables, "but the White House persuaded the network that Conein had vital new information to provide and the interview [of Conein] was filmed over again." In addition, Hunt "briefed the producer of the program . . . on the secret telegram, which shaped the program in such a way as to imply Kennedy's complicity in the murder." All that may seem like an extreme—and risky—length to go to in order to smear a long-dead President, but Nixon may have thought that if his own complicity in the CIA-Mafia plots came out during the campaign, it might not look as bad if JFK had apparently done something similar. After Watergate, when the phony cables became known, Nixon tried to tell Ehrlichman he hadn't known of the Diem cable operation, but Ehrlichman told him that wasn't the case, and "my recollection is that this was discussed with you."[41]

President Nixon's relations with the press in 1971 were generally good, with several notable exceptions. Columnist Jack Anderson continued to be a thorn in the President's side, a situation that would continue to worsen as time went on. On August 6, 1971, Anderson had published the first article revealing that Howard Hughes had—earlier in Nixon's term—arranged for Bebe Rebozo to get an illegal contribution of $100,000 in cash for Richard Nixon. This was the first of what would be a slowly rising tide of stories about financial scandals and corruption that would start to dog Nixon even before Watergate.[42]

Nixon's coverage by the three television networks had been largely favorable and respectful, and it included a steady stream of information originated by the White House. But some cracks were starting to appear, especially at CBS News. There, Nixon especially resented the reporting of anchor Walter Cronkite, White House correspondent Dan Rather, and especially Washington correspondent Daniel Schorr, who talked about Nixon's actions in an exclusive interview with this author. In August 1971, Schorr had heard from some of his associates that he was being considered for some type of federal "environmental board," and that they had been interviewed by the FBI as part of a routine background check. While that seemed highly unlikely to Schorr, the environment was one of the few areas where Nixon was almost progressive. In actuality, Nixon—angry at Schorr's coverage—had asked Hoover to investigate Schorr, and the Director had agreed. The "environmental board" ruse was just a cover story for an operation begun after the Bureau had looked through its files on Schorr and found no derogatory information. In an attempt to get Nixon information he could use against the reporter, Hoover had sent his agents out to interview Schorr's family, neighbors, friends, and associates. Nixon told Haldeman that the point was to "Pound these people," to which Haldeman added, "Just give them something to worry about."[43]

On October 23, 1971, *CBS Evening News* anchor Walter Cronkite showed that Jack Anderson wasn't going to be the only journalist looking into the close financial ties of President Nixon and Bebe Rebozo. Cronkite said that "Nixon and his close friend, Bebe Rebozo, had profited handsomely in Florida land transactions," selling "shares in a land company back to the company at $2 a share, when the market price was $1." (That was the Fisher Island deal, detailed in Chapter 19.) "Nixon bitterly resented the coverage" by Cronkite, according to "a White House aide." When stories like this continued to sporadically appear, Nixon's aides ordered E. Howard Hunt and Bernard Barker to look for derogatory information on a possible source, Hoke Maroon, described as "Rebozo's banker colleague" in Miami. However, Hunt and Barker reported back to Nixon's aides that Maroon "was regarded by the financial community as a man of 'unimpeachable integrity,' while Rebozo was 'not well thought of.'" Given Rebozo's close financial ties to Nixon—and the business ties of Barker and Eugenio Martinez to Rebozo—Summers wrote, "This was not the report the White House wanted."[44]

By the end of 1971, *Newsday* would follow up Cronkite's and Anderson's stories with a series of articles focusing on the Nixon-Rebozo real estate deals. *Newsday*'s publisher at that time was William Attwood, a former JFK aide who had handled President Kennedy's secret negotiations with Fidel back in 1963. Nixon ordered massive retaliation against *Newsday*, some of it obvious, but most of it not. Nixon cut off access to *Newsday*'s White House reporter, sending a signal to other news organizations that depended on such access for their regular coverage. But Nixon also ordered illegal "tax probes" by the IRS of Attwood and his top editor, and having "FBI and Secret Service agents [run] surveillance on *Newsday* reporters." It was later documented that Nixon "himself was behind [those] measures." William Safire, one Nixon's speechwriters at the time, later said that "Nixon could not take it when it came to an attack on Bebe." Now it's clear that Nixon felt that way because any investigation of Bebe risked exposing Nixon's own crimes and his longtime questionable business dealings with his best friend. Charles Colson would later say he'd heard the Mafia "owned Bebe Rebozo," and President Nixon himself was continuing his longtime dealings with the Mafia in 1971.[45]

The New York Times was also subjected to Nixon's wrath. *The Washington Post* would later report that Tad Szulc, the *Times* Latin American expert who had been close to JFK, and "Neil Sheehan . . . the *Times* correspondent who had obtained the Pentagon Papers [from Ellsberg,] had been wire tapped at least for several months in 1971 and that information from these tapes had been received by the 'Plumbers.'"[46]

President Nixon was a man with many secrets to hide, which is one reason he saw CBS's Schorr, Cronkite, and Rather; Jack Anderson; and *The New York Times*, *Newsday*, and *The Washington Post* as adversaries. There was also a small, progressive press in America that constantly challenged the spin of Nixon and his spokesmen, epitomized by *Ramparts* magazine, which ran stories on Nixon's efforts to stop LBJ's fall 1968 peace plan and on the ties of South Vietnamese leaders to the heroin trade. But most of America's press—especially in middle America—was still surprisingly supportive of Nixon and the office of the President in those pre-Watergate days. All three major television networks, including CBS, were cautious and careful in their coverage of Nixon, always presenting his side of major stories. It was largely through the personal efforts of Cronkite, Schorr, and Rather that CBS allowed probing questions to be raised and reported, even before Watergate.*[47]

* After one interview with Rather, Nixon complained to one of his daughters that the newsman was a "bastard."

. . .

Nixon's anti-drug policy—particularly his attempts to deal with the growing epidemic of heroin use in America—helped to obscure the organized crime ties of some men working for the White House. Nixon's drug policies were the subject of a book-length study—*Agency of Fear*, by noted journalist Edward J. Epstein—and those policies were enlightened in some ways, repressive in many other ways, and often spectacularly ineffective. In Nixon's administration, an "ad hoc committee" of roughly eight officials had been formed to look at the problem. The members included Attorney General John Mitchell and Richard Helms, and though the committee was officially chaired by Henry Kissinger, it was usually chaired by his Deputy, Alexander Haig, because Kissinger "rarely attended" the meetings. Kissinger and Haig "spent most of their efforts dampening the efforts of White House zealots to launch a new heroin crusade," which, while good for publicity, could "threaten diplomatic relations with important allies." As noted earlier, the heroin issue was problematic in Southeast Asia, because even though heroin use was a rising problem for U.S. troops, South Vietnamese government officials—and warlords helping the United States in Laos and Cambodia—were also involved in the drug trade.[48]

In the summer of 1971, G. Gordon Liddy proposed creating "a new special narcotics unit which would report directly to the White House," as a way to avoid the problems with the competing government bureaucracies of the FBI, Justice, CIA, State, the Bureau of Narcotics and Dangerous Drugs (BNDD), and others. It advocated using "CIA agents for 'the more extraordinary missions,'" something Richard Helms would not have wanted. But through his Deputy Director, General Cushman, Helms "agreed to provide [the White House unit] financing for 'narcotics work,'" provided "that the CIA" not be "involved in . . . domestic investigation[s]." Thus, "the White House agents" such as Liddy and Hunt "would now act under the cloak of combating the drug menace."[49]

Congressional investigator Gaeton Fonzi wrote that "It has been suggested that Nixon's anti-drug campaign was, in actuality, a bid to establish his own intelligence network," a view supported by the fact that key members of the White House Special Investigations Unit—the Plumbers—were involved. Though the White House's "Office of Drug Abuse Law Enforcement" would not be officially created until December 1971, Hunt and his men went into action well before that date. Hunt and Barker recruited new members for their group, including former CIA contract agent and future Watergate burglar Frank Fiorini, by then often using the name Frank Sturgis. Fiorini's activities in 1969, 1970, and 1971—after the car-smuggling incident described earlier—are not documented, though he continued to have ties to Santo Trafficante's Mafia organization in Miami. According to Epstein, Fiorini said "he undertook several missions for Hunt involving tracking narcotics, and he assumed [the activities of Hunt's drug unit] would be expanded after Nixon's [re]election."[50]

Egil Krogh officially oversaw the drug efforts for Nixon, which the President talked about on the White House tapes. However, even though Krogh supposedly supervised the effort and the idea apparently originated with G. Gordon Liddy, E. Howard Hunt quickly became the dominant force on the covert side of the operation. The exact size of the drug operation in 1971 and 1972 has never been established. John Dean, for example, wrote that "Liddy . . . and Hunt had recruited hundreds of operatives—most had CIA training—and had promised them service after the election." Many of Hunt's recruits were Cuban exiles based in Miami, including some operatives who had worked for the Federal Bureau of Narcotics (the forerunner of Nixon's reorganized BNDD) under Tom Tripodi, as described in Chapter 21. To recruit and motivate the Cuban exiles—something Barker had been doing since the Bay of Pigs—Barker told them all that all their work was building toward action to remove Fidel Castro. Barker also said that Hunt "mentioned something about planning for the second phase of the Bay of Pigs around the beginning of Nixon's second term." This also created a pool of operatives that Hunt could use for additional Plumbers-type domestic break-ins that investigators would later uncover.[51]

With E. Howard Hunt taking effective control of the covert side of the "anti-drug" operation, it's no surprise that in the fall of 1971, Hunt recruited his best friend, Manuel Artime, the former Bay of Pigs leader whose AMWORLD operation had been supported by the CIA from 1963 to 1966. Like Barker and Fiorini, Artime also worked with Santo Trafficante. Artime was involved with drug trafficking for the godfather's network and would later become one of Nixon's hush-money paymasters after the Watergate arrests. With three Trafficante operatives involved in the White House anti-drug unit, it's also not surprising that the godfather's operations—and those of his associates—flourished under the new regime.[52]

Nixon's anti-drug efforts had the odd effect of increasing both drug consumption and the coffers of Santo Trafficante. Author Henrik Krüger wrote an entire book documenting how Nixon's drug policies—including his reshuffling of federal drug enforcement and involving his Plumbers in "drug enforcement"—weakened some of the traditional French Connection distributors while building up the Miami-based arm of the network, run by Cuban exiles working for Trafficante. Krüger built his case utilizing many mainstream news reports, including a Pulitzer Prize–winning series on heroin trafficking by *Newsday*.[53]

It's important to point out that Nixon probably had no idea his anti-drug operation was being compromised in such a fashion by those outside of the Oval Office. On the other hand, author Joseph Trento documented that "the BNDD could not get the Nixon administration to go after Trafficante directly," as noted previously. It's also possible that E. Howard Hunt was simply using men he trusted and didn't realize the degree to which his actions were being compromised because some of his men were associates of Santo Trafficante (toward that end, it's worth pointing out that it was Fiorini who first approached Hunt in 1971, via Barker). As for Trafficante, his initial interest was probably in making sure his drug network wasn't harmed by the White House's efforts, and any positive effect was simply a bonus.[54]

Hunt's "anti-drug" unit (which included most of his Plumbers) also worked with Lou Conein, the former CIA man Hunt used in the JFK-Diem smear. Conein would soon run a Special Operations group for the Bureau of Narcotics and Dangerous Drugs whose duties included, according to Congressional investigator Fonzi, "assassinating the key drug suppliers in Mexico." While Conein was working with Hunt, *The Washington Post* later reported their operations "stretched . . . far over the boundaries of legality." Five years after he began working with Hunt, Lucien Conein told *The Post* "that he had been brought to the Bureau of Narcotics and Dangerous Drugs to superintend a special unit which would have the capacity to assassinate selected targets in the narcotics business."[55]

Apparently, the original plan had been only to kidnap drug traffickers and bring them to the United States for trial. John Dean wrote that Egil Krogh—who, as noted, officially ran the anti-drug unit for Nixon—"had asked my office to resolve a dispute among the Pentagon, the State Department, and the Bureau of Narcotics over the legality of kidnapping drug traffickers abroad." However, at some point after that, Dean said that "Krogh had called me in and treated me to a mysterious denial that the White House narcotics office had been involved in the assassination of drug traffickers in Latin America" even though "no such story had appeared in print" at that time. Dean also noted that "Krogh has described to me how, when he was bored with his desk work, he had carried bars of gold bullion through Asia's 'Golden Triangle' in CIA planes and bargained with drug chieftains."[56]

There are other reports that Hunt's men did plan drug-related assassinations, including a plot to kill Panamanian dictator Omar Torrijos. Jack Anderson later wrote, well after Watergate, that "Hunt told a Boston television interviewer that there was 'concern' over Panama's drug smuggling and therefore, that 'if Torrijos didn't shape up and cooperate, he was going to be wasted.'" Hunt said, "the people in the Plumbers unit . . . had that as part of their brief." Anderson found that a "Dade Country, FL, investigation [had interviewed] Manuel Artime," who tied Barker to the plot. Artime said that "he was working with Barker in Panama." Anderson quoted Senate investigator Michael Ewing as saying they'd discovered "a front, with a fictional subsidiary in Panama, linked to . . . Barker." During a later deposition, when Hunt was asked, "Did you indicate to the press that you had knowledge of a plot to kill Omar Torrijos?" Hunt answered, "Well, I probably did." Jack Anderson's old friend, Frank Fiorini, independently confirmed the drug assassination component of the Plumbers Unit.[57]

Torrijos wasn't assassinated by Hunt and Barker's crew—and neither was Jack Anderson, who was himself the reported target of an aborted assassination plot by Hunt and Barker in 1972. However, other killings may have been linked to members of the Plumbers, such as one reported in *The New York Times* in 1972. That assassination involved an official who was shot in a Guatemala City restaurant by two men with pistols, as almost happened to Harry Williams nine years earlier when he went to visit Manuel Artime. The slain official had recently begun dealing with Artime.[58]

It would have been easy for Bernard Barker to motivate exile members of the Plumbers by telling them that sniper teams trained to slay drug lords could eventually be turned against Fidel. And if the slain drug kingpins had been competition for Trafficante, so much the better for the ultimate superior of Barker (and Artime and Fiorini).

Amid the start of Hunt's anti-drug activity, he was still getting help from the CIA, which was funding part of the White House narcotics effort. In addition to the fall 1971 help with the Ellsberg profiles mentioned earlier, "in mid-October [1971], Hunt had lunch with Thomas Karamessines, the CIA's Deputy Director for Plans," who had been Helms's top assistant. Hunt had a cover story for the CIA meeting, but *New York Times* reporter J. Anthony Lukas found Hunt's cover story unconvincing and noted that Karamessines was then "one of the CIA's most powerful figures."[59]

It's important to remember that Hunt's drug operations that began in 1971 would continue into 1972, through the arrests at the Watergate, and—without Hunt, Barker, and Fiorini—even after that. It was one more thing that Nixon would have to cover up after the arrests of the burglars. It's also possible that Nixon's drug operations were used as a cover for the payments from Southeast Asia later uncovered by Alexander Haig's probe by the Army's Criminal Investigation Command.

There was one well-documented, related operation near the start of Hunt's drug operation that might explain how Frank Fiorini came to become involved with Hunt again. According to Congressional investigator Michael Ewing, in June 1971 Fiorini had gone to Hunt with information that a female Cuban exile had information about Castro's reaction to JFK's assassination. Hunt, Fiorini, and Barker investigated the matter. The woman had been a servant in Castro's household at the time of JFK's assassination. Barker later told NBC News that

> I spoke to the lady in Spanish and brought—took her—to Mr. Hunt. Mr. Hunt personally examined her, in the sense that he questioned her, and he took it down on tapes.[60]

Hunt later testified to Ewing's committee that "I provided a raw report and submitted it to the Chief of the Western Hemisphere Division." After confirming Barker's role in the woman's interview, Hunt continued his testimony, saying, "I had part of that typed up in the White House and eventually sent a summary of it or a transcript over to CIA, and I may have accompanied that with a cassette tape." Hunt kept a copy of the report in his White House safe, while the CIA's copy wound up with "CIA Director Richard Helms." In addition, Hunt said he gave a copy to Charles Colson. Hunt's copy was apparently destroyed, along with the rest of the contents of his safe, after his name surfaced in the Watergate scandal. The CIA has never produced its copy for any of the Congressional investigations into Hunt or JFK's assassination—just one example of the many files involving Hunt and Barker that either are still withheld or were destroyed by Richard Helms, before he was forced to step down as CIA Director in early 1973.[61]

E. Howard Hunt had so far been a covert action "jack of all trades" for the Nixon White House, and he still had more roles yet to play. Some writers depict Hunt as a minor figure, bumbling his way from one small White House operation to the next. However, a review of all the evidence shows that Hunt was consistently working on important tasks for the Nixon White House, on matters that interested the President. Hunt also kept expanding (or wanting to expand) his operations, which often overlapped with other projects that he sought out or pushed. The more Nixon operations Hunt became involved in, the higher his status in the White House and the better for his future there. It was also good for his mentor, Richard Helms, since it gave him more access to White House (and FBI) information and operations. The President's White House staff was expanding its illegal operations on his behalf so rapidly that Hunt had no problem finding Nixon aides who wanted Hunt's services, to help them achieve the illicit goals the President wanted. That symbiotic relationship would soon grow so rapidly that it would start to spiral out of control, with disastrous results for all concerned.

CHAPTER 27

Nixon, the Mafia, Hoffa, the CIA, and Castro in 1971: Echoes of September 1960

The Nixon administration had an extremely mixed record when it came to prosecuting organized crime. Nixon's defenders point to Attorney General John Mitchell doubling "the number of organized crime strike forces," and they claim that Mitchell secured "indictments or convictions against half the top bosses in the nation's two dozen largest organized crime syndicates." However, those efforts stand in contrast to the brief prison hospital stay of mob boss Carlos Marcello (for his 1966 arrest), who was allowed to return home without being deported. In addition, over eight hundred organized crime indictments—including some major ones—had to be voided because Attorney General John Mitchell used "improper procedures" to get court approvals for wiretaps.[1]

Mitchell does deserve credit for proposing what came to become known as the RICO law, the Racketeer-Influenced and Corrupt Organizations Act. Historian David Kaiser wrote that the new law "made it easier to prosecute leading mobsters, without tying them directly to illegal acts." That statute was "largely written" by G. Robert Blakey, a former Mafia prosecutor for Robert Kennedy who later directed the House Select Committee on Assassinations that investigated Helms, Hunt, Barker, and other Watergate figures.[2]

However, President Nixon made sure the Attorney General didn't pursue mobsters in ways that could hurt him politically. For example, on July 13, 1970, Nixon ordered Mitchell to wait on any Mafia prosecutions until after "the midterm elections." Nixon's note, unpublished until 2008, said, "Mitchell—no prosecutions whatever re Mafia or any

Italians until Nov." Of all Nixon officials and White House aides, John Mitchell was the only one (aside from Helms) who knew about the CIA-Mafia plots, and likely Nixon's role, thanks to Mitchell's talk with Robert Maheu (documented in Chapter 25). Thus, Mitchell—soon to become Nixon's campaign manager—knew how politically sensitive Mafia prosecutions could be.[3]

Despite the gains that John Mitchell made in some areas of fighting crime, he would later become the first Attorney General to go to prison. Mitchell's Deputy, Richard Kleindienst—who would become Attorney General after Mitchell resigned to run Nixon's campaign—was "offered a $100,000 bribe to stop prosecution of several underworld figures . . . but he reported [the attempted bribe] a week later only when he learned that federal agents were investigating the" bribe attempt. Kleindienst was later convicted for an illegal insurance scam involving the Teamsters that eventually led to the arrest of mob boss Santo Trafficante. Another Nixon official, who screened "potential appointees to the Justice Department," was later arrested in the same "drug-money-laundering" scheme as a brother of Louisiana/Texas godfather Carlos Marcello.[4]

Other Nixon appointees also had links to the Mafia. Peter Brennan, who would become Nixon's Secretary of Labor, was described by organized crime expert David E. Scheim as "boss of New York City's Mob-linked Building and Trades Council, who traveled around carrying a loaded gun, accompanied by a pack of bodyguards." In addition, "a Justice Department official" told Dan Moldea about "several allegations before Brennan's confirmation that he was closely associated with members of the criminal syndicate." Brennan even brought a friend "convicted of labor racketeering" to meet Nixon at the White House. However, Brennan was important for helping Nixon generate support among traditionally Democratic union workers across the country, creating a voting bloc known as "hard-hat Republicans." Before being offered the position, Brennan was told he would have to keep the Labor Department from investigating Teamsters leader Frank Fitzsimmons, and Brennan complied.[5]

Nixon aide Chuck Colson would later tell journalist Dick Russell he'd heard that the Mafia "got their hooks into Nixon early, and of course, that ties into the overlap of the CIA and the mob," as mentioned earlier. While most of Nixon's dealings with the Mafia were handled through longtime trusted confidants (and mob associates) like Bebe

Rebozo and Murray Chotiner, some of Nixon's White House aides did see and hear things that made them suspicious about Nixon's mob ties. As with Nixon in September 1960, those ties were leading Nixon back to yet another huge Mafia bribe involving Jimmy Hoffa and a Presidential election. (Also like in September 1960, another CIA attempt to assassinate Fidel Castro was brewing, as described shortly.)[6]

In 1971, President Richard Nixon's biggest scheme with the Mafia was a new attempt to release Jimmy Hoffa from prison, a long-sought-after goal for the mob since 1966, when Carlos Marcello was given control of the Mafia's $2 million "spring Hoffa" fund. But much had changed for the Teamsters, Hoffa, and the Mafia by 1971—with the biggest change being the unexpected emergence of Frank Fitzsimmons as the new leader of the Teamsters. Originally, the Teamsters Vice President was seen as little more than a flunky, carrying out the orders of the imprisoned Jimmy Hoffa. However, the longer Hoffa stayed behind bars, the more powerful the large and amiable Fitzsimmons became.

Hoffa had appointed a corrupt Teamsters official named Allen Dorfman to dole out loans to the Mafia from the huge Teamsters pension fund. (Dorfman's father had been involved in a Chicago murder that forged the first ties between the Teamsters and the mob.) Mafia leaders outside the South felt that Hoffa had especially favored the mob families of Carlos Marcello and Santo Trafficante, and now Dorfman was open to payoffs to rectify that imbalance. However, after a shooting incident was arranged to intimidate Dorfman, an accommodation was reached that satisfied all the mob bosses. According to one account, "under Fitzsimmons and Dorfman . . . Frank Ragano, Santo Trafficante's lawyer, received [an] $11 million" loan, and a Marcello associate "received [a] $7 million" loan from the Teamsters. In all, the Teamsters' "pension fund controlled by Allen Dorfman had loaned over $500 million in Nevada, to the [Mafia's] favored casinos."[7]

Aside from Marcello and Trafficante, most of the other mob bosses and corrupt Teamsters leaders would have been happy to see Frank Fitzsimmons remain in charge of the union. But Fitzsimmons soon developed close ties to the Nixon White House that even Marcello and Trafficante must have realized were beyond anything Hoffa could have engineered. Attorney General John Mitchell began communicating regularly with Fitzsimmons, and by 1971, Nixon's aides were also "pressuring the Justice Department to ease up on prosecutions of crooked Teamsters, as a way to ensure the union's backing in the coming presidential election."[8]

A new deal to release Jimmy Hoffa from prison was being planned in 1971, one that had several goals. First, it had to be done carefully, so it didn't look like an obvious bribe or quid pro quo. Second, it had to involve a way to keep Frank Fitzsimmons in power, and Jimmy Hoffa out of the Teamsters, for a long time. That was needed not only for the Mafia bosses, but also because it was possible for President Nixon to be close to Fitzsimmons in public in a politically advantageous way that simply wasn't possible with the controversial Hoffa. Third, the bribe needed to structured more carefully than the 1960 Nixon-Mafia-Hoffa $500,000 bribe, since by 1971 Nixon almost certainly knew the Justice Department and FBI were aware of his 1960 bribe. Finally, the 1971 deal had to overcome the problems of the previous arrangement to free Hoffa in 1969, which had stalled in the first year of Nixon's term, as mentioned in Chapter 23.

The 1969 "spring Hoffa" attempt had involved Murray Chotiner, whom Teamsters expert Dan Moldea pointed out "had numerous known connections with the underworld, particularly . . . among the Marcello clan." On at least three occasions, Marcello and Trafficante had their associates try to bribe key Hoffa witness Edward Partin to recant his testimony against Hoffa, but without success. Their efforts quickly shifted to getting newly elected President Nixon to pardon Hoffa. Murray Chotiner told Marcello's Washington lobbyist that "Hoffa would be out of jail by Thanksgiving" and said "approval had come directly from the Oval Office." The price was a rumored $100,000; Summers reported that Allen Dorfman—later killed in a mob hit—"had a receipt, purportedly signed by John Mitchell, for one hundred thousand dollars."[9]

However, back in 1969 word had spread quickly, not just to Hoffa's family, Teamsters leaders, and the Mafia, but also to Walter Sheridan, the former Justice Department prosecutor who had worked so long to put Hoffa behind bars. Sheridan called an old friend, Clark Mollenhoff, who worked in the Nixon White House, telling him

> It's all set for the Nixon Administration to spring Jimmy Hoffa . . . I'm told Murray Chotiner is handling it with the Las Vegas mob. John Mitchell and John Ehrlichman have something to do with it, and I'm told that it has been cleared with Nixon.[10]

Sheridan's friend Mollenhoff was described as a "decent man opposed to" criminal activity. In September 1969, when Mollenhoff checked with his associates at the Nixon White House, John Ehrlichman told him, "The President does not want you in this. It is highly sensitive. John Mitchell and I have it under control." However, Hoffa's release that year was thwarted, for several reasons. Moldea pointed to the growing friendship between Attorney General Mitchell and Fitzsimmons in 1969, indicating that Fitzsimmons prevailed upon Mitchell to stop Hoffa's early release, because Fitzsimmons's own power kept expanding only as long as Hoffa remained in prison. In addition, the fact that Clark Mollenhoff was able to find out about the deal—even though he wasn't part of Nixon's inner circle—showed White House aides the deal wasn't secure and could leak to others. Finally, Marcello's lobbyist said that "Charles Colson had persuaded Nixon to scuttle the idea." According to Stephen Ambrose, Colson didn't want Hoffa released "until after the union election in 1971, so that Hoffa could not challenge Fitzsimmons for the [Teamsters] presidency."[11]

While Hoffa remained in prison into 1970 and 1971, Frank Fitzsimmons consolidated his power and developed new ties to the White House and to Nixon himself. Fitzsimmons is said to have met Nixon in late 1970, but even before that, Nixon's aides were busy seeing how they could exploit the Nixon-Fitzsimmons-Teamsters relationship—and the new price would be much more than $100,000. On June 7, 1970, Charles Colson sent a memo to Egil Krogh, saying "substantial sums of money, perhaps a quarter of a million dollars" could be obtained if Nixon "arrang[ed] to have James Hoffa released from prison." Five months later, on November 8, Nixon's Chief of Staff H.R. Haldeman sent a memo to Colson saying, "The President wants you to take on the responsibility for working on developing your strength with the labor unions . . . by picking them off one by one . . . The President specifically has in mind the Teamsters [since] there is a great deal of gold there to be mined."[12]

On March 8, 1971, Jimmy Hoffa's wife suffered "a heart attack and stoke," according to Frank Ragano. Soon after that, Hoffa summoned Frank Ragano to be present when he confronted Frank Fitzsimmons and Allen Dorfman about not securing his release from prison. At the meeting, Fitzsimmons told Hoffa he'd been trying to arrange his release through his White House connections, but Nixon's aides wanted to wait until after the 1972 election, to avoid any bad publicity. Hoffa then "unleashed a torrent of curses at Fitzsimmons, telling him his wife

> is very sick, and needs me. I'm going to give you until Christmas to get me out of prison. If I'm not out before Christmas Day, you won't be around to celebrate New Year's. Don't forget, I still have friends on the outside."[13]

Ragano later said he was there to remind Fitzsimmons that "I was the surrogate for Santo and Carlos Marcello, and they represented the brute force [Hoffa] could command to kill or maim [Fitzsimmons]." The men reached an arrangement whereby Hoffa would resign as Teamsters President, Fitzsimmons would be elected to replace him, but then Fitzsimmons would step down as soon as Hoffa was released. Ragano said that Santo Trafficante allowed Hoffa's threat to Fitzsimmons to remain in place, forcing Fitzsimmons and Dorfman into increasing action with the Nixon White House as the Christmas deadline loomed.[14]

Hoffa kept his part of the bargain, announcing "on June 3, 1971 [that] he would not be a candidate in the July [Teamsters] election," and he officially tendered his resignation as Teamsters President on June 20. On June 21, 1971, Frank Fitzsimmons was elected the new Teamster President, at the executive board's meeting in Miami.[15]

Richard Nixon personally welcomed Fitzsimmons into office, having "driven up from Key Biscayne." In a private meeting with the board, Nixon didn't mention Hoffa, but he proclaimed, "my door is always open to President Fitzsimmons." Ambrose notes that "Fitzsimmons became a golfing partner of the President's and the Teamsters pledged financial support and an endorsement for Nixon in" the 1972 election. Nixon even appointed Fitzsimmons to a government board dealing with wage and price controls. But there was "still no pardon for Hoffa" in the summer of 1971.[16]

Many details remained to be worked out before Hoffa could be released. Fitzsimmons wanted to make sure he wouldn't have to keep his promise to resign upon Hoffa's release. He and his allies also needed a way to prevent Hoffa from challenging Fitzsimmons's Presidency through the Teamsters membership (where Hoffa remained popular) or through the courts. Other considerations included how much money would be required to release Hoffa with the proper conditions, when to release him, how to make it look good to the press, and how to keep the secret deal from becoming known. The new relationship of trust between Nixon, Fitzsimmons, and John Mitchell opened up several new possibilities, such as paying much of the money well after Hoffa's release so as not to arouse suspicion.[17]

Time magazine, in 1977 and 1981, published the results of investigations by the IRS and FBI, detailing how the Mafia-Teamsters bribe to release Hoffa in 1971 was arranged and paid. The amounts are staggering: *Time* said that "the Teamsters contributed an estimated $1 million" to Nixon's campaign. And there was an additional $500,000 for Nixon, personally. The information came from "IRS agents' interviews with Fitzsimmons and some of his Teamsters colleagues, who had cooperated in hope of avoiding prosecution on other matters." In addition, there was an informant, Harry Hall, "who acted as their go-between with [the] IRS." Hall later told Anthony Summers that "a large amount of money was given by the Teamsters to the Committee to Re-Elect the President . . . I was told they gave the money to Chotiner that was to go to Nixon. I think it was close to five hundred thousand dollars." Hall points out that "five hundred thousand dollars" was "intended for Nixon personally" and "was separate from the sum [of $1 million] donated to CREEP." Murray Chotiner worked with "an associate of Mafia boss Carlos Marcello" to arrange part of the Hoffa deal, and in "a file on the negotiations . . . Chotiner was referred to by the code name [of] Mr. Pajamas."[18]

Because of the good relationship between Richard Nixon and Frank Fitzsimmons, *Time* found indications that some of the money was paid a year after Hoffa's release. That transaction involved both Fitzsimmons and Tony Provenzano, a captain in the Genovese crime family and vice president of a New Jersey Teamsters local. Provenzano had also been involved with Marcello in Nixon's 1960 Mafia-Hoffa bribe and remained friendly with the New Orleans godfather. According to *Time*, citing "government informants," Allan "Dorfman provided half of the bribe for Nixon on Fitzsimmons's orders. The other $500,000 was handled by Provenzano, again at Fitzsimmons's behest, and delivered to a White House courier in Las Vegas . . . The FBI believed Charles Colson received the money in Las Vegas on January 6, 1973."*[19]

*Charles Colson denied being part of any such bribe attempt

Richard Nixon was careful not to document his illicit dealings with the mob, but years later, the *New York Post* described the FBI's discovery of a diary belonging to a New Orleans associate of Carlos Marcello. An entry in the diary for January 5, 1973, said, "Fitz OK Al Dorfman chi ok.—Tony Pro Jersey ok ($500—to C. C. = nix OK)." This indicates that "a payment [of possibly $500,000] was made to Nixon through Charles Colson and had been okayed by Teamsters Allen Dorfman, Tony Provenzano, and Frank Fitzsimmons," according to Anthony Summers and A.J. Weberman.[20]

Nixon was involved in the deal, not just through Murray Chotiner but also apparently through Charles Colson. Colson later testified in a civil deposition that "the President" had asked him at one point in 1971 to give advice with respect to the commutation of Mr. Hoffa, which I did." Colson also admitted "that he had discussed the Hoffa case with Fitzsimmons before the White House commuted the sentence." Moldea points out that when Colson was questioned about the Hoffa release "by the Senate Watergate Committee, Colson invoked the Fifth Amendment" against self-incrimination.[21]

One person who was not involved with the 1971 Hoffa release and Mafia bribe for Nixon was E. Howard Hunt, even though he did have a meeting with Frank Fitzsimmons. Moldea found that "according to federal investigators, Hunt met Fitzsimmons at least once and was told by Colson that the Teamster president was providing 'derogatory information' about [Senator Edward] Kennedy. Hunt told the investigators that Colson said the material came from Teamster sources in Las Vegas." But "a federal investigator said it was the usual Teamster crap—probably invented by Fitzsimmons to try and ingratiate himself with the White House even more." It is interesting that three days after the Watergate break-in, on the day Hunt's name first surfaced in the press, President Nixon—less than an hour after concluding the tape with the infamous "18 minute gap"—made a still unexplained call to an associate of Tony Provenzano.* Just over six months after that call, Nixon would apparently consider using some of the Mafia-Hoffa money from Provenzano as hush money for Hunt and his Watergate burglary team.[22]

*An article in the *Manchester Union Leader* claimed that Hunt and G. Gordon Liddy had been couriers for the Mafia-Hoffa bribe, but Chotiner sued and the article was retracted. None of the information in that story was used in the *Time* articles or any of the other material cited in this book.

Richard Nixon's 1971 Mafia-Hoffa bribe was not without risk, both in terms of angering Hoffa and having the deal possibly uncovered by the press in the upcoming election year. But with union support in short supply for the Republican President—who was facing what he felt would be another tight race—the risk could be worth it. And the money, both for his campaign and himself, was a golden opportunity. The $500,000 Nixon received for himself would likely have been handled by Bebe Rebozo, like Nixon's other sensitive, personal financial matters. Rebozo was also one of the only people Nixon could talk to completely candidly about the Hoffa matter. On December 4, 1971, Nixon went without his family to his Key Biscayne house, next to Rebozo's home in the Presidential compound. The White House prepared daily logs (called "Nixon's Daily Diary") of the President's activities each day, and they show that Nixon and Rebozo spent two hours together alone on the beach and Rebozo's yacht in the afternoon. That evening, Nixon and Rebozo spent several hours alone together, having dinner and talking. Apparently, Nixon had made his decision about Hoffa and was satisfied with the arrangements. The following day, Nixon talked to Charles Colson by phone, then returned to the White House. On December 8, 1971, Attorney General John Mitchell talked with Nixon about the Hoffa arrangement. Chief of Staff H.R. Haldeman heard about Hoffa's release date on December 9, 1971, when he wrote in his own diary, "The P[resident] apparently met with the Attorney General yesterday and agreed to pardon Jimmy Hoffa." Technically, it wouldn't be a full pardon, but a commutation of the remainder of Hoffa's sentence.[23]

Nixon planned to release Hoffa from prison two days before Christmas. It would look like a humanitarian gesture, good for Hoffa's family, and the official reason for the pardon was Hoffa's "wife's health." Plus, it was a slow time in the news cycle, with most of the Washington press corps on holiday, which would help to mute any criticism or press investigation. On December 22, Hoffa signed the commutation agreement. It specified that he would remain on federal probation until March 1973—but Hoffa says the agreement mentioned nothing limiting his activities with the Teamsters. However, the following day, when President Nixon "signed the papers that freed Hoffa," Moldea points out that "a proviso was added to Hoffa's commutation that barred him from union activities until March 6, 1980, when he would be sixty-seven years old." That special provision was the result of the dealings between Nixon, his aides, the Mafia, and Fitzsimmons.[24]

On December 23, 1971, Jimmy Hoffa walked out of the gates of the Lewisburg Federal Penitentiary, tasting freedom for the first time in more than four years. Reporters swarmed around the smiling Hoffa, who initially stuck to his script, saying, "I have no intention of returning to the Teamsters . . . Frank Fitzsimmons is doing a good job."[25]

Then a reporter asked, "What about the [special] restrictions Nixon put on you, forbidding you from running for union office until 1980?"[26]

Hoffa was stunned. His "smile disappeared and he replied that he was unaware of any restrictions." He told the reporters "the document he had signed" the previous day "made no mention of them." Fitzsimmons greeted Hoffa at the airport, and the two talked privately in a car. One can only imagine what was said between a furious Jimmy Hoffa and Fitzsimmons, now the Teamsters President. Frank Fitzsimmons probably tried to lay the blame for the special provision on the Nixon White House. In addition, Fitzsimmons had arranged for the Teamsters Board to pay Hoffa a "lump-sum $1.7 million pension" to help placate the angry Hoffa. As Hoffa left, Fitzsimmons told him they could talk again after the holidays, to which Hoffa replied, "We'll see about that."*[27]

Hoffa's fury over the special restrictions no doubt eclipsed that of his anger after the September 1960 $500,000 Mafia bribe to Nixon, when Hoffa was indicted after Nixon lost the November 1960 election. But Fitzsimmons—and President Nixon—had all the power at this point, so Hoffa would have to be careful about anything he said or did in public. He was on federal parole, and he faced having to serve more than an additional eight years if he violated the special restrictions.[28]

When pressed in a civil deposition, Hoffa would only blame Charles Colson for the special restrictions. However, Hoffa learned more about the deal from Carlos Marcello's Washington lobbyist. Jimmy Hoffa told Frank Ragano that "Nixon and Fitz[simmons] had become friends and Nixon sure as hell knew" about the special restriction. After all, Nixon could have easily overruled Colson if he'd wanted to. Hoffa also told Ragano, "We had to pay $1 million" for his release. The $1 million payment was also confirmed to Ragano by Allen Dorfman, who said "the money had been given to John Mitchell . . . under the table."[29]

*One of Hoffa's codefendants was released the same day as Hoffa, after arranging to donate $30,000 to Nixon's reelection campaign.

Jimmy Hoffa would bide his time, looking for a way to get some measure of revenge on Richard Nixon. Two years after his release, still under the special conditions he hated, Hoffa would tip off the Senate Watergate Committee about one of Nixon's darkest secrets: Johnny Rosselli and the 1960 CIA-Mafia plots. Hoffa's disclosure would result in Rosselli being forced to testify about the plots to Committee investigators. Hoffa's attempt to get revenge on Nixon would lead directly to Rosselli's gruesome murder and contribute to Hoffa's own death.[30]

The deal between President Nixon and Frank Fitzsimmons produced benefits for both men. Just over six months after Hoffa was released—long enough so that it wasn't an obvious quid pro quo—Fitzsimmons and the Teamsters would officially endorse Nixon. In the year after that endorsement, Fitzsimmons would be flying on Air Force One with Nixon while the White House intervened to halt Teamsters investigations at least six times, protecting Fitzsimmons, Dorfman, and others (including Dave Beck, the first Teamsters leader to endorse a Nixon ticket). Those actions became so brazen they would lead to a major *Los Angeles Times* editorial titled "Nixon, the Teamsters, and the Mafia."[31]

A celebrated reporter for the *Los Angeles Times*, Jack Nelson, interviewed "an FBI agent who has been investigating widespread Teamster-Mafia deals." The worried agent told them: "This whole thing of the Teamsters and the mob and the White House is one of the scariest things I've ever seen." There were other controversial Mafia-linked pardons and commutations as well, including that of "Angelo DeCarlo, a killer [and] top rackets figure in New Jersey," where Nixon aides and officials took action outside of normal channels.[32] A Justice Department official told Dan Moldea:

> The whole goddamn thing is too frightening to think about . . . We're talking about the President of the United States . . . a man who pardoned organized crime figures after millions were spent by the government putting them away, a guy who's had these connections since he was a congressman in the 1940s.[33]

There are striking parallels between Richard Nixon's bribe to release Hoffa in 1971 and Nixon's actions in September 1960, when some of the same players gave then–Vice President Nixon $500,000 to stall charges against Hoffa. Carlos Marcello, Santo Trafficante, and Tony

Provenzano were involved in both the 1971 deal and the 1960 bribes. In each case, the bribes were politically expedient, both for Teamsters political support and to help fund Nixon's Presidential campaign. Remarkably, just as in 1960—when the Mafia-Hoffa bribe coincided with Nixon's CIA-Mafia plots to kill Fidel before the elections—in December 1971 the CIA was attempting a new Castro assassination plot.[34]

In late 1971, CIA Director Richard Helms was still under intense pressure from Nixon to undermine the Socialist President of Chile, Salvador Allende. The White House effort involved Henry Kissinger and Alexander Haig, but most of the work fell to Helms and the CIA, as documented earlier. Originally called "Project Camelot," the plan to overthrow Allende was now called "Track II," another code name from 1963 (when it was used to cover U.S. support for exile leaders in the JFK-Almeida coup plan such as Manuel Artime and Eloy Menoyo).[35]

The head of the CIA's Chile Task Force was David Atlee Phillips, now in charge of all of the CIA's Latin American operations. That meant at the same time Phillips was being pressed for results in Chile, he was also responsible for continuing some level of operations to undermine Fidel Castro and Cuba. Apparently, Phillips came up with an operation that could deal with Nixon's goals for both countries. It would be "an attempt to assassinate Castro in Chile in 1971," one that was later extensively documented by the House Select Committee on Assassinations (HSCA).[36]

Congressional investigator Gaeton Fonzi discovered that the assassination plot had been organized by David Atlee Phillips, using the cover name of "Maurice Bishop." Phillips used the founder of the Alpha 66 Cuban exile group—CIA asset Antonio Veciana—in the operation. As explained in Chapter 11, Veciana was reluctant to publicly identify Phillips as Bishop to Congressional investigators in the late 1970s, perhaps due to the spate of killings in the mid-1970s of Cuban exile leaders and others connected to the 1960 CIA-Mafia plots. Veciana himself was shot in the head soon after the HSCA's report naming him was published. In an interview with this author's research associates, Veciana remained reluctant to change his earlier sworn testimony, only implying that Phillips was Bishop (saying he named "Alpha 66" after the "Phillips 66" gas stations). But Gaeton Fonzi compiled overwhelming evidence showing that Phillips was

Bishop. His conclusion was later confirmed when E. Howard Hunt—in a CIA-approved account—stated that Phillips had supported Alpha 66 for the CIA, including dealing with Alpha 66's "founder, Antonio Veciana." So this account will dispense with the "Bishop" cover name and will use Phillips's actual identity.[37]

The CIA's December 1971 plot to kill Fidel Castro during his state visit to Chile was first revealed in the secret Cuban Dossier of CIA attempts to assassinate Fidel. Just five months after the CIA attempted to assassinate Fidel in Chile, the Cuban Dossier would become the primary goal of the Watergate burglars—not just at the Watergate building, but in their first burglary, at the Chilean embassy in Washington. The Dossier detailed many CIA attempts to kill Castro, starting with a 1960 plot involving a "gangster" and ending with the December 1971 attempt in Chile. In addition to the Dossier's concise account, more details about the Chile attempt come from the HSCA's inquiry and additional reporting by its investigator, Gaeton Fonzi.[38]

David Atlee Phillips officially reported to the CIA Deputy Director for Plans (DDP) Thomas Karamessines, but Phillips also worked with CIA Director Richard Helms. If any CIA officer admired Helms as much as E. Howard Hunt, it was Hunt's good friend David Atlee Phillips, who later wrote glowingly of Helms and would have done anything the Director asked. According to a Senate report, "Helms ran the DDP out of his hip pocket." Thus it was Helms who had final say on sensitive operations, not his former assistant, Karamessines. And in 1971, Helms was being pressured on Chile in much the same way John and Robert Kennedy had pressured him over Cuba in 1963.[39]

Earlier in 1971, when Fidel Castro announced plans for a lengthy state visit to Chile, it presented a rare opportunity for Helms and Phillips. Nixon's formal agreement to a "no invasion" pledge for Cuba had limited the types of action the CIA could plan against Fidel. The CIA had few viable assets inside Cuba capable of mounting significant operations. However, several important CIA Cuban exile agents and assets were now based in countries neighboring Chile, and the Agency still had ties to right-wing elements in the Chilean military and intelligence services. The CIA's Station Chief in Chile was anti-Castro veteran Henry Hecksher, Manuel Artime's former case officer for AMWORLD. If Fidel Castro were killed in Chile, it would not only achieve that long-sought-after goal for Helms and the CIA, but would also disrupt Chilean President Allende's government, and probably end any alliance between Chile and Cuba.[40]

Helms and Phillips knew that Commander Juan Almeida remained alive, unexposed, and high in the government in Cuba. Almeida was no longer as powerful as he had been in 1963—no Cuban official was, save for Fidel and Raul Castro—and Almeida hadn't been actively engaged with U.S. anti-Castro efforts since his last contact with Harry Williams in January 1964. But, hoping something might develop in the future, the CIA had continued to support Almeida's wife and two of his children outside of Cuba in an operation now overseen by Phillips. Almeida was still immensely popular in Cuba and remained essentially the No. 3 official after Fidel and Raul Castro. For Helms and Phillips, seeing Almeida move up to at least No. 2 would have been an enticing prospect.[41]

When CIA anti-Castro operations in the United States had wound down in the late 1960s, David Atlee Phillips had helped Alpha 66's Antonio Veciana get a job with the U.S. Agency for International Development (AID) in Bolivia, supposedly "as a banking advisor to Bolivia's Central Bank." However, Veciana spent much of his time working for Phillips, traveling for the CIA "around Latin America . . . involving himself in propaganda ploys aimed at the character assassination of leading communist politicians or weakening the financial stability of left-leaning governments."[42]

It was Phillips who told Veciana about Fidel's upcoming trip to Chile and asked him to "begin planning another assassination attempt." Phillips explained "that it was an opportunity to make it appear that the anti-Castro Cubans killed Castro without American involvement." As had been the case for the CIA since the 1960 plots with Johnny Rosselli and Santo Trafficante, the point for the Agency wasn't just to kill Fidel, but to do it in a way that someone else could be blamed besides the U.S. government and the CIA.[43]

Antonio Veciana and his exile associate in the operation, Luis Posada, had some links to the Mafia in their pasts (Veciana through his associates), but they were primarily creatures of the CIA. Both men had worked on the anti-Castro operations of Desmond FitzGerald. Veciana's close partner from 1962 through 1964 was Eloy Menoyo, whom the Kennedys and Harry Williams had tried to woo away from Veciana in 1963 so that Menoyo could join the JFK-Almeida coup plan. Also involved in the December 1971 plot against Fidel was Luis Posada, a longtime CIA agent and asset who had begun his work with the Agency during the Bay of Pigs planning (though not as an invader). Posada became part of the Fort Benning troops who were to be the first into Cuba as part of the JFK-Almeida coup plan; after that ended, Posada had joined the exile group of Manolo Ray, until it dissolved.[44]

In 1971, Posada was still a contract agent with the CIA, and to Congressional investigators "Phillips admitted that Posada had been one of his operatives and had worked with him closely on Chilean activities." The CIA had helped Posada become "the chief of security and counterintelligence in the Venezuelan secret police," which put him in an excellent position to help Veciana and Phillips with the Castro plot.[45]

Antonio Veciana said that Phillips "not only suggested the operation, he had a major role in setting it up." While Phillips had numerous duties in Washington, his role as Latin American Chief for the CIA allowed him to travel extensively throughout the region, and he'd retained his decade-plus deep cover relationship with Veciana.[46]

The Cuban Dossier soon to be at the heart of the Watergate burglaries provides a concise summary of the Chile operation. It says the plot involved "the CIA and Cuban [exiles] from 'Alpha 66.'" The Dossier explains that one of the shooters "obtained false documents which identified him as a Venezuelan newspaper man, which permitted him to report [on Castro's] visit in that country." After scouting Castro's security arrangements, the next step would occur in Chile, where "the plan would be carried out using a gun—camouflaged into a television camera." According to Veciana and investigator Fonzi, "Posada . . . provided all the credentials and documents necessary to enable the selected assassins to establish their false identities and get into place in Chile.*[47]

Antonio Veciana planned to use two other Cuban exiles to actually carry out the assassination of Fidel. Veciana said they "arrived in Santiago de Chile 'long before Castro was due to arrive. . . and began interviewing the Chilean government as if they were Venezuelan journalists.'" Veciana said "the plan was [then] to convert the two [assassins] into Venevisión cameramen to subsequently infiltrate them into a press conference to be given by [Castro] in Santiago de Chile." Veciana said that idea came from the CIA, to take "advantage of the conference where 600 or 700 journalists would be present, for

*Posada would later tell HSCA investigators "that he was not involved in the Castro assassination attempt in Chile in 1971," though he admitted "he did talk to Veciana about the time the Chile plot was being planned."

the assassination." As Veciana explained, "we had somebody who knew about the workings of Cuban press conferences . . . by using a small weapon and hiding it in a certain section of the camera . . . the weapon wouldn't be detected." It was Veciana who "left La Paz . . . in a diplomatic car from the U.S. embassy with the weapons."[48]

However, Veciana and his associates came up with an idea they didn't completely explain to Phillips. The exiles had wondered "who's going to be blamed for Castro's death?" Just as the CIA didn't want to be blamed, Veciana and his fellow exile leaders also didn't want to be blamed. So they came up with a plan to "put the blame on the Soviet Union." Without telling Phillips, they used photos and other methods—fake passports, diaries, etc.—to link the two shooters to a couple of alleged KGB agents, so Fidel's murder could be blamed on the Soviets (evoking a strategy used by the CIA on some of their Castro plots in the 1960s).[49]

The way Phillips had originally planned for the operation to work, after the two exile assassins had shot Fidel, they would be taken into custody by Chilean military security, before Castro's guards could grab them. Later, the two assassins would be taken out of the country. Clearly, Veciana—with his "blame the Soviets" ruse—felt there was a chance the two assassins would be killed by security, even before they got out of the press conference. That thought must have also occurred to the two assassins. Veciana explained that while he knew Phillips had the clout to be able to arrange for the two to be quickly arrested by Chilean military security, the two assassins were skeptical. In any event, the two men—according to different accounts—either lost their nerve or one became ill, and shots were never fired.[50]

Veciana made one last attempt to salvage the operation by trying to talk Luis Posada into assassinating Fidel when he made "a stop in Quito, Ecuador, on his return to Cuba." But Posada couldn't see any "assured escape route, and declined Veciana's assassination offer." Phillips was angry when he found out the details of Veciana's "blame the Soviets" strategy. As Veciana told this author's researchers, Phillips "thought I'd stabbed him in the back [and he] told me, why did you do this without consulting me?" Phillips said, "If it would have occurred it would have been a major problem for the US." That dispute led to the end of the Phillips-Veciana relationship.[51]

Later, the HSCA "probed the anti-Castro Cuban community in Miami and found that Veciana's involvement in the [1971] plot was known by many of the active exiles." In fact, the "editor and publisher of . . . the most prominent Spanish-language weekly publication in the community, said he was aware of Veciana's involvement in the assassination attempt at the time" of the attempt and thought "that Veciana must have had 'some high Government contacts, probably CIA.'" If "many of the active exiles" in Miami knew about the attempt, experience shows that Cuban intelligence knew as well, which explains how an account of the December 1971 attempt came to be included in the Cuban Dossier of CIA assassination attempts. In fact, knowledge of the December 1971 attempt could have been what prompted the first preparation of the Cuban Dossier in the months following the failed Chile attempt.[52]

David Atlee Phillips would not have undertaken such a risky move without the approval of CIA Director Richard Helms, since it could have impacted the situation with two sensitive, high-priority countries. It's also possible that the idea for the operation originated with Helms, given his previous four-year-long campaign (1962–1965) to assassinate Fidel Castro.

More importantly, did President Richard Nixon approve the operation, or know about it ahead of time? The answer to that question is less clear. A year earlier, "Nixon [had] demanded an immediate CIA briefing on '*any* kind of action which will irritate Castro," as mentioned in the previous chapter. (Emphasis in original.) While assassinating the Cuban leader was a leap beyond that, ordinarily it would be hard to imagine a CIA Director not giving the President any indication a major assassination attempt was being planned that involved two of Nixon's target countries, Cuba and Chile. However, Helms did have a documented, self-admitted track record of pursuing Castro assassination attempts without informing Presidents, from Kennedy to Johnson. On the other hand, Nixon himself had a documented track record of also pressing for Fidel's assassination, so the answer may never been known.[53]

Assassinating foreign leaders was not out of the question for President Nixon and his inner circle. Sy Hersh reported that Nixon aide Alexander Haig, when talking about Chile, "once told John Court, an NSC staff aide, that . . . 'if we have to take care of somebody, we could do it.'" And it's now well documented that, as cited earlier, Nixon and Helms's operations led to the assassination of Chile's Commander-in-Chief, General René Schneider, a year before the Castro attempt in

Chile. Even though U.S. covert operations against Chile have been investigated since 1973, many files have taken decades to be declassified, and numerous important files about Chile from 1970 to 1973 remain secret today. (General René Schneider's family is still seeking justice, and information, from the United States in 2012.) Not that Nixon would have signed an order or recorded a conversation about having Fidel assassinated in Chile, but a full disclosure might reveal meetings or memos that could provide clues to Nixon's knowledge, or lack of it. If Nixon did approve the attempt, he might have done so hoping that Fidel's death, and a new U.S. focus on post-Castro Cuba, would give him cover for more rapid disengagement from Vietnam without appearing weak.[54]

Even if Richard Nixon hadn't approved the operation in advance, he almost certainly would have been informed by Richard Helms about its failure, probably soon after the fact, since "the plot was known by many of the active exiles" in Miami. Bebe Rebozo had numerous contacts and business associates in the exile community, including those he shared with Bernard Barker and Eugenio Martinez. It would have been a disaster for Helms if Nixon had heard about the failed plot through Rebozo, instead of from his own CIA Director, especially given the important status of Chile to Nixon at that point. Given the earlier-noted incident in one of Nixon's first Cabinet meetings—when Nixon corrected Helms for leaving out relatively minor information about a small African country—Helms would have told Nixon something about the Chile attempt, at least after it occurred. If Helms told Nixon after the fact (and had acted without approval), Helms could have covered himself by simply saying he had received a report about a failed plot by Cuban exiles to kill Fidel in Chile. Still, given the enormous U.S. effort against Chile—and Nixon's and the CIA's long history with Cuba—Nixon would have known or at least suspected that the CIA was probably involved to some degree.

It's remarkable that the only documented CIA attempt to kill Fidel Castro during Nixon's time in office occurred in December 1971, the same month Nixon had completed a new bribery deal with the Mafia regarding Hoffa, echoing the September 1960 Nixon-Mafia-Hoffa bribe and CIA-Mafia plots. The exposure of any of those secret operations could imperil Nixon's reelection chances, and the exposure of one could also lead to uncovering some or all of the others. Even if Nixon didn't authorize the 1971 Chile attempt, it was still part of a series of events that would lead to even more dangerous operations by E. Howard Hunt and Nixon's Plumbers, including the Watergate break-in.

According to a probation official for Bernard Barker, E. Howard Hunt told the exile Watergate burglars that "another 'assassination team' was being readied in Spain" to kill Fidel Castro. Hunt also told them "about planning for the second phase of the Bay of Pigs around the beginning of Nixon's second term" to motivate them, as mentioned previously. With Nixon's "no invasion pledge," a Bay of Pigs–style invasion was no longer an option—but an assassination plot was. Whether Hunt was serious or just telling that to his exiles to spur them on, any word they heard about the failed Chile plot in Miami would only serve to make them think the U.S. government and the CIA were still serious about trying to eliminate Fidel.[55]

Antonio Veciana would not be part of those operations. Though he pressed David Atlee Phillips to continue plans to assassinate Fidel, Phillips—wary and more cautions after the failure of his Chile plot—refused, and would soon terminate his relationship with Veciana. Luis Posada, however, would continue working for the CIA for at least another five years, and would later be accused of committing several terrorist acts.

For reasons still unclear, at the end of December 1971, Deputy CIA Director Lieutenant General Robert Cushman resigned. He was promoted to General and became the Marine Corps Commandant, but it's not known if he wanted to leave or if he was forced out. His replacement would be Lieutenant General Vernon Walters, whose work for Nixon dated back to the 1950s. (Chapter 4 described the meeting between Vice President Nixon, Walters, Cushman, and Hunt in Uruguay.) Since 1967, Walters had been the U.S. military's attaché in Paris. His duties there included helping to sneak Nixon's National Security Advisor Henry Kissinger into France for secret meetings with senior North Vietnamese officials, as the U.S. tried to reignite the type of peace talks that Nixon had helped to stall back in November 1968.

In the wake of the failed December 1971 attempt to kill Fidel Castro in Chile, the CIA and Nixon increased their efforts to undermine and overthrow President Allende. The Chile operations of Helms and Phillips involved one of the same groups involved in funneling illegal money to Nixon and his reelection campaign: International Telephone and Telegraph (ITT). The conglomerate owned 60 percent of Chile's telephone company and, as noted earlier, had pushed for Nixon to take strong action against Allende. According to *The New York Times*, "Congressional investigators eventually established . . . that the CIA had used ITT as a conduit to funnel at least $8 million to anti-Allende groups over the years." Within weeks of the failed Castro assassination attempt, ITT would also be at the heart of a $400,000 scandal involving Nixon, Jack Anderson, Richard Helms, and E. Howard Hunt.[56]

CHAPTER 28

The 1972 Campaign: Why Nixon Ordered the Watergate Break-Ins

Richard Nixon's quest for the Presidency in 1972 would dominate his most important decisions, yielding enormous consequences for himself that would only start to transform the country the following year. The election overshadowed everything else for Nixon in 1972, as he showed a drive that mirrored his desperation to win his first race back in 1946, when he had said, "I had to win . . . the important thing is to win." In 1972, Nixon would do what he'd been doing since 1946, only on a massive scale, from a position of immense power.[1]

The result of Nixon's self-imposed pressure to win at any cost would be an amazing range of criminal activity that exceeded anything in his long political career. Nixon was not the only politician engaging in shady fund-raising and "pay for favors" contributions. But by 1972, Nixon had taken a system that had long existed for both parties in Washington and raised it to new heights of brazen criminality, both in how he raised huge sums of money and how he used it in his campaign operations.

Given his extremely close races in 1960 and 1968, Nixon's zeal is almost understandable. In trying to ensure he had all the resources he needed, Nixon raised—through legal and illicit means—what his own aides sometimes saw as "too much money." Nixon feared a strong opponent so much that he had five "dirty tricks" teams operating against the Democratic front-runner, Maine Senator Edmund Muskie. But there were other candidates too, so Nixon's operation also had to be able to attack Senator Henry "Scoop" Jackson, Nixon's old nemesis Senator Hubert Humphrey, and moderate North Carolina Governor Terry Sanford. It was in part because of the prospect of running against Sanford—but also to harm the Democrats in general—

that Nixon convinced Alabama Governor George Wallace to run as a Democrat, instead of as an Independent. Nixon realized that even though Wallace could wreak havoc in some of Democratic primaries and the Democratic National Convention, in the fall Nixon might still have to contend with an independent Wallace, siphoning conservative votes from him. Yet it many ways, the opponent Nixon feared most wasn't even a declared candidate; it was the possibility that Senator Edward Kennedy might enter the race or somehow emerge from the convention as the nominee. Nixon felt he needed a "dirty tricks" campaign apparatus that could hinder—or destroy—the campaigns of all those real and imagined candidates, so that Nixon could face the one challenger he felt he stood the best chance against, peace candidate South Dakota Senator George McGovern.[2]

Nixon's initial covert campaign operations in early 1972 would be successful, which allowed them to continue and expand, until they resulted in the Watergate break-ins. When seen in context, those break-ins are not an isolated, unusual event, but a logical progression in Nixon's Presidency. The break-ins also had an important national security aspect that has mostly remained hidden until now. In addition, the break-ins were just part of a broad range of Nixon crimes, and there were so many that only the most important can be detailed here, mainly those directly related to Watergate. That tight focus makes the crimes of Watergate much clearer, and answers most—perhaps all—of the lingering questions about the scandal.

Irony seems to permeate Nixon's political life, and that was never more apparent that in 1972. Nixon's efforts to gain political advantage in 1960 had resulted in the CIA-Mafia plots with Rosselli and Trafficante, and those plots would once more be a critical factor in his 1972 race. There is also the irony that Nixon would win the battle of the '72 election, but in doing so, he sowed the seeds that would later cause him to lose the war he'd fought to become President.[3]

Perhaps the ultimate irony is that the Watergate break-ins weren't needed for Nixon to win in 1972, and the same might be true for all of his many campaign crimes. Nixon thought burglaries like those at the Watergate were a political necessity, but they were actually born out of Nixon's fear, paranoia, and guilt. In reality, Nixon's political instincts, abilities, and intelligence had positioned him to wage—and probably win—a fair contest for President, if he had chosen to do so. The foreign policy triumphs he planned and achieved in 1972 would have likely cemented that winning status. Yet Nixon either lacked the confidence that he could win a fair election, or his pattern of criminal behavior had gone on for so long that by 1972 it was simply an unavoidable part of his political life.

President Nixon's 1972 campaign got off to an auspicious start when he was named *Time* magazine's "Man of the Year," even though what most would consider his most notable Presidential accomplishments (the opening to China, his visit to Russia, ending the Vietnam War) were still ahead of him. While Nixon was still a controversial, polarizing figure to liberals and young people, his masterful use of the press had helped to make him popular in many parts of America, especially the burgeoning "white flight" suburbs that harbored increasing numbers of voters. Nixon had learned how to use the old techniques of "fear, ignorance, bigotry, and smear" more subtly than in the early 1950s. Nixon played on racial fears by opposing "busing" to integrate schools and not aggressively enforcing civil rights laws, instead of openly opposing equal rights.

Most of the mainstream press still supported—or at least rarely attacked—President Nixon. While there were those in the media who balanced their reporting of Nixon and his administration's announcements, accomplishments, and spin with more assertive journalism (CBS, *The New York Times*, *The Washington Post*, *Newsday*, and some other daily newspapers), Nixon had even learned how to use them to his advantage. The White House tapes show repeated examples of Nixon planning to put out a certain story, fully anticipating how his critics would attack it, and when they did, Nixon put out another story that built upon his critics' reactions to get across the points he really wanted to convey all along. It's not hard to see why Nixon made an advertising man like Haldeman his Chief of Staff, since Nixon himself was a political marketing strategist perhaps unsurpassed in the era since Franklin Roosevelt. Nixon's skills with the media—never better than in 1972, when he orchestrated the tremendous coverage of his groundbreaking trips to China and Russia—would be a major reason the Watergate arrests in June 1972 would not become a major news story in most of the country until months after the November election.

For much of his 1972 campaign, Nixon planned to appear "Presidential" and above the fray as the Democrats battled for the nomination. That was the rationale for Nixon's major foreign trips in the first half of 1972, to China in February and to the Soviet Union in late May. While they certainly paid huge dividends in burnishing Nixon's Presidential image, those trips also took him out of the country at crucial times during his covert campaign activities, which involved illicit money and illegal operations. It's possible Nixon might have asserted firmer control if he hadn't gone on those trips, but it's also possible he wanted to be out of the country at times when his criminal operations were reaching new levels.

Raising money was even more of a prime concern for Nixon in the early months of 1972 than it had been for the past two years. Fearing another close race, Nixon wasn't just thinking about 1968. He told his aides, "Remember 1960 . . . I never want to be outspent again." A new campaign finance law was set to take effect on April 7, so Nixon and his men tried to raise as much money as possible before that date. In all, CREEP would raise "$60 million, the largest amount of money that had ever been spent in a political campaign." The money Nixon and his men raised basically fell into three categories. First, there were entirely legal campaign contributions from individuals. Second, there were basically illegal contributions that were received in a way to technically skirt the law. For example, the Dairy industry contribution detailed earlier was originally going to be split into many dozens of small contributions from many dozens of small phony front organizations, each donating $2,500. Robert Bennett of the Mullen Company reportedly helped with that scheme. The third category of contributions to Nixon for 1972 were simply illegal, often with no pretense made to hide their illicit origins. This included contributions made directly by U.S. corporations and those made by foreign governments and their agents, both types illegal then as they still are now.[4]

Many of America's largest companies were pressured by the Nixon administration and CREEP for donations, and some came through. Prosecuted later for making such donations were "Phillips Petroleum, Ashland Oil, Occidental, Goodyear Tire and Rubber, Braniff [Airlines], and American Airlines." Other companies found to have given illegal contributions were 3M, Greyhound, and military contractor Northrop. Another contractor, Grauman, was pressured "to make a million-dollar contribution in return for Nixon's 'assistance' in arranging an aircraft sale to Japan." Government action against fast-food purveyor McDonald's "was reversed—after the company's chairman had donated $235,000" to CREEP. Anthony Summers points out that "Oilmen alone gave five million dollars" to Nixon's reelection effort. He quoted "officials of Gulf Oil"—which was "later fined"—as saying, "I certainly considered it pressure when two cabinet officials asked me for funds." Another Gulf official "recalled having withdrawn money in hundred-dollar bills from a Swiss bank and handing the cash to [Maurice] Stans stuffed in an envelope." Stans, Nixon's Commerce Secretary, had "become CREEP's chief fund-raiser."[5]

One of Nixon's attorneys told George Steinbrenner, the chairman of American Shipbuilding and later owner of the New York Yankees, that "if you're thinking of coming in for under a hundred thousand dollars, don't bother. We work up to a million around here." Substantial sums smaller than a million could still get results, as in the case of financier Robert Vesco, who remained a fugitive for decades because of charges stemming from "an illegal two-hundred-thousand-dollar contribution to Nixon's 1972 campaign." In early 1972, Vesco had been "arrested in Switzerland on charges of fraud and embezzlement," but "John Mitchell intervened personally, ordering U.S. diplomats in Berne to being 'all possible pressure to secure his release.'" At the time, Mitchell was moving from being Attorney General to heading CREEP.[6]

Foreign dictators were another major source of illegal funds for President Nixon in 1972. After Nixon gave the U.S.-backed Shah of Iran "carte blanche to buy any American conventional weapon he wished," in return, the Shah "provided hundreds of thousand of dollars, perhaps more than a million [to Nixon] through the Swiss Bank Corporation and the Banco de Londres y Mexico in Mexico City." Nixon's Secretary of State, William Rogers, personally "blocked" one journalist's investigation into the Shah's donations.[7]

Other illegal donations from foreign dictators reportedly included President Ferdinand Marcos of the Philippines, South Vietnam's Diem, the Somozas of Nicaragua, and the Greek military Junta. Saudi businessman Adnan Khashoggi is said to have told his friend Pierre Salinger that after "a secret meeting with Nixon . . . he'd given a million dollars to help with the campaign" in 1972. Khashoggi denied any contribution that large, but Anthony Summers points out that "Watergate . . . prosecutors were 'cautious' in their questioning [of Khashoggi] because of the witness's high-level connections in the Saudi government." If Salinger's account is true, the money could be seen as more of a Saudi government contribution than one from

Khashoggi. In addition, Khashoggi sold Summers "he had given jewelry worth sixty thousand dollars to Nixon's daughters and later donated two hundred thousand dollars to the Nixon [Presidential] Library. Khashoggi added that Bebe Rebozo was "very fine, very secretive, you know, the type you can trust."[8]

President Nixon's illegal campaign contributions—which were hard to track or were untraceable—were also ripe for use in Nixon's illegal campaign operations. In the summer of 1971, when Nixon was told by Haldeman they had only "about $1,000,000" that was "stashed away for special operations," Nixon had replied, "Jesus God! We need two million . . . at least two million." By 1972, Nixon was still gathering money for those operations, which were quickly expanding as the campaign got underway. But before detailing those new operations, it's important to look at two little-known incidents that would overshadow—and in some ways influence—the Watergate political spying operations to come.[9]

Unfolding for Nixon in the early weeks of 1972 was a White House scandal that had first come to light on December 21, 1971. Only this wasn't a crime perpetrated by Nixon or his operatives, but in which Nixon was the victim: The President and his staff were the targets of spying by his own Joint Chiefs of Staff.

The fact that the Pentagon was spying on President Nixon had come to light because of several Jack Anderson articles "in mid-December" that contained "material from the minutes of the Washington Special Action Group," which were at odds with Nixon's public pronouncements about a war between India and Pakistan. Nixon was furious "and the Plumbers were directed to investigate," according to J. Anthony Lukas, who says the Plumbers used "secret wiretapping for [this] investigation." Egil Krogh says John "Ehrlichman dismissed him from the Plumbers . . . because he refused to authorize a wiretap" for the investigation, but Nixon simply turned to John Mitchell, who was still Attorney General at the time. The FBI "disclosed that on John Mitchell's instructions, it placed four tapes during this investigation."[10]

In this case, unlike Watergate five months later, the Plumbers were apparently using the results of FBI wiretapes, not bugs that the Plumbers themselves had placed. The Plumbers discovered that a "Yeoman First Class Charles E. Radford, a . . . clerk in the Joint Chiefs of Staff liaison office with the National Security Council," was the likely culprit.

He was soon reassigned to Oregon and never charged, but "the Plumbers turned up . . . evidence that Radford had taken other highly sensitive documents, never intended for transmittal to the Pentagon, and funneled them through the liaison office to Admiral Thomas H. Moorer, Chairman of the Joint Chiefs of Staff." Radford said "he was carefully trained and instructed by his immediate superiors—including Admiral Robert O. Welander—to take 'anything I could get my hands on.'"[11]

"In all, perhaps a thousand top-secret documents were stolen and transmitted to Moorer's office" by Radford, "on orders of Adm. Robert Welander," according to a recent account by author Jim Hougan. While Nixon was furious at being the target of spying by the Pentagon, he kept Moorer on as Chief of Staff, as well as others implicated in the affair. It's hard to say whether Nixon's inaction was because it was an election year with the Vietnam War still raging, or because he couldn't be sure of what secrets Moorer now possessed. Regardless of the reason, "Nixon was determined to keep the affair secret, telling [one] Kissinger aide . . . 'If you love your country, you'll never mention it,'" and "the affair did not become public until almost three years later," after Nixon had resigned and the story of Watergate was essentially over.[12]

In addition to Admiral Moorer and Admiral Welander, Alexander Haig was also suspected in the spying scandal. As mentioned in Chapter 24, Haig was very close to Moorer, saying the two had "daily contact." However, Nixon took no action against Haig. He was not only allowed to remain as a Deputy National Security Advisor, but soon after the Admiral Moorer spying affair, Nixon made Haig the extraordinary recipient of a promotion to "major general—at forty-seven, one of the youngest in the army." Nixon's favorable treatment of Haig might be explained by Haig's crucial duties in early 1972: He was helping Nixon and Henry Kissinger secretly prepare the way for Nixon's upcoming landmark trip to China, which would mark the beginning of the end of twenty-five years of hostility between the two countries. Haig has said he was the "keeper of the details" about the complex negotiations that preceded the trip, and he "frequently took part in clandestine meetings with our principal Chinese contact in the United States, U.N. Ambassador Huang Hua, in a seedy CIA safe house in Manhattan." Since President Nixon's trip to China would be a unique publicity coup to help kick off his reelection campaign,

Nixon apparently felt it was best not to press Haig on the Moorer spying affair.[13]

The Pentagon's spying on Nixon echoes that of Haig's mentor, Joseph Califano, and their superior in 1963, Secretary of the Army Cyrus Vance, on President Kennedy. As described in Chapter 14, Califano wrote about himself and Vance in 1963 "sitting in the Army war room at the Pentagon, with sophisticated communications . . . capabilities" so they would "know everything the White House and Justice Department were doing" by secretly running "all their communication lines though the Army war room. Sitting there, Vance and I were able to listen to any conversations the President or Attorney General had." If that was going on in 1963, one has to wonder if the relatively simple spying by Yeoman Radford was the only Pentagon surveillance being conducted on President Nixon. As for Califano, by early 1972, he was settling in as the new attorney for *The Washington Post*, and was still the attorney for the Democratic National Committee, whose offices were at the Watergate complex.[14]

The Admiral Moorer spying incident (sometimes known as the "Moorer-Radford affair") is important because it helped to foreshadow Watergate in three ways. First, it shows that Nixon's first impulse was to turn to the Plumbers when he was faced with a serious crisis that needed to be kept secret. Second, as part of the Plumbers investigation, wiretaps were used to identify the suspects and then to keep them under surveillance even after the basic facts were known (Radford was wiretapped not just in Washington, but even after he was transferred to Oregon). Third, Nixon's discovery that he had been the target of spying himself probably made it easier for him to rationalize political espionage against the Democrats several months later, which resulted in the Watergate burglaries.*

Another often-overlooked episode that would have ramifications for Watergate was also unfolding in January of 1972, and it involved a young Karl Rove, then the President-elect of the National College Republicans. That month, Rove received a complaint from the head of

*Jim Hougan in *Secret Agenda* pointed out that Moorer's aide Admiral Welander, heavily involved in the spying scandal, "was also a mentor of Lt. Bob Woodward." Welander had commanded Woodward's ship and "reportedly, it was at the urging of Welander . . . that Woodward extended his tour of duty in 1969, going to the Pentagon to serve as Communications Duty Officer to" Admiral Moorer. While serving under Moorer, Woodward met FBI Assistant Director Mark Felt, who later became Deep Throat.

the Wisconsin College Republicans, Tim Gratz, that a political trickster had been trying to recruit people there for a "dirty tricks" campaign against the Democrats, especially "to find a college student to plant as a spy in the" campaign of Democratic front-runner Senator Edmund Muskie. As Gratz told the author in an exclusive interview (and later confirmed by Senate investigators), he stressed to Karl Rove that he feared the operative might be a "plant" by the Democrats, to embarrass the Nixon campaign. Rove replayed Gratz's story to CREEP, which seemed at first uninterested. But Rove didn't let the matter drop, and he pressed CREEP again about it. This time, in response to Rove's concern, White House aide Jeb Magruder dispatched an investigator to Wisconsin to talk to Gratz. But Magruder's investigator was soon called by John Caulfield, the former New York City policeman, now one of Nixon's covert operatives, who ordered Magruder's investigator to "back off," since the man that had concerned Rove and Gratz "is Haldeman's man."[15]

The trickster in Wisconsin was using an alias, but he turned out to be Donald Segretti, an attorney and former Army JAG Captain who had been hired on Haldeman's approval back in June 1971. But it was becoming clear that the White House had so many covert operatives approved at the highest levels that lower-ranking aides sometimes didn't know who was doing what or working for whom. So, E. Howard Hunt and G. Gordon Liddy were ordered to take on supervision of Segretti. After an intimidating interview with him on February 11, 1972, Hunt took on a supervisory role for him, and Segretti became one of Nixon's most active "dirty tricks" operatives against the potential Democratic nominees. Four months after Watergate, Segretti would be an important link for Bob Woodward and Carl Bernstein in tracking Watergate back to the high levels of the White House, and he figures prominently in both the book and movie of *All the President's Men*. Segretti would eventually serve four and a half months in prison for his Nixon "dirty tricks." As for Karl Rove, two years after he inadvertently helped to bring Segretti and Hunt together, *The Washington Post* would report in 1974 that Rove was training college Republicans in Nixon-style "dirty tricks." Their report resulted in an investigation by Republican National Committee chairman George H.W. Bush, which cleared Rove despite what *Salon* called "strong taped evidence against him." Rove would later use tactics evocative of Nixon's to guide Bush's son to two terms as Texas Governor and two terms as President.[16]

. . .

The Segretti episode showed that the White House political espionage efforts needed more structure, and that's what was proposed on January 27, 1972, at a meeting in Attorney General John Mitchell's office. Mitchell was set to leave his post just over a month later, to become the head of CREEP, and he was being pitched a massive, detailed political espionage plan—code-named GEMSTONE—by G. Gordon Liddy. Also present were Nixon aide Jeb Magruder and White House Counsel John Dean.[17]

The effort Liddy pitched to Mitchell that day had been building for months. Almost four months earlier, a "Talking Paper" for H.R. Haldeman stated "that a budget of '800-300 [thousand dollars]' for 'surveillance' was on the agenda for a meeting with" Attorney General Mitchell. In December 1971, just after Liddy became the counsel of CREEP, Liddy revealed to Hunt that "the AG [Attorney General Mitchell] wants me to set up an intelligence organization for the campaign. It'll be big, Howard . . . there's plenty of money available—half a million dollars for openers, and there's more where that came from." Jeb Magruder's version is a bit different; he says Liddy told him in mid-December 1971 that "he had been promised $1 million for a 'broad-gauged intelligence plan.'" Magruder tells Liddy if he "could document and justify such a budget" he could "present it to Mitchell." Hunt and Liddy strategized about the plan over the holidays, which led to Liddy's formal pitch to Mitchell.[18]

John Mitchell would later describe the "GEMSTONE Plan" that Liddy pitched to him on January 27, 1972, as involving "mugging squads, kidnapping teams, prostitutes to compromise the opposition and electronic surveillance." There were numerous parts in Liddy's elaborate plan, each with its own code name. They included DIAMOND, which planned to neutralize the "urban guerillas expected to disrupt the Republican convention" by having them kidnapped, drugged, and taken to Mexico. Liddy boasted that for this job, he would be using "professional killers who had accounted between them for twenty-two dead [including] members of organized crime." More practical—and relevant for Watergate—were "OPAL, for clandestine entries to place bugs" and "TOPAZ for photographing documents." There were seven other parts of the GEMSTONE plan, including "a scheme to infiltrate spies into the Democratic camp," called RUBY. Liddy told Mitchell, Magruder, and Dean that the budge it for his plan was approximately $1 million.[19]

Mitchell's response was to tell Liddy to come back with a more "realistic plan," both in terms of what it attempted to do and the cost. The next day, Mitchell met with President Nixon "to discuss 'the overall political plan'" for the campaign. A week later, Liddy was back to pitch Mitchell a revised, scaled-down political "espionage proposal, a $500,000 plan focusing on wiretapping and photography." Jeb Magruder and John Dean once more joined Liddy and Mitchell in this February 4, 1972, meeting. However, Mitchell put off making a final decision, and Liddy would need to revise—and scale back—his plan once more. But according to *The New York Times*, Jeb Magruder would later say that at the meeting, "Mitchell chose the Democratic National Committee (DNC) headquarters at the Watergate and other top priority targets for surveillance" at that meeting, but Mitchell denied doing so. Magruder and Dean both "agree that the targets" included not only "Larry O'Brien's office at the Democratic National Committee," but also "O'Brien's hotel suite in Miami Beach during the convention; the [hotel] rooms of other prominent Democrats . . . and ultimately, the campaign headquarters of whichever Democrat" was the nominee. Providing some support for Magruder and Dean is the fact that around this time, Liddy asked James McCord—recently appointed as the full-time Security Coordinator for CREEP and the RNC—if "he would be willing to join an operation to bug Democratic headquarters if it was approved." McCord said "yes," because he assumed "that Mitchell would consult the President [about the operation] as he did about all major and many minor campaign decisions."[20]

This type of "he said, no I didn't" between Magruder and Mitchell becomes very common in the Watergate story from this point forward for all the participants, creating a type of *Rashomon*-like mosaic of claims, counter-claims, and blame. So many people would be prosecuted (by historian Stanley Kutler's count, seventy in all) in the coming years that many wanted to blame others so they wouldn't face additional charges themselves. In general after Watergate, there would be many efforts to divert blame from President Nixon, since only he had the power to pardon the participants, and he implied that he was willing to use that power to help those who helped him. Even in the years and decades since, various participants still sometimes seek to settle old scores, or—in the cases of Haldeman and others—years later wanted to make amends with Nixon, so they later softened some of their accounts. To avoid getting bogged down by the welter of claims and denials, this book will focus on the most basic and well-documented events, especially those backed up by recently released tapes, files, and credible accounts.

Political espionage continued to be undertaken by the Nixon White House and CREEP even while Liddy's plans were being discussed and revised. In other words, approval of Liddy's plans weren't required for political crimes to be undertaken. There was plenty of money for such ongoing operations; one "secret trust fund [had] $915,037.68," and there were other slush funds as well, including at least one controlled by Bebe Rebozo.[21]

At this critical time in organizing the campaign, Nixon left the country for eleven days, on February 17, 1972. Since the 1950s, Nixon had always viewed foreign policy as his biggest strength, but the situation in Vietnam had continued to be problematic for Nixon. Actual peace talks to end the Vietnam War continued to elude Nixon and his National Security Advisor, Henry Kissinger. Nixon had continued to withdraw U.S. ground forces, in the hopes that South Vietnamese forces could assume control. But real progress was slow and corruption in South Vietnam's government—especially at the highest levels—continued to be a problem. Nixon needed a foreign policy breakthrough somewhere else to boost his 1972 Presidential campaign, and his secretly arranged trip to China was the result. That trip has been well covered hundreds of times, and all this book can add is the observation that—based on Nixon's rhetorical track record—it's not difficult to imagine what Nixon would have said to the press if a liberal or Democratic President had attempted such a bold move with a Communist former enemy like China.

The day after Nixon returned from China, Jack Anderson hit the Nixon administration with a bombshell—and this time, the mainstream media would finally follow up on his reports, in a big way. On February 29, 1972, Anderson published "an internal memo written by International Telephone & Telegraph (ITT) lobbyist Dita Beard [saying] that the Nixon Justice Department had dropped three antitrust suits against the firm in return for its $400,000 pledge to help finance the GOP convention in 1972." Because Anderson claimed to have the actual memo, and because he played up the story over four consecutive days—his story on March 1 implicated Attorney General-designate Richard Kleindienst in the Nixon-ITT bribe—Anderson's bombshell was soon being repeated by the mainstream media.[22]

CBS Evening News anchor Walter Cronkite reported the story on

March 3, 1972, saying it "could be the biggest political scandal of the year," and in a way he was right, since the ITT story would get more intense press coverage (and Congressional scrutiny) in 1972 than Watergate. ABC News covered the story that day as well, and by March 7, all three network news shows led with coverage of Congressional hearings looking into the matter. The Senate Judiciary Committee had just unanimously approved Richard Kleindienst to take Mitchell's place as Attorney General, but Kleindienst asked that the hearings be reopened, to clear his name. Conservative Democratic Chairman James Eastland tried to use the hearings to discredit Anderson, but Anderson's grandstanding had the opposite effect. The hearings would drag out for two months and start to unveil a small part of the huge mountain of illegal money Nixon had been raising.[23]

President Nixon was outraged at the story and the way it had gained traction, erasing the afterglow from the almost uniformly positive press coverage of his China trip. Nixon had his aides assemble an "ITT Task Force" to counterattack Anderson. Nixon himself directed much of the attack strategy, encouraging sympathetic members of Congress and the media to paint the whole matter as a political "smear" against him. Nixon told Charles Colson, "Just continue to hit [Anderson and the Democrats by saying] smear, smear, smear, smear." Nixon's press strategy worked to a degree, but this time the press coverage was clearly in Anderson's favor, and the muckraking reporter was becoming part of the story—and a celebrity—himself.[24]

Nixon and his men broke more laws in going after Anderson, "as White House aides secretly huddled with ITT lawyers and CREEP operatives" to plot attacks. John Mitchell—now heading CREEP—the Justice Department, and the FBI were all used to smear or counterattack Anderson. Kleindienst's nomination as Attorney General seemed in jeopardy, and Nixon's counsel Donald Rumsfeld advised Nixon that "we should take our losses and get out." But Nixon's new Treasury Secretary, John Connally, advised the President not to back down and repeated the same advice that Murray Chotiner had been giving Nixon since 1946: "hit 'em, hit 'em, hit 'em, that's the only way."[25]

Just as Nixon had first thought of E. Howard Hunt when he wanted someone to burglarize the Brookings Institute, and Hunt was the one the White House turned to when it needed someone to break into the office of Daniel Ellsberg's psychiatrist, Hunt was now brought into the sensitive ITT affair. Hunt had started working for CREEP at the end of February, and on March 15, 1972, he was called into a meeting of the ITT Task Force in Charles Colson's office. He was asked to fly to Denver, to talk to Dita Beard herself, to try to get her to repudiate the ITT memo published by Anderson. The goal was to get her to call it a "hoax" and deny she had written it. They also wanted her to return to Washington and hold a press conference to publicly state her denial.[26]

Colson wanted Hunt to talk to Dita Beard "in a physical disguise with a phony ID because 'we don't want you traced back to the White House,'" and "for his expenses, he was handed an envelope filled with cash from Nixon's reelection campaign." Perhaps as a precaution, that same day the telephone with Hunt's "White House number [was] removed from Hunt's office in the [Old] Executive Office Building." However, some precautions were missed, because Hunt's "flight to Denver was booked by a White House secretary." Hunt used his CIA-supplied "Edward J. Hamilton" alias and identification for the trip. He also wore the disguise he'd been given by the CIA, consisting mainly of a red wig, and used a CIA voice modification device (which fit inside his mouth to alter the way he talked). Hunt was unable to convince the ailing Dita Beard to return to Washington, even after telling her she could simply "collapse" at the end of her press conference, both to avoid having to answer questions and to gain sympathy. But after the promise of money, in a "disjoint" conversation, she supposedly gave him a sort of denial that she had written the ITT memo (though other accounts say she refused to call it a hoax). In any event, J. Anthony Lukas reports that "back in Washington, Hunt found Bob Bennett coordinating a rush effort to get Mrs. Beard's denial out to the press." Bennett drafted her statement, "checked it with her lawyers, officials at ITT, and" the Senate minority leader, then had the statement—"branding the memo a 'hoax,' a 'forgery,' and a 'cruel fraud'"—issued by the minority leader and Dita Beard's attorney.[27]

The "denial" Hunt obtained had an immediate effect, since the mainstream press had to report the denial as issued. That took much of the pressure off Nixon, meaning that Hunt's work had kept the ITT/Dita Beard scandal from truly threatening Nixon's Presidency or reelection. Even Kleindienst was eventually able to be confirmed. It's interesting that in the wake of Watergate, and the well-crafted post-Watergate image of Hunt as a bumbling nobody, many accounts after Watergate depicted his mission to Dita Beard as a complete failure, and dwelled mainly on his ill-fitting wig. However, Hunt's accomplishment was actually very important for Nixon, as shown by a recent analysis, by Mark Feldstein, the Peabody and Murrow Award–winning veteran correspondent for CNN and ABC, who authored a recent book about Anderson and his battles with Nixon. As for the involvement of Robert Bennett and his PR firm in quickly pushing out Dita Beard's "denial" to the press, that can be explained in part by the work Bennett's PR firm did for the CIA. The Agency's deep involvement with ITT in Chile was something the CIA wouldn't want Anderson or Congressional investigators stumbling across in pursuit of the Dita Beard story.[28]

Unfortunately for President Nixon and CIA Director Richard Helms, in the second week of March 1972, the CIA was contacted by Jack Anderson's assistant, Brit Hume (later to work for Fox News). Hume and Anderson had obtained "twenty-six internal memos . . . written on the letterhead of ITT [that] revealed a conspiracy between the CIA and ITT to overthrow Salvador Allende, the . . . president of Chile," and Hume told the CIA he had "'urgent' questions" about the matter. Hume's inquiry immediately generated a "flurry of CIA memos" within the Agency, which were reviewed by Mark Feldstein. The CIA quickly "discussed the problem [of Hume's call] with General Haig, at the White House, which Feldstein wrote "immediately set off alarms inside the Nixon administration."[29]

To demonstrate how serious the matter was for both Nixon and Helms, "Within two hours of Hume's call to the CIA, its Director [Helms] crossed the Potomac River from his Virginia headquarters for an emergency lunch with Anderson in downtown Washington." The clout and fear Jack Anderson inspired at this point is remarkable. Then again, Helms knew that Anderson also harbored information about the CIA-Mafia plots, though the CIA Director didn't know how much Anderson knew about Helms's role in continuing them. The charm Helms usually found effective with most reporters failed to work on Anderson, who had a big scoop and wasn't about to hold the story.[30]

On March 21, 1972, Jack Anderson dropped his bombshell, trumpeting in his column that "Secret [ITT] documents that escaped shredding show that the company maneuvered at the highest levels" against Chile's President, Salvador Allende. Anderson cited documents describing the involvement of the White House, John McCone, and the State Department. The columnist quoted more of the explosive files in his column the next day, and his stories "ignited a firestorm"—in part because Anderson had learned how to maximize his press coverage by "selectively parcel[ing] out copies of his secret memos to *The New York Times* and *The Washington Post* for prominent play." The story also became huge in Chile, where CIA agents noted that "Anderson gave a lengthy interview to Chilean television." Helping that campaign was Allende's ambassador to the United States, Orlando Letelier, who "rushed" copies of the memos from Washington "to his home country," where they were translated, and a booklet of them was distributed "on the streets of Santiago."[31] Democratic Senator Frank Church of Idaho soon "launched an official probe of the" matter and called upon CIA Director Helms to testify. Under oath, Helms answered "No" when asked questions such as "Did you try in the Central Intelligence Agency to overthrow the government of Chile?" and "Did you have any money passed to opponents of Allende?" Helms's lies to Congress not only protected himself but also protected Nixon, and the whole ITT-Chile matter helped to bring the CIA Director and President Nixon together more as allies. However, it would not be the last time Helms would be asked about the Chilean matter by a Congressional committee, and his lies about Chile would eventually result in his indictment for providing false information to Congress.[32]

Richard Nixon once again tried to retaliate against Jack Anderson, knowing that if the truth came out about his massive effort to prevent Allende's election, and then to overthrow him, it could be a major problem in his own reelection campaign, especially if he faced a strong opponent. But when "the President's men tried to plant derogatory stories about Anderson in the media . . . the move backfired." Instead of running Nixon's planted stories, some newspapers—like *The Washington Post*—reported on Nixon's tactics, with *The Post*'s front page blaring that "the White House 'is directing a major effort to discredit columnist Jack Anderson.'" Nixon's aides also hired someone to infiltrate Jack Anderson's office, a former investigator for the House Un-American Activities Committee that Nixon had worked with on the Hiss case named Lou Russell. Russell, now a private detective, was successful for a time, and filed "secret reports on Anderson with the Nixon campaign's security director, James McCord." Anderson's secretary soon became suspicious of Russell, and he was fired, but then Anderson hired "an intern who turned out to be the son of another spy hired by the Nixon campaign." Mark Feldstein points out that "to this day, it is unclear what Nixon's men learned from their infiltration of Anderson's office."[33]

Richard Helms and the CIA also went to extraordinary lengths to get information about Anderson. According to a 1975 memo prepared by Dick Cheney when he was President Ford's Chief of Staff, the CIA admitted that "from February 15 to April 12, 1972, 'personal surveillances' were conducted by the CIA on Jack Anderson and members of his staff [including] Brit Hume . . . the physical surveillances were authorized by Helms."* But the Agency's illegal surveillance didn't produce any information that could be used to stop or discredit Anderson.[34]

From the perspective of the Nixon White House, something clearly had to be done about Anderson. But what? As with Brookings, Ellsberg's psychiatrist, and Dita Beard, Nixon and his men turned to E. Howard Hunt for yet another sensitive mission. In March 1972, Charles Colson summoned Hunt "to the Old Executive Office Building, across from the White House." Hunt says that "Colson had apparently 'just come from a meeting with President Nixon,' whose hideaway office was next door." Colson looked "uncharacteristically 'nervous' and 'agitated' about [telling] Hunt that Nixon 'was incensed over Jack Anderson's frequent publication of leaks [and the] son of a bitch [Anderson] had become a great thorn in the side of the President [so they needed to] stop Anderson at all costs."[35]

According to Hunt, "Colson proposed assassinating Anderson in a manner that would appear accidental, perhaps by using a special poison that could not be detected during an autopsy. Colson also asked Hunt if he "could explore the matter with the CIA," saying "that neutralizing Anderson was 'very important' to the White House"—meaning Nixon—"and Hunt was 'authorized to do whatever was necessary' to eliminate [Anderson]." Colson has denied Hunt's account, but Liddy—whom Hunt turned to for assistance on the plot—has confirmed it. Feldstein's conclusion after his recent analysis was that "it is difficult to imagine Nixon's closest advisors plotting to execute America's leading investigative reporter without at least the tacit approval of their president. Historian Kutler pointed out that "Colson rarely acted on his own initiative [and] his deeds . . . correlate

* In the Nixon White House, Dick Cheney was deputy to White House Counsel Donald Rumsfeld.

with his notes of his regular meetings with the President." Feldstein writes that "Nixon was a micromanager who hired zealous younger subordinates to ensure that they would carry out his will." He cites H.R. Haldeman, who said that "the chain of command was clearly established . . . 'Nixon tells Colson, Colson orders Hunt, Hunt executes [the operation].'" That chain of command is important to remember for Watergate.[36]

In the case of Jack Anderson, Nixon may well have ordered Colson to "neutralize" Anderson, in the same way Nixon ordered the Brookings Institute burglarized, only to either change his mind or be talked out of it by his subordinates. Hunt and Liddy both seriously pursued Anderson's assassination for a time, even meeting with "Dr. Edward Gunn, a CIA physician involved in the" CIA-Mafia plots to assassinate Fidel Castro, both in 1960 and in 1963. Gunn had officially "retired" from the Agency, but Liddy said he "took 'retired' to be in quotes, since that is a standard technique used to give the [CIA] deniability in clandestine operations." After exploring but abandoning a plan with the CIA physician to kill Anderson in a car wreck, "Hunt decided to subcontract the job to [men] he had previously signed up for the CIA invasion of Cuba's Bay of Pigs, men who were now working for the Nixon campaign." But Feldstein points out that Anderson "actually knew two of the [men] selected to execute him." And "one of those assassins"—Frank Fiorini—"turned out to be a longtime friend and source of the columnist who had even stayed in the Anderson home as a house guest." Since using Fiorini or the other Cubans like Barker looked problematic, Liddy offered to assassinate Anderson himself.[37]

In late March 1972, possible ways to kill Anderson were "written up in a memo and sent to the White House" by Hunt. According to Liddy, Hunt was told "the White House [had] decided it would be 'unproductive'" to kill Anderson after all. *The Washington Post* said Hunt's order from a senior White House official "to assassinate [columnist] Jack Anderson . . . was cancelled at the last minute."[38]

Unfolding at the same time as the ITT scandals was another matter involving Jack Anderson, Hunt, and Liddy, as well as Bebe Rebozo, that was of great concern to Richard Nixon. On January 24, 1972, Jack Anderson had published an update to his story from the previous summer about Rebozo receiving $100,000 in cash for Nixon from Howard Hughes, saying "he now had 'documentary evidence' to back it up." Lukas points out "this must have aroused something approaching panic in the White House—visions of Anderson getting memos or other documents about the contribution," either from Anderson's friend Robert Maheu, or from their mutual friend, Las Vegas newspaper publisher Hank Greenspun.[39]

After Howard Hughes fired Robert Maheu in late 1970, Hank Greenspun had sided with Maheu in the ensuing legal battle. Anderson and Greenspun were so close that "Anderson even owned a small piece of the *Las Vegas Sun*," Greenspun's newspaper. Anderson, Greenspun, and Maheu were all involved with the now-imprisoned Johnny Rosselli, and all of them knew about the CIA-Mafia plots to kill Castro (Greenspun had published the first small article about them).[40]

E. Howard Hunt says the idea of targeting Hank Greenspun came up "several days before the February 4," 1971, meeting between Mitchell, Liddy, Dean, and Magruder, about Liddy's revised GEMSTONE political espionage plan. According to Robert Bennett, the idea of targeting Greenspun originated with Hunt. Bennett says that Hunt wanted him to ask for "the help of the Hughes organization."[41]

On February 3, 1972—just over a week after Jack Anderson's newest column about the $100,000 Hughes-Rebozo-Nixon bribe—"*The New York Times* reported that Greenspun had Hughes memos in his safe . . . 200 individual items.'" J. Anthony Lukas thinks "the President's men" most likely wanted to know what "the memos contained about the dealings between Hughes and Richard Nixon, particularly the $100,000 funneled through Bebe Rebozo."[42]

Whether it was Hunt, *The New York Times*, or the Jack Anderson article—or a combination of all three—the Greenspun matter got the attention of John Mitchell, then in his last weeks as Attorney General. At the February 4, 1972, meeting to review Liddy's revised GEMSTONE espionage plan, Mitchell himself mentioned Hank Greenspun as a "possible target," along with the priority target of Larry O'Brien and the DNC.[43]

James McCord adds another piece of the puzzle—the Mafia—with his sworn testimony to the Senate Watergate Committee the following year. McCord testified that he was told by Liddy in early 1972 "that Attorney General John Mitchell has told him that Greenspun had in his possession blackmail type information . . . that Mitchell wanted that material, and . . . this material was in some way racketeer-related, indicating that if this candidate became President, the racketeers or national crime syndicate could have a control or influence of him as

President." That description sounds amazingly like the situation for Richard Nixon, given his involvement in the CIA-Mafia plots with Johnny Rosselli, Greenspun's friend. However, McCord testified that he'd been told the "crime syndicate" information referred to "a Democratic candidate for President," later identified as Senator Edmund Muskie. However, Muskie had no Mafia ties, and Greenspun later said the only crime Muskie had committed was a minor duck hunting violation, for which Muskie had paid a small fine. However, in McCord's testimony to the Senate Watergate Committee, the former CIA officer said he no longer believed the cover story about "the Democratic candidate" and now believed "there was in reality some other motive for wanting to get into Greenspun's safe."[44]

E. Howard Hunt says that even though the Hughes organization provided some help (including a diagram of Greenspun's office), there was no burglary, and Liddy says the same thing. However, McCord testified that Liddy told him on two occasions in early 1972 about going to Las Vegas to case Greenspun's office. The following year, John Ehrlichman would tell Nixon "that the Hunt-Liddy team 'flew out, broke his safe, got something out.'" But Greenspun was not aware of a burglary in that time frame (only a burglary two months after the Watergate break-in). Adding more mystery, McCord said that Hunt and Liddy had handled contributions to CREEP from Hughes in 1972, and that Hunt had even asked him if he'd like to work for the Hughes organization after the election.[45]

While the only thing that everyone agrees on is that Greenspun was targeted, J. Anthony Lukas points out the importance of another Mitchell target of even higher priority tied to Maheu and Hughes: Larry O'Brien, the former Hughes consultant now heading the DNC at the Watergate. While Greenspun was a Nixon supporter, because of the President's support for Israel, O'Brien would have the maximum incentive to put out Hughes information from Maheu—or information that O'Brien had gotten while working for Hughes—that was damaging to Richard Nixon. Lukas concluded that "the Nixon White House may well have decided that it should burglarize Hank Greenspun and Larry O'Brien to find out just what each man knew about 'Republican skeletons' in the closet," including the $100,000 Hughes-Rebozo-Nixon payment. The same could apply to the 1960 CIA-Mafia plots under Nixon that Maheu had worked on and revealed to Hughes (either man could have then told O'Brien), which might account for the "racketeer" cover story that McCord was told. It was only a year earlier that Maheu's account of those plots to John Mitchell had left the Attorney General "shaking." But Liddy's espionage plan, which would have implemented Mitchell's targeting of O'Brien, had not yet been approved. But that was about to change.[46]

On March 27, 1972, Liddy moved slightly within the Nixon campaign organization, from CREEP to become Counsel for the Finance Committee to Reelect the President, after a dispute with Jeb Magruder over what floor his office was on and other matters. But Liddy continued "to report to Magruder as CREEP's intelligence chief." As a result of pressure on Magruder from Colson—who told Magruder "we need information, particularly on Mr. [Larry] O'Brien," Liddy's revised-yet-again GEMSTONE espionage plan was finally going to be presented to Mitchell one more time. Now, this third version of the plan involved mainly "electronic surveillance and photography of documents," with a budget of $250,000.[47]

On March 30, 1972, Liddy's proposal would be discussed at a small planning meeting at Key Biscayne, where John Mitchell was vacationing with his wife, Martha. In addition to Magruder, the other participants would include Mitchell's chief deputy at CREEP, Fred LaRue, and Mitchell's "protégé," Harry Flemming. There were more than two dozen items on the meeting's agenda, with Liddy's plan saved for last. Because the plan was so sensitive—and "we knew it was illegal"—Magruder had Flemming leave the meeting before it was discussed.[48]

As Magruder later testified to the Senate Watergate Committee, that left Mitchell, LaRue, and himself in the Key Biscayne meeting to discuss Liddy's espionage plan against the Democrats. The plan included targeting the office of DNC Chief Larry O'Brien, who had been a priority target for John Mitchell since at least the February 4 meeting about an earlier version of the plan. Magruder testified that "I can honestly say that no one was particularly overwhelmed with the project." He stressed in his testimony that none of the three in the meeting had "any great feeling of acceptance to this plan." And Mitchell's approval of the plan would be "a reluctant decision." During the Watergate Hearings, Senator Howard Baker told Magruder he couldn't "come to grips with why you all had an expressed reservation about this [plan] and you still went ahead with it." Instead of giving a direct answer at the time, Magruder gave a very long, rambling discourse about anti–Vietnam War demonstrations and a college professor he admired, William Sloane Coffin, that in no way dealt with Senator Baker's question. After his lengthy, unrelated speech, Magruder finally came back to the topic and said, "I didn't make the decision" to approve the plan, "but [I] certainly participated in it."[49]

Magruder fully confessed his own guilt in various crimes at the Watergate hearings—unlike many witnesses, such as H.R. Haldeman—but Magruder never fully answered Baker's question of why Mitchell had approved a plan that none of the three in the Key Biscayne meeting liked and that all had reservations about. However, Magruder's testimony was relatively early in the hearing process, and many viewed the scandal as one that would blow over for Nixon, since it wouldn't be until a month after Magruder testified that Alexander Butterfield's revelation of Nixon's taping system finally started Nixon on the road to his resignation, more than a year later.[50]

Jeb Magruder finally fully answered Senator Baker's question thirty years later, in 2003, in interviews for a PBS special, *Watergate Plus 30: Shadow of History*, and in additional interviews for the Associate press and *PBS NewsHour*. According to those reports, at the March 30, 1972, Key Biscayne meeting with Mitchell, Magruder, and LaRue, the three were discussing Liddy's problematic espionage proposal, slated to start with breaking into Larry O'Brien's DNC office at the Watergate. Magruder told PBS

> We didn't like the idea, it was going into Watergate Democratic National Committee headquarters and bugging Larry O'Brien's phone. So Mitchell said call Haldeman, find out do we really have to, is this really important—so I called Haldeman and he talks to me, and I say, "you know, we're not sure it's worth doing." And Haldeman said "yes, the president wants it done." He said, "is John there?" I said, "yes," and I give the phone to John, and Haldeman talks to him. And then the president comes on the line and talks to Mitchell. I could hear the president talking to him, and it was simply, you know, "John, we need to get the information on Larry O'Brien, the only way we can do that is through Liddy's plan, and you need to do that." Nixon was saying we want Liddy to break into the Watergate. Mitchell gets off the phone, and says to me, he says, "well, Jeb, tell Maurice [Stans] to give Libby $250,000 and let's see what happens."[51]

Magruder told the Associated Press he was sure it was Nixon on the phone with Mitchell "because his voice if very distinct, and you couldn't miss who was on the phone." Magruder "concedes that he did not hear every single word while Nixon was on the phone with Mitchell, but 'I heard the import.'" When asked why he waited until 2003 to reveal hearing the Nixon-Mitchell call during the meeting, Magruder said he'd wanted to come clean because of a recent heart attack and the fact that he'd become a Presbyterian minister after Watergate. At the time of Watergate, he said he didn't mention the Nixon-Mitchell call—instead revealing only its result, that Mitchell approved Liddy's plan—because "I was really never asked in a specific way—certainly not during my testimony at the Watergate trials." Magruder's 2003 disclosure of the Nixon-Mitchell call helps to explain his rambling non-answer to Senator Baker in the 1973 Senate Watergate hearings. There is another reason Magruder may have also not fully answered Baker's question at the time by implicating Nixon: Nixon was still the President, and for more than another year, Nixon could have granted Magruder—and other Watergate defendants—pardons, something Nixon had arranged to offer to several defendants if they protected him.[52]

There is information to back up Magruder's statements to PBS and the AP. After the Key Biscayne meeting ended, Magruder called H.R. Haldeman's assistant, who wrote up a memo for Haldeman saying CREEP "now has a sophisticated intelligence-gathering system including a budget of $300[000]." Haldeman's assistant "also prepared a 'talking paper' (with an item about the intelligence system) for a meeting Haldeman and Mitchell were to have on April 4, 1972." The talking paper told Haldeman that "you may want to cover with Mitchell, who will be privy to the information." After Magruder returned to Washington, he[53]

> discussed the plan's approval with Liddy, who relayed the news to Hunt and McCord. When Liddy went to Hugh Sloan to get the first installment of $83,000 for the espionage program, Finance Chairman Maurice Stans checked with Mitchell, and then told Sloan to pay it and as to the purpose of the money "I do not want to know; you do not want to know."[54]

Mitchell claimed he didn't approve the plan at the March 30, 1972, Key Biscayne meeting, and while Fred LaRue admits the plan was discussed and did include breaking into the DNC, he said that "the decision was tabled" at the time. However, J. Anthony Lukas points out that "most investigators" during Watergate didn't accept Mitchell's denial or LaRue's version "because of the events that followed" the meeting, quoted above. Instead, Lukas says Watergate investigators "largely accept[ed] Magruder's [original] version of the meeting," which included Mitchell's approval, but not Nixon's call that preceded it. LaRue—the only other meeting participant still alive in 2003—denied Magruder's new account of the call in 2003, but former Nixon Counsel John Dean "said Mr. Magruder's [new] account was credible." Dean told interviewers, "I have no reason to doubt that it happened as [Magruder] describes it," and, "It's not something that strikes me as something Nixon would never do."[55]

During Watergate and until his death, John Mitchell would always deny authorizing—or even knowing about—the illegal Watergate operation. But in April 1973, "in a scotch-laced conversation with Washington correspondent Winzola McLendon, one that she did not publish at the time," Mitchell admitted knowing about "a whole espionage operation." In *All the President's Men*, Carl Bernstein recounted a talk he had about Nixon's political espionage with a Justice Department attorney, who told him that "John Mitchell . . . can't say he didn't know about it, because it was strategy—basic strategy that goes all the way to the top. Higher than him, even." While someone like Haldeman might convey an order to Mitchell from Nixon, the only person who was really higher than Mitchell and could tell Mitchell what to do—as Attorney General or the head of CREEP—was Richard Nixon.[56]

President Nixon's order to a reluctant Mitchell to approve the plan fits with other evidence and statements about Nixon's concerns at the time, and the way the White House operated. Nixon himself had publicly stated, "when I am the candidate, I run the campaign," and as pointed out earlier, Feldstein stated that "Nixon was a micromanager" who used his staff to "carry out his will."[57]

False statements by Nixon about his political crimes are abundant. He later claimed, "I didn't talk to Mitchell about this matter," and even declared, "I never met with him alone." However, Alexander Butterfield—responsible for tracking the President's daily movements—says that during 1972, "the president met with John Mitchell almost every night, over in the [Old] Executive Office Building." In addition, Mitchell later told Nixon supporter Rabbi Baruch Korff that he met with Nixon where there were no microphones or others present: "I usually met with the President in his living quarters," such as the White House's kitchen and solarium, when "no one was present." Mitchell told Korff that "no one was allowed" to be present for those private talks with Nixon, even including "family members and Nixon's valet." Mitchell also told the Rabbi, "I never did anything, without his approval."[58]

A year after the March 30, 1972, Nixon-Mitchell call approving the break-in, President Nixon himself made an amazing admission to H.R. Haldeman. On the day the President fired Haldeman and Ehrlichman, Nixon had separate, highly emotional meetings with each man and even "began crying uncontrollably" at one point. In their meeting, Nixon told Haldeman that he—Nixon—"was 'really the guilty one'" because "he's the one that started Colson on his projects [and] he was the one who made Mitchell Attorney General and later his campaign manager."[59]

It's also important to remember that Nixon's various campaign crimes were going on long before Liddy's plan was approved on March 30, and they simply continued under a somewhat new structure afterward. Nixon's razor-thin popular vote victory in 1968—coupled with the unpredictable revelations by Jack Anderson, and the possibility that Larry O'Brien knew some of Nixon's secrets shared by Howard Hughes and Robert Maheu—made extreme steps necessary, from Nixon's perspective.

The close Nixon-Mitchell relationship also adds credence to Magruder's revelation of the Nixon-Mitchell phone call. Nixon trusted Mitchell more than any other high-ranking White House official. Mitchell was the only one of those officials who shared some of the President's darkest secrets, like the 1960 CIA-Mafia plots. It's likely that Mitchell could have avoided prison if he had blamed Nixon for the crimes he was charged for, but Mitchell didn't and continued to protect Nixon during and after his sentence. A grateful Nixon even held a celebration for Mitchell after his release from prison.[60]

One skeptic of Magruder's more complete account of his March 30, 1972, meeting with Mitchell is Stanley Kutler, who points out that there is no tape of Nixon authorizing the plan or the break-ins. However, there is evidence for numerous crimes that Nixon committed while his taping system was in operation that aren't reflected on the tapes at all—which is no surprise, since Nixon knew he was being recorded. Plus, the well-documented large sums of money that began to flow immediately after the March 30, 1972, meeting show that someone approved something major, and it's hard to imagine that any of Nixon's devoted, ambitious aides and officials would have risked their careers by doing something like that without telling Nixon.[61]

President Nixon himself summed up his thinking best, a year after the first Watergate break-in, when he said to Alexander Haig on May 23, 1973,

> I ordered that they use any means necessary, including illegal means, to accomplish this goal. The President of the United States can never admit that.[62]

At the time, Nixon was talking about the Huston Plan, the President's attempt in 1970 to set up a national domestic intelligence network controlled by the White House. In his talk with Haig, Nixon seemed more concerned with stressing to Haig that the President could never publicly admit that "I ordered the use of illegal means or that I condoned it," rather than the fact that Nixon had done exactly that. Nixon's thinking helps to explain not only the Watergate burglaries but also his extensive denials and cover-ups that followed.*[63]

The New York Times reported that the author of the Huston Plan for Nixon, Lawrence Huston, said "that [Nixon's] authorization [for the Huston Plan] was never formally rescinded." In some ways, Nixon simply implemented the Huston Plan on a smaller scale, using former CIA operatives like Hunt and former FBI men like Liddy, instead of using the actual CIA and FBI.

CHAPTER 29

Nixon, the CIA-Mafia Plots, and Break-Ins: From the Chilean Embassy to Watergate

From Richard Nixon's perspective in the spring of 1972, the new political espionage plan he had ordered Mitchell to approve was just a few minutes out of his massive campaign effort, itself only part of a full plate of foreign and domestic issues that filled Nixon's days. The President's ongoing "dirty tricks" operations were already producing results against early front-runner Edmund Muskie, as well as moderates Henry "Scoop" Jackson, Terry Sanford, and Hubert Humphrey. That left Nixon's preferred choice—Senator George McGovern of South Dakota, running on a peace platform—starting to emerge as the new front-runner. McGovern would soon become the main target of Nixon's political espionage, along with Larry O'Brien's Democratic National Committee offices at the Watergate.

President Nixon was also busy dealing with the aftermath of his trip to China, whose leaders' reassurance to him about North Vietnam allowed Nixon to respond aggressively to an Easter offensive by the Communist forces in South Vietnam. On April 16, 1972, Nixon resumed bombing Hanoi and the port city of Haiphong, hoping to force the North Vietnamese into peace talks; three weeks later he would begin mining Haiphong and other ports. This inflamed the antiwar movement in the United States, energizing McGovern's supporters even more. Nixon was also busy planning his next foreign policy and PR offensive, a late May trip to the Soviet Union, the first by an American President.[1]

Domestically, in addition to a variety of legislative and regulatory issues—some involving his major contributors—Nixon was also still dealing with the ITT scandals that Jack Anderson had exposed. But the "denial" Hunt had secured from lobbyist Dita Beard about ITT's

$400,000 "contribution" was gradually helping to get that issue off the front pages. The same was true for the Nixon administration and ITT's use of the CIA to undermine Chile's President, a scandal that began to fade from the headlines after Richard Helms's denials to Congress about the matter.[2]

An earlier Jack Anderson exposé—a January 24, 1972, update to his August 1971 revelation of the $100,000 Howard Hughes gave to Bebe Rebozo for Nixon—should have generated coverage by other news organizations and an FBI investigation. But the press's attention had been diverted by the ITT scandals, and it appeared that J. Edgar Hoover at the FBI was protecting Nixon. Hoover had previously met Rebozo, at Nixon's Key Biscayne home, and didn't seem inclined to investigate the two men. When the FBI finally interviewed Rebozo on March 9, 1972, it wasn't about the $100,000 from Hughes. The interview appears to have been about several Cuban exiles, and Rebozo at first told the FBI agents he couldn't help because "his immediate circle of friends does not include any Cubans." That wasn't true, as Rebozo himself later indicated to the agents, when he "suggested" they talk to "Mr. Edgardo Buttari [Sr.], who is Cuban and whom he considers a close personal friend." It's hard to tell what the matter was really about because even in 2012, much of Rebozo's released FBI file is still heavily censored, with many parts totally blocked out.[3]

Rebozo's friend Buttari was a mutual business partner and friend of Cuban exile Bernard Barker, at the same time Barker was becoming more heavily involved in Nixon's new political espionage plan. Liddy had gone to Hunt in "early April," showing Hunt "checks for large amounts of money," and asking if Barker could launder them "through his business in Miami." Hunt called Barker, who agreed, since he'd been laundering money for Hunt since well before the Bay of Pigs operation. Liddy took checks totaling $114,000 to Miami, where Barker deposited them in the bank his business used. However, the bank initially refused one $25,000 cashier's check, until Barker gave the bank a "falsely notarized statement." Then, Barker "withdrew cash "over the next three weeks" and returned the money to Liddy—"minus $2500," as a kind of commission. Most of the money—$89,000 of the $114,000—had been obtained from a Houston company, as an apparently illegal corporate contribution. That money had previously been laundered through a Mexican bank, leaving an important paper trail that would be discovered after Watergate. The rest of the money had been a cash contribution from Nixon supporter "Dwayne O. Andreas, president of the Archer-Daniels-Midland Company," that had been passed on a golf course to CREEP's Kenneth Dahlberg, who then converted the cash into Barker's initially problematic cashier's check. Some of the money Barker laundered would be used for the Watergate break-ins, and he would actually be carrying some of the cash when he was arrested.[4]

Barker's supervisor, E. Howard Hunt, was extremely busy in the spring of 1972. Hunt was supervising three of the five "dirty tricks" teams working against Senator Edmund Muskie. One team involved Donald Segretti, while another had planted two spies in Muskie's campaign who were able to get advance copies of "hundreds of Muskie's interoffice memos, itineraries, drafts of speeches, and position papers." Xerox machines were not as common in 1972 as they would become, so many of the files had to be photographed on 35mm film, the same technique that would be used in the Watergate break-ins. Hunt also helped to place a spy in Muskie's Washington headquarters: Thomas Gregory, a friend of Robert Bennett's nephew. In return for $175 a week, Gregory gave Hunt reports each Friday, which Hunt passed on to Liddy.[5]

In addition to Hunt's anti-Muskie operations, Nixon's other efforts were run by Murray Chotiner and Jeb Magruder. Most of Nixon's "dirty tricks" against Muskie remained below the radar of the mainstream press at the time, except for the infamous "Canuck letter" in the *Manchester Union Leader,* which claimed that Muskie had insulted French-Canadians. Much later, the letter was shown to be a forgery, created by Nixon's operatives, but at the time the fake letter had an effect in New Hampshire, where a sizable minority of the small state had French-Canadian roots. In addition, the conservative *Union Leader* ran excerpts from a *Women's Wear Daily* interview with Muskie's wife, focusing on quotes saying that she liked to drink, smoke, and tell "dirty jokes." Muskie's emotional response in the falling snow marked a turning point for his campaign. Some reports claimed Muskie cried, and even though he said what looked like tears were melting snowflakes, the damage was done. Though Muskie won the New Hampshire primary, his margin was not as large as expected. However, it's often overlooked that Nixon's "dirty tricks" operations with Hunt and others did not let up on the candidate, and even as

Muskie's campaign faltered, he continued to be targeted, lest he stage a comeback.* [6]

Perhaps to provide cover for Hunt's espionage operations, his White House phone in the Old Executive Office building was removed on March 15. But Hunt continued to be employed by the White House and CREEP, and his work for Nixon's campaign not only continued, but increased. (Hunt's White House employment would not be officially terminated until June 19, 1972, two days after the final Watergate break-in.) A week before Muskie withdrew from the race on April 24 (after a last-place finish in Pennsylvania, losing to McGovern, Humphrey, and Wallace), Hunt and Liddy had been told to start targeting their resources against the new front-runner, George McGovern. McGovern was proving to be a savvy campaigner; he and his campaign manager, Gary Hart, were taking full advantage of the rule changes for primaries and delegates that had been passed in the wake of the 1968 Democratic convention. Still, the McGovern campaign wasn't close to locking down the nomination, and Nixon continued to worry that a candidate with wider appeal—either a moderate or Senator Edward Kennedy—would emerge as the nominee. But for now, McGovern was the top target for Nixon's "dirty tricks" operation, so Hunt reassigned his spy, Thomas Gregory, from Muskie's headquarters to McGovern's Washington headquarters.[7]

April 1972 is supposedly when Hunt met Frank Fiorini for the first time, as both men would publicly claim and testify for years. However, that claim ignores Fiorini's admitted work on Hunt's "anti-narcotics" operation, as well as Hunt's June 1971 JFK-Castro investigation with Fiorini and Barker (covered in Chapter 26). Near the end of Hunt's life, he admitted on tape to his son David that he had known Fiorini by 1963. In a talk with journalist and longtime friend Andrew St. George shortly after Watergate—an interview not intended for publication—Fiorini slipped up and admitted that he and Hunt had met during the planning for the Bay of Pigs operation. The first meeting between Hunt and Fiorini was probably around the time of Fiorini's role in the

* The there is no truth to reports that Nixon's operatives slipped LSD to Muskie before he gave the speech defending his wife. The rumor may have been inspired by Hunter S. Thompson's claim in a *Rolling Stone* article that Muskie had used another psychedelic substance, something that Thompson later admitted he'd simply made up.

CIA-Mafia plots in October 1960, just after Hunt had been assigned a new assistant: Bernard Barker, Fiorini's longtime associate.[8]

James McCord also testified that he first met E. Howard Hunt in April 1972. If the accounts of *Vanity Fair*, *New York Times* journalist Tad Szulc, former FBI agent William Turner, and aides to Robert Kennedy are correct, their first meeting would have been during Cuban operations in the 1960s, including in 1963 for the JFK-Almeida coup plan. However, that plan was still classified—and parts of it were still in operation—every time McCord (and Hunt) testified, which could account for the discrepancy in dates. On April 12, 1972, Liddy gave McCord, CREEP's Security Director, "a stack of $100 bills totaling $65,000," saying, "This is for the electronic equipment" for the newly approved espionage program. Then "Liddy took McCord across the street to" the Mullen Company, "where he introduced him to Hunt." Given the top secret nature of the CIA's work with Commander Almeida and his family, it's not surprising that Hunt wouldn't tell Liddy that he already knew McCord. Unknown to Liddy, Hunt was still secretly feeding information to Richard Helms, and protecting the Agency was still a prime concern for Hunt.[9]

McCord also appeared to have strong feelings for the CIA, more so than for Nixon. John Mitchell's biographer quoted "a former CREEP employee" as saying, "I could actually sense a fear of Richard Nixon with Jim McCord [because McCord felt that] Nixon wasn't a team player, wasn't an American, wasn't, you know, 'one of us.'" But McCord was valuable to Nixon's campaign and its espionage program. "McCord was not just somebody's little wiretapper or debugging man . . . He's a pro, he's a master. Allen Dulles [once] said: 'This man is the best man we have,'" according to "an Air Force colonel" quoted in Mitchell's biography.[10]

To join the espionage plan, "Liddy offered McCord an extra $2,000 in salary each month, plus $2,000 per surreptitious entry." (Hunt would get $3,000 per entry.) Later, Cuban exile Felipe De Diego—part of the burglary team that ransacked the office of Ellsberg's psychiatrist and a member of the initial Watergate crew—would tell "investigators he instantly recognized McCord as the same man who a decade earlier, in Florida, had helped organize 'an infiltration group . . . of Cubans working for the CIA.'" On May 1, 1972, McCord hired as his assistant Alfred Baldwin, a thirty-five-year-old attorney and former FBI agent. Three days later, McCord would rent room 419 at the Howard Johnson motel across the street from the Democratic National Committee headquarters at the Watergate. McCord would move Baldwin into that room on May 11, but another operation would intervene before it could be used as a base for the Watergate break-ins.[11]

McCord does not appear to have been part of some of the other operations Hunt was still running in the spring of 1972, such as Hunt's portion of the White House's "anti-narcotics" program. Hunt was still working with Barker, Fiorini, and Manuel Artime on the drug operation, though few details have ever been uncovered about their activities, aside from the drug trafficker assassination component mentioned earlier. Many of the White House files about the drug operation were probably among those destroyed after the Watergate arrests. In March of 1972, Hunt seems to have been very involved with Manuel Artime, his close friend from the days of the CIA-Mafia plots and the Bay of Pigs operation—so much so that CIA agent Eugenio Martinez prepared a report for the CIA about their activities.

Martinez's report on Hunt and Artime was prepared at the request of Jacob Esterline, the Chief of the CIA's Miami station. Martinez's case officer had referred Martinez to Esterline after becoming concerned at some of the things Martinez told him about Hunt. Esterline had known Hunt since at least 1960, when they had worked together on CIA efforts to topple Castro, and he immediately asked CIA headquarters about "Hunt's White House status." However, Esterline was baffled when he received a reply from the "Assistant Deputy Director of Plans" that told him "not [to] concern himself with the travels of Hunt in Miami, that Hunt was on domestic White House business of an unknown nature and that the Chief of Station should 'cool it.'" According to the Senate Watergate Report, "the letter infuriated the Chief of Station and left him uneasy about [Hunt's activities, so] the Chief of Station requested that Martinez prepare in Spanish a report on the Hunt information." But Martinez's own case officer cautioned him "that he should instead compile a 'cover story,' and that he should not put anything in the report 'which might come back to haunt him.'" Martinez's resulting report was thus described as "a vague account." After the Hunt matter arose, Martinez's case officer was quickly replaced by a CIA officer "dispatched" to Miami from CIA headquarters.[12]

On April 5, 1972, the CIA's Inspector General's office prepared—as part of an "Internal Review"—an index card that listed some of the names mentioned in Martinez's report. The index card, and apparently Martinez's report, was titled "Activities of Howard Hunt and Dr. Manuel Artime in Miami and Nicaragua [English translation of Martinez's report]" (brackets in original). According to the CIA index card, in addition to Hunt and Artime, Martinez's report also covered "Barker, Mrs. Hunt, Tony Varona . . . Carlos Prio," and two other exiles. Hunt had worked with Tony Varona on the 1960 CIA-Mafia plots with Trafficante and Rosselli, while Prio—like Barker—was also a Trafficante associate. It's likely that Martinez, who was not tied to Trafficante, had grown concerned about some aspect of Hunt's drug operation, which involved "Artime in Miami and Nicaragua." After Watergate, Artime admitted that Hunt called him in April 1972, but he made it sound like Hunt was simply interested in pursuing business for his PR firm. However, that type of activity would not have alarmed Martinez or the Miami CIA men. Senate investigators were stymied by the CIA when they tried to find out more about the Hunt-Artime-Martinez matter, and authors like Jim Hougan say it's obvious "that someone in CIA headquarters was working overtime to protect Hunt's operations." That person was almost certainly Richard Helms, who would have been protecting both his protégé and his pipeline into the White House, which gave him access to FBI reports the CIA couldn't obtain from Hoover and the Bureau.[13]

In the spring of 1972, Richard Helms had additional reasons to protect E. Howard Hunt and his White House operations. As amazing as it might sound, CIA files confirm that Helms was personally pitching major Hollywood figures a television show based on Hunt's series of paperback spy novels. Declassified CIA memos show that in late April and early May 1972, Helms was pitching the TV series to Jack Valenti, a former aide to LBJ who had become the head of the powerful Motion Picture Association of America (MPAA). Hunt wrote his spy novels under the pseudonym of "David St. John." According to the Agency files, Valenti said that "Helms, a personal friend of David St. John, said he would like to help St. John get the books made into movies or a TV series." In talking to Valenti about the Hunt novels in late April, Helms was following up an earlier conversation he had with Valenti about the matter "about six months ago," in the latter part of 1971. Helms himself admitted in a CIA memo that he had first approached Valenti even before that, perhaps in 1969, to say that Hunt's "books gave a favorable impression of the Agency and might be exploitable for the movies." In early May or late April 1972, Jack Valenti told "Marvin

S. Davis, senior vice president of Gulf & Western, a conglomerate which owned Paramount Pictures," that "he had interviewed David St. John . . . at the request of Helms."[14]

It's simply astonishing to see that just weeks before the first Watergate break-in, the Director of the CIA was personally pitching a powerful industry figure such as Jack Valenti a TV series based on Hunt's novels. One can only imagine what Valenti must have thought after Watergate when the man he'd interviewed at Helms's behest turned out to be the infamous E. Howard Hunt. Like the other media and publishing figures who had met Hunt before Watergate, Valenti apparently kept that knowledge to himself.[15]

By May 8, 1972, Helms was still pressing for a Hunt TV show, at a special screening of *The Godfather* at Valenti's MPAA headquarters. The showing was "held under unspecified CIA 'cover arrangements.'" Among those at the screening were CIA officials such as Helms, White House officials like John Ehrlichman, and "Charles Bluhdorn, the President of Paramount Pictures." At the *Godfather* screening, Helms (or Valenti on Helms's behalf) gave the Paramount Pictures president "a stack of David St. John's books . . . as evidence of the CIA's continued interest in a TV series" based on the novels. One reason for Helms's interest in pushing Hunt's books for a TV series was the rivalry between the CIA and the FBI. In 1972, *The FBI* was a popular, long-running primetime TV drama show that gave a weekly publicity boost to the Bureau, always presenting it in a good light. Helms apparently wanted the same thing for the CIA.[16]

The Helms-Valenti-Hunt matter is important for two reasons. First, it is more confirmation that the close relationship between Hunt and Helms continued even while Hunt was working for the Nixon White House. Second, some authors and officials over the years have proposed or insinuated that the arrests at the Watergate were engineered by Helms and the CIA to bring down President Nixon. However, the fact that Helms was personally pushing Hunt's book for a TV series just over two weeks before the first Watergate break-in attempt is totally inconsistent with Helms trying to engineer Hunt's arrest soon after that. (In addition, the "CIA was behind Watergate to bring down Nixon" theory fails to explain why Helms did not use the Agency's extensive media contacts to expose Nixon's involvement in Watergate prior to the November 1972 election, in which Watergate wasn't a factor.)

In the spring of 1972, President Nixon helped Richard Helms deal with an extremely difficult situation involving a former Agency employee, beginning at least a temporary era of cooperation between Nixon and Helms. Victor Marchetti was described by Helms's biographer, Thomas Powers, as being "a former Russian-language specialist, analyst, and aide in the Director's own office." Marchetti was quoted in earlier chapters regarding Helms's reaction to David Ferrie's name surfacing in the Jim Garrison investigation, because Ferrie had worked for the Agency. Marchetti had since left the CIA, and in March 1972, the CIA learned that he was circulating to publishers a "tell all" outline for a book about the CIA. Helms wanted publication stopped, but the Justice Department was in a state of flux at that time, since Mitchell had resigned to run CREEP, while the confirmation hearing for his successor, Kleindienst, was bogged down due to the ITT scandals.[17]

So, "Helms decided to approach Nixon directly, to ensure that the Justice Department would take the problem seriously." Powers wrote that Nixon "listened to Helms's argument, promised his support," and referred the matter to John Ehrlichman for action. Despite the difficult time Helms had given Nixon and Ehrlichman over the Bay of Pigs material, "Nixon and Ehrlichman went out of their way to help keep the secrets" of Helms and the CIA. "The Justice Department pressed its suit" against Marchetti "vigorously and eventually forced Marchetti to drop 168 passages from his book." Marchetti didn't know about tightly held secrets such as the CIA-Mafia plots to kill Castro, but he did know about many matters that could have embarrassed the Agency. Nixon's assistance to Helms marked a turning point in their relationship, making it less adversarial and more cooperative. While Helms still didn't give Nixon the CIA material he wanted about "the Bay of Pigs thing"—the CIA-Mafia plots—Hunt would soon oversee an effort beneficial to both Nixon and Helms to keep the plots secret.[18]

The espionage plan that Nixon had Mitchell approve had been drawn up by G. Gordon Liddy—in response to requests from Nixon, aides, and officials—but it was E. Howard Hunt who took the leading role in implementing the plan in May and June 1972. Hunt and his aide Barker recruited most of the operatives for the plan, and at times Liddy appears to have been relatively out of the loop about what Hunt was actually doing and why, something Liddy realized only in hindsight. Indeed, Liddy was the only one in the group without anti-Castro and/or CIA experience (most had both), which became more evident as Hunt recruited more men for the program. Hunt's operatives were more numerous than most people realize and go far beyond the burglars caught at the Watergate. Hunt was soon working with at least ten Cuban exiles, and there were still more involved with his "anti-narcotics" program. It's also possible some of Hunt's lesser-known burglars were drawn from his narcotics operations.

On May 1, 1972, Jack Anderson's column revealed that the FBI had kept files "on the private lives of political figures, black leaders, newsmen, and show business people." Anderson ran the column to coincide with his testimony to a Congressional committee, where he proclaimed that "J. Edgar Hoover has demonstrated an intense interest in who is sleeping with whom in Washington . . . I have seen FBI reports; I have examined FBI files [and] am willing to make some of these documents available to the Committee."[19]

The following morning, on May 2, 1972, the body of Hoover, the only Director the FBI had ever known, was discovered at his home. Hoover's death set off a scramble to get his legendary secret files, both the "Official and Confidential files" and the even more sensitive "Personal and Confidential files." Liddy and Hunt contacted Ehrlichman and Colson, and the rush was on. The undertaker who arrived at Hoover's home shortly after noon saw "men in suits, fifteen or eighteen of them, swarming all over the place, ransacking it, going through everything he had. I assumed they were government agents. They were going through Hoover's books, desk, drawers, like they were looking for something." Richard Kleindienst, the acting Attorney General who was still undergoing confirmation, ordered that Hoover's FBI office "be sealed—to secure [Hoover's] files."[20]

The secret files were Nixon's top concern when he heard of Hoover's death, according to Haldeman and Ehrlichman. John Mitchell ordered Haldeman "to hunt down the 'skeletons'"—the dark secrets that could harm Nixon's campaign. Mitchell and Nixon knew there were many, from the 1960 $500,000 Nixon-Mafia-Hoffa bribe to the CIA-Mafia plots to kill Fidel to Nixon's array of illegal money, and even Nixon's fall 1968 interference with LBJ's Vietnam peace deal. Nixon quickly appointed L. Patrick Gray, previously the Deputy Attorney General–designate, as the new acting FBI Director. That was a crushing blow to Assistant FBI Director Mark Felt, who felt he deserved the top post. But Nixon had worked with Gray since he'd been Vice President, and he wanted someone he could trust to handle any information that could harm his reelection chances.[21]

When new Acting Director L. Patrick Gray arrived at FBI headquarters to secure the secret files, he was shocked and angry when he was told no such files remained. Only Hoover's personal office had been sealed per Kleindienst's orders, but it contained no files. However, that meant "the other nine rooms in [Hoover's] office suite," which had been "bulging with documents, remained unsecured." Congress later tried to determine what happened to many of the files, but without success. Some files were destroyed by Gray and Mark Felt "a week after" Hoover died. Congressional investigators found that "a mass of documents were trucked to [Hoover's] home in the weeks that followed his death." *Newsweek* would later report that Clyde Tolson, Hoover's longtime companion, had files "very, very damaging to the Nixon White House."[22]

Aside from the relatively few sensitive files Gray was able to find and destroy, either to protect Nixon or the Bureau, the President had once more been frustrated by Hoover. For a Chief Executive who wielded vast power in many ways, it's amazing that Nixon had been stymied in his quest for information—especially damaging information about himself—by both his FBI Director, Hoover, and by his CIA Director, Helms.

At Hoover's funeral on May 4, Richard Nixon delivered an eulogy laced with irony, saying, "The American people today are tired of . . . disrespect for law. America wants to come back to the law as a way of life." Nixon's words were especially ironic in light of what some of his men had done the day before in Washington, while Hoover's body lay in state at the U.S. Capitol building.[23]

E. Howard Hunt later claimed that he had Barker bring a group of Cuban exile operatives up from Miami to prevent "an anti-war demonstration being held on the Capitol steps from disturbing" the thousands of mourners viewing Hoover's body. Another rationale given later by Nixon aides was that Hunt's operatives were supposed to steal a Viet Cong flag from the demonstrators, so it could be given to Nixon as a trophy—but that has the whiff of an after-the-fact cover story. Noted Watergate authority Fred Emery is skeptical, saying that "it is equally possible that the antiwar demonstration, regardless of Hoover, was the target of Nixon's fury" since "[Daniel] Ellsberg was listed among those attending." On Nixon's orders, Ellsberg was being aggressively prosecuted by the Justice Department and would face twelve felony charges with a combined "sentence of 115 years."[24]

Based on accounts by Barker and other Cuban exile operatives, Ellsberg was clearly their target. One said that Barker showed him "a picture of Ellsberg [and] they were told: 'Our mission is to hit him, call him a traitor, and punch him in the nose. Hit him and run.'" Some of the exiles "were told they were going on a 'government mission.'" The day after Hoover's body was discovered, Barker led nine other Cuban exiles to Washington. They included Eugenio Martinez and Felipe De Diego, who had participated in the burglary eight months earlier of Daniel Ellsberg's psychiatrist. There was also CIA veteran Frank Fiorini, Bay of Pigs veteran Reinaldo Pico, and Pablo Fernandez, described as "a former CIA operative in South America." Also in the group were anti-Castro activists Angel Ferrer, Iran Gonzalez, and Humberto Lopez. Rounding out the group was expert locksmith Virgilio Gonzalez, who would later be arrested with Barker, Fiorini, and Martinez at the Watergate.[25]

For some of the men, their mission was a dry run for the disruptions they were planning to stage for Hunt and Liddy at the summer's Democratic National Convention in Miami. For the May 3 Washington operation targeting Ellsberg, the men were paid $100 each. According to Fenandez, "Barker ordered the men to 'get' Ellsberg and [attorney William] Kunstler." The men were not able to get close to Ellsberg, but Fiorini and Pico actually managed to hit several demonstrators and were grabbed by "Capitol Police," but "Pico saw a man in a gray suit give a signal to the policeman [who] took us down to the street and told us we could go away." After the mission, Barker was "debriefed" by Hunt and Liddy.[26]

The whole mission seems odd: pulling together so many men so quickly, and spending so much time and money for such a small result—all only three weeks before the first Watergate burglary attempt, by many of the same people. In addition to all the expenses, Liddy received extra money for the mission above what was already in his budget. Was there something more to the mission? Nixon had talked to Haldeman before about using "goon squads" to "rough up hecklers . . . and silence them [since Nixon] approved of strong arm tactics." Nixon had talked on tape about having thugs "go in and knock their heads off."[27]

Daniel Ellsberg put a more ominous spin on the mission, when he was later told by one of the Watergate prosecutors that "a dozen Cuban assets were brought up from Miami with orders, quoting the prosecutor, to incapacitate [me] totally, on the steps of the Capitol." Ellsberg says he "asked the prosecutor, what does that mean, kill me? And he said, the words were 'to incapacitate you totally.'" Ellsberg told MSNBC, "I actually think it was to silence me at that particular time," and Ellsberg has told other interviewers that he felt the men were supposed "to kill me." Ellsberg said they didn't because the large crowd "was friendly to him" and perhaps "they smelled that they were being set up" to take the blame.[28]

Ellsberg's biographer—Tom Wells—felt that Ellsberg "blew the operation out of proportion," and Barker denied they intended to kill Ellsberg. However, Wells did quote testimony showing that Barker told the Watergate Special Prosecution Force that "'the heads at the top' wanted the demonstration terminated 'at any cost.'" Neither Ellsberg nor his skeptical biographer knew about Barker's, and Fiorini's, ties to Santo Trafficante or to the plots to kill Fidel Castro. Also, recall Liddy's boast at the first GEMSTONE meeting with Mitchell, Magruder, and Dean, that he planned to use "professional killers who had accounted between them for twenty-two dead [including] members of organized crime." There is also E. Howard Hunt's earlier boast to Liddy that his operatives "had accounted among them for a substantial number of deaths [and] he indicated that these . . . Cuban individuals were connected in some way with organized crime."[29]

Daniel Ellsberg's charge that he was going to be murdered cannot be proved, but it is clear that if Barker and his men could have gotten close to him, he could have been injured, perhaps seriously. The May 3 Ellsberg incident is also important because members of this same group would soon be involved in the Watergate break-ins. The approach of unleashing operatives to beat up demonstrators would also be repeated after Watergate, when former Cuban President Carlos Prio filled in for Hunt and Barker, by directing "a goon squad that roughed up antiwar demonstrators." As mentioned earlier, Prio had become involved again with Hunt and Artime by March 1972, and he had known them since 1960. Prio had also been part of Nixon's fall 1963 effort to learn about the JFK-Almeida coup plan, and in the summer of 1972, Prio would be the leader of a group named "Cuban-Americans for Nixon-Agnew."[30]

Most accounts of the Ellsberg incident end with Liddy telling Barker that their next target would be the Watergate, though some accounts have Liddy saying their next target would be the campaign headquarters of Senator George McGovern. But there would be another well-documented—but little known—burglary before those attempts, one that men like Hunt, Barker, and Fiorini were especially well suited for.

In May 1972, Richard Nixon would have been concerned about a new book by Walter Sheridan, *The Fall and Rise of Jimmy Hoffa*, that was well into production. Sheridan was the former leader of the Justice Department's "Get Hoffa Squad" for Robert Kennedy. After finishing his work for NBC News on the Garrison case, Sheridan had done various types of private investigation work. Sheridan apparently began his book project even before Hoffa's December 1971 release, since he said that he "decided to write this book when it became apparent that the attempts to corrupt government witnesses and others were going to continue until Hoffa somehow obtained his freedom." However, when "Hoffa [was] finally . . . released through the intervention of President Nixon," Sheridan's book project became more commercially viable, since Hoffa was back in the news.[31]

Sheridan's *The Fall and Rise of Jimmy Hoffa* is not really a biography, and it is not like any book ever written before or since. It is basically a massive criminal history of Hoffa, a dramatic retelling of the various Hoffa investigations and trials, many of which involved Sheridan. The densely written book is also an indictment of Hoffa's associates, including the politicians that aided Hoffa. In preparing the book, Sheridan was no doubt helped by many of his former Justice Department associates, and possibly even some still working for the Justice Department. The first person Sheridan thanked in the book was Jack Miller, who had headed Robert Kennedy's overall effort against organized crime, which included both the "Get Hoffa Squad" and the group that targeted Mafia figures like Carlos Marcello. Jack Miller was then in private practice in Washington, as were many veterans of RFK's Justice Department. They were just as angry at Hoffa's release as Sheridan was, mirroring the Justice Department official quoted earlier who said, "the President of the United States . . . pardoned organized crime figures after millions were spent by the government putting them away."[32]

The Fall and Rise of Jimmy Hoffa reads as if various Congressional and Justice Department reports were turned into a somewhat dry nonfiction book. How Sheridan obtained much of the material—especially after he'd left the Justice Department—is not clear. The same is true for the book's ghostwriter (or writers), though three editors are credited, including best-selling author Peter Maas. The book has no endnotes, but it is worded very carefully and precisely and makes a remarkable number of criminal charges against individuals who were alive at the time.

By May 1972, the lengthy book (eventually 554 pages, plus an introduction) would have been well into production, since sales and marketing to the trade usually began six months before the publication date. News of the book was probably known in publishing circles before that, when the book was first shopped to publishers. The book's introduction by writer Budd Schulberg is dated July 4, 1972, and he refers to having read the manuscript. Schulberg viewed the book as important to the 1972 Presidential campaign, pointing out that it was "an election year, when Nixon has become anathema to the legitimate labor movement and the Teamsters wind up as his only big-labor supporters." Schulberg concludes his introduction by stating, "Whether or not a Jack Anderson [or] a Walter Sheridan can arouse our people from their complacency is the question on which the future course of America may depend." A major impetus for Walter Sheridan to write his book was probably so that it could come out before—and thus affect—the 1972 election. Sheridan didn't want to see Nixon reelected, and he would soon begin working directly for Senator McGovern's campaign, even while his Hoffa book was still in production.[33]

Richard Nixon certainly knew about Walter Sheridan's Hoffa book by May 1972, since it was going to be a major hardback book for a noted publisher, Saturday Review Press. In addition, interviews were conducted for the book, and word of Sheridan's new investigation would have become known in Teamsters and organized crime circles, especially by those Sheridan was targeting. Sheridan's book would have been a major concern for Nixon because by 1972 Nixon realized that the Justice Department—and some who had worked there under Robert Kennedy, such as Sheridan—knew about the $500,000 bribe he'd gotten in September 1960 from the Mafia, on behalf of Jimmy Hoffa. There is no way to know with certainty how much Nixon knew about Sheridan's project, which no doubt also concerned Hoffa, Fitzsimmons, and others. But Nixon had the most to lose if his $500,000 bribe from 1960 were revealed. That crime would be bad enough to have exposed, but Hoffa's December 1971 release would also raise additional questions—and Nixon knew that even more money had been paid (and promised) to arrange that specially conditioned commutation.[34]

Because so many living criminals and criminal associates were named in the book, Sheridan and his publisher probably kept the book's actual manuscript tightly under wraps, while releasing enough provocative information to entice booksellers and distributors to order it. That meant that Nixon couldn't have known exactly what the book said—or didn't say—about his crimes. Sheridan knew every detail about Nixon's 1960 bribe, and if Nixon had been able to see the manuscript, the President would have cringed at passages like, "Hoffa's apparent immunity from prosecution had ended with the defeat of Nixon" in the 1960 election, and Sheridan's description of how Hoffa felt "double-crossed" after he was indicted following Nixon's loss. Sheridan even included much information about Murray Chotiner's help in arranging Hoffa's 1971 release.[35]

Richard Nixon could not know what, if anything, Sheridan might include about the September 1960 CIA-Mafia plots, given what had been in Jack Anderson's 1967 and 1971 articles. Nixon knew the bribe and the plots unfolded at the same time, and with some of the same participants (Nixon, Marcello, Trafficante). The perfect storm for Nixon would have been if the $500,000 September 1960 bribe came out during the 1972 campaign, along with Nixon's role in the ramped-up 1960 CIA-Mafia plots. That would destroy Nixon's "law and order" image and would set journalists and Congress digging into Hoffa's recent release, which Nixon knew could uncover an even larger bribe. In May 1972, that perfect storm became a very real possibility for Richard Nixon, one that he would have to prevent no matter what the risk.

The first well-documented burglary for E. Howard Hunt's crew, as part of Nixon's new political espionage plan, was not the initial attempt at the Watergate, on May 26, 1972. Instead, it was on May 13, 1972, at the Chilean embassy in Washington, D.C., where the crew committed a political burglary using a "national security" cover, just as it would soon do at the Watergate, in May and June. The Chilean embassy break-in has been overlooked in most Watergate books and articles, in part because of what Nixon called "national security reasons"—the same reasons he thought would prevent a full investigation of the Watergate burglaries.[36]

President Nixon talked about the Chilean embassy break-in on a White House tape that was not released until 1999. *The New York Times*, one of the only newspapers to mention the tape's release, said it had been withheld on "national security grounds," according to the National Archives. *The Times* reported that a year after the May 13, 1972, break-in, Nixon was talking with his "his legal aide, J. Fred Buzhardt." Nixon told him that "the break-in, the Chilean Embassy—that thing was a part of the burglars' plan, as a cover . . . a CIA cover."[37]

Nixon's reference to "the burglars" refers to the Plumbers group of Hunt, Bernard Barker, Frank Fiorini, and—according to an FBI memo about Fiorini—Eugenio Martinez and Felipe De Diego. All were current (Martinez) or former CIA agents and officers, which explains why Nixon said he was using "a CIA cover." It was essentially the same group that Nixon and his aides had used to burglarize the office of Daniel Ellsberg's psychiatrist the previous year, with the addition of CIA contract agent Fiorini and without G. Gordon Liddy. It's not known if James McCord actively participated in the break-in, but in a 1999 interview with *The New York Times*, Nixon's former counsel John Dean "said one of the Plumbers, James W. McCord Jr., a former CIA officer, was thought to have used his knowledge of American espionage against the Chilean Embassy as a bargaining chip, after his conviction for the Watergate break-in." The main researcher for Woodward and Bernstein on *All the President's Men*, Robert Fink, wrote that CIA veteran James McCord—later arrested at the Watergate—"expressed a belief that the Chilean embassy was bugged by the Administration, a belief then shared by officials of the embassy, and strengthened by the intruders' apparent knowledge of the diplomats' movements."*[38]

Eleven days after the final Watergate break-in, a June 28, 1972, memo by Deputy CIA Director General Vernon Walters reported that John Dean "believed that Barker had been involved in a clandestine entry into the Chilean embassy." According to an Agency memo in one of Barker's CIA files, someone at *The New York Times* "believe[s] that Watergate, the break-in at the Chilean Embassy and [the] attempt to beat up Ellsberg on Capitol grounds [are] all related [and they] believe Barker is the 'key man.'" Barker was the key man in the sense that he was E. Howard Hunt's top Cuban exile in the operation, and

*McCord, Martinez, and De Diego have never acknowledged or been charged with the Chilean embassy break-in.

the one who had recruited most of the others. Hunt's role in overseeing the Chilean embassy break-in is simply a logical extension of what he'd been doing for the CIA since the early 1950s, when he broke into embassies in Mexico City and Uruguay.[39]

Frank Fiorini's extensive remarks about his involvement in the Chilean embassy burglary were recorded in an FBI memo about a related investigation that was sent to the FBI Director the following year. The memo states that Fiorini "confirm[ed] his participation in the Chilean break-ins" to the "Washington DC Bureau Chief of the publication *Newsday*." Fiorini also repeated "his disclosure regarding his involvement in Chilean break-ins" on November 5, 1972, at a dinner meeting with a representative of NBC. Several of Fiorini's remarks about the embassy break-in were made to his friend, Andrew St. George, whom Fiorini had known since 1958. After Watergate, St. George had been surprised to see the man he'd always known as Fiorini using the name "Frank Sturgis." St. George told the FBI that "Sturgis remarked to the effect that he had been involved in an entry made at the Chilean Embassy, Washington, DC." He added that "with regard to Sturgis's entry at the Chilean Embassy . . . it is St. George's recollection that Sturgis mentioned that Felipe (De Diego) and Rolando (Martinez) went in with him." As for what Fiorini was doing there, the FBI memo states that he "said his function was 'document acquisition,' the theft and/or duplication of documents. He also indicated that it took a team of three men to acquire documents."[40]

When Hunt's crew broke into the Chilean embassy on May 13, 1972, "drawers were forced open [and] papers were examined," but only a few items were taken, like the press attaché's "passport and a mailing list," while "many valuables remained untouched." According to Woodward and Bernstein's researcher, "the only offices entered were those of Ambassador [Orlando] Letelier on the third floor," a political aide's "on the fourth floor and" the press attaché's office "on the second floor." All three officials "habitually worked off hours of the night and weekends," but somehow the burglars knew that "all three were out of town the weekend" of the break-in, with "Ambassador Letelier . . . 100 miles from Washington." That lends credence to the previous comment about veteran CIA official James McCord's "belief that the Chilean Embassy was bugged by the Administration." It's possible that as few as three anti-Castro veterans (Fiorini, Martinez, De Diego) went inside, while Hunt and Barker watched for problems outside the embassy (just as Hunt and Liddy had remained outside during the burglary of Ellsberg's psychiatrist). If Fiorini and the others had been caught inside, they could have claimed to police they were angry at Chile's new, close relationship with Fidel Castro and Cuba, with the burglary being a way to strike back. That would have been a logical explanation, given the burglars' long anti-Castro track records. Plus, none of the men were involved in the CIA's current clandestine anti-Allende operations, which would have also helped to keep things "deniable" for the Agency and the Nixon White House. But no one was caught that night, and after the burglary was discovered, Ambassador Letelier and the embassy staff reported the break-in to the Washington, D.C., police, though no suspects or other evidence were found.[41]

The May 13 break-in at the Chilean embassy was a political operation by the Plumbers, but with an important CIA cover involving national security. If it had been a genuine national security operation, the CIA could have done it without involving the White House's Plumbers, or Nixon could have had new FBI Director L. Patrick Gray order his agents to do it (*Newsweek* later reported that the FBI "had conducted about 1,500 break-ins," including those at "foreign embassies"). Just as Nixon knew about the break-in by the same crew at Ellsberg's psychiatrist's office, his White House tapes show he knew about this one, and it is one more piece of important evidence that he also knew in advance about the Watergate burglaries, where the same White House group was after the same information, a document that was critical for both President Nixon and CIA Director Helms. The involvement of Helms protégé Hunt, and active CIA agent Eugenio Martinez, shows that the operation was also no doubt approved by CIA Director Helms. That type of cooperation was part of the improved relationship between the President and the Agency's Director, in the wake of Nixon's help for Helms in the Victor Marchetti case.[42]

The Chilean embassy burglary occurred just six weeks after Nixon had ordered John Mitchell to approve the new political espionage program. Even with careful planning and a "CIA cover" for the "burglar's plan" involving national security, the break-in was still a huge risk for Nixon, one that could have triggered a major diplomatic incident if the burglars had been caught and Hunt's participation had been discovered. The revelation that the CIA or the Nixon White House was involved in the break-in wouldn't have been bad just for U.S.-Chile relations but also for the entire Washington diplomatic community—and how U.S. embassies were treated abroad. What could Nixon have wanted so desperately at the Chilean embassy that he was willing to jeopardize so much if the operation had been uncovered?

Thanks to the Senate Watergate Committee, and the FBI memo about Frank Fiorini quoted earlier, we know exactly what Nixon and Helms had Hunt and his crew looking for at the Chilean embassy—and at the Watergate offices of the Democratic National Committee (DNC) two weeks later. On February 20, 1974, Johnny Rosselli was interviewed by three investigators for the Senate Watergate Committee at the office of Roselli's attorney, Tom Wadden. Washington lawyer Leslie Sherr helped Wadden represent Rosselli during his testimony to Watergate Committee investigators. Sherr told Rosselli's biographers that based on questions asked by the Congressional investigators, "the reason the break-in occurred at the Democratic Party headquarters was because Nixon or somebody . . . suspected that the Democrats had information as to Nixon's involvement with the CIA's original contact with Rosselli [and] felt that a document existed showing Nixon was involved with or knew what was going on with the CIA and the assassination of Castro and Rosselli's involvement. [The Watergate burglars] wanted to try to get this information that Nixon suspected [the Democrats] were going to use against him."[43]

E. Howard Hunt's crew was trying to find a specific Cuban Dossier about the CIA's plots to kill Castro. Soon after the final Watergate break-in, Frank Fiorini described the secret Cuban Dossier to his friend, journalist Andrew St. George, saying that what

> they were looking for in the Democratic National Committee's files, and in some other Washington file cabinets, too, was a thick secret memorandum from the Castro government, addressed confidentially to the Democrats . . . we knew that this secret memorandum existed—knew it for a fact—because the CIA and the FBI had found excerpts and references to it in some confidential investigations . . . But we wanted the entire document [which was] a long, detailed listing [of the] various attempts made to assassinate the Castro brothers.[44]

Fiorini told St. George the Dossier was approximately a hundred pages long and had "two main parts," including information about "espionage and sabotage [by] the CIA and the DIA." Fiorini's information—obtained from Hunt, who must have gotten it from the CIA—would later be confirmed as remarkably accurate. Fiorini told St. George that in a non-Watergate break-in, "we found a piece of" the secret Cuban Dossier of CIA Castro assassination attempts, but not "the entire thing." That portion almost certainly came from the Chilean embassy, which was one of those "other Washington file cabinets" where Fiorini says "they were looking for" the Dossier.[45]

There is good reason to believe Fiorini about the Dossier, in addition to the confirmation from the Watergate Committee investigators' questioning of Rosselli: Fiorini described the Dossier to Andrew St. George soon after the Watergate break-in, in the summer of 1972; and though Fiorini didn't want his comments published, St. George put them in an article published in *True* magazine in August 1974. That was one year before anyone else had ever publicly talked about such a Dossier, or shown it to the world. That finally occurred on July 30, 1975, when George McGovern issued a press release about the Cuban Dossier of CIA attempts to kill Fidel that he had just received from Castro, following his visit to Cuba earlier that year.[46]

That secret Cuban Dossier is very much as Fiorini described to St. George almost three years earlier. It is filled with detailed accounts of U.S.-backed assassination attempts against Fidel. Almost a hundred pages long (the version adapted in this book is ninety pages, including covers), it has the dates, names, and photos of those captured, and photos of the sometimes quite sophisticated arms and explosives used in the CIA's attempts to kill Fidel Castro. A couple of pages appear to have been added to the Dossier in 1975, reflecting then-ongoing Congressional hearings, but otherwise the Cuban Dossier looks like the one Hunt described to Fiorini in 1972. It has two parts, like Fiorini said, one in Spanish and one in English.[47]

The Cuban Dossier lists familiar names and shows why Nixon, Helms, and Hunt—as well as godfather Santo Trafficante—would have been worried in 1972 about the report becoming public: Those named include these CIA assets, all linked to Trafficante: Tony Varona (named three times, the first during the CIA-Mafia plots), Hunt's best friend Manuel Artime (and several of his associates), Rolando Cubela as well as his CIA contact Carlos Tepedino, and Trafficante henchman

Herminio Diaz. The Dossier begins with a mid-1960 attempt (involving "a gangster . . . equipped by the CIA"), at the time when Vice President Nixon and Hunt were involved with the CIA's anti-Castro operations. The Dossier lists twenty-eight attempts in all, ending with the December 1971 attempt to assassinate Fidel in Chile. It included two attempts that Rosselli had hinted at in his disclosures to Jack Anderson: Helms's unauthorized plots to kill Fidel on March 13, 1963 (at the University of Havana), and on April 7, 1963 (at the Latin American Stadium). Johnny Rosselli's name is in the few pages added to the 1975 version of the Cuban Dossier, but there is no way to know if he was named in the original 1972 version.[48]

Hunt used Cuban exiles (and Fiorini) to look for the document during the May and June 1972 break-ins because when going through files, they would immediately recognize relevant names like Varona, Cubela, and Artime. Their anti-Castro backgrounds would also ensure their silence if they learned details of CIA assassination operations directed at Fidel. In addition, Hunt, Barker, and Fiorini had actually worked on the CIA-Mafia plots.

Fiorini was unusually candid with Andrew St. George because they had known each other since 1958, and their talks were conducted with no attorney or spin doctor present. In addition, Fiorini told St. George, "If you attempt to publish what I've told you, I am a dead man." That may be why St. George waited almost two years to publish an article based on his talks with Fiorini. It's possible Fiorini was thinking about his longtime employer Santo Trafficante when he made the "dead man" remark. It is interesting that two of Trafficante's men—Fiorini and Barker—were on the Chilean embassy break-in crew, but as noted, the godfather wouldn't have wanted his role in the CIA-Mafia plots becoming known.[49]

Given the huge U.S. covert campaign that Nixon had ordered against Allende's government in Chile, the Chilean embassy in Washington, D.C., was certainly targeted for surveillance by the CIA. It's well documented how the Agency had long targeted the Cuban and Russian embassies in Mexico City, and some of the same techniques (wiretaps, bugs, developing informants inside the embassy) were probably used against the Chilean embassy in Washington. The CIA—and eventually Nixon—probably heard about the Cuban Dossier through a wiretap, bug, or a tip, but didn't actually have a copy of it (only the "excerpts and references" Hunt had told Fiorini about).

The Dossier was prepared in Havana, and if it were passed from a Cuban diplomat to a Chilean diplomat—either in New York at the U.N. or outside of the United States—the CIA would have no way to actually get its hands on a copy, at least not without taking extraordinary steps.[50]

Even if the CIA's source only heard about or glanced at a copy of the Dossier—or the CIA got its description from a wiretap or bug—that would have been enough to trigger desperate action by Richard Helms. After all, the Dossier started in 1960 and continued chronologically with twenty-eight assassination attempts, including the CIA's December 1971 attempt to kill Fidel in Chile. It had only been five months since that attempt, but that was plenty of time for word of it to spread among the notoriously talkative anti-Castro exile activists in Miami. Cuban intelligence had thoroughly penetrated the exile community, which would have allowed them to compile the accurate information about the December 1971 attempt that is in the Dossier. As mentioned previously, it's possible that attempt is what prompted an angry Fidel Castro to prepare the Cuban Dossier of CIA attempts to kill him. After finally getting the "no invasion" pledge from Nixon, which had never taken effect under JFK, the recent CIA attempt to kill him in Chile might have seemed to Castro like a return to the early 1960s—and one way to prevent that would be to expose the December 1971 attempt and all the attempts he knew about, going back to 1960.[51]

Once Richard Helms had information that Chilean Ambassador Letelier had a copy of the Cuban Dossier, Helms would worry that it could be given to others in Washington, like Jack Anderson or, because it was an election year, the DNC. If Helms couldn't obtain a copy of the Dossier through the CIA's usual means, it's logical that he would then turn to his protégé, E. Howard Hunt, and to the man he'd turned to for help earlier in the spring, President Nixon. Helms could privately talk to Nixon before or after meetings of the National Security Council, and given the highly sensitive nature of the CIA-Mafia plots and the 1971 Castro attempt, Helms would want to talk to Nixon with no witnesses present. Helms taped his own meetings and phone conversations at the CIA, so he would probably try to talk to or meet with Nixon in a way that Helms felt couldn't be recorded. Nixon likewise wouldn't want such a meeting recorded, since he didn't want his staff to know about the CIA-Mafia plots (even John Mitchell had first learned about them not from Nixon, but from Robert Maheu).

All Helms would have needed to do initially was to communicate to Nixon that he needed to see him about "the Bay of Pigs thing"—meaning the CIA-Mafia plots—and that would have gotten the President's immediate attention. That also helps to explain why that term came up on Nixon's tapes when Hunt's name surfaced in the Watergate affair, and the term was then thrown back at Helms, to get him to force the FBI to back off on the Watergate investigation.[52]

Recall that Helms and Hunt also had ways to communicate in private, described earlier by the "CIA liaison to the National Security Council," who said that "Hunt made frequent, secret reports to CIA Director Richard Helms and others at the agency, using CIA channels on the [NSC], while supposedly working exclusively for the Nixon administration." It's not hard to imagine Hunt's reaction when he heard about the Cuban Dossier, since he'd been involved in attempts to kill Fidel from 1960 to 1965. The same is true for his assistant, Bernard Barker—and for Barker's longtime boss, Santo Trafficante. The godfather would not only have no objection to Barker and Fiorini's involvement in trying to get a copy of the Dossier, but would probably have encouraged their participation as a way to know what was going on.[53]

Historian David Kaiser wrote that since "the CIA-Mafia plots against Castro [were] planned at the highest level, it took place in such complete secrecy that the American people might never have heard of it at all." In 1972, Richard Nixon and Richard Helms needed those plots to remain a complete secret from "the American people" if they wanted to retain their powerful positions. The question was, how to make that happen?[54]

In a taped talk between Nixon and Alexander Haig a year after the Chilean embassy break-in, Nixon told Haig, "There are times, you know, when, good God, I'd authorize any means to achieve a goal," including "the breaking-in of embassies." Like Nixon's admission about the Chilean embassy break-in, that tape was also withheld until 1999 on "national security grounds." Nixon and Helms actually found a national security justification for the Chilean break-in, one that they also used for their further searches for the Cuban Dossier at the Watergate complex. In fact, until just before his resignation, Nixon would still privately be insisting that legitimate "national security" concerns were behind the Watergate break-ins and the cover-up. Nixon was specifically talking about the highly incriminating "Smoking

Gun" tape, in which the President talked about the Watergate cover-up and the "Bay of Pigs thing," and the fact that "Hunt, ah, he knows too damn much, and he was involved." Just over a week before Nixon's resignation, Woodward and Bernstein wrote in *The Final Days* that "Nixon insisted [the tapes] demonstrated that national-security purposes were real," which required the CIA to stop the FBI's investigation of Watergate. The President insisted to one of his attorneys, Fred Buzhardt, "I know what I meant . . . and regardless of what's on the tapes, it was done for national-security reasons." Those same national security reasons explain why Nixon also wanted to press for a trial after his resignation—before he was pardoned—as first revealed in a 2009 *Washington Post* report. As explained in Chapter 32, after Nixon resigned he was confidant he could "clear his name" because any charges against him would have to be dropped or not pursued, because he could raise national security considerations involving Cuba.[55]

Nixon never explained—to his aides or in public—just what those "national security reasons" were, and how they related to Hunt and the "Bay of Pigs thing." Ongoing CIA operations are exempt from some disclosure requirements to Congress, an important consideration since both houses were controlled by the Democratic Party. (Ongoing operations only have to be disclosed to four members, two leaders from each party in each house of Congress, and the CIA's descriptions can be so vague and general as to be virtually meaningless.) But the CIA-Mafia plots were five years in the past by 1972, and even the CIA's December 1971 Castro attempt couldn't be called an "ongoing" operation, certainly not one that Democratic leaders would consider legitimate or want to protect.

But there was an important, ongoing CIA operation that could have been endangered if it were listed in the Cuban Dossier, or if it were uncovered because public exposure of the Dossier led to more investigations. That ongoing operation had involved Richard Helms since its inception, and had also involved E. Howard Hunt and Bernard Barker. It was the JFK-Almeida coup plan, or, rather, what was left of the operation, which was the CIA's ongoing support for Commander Juan Almeida's wife and at least two children outside of Cuba. Plus the fact that Commander Almeida—in some ways the No. 3 official in Cuba—could still be favorably disposed to helping the United States if anything should happen to Fidel Castro (who had already ruled longer than most Latin American dictators). There was also the fact that Almeida could always be blackmailed into helping the United States (because of his work for JFK), even if he didn't want to do so willingly. Hunt and Barker had even handled the $50,000 payment to Almeida in 1963, when they had helped arrange for his wife and two children to first leave Cuba under a seemingly innocent pretext. And the two CIA men had helped to surreptitiously provide Almeida's wife with U.S. funds on a regular basis ("like a pension") for a time, a task now overseen by Hunt's good friend David Atlee Phillips.[56]

Protecting Commander Almeida and the CIA's ongoing help for Almeida's family gave Richard Helms—and Nixon—a thin reed of national security justification for their break-ins at the Chilean embassy and the Watergate. It was one that even Democratic leaders in Congress would not be able to ignore, if it came to that. In hindsight, it might also be called a rationalization on the part of Nixon and Helms. But the two would have been desperate to keep the information in the Dossier from becoming public, and their desperation is understandable, given recent events of the time and the high positions both men could lose if certain information about their past activities were exposed.

Some of the worries of Nixon and Helms were the same. For example, both would have worried about what Jack Anderson might write if he obtained the Cuban Dossier or what DNC Chairman Robert O'Brien might have learned about the plots from the Chilean embassy or his contacts with Robert Maheu and Howard Hughes. Even though Jack Anderson's 1967 and 1971 articles about the CIA-Mafia plots had originally generated no follow-up in the mainstream press, by May 1972, Anderson was a widely respected and quoted figure by the nation's media. Even more, Anderson already had a relationship with Chilean Ambassador Orlando Letelier—only a few months earlier, Anderson had given Letelier and the Chilean government files about the ITT/CIA/Nixon efforts against Allende, which had created such a stir in Chile. If Letelier returned the favor by giving Anderson the secret Cuban Dossier of Castro assassination attempts, that could cost Richard Nixon the election. To most Americans in 1972, it was inconceivable that the CIA would try to assassinate a foreign leader, let alone use the Mafia to do it. Nixon would be worried that the press would pounce if they got access to that information, especially in an election year, and especially journalists that Nixon viewed as "enemies," like Jack Anderson; CBS's trio of Walter Cronkite, Daniel Schorr, and Dan Rather; *The New York Times*; and, increasingly, *The Washington Post.*

Richard Helms knew the exposure of the CIA-Mafia plots and the other assassination attempts would cost him his career and reputation. Pressure from Helms and Nixon hadn't worked so far on curtailing the revelations from Jack Anderson. So, it's only logical that Nixon and Helms would once more enlist E. Howard Hunt, as they had in the past when White House and CIA secrets seemed threatened in the cases of Ellsberg's psychiatrist and Dita Beard's ITT memo. (Also recall that Hunt was the first name Nixon thought of when he wanted the Brookings Institute broken into.) Hunt knew the risks involved for his mentor and for the President he both admired and worked for. Since Hunt wouldn't want his own involvement in the CIA-Mafia plots exposed, it's no surprise that he was willing to undertake such a risky mission, first at the Chilean embassy and then at the DNC offices at the Watergate.

The search for the Cuban Dossier explains why the burglars at the Chilean embassy and the Watergate were all former CIA agents, officers, or assets experienced in anti-Castro operations. The only exception was G. Gordon Liddy, who helped Hunt supervise the Watergate break-ins from across the street.

National security considerations might also explain why Congress didn't thoroughly investigate the Chilean embassy break-in, even after articles linking Watergate figures to the burglary appeared in the media (in January 1973 in *The New York Times* and St. George's 1974 article). In addition, any Congressional investigation of the Chilean matter would have caused havoc with other countries, prompting them to worry about the security of their embassies in Washington. It's also possible that Congressional investigators did look into the matter discreetly, after they learned the Watergate burglars were looking for information on the CIA-Mafia plots. But they might have only used that information out of the public eye, such as in their private interview of Johnny Rosselli, which was not open to the press or public. Memos concerning Rosselli's 1974 Watergate Committee staff interview about the CIA-Mafia plots were considered so sensitive that they were kept secret for decades, and are published in this book for the first time.[57]

Richard Nixon's national security rationale/excuse for the Chilean embassy and Watergate break-ins would initially be effective in forcing CIA Director Richard Helms to ask the FBI not to fully investigate the final Watergate break-in. It also kept Nixon's taped admission about his knowledge of the Chilean Embassy break-in secret until 1999. That was good for Nixon, since in 1976, he provided a written answer to the Senate Church Committee denying any such knowledge, saying that

> I do not remember being informed while President, that at any time during my Administration an agency or employee of the United States Government, acting without a warrant, engaged in a surreptitious or otherwise unauthorized entry into the Chilean Embassy in the United States.[58]

Then again, Nixon could have been relying on his national security justification to avoid giving the Senate Church Committee a straight answer, since at that time Commander Almeida was still in place and unexposed—and his first wife was still receiving ongoing secret CIA support—which technically made it an ongoing CIA operation. The Agency hid Almeida's secret work for JFK from the Church Committee, as it had from the Senate Watergate Committee. That same national security excuse/justification was used by the CIA to withhold important Agency files about Hunt and Barker from the Watergate Committee, the Church Committee, and other Congressional investigations. Many important files about Hunt and Barker from 1960 to 1965 remain unreleased today, despite the 1992 law (the JFK Act) requiring their release.[59]

In files released so far, there is no indication the FBI made a real investigation of the May 13, 1972, Chilean embassy break-in, though it's hard to say whether that was because of national security reasons or due to pressure from the Nixon White House. The FBI did finally investigate three earlier break-ins involving Chilean diplomats in New York City. The Bureau apparently did not begin the New York investigation until a year after those additional break-ins, when it looked briefly at Frank Fiorini as a suspect, but quickly cleared him—as well as Barker, Martinez, De Diego, and Virgilio Gonzalez—by saying there was no evidence in New York FBI files that any of the men had been in the state during the additional break-ins. It's odd the FBI didn't mention checking Miami FBI files for the whereabouts of

Fiorini and the others, especially once the Bureau received information that Fiorini had visited New York City from time to time. The FBI was also told that Fiorini had "remarked he had been in and checked out the Chileans twice," which could have referred to either an additional undetected burglary at the Chilean embassy or one of the New York City break-ins. It's also unclear why the Bureau's investigation of the attempted burglaries of the three New York City Chilean diplomats wasn't expanded to include the Chilean embassy break-in.[60]

Clearly related to the Chilean embassy break-in was yet another burglary attempt, only six days earlier, at the home of Andres Rojas, the embassy's press attaché. Rojas's office was one of those burglarized at the Chilean embassy on May 13, but on May 7, 1972, "he was awakened by noises" around 2 am. "Looking out the window he saw the silhouettes of three white males trying to get inside" his house. The three "men appeared to be middle-aged and well-dressed," and when he yelled at them, they fled in "a late-model, dark-blue sedan." (When arrested, the Watergate burglars would also be described by police as being middle-aged and well-dressed.)[61]

The burglaries at the Chilean embassy and the Watergate weren't the only burglaries planned—or possibly completed—by the Plumbers in May 1972. Liddy, Hunt, and others admit planning the burglary of George McGovern's Washington campaign headquarters, but they say it was never carried out. J. Anthony Lukas wrote that in May 1972, just prior to the initial unsuccessful Watergate break-in, Hunt and Barker's team cased and made plans to bug "the offices of McGovern's two top aides, Frank Mankiewicz and Gary Hart." (Five years earlier, Mankiewicz had secretly investigated JFK's assassination for Robert Kennedy, while Hart would soon be part of the Senate Church Committee that first exposed the CIA-Mafia plots.) According to Lukas, Hunt ordered Barker to get ready for a break-in to bug Mankiewicz's and Hart's offices on Memorial Day 1972 and told him that photographing documents would be part of the mission. Lukas also pointed out that Barker and the other Watergate burglars were "mentioned in connection with a May 16 burglary of a prominent Democratic law firm in the Watergate, whose members included . . . Sargent Shriver, [Senator Edward] Kennedy's brother-in-law." That burglary was discovered when an early-arriving employee "noticed the entry door was . . . taped so the door would not lock," similar to what happened on the final two Watergate burglaries. After the Watergate arrests, the offices of Shriver's firm were checked for "bugs," and one was found. In addition, the FBI was told that Fiorini had said that "One unsuccessful attempt was made to 'bug' Senator Kennedy's office." From the perspective of Nixon, Helms, and Hunt, all of those targets make sense in terms of who the Chileans might have given copies of the Cuban Dossier to, in addition to the other political value the targets had for Nixon.[62]

After the Plumbers failed to obtain a complete copy of the Cuban Dossier at the Chilean embassy, there would be a significant change in mission for the upcoming burglary of the Democratic National Committee headquarters at the Watergate. No longer would it be primarily a small bugging operation; now, having a larger crew photographing documents would become its primary goal. One can only imagine the reaction of Nixon, or Helms, if they heard that the Cuban Dossier started in 1960 with a CIA plot to kill Fidel involving a "gangster," or that the Dossier continued until the December 1971 attempt to kill Fidel in Chile. Hunt had told Fiorini the Dossier was approximately one hundred pages long, yet they only had a piece of it, so they had no way of knowing what was on the other pages that could harm the CIA's reputation or Nixon's reelection campaign.[63]

Nixon would have been most worried about what the Dossier might contain about 1960, 1963, and anything during his Presidency. Helms would share those worries, in addition to any information the Dossier might contain about the entire period from 1962 to 1965, when he continued the CIA-Mafia plots without authorization from JFK, LBJ, and two different CIA Directors. Plus, it would look terrible for Helms if Larry O'Brien at the DNC wound up with information about the CIA-Mafia plots that Helms had refused to give to President Nixon. Nixon would have feared O'Brien and the DNC getting the Dossier, and any significant information about the CIA-Mafia plots, since they could leak the story accurately, in a way that would severely damage Nixon's reputation and reelection. In contrast, Jack Anderson—dependent upon Rosselli for his information—had conflated the CIA-Mafia plots with Robert Kennedy's separate anti-Castro operation in 1963, which made Anderson's public stories damaging to RFK and not to Nixon.[64]

Nixon couldn't talk about the CIA-Mafia plots and the Cuban Dossier—and what to do about the matter—with any of his aides, except for John Mitchell. And Mitchell only knew what Robert Maheu had told him and what was in the Justice Department file he looked at (and discussed with Nixon) in January 1971. Even that information was only part of what Nixon would have worried might come out. Nixon would largely have to depend on Helms and Hunt in the matter.[65]

Some writers have speculated that Watergate was all about the $100,000 cash contribution from Howard Hughes to Nixon, via Bebe Rebozo, and what DNC Chairman Larry O'Brien might have known about the payment. But there had already been two Jack Anderson articles about the $100,000, and it would have been hard—if not impossible—for Larry O'Brien to use that issue against Nixon without opening himself up to charges about his own lucrative work for Hughes. In addition, there was nothing about the $100,000 Hughes money at the Chilean embassy, where the Watergate crew staged a similar burglary. The Watergate Committee investigators' questioning of Rosselli, coupled with Fiorini's admission to his trusted friend, make it clear that the main goal of the Watergate break-ins was the Cuban Dossier, and any information about the CIA-Mafia plots—and the December 1971 Castro assassination attempt—that it might contain. As detailed in the following chapter, the Watergate crew would also be looking out for any politically useful information that could be used to harm the Democrats, or that the Democrats could use to harm Nixon's reelection campaign. The latter especially included any material damaging to Nixon that O'Brien might have gotten from Hughes (O'Brien could have information about the CIA-Mafia plots from Hughes or Maheu, independent of the Cuban Dossier). All of those considerations made O'Brien's office at the Watergate an irresistible and critical target for Nixon, Helms, and Hunt.[66]

CHAPTER 30

Mid-May to Mid-June 1972: The First Three Watergate Burglary Attempts

Word of the secret Cuban Dossier that triggered the May 13, 1972, Chilean embassy break-in by Hunt's Plumbers, and that burglary's results, caused a major change in plans for Hunt and his men. Since the burglars had only "found a piece of" the Cuban Dossier and not "the entire thing," President Nixon and CIA Director Helms still needed to know what the whole Dossier said—and if the Democrats had any part of it. The focus of the long-planned burglaries of the Democratic National Committee (DNC) at the Watergate and of front-runner George McGovern's campaign office was now on finding the Dossier, while bugging became a secondary goal.[1]

In a later civil trial, G. Gordon Liddy gave testimony about their mission's change. The Associated Press reported that Liddy "testified that he was kept in the dark about the 1972 break-in he helped organize . . . he learned afterward that the 1972 burglary was not [primarily] an attempt to tap phones." Instead, "Liddy testified that the break-in mysteriously turned from one of a skeleton crew quickly bugging the office to one with a full crew of burglars and a load of photographic equipment." Although Liddy's statement is at odds with some conventional accounts of Watergate, it is completely consistent with Frank Fiorini's account to journalist Andrew St. George.[2]

For a bugging operation, only two or three men would have been needed, one expert to place the bug with perhaps another one (or two) to act as a lookout after picking the lock. In fact, the fewer men the better, both to escape detection and to have a more credible cover story if seen by guards. However, each of the Watergate burglaries would put five men in the DNC offices, a risky and unnecessary move if bugging were the only goal. In addition, with J. Edgar Hoover dead, and a Nixon loyalist like L. Patrick Gray now running the FBI, it's possible that Nixon could have at least tried to order Gray to have the DNC bugged by the Bureau on national security grounds, if bugging had been the main goal.

The Watergate burglaries—and those attempted at McGovern's campaign office—were now primarily to search for the secret Cuban Dossier and any related information damaging to Nixon; hence the new plan for a "full crew of burglars and a load of photographic equipment." Even though Liddy was ostensibly in charge of the Plumbers, Hunt was really calling the shots for the Chilean embassy, DNC, and McGovern operations. The exiles were his men, loyal to him, along with James McCord who—like Hunt—was loyal to Helms and the CIA. Helms was clearly in favor of the new mission for the DNC, risky though it might be; otherwise the CIA would have barred active CIA agent Martinez from his repeated participation in the break-ins.

The fact that Nixon, Helms, and Hunt were willing to risk several break-ins in the span of just a few weeks shows a level of desperation missing from most Watergate accounts. However, the possibility of the CIA-Mafia plots becoming public during the campaign was simply too great to ignore. Ultimately, in trying to obtain a full copy of the Dossier and learn what the Democrats knew, Nixon would cost himself the Presidency, Helms would end his career, and Hunt would go to prison.

President Nixon's outlook on the campaign underwent a major shift on May 15, 1972, when Alabama Governor George Wallace was shot during a campaign appearance in Laurel, Maryland. Twenty-two-year-old Arthur Bremer was immediately arrested at the scene. As soon as Nixon heard about the shooting, he "voiced immediate concern that the assassin might have ties to the Republican Party or, even worse, to the President's Re-election Committee." The latter concern was probably because Nixon was at least generally aware of the numerous operatives and teams CREEP was using against his Democratic opponents. There was no way to know in those early hours if one of those operatives had been unstable or simply tried to take things too far. Nixon told aide Charles Colson, "Wouldn't it be great if they had left-wing propaganda in [the assassin's] apartment? . . . Too bad we couldn't get somebody in there to plant it."[3]

That's exactly what Colson tried to do, calling once more upon the White House's main operative for important missions, E. Howard

Hunt. Colson wanted Hunt "to fly to Milwaukee, where the would-be assassin had lived," where "Hunt could 'bribe the janitor or pick the lock'" to enter Bremer's apartment. Hunt said he told Colson that "it was too late, [since] the apartment would now be sealed" by the authorities, so he didn't make the trip. In the years that followed, many investigators looked for some connection between Bremer and any of Nixon's men, but none was found.[4]

Wallace survived the attack—as did the three others hit by gunfire—but the Governor's spine was severed, and he would be paralyzed the rest of his life.* Prior to the shooting, Nixon's support in the polls had been around 43 percent, but afterward it climbed by five to seven points against either McGovern or Hubert Humphrey—if Wallace stayed out of the race. However, the injured Wallace remained in the race. Though Wallace had reached new heights of racial rhetoric in his 1970 gubernatorial campaign, in 1972 he claimed to be more moderate, and that—along with sympathy votes—helped him win Democratic primaries not just in Tennessee and North Carolina, but also in Michigan and Maryland. For Nixon, as long as Wallace remained a candidate, the race for the Presidency would remain tight, especially since Nixon still wasn't sure whether his eventual Democratic opponent would be McGovern, Humphrey, or a compromise choice of a deadlocked convention, such as Edward Kennedy or Terry Sanford.[5]

Hunt and Nixon's other operatives had narrowed the field by forcing out Edmund Muskie and helping to make sure Henry "Scoop" Jackson was no longer a factor in the race. Hunt and his men were still needed to make sure that McGovern won the nomination, since he was Nixon's preferred opponent. Nixon and his aides felt the President would do well against McGovern, who was mainly known for his pledge to end the war, something Nixon was finally trying to do by continuing to draw down the number of U.S. combat troops in Vietnam. In addition, Nixon was convinced that McGovern was too liberal for the moderate and independent voters necessary for a victory in November.[6]

One of Hunt's men, CREEP Security Director James McCord,

*Arthur Bremer, convicted of the shootings, was paroled on November 9, 2007. Until his own death, Wallace remained skeptical that Bremer had acted alone, asking how a man who rarely "made $30 a week [could] buy an automobile, buy two guns? Stay at the Waldorf-Astoria, go to massage parlors, rent limousines, go to Canada, went all over Michigan, followed me around?" In addition, William Turner points out that "Wallace was also skeptical of Bremer's diary found in his car after the shooting," in which Bremer claimed to have initially stalked Richard Nixon.

"reconnoitered the McGovern [campaign headquarters] on the evening of the day Wallace was shot," May 15, 1972. An attempt to break in to McGovern's headquarters was planned using the same crew, on the same Memorial Day weekend as the burglary scheduled for the DNC offices at the Watergate. In addition to targeting DNC offices in general, especially that of Chairman Larry O'Brien, another target was added: the DNC office of Spencer Oliver, "the 34-year-old . . . executive director of the Association of State Democratic Chairmen."[7]

There were several reasons for targeting Spencer Oliver's Watergate office and phone. Former Associated Press reporter Robert Parry pointed out that Oliver's father "worked with Robert R. Mullen, whose Washington-based public relations firm [still officially] employed Hunt," even as most of Hunt's time was consumed by his work for Nixon. The Mullen firm, and new owner Robert Bennett, worked extensively for Howard Hughes, and "Oliver's father had represented Hughes." That meant in addition to the secret Cuban Dossier, Oliver could have information damaging to Nixon that his father could have gotten from Hughes or his representatives.[8]

In addition, Parry uncovered another long-overlooked role Oliver had for the DNC: heading the "Stop McGovern" movement for some Democratic leaders. Some party heads, including many of the state Democratic chairmen from moderate or conservative states, realized that McGovern stood little chance of carrying their states, so they wanted a more electable alternative. That would remain a realistic possibility until at least June 16, and even later, because—as Oliver pointed out—"in those days not all primaries were binding and not all delegates were bound." Humphrey, Muskie, Jackson, and Sanford all had a sizable number of delegates, "while scores of other delegates were uncommitted or tied to favorite sons." Additionally, many of the delegate selection rules enacted after 1968 had never been tested at the convention, or in court. The hope was that a more electable "unity candidate" such as Sanford or Humphrey might emerge "from a deadlocked convention." Since Oliver coordinated that effort, his phone was slated to be bugged, in addition to that of O'Brien's secretary.[9]

While the President's aides and operatives busied themselves with both the covert and the aboveboard aspects of his campaign, Nixon prepared to depart on another historic trip, designed to make him look "Presidential." Taking advantage of what Nixon had seen as his greatest political strength since 1960—his foreign policy experience—

Nixon had arranged an almost two-week trip to become the first U.S. President to visit the Soviet Union. The trip also included a visit to Nixon's financial supporter, the Shah of Iran, whose brutal and repressive regime was viewed as an important U.S. ally in the region. Nixon planned to leave on May 20 and to stage a triumphant return on June 1 followed by an address to Congress. As with Nixon's visit earlier in the year to China, there were many ironies in his trip to Russia, from Nixon's longtime Red-baiting to how he would have likely reacted if a Democratic President had planned a visit to Moscow. The biggest irony is that Nixon would be out of the country when the most important domestic event of his Presidency began: the Watergate break-ins.

Even as E. Howard Hunt and the other current and former CIA agents were planning their assault on the Watergate, Richard Helms had a sudden change of heart about pushing a television show based on Hunt's spy novels. Helms had been enthusiastic about Hunt's TV project at the May 8, 1972, *Godfather* screening with Jack Valenti and other top entertainment executives, even arranging for Valenti to interview Hunt (using his "David St. John" alias). But the risky Chilean embassy break-in by Hunt and his men on May 13—and Hunt's upcoming covert operations for Nixon—apparently made Helms realize the time was not right to be pushing a television show that could shine a media spotlight on his protégé. On May 19, Helms met with "Martin J. Lukoskie, Chief of the Corporate Cover Branch of the CIA's Cover and Commercial Staff." Lukoskie told Helms he had been contacted three days earlier by Marvin Davis—senior vice president of Gulf+Western, the corporate parent of Paramount Pictures—about the television project. Lukoskie wanted Helms to tell him "whether Davis and Paramount had a commitment from the CIA 'concerning a TV series'" based on Hunt's novels.[10]

In stark contrast to Richard Helms's advocacy of Hunt's TV project just over a week earlier, Helms now told his CIA subordinate Lukoskie "flatly that he had made no commitment to anyone regarding the possibility of a TV series" based on Hunt's books. Helms went much further, saying that now "as a matter of fact, [he] opposed presentation of such a series." In addition, Helms even tried to tell Lukoskie he had not promoted the TV series at all, though Helms's claim is contradicted by earlier CIA memos and statements from Valenti and the other executives. In hindsight, Helms made the right decision to stop pushing Hunt's TV show at that time; one can only imagine the consequences for Helms—and the history of Watergate—if an announcement about Hunt's TV show had appeared in *Variety* just before the Watergate arrests. However, the ease with which Helms could lie even to his own CIA subordinate about such a relatively small matter foreshadowed the later lies and cover-ups of Helms in the wake of Watergate.[11]

E. Howard Hunt had his Miami crew return to Washington, D.C., on May 22, 1972, to begin preparations for the break-ins at the Watergate offices of the DNC and at McGovern's campaign headquarters. From this point forward in the story of Watergate, it's important to stress that accounts from the participants vary widely, as do even authoritative accounts. This book will stick to the most basic and verifiable facts, especially those not widely known.

Hunt's group now included Frank Fiorini, plus Cuban exiles Bernard Barker, Eugenio Martinez, Felipe De Diego, Virgilio Gonzalez, and Reinaldo Pico. Hunt motivated the Cuban exiles to help the White House by telling them their actions would help to defeat Fidel Castro, indicating that if Nixon won reelection, he could take stronger action against the Cuban leader. In addition, George McGovern's professed desire to negotiate with Castro made his possible victory anathema to the conservative exiles. Hunt also lied to the exiles, telling them McGovern was getting money from Castro and that to obtain proof they needed to break into McGovern's campaign office and the Watergate offices of the Democratic National Committee. Supervising the group with Hunt were G. Gordon Liddy and James McCord, who was introduced to the group as "Jimmy" by Hunt. Former FBI agent Liddy didn't fit the mold of the rest of the Plumbers—and knew less than Hunt and some of the others—because he wouldn't actually be entering targets such as the DNC offices.[12]

The seemingly odd assortment of men that made up the Plumbers has perplexed investigators and historians for decades. However, since the Plumbers' main goal was still the secret Cuban Dossier of CIA assassination attempts, it's now clear that the group was extremely well suited to the task that was so important to Nixon and Helms. There were two former high-ranking CIA officials: Hunt, who had been the "Chief of Covert Action for Western Europe," and McCord, previously "Assistant Director for Security for the entire Central Intelligence Agency." Both were loyal to the Agency, and Hunt was close to Helms personally. McCord had made sure to buy all of his bugging equipment "off the shelf," so none of it could be traced to—or implicate—the CIA. In addition, McCord was a veteran of the CIA's Office of Security, which had run the CIA-Mafia plots under Nixon and was responsible for keeping those plots secret. The later testimony of CIA Deputy Director Vernon Walters verified that all of the Watergate burglars had been CIA agents. Hunt, Barker, and Fiorini had actually worked on the CIA-Mafia plots that started in 1960 and grew into the Bay of Pigs invasion. Martinez and Gonzalez had worked on a related operation, the Johnny Rosselli–William Pawley mission in 1963. According to *The New York Times*, "McCord . . . is believed to have played a role in the abortive Bay of Pigs invasion." Pico and De Diego were veterans of the CIA's anti-Castro covert operations of the early 1960s.[13]

All of those men could be trusted to immediately zero in on any files they might see that could be related to Fidel Castro or Cuban exiles. They all knew about—and many had worked with—key figures in the CIA-Mafia plots such as Tony Varona and Manuel Artime, who might be listed in the Cuban Dossier or a related file. Since all were from Miami, they would also be familiar with the name of Santo Trafficante, if they encountered it.

Trafficante no doubt welcomed the chance to have two of his men—Barker and Fiorini—in Hunt's operation. The godfather would have needed to know anything the Dossier might say about his role in the CIA-Mafia plots, especially since he knew what other criminal actions he'd used the plots as cover for. From Trafficante's point of view, it was good to have Barker and Fiorini on the mission because the seemingly successful real estate man and the soldier of fortune didn't have obvious ties to his organization if anything should go wrong.

There is evidence that Barker and Fiorini were told more about the mission than the other exile Plumbers—who may have been given only more general instructions on what to look for (i.e., anything about Castro or Cuban exiles)—keeping the Dossier's existence from having to be revealed to the other exiles. On the other hand, all of the exiles may have been fully informed, and the others simply maintained their prearranged cover story—about Castro funding McGovern—after their arrests, in public and private. Even Fiorini maintained the cover story about McGovern and Castro in his testimony and public statements, only confiding the truth to his friend Andrew St. George.[14]

The first break-in wasn't scheduled until May 26—so why did Hunt have the men fly into Washington on May 22? It's possible the extra time was needed to get their cover stories straight, and to make sure the men knew what additional information to look for at the Watergate and McGovern headquarters. As Fiorini told St. George, in addition to their main goal of looking for the Cuban Dossier, they were also keeping their eyes open for other material to photograph, some related to the Dossier and some not: "any document with money on it . . . anything that had to do with Howard Hughes . . . damaging rumors about Republican leaders [and] everything that could be leaked to the press with a damaging effect to the McGovern people." Those items would be icing on the cake, but they weren't the kinds of things for which Nixon would have risked his Presidency.[15]

Though E. Howard Hunt later admitted that "photography [of documents] had been the priority mission" of the break-ins, at the Watergate they also planned to bug the telephones of Spencer Oliver and the secretary for Larry O'Brien, since O'Brien would be presumably checking in frequently by phone from his new base in Miami. The specific bugging targets at McGovern headquarters are less clear, but probably would have included the phone of McGovern's campaign manager, Gary Hart. It's ironic the burglars planned to look for the Cuban Dossier at Hart's office, since three years later he would be serving on the Senate Committee that first officially exposed the CIA-Mafia plots to kill Castro.[16]

There are at least three different versions of the first attempt to burglarize the Watergate offices of the DNC, on Mary 26, 1972. All agree only on some basic information: After initially staying at the Hay-Adams hotel, the burglars had been moved to the Watergate Hotel. James McCord had his headquarters set up in room 419 of the Howard Johnson's motel across the street from the Watergate office building. His room had a partial view of the windows of the DNC offices, and manning McCord's post would be former FBI agent Alfred Baldwin, recruited by McCord earlier that month. The "cover" for the burglary was going to be a supposed "board meeting" banquet and film screening for Ameritas, a real estate company affiliated with Barker. The small banquet would be held in the basement of the Watergate Hotel, which had access—via a corridor and a courtyard—to a garage and stairwell in the Watergate office building where the DNC headquarters was located.[17]

The primary story as told by E. Howard Hunt and most of his men—later shown to be impossible—was that after the banquet, Hunt would be notified by McCord via walkie-talkie when the last DNC employee had left the office (McCord would leave the banquet early to return to his room at the Howard Johnson's motel). Then the "entry team" would head for the garage, meet up with McCord after he'd returned, and then go up the stairwell to the DNC offices. Supposedly, the plan was thwarted because a banquet room corridor alarm was automatically set at 11 PM, and someone remained working in a DNC office past that time. Hunt's later cover story was that after the others left, he and Gonzalez wound up trapped in the banquet room's closet. They supposedly had to stay all night, until after 6 AM, because they didn't want to trip the alarm and because Gonzalez couldn't pick the lock of the banquet room door, which had been locked by a security guard at 11 PM.[18]

Hunt's story isn't possible because there was no alarm outside the banquet room "or anything that could be mistaken for an alarm," something first documented by Jim Hougan in 1984. In addition, when security guard Frank Willis made his rounds "between 1:00 and 2:00 AM," the banquet room was still in use, and it wasn't closed until "2:10 AM." These discrepancies with Hunt's cover story weren't noted earlier because, as Hougan points out, there was no real police investigation of the May Watergate break-ins as there was for the final one, on June 17.[19]

Most accounts agree that McCord and the remaining exiles intended to burglarize George McGovern's campaign office that same night, but British journalist Fred Emery writes that "they were also thwarted there." Some accounts say the problem was "a derelict's presence on the front steps of McGovern headquarters." Lukas gives a more detailed account, saying that at McGovern headquarters, "an upstairs light was on and a man—evidently a campaign volunteer—was standing by the front door." A few days earlier, "Liddy had shot out a [street]light" near the headquarters to make the area darker, and he asked McCord if he should do it again, but "McCord said it wasn't necessary." Finally, around "5:00 AM, with the man still lingering around the front door" of McGovern headquarters, the mission was called off. The only thing that can be said with certainty about that night is that there was some plan to burglarize both targets, and neither burglary was apparently successful. Hougan speculates that Hunt's cover story might have been meant to hide another burglary attempt (or even a success).[20]

The next night, the Plumbers tried a different approach: going in through the main Watergate office building entrance, signing the register (using aliases) indicating they were going to the Federal Reserve offices on the eighth floor, then walking down two flights of stairs to the DNC offices. McCord was with Fiorini and the exiles, while Hunt and Liddy waited with Baldwin across the street. Eugenio Martinez thought the plan strained credibility—what were so many men doing going to the Federal Reserve office at midnight, on Saturday, during the Memorial Day weekend? Still, all went according to plan, until Virgilio Gonzalez was unable to open the doors to the DNC offices with the lock-picking tools he had brought.[21]

Hunt was furious when he learned of the failure, and he demanded that Gonzalez fly back to Miami, get his tools, and return by Sunday night, for a third attempt. Martinez thought that Hunt was being too hard on Gonzalez, but when he complained, Barker relayed a blunt message from Hunt: "You are an operative. Your mission is to do what you are told and not to ask questions." One starts to get a sense of desperation on Hunt's part, but according to the conventional story of Watergate, there was no particular urgency or pressing deadline. Yet for Hunt—and Helms and Nixon—there was a looming threat: the exposure of the Cuban Dossier that could end all of their careers. That was especially true if the Dossier contained details of the CIA-Mafia plots, or if O'Brien had information about the plots from Hughes or Maheu. Eugenio Martinez had noticed this pressure in the briefing before the first Watergate attempt, when he said that "throughout the briefing, McCord, Liddy, and Eduardo [Hunt] would keep interrupting each other, saying, 'Well, this way is better,' or, 'That should be the other way around.'"[22]

According to some accounts, there was another attempt at McGovern headquarters very late on the night of the second failed Watergate attempt. J. Anthony Lukas wrote that "the mission was aborted because some volunteers were working late, and [Hunt's spy at McGovern's office, Thomas] Gregory, who had been stationed outside, was asked to 'move along' by a policeman."[23]

On Sunday night, May 28, 1972, the burglars tried a different route into the Watergate, and they finally were successful. While Hunt, Liddy, and Baldwin waited in the Howard Johnson's motel across the street, this time the burglars entered the Watergate office building through the garage, with McCord taping open "the basement stairwell door." Emery wrote that "once on the sixth floor, Gonzalez . . . used a pressure wrench to twist the lock on the rear door to the DNC and they were in." As McCord placed the bugs, "Barker and Martinez started photographing documents, while . . . Pico and De Diego served as corridor lookouts."[24]

It's often overlooked that "De Diego was confronted by a guard and escorted out of the building." But the guard did not call the police, which might have uncovered the whole operation. Some accounts state that De Diego was on a lower floor, not the sixth floor with the DNC, but it's still amazing just how close the entire Watergate saga came to unraveling that night. It also shows how just one or two men on a bugging mission might have been able to talk their way out of trouble, like De Diego, but not the large photography crew that Hunt—and apparently also John Mitchell—wanted.[25]

In the DNC offices, two telephone bugs were placed and tested by McCord in approximately fifteen minutes. Fiorini said that "we looked high and low for" the Cuban Dossier, but they didn't find it. Accounts again differ as to what happened next. McCord said that "the photographic team had finished" before he did, and they all left at the same time. McCord also reported that "Liddy . . . was elated with the success," which Liddy confirmed in his account. But Liddy was in some ways the least informed of the Plumbers, and Bernard Barker and Hunt had a different version of the events. Hunt said he "had expected that Barker and his men would remain inside the DNC, photographing documents, throughout the night," since to Hunt "the photography mission had been even more important . . . than McCord's placement of eavesdropping devices." According to Barker, after "he and Martinez had photographed some of the correspondence on Larry O'Brien's desk [but] before they could break into the filing cabinets as instructed . . . McCord had ordered them to leave." That meant Barker and Martinez had photographed fewer than fifty pages of files. Hunt said that he was surprised and astonished by Barker's premature departure and the lack of photographed files. Hunt wrote that he "was livid, wanting to jump down Barker's throat, because he should have just let McCord leave . . . because in my mind, the photography had been the priority mission and the team had . . . only a fraction of the amount of photographs that I had expected."[26]

The discrepancy in accounts could be explained by Hunt's greater need to know about the Cuban Dossier and either McCord's sense of caution or the former CIA security officer's possible growing reluctance to be part of such clearly illegal political spying. The break-in at the Chilean embassy was standard CIA fare; in some ways it was a typical CIA security operation to ensure that Agency secrets weren't in the wrong hands. But the DNC break-in was something else, a grossly illegal political operation with a thin national security cover of protecting CIA secrets and Agency assets like Commander Almeida. After the successful May 28 break-in, Liddy planned for McCord to develop the two rolls of film. But after a week, McCord had made no progress, which could be another sign of his unease about the whole project. Liddy then gave the film to Hunt and asked if Barker could get it developed.[27]

The fact that McCord was supposed to use his contact to develop the Watergate film raises interesting questions. Who developed the film from the Chilean embassy break-in? The CIA? And who was McCord's contact who was supposed to develop the Watergate film? Someone with Agency contacts? Those questions would only deepen after Barker had the film developed.

In early June 1972, in the wake of the first round of Watergate burglaries, E. Howard Hunt was extremely busy in Washington and in Miami, which was soon to be the site of the Democratic National Convention. Hunt was still involved with Donald Segretti in the "dirty tricks" campaign that had helped to destroy Muskie's candidacy, only Hunt was now focused on McGovern and the Convention. In addition, Hunt still helmed one of the White House's "anti-drug" operations, which included exile Manuel Artime as well as Barker, Fiorini, and an undetermined number of additional former CIA exile operatives. Finally, there remained matters to follow up from the Watergate burglaries. All three of Hunt's roles for the White House were involved in his trip—or trips—to Miami in early June.

"In early June, Hunt met with [Donald] Segretti . . . in Miami," telling him to arrange some "peaceful demonstrators to picket" McGovern's convention headquarters at Miami's Doral Hotel. According to Lukas, Hunt planned to have them attacked "by an unruly group" to "create a 'disruption' that would be blamed on McGovern." Hunt turned to his trusted aide Bernard Barker to arrange the "unruly" attackers, who were supposed to appear to be "'hippies' who were to throw rocks, break glass, defecate and urinate outside the Doral." Barker enlisted the aide of Eugenio Martinez, who turned to "a former

CIA operative" named Pablo Fernandez to provide the disruptive "hippies." But Fernandez turned down the opportunity, since it also involved infiltrating "protest groups and [spying] on McGovern's movements around Miami Beach." It's interesting to read Hunt's own account of the plans in his autobiography, which minimizes the operation and leaves out the attacks and the spying that others testified were part of the plans.[28]

While making those plans, and dealing with Artime in Miami on the narcotics operation, Hunt gave the DNC film from the third Watergate burglary attempt to Barker to get developed. Hunt later said that somehow Barker didn't understand the film was from the Watergate job, so Barker took it to a local camera shop to have the film developed and enlargements made. Why Barker wouldn't realize—or even assume—the two rolls were from the Watergate mission has never been clear. As Hunt and Barker later told the story, once Barker realized it was the Watergate film, he became frantic. To the Hunt/Barker account, Martinez added a scene where an anxious Barker came to his real estate office, where Martinez just happened to be talking to two other Watergate burglars, Fiorini and De Diego. The three supposedly rushed to Rich's Camera Shop, where the other two covered "each door to the shop" while Barker tipped the owner "$20 or $30" when the owner said about the photos: "It's real cloak-and-dagger stuff, isn't it?"[29]

A different—and probably more accurate—story emerged from the camera shop owner, who said that when Barker first came in, he was anxious to get the film developed and printed quickly. Since it was Saturday near closing time, the owner told Barker it would be an extra $40, and "Barker told him to go ahead, and several times in the next few hours [Barker] called . . . urging speed." The owner "produced thirty-eight seven-by-ten glossy prints, which showed gloved hands holding documents against a shag rug." There was just one problem—the DNC offices had no shag carpeting, and neither did the Watergate Hotel. However, there was shag carpeting at the Howard Johnson's motel across the street from the Watergate, where McCord had his listening post with Alfred Baldwin, which was also where Liddy and Hunt had waited during the break-in. Lukas said the carpet in the photos was later matched to McCord's room 419 at the Howard Johnson's.[30]

Clearly, Barker knew from the start that the film was important and—once he saw the photos—that they weren't the pictures he had taken at the DNC offices. The developed photos were of innocuous DNC notes and memos, and the camera shop owner said that "some of the documents had an emblem and were headed 'Chairman Democratic National Committee.'" The owner recalled that "one document mentioned either Robert or Edward Kennedy." One of several things could have happened. The Watergate burglars could have stolen some documents and photographed them later in the Howard Johnson's motel room. But few papers—and none of importance—could have been taken, since the DNC staff didn't realize anything had been taken from the office. Some authors, like Hougan, think that McCord could have switched the film canisters and had the real photos developed by the CIA, while giving Liddy and Hunt innocuous files photographed at the Howard Johnson's. Given McCord and Hunt's relationship and mutual CIA background, that seems unlikely. Hougan also thinks it's possible that Hunt himself switched the film, perhaps sending the real film to Richard Helms in "the packages that Hunt was sending to CIA headquarters."[31]

The bottom line for the whole affair is that the photos Hunt gave to Liddy, which Liddy gave to Nixon's aides, were not the photos Barker had taken at the DNC offices. Only former CIA officials McCord or Hunt could have effected the switch, since Liddy had no motivation and wouldn't have given Barker photos the Cuban exile would have recognized weren't the ones he had taken. Liddy, who hadn't been in the DNC offices and didn't know what kind of carpet it had, wouldn't have noticed they weren't the right photos, and neither would Nixon's aides. This scenario is consistent with the burglars looking for the secret Cuban Dossier, something of great interest to Hunt, Barker, Helms, and Nixon because of the CIA-Mafia plots that involved them all. None of Nixon's aides (save for John Mitchell) even knew about the CIA-Mafia plots, so it makes sense they wouldn't be given the real photographic "take" from the third Watergate burglary. The actual photos would need to be studied carefully for any reference, no matter how small, to Chile, Cuba, Maheu, Hughes, Rosselli, Trafficante, Pawley, Rebozo, and a variety of other telling names or terms or dates. That meant a fake set of document photos would need to be created for Nixon's aides, which is exactly what happened. Also, in hindsight, it makes no sense for it to have taken so long for photos to be developed for such a large and risky mission; the real photos were probably developed soon after the break-in. The faked photos, given by Liddy to Nixon's aides, were destroyed after the Watergate arrests, leaving the camera shop owner's consistent testimony—about an unusual task and photos that stood out among his usual work—as the only definitive account.[32]

Around the time of Hunt's dealings with Barker and Segretti in Miami, Hunt also made a trip to the city to see his best friend, Manuel Artime, for an overnight visit at Artime's house. Artime's later account of the story to the FBI, after the Watergate arrests, makes it sound like a purely social visit, perhaps with some vague connection to Artime's business interests in Nicaragua (where Artime was partners with that country's corrupt dictator, a fact the exile didn't tell the FBI). However, Artime was still working on Hunt's "anti-drug" operation at the time, along with other Trafficante associates like Barker and Fiorini, so that was probably the real subject of Hunt's overnight visit.[33]

In June 1972—as had been the case since at least 1964, and would continue until Artime's death—Artime had a role in Trafficante's drug trafficking network. CIA official Jake Esterline, who worked with Artime and Hunt during the Bay of Pigs operation, would say in his CIA exit interview in 1975 that "Artime . . . probably made, in addition to stealing money from us, probably made a lot of money in the drug traffic in the last few years." Four months after Artime's June 1972 Miami meeting with Hunt, a CIA memo about Artime would make reference to the "source of info on drugs," and then name two drug trafficking figures, calling one a "confidante of Artime." It's unclear from the memo if Artime was providing the "info on drugs" or if someone were informing on Artime's drug activities. By the following year, *Newsday* would report that "at least eight percent of the 1500-man [Bay of Pigs] invasion force [had] been investigated or arrested for drug-dealing." However, as a highly respected former leader of the Bay of Pigs operation, a seemingly successful business partner with the rulers of Nicaragua, a psychiatrist, and the best friend of White House consultant E. Howard Hunt, Artime could play a uniquely valuable role in Trafficante's drug network. His frequent travels to Central America and especially his longtime skills in laundering large sums of money from his AMWORLD days made him extremely useful to Trafficante—and would soon also make Artime useful to Richard Nixon.[34]

In June 1972, Richard Helms was all too aware of press reports about the drug trafficking activities of so many of his former—and some said current—agents and assets. The negative publicity for the Agency was the opposite of the positive spin Helms had tried to achieve just a month earlier, when pitching the TV show based on Hunt's spy novels. More drug activities by CIA personnel were going to be exposed in *The Politics of Heroin in Southeast Asia*, a soon-to-be-published book by Alfred McCoy, who had just testified to Congress about the heroin problem. Helms had turned to Nixon to help stop Victor Marchetti's CIA exposé, but to stop McCoy's book, Helms unleashed high-ranking CIA official Cord Meyer in June 1972. Meyer tried to prevail upon the head of McCoy's publisher, Harper & Row, to halt publication of the book because it was "a threat to national security." Over the protests of McCoy, Harper & Row actually submitted the thoroughly documented book to the CIA for a pre-publication review.[35]

But Helms's attempt to stop the book backfired. McCoy's agent knew "Seymour Hersh, recently hired as an investigative reporter for *The New York Times*." Hersh ran a story about "the CIA's attempt to suppress the book" on the front page of the *Times*. *The Washington Post* followed up with an editorial about the matter, augmented by "an hour long" NBC News program about "the Agency's complicity in the Laotian drug trade." Harper & Row published McCoy's book without any changes. Helms may not have stopped the book, but he did learn important lessons from the incident that apply in dealing with the scandals for him and the Agency that followed, including some exposed by Sy Hersh.[36]

In June 1972, information was flowing from the DNC offices to CREEP, thanks to one of McCord's bugs placed during the Watergate burglary. Unlike the Chilean embassy, the DNC staff didn't realize their offices had been victimized by a break-in, since the burglars hadn't broken into file cabinets and had left the offices as they had found them. Watergate building security did notice the lock on the office's front door had been tampered with, and a police report was filed. But "the police concluded entry had not been gained to the DNC," so no attempt was made to sweep the office for bugs.[37]

Some writers have pointed out that O'Brien had been warned in March 1972 of "disturbing stories about GOP sophisticated intelligence techniques." The matter was pursued at the time of the warning, but no information or specifics could be confirmed. It was only decades later that the source of the detective that warned the Democrats was finally identified as John Ragan, essentially James McCord's predecessor at CREEP. Even if O'Brien and the DNC had been able to confirm more information in March of 1972, there is little they could have done aside from either closing their offices entirely or doing a time-consuming sweep for bugs every day until the election.[38]

However, there was a problem with one of the bugs in the DNC offices, the one on the phone of Larry O'Brien's secretary. McCord and Baldwin moved their listening post in the Howard Johnson's to a room three floors higher (No. 713) with a better sight line, but it didn't help. That meant that only the bug on Spencer Oliver's phone was sending data to Baldwin's receiver. McCord did not have Baldwin record the bug's information on a tape recorder because of an electronic resistance problem between the receiver and the recorders. Instead, Baldwin typed up summaries of what he heard on his headphones, including any information he thought was of value. Later, Liddy told McCord he wanted everything that was said transcribed. Some authors have wondered how McCord's system would have worked if both bugs had been operating—with just one man listening—and what was missed when Baldwin had to be away from his listening post. Obviously, bugging had not been the highest priority of the mission.

Liddy gave Baldwin's typed summaries to Nixon aide Jeb Magruder, and they eventually covered two hundred calls. Information gets murky after that, in part because of "the federal wiretap statute," which criminalizes not just listening to a bugged conversation or reading a transcript, but even looking at a summary of the conversation or a memo written about that summary. Because any of those activities is a felony, many Nixon aides, officials, and their assistants have given conflicting accounts about who saw or read the DNC call summaries. Magruder says he passed them on to John Mitchell, and Liddy says he gave some to Mitchell, but Mitchell denies ever seeing them, or knowing about any bugging. Yet Mitchell made what Emery considers a "damning" remark about bugging in general on June 14, when Mitchell was talking to Charles Colson about a Democratic strategy meeting. Mitchell said, "tell me what room they are in and I will tell you everything that is said in that room." Other Nixon aides who logically should have seen the summaries denied having done so. For example, H.R. Haldeman hedged when he testified to the Senate Watergate Committee that "to the best of my knowledge I did not see any material produced by the bugging," but when questioned about it in court, "he refused to reply 'on advice of counsel.'"[39]

Magruder and Liddy, among the few who acknowledged reading

the summaries, say they were of little value. However, the man whose phone was bugged, DNC official Spencer Oliver, revealed twenty years later how some of his comments were used by Nixon's aides, and why the Democratic nominee was still uncertain in mid-June 1972. Many people think that George McGovern clinched the Democratic nomination when he won the California primary in the first week of June, but that's not the case. The new winner-take-all rule for the California primary had never been tested and was subject to challenge, and it still left McGovern short of enough delegates to secure the nomination. Oliver, the head of the DNC's "Stop McGovern" movement, looked ahead to the Texas Democratic Convention, which started on June 13. Conservative Democrats held much power there, and they didn't want to see McGovern—who was supported by only one-third of the Texas delegates—become the nominee. The Texas Democratic Convention could give all of the state's delegates to one candidate, instead of using proportional representation, keeping McGovern from locking up the nomination and giving a boost to one of his rivals, like Humphrey. Oliver still hoped for a deadlocked convention that would turn to Humphrey, Terry Sanford, or "Scoop" Jackson—anyone but McGovern.[40]

Spencer Oliver said that through the DNC bug, Nixon's men were essentially "listening to me on that phone do a vote count" about Texas, and planning "a project to block McGovern's nomination. Now, how do you block that?" In the case of Texas, Nixon turned to John Connally, the conservative Texas Democrat who had become Nixon's Treasury Secretary two years earlier. According to Oliver, Connally's protégé unexpectedly showed up at the Texas Democratic Convention and helped to broker an unlikely deal between McGovern's backers and George Wallace's supporters. As a result, Wallace and McGovern split most of the Texas delegates. That surprising coalition, which Oliver felt was engineered by Nixon and Connally, gave McGovern important delegates and momentum, with *The New York Times* reporting it "put McGovern about two-thirds of the way toward [the] 1,509 needed for a first-round nomination."[41]

McGovern had beaten Humphrey in the California primary by only 44 percent to 39 percent, which, according to some interpretations, could have kept McGovern from getting all the delegates, since he didn't get a majority of the vote. One ruling gave McGovern 120 delegates and Humphrey 106, but that was challenged by McGovern's supporters, who wanted all 271 of California's delegates for McGovern to assure him of the nomination. DNC attorney Joseph Califano then became involved in legal and party disputes that could have kept McGovern from securing the nomination. Califano's involvement in these disputes would last all the way until the Democratic National Convention, but the bottom line is that while Nixon's Democratic opponent was probably going to be McGovern, that wasn't certain in mid-June 1972. There was also still the Wallace factor. In a poll without Wallace, Nixon beat McGovern 53 percent to 34 percent, but that could change if Wallace ran as an independent and drew conservative votes from Nixon.[42]

In mid-June 1972, the decision was made to have James McCord return to the Watergate offices of the DNC, to fix the bug in the telephone of Larry O'Brien's secretary. Most accounts say the decision was made to return because the summaries obtained from Spencer Oliver's phone had been of no value. However, since no one could admit knowing what the summaries said without opening themselves up to felony prosecution, that may not be accurate. If Spencer Oliver is correct that his bugged conversations helped to torpedo his "Stop McGovern" movement in Texas, then White House officials might have wanted more information that could help them ensure that McGovern became the nominee.

The question of who made the decision to have the Watergate burglars return—and why—has been a source of great debate for decades. Jeb Magruder said that CREEP Chairman John Mitchell made the decision, after Mitchell told him the bugging material produced so far "isn't worth the paper it's printed on." Mitchell denied any involvement. However, Magruder's account is "backed up by testimony from his assistant," and J. Anthony "Lukas . . . reported that most contemporary investigators seemed to believe Magruder's version rather than Mitchell's denial." If Mitchell knew about the Watergate burglars' return, then it's likely that Nixon knew as well, at least in a general sense. The Cuban Dossier was still an open issue that could harm or end Nixon's reelection chances, unless they could find out what the DNC had—or didn't have—about the CIA-Mafia plots. However, those were concerns that Nixon and Mitchell couldn't share with the other White House aides, but Mitchell could apply general pressure on Liddy and Magruder to go back in. As an added incentive, another break-in might uncover additional political information, and Nixon seemed to want as much intelligence on his opponents as possible. For example, "the Nixon tapes show that the President urged Colson at this time to get the Secret Service to spy on McGovern. Confidential information was subsequently picked up by an agent on the Senator's detail and passed to the White House."[43]

Magruder said that Liddy told him on June 12 "that he was planning to 'hit McGovern headquarters' within days." At a June 15 meeting, Liddy says he told Mitchell "'the problem we have, will be corrected this weekend, sir.' Mitchell just nodded." Liddy and Magruder are at odds on many details about the decision to return to the Watergate, though Liddy made no statements about the matter until his 1980 book, *Will*, while Magruder testified about the events much earlier, after he had admitted being part of the whole criminal operation.[44]

However, the final Watergate mission wasn't just about bugging, and in fact most accounts say that wasn't the primary reason for the return. Liddy said that Magruder "placed the new emphasis on photography [of documents] rather than bugging." On June 14, E. Howard Hunt said that Liddy told him "they want a lot more photographs. Have Macho [Barker] buy another camera and bring up a lot of film. They want everything in those file cabinets photographed." Liddy "explained to Hunt that this time McCord was merely to be a 'hitchhiker' [since] the main mission was to be a photo mission" targeting documents.[45]

There were so many files to photograph that, according to Hunt, the burglars would "use an assembly-line method in photographing documents at the DNC [with] two people [selecting] documents while a third person turned each page for the photographer." While McCord fixed or replaced the defective bug, the four men on the photography team were "expected to expose perhaps five frames a minute (or about eight rolls of film each hour). And their mission wouldn't just be at the Watergate.[46]

Hunt says Liddy told him his superiors "wanted the McGovern office operation completed, too," either "the same night" or "the night after Watergate." When Hunt remarked that hitting both the Watergate and McGovern's office sounded like a lot of work in a short amount of time for his crew, Liddy replied that "The Big Man [Mitchell] says he wants the operation." Given everything that's known about the relationship between Nixon and Mitchell, it's hard to imagine Mitchell would order two risky operations, potentially in one night, without at least the tacit approval of Nixon. Even the usually circumspect Hunt wrote that "Watergate . . . was a political intelligence-gathering operation from start to finish, possibly personally ordered by the president himself."[47]

Present in the accounts of most of the participants—but usually missing from conventional histories of Watergate—is the sense of desperation on the part of whoever was pushing for the next Watergate mission, which also included another attempt on McGovern's headquarters. Everyone who has testified or written on the record has tried to pass the buck to others regarding responsibility for the next break-in. They usually add that they had doubts about the wisdom of the final mission, but they nonetheless went ahead with it for reasons that aren't clear. With McGovern closer to securing the nomination, and the convention still weeks away, what was the rush? Why not take an extra week, even two, to make sure the operation was planned and executed as carefully as possible? It's odd that wasn't a major consideration, especially since it had taken three attempts at the Watergate the first time—and one of the participants had been caught and was simply lucky to be let go. As Liddy told Magruder, the bug could be quickly fixed with just "McCord and a couple of others," not the group of five that would be required for the massive photo-document operation that would last for hours.[48]

The sense of urgency for the final Watergate mission is, however, consistent with looking for the secret Cuban Dossier, the goal explicitly described by Frank Fiorini and indicated by Watergate Committee investigators to Johnny Rosselli. After all, the CIA-Mafia plots spawned under Nixon—that had grown into the Bay of Pigs operation—were the dark secret that tied together Nixon, Helms, Hunt, Barker, Fiorini, Artime, and, in some ways, McCord. Even G. Gordon Liddy, the least informed of the Watergate crew, emphasized in his book that "the purpose of the second Watergate break-in was to find out what O'Brien had of a derogatory nature about us, not for us to get something on him." In addition to the Dossier, the burglars—and those who ordered the final break-in—wanted any other information Larry O'Brien might have gotten from his friend Robert Maheu or Howard Hughes. Also, by mid-June, Walter Sheridan's upcoming Hoffa exposé would have been known by more people, especially Kennedy loyalists. Sheridan would soon be working for the McGovern campaign, and Nixon no doubt worried about what Sheridan might have told or shown to O'Brien about the 1960 or 1971 Nixon-Mafia-Hoffa bribes.[49]

The worst thing Nixon could face in the campaign was the exposure of the CIA-Mafia plots and one or both of his Mafia-Hoffa bribes. That perfect storm was still a very real possibility in mid-June, and could even make a race with George McGovern difficult. Worse still, if the information came out before the Democratic National Convention, it might spur a more electable challenger to try to secure the nomination in a floor fight. Almost all of the participants—including Hunt, McCord, and Liddy—expressed doubts or misgivings about the operation, yet not one tried to postpone it or even tell their superiors they shouldn't attempt two massive jobs at two risky targets in just one or two nights. If Hunt's accounts about his worries and doubts about the operation are true, why didn't he just refuse, or quit his White House position, since he was still receiving a full-time salary from the Mullen Company? If the pressure for the final mission was coming from Nixon or Helms—or both—the answer is clear. Hunt couldn't say no; he only had his salary at the Mullen Company because of Helms, who would have also wanted Hunt to stay in the White House. As with the previous Watergate mission, there is no way Hunt—or Martinez—would have participated if Helms hadn't wanted him to. Once more, all of those participating—except for Liddy—would be current or former CIA agents and officials. Helms and Nixon stood to lose far more than Hunt if the CIA-Mafia plots were exposed, and Nixon would lose more than Helms. Hence, the operation had to go forward, and quickly, despite the risks and doubts.[50]

CHAPTER 31

June 16 to Late June 1972: Another Watergate Burglary, Nixon, and "the Bay of Pigs Thing"

The next Watergate burglary was originally scheduled for Friday night, June 16, 1972, with the McGovern operation slated for later that night, or the following night. However, problems surfaced that day, June 16, when "Hunt met with McCord and Thomas Gregory, the student plant, to settle the final details of the entry into McGovern's headquarters." The young man "surprised them by saying he wanted out: 'This is getting too deep for me.'" The following year, H.R. Haldeman would tell Nixon that even after being "paid $3,500" to spy for the White House, Gregory had "finally broke off with Hunt because he refused to bug Gary Hart's telephone over at McGovern headquarters." Gregory's departure would seem to have been the logical time to at least cancel the McGovern mission, but it wasn't. It's ironic that Gregory quit, while the far more experienced Hunt and McCord forged ahead with both the Watergate and McGovern operations, with the blessings of the Nixon White House.[1]

Even before Bernard Barker, Eugenio Martinez, Frank Fiorini, and Virgilio Gonzalez left Miami and headed to Washington for the mission, Martinez had severe misgivings about continuing his work for Hunt and the White House. Martinez said he had talked about quitting with Fiorini and Felipe De Diego (who, after being caught the last time, was not part of the final Watergate crew). In fact, Martinez was getting ready to write a letter of resignation when Barker told him about the new Watergate mission, saying they were to leave for Washington on June 16. Even though Martinez said he "had just gotten my divorce that day," he complied with Barker's request and went to Washington with the others.[2]

Even their arrival at Washington's National Airport was problematic. Frank Fiorini was walking with Virgilio Gonzalez, who was carrying his locksmith tools in his suitcase. Suddenly, Fiorini heard someone calling for him, yelling, "Frankie!" It was his old friend, columnist Jack Anderson, who was at the airport "to catch a plane to Cleveland to speak to a college journalism fraternity." Fiorini introduced Gonzalez to Anderson, but demurred when Anderson asked, "What are you doing in town?" Fiorini cautiously replied, "I'm going to see friends." Anderson said later he sensed Fiorini "was 'chagrined to meet me, so I suspected something was up.'" Fiorini muttered "'Private business. Top secret. Top secret' . . . with a conspiratorial smile." That was enough to ensure that Anderson wouldn't casually mention running into his soldier-of-fortune friend, and the men parted ways. Some authors have thought the Fiorini-Anderson meeting was too much of a coincidence, but later investigations proved that Anderson was indeed going to his long-planned speaking engagement.[3]

Once all the men reached the Watergate Hotel, the problems and pressure mounted. Martinez says he was surprised when Hunt told them there were two operations "and we were supposed to perform them both that night. There was no time for anything, it was all rush." Hunt said they "were going to photograph more documents at the Democratic headquarters and then move on to another mission at the McGovern headquarters after that." Martinez wrote that "McCord was critical of the second operation. He said he didn't like the plan. It was very rare to hear McCord talking because usually he didn't say anything and when he did talk he only whispered."[4]

Hunt told the exiles "to buy surgical gloves and forty rolls of film with thirty-six exposures on a roll," and Martinez thought, "Imagine, that meant 1,440 photographs." Martinez "told Barker it would be impossible to take all those pictures," but his concerns were ignored. All the men were given false identification, and Hunt gave Fiorini and McCord some of the CIA-supplied IDs he'd used in the past.[5]

The DNC break-in was originally scheduled to begin at 10 PM on Friday night, June 16, to allow enough time for the break-in at McGovern campaign headquarters a few hours after midnight. However, by 11:30 PM, a light was still burning at the sixth-floor offices of the DNC, so the decision was made to wait until after the midnight guard inspection before beginning the break-in attempt. McCord had already taped open a stairwell door in the garage, by using the same ruse as in the previous successful attempt in May: He'd signed in (using an alias) at the main entrance of the Watergate building as if going to the Federal Reserve office on the eighth floor, and, once there, he had walked down the stairwell to the parking garage, where he'd taped the door. In contrast to latter accounts, Jim Hougan's research showed that McCord didn't tape the door locks horizontally, so the tape was obvious, but vertically, so it was almost impossible to see.[6]

From this point forward, the various accounts by all of the participants in the break-in, and the cover-up, multiply by almost exponential proportions. As Fred Emery points out, many accounts about the various events are often "totally at odds." Often, a single participant told different stories about a single event at different times, first as part of the cover-up, then a different version to investigators or at hearings, followed by yet another version in later books or articles, and still another version years or decades later in lawsuits or interviews. The reasons participants gave these different versions include avoiding prosecution, diverting blame, or simply presenting themselves in the best possible light. In addition, the burglars were probably given cover stories by Hunt at the very start of the operation, to use in case any problem arose. After the arrests, all of the participants—the burglars and those in the White House—had months to coordinate further cover stories with each other, and to update those stories to match evidence as it emerged.[7]

Attempts by journalists and historians to reconcile all of those varying stories with the actual evidence and documentation consumed much of the first two decades of Watergate research, and they continue today. However, as Emery pointed out in his 1994 book and BBC documentary series, many of those discrepancies are "impossible to reconcile" and in any event "are not, in the end, very important." It's now also clear that all that effort has served to distract from basic issues that are important, such as what the burglars were after, why President Nixon and Richard Helms wanted it so badly, and how their cover-up kept the Watergate arrests from becoming a factor in the 1972 Presidential election. For those reasons, this book combines the most basic, documentable facts about the break-in and its aftermath with the newest information about Nixon, Helms, Hunt, and others, to illuminate the most important parts of the Watergate story in a new way.

Watergate security guard Frank Wills discovered McCord's tape on the garage door and removed it. While taping doors was not uncommon for maintenance men, Wills began the process of checking with his superior for further instructions, and he left the garage. When the burglars arrived at the un-taped garage door about 1:10 AM, they were unable to enter the stairwell. The participants' accounts begin to differ wildly at this point, but all agree that the decision was made to proceed with the operation. Gonzalez was able to pick the lock on the stairwell door in the garage. One of the crew—some accounts say it was Fiorini—re-taped the door locks, and the burglars proceeded up to the sixth floor and were soon joined by McCord. This time, Hunt and Liddy waited in their room at the Watergate Hotel during the break-in, while Alfred Baldwin alone kept an eye on the sixth floor from the listening post at the Howard Johnson's motel (when Baldwin wasn't distracted by going out for food or watching a movie on the room's television). Hunt, Baldwin, Barker, and McCord each had a walkie-talkie for communication.[8]

Once the men had climbed the stairs to the sixth floor, locksmith Virgilio Gonzalez had problems opening the locked rear door to the DNC offices. Fiorini decided they should remove the entire door, a drastic step that again shows a sense of urgency or desperation. (Fiorini had not only been told by Hunt about the secret Cuban Dossier, but as a participant in the CIA-Mafia plots, Fiorini might have worried he might be named in the Dossier.) When McCord joined the men at 1:40 AM, he was worried that by removing the door they were making too much noise. But the door was finally dislodged, and they were able to enter the DNC offices.[9]

In the Watergate building's garage, guard Frank Wills checked the doors again as ordered by his supervisor and was surprised to find the locks had been re-taped. Realizing it couldn't be the work of a maintenance man at that hour, he called the Washington, D.C., police at 1:47 AM. A police call went out at 1:52 AM, and a squad car with three plainclothes officers responded. Officer Carl Shoffler, who had almost shoulder-length hair as part of his undercover work, told the dispatcher they were only a block and a half away, and they were soon at the Watergate, talking to Frank Wills. At that moment, the burglars had likely not yet even finished removing the door to the DNC offices.[10]

The officers first went up to the eighth floor, since there had been a burglary attempt at the Federal Reserve offices several weeks earlier. From there, they began working their way down toward the sixth floor. Eugenio Martinez had heard the men, but McCord told him it must be the security guard making his rounds. At the Howard Johnson's motel across the street, Alfred Baldwin had noticed the lights coming on, first on the eighth floor, then on the seventh. Baldwin—spotting Shoffler's long hair and casual clothes—radioed Liddy, asking, "Are any of your men wearing hippie clothes?" Liddy replied, "No, they are all in business suits." Baldwin then breathlessly told Liddy over the walkie-talkie, "They're on the sixth floor now. Four or five guys"—the officers had been joined by a Federal Reserve guard—"it looks like . . . guns! They've got guns. It's trouble!"[11]

Hunt and Liddy tried to radio a warning to Barker, but there was a problem. Frank Fiorini later told Andrew St. George that Barker's

> job was to keep his ear to that goddamn walkie-talkie, listening to our lookout across from the Watergate in case there was any outside problem . . . But Barker [was] too cheap to install a fresh battery in the thing before an operation; no, he keeps the old battery going week after week by never turning up the volume . . . the night we got arrested, the minute we get safely inside the [Democratic National Committee office at the Watergate,] Macho turns the volume of his walkie-talkie all the way down . . . saving the battery. He also kept us from picking up the first warning calls from the lookout across the street [who] saw the unmarked police car arrive, saw the cops begin turning up the lights on one floor after another . . . we suspected nothing until finally Barker heard the footsteps of the cops pounding outside our door and [he finally] turned up his walkie-talkie. Hunt was stationed in another section of the Watergate complex and his voice came in, squeaky with tension, "Alert! Alert! Do you read me? Clear out immediately" . . . but by then it was too late: the cops were in the corridor. Barker saved his damn walkie-talkie battery and blew our team.* [12]

At approximately 2:30 AM on June 17, 1972, Shoffler and the other officers entered the Watergate offices, finding the burglars hiding "behind a desk in the secretarial cubicle adjacent to Larry O'Brien's office." McCord radioed to Baldwin, "They got us."[13]

It must have been an odd scene, Shoffler and his two fellow plainclothes officers, dressed "like hippies," guns drawn, arresting the

*Some of the burglars, including Fiorini, later claimed that McCord had told Barker to turn down his walkie-talkie, as part of an attempt to blame McCord for the mission's failure. However, Fiorini's early account to his friend St. George—not intended for publication—is probably more accurate.

unarmed, middle-aged, well-dressed burglars. The officers later described the burglars as looking like "'Mafia types' because of their swarthy complexions, business suits, and surgical gloves." The officers were jumpy and nervous, but the mature burglars offered no resistance and went quietly. Once at the police station, Martinez said that "McCord was the senior officer, and he took charge. He was talking loudly now. He told us not to say a thing. 'Don't give your names. Nothing. I know people. Don't worry, someone will come and everything will be all right. This thing will be solved.'"[14]

E. Howard Hunt and G. Gordon Liddy could not see the DNC offices on the sixth floor from their Watergate Hotel room, but they saw the commotion on the street as "squad cars began pulling up in front of the [Watergate] office building with lights flashing." Both seemed to panic, especially after Hunt told Liddy, "We gotta get out fast," since Barker had a key to their hotel room. In their haste to flee, "they neglected to sanitize either their own room or the [Cubans' hotel] room," which contained more material from the burglars. After dropping off Liddy at his parked jeep, Hunt went to the Howard Johnson's motel to meet Alfred Baldwin. Hunt told Baldwin to "load" all "of the electronic equipment" into McCord's "van and get out of town." Baldwin says Hunt told him to take it to McCord's house, while Hunt claims he told Baldwin to take it "anyplace but" McCord's. Baldwin drove the van to McCord's home, where it would sit, undisturbed, for days.[15]

Hunt and Liddy's panicked failure to sanitize the burglars' hotel room was a disaster. Shoffler and the other officers would be searching it approximately twelve hours after the arrests, finding "more surgical gloves, electronic equipment, $3,200 in sequentially numbered $100 bills, an address book belonging to Barker that contained the initials 'H.H.—W.H.,' and Hunt's telephone number of the White House." The "H.H." was easy for police to figure out, since they also recovered "a check for $6.36 made out by E. Howard Hunt to the Lakewood Country Club."*[16]

The men had been arrested carrying even more incriminating evidence, including

*Some writers have raised suspicions about the background and presence of Officer Shoffler, but those claims were thoroughly investigated by author Jim Hougan, who found innocent explanations for those concerns.

> thirty-nine roles of [unexposed] film, two Minolta cameras, a light stand for document photography, the . . . key to [O'Brien's secretary's] desk, and . . . a pop-up telephone desk directory . . . that belonged to Martinez and contained a listing for "Howard Hunt—W. House."[17]

When taken into custody, the burglars also had "$2,400 in sequentially numbered new $100 bills, assorted blank keys and screwdrivers." In addition, "three miniature electronic transmitters (bugs)" had been recovered from James McCord, as well as a "smoke detector converted into a room bug." Oddly, later on the day of the burglars' arrests, two FBI agents "conducted 'a physical check' of the DNC's headquarters 'in an effort to locate hidden electronic surveillance equipment,'" and the "results of the check were negative." In addition, the "chief of security for the Chesapeake and Potomac Telephone Company, and his assistant . . . conducted a security check on all telephones and communications equipment in the DNC . . . [and] no bugs were found." (Emphasis in original.) Almost three months later, "a bug did turn up in Spencer Oliver's office phone . . . following a report of a malfunction by an Oliver secretary. The bug was defective however," and some say it couldn't have made the transmissions logged by Alfred Baldwin. McCord wrote and testified that the other bug he'd installed back in May "remained in place—'on an extension . . . carrying Larry O'Brien's lines'—until April 1973," even though an FBI check on "April 9, 1973 . . . of all DNC phones found no second device."[18]

How to explain the anomalies? "Acting U.S. Attorney Earl Silbert [the main prosecuting attorney for the Watergate cases] thought the FBI 'goofed' in its initial check of the DNC phones." Since the bugs had been installed by a former CIA official, another possibility is that the Agency had information about the bugs suppressed. After all, the bugs had been placed for reasons at least tangentially related to national security (preventing the disclosure of information that could reveal or harm CIA operations and assets). At least two other documented pieces of evidence obtained by the FBI would go missing, one on June 17, 1972, from McCord, and another later that week that had belonged to CIA agent Eugenio Martinez. With Hoover no longer running the FBI, cooperation had started to resume between the Agency and the Bureau, which might help to explain the missing evidence.[19]

For example, Hougan points out that on June 17, 1972, "[James] McCord would be arrested and booked under a Hunt alias, 'Edward Martin,' producing a phony ID on which the birth date was identical with Howard Hunt's own." What's also interesting is "that the identification papers in McCord's possession at the time of his arrest . . . disappeared from police and prosecution files. The false ID was issued by the CIA to Howard Hunt, and vanished immediately after McCord's fingerprinting by Washington police."[20]

The disappearance of the CIA-supplied McCord/Hunt ID was no accident. Hougan found that "a file on Hunt's activities" using the Edward Martin alias and "maintained 'outside the normal CIA filing system,' was [later] requested from the CIA by the [Senate Watergate] committee." But "the CIA's initial response was to claim that the 'Mr. Edward file' could not be located and might not exist. Repeated requests from the committee, however, were eventually satisfied when the Agency provided it with access to a rather uninteresting [file] concerning Howard Hunt. Minority staff members on the committee speculated that this Dossier was a surrogate created in an effort to mollify the committee, and that the authentic 'Mr. Edward file' concerned the activities of both Hunt and McCord while using the Mr. Edward/Don Eduardo alias." All of that was documented in the Watergate Committee's Final Report, but the last portion is especially important. Hunt's use of the "Don Eduardo" alias dated from his time working on the CIA-Mafia plots in 1960, when Nixon was Vice President, and continued during Hunt's time working on the JFK-Almeida coup plan in 1963 (when, according to Harry Williams, McCord also used the "Eduardo" cover identity). Thus, to protect an ongoing CIA operation, the Agency could legally ask the FBI and Washington, D.C., police to suppress the Edward ID and any related evidence.[21]

Other evidence that would disappear concerned active CIA agent Eugenio Martinez. On June 17, 1972, after Martinez's arrest, his car was driven by someone (never identified) to the parking lot at the Miami airport, where they received a parking receipt with that date. Two days later, the CIA claims it was notified by an unidentified "informant or agent" that Martinez's car was at the airport parking lot. The CIA admitted it then waited two more days before telling the FBI, which then searched Martinez's car. Among the items the Bureau recovered was a "notebook containing various names and numbers [and] Spanish writing." However, that notebook—"thought to have been the operational diary that Martinez was required to keep as a contract agent to the CIA . . . disappeared without a trace," just like McCord's CIA-supplied ID.[22]

On the morning of their arrest, McCord, Martinez, and all of the Watergate burglars had given only their aliases, and almost no other information. However, months earlier, McCord—in his role as CREEP's Security Director—had established a liaison with the Washington, D.C., Police Intelligence Division. The liaison officer for McCord, Gary Bittenbender, just happened to see the arrested McCord in "a chance encounter at the police station" that morning. The two associates briefly spoke, and "Bittenbender would [later] be quoted in Senate [hearings] as having said that McCord told him, on the day of the arrests, that the Watergate break-in was 'a CIA operation'—an allegation that McCord would later vehemently deny." Technically, both McCord's denial and Bittenbender's allegation could be correct. Like the Chilean embassy break-in described by Nixon on his tapes, the Watergate burglaries were essentially a White House operation using "a CIA cover."[23]

According to journalist Carl Rowan, then with *The Washington Star*, Richard Helms told him a few days after the arrests that early on June 17, "he was awakened before dawn by a telephone call from someone at the Agency who told him about the events at the Watergate." The CIA has always claimed it was unaware of the arrests of five of its current and former agents until much later in the day, at 5 PM. Helms asserted that he didn't learn about the men until 10 PM that night, sixteen hours after the arrests, when the CIA's Director of Security called him at home, saying that "McCord was in jail and Howard Hunt was somehow involved in the affair." Since the 1970s, many authors like J. Anthony Lukas have been skeptical of the CIA's and Helms's accounts of how long it took them to learn about the arrests. Helms's casual admission to Carl Rowan seems much more likely. Helms knew Rowan, who was the former head of the U.S. Information Agency, and made the admission in passing when they met briefly at a film screening, well before cover stories protecting Helms had to be devised and implemented. Helms would soon start withholding information about Hunt and McCord even from his own Counterintelligence Chief, James Angleton. As for the pre-dawn call that alerted Helms about the Watergate arrests of CIA personnel, Hougan raises the point that the men had only been identified by aliases at that point. Arrests of CIA agents and assets, or those using CIA-supplied ID and aliases, was also not so rare (or so serious) that they would necessitate an early-morning call to the CIA Director's home by "a lowly watch officer at CIA headquarters." Instead, Hougan suggests that, given the already documented flow of information going from Hunt to Helms, that "it was Helms's friend E. Howard Hunt" who first called the CIA Director.[24]

One person who admitted he was informed very early about the Watergate arrests is Joseph Califano, whose key role in focusing attention on the Watergate story has been overlooked by most historians and journalists. At 5:00 AM on the morning of the arrests, Califano was called with news of the break-in at the offices of his client, the Democratic National Committee. According to *Newsweek* editor Evan Thomas, Califano was told that "the burglars had been caught copying files and bugging telephones. Califano hung up and called another of [his] firm's clients, *The Washington Post*. Califano suggested to . . . the managing editor that the Watergate burglary might be a good story," setting in motion the coverage that would make Bob Woodward and Carl Bernstein famous. Califano's instincts and timing continued to be amazing later that morning, because after "Califano was told that the police had found the phone number of the Committee to Re-Elect the President on one of the burglars," Califano asked his law partner, Edward Bennett Williams, "What if this goes all the way to the White House?"[25]

Califano didn't stop there. The following evening, "Califano decided to file a suit for the Democrats against [CREEP]." Though little-remembered today, the suit would be extremely important, because the pre-trial discovery process would keep the story barely alive throughout the summer and fall, when most American journalists—aside from those at *The Washington Post* and a few others—kept Watergate off their front pages or ignored it all together. Califano himself would later write about how he was

> struck by his own involvement in so many sides of the Watergate drama. I . . . personally represented the Democratic Party and *The Washington Post*. I found myself advising [Alexander] Haig and [Alexander] Butterfield. I [also] worked with Democratic Senators pressing for a special prosecutor and establishment of the Senate Watergate Committee. I [even] conferred with . . . the [Watergate] Special Prosecutor, when he needed a messenger.[26]

The many pivotal roles of Califano aren't more widely known because he wouldn't detail them until his 2005 autobiography, appropriately named *Inside*. In addition, he wrote that he "tried to be discreet" during the Watergate era and after, not telling "one client or friend what another told me." At the time of the Watergate break-in, Califano's longtime associates from 1963—Haig and Butterfield—were still in the White House positions he'd helped them secure.[27]

As a result of Califano's call to his client, *The Washington Post*, the newspaper went after the story aggressively, and "eight reporters would work the Watergate story that first day, including Carl Bernstein." Bernstein was not yet partnered with Bob Woodward, who wrote that he was also "summoned . . . to the *Post* that Saturday morning." Woodward had been with the *Post* as "a police reporter for [only] nine months," and he was "sent . . . to the local courthouse to cover the arraignment of the five burglars," who had been charged with second-degree burglary. There, Woodward happened to encounter one of the two attorneys that E. Howard Hunt had arranged for his crew. When Judge James A. Belson asked the defendants "what they did for a living," one said they are "'anti-Communists' . . . and the others nodded in agreement." James McCord was the first to be questioned by the Judge, who asked for his occupation. McCord replied, "Security consultant." Woodward wrote that "in a low voice, McCord said that the was recently retired from government service . . . sending a strong message that he wanted this to be between the judge and him." However, since "it was an open courtroom," Woodward said that he "moved to the front row and leaned as far into the conversation as possible without joining in."[28]

Woodward wrote that the Judge asked, "Where in government?"

> McCord's "barely audible" reply was "CIA."
>
> The judge flinched.
>
> Holy shit, I said half aloud. It was like a 10,000-volt jolt of electricity. I was amazed.

The Washington Post's story the next day, in which Woodward was credited as only one of several contributors, stated that "Five men, one of whom said he is a former employee of the Central Intelligence Agency, were arrested at 2:20 a.m. yesterday in what authorities described as an elaborate plot to bug the offices of the Democratic

National Committee here." Very early the following day, another *Post* police reporter told Woodward that "the address books of two of the burglars contained the phone number of an E. Howard Hunt Jr. with small notations 'W. House' and 'W.H.' by his name." After getting some sleep, Woodward made a call to his friend, Mark Felt, the FBI Assistant Director he'd met two years earlier, while he was on a White House briefing run for Admiral Moorer. Felt said "he disliked phone calls at the office, but told Woodward that the burglary case was going to 'heat up' for reasons he could not explain. He hung up abruptly." That brief call was the start of Woodward's use of Felt as the Watergate source that would later be named "Deep Throat."[29]

Bob Woodward then called "the White House—and asked for Howard Hunt. There was no answer but the operator said helpfully he might be in the office of Charles Colson, Nixon's special counsel. Colson's secretary said Hunt was not there but might be at a public relations firm where he worked as a writer."

> I called the firm, reached Hunt, and asked why his name was in the address books of two of the Watergate burglars.
>
> "Good God!" Hunt shouted, [then] said he had no comment and slammed down the phone.[30]

The next call Woodward made was to "the president of the public relations firm, Robert F. Bennett." Woodward was in for another shock after he asked Bennett about Hunt.

"'I guess it's no secret that Howard was with the CIA,' Bennett said blandly."[31]

Woodward was stunned, and he wrote, "There it was again—CIA. It had been a secret to me, but a CIA spokesman openly confirmed that Hunt had been with the Agency from 1949 to 1970." That prompted another call from Woodward to Felt, who said "that Hunt was a prime suspect in the Watergate burglary for many reasons beyond the address books. So reporting the connections forcefully [in the *Post*] would not be unfair." Woodward went to work on his next story, which would reveal Hunt's CIA past and his connection to the Watergate break-in. But after that article, despite the dramatic revelations of the Agency connections of McCord and Hunt, the CIA side of Watergate would soon fade into the background of Woodward's Watergate reporting, and his subsequent books.[32]

There are several possible reasons for Woodward and the *Post*'s subsequent lack of focus on the CIA and its Director, Richard Helms. Woodward would maintain his contact with Robert Bennett, unaware that Bennett had played a role in some of Hunt's operations with the White House. Just three weeks after Woodward first talked to Bennett, "Bennett met with this CIA case officer, Martin Lukoskie, [and] bragged that he had dissuaded reporters from the *Post* and *Star* from pursuing [stories] implicating the CIA in a Watergate conspiracy." Bennett's CIA case officer considered that information so sensitive "that he hand-carried it to CIA Director Helms," indicating Helms's level of concern about the whole matter (Bennett told his case officer that he'd originally hired Hunt because "Helms, wished him to employ Hunt [and] Helms . . . later personally expressed his appreciation").[33]

The following year, an Agency memo described Bennett as boasting to his CIA case officer

> that he has been feeding stories to Bob Woodward of the *Washington Post* with the understanding that there be no attribution to . . . Bennett. Woodward is suitably grateful for the fine stories and by-lines which he gets and protects Bennett, and Mullen and Company.[34]

It wasn't just the *Post*—and the *Star* and also *Newsweek*—that Bennett was feeding stories and information to in order to protect his CIA proprietary firm. In the first CIA memo quoted above, from three weeks after the Watergate arrests, his case officer said that "Mr. Bennett related that he has now established a 'back door entry' to the Edward Bennett Williams law firm which is representing the Democratic Party . . . to kill off any revelation by Ed Williams of Agency association with the Mullen firm." At that time, Edward Bennett Williams was working with his partner Joseph Califano on the DNC's lawsuit against CREEP for the break-in.[35]

Robert Bennett was probably just one of many CIA assets that Richard Helms had the Agency use to move the news media away from a focus on the CIA. Helms had learned from his difficult, more direct approaches with Jack Anderson and in sending Cord Meyer to try to suppress *The Politics of Heroin in Southeast Asia* that a more indirect approach—more carrot than stick—could be more effective in some instances.

As for *The Washington Post*, Richard Helms had apparently known editor Ben Bradlee for more than a decade at that point, and the *Post*'s friendly relationship with the Agency had existed long before Helms or Bradlee had ascended to their top posts. In terms of Bob Woodward's reporting, the relatively inexperienced reporter's main inside source of exclusive information was Mark Felt, who had access to all of the Bureau's information, but little from the CIA—a legacy of the strained relationship between the two agencies. Felt did not even share with Woodward all of the relevant information from FBI files, such as the Bureau's knowledge of the organized crime connections of Bernard Barker and Frank Fiorini [36]

For E. Howard Hunt and his Watergate compatriots, as well as some White House officials, the time between the arrests and Bob Woodward's call had been a nightmare. Hunt and Liddy had immediately realized the seriousness of what had happened. Liddy had told his wife at 3 AM on the morning of June 17, 1972, "There was trouble. Some people got caught. I'll probably be going to jail." Instead of going home to get some sleep like Liddy, Hunt had headed for "his White House office" in the Old Executive Office Building. There, "he stuffed the case containing McCord's extra electronic gear into his safe, along with address books, notebooks, and other items." Hunt also removed $10,000 given to him by Liddy from CREEP funds, then used most of it to pay one of the two lawyers he quickly arranged for his jailed crew.[37]

After Liddy woke up, he headed to his CREEP office, where he "began shredding the GEMSTONE files and anything else that might prove incriminating . . . even stacks of hundred-dollar bills, surplus from GEMSTONE funds." Unfortunately, the "sequenced $100 bills" that Barker was carrying when he was arrested were "part of Barker's $89,000 withdrawals from his April" money laundering for Liddy, funds that would prove a valuable tool for investigators in "following the money." Later that day, still on June 17, Liddy used "his White House pass" to get into "the Situation Room in the basement of the West Wing." There, Liddy "placed a scrambler call through the White House switchboard to [Jeb] Magruder," who was in California.[38]

Much controversy exists about exactly who was called when, and what their reaction was, regarding Liddy, Magruder, and John Mitchell, who was also in California. Either Magruder or Mitchell, depending on whose account you believe, wanted the relatively new Attorney General Richard Kleindienst to intervene and have all the men—or at least McCord—released. But Kleindienst refused, saying, "What happens to the President if I try a fool thing like that? It's the goddamnedest thing I ever heard of. For the President's sake I'm going to handle this like any other case." He would not always follow through on that commitment, but Kleindienst was standing up for the President who had fought so long and hard for his confirmation, which had appeared all but dead in the spring due to the ITT scandals.[39]

Conflicting accounts and evidence swirl around exactly how and when President Nixon—and his top aides—first heard about the Watergate arrests of McCord and the others. In an "address to the nation about Watergate" the following spring—after the scandal had finally become a major national story—Nixon said "he found out [about the break-in] from news reports within hours" of the arrests, on Saturday, June 17. However, in his memoirs, Nixon changed his story, claiming he didn't hear about the arrests until Sunday morning, June 18, when he arrived back at Key Biscayne after spending Friday evening and all day Saturday at Walker's Cay in the Bahamas, at the private island home of Nixon's millionaire friend Robert Abplanalp. Bebe Rebozo was with Nixon in the Bahamas, and Rebozo said "that Nixon got the news . . . on Saturday." But Rebozo said he and Nixon were at Key Biscayne when they heard the news, while the President's Daily Dairy shows that both men were still in the Bahamas. Nixon's friend Abplanalp later said "he was with Nixon when he heard about Watergate and that Nixon was very surprised and angry."[40]

Nixon's aides have given often-problematic accounts of when they first learned about the break-in and what their reactions were. Haldeman said he was in Key Biscayne on the beach with an aide when Nixon's Press Secretary walked up with a wire story about the break-in. Haldeman claimed he and Ziegler didn't think it was important enough to call the President, and he thought that Ehrlichman, back in Washington, would do it. Haldeman did talk to Nixon briefly that day, but he—and Nixon—claimed they didn't talk about Watergate. Ehrlichman said he was called by the Secret Service at his home on the evening of Saturday, June 17, and was told that Hunt's name and a check had been found in the effects of the burglars. Ehrlichman called Colson, who claimed "Hunt no longer had any connection with the White House" and that "he did not know why Hunt still had a White House phone." Ehrlichman then called Ziegler in Key Biscayne. Also on Saturday, the FBI reached Alexander Butterfield, who "confirmed that

Hunt had been a White House consultant on 'highly sensitive confidential matters,' but claimed it had been nine months previously." Yet Haldeman, Ehrlichman, Colson, Ziegler, and Butterfield all said they didn't think to call Nixon about the matter. It strains credibility that not one of those White House aides thought that the arrest of CREEP's Security Director for burglarizing the DNC—an arrest linked to White House consultant Hunt—was worth a call to the President.[41]

What is well documented is that various types of evidence began to be destroyed that day and in the days that followed. As summarized by Anthony Summers, "Papers McCord kept at the office were removed by his secretary for burning, while others were destroyed by his wife in the living room fireplace. Howard Hunt also burned documents at home. John Dean and a colleague, wearing surgical gloves to avoid leaving fingerprints, picked over the contents of [Hunt's] White House safe . . . papers they found . . . would eventually be burned by Nixon's compliant acting FBI Director, Pat Gray." John Mitchell told Jeb Magruder "maybe you ought to have a little fire at your home," and Magruder complied. Even Mitchell destroyed "his campaign correspondence with Nixon and Haldeman," which could have included information on a wide range of illegal matters. After Haldeman told his aide to "make sure our files are clean," more files were shredded. It's impossible to know what paper trails, or evidence of other crimes, literally went up in smoke or through the shredder.[42]

The Watergate burglars themselves seemed almost forgotten on June 17 and the days that immediately followed. Bail was "set at $50,000 for the four Miami men and $30,000 for McCord." On June 18, Jack Anderson managed to get into the jail to speak to Frank Fiorini. The columnist offered to post Fiorini's bail if he would stay at his home, where Anderson intended to pump him for information about the crime. Fiorini was agreeable, though he said he wouldn't discuss the break-in, since "we swore not to discuss this [with anyone] and we're sticking together." Anderson felt he could get Fiorini to talk, so he went before the Judge and argued that Fiorini should be released into his custody. However, "the Justice Department . . . vigorously objected," and the Judge refused Anderson's request.[43]

Carl Shoffler continued trying squeeze information out of the jailed Fiorini, who remained tight-lipped about the crime. However, in an exclusive interview with this author, Shoffler said that Fiorini later talked "off the record" about his organized crime connections, and admitted "knowing and working with Trafficante." Once Fiorini's real name had been established, the FBI quickly uncovered his criminal connections. By June 19, acting FBI Director Gray had written a memo to Haldeman, saying that "sources in Miami say he is now associated with organized crime activities"—but for some reason, Gray decided not to send Haldeman the memo. The FBI would continue to receive reports about Fiorini's mob ties, such as one stating that "in Miami [Fiorini] has the reputation of being a mercenary with Mafia type connections." Yet Fiorini's work for Trafficante and the Mafia would not become part of the Watergate story. Fiorini's use of the name "Frank Sturgis" during and after Watergate may have helped to obscure his criminal past, but that wasn't a factor for Bernard Barker.[44]

In the first *Washington Post* story about Watergate, Barker was "identified [only] as a wealthy real-estate man with important GOP links in Florida." But an FBI summary prepared for Gray a week after the arrests stated that "during the late 1940's, [Barker] became associated in gangster activities in Cuba." Other FBI files, including those about Bebe Rebozo, noted the ties of Barker and his associates to organized crime, and drug trafficking in particular. As with Fiorini, FBI Assistant Director Mark Felt would have seen these reports, but he apparently never mentioned the mob ties of Fiorini and Barker to Bob Woodward. In a way, that helped to keep the focus of a complex story on Nixon and the White House. On the other hand, it left a huge part of the Watergate story—the Mafia, and specifically the Mafia's work with the CIA on the anti-Castro plots—out of not just Woodward's books, but all conventional Watergate histories.[45]

Barker's full FBI file has never been released, likely because at certain times—such as from the fall of 1960 to the spring 1961 Bay of Pigs operation, and again from May 1963 until JFK's assassination—Barker was involved in sensitive covert operations like the CIA-Mafia plots and the JFK-Almeida coup plan. Because the FBI was helping the Agency hide the CIA-Mafia plots from the public in 1972, Barker and Fiorini's Mafia ties were also concealed. Conversely, because most journalists weren't investigating the mob ties of the two men, it also kept the press from finding out about the CIA-Mafia plots at that time.

Monday, June 19, 1972, was the first in a series of increasingly important days in the Watergate cover-up. That morning, Nixon's Press Secretary, Ron Ziegler, proclaimed that the Watergate break-in was nothing more than "a third rate burglary," a term some still use today. Ziegler also cautioned the press, saying that "certain elements may try to stretch this beyond what it is," and much of the press corps took his caution seriously. After news coverage that was fairly extensive for the first several days, Emery observed that "the break-in was [widely] dismissed as a 'caper'" for months, until well after the election and into the spring of 1973. With the exception of *The Washington Post*, *The New York Times*, the *Los Angeles Times*, and a few others, most "newspaper and television networks swallowed the line" that the White House wasn't responsible for the break-in. Of the TV networks, only a few CBS correspondents such as Schorr, Rather, and eventually Cronkite would buck the tide of relative media disinterest for the remainder of 1972.[46]

However, Ziegler's deputy—former *Washington Post* reporter Ken Clawson—later admitted that E. Howard Hunt's White House "employment was terminated on" June 19, after initially claiming to the press that Hunt hadn't worked for Nixon's team since March. James McCord was also fired, with John Mitchell announcing that McCord's "apparent actions [are] wholly inconsistent with the principals upon with we are conducting our campaign." The previous day, Mitchell had admitted to Magruder and CREEP's deputy manager, Robert Mardian, that he had, in fact, "authorized two hundred thousand dollars" for the political espionage plan that resulted in the break-in.[47]

Once Nixon was back in Washington, the worried President started taking charge of a counteroffensive, telling Haldeman to have Colson "go through his opponent's attacks and 'collect the worst smear stuff on Nixon'" to have as "a counterattack available to challenge" his critics. Nixon also wanted Mitchell to hire "an executive officer," so that Mitchell "would be free for decision making." That same day, a Watergate strategy "meeting [was] held in Mitchell's Watergate apartment, with Mitchell, Dean, Magruder, Mardian, and [Fred] LaRue." According to Magruder and LaRue, "Mitchell suggested the destruction of incriminating files."[48]

Also on June 19, the Supreme Court dealt a serious blow to Nixon when it unanimously ruled that "bugging of U.S. citizens in internal security cases must be first authorized by a court-ordered warrant." Basically, Nixon and Mitchell had argued that if the President wanted someone bugged, the President had the "inherent power" to do so, which the Supreme Court rejected. Hence any contact with the bugging results was now even more clearly a felony, which helps to explain why so many White House aides and officials who probably saw bugging transcripts later denied doing so. The Supreme Court's ruling also meant that any "national security" justification Nixon felt he could use to ultimately cover his political bugging was no longer valid, a concept that Nixon would still be struggling to accept until his resignation.[49]

On June 19, *Washington Post* reporters Bob Woodward and Carl Bernstein—in their first joint article—revealed that James McCord was CREEP's "security coordinator." The article also disclosed that Republican National Committee Chairman Bob Dole had admitted that McCord also provided services to the RNC. Woodward and Bernstein reported that McCord had "retired" from the CIA in 1970, and pointed out that Barker and Fiorini—like most reporters, they used his "Frank Sturgis" name—"are known to have had extensive contracts with the Central Intelligence Agency," based on "exile sources." They added that Barker "was closely associated with . . . Brigade 2506, the Bay of Pigs invasion force."[50]

"After seeing the *Post* story" on June 19, Joseph Califano, attorney for both the Democratic National Committee and *The Washington Post*, called DNC chairman Larry O'Brien "and told him that we had enough to file suit on behalf of the DNC against [CREEP], as well as McCord and the others caught breaking in." O'Brien agreed, and Califano wrote that "the following morning O'Brien and I announced the lawsuit, seeing $1 million in damages," in a press conference, where "O'Brien said that responsibility for the break-in went right to the White House." In private, O'Brien told Califano, "I've no doubt that the trail will lead to the Oval Office, if we can hang in there long enough." Califano knew that even if it were true, proving it in court would be extremely difficult, since "I had seen President Kennedy maintain his ability to deny any involvement in" Cuban operations back in 1963. In the coming weeks, Califano would learn "that two of the burglars were Cuban Brigade members, trained by the U.S. Army" in 1963, when "I had been in charge of the program!" Thinking back to the time when he worked on the program with Alexander Haig and Alexander Butterfield, Califano thought it "ironic [that] we may have taught these guys the techniques of . . . document photography that they had tried to use at the Watergate."[51]

. . .

Califano and O'Brien's press conference was not, in fact, the worst news President Nixon faced on the morning of Tuesday, June 20, 1972, three days after the final Watergate break-in. Their announcement was bad enough, since—as a longtime attorney—Nixon knew the DNC lawsuit could be used as a fishing expedition during the deposition phase to try to uncover a wide range of White House wrongdoing. However, that would have only added to Nixon's grave concern over that morning's new *Washington Post* article by Bob Woodward, which publicly identified E. Howard Hunt's connection to the break-in for the first time. It even included Hunt's "Good God!" comment when Woodward had called Hunt—hardly the reaction of someone with nothing to hide. The article described Hunt as working for the White House as "a consultant in [the] declassification of the Pentagon Papers and most recently on narcotics intelligence," with the latter descriptions coming from Ziegler's aide, Ken Clawson. Nixon would have flinched at the mention of the Pentagon Papers, since he was aware of Hunt's illegal break-in of Ellsberg's psychiatrist.[52]

However, the worst development that morning for Nixon would have been Tad Szulc's article in *The New York Times*. It not only revealed that Hunt's name and check had been found in the burglar's belongings, but also that Hunt had met with still-jailed burglar Bernard Barker two weeks before the break-in. But the revelation that would have had the biggest impact on Nixon was Szulc's disclosure that "Hunt, using the code name 'Eduardo,' was the CIA official in charge of the abortive Bay of Pigs invasion of Cuba in 1961. He was the immediate superior of Bernard Barker in the preparations for the Cuban invasion." Tad Szulc's longtime experience in Latin American affairs, combined with his insights from his work with John and Robert Kennedy on the CIA's AMTRUNK operation in early 1963, had helped Szulc ferret out the key part of Hunt's CIA background that could tie him to Richard Nixon.[53]

In Watergate lore, however, June 20, 1972, is mainly remembered as the date of the infamous "eighteen-and-a-half-minute" gap in one of Richard Nixon's White House tapes, which later investigations proved was a deliberate erasure. Many authors have speculated as to why that portion of that particular tape, a conversation between Nixon and H.R. Haldeman, was erased when other very incriminating tapes were not, such as the June 23, 1972, "Smoking Gun" tape, whose release forced Nixon's resignation. A close look at all of Nixon's activities that day, and what he would have been talking about to aides, helps to show why that tape was probably erased—and why it isn't the only record of Nixon's talks that day that is missing.

On the morning of June 20, "Nixon sat alone for more than an hour, neither making nor receiving calls." Given recent events, and that morning's revelations about Hunt, it's not hard to imagine why Nixon needed time alone to ponder. The break-ins at the Watergate and the Chilean embassy had been about trying to limit any damage that could come from information in the secret Cuban Dossier of CIA assassination attempts. If the Dossier, or other information Larry O'Brien had obtained from Robert Maheu, had mentioned anything about Nixon's role in the CIA-Mafia plots that had grown into the Bay of Pigs operation, it could have made the ITT scandal look minor in comparison. It might have also led to investigations that could have uncovered Nixon's bribes from the Mafia. Now, in trying to deal with those possibilities, another huge problem for Nixon had been created. Hunt, his leading role in the Bay of Pigs operation, and his work for the White House was now public knowledge. If any journalist or investigator started putting that information together with Jack Anderson's articles about the CIA-Mafia plots from January 1971 that had so concerned Nixon and Mitchell, the results could be disastrous for Nixon's reelection chances.[54]

For Nixon, trying to limit the damage by coming clean was not an option. He knew that the Watergate arrests were just the tip of the iceberg, of actions involving Hunt that included not just the burglaries of the Chilean embassy and Ellsberg's psychiatrist, but also Hunt's role in Nixon's extensive—and often illegal—"dirty tricks" operations. Any unfettered government investigation would eventually reveal those schemes and more, including Nixon's millions in illegal contributions and bribes. Yet, Nixon could talk freely only to John Mitchell about some of the matters, such as the CIA-Mafia plots. Knowledge and more direct supervisory responsibility for the various operations were spread among several aides, none of whom knew about the CIA-Mafia plots, the Mafia-Hoffa bribes (except for Colson), or other secrets Nixon needed to keep.

Nixon may have decided to tell John Ehrlichman a little about the CIA-Mafia plots, because after his time alone, Nixon met with him. Nixon later wrote that Watergate wasn't talked about at the meeting, but Ehrlichman says it was briefly discussed, along with wiretapping. As Summers points out, "no tape of that meeting has ever been produced. The tape of the President's next meeting that morning, with Haldeman," contains the eighteen-and-a-half-minute gap. Prosecution and White House experts "would later conclude that the tape's long stretch of buzzing, clicks, and pops reflected a series of overlapping erasures. Someone had manually set the machine to erase at least five times, suggesting that tape was intentionally wiped." Leon Jaworski, the second Watergate Special Prosecutor, said that "only the President had access to both the tape and the machine [at the time of its later erasure, and knew] what was on the tape, and what portion might be incriminating." One lower-level Watergate prosecutor, Jill Wine-Banks, agreed that "most likely it was the President" who erased the tape.[55]

Haldeman's notes of the talk are of little help, since he "emphasized in his own memoirs—and in the context of the eighteen-and-one-half-minute gap—that his notes were often incomplete," and were not about topics discussed, but were "devoted to actions to be assigned or executed." The unusually brief two pages of notes do show that Watergate was the topic at the time of the gap. Haldeman's diary does mention that Nixon "raised [the break-in] in considerable detail today." Looking at Haldeman's concerns for the rest of the day is also revealing, since historian Stanley Kutler points out that "Haldeman's diary entry for this date talked about lengthy meetings with John Ehrlichman, John Mitchell, and John Dean, which concluded that it was necessary to keep the FBI from going 'beyond what's necessary in developing evidence and we can keep a lid on that.'" Those meetings probably reflected Nixon's deep concern that the break-in investigation should not expose his other secrets. In a matter that has never been explained, Dan Moldea found that just "fifty-three minutes" after the eighteen-and-a-half-minute gap, "Nixon placed a long-distance call to . . . an associate of Anthony Provenzano . . . that lasted only one minute." Provenzano had been part of both Nixon-Mafia-Hoffa bribes, for Jimmy Hoffa's December 1971 release and also in September 1960 (at the same time the CIA-Mafia plots with Johnny Rosselli were beginning).[56]

Nixon and Haldeman had another conversation four hours after the one with the eighteen-and-a-half-minute gap, which Nixon started by asking, "Have you gotten any further on that Mitchell operation?"

That remark demonstrates that Nixon felt John Mitchell was really running, at a high level, the Plumbers operation. Nixon and Haldeman talked about the DNC lawsuit, and the President was worried that "they want to get depositions" from those involved—and with that day's developments, he knew that could mean not just Barker, but also Hunt. Haldeman told Nixon that "Hunt disappeared or is in the process of disappearing. He can undisappear if we want him to. He can disappear into a Latin American country. But at least the original thought was that he would do it, that he might want to disappear . . . [unintelligible] on the basis that these guys, the Cubans—see, he was in the Bay of Pigs thing," something Nixon had essentially known since 1960. Haldeman said that "One of the Cubans, Barker . . . was his deputy in the Bay of Pigs operations," though it's not clear if Haldeman was referencing *The New York Times* or knew that already. When Haldeman seemed vague on some of Hunt's activities for the White House, Nixon quickly added "Intelligence." Since McCord worked for CREEP and not the White House, Nixon and Haldeman talked for a bit about exactly which entity actually employed Hunt. Haldeman said he wasn't sure—which seems odd, since even the *Post* had reported that Hunt was a White House consultant.[57]

That evening, "Nixon spoke on the telephone with John Mitchell," the first officially documented "contact between the two since the Watergate arrests." Nixon said they discussed Watergate, and Mitchell essentially apologized, saying that he was "terribly chagrined that the activities of anybody attached to his committee should have been handled in such a manner and that he only regretted that he had not policed all of the people more effectively." However, no recording was made of the call, supposedly "because the call had been placed on a line from the president's private quarters, one that was not hooked into the recording system"—at least, that was what Nixon later told one of his attorneys. Eventually, it was discovered "that Nixon had made a note of the [unrecorded Mitchell] conversation on the Dictabelt machine on which he recorded his daily diary." Even in Nixon's own summary of his conversation with Mitchell, "there is a forty-two-second break in the dictation," and the Watergate Special Prosecution Force stated that Nixon's "Dictabelt appears to have been tampered with" at the time of the break. The tampering was likely because Mitchell's apology—or Nixon's comment about it on the Dictabelt—might have included a reference to the fact Nixon had ordered a reluctant Mitchell to approve the whole political espionage plan in the first place.[58]

There is even more missing evidence from the day of the eighteen-and-a-half-minute gap that is often overlooked. Summers discovered that there are "no tapes of four other calls Nixon received that evening from Haldeman and Colson, even though three of them were made from an office where recording was automatic." From Haldeman's autobiography, we know that Nixon told him that "Watergate might now be 'under control' because of the Cuban involvement." Nixon explained to Haldeman that

> A lot of people think the break-in was done by anti-Castro Cubans . . . I'm going to talk to Bebe and have him round up some anti-Castro Cubans . . . Those people who got caught are going to need money . . . I'm going to have Bebe start a fund for them in Miami. Call it an anti-Castro Fund and publicize the hell out of the Cuban angle. That way we kill two birds with one stone. Get money to the boys to help them, and maybe pick up some points against McGovern on the Cuban angle.[59]

The fund proposed by Nixon for "the boys, " later referred to as the "Cuban Defense Fund," would in fact be created—but not by Rebozo. It would be run by Manuel Artime and would literally be his ticket to Nixon's inauguration, even though Haldeman points out that Nixon would later disingenuously "deny all knowledge of fund-raising activities for the burglars."[60]

Nixon's evening call to Haldeman then veered into "the Bay of Pigs thing" again, in a way that left Haldeman perplexed. The President ordered Haldeman to "tell Ehrlichman this whole group of Cubans is tied to the Bay of Pigs." A confused Haldeman asked, "The Bay of Pigs? What does that have to do with this?" Nixon simply said, "Ehrlichman will know what I mean." This might help to explain Nixon's unrecorded call to Ehrlichman earlier that day. Recall that Ehrlichman had taken the lead in trying to get Helms to give Nixon the Bay of Pigs material starting in 1969, soon after Nixon's Assistant Attorney General had checked out the Justice Department's file on the CIA-Mafia plots involving Johnny Rosselli.[61]

We have only Haldeman's account of this call, in which Nixon could have discussed other subjects or could have given Haldeman more indication of what he meant about the Bay of Pigs. When Haldeman relayed Nixon's message the following day, Haldeman says Ehrlichman was cryptic, and replied, "message accepted." But Ehrlichman said he wanted "to stay out of this one."[62]

However, Nixon's Bay of Pigs comment regarding Ehrlichman—and the eighteen-and-a-half-minute gap—become clearer when we look at Nixon's recorded comments the following morning, June 21, in a meeting with Haldeman. That fact that Hunt's background and involvement in the Watergate break-ins was now in the press "filled Nixon with foreboding," according to Kutler. In the meeting, Nixon talked extensively about Hunt, while Haldeman's mention of Liddy's name brought a "Who's he?" response from Nixon. In contrast, Nixon knew a lot about Hunt, especially his past, saying on tape that Hunt "worked for Kennedy, he worked for Johnson . . . and he worked for the CIA. He worked in the Bay of Pigs. I mean, he's done a lot of things." Nixon brought up Hunt's involvement in ITT, though in some ways, Nixon seemed more familiar with, and concerned by, Hunt's 1960-era work in this and later tapes. Nixon also said that "I think you're going to have Hunt on the lam, if he is, and that's going to be quite a story." Emery observed that Nixon later wrote "in his memoirs" that "It has always been my habit to discuss problems a number of times often in almost the same terms and usually with the same people." That means Nixon's recorded talks with Haldeman that day, and the previous day, likely indicate what was discussed in their talk whose recording was obliterated by the gap.[63]

A review of all of Nixon's known comments and meetings yields clues about what might have been talked about during the eighteen-and-a-half-minute gap on June 20. The press's naming of Hunt, particularly his leading role in the Bay of Pigs operation, seems to have been a concern for Nixon that day. In addition, two of the unrecorded calls from that day involved Mitchell, who knew about the CIA-Mafia plots, and Ehrlichman, who apparently knew more about the Bay of Pigs matter—a euphemism for the CIA-Mafia plots—than Haldeman. The call to the Provenzano associate less than an hour after the eighteen-and-a-half-minute gap also raises the possibility that the gap concerned one or both of the Nixon-Mafia-Hoffa bribes, which were known by John Mitchell. So, it appears likely that the eighteen-and-a-half-minute gap—like other conversations that day—involved some discussion about Hunt and something about the Bay of Pigs (which to Nixon meant the CIA-Mafia plots); it could have also included a reference or allusion to one or both of the Nixon-Mafia-Hoffa bribes. The next time Nixon talked extensively about Hunt, Helms, and the Bay of Pigs would be on the "Smoking Gun" tape, three days later—which also has less-known unexplained erasures.

Richard Helms must have also been very worried about the naming of Hunt and the exposure of his CIA background in the *Times* and the *Post*. Less than six weeks earlier, Helms had been personally pitching Hunt's spy novels to major players in television and films, and now Hunt was—in Nixon's words—"on the lam." Hunt had gone from being an asset to his mentor, Helms, just a week earlier, to now being a major liability and problem. Hunt wrote almost wistfully in his final autobiography about his "enduring friendship" with Helms "that would last until my name was broadcast in connection with Watergate." While Hunt had once been Helms's protégé and "confidant," he lamented that "in the end . . . when the time came when he might have been able to help me and come to my defense, Dick said, 'Oh Hunt . . . Oh, well, I sort of know him. He was a romantic.' And that was all he had to say about me. He pretended that he barely knew me when in fact he had known me for years."[64]

Hunt and McCord would soon be depicted to the press and investigators as minor, bumbling figures in the Agency, scarcely known to Helms. In addition, Helms would have been worried about the other current and former CIA agents still in jail. But from the time of the Bay of Pigs operation, Helms always seemed to have an instinct for self-preservation, which he would demonstrate in the coming weeks and months. As part of that, the Agency backgrounds and positions of all of the CIA men involved in Watergate would be minimized by the press or, in the case of Fiorini and Gonzalez, would almost disappear entirely.

One related matter Nixon talked about in his June 21 meeting with Haldeman was Jack Anderson's most recent column. Anderson stated that "President Nixon's favorite Cuban, Bebe Rebozo . . . has been associated . . .with the Cuban bugging crew." Anderson offered no real specifics, but he might have been tipped off about the business dealings between Rebozo and the real estate companies of Bernard Barker and Eugenio Martinez. The President was angry that "Anderson said Rebozo was involved in it with the Cubans, one of the Cubans." Nixon tried to make it sound like Anderson accused Rebozo of being part of the break-in, but Haldeman pointed out that Anderson hadn't said that. Of course, the real reason Nixon was angry was because he knew or suspected that some of his own business dealings with Rebozo—such as his Key Biscayne estate—were linked to Barker, Martinez, and their associates. We may never know how much Nixon knew about Barker's ties to Rebozo, if Nixon knew that Barker had worked on the CIA-Mafia plots with Hunt in 1960, or if Nixon knew about Barker's ties to Santo Trafficante. Some of that information Nixon would have to have learned from Rebozo, so it's beyond the usual White House tapes and Watergate testimony. It's plausible that Nixon learned at least some of Barker's connections after the fact, because Rebozo would want help in making sure they weren't exposed. Anthony Summers cited Nixon's White House tapes, which showed that

> Bebe Rebozo's name kept being mentioned on the tapes . . . in a way that suggests Nixon was nervous about his friend's vulnerability. At one point, while discussing the fact that Howard Hunt's name had turned up in two of the burglars' contact books, [Nixon] suddenly asked an odd question: "Is Rebozo's name in anyone's address book?"[65]

Nixon's aides likely never realized the extent of Nixon's business ties to Rebozo, and thus to Barker and Martinez, but they wanted to attack Anderson for the angered President. Haldeman soon told Nixon that "'we started a rumor . . . that this whole thing is a Jack Anderson thing, that Jack Anderson did it . . . he was bugging the Democratic offices." Haldeman boasted to Nixon that "the great thing about this [is that the burglary] is so totally fucked up and so badly done that nobody believes—," and Nixon himself added, "That we could have done it."[66]

Nixon's comment was right, because "by Thursday, June 22, the Watergate affair was already sliding down the news agenda," according to Emery. That was illustrated by "Nixon's first news conference [since] the break-in," in which only one question was asked about Watergate, the first one posed. Nixon answered by saying "the White House has had no involvement whatever in this particular incident. As far as the matter now is concerned, it is under investigation, as it should be by the proper legal authorities, by the District of Columbia police, and by the FBI. I will not comment on those matters, particularly since possible criminal charges are involved." Emery stressed that "Amazingly, there was not a single follow-up question from the White House press corps." That tactful tone would start to change the following year, especially by CBS's Dan Rather, but for the first eight months after the break-in, such careful treatment of the President would be the norm.[67]

Meanwhile, Nixon's aides—including John Dean, Ehrlichman, and Haldeman—were trying to come up with a way to limit the investigation, and keep it out of the White House. An early ploy they discussed was to have Liddy take full responsibility. But the problem was that Liddy had been given a lot of money, and that might lead to John Mitchell. Both Haldeman and Ehrlichman thought that Mitchell might be involved, something that Mitchell didn't clearly deny to Haldeman. However, a new problem—and a possible solution—surfaced when acting FBI Director Gray told John Dean that "the FBI had just found out that checks totaling $114,000 had been passed through Barker's account," including four from a Mexican bank.[68]

One local Washington FBI official had passed information up the chain of command suggesting that the Watergate break-in might be a CIA operation. However, that official's superior, "Robert Kunkel, in charge of the Washington field office" of the FBI, had a different theory that he sent to his superiors: "that the Watergate break-in 'was in furtherance of the White House efforts to locate and identify 'leaks.''" Emery notes that Kunkel was right, but his theory "was never explored [and] Kunkel was later demoted [and] died in 1992." Gray may have known Kunkel's theory was too close to the truth, but the Nixon loyalist helpfully passed along the "Watergate was a CIA operation" theory to Dean, to help explain the Mexican checks that Barker had laundered. Dean liked Gray's suggestion, and talked to Mitchell about the Barker check problem and Gray's suggested CIA solution. The claim that the FBI had to stop its investigation to avoid exposing a "CIA operation in Mexico" could "restrict the scope of the [FBI's] investigation to the five men arrested." Dean said that Mitchell and he "hatched the" plan, and Dean called Haldeman about it "first thing the next morning."[69]

On June 23, 1972, in three meetings, Richard Nixon and H.R. Haldeman discussed the Watergate cover-up extensively on what has come to be known as the "Smoking Gun" tape. Nixon was very receptive to using the CIA to block the FBI investigation because he knew secrets about the CIA, Hunt, and Richard Helms that his aides like Haldeman and Dean didn't know or only suspected. In a way, we're lucky that the "Smoking Gun" tape exists at all, and that it involved a conversation with Haldeman—as opposed to the more-informed Mitchell, who already knew about the CIA-Mafia plots. Nixon, not wanting to spread the knowledge of those plots further than it already had been disseminated, kept having to repeatedly imply things about Helms, Hunt, and the plots to Haldeman, leaving a revealing audio trail. Dean and Gray's suggestion was to use the protection of a possible Mexican CIA operation as the excuse to have the CIA limit the FBI investigation, but Nixon quickly went in a very different and telling direction. Nixon's comments on the tape about the CIA weren't fully appreciated when it was finally made public on August 5, 1974, because just the fact that it showed Nixon was actively involved in the cover-up forced the President to resign three days later, on August 8. In addition, the CIA-Mafia plots wouldn't become widely known and documented until the year after the tape's release, and the CIA would continue to withhold important information about the plots for decades after that.[70]

The information documented in this book about Nixon's ties to the 1960 CIA-Mafia plots that grew into the Bay of Pigs operation—and to Hunt and Barker—puts a new spin on Nixon's willingness to have the CIA staunch the FBI's investigation. In the meeting, Nixon refers to Hunt by name, while Barker is simply lumped in with "the Cubans." After Haldeman outlined to Nixon the proposal to use the CIA to limit the FBI, he told Nixon that he wanted to discuss the matter with Richard Helms and CIA Deputy Director Vernon Walters (Nixon's aide when he was Vice President). Nixon's replies on the tape are revealing, especially when compiled below without interruptions from Haldeman, or by brief side comments:[71]

> PRESIDENT NIXON: All right, fine . . . you call him in, I mean you just—well, we protected Helms from one hell of a lot of things.

> PRESIDENT NIXON: Of course, this Hunt will uncover a lot of things. You open that scab, there's a hell of a lot of things and

that we just feel that it would be very detrimental to have this thing go any further. This involves these Cubans, Hunt, and a lot of hanky-panky that we have nothing to do with ourselves.

PRESIDENT NIXON: When you get these people [Helms and Walters] say: "Look, the problem is that this will open the whole, the whole Bay of Pigs thing and the President just feels that . . . The President's belief is that this is going to open the whole Bay of Pigs thing up again. And, because these people are plugging for, for keeps and that they should call the FBI in and say that we wish for the good of the country, don't go any further into this case," period . . .

PRESIDENT NIXON: Hunt . . . knows too damn much and he was involved, we have to know that. And that it gets out . . . this is all involved in the Cuban thing, that it's a fiasco, and it's going to make the FB—ah CIA—look bad, it's going to make Hunt look bad, and its likely to blow the whole, uh, Bay of Pigs thing, which we think would be very unfortunate for the CIA and for the country at this time, and for American foreign policy and he's [Helms] just gotta tell 'em "lay off."

PRESIDENT NIXON: I would just say, "Look it's because of the Hunt involvement."[72]

Clearly, Nixon has his own agenda here, one to pressure Helms by using Hunt's involvement in "the whole, uh, Bay of Pigs thing." Of course, Hunt's leading role in the actual Bay of Pigs invasion and even his cover identity as "Eduardo" had already been announced in *The New York Times* three days earlier, so that wasn't a secret any more. What was left to "blow" about "the whole Bay of Pigs thing" that involved Helms (and Nixon) except the CIA-Mafia plots? After all, neither man was officially involved in the April 1961 invasion. Nixon's comments about "for the good of the country" and "for American foreign policy" are also telling, but they make sense in terms of the harm revealing the CIA-Mafia plots could do, especially if it led to the exposure of Commander Almeida and his secret work for JFK. Also, Nixon was the one that brought up the Bay of Pigs angle on the "Smoking Gun" tape, not Haldeman—the original plan the Chief of

Staff was pitching to Nixon had only involved a possible Mexican CIA operation.[73]

Nixon knew that Helms could be difficult to deal with from his previous fights to try to get "the Bay of Pigs" material. So, the President felt that he needed to give Haldeman more ammunition to pressure Helms, using terms that Helms would understand without Nixon having to fully explain them to Haldeman. It's possible that Nixon had used the "Bay of Pigs" euphemism before when talking with Helms about the CIA-Mafia plots, and felt that Helms would immediately realize what Haldeman was relaying from Nixon. In a later taped conversation with Nixon, Haldeman himself would frame Nixon's orders to him on June 23 by telling the President that "you had some knowledge that I didn't know about—that Helms was concerned about some Bay of Pigs stuff at that point in time." The détente and cooperation that came after Nixon had helped Helms with the Victor Marchetti book situation was now replaced by a new, tough stance on the part of Nixon. The President told Haldeman on June 23: "You call them in . . . Play it tough. That's the way they play it and that's the way we are going to play it."[74]

Nixon apparently wanted Helms to help him solve two problems. First, to use the CIA to limit the FBI's investigation. The second problem was that Nixon no longer had a way to find out more about—or stop the leak of—the Cuban Dossier and anything it might say about Nixon's role in the CIA-Mafia plots. That could still be devastating if it came out before the election, especially if it caused journalists and investigators to look for other ties between Nixon and the mob. Nixon seemed to want Helms to take responsibility for the Cuban Dossier matter as well, and appears to be trying to convey that through Haldeman.

One sign that the "Smoking Gun" tape's conversations between Nixon and Haldeman might indicate the contents of their conversation three days earlier, on the eighteen-and-a-half-minute-gap tape, is that portions of the "Smoking Gun" tape also appear to have been erased. When Anthony Summers had two researchers repeatedly listen to a copy of the tape at the National Archives, they found that it "appears to have at least six unexplained erasures," of apparently brief duration. It is surprising that Haldeman, at least on the tape as it exists today, never thought to ask Nixon what it was about "the Bay of Pigs" that would pressure Helms.[75]

As for Nixon's comment that "we protected Helms from one hell of a lot of things," Nixon later said he was referring to his help for Helms regarding suppressing parts of Victor Marchetti's book. But Nixon didn't say "one thing" on the tape, he said "one hell of a lot of things," which led investigators to wonder what else Nixon could have been referring to. Helms's Chilean and domestic spying operations had all been done for Nixon, so those hardly seem like instances in which Nixon "protected" Helms. Congressional investigator Michael Ewing looked at the matter in a report for the House Select Committee on Assassinations in the late 1970s. Ehrlichman claimed not to know what Nixon had protected Helms from, or what the "whole Bay of Pigs thing" was referring to. But Ewing found it interesting that Ehrlichman had just published a "new 'political novel' [in which] he writes about a President (not unlike Nixon) who blackmails a CIA Director (not unlike Helms) over a secret CIA Inspector General's Report about CIA-connected assassination plotting." (Parentheses in original.) The following year, Ehrlichman would finally tell Haldeman that "the CIA was very concerned about the Bay of Pigs" because when Ehrlichman had investigated the matter for Nixon, he discovered "there is a key memo missing that CIA or somebody"—meaning Helms—"has caused to disappear [regarding] what really did happen on the Bay of Pigs."[76]

That comes back yet again to the CIA-Mafia plots. While Nixon would have been most worried about his involvement with Maheu in getting the CIA to hire Johnny Rosselli in September 1960 (which then led to the involvement of Santo Trafficante, Sam Giancana, and others), Helms would have been most worried about 1963. Jack Anderson had already written more than once that the plots with Rosselli continued into 1963, and Nixon would have realized they could not have continued without Helms's authorization. Nixon had only slight contact with the plots in 1963, but Helms would have learned (or strongly suspected) that those operations had apparently somehow been involved in JFK's assassination, as shown by the later JFK confessions of Rosselli and Trafficante.

Haldeman himself made that point in his 1978 autobiography, writing that "in all those Nixon references to the 'Bay of Pigs,' he was actually referring to the Kennedy assassination." In other words, Haldeman explained, "when Nixon said, 'It's likely to blow the whole Bay of Pigs thing,' he might have been reminding Helms, not so gently, of the cover-up of the CIA assassination attempts on . . . Fidel Castro—a CIA operation that may have triggered the Kennedy tragedy, and which Helms desperately wanted to hide." Haldeman went on to say that "as an outgrowth of the Bay of Pigs, the CIA made several attempts on Fidel Castro's life," including at a time when "the Deputy Director of Plans at the CIA . . . was a man named Richard Helms." Haldeman also wrote that when he "first entered the [Nixon] White House," he "suggested" an "investigation of the Kennedy assassination . . . but Nixon turned me down." The bottom line is that Haldeman felt that Nixon had protected Helms on those sensitive matters.[77]

Just how sensitive those matters were to Helms would soon become all too obvious to Haldeman. The same day as the "Smoking Gun" tape's conversations, Haldeman and Ehrlichman met with CIA Director Helms and Deputy Director Walters in Ehrlichman's office at the White House. The two Nixon aides made their pitch, approved by the President and crafted by Dean and Mitchell, to have the CIA ask the FBI to limit the Bureau's investigation to just the five burglars, because doing otherwise would compromise a current CIA operation in Mexico. Haldeman and Ehrlichman wanted Walters to go see Gray and ask him to limit the investigation. But Helms told them "no way," and "they're not connected," referring to the Watergate break-in and any CIA operation in Mexico.[78]

Haldeman said he then "played Nixon's trump card," and relayed the message the President had ordered him to convey to Helms: "The President asked me to tell you this entire affair may be connected to the Bay of Pigs and if it opens up, the Bay of Pigs may be blown."[79]

Helms erupted in rage. According to Haldeman, there was suddenly "turmoil in the room, Helms gripping the arms of his chair leaning forward and shouting, 'The Bay of Pigs had nothing to do with this! I have no concern about the Bay of Pigs!'" Haldeman was "absolutely shocked by Helms's violent reaction [and] wondered what was such dynamite in the Bay of Pigs story?" Haldeman then told Helms, "I'm just following my instructions, Dick. This is what the President told me to relay to you." Haldeman wrote that Helms then calmed down, settled back and said, "All right."[80]

(The next time Helms would explode in rage would be a public, profanity-laced tirade against Daniel Schorr in 1975, after Helms had finally been forced to testify to Congress about the CIA-Mafia plots, as detailed in Chapter 32.)

Haldeman said that Helms's whole attitude about his request "had changed. Now surprisingly, the two CIA officials expressed no concern about the request that Walters go to see Gray. And Walters later testified that when he and Helms went downstairs they talked briefly and Helms said, 'You must remind Mr. Gray of the agreement between the FBI and the CIA that if they run into or expose one another's 'assets'... they will not interfere with each other.' Meaning 'FBI, stop the investigation.' Just what Nixon wanted."[81]

Helms went along with Nixon's request, writing a memo to Walters saying that the CIA was requesting the FBI to "confine themselves to the personalities already arrested... and that they desist from expanding the investigation into other areas which may well, eventually, run afoul of our operations." In later years, Richard Helms would make a point of telling journalists that he had never succumbed to pressure to get the FBI to back off from its Watergate investigation, something repeated by many journalists and several historians. But the record clearly shows Helms did call off the FBI, at least for a time. Summers points out that "key interviews were stalled" by the FBI because of Helms. Even after the CIA would finally allow the FBI to resume a somewhat more thorough investigation by mid-July, Helms still withheld crucial information about the backgrounds of Hunt, Fiorini, and other Watergate participants from the Bureau, other government investigators, the DNC/Califano lawsuit, and eventually from Congress.[82]

Because Nixon had Haldeman evoke "the whole Bay of Pigs thing," Helms delayed the FBI's investigation at a critical time. That not only prevented the Watergate scandal from expanding, but also kept it from gaining traction in the press, and the whole matter soon began to fade from the headlines.

CHAPTER 32

Late June 1972 to December 1972: The Cover-Up Holds and Reelection

"I ordered the Plumbers operation . . ."
President Richard Nixon, taped phone call to H.R. Haldeman

Richard Nixon's guiding role in defining the Watergate cover-up from the top down is missing from many Watergate accounts because the Smoking Gun tape was released so late in the process. The public would only hear the tape after the Senate Watergate Committee had completed its hearings and investigation, once *All the President's Men* was a bestseller, and after various aides and officials had testified about the cover-up, often trying to avoid responsibility or blaming other aides. Like any Chief Executive, Nixon didn't usually know the details of how his policies and directives were implemented, but he set the tone for the cover-up in the week after Watergate for his aides and officials to follow: Stall investigations and the release of information, even if it meant breaking more laws. Amazingly, even beyond the cover-up, Nixon would also continue to commit new crimes both before and after the election. In doing so, Nixon was continuing a pattern he had begun during his first run for office back in 1946.

After Watergate, CIA Director Richard Helms not only limited the FBI's investigation at a critical time, but he would also withhold information from investigators and lie to Congress. Helms was continuing the pattern he began in 1962, when he started withholding information on his continuation of the CIA-Mafia plots from Presidents and two CIA Directors, before he ascended to that same office. Like Nixon, Helms would set the tone for the CIA's lack of compliance with Congressional investigations, but in Helms's case it would far outlast his own tenure as CIA Director. In some ways, the cover-ups Helms began in the week after Watergate are maintained by the Agency today: Current estimates of the number of relevant CIA files that remain unreleased in 2012 despite the 1992 JFK Act—including important files about Hunt, Barker, Rosselli, Almeida, and AMWORLD—range from fifty thousand pages to over a million. Estimates have to suffice, since the CIA and the National Archives have not revealed the exact number. However, files that have been released indicate that most of those unreleased files are in some way connected to people involved in the CIA-Mafia plots, including participants such as Santo Trafficante and Manuel Artime. That demonstrates the sensitivity about the issue that remains even today, which helps to explain why so much was hidden or withheld in the aftermath of the Watergate arrests.[1]

In late June 1972, E. Howard Hunt was keeping a low profile, and he had not yet been charged or arrested. G. Gordon Liddy's name had not yet surfaced in public, and it wouldn't for three more weeks. Nixon wanted to make sure that they, and the other defendants, remained quiet and didn't implicate the White House. As Fred Emery wrote, that would take "large cash sums and promises of clemency." On June 30, the tapes reveal that Nixon told H.R. Haldeman, "I'll pardon the bastards," and executive clemency for the burglars and others involved would be a recurring theme for Nixon in the coming months. On June 29, Nixon's personal attorney, Herbert Kalmbach, gave John Caulfield's partner $75,000 in cash to deliver to "the defendants and their lawyers." Some $219,000 would be distributed to them in less than three months, with at least another $237,000 after that.[2]

A month later, on a White House tape of a meeting with Haldeman, Nixon called the hush money for Hunt and the others "a considerable cost," but said that "It's worth it." Haldeman protested that "it's very expensive. It's a costly—," but Nixon interrupted him to say, "That's what the money is for . . . they have to be paid. That's all there is to that." For Nixon, "keeping Hunt happy"—as Haldeman put it—was a high priority. The tapes make it clear that Nixon, and aides such as Colson, admired some of Hunt's exploits while dreading what he could reveal.[3]

Nixon would tell John Dean the following year that "Well, your major guy to keep under control is Hunt. Because he knows—about a lot of other things." In October 1972, Nixon would allude to one of those "other things" in a taped meeting with Haldeman and Treasury Secretary John Connally, saying that Hunt "was working the Pentagon Papers, trying to make sure it was Ellsberg. He found out about his girlfriend." Nixon's "girlfriend" comment might have been a reference to Ellsberg's close friendship with the daughter of Desmond FitzGerald, the CIA official who continued the CIA-Mafia plots with Richard Helms—a connection that had alarmed CIA officials. Given Hunt's role in the CIA-Mafia plots, for a time nothing Hunt did seemed to surprise Nixon. In a June 30, 1972, meeting, the President told Haldeman "About this fellow [Hunt]—I mean, after all, the gun [found in Hunt's White House office safe] and the wiretapping doesn't bother me a bit with this fellow. He's in the Cuban thing, the whole Cuban business." In transcripts of Nixon's taped conversations days after the Plumbers' arrests, when Colson told Nixon on July 1, 1972, that Hunt had "certainly done a lot of hot stuff . . . Oh, Jesus. He pulled a lot of very fancy stuff in the sixties," that was followed by a notice from the National Archives: "[Withdrawn item. National security.]" After the censored portion, Nixon then said, "If anything ever happens to him, be sure that he blows the whistle, [on] the whole Bay of Pigs."[4]

In addition to the hush money flowing to Hunt and the others from Kalmbach and White House operatives, there was also another channel of money. Nixon had wanted Bebe Rebozo to set up a fund for "the boys," but it had to be done in a deniable way that could not be traced to the President. That task fell to Manuel Artime, an office tenant in Rebozo's mob-built shopping center. Lukas wrote that Artime "formed an informal committee to aide the Miami defendants." He pointed out since Artime was "a leader of the Cuban exile community and the godfather of Hunt's youngest son, he was an ideal man to assume the role" of a hush money paymaster without arousing suspicion.[5]

Artime's hush money fund also helped to ingratiate Artime with Nixon. Former Congressional investigators Bud Fensterwald and Michael Ewing documented that "the Senate Watergate Committee investigation disclosed that President Nixon had personal knowledge of Manuel Artime's early hush money payments to the Watergate burglars," which is probably why "Artime was invited by the Nixon Administration to attend the second inauguration of President Nixon." Nixon talked on tape about some of the hush money being "under the cover of a Cuban Committee," and he wanted to keep it going into the spring of 1973. Journalist Haynes Johnson later wrote that Artime's assistant at the time, Milian Rodriguez, said that the amounts Artime distributed to Barker and the others were much larger than most investigators realized. As documented by PBS, Milian Rodriguez later used the skills he first learned with Artime by handling the Watergate hush money to become one of Miami's largest drug traffickers. Artime would have to testify to the Watergate grand jury, but he would never be charged for his Watergate involvement or for his drug trafficking (documented in earlier chapters).[6]

It was initially difficult to get the Watergate defendants' attorneys to take the envelopes stuffed with cash. Finally, after two weeks, Hunt's second attorney—William Bittman—"accepted a bizarre delivery of $25,000 in an envelope left on a ledge in the downstairs lobby of" his law firm. Bittman had been a Mafia prosecutor for Robert Kennedy's Justice Department before leaving in 1967 to enter private practice. Liddy had no qualms about accepting the hush money, and a money drop for him was arranged "at National Airport, where the cash was in a luggage locker."[7]

Hunt's wife, Dorothy, gave the White House money courier "a five-month 'budget' for all seven men involved [that] totaled $450,000," while Hunt sent Colson a personal note saying that "re-electing the President" was of "overwhelming importance [and] you may be confident that I will do all that is required of me toward that end." That was no doubt reassuring for Colson and the President, after the FBI began a nationwide manhunt for Hunt on July 1. Because Hunt and his involvement had been publicly disclosed by *The New York Times* and *The Washington Post* so soon after the break-in, it wasn't really possible for Helms to protect his now former protégé. So Hunt remained a wanted fugitive for only six days before sending word through his attorney that he would turn himself in.[8]

After Hunt's arrest, the American publishers and press that Hunt had previously dealt with never revealed their ties to the former CIA official. They simply had no incentive to tout their own links to Hunt, especially if they wanted to maintain their own credibility with the public or their relationships with the CIA. Their silence was made easier by the steady leak of stories that would soon begin, emphasizing the gaffes Hunt had made over the years while ignoring his high-ranking posts, sensitive assignments, and friendship with CIA Director Helms.

Hunt's actions after his arrest seem primarily concerned with watching out for his own self-interest while still protecting Nixon and the CIA. His friend and assistant Barker also had to protect his longtime boss, Santo Trafficante. The latter was also true for Frank Fiorini, which is why he almost never talked publicly about his ties to the mob, except for those he had before leaving Cuba in 1959.

Nixon's men continued to plan and coordinate the Watergate cover-up in July 1972, even after John Mitchell resigned as CREEP Director on July 1. Mitchell claimed he resigned so he could spend more time with his troubled wife, Martha. In actuality, Martha Mitchell had grown increasingly frustrated with her husband's activities for Nixon and wanted to speak out about it. A week before her husband resigned, she had called "Helen Thomas of UPI" to tell her about some of the things she knew about—until "the phone [was] ripped out of the wall by" her husband's security guard. Martha Mitchell's claims to Helen Thomas and other reporters that "Nixon is involved with the Mafia. The Mafia was involved in his election," would soon be widely derided in the press as the delusions of a mentally ill alcoholic, even though many of her claims were later shown to be true.[9]

After his resignation, John Mitchell continued to lead the cover-up for Nixon from "his office in his law firm, which was just across the hall from CREEP." Jeb Magruder wrote that meetings about the cover-up led by Mitchell included not only himself, but also Fred LaRue "and sometimes Dean and [Robert] Mardian," CREEP's Deputy Director. After a couple of weeks, some problems surfaced with the CIA-FBI deal to limit the Watergate investigation. At the Bureau, Assistant FBI Director Mark Felt resented the fact that the man who had taken the top position he felt he deserved was now limiting the Watergate investigation. At the Agency, CIA Deputy Director Vernon Walters was not the complete Nixon loyalist his predecessor, General Cushman, had been. Walters later testified that John Dean had first tried to get him to use CIA funds to pay the Watergate defendants, but he had refused. Within limits, Walters tried to be helpful, even suggesting to Dean an "anti-Castro" cover story to explain the break-in. A story like that was floated for a while but failed to gain traction, though it did serve to distract reporters and the public.[10]

However, when FBI Director L. Patrick Gray—under pressure from Felt and others in the Bureau—told Walters that "he will need written CIA authorization [to keep] restricting the FBI's investigation,"

Walters began to balk, lest he be drawn personally into the cover-up. Walters told Gray he couldn't put the authorization in writing, which led Gray to talk to Nixon directly. Gray later said that at the time, he still thought the Watergate operations were entirely the idea and work of Nixon's aides, so he told Nixon he should fire those responsible. Nixon didn't reveal his own culpability to Gray, and following more conversations between Gray and Walters, by July 13 the FBI was conducting a somewhat more expansive Watergate investigation. However, Gray continued to keep Nixon's White House informed of the FBI's progress by supplying transcripts of interviews to John Dean, as reported much later by *The New York Times*. This no doubt stiffened Mark Felt's resolve to continue leaking information to Bob Woodward. The flow of Gray's FBI information to the White House often went through Attorney General Richard Kleindienst, who would publicly promise the following month "that the Justice Department will undertake 'the most extensive, thorough and comprehensive investigation since the assassination of President Kennedy.'"[11]

During the Watergate cover-up, Nixon's White House continued to mount new operations against the Democrats. Nixon talked on tape with Charles Colson about staging a fake break-in at RNC "headquarters to make people think the Democrats were as guilty as the Republicans." Nixon told Colson "there would be a rifling [of files and] missing files . . . something where it's really torn up, where pictures could be taken." In making those plans, Nixon accurately mirrored what happened when his Plumbers had broken into Daniel Ellsberg's psychiatrist's office the previous year. While no RNC break-in occurred, Anthony Summers pointed out that before the election there was "an apparent break-in at the office of the President's California physician . . . cash was ignored, but a file containing Nixon's patient records [was] left disordered on the floor. Haldeman and an aide called the FBI at the highest level fifteen times, urging that the Bureau issue a press release on the case." But "Mark Felt turned down the request, saying it was a matter for the local police." However, "Felt came to suspect someone at the White House" was behind the break-in, so they could "show that President Nixon had also been a victim of such tactics."[12]

Even as Jeb Magruder was plotting cover-up strategy with John Mitchell about one failed operation, Nixon Chief of Staff H.R. Haldeman called Magruder and asked "him to 'get someone into

McGovern's headquarters in July.'" Richard Gerstein, "the state's attorney for the Miami area . . . concluded that the Fontainebleau Hotel, headquarters for the Democratic convention, was bugged [and that] ground work for the operation had been laid by [E. Howard] Hunt before his arrest." Even Gerstein's "own office had been broken into within weeks" after he started to investigate the "Miami-based" burglars. Summers found that "there had also been a break-in at the Texas home of Lawrence O'Brien's close colleague Robert Strauss," who would later become DNC Chairman. Strauss's "house had been ransacked, but jewelry worth [over $100,000 was] left untouched."[13]

On his tapes, Nixon also talked about using the IRS against O'Brien, and hoped McGovern "might have feet of clay . . . kick him again . . . keep whacking, whacking, whacking [and] on O'Brien [see if] you could dirty up O'Brien." Nixon said to "get everything you possibly can . . . any little crumb or lead involving anyone." Unfortunately for Nixon, "O'Brien's [tax] records were in order." Given Nixon's problems with Watergate, it's surprising that "even months after the Watergate arrests, when discussing with Haldeman and [John] Dean how to obtain the tax files of political enemies, President Nixon would unhesitatingly suggest a break-in. 'There are ways to do it . . . Goddamnit, sneak in in the middle of the night,'" Nixon said on tape. Apparently, the pervasive sense of lawlessness in the Nixon White House had changed little after the Watergate arrests. That was especially surprising since the federal trial of Daniel Ellsberg and his codefendant, Tony Russo, had been stayed on July 29, 1972, by Supreme Court Justice William O. Douglas. He ruled that defense attorneys should be allowed to appeal to the full "Court their contention that the government should be required to divulge details of [a] wire tapped conversation" involving Ellsberg. However, Nixon was determined to see Ellsberg prosecuted, and the trial would eventually be allowed to proceed.[14]

The possibility that the final Watergate break-in had been sabotaged by one or more of the perpetrators soon began showing up in Nixon's taped conversations. However, that possibility was usually brought up by aides, often those who hadn't been closely involved with the burglaries. The CIA was considered as a source of the sabotage, though Nixon himself immediately ruled out Hunt as a possible saboteur, likely because he or aides such as General Cushman had worked with Hunt for more than a decade. Nixon's attitude toward

Hunt would eventually change, but aside from indulging the speculations of his aides, the President didn't seem to really embrace sabotage as a likely option.[15]

Many authors have promoted the idea that the final Watergate burglary was sabotaged from the inside, though most of those theories were formed before the release of additional Nixon audiotapes in the 1990s that made his culpability clearer. Some of the Watergate burglars themselves—especially Fiorini, and exiles such as Barker—promoted their own sabotage theories, usually directed at the CIA and James McCord. However, British researcher John Simkin compiled a list of the mistakes committed by each of those involved with the burglaries, which showed that while McCord committed seven critical errors, so had G. Gordon Liddy, who had no connection to the CIA. Simkin listed Barker as committing six critical errors, along with eight by Hunt. Fiorini himself committed several key errors, including the final taping of the garage stairwell door and insisting the burglary go forward even if it required the time-consuming step of removing the rear door to the DNC offices. Fiorini initially blamed his longtime associate Barker for the mission's failure (though not from sabotage), but he later fell in line with the exile burglars in blaming McCord. In the final analysis, there wasn't one error, but many, and they were not made by one person, but by several (including those making claims of sabotage against other people or agencies). In addition, if Helms and the CIA had sabotaged the final break-in to remove Nixon from office, Helms would have used his—and the Agency's—considerable media clout to expose Nixon's role before the election, instead of doing just the opposite and helping to contain the scandal.[16]

In reality, no sabotage was necessary for the final mission's failure. After all, it took three attempts just to gain access to the DNC offices in the first place, and one of that crew was caught by a guard on the third attempt (only to be released). With so many planned and attempted break-ins in such a relatively short span of time—not just at the Watergate, but at the Chilean embassy and other targets too—it was almost inevitable that one was bound to fail in a major way.

It was Nixon's desperation to learn the contents of the full Cuban Dossier that pressed the break-in efforts forward, probably through his pressure on John Mitchell, who then pushed Magruder, Liddy, and others. Nixon himself essentially explained to Haldeman how such matters worked, in a June 29, 1972, meeting at Nixon's hideaway office in the old Executive Office Building, which was near Hunt's office. Regarding John Mitchell's orders to the Plumbers, Nixon said, "I think . . . John said well, we're trying to get information, [and] he said well, don't tell me anything about it. You know, that's the way you do it." That's probably also "the way" Nixon gave his orders about the matter to Mitchell, saying they needed to get certain information and "don't tell me anything about" how it was going to be done.[17]

Most people don't realize that Nixon admitted on his White House tapes some of his own role in the scandal. The following spring, on May 20, 1973, as he desperately sought a way out of what had finally become a serious public crisis, Nixon told Haldeman in a taped phone call,

> I'm going to put out all of the national security kind of stuff . . . because I'm going to take—say that I ordered the Plumbers operation, that I ordered the meeting. I'm going to say that I directed that you and John [Ehrlichman] meet with Helms and Walters . . .[18]

However, Nixon didn't follow through with what he told Haldeman, either in 1973 or at any other time, and he never really took responsibility for his role in the scandal. Practically speaking, Nixon could not state his real national security rationale for the break-ins at the Watergate (and the Chilean embassy), which was to prevent the exposure of the CIA-Mafia plots to kill Fidel Castro, and his role in them. Nixon also couldn't publicly use the national security justification of protecting the CIA's past work with Commander Juan Almeida without risking Almeida's life and high-ranking position in Castro's government.

Instead, even in private, Nixon would usually try to blame others. When Ehrlichman would tell Nixon in December 1972 that if they "dump" the responsibility on Mitchell, then his subordinates will say that "Mitchell was in eighteen meetings where this was discussed, ratified, approved, authorized, financed." Nixon asked, "Was he?" Ehrlichman replied, "I gather so." Nixon then pronounced, "Well, Mitchell then did it . . . " The following year, in a taped talk with John Dean, Nixon kept stressing to him, "I know very well it had to be a higher-up" who gave the order to go back into the Watergate. "They wouldn't have done it because Magruder told them to, or Hugh

Sloan told them, and we've just got to recognize that." Of course, the "higher-up" who gave Mitchell his orders was Nixon. In that same conservation with Dean, Nixon revealed his own thinking that played a role in the Watergate scandal, when he said that "Espionage and sabotage is illegal only if against the government."[19]

Tape transcripts from the summer of 1972 and into the following spring reveal a striking number of meetings held by Nixon and his aides, as they attempted to find a permanent way out of the Watergate scandal—only for them to realize there was no really viable option. In addition, just weeks after the final break-in, Nixon started lying about the affair to less-informed aides and officials, one day admitting on tape various problems, and the next day denying to someone like the new head of CREEP that he even knew those problems existed. That tendency would accelerate the following year, to the point where—by spring 1973—Nixon was lying not only to new aides, but to old ones like Haldeman and Ehrlichman, who would then have to point out to Nixon that he had, in fact, ordered or discussed matters that he claimed to no longer recall. However, Nixon would usually remember enough—or have refreshed his memory from notes or the tapes—to always spin specific details in his favor, in a way that cast him in the most non-culpable light.[20]

While Nixon and his men kept the Watergate scandal largely contained in the summer and early fall of 1972, attorney Joseph Califano was trying hard to keep it in the public eye and stop Nixon's reelection. He was involved in some of the delegate wrangling leading up to the 1972 Democratic National Convention in Miami, which—while not as fractious as the 1968 convention—was still beset by dissension. Because George Wallace had won several Democratic primaries, he had to be given a speaking slot at the convention, making an odd contrast with George McGovern, the peace candidate who finally secured the nomination. That contrast, and Wallace's extremism, helped make Nixon even more appealing to independent voters.

McGovern wounded his candidacy from the start when he named Missouri Senator Thomas Eagleton as his running mate, without realizing he had undergone psychiatric hospitalization "three times [which] included electroshock treatments." In 1972, being treated—let alone hospitalized—for depression as was Eagleton was not considered widely acceptable, as it is today. In addition, there is plenty of evidence that Nixon's operatives helped to inflame the Eagleton crisis. Mark Felt later told Bob Woodward that "the business of Eagleton's . . . health records, I understand, involves the White House and Hunt somehow," possibly referring to Miami operatives Hunt had in place before his arrest. Felt told Woodward that "Senator Eagleton's health records had arrived in John Ehrlichman's office before they were leaked to the press." The tip might have originated with a "CREEP . . . private detective" who had been planted "in the McGovern camp at the Democratic convention . . . who later admitted having overheard a discussion about Eagleton's personal history." Decades later, Alexander Butterfield confirmed that "Haldeman once intimated to me that they had stuff on Eagleton [about his treatment and] were just waiting to spring it, waiting for the right time."[21]

Someone leaked the story to a newspaper reporter, who asked Eagleton about the matter. When Eagleton answered truthfully, the storm broke and Nixon talked on tape about how to exploit the situation. Haldeman suggested planting hecklers to shout remarks at Eagleton appearances, and Nixon said they should say, "Why did you lie to McGovern? Why did you lie to McGovern about your heath?" When the news about Eagleton broke, McGovern vacillated, first publicly proclaiming he was behind Eagleton "one thousand percent," only to ask DNC attorney Califano the next day to advise him on how to replace a Vice Presidential candidate. McGovern was then turned down by several Democratic heavyweights that he wanted on the ticket, including Senators Edward Kennedy, Hubert Humphrey, and Edmund Muskie. McGovern finally settled on, and announced, the selection of former Peace Corps Director Sargent Shriver. After the convention, Califano resigned as "counsel for the Democratic National Committee," though he continued to help with "the lawsuit [he'd] filed against [CREEP]." Califano kept working on the lawsuit because he "believed that Richard Nixon was deeply involved in the Watergate break-in [and] now I would try to prove it."[22]

Larry O'Brien also resigned after the convention, while continuing to tell Califano "that Nixon was personally involved [in the Watergate break-in] but that as yet [he] couldn't prove it." Califano tried to persuade McGovern's campaign managers Frank Mankiewicz and Gary Hart to make a major issue of the Watergate break-in, since Califano thought it "could prove to be Richard Nixon's Achilles' heel." Back in Washington, at a July 21 meeting at the Mayflower Hotel, Califano wrote that he told Mankiewicz and Hart "everything I knew, plus what I suspected we might learn over the summer and fall," including O'Brien's belief that Nixon was involved. However, unlike *The Washington Post*—which had immediately followed Califano's advice about pursuing the Watergate story, and in a big way—Mankiewicz and Hart proved reluctant. They indicated to Califano they weren't interested, since they were "convinced that McGovern's commitment to pull out of Vietnam would win the election."[23]

Unknown to Califano, Frank Mankiewicz might have had another reason for being initially reluctant to focus on the Watergate issue. As described in Chapter 20, five years earlier Robert Kennedy had asked Mankiewicz to privately investigate the assassination of John F. Kennedy. Mankiewicz had come "to the conclusion that there was some sort of conspiracy, probably involving the mob, anti-Castro Cuban exiles, and maybe rogue CIA agents." As a Kennedy and Washington insider and savvy PR man, Mankiewicz certainly would have been aware of Jack Anderson's 1967 and 1971 articles about the CIA-Mafia plots, which blamed Robert Kennedy for the plots that had lasted from the Bay of Pigs until 1963. Given the then-recent *New York Times* story about the key roles of Hunt and Barker in the Bay of Pigs operation—and the Watergate arrests of other Cuban exiles and former CIA agents such as Fiorini—Mankiewicz might not have wanted to cast extra light on the scandal at that time, not knowing what else might emerge. However, he would soon change his mind.[24]

Within weeks of telling Califano that they weren't interested, Mankiewicz and the McGovern campaign completely changed their Watergate strategy. The campaign decided to make Watergate a major issue, and McGovern was soon denouncing "Watergate in most of his speeches and suggest[ing] in no uncertain terms that the White House was behind the burglary." The reason for the complete reversal isn't clear. It could have resulted from information Mankiewicz received from a Kennedy aide familiar with the 1963 Cuban operations (including the involvement of Hunt and Barker), or for some other reason. In any event, according to Edward Epstein, the McGovern campaign that Mankiewicz and Hart were running decided to hire someone "to help 'get out' the story" of Watergate to the press and public. That person was someone else who, like Mankiewicz, had conducted for Robert Kennedy a secret investigation of JFK's murder: Walter Sheridan.[25]

In many ways, Walter Sheridan seemed an ideal choice to "get out" the Watergate story for McGovern's campaign. His experience working for NBC should have left him with good contacts at the network, and he knew many of Robert Kennedy's former aides and associates. In addition, Sheridan's own book exposé on the crimes of Jimmy Hoffa was being prepared for publication, and it would focus attention on the unusual circumstances of Hoffa's release by Nixon the previous year. Teamsters President Frank Fitzsimmons had announced his union's support for Nixon on July 17, so the time seemed ripe to start releasing the information in Sheridan's book, which called into question Hoffa's release and the Nixon-Teamsters-Mafia relationship.[26]

However, Walter Sheridan didn't release or leak any of the Hoffa information during the campaign, and it's not known why. In addition, Walter Sheridan was spectacularly unsuccessful in bringing media attention to the Watergate story. It's possible he tried and simply couldn't arouse any interest. But that doesn't explain why he didn't leak or publish before the election his information about Nixon's illegal dealings with the Mafia in 1960 involving Hoffa and the Teamsters.

Sheridan might have felt that once he was working for the McGovern campaign, leaking that information might have looked too partisan and political. It could also have given Hoffa new grounds to appeal his conviction—which, if overturned, could allow Hoffa to immediately resume his involvement in Teamsters activities. Regardless of the reason, a huge opportunity was lost for Watergate and the Nixon-Mafia-Hoffa relationship to become issues in the final months of the 1972 campaign.

That pretty much left it up to Joseph Califano, his client *The Washington Post*, and a few other media outlets to expose as much of the Watergate story as possible before the election. But Califano's lawsuit for the DNC against CREEP was stymied at every turn. At first, Hunt, Colson, and the Watergate burglars refused to show up for depositions. Califano got "U.S. district court Judge Charles Richey" to "compel testimony," but suddenly "on his own, Richey issued an order sealing all depositions." Even though the defendants were sticking to their cover stories, their depositions could still have been useful in Califano's effort to keep Watergate alive in the press. Califano thought the judge was "trying to protect the Nixon administration from any embarrassment before the election." Califano became even "more suspicious when [he] learned that Richey had called . . . Carl

Bernstein, whom he had never met, to justify his ruling," with the judge claiming to Bernstein, "I haven't discussed this case outside the courtroom with anyone, and that political considerations played no part whatsoever" in his decision.[27]

Califano and the DNC were fortunate when they learned about, and gained access to, Alfred Baldwin, James McCord's surveillance assistant. But they still couldn't publicize what he said in his deposition, because of Judge Richey's ruling. To try to get some press attention, Califano amended his original complaint, adding more defendants (such as Maurice Stans) and calling more people to give depositions. However, Judge Richey himself suggested to Stans that he file a libel suit against the DNC, which Stans promptly did. Next, Califano wrote that Judge Richey "pressured me to join [the RNC] attorneys in [announcing] that we would postpone all activity in the case until after the election!" When Califano refused, Judge Richey "asked that [Califano] agree to stop all depositions until after the election." When Califano refused yet again, Judge Richey ordered "an indefinite stay of all proceedings" and halted "more than forty depositions" that Califano was ready to take "until completion of the Watergate criminal trial." With those actions, Califano wrote that "Judge Richey's stay had effectively shielded Nixon from any potential embarrassment as a result of the civil suit, until after the election."[28]

The intervention of Judge Richey to protect Nixon was no accident. Two days after Joseph Califano first filed the suit, Haldeman pointed out to Nixon that Califano had erred in filing "the suit on behalf of all Democrats" because that disqualified "any Democratic judge from hearing" the case. In fact, "the next judge up was a Democratic judge," but instead the case had to be assigned to Judge Richey, who Haldeman told Nixon "has a very solid—." Nixon then interrupted Haldeman to say of Judge Richey, "I know him." In the tape transcripts, the National Archives has "withdrawn" the rest of Nixon's comments about Richey on "privacy" grounds. However, later tapes show that "[Judge] Richey was actively <u>seeking</u> guidance from Nixon" while he dealt with the case. (Emphasis in original.) On September 15, 1972, "John Dean told Nixon" that Richey "made several entrées, uh, off the bench to, uh, one, Kleindienst" and to an "old friend" who was "the general counsel of the Republican National Finance Committee." With contacts like those, Dean was able to tell Nixon "that Richey would put [Califano's] civil trial on hold" a full "week before Richey" issued his order.[29]

Judge Richey's tactics left just *The Washington Post* and a few journalists at other newspapers to take on Nixon and the Watergate story, but it was a tall order. The Republican National Convention had been an elaborate coronation of Richard Nixon, a PR man's dream—which it was, since it was conceptualized and staged by former adman H.R. Haldeman. Clean-cut young people chanted their support for Nixon at the convention and "were praised by Ehrlichman as individuals who had 'come here spontaneously, sometimes at great hardship to support Nixon.' The truth was that a party committee had subsidized their attendance, and a cheerleader orchestrated their chants." And that was only the start. As summarized by Anthony Summers,

> A television audience of some sixty million . . . was treated to packaged movies tracing the high points of Nixon's presidency, from grandeur in the White House to the Beijing and Moscow summit meetings. At the crowning moment the President himself appeared in triumph on a podium designed . . . to rise or fall at the flick of a switch, to ensure that no other speaker could appear taller than Nixon.[30]

After the convention, "a Gallop poll . . . gave Nixon 64 percent to McGovern's 30 percent." Nixon also announced that the last American combat troops had left Vietnam, undercutting McGovern's main campaign platform. If Nixon had only possessed confidence in his own political abilities, he might not have needed his election crimes to sail toward an easy victory in the fall.

The Watergate cover-up by Nixon and his aides continued to hold throughout the summer. Judge Richey had stalled Califano's DNC lawsuit, and John Dean had "coached [Jeb] Magruder," who then perjured "himself before the [Watergate] grand jury" on August 16. At his press conference on August 29, President Nixon confidently proclaimed that "Dean has conducted a complete Watergate investigation and I can state categorically that his investigation indicates that no one in the White House staff, no one in this Administration, presently employed was involved in this very bizarre incident." Dean would later testify that Nixon's speech was "the first time he [had ever] heard about" his alleged report to Nixon.[31]

One of the few small cracks in Nixon's mostly tight cover-up was Bernard Barker's upcoming trial in Florida, on charges related to the

$25,000 cashier's check Barker had deposited in April using a "falsely notarized statement." Bob Woodward and Carl Bernstein used information from the Florida investigation, as well as other leaks and investigations, to put out a string of strong Watergate stories in *The Washington Post* from August to October. Their "scoops" included "the financial link between CREEP and the Watergate burglary [including] the 'secret fund' controlled by Maurice Stans and CREEP aides [and] Mitchell." Journalist J. Anthony Lukas pointed out that Woodward and Bernstein's October 10 story was "a blockbuster" because it reported that "FBI agents had established that the Watergate bugging incident stemmed from a massive campaign of political spying and sabotage conducted on behalf of President Nixon's reelection and directed by officials of the White House and [CREEP]." Woodward's confidential source, FBI Assistant Director Mark Felt, enabled the *Post* to be aggressive in such reporting, allowing the daily to distinguish itself from the few other newspapers that were really making an effort to cover Watergate.[32]

Woodward and Bernstein knew they were telling an important and timely story, so they "put together a book proposal in the fall." Their initial attempt wasn't like *All the President's Men*, and according to their literary agent Mark Obst, "it began: 'Martha Mitchell reached across the bed to John. He wasn't there. He was on the phone to the western White House. There was trouble.'" In addition, "in the original proposal . . . Deep Throat did not exist," according to Obst. No publisher bid on the book, but Obst eventually prevailed upon Simon & Schuster to buy it. Obst says that "the boys got a $55,000 advance in fall 1972." However, "they were chasing the story, so they couldn't work on the book," which was then called *Reporting Watergate*. According to Stephen Ambrose, the book editor he shared with Woodward and Bernstein—Alice Mayhew—told him that after looking at the initial manuscript, "she told [Woodward and Bernstein that] the book needed a strong plot device." As a result, Mark Felt became Deep Throat.[33]

Actor Robert Redford also played an important role in shaping the book. Redford said that he "read a little article in some publication, and it hit me. They were two guys on the low end of the totem pole, and they couldn't be more different . . . How in the hell could they work together? I was only interested in a character-driven piece . . . I began to think of a low-budget black-and-white film that I would just produce, centering on investigative journalism and how it worked. I called these guys to see if I could get the rights to their story. That was in October 1972. I called Carl first, largely because he was the more flamboyantly drawn character . . . He never called back. Then I called Bob. That didn't work, either." It would be two more months before Redford and Woodward began to connect, eventually leading to a deal for a feature film. Meanwhile, the book was still taking shape, and Obst said that "Redford came up with the idea to write about how the boys broke [the Watergate story]. It was an unusual focus at the time, particularly for Bob. He didn't want to become part of the story." But writing the book with a focus on the two reporters, and the addition of Felt's Deep Throat character, was still many months away, and in the fall of 1972 the Watergate story itself was struggling to stay alive.[34]

Nixon had begun a fierce counterattack against *The Washington Post*. On September 15, 1972, Nixon told Dean that "the *Post* is going to have damnable, damnable problems out of this one. They have a television station." Lukas wrote that the *Post* "had several stations" and that "license challenges" to three of them "were instigated by the Nixon administration." The Nixon White House also unleashed a barrage of public criticism of the *Post*, which included calling its stories "a senseless pack of lies" full of "unfounded and unsubstantiated allegations." When Woodward and Bernstein finally made two relatively small errors in their October 6 and October 25 stories, Nixon's men pounced, using those errors as a way to challenge the accuracy of all their other articles. The *Post*'s editors "were now on the defensive," and thus in the critical days before the election, the *Post* "went quiet on Watergate."[35]

Remarkably, Richard Nixon even discovered that Mark Felt was leaking information to *The Washington Post*, and his reaction to that development would have a major impact on Watergate's press coverage. Nixon heard about Felt and the *Post* from H.R. Haldeman in a White House meeting on October 19, 1972, that was recorded on tape. That tape was released in 1996 and was first published by historian Stanley Kutler in 1997. But because Felt had been named frequently as a candidate for Deep Throat in the 1970s, he apparently was considered "old news" by the mid-1990s, so most journalists and historians overlooked that tape's startling revelation.[36]

In the October 19 meeting, Nixon complained to Haldeman that "they've got a leak down at the FBI." Haldeman replied that "we know what's leaked and we know who leaked it . . . it's pretty high up . . . Mark Felt." Nixon said, "Now why the hell would he do that?" Without answering that question, Haldeman cautioned Nixon about how secret the information about Felt was, that "Mitchell is the only one that knows this and he feels very strongly that we better not do anything because . . . If we move on him, he'll go out and unload everything. He knew everything that's to be known in the FBI. He has access to absolutely everything." Haldeman told Nixon that Dean had warned, "you can't prosecute him, that he hasn't committed any crime . . . Dean's concerned [that] if you let [Felt] know now, he'll go out and go on network television."[37]

Haldeman's comments about Felt having "access to absolutely everything" in the FBI helps to explain why Nixon went along with Haldeman, Mitchell, and Dean's suggestion of doing nothing, in order to keep Felt from revealing "everything." Nixon, like Mitchell, knew the FBI had information about the 1960 Nixon-Mafia-Hoffa bribe, the CIA-Mafia plots, and probably other Nixon crimes as well—so there was literally nothing Nixon could do about Felt's leaking to *The Washington Post*. Nixon apparently didn't even tell FBI Director Gray or Attorney General Kleindienst that Felt was leaking.[38]

After Haldeman told Nixon that "the conveyor belt for Felt" was "the *Post*," Nixon asked: "how did we stumble on [that information]?" Haldeman said that the information came "through an official in a publication who knows where a reporter in the publication is getting his stuff." *Washington Post* reporter James Mann later said that "Woodward was quite open with those directly involved in the Watergate coverage, speaking about 'my source at the FBI' or 'my friend at the FBI' and 'making it plain that this was a special, and unusually well-placed, source.'" Haldeman said the official at the publication (apparently the *Post*) who informed on Felt was "a legal guy" who "has stronger ties here than he does to the publication." Which raises the ironic possibility that the publication official who informed on Felt might have actually worked at times with the *Post*'s outside counsel, Joseph Califano, who was anything but a Nixon partisan. The official connected to the *Post* (or perhaps one of its sister companies) has never been identified.[39]

The *Post*'s attempts to cover Watergate thoroughly were an all-too-rare exception to the generally favorable press coverage Nixon received. In addition to the *Post*, Lukas said the only other mainstream publications covering Watergate extensively by the fall of 1972 were "*Time* . . . the *Los Angeles Times*; and sporadically, *The New York Times*, *Newsday*, [and] *Newsweek*. Newspapers overwhelmingly supported Nixon over McGovern by a margin far larger than the general public, with more than thirteen times as many supporting Nixon as his challenger (753 to 56). As a result, an October 1972 "Gallup Poll found that 48 percent of Americans had never heard of the Watergate affair." The good press relations, and spin control, of Nixon and Helms (and their organizations) had kept Watergate not only from mushrooming into a large scandal before the 1972 election, but ensured it wasn't a factor at all.[40]

Also suppressing press coverage of Watergate was the fact that Nixon and his men had stymied any Congressional investigation of the affair. When a Government Accounting Office (GAO) investigation was pressed by "Speaker of the House Carl Albert," Nixon and Haldeman discussed ways to stop him using pressure or threats. In the end, though "the GAO continued its probe into the financial aspects of Watergate [it produced] only meager results." Nixon also tried to stall "the House Banking and Currency Committee investigation [led by] Chairman Wright Patman." To stop him, "the White House brought heavy political pressure to bear on committee members through Michigan Representative Gerald R. Ford, Jr., the House minority leader." Ford and others claimed that "a public investigation at that time could jeopardize the rights of the Watergate defendants . . . the committee voted 20–15 against issuing the necessary subpoenas" for its investigation. Angry at Patman's treatment, "Senator Edward Kennedy [began] his own private inquiry [by] using the staff of his Subcommittee on Administrative Practices and Procedures." But Kennedy's small inquiry would take months to produce results, so it had no influence on Watergate's press coverage or the election.[41]

With all polls showing that Nixon was the overwhelming favorite, he had no reason to fear that any of the Watergate defendants would break their silence or cover stories. With his reelection assured, they all stood to gain pardons and other special treatment once Nixon had secured another term. When the seven Watergate defendants (Hunt, Liddy, McCord, Barker, Fiorini, Gonzalez, Martinez) were indicted on September 15, the grand jury completely ignored "the officials of [CREEP] who had paid them and given them their orders." Even Barker's conviction in Miami on November 1, 1972, brought no reason for

Nixon to worry, especially since his brief "two and a half hour trial" had not revealed any evidence linking Barker to the White House or Barker's business ties to Bebe Rebozo.[42]

There were only two sour notes for Nixon in the days before the election. "In late October," *CBS Evening News* anchor "Walter Cronkite . . . ran special Watergate segments" on his show, "spending fourteen minutes [carefully] guiding viewers through charts that explained the Watergate scandal" clearly to viewers for the first time. Cronkite's coverage didn't affect the election, but Califano pointed out that it did serve to vindicate the *Post*'s coverage, allowing its aggressive coverage to soon resume.[43]

In an ironic twist to the 1968 election, Nixon had hoped to secure a peace deal with North Vietnam before November. But Henry Kissinger prematurely announced that "peace is at hand" on October 26, even though "President Thieu of South Vietnam" had not yet agreed to the arrangement that Nixon and Kissinger had struck with North Vietnam. In 1972, as in 1968, there would be no pre-election deal, but Nixon was so far ahead in the polls that it didn't matter.[44]

On November 7, 1972, Richard Nixon won a resounding victory, carrying all but one state; Senator McGovern even lost his home state of South Dakota. Nixon had "his public relations staff . . . prepare propaganda pointing out that he had run 'one of the cleanest campaigns in history.'" Soon after the election, Colson and Hunt discussed in a recorded conversation how Watergate wasn't a factor in the election. After mutual laughter, Colson commented on the Democrats, saying, "Dumb bastards were on an issue the public couldn't care less about—really."[45]

After his massive win, Nixon was surprisingly downbeat in many ways. He demanded the resignations of all of his top officials and political appointments, saying that he wanted a fresh start, and that some would retain their positions, while others wouldn't. In one of his last acts of insubordination, Richard Helms didn't submit his resignation and told CIA Deputy Director Vernon Walters not to submit his, either. Helms apparently felt that the same hold he had over Nixon that had allowed him to withhold the CIA's most important material on "the Bay of Pigs thing"—and to have fully complied for only a few weeks with Nixon's desire for the CIA stall to the FBI's Watergate investigation—would still be effective with the President. He was wrong.[46]

Now that Nixon had won reelection and faced no more campaigns, his fears about whatever Helms could release about his past were greatly diminished. In addition, Helms had committed so many illegal acts for Nixon—from Chile to domestic surveillance to stalling for a time the Bureau's Watergate investigation—that Helms was vulnerable to much of what he could leak about Nixon, including the CIA-Mafia plots.[47]

In a thirty-minute meeting at Camp David, Nixon fired Helms, telling him he was going to appoint a new CIA Director. Helms told Nixon he hoped to stay on until March, when he would be sixty, the Agency's usually mandatory retirement age—despite the fact that just a week earlier, Helms had told Haig over lunch that he planned to remain Director for another year or two. Nixon made a point of telling Helms that he hadn't known about the March mandatory retirement date, as if to emphasize to Helms that he was being fired for another reason. Helms still knew a lot of secrets, so Nixon made sure to ask if he'd like another position in the administration. Helms suggested that he might like to be Ambassador to Iran, a crucial American base in the Middle East that also bordered the Soviet empire, and Nixon was agreeable.[48]

Helms was apparently very surprised by his firing, and his biographer, Thomas Powers, wrote that "Helms returned to the CIA in a state of shock. General Walters look one look at his face and knew he'd been fired." It would take five months, but Nixon's firing of Helms would prove to be a tactical mistake that would come back to haunt the President four months later, when it would escalate the Watergate scandal to a whole new level.[49]

CHAPTER 33

January to Early May 1973: Nixon's Pinnacle and the Gathering Storm

Richard Nixon began 1973 as one of America's most popular Presidents. With Watergate no longer a major story, and a peace deal finally in place for the Vietnam conflict, Nixon was poised to reach new heights of public acclaim in this second term. However, his firing of CIA Director Richard Helms meant that the dark undercurrent of crime and corruption just below the surface of Nixon's carefully crafted public image would soon start to become exposed. Just four months into his new term, Nixon would be forced into major action to save his Presidency, and in less than a year his impeachment would appear inevitable.

On the surface, there seemed to be nothing but positive news for Richard Nixon when he was inaugurated on January 20, 1973. His approval rating in a Gallup poll was 68 percent, and three days after he took his second oath of office, his peace deal for Vietnam became final. The settlement was reached after a massive bombing campaign of North Vietnam that Nixon had begun in December, along with intense pressure from Nixon on President Thieu, still the U.S.-backed dictator of South Vietnam. Lyndon Johnson had died the day before the peace deal took effect, and Nixon could claim public credit for ending what he liked to depict as Johnson's war. Henry Kissinger was awarded a joint Nobel Peace Prize for his efforts (with North Vietnam's Le Duc Tho), an honor Nixon might have shared had he not withdrawn his name from consideration. American POWs were finally starting to return home, boosting Nixon's image even more.[1]

Nixon was almost free of the headstrong Richard Helms, who was set to leave office on February 14. Nixon continued to reshuffle his other Cabinet officials and aides, but Haldeman and Ehrlichman retained their key White House roles. Some aides with possible Watergate exposure were reassigned, with Jeb Magruder going to the Commerce Department, Egil Krogh to the Department of Transportation, and Fred LaRue returning to Mississippi. Alexander Haig returned to the Pentagon, as the Army's Vice Chief of Staff, where he was said to have been "catapulted by Nixon over the heads of two hundred senior officers." Alexander Butterfield went to the Federal Aviation Administration. As a result of all those shifts, John Dean became a "central figure" in Nixon's second-term White House. After only having three meetings with Nixon in the first eight months of 1972, Dean would soon have "31 meetings and telephone calls with Nixon" in less than a one-month span, starting in late February.[2]

Nixon received surprisingly good news when Walter Sheridan's exposé *The Fall and Rise of Jimmy Hoffa* was finally published in mid-January 1973. Jack Anderson had run a story "from a bootleg copy" on January 10, a week before its release, but Anderson's article—like Sheridan's book—didn't contain any of the bombshells Nixon would have feared. Not only was Sheridan's book too late to affect the election, but there was also no mention of the September 1960 $500,000 Nixon-Mafia-Hoffa bribe that Sheridan had originally helped to uncover. The book did contain plenty about Nixon, including much about his aides' chicanery in trying to arrange Hoffa's December 1971 release. But again, there was no direct mention of the 1971 bribe, either. While Sheridan probably lacked details or proof about the December 1971 deal, he had all the information needed to expose Nixon's September 1960 bribe, and it's still unclear why he didn't include it (it would have fit perfectly in the book's Chapter 5). It's possible that Nixon had been such an overwhelming favorite in the election by the fall of 1972 that Sheridan feared that including or leaking Nixon's 1960 bribe would not only be dismissed as an election year ploy, but could also help Hoffa in his quest to have his conviction reversed. After the election, trying to expose Nixon's 1960 crime while men loyal to him controlled the FBI and the Justice Department might have seemed to Sheridan to be of little use. While there was much damaging information about Nixon, his aides, and their associates spread throughout Sheridan's 554-page book, the lack of a clear crime like a direct bribe kept his more-complicated Nixon revelations from gaining any significant traction in the press at the time. However, as journalists worked their way through the lengthy book and its many leads, it would start to have an effect. Five months later, other writers would start to take up Sheridan's cause, with reverberations that would continue until the 1960 Nixon-Mafia-Hoffa bribe would finally be made public—with Sheridan's help—in Dan Moldea's 1978 book *The Hoffa Wars*.[3]

President Nixon, perhaps emboldened by his resounding victory and his still-solid Watergate cover-up, began engaging in what some might call arrogant or vindictive behavior. In late January, the Nixon administration engineered the arrest of Jack Anderson's aide, Les Whitten. The charges would eventually be dropped, but it seemed perhaps a warning to other journalists who might try to investigate the seamier side of the immensely popular President.[4]

In a bizarre scenario that brought together Watergate and Nixon's Hoffa bribes, "on February 10-11, 1973 . . . two meetings were held simultaneously on the grounds" of the La Costa Country Club in Southern California: one for Nixon's aides plotting their Watergate cover-up strategy and the other between Teamsters President Frank Fitzsimmons and several Mafia leaders. One of the owners of the 5,600-acre posh La Costa resort was mobster Moe Dalitz, who had sold Howard Hughes his first Las Vegas casino in the deal brokered by Johnny Rosselli (see Chapter 19). According to Sheridan, $27,200,000 in loans to finance the La Costa resort came from the Teamsters pension fund.[5]

At the Mafia's La Costa meeting, joining Fitzsimmons were Allen Dorfman (who would head to prison in a month) and Mafia figures from California, Cleveland, and Chicago, the latter including Tony Accardo, the elder statesman of the Chicago mob. According to "government wiretaps on a Los Angeles underworld front [company]," their meeting was primarily to finalize "a massive fraud scheme" involving the "Teamsters health and welfare fund," which spent "$1 billion per year." Under the scheme, "the California mob" would get a 7 percent annual commission, with "the boys in Chicago taking 3 percent of the kickback. According to other FBI data . . . Fitzsimmons gave his personal approval to the multimillion-dollar swindle."[6]

While Frank Fitzsimmons and the mob bosses were hammering out their deal at La Costa, "after meeting with the President at San Clemente [the "Western White House"], Haldeman, Ehrlichman, and . . . John Dean . . . drove south to La Costa and met at Haldeman's villa" in the resort. "According to Dean, the purpose of [their] meeting . . . was 'to deal with [the] investigation of Watergate.'" Dan Moldea interviewed "two former Nixon aides" who "confirm[ed] that the La Costa meetings were regarded as 'very strange' even by other members of the Nixon staff." One aide explained that "the meetings were going on in a setting which obviously had the Secret Service, FBI, and Justice people climbing the wall . . . I say it was no secret. What I still don't know is if it was no accident." Another aide said that "Word came down from Haldeman to the Secret Service to make sure the agents for that trip kept their mouths shut—about the appearance of impropriety of these [meetings] being held in the midst of Fitzsimmons's Apalachin affair"—a reference to the historic mob conference described in Chapter 4. The Nixon aide told Moldea the Secret Service "agents and a couple of other officials knew all about it and knew how rotten it looked."[7]

Amazingly, after Fitzsimmons finished his mob conference at La Costa, "Nixon invited Fitzsimmons to meet him at the Marine Air Station near the Western White House and accompany him on the Air Force One flight back to Washington. Fitzsimmons accepted and they flew back on February 12." The story soon took another intriguing twist when *The New York Times* and the *Los Angeles Times* reported that "Attorney General Kleindienst refused to authorize continuation of electronic surveillance on" the "Los Angeles underworld front [company]" involved in the Teamsters-Mafia scheme Fitzsimmons had just finalized. Even though "government wiretaps on" the front company had uncovered the scheme, Kleindienst's assistant said the wiretaps weren't being continued because "prior electronic interceptions were unproductive in obtaining evidence . . . "[8]

Adding more intrigue to the February 1973 Nixon-Fitzsimmons-Mafia matter is that the previous month—on January 6—the FBI had found that Charles Colson had received a $500,000 bribe for Nixon that had been authorized by Fitzsimmons, Dorman, and mobster Tony Provenzano (as documented in Chapter 27). The money given to Colson for Nixon was apparently the last installment of the $1 million bribe for Hoffa's release, with the special conditions demanded by Fitzsimmons and the Mafia; the deal had also included the support of Fitzsimmons and the Teamsters in the last election. However, the Fitzsimmons-Mafia meeting, followed by the Nixon-Fitzsimmons Air Force One meeting and Nixon's Attorney General ending the surveillance on the company involved in the new multimillion-dollar fraud scheme, raises the possibility that Nixon's January 1973 $500,000 payment was also part of a new deal between Nixon, Fitzsimmons, and the Mafia.[9]

Time magazine later reported that the "$500,000 had been approved for Nixon" and "the cash had been requested by White house aide Charles Colson, who handled the Administration's relations with the Teamsters." Less than four weeks after Nixon flew with Fitzsimmons on Air Force Once, Colson resigned his White House position and joined a small law firm. Frank Fitzsimmons then pressured the Teamsters' current attorney—Edward Bennett Williams, Califano's partner—to drop the DNC lawsuit against CREEP. When Williams refused, Fitzsimmons "fired Williams and gave the $100,000-a-year business to Colson" and his law partner.[10]

Was Nixon being arrogant in continuing his illegal dealings with Fitzsimmons and the Mafia in his new term, since he would not have to face another election? Was the relatively young President simply interested in accumulating as much money as possible, looking ahead to his post-Presidency years? According to the *Time* article, Nixon might have just been being practical. It pointed out the "crucial timing" that just three days before Colson received the $500,000 authorized by Fitzsimmons, Dorfman, and Provenzano, there had been a meeting between [E. Howard] Hunt's lawyer and Colson" regarding "demands for payoffs by [the] Watergate" figure."[11]

Bubbling below the surface, often out of public view, there had been a small but growing tide of troubling news for Richard Nixon regarding Hunt, James McCord, and other aspects of Watergate. E. Howard Hunt, then fifty-four years old, must have been crushed when Nixon fired his former mentor, Richard Helms. Though Helms had been of little help to Hunt since the burglaries, the possibility of help had remained as long as Helms was Director, plus Hunt knew enough about Helms that he could always force the issue, if need be. Now, that possibility no longer existed. Hunt had been trying to exert pressure on the White House and Charles Colson since November, in an attempt to have them live up to their promises of hush money, expense money, and lawyers' fees for himself and the other defendants. His wife, Dorothy Hunt, played a major role in helping to solicit and distribute funds, often giving money to Manuel Artime so he could disburse it to the Cuban exile defendants and Frank Fiorini.

On December 8, 1972, Dorothy Hunt had flown to Chicago, carrying $10,000 in cash in $100 bills, the same type of money she'd been distributing to the other defendants "for more than four months." On its approach to "Chicago's Midway Airport through drizzle and fog . . . the plane suddenly nose-dived into a neighborhood . . . a mile and a half short of [the] runway . . . Forty-three of the fifty-five people on board were killed, including Mrs. Hunt." Her death briefly made the headlines, especially after the cash she was carrying was recovered, and conspiracy theories soon flourished. However, Peter Dale Scott pointed out that "the crash was investigated for possible sabotage by both the FBI and a Congressional committee," but none was found.[12]

Controversy remains as to exactly what the money, and her trip, was for. White House tapes show that "Dean later told the President that Mrs. Hunt had gone to Chicago 'to pass that money to one of the Cubans, to meet him in Chicago.'" The FBI was later told that the money was intended for the "Chicago wireman" who had apparently sold James McCord the bugging devices he was arrested with at the Watergate. Hunt claimed the cash was to be invested in a small hotel "company controlled by Dorothy's cousin-in-law," in hopes of an eventual job. Yet given Hunt's self-stated precarious financial condition at the time, his need for immediate money, and the trial he was facing the following month, his explanation strains credibility.[13]

Even Hunt admitted in his last autobiography that "there are stories that [Dorothy] was meeting with CBS reporter Michelle Clark, who was also a passenger on the flight." Some have thought it suspicious that Egil Krogh moved to the Department of Transportation as an Undersecretary a month after the crash. The same might apply to Alexander Butterfield's appointment in March 1973 to become Administrator of the Federal Aviation Administration, where *The New York Times* reported that Butterfield "read all the accident reports himself." However, Nixon probably just wanted his people in place so he could know immediately if information about his hush money surfaced in the FAA's crash investigation.[14]

E. Howard Hunt was devastated by his wife's death, and he increased his efforts to pressure the White House for money and clemency. Even before the crash, Hunt had sent a threatening letter to a CREEP attorney, stating that "The Watergate bugging is only one of a number of highly illegal conspiracies engaged in by one or more of the defendants at the behest of senior White House officials. These as yet undisclosed crimes can be proved." According to Emery, Hunt was given $50,000 from a "secret $350,000 fund . . . [that] had been kept in a bank safe-deposit box by a friend of Alexander Butterfield's." Ferrying that $50,000 from his friend to Haldeman's aide was as close as Butterfield got to the Watergate scandal, something he would make clear to Watergate investigators several months later. Hunt's wife had bought, on the spur of the moment, a $225,000 insurance policy before the crash, but Hunt also wanted to make sure his Cuban exile friends were taken care of.[15]

As the despondent Hunt increased his demands for clemency and cash, Nixon was very receptive to the idea. In his diary, Nixon wrote that "Colson told me on Friday that he had tried to do everything he could to keep Hunt in line [to keep] from turning state's evidence. After what happened to Hunt's wife, etc., I think we have a very good case for showing some clemency." In a taped discussion with Colson, Nixon said that on the "Question of clemency—Hunt's is a simple case. I mean, after all, the man's wife is dead, was killed; he's got one child that has—." Colson added, "Brain damage from an automobile accident." Nixon said, "We'll build, we'll build that sonofabitch up like nobody's business. We'll have [William] Buckley write a column and say, you know, that he, he should have clemency." Colson met with Hunt's lawyer, William Bittman (who had worked with Walter Sheridan on the Hoffa prosecutions) "on January 3, and the next day told the lawyer he had spoken to 'people' about Hunt's plight." According to Dean, "on January 5 Colson met with him and Ehrlichman . . . and reported that the had indeed given Bittman a 'general assurance' that Hunt would get clemency" from Nixon. The next day, according to the FBI, Colson got the Mafia-Teamsters bribe of $500,000 for Nixon.[16]

The clemency message was conveyed to Hunt, who was willing "to plead guilty but would do so only if he got a White House promise of executive clemency." The White House wanted the guilty plea, to avoid a potentially problematic trial, and that's what Hunt gave them. In addition, he convinced Barker and the other exile defendants, and Fiorini, to plead guilty as well, "to seven charges of conspiracy, burglary and wiretapping." It's interesting that Hunt received special treatment from Nixon over the other defendants, with the President saying in a conversation with Colson on January 8, 1973, that when it came to clemency, "I would have difficulty with some of the others." Nixon agreed with Colson's line of reasoning that the others "can't hurt us [but] Hunt and Liddy [had] direct meetings, discussions [that] are very incriminating to us."[17]

Colson was wrong when he said the other Watergate defendants "can't hurt us," because the firing of CIA Director Richard Helms had apparently been the last straw for Agency veteran James McCord. Unlike Hunt, McCord was strongly resisting the White House pressure to plead guilty to avoid a trial. In addition, McCord resented the pressure to blame the whole affair on the CIA, which he felt was coming even from his own attorney. McCord had written to Richard Helms back on July 30, 1972, saying that "From time to time I'll send along things you might be interested in from an info standpoint," and he included "a copy of a letter that went to my lawyer."[18]

James McCord also sent several letters from the fall until January 5, 1973, to Paul Gaynor, his former boss at the CIA's Office of Security. McCord told him that "there is tremendous pressure to put the operation off on the [CIA]." In addition, McCord wrote that he resented the influence that Nixon was trying to exert on the CIA with the firing of Helms: "When the hundreds of dedicated fine men and women of the CIA can no longer write intelligence summaries and reports with integrity, without fear of political recrimination—when their fine Director is being summarily discharged in order to make way for a politician . . . our nation is in the deepest of trouble and freedom itself was never so imperiled. Nazi Germany rose and fell under exactly the same philosophy of government operations." He even told Gaynor, "I have the evidence of the involvement of Mitchell and others, sufficient to convene a jury, the Congress and the press."[19]

Unlike Hunt, McCord wasn't willing to serve time and then be pardoned. In the fall of 1972, McCord had come up with a unique and telling strategy to avoid conviction: He had called the Chilean embassy, "stating that he was involved in the Watergate scandal and inquiring about visas. " McCord maintained that the embassy was "subject to national security wiretapping . . . A motion made in court to have wiretap evidence against him produced would force the government to dismiss the charges rather than be embarrassed to admit it was bugging embassies." However, the government simply refused to admit bugging the Chilean embassy—especially since it was in the midst of a highly secret CIA covert war against Chile's Allende administration—so as a legal strategy, McCord's ploy failed. However, McCord's strategy was probably also meant to pressure the

Nixon White House, since Nixon knew about the Chilean embassy burglary the previous May.[20]

McCord wrote to former White House investigator John Caulfield, saying that "If Helms goes and if the WG [Watergate] operation is laid at the CIA's feet, where it does not belong, every tree in the forest will fall. It will be a scorched desert." That began a series of exchanges between McCord, Caulfield, and others passing McCord's demands along to the White House. Clemency was offered, but that wasn't what McCord wanted. Along with Liddy, McCord stood trial in front of Judge John Sirica—a conservative Republican judge known for his harsh sentences—who seemed determined to get to the bottom of the Watergate morass. "At a pretrial hearing [Judge Sirica] put the prosecutors on notice that they had to get to the bottom of who had hired the men to go into the Watergate. 'The jury is going to want to know: . . . What did these men go into that headquarters for?'" Sirica would be continually frustrated by the lack of information presented at trial. When McCord and Liddy were convicted on January 30, 1973, after no real evidence implicating higher-ups had been presented, Judge Sirica "castigated the prosecutors, saying: 'I have not been satisfied, and I am still not satisfied that all the pertinent facts that might be available . . . have been produced before an American jury." Sirica delayed sentencing all the defendants—including Hunt and the others who had pleaded guilty—to see if any of them were willing to cooperate with prosecutors.[21]

Richard Helms's last day at the CIA was supposed to be February 14, 1973, but Nixon moved the date up to February 2 on just two weeks' notice, so that new CIA Director James Schlesinger—moving over from the Atomic Energy Commission—could take office. Helms and his secretary spent the next ten days destroying four thousand pages of transcripts from Helms's own office taping system, plus the tapes themselves. According to Helms biographer Thomas Powers, the destruction also included all of Helms's "personal records from six and a half years as Director." That probably included everything relating to Watergate and Helms's close relationship with Hunt, even though Helms and the CIA had received an order by Senator Mike Mansfield on January 18, 1973, to preserve "all materials having to do with the Watergate affair." Because so many of the figures involved in Watergate had also been involved in the JFK-Almeida coup plan, the Mafia's infiltration of the plan, or the CIA-Mafia plots, this effectively allowed Helms to complete the cover-up he'd been conducting since 1963. There was no way his successor would have the information needed to really expose Helms, even if the new Director were so inclined.[22]

Helms didn't destroy the only copy of the IG Report because it had left out so much crucial information, and all of its supporting files had already been destroyed in 1967. When coupled with that earlier file destruction, Helms's 1973 housecleaning put some details about the CIA-Mafia plots permanently beyond the reach of easily documented history. However, some top secret operations that involved Helms—like AMWORLD—were so large that many related files probably still exist. Helms still had trusted associates in high-ranking positions at the CIA who could protect his secrets, including Hunt's friend David Atlee Phillips (likely still handling Almeida's family), Ted Shackley, and Thomas Karamessines.[23]

As a parting shot at Nixon, Helms also apparently had CIA official William Colby give to the Justice Department one of the CIA-developed photos of G. Gordon Liddy standing outside of Ellsberg's psychiatrists office. That action alarmed White House aides, who tried to get the photo back, but it was too late. Neither the public nor the court involved in Ellsberg's trial as yet knew about the Plumbers' break-in at the psychiatrist's office.[24]

It was perhaps poetic justice for Richard Helms that on February 7, 1973—five days after he finished destroying files and had stepped down as CIA Director—Helms found himself testifying to Congress when the subject of Chile came up. Helms lied when asked if the CIA had provided help to those who opposed Allende in Chile. Helms had lied to Congress before, about Chile and other matters, but it would be that particular false statement that would eventually bring him a criminal conviction. However, Helms at times was unusually candid when he testified to the Senate Foreign Relations Committee, saying the CIA had "fired" Barker because "we found out he was involved in certain gambling and criminal elements." Helms probably realized that the FBI must have files documenting Barker's longstanding criminal ties, which accounts for his candor in that instance. However, Helms's testimony about Barker's mob ties would not be released for more than a year, after *All the President's Men* had been completed, which kept Barker's criminal connections from becoming part of the conventional story of Watergate.[25]

James Schlesinger, who became CIA Director on February 23, 1973, was not part of the "old boy" intelligence network like Helms, and he relied on the man who was the CIA's No. 3 official, William Colby, for guidance. Richard Nixon wasted no time in pressing Schlesinger for the files about "the Bay of Pigs thing" that Helms had denied him for so long. Schlesinger would later call Nixon's demands for that information an "obsession." Schlesinger was soon hearing about various illegal and potentially illegal CIA operations, so he issued "an order, drafted and urged on him by Colby, ordering [all] employees of the CIA to report all suspected violations of the law or the CIA's charter to the office of the Inspector General."[26]

The resulting file would come to be known as the CIA's "Family Jewels," and the CIA would resist releasing the full 693-page document until 2007. However, when the file was finally declassified, far from being a definitive compendium of the CIA's illegal operations, it turned out to be a grossly incomplete account of several illegal programs or operations. Numerous Congressional investigations, lawsuits, and declassification efforts had turned up much information showing how incomplete the "Family Jewels" really were. In hindsight, it was naïve of Schlesinger to think that CIA employees would risk ending their careers by informing on themselves and their friends, bosses, and subordinates. Key Agency officials such as Phillips and Shackley who owed their careers to Helms had no incentive to reveal anything to novice Director Schlesinger that might damage Helms's reputation—especially because they had worked on many of those questionable or illegal operations themselves. In addition, veteran CIA officials close to Helms knew how well the former Director had essentially buried, or destroyed, the biggest secrets. In some cases, Schlesinger's attempt may have resulted in more files being destroyed or buried more deeply. In addition, Schlesinger's effort really only lasted two weeks and was entirely voluntary, which helps to account for the effort's relative failure.[27]

One reason that Richard Helms spent ten days destroying his files and tapes—and that CIA personnel would be less than fully revealing when disclosing files for the "Family Jewels"—was that in January 1973, more information that might uncover the CIA-Mafia plots or the JFK-Almeida coup plan had started to emerge. Of all the millions of words written about Watergate as the scandal unfolded, only one largely ignored article mentioned an important part of Hunt's background that Helms had withheld from investigators: Hunt's work on the plots to assassinate Fidel Castro in the mid-1960s. Tad Szulc's February 1973 *Esquire* magazine article—on the stands in January, before Helms began his housecleaning—briefly described those operations. Szulc's article focused primarily on the Cubela assassination plots, stating they involved Hunt, Barker, and Artime. No mainstream journalist followed up on Szulc's 1973 revelations, so he would expand on them the following year in a short biography of Hunt, which said that in the mid-1960s Hunt was "helping to coordinate [an] assassination plot" against Castro, which would be followed by Artime's arrival in Cuba. But Szulc couldn't write too much about the subject—in his article or book—without potentially drawing attention to his own covert work for President Kennedy, and with the CIA, on the AMTRUNK attempt to find a Cuban official to overthrow Castro.[28]

Szulc's article was not the only explosive information about Hunt that started to emerge in early in 1973. Pulitzer Prize winner Haynes Johnson, then working for *The Washington Star*, was interviewed by researcher Richard E. Sprague on January 12, 1973, and the following quotes come from Sprague's handwritten notes. According to the notes, Haynes said that "CIA-backed plans for [a] second Cuban invasion were going on in 1963." Haynes "knew RFK very well. He and Harry Williams called RFK a lot in 1963, because RFK had the CIA reporting to him and JFK." Harry was "the prime contact with the Cubans and other Florida groups by 1963 [and he] knew and met all of the CIA people in Wash[ington] & Miami."[29]

In the interview, Haynes told Sprague that "A meeting was held on Nov. 22, 1963 in Wash[ington] D.C. to discuss plans for Cuban operation . . . it was the most important meeting they had . . . at [the] meeting were [CIA Executive Director Lyman] Kirkpatrick, Helms, Hunt, and Williams. Word of [JFK's] assassination came in [during the] meeting." Haynes knew something had been about to happen with Cuba, but he hadn't been told about Almeida or the coup plan. If any of Haynes's information involving Hunt and Helms had become widely known at that time, it would have radically changed the Watergate investigations. Instead, when some of the interview was finally published in a small newsletter in 1975—after Watergate had faded from the headlines—it passed without notice.[30]

According to the interview notes, Haynes also said that "Bernstein & Woodward at *Wash*[*ington*] *Post* have a contract for a Watergate book with Simon & Schuster," which would become *All the President's Men*. Haynes added that "the *Post* has a lot of sensitive, unpublished material on Watergate. They're protecting their sources." The notes say that Haynes revealed that "Ben Bradlee and his wife know Fiorini very well," something that—if true—neither Bradlee nor Fiorini ever apparently disclosed. That contact might have developed because of Fiorini's penchant for publicity in the early 1960s, and Fiorini's long friendship with Jack Anderson. Haynes didn't mention Fiorini's Mafia ties, but he did state in the interview that "Fiorini's money raising activities in 1963 were not CIA-backed."[31]

Later in 1973, journalist and former FBI agent William Turner interviewed Harry Williams, who had been Robert Kennedy's close friend and top Cuban exile aide in 1963. This author asked Williams why he agreed to talk to Turner, since Williams usually avoided publicity. Williams said he had been shocked when the Watergate scandal erupted and he recognized former associates from the 1963 JFK-Almeida coup plan, such as Hunt and Barker. In the ten years since JFK's murder, Williams had learned about Barker's ties to godfather Santo Trafficante and had come to believe that Barker had sold out the coup plan to Trafficante, and that both men had played a role in JFK's assassination. Now, Williams saw that Barker was involved with Hunt, James McCord, and other notable Cuban exiles in Watergate. Williams also heard in Miami's Cuban exile community about the efforts of his former friend and rival, Manuel Artime, to provide financial assistance to the burglars. Hunt, McCord, Barker, Artime, and Watergate—it seemed beyond coincidence. When contacted by Turner, Williams tried to tell the investigative journalist as much as he could without revealing or endangering Commander Almeida, who was still high in the Cuban government in 1973.[32]

In his long interview with Turner on November 28, 1973, Williams confirmed much of what Haynes Johnson had told Sprague. Without mentioning Almeida or a specific coup plan, Harry provided a wealth of additional information about Robert Kennedy's control of Cuban operations in 1963, their work together, and Williams's activities with Cyrus Vance, Joseph Califano, Alexander Haig, Hunt, McCord, and Barker. The names of Hunt, McCord, and Barker were still big news items in November 1973 as Watergate continued to unfold, and an article about them by Turner at that time would have been major news. However, Turner's 1973 interview with Williams wasn't published until eight years later, in 1981, when parts of it appeared in Turner's book *The Fish Is Red*, about the covert U.S. war against Castro.[33] In hindsight, Szulc's *Esquire* article and the interviews with Haynes Johnson and Harry Williams represent a fascinating lost opportunity that could have changed the way Watergate was viewed, investigated, and reported at the time.[34]

February and March of 1973 saw several important developments in the Watergate investigations. Joseph Califano, feeling the DNC lawsuit against CREEP "was fixed . . . appealed to Senators Ted Kennedy . . . Phil Hart . . . and Birch Bayh . . . to press for creation of a special Senate Committee." There was already sentiment in Congress for just such an investigation, and the Senate voted on February 7, 1972, to create a committee to investigate Watergate. The vote was 77–0, and the Republican support was in part due to the fact that Nixon had not tried to help a number of GOP candidates in the past fall's Congressional races. The new committee was officially called the Select Committee on Presidential Campaign Activities, and it would be composed of four Democrats and three Republicans, with a more predominantly Democratic staff.[35]

The Committee's Chairman was longtime North Carolina Senator Sam Ervin, who in 1970 had been frustrated by Nixon and his officials when Ervin had tried to hold hearings about the U.S. military's extensive domestic surveillance operations. Now, Senator Ervin was in a much stronger position, and he wouldn't waste his opportunity in the spotlight while he tried to uncover who in the White House had been behind the Watergate break-ins. Ervin was a good choice to chair the Committee because he was a Southern Democrat who sometimes voted conservative and other times liberal. In addition, his folksy manner and Southern drawl made the hearings seem less like a vendetta or political witch hunt, helping to blunt two ways that Nixon might have tried to criticize the hearings. Other Democratic Senators on the Committee included Herman Talmage of Georgia, Hawaii's Daniel Inouye, and New Mexico's Joseph Montoya. The top Republican on the Committee was Tennessee's Howard Baker, and the others were Florida's Edward Gurney and the relatively liberal Lowell Weicker of Connecticut.[36]

The White House's strategy for dealing with the Senate Watergate Committee, as it would come to be known, was to "take a public posture of full cooperation but privately . . . attempt to restrain the investigation and make it as difficult as possible to get the information and witnesses" that Ervin wanted. As part of that strategy, some of which was developed at the La Costa meeting of Nixon aides, "a behind-the-scenes media effort would be made to make the Senate inquiry appear very partisan. The ultimate goal would be to discredit the hearings," according to John Dean.[37]

In addition to Joseph Califano's DNC lawsuit against CREEP being overseen by Judge Richey, Califano also had to represent *The Washington Post* when Nixon had CREEP try to subpoena Woodward, Bernstein, *Post* editor Howard Simons, and *Post* owner Katherine Graham. CREEP also demanded all of "their notes, internal memoranda, and phone logs," since "CREEP wanted to uncover the identity of the reporters' anonymous source or sources." Nixon and Haldeman already knew that Mark Felt was providing information to the *Post*, but they couldn't be sure of how much or if other officials might be doing the same.[38]

Joseph Califano and Ben Bradlee were determined not to give in to CREEP's attempt to stifle the *Post*'s reporting. Califano had all of the reporters' notes given to the mature, gray-haired Katherine Graham, feeling that Judge Richey was far less likely to send her to jail for contempt than the others. On March 5, Judge Richey demanded that Califano choose between representing the *Post* and representing the DNC in its lawsuit, saying there was "a serious conflict" in representing both. Califano resigned his DNC position, saying he felt "more comfortable" just handling the *Post* as a client. At the *Post*, Califano said he "was becoming involved on an almost daily basis in clearing Watergate stories for the paper or advising [them] on legal issues the paper's aggressive coverage raised." Surprisingly, replacing Califano as counsel for the DNC lawsuit would be Edward Morgan, Johnny Rosselli's longtime friend. On March 21, Judge Richey quashed CREEP's subpoena against the *Post* "on First Amendment grounds." In addition, two weeks earlier, Richey had finally released the depositions the DNC had taken in its lawsuit; while most of those deposed—such as the Watergate defendants—had stuck to their cover stories, some good information was obtained that would at least provide a starting point for the new Senate Watergate Committee.[39]

Califano finally wrote about his role in so many aspects of Watergate in his 2004 autobiography. In 1973 and into 1974, even after dropping the DNC as a client, Califano wrote that he stayed busy: "At night I was meeting with Ted Kennedy to plot strategy as the Senate Watergate Committee investigation proceeded and [eventually] as the House Judiciary Committee looked into Nixon's [possible] impeachment . . . in the late afternoon I found myself at the [*Post*] vetting Woodward and Bernstein Watergate stories." He said that he "viewed my activity during Watergate . . . as part of a citizen's crusade to protect democracy and eventually to bring down Nixon." The reason, Califano explained, was "to keep the Constitution from being subverted by stop-at-nothing use of government power."[40]

Despite all of the efforts of Califano, Woodward, Bernstein, Bradlee, Senator Ervin, and Judge Sirica—as well as reporters such as Tad Szulc, Sy Hersh, Jack Nelson, and Bob Jackson—the Watergate cover-up by Nixon and his aides continued to hold. None of the Watergate defendants had implicated those higher up or had agreed to help prosecutors, and they largely maintained their cover stories as they awaited sentencing by Judge Sirica, slated for March 23, 1973.

However, the entire Watergate cover-up started to unravel on March 19, 1973, when James McCord wrote his explosive letter to Judge John Sirica. In his obscure Watergate autobiography, McCord wrote that his reason for writing the letter was that he "believed that the whole future of the nation was at stake." There were other reasons as well. McCord didn't want to go to prison, and in his presentencing interview with his probation officer, it was made clear to him that providing information and cooperating could lessen his sentence.[41]

McCord might have felt free to act because of Richard Helms's firing from the CIA. Helms was preparing to assume his post as Ambassador to Iran, and an outsider, loyal to Nixon, now ran McCord's beloved Agency. There were still many CIA secrets McCord would protect, but McCord viewed Watergate as a Nixon White House operation, "not a CIA operation." As McCord would later testify, he "believed that President Nixon gave the final approval, and set the Watergate operation in motion."[42]

It's not known what other Nixon crimes McCord may have become aware of or suspected, or heard about from Hunt. McCord wrote in his book that Hunt had "information which would impeach the President." In his Watergate book, McCord did go out of his way to decry "the volume of heroin illegally entering the U.S.," but there is no indication if he ever learned about or suspected the Trafficante-linked money that Al Haig's Army investigation would uncover the following year. McCord saw himself as different from his fellow ex-CIA officer Hunt, and certainly from Fiorini and Barker, and seems to have resented having to work with—and being lumped in with—the latter. In his letter to Sirica, McCord was careful to stress that "my motivations were different than those of the others involved, but were not limited to . . . those offered in my defense during the trial." In his book, McCord doesn't make clear exactly what those motivations were, or why he got involved in a seemingly purely political operation.[43]

Within days of writing his letter, McCord would jettison his original attorney, who he felt was compromised by the White House (which is why McCord didn't tell him about the letter to Sirica in advance). McCord chose as his new attorney Bud Fensterwald, a former Senate investigator. Fensterwald had almost come into contact with the CIA-Mafia plots back in 1966, when Robert Maheu was supposed to testify before the committee he worked for (described in Chapter 19). It is interesting to note that when hired by McCord, Fensterwald was best known for heading the Committee to Investigate Assassinations, dedicated to uncovering more information about JFK's murder.*[44]

On March 20, 1973, James McCord tried to deliver his sealed letter to Judge Sirica. Afraid it might be a bribe attempt or some type of evidence, Sirica's clerk refused to accept it and had McCord give it to his probation officer. It was then delivered to Sirica, who called the two U.S. Attorneys handling the Watergate prosecutions to come "to his office to witness the opening of the letter, " but they declined. McCord felt that one of the U.S. Attorneys must have then called Attorney General Richard Kleindienst or the White House, since Nixon appears to have found out about the letter, perhaps before it was even opened. On March 20, 1973, Nixon made "curious, garbled taped remarks" when he said that "McCord didn't want to go to jail . . . [unintelligible] jail sentence . . . [unintelligible] decided to talk [so] I said, 'What the hell's he doing?'" Nixon also said that McCord "might crack . . . and might say to the judge he is willing to tell all [and that McCord] knows a hell of a lot about Mitchell. Mitchell is the one I am

*When this author asked Fensterwald about James McCord in 1991, Fensterwald pointed to the publicly available information of McCord's alleged involvement with Hunt in the anti-Castro operation of Harry Williams and Robert Kennedy as being especially important.

most concerned about." Nixon didn't know what McCord's letter said, but he could imagine what it might contain. Sirica, after reading the letter on March 20, had "resealed it and decided to sit on it until the sentencing, scheduled for March 23."[45]

However, Nixon's main focus the following day was on E. Howard Hunt, and making sure Hunt had enough hush money to remain silent even after he was sentenced. On March 21, 1973, Nixon talked with John Dean about the matter, in the famous conversation that began with Dean telling Nixon, "We have a cancer—within—close to the Presidency, that's growing." As mentioned earlier, this is the conversation where Nixon told Dean that "Your major guy to keep under control is Hunt. Because he knows . . . about a lot of other things." The two discussed the fact that some of the money had gone through "the cover of a Cuban Committee," the one Nixon had planned to use Rebozo for but that had actually been implemented by Cuban exile Manuel Artime. Dean said that "this is . . . going to be a continual blackmail operation by Hunt and Liddy and the Cubans," though "McCord . . . has asked for nothing." (It is not clear from their conversation if Nixon had told Dean about McCord's sealed letter to Judge Sirica.) Dean also reminded Nixon that "as you know, Colson has talked to, indirectly to Hunt about commutation." But the immediate need was for money, since Dean told the President that "the blackmail is continuing . . . Hunt now is demanding another $72,000 for his own personal expenses [plus] $50,000 to pay his attorney's fees [and he] wanted it by the close of business yesterday. 'Cause he says, 'I am going to be sentenced Friday, and I've got to be able to get my financial affairs in order.'" Hunt backed up his threat by saying, "I will bring John Ehrlichman down to his knees and put him in jail. Uh, I have done enough seamy things for he and [Egil] Krogh that they'll never survive it."[46]

Dean told Nixon that keeping Hunt and the others quiet will "cost money. It's dangerous. Nobody, nothing—people around here are not pros at this sort of thing. This is the sort of thing Mafia people can do: washing money, getting clean money, and things like that . . . we just don't know about those things . . . we are not criminals." The irony of the last statement is lost on Nixon and Dean, who then told the President, "these people are gong to cost, huh, a million dollars over the next, uh, two years."[47]

After a pause, President Nixon told Dean:

> We could get that . . . if you need the money . . . you could get the money . . . What I mean is, you could, you could get a million dollars. And you could get it in cash. I, I know where it could be gotten . . . I mean it's not easy, but it could be done."[48]

Nixon later added, "Suppose that you get, you, you get the million bucks, and you get the proper way to handle it, and you could hold that side. It would seem to me that would be worthwhile . . . " When Dean expressed doubts about paying so much money, Nixon reassured him that the money was "no problem, we could, we could get the money. There is no problem in that. We can't provide the clemency. The money can be provided." Dean then brought up Mitchell's recent talks with Nixon's friend Thomas Pappas, whom Nixon had recently met with in the Oval Office on March 7, 1973. Pappas was close to the U.S.-backed military junta that ran Greece, and he had been a major donor to Nixon before. In addition, recall that just two months earlier, Nixon had gotten $500,000 from the Mafia for the Teamsters deal, which was only part of a $1 million total.[49]

After his meeting with Dean, Nixon then told his longtime secretary, Rose Mary Woods, that "We at the present time may have a need for substantial cash for a personal purpose for some things . . . how much do you have at this point . . . ?" After that, Nixon met with H.R. Haldeman in the old Executive Office Building. Nixon told him that "the first consideration . . . is what to do about Hunt." The bottom line for all of these discussions is that Nixon authorized another hush money payment to Hunt—while Nixon should have been equally worried about McCord.[50]

March 23, 1972—when Hunt, McCord, and the other Watergate defendants were to be sentenced—would be a watershed day in the Watergate scandal. It was on that day that Judge Sirica created a firestorm when he read James McCord's letter in open court. From that moment forward, Watergate once again was front-page news, and Nixon would be forced to take a series of drastic, public steps to deal with the crisis in the coming weeks. McCord said, "the air was electrified" in the courtroom when Sirica read his letter aloud. Its main points were that "there was political pressure applied to the defendants to plead guilty and remain silent," and that "perjury occurred during the trial in matters highly material to . . . the government's case, and to the motivation and intent of the defendants." McCord's letter also said that "Others involved in the Watergate operation were not identified during the trial, when they could have been by those testifying." Trying to indicate the wide nature of the corruption surrounding the Watergate conspiracy and cover-up, McCord's letter stated that "I cannot feel confident in talking with an FBI agent, in testifying before a Grand Jury whose U.S. Attorneys work for the Department of Justice, or in talking with other government representatives." Finally, McCord had added in his letter protection for his Agency, and a means to short-circuit any CIA or national security excuse the Nixon White House might offer, by stating: "The Watergate operation was not a CIA operation. The Cubans may have been misled by others into believing that it was a CIA operation. I know for a fact that it was not."[51]

Judge Sirica then sentenced the defendants, giving "forty years each to Bernard Barker, Eugenio Martinez, Virgilio Gonzales, and Frank [Fiorini, and] thirty-five years to Howard Hunt," who had made an extraordinary plea for mercy in his statement to the court. However, Sirica made their "sentences 'provisional' and said he would review them after three months, and after the defendants had had an opportunity to cooperate with other investigations." Sirica gave a non-provisional sentence to G. Gordon Liddy of at least "six years eight months to a maximum of twenty years."[52]

McCord's revelations invigorated the recently created Senate Watergate Committee investigation and gave the Committee its first star witness. Suddenly, the entire American press corps was putting the Watergate story on its front pages, and the drumbeat of pressure on Nixon would continue to mount over the coming months. Now that McCord had made it clear that higher-ups were involved, some of Nixon's aides began reassessing their own positions. On April 12, 1972, there was another breakthrough when former Nixon aide Jeb Magruder confessed to U.S. Attorneys that he had committed perjury in his earlier testimony. Just four days prior to that, John Dean had begun talking to Watergate prosecutors. The day after Dean met with the prosecutors, Nixon told Haldeman they ought to get rid of the White House tapes, but nothing was done and Nixon continued his recording. However, Nixon greatly increased his use of the tapes to try to spin or simply lie about past events to new and old aides.[53]

The ensuing media storm sparked by McCord's letter and its fallout continued to build momentum in April, putting ever-increasing pressure on President Nixon. Finally, Nixon had no choice but to make a major effort to try to staunch the crisis. To divert blame and responsibility from himself, Nixon had to use the strategy of essentially blaming Watergate on his staff, implying they might not have supervised their underlings properly. To make that approach work, he would have to take dramatic action by shaking up his staff and top officials.

After much soul-searching and emotion, Nixon told H.R. Haldeman and John Ehrlichman they would have to go. On April 30, 1973, in a dramatic speech, Nixon announced their resignations, while calling them "two of the finest public servants it has been my privilege to know." That same day, Nixon also announced the resignations of John Dean and Attorney General Kleindienst. L. Patrick Gray had resigned three days earlier, so William Ruckelshaus left the Environmental Protection Agency (the creation of which was one of Nixon's most notable domestic achievements) to become the new FBI Director. Nixon said that Elliot Richardson would move over from the Defense Department to become his new Attorney General, and Nixon stressed that he would be free to appoint a Special Prosecutor for the Watergate matter. In addition, James Schlesinger was soon moved from the CIA to the Defense Department, with William Colby becoming the new Agency Director. In all, it was an astonishing official shake-up by a President, meant to divert attention from Nixon's own guilt in the affair. To a degree, it was successful, since Nixon would not have to resign for almost a year and a half. (After his speech, only 13 percent of the America public thought he should resign.) However, Nixon's drastic actions convinced some that there must be much more to the scandal.[54]

Richard Nixon had been forced to take such public and extreme actions not just because of public pressure, but, because he knew his own culpability. When he met privately with Haldeman to tell him he was going to have to resign, Nixon admitted that "he was 'really the guilty one . . . he's the one that started Colson on his projects. He was the one who told Dean to cover up, he was the one who made Mitchell Attorney General and later his campaign manager . . . and now he has to face that and live with it." In private, before his April 30 speech, Nixon had told Press Secretary Ron Ziegler that "It's all over," and Ziegler said he knew that Nixon "was referring to himself and the Presidency." The day after Nixon's speech, Ziegler apologized "to *The Washington Post* and its reporters Woodward and Bernstein for his criticisms of their Watergate articles."[55]

Part of the furor that led to Nixon's April 30 speech was due to disclosures in the trial of Daniel Ellsberg and his codefendant, revelations that escalated after Nixon's speech. When Ellsberg's trial had resumed in January, he faced "twelve felony counts [and a] possible sentence of 115 years." As if to help ensure a guilty verdict and even before L. Patrick Gray's resignation, on April 5 in San Clemente, Nixon met with the judge in the case, William Matthew Bryne, and Ehrlichman offered to make him Director of the FBI. On April 18, the Assistant Attorney General told Nixon that Watergate prosecutors had "learned of the burglary of" Ellsberg's psychiatrist's office, but that "Judge Byrne does not yet know of it." Nixon told the official that "this is a national security matter" and ordered him to "stay out of it."[56]

However, Nixon was soon forced to allow Judge Byrne to be informed about the burglary; he was told on April 26, and that information was also provided to Ellsberg's defense. On May 2, Judge Bryne admitted that his meetings with Ehrlichman were about the FBI Directorship, and he requested that motions be filed for a mistrial. After more illegal wiretapping of Ellsberg was revealed on May 9, the government claimed its records couldn't be located. Finally, on May 11, Judge Bryne dismissed all charges against Ellsberg and his codefendant, due to government misconduct. However, the revelations about the break-in and surveillance, when paired with McCord's disclosures and Nixon's official shake-up, added even more fuel to the Watergate publicity fire.[57]

Nixon's longtime friend John Mitchell was indicted on May 10, 1973, along with Maurice Stans, "on charges of accepting a $200,000 campaign contribution from financier Robert L. Vesco, in return for a promise to intercede with the government on his behalf." With that indictment, Nixon no longer had Mitchell to confide in, or get advice from, on secrets the two men shared, such as the CIA-Mafia plots. Soon after the Watergate scandal, Nixon had wanted to protect Mitchell, but in recent months, Nixon had been increasingly willing to have Mitchell take the blame for the whole affair. Mitchell hired attorney William Hundley to handle his case, an interesting choice since Hundley had formerly been a top Mafia prosecutor for Robert Kennedy, on cases such as those against Sam Giancana. Hundley was also friends with Johnny Rosselli's current attorney, Tom Wadden. Hundley said that Mitchell "was very fatalistic about what was going to happen. I didn't get a story telling me how innocent he was or anything like that." Mitchell would be acquitted of the Vesco charges the following year, but his "fatalistic" attitude was likely because he knew he could well be charged with, and convicted of, Watergate crimes. In fact, John Mitchell would be the first former Attorney General—and the highest-ranking Nixon official—to be sent to prison.[58]

CHAPTER 34

May 1973 to August 1974: Nixon, Rosselli, and Resignation

To help calm the Watergate storm, Nixon offered the position of Chief of Staff to General Alexander Haig, his former National Security Advisor. Haig was uncertain about stepping back into the Nixon White House at such a difficult time, so he called his old friend Joseph Califano for advice on May 3, 1973. Califano initially told Haig that "Nixon will either be impeached or resign, Al. It's just a matter of time . . . If guys like Haldeman and Ehrlichman face jail time, they'll spill on Nixon." Haig told his friend the country needed a strong Presidency, and in the end, Califano agreed, saying, "'this isn't what you or I would wish for you. But it's what the country needs.' The next day [May 4] Haig became Nixon's White House Chief of Staff." In that role, Haig would play a crucial role in essentially running the country in Nixon's last months in office, before helping to engineer the President's resignation.[1]

Nixon had just named Leonard Garment, a Democrat, to replace Dean as White House counsel. But Haig thought Nixon also needed another attorney, someone to "devote his entire attention to the legal aspects of Watergate." Surprisingly, one of the first attorneys Haig suggested to Nixon was Joseph Califano—the man who had, until recently, been pressing the DNC lawsuit over Watergate. It's amazing that Haig would even suggest Califano, but Nixon turned down the idea, saying, "we've got to have a man who's with us, a man we can trust." Instead, Nixon agreed with Haig's next suggestion of the low-profile "J. Fred Buzhardt, the acting general counsel of the Defense Department," whose new appointment as White House counsel was announced on May 10, 1973. The White House tapes show that amid talk of resignation or impeachment, Nixon began lying extensively to both Haig and Buzhardt about his involvement in Watergate, saying on May 18 "that he knew nothing about the Plumbers, Hunt [or] Liddy." In contrast, in a private talk with former aide H.R. Haldeman two days later, Nixon admitted that "I ordered the Plumbers operation" and "the whole Plumbers operation, I'm going to take [responsibility for] that."[2]

Even as Nixon shored up his defenses, in May 1973, developments were proceeding rapidly for the Senate Watergate Committee and the Watergate grand jury. E. Howard Hunt testified to the Watergate grand jury on May 2. He was only partially truthful, so on May 7 Judge Sirica tried to give him more incentive to be honest by granting him immunity from further prosecution for anything he might say in his testimony. However, Hunt was still torn between wanting a reduced sentence from Sirica and wanting his promised clemency from President Nixon, so in his testimony he only implicated Nixon aides, not the President.[3]

Far more media attention was on Hunt's former CIA and Plumbers compatriot James McCord, the star witness in the first day of televised hearings by Sam Ervin's Senate Watergate Committee. That day, May 18, 1973, McCord was quite forthcoming in many ways, and he made it clear that the final Watergate mission was primarily a "photographic operation," with his bugging only added on "as long as the team was going in" anyway. Ironically, McCord's attorney, Bernard Fensterwald, said that the Senate Watergate Committee "never asked McCord [exactly] what they hoped to get from [the office of] Larry O'Brien." The House had begun often-overlooked hearings into Watergate, chaired by Representative Lucien Nedzi, seven days earlier, but it was the Senate hearings that received the attention of the news media, and they soon became an integral part of the Watergate story. The same day as McCord's explosive testimony, Archibald Cox was chosen by acting Attorney General Eliot Richardson to be the Watergate Special Prosecutor; both Cox and Richardson were sworn in the following week. Cox had been the Solicitor General during John F. Kennedy's administration, and the tapes show that Nixon soon regarded Cox as "an adversary," and the President had no intention of cooperating with Cox's investigation.[4]

On May 22, Nixon issued a "White Paper" to the press, in which he "denied prior knowledge of the Watergate break-in or cover-up" and claimed he didn't even know about the cover-up until March 21, 1973.

However, Nixon did admit to "ordering some aides to restrict the burglary probe because of national security considerations." Nixon would continue to justify his actions by citing "national security" until shortly before his resignation, though he would never explicitly state what those "considerations" were. To his new counsel, Fred Buzhardt, Nixon would only say that these national security considerations "had nothing to do with . . . the Mexican connection," but "something about the Bay of Pigs operation may have figured into his decision." Nixon couldn't be more specific without causing himself (and the country) more problems. For Nixon, hiding the 1960 CIA-Mafia plots was his top concern, but judges and Democratic leaders wouldn't see that as a legitimate national security issue. The real national security consideration was the U.S. government's past ties with, and current CIA family support for, Cuba's Commander Juan Almeida. His work for the United States had never been exposed, and he was still essentially the third-highest-ranking official in Cuba. But there was almost no way for Nixon to use that—and the past work of Hunt, Barker, and allegedly McCord on the JFK-Almeida coup plan—without potentially exposing Almeida. That's why Nixon couldn't reveal his actual national security consideration.[5]

Bernard Barker testified to Ervin's Watergate Committee on May 24, 1973, but he was not asked anything about his Mafia ties. The Senate and House Watergate Committees only had access to some FBI information, not the Bureau's full file, so the subject of his organized crime ties wasn't raised to Barker, and the same was true when the Committee questioned Frank Fiorini. That meant that organized crime was completely missing from the public Watergate hearings, which was ironic, since the chief investigator for Ervin's Watergate Committee was Carmine Bellino, who had worked on organized crime cases for Robert Kennedy's Justice Department. Before that, Bellino had been an investigator for the Senate crime hearings in the late 1950s that had propelled John F. Kennedy to prominence (Senator Sam Ervin had been on that committee with JFK). In the mid-1950s, Bellino had also been partners for a time with Robert Maheu, which would put him in an unusual and potentially awkward position the following year, once Maheu—and the CIA-Mafia plots with Rosselli—became a quiet subject of investigation by the Watergate Committee.[6]

Walter Sheridan's book had slowly started to cause more journalists to look into Nixon's organized crime ties, and on June 1, 1973, the

Los Angeles Times ran a lead editorial entitled "Nixon, the Teamsters, the Mafia." However, even those investigations didn't link Nixon's mob connections to Watergate. Also on newsstands in June was the July-dated issue of *The Atlantic* magazine, with Lyndon Johnson's final interview, in which he stated that "when he had taken office he found that 'we had been operating a damned Murder Inc. in the Caribbean," involving "a CIA-backed assassination team." LBJ speculated in the interview that Castro had killed JFK in retaliation. As with Jack Anderson—whose Rosselli-derived information may have influenced LBJ's remarks—the blame for the CIA-Mafia plots was being placed on the Kennedys, instead of on Nixon (who originated them) or Richard Helms (who continued them without authorization into 1962 and 1963). However, LBJ's published opinion no doubt fed the feeling of officials like Alexander Haig, and his influential friend Joseph Califano, that Castro had killed JFK (not realizing that those reports were linked to associates of Johnny Rosselli). For Haig, who knew about Commander Almeida and that his exposure could trigger a new Cuban crisis while Nixon was battling for his political life, keeping a lid on anything that might expose past U.S. operations against Cuba would be a priority. In addition, Haig himself had worked on some of those failed operations, so their exposure could only dim his upward career trajectory.[7]

Senator Ervin's Watergate Committee got another crucial break when John Dean agreed to testify in open hearings against Nixon on June 25, 1973. His testimony brought the Watergate cover-up into the Oval Office and directly implicated Nixon, something even McCord's testimony hadn't been able to do. Dean's testimony raised the media furor to an even higher level, but it was still just his word against the President's. That was about to change, however, in a dramatic fashion.

On July 13, 1973, Nixon's former close aide Alexander Butterfield was questioned in private by investigators for the Senate Watergate Committee, in preparation for his upcoming testimony. Three months earlier, Butterfield had gone to the Watergate grand jury to tell it about the $50,000 he had been asked to take to Haldeman's aide. Butterfield seemed willing to tell the truth, in contrast to most of Nixon's other aides. Now, on July 13, he was similarly forthcoming in his answers as investigator Scott Armstrong asked Butterfield a series of questions. According to *The Boston Globe*, Armstrong then turned the questioning over to "Republican staffer Don Sanders, who asked Butterfield the question that led to [Butterfield's] mention of [Nixon's] taping system. To the astonishment of everyone in the room, Butterfield admitted the taping system existed."[8]

Butterfield's revelation of Nixon's taping system quickly became the focus of the Senate Watergate Committee, and it triggered an internal Committee power struggle. The Committee's chief counsel was Sam Dash, a progressive Democrat, while the minority counsel was Fred Thompson, who had been chosen by Republican Senator Howard Baker.* Since a Republican staffer had asked the question that led to Butterfield's admission, Senator Baker wanted Fred Thompson to ask Butterfield the key question during the live, televised hearing. Scott Armstrong and others protested. *The Boston Globe* noted that "Armstrong . . . and other Democratic staffers had long been convinced that Thompson was leaking information about the investigation to the White House." But Dash agreed to let Thompson asked the fateful question on live TV.[9]

The day before Butterfield's testimony, Thompson admitted in his own autobiographical Watergate book that "'Even though I had no authority to act for the committee, I decided to call Fred Buzhardt at home' to tell him that the committee had learned about the taping system. 'I wanted to be sure that the White House was fully aware of what was to be disclosed so that it could take appropriate action.'" In contrast to that questionable act, Thompson would later take the lead in investigating the CIA's withholding of important information from the Committee, which raised important unanswered questions about the CIA, Helms, Hunt, and McCord. Thompson's book and his Minority Report in the Committee's Final Report added crucial information such as Hunt's NSC backchannel to Helms, the missing "Mr. Edward/Don Eduardo" file of Hunt and McCord, and Robert Bennett's work for the CIA.[10]

On July 16, 1973, a nervous Alexander Butterfield called his associate, Joseph Califano, for advice. Butterfield asked Califano if he would represent him at the hearing. But Califano said that as counsel for *The Washington Post*, and having filed the original DNC lawsuit, he couldn't be his attorney. Califano suggested that he call Leonard Garment, the White House counsel. Butterfield did so, but Garment declined to represent Butterfield "because he was the President's lawyer."

*Fred Thompson is best known today as a character actor in films and television.

When Butterfield called Califano again, the attorney advised him to "testify without counsel" since he "had nothing to hide" and it would "make a much better impression on the Committee."[11]

Later that day, before a nationwide television audience, Fred Thompson asked Butterfield, "Are you aware of the installation of any listening devices in the Oval Office of the president?" Butterfield replied, "I was aware of listening devices, yes, sir." As Butterfield went on to describe Nixon's taping systems in great detail, those in the hearing room—and in newsrooms and living rooms across America—realized that Watergate would no longer be Dean's or McCord's word against the President. Now, Nixon's tapes would become the focus, as investigators, journalists, and citizens wanted to hear in the President's own words what he knew and what he had done. From that time forward, it was simply a matter of time before Nixon would have to face some type of justice—if the tapes survived, and could be obtained.[12]

The day after Butterfield's bombshell revelation, his friend and former co-worker Alexander Haig called their mutual friend, Joseph Califano. Like Butterfield, Chief of Staff Haig had called Califano looking for advice. "What, he asked, should he advise the President to do about the tapes? The Senate Watergate Committee wanted them, but neither the Committee nor the grand jury had yet subpoenaed them." Surprisingly, Califano told Haig that "If I were in your shoes, I'd tell the President to burn the tapes immediately and then proclaim he'd done so as a matter of national security and executive privilege and out of an obligation to protect the office of the Presidency." Apparently, Califano's advice made Nixon view Califano differently, because "a few days later [Haig] called and again asked if [Edward Bennett] Williams and I could represent President Nixon. He said he had recommended that Nixon retain us"—but Califano declined. As Califano summarized the next year in the Watergate saga, Special Prosecutor Archibald "Cox and the Senate Committee both demanded the tapes. President Nixon was subpoenaed to produce them [and] his . . . refusal set off a constitutional battle that would wind up in the Supreme Court."[13]

The battle for the tapes that pitted the Senate Watergate Committee and Special Prosecutor Cox against the White House intensified, and would last for another year. In response, Nixon tried to counterattack in various ways. Haldeman, still apparently hoping for clemency from

Nixon in the future, was still not being honest in his testimony and claimed "that the tapes he had listened to proved that Nixon was telling the truth" about his lack of involvement in Watergate and the cover-up. In early August 1973, George H.W. Bush—now head of the Republican National Committee—"released an affidavit that linked the [Watergate] Committee's chief investigator, Carmine Bellino, to a 1960 wiretapping" during the 1960 Nixon-JFK election battle. Bellino had been a thorn in Nixon's side in 1956, when he'd helped Robert Kennedy go after Murray Chotiner. Even though "a Senate subcommittee that probed" Bush's 1973 allegation "found no proof of election eavesdropping" by Bellino in 1960, Bush's tactic for Nixon still served to distract the Committee and the press, and it gave hope to Nixon's supporters.[14]

When Nixon made a nationally televised address on August 15, 1973, the strain of the scandal was starting to show, and Stephen Ambrose described him as looking "drawn and a little sad." While taking "full responsibility for any abuses" and regretting "that these events took place," he still claimed that "I had no prior knowledge of the Watergate break-in. I neither took part in nor knew about any of the subsequent cover-up activities; I never authorized or encouraged subordinates to engage in illegal or improper campaign tactics." As with past major addresses, Nixon's "own aides" made sure that "manufactured" telegrams and calls of support flooded the White House. A poll that month showed that even with the stunning revelations of McCord, Dean, and Butterfield, most of the country was still behind Nixon, with 60 percent of those surveyed wanting him to continue as President. Only 20 percent were in favor of resignation, and 10 percent ready for impeachment.[15]

In August, Richard Helms had to testify to the Senate Watergate Committee. His biographer described him as looking "hard and angry" at times during his testimony. Helms's lies were starting to catch up with him, as Haldeman and Ehrlichman had started to reveal more of their dealings with him, even as the two aides still tried to protect Nixon. In addition, General Vernon Walters, still the CIA's Deputy Director, made statements that began to sometimes contradict those of Helms. Simply put, Helms had lied too many times to too many Congressional committees to keep his stories consistent. In testimony to the Armed Services Committee in May, Helms had said there was no discussion of Watergate at the pivotal June 23, 1972, meeting between himself, Walters, Haldeman, and Ehrlichman (the meeting at which Helms exploded in rage at the mention of "the Bay of Pigs thing"). All three of the other participants testified that Watergate had been raised, and Helms struggled to reconcile his past testimony with theirs. When Walters testified to the Watergate Committee, he slipped when discussing the burglars, admitting that when a Nixon aide told him "these people all used to work for the CIA . . . I said maybe they used to but they were not" during the Watergate burglary. The past CIA employment of Frank Fiorini was hidden from the Committee and the public. It would not be admitted by Helms until twenty years later, in a deposition. However, in 1973 Colby told another CIA official Fiorini had been "on the payroll" of the CIA "years" earlier.[16]

The fates of Helms's former protégé, E. Howard Hunt, and his friend David Atlee Phillips could not have been more different. Phillips was leading Nixon's effort to overthrow Chilean President Salvador Allende in his role as Chief of Latin American Operations for the CIA. On September 4, 1973, a U.S.-backed coup in Chile, led by Chilean General Augusto Pinochet, resulted in the death of Allende. Most accounts, and his family, say Allende committed suicide using an AK-47 given to him by Fidel Castro, and the most recent forensic investigation confirmed that.* Allende's death ushered in many years of a repressive and bloody Pinochet dictatorship in Chile, a legacy the country still struggles to come to terms with today. David Atlee Phillips's stewardship of Nixon and the CIA's Chile effort earned him a promotion to be the CIA's Chief of Western Hemisphere Operations.[17]

Before his dubious "success" in Chile, Phillips had taken care of a loose end from his past, his longtime Cuban exile operative Antonio Veciana, whose most recent effort for Phillips had been the assassination attempt of Fidel Castro in Chile in December 1971. According to a later Congressional investigator, Gaeton Fonzi, and author Dick Russell, Phillips had ended his relationship with Veciana by giving him a suitcase containing "$253,000 in cash" at a dog track in Miami. Soon afterward, Veciana was arrested in a drug bust that he indicated was a setup linked to the end of his work for the CIA. As a high-ranking CIA official, Phillips no longer had time to personally run operatives like Veciana, or to worry about what those operatives might reveal.[18]

*Castro and others say Allende was executed, and point to two bullet wounds as evidence.

In stark contrast to the success of his friend Phillips, E. Howard Hunt faced having to testify to the Watergate Committee, and he would soon have his sentence reviewed by Judge Sirica. On September 14 and 17, 1973, Hunt, Barker, Fiorini, Gonzales, and Eugenio Martinez tried a new strategy, filing petitions to change their guilty pleas to "not guilty." The three exiles and Fiorini claimed they had only pleaded guilty "to keep from exposing national security operations." Hunt's petition claimed "that he thought he had acted lawfully to protect the national security."

Hunt made the same "national security" claim when he testified to the Senate Watergate Committee on September 24 and 25, 1973. Hunt testified honestly in some regards but was not forthcoming about other matters, and he generally stuck to the "McGovern was getting money from Castro" cover story. He also floated a conspiracy theory that McCord's assistant Alfred Baldwin had been a "double agent" for the Democrats who "exposed" the final burglary on purpose because—Hunt claimed—Baldwin had an uncle who was a Democratic judge. But on Hunt's last day of testimony, Senator Lowell Weicker revealed that Baldwin's only relative who was a judge was not a Democrat, but had been a "Republican Senator from Connecticut, who was also the Republican Governor of Connecticut."[19]

Hunt's performance during his testimony did him no good. If his "national security" claim was meant to foster help for him from the CIA, it failed. Helms was no longer in a position to help, and Colby, Walters, and Phillips needed to keep an arm's length from the matter, lest they be drawn into the cover-up. In addition, Hunt and Barker were fiercely anti-Castro, which meant they couldn't actually play their ultimate national security justification of protecting Cuba's Commander Almeida. Hunt's testimony, cover stories, lack of candor, and easily exposed conspiracy story also apparently made an impression on Judge Sirica. When Hunt and his compatriots were given their final sentences by Judge Sirica in November, Hunt fared the worst. "Gonzales, Martinez, and [Fiorini] each [received] one-to-four-year terms." Barker's sentence was a little longer, but all would be released after serving approximately one year. Hunt, however, would serve a total of "thirty-three months" in prison. In contrast, Egil Krogh, Hunt's original supervisor for the Plumbers unit, would be incarcerated for only four and a half months. James McCord had to serve "only three months and twenty-one days."[20]

. . .

Also coming to a head in the fall of 1973 was an investigation of Nixon's Vice President Spiro Agnew. In a matter that didn't involve Watergate, Nixon had been told six months earlier that Agnew was under investigation by the Justice Department. In August, "*The Wall Street Journal* [had] reported that Agnew was suspected of extortion, bribery, and tax evasion [involving] kickbacks paid by contractors architects and engineers" to Baltimore and Maryland officials. As noted earlier, when Nixon had chosen the racially divisive Agnew as his running mate, he knew "that his running mate was corrupt," so the news of Agnew's crimes should have been no surprise. On October 9, 1973, Vice President Agnew told Nixon that he was resigning, after striking a "deal with the Justice Department [to plead] nolo contendere to one count of having knowingly failed to report income for tax purposes." Agnew would get "three years probation and a $10,000 fine [and] no further prosecution."[21]

On October 12, 1973, Nixon chose House Minority Leader Gerald Ford as his new Vice President. In addition to Ford's popularity in Congress, Nixon chose Ford because "Nixon had Ford totally under his thumb. He was the tool of the Nixon Administration," according to Alexander Butterfield. To Nixon's way of thinking, Agnew's resignation somehow gave him an excuse to fire Special Watergate Prosecutor Archibald Cox, so the President said, "Now that we've taken care of Agnew, we can get rid of Cox." The Special Prosecutor had been pressing for the tapes for several months, and he was reported to be investigating Nixon's financial affairs with Bebe Rebozo, so Nixon felt he had to be removed.[22]

On Saturday, October 20, 1973, a critical part of the Watergate saga began. Richard Nixon ordered Attorney General Elliot Richardson to fire Special Prosecutor Cox. However, Richardson resigned rather than obey Nixon's orders. Richardson's deputy, former FBI Director William Ruckelshaus, also resigned. That left "Solicitor General Robert Bork . . . temporarily promoted to acting Attorney General, [to] obediently [send] the letter of dismissal" to Cox. The dramatic resignations and the firing of Cox became known as "the Saturday Night Massacre."[23]

The press and public learned about it from an 8:25 RO announcement by Ron Ziegler, who said "the office of the Watergate Special Prosecution Force has been abolished." It seemed like something out of a movie when FBI agents rushed to seal Cox's offices and those of Elliot Richardson and William Ruckelshaus while "network TV was crackling with bulletins and instant specials were preempting the Saturday night schedules."[24]

Cox's firing related mainly to Nixon's tapes, but there were other matters as well. "Just days earlier," Cox's prosecutors had obtained "covertly recorded conversations of [a] Rebozo bank vice president... saying he managed Nixon's 'buried' financial portfolio." In addition, "ten days earlier, Rebozo had admitted receiving one hundred thousand dollars in cash from Howard Hughes on Nixon's behalf."[25]

Due to an outcry from the public, the press, and especially Congress, Nixon was forced to agree to a package deal with Congressional leaders to assure confirmation of Ford and a new Attorney General. The deal included a new Special Prosecutor, whom Nixon agreed "could sue him in the courts for evidence" and who couldn't be fired without the approval of key Congressional leaders from both parties. Haig suggested Texan Leon Jaworski, "an old friend of Lyndon Johnson and of John Connally and a former president of the American Bar Association." Jaworski had also been "Special Counsel to the Warren Commission," whose members included the new Vice President, Gerald Ford. However, because Jaworski emerged with more power than Cox, his appointment marked another milestone. Nixon had lost control of the Watergate investigation, which was now centered on the tapes. If he lost control of the tapes, Nixon knew his Presidency was over. That process began three days after the Saturday Night Massacre, when Nixon agreed to comply with an appeals court ruling to turn over seven tapes that had been subpoenaed by Sirica's court, for the grand jury.[26]

The Bebe Rebozo investigation may have been stalled by Cox's firing, but word soon started to leak. By early December 1973, two weeks after Barker's sentencing, NBC News was reporting that the Miami-Dade County prosecutor was seeking "more information on Bebe Rebozo's bank [from] Bernard Barker." At that point, the IRS had been investigating Rebozo for over six months. In October, *The Washington Post* had run an article about the Rebozo "stock theft case," in which Rebozo handled stock he knew was stolen. Rebozo's finances were entwined with those of Nixon, and the staff of the new Watergate Special Prosecutor was being "bombarded" with tips about Nixon's "ill gotten gains." "'We're not talking about twenty [tips] a week,' recalled Carl Feldbaum, a Watergate Special Prosecution Force attorney. 'We're talking about twenty a day' . . . There was not enough time or money to follow up on everything."[27]

There are several reasons why the Nixon-Rebozo financial entanglements didn't become a huge scandal in the following months. An investigative report in *Rolling Stone* reported that "Bebe Rebozo escaped indictment in Watergate despite strong circumstantial evidence of tax evasion and bribe taking. One reason, according to CIA sources, is that CIA officials sanctioned his plea of 'national security' when the Special Prosecutor's office began investigating Rebozo's" business affairs. (Rebozo's only real "national security" activity had been money laundering for the Bay of Pigs.) In addition, Rebozo sued *The Washington Post* for "ten million dollars in damages" for its stock story, and he then dragged the case out for a decade, until a settlement was reached (in which the *Post* paid Rebozo no damages). Rebozo's suit eventually had a chilling effect on other news outlets, so his financial crimes and Mafia ties were soon rarely mentioned in the press. In short, Rebozo and Nixon had enough money to make reporting the Nixon-Rebozo story very expensive for media outlets—at a time when there was plenty of other Watergate news to cover. There were other forms of intimidation as well. House Judiciary Committee counsel Jerry Zeifman wrote that John Dean told him that "when I was first placed in the witness protection program, a Justice Department official had warned me that they were in fear for my life. They were afraid that the President's friend Bebe Rebozo would arrange to have me encased in concrete and buried . . . off the Bahamas." The Senate Watergate Committee would soon begin a "Hughes-Rebozo Investigation," which gave *The New York Times* cover to run headlines such as "Rebozo denies shifting funds to Swiss banks for President." However, the Committee's investigation would simply be overshadowed by the slowly building drumbeat for Nixon's resignation or impeachment.[28]

In the wake of Nixon's Saturday Night Massacre, his problems continued to mount. At Disney World, where Nixon answered questions "at an . . . editor's meeting," the President was forced to proclaim, "I am not a crook." He made that statement after making "gaffe after gaffe as he responded to a volley of sharp questions: on missing tapes, on the tiny income taxes he had paid; on the rumors that Rebozo kept a secret trusts fund for him."[29]

A new Watergate scandal erupted on December 7, 1973, when the public learned about the eighteen-and-a-half-minute gap on Nixon's June 20, 1972, tape. Though Nixon had turned over the seven subpoenaed tapes, only three had been sent to the grand jury, since he was claiming executive privilege on four, which remained with Sirica. Nixon knew that other tapes would be subpoenaed, so he was having them transcribed for his own use and reference. As part of that process, Nixon's lawyers had first learned about the mysterious gap on November 14, and they waited a week before telling Judge Sirica. The President's longtime secretary, Rose Mary Woods, claimed she might have made the erasure accidentally when she tried to answer the phone while transcribing the tapes. But the odd stretch she demonstrated that would have been required to do that didn't convince investigators, and soon even she backed off, saying that perhaps "she was responsible for the loss of only five minutes of dialogue," not the whole gap. The gap controversy made it look like Nixon had something to hide, and it fed the public's appetite for press coverage of Watergate news even more. (The gap was detailed in Chapter 31.)[30]

While the Watergate scandal filled the airwaves and newspapers in December 1973, the coverage completely ignored the men involved in the CIA-Mafia plots who were really at the root of the scandal. Due to political intervention from an unknown Washington official, Johnny Rosselli had been moved to a much more comfortable prison before he was finally released on October 5, 1973. At sixty-eight, Rosselli faced a relatively bleak future. Sam Giancana was still in Mexico—where he was primarily concerned with the drug network and gambling—and the mob powers in Chicago had Rosselli officially turn over his Las Vegas role to Tony "The Ant" Spilotro.* With no part left to play in Las Vegas or Los Angeles, Rosselli moved to Florida, where he had family—and Santo Trafficante. Without his income from Las Vegas, or his power from the old days, Rosselli moved in "with his sister and brother-in-law" in Plantation, Florida.[31]

Rosselli's Chicago associate from the 1960 CIA-Mafia plots, Richard Cain, had started providing information to FBI agent William Roemer. Cain was the "made" member of the Mafia and former CIA asset, who had once been the Chief Investigator for the Cook County–Chicago

*Spilotro inspired Joe Pesci's character in the film *Casino*

Sheriff's Office. Though Cain had been careful not to tell Agent Roemer too much, the men developed a friendship, and Roemer once described Cain "as his best friend." Like Rosselli, Cain's power had flowed from Sam Giancana, and with Giancana in Mexico, Cain no longer had the protection he once enjoyed. On December 20, 1973, Cain was gunned down in a Chicago sandwich shop. Cain was murdered by the same mobster who would eventually face prosecution for killing Tony "The Ant" Spilotro. Richard Cain's slaying was a reminder that talking to federal authorities could be fatal, if your mob associates found out.[32]

By Christmas 1973, Jimmy Hoffa had been out of jail for almost two years, but he still chafed at not being able to hold any Teamsters office, which he blamed on Nixon. Hoffa had to sit at home in Michigan, frustrated, while his replacement, Frank Fitzsimmons, was so close to President Nixon he had even flown on Air Force One. Hoffa felt that he had been betrayed—and someone had to pay. According to Dan Moldea, America's leading Hoffa authority, he "can document that during the Senate Watergate Committee hearings Hoffa was leaking information to [Senator] Ervin's Committee, via a source in Washington, as a means of getting even with Nixon."[33]

It's possible that news of the murder of Richard Cain, a participant with Rosselli in the 1960 CIA-Mafia plots, prompted Hoffa to look to Rosselli as a way to get revenge on Nixon and Fitzsimmons. Unlike Hoffa's close associate Santo Trafficante, Hoffa had never really been involved with Rosselli. In addition, Rosselli's power in the mob was largely a thing of the past and, because of the Jack Anderson articles, some information about Rosselli was already in the public sphere. Hoffa appears to have tipped off someone with the Senate Watergate Committee about Rosselli and the 1960 CIA-Mafia plots. It's also possible that because of the Hughes-Rebozo $100,000 investigation, Watergate Committee investigators were already starting to make the connection between Hughes, his former aide Robert Maheu, and Jack Anderson's articles about Johnny Rosselli.

Quoted in detail here for the first time is a "Memorandum Personal and Confidential" written by two Watergate Committee investigators "to Senator Ervin, about "the Relevance . . . of John Rosselli's testimony about his CIA activities." (See Appendix for the "Ervin-Rosselli-Watergate memo.") This memo is undated, but from the results that followed, it appears to have been written in January or early February of 1974. Committee investigators Terry Lenzner and Marc Lackritz told Senator Ervin that "John Rosselli and his attorney, Tom Wadden, object to testifying about Rosselli's involvement with Robert Maheu in a CIA-financed plot to assassinate Fidel Castro in the early 1960s. The objection is based upon national security grounds as well as an assertion . . . that the material is not relevant" to the Committee's work. The investigators asserted that the "Testimony of Mr. Rosselli about his matter is relevant and necessary to our investigation," and they detailed a compelling case.[34]

The Committee investigators pointed out that "during the last year of the Eisenhower Administration, the CIA apparently financed and organized a plot to assassinate Fidel Castro." They didn't have to point out to Ervin that of course Nixon was Vice President at that time, but they did say that "only a few officials in the government knew of the existence of the plot . . . " The investigators stated that "among the participants in this plot were Robert Maheu and John Rosselli." They said "the plot continued into the early 1960s even after the abortive Bay of Pigs invasion." The memo said the Justice Department developed a file on the plots because of the Sam Giancana "wiretap" incident.[35]

Nixon's interest in the CIA-Mafia plots with Rosselli is shown in the memo, because soon after taking office 1969, his "Assistant Attorney General Will Wilson requested the file [on Rosselli and the CIA-Mafia plots] from the Deputy Chief of the Organized Crime Section." The file was certainly shared with Attorney General Mitchell, who no doubt told Nixon what it said. After the file was returned, it next became of interest to the Nixon White House in January 1971 "only one day after Jack Anderson published his first column linking both Maheu and Rosselli to the CIA plot to kill Castro." Originally, Anderson's two January articles were attached to this Watergate memo.[36]

The memo then details the concerns of Nixon aides such as H.R. Haldeman, Jack Caulfield, and John Dean to Anderson's article. Assistant Attorney General Will Wilson once more "requested the secret Justice file," and he "showed the sensitive 'Castro' file to Attorney General Mitchell, in January 1971, and discussed with him the political implications of the information." Then, "Attorney General Mitchell discussed the contents of the sensitive file with President Nixon." Missing from the Watergate investigator's memo is the fact that Maheu said he met privately with Mitchell and told him enough about the CIA-Mafia plots that it left the Attorney General "shaking." Such a Maheu-Mitchell meeting is logical because the memo said that when "Maheu was interviewed privately by [Assistant Attorney General] Wilson concerning his prior CIA activities with John Rosselli [Robert] Maheu was <u>not</u> forthcoming with information about the plot . . . " (Emphasis in original.)[37]

The Committee investigators concluded their memo by saying that "the obsession of the Administration . . . on Larry O'Brien in 1971 and 1972 . . . was in part motivated by a fear that Maheu would impart some of this sensitive information about the plot to O'Brien . . . and these concerns could have been a possible motivation for the break-in to the office of the DNC and Larry O'Brien . . . especially since their directions were to photograph any documents relating to Cuban contributions or Cuban involvement in the 1972 Democratic campaign." Clearly, the investigators were getting very close to uncovering the Plumbers' goal of the Cuban Dossier, which could easily fall into the category of "Cuban involvement in the 1972 Democratic campaign." They end the memo by saying "it is for these reasons that we wish to question John Rosselli about the nature and scope of his activities with Robert Maheu in the early 1960s."[38]

The memo worked, and Ervin approved their interview of Rosselli, again putting the Mafia don in a difficult position. Deportation proceedings against Rosselli had mysteriously stopped while he was in prison, but now that Richard Helms no longer ran the CIA, by January 4, 1974, the INS was again targeting Rosselli. The INS pressure left Rosselli with little choice but to talk to the Watergate Committee investigators. Setting a pattern that would last until his death, as long as Rosselli at least talked to government investigators, he wouldn't be deported.

In another important Watergate memo quoted here for the first time, Committee investigator Bob Muse summarized his interview of Johnny Rosselli on "February 20, 1974," when he was accompanied by two other Committee investigators, "Scott Armstrong [and] Marc Lackritz." Rosselli was interviewed "at the office of Rosselli's attorney, Thom Wadden . . . in Washington, DC . . . also present were Wadden's associates Bryan B. McMenamin and Leslie Scherr." (See Appendix for "Watergate Committee investigators' Rosselli interview.")[39]

Wadden warned the investigators that having "discussed with Rosselli the Maheu Cuban matter . . . it presented a great problem of national security." He admitted he'd tried "to reach Senator Ervin, an old acquaintance [to] persuade the Senator" to stop the interview. Wadden was unable to talk to Ervin, but the attorney said "that Rosselli was insistent upon not giving any information about his Cuban activities and would rather go to jail than be compelled to testify about the matter." However, that didn't stop the investigators from trying to get the information they wanted from Rosselli, either directly or by having him talk about related matters.[40]

Attorney Leslie Scherr, Wadden's associate, was present for the entire interview. As noted in Chapter 29, Scherr said that

> judging from the questions posed to Rosselli . . . the prosecutors felt that "the reason why the break-in occurred at the Democratic Party headquarters was because Nixon or somebody in the Republican Party suspected that the Democrats had information as to Nixon's involvement with the CIA's original contract with Rosselli."[41]

As a result, Nixon and his Republican associates, and the Watergate burglars,

> felt that a document existed showing Nixon was involved with or knew what was going on with the CIA and the assassination of Castro and Rosselli's involvement, et cetera. It's for that reason that they wanted to try to get this information that Nixon suspected they were going to use against him.[42]

Scherr added that Rosselli "offered nothing that would confirm Nixon's involvement in the CIA plots, or shed any light on the motivations of the Watergate burglars." Scherr's remarks about Rosselli—made to Rosselli's biographers and published in 1991—are borne out by the memo of the Watergate committee investigators, who wrote that "the interview was not productive insofar as Rosselli's involvement with Maheu in 1960 was concerned." However, in many ways what is most important is Scherr's observations of the investigators' questioning, which apparently referred to a "document" that could have shown "Nixon was involved with . . . the CIA and the assassination of Castro and Rosselli's involvement." As part of their Hughes-Rebozo investigation, some of these same Watergate investigators had talked, or would talk, to Frank Fiorini in a non-public executive session, and it's not known if he may have indicated to them what he'd told journalist Andrew St. George about the secret Cuban Dossier.[43]

The Watergate Committee investigators had been stymied about getting direct confirmation of Nixon's involvement of the CIA-Mafia plots from Rosselli, but they were able to extract some additional information from him. They also continued to press Rosselli for more information about the plots. When the Mafia don told them how "he met Maheu for the first time . . . questions were asked as to what his subsequent involvement with Maheu was," and those are likely the questions that Scherr referred to. However, Wadden stopped Rosselli from answering "on the ground[s] of national security."[44]

Johnny Rosselli did talk more freely about how he brokered the sale of the Desert Inn hotel and casino to Howard Hughes, with the help of Maheu and attorney Ed Morgan. In addition, Rosselli talked about his other dealings with Morgan and the last time he claimed to have seen Maheu. Rosselli said that "he has no recollection of ever having met Bebe Rebozo," and said that "with regard to political contributions, he has never had any discussions with Rebozo, or had any conversations with anyone about any contributions (of over $10,000) to a Presidential campaign." (Parenthesis in original, and one wonders about contributions of less than $10,000.)[45]

At one point, Rosselli's attorney Wadden "chimed in by noting that he had been an old associate of [William] Hundley and had gone to Paradise Island with Hundley about 7 years ago." That admission is important, because Wadden would later confide to Hundley that Rosselli had admitted his involvement in JFK's murder, before Rosselli's own gruesome slaying two years later.[46]

Rosselli omitted much information about topics he was willing to talk about, and he lied and hedged at other times. At first, Rosselli said "that he has never met Gordon Liddy [or] Howard Hunt." Then, Rosselli admitted he had seen Liddy once, when Liddy "was acting as a prison librarian." Rosselli hedged when he said "he is fairly certain" that "he has never met Hunt with regard to any CIA involvement of his own." As cited previously, former CIA agent—and *Newsweek* bureau chief—Bayard Stockton wrote in a CIA-approved account that "in March 1961"—when the CIA-Mafia plots were very active, just weeks before the Bay of Pigs invasion—"Rosselli went to the Dominican Republic, accompanied by Howard Hunt of the CIA."

Rosselli lied when he told the Watergate Committee investigators "that he has never had any property or business dealings in Cuba." His biographers found that Rosselli operated "for a time in a management capacity at [Santo] Trafficante's Sans Souci" casino in Havana.[47]

The Watergate Committee investigators' "interview concluded with the serving of a subpoena upon Mr. Rosselli and the decision to hold a further meeting under oath at a later date." That presented a problem for Rosselli. When Rosselli returned to Miami on February 25, 1974, he no doubt wasted no time in telling Santo Trafficante that he hadn't given investigators Trafficante's name or anything of importance. But refusing to comply with the subpoena could put Rosselli back in prison, or even result in his deportation.

In the immediate wake of their Rosselli interview, the Hughes-Rebozo aspect of the Watergate investigation forged ahead. The knowledge the Committee investigators had developed about the CIA-Mafia plots was used when Nixon's former operative John Caulfield testified on March 16, 1974. At one point—after going "off the record"—they were able to get Caulfield to admit that he was concerned specifically about the CIA-Mafia plots when he wrote a January 1971 memo. However, the Committee investigators soon found themselves "stalled" in trying to bring Rosselli back for sworn testimony. Anthony Summers wrote that "when they asked the CIA for information they were given none. When they [the investigators] asked Senate Watergate Committee Sam Ervin to let them subpoena key witnesses he turned them down."[48]

Why did the Rosselli aspect of the Watergate investigation suddenly end? Assistant Chief Counsel Terry Lenzner told Summers that he didn't know. In hindsight, there are several possibilities. Most obvious was the fact that Rosselli's friend Ed Morgan was now an attorney for the Democratic National Committee. In addition, Morgan was dealing with Watergate counsels at the time, because he was representing Herbert Kalmbach, who testified the same day as Caulfield. Morgan could have brought pressure to bear on Senator Ervin. The same is true for Tom Wadden, who might have revealed or hinted to Ervin the actual national security concerns regarding Rosselli that Wadden wasn't willing to share with Watergate Committee investigators. In addition, the CIA had quietly intervened for Rosselli before, and the Agency could have done so again. Finally, Rosselli knew secrets that Kennedy loyalists wouldn't want exposed, such as John F. Kennedy's liaisons with Rosselli's close friend, Judith Campbell—a secret Rosselli would leak the following year when dealing with the Senate Church Committee. A former Kennedy associate with the Watergate Committee, such as Carmine Bellino, could have intervened to keep Rosselli from testifying, to make sure JFK's secret wasn't revealed. The bottom line is that Rosselli wasn't forced to testify about the CIA-Mafia plots to Watergate investigators, and he wasn't deported.[49]

As a result, the fact that Rosselli had been interviewed by Watergate investigators at all—let alone the fact that he was viewed as key to the Watergate burglar's motivation—remained largely unknown. Woodward and Bernstein had finished the manuscript for *All the President's Men* the previous month, so it contained nothing about Rosselli or the Mafia. Oddly, Scott Armstrong—one of the Committee investigators who interviewed Rosselli—later did extensive work for Woodward and Bernstein on their next book, *The Final Days*. However, *The Final Days* also contains nothing about Rosselli or the Mafia.[50]

Bernard Barker's mob ties briefly became news on March 10, 1974. A CIA memo says on that day, Barker called the CIA, saying he was worried because a "newsman had just . . . indicated that Ambassador [Richard] Helms testified that Mr. Barker [was] formerly associated with criminal and gambling elements." In fact, Helms had so testified a year earlier, while being confirmed as Ambassador to Iran, but his testimony had just been released on March 5, 1974. However, Helms worked with the CIA to quickly issue a retraction before the news media started investigating Barker's links to the Mafia. As a result, Barker's work for the mob didn't become part of the conventional Watergate story.[51]

By the spring of 1974, the battle over Watergate had become a battle for the tapes that would decide Nixon's fate, since impeachment was now a very real possibility. Earlier in the year, Special Prosecutor Jaworski had "requested twenty-two more tapes," but Nixon had turned him down. (Unknown to Nixon, on February 25, after the President had refused to talk to the Watergate grand jury, it had named Nixon as an "unindicted co-conspirator," though that wouldn't become public for almost four months.) Jaworski soon subpoenaed "sixty-four more tapes," and he included in his request the June 23, 1972, "Smoking Gun" tape. Naturally, Nixon didn't comply. On April 11, the House Judiciary Committee subpoenaed forty-two tapes, but Nixon resisted releasing additional tapes.[52]

To deal with legal, Congressional, press, and public pressure, Nixon decided to release edited transcripts of forty-six of his White House tapes. The effort became an intense, mad dash by Nixon and his aides to release enough to make it look like a good faith effort, without revealing anything criminal. Worried about the outcome, Press Secretary Ron Ziegler "assigned his two personal assistants—Diane Sawyer and Frank Gannon, to review the editing and report back to him." Diane Sawyer was "dismayed at the sloppy presentation [where] lines spoken by the President were mistakenly divided and attributed in part to Ehrlichman." Much worse was the fact that "certain passages referred back to matters that had been excised [and] could not fail to convey the impression that the really damaging parts had been eliminated." Sawyer and Gannon "pleaded for more time" to prepare things more properly. Haig said that Nixon's "lawyers were firm," and they had to meet an agreed-upon extended deadline of April 30 to turn them over to the House Judiciary Committee. "No matter how sloppy the transcripts were, or how serious the inconsistencies and inaccuracies, the transcripts would have to reach the Committee on the thirtieth." Sawyer had no choice but to resume her "proofreading and editing."[53]

When Nixon revealed the tape transcripts to the nation in a televised address on April 29, 1974, they were in neat, uniform, nicely bound volumes that belied the problems within. Criminal references had been removed, and some tapes—like the June 23 "Smoking Gun" tape—were withheld entirely. So the tape battles continued, and pressure continued to mount on Nixon to release more.

Even what was left in the volumes—when paired with other testimony or evidence—was still damaging to Nixon, and the tide toward impeachment continued to climb. By April, polls showed that more people wanted Nixon to resign or be impeached (55 percent) than wanted him to remain President (37 percent). Adding fuel to the fire was Woodward and Bernstein's new book, *All the President's Men*, which quickly became a bestseller. As the House Judiciary Committee began to consider impeachment more seriously, it hired additional staff. One of those added was twenty-six-year-old Hillary Rodham, thanks to a recommendation by one of her professors, Burke Marshall, who had served in Robert Kennedy's Justice Department.[54]

According to David Brock, Hillary was "involved . . . in two important projects. Under the direction of Bernard W. Nussbaum, another Kennedy Justice Department lawyer, she was responsible for drawing up highly restrictive rules of procedure that were to govern the impeachment process." In addition, she helped "to oversee the preparation of a confidential history of Presidential abuse of power." The thinking was "that Nixon would mount a defense to the effect that actions in the Watergate affair were not inconsistent with those of many previous administrations." The report was "drafted under the direction of Yale historian C. Vann Woodward, a colleague of Burke Marshall's," and he and Hillary were aided by "twelve legal scholars."[55]

However, the report became controversial because "it was kept from House Committee members and staff," and it "was attacked by Nixon supporters for . . . omitting many well-established presidential abuses of authority." In many ways, the project was a no-win situation for Hillary Rodham and her co-workers. Nixon supporters could always claim that abuses by Democratic Presidents had been omitted, both to help reputations of the former Chief Executives and to make Nixon look worse. On the other hand, including alleged abuses against recent Presidents, without giving members of that administration a chance to defend themselves, would hardly be suitable either. Those are probably the reasons it was decided not to release the report to the full Committee; though several months later it was published as a paperback book.[56]

In the spring of 1974, Nixon's Chief of Staff, Alexander Haig, faced having to answer questions in the Hughes-Rebozo investigation. On April 24, he once again asked Joseph Califano for advice. As they discussed Haig's options and the tape situation, "Califano asked his friend why he seemed so unusually troubled," even beyond the issues they were discussing. Haig claimed it was because world affairs were being neglected while Nixon dealt with Watergate, but "Califano believed his friend was holding something back [and] his manner indicated that he thought things were worse than he was willing to admit." Haig said, "We've got to get rid of the Watergate problem."[57]

Haig had two major concerns that he was "holding . . . back" from Califano. A problem that would only increase in the coming months was that "the details of running the country had been left to General Haig as the President withdrew more and more into himself to reflect on his Watergate options." As later reported by Woodward and Bernstein, "Nixon had lost interest in domestic affairs, and he gave only occasional bursts of attention to foreign policy." Their book *The*

Final Days shows how Haig had to take on more and more executive responsibility. Another concern for Haig was his suspicions about Nixon's illicit money from overseas, which would soon cause him to order the "secret [Army] investigation of any Nixon connections with huge cash contributions from countries in the Far East [or] organized crime." As a result, *The Washington Star* reported that the "Army's Criminal Investigation Command [found] strong indications of a history of Nixon connections with money from organized crime." (That investigation was detailed at length in Chapter 24, so it won't be repeated here.) The President's increasingly erratic behavior, despondency, and drinking worried Haig—and some have suggested that the Army investigation Haig finally ordered in June 1974 was meant to give him leverage to force Nixon's resignation, if that became necessary "for the good of the country."[58]

As the summer progressed, the battle for the tapes that riveted the country headed to the Supreme Court, even as journalists and the public tried to guess the identity of *All the President's Men*'s "Deep Throat" character. The leading candidate was Mark Felt, named in June articles in both the *Washingtonian* and *The Wall Street Journal.* Away from the public spotlight, a June 28, 1974, internal CIA memo showed that the Agency had recently found that "James McCord's service records [reveal] that he was involved in Cuban operations" in the 1960s, "contrary to earlier reports by this Agency to the various investigating authorities." In the memo, Agency officials debated whether or not to tell the Senate Watergate Committee "before it ceases its operations."[59]

The CIA only had two days to wait, because Senator Ervin's Watergate Committee came to an end on June 30, 1972. The Committee "quickly issued its damning Final Report on the President," as well as its own transcripts of eight Nixon tapes, which showed how selective Nixon's edited transcripts had been. On July 8, 1972, the Supreme Court heard oral arguments in Special Prosecutor Jaworski's effort to obtain sixty-four important tapes. One would turn out to be the soon-to-be-infamous "Smoking Gun" tape that clearly documented Nixon's leading role in the cover-up (detailed in Chapter 31). In the following days, the cumulative effect of news reports about the case made it clear to the country that the Supreme Court's ruling would essentially decide Nixon's fate.

On July 24, 1974, the Supreme Court made its anxiously awaited ruling: In a unanimous decision, the Court ordered President Nixon to turn over all sixty-four tapes. By that time, it was obvious to the public what the decision meant, and that included Jimmy Hoffa. His longtime associate Dave Johnson said that Hoffa was "happy as hell when the Supreme Court told Nixon he had to give up those tapes . . . Hoffa called me up and said, 'it looks like Nixon's out and we're in!'"[60]

Three days after the Supreme Court's decision, the House Judiciary Committee passed its first article of impeachment, for obstruction of justice. Now, the end of Nixon's Presidency was only a matter of time. Alexander Haig increased his pressure on Nixon to resign. On July 30, 1974, as Nixon's counsel Fred Buzhardt discussed the "Smoking Gun" tape with the President, Nixon still claimed everything "was done for national security reasons," saying, "I know what I meant . . . regardless of what's on the tapes." When Buzhardt asked Nixon about those national security reasons—"What were they?"—Nixon "didn't really reply."[61]

Bebe Rebozo was probably the only person in the world that the President could truly confide in, something that was just as true before Watergate as during the scandal. On August 8, 1974, Rebozo was with Nixon at the White House when the President made his decision to resign, largely in response to the actions of Alexander Haig and Vice President Gerald Ford. That night, at 9:01 RO , Richard Nixon finally announced his resignation to a nationwide television audience. The speech was filled with emotion, the most Nixon had ever shown in public, as he rambled through passages that spun from homilies to almost—but never quite—accepting responsibility. Nixon said that "if some of my judgments were wrong—and some were wrong—they were made in what I believed at the time to be the best interest of the nation."[62]

Much has been written about Nixon's decision to resign, his resignation speech, and his well-documented last morning at the White House. What remains hidden forever is Nixon's own thoughts, and what he might have said to Bebe Rebozo about how he had come to this point. All of Nixon's promise and effort and ambition had been reduced to the disgrace of resignation. Like the four break-ins at the Watergate that ultimately ended in disaster, Nixon's almost three decades of flirting with organized crime, corruption, and secret intelligence had ultimately taken their toll. In hindsight, Nixon's crash seems almost inevitable. In reality, if not for one Watergate break-in too many, he might have gotten away with everything.

The morning after Nixon's resignation speech, he said goodbye to his aides and the White House staff, and he made a final, sometimes poignant, speech. Nixon and his family then helicoptered away from the White House, to Andrews Air Force Base and then—on Air Force One—to his home at San Clemente. Nixon hadn't waited to see Gerald Ford take the oath of office. Nixon was halfway across the country as Ford proclaimed in his inaugural address that "Our long national nightmare is over."[63]

EPILOGUE

Late 1974 to 1979: Nixon Golfs with Mobsters, Investigations Continue, and Rosselli Is Murdered

Even before Nixon left the White House, Ambrose found that "the process of . . . destroying documents had already begun." A Ford aide found that Rose Mary Woods's former office was "heavy with the acrid smell of paper recently burned in the fireplace." More serious was that "the Burn Room of the White House . . . was so jammed with bags of paper waiting to be destroyed that the overflow was piling up in the corridor." In addition, "the paper shredder was also working overtime"—and the destruction didn't end until August 10. Nixon had begun having papers taken out in "suitcases and boxes" for at least a week before that, but he now began his most audacious move.[64]

On the night of August 10, Ford aide Benton Becker "found three military trucks lined up outside the basement entrance to the West Wing, stuffed with boxes and file cabinets, about to depart for Andrews Air Force Base." When Becker told them to stop, the Air Force Colonel in command of the convoy said, "I take my instructions from General Haig." Becker found and confronted Haig, who "claimed ignorance of what was happening and ordered the colonel to unload the trucks." Ford's aides felt that "as Haig and his friends took possession of or destroyed documents, they were protecting themselves as well [as Nixon]."[65]

Haig remained as Ford's Chief of Staff for a time, and he had an important role to play in the coming weeks. Just as he had helped—by some accounts—to engineer Nixon's resignation, Haig now seemed determined that the former President not try to clear his name by demanding a trial, one that could reveal the national security secrets that Nixon had been referring to for so long. Some of those secrets, like the JFK-Almeida coup plan, involved Haig, so it makes sense that Haig wouldn't want to see them exposed. Haig soon gained an unlikely ally in his cause.

After his resignation, Nixon made the unlikely choice of Herbert J. Miller to represent him in his legal battles regarding his papers, tapes, and possible criminal charges. Miller had been "chief of the Justice Department's criminal division under Attorney General Robert F. Kennedy from 1961 to 1965," where "he directed the successful prosecutions of Teamsters leader Jimmy Hoffa and members of organized crime." Only after Miller's 2009 death did *The Washington Post* reveal that Nixon had actually "wanted to fight the pending corruption charges in court, but Mr. Miller convinced him that a legal battle over Watergate would not be in his or the country's best interests." If he faced charges, Nixon could have used the same national security defense he'd been talking about since the scandal broke, and he might have been successful. The government couldn't allow Nixon to reveal their most sensitive anti-Castro operations of the early '60s—especially with Almeida still alive, in place, and unexposed—so any charges would probably have been dropped. Nixon's desire for a trial would also motivate Miller to help the ex-President, since Miller wouldn't want secret Kennedy-era Cuban operations exposed. Nixon's stance also gave him bargaining leverage with new President Gerald Ford for an unconditional pardon as well as more control of his papers and tapes.[66]

Thanks to Nixon's approach and Herbert Miller, that's exactly what Nixon got from Ford on September 8, 1974, when Ford issued a full pardon to Nixon, which was "unconditional for all crimes Nixon may have committed in the White House." For the numerous prosecutions of Nixon aides and officials that were still ongoing, Nixon's pardon presented a problem. Ford's pardon of the former President removed the leverage prosecutors needed to get Nixon to testify in those existing cases, or about other officials who could only be indicted and prosecuted with Nixon's testimony. The deal arranged by Jack Miller helped to ensure that many of Watergate's mysteries would remain just that, until after Nixon's death. Only sixty hours of tapes were released in the 1970s—out of thousands of hours—and Miller aggressively represented Nixon (and his estate) in his fights to prevent the release of more tapes and documents for decades, while Miller continued to represent clients like Senator Edward Kennedy.[67]

Even without Nixon's testimony, Stanley Kutler wrote that "more than seventy persons were convicted or offered guilty pleas as a consequence of the Age of Watergate." Without a Nixon trial or testimony to bring attention to them, some major disclosures passed unnoticed, such as when Andrew St. George finally revealed in the August 1974 issue of *True* magazine that Frank Fiorini had admitted that the Watergate burglars were primarily looking for the Cuban Dossier of CIA attempts to assassinate Fidel Castro.[68]

Nixon remained in seclusion, essentially in exile at San Clemente, as Herbert Miller fought against the release of his tapes and papers, in battles that began immediately after his pardon. Some of Nixon's staff went with him to California, including Ron Ziegler and his aide Diane Sawyer. From most accounts, Nixon suffered from depression and health problems in the aftermath of his resignation.

Soon after taking office, Gerald Ford would have been briefed by CIA Director William Colby on covert U.S. operations against Fidel Castro. That should have included information on Commander Almeida and material from the 1967 IG Report about the CIA-Mafia Castro assassination plots. Unlike Richard Helms, Colby hadn't worked on those operations, so the important differences between them would have been difficult for him to convey to Ford. It's not known what, if anything, Haig may have told Ford about his own work on the 1963 JFK-Almeida coup plan.

As Gerald Ford consolidated his Presidency, it became clear that Alexander Haig wasn't a good fit, and he was replaced as Chief of Staff by Donald Rumsfeld. Dick Cheney soon joined Rumsfeld as a top Ford aide. Haig was named Commander of NATO and all U.S. forces in Europe. Ford chose as his Vice President Nelson Rockefeller, but the political climate was such that it took "four months of investigation by 300 FBI agents" before he could be confirmed by Congress.[69]

By late 1974, the intense press and Congressional interest in Watergate began to fade, especially after a revelation by *New York Times* reporter Sy Hersh ignited a new round of government investigations. Sy Hersh's December 22, 1974, *Times* article began to expose what its headlines called the "Huge CIA [Domestic Surveillance] Operation" directed against antiwar critics in the U.S. CIA Director William Colby fired Counterintelligence Chief James Angleton the next day, but the firestorm had begun. To quell the furor, President Ford appointed a blue ribbon commission headed by Vice President Nelson Rockefeller to look into the CIA's domestic activities. However, since most of the Rockefeller Commission's members were conservative establishment figures such as Ronald Reagan, many in Congress didn't trust the panel, and both the House and Senate prepared their own investigations.[70]

On January 1, 1975, in Judge John Sirica's courtroom, John Mitchell, H.R. Haldeman, and John Ehrlichman were all found guilty on five counts for crimes related to the cover-up of Watergate. But that news was quickly overshadowed by a dramatic admission from President Ford. When Ford met with a group of editors from *The New York Times* on January 16, 1975, he told them that the Rockefeller Commission had to be careful not to expose certain past CIA operations, "like assassinations." Ford quickly tried to qualify his remark, saying it was off the record, but word raced through journalistic circles, soon reaching Congress, where members added CIA assassinations to their investigative agenda.[71]

The Senate Select Committee on Intelligence was created on January 27 and chaired by Idaho Senator Frank Church. The Church Committee would look into matters such as domestic spying and CIA attempts to assassinate foreign leaders, including the CIA-Mafia plots against Castro. The Church Committee also created a subcommittee devoted to the JFK assassination, headed by moderate Pennsylvania Republican Senator Richard Schweiker, which also included Colorado Senator Gary Hart. On February 19, 1975, the House created the Nedzi Committee, soon to be called the Pike Committee, to delve into CIA assassinations.[72]

The general public finally heard about President Ford's "assassinations" comment on February 28, 1975, during Daniel Schorr's CBS news broadcast. Schorr had also obtained from CIA Director William Colby an indirect confirmation of CIA assassination attempts against foreign leaders. When Jack Anderson weighed in with new articles about the CIA-Mafia plots on March 10 and 13—having already named Johnny Rosselli as one of those involved—the floodgates were beginning to open. Four days later, *Time* magazine advanced the story by adding Sam Giancana to the plots with Rosselli and the CIA.[73]

Richard Helms was called back from his ambassadorial post in Iran to begin a series of increasingly intense rounds of testimony to the investigating committees. The Church Committee interviewed Helms on April 23, followed by the Rockefeller Commission staff on

April 27, and culminating with a four-hour private session with the Rockefeller Commissioners on April 28, 1975. Upon leaving, Helms saw CBS newscaster Daniel Schorr. Fearing that the secret cover-ups he had maintained since 1962 were about to unravel, Helms exploded in fury at the man he blamed for making them public—Daniel Schorr. As described by Schorr:

> Helms['s] face, ashen from strain and fatigue, turned livid. "You son-of-a-bitch!" he raged. "You killer! You cocksucker! 'Killer Schorr'—that's what they ought to call you!" Continuing his string of curses, he strode toward the press room.[74]

Helms was furious that some of his most important long-hidden secrets were being exposed, and his use of the term "killer" indicated his worry that the revelations of Schorr and the investigations might result in the death of a CIA asset. The questioning of Helms focused on the plots to assassinate Fidel Castro in the early 1960s, but most of the non-Mafia CIA assets from those operations were either out of harm's way or already convicted and in Cuban prisons, like Rolando Cubela. In addition to his own self-interest, Helms's biggest concern would have been that a valuable asset like Almeida could be exposed and killed.[75]

Declassified files now make it clear that Helms lied to both committees about his unauthorized Castro assassination plots (admitting only a limited amount of information) and he completely hid the JFK-Almeida coup plan and most of AMWORLD (including its code name and immense size). However, he wasn't the only CIA official to hide important information from the Committee. In contrast to CIA Director William Colby's carefully cultivated public image as being almost too forthcoming with Congress, according to the Church staff, "when it came to the assassination plots . . . Colby closed the door" and wouldn't cooperate. (The situation would not change when Ford replaced Colby as Director with George H.W. Bush in 1976, and made Donald Rumsfeld Secretary of Defense and Dick Cheney his Chief of Staff. Files show that much CIA, FBI, and military information was withheld from the Church Committee, including everything about AMWORLD and Manuel Artime's ties to the CIA-Mafia plots with Rosselli and Trafficante.)[76]

Even as the Rockefeller Commission issued its final report on June 11, 1975, the Church Committee intensified its efforts. On June 13, the

Church Committee again grilled Helms, this time exclusively about CIA assassination plots, including those with the Mafia. His testimony was in closed session, so the public had no way to know what Helms said—or didn't say—about those involved in the plots. Johnny Rosselli's friend, former CIA agent William Harvey, also had to testify.[77]

Other participants in the CIA-Mafia plots, such as Santo Trafficante, must have worried about what might come out concerning the CIA's assassination plots. Trafficante would have been especially worried when Sam Giancana was subpoenaed and slated to testify on June 26. Giancana had finally returned to the United States the previous year, but he was no longer a major force in the Mafia.[78]

On June 19, 1975, Sam Giancana became the first of several Congressional witnesses to be murdered. The former mob boss was cooking a late-night meal for a trusted friend who was visiting his home in the Chicago neighborhood of Oak Park. His friend shot Giancana seven times with a silenced .22-caliber pistol, an unusually small gun for a mob hit. Five of the shots were around Giancana's chin and mouth, a sign that mafiosi shouldn't talk. The crime was never officially solved, but the gun was eventually traced to Florida, and some pointed to Trafficante.[79]

Giancana's murder made headlines across the country, adding an urgency to the Committees' investigations. The day after Giancana's death, William Colby testified about CIA assassination plots, followed four days later by Johnny Rosselli. The transcripts—kept secret until the 1990s—show that Johnny Rosselli had mastered the art of saying a lot while revealing little, sticking to an incomplete version of the CIA-Mafia plots that mirrored the whitewashed version Helms had promulgated in his own testimony and in the 1967 Inspector General's Report. Jack Anderson wrote once more about Rosselli on July 7, and *Time* magazine ran an article touching on the original 1959 CIA Mafia plots brokered by Hoffa—a story Hoffa himself had just leaked to someone with the Church Committee. On July 17 and 18, the Church Committee once more interrogated Helms about assassination plots, in closed sessions.[80]

Jimmy Hoffa was now in the crosshairs of the Church Committee, because of *Time*'s article about Hoffa's role in the 1959 CIA-Mafia plots. Trafficante, Marcello, and others couldn't afford to let Hoffa testify under oath about those or related matters like the Mafia-Hoffa-Nixon bribes. On July 30, 1975, Jimmy Hoffa was spotted leaving a restaurant near Detroit, heading for what he thought was a meeting with New Jersey mobster Tony Provenzano. Immediately, Provenzano became the government's top suspect for having arranged Hoffa's murder, with Frank Fitzsimmons not far behind.[81]

Hoffa's disappearance, quickly assumed to be a homicide, immediately became a huge national story, generating headlines for weeks. Though Provenzano was the leading suspect in Hoffa's murder, he and the other Mafia and Teamsters figures under suspicion managed to evade arrest. Clearly, Hoffa's murder had been well planned, as it had to be for such a high-profile public figure. Hoffa was never seen again, and no body was ever found, though his disappearance would continue to generate headlines for months and into succeeding decades. However, at the time, few of those headlines tied Hoffa's murder to the recent sensational stories about Sam Giancana's murder and the Church Committee's hearings into the CIA-Mafia plots. In the same way, stories about Tony Provenzano and his likely role in Hoffa's murder didn't mention his involvement in both the 1960 and 1971 Nixon-Mafia-Hoffa bribes, since neither was public knowledge at that point.

On the same day that Hoffa disappeared, Senator George McGovern had a press conference to show a copy of the secret Cuban Dossier that he had just received from Fidel Castro. (See Appendix.) McGovern had traveled to Cuba the previous May, and Castro may have been inspired to send him the copy because of the hearings then going on in Washington. McGovern's version of the Cuban Dossier had two pages that were added to reflect those hearings. Otherwise, it is very much as Frank Fiorini had described it back in 1972, when he and the other Watergate burglars had been ordered to look for it. The Dossier looked like a large photo album, with dark covers (one reason the CIA called it "the Black Book") and high-quality photos of the assassins and weapons captured during the assassination plots described in its bilingual text.[82]

After a brief flurry of publicity in newspapers like *The Miami Herald*, the Cuban Dossier quickly faded from the press. The CIA issued denials to the press and to Congress regarding most of the plots, saying that "of the twenty-four incidents described in Castro's report . . . CIA had no involvement in fifteen of the cases . . . in the remaining nine cases, CIA had operational relationships with some of the individuals . . . but not for the purpose of assassination." However, even internal CIA documents about the Cuban Dossier make false claims, such as one discussing "Tony Varona" that said, "There is no indication in his [Varona's] file that he attempted to assassinate Castro or sought CIA assistance for this purpose." However, the 1967 Inspector General's Report had already been given to the Church Committee, and it showed that Varona was very involved in the CIA-Mafia plots with Rosselli. The same is true for other exiles listed in the Dossier, such as Manuel Artime. While it appears the CIA was deliberately attempting to deceive the public and Congressional Committees, it's possible that Richard Helms had destroyed so many of the relevant files—and his associates in the Agency knew where to hide the rest in the CIA's vast filing systems—that routine CIA reviews failed to turn up the relevant information.[83]

Because of the CIA's denials, and the fact that so many Castro assassination attempts were detailed, no special attention was paid by the press to the Cuban Dossier's description of the December 1971 attempt in Chile, or the possible roles of Nixon and Helms. In many ways, the Dossier was not as bad as Nixon had probably feared back in 1972, when the Plumbers were searching for it at the Watergate and the Chilean embassy. While the Dossier did begin with a 1960 CIA plot involving a "gangster," it did not describe the plot with Johnny Rosselli and Robert Maheu that Nixon had instigated. When later plots were mentioned that had involved Rosselli—like those in March and April 1963—Rosselli wasn't named. When the Cuban Dossier described plots with Varona, Manuel Artime, and Rolando Cubela, it didn't mention Varona's ties to Rosselli and Santo Trafficante, or Artime and Cubela's ties to Trafficante. For those same reasons, Richard Helms was also no doubt relieved when he finally learned the Dossier's full contents. However, neither Nixon nor Helms could have known what the complete Cuban Dossier said—or didn't say—back in 1972, when both had taken such huge risks to get it.[84]

While Nixon had paid a high price for his pursuit of the Cuban Dossier, at least he was fortunate that it wasn't released until five days after he had finally been forced to testify to the Watergate grand jury. Nixon's two-day testimony had begun on June 23, 1975, four days after Giancana's murder, and five weeks before Hoffa's slaying. It was the only time Nixon had to testify under oath about the Watergate scandals surrounding his Presidency.

Nixon had successfully avoided having to testify in any of the trials of his former aides and officials, generally pleading ill health from circulation problems in his legs. A resulting blood clot had been a serious matter in the months after his resignation, but by 1975, his health had improved. When the Church Committee wanted Nixon to testify about his knowledge of CIA assassination plots, "in months of negotiation" Nixon repeatedly refused to testify in person, invoking "the Fifth Amendment . . . and the principle of executive privilege." Finally, Nixon and Miller secured an agreement that he would "respond, in writing, to a number of agreed upon questions [but] none of them dealt with Cuba or specifically with the Castro plots." Since those plots were a prime focus of the Church Committee—especially the CIA-Mafia plots with Rosselli that began when Nixon was Vice President—their exclusion was certainly at the insistence of Nixon.*[85]

The Watergate Special Prosecutors also wanted Nixon's testimony, and after extensive negotiations with Nixon's attorney, Herbert Miller, an agreement was finally reached. Several prosecutors and two members of the grand jury would go to San Clemente to interview Nixon near his home. Miller and his associate would be present, and once more the questioning was limited to an approved list of topics negotiated by Nixon and Miller. Surprisingly, the actual Watergate break-in was not one of the topics. Questions involving Larry O'Brien were limited to those about the use of the IRS against him, not the burglary of his offices at the Watergate.

Because the permitted topics included subjects like the eighteen-and-a-half-minute gap and the Hughes-Rebozo $100,000 payment, Nixon's grand jury testimony was of great interest to the press, especially since it remained sealed until 2011. As a result of a lawsuit, his testimony was finally ordered released on July 29, 2011. While devoid of dramatic revelations, it does provide a fascinating snapshot of Nixon in 1975, and it shows how he probably would have handled questions about the Watergate break-in if he ever had to answer them in a legal setting.[86]

Over his two days of testimony, Nixon gave a masterful legal and political performance. Even though his appearance was "voluntary," any provably false answer was still a crime. So Nixon often

* As noted in Chapter 29, Nixon apparently lied when he answered a question about the Chilean embassy break-in when he said he did "not remember being informed" about the break-in, even though a White House tape released in 1999 showed him talking about it.

prevaricated in his answers, making comments such as "Hard as that may seem to believe, this is the best recollection I have" or "I simply can't tell you." He would often try to avoid answering questions by giving extremely long, complicated answers unrelated to the question. Nixon was forceful, and often seem to take charge of the session. Nixon almost lost his composure when questioned about the Hughes-Rebozo money, and several times he tried to intimidate the prosecutor who was questioning him.[87]

Unlike the Senate Watergate Committee, which pursued information on the CIA-Mafia plots because they related to Robert Maheu and Howard Hughes, the Watergate Special Prosecutors didn't delve into the plots at all. (It's possible they hadn't been tipped off by Hoffa as had the Watergate Committee.) The only mention of assassination during the proceedings came in Nixon's opening statement, when he remarked on the news "in recent weeks" about "former presidents . . . being accused of approving or participating in . . . assassination." Safe from being questioned about the topic, Nixon's comment might have been intended as a subtle reminder of the national security secrets he still held.[88]

As *The Washington Post* reported more than three decades later, "Ten days after Nixon testified, the grand jury was dismissed without making any indictments based on what he told them." The most important person not indicted was Richard Nixon, as a result of his adroit testimony that had skirted any possible perjury charges. Nixon was now completely free of any criminal charges because of Watergate.

For Nixon, clearing his last legal hurdle must have been a huge relief. His health was much better, and he was able to enjoy the perfect San Clemente climate by playing the occasional round of golf. His fourteen-room San Clemente home had a spectacular cliff-side setting overlooking the ocean. Nixon had done well financially, with an official net worth of $1 million ($4 million today). There were unofficial funds as well, including indications of substantial Swiss bank accounts—some later confirmed by Anthony Summers totaled $11 million or more. Bebe Rebozo had made and managed money for both of them while Nixon was President, so Rebozo's official net worth had grown to $16 million in today's dollars. Four years later, Rebozo would begin paying Nixon his share, "giving" Nixon clear title to the entire San Clemente estate, a gift worth $2 million in today's dollars.

In the meantime, on August 9, 1975, Nixon signed a $600,000 deal with British television producer David Frost for a series of interviews to be televised more than a year later.[89]

Nixon may have been in a self-imposed exile, but at least he wasn't in prison like his former close associates John Mitchell, H.R. Haldeman, and John Ehrlichman. Rebozo was even safe from prosecution, since the Justice Department decided in 1975 not to indict him for the $100,000 he'd gotten from Howard Hughes. That also meant that none of Nixon's own dealings with Hughes or Maheu could come out at a trial. Even the deaths of Giancana and Hoffa hadn't led to any public inquiries about Nixon's role in the 1960 CIA-Mafia plots or the Hoffa bribes, and now those two could never provide information to authorities. The concerns of the mob bosses who silenced them had inadvertently helped Nixon, and, ironically, the same was true in a different way for Richard Helms. Despite all of the past tension between Nixon and Helms, when the former CIA Director protected himself by lying to the Church Committee, Helms had also protected Nixon from having to deal with a new round of scandals.

On October 9, 1975, Nixon finally made his first public appearance, "thirteen months after his resignation," in a place that struck some as unusual, but which makes perfect sense when viewed in the light of Nixon's and Watergate's hidden history. As recounted by historian Stephen Ambrose,

> It was a charity golf tournament . . . held at the La Costa Country Club [where Nixon's] playing companions included Frank Fitzsimmons (a prime suspect in the . . . murder of Jimmy Hoffa . . .), Allen Dorfman (a convicted felon who would later be executed gangland-style), Anthony Provenzano (New Jersey Teamster leader later convicted of murder), and others of that ilk. [Parentheses in original.][90]

Ambrose didn't mention that Provenzano was the top suspect in Hoffa's murder, or that he was a captain in the Genovese Mafia family. Since Ambrose's otherwise excellent three-volume biography of Nixon had left out almost all of Nixon's mob dealings, he simply considered Nixon's association with the men "odd," while "it just seemed inexplicable to most reporters and editors that Nixon would make his first public appearance with such a crowd."[91]

Given Provenzano's role in the huge 1960 and 1971 Nixon-Mafia-

Hoffa bribes, the approval given to the $1 million in total payments for the 1971 Hoffa deal by Dorfman and Fitzsimmons, and Fitzsimmons's delivery of Teamsters support for Nixon, the golf outing seems very consistent with Nixon's previous—but not often reported—history. After all, La Costa had been where Nixon's own aides had plotted Watergate cover-up strategies at the same time Fitzsimmons had been plotting with Mafia leaders at the resort.[92]

Richard Nixon's mob golf outing was the logical culmination of his political career. Nixon was no longer the nervous young man running for his first Congressional seat, speaking a few words to a hotel ballroom full of mobsters before leaving as quickly as he could. Now he was confident, wealthy, and comfortable with the type of men who—like him—understood how money and power sometimes worked in Washington. Nixon was not the first to blend the worlds of politics, organized crime, and illegal money, and he certainly wouldn't be the last, but for almost thirty years, he had done it better than anyone else.

As Ambrose pointed out, Nixon seemed "stung by the criticism" in the press of his mob golf outing, and "perhaps surprised by it." Nixon had been on the fringe of that corrupt world for so long that he possibly didn't understand how it would look. The criticism caused Nixon to withdraw from public appearances for a few months, but he was soon letting "selected reporters and photographers in, to do feature stories on his life in retirement," resulting in glowing coverage from *Time* and *Newsweek*.[93]

The rehabilitation of Nixon's public image had begun, an effort that would last for the rest of his life.

The main Church Committee investigation ended in early 1976 due to pressure from the CIA and David Atlee Phillips, but Senator Schweiker's JFK subcommittee continued with its investigation. Schweiker's subcommittee heard more testimony from Johnny Rosselli on April 23, 1976, and planned to recall him in the future. On July 27, 1976, Rosselli met with Santo Trafficante, his longtime associate who had joined him in the CIA-Mafia plots in September 1960. Less than two weeks later, on August 7, 1976, Rosselli's body was found in a fifty-five-gallon oil drum in a canal near Miami. Rosselli had been shot and stabbed, his legs had been cut off, and he had been stuffed in the oil drum. His slaying was never solved, but three of Rosselli's associates said Trafficante had ordered the hit.[94]

In response to Rosselli's sensational murder, and revelations from the Church Committee about the CIA-Mafia plots, the House Select

Committee on Assassinations (HSCA) was created on September 17, 1976. Six men sought by the HSCA to testify had either been murdered, committed suicide, or died unexpectedly. Chicago hit man Charles Nicoletti (a veteran of the CIA-Mafia plots) was the victim of a mob execution on March 29, 1977; that same day, George De Mohrenschildt (Oswald's unlikely best friend in Dallas) committed suicide. Seven days later, former Cuban President Carlos Prio, the mutual associate of Trafficante, Nixon, and E. Howard Hunt, committed suicide before he could be interviewed. Nixon's friend during the anti-Castro plots in the early 1960s William Pawley committed suicide on January 7, 1977. On November 18, 1977, Cuban exile and AMWORLD veteran Manuel Artime died of natural causes after an HSCA investigator talked to him, but before he could testify. On March 8, 1978, David Morales, retired CIA officer and friend of Johnny Rosselli, died of apparently natural causes while the HSCA was seeking his testimony.[95]

Richard Helms testified to the HSCA after his attorney Edward Bennett Williams negotiated a small fine to settle his charge of lying to Congress. Helms hinted at the JFK-Almeida coup plan in his HSCA testimony, but the CIA withheld all information about the coup plan from the HSCA. Hunt, Phillips, and Bernard Barker also had to testify.[96]

Joseph Califano became President Jimmy Carter's Secretary of Health, Education, and Welfare, while Cyrus Vance was named Secretary of State. Vance's representative met with Commander Juan Almeida at the U.N. on April 22, 1978, and Almeida's name never surfaced in the HSCA hearings. In 1979, the HSCA concluded that JFK was likely killed by a conspiracy, and "Trafficante, like Marcello, had the motive, means, and opportunity to assassinate President Kennedy."[97]

In 1978, with the help of Walter Sheridan, Dan Moldea's book *The Hoffa Wars* finally revealed the September 1960 Nixon-Mafia-Hoffa bribe. But news about the ongoing investigations of the HSCA and those looking into Hoffa's disappearance overshadowed that important revelation.

With the airing of the Nixon-Frost interviews in 1977 and the publication of Nixon's massive memoir in 1978, Richard Nixon was well on his way to rehabilitating his image. In 1981, his former Chief of Staff Alexander Haig became President Reagan's Secretary of State and began a new plan of covert action against Fidel Castro.

By the early 1990s, Nixon's involvement with the Watergate exhibit at the then-private Richard Nixon Library showed that he viewed the scandal as an attempt by the press, especially *The Washington Post*, to bring him down. Nixon died on April 22, 1994. Thanks to his attorney Herbert Miller, many of Nixon's "abuse of power" tapes were only released in 1996, and more tapes continue to be released today. In 2011, the Nixon Presidential Library—now overseen by the National Archives—opened an accurate Watergate exhibit. Over four million pages of files were released in the 1990s under the JFK Act, but thousands of pages of important CIA files about Hunt, Barker, Helms, Almeida, AMWORLD, and the 1960s anti-Castro plots remain unreleased today.[98]

For more detailed information about many of the people and subjects in this book from 1979 to 2012, please see the free Author's Afterword at watergatethehiddenhistory.com. It also has additional information resources, since the saga of Watergate remains an ongoing, developing story, with new tapes being released and files being declassified every year.

APPENDIX

Key Declassified Documents and Files Linking Watergate, the Mafia, and the CIA

The following important declassified files are a small sample of the hundreds of documents cited and quoted in this book. More files, and other portions of these documents, will be available on watergatethehiddenhistory.com by June 17, 2012. All marks on the documents were on the originals, and no typos have been corrected.

The following files—and most of the documents cited in this book—originated from the National Archives. Many of those files and reports are online at the non-profit Mary Ferrell Foundation (maryferrell.org). Special thanks also goes to the Library of Congress and the Center for Legislative Archives for their help in obtaining the Rosselli-Watergate memos, published here for the first time ever.

As the book documents, the primary goal of the four Watergate burglary attempts in May and June 1972 was to obtain information about the plots between the CIA and the Mafia to assassinate Fidel Castro that began in 1960, when Richard Nixon was Vice President. The revelation of those plots could have harmed President Nixon's reelection chances in 1972.

Nixon had been supported by billionaire Howard Hughes since the start of his political career. Hughes operative Robert Maheu admitted that in 1960—as Nixon faced a close election with Senator John F. Kennedy—"the CIA had been in touch with Nixon, who had asked them to go forward with this project . . . It was Nixon who had him do a deal with the Mafia in Florida to kill Castro."

As a result of Vice President Nixon's pressure, in the summer of 1960 the CIA used Robert Maheu as an intermediary to have Mafia don Johnny Rosselli help them plot the assassination of Fidel Castro. In September 1960, Rosselli brought Chicago mob boss Sam Giancana and Florida-based godfather Santo Trafficante into that CIA-Mafia plot.

I: Ervin-Rosselli-Watergate memo

Published here for the first time, this early 1974 memo to Senator Sam Ervin, Chairman of the Senate Watergate Committee, explains why his Watergate investigators considered "Rosselli's involvement with Robert Maheu in a

CIA-financed plot to assassinate Fidel Castro in the early 1960s" to be "relevant and necessary to our investigation." Page 2 shows that in early 1969, after President Nixon's inauguration, his Assistant Attorney General reviewed the Justice Department's file about the CIA-Mafia plots. Pages 2 and 4 show that in 1971, articles about Rosselli and the plots prompted concern by Nixon's aides and Attorney General John Mitchell. Mitchell himself then showed the Rosselli file to President Nixon.

II: Watergate Committee investigators' Rosselli interview

Also published for the first time, this memo summarizes three Watergate Committee investigators' "Interview of John Rosselli on Wednesday, February 20, 1974." (Pages 1, 2, and 4; page 3 will be online.) Rosselli refused to answer their questions about the CIA-Mafia plots with Robert Maheu because of "national security," but he did provide other information.

However, one of Rosselli's three attorneys at the interview later said that based on the questions posed by the Watergate investigators, "the reason the break-in occurred at the Democratic Party headquarters was because Nixon . . . suspected that the Democrats had information as to Nixon's involvement with the CIA's original contact with Rosselli [and] felt that a document existed showing Nixon was involved with...the CIA and the assassination of Castro."

On the final page of the Watergate investigator's memo, Rosselli—who was not under oath—lied when he said "he has never had any...business dealings in Cuba" and hedged when he claimed "he is fairly certain he has never met Hunt." Dissatisfied with Rosselli's answers, the Watergate investigators served him with "a subpoena" for "a further meeting under oath," which apparently never occurred. However, the following year (1975) Rosselli had to testify under oath to the Senate Church Committee. In 1976, while preparing for another round of questioning by the Church Committee, Rosselli was gruesomely murdered shortly after his final meeting with Santo Trafficante.

III. CIA Inspector General's Report on the CIA-Mafia Plots

This 1967 CIA Inspector General's Report was the Agency's top-secret, 133-page internal summary of the CIA-Mafia plots, prepared on the orders of CIA Director Richard Helms for then-President Lyndon Johnson. After Nixon became President, he was obsessed with getting the CIA's extensive information on the CIA-Mafia plots, which Helms consistently refused to give him. Nixon referred to the CIA-Mafia plots as "the Bay of Pigs thing"—since the plots became part of that operation—and Nixon used that phrase repeatedly on the "Smoking Gun" tape, the release of which forced his resignation.

The cover page shows the sensitivity of the "Secret Eyes Only" Report, while pages 18 and page 19 describe a September 25, 1960, meeting in Miami involving Rosselli, CIA official Jim O'Connell, Maheu, and also Sam Giancana and Santo Trafficante.

The CIA resisted making the full, uncensored report available for decades. When finally released, it was notable for how much the CIA had left out of the original report. For example, it does not say who in the Executive Branch authorized the plots in 1960 (it was Nixon), and it obscures the fact—later admitted by Helms—that he continued the CIA-Mafia plots into 1962 and 1963 without telling President Kennedy.

IV: Cuban Dossier of CIA attempts to kill Fidel Castro

This is the secret Cuban Dossier that E. Howard Hunt told Watergate burglar Frank Fiorini (Sturgis) "they were looking for in the Democratic National Committee's files . . . a thick secret memorandum from the Castro government . . . a long, detailed listing [of the] various attempts made to assassinate the Castro brothers." Fiorini confided to a friend that the Dossier was approximately a hundred pages long and had "two main parts," including information about "espionage and sabotage [by] the CIA." The version published here was ninety pages long, including covers, and was in two parts, Spanish and English, with text as well as many photos of captured CIA agents and assets, their weapons, explosives, and communications equipment.

Fiorini described the Dossier to his friend, journalist Andrew St. George, in the fall of 1972. St. George waited until August 1974—just before Nixon's resignation—to publish the information. A year later, on July 30, 1975, Senator George McGovern briefly made the Dossier public, after receiving a slightly updated version from Fidel Castro. Two pages (3 and 4) were added in 1975, but otherwise the document is much as Fiorini described it in 1972. It begins in 1960—when Nixon was Vice President—with a plot involving a "gangster," and it ends in 1971, with a CIA plot during President Nixon's administration to kill Castro in Chile. It includes two 1963 Castro assassination attempts, on March 13 and April 7, that Rosselli hinted at in his disclosures to journalist Jack Anderson. The Dossier also details a CIA plot involving Manuel Artime, one of Nixon's Watergate hush money paymasters, and Rolando Cubela, who began working on the plots while Nixon was Vice President.

At the time of the Watergate break-ins, Hunt—a White House consultant—and the CIA only had "a piece of" the Dossier, but Nixon and CIA Director Helms needed "the entire thing" to see if it could damage their reputations.

The first seven pages of the Dossier have been reproduced exactly as originally printed, with photos of the captured CIA assets and their weapons. The remainder of the Dossier's text has been typeset so that it can be read more easily. This is the first time the entire text has been printed in any book. The dozens of pages of photos (all of poor quality) have been omitted to save space, but are available online.

I: Ervin-Rosselli-Watergate Memo

SAM J. ERVIN, JR., N.C., CHAIRMAN
HOWARD H. BAKER, JR., TENN., VICE CHAIRMAN
HERMAN E. TALMADGE, GA. EDWARD J. GURNEY, FLA.
DANIEL K. INOUYE, HAWAII LOWELL P. WEICKER, JR., CONN.
JOSEPH M. MONTOYA, N. MEX.

SAMUEL DASH
CHIEF COUNSEL AND STAFF DIRECTOR
FRED D. THOMPSON
MINORITY COUNSEL
RUFUS L. EDMISTEN
DEPUTY COUNSEL

Rosselli file

United States Senate

SELECT COMMITTEE ON
PRESIDENTIAL CAMPAIGN ACTIVITIES
(PURSUANT TO S. RES. 60, 93D CONGRESS)

WASHINGTON, D.C. 20510

MEMORANDUM
PERSONAL AND CONFIDENTIAL

To: Senator Ervin

From: Terry Lenzner and Marc Lackritz

Subject: Relevance to S. Res. 60 of John Rosselli's testimony about his CIA activities

<u>Summary:</u>

John Rosselli and his attorney, Tom Wadden, object to testifying about Rosselli's involvement with Robert Maheu in a CIA-financed plot to assassinate Fidel Castro in the early 1960's. The objection is based upon national security grounds as well as an assertion by Mr. Wadden that the material is not relevant to our inquiry under S. Res. 60.

Testimony of Mr. Rosselli about this matter is relevant and necessary to our investigation for a variety of reasons.

<u>Facts:</u>

During the last year of the Eisenhower Administration, the CIA apparently financed and organized a plot to assassinate Fidel Castro. Among the participants in this plot were Robert Maheu and John Rosselli. Maheu had a public relations business at the time, and Rosselli was associated with some alleged organized crime figures (e.g. Sam Giancana) who had lost substantial gambling investments when Castro came to power. Apparently, the plot continued into the early 1960's even after the abortive Bay of Pigs invasion, but it failed in attaining its objective of killing Castro.

Only a few officials in the government knew of the existence of the plot at that time.

Justice Department officials stumbled across this information about the plot as a result of their investigation into an illegal wiretap by Sam Giancana in the early 1960's.

I: Ervin-Rosselli-Watergate Memo

-2-

The sensitive information was brought to the attention of FBI Director J. Edgar Hoover, and either he or then-Attorney General Robert Kennedy ordered the prosecution of Giancana dropped in order not to compromise national security considerations.

The information about the alleged assassination plot then lay dormant in a secret file in the Department of Justice until early 1969, when Assistant Attorney General Will Wilson requested the file from the Deputy Chief of the Organized Crime Section. The file was returned to Central Files shortly after it was taken out.

Assistant Attorney General Wilson next requested the secret Justice file in early 1971 in connection with his interview of Robert Maheu on January 27, 1971 (see attached chronology). This interview at the Department of Justice, in lieu of a grand jury appearance, was arranged by a telephone call to Attorney General Mitchell on January 19, 1971, only one day after Jack Anderson published his first column linking both Maheu and Rosselli to the CIA plot to kill Castro. (see attached)

However, the significance of Anderson's column on January 18, 1971, was that on the same day, Haldeman requested Dean to find out what he could about the Hughes - Maheu - O'Brien relationship.

In the follow-up memos from Caulfield to Dean on the Maheu-O'Brien link, Caulfield notes Maheu's prior "covert activities" for the CIA and advises Dean that a check into CIA, FBI, and IRS files on Robert Maheu is advisable to avoid a "counter-scandal."

In addition, Assistant Attorney General Wilson showed the sensitive "Castro file" to Attorney General Mitchell, in January, 1971, and discussed with him the political implications of the information. Following the on-the-record interview of Maheu on January 27, 1971, by Lynch, Wilson and Petersen, Maheu was interviewed privately by Wilson concerning his prior CIA activities with John Rosselli. Maheu was not forthcoming with information about the plot at that time. Attorney General Mitchell discussed the contents of the sensitive file with President Nixon, according to Wilson, who had advised him to do so.

Conclusion:

Therefore, the obsession of the Administration in keeping tabs on Larry O'Brien in 1971 and 1972 was in part motivated by a fear that Maheu would impart some of this sensitive information about the plot

I: Ervin-Rosselli-Watergate Memo

-3-

to O'Brien. Alternatively the objective was to discover if there was any information about the plot that might be damaging to the Democrats that O'Brien might possess from Maheu. And these concerns could have been a possible motivation for the break-in to the offices of the DNC and Larry O'Brien by four Cuban-Americans on June 17, 1972, especially since their directions were to photograph any documents relating to Cuban contributions or Cuban involvement in the 1972 Democratic campaign.

It is for these reasons that we wish to question John Rosselli about the nature and scope of his activities with Robert Maheu in the early 1960's.

Maheu recruited John Rosselli, a [illegible]

I: Ervin-Rosselli-Watergate Memo

CHRONOLOGY OF EVENTS

Thanksgiving, 1970	Hughes leaves Las Vegas.
December 4, 1970	Maheu is fired.
January 18, 1971	Jack Anderson column published linking Mah and Rosselli to plot to kill Castro.
January 18, 1971	Haldeman sends memo to Dean requesting inf mation on O'Brien-Maheu-Hughes relationshi
January 19, 1971	Jack Anderson column appears with more deta on Maheu's involvement in plot to assassina Castro.
January 19, 1971	Attorney General John Mitchell called Robert Maheu in Las Vegas at 5:12 p.m. and talked.
January 25, 1971	Caulfield to Dean memo discussing Danner relationship with Maheu, O'Brien relationshi with Maheu, and request for investigation in CIA, FBI, IRS files for information to avoid a "counter-scandal."
January 25, 1971	John Rosselli enters prison.
January 26, 1971	Dean to Haldeman memo on Maheu-O'Brien-Hughes relationship
January 27, 1971	Maheu interviewed at Department of Justice A.A.G. Will Wilson, Henry Petersen and Bil Lynch, in lieu of an appearance before the Grand Jury. Interview is about "skimming" Las Vegas.
January 27, 1971	A.A.G. Wilson and Petersen meet with Mahe privately to discuss Maheu's prior CIA activ
February 1, 1971	Caulfield to Dean memo noting that Maheu w involved in "covert activities" for the CIA ir early 1960's.
February 12, 1971	Rosselli's attorney files a Motion to Reduce Sentence based on Rosselli's prior CIA activ

II: Watergate Committee investigators' Rosselli interview

Memorandum

To : Terry Lenzner

From : Bob Muse

Subject: Interview of John Roselli

File

On Wednesday February 20, 1974, Scott Armstrong, Marc Lackritz and Bob Muse interviewed John Roselli at the office of Roselli's attorney, Tom Wadden, 888 17th Street, N. W., Washington, D. C., telephone 833-1440. Also present were Wadden's associates Bryan B. McMenamin and Leslie Scherr.

Wadden began the interview by noting that for the first time, he had discussed with Roselli the Maheu Cuban matter with which we were concerned; and found that it presented a great problem of national security. Accordingly he had tried to reach Senator Ervin, an old acquaintance, and see if he could persuade the Senator from allowing this interview to go forward. He did not get in touch with Ervin directly but talked to a staff member in Ervin's office, whom he would not identify. He further noted that Roselli was insistent upon not giving any informatio[n] about his Cuban activities and would rather go to jail than be compelled to testify about the matter. Thus the interview was not productive insofar as Roselli's involvement with Maheu in 1960 was concerned. However Wadden did allow us to interview Roselli about his background and we reserved the right to have an executive session before a Senator where John Roselli might be compelled to testify about his involvement with Maheu in Cuba. (It should be noted that Wadden would not identify his privilege claim other than saying it related to national security.)

John Roselli presently resides with his sister and brother-in-law, a Mr. and Mrs. Joseph Daigle at 522 Southwest Temp Corner, Plantation, Florida 33314. His telephone number there is area 305 581-6585. He has been living in retirement with them since he left jail at the end of last summer. Prior to moving to Florida he had been in the federal prison for thirty-three months, having been convicted in the Friar's Club case, a conspiracy in which he was charged along with Maurice Friedman, Benjamin Teitlebaum, and Manuel Jacobs. (He noted that Hank Greenspun had no involvement either as a co-defendant or unindicted co-conspirator in that case.)

With regard to Bob Maheu, he met Maheu for the first time in the mid-50's in either Washington or California through a mutual acquaintance, Herman Spitzel. When questions were asked as to what his subsequent involvement with Maheu was, Roselli's attorney instructed him not to answer any questions on the ground of national security.

Roselli did however indicate how he and Maheu had made arrangements for Hughes to live at the Desert Inn when Hughes first arrived there in late 1966. He said that he had received a call from Maheu, who needed to make arrangements for Hughes to move to Las Vegas from Boston. According to Maheu, no one wanted to give Hughes any rooms. Roselli at the request of Maheu left his residence in Los Angeles and went up to Las Vegas and asked his acquaintance Ruby Kolod, who owned 13% of the Desert Inn, to accommodate Hughes and allow him to take two of the penthouses at the Desert Inn. At the time Maheu was in charge of security and responsible for seeing that Hughes arrived unnoticed in Las Vegas. Kolod acquiesced and told Roselli that the top floor of the Desert Inn would be available at the going rate, but that they would have to leave the hotel by New Years. When the New Years date was approaching, Maheu called and said that they had received notice from Kolod and were suppose to leave their premises. Roselli then convinced Kolod to allow them to stay. At the same time he told Maheu that Hughes should buy the Hotels and avoid any problems. Maheu responded that he was of the impression that Hughes didn't

II: Watergate Committee investigators' Rosselli interview

2.

want to get involved in any of the gambling businesses and would not therefore want to purchase the hotel. It was at this point that Roselli conceived of the idea of trying to sell the hotel, and approached Kolod and asked if he would be willing to sell it. Kolod replied that if Roselli could make arrangements to sell it he would receive a finder's fee. Roselli then turned around and asked Maheu if he wanted to purchase it. Maheu responded that he would and Roselli turned the matter over to his attorney Ed Morgan who then handled the matter until the end. Roselli also instigated some talk about the possibility of purchasing the Sands and, while he did not negotiate it, received at a later date from Ed Morgan a check for $95,000 which represented his finder's fee for the sale of both the Desert Inn and the Sands.

Roselli noted that while Moe Dalitz was the owner of the Desert Inn, he did not negotiate with him because he found him less agreeable than Kolod. He said that he had some minor dealings with Dalitz but none of them related to matters concerning the Las Vegas hotel industry.

With regard to Ed Morgan, Roselli met him in the middle 50's. Since that time Morgan has represented him in different Las Vegas interests. He noted that Morgan did not represent him in his Friars' Club defense(~~but did arrange for Jim~~ Cantillion, a Los Angeles attorney to handle the matter). He said that he had no trouble with Morgan's handling of the Desert Inn finder's fee, since he trusted Morgan implicity. He noted that Morgan had arranged for John Roselli to be represented by Tom Wadden, his present attorney. This representation first began on the appeal from the Friar's Club.

Roselli indicated that his only present interest in Las Vegas concerns his holdings in the gift shop at the Frontier hotel. His involvement there started in 1967 when he had an arrangement with Mr. Friedman. This set-up did not work out and Roselli resigned as President of the gift shop. Thereafter he made an arrangement with a Mr. Breen whereby he would furnish Breen with money and indemnify him against any losses if Breen would run the gift shop. This arrangement has worked out fairly well and he continues to receive his share of the profits each year from the gift shop. He mentioned that it was his opinion that Breen had been poorly treated by the Hughes enterprises, since Hughes first purchased the Frontier. He recalls, at his last meeting with Maheu, asking Maheu to lend Breen $60,000 for the gift shop. Maheu said he would get back to him but never did. Ultimately a loan was arranged through Perry Thomas at the Valley Bank of Nevada.

Since 1967 Roselli has seen Maheu only once. And while he does not recall the date of that meeting he remembers that it was in Los Angeles before Maheu had terminated with Hughes. He recalls that Maheu was in Los Angeles at the time while his wife was having a foot operation, and that he called Roselli to have supper. Roselli has no recollection of the conversation that the two had at supper other than that they discussed, as noted above, the possibility of arranging a loan for Breen at the Frontier Hotel Gift Shop.

He said he has known Peter Maheu since the middle 1950's and that he went to Peter's wedding reception. His only involvement with Peter occurred whenever Robert Maheu wanted a message conveyed to Roselli. He recalls no ~~subsequent~~ [substantive] discussions with Peter Maheu.

He indicated he knew nothing about Larry O'Brien, Tony Hatsis, or Jack Cleveland. Similarly he has no recollection of ever having met Bebe Rebozo, and knows of the person only through newspaper articles.

With regard to his appearance before the Frontier Hotel grand jury in

II: Watergate Committee investigators' Rosselli interview

With regard to Hank Greenspun, Roselli has known him since the 50's. The last time he met Greenspun was when he ran into Greenspun in Los Angeles shortly after he got out of prison, at which time they talked a few minutes. No questions were asked and there was no discussion with Greenspun about his involvement with Maheu. He noted that Greenspun has never questioned him about any matters.

He noted that he has never met Gordon Liddy, Howard Hunt or any of the Cuban Americans who were involved in the Watergate break-in. He said however that he has been Liddy once, and that was at Terminal Island when he was acting as a prison librarian. There were no discussions with Liddy. He is fairly certain he has never met Hunt with regard to any CIA involvement of his own. He also noted that he has never had any property or business dealings in Cuba.

The interview concluded with the serving of a subpoena upon Mr. Roselli and the decision to hold a further meeting under oath at a later date.

III. CIA Inspector General's Report on the CIA-Mafia Plots

CIA HISTORICAL REVIEW PROGRAM
RELEASE AS SANITIZED
1997

~~SECRET EYES ONLY~~

CIA HISTORICAL REVIEW PROGRAM
Release As Sanitized

23 May 1967

MEMORANDUM FOR THE RECORD

SUBJECT: Report on Plots to Assassinate Fidel Castro

This report was prepared at the request of the Director of Central Intelligence. He assigned the task to the Inspector General on 23 March 1967. The report was delivered to the Director, personally, in installments, beginning on 24 April 1967. The Director returned this copy to the Inspector General on 22 May 1967 with instructions that the Inspector General:

Retain it in personal, EYES ONLY safekeeping

Destroy the one burn copy retained temporarily by the Inspector General

Destroy all notes and other source materials originated by those participating in the writing of the report

The one stayback burn copy, all notes, and all other derived source materials were destroyed on 23 May 1967.

This ribbon copy is the only text of the report now in existence, either in whole or in part. Its text has been read only by:

Richard Helms, Director of Central Intelligence
J. S. Earman, Inspector General
K. E. Greer, Inspector (one of the authors)
S. D. Breckinridge, Inspector (one of the authors)

All typing of drafts and of final text was done by the authors.

Filed with the report are:

Office of Security file used as source material
Memorandums concerning William Harvey
Certain MONGOOSE papers
Drew Pearson columns

J. S. Earman
Inspector General

~~SECRET EYES ONLY~~

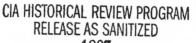

III. CIA Inspector General's Report on the CIA-Mafia Plots

SECRET EYES ONLY

deliberately avoided the use of any "bad words." The descriptive term used was "an intelligence operation." Edwards is quite sure that the DCI and the DDCI clearly understood the nature of the operation he was discussing. He recalls describing the channel as being "from A to B to C." As he then envisioned it, "A" was Maheu, "B" was Roselli, and "C" was the principal in Cuba. Edwards recalls that Mr. Dulles merely nodded, presumably in understanding and approval. Certainly, there was no opposition. Edwards states that, while there was no formal approval as such, he felt that he clearly had tacit approval to use his own judgment. Bissell committed $150,000 for the support of the operation.

(Comment: In the light of this description of the briefing, it is appropriate to conjecture as to just what the Director did approve. It is safe to conclude, given the men participating and the general subject of the meeting, that there was little likelihood of misunderstanding--even though the details were deliberately blurred and the specific intended result was never stated in unmistakable language. It is also reasonable to conclude that the pointed avoidance of "bad words" emphasized to the participants the extreme sensitivity of the operation.)

During the week of 25 September 1960, O'Connell and Maheu went to Miami where Roselli introduced only Maheu to "Sam Gold" at a meeting

- 18 -

SECRET EYES ONLY

III. CIA Inspector General's Report on the CIA-Mafia Plots

SECRET EYES ONLY

in the Fontainbleau Hotel. "Gold" said he had a man, whom he identified only as "Joe," who would serve as courier to Cuba and make arrangements there. Maheu pointed out "Gold" to O'Connell from a distance, but O'Connell never met either "Gold" or "Joe." He did, however, learn their true identities. An Office of Security memorandum to the DDCI of 24 June 1966 places the time as "several weeks later." O'Connell is now uncertain as to whether it was on this first visit to Miami or on a subsequent one that he and Maheu learned the true identities of the two men. Maheu and O'Connell were staying at separate hotels. Maheu phoned O'Connell one Sunday morning and called his attention to the Parade supplement in one of that morning's Miami newspapers. It carried an article on the Cosa Nostra, with pictures of prominent members. The man Maheu and O'Connell knew as "Sam Gold" appeared as Mom Salvatore (Sam) Giancana, a Chicago-based gangster. "Joe, the courier" (who was never identified to either Maheu or O'Connell in any other way) turned out to be Santos Trafficante, the Cosa Nostra chieftain in Cuba.

At that time the gambling casinos were still operating in Cuba, and Trafficante was making regular trips between Miami and Havana on syndicate business. (The casinos were closed and gambling was banned effective 7 January 1959. On 13 January 1959, Castro announced that the casinos would be permitted to reopen for tourists and foreigners

- 19 -

SECRET EYES ONLY

IV: Cuban Dossier of CIA attempts to kill Fidel Castro

000593

La Agencia Central de Inteligencia(CIA) de Estados Unidos, ha jugado el papel - principal en la historia de las agresiones contra Cuba, promoviendo, organizando, financiando y en muchos casos dirigiendo acciones vandálicas, no sólo contra el territorio cubano sino también - contra nuestras representaciones e intereses en países extranjeros o en aguas-internacionales.

En esta amplia gama de actividades desplegadas por la CIA, y demás órganos -- subversivos de Estados Unidos contra -- nuestro país, se destacan por su peli-- grosidad, los reiterados planes dirigidos a la eliminación física de los principales dirigentes de la Revolución y,- en especial, contra la figura de nuestro Primer Ministro.

Las pruebas que aportamos evidencian -- que, desde 1959, éste ha sido uno de sus objetivos principales, mediante el em-- pleo de los más variados métodos técnicos de precisión.En los casos de agen-- tes radicados en el exterior, les han - facilitado medios de traslación y comunicación.

The United States Central Intelligence Agency (CIA) has played the leading role in the history of the agressions against Cuba,promoting, organizing, financing, and, in many cases,--- directing vandalic actions, not only against- the Cuban territory, but also against our --- representations and interest in foreign countries, or in international waters.

In this wide variety of activities carried -- out by the CIA and by other United States --- subversive bodies against our country ,the --- reiterated plans toward the physical elimination, of the principal leaders of the Revolution, and specially, against our Primer Minister, stand out because of their dangerousness.

The proofs we provide, evidence that, since - 1959, this has been one of its major aims, by using the most varied technical precision --- methods. In the case of agents living abroad, they have been given means of transportation- and communication.

IV: Cuban Dossier of CIA attempts to kill Fidel Castro

Es de destacar que en las innumerables-infiltraciones organizadas por la CIA,-utilizando miembros de organizaciones -contrarrevolucionarias, uno de los obje tivos constantes ha sido también la eli minación física del Comandante en Jefe-Fidel Castro Ruz.

La CIA, para la ejecución de sus planes, ha utilizado elementos contrarrevolucio narios en el interior y exterior del --país.No sólo ha tenido como colaborado-res a los desplazados del poder, sino -también a elementos de distinta proce--dencia social, incluyendo a exponentes-de todo tipo de lacras.

Igualmente, no han tenido reparo en re-clutar a destacados jefes y elementos -de la maffia norteamericana, a quienes-les han conmutado fechorías a cambio de su participación en los planes de aten-tado contra nuestros dirigentes.

No han vacilado tampoco en tratar de --ejecutar sus acciones en lugares públi-cos, donde el número de víctimas inocen tes hubiese sido incalculable, como fue ron: los atentados planificados en el -Stadium Latinoamericano, Plaza de la Re volución y escalinata de la Universidad de La Habana.

It is worth noticing that, in the innumerable infiltrations organized by the CIA, using ---members of counterrevolutionary organizations, one of the permanent goals has also been the-physical elimination of Commander in Chief,-Fidel Castro Ruz.

The CIA, in orden to carry out its plans, has-used counterrevolutionary individuals inside-and outside the country. It has had as collaborators, not only those who had been shifted fron power, but also individuals of different social origins, including samples of all types of viciousness.

In the same way, they have had no objection -to recruting well-known leaders and members-from the American maffia, to whom they have -barred their offences, in exchange for their-participation in the plots against our leaders.

Nor have they hesitated in trying to carry --out their actions in public places, where the number of innocent victims would have been --incalculable, as were the crimes planned to -take place at the Latin American Stadium, the Revolution Square and the University of Ha--vana.

IV: Cuban Dossier of CIA attempts to kill Fidel Castro

Durante los últimos meses, la prensa norteamericana ha publicado una creciente y amplia información sobre la realización de estas actividades, ofreciendo en detalles la participación de la Agencia Central de Inteligencia en la elaboración y ejecución de los planes de atentado.

En los informes rendidos por la llamada Comisión Rockefeller y la presidida por el senador Frank Church, para las investigaciones sobre las actividades ilegales de la CIA, ha quedado demostrado de forma categórica lo antes expuesto.

Un ex-agente hizo públicas declaraciones sobre la participación de dicha agencia en el criminal atentado perpetrado contra el vapor francés "La Coubre", donde más de un centenar de cubanos resultaron muertos y alrededor de 200, heridos graves.

Brinda detalles pormenorizados sobre su realización, tratando de "justificar" esta matanza por un desperfecto en el mecanismo del equipo explosivo utilizado.

During the last month, the American press has published an increasing and extensive information about the accomplishment of these activities, offering details about the participation of the Central Intelligence Agency in the elaboration and execution of the criminal plans.

In the reports of the so-called Rockefeller Commission, as well as the one headed by Senator Frark Church, for the researches on the illegal activities of the Central Intelligence Agenci (CIA), all that we have stated above, has been undoubtedly demonstrated.

A former agent made public statements about the participation of this Agency in the criminal act carried out against the French steamship "La Coubre", where more than one hundred Cubans were killed and about 200, were seriously injured. He offers details about his accomplisments trying to "justify" this killing by blaming a slight damage in the mechanism of the blowing equipment which was used.

IV: Cuban Dossier of CIA attempts to kill Fidel Castro

Resulta significativa la información --- aportada por el columnista Jack Anderson en el diario "The Washington Post" sobre la intervención del ganster John Rosselli en varios planes de atentados contra el-Primer Ministro Fidel Castro, algunos de ellos mediante envenenamiento con pastillas entregadas por la CIA. Posteriormen te, según la propia prensa norteamericana, Rosselli admitió ante la Comisión de Inteligencia del Senado su participación con esta Agencia en varios complots para asesinar al Primer Ministro Cubano.

Paulatinamente, funcionarios, senadores, jefes, oficiales y ex-agentes de la CIA, así como conocidos columnistas de la --- prensa norteamericana, han hecho categóricas declaraciones, que coinciden con - las denuncias formuladas, oportunamente - por el gobierno de Cuba.

Sin pretender relacionar todos los pla-- nes de atentados fraguados, exponemos a-continuación algunos casos, que en su -- casi totalidad no han sido de conocimien to público y prueban la diversidad y rei teración de la participación de la CIA y otras agencias subversivas en estos he-- chos:

Very significant is the information given by-the journalist Jack Anderson from"The Washing ton Post" about the gangster John Rosselli's-participation in various plots against Prime-Minister Fidel Castro, somo of them by means-of poisoning, with pills handed to him by the CIA. Afterwards, according to the American -- press itself, Rosselli, before the Senate --- Intelligence Commission,conceded having parti cipated with this Agency in various plots for assassinating the Cuban Prime Minister.

Gradually, officials, Senators, chiefs, offi-cers and former CIA agents, as well as well known American press press journalists, have-made categorical statements, which coincide-- with the denounces expressed, apropos,by the-Cuban Government.

Without pretending to mention all the plots-- attempted, we expose some of them the majority of which have not been publicly known.
They prove the diversity and recurrence of -- the CIA as well as other subversive agencies participation in these actions:

IV: Cuban Dossier of CIA attempts to kill Fidel Castro

A mediados del año 1960,los elementos contrarrevolucionarios Armando Cubría Ramos-y Mario Tauler Sagué,miembros de la organización contrarrevolucionaria"La Cruz",-se infiltraron por la zona de Punta de Hicacos, Matanzas.

Tauler Sagué, elemento gansteril,junto a-Cubría Ramos traían la misión de realizar un atentado a nuestro Primer Ministro,así como perpetrar distintas acciones de sabotaje y terrorismo. Para cumplirla fueron-pertrechados por la CIA de gran cantidad-de material bélico y equipos, los que fueron ocupados al ser detenidos.

In mid 1960,the counterrevolutionary Armando - Cubría Ramos and Mario Tauler Sagué, members-- of the "La Cruz" counterrevolutionary organization, were infiltrated through the Punta Hicacos zone, in Matanzas Province.

Tauler Sagué,a gangster,together with Cubría - Ramos, were instructed to carry out a plot --- against our Prime Minister, as well as to ---- commit various sabotage and terrorism actions. For accomplishing this, they were given great quantity of warlike material and equipment by-the CIA,which were taken from them when arrested.

IV: Cuban Dossier of CIA attempts to kill Fidel Castro

Reference copy, JFK Collection: HSCA (RG 233)

IV: Cuban Dossier of CIA attempts to kill Fidel Castro

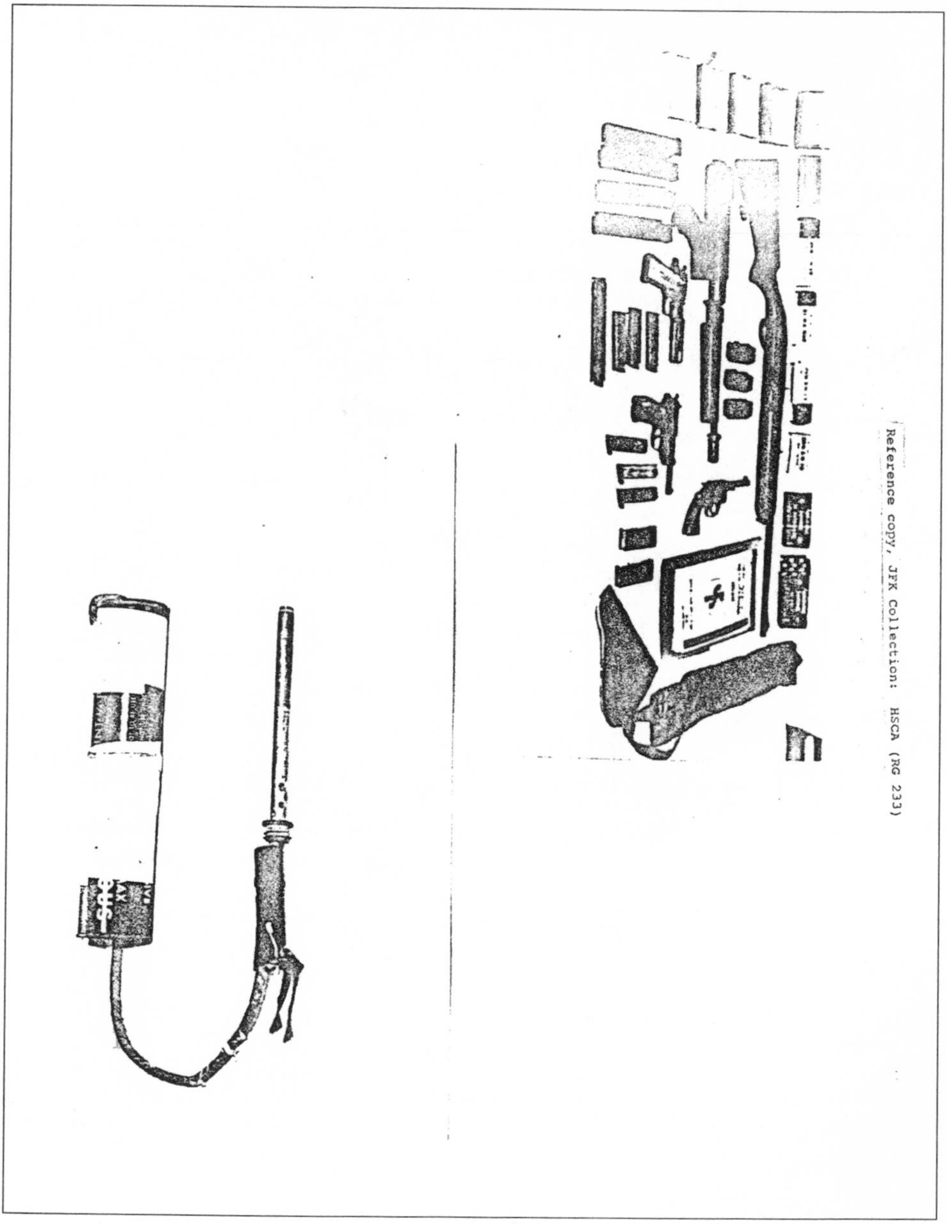

IV: Cuban Dossier of CIA attempts to kill Fidel Castro continued: The traitor Humberto Sorí Marín with four other counterrevolutionaries, were infiltrated in March 1961, through the north coast of Havana, with the purpose of grouping the counterrevolutionary organizations, of carrying out the assassination of Commander in Chief and of developing all types of subversive activities in order to support the Playa Girón invasion.

For this purpose, they were trained and armed by the Central Intelligence Agency. A great quantity of warlike material and other equipment were taken from them when arrested.

Among the participants were Rogelio González Corcho, Manuel Lorenzo Puig Millán, Nemesio Rodríguez Navarrete, Gaspar Domínguez Trueba Varona, Eufemio J. Fernández Ortega and Rafael Díaz Hanscons, heads of various counterrevolutionary groups and organizations directed by the CIA.

In June 1961, a meeting was celebrated with the attendance of an individual infiltrated in Cuba by the "Frente Revolucionario Democrático" (FRD) counterrevolutionary organization, who was instructed to carry out a plot against Commander in Chief Fidel Castro Ruz.

To accomplish this action, Juan Basigalupe Hornedo, Higinio Menéndez Beltrán, Guillermo Coula Ferrer and others were appointed, and they were given money to meet the expenses of the operation.

The plan was to place two jeeps with bazookas in the garage which is at Rancho Boyeros and Santa Catalina Avenues, and a light truck at the Ciudad Deportiva (Sports City) with men carrying grenades. When our leaders would pass by, they would stop the traffic and open fire.

When they were arrested, Guillermo Caula Ferrer and Higinio Menéndez accused the CIA of being the principal director of the plot. The indicted kept contacts through Guantánamo Naval Base and the Swiss Embassy, with members of the CIA and American authorities, who gave them means and instructions to carry out their activities.

After the Playa Girón defeat, the Central Intelligence Agency continued its subversive activities against our country, starting the regrouping of the dispersed counterrevolutionary organizations, under the "Unidad Resistencia" organization.

This task was carried out by the infiltrated CIA agents Emilio Adolfo Rivero Caro (Brand), Adolfo Mendoza (Raúl) and Jorge García Rubio (Tony) among others. Aterwards, they tried to develop all types of subversive activities, including a plot against Division Commander (Lieutenant Colonel) Raúl Castro Ruz, during the provincial celebration of July 26 at Oriente Province in 1961; the self-aggression to Guantánamo Naval Base, with the purpose of justifying the aggression by the American Armed Forces, as well as attacks to neighboring republics, in order to provoke an international conflict.

The plans included also a plot against the Commander in Chief, during the central rally the same day, at the Revolution Square. For this purpose, the counterrevolutionary José Pujals Mederos made an undercover visit to the United

States, in order to coordinate this action. There, he met CIA officers Jim Bender, known as Jim Boulding, Harold Bischop and Carl Hitch. During this meeting, Mederos was appointed chief of the CIA officers, who operated in Cuba, substituting Alfredo Izaguirre, known as Tito, who was arrested.

The conspiratory meetings were carried out at the Guantánamo Naval Base, and its authorities (Captain Schenweias) supplied a lot of warlike material and equipment for the accomplishment of these plans.

The mentioned Captain Carl E. Schenweias, former chief of the Naval Base, was one of the most active organizers of the aggresions.

When all the indicated were arrested, a great number of warlike material and equipment was taken from them.

It is worth noticing that all these subversive plans were denounced opportunely by Commander Ernesto Guevara at Punta del Este.

During the second fortnight of July, 1961, a group of counterrevolutionaries from "30 de Noviembre", "Movimiento Revolucionario del Pueblo" and "Frente Revolucionario Democrático" organizations, were plotting against our Commander in Chief and other leaders.

They received CIA instructions through contacts abroad with Tony Carona, Manuel Ray and Aureliano Sánchez Arango, and with Admiral Burke and CIA agents in Guantánamo Naval Base. The plot would be carried out in the proximity of Celia Sánchez Manduley's house, in Vedado. Mario Chanez de Armas, Francisco Chanez de Armas, Roberto Coscuyuela Valcárcel, Orlando Ulacia Valdés, Francisco Gil Cruz, Segundo González González and others were arrested and weapons and explosives were taken from them.

Among their plans was also the failed plot against Dr. Carlos Rafael Rodríguez, which was attempted on September 13th, 1961, when he was coming back from Matanzas to Havana. With that purpose, a group of counterrevolutionary individuals, belonging to the organizations mentioned above, contacted representatives of the "Movimiento de Recuperación Revolucionaria" (MRR). The group's leader was Juan José Martore Silva.

These individuals kept close relation with a CIA agent as well as with the chief of a band in Matanzas Province. When arrested, warlike material was taken from them.

In October 1961, "II Frente del Escambray" and "Movimiento de Recuperación Revolucionaria" (MRR) counterrevolutionary organizations, directed by the Central Intelligence Agency (CIA), approved a joint plan for a sabotage in the capital, in order to cause people's indignation and to influence on the mass gathering to welcome the President of the Republic Osvaldo Dorticós Torrado, on his arrival from Punta del Este.

This tactic was aimed to facilitate the plot, which would be carried out on the 4th of the same month, shooting with a bazooka in the direction of the tribune located on the terrace of the former Presidential Palace, from an apartment located in a nearby building. The withdrawal would be covered by the criminal launching of grenades against the public, in order to cause confusion and panic.

Their purposes were frustrated when all of the indicted were arrested and a great number of warlike material was taken from them.

In early 1962, following instructions from the CIA and the Guantánamo Naval Base, the counterrevolutionary Jorge Luis Cuervo Calvo reorganized several groups and counterrevolutionary organizations, and created the "Unión de Unidades Revolucionarias" (UDUR).

Cuervo Calvo, Humberto Gómez Peña, Raúl Cay Hernández, Raúl Cay Gispert and others met in order to prepare plans for uprising and inform about the contacts established with the Guantánamo Naval Base for receiving warlike material and equipment.

The Central Intelligence Agency insisted on its plots against the Prime Minister's life, and to carry out a self-aggression to the Naval Base. Following these instructions, the counterrevolutionary Cuervo Calvo made contacts with the DRE organization, and elaborated what would be known as "Plan Z", which consisted of an attempt against the life of the Minister of Foreign Relations Raúl Roa, what would enable them to carry out another plot of bigger proportions against the Prime Minister and other revolutionary leaders who would attend the burial.

it is worth noting that the intellectual authors of this plan were the counterrevolutionaries Cay Hernández and Cay Gispert, members of the DRE organization, which was headed by Julio Hernández Rojo, a CIA agent infiltrated into our country.

The "Resistencia Cívica Anticomunista" organization (RCA), to which "Ejército de Liberación Nacional" (ELN), "Movimiento de Recuperación Revolucionaria" (MRR), "Agrupación Montecristi" and others were joined, was directed from abroad by the CIA, through its agent Nino Díaz.

In 1963, the CIA gave instructions to the RCA block for organizing and carrying out internal actions in order to give the impression of the existence of a popular civic resistence, and therefore, demanding an armed intervention in Cuba, at the meeting of the Presidents of countries who were members of the OAS.

The instructions were given by the CIA through Guantánamo Naval Base. Since then, the RCA elaborated new plans for actions and crimes, for supporting the armed invasion which was expected in July.

On the occasion of the acts commemorating the 14th of March, they planned to assassinate the Commander in Chief, from a house near the University of Havana, shooting with a mortar in the direction of the tribune. The principal persons indicted were Samuel Carballo Moreno (CIA agent), Luis David Rodríguez González, Ricardo Olmedo Moreno, José A. López Rodríguez, Juan Lucio Morales Sosa and others.

Simultaneously with this plot, attacks on the Committees of Defense of the Revolution and the National Revolutionary Militias sites, were planned to be carried out.

Having failed, the RCA elaborated a new plot against the Prime Minister, this time at the Latin American Stadium on April 7th, 1963. Sixteen men armed with pistols and fragmentation grenades would participate in it.

Among the principal persons indicted were Enrique Rodríguez Valdés, known as "Mulgado", Ricardo López Cabrera, Onorio Torres Perdomo and Jorge Carlos Espinosa Escarles.

They elaborated another plot, this time against the life of the Minister of the Armed Forces, Division Commander (Lieutenant Colonel) Raúl Castro Ruz, at the Revolution Square, during the celebration of the 26th of July. Four groups led by René Sigler Sánchez Evias, Jesús Montes de Oca Cruz, Oscar Sibila Soria and Eliecer Rodríguez Suárez, would participate. The head of these groups was Ibrahim Machin Hernández.

All these actions, organized and promoted by the CIA through the RCA block, were frustrated, the persons indicted were arrested and a great number of weapons and equipment were taken from them.

For September the 28th, 1963, anniversary of the Committees of Defense of the Revolution, the counterrevolutionary Orlando Martiniano de la Cruz Sánchez, Juan Israel Cazañas León, Jesús Plácido Rodríguez Mosquera, Luis Beltrán Arencibia Pérez, Francisco Vlanco de los Cuetos, Federico Hernándes González and others, related to the CIA agent Pierre Owen Diez de Ure, prepared a plot against our Prime Minister.

These individuals grouped into the "Frente Interno de Unidad Revolucionaria" (FIUR), "Triple A", "Movimiento Democrático Revolucionario" (MDR), "Ejército de Liberación Nacional" (ELN) counterrevolutionary organizations, had CIA advice and support.

The plan was to dynamite the sewage pipes which pass under the presidential tribune. Once the plan frustrated and the authors arresteed, the agent Pierre Owen Diez de Ure, French citizen living in our country, confessed that he had been working for the CIA for approximately two years, and that he had given this Agency information of various sorts.

In March 1964, another plot against Commander in Chief was elaborated. The principal indicted Mario Salabarría Aguiar, a gangster, had contacts with the CIA through the agent Dr. Bernardo Milanés López head of a network who informed the CIA center of the plan and sought, from Spain, the support of Salabarría's friends, Tony Varona and Juan Bosch.

The plan consisted of installing a machine gun caliber of 30 or 50 in a vehicle and waiting for the occasion when the Commander in Chief would pass by, in order to attempt against his life. The CIA gave Salabarría the necessary weapons and means, including great sums of money.

In mid-1964, the counterrevolutionaries Osvaldo Valentín Figueroa Gálvez, known as "Mnakeca", Reinaldo Figueroa Gálvez, Relipe Alonso Herrera and José Manuel Rodríguez Cruz, known as "Lolo", members of the "Movimiento de Liberación Nacional", which belonged to the RCA block of organizations, directed by the CIA, began to prepare a plot against the Prime Minister.

These persons were related to the CIA agents Alberto and Ramón Grau Sierra, who berlonged to the net headed by Ramón and María Leopoldina Grau Alsina, who later in June 1965 attempted to poison the Prime Minister.

The plan consisted of throwing grenades against our Prime Minister at the Latin American Stadium, by a group of nine men who were arrested and whose warlike equipment was taken from them.

In September of this same year (1964), a group of counterrevolutionaries from the "Ejército de Liberación Nacional" (ELN), and "Frente Interno de Liberación" (FIL) organizations, who were accomplishing instructions of obtaining information for the CIA, began to seek unification, according to the CIA's orders.

While accomplishing these tasks for achieving unity, the counterrevolutionary Nemesio Cubillas Pérez informed Angel Miguel Arencibia Virán, Rolando Galdós Ranzola and others about the plot they were elaborating against our Prime Minister at 11 St., Vedado, according to the CIA instructions.

At the beginning of 1965, the counterrevolutionaries Julio Omar Cruz Cecilia, Fermín González Carballo and Giraldo Reynaldo Diego Solano, members of the "Ejército de Liberación Nacional" (integrated into the RCA block, directed by the CIA) began to complete details of a plot against the Commander in Chief in Santiago de las Vegas.

They gave up this first plan and devised another plot, which would be committed by armed men with fragmentation grenades at the Latin American Stadium, and in a nearby building, there was another group which would open fire with machine guns against the people, producing panic and confusion and thus guaranteeing the withdrawal.

As it has been said before, in June of this same year, a net of CIA agents, headed by Ramón and María Leopoldina Grau Alsina (known as Polita) were devoted to all type of enemy activities, as well as others of antisocial nature. For this purpose, they made use of contacts with capitalist representations in the country, which were used as liaisons with the Central Intelligence Agency.

These individuals were part of the organizations "Rescate", "Movimiento Anticomunista Revolucionario" (MAR) and other organizations directed and sponsored by that Agency.

María Leopoldina Grau was given instructions by the CIA to plot for poisoning Prime Minister Fidel Castro, thereby she was sent a poisonous pill bottle, which was given to Alberto Cruz Caso, who in turn, gave it to Jesús Campanioni Souza and Santos de la Caridad Pérez Núñez, members of the Organization (MAR), so that they would commit the attempted crime at the Havana Libre Hotel.

The counterrevolutionary Tony Varona sent another bottle with 500 capsules when this attempt failed, in order to try to carry out the act again.

Likewise, "Polita" received from the CIA some weapons with mufflers and special projectiles for personal assassinations, which were taken from them when arrested in June 1965.

Once more, in 1965, the Central Intelligence Agency attempted to regroup the dispersed counterrevolutionary organizations, under the name "Unidad Resistencia" (UNARE). In these activities, the counterrevolutionaries Enrique Abreu Vilahu, known as Henry, Carlos Vicente Sánchez Hernández, Julio de las Nieves Ruiz Pitaluga and others, plotted against the Commander in Chief, taking advantage of his visit to Vita Nouva's restaurant, in the Vedado. In this place, Abreu Vilahu would open fire with a Thompson machine gun against the Prime Minister and the guards of the Ministry of the Interior building located across the restaurant, in order to create confusion and escape.

On being arrested in July of that same year, warlike material they had for the fulfillment of their purposes was taken from them.

Being the principal indicted in a plan to kill the Prime Minister, the former Commander Rolando Cubela Secades was also arrested in 1966. That plan was prepared by the CIA, taking advantage of Cubela's trip to Madrid, where he was recruited by the CIA agents Manuel Artime, Jorge Robreño known as "The Magician" (El Mago), Luis Enrique Trasancos and Carlos Tepedino.

Others that also participated in the plot, were the traitors José Luis González Gallarreta ,official at the Cuban Embassy in Madrid, and Alberto Blanco known as "The Crazy" (El Loco).

In the interview of Cubela with Manuel Artime, the later guaranteed the delivery of pirate crafts, weapons and men for an invasion which would support the plan for the assassination of the Prime Minister in less than 72 hours.

For that purpose, before Cubela came back to Cuba, he received from José Luis González Gallarreta a rifle with telescopic peephole and muffler, which was taken from him when arrested, together with a great number of weapons and equipment that the CIA had sent to him. Alberto Blanco Romariz and José Luis González Gallarreta were also arrested.

The "Comandos L" and the "Movimiento 30 de Noviembre", with representation in the U.S. territory, directed by the CIA, undertook the task of making ready two crafts equipped with guns to be infiltrated, and commit subversive activities in our country, about mid-1965.

They gave up the infiltration and decided to shoot at the scholarship zone in Miramar and at the Riviera Hotel, mainly in the direction of the residence of the President of the Republic. After this action they returned to the United States.

In May, 1966, these men were infiltrated by the Monte Barreto zone, in the capital, with the mission of assassinating the Prime Minister. Armando Romero Martinez and Sandalio Herminio Díaz García were killed in action, and Antonio Cuesta Valle, principal head of the "Comandos L", and Eugenio Enrique Zaldívar Cárdenas, were arrested and a great number of equipment and warlike material were taken from them.

These men were trained by the CIA in Puerto Rico, and some of them were the authors of the bombardment of the "San Pascual" merchant vessel anchored at the Caibarién Port, in Las Villas Province.

Félix Asencio Crespo, Wilfredo Martínez Díaz and Gustavo Areces Alvarez were arrested on March 17th, while they tried to infiltrate through the Cayo Fragoso zone, coming from the United States.

The main objective they should carry out was to assassinate our Prime Minister and launch a systematic activity of sabotage with plastic explosives, all that supported by pirate attacks, in order to give abroad an image of the existence of subversive activities in different areas and thus to create a situation which would permit the counterrevolutionary organizations located in the United States to succeed in getting official support.

In order to carry out their activities in Cuban territory, they were trained by the CIA through the "M-30-11", "RECE", "Los Pinos Nuevos", "Comandos L", "Alpha-66" and other organizations. For this mission they were given all the necessary warlike material.

In 1971, due to Commander in Chief's trip to Chile, a plot was elaborated in that country for which the CIA, the Chilean fascists and Cuban counterrevolutionaries from "Alpha-66" organization came together.

The major indicted in this plan was Jesús Domínguez Benítez, known as "The Islander". Through Cuban counterrevolutionaries settled down in Venezuela, he obtained false documents which identified him as a Venezuelan newspaper man, which permitted him to report our Prime Minister's visit in that country.

The plan would be carried out using a gun camouflaged into a television camera, but they gave this up on considering there were no guarantees for the preservation of their lives.

Domínguez Benítez, belonged to the "Poder Cubano" terrorist organization. He was accused by the American authorities of promoting terrorist actions inside the United States and other countries, as a member of that organization, and was arrested by the FBI in 1968.

However, in 1970 he participated in the "Alpha-66" unsuccessful attempt of infiltration through Oriente Province, and sought refuge at the Naval Base, where he was arrested again, this time because he violated the conditions of a bond over an 18 months condemn due to the trial just mentioned before.

Nevertheless, he is set free and leaves the United States without any difficulty, and moves to South America in order to participate in the plot. Afterwards, he returns to the United States.

We consider that the analysis of the information we offer, the publicly known, and the ones that the American authorities possess and have not been published, allow us to affirm that the physical elimination of Cuban Revolutionary leaders, specially the Prime Minister Fidel Castro Ruz, has been a reiterated policy of the United States through its subversive agencies, making use of Cuban counterrevolutionaries, U.S. citizen and all kinds of corrupted individuals, inside the country as well as abroad, without taking into consideration the victims that would result from these actions.

With this purpose, they have provided the participants with a great number of weapons, explosives, technical means of transportation and communication for the accomplishment of their plans.

These are some of the co-noted and proved facts of the numerous subversive activities that the CIA has carried out aimed to the assassination of the leaders of the Revolutionary Government of Cuba.

ACKNOWLEDGMENTS

As with each of my non-fiction books, so far, *Watergate: The Hidden History* turned out to be three times as large as planned and took three times as long to write. But somehow, the amazing crew at Counterpoint have managed to get the book out on time, on a schedule that was a fraction of the usual time for the production any book, let alone one of this size.

Charlie Winton is a true developmental editor who deserves much of the credit for this and my other books. Kelly Winton is carrying on his publishing tradition, and everyone at Counterpoint is great to work with, from Liz Parker in Marketing to Editorial Assistant Jodi Hammerwold. Also helping this book to look and read as well as possible were Copyeditor Matthew Grace, Interior Designer David Bullen, Cover Designer John Yates, Proofreaders Julie Pinkerton and Barrett Briske, Indexer Susan Clements and Lorna Garano helming Publicity.

Editor Brad Strickland always takes makes my work read better, and Susan Barrows did an amazing job helping to pull together the two thousand endnotes.

Special thanks are due to these two gentlemen for helping me finally obtain the Johnny Rosselli Watergate memos: Thomas Mann at the Library of Congress and William H. Davis of the Center for Legislative Archives at the National Archives. The folks at the Richard Nixon Presidential Library were extremely helpful, and many of the documents cited in this book couldn't have been uncovered without the help of the staff of Archives II in College Park, Maryland. The National Security Archive is also a valuable resource for files and for trying to make the government finally declassify decades-old files that are still needlessly withheld.

This book wouldn't exist with the aid and effort over the years of Thom Hartmann, my original collaborator and now one of the best radio and TV political hosts in the country. He and Louise Hartmann are two of the finest people I've ever known. Producer Shawn Taylor always makes any visit to their show a pleasure.

Always helping to spread the word are Mark Crispin Miller, Mark Karlin, and Margie Burns, outstanding purveyors of progressive news and views. Liz Smith remains an icon of good journalism and always has a fresh viewpoint. Henry and everyone at Scribe have helped to broaden the reach of my work to the wonderful people of Australia.

More than two dozen associates of John and Robert Kennedy have gone out of their way to aid my efforts over the years, but special thanks go to Ron

Goldfarb, G. Robert Blakey, Abraham Bolden, Rep. John Lewis (and his Communications Director, Brenda Jones), and Gore Vidal.

For research and the sharing of important information, you can't beat Larry Hancock, Stuart Wexler, Debra Conway, Rex Bradford, Jim Lesar, Mike Cain, Gordon Winslow, Paul Hoch, Robert Dorff, Vince Palamara, and Kate Willard.

George DiCaprio, Leo DiCaprio, everyone at Appian Way are wonderful to work with and will soon be bringing you more of America's hidden history on the big screen. Thanks is also due to producer Earl Katz, for helping to clear the Watergate documentary rights for this book. And Jack Van Laningham is both living history and a good friend.

When I'd written something as concisely as possible in *Legacy of Secrecy*, I sometimes used some of that wording in this book, so I'd like to thank everyone who made that book possible as well.

Thanks also go to my supportive family, from my father to my siblings, niece and nephews, and my many aunts, uncles, and cousins, in particular my recently departed uncles, Billy and Elijah.

Finally, I'd like to thank anyone I may have forgotten and all those who spend long hours digging through files and searching for the truth.

Lamar Waldron
May 11, 2012

NOTES

All government files cited in these endnotes have been declassified and are available at the National Archives. Many can be viewed at maryferrell.org, by using document numbers or other information.

Usually, one endnote number is placed at the end of a paragraph, for all references in that paragraph. In the endnote, references are usually either alphabetical by author's last name, or in the order the references appeared in the book's main text.

Several key names have been simplified in this book. "Jr." has been dropped for Dr. Martin Luther King, Joseph Califano, and Santo Trafficante. The names of important Cuban exiles were standardized to: Manuel Artime, Manolo Ray, Eloy Menoyo, Tony Varona, Harry Williams, and Carlos Prio

All Author interviews prior to 1995 were done in close collaboration with Thom Hartmann.

For updates to these endnotes, check out watergatethehiddenhistory.com.

NARA = National Archives and Records Administration

JCS = Joint Chiefs of Staff.

HSCA = House Select Committee on Assassinations

DIA = Defense Intelligence Agency

CHAPTER 1

1. Rappleye, Charles, and Ed Becker. *All American Mafioso: The Johnny Roselli Story.* (New York: Doubleday, 1991), 307; St. George, Andrew Frank Sturgis (Fiorini) interview, *True* magazine, August 1974; HSCA: 180-10090-10232.
2. Summers, Anthony, with Robbyn Swan. *The Arrogance of Power: The Secret World of Richard M. Nixon.* (New York: Viking Press, 2000), 196, 197; more references in Chapter 7.
3. CIA. Inspector General's Report, 1967; Moldea, Dan. *The Hoffa Wars.* (New York: S.P.I. Books, 1993), 320, 321, 396, 397; Summers, Anthony, with Robbyn Swan. *The Arrogance of Power: The Secret World of Richard M. Nixon.* (New York: Viking Press, 2000), 196, 197.
4. Author's interviews with Harry Williams, 2-24-92, 7-24-93; Fonzi, Gaeton. *The Last Investigation.* (New York: Thunder's Mouth Press, 1993), 136–138, 272, 273; House Select Committee on Assassinations, vol. X;.Haynes Johnson, *Sleepwalking Through History* (New York: W. W. Norton, 2003), 271; Moldea, Dan. *The Hoffa Wars* (New York: S.P.I. Books, 1993), 260–322; author's phone interview with Carl Shoffler, 12-14-93; Stockton, Bayard. *Flawed Patriot: The Rise and Fall of CIA Legend Bill Harvey.* (Dulles, Virginia: Potomac Books, 2006), 175; Valentine, Douglas. *The Strength of the Pack: The Personalities, Politics, and Espionage Intrigues That Shaped the DEA.* (Walterville, Oregon: Trine Day, 2009), 198, 473.
5. Rappleye, Charles, and Ed Becker. *All American Mafioso: The Johnny Roselli Story.* (New York: Doubleday, 1991), 307; St. George, Andrew Frank Sturgis (Fiorini) interview, *True* magazine, August 1974; HSCA: 180-10090-10232.
6. Epstein, Edward. "Did the Press Uncover Watergate?" *Commentary*, July 1974.
7. Woodward, Bob. *The Secret Man: The Story of Watergate's Deep Throat.* (New York: Simon & Schuster, 2005), 15, 16.
8. For example, see Colodny, Len, and Robert Gettlin. *Silent Coup.* (New York: St. Martin's Press, 1992), 77–91, 288–310.
9. O'Leary, Jeremiah, "Haig Probe: Did Nixon Get Cash from Asia?" *Washington Star*, December 5, 1976.
10. Shudel, Matt. "Top D.C. lawyer secured Hoffa conviction, Nixon's pardon." *Washington Post* 11-19-2009. Information about Haig's role in 1963 anti-Castro operations can be found in later chapters of this book, and in the author's udpated editions of *Ultimate Sacrifice* (Berkeley: Counterpoint, 2006) and *Legacy of Secrecy* (Berkeley: Counterpoint, 2009); Anthony and Robbyn Summers, "The Ghosts of November," *Vanity Fair*, 12-94; Warren Hinckle and William Turner, *The Fish Is Red: The Story of the Secret War Against Castro* (New York: Harper & Row, 1981), 153, 299, 303, 304.
11. Bernstein, Carl, and Bob Woodward. *All the President's Men.* (New York: Simon & Schuster, 1974), 318; Szulc, Tad."Cuba on Our Mind," *Esquire*, 2-73.
12. Final Report of the Senate Select Committee on Presidential Campaign Activities, 1974, 1123–1128. Hougan, Jim. *Secret Agenda.* (New York: Random House, 1984), 264, 328–335; Final Report of the Senate Select Committee on Presidential Campaign Activities, 1974, 1123–1128.
13. Hougan, *Secret Agenda, op. cit.*, 264, 328–335; Final Report of the Senate Select Committee on Presidential Campaign Activities, 1974, 1123–1128.
14. Moldea, *Hoffa Wars, op. cit.*, 260–322.
15. *New York Times* October 13, 1975.
16. Rosselli memo to Senator Ervin by Lenzner and Lackritz, February 1974—Senate Select Committee on Presidential Campaign Activities (Ervin Committee), staff files; Lenzer to Muse Rosselli Watergate Committee memo, February 1974—Senate Select Committee on Presidential Campaign Activities (Ervin Committee), staff files.

17. Sussman, Barry. "Watergate 25 Years Later," June 17, 1997.
18. FBI 124-10280-10440; HSCA 124-10289-10440.
19. Califano, Joseph. *Inside: A Public and Private Life*. (New York: Public Affairs, 2004), many passages.
20. Califano, *Inside, op. cit.*, 267–308; Evan Thomas, *The Man To See* (New York: Simon & Schuster, 1991), p. 269.
21. Califano, *Inside, op. cit.*, 285–288.
22. Califano, *Inside, op. cit.*, 307–309.
23. Shudel, "Lawyer re: Hoffa, Nixon," *op. cit.*
24. Ambrose, Stephen, *Nixon, Vol. 3: Ruin and Recovery*. (New York: Simon & Schuster, 1991), 449–451.
25. Lukas, J. Anthony. *Nightmare: The Underside of the Nixon Years*. (New York: Random House, 1976), 411–414; McCord, James W. Jr. *A Piece of Tape: The Watergate Story—Fact or Fiction?* (Rockville, Maryland: Washington Media Services, Ltd., 1974), 59–63.
26. Anthony and Robbyn Summers, "The Ghosts of November," *Vanity Fair*, 12-94; Hinckle, Warren, and William Turner, *The Fish Is Red: The Story of the Secret War Against Castro* (New York: Harper & Row, 1981) pp. 153, 299, 303, 304; CIA104-10315-10004, AMWORLD memo 6-28-63, declassified 1-27-99.
27. McCord, James W. Jr. *A Piece of Tape: The Watergate Story—Fact or Fiction?* (Rockville, Maryland: Washington Media Services, Ltd., 1974), many passages.
28. Kutler, Stanley I. *Abuse of Power: The New Nixon Tapes*. (New York: The Free Press, 1997), 3–13. For references documenting Nixon's pre-Pentagon Papers crimes, see Chapters 23–25 in this book.
29. Weiner, Tim. "In tapes, Nixon muses about break-ins at foreign embassies," *The New York Times* February 26, 1999.
30. Epstein, Edward Jay. *Agency of Fear: Opiates and Political Power in America*. (London and New York: Verso, 1990), 206.
31. Kutler, *Tapes, op. cit.*, many passages; Summers and Swan, *Nixon, op. cit.*, many passages.
32. Fulsom, Don. "The Mob's President: Richard Nixon's Secret Ties to the Mafia." *Crime Magazine* February 5, 2006.; Scheim, David. *The Mafia Killed President Kennedy*. (Kent, England: S.P.I. Books, 1974), 368. "Nixon, the Teamsters, the Mafia," Los Angeles Times, June 1, 1973.
33. Fulsom, "Mob's Prez," *op. cit.*; Scheim, *Mafia Killed, op. cit.*, 368.
34. Fulsom, "Mob's Prez," *op. cit.*
35. Davis, John H. *Mafia Kingfish: Carlos Marcello and the Assassination of John F. Kennedy*. (New York: McGraw-Hill, 1989), 566, 567.
36. Anson, Robert Sam. *"They've Killed the President!"* (New York: S.P.I., 1993), 295, 296.
37. Dick Russell, "Charles Colson," *Argosy*, 3-76.
38. Scheim, *Mafia Killed, op. cit.*, 370.
39. *Ibid.*, 365.
40. Scheim, *Mafia Killed, op. cit.*, citing *Life* magazine 9-1-67.
41. President Richard Nixon's Daily Diary, 1969 to 1974, available at the Richard Nixon Presidential Library.
42. Scheim, *Mafia Killed, op. cit.*, 364, citing *The New York Times* 1-21-74 and *Life* magazine 2-3-67.
43. Summers and Swan, *Nixon, op. cit.*, 114.
44. Dick Russell, "Charles Colson," *Argosy*, 3-76., Summers and Swan, *Nixon, op. cit.*, 106–115, 376, 377.
45. Kutler, *Tapes, op. cit.*, several passages detailed in later chapters of this book.
46. Powers, Thomas. *The Man Who Kept the Secrets: Richard Helms and the CIA*. (New York: Alfred A. Knopf, 1979), 62; Hunt, E. Howard, and Greg Aunapu. *American Spy: My Secret History in the CIA, Watergate, and Beyond*. (Hoboken, New Jersey: John Wiley & Sons, Inc., 2007) 97, 143, 144; Kaiser, David. *The Road to Dallas: The Assassination of John F. Kennedy*. (Cambridge, Massachusetts: Belknap Press of Harvard University Press, 2008), 430.
47. CIA. Inspector General's Report, 1967; Church, Senator Frank. *Alleged Assassination Plots Involving Foreign Leaders*. (New York: W.W. Norton & Company, 1976), many passages.
48. Hunt, E. Howard, and Greg Aunapu. *American Spy: My Secret History in the CIA, Watergate, and Beyond*. (Hoboken, New Jersey: John Wiley & Sons, Inc., 2007), many passages; Szulc, Tad. *Compulsive Spy: The Strange Career of E. Howard Hunt*. (New York: Viking Press, 1974), many passages; many more detailed references about the Helms-Hunt friendship are contained in the later chapters of this book.
49. Hunt, E. Howard, and Greg Aunapu. *American Spy: My Secret History in the CIA, Watergate, and Beyond*. (Hoboken, New Jersey: John Wiley & Sons, Inc., 2007), 157.
50. Kutler, *Tapes, op. cit.*, 6; Tad Szulc, *Compulsive Spy: The Strange Career of E. Howard Hunt* (New York: Viking, 1974), pp. 128, 129; Senate Watergate Committee testimony of Bernard Barker, May 24, 1973; "A Man Called Macho by Marcelo Fernandez-Zayas," *Guaracabuya*, www.amigospais-guaracabuya.org.
51. Hougan, *Agenda, op. cit.*, 328, 329; Powers, *Helms, op. cit.*, 62.
52. Califano, *Inside, op. cit.*, 268–270.
53. Morley, Jefferson. "What Jane Roman said." Accessed at mcadams.posc.mu.edu/morley1.htm on December 2, 2002; Powers, *Helms, op. cit.*, many passages; Hunt, E. Howard, and Greg Aunapu. *American Spy: My Secret History in the CIA, Watergate, and Beyond*. (Hoboken, New Jersey: John Wiley & Sons, Inc., 2007), 148–151.
54. Epstein, *Fear, op. cit.*, 236; Kaiser, *The Road to Dallas, op. cit.*, 430.
55. Lukas, *Nightmare, op. cit.*, 373, 374.
56. Kutler, *Tapes, op. cit.*, 7–10, 18, 22–23, 27, 92, 93, 105, 137, 138, 214–216, 222, 261, 268, 438, 583.

CHAPTER 2

1. The Pecora Commission Hearings, sometimes called the Stock Exchange Practices Hearings, Committee on Banking and Currency.
2. The Senate Special Committee on Investigation of the Munitions Industry.
3. Denton, Sally. The Plots against the President: FDR, a Nation in Crisis, and the Rise of the American Right. (New York: Bloomsbury Press, 2012), many passages.
4. Wall, Joseph Frazier. *Alfred I du Pont: The Man and His Family*. (New York: Oxford University Press, 1990

5. Higham, Charles. *Trading with the Enemy*. (New York: Dell Books, 1983), many passages.
6. Trento, Joseph J. *The Secret History of the CIA*. (New York: Basic Books, 2001), 25, 26.
7. Summers and Swan, *Nixon*, *op. cit.*, 62, 63, 489.
8. *Ibid*., 62, 63, 489.
9. Ambrose, Stephen, *Nixon, Vol.1: The Education of a Politician*. (New York: Simon & Schuster, 1987), 44–53.
10. Ambrose, *Vol. 1*, *op. cit.*, 44–53.
11. Ambrose, *Vol. 1*, *op. cit.*, 52, 53.
12. Ambrose, *Vol. 1*, *op. cit.*, 52, 53.
13. Ambrose, *Vol. 1*, *op. cit.*, 69; Summers and Swan, *Nixon*, *op. cit.*, 15–20.
14. Ambrose, *Vol. 1*, *op. cit.*, 70–75.
15. Summers and Swan, *Nixon*, *op. cit.*, 21; Ambrose, *Vol. 1*, *op. cit.*, 70–81.
16. Summers and Swan, *Nixon*, *op. cit.*, 22; Ambrose, *Vol. 1*, *op. cit.*, 70–81.
17. Summers and Swan, *Nixon*, *op. cit.*, 32.
18. *Ibid*., 27.
19. Ambrose, *Vol. 1*, *op. cit.*, 92; Summers and Swan, *Nixon*, *op. cit.*, 42.
20. Ambrose, *Vol. 1*, *op. cit.*, 101–108.
21. Ambrose, *Vol. 1*, *op. cit.*, 114, 115.
22. *Ibid*., 113, 114.
23. *Ibid*., 117–119.
24. Ambrose, *Vol. 1*, *op. cit.*, 117, 118; Summers and Swan, *Nixon*, *op. cit.*, 46–49, 63.
25. Ambrose, *Vol. 1*, *op. cit.*, 117, 118; Summers and Swan, *Nixon*, *op. cit.*, 46–49, 63.
26. Summers and Swan, *Nixon*, *op. cit.*, 153.
27. Summers and Swan, *Nixon*, *op. cit.*, 46–49.
28. *Ibid*., 47, 48.
29. Bernays, Edward. *Propaganda*. (Brooklyn, New York: Ig Publishing—book by Bernays, 1928; introduction by Mark Crispin Miller, 2005), many passages.
30. Voorhis, Jerry. *The Strange Case of Richard Milhous Nixon*. (New York: Popular Library, 1973), 12, 13.
31. Summers and Swan, *Nixon*, *op. cit.*, 50–59.
32. Rappleye and Becker, *All American*, *op. cit.*, 60–73; Summers and Swan, *Nixon*, *op. cit.*, 54, 55, 489.
33. Many examples can be found in Davis, John H. *Mafia Kingfish: Carlos Marcello and the Assassination of John F. Kennedy*. (New York: McGraw-Hill, 1989) and Kennedy, Robert Francis. *The Enemy Within*. (New York: Popular Library, 1960).
34. Ambrose, *Vol. 1*, *op. cit.*, 427; Summers and Swan, *Nixon*, *op. cit.*, 153–158.
35. Summers and Swan, *Nixon*, *op. cit.*, 42, 43, 52, 54, 55; Voorhis, *Strange Case*, *op. cit.*, 12–17, 20.
36. Summers and Swan, *Nixon*, *op. cit.*, 44, 45; Voorhis, *Strange Case*, *op. cit.*, 11–20.
37. Summers and Swan, *Nixon*, *op. cit.*, 44, 45; Voorhis, *Strange Case*, *op. cit.*, 11–20.
38. Summers and Swan, *Nixon*, *op. cit.*, 43–45; Voorhis, *Strange Case*, *op. cit.*, 15, 16.
39. Voorhis, *Strange Case*, *op. cit.*, 11–20.
40. Summers and Swan, *Nixon*, *op. cit.*, 48, 49.
41. Voorhis, *Strange Case*, *op. cit.*, 16.

CHAPTER 3

1. Thomas, Evan. *Robert Kennedy: His Life*. (New York: Simon & Schuster, 2000), many passages.
2. Ambrose, *Vol. 1*, *op. cit.*, 157–159.
3. Ambrose, *Vol. 1*, *op. cit.*, 149–159.
4. Ambrose, *Vol. 1*, *op. cit.*, 149–159.
5. Though widely-acclaimed today, *It's a Wonderful Life* was not considered a success when first released in 1946, but it was still playing in smaller towns and second-run houses in 1947.
6. Summers and Swan, *Nixon*, *op. cit.*, 490.
7. Trento, Joseph J. *The Secret History of the CIA*. (New York: Basic Books, 2001), 42, 43; Higham, *Trading*, *op. cit.*, 246.
8. Summers and Swan, *Nixon*, *op. cit.*, 65, 66, 490.
9. Summers and Swan, *Nixon*, *op. cit.*, 67.
10. Summers and Swan, *Nixon*, *op. cit.*, 65, 66, 490.
11. Kutler, *Tapes*, *op. cit.*, 7–10, 18, 22–23, 27, 92, 93, 105, 137, 138, 214–216, 222, 261, 268, 438, 583.
12. Voorhis, *Strange Case*, *op. cit.*, 17,18.
13. Ambrose, *Vol. 1*, *op. cit.*, 212.
14. Summers and Swan, *Nixon*, *op. cit.*, 81–83, other passages.
15. Daniel, Clifton and John Kirshon, editors. *Chronicle of America*. (Liberty, Missouri: JL International Publishing, 1993), 756.
16. Summers and Swan, *Nixon*, *op. cit.*, 55, 83–87; Voorhis, *Strange Case*, *op. cit.*, 20.
17. Summers and Swan, *Nixon*, *op. cit.*, 83–87.
18. *Ibid*., 83–87.
19. *Ibid*., 83–87.
20. *Ibid*., 83–87.
21. *Ibid*., 83–87.
22. *Ibid*., 122–124.
23. *Ibid*., 122–124.
24. *Ibid*., 122–124.
25. "War Views: Afghan heroin trade will live on" BBC News 10-10-2001.
26. Rappleye and Becker, *All American*, *op. cit.*, 120, 121.
27. Rappleye and Becker, *All American*, *op. cit.*, 132, 133.
28. Summers and Swan, *Nixon*, *op. cit.*, 124–126.
29. *Ibid*., 124–126.
30. English, T. J. *Havana Nocturne* (New York: HarperCollins 2008) 93–100.
31. Summers and Swan, *Nixon*, *op. cit.*, 100–115.
32. *Ibid*., 102, 112, 114, 115, 128.
33. *Ibid*., 127, 128.
34. *Ibid*., 100–115.
35. It's now known that Eisenhower's affair with his aide Kate Sommersby before the D-Day invasion was far more torrid than its mild description in the published version of Sommersby's book, *Past Forgetting*. If General Eisenhower's affair had been discovered and exposed by the Germans, it could have played havoc with Allied plans. The second scandal in Eisenhower's past was the failed practice landing for D-Day on the coast of England, codenamed Operation Tiger. On April 28, 1944, the exercise was accidently discovered by the Germans, resulting in the deaths of 946 American servicemen, most of whom were killed when their landing craft was hit at sea. Under General Eisenhower, the true cause of their deaths was covered up at the time, and the casualties were simply included in the overall figures for D-Day. The biggest part of the scandal was that 308 of the Americans who fell on the beach died by friendly fire, because Eisenhower had ordered a British ship to fire on them with live ammo. The whole incident didn't become widely known in England until the 1980s and in the US until the

1990s. See Associated Press "U.S. GIs in British WWII Disaster Honored" *Newsday*, 4-25-2004.
36. Ambrose, *Vol. 1, op. cit.*, 271–299.
37. Ambrose, *Vol. 1, op. cit.*, 276–295; Summers and Swan, *Nixon, op. cit.*, 118–123.
38. Ambrose, *Vol. 1, op. cit.*, 276–295; Summers and Swan, *Nixon, op. cit.*, 118–123.
39. Summers and Swan, *Nixon, op. cit.*, 116–124.
40. Ambrose, *Vol. 1, op. cit.*, 285.

CHAPTER 4

1. *New York Times* November 10, 1999; *The Guardian* December 19, 2010.
2. Ambrose, *Vol. 1, op. cit.*, 321–340; Summers, Anthony. *Official and Confidential: The Secret Life of J. Edgar Hoover*. (New York: G.P. Putnam's Sons, 1993),179–182, 191, 444.
3. Anslinger, Harry Jacob and Will Oursler. *The Murderers: The Story of the Narcotic Gangs*. (New York: Farrar Straus & Cudahy, 1961); Cheshire, Maxine. "Drugs and Washington, D.C." *Ladies Home Journal* December 1978.
4. Ambrose, Vol. 1, *op. cit.*, 339–341.
5. Summers and Swan, *Nixon, op. cit.*, 195, 196.
6. Ambrose, Vol. 1, *op. cit.*, many passages.
7. Summers and Swan, *Nixon, op. cit.*, 164–166.
8. Summers and Swan, *Nixon, op. cit.*, 164, 165.
9. Hunt and Aunapu, *American Spy, op. cit.*, 5, 6; 62–66.
10. Hunt and Aunapu, *American Spy, op. cit.*, many passages; Phillips, David Atlee. *The Night Watch.* (New York: Atheneum, 1977), many passages.
11. Newton, Jim. *Eisenhower: The White House Years.* (New York: Doubleday, 2011), Trefousse, Hans Louis. *Dwight D. Eisenhower*, 40, 41.
12. Bardach, Ann Louise. "Scavenger Hunt" Slate 10-6-04; *CIA and Assassinations: The Guatemala 1954 Documents* by Kate Doyle and Peter Kornbluh, National Security Archives website.
13. Ambrose, *Vol. 1, op. cit.*, 366.
14. Ambrose, *Vol. 1, op. cit.*, 427; Summers and Swan, *Nixon, op. cit.*, 153–158.
15. Ambrose, *Vol. 1, op. cit.*, 427; Summers and Swan, *Nixon, op. cit.*, 153–158.
16. Summers and Swan, *Nixon, op. cit.*, 155–158.
17. Ambrose, *Vol. 1, op. cit.*, 397, 398; Summers and Swan, *Nixon, op. cit.*, 51, 56, 149.
18. Ambrose, *Vol. 1, op. cit.*, 397, 398; Summers and Swan, *Nixon, op. cit.*, 51, 56, 149.
19. Ambrose, *Vol. 1, op. cit.*, 397, 398; Summers and Swan, *Nixon, op. cit.*, 51, 56, 149.
20. Ambrose, *Vol. 1, op. cit.*, 397, 398; Summers and Swan, *Nixon, op. cit.*, 51, 56, 149.
21. Ambrose, *Vol. 1, op. cit.*, 397, 398; Summers and Swan, *Nixon, op. cit.*, 56, 149.
22. Summers and Swan, *Nixon, op. cit.*, 52.
23. Ambrose, *Vol. 1, op. cit.*, 397, 398; Summers and Swan, *Nixon, op. cit.*, 56, 149.
24. Ambrose, *Vol. 1, op. cit.*, 384–426; Daniel and Kirshon, eds., *Chronicle of America, op. cit.*, 779; Summers and Swan, *Nixon, op. cit.*, 51–53.
25. Ambrose, *Vol. 1, op. cit.*, 420–423; Daniel and Kirshon, eds., *Chronicle of America, op. cit.*, 771–773.
26. Rappleye, Charles, and Ed Becker. *All American Mafioso: The Johnny Roselli Story*. (New York: Doubleday, 1991), 148–151.
27. Ed Reid, *The Anatomy of Organized Crime in America: The Grim Reapers* (Chicago: Regnery, 1969), pp. 93–95; Carl Sifakis, *The Mafia Encyclopedia* (New York: Facts on File, 1987) 11–13; Douglas Valentine, *The Strength of the Wolf: The Secret History of America's War on Drugs* (London, New York: Verso, 2004), 176.
28. Valentine, *Wolf, op. cit.*, 176.
29. Mahoney, Richard D. *Sons & Brothers*. (New York: Arcade Books, 1999), 26.
30. Summers and Swan, *Nixon, op. cit.*, 107, 128.
31. Ambrose, *Vol. 1, op. cit.*, 570; Summers and Swan, *Nixon, op. cit.*, 178, 179.
32. Ambrose, *Vol. 1, op. cit.*, 570; Summers and Swan, *Nixon, op. cit.*, 178, 179.
33. Ambrose, *Vol. 1, op. cit.*, 448–452.
34. *Ibid.*, 448–452.
35. *Ibid.*, 366, 462.
36. Ambrose, *Vol. 1, op. cit.*, 473–477; Summers and Swan, *Nixon, op. cit.*, 166–170.
37. Hunt and Aunapu, *American Spy, op. cit.*, 110.
38. Hunt, *Undercover, op. cit.*, 126.
39. Hunt, E. Howard. *Undercover: A Memoir of an American Secret Agent*. (New York: Berkley Publishing Corp., 1974), 126, 127; Szulc, Tad. *Compulsive Spy: The Strange Career of E. Howard Hunt*. (New York: Viking Press, 1974), 74–78.
40. Hunt and Aunapu, *American Spy, op. cit.*, 111, 112.

CHAPTER 5

1. Summers and Swan, *Nixon, op. cit.*, 180, 501.
2. Deitche, Scott M. *Silent Don, op. cit.*, 141–146; Richard Helms deposition 1984 Hunt vs. Spotlight trial, *Miami Herald* 1-31-85 cited by A.J. Weberman; Hunt, Jim, and Bob Risch. *Warrior: Frank Sturgis, the CIA's #1 Assassin-Spy Who Nearly Killed Castro But Was Ambushed by Watergate.* (New York: Tom Doherty Associates, 2011), many passages; Kaiser, *Road to Dallas, op. cit.*, 430. Fiorini took the name Sturgis when he came to the United States; it was under this name, Frank Sturgis, that he became infamous as one of the "White House Plumbers."
3. Allen Friedman and Ted Schwarz, *Power and Greed: Inside the Teamsters Empire of Corruption* (New York: F. Watts, 1989), pp. 132, 154; Joseph Franco with Richard Hammer, *Hoffa's Man: The Rise and Fall of Jimmy Hoffa as Witnessed by His Strongest Arm* (New York: Prentice Hall, 1987), pp. 197, 198.
4. Hunt, Jim, and Bob Risch. *Warrior, op. cit.*, 51–54.
5. Summers and Swan, *Nixon, op. cit.*, 181–183; Brodie, Fawn M. *Richard Nixon: The Shaping of His Character* (New York: Norton, 1981), 396–399.
6. Summers and Swan, *Nixon, op. cit.*, 181–183; Brodie *Nixon: Shaping op. cit.*, 396–398.
7. Summers and Swan, *Nixon, op. cit.*, 181–183.
8. Nixon, Richard Milhous. *Six Crises*. (Garden City, New York: Doubleday, 1962).
9. Kennedy, Robert Francis. *The Enemy Within*. (New York: Popular Library, 1960), 33, 286.
10. *Ibid.*, many passages.
11. *Ibid.*, 44–48.
12. *Ibid.*, 48.
13. *Ibid.*, 62–65.
14. Moldea, Dan. *The Hoffa Wars.* (New York: S.P.I. Books, 1993), 77–121.
15. *Ibid.*, 77–121.
16. RFK, *Enemy Within, op. cit.*, many passages.
17. RFK, *Enemy Within, op. cit.*, many passages; Valentine, *Wolf, op. cit.*, 177, 178, 253, 254.

18. RFK, *Enemy Within*, *op. cit.*, 78, 286.
19. HSCA Vol. V, 294; plus other information from A.J. Weberman; Schlesinger, Stephen, and Stephen Kinzer. *Bitter Fruit: The Story of the American Coup in Guatemala*. (Garden City, NY: Doubleday, 1982), 234.
20. Investigation of Improper Activities in the Labor or Management Field, Senate Select Committee Hearings June 1959; Mahoney, Richard D. *Sons & Brothers: The Last Days of Jack and Bobby Kennedy*. (New York: Arcade Books, 1999), 33, 34; additional research by Jonathan Marshall.
21. Investigation of Improper Activities in the Labor or Management Field, Senate Select Committee Hearings March 1959; Davis, *Mafia Kingfish*, *op. cit.*, 86–92.
22. Investigation of Improper Activities, US Senate, 6-59, *op. cit.*, cite Ultimate, at least 337–361, 380
23. Scaduto, Tony. "The CIA-Mafia Connection." *Genesis* 1–76.
24. Investigation of Improper Activities, US Senate, 6-59, *op. cit.*; Kohn, Howard. "Execution for the Witnesses." *Rolling Stone* 6-2-77; Moldea, *Hoffa Wars*, *op. cit.*, 5, 12.
25. Investigation of Improper Activities, US Senate, 6-59, *op. cit.*
26. Reid, *Grim Reapers*, *op. cit.*, 288, 289.
27. CIA document RCD 5.6.75 that was mistakenly labeled by the National Archives as HSCA 180-10107-10419, cited by A.J. Weberman; Hunt, Jim, and Bob Risch. *Warrior*, *op. cit.*, 59, 60; Summers and Swan, *Nixon*, *op. cit.*, 180, 181, 498.
28. Friedman, Allen, and Ted Schwartz. *Power and Greed: Inside the Teamsters Empire of Corruption*. (New York: F. Watts, 1989), 132; Hunt, Jim, and Bob Risch. *Warrior*, *op. cit.*, 59, 60; Summers and Swan, *Nixon*, *op. cit.*, 180, 181.
29. Church, *Plots*, *op. cit.*, 92; Moldea, *Hoffa Wars*, *op. cit.*, 126, 127; Summers and Swan, *Nixon*, *op. cit.*, 498.
30. Deitche, Scott M. *Silent Don*, *op. cit.*, 98–105; Ragano and Raab, *Mob Lawyer*, *op. cit*, 53.
31. Ragano and Raab, *Mob Lawyer*, *op. cit*, 60, 61.
32. Hunt, Jim, and Bob Risch. *Warrior*, *op. cit.*, 62, 63; Malone, William Scott. "The Secret Life of Jack Ruby." *New Times* 1-23-78; Phillips, *Night Watch*, *op. cit.*, 77.
33. Gaeton Fonzi, *The Last Investigation* (New York: Thunder's Mouth, 1994), 77; Wyden, Peter. *The Bay of Pigs: The Untold Story*. (New York: Touchstone Books, 1979), 115.
34. CIA 180-10144-10219; additional Barker CIA memos cited by A. J. Weberman.

CHAPTER 6

1. Beschloss, *Crisis*, *op. cit.*, 134–137; Moldea, *Hoffa Wars*, *op. cit.*, 126, 127.
2. Hunt and Aunapu, *American Spy*, *op. cit.*, 111, 112.
3. Moldea, *Hoffa Wars*, *op. cit.*, 126, 127.
4. Ambrose, *Vol. 1*, *op. cit.*, 553, 541, 542.
5. *Ibid.*, 545.
6. *Ibid.*, 554.
7. Ambrose, *Vol. 1*, *op. cit.*, 69; Summers and Swan, *Nixon*, *op. cit.*, 183, 184.
8. Hunt, *Undercover*, *op. cit.*, 131; Summers and Swan, *Nixon*, *op. cit.*, 185.
9. Beschloss, *Crisis*, *op. cit.*, 134–137; Church, Senator Frank. *Alleged Assassination Plots Involving Foreign Leaders*. (New York: W.W. Norton & Company, 1976), 64, 65, 109–110; Summers and Swan, *Nixon*, *op. cit.*, 189.
10. Summers and Swan, *Nixon*, *op. cit.*, 181.
11. Summers and Swan, *Nixon*, *op. cit.*, 181.
12. Beschloss, *Crisis*, *op. cit.*, 136.
13. Summers and Swan, *Nixon*, *op. cit.*, 190.
14. Canfield, Michael, and Alan J. Weberman. *Coup d'Etat in America: The CIA and the Assassination of John F. Kennedy*. (New York: Third Press, 1975), 171.
15. Scheim, Mafia Killed, *op. cit.*, 118, 119.
16. Canfield and Weberman. *Coup d'Etat*, 171.
17. Scheim, *Mafia Killed*, *op. cit.*, 118, 119.
18. Church, *Plots*, *op. cit.*, 93, 114, 115.
19. Beschloss, *Crisis*, *op. cit.*, 102; Church, *Plots*, *op. cit.*, 93, 114, 115.
20. Franklin, Jane. *Cuban Revolution and the United States*. (Melbourne, Australia: Ocean Press, 1992), 30. It should be noted that it is possible that the explosion was some sort of accident.
21. Brodie, Fawn. *Richard Nixon: The Shaping of His Character*. (New York: Norton, 1981), 396; Church, *Plots*, *op. cit.*
22. Beschloss, *Crisis*, *op. cit.*, 102.
23. Beschloss, *Crisis*, *op. cit.*, 102; Hunt and Aunapu, *American Spy*, *op. cit.*, 117; Summers and Swan, *Nixon*, *op. cit.*, 191.
24. Moldea, *Hoffa Wars*, *op. cit.*, 126, 127; Wyden, *Bay: Untold*, *op. cit.*, several passages.
25. Summers and Swan, *Nixon*, *op. cit.*, 191.
26. Hunt, *Undercover*, *op. cit.*, 131.
27. Scott, Peter Dale. *Crime and Cover-Up: The CIA, the Mafia, and the Dallas-Watergate Connection*. (Santa Barbara, California: Open Archive Press, 1993), 55; Summers and Swan, *Nixon*, *op. cit.*, 185.
28. Summers and Swan, *Nixon*, *op. cit.*, 191.
29. *Ibid.*, 189.
30. Stockton, Bayard. *Flawed Patriot: The Rise and Fall of CIA Legend Bill Harvey*. (Dulles, Virginia: Potomac Books, 2006), 27; Summers and Swan, *Nixon*, *op. cit.*, 189.
31. Hunt, *Undercover*, *op. cit.*, 115; Powers, *Helms*, *op. cit.*, 115.
32. Wyden, *Bay: Untold*, *op. cit.*, 33, 34.
33. 1967 CIA Inspector General's Report on the CIA-Mafia plots.
34. Hougan, *Secret Agenda*, *op. cit* 18; Szulc, "Cuba on Our Mind," *op. cit*
35. Ambrose, *Vol. 1*, *op. cit.*, 550.
36. Summers and Swan, *Nixon*, *op. cit.*, 185.
37. *Ibid.*, 185
38. Beschloss, *Crisis*, *op. cit.*, 109; Escalante, Fabián. *The Secret War*. (Melbourne, Australia: Ocean Press, 1995), 162.
39. Summers and Swan, *Nixon*, *op. cit.*, 190.
40. *Ibid.*, 191, 192.
41. *Ibid.*, 192.
42. Escalante, *Secret War*, *op. cit.*, 162, 163.
43. Ambrose, *Vol. 1*, *op. cit.*, 554.
44. Ambrose, *Vol. 1*, *op. cit.*, 550; Summers and Swan, *Nixon*, *op. cit.*, 185.

CHAPTER 7

1. Summers and Swan, *Nixon*, *op. cit.*, 194.
2. Beschloss, *Crisis*, *op. cit.*, 140.
3. Deitche, Scott M. *Silent Don: The Criminal World of Santo Trafficante Jr.* (Fort Lee, New Jersey:

Barricade Books, 2009), 134; Wyden, *Bay: Untold, op. cit.*, 40.
4. Wyden, *Bay: Untold, op. cit.*, 40–41.
5. Wyden, *Bay: Untold, op. cit.*, 40–41.
6. Church, *Plots, op. cit.*, 74–77; Campbell, Rodney. *The Luciano Project*. (New York: McGraw-Hill, 1977), 27.
7. Church, *Plots, op. cit.*, 74–77.
8. Summers and Swan, *Nixon, op. cit.*, 196, 197.
9. Kohn, Howard. "Strange Bedfellows: The Hughes-Nixon-Lansky Connection," *Rolling Stone*, 5-20-76; Summers and Swan, *Nixon, op. cit.*
10. *Ibid.*, 188, 189.
11. Ambrose, *Vol. 1, op. cit.*, 569.
12. Church, *Plots, op. cit.*, 75; Maheu, Robert, and Richard Hack. *Next to Hughes*. (New York: HarperCollins, 1992), 113–115; Summers and Swan, *Nixon, op. cit.*, 196, 197.
13. Wyden, *Bay: Untold, op. cit.*, 41.
14. Church, *Plots, op. cit.*, 76; Maheu, Robert, and Richard Hack. *Hughes, op. cit.*, 114–116; Wyden, *Bay: Untold, op. cit.*, 42–44, 109.
15. Roemer, William F. Jr. *Accardo: The Genuine Godfather*. (New York: D.I. Fine, 1995); Summers and Swan, *Nixon, op. cit.*, 213; Wyden, *Bay: Untold, op. cit.*, 42–44, 109.
16. Church, *Plots, op. cit.*, 75–78; CIA IG Report, 1967, *op. cit.*, 15–17.
17. Hougan, *Secret Agenda, op. cit.*, 18. The full list of names assigned to Hunt on September 20, 1960, were "Eduardo J. Hamilton," "Mr. Edwards," and "Edward J. Hamilton."
18. CIA 104-10408-10029; CIA 104-10308-10080; Warren Commission Exhibit #3063.
19. Stockton, *Flawed Patriot, op. cit.*, 175; Church, Senator Frank. *Alleged Assassination Plots Involving Foreign Leaders*. (New York: W.W. Norton & Company, 1976), 191–216.
20. Harry Williams interviews, 2-24-92, 7-24-93; Davis, *Mafia Kingfish, op. cit.*, 401, 410; Fensterwald and Ewing, *Coincidence, op. cit.*, 512, 513.
21. Bernard Fensterwald, Jr., and Michael Ewing, *Coincidence or Conspiracy* (New York: Zebra Books, 1977), p. 512; 1967 CIA Inspector General's Report on the CIA-Mafia plots.
22. Warren Hinckle and William Turner, *Deadly Secrets* (New York: Thunder's Mouth, 1992), p. 56; Haynes Johnson interview notes by Richard E. Sprague, 1-12-73; Frank Sturgis interview by Andrew St. George, *True* magazine, 8-74.
23. CIA 180-10144-10219; E. Howard Hunt with Greg Aunapu, *American Spy* (Hoboken, NJ: John Wiley & Sons, 2007), several passages; Marcelo Fernandez-Zayas, "AMan Called Macho," *Guaracabuya*, www.amigospais-guaracabuya.org.
24. CIA document #104-10110-10498; Wyden, *Bay: Untold, op. cit.*, 33.
25. Howard Kohn, "Strange Bedfellows: The Hughes-Nixon-Lansky Connection," *Rolling Stone*, 5-20-76; Summers and Swan, *Nixon, op. cit.*, p. 496; Richard D. Mahoney, *Sons & Brothers: The Days of Jack and Bobby Kennedy* (New York: Arcade, 1999), pp. 383–385.
26. Church, *Plots, op. cit.*, 76, 77.
27. Wyden, *Bay: Untold, op. cit.*, 43.
28. Church, *Plots, op. cit.*, 76, 77; CIA IG Report, 1967, *op. cit.*
29. CIA IG Report, 1967, *op. cit.*, 19.
30. Church, *Plots, op. cit.*
31. Beschloss, *Crisis, op. cit.*, 135; Church, *Plots, op. cit.*, 80; CIA IG Report, 1967, *op. cit.*, 24, 25.
32. Church, *Plots, op. cit.*, 76–79; Wyden, *Bay: Untold, op. cit.*, 44, 45.
33. Summers and Swan, *Nixon, op. cit.*, 192, 193, 567.
34. *Ibid.*, 192, 193, 567.
35. Hunt, Jim, and Bob Risch. *Warrior, op. cit.*, 33.
36. Summers and Swan, *Nixon, op. cit.*, 192, 193, 567.
37. Hunt, Jim, and Bob Risch. *Warrior, op. cit.*, 69; Summers and Swan, *Nixon, op. cit.*, 192, 193, 567.
38. Beschloss, *Crisis, op. cit.*, 135; Cain, Michael. *The Tangled Web: The Life and Death of Richard Cain*. (New York: Skyhorse Publishing, 2007), 72; Church, *Plots, op. cit.*, 19–22, 73.
39. Beschloss, *Crisis, op. cit.*, 135; Cain, *Tangled Web, op. cit.*, 72; Church, *Plots, op. cit.*, 19–22, 73.
40. Escalante, *Secret War, op. cit.*, 53, 164; Article by Eugenio Martinez, *Harper's* 10-74.
41. Church, *Plots, op. cit.*; Escalante, *Secret War, op. cit.*, 53, 164; CIA IG Report, 1967, *op. cit.*; Kurtz, Michael L. *The JFK Assassination Debate*. (Lawrence, Kansas: University of Kansas Press, 2006), 176.
42. Cain, *Tangled Web, op. cit.*, 1–62.
43. *Ibid.*, 72–82.
44. *Ibid.*, 72–82.
45. Cain, *Tangled Web, op. cit.*, 81, 82; Church, *Plots, op. cit.*, 73.
46. Cain, *Tangled Web, op. cit.*, 81, 82.

CHAPTER 8

1. Moldea, *Hoffa Wars, op. cit.*, 107–109, 430–432; Summers and Swan, *Nixon, op. cit.*, 213, 214, 507.
2. Moldea, *Hoffa Wars, op. cit.*, 107–109, 430–432; Summers and Swan, *Nixon, op. cit.*, 213, 214, 507.
3. Moldea, *Hoffa Wars, op. cit.*, 107–109, 430–432; Summers and Swan, *Nixon, op. cit.*, 213, 214, 507.
4. Moldea, *Hoffa Wars, op. cit.*, 107–109, 430–432;Summers and Swan, *Nixon, op. cit.*, 213, 214, 507.
5. Moldea, *Hoffa Wars, op. cit.*, 107, 108; Summers and Swan, *Nixon, op. cit.*, 213, 214, 507.
6. Moldea, *Hoffa Wars, op. cit.*, 107, 108; Summers and Swan, *Nixon, op. cit.*, 213, 214.
7. Moldea, *Hoffa Wars, op. cit.*, 107, 108; Summers and Swan, *Nixon, op. cit.*, 213, 214.
8. Moldea, *Hoffa Wars, op. cit.*, 4, 107, 108, 109; Summers and Swan, *Nixon, op. cit.*, 213, 214, 507.
9. Moldea, *Hoffa Wars, op. cit.*, 4, 107, 108; 109; Summers and Swan, *Nixon, op. cit.*, 213, 214, 507.
10. Moldea, *Hoffa Wars, op. cit.*, 4, 107, 108; 109; Summers and Swan, *Nixon, op. cit.*, 213, 214, 507.
11. Moldea, *Hoffa Wars, op. cit.*, 4, 107, 108; 109; Summers 213, 214, 507.
12. Moldea, *Hoffa, op. cit.*, 320, 321, 396, 397; Scheim, *Mafia Killed, op. cit.*, 368. Sheridan, Rise of Hoffa, op. cit, 406–408; Rosselli memo to Senator Ervin by Lenzner and Lackritz, February 1974—Senate Select Committee on Presidential Campaign Activities (Ervin Committee), staff files; Lenzer to Muse Rosselli Watergate Committee memo, February 1974—Senate Select Committee on Presidential Campaign Activities (Ervin Committee), staff files.
13. Moldea, *Hoffa, op. cit.*, 320, 321, 396, 397; Scheim, *Mafia Killed, op. cit.*, 368. Sheridan, Rise of Hoffa, op. cit, 406–408; *Time* magazine 8-8-77.

14. Wyden, *Bay: Untold, op. cit.*, 68; Summers and Swan, *Nixon, op. cit.*, 206–208.
15. Summers and Swan, *Nixon, op. cit.*, 206–208.
16. Wyden, *Bay: Untold, op. cit.*, 45, 46.
17. *Ibid.*, 45, 46.
18. Escalante, *Secret War, op. cit.*, 165.
19. Ambrose, *Vol. 1, op. cit.*, 590–598; Wyden, *Bay: Untold, op. cit.*, 65–67.
20. Ambrose, *Vol. 1, op. cit.*, 590–598; Wyden, *Bay: Untold, op. cit.*, 65–67.
21. Ambrose, *Vol. 1, op. cit.*, 590–598; Wyden, *Bay: Untold, op. cit.*, 65–67.
22. Ambrose, *Vol. 1, op. cit.*, 590–598; Wyden, *Bay: Untold, op. cit.*, 65–67.
23. Beschloss, *Crisis, op. cit.*, 134, 135; CIA 1961 Kirkpatrick IG Report. Escalante, *Secret War, op. cit.*, 165; Wyden, *Bay: Untold, op. cit.*, 31, 68, 73.
24. Ambrose, *Vol. 1, op. cit.*, 590–598; Wyden, *Bay: Untold, op. cit.*, 65–67.
25. Ambrose, *Vol. 1, op. cit.*, 594, 595.
26. *Ibid.*, 594, 595.
27. *Ibid.*, 594, 595.
28. Wyden, *Bay: Untold, op. cit.*, 45, 46.
29. Church, *Plots, op. cit.*, 76–79; Wyden, *Bay: Untold, op. cit.*, 44–45.
30. Church, *Plots, op. cit.*, 76–79; Wyden, *Bay: Untold, op. cit.*, 44–45.
31. Summers and Swan, *Nixon, op. cit.*, 178.
32. Ambrose, *Vol. 1, op. cit.*, 429, 561; Gus Russo, *Live by the Sword: The Secret War against Castro and the Death of JFK* (Baltimore: Bancroft Press, 1998), 422; Summers and Swan, *Nixon, op. cit.*, 311–312.
33. Ambrose, *Vol. 1, op. cit.*, 561; Gus Russo, *Live by the Sword, op. cit.*, 422; Summers and Swan, *Nixon, op. cit.*, 311–312.
34. Summers and Swan, *Nixon, op. cit.*, 209–212.
35. *Ibid.*, 209–212.
36. *Ibid.*, 209–212.
37. *Ibid.*, 209–212.
38. Ambrose, *Vol. 3, op. cit.*, 202, 203, Summers and Swan, *Nixon, op. cit.*, 212.
39. Summers and Swan, *Nixon, op. cit.*, 215, 216.
40. *Ibid.*, 215, 216.
41. *Ibid.*, 215, 216.
42. Church, *Plots, op. cit.*, 76; Summers and Swan, *Nixon, op. cit.*, 215, 216.
43. CIA Kirkpatrick Inspector General Report, 1961; CIA IG Report, 1967, *op. cit.*
44. Ambrose, *Vol. 1, op. cit.*, 596, 597; Thomas, *RFK, op. cit.*, 100–103.
45. Ambrose, *Vol. 1, op. cit.*, 596, 597; Thomas, *RFK, op. cit.*, 100–103.
46. Ambrose, *Vol. 1, op. cit.*, 596, 597; Thomas, *RFK, op. cit.*, 100–103.
47. Ambrose, *Vol. 1, op. cit.*, 596, 597; Thomas, *RFK, op. cit.*, 100–103; Summers and Swan, *Nixon, op. cit.*, 354.
48. Ambrose, *Vol. 1, op. cit.*, 596, 597; Thomas, *RFK, op. cit.*, 100–103.
49. Ambrose, *Vol. 1, op. cit.*, 596, 597; Thomas, *RFK, op. cit.*, 100–103.
50. Ambrose, *Vol. 1, op. cit.*, 596, 597; Thomas, *RFK, op. cit.*, 100–103.
51. Ambrose, *Vol. 1, op. cit.*, 596, 597; Thomas, *RFK, op. cit.*, 100–103.
52. Summers and Swan, *Nixon, op. cit.*, 217, 508.
53. Summers and Swan, *Nixon, op. cit.*, 217, 508.
54. Beschloss, *Crisis, op. cit.*, 141; Summers and Swan, *Nixon, op. cit.*, 217, 508; Evan RFK p410; Kaiser, David. *The Road to Dallas: The Assassination of John F. Kennedy*. (Cambridge, Massachusetts: Belknap Press of Harvard University Press, 2008), 88, 89.
55. Beschloss, *Crisis, op. cit.*, 141; Arthur Schlesinger, Jr., *Robert Kennedy and His Times* (New York: Ballantine, 1979), 237; Summers and Swan, *Nixon, op. cit.*, 217, 508.
56. Rappleye and Becker, *All American, op. cit.*, 208–215, 229, 235, 243, 249–253

CHAPTER 9

1. CIA Kirkpatrick IG Report, 1961, *op. cit.*; Summers and Swan, *Nixon, op. cit.*, 115, 496.
2. Wyden, *Bay: Untold, op. cit.*, 46.
3. Beschloss, *Crisis, op. cit.*, 102, 103; Wyden, *Bay: Untold, op. cit.*, 68–71. Note that some sources give the date of the JFK-Dulles-Bissell meeting as November 27, 1960.
4. Beschloss, *Crisis, op. cit.*, 102, 103; Church, *Plots, op. cit.*, 120, 121; Wyden, *Bay: Untold, op. cit.*, 68–71.
5. Beschloss, *Crisis, op. cit.*, 102, 103; Church, *Plots, op. cit.*, 120, 121; Wyden, *Bay: Untold, op. cit.*, 68–71.
6. ABC News website. "Friendly Fire: U.S. Military Drafted Plans to Terrorize U.S. Cities to Provoke War with Cuba." 11-7-2001; Hinckle and Turner, *Deadly Secrets, op. cit.*, 84, 85, 89, 93–94.
7. CIA file from the National Archives with no RF number, 10-8-76 memo to Director of Security by Curtis R. Rivers, handwritten note at bottom of RIF sheet: "To NARA—Please replace previously released version of this document with the attached." From Miami-Dade Archivist Gordon Winslow at www.cuban-exile.com.
8. 7-29-82 Department of the Navy release to Bernard Fensterwald, #110-6-21258; Hinckle and Turner, *Fish Is Red, op. cit.*,
9. FBI 62-109060-4759 and CIA MFR 2.14.68 cited by A.J. Weberman; Russo, *Live by the Sword, op. cit.*, many passages.
10. CIA Kirkpatrick IG Report, 1961, *op. cit.*
11. CIA IG Report, 1967, *op. cit.*, 25; Summers and Swan, *Nixon, op. cit.*, 192, 193, 567.
12. CIA IG Report, 1967, *op. cit.*, 113; Kaiser, *Road to Dallas, op. cit.*, 64.
13. Kaiser, *Road to Dallas, op. cit.*, 69.
14. Moldea, *Hoffa Wars, op. cit.*, 109; Summers and Swan, *Nixon, op. cit.*, 214.
15. Moldea, *Hoffa Wars, op. cit.*, 109; Summers and Swan, *Nixon, op. cit.*, 214.
16. Ambrose, *Vol. 1, op. cit.*, 608; Moldea, *Hoffa Wars, op. cit.*, 109; Summers and Swan, *Nixon, op. cit.*, 214.
17. Ambrose, *Vol. 1, op. cit.*, 608; Moldea, *Hoffa Wars, op. cit.*, 109; Summers and Swan, *Nixon, op. cit.*, 214.
18. Stockton, *Flawed Patriot, op. cit.*
19. Franklin, *Cuban Revolution, op. cit.*, 38.
20. Rodriguez, Felix I., and John Weisman. *Shadow Warrior*. (New York: Simon & Schuster, 1989), 65–67.
21. Rodriguez and Weisman. *Shadow Warrior, op. cit.*, 65–67.
22. *Ibid.*, 65–67.
23. Beschloss, *Crisis, op. cit.*, 79, 81; Church, *Plots, op. cit.*, 19–70; Stockton, *Flawed Patriot, op. cit.*,

148, 160, 161; Summers and Swan, *Nixon*, *op. cit.*, 188, 501, 502; Trento, Joseph J. *Secret History*, *op. cit.*, 196, 197.
24. Beschloss, *Crisis*, *op. cit.*, 79, 81; Church, *Plots*, *op. cit.*, 19–70; 1967 CIA IG Report, 27; Stockton, *Flawed Patriot*, *op. cit.*, 148, 160, 161; Summers and Swan, *Nixon*, *op. cit.*, 188, 501, 502; Trento, Joseph J. *Secret History*, *op. cit.*, 196, 197.
25. Wyden, *Bay: Untold*, *op. cit.*, 56, 57.
26. *Ibid.*, 46, 47.
27. *Ibid.*, 56, 57.
28. Ambrose, *Vol. 1*, *op. cit.*, 630.
29. *Ibid.*, 630.
30. Beschloss, *Crisis*, *op. cit.*, 104.
31. *Ibid.*, 104, 105.
32. *Ibid.*, 134.
33. *Ibid.*, 105.
34. Wyden, *Bay: Untold*, *op. cit.*, many passages; Johnson, Haynes, with Manuel Artime, José Pérez San Román, Erneido Oliva, and Enrique Ruiz-Williams. *The Bay of Pigs: The Leader's Story of Brigade 2506*. (New York: W.W. Norton & Company, 1964), many passages.
35. CIA memo 2-20-61, page 28 of CIA Sensitive Study, 1978, CIA #104-10400-10200, declassified 10-31-98.
36. Hinckle and Turner, *Deadly Secrets*, *op. cit.*, many passages; FBI 62-109060-4759 & FBI Bufile 105-89923, New Orleans file 105-1446 both cited by A.J. Weberman along with: David Phillips memo to Chief, CI/R & A: CIA OGC 67-2061, CIA MFR 2.14.68 Sarah K. Hall.
37. CIA IG Report, 1967, *op. cit.*, 28–31.
38. CIA IG Report, 1967, *op. cit.*, 29–33; CIA Office of Security Varona File Summary, Record Number 180-10144-10405, declassified 8-23-95; CIA Confidential Information Report, 8-30-63; Document ID number1993.07.29.17:58:19:340059, declassified 7-29-93.
39. CIA IG Report, 1967, *op. cit.*, 29, 31.
40. Summers, *Hoover*, *op. cit.*, many passages; Author's phone interview with Courtney Evans, former FBI liaison between Hoover and Robert Kennedy.
41. Summers, *Hoover*, *op. cit.*, many passages; Shudel. Matt. "Top D.C. lawyer secured Hoffa conviction, Nixon's pardon." *Washington Post* 11-19-2009.
42. Author's phone interview with Courtney Evans, former FBI liaison between Hoover and Robert Kennedy; Moldea, Hoffa Wars, *op. cit.*, 107–109
43. Davis, Mafia Kingfish, *op. cit.*, 94.
44. *Ibid.*, 94–100.
45. HSCA: 180-10090-10232.

CHAPTER 10

1. Author's interviews with Harry Williams, 2-24-92, 4-92, 7-24-93, 2-21-95; Wyden, *Bay: Untold*, *op. cit.*, 114.
2. Schlesinger, Arthur Jr. White House memo to Richard Goodwin in SSCIA 157-10002-10057. June 9, 1961.
3. Canfield, Michael Interview with Frank Fiorini; Schlesinger, memo to Goodwin, 6-9-61, *op. cit.*; Frank Fiorini (Sturgis) Rockefeller Commission interview, NARA SSCIA 157-10005-10125, March 3, 1975; Olsen, Robert B. Rockefeller Commission memo, SSCIA 157-10005-101-46, April 23, 1975.
4. Frank Sturgis interview by Andrew St. George, *True* magazine, 8-74
5. Haynes Johnson interview notes by Richard E. Sprague, 1-12-73, donated to the Assassination Archives and Records Center; Warren Hinckle and William Turner, *Deadly Secrets* (New York: Thunder's Mouth, 1992), p. 56; Lukas, *Nightmare*, *op. cit.*, 193, 194, 258; *NYT*, *Watergate Hearings*, *op. cit.*, 71, 72.
6. CIA IG Report, 1967, *op. cit.*; Summers and Swan, *Nixon*, *op. cit.*, 193, 194.
7. Szulc, Tad. *Compulsive Spy*, *op. cit.*, 93; Wyden, *Bay: Untold*, *op. cit.*, 116.
8. Szulc, Tad. *Compulsive Spy*, *op. cit.*, 93; Wyden, *Bay: Untold*, *op. cit.*, 116.
9. Szulc, Tad. *Compulsive Spy*, *op. cit.*, 93; Wyden, *Bay: Untold*, *op. cit.*, 116.
10. Wyden, *Bay: Untold*, *op. cit.*, 114–116 (Wyden uses a pseudonym of "Nobel" for "Noel")
11. **237 FOOTNOTE MISSING**
12. **238 FOOTNOTE MISSING**
13. Szulc, Tad. *Compulsive Spy*, *op. cit.*, 93, 94; Wyden, *Bay: Untold*, *op. cit.*, 118, 146, 206–208.
14. Confidential interivew with Cuban exile, 1990.
15. Szulc, Tad. *Compulsive Spy*, *op. cit.*, 88; Wyden, *Bay: Untold*, *op. cit.*, 117.
16. Beschloss, *Crisis*, *op. cit.*, 109; Franklin, *Cuban Revolution*, *op. cit.*, 42; Hunt and Aunapu, *American Spy*, *op. cit.*, 120.
17. Hunt and Aunapu, *American Spy*, *op. cit.*, 120; Wyden, *Bay: Untold*, *op. cit.*, 161.
18. Hunt and Aunapu, *American Spy*, *op. cit.*, 120; Hinckle and Turner, *Deadly Secrets*, *op. cit.*, 82–94.
19. Hinckle and Turner, *Deadly Secrets*, *op. cit.*, 82–94.
20. CIA 104-10315-10003, 12-19-60, declassified 1-27-99, provided by Larry Hancock; Hinckle and Turner, *Deadly Secrets*, *op. cit.*, 81, 93.
21. Wyden, *Bay: Untold*, *op. cit.*, many passages.
22. *Ibid.*, 199, 200.
23. Hinckle and Turner, *Deadly Secrets*, *op. cit.*, 102, 103.
24. Hinckle and Turner, *Deadly Secrets*, *op. cit.*, 81, 93.; Wyden, *Bay: Untold*, *op. cit.*, many passages.
25. Hinckle and Turner, *Deadly Secrets*, *op. cit.*, 81, 93; Wyden, *Bay: Untold*, *op. cit.*, many passages.
26. Hinckle and Turner, *Deadly Secrets*, *op. cit.*, 84–86, 89, 93, 94.
27. *Ibid.*, 84–86, 89, 93, 94.
28. *Ibid.*, 84–86, 89, 93, 94.
29. Wyden, *Bay: Untold*, *op. cit.*, 206–209.
30. Hunt and Aunapu, *American Spy*, *op. cit.*, 122.
31. Carbonell, Nestor T. *And the Russians Stayed: The Sovietization of Cuba: A Personal Portrait.* (New York: Morrow, 1989), many passages; Johnson, Haynes, with Manuel Artime, José Pérez San Román, Erneido Oliva, and Enrique Ruiz-Williams. *The Bay of Pigs: The Leader's Story of Brigade 2506*. (New York: W.W. Norton & Company, 1964), many passages.
32. Johnson, Artime, San Román, Oliva, and Ruiz-Williams, *Bay: Leader*, *op. cit.*, many passages.
33. Author's interviews with Harry Williams, 2-24-92, 4-92, 7-24-93, 2-21-95.
34. Wyden, *Bay: Untold*, *op. cit.*, 292–295; Beschloss, Michael. *The Crisis Years: Kennedy and Khrush-*

chev, 1960–1963. (New York: Edward Burlingame Books, 1991), 143, 144.
35. Ambrose, *Vol. 1*, *op. cit.*, 631, 632; Wyden, *Bay: Untold*, *op. cit.*, 293.
36. Ambrose, *Vol. 1*, *op. cit.*, 631, 632; Wyden, *Bay: Untold*, *op. cit.*, 293.
37. Ambrose, *Vol. 1*, *op. cit.*, 632–633, Hinckle and Turner, *Deadly Secrets*, *op. cit.*, *82–94.
38. Ambrose, *Vol. 1*, *op. cit.*, 632–633.
39. *Ibid.*, 632–633.
40. *Ibid.*, 632–633.
41. *Ibid.*, 633, 634.
42. *Ibid.*, 633, 634.

CHAPTER 11

1. Wyden, *Bay: Untold*, *op. cit.*, 306, 307.
2. Church, *Plots*, *op. cit.*; Wyden, *Bay: Untold*, *op. cit.*, 98; 121–123; 1961 Maxwell Taylor Bay of Pigs Report, 30.
3. Church, *Plots*, *op. cit.*
4. Hinckle and Turner, *Deadly Secrets*, *op. cit.*, 111; Stockton, *Flawed Patriot*, *op. cit.*, 175.
5. Spindel, Bernard. *The Ominous Ear*. (New York: Award House, 1968), 74, 79.
6. Hinckle and Turner, *Deadly Secrets*, *op. cit.*, 191–193.
7. Summers and Swan, *Nixon*, *op. cit.*, 188; Benson, Michael. *Who's Who in the JFK Assassination*. (New York: Citadel Press, 1993), 208, Frank Sturgis interview by Andrew St. George, *True* magazine, 8-74.
8. Summers and Swan, *Nixon*, *op. cit.*, 491.
9. Author's interviews with Harry Williams 2-24-92 and confidential Kennedy aide source 3-17-92.
10. Kaiser, *Road to Dallas*, *op. cit.*, 151, Wyden, *Bay: Untold*, *op. cit.*, 303.
11. Johnson, Artime, San Román, Oliva, and Ruiz-Williams, *Bay: Leader*, *op. cit.*, 237, 238; Kaiser, *Road to Dallas*, *op. cit.*, 151.
12. CIA IG Report, 1967, *op. cit.*, 17, 43.
13. CIA Task Force Report, 1977, 20.
14. Church, *Plots*, *op. cit.*; CIA Task Force Report, 1977, *op. cit.*, 20.
15. HSCA: 180-10090-10232, *op. cit.*
16. *Ibid.*
17. CIA IG Report, 1967, *op. cit.*, 20; Fonzi, *Last Investigation*, *op. cit.*, many passages; Scott, Peter Dale. *Crime and Cover-Up: The CIA, the Mafia, and the Dallas-Watergate Connection*. (Santa Barbara, California: Open Archive Press, 1993), 57.
18. Interview with Antonio Veciana, 6-2-93.
19. HSCA v.10
20. Rappleye and Becker, *All American*, *op. cit.*, 198; Stockton, *Flawed Patriot*, *op. cit.*, 144.
21. Riebling, Mark. *Wedge: From Pearl Harbor to 9/11: How the Secret War between the FBI and the CIA Has Endangered National Security*. (New York: Simon & Schuster, 2002), 186.
22. Church, *Plots*, *op. cit.*, 99–103; Powers, *Helms*, *op. cit.*, 150, 151; Stockton, *Flawed Patriot*, *op. cit.*, 144.
23. Thomas, Evan. *The Very Best Men: Four Who Dared: The Early Years of the CIA* (New York: Simon & Schuster, 1995), 151; Hersh, Seymour M. *The Old Boys*. (New York: Charles Scribner's Sons, 1992), 160; Powers, *Helms*, *op. cit.*, 21, 30–35.
24. Davis, *Katharine*, *op. cit.*, 128–131; 134, 279.
25. CIA IG Report, 1967, *op. cit.*, many passages; Powers, *Helms*, *op. cit.*, 137–141, 168–177, 238, 396-400.
26. Powers, *Helms*, *op. cit.*, 150-163.
27. Powers, *Helms*, *op. cit.*, 175, 176.
28. Church, *Plots*, *op. cit.*, 83; CIA IG Report, 1967, *op. cit.*, 43, 44, 48; Powers, *Helms*, *op. cit.*, 168–171.
29. Church, *Plots*, *op. cit.*, 82-84, CIA IG Report, 1967, *op. cit.*, 42-48; Powers, *Helms*, *op. cit.*, 168–171; Marcello Border Patrol report.
30. Powers, *Helms*, *op. cit.*, 170.
31. Rappleye and Becker, *All American*, *op. cit.*, 235.
32. Church, *Plots*, *op. cit.*, 99, 100; 131–134.
33. Church, *Plots*, *op. cit.*, 99, 100, 131–134; Powers, *Helms*, *op. cit.*, 176; Jonathan Marshall Watergate article, *West* magazine 11-20-83.
34. Thomas, *RFK: His Life*, *op. cit.*, many passages; HSCA *Final Report* and volumes, many passages.
35. Church *Plots*, *op. cit.*, 99, 100; 131–134; 1967 IG 51, 104.
36. Szulc, *Compulsive Spy*, *op. cit.*, many passages; Hunt and Aunapu, *American Spy*, *op. cit.*, many passages.
37. There many CIA files about Barker (though key CIA and FBI files are still withheld), and the most important include: NARA 1994.03.08.09.-46:690007 CIA/DCD File on Bernard Barker; HSCA 180-10144-10219 (the CIA notes Barker's underworld connections); CIA 1993.07.22.18:36:08:560390 (the notes Barker's long-time gangster activities); CIA 1993.07.22.18:36:08:560390; CIA 1994.03.03.15:12:02:470005; HSCA FBI 124-10289-10440; HSCA 180-10145-10362; HSCA 180-10142-10061; plus his individually released CIA files for 1960, 1961,1962, 1963, though those are clearly incomplete based on other files and the later accounts of Barker and E. Howard Hunt. Frank Fiorini shows up frequently in Barker's CIA files, though those files—and Fiorini's own CIA files—don't contain his contract agent work for the CIA that Richard Helms and William Colby later admitted, after withholding that information from the Senate Watergate Committee.
38. ABC News web site, "Friendly Fire: US Military Drafted Plans to Terrorize US Cities to Provoke War with Cuba" 5-1-01 and 11-7-01; Northwoods file in JCS files at the National Archives.
39. ABC News web site, "Friendly Fire: US Military Drafted Plans to Terrorize US Cities to Provoke War with Cuba" 5-1-01 and 11-7-01; Northwoods file in JCS files at the National Archives.
40. Hersh, Seymour M., *The Dark Side of Camelot* (Boston: Little, Brown, 1997) 285.
41. CIA IG Report, 1967, *op. cit.*, 17.
42. Chang, Laurence and Peter Kornbluh. *The Cuban Missile Crisis, 1962*. (New York: The New Press, 1992), 352–366.
43. *Ibid.*, 352–366.
44. Meskil, Paul. "How US made unholy alliance with the Mafia." *New York Daily News* 4-23-75; Powers, *Helms*, *op. cit.*, 162.
45. Chang and Kornbluh, *Missile Crisis*, *op. cit.*, 352–366.

CHAPTER 12

1. Ambrose, *Vol. 1*, *op. cit.*, 629; Summers and Swan, *Nixon*, *op. cit.*, 221, 222.
2. *Ibid.*
3. *Ibid.*
4. *Ibid.*
5. Ambrose, *Vol. 1*, *op. cit.*, 629; Summers and Swan, *Nixon*, *op. cit.*, 107, 221, 222.
6. Summers and Swan, *Nixon*, *op. cit.*, 224–226.
7. Ambrose, *Vol. 1*, *op. cit.*, 637, 639, 640, 641.
8. Ambrose, *Vol. 1*, *op. cit.*, 637, 639, 640, 641; Nixon, Richard Milhous. *Six Crises*. (Garden City, New York: Doubleday, 1962), many passages.
9. Summers and Swan, *Nixon*, *op. cit.*, 226.
10. *Ibid.*, 226–229.
11. Lewis, Bradley. *Hollywood's Celebrity Gangster: The Life and Incredible Times of Mickey Cohen*. (New York: Enigma Books, 2007), many passages.
12. *Ibid.*
13. Summers and Swan, *Nixon*, *op. cit.*, 226, 227.
14. Mankiewicz, Frank. *Perfectly Clear: Nixon from Whittier to Watergate*. (New York: Quadrangle Books, 1973), 65–75, 219–232.
15. *Ibid.*, 65–75, 219–232.
16. Lewis, *Celebrity Gangster*, *op. cit.*; Summers and Swan, *Nixon*, *op. cit.*, 226.
17. Moldea, Hoffa Wars, *op. cit.*, 148.
18. Chang, Laurence and Peter Kornbluh. *The Cuban Missile Crisis, 1962*. (New York: The New Press, 1992), 385.
19. Summers and Swan, *Nixon*, *op. cit.*, 230, 231.
20. Ambrose, *Vol. 1*, *op. cit.*, 670–674; Summers and Swan, *Nixon*, *op. cit.*, 230, 231.
21. Ambrose, *Vol. 1*, *op. cit.*, 670–674.
22. Chang and Kornbluh, *Missile Crisis*, *op. cit.*, 235, 236; Chase, Harold William, and Allen H. Lerman. *Kennedy and the Press: The News Conferences*. (New York: Crowell, 1965), 333-339.
23. Author's interview with Dean Rusk, 1-5-90; Chang and Kornbluh, *Missile Crisis*, *op. cit.*, Document 72.
24. Author's interview with Dean Rusk, 1-5-90;. Chase, Harold William, and Allen H. Lerman. *Kennedy and the Press: The News Conferences*. (New York: Crowell, 1965).
25. Author's interview with Dean Rusk, 1-5-90; Chang and Kornbluh, *Missile Crisis*, *op. cit.*, 391, 396.
26. Author's interview with Dean Rusk, 1-5-90; Gedda, George. "Kennedy backed off pledge not to invade Cuba, documents show." Associated Press, 4-6-97.
27. Author's interviews with Harry Williams (some via Thom Hartmann), 2-24-92, 4-92, 11-13-92, 7-24-93, 2-21-95; Johnson, Artime, San Román, Oliva, and Ruiz-Williams, *Bay: Leader*, *op. cit.*, many passages.
28. Author's interviews with Harry Williams (some via Thom Hartmann), 2-24-92, 4-92, 11-13-92, 7-24-93, 2-21-95; Johnson, Artime, San Román, Oliva, and Ruiz-Williams, *Bay: Leader*, *op. cit.*, many passages.
29. Author's interviews with Harry Williams (some via Thom Hartmann), 2-24-92, 4-92, 7-24-93, 11-13-92, 2-21-95, Johnson, Artime, San Román, Oliva, and Ruiz-Williams, *Bay: Leader*, *op. cit.*, many passages.
30. Franklin, *Cuban Revolution*, *op. cit.*, 60; Johnson, Artime, San Román, Oliva, and Ruiz-Williams, *Bay: Leader*, *op. cit.*, many passages; Kaiser, *Road to Dallas*, *op. cit.*, 151.
31. Carbonell, *Russians Stayed*, *op. cit.*, 191; Johnson, Artime, San Román, Oliva, and Ruiz-Williams, *Bay: Leader*, *op. cit.*, many passages.
32. Carbonell, *Russians Stayed*, *op. cit.*, 191.
33. Bradlee, Benjamin C. "What was lost" *Newsweek* November 2, 1963; Summers and Swan, *Nixon*, *op. cit.*, 218.
34. Moldea, *Hoffa Wars*, *op. cit.*, 148–151.
35. Moldea, *Hoffa Wars*, *op. cit.*, 148–151.
36. Moldea, *Hoffa Wars*, *op. cit.*, 148–151.
37. Davis, *Mafia Kingfish*, *op. cit.*, 114; Moldea, *Hoffa Wars*, *op. cit.*, 148–151.
38. Rappleye and Becker, *All American*, *op. cit.*, 237, 238.
39. Ragano and Raab, *Mob Lawyer*, *op. cit.*, several passages; Rappleye and Becker, *All American*, *op. cit.*, 237, 238.
40. Hinckle and Turner, *Fish Is Red*, *op. cit.*, 297.
41. HSCA, *op. cit.*, 173.
42. Author's interview with Courtney Evans; HSCA, *op. cit.*, 173.
43. Author's interview with former FBI supervisor Thomas Kimmel, 3-19-07 and Jack Van Laningham (many, 2009 to 2012); *Did the Mob Kill JFK?* Discovery Channel special produced by NBC News/Dateline; McNary, Dave "Leo nabs JFK tale," *Variety*, 11-19-10.
44. Author's interview with Richard Goodwin, 4-15-98; Newfield, Jack. "I Want Kennedy Killed." *Penthouse*, 5-92.
45. Summers and Swan, "The Ghosts of November," *Vanity Fair*, 12-94.
46. The *Warren Report*.
47. HSCA *Final Report* US government printing office, 172, 173.
48. Hinckle and Turner, *Deadly Secrets*, *op. cit.*, 194–197; Jack Anderson TV Special 1988; Rappleye and Becker, *All American*, *op. cit.*, 307.
49. Kaiser, *Road to Dallas*, *op. cit.*, 135; Mahoney, *Sons & Brothers*, *op. cit.*, 230.
50. Hinckle and Turner, *Deadly Secrets*, *op. cit.*, 194–197; Jack Anderson TV Special 1988; Rappleye and Becker, *All American*, *op. cit.*, 307.
51. Haldeman and DiMona, *Ends of Power*, *op. cit.*, 67–70; HSCA *Final Report* US government printing office, 172, 173.

CHAPTER 13

1. Ambrose, Stephen, *Nixon*, *Vol. 2: The Triumph of a Politician*. (New York: Simon & Schuster, 1989), 13, 14.
2. *Ibid.*, 16–18, 21, 22.
3. *Ibid.*, 18.
4. *Ibid.*, 18.
5. *Ibid.*, 19.
6. *Ibid.*, 19, 29.
7. HSCA Vol. X March 1979, 11; Kaiser, *Road to Dallas*, *op. cit.*, many passages; Powers, *Helms*, *op. cit.*, 150–163.
8. Kaiser, *Road to Dallas*, *op. cit.*, 147; Thomas, *Best Men*, *op. cit.*; Russell, *Man Who Knew*, *op. cit.*, 148.
9. Church, *Plots*, *op. cit.*, 144–190.
10. Church, *Plots*, *op. cit.*, 44–190; Powers, *Helms*, *op. cit.*, many passages.
11. Hunt and Aunapu, *op. cit.*, 148; Cable [JM]Wave 3058 1-6-63 in HSCA 180-10142-10307.

12. Hunt CIA file dated June 19, 1972, containing biography, biographic profile, from "Box 36, folder," "IG File 12, Tab 2," declassified 1993; Church Report hearings on domestic intelligence activities, book I, 206, 207.
13. Hinckle and Turner, *Deadly Secrets*, *op. cit.*, 164–167; Kaiser, *Road to Dallas*, *op. cit.*, 152.
14. CIA 104-10308-10198; Fabian Escalante at Nassau Conference, cited in *AARC Quarterly*, Fall 95/Winter 1996 issue; *Foreign Relations of the United States*, Vol. XI, Department of State #376, 11-12-63.
15. Kaiser, *Road to Dallas*, *op. cit.*, 148.
16. Mahoney, *Sons & Brothers*, *op. cit.*, 170, 171, 400.
17. FBI report on Jon Martino 7-31-59; *Human Events* article by John Martino; Rappleye and Becker. *All American*, *op. cit.*, several passages.
18. FBI memo re: Rebozo release #6, 8-31-76, available at fbi.gov.
19. Kaiser, *Road to Dallas*, *op. cit.*, 160.
20. FBI memo re: Rebozo release #6, 8-31-76; Hancock, Larry. *Someone Would Have Talked*. (Southlake, Texas: JFK Lancer Productions and Publications, 2010), many passages.
21. Kaiser, *Road to Dallas*, *op. cit.*, 160–165; Hancock, Larry. *Someone Would Have Talked*. (Southlake, Texas: JFK Lancer Productions and Publications, 2010), 21.
22. Kaiser, *Road to Dallas*, *op. cit.*, 160–165.
23. Kaiser, *Road to Dallas*, *op. cit.*, 160–165.
24. Hinckle and Turner, *Fish Is Red*, *op. cit.*, 169.
25. Kaiser, *Road to Dallas*, *op. cit.*, 163, 454.
26. Kaiser, *Road to Dallas*, *op. cit.*, 160–165, 454.
27. Kaiser, *Road to Dallas*, *op. cit.*, 159–165, 454.
28. FBI memo re: Rebozo release #6, *op. cit.*
29. Mahoney, *Sons & Brothers*, *op. cit.*, 124, 125.
30. HSCA: 180-10090-10232, *op. cit.*; *Miami Herald*, 7-31-75.
31. Kaiser, *Road to Dallas*, *op. cit.*, 154
32. HSCA: 180-10090-10232, *op. cit.*; *Miami Herald*, 7-31-75.
33. Kaiser, *Road to Dallas*, *op. cit.*, 154, 155; Mahoney, *Sons & Brothers*, *op. cit.*, 272, 273.
34. Kaiser, *Road to Dallas*, *op. cit.*, 154, 155; Mahoney, *Sons & Brothers*, *op. cit.*, 272, 273.
35. HSCA *Final Report* and volumes, many passages; G. Robert Blakey and Richard N. Billings, *The Plot to Kill the President* (New York: Times Books, 1981), many passages; John H. Davis, *Mafia Kingfish* (New York: Signet, 1989); Frank Ragano and Selwyn Raab, *Mob Lawyer* (New York: Scribners, 1994), many passages.
36. Kaiser, *Road to Dallas*, *op. cit.*, 151–166.
37. *Ibid.*, 158.
38. Kaiser, *Road to Dallas*, *op. cit.*, 156.
39. Church, *Plots*, *op. cit.*, 85, 86; Hinckle and Turner, *Deadly Secrets*, *op. cit.*, 214, 215; Kaiser, *Road to Dallas*, *op. cit.*, 155, 304; Wise, David, and Thomas B. Ross. *The Invisible Government*. (New York: Random House, 1964), 275, 276.
40. Church, *Plots*, *op. cit.*, 85, 86; Hinckle and Turner, *Deadly Secrets*, *op. cit.*, 214, 215; Kaiser, *Road to Dallas*, *op. cit.*,155, 304; Wise and Ross, *Invisible*, *op. cit.*, 275, 276.
41. Church, *Plots*, *op. cit.*, 85, 86; Hinckle and Turner, *Deadly Secrets*, *op. cit.*, 214, 215; Kaiser, *Road to Dallas*, *op. cit.*, 155, 304; Wise and Ross, *Invisible*, *op. cit.*, 275, 276.
42. Kaiser, *Road to Dallas*, *op. cit.*, 156-158.
43. Author's interviews with Harry Williams (some via Thom Hartmann), 2-24-92, 4-92, 11-13-92, 7-24-93, 2-21-95; RFK Oral History at the JFK Library; Edwin O. Guthman and Jeffrey Shulman, eds., *Robert Kennedy: In His Own Words: The Unpublished Recollections of the Kennedy Years* (Toronto, New York: Bantam, 1988), pp. 376, 377; Robert Kennedy phone logs at the National Archives; Evan Thomas, *Robert Kennedy: His Life* (New York: Simon & Schuster, 2000), pp. 238–239; Haynes Johnson, "One Day's Events Shattered America's Hopes and Certainties," *Washington Post*, 11-20-83; Mahoney, Richard D. *Sons & Brothers*. (New York: Arcade Books, 1999), 170, 174, 217–220, 264-265, 294.
44. Author's interviews with Harry Williams (some via Thom Hartmann), 2-24-92, 4-92, 11-13-92, 7-24-93, 2-21-95.
45. "Cuban Exiles in New Drive for Unity to Topple Castro," *New York Times* 5-11-63, citing 5-10-63 AP report. This was one of three similar articles that came out around the same time.
46. *NYT*, "Cuban Exiles," *op. cit.*; "Bobby's Friend Another Hope," *Miami News* 5-19-63.
47. Robert Kennedy phone logs at the National Archives; Author's interviews with Harry Williams (some via Thom Hartmann), 2-24-92, 4-92, 7-24-93, 11-13-92, 2-21-95.
48. Author's interviews with Dean Rusk 1-5-90 and confidential Kennedy aide source 3-17-92; Anthony and Robbyn Summers, "The Ghosts of November," *Vanity Fair*, 12-94; CIA 104-10163-10258; CIA Dispatch from Chief of Station Caracas to Chief, SAS, 2-28-64.
49. Califano Papers 198-10004-10001, declassified 10-7-97; 198-10004-10072, declassified 7-24-97; JCS 202-10002-101116, declassified 10-7-97; Interview with confidential Defense Dept. source 7-6-92; Author's interviews with Harry Williams 2-24-92 and confidential Kennedy aide source 3-17-92; HSCA vol. X, page 77.
50. Declassified "top secret" memo by General Maxwell Taylor, 5-29-63, CM-605-63, "Actions Related to Cuba."
51. Califano Papers 198-10004-10001, declassified 10-7-97; 198-10004-10072, declassified 7-24-97; JCS 202-10002-101116, declassified 10-7-97.
52. Califano Papers 198-10004-10001, declassified 10-7-97; 198-10004-10072, declassified 7-24-97; JCS 202-10002-101116, declassified 10-7-97.
53. HSCA vol. X, page 77.
54. Califano Papers 198-10004-10001, declassified 10-7-97; 198-10004-10072, declassified 7-24-97; JCS 202-10002-101116, declassified 10-7-97; Author's interviews with Harry Williams (some via Thom Hartmann), 2-24-92, 4-92, 7-24-93, 11-13-92, 2-21-95.
55. Califano Papers 198-10004-10001, declassified 10-7-97; 198-10004-10072, declassified 7-24-97; JCS 202-10002-101116.
56. Author's interviews with Harry Williams (some via Thom Hartmann), 2-24-92, 4-92, 11-13-92, 7-24-93, 2-21-95; Interview with confidential Defense Dept. source 7-6-92.
57. JCS 202-10001-10171.; Hunt and Aunapu, *American Spy*, *op. cit.*, 153, 154.
58. Califano Papers 198-10004-10001, declassified 10-7-97; 198-10004-10072, declassified 7-24-97; JCS 202-10002-101116; Author interviews with

Dean Rusk 1-5-90; Anthony and Robbyn Summers, "The Ghosts of November," *Vanity Fair*, 12-94;

59. Haig, Alexander M. Jr., *Inner Circles: How America Changed the World* (New York: Warner Books, 1992), 109; Interview with confidential Defense Dept. source 7-6-92.
60. Thom Hartmann interview with Dave Powers 6-5-91 at the John F. Kennedy Presidential Library; Author's interviews with Harry Williams 2-24-92 and confidential Kennedy aide source 3-17-92.
61. Ambrose, *Vol. 2*, *op. cit.*, 23.
62. Joint Chiefs of Staff document. "Courses of Action Related to Cuba," Record Number 202-10002-10018. 5-1-63 (revised 5-13-63); Author's interviews with Harry Williams (some via Thom Hartmann), 2-24-92, 4-92, 11-13-92, 7-24-93, 2-21-95.
63. Author's interviews with Harry Williams (some via Thom Hartmann), 2-24-92, 4-92, 11-13-92, 7-24-93, 2-21-95; Califano Papers 198-10004-10001, declassified 10-7-97; 198-10004-10072, declassified 7-24-97; JCS 202-10002-101116.
64. Evan Thomas, *Robert Kennedy: His Life* (New York: Simon & Schuster, 2000), p. 159.; Gus Russo, *Live by the Sword: The Secret War against Castro and the Death of JFK* (Baltimore: Bancroft Press, 1998).

CHAPTER 14

1. Summers and Swan, "The Ghosts of November," *Vanity Fair* 12-94; Hinckle and Turner, *Deadly Secrets*, *op. cit.*, many passages; Author's interviews with Harry Williams (some via Thom Hartmann), 2-24-92, 4-92, 11-13-92, 7-24-93, 2-21-95 and confidential Kennedy aide source 3-17-92.
2. Author's interviews with Harry Williams (some via Thom Hartmann), 2-24-92, 4-92, 7-24-93, 11-13-92, 2-21-95.
3. NARA 1994.03.08.09.-46:690007 CIA/DCD File on Bernard Barker, declassified 3-8-94; WPLG-TV (Miami) Wright and Rinker interview Bernard Barker and Eugenio Martinez, 5-22-76.
4. Haynes Johnson interview notes by Richard E. Sprague, 1-12-73, donated to the Assassination Archives and Records Center; Warren Hinckle and William Turner, *Deadly Secrets* (New York: Thunder's Mouth, 1992), p. 56; NARA 1994.03.08.09.-46:690007 CIA/DCD File on Bernard Barker, declassified 3-8-94; Author's interviews with Harry Williams (some via Thom Hartmann), 2-24-92, 4-92, 7-24-93, 11-13-92, 2-21-95.
5. Author's interviews with Harry Williams (some via Thom Hartmann), 2-24-92, 4-92, 7-24-93, 11-13-92, 2-21-95; Author's interviews with Dean Rusk 1-5-90 and confidential Kennedy aide source 3-17-92; Interview with confidential Defense Dept. source 7-6-92.
6. There many CIA files about Barker (though key CIA and FBI files are still withheld), and the most important include: NARA 1994.03.08.09.-46:690007 CIA/DCD File on Bernard Barker; HSCA 180-10144-10219; CIA 1993.07.22.18:36:08:560390; CIA 1993.07.22.18:36:08:560390; CIA 1994.03.03.15:12:02:470005; HSCA FBI 124-10289-10440; HSCA 180-10145-10362; HSCA 180-10142-10061.
7. HSCA 180-10145-10362.
8. Author's interviews with Harry Williams (some via Thom Hartmann), 2-24-92, 4-92, 11-13-92, 7-24-93, 2-21-95.
9. FBI Rebozo files online at fbi.gov); NARA 1994.03.08.09.-46:690007 CIA/DCD File on Bernard Barker; HSCA 180-10144-10219; CIA 1993.07.22.18:36:08:560390; CIA 1993.07.22.18:36:08:560390; CIA 1994.03.03.15:12:02:470005; HSCA FBI 124-10289-10440; HSCA 180-10145-10362; HSCA 180-10142-10061.
10. Hinckle and Turner, *Deadly Secrets*, *op. cit.*, many passages; Author's interviews with Harry Williams (some via Thom Hartmann), 2-24-92, 4-92, 11-13-92, 7-24-93, 2-21-95; Szulc, *Compulsive Spy*, *op. cit.*, many passages.
11. *New York Times* 9-1-63 and 9-7-63; 5-8-67 CIA memo cited by Russo, Gus. *Live by the Sword: The Secret War against Castro and the Death of JFK.* (Baltimore: Bancroft Press, 1998), 548; HSCA vol. X 67, 68; Burt, Al "Cuban Exiles: The Mirage of Havana," *The Nation* 1-25-65.
12. *New York Times* 9-1-63 and 9-7-63; 5-8-67 CIA memo cited by Russo, Gus. *Live by the Sword: The Secret War against Castro and the Death of JFK.* (Baltimore: Bancroft Press, 1998), 548; HSCA vol. X 67, 68; Burt, Al "Cuban Exiles: The Mirage of Havana," *The Nation* 1-25-65.
13. Author's interviews with confidential Kennedy aide source 3-17-92 and with Harry Williams (some via Thom Hartmann), 2-24-92, 4-92, 11-13-92, 7-24-93, 2-21-95; Interview with confidential Defense Dept. source 7-6-92; CIA104-10315-10004, AMWORLD memo 6-28-63, declassified 1-27-99.
14. Robert Kennedy phone logs at the National Archives; CIA104-10315-10004, AMWORLD memo 6-28-63, declassified 1-27-99.
15. Kaiser, *Road to Dallas*, *op. cit.*, 165.
16. John Simkin, David Morales biography at the British educational website www.spartacus.schoolnet.co.uk; see also Larry Hancock, *Someone Would Have Talked* (Southlake, TX: JFK Lancer, 2006), many passages; Wayne Smith comments on BBC "Newsnight" report 11-20-06; Eric Hamburg, *JFK, Nixon, Oliver Stone, and Me* (New York: Public Affairs, 2002); David Corn, *Blond Ghost* (New York: Simon & Schuster, 1994), 85.
17. Anthony and Robbyn Summers, "The Ghosts of November," *Vanity Fair*, 12-94; Hinckle and Turner, *Deadly Secrets*, *op. cit.*, Author's interview (with Thom Hartmann) with Harry Williams 2-24-92.
18. Albarelli, H.P. Jr. *Terrible Mistake: The Murder of Frank Olson and the CIA's Secret Cold War Experiments.* (Walterville, Oregon: Trine Day, 2007), 340; McCord family website at mccord-familyassn.com/endpage.htm; John Simkin, McCord biography at the British educational website www.spartacus.schoolnet.co.uk; James McCord CIA files and biographical profile.
19. CIA 1993.07.15.20:17:15:590380 and others in that series; additional files cited by A. J. Weberman; Newman, John. *Oswald and the CIA* (New York: Carroll & Graf, 1995), 240–241.

20. Anthony and Robbyn Summers, "The Ghosts of November," *Vanity Fair*, 12-94; Hinckle and Turner, *Deadly Secrets*, *op. cit.*, Author's interview (with Thom Hartmann) with Harry Williams 2-24-92.
21. Anthony and Robbyn Summers, "The Ghosts of November," *Vanity Fair*, 12-94; Hinckle and Turner, *Deadly Secrets*, *op. cit.*, many passages; Author's interviews with Harry Williams (some via Thom Hartmann), 2-24-92, 4-92, 11-13-92, 7-24-93, 2-21-95.
22. HSCA 157-10014-10046; Hougan, *Agenda*, *op. cit.*, many passages; Conspire Interview with Jim Hougan about Watergate, Deep Throat and the CIA www.conspire.com; Author's interviews with Harry Williams (some via Thom Hartmann) 2-24-92, 4-92, 11-13-92, 7-24-93, 2-21-95; Evan Thomas, *Robert Kennedy: His Life* (New York: Simon & Schuster, 2000), 238.
23. Anthony and Robbyn Summers, "The Ghosts of November," *Vanity Fair*, 12-94; Hinckle and Turner, *Deadly Secrets*, *op. cit.*, many passages; Author's interviews with Harry Williams (some via Thom Hartmann), 2-24-92, 4-92, 7-24-93, 2-21-95.
24. 2-24-92, 4-92, 11-13-92, 7-24-93, 2-21-95; CIA 104-10308-10045 is a summer 1963 memo that generally describes godfather Santo Trafficante's attempts to influence CIA anti-Castro operations and also describes Harry Williams operation with Robert Kennedy.
25. 2-24-92, 4-92, 7-24-93, 2-21-95; CIA 104-10308-10045.
26. 2-24-92, 4-92, 7-24-93, 2-21-95; CIA 104-10308-10045 also contains FBI reports that were sent to the Agency.
27. Haig, Alexander M. Jr., *Inner Circles: How America Changed the World* (New York: Warner Books, 1992), many passages; Morris, Roger, *Haig: General's Progress* (New York: Playboy Press, 1982), many passages.
28. Gus Russo, *Live by the Sword: The Secret War against Castro and the Death of JFK* (Baltimore: Bancroft Press, 1998), 163; Joseph A. Califano, Jr., *Inside: A Public and Private Life* (New York: Public Affairs, 2004), 115–129; Evan Thomas, *Robert Kennedy: His Life* (New York: Simon & Schuster, 2000), 159. ABC's *Nightline* 12-29-97 cited by Russo; CIA document, from Director to (censored) and JMWAVE, 11-30-63 #86031 released in 1994 from "Carlos Prio Socarras [soft file]."
29. Author's interviews with Harry Williams (some via Thom Hartmann) 2-24-92, 4-92, 11-13-92; 7-24-93, 2-21-95; Joseph A. Califano, Jr., *Inside: A Public and Private Life* (New York: Public Affairs, 2004), 115–129.
30. Key passages from those hundreds of pages are cited in the author's previous volumes *Ultimate Sacrifice* and *Legacy of Secrecy*; copies also are available from the National Archives.
31. Anthony and Robbyn Summers, "The Ghosts of November," *Vanity Fair*, 12-94.
32. Califano, *Inside*, *op. cit.*, 109.
33. David Corn, *Blond Ghost* (New York: Simon & Schuster, 1994), 98; CIA 104-10110-10243.
34. CIA 10410308-10113.
35. CIA Office of Security Varona File Summary, Record Number 180-10144-10405, declassified 8-23-95; CIA Confidential Information Report, 8-30-63; Document ID number 1993.07.29.17:58:19:340059, declassified 7-29-93.
36. CIA 104-10308-10045; Author's interviews with Harry Williams (some via Thom Hartmann) 2-24-92, 4-92, 11-13-92, 7-24-93, 2-21-95; *New York Times* 6-18-72 p. 11, 6-27-72 p. 43, 7-13-72 p. 9 all cited by A. J. Weberman.
37. HSCA 180-10144-10219; Author's interviews with Harry Williams (some via Thom Hartmann) 11-13-92; 2-21-95.
38. Author's interviews with Harry Williams (some via Thom Hartmann) 11-13-92; 2-21-95.
39. Rappleye and Becker, *All American*, *op. cit.*, 236.
40. Kaiser, *Road to Dallas*, *op. cit.*, 328; Rappleye and Becker, *All American*, *op. cit.*, 236, 237; Washington Post 3-7-99.
41. CIA IG Report, 1967, *op. cit.*; Kaiser, *Road to Dallas*, *op. cit.*, 64, 113, 435.
42. CIA IG Report, 1967, *op. cit.*, 12-7 & 12-8-95 Nassau Conference transcript and reported in *AARC Quarterly*, Fall 1995; Fonzi, *Last Investigation*, *op. cit.*, many passages.
43. Author's interview with Dean Rusk, 1-5-90 and confidential Kennedy Foreign Policy Advisor source 4-18-96.
44. CIA cable from (censored) to Director 10-30-63.
45. CIA104-10308-10198; CIA 104-10309-10008; HSCA Rolando Cubela interview; Fabian Escalante at Nassau Conference, cited in *AARC Quarterly*, Fall 95/Winter 1996 issue.
46. Bradley Ayers, *The War that Never Was* (Canoga Park, Calif.: Major Books, 1979), 58, 59; Fensterwald affidavit for the Justice Department, 7-7-82; *Miami Herald*, 4-1-77; Michael Benson, *Who's Who in the JFK Assassination: An A-to-Z Encyclopedia* (New York: Citadel, 1993), 313; John M. Lesar, "Ed Arthur—Soldier of Fortune," *Soldier of Fortune*, 5-78; Mike Wales, *Ed Arthur's Glory No More: Underground Operations from Cuba to Watergate* (Westerville, O.: Dakar, 1975), pp. 80–84; Rappleye and Becker, *All American*, *op. cit.*, 245.
47. *New York Times* 9-24-63.
48. Examples in *New York Times* 5-20-63; 5-23-63; 6-7-63; 7-18-63; 7-23-63; 9-6-63; 9-12-63; 9-21-63; also HSCA vol. X p. 13.
49. Ambrose, *Vol. 2*, *op. cit.*, 24, 25, 27, 28.
50. Hendreix, Hal "Backstage with Bobby," *Miami Herald 7-14-63.*
51. CIA 1993.08.04.16:20:46:530028; CIA document, JMWAVE to Director, 12-5-63, and other files released in 1994 by the CIA Historical Review Program from "Carlos Prio Socarras [soft file]."
52. CIA document, JMWAVE to Director, 12-5-63, and other files released in 1994 by the CIA Historical Review Program from "Carlos Prio Socarras [soft file]."
53. Hinckle and Turner, *Deadly Secrets*, *op. cit.*, 356, 357.
54. Ambrose, *Vol. 2*, *op. cit.*, 11-37; Nixon, Richard Milhous. *The Memoirs of Richard Nixon.* (New York: Grosset & Dunlap, 1978), 252.
55. Author's interviews with Dean Rusk 1-5-90 and confidential Kennedy aide source 3-17-92; Anthony Summers, *Not In Your Lifetime* (New York: Marlowe & Co., 1998), 247.
56. *Foreign Relations of the United States*, vol. XI, Department of State, #370; Anthony Summers,

Conspiracy (New York: McGraw-Hill, 1980), p. 453.

57. Arthur Schlesinger, Jr., *Robert Kennedy and His Times* (New York: Ballantine, 1979), p. 598-600; *Foreign Relations of the United States*, vol. XI, Department of State, #373, 11-5-63.
58. Author's interviews with Dean Rusk 1-5-90 and confidential Kennedy aide source 3-17-92; Anthony and Robbyn Summers, "The Ghosts of November," *Vanity Fair*, 12-94.
59. *Foreign Relations of the United States*, vol. XI, Department of State, #373, 11-5-63.

CHAPTER 15

1. Hendreix, Hal "Backstage with Bobby," *Miami Herald* 7-14-63.
2. Department of the Army documents dated 9-14-63 and 9-27-63, provided by the State Department, in SSCIA record number 157-10005-10372 dated 3-27-76, declassified 2-18-94; 11-12-63 the John F. Kennedy Presidential Library, NLK 78-473, declassified 5-6-80; Army document, summary of plan dated 9-26-63, Califano Papers, Record Number 198-10004-10001, declassified 10-7-97.
3. Department of the Army documents dated 9-14-63 and 9-27-63, provided by the State Department, in SSCIA record number 157-10005-10372 dated 3-27-76, declassified 2-18-94; 11-12-63 the John F. Kennedy Presidential Library, NLK 78-473, declassified 5-6-80; Army document, summary of plan dated 9-26-63, Califano Papers, Record Number 198-10004-10001, declassified 10-7-97.
4. Department of the Army documents dated 9-14-63 and 9-27-63, provided by the State Department, in SSCIA record number 157-10005-10372 dated 3-27-76, declassified 2-18-94; 11-12-63 the John F. Kennedy Presidential Library, NLK 78-473, declassified 5-6-80; Army document, summary of plan dated 9-26-63, Califano Papers, Record Number 198-10004-10001, declassified 10-7-97.
5. Department of the Army documents dated 9-14-63 and 9-27-63, provided by the State Department, in SSCIA record number 157-10005-10372 dated 3-27-76, declassified 2-18-94; 11-12-63 the John F. Kennedy Presidential Library, NLK 78-473, declassified 5-6-80; Army document, summary of plan dated 9-26-63, Califano Papers, Record Number 198-10004-10001, declassified 10-7-97.
6. 11-12-63 the John F. Kennedy Presidential Library, NLK 78-473, declassified 5-6-80; Author's interview with confidential Kennedy aide source 3-17-92.
7. Author's interview with Pierre Salinger 4-10-98; Author's interviews with Abraham Bolden 4-15-98 and Confidential Kennedy Foreign Policy Advisor source 4-18-96; CIA 104-10309-10008; HSCA Document #180-10070-10273, interview of Secret Service Agent Abraham Bolden by HSCA staffers Jim Kelly and Harold Rese; Bernard Fensterwald interview of Abraham Bolden 3-29-68; *Chicago Daily News* interviews 5-28 and 5-29-68, from the files of Bud Fensterwald at the Assassination Archives and Research Center in Washington, D.C.
8. Edwin Black article, *Chicago Independent*, 11-75; CIA memo for Director of Security, subject: Cain, Richard Scully, 12-19-69, declassified 1992; HSCA 180-10105-10393; Bud Fensterwald, "The Case of Secret Service Agent Abraham W. Bolden," *Computers and Automation*, 6-71.
9. Author's interviews with Pierre Salinger 4-10-98; HSCA Document #180-10070-10273, interview of Secret Service Agent Abraham Bolden by HSCA staffers Jim Kelly and Harold Rese; CIA F82-0272/1,82-165 (4); CIA F82-0272/2; 1-64 CIA cable to Director from (censored); CIA F82-0278 (might be 02781); Joseph J. Trento, *The Secret History of the CIA* (Roseville, CA: Prima, 2001), 226, 227.
10. Author's interviews with Pierre Salinger 4-10-98, Jim Allison 4-15-98 and 4-16-98, Abraham Bolden 4-15-98.
11. 11-12-63 the John F. Kennedy Presidential Library, NLK 78-473, declassified 5-6-80; Author's interviews with confidential Kennedy aide source 3-17-9 and confidential Kennedy Foreign Policy Advisor source 4-18-96.
12. *Chicago Daily* news 11-2-63; Author's interview with Pierre Salinger 4-10-98; Vincent Michael Palamara, *The Third Alternative* (Pennsylvania: 1993) 73.
13. Ambrose, *Vol. 2*, *op. cit.*, 37.
14. Author's interviews with Harry Williams (some via Thom Hartmann) 2-24-92, 4-92, 11-13-92, 7-24-93, 2-21-95.
15. Church Committee Report, vol. V, 20, 21, 31, citing CIA Memorandum for the DCI, "Considerations for US Policy Toward Cuba and Latin America," 12-9-63; Hersh, Seymour M. *The Old Boys*. (New York: Charles Scribner's Sons, 1992); Schlesinger, Jr., *RFK: His Times*, *op. cit.*, 598.
16. Miami Police Intelligence files; Michael L. Kurtz, *The JFK Assassination Debates* (Lawrence, KS: University Press of Kansas, 2006), 209–219; Dan Christensen, "JFK, King: The Dade County links," *Miami* magazine, 12-76; HSCA Report, p. 232; Miami Police Department transcript of 11-9-63 Milteer conversation with William Somersett; Author's phone interview with confidential high Florida law-enforcement source 12-10-96; Miami Police interview with William Somersett transcribed 11-26-63; Author's phone interview with Don Adams, the FBI agent who investigated Milteer just before JFK's murder, 6-14-06.
17. "Threats on Kennedy Made Here," *Tampa Tribune*, 11-23-63; "Man Held in Threats to JFK," *Miami Herald*, 11-24-63: It is bylined, "Tampa (UPI)," so it may well have appeared in other newspapers; Author's phone interviews with J. P. Mullins 12-10-96 and high Florida law-enforcement source 12-10-96.
18. Author's phone interviews with J. P. Mullins 12-10-96 and high Florida law-enforcement source 12-10-96.
19. *New York Times* 11-19-63.
20. Haynes Johnson, "One Day's Events Shattered America's Hopes and Certainties," *Washington Post*, 11-20-83; Author's interviews with Harry Williams (some via Thom Hartmann) 2-24-92, 4-92, 11-13-92, 7-24-93, 2-21-95; Interview with confidential Defense Dept. source 7-6-92; Author's interviews with Harry Williams (some via Thom Hartmann) 2-24-92, 4-92, 11-13-92, 7-24-93, 2-21-95.

21. *New York Times*, 12-3-63 (87:4); Author's interview with Harry Williams, 2-24-92.
22. Helms and Hood, *Over My Shoulder*, 226, 227; Kaiser, *Road to Dallas, op. cit.*, 298; Church Committee vol. V pp. 19, 101.
23. CIA Document 12-6-63, from Director, released during the 1993 CIA Historical Review Program, courtesy Dr. John Newman.; Gus Russo, *Live by the Sword* (Baltimore: Bancroft Press, 1978), 272.
24. Joint Chiefs of Staff, "Action Re: Cuba," *op.cit*.
25. CIA 104-10098-10093, 10-31-63 AMWORLD Dispatch, declassified 6-20-96; Morley, Jefferson. "What Jane Roman said." Accessed at mcadams.posc.mu.edu/morley1.htm 12-2-02; Newman, John. *Oswald and the CIA*. (New York: Carroll & Graf, 1995), several passages.
26. Phone interview with wife of Gilberto Policarpo Lopez 3/2/96; Skip Johnson and Tony Durr, "Ex-Tampan in JFK Plot?" *Tampa Tribune*, 9-5-76; CIA 104-10075-10006. 9. HSCA Report, pp. 118-21; 12-4-63 "secret" "classified message" from the office of CIA Director John McCone (though signed by Richard Helms) about the Tampa suspect and not wanting "to blow the [censored] operation," declassified 4-6-94, Document ID 1994.04.06.10:28:12:530005; numerous Lopez files from the CIA Russell Holmes work files collection; Anthony Summers, *Not In Your Lifetime* (New York: Marlowe & Co., 1998), 442, 443; Fonzi, Gaeton. *The Last Investigation*. (New York: Thunder's Mouth Press, 1993), 141, 142; HSCA Lopez Mexico City Report, many passages; HSCA vol. X Veciana section.
27. Phone interview with wife of Gilberto Policarpo Lopez 3-2-96; Skip Johnson and Tony Durr, "Ex-Tampan in JFK Plot?" *Tampa Tribune*, 9-5-76; CIA 104-10075-10006. 9. HSCA Report, 118–121; 12-4-63 "secret" "classified message" from the office of CIA Director John McCone (though signed by Richard Helms) about the Tampa suspect and not wanting "to blow the [censored] operation," declassified 4-6-94, Document ID 1994.04.06.10:28:12:530005; numerous Lopez files from the CIA Russell Holmes work files collection; Anthony Summers, *Not In Your Lifetime* (New York: Marlowe & Co., 1998), 442, 443; Fonzi, Gaeton. *The Last Investigation*. (New York: Thunder's Mouth Press, 1993), 141, 142; HSCA Lopez Mexico City Report, many passages; HSCA vol. X Veciana section.
28. Declassified ZR/RIFLE notes of William Harvey also cited in Church, Senator Frank. *Alleged Assassination Plots Involving Foreign Leaders*. (New York: W.W. Norton & Company, 1976).
29. Author's phone interview with Carlos Marcello's Justice Department prosecutor John Diuguid, 9-30-04; talks with Ronald Goldfarb, former Mafia prosecutor and several passages of his book: Ronald Goldfarb, *Perfect Villains and Imperfect Heroes* (New York: Random House, 1995); Author's interview with confidential Kennedy aide source 3-17-92, Courtney Evans, and "Get Hoffa Squad" prosecutors Tom Kennelly and Marvin Lowey.
30. Noel Twyman, *Bloody Treason* (Rancho Sante Fe, CA: Laurel Publishing, 1997), 451; Gaeton Fonzi, *The Last Investigation* (New York: Thunder's Mouth, 1994), 389, 390, other passages; David Corn, *Blond Ghost* (New York: Simon & Schuster, 1994), 85; Wayne Smith comments on BBC "Newsnight" report 11-20-06.
31. Hancock, Larry. *Someone Would Have Talked*. (Southlake, Texas: JFK Lancer Productions and Publications, 2010), many passages.
32. 5-22-76 WPLG-TV interview with Barker (Miami ABC affiliate); Author's interviews with Harry Williams (some via Thom Hartmann) 2-24-92, 4-92, 11-13-92, 7-24-93, 2-21-95.
33. Mahoney, Richard D. *Sons & Brothers*. (New York: Arcade Books, 1999), many passages; Kaiser, David. *The Road to Dallas: The Assassination of John F. Kennedy*. (Cambridge, Massachusetts: Belknap Press of Harvard University Press, 2008), many passages; Blakey, G. Robert, and Richard N. Billings. *The Plot to Kill the President*. (New York: Times Books, 1981), many passages; Author's phone interview with confidential high Florida law-enforcement source 12-10-96; Davis, John H. *Mafia Kingfish: Carlos Marcello and the Assassination of John F. Kennedy*. (New York: Signet Books (pb), 1989), many passages; HSCA *Final Report* and volumes (1979) many passages.
34. Cain, Michael. *The Tangled Web: The Life and Death of Richard Cain, Chicago Cop and Mafia Hitman*. (New York: Skyhorse Publishing, 2007), many passages; Author's confidential interview with close family member of Lt. Vernon S. Smart and with confidential high Florida law-enforcement source 12-10-96.
 * The JFK-Almeida coup plan remained secret for forty-two years, while the mobsters' confessions were not revealed until 1992 (Trafficante), 1999 (Rosselli), and 2008 (Marcello).
35. Michael L. Kurtz, *The JFK Assassination Debates* (Lawrence, KS: University Press of Kansas, 2006), 209–219 & other passages; Fonzi, Gaeton. *The Last Investigation*. (New York: Thunder's Mouth Press, 1993); Author's interview with Harry Williams (via Thom Hartmann) 11-13-92; Cain, Michael. *The Tangled Web: The Life and Death of Richard Cain, Chicago Cop and Mafia Hitman*. (New York: Skyhorse Publishing, 2007), many passages.
36. CIA Document 12-6-63, from Director, released during the 1993 CIA Historical Review Program, courtesy Dr. John Newman; CIA #104-10308-10098, declassified 9-18-98; CIA #104-10308-10098, declassified 9-18-98; David Atlee Phillips has outlined the scenario in an autobiographical novel proposal that has not been published, but portions have appeared in other sources, such as Anthony and Robbyn Summers, "The Ghosts of November," *Vanity Fair*, 12-94, p. 139. While Phillips' unsold proposal appears to be for a novel, it could also be for a movie or play.
37. CIA 104-1040810029; CIA104-10308-10080.
38. CIA Document 12-6-63, from Director, released during the 1993 CIAHistorical Review Program, courtesy Dr. John Newman.
39. HSCA *Final Report* and supporting volumes, many passages; Davis, John H. *Mafia Kingfish: Carlos Marcello and the Assassination of John F. Kennedy*. (New York: Signet Books (pb), 1989), many passages; Ragano, Frank, and Selwyn Raab. *Mob Lawyer*. (New York: Scribners, 1994), many passages; Rappleye, Charles, and Ed Becker. *All American Mafioso: The Johnny Roselli*

Story. (New York: Doubleday, 1991), many passages.

40. Summers, *Official: Hoover, op. cit.*, 303, 309–313, 336.
41. Summers, *Official: Hoover, op. cit.*, 303, 309–313, 336.
42. *The Dallas Times Herald* 11-22-63, A25; *The Dallas Morning News* 11-22-63, Section 1-19, both references courtesy of Dave Perry.
43. Johnson, Haynes, "One day's events shattered America's hopes and certainties." *Washington Post* 11-20-83; Haynes Johnson interview notes by Richard E. Sprague, 1-12-73; Anthony and Robbyn Summers, "The Ghosts of November," *Vanity Fair*, 12-94; Hinckle and Turner, *Deadly Secrets, op. cit.*, many passages.
44. Mahoney, *Sons & Brothers, op. cit.*, 290; Beschloss, Michael. *The Crisis Years: Kennedy and Khrushchev, 1960–1963*. (New York: Edward Burlingame Books, 1991), 670, 671; Anthony Summers, *Conspiracy* (McGraw-Hill, 1980), 36.
45. CIA document, JMWAVE to Director, 12-5-63, released 1994 from "Carlos Prio Socarras [soft file]"; Fensterwald and Ewing, *Coincidence, op. cit.*, 530.
46. Mahoney, *Sons & Brothers, op. cit.*, 290; Summers and Swan, *Nixon, op. cit.*, 262.

CHAPTER 16

1. Fensterwald and Ewing, *Coincidence, op. cit.*, 528.
2. Fensterwald and Ewing, *Coincidence, op. cit.*, 528; Fulsom, "Mob's President," *op. cit.*
3. Summers and Swan, *Nixon, op. cit.*, 262.
4. Manchester William. *The Death of a President, November 20–November 25, 1963*. (New York: Harper & Row, 1967), 196.
5. *Ibid.*
6. Helms, Richard, and William Hood. *A Look Over My Shoulder: A Life in the Central Intelligence Agency* (New York: Random House, 2003), 226–244. The author faults Helms for providing incomplete information to his co-writer.
7. Church Committee Report, Vol. V, *op. cit.*, many passages; Church, *Plots, op. cit.*, many passages; CIA IG Report, 1967, *op. cit.*
8. CIA 104-10306-10017; PFIAB 11-22-63 notes at National Archives and at maryferrell.org.
9. Richard Helms with William Hood, *A Look Over My Shoulder: A Life in the Central Intelligence Agency* (New York: Random House, 2003), 228.
10. CIA IG Report, 1967, *op. cit.*; CIA "Response to Item Comments on Draft Report," 6-13-76, in the National Archives, from the files of Anna-Marie Kuhns-Walko; CIA10410434-10267 and CIA104-10434-10283, both declassified 11-18-98; Ayers, Bradley. *The War that Never Was*. (Canoga Park, CA: Major Books, 1979), 58, 59; William Scott Malone, "The Secret Life of Jack Ruby," *New Times* 1-23-78; Many QJWIN files at the National Archives, including his November 1963 payroll records in 1994.04.06.10:47:29:710005 and his 1964 termination notice in 1993.08.13.08:39:48:560024.
11. Phillips' entire novel proposal has not been published, but portions have appeared in other sources, such as Anthony and Robbyn Summers, "The Ghosts of November," *Vanity Fair*, 12-94, 139.
12. CIA 104-10004-10199.
13. For the conventional view of the teenaged Communist Oswald, see the Warren Report and volumes (1964); for more recent research, see Newman, John. *Oswald and the CIA* (New York: Carroll & Graf, 1995), many passages; Benson, *Who's Who, op. cit.*, 63, 329, 331; also Robert Oswald testimony Warren Commission vol. 1, 264–469; John Edward Pic testimony Warren Commission vol. VIII, 196–202; Robert L. Oswald "We Was My Brother," *Look* 10-17-67; Anthony Summers, *Conspiracy* (McGraw-Hill, 1980),142, 296 and updated edition (New York: Paragon House, 1989) 61, 122, 123, 125; Dick Russell, *The Man Who Knew Too Much* (New York: Carroll & Graf/R. Gallen, 1992),178, 179; Henry Hurt, *Reasonable Doubt* (New York: Henry Holt, 1987), 243.
14. Benson, *Who's Who, op. cit.*, 331, 332; Summers, *Conspiracy, op. cit.*, 125, 154, 155; Summers, Anthony, *Not in Your Lifetime*, (New York: Marlowe & Co., 1998), 234, 235; Dick Russell, *Man Who Knew, op. cit.*, 126.
15. Warren Commission Vol. 16, Exhibit 102, 441–442. In these notes for a speech, Oswald makes it clear that he doesn't want to be just a "pseudo-professional communist like Herbert Philbrick or [former senator] Joe McCarthy." It's important draw a distinction between what Philbrick did—befriend numerous people for years, only to turn on them in court—and what Oswald did. That may be yet another reason why Oswald avoided Communist Party meetings in the US—because he saw befriending and developing close, personal relationships with people—only to betray those individuals, even for a good cause—as being different from the type of undercover work he was doing. On a more practical level, in giving speeches like the one these notes were for, Oswald would have been competing with Philbrick for speaking engagements, so distinguishing himself from his competition would also make sense.
16. Russell, *Man Who Knew, op. cit.*, 718, 719; Summers, *Conspiracy, op. cit.*, 205–217.
17. Russell, *Man Who Knew, op. cit.*,400, 401; WDSU news footage, 8-23-63, cited by Oliver Stone and Zachary Sklar in *JFK: The Book of the Film*. (New York: Applause Books, 1992), 36.
18. Interview with Anthony Veciana 6-2-93; Fonzi, *Last Investigation, op. cit.*, 141; Hunt, E. Howard, and Greg Aunapu. *American Spy: My Secret History in the CIA, Watergate, and Beyond*. (Hoboken, New Jersey: John Wiley & Sons, Inc., 2007), 135–138; HSCA Veciana summary vol. X.
19. CIA document to Director (John McCone) from JMWAVE (Miami CIA Station 11-23-63, provided by Dr. John Newman; CIA 104-10098-10093, 10-31-63 AMWORLD Dispatch, declassified 6-20-96.
20. CIA Record Number 104-10125-10239, "Mr. Phillips will arrive." 10-4-63, declassified 8-11-93; CIA Record Number 104-10100-10134, "Arrival of David Phillips C/Cuba Ops for Consultation." 10-4-63, declassified 3-7-94.
21. Author's interviews with Mike Cain; Cain, *Tangled Web, op. cit.*, many passages; Newman, John. *Oswald and the CIA* (New York: Carroll & Graf, 1995), 354, 356; John Newman, "Oswald, the CIA, and Mexico City," at pbs.org; Scott,

Peter Dale. *Deep Politics III* (online excerpt available at maryferrell.org).

22. Fonzi, *Last Investigation, op. cit.*, 295; Morley, Jefferson. "What Jane Roman Said." Accessed at mcadams.posc.mu.edu/morley1.htm 12-2-02; Newman, *Oswald & CIA, op. cit.*, 369.
23. Warren Commission draft by David Belin 7-11-64, cited in Seth Kantor, *The Ruby Cover-Up*. (New York, Zebra Books, 1978), 386–389; Kaiser, David, *The Road to Dallas: The Assassination of John F. Kennedy*, (Cambridge, Massachusetts: Belknap Press of Harvard University Press, 2008), many passages.
24. Fonzi, *Last Investigation, op. cit.*, many passages.
25. BI 62-109060-251; FBI 62-109060-7077 2.26.73; FBI 62-109060-5815 10.13.67 cited by A. J. Weberman; *Independent American*, 8-12-63.
26. Warren Commission internal memo 4-30-64 (document #674-279); CIA 1994.04.06.10:28:12:530005. For the full list of parallels, see this author's previous volume *Ultimate Sacrifice* (updated trade paperback, Counterpoint, 2006) 501, 502.
27. HSCA *Final Report* 231; HSCA 180-10070-10276; HSCA 180-10080-10154; Edwin Black article, *Chicago Independent*, 11-75 Davis, *Mafia Kingfish, op. cit.*, 162; Kantor, *Ruby Cover-Up, op. cit.*, 62; Warren Commission document #1016; Vincent Michael Palamara, *The Third Alternative* (Pennsylvania: 1993), many passages.
28. CIA 10410306-10017, 4-10-64 interview with McCone, declassified 9-19-98, later partially used in: Manchester, William, *Death of a President*, (New York: Harper & Row, 1967).
29. Arthur Schlesinger, Jr., *Robert Kennedy and His Times* (New York: Ballantine, 1979), 655, 656.
30. CIA 104-10306-10017; Arthur Schlesinger, Jr., *Robert Kennedy and His Times* (New York: Ballantine, 1979), 665.
31. Anthony and Robbyn Summers, "The Ghosts of November," *Vanity Fair*, 12-94.
32. CIA 104-10306-10018.
33. Talbot, David. *Brothers: The Hidden History of the Kennedy Years.* (New York: Free Press, 2007), 6.
34. NARA #179-40005-10028; Talbot, *Brothers, op. cit.*, 8, 21, 414.
35. CIA10410236-10350; Author's interviews with Harry Williams (some via Thom Hartmann), 2-24-92, 4-92, 11-13-92, 7-24-93, 2-21-95;
36. Author's interviews with Harry Williams (some via Thom Hartmann), 2-24-92, 4-92, 11-13-92, 7-24-93, 2-21-95.
37. Anthony and Robbyn Summers, "The Ghosts of November," *Vanity Fair*, 12-94; Johnson, Haynes, "One day's events shattered America's hopes and certainties." *Washington Post* 11-20-83; Author's interviews with Harry Williams, 2-24-92, 4-92, 11-13-92, 7-24-93, 2-21-95 (some via Thom Hartmann).
38. Author's interviews with Harry Williams, 2-24-92, 4-92, 11-13-92, 7-24-93, 2-21-95 (some via Thom Hartmann); Johnson, Haynes, "One day's events shattered America's hopes and certainties," *Washington Post* 11-20-83.
39. Johnson, Haynes, "One day's events shattered America's hopes and certainties," *Washington Post* 11-20-83; Author's interviews with Harry Williams, 2-24-92, 4-92, 11-13-92, 7-24-93, 2-21-95 (some via Thom Hartmann).
40. Haynes Johnson, Haynes. *Sleepwalking Through History*. (New York: W. W. Norton, 2003), 271.
41. Larry Hancock, *Someone Would Have Talked* (Southlake, Tex.: JFK Lancer, 2003), 92. Hosty has denied making the remark.
42. Ambrose, *Vol. 2, op. cit.*, 32, 33.
43. Ambrose, *Vol. 2, op. cit.*, 32, 33.
44. G. Robert Blakey and Richard N. Billings, *Fatal Hour* (New York: Berkley Books, 1992); John Newman, *Oswald and the CIA* (New York: Carroll & Graf, 1995); Anthony Summers, *Not In Your Lifetime* (New York: Marlowe & Co., 1998); Kaiser, David, *The Road to Dallas: The Assassination of John F. Kennedy* (Cambridge, Massachusetts: Belknap Press of Harvard University Press, 2008); Meagher, Sylvia, *Accessories after the Fact* (New York: Vintage Books, 1992); Kurtz, Michael L., *The JFK Assassination Debate* (Lawrence, Kansas: University of Kansas Press, 2006); Hancock, Larry, *Someone Would Have Talked* (Southlake, Texas: JFK Lancer Productions and Publications, 2010); Davis, John H., *Mafia Kingfish: Carlos Marcello and the Assassination of John F. Kennedy* (New York: Signet Books (pb), 1989); Moldea, Dan, *The Hoffa Wars* (New York: S.P.I. Books, 1993); Scheim, David, *The Mafia Killed President Kennedy* (Kent, England: S.P.I. Books, 1974); Scott, Peter Dale, *Deep Politics and the Death of JFK* (Berkeley, California: University of California Press, 1993); Scott, Peter Dale, *Crime and Cover-Up: The CIA, the Mafia, and the Dallas-Watergate Connection* (Santa Barbara, California: Open Archive Press, 1993); Noyes, Peter, *Legacy of Doubt* (New York: Pinnacle Books, 1973); all of the preceding laid the groundwork for the new research found in the updated trade paperbacks of: Waldron, Lamar with Thom Hartmann, *Legacy of Secrecy* (Berkeley, CA: Counterpoint, 2009); Waldron, Lamar and Thom Hartmann, *Ultimate Sacrifice* (New York: Counterpoint, 2006)
45. Lifton, David S., *Best Evidence: Disguise and Deception in the Assassination of John F. Kennedy* (New York: Carroll & Graf, 1988), many passages; Thompson, Josiah, *Six Seconds in Dallas* (New York: Bernard Geis, 1967), many passages; in Waldron and Hartmann's updated trade paperback of *Ultimate Sacrifice*, 738–753, is a minute-by-minute timeline account of the events in Dealey Plaza.
46. Benson, Michael, *Who's Who in the JFK Assassination: An A-to-Z Encyclopedia* (New York: Citadel, 1993), 172, 173; Kurtz, Michael L, *The JFK Assassination Debates*, 25, 47, 48; Warren Commission Decker Exhibit #5323, 540.
47. Summers, *Conspiracy, op. cit.*, 50; Thompson, Josiah, *Six Seconds, op. cit.*, 163, 164.
48. Canfield and Weberman, *Coup d'état, op. cit.*, 56, 57; at www.ajweberman.com, Weitzman is quoted in an interview as saying, "I can't remember for sure, but it looked like him. Couldn't swear it was him though . . . anyway so many witnesses are dead . . . two Cubans once forced their way into my house and waited for me when I got home. I had to chase them out with my service revolver . . . I feared for my life."
49. Michael Benson, *Who's Who, op. cit.*,172; Anthony Summers, *Conspiracy* (New York:

Paragon House, 1989), 50, 51; Anthony Summers, *Conspiracy* (New York: McGraw-Hill, 1980) 58, 59.

50. Barker's lawsuit deposition is at: www.ajweberman.com/nodules2/nodulec22.htm.
51. *Ibid.*
52. *Ibid.*
53. Many years later, after frequent showings of the restored version on television and in the Oliver Stone *JFK* film, some people convinced themselves they'd seen the JFK assassination televised live. Shelly Winters, in her autobiography, is one documented example. But at the time of Barker's deposition, because the Zapruder movie was so infrequently shown and the film's quality before restoration was so much poorer compared to that of a typical TV newscast, this scenario was highly unlikely.
54. Author's interviews with Jack Van Laningham, 2009-2012.
55. There is an unconfirmed report that shortly before his death, David Atlee Phillips told his brother that he had been in Dallas at the time of JFK's murder. However, Phillips didn't confess to participating in JFK's assassination, and it should be noted that Phillips—from Fort Worth—had used Dallas in his anti-Castro operations, such as his public meeting with Oswald and Veciana in Dallas in the summer of 1963, detailed earlier, which leaves his remarks open to interpretation.
56. Author's interviews with Harry Williams (some via Thom Hartmann), 2-24-92, 4-92, 11-13-92.
57. Rappleye and Becker, *All American Mafioso, op. cit.*, several passages.
58. Davis, *Mafia Kingfish, op. cit.*, 198, 199; phone interview with John Diuguid 9-30-04.
59. Davis, *Mafia Kingfish, op. cit.*, 199.
60. Ragano and Raab, *Mob Lawyer*, 146.
61. *Ibid.*, 147, 148.
62. *Ibid.*, 148.
63. Author's interview with Dave Powers 6-5-91 at the John F. Kennedy Presidential Library; Hurt, Henry, *Reasonable Doubt* (New York: Henry Holt, 1987), 49; Kurtz, *JFK Assassination Debates*, *op. cit.*, 39; Novak, William, *Man of the House: The Life and Political Memoirs of Speaker Tip O'Neill* (New York: Random House, 1987), 17.
64. Dr. George Burkley's Oral History at the JFK Presidential Library; Law, William Matson, *In the Eye of History* (Southlake, TX: JFK Lancer Productions, 2005), 35, 43, 51, 84, 124, 125, 130; Russo, *Live by the Sword, op. cit.*, 325.
65. Benson, *Who's Who, op. cit.*, 138; Kurtz, *JFK Assassination Debates*, *op. cit.*, 86; Law, *Eye of History, op. cit.*, 132, 133; Lifton, *Best Evidence, op. cit.*, 403–407.
66. David S. Lifton, *Best Evidence: Disguise and Deception in the Assassination of John F. Kennedy* (New York: Carroll & Graf, 1988), 590, 595, 646, 647, 651; HSCA vol. VII, p. 15; William Matson Law, *In the Eye of History* (Southlake, TX: JFK Lancer Productions, 2005), 132, 133, 258, 259;
67. Califano, Joseph A. Jr., *The Triumph & Tragedy of Lyndon Johnson: The White House Years* (New York: Simon & Schuster, 1991), 13, 14; Haig and McCarry, *Inner Circles, op. cit.*, 113, 114.
68. Department of the Army documents dated 9-14-63 and 9-27-63, provided by the State Department, in SSCIA record number 157-10005-10372 dated 3-27-76, declassified 2-18-94; 11-12-63 the John F. Kennedy Presidential Library, NLK 78-473, declassified 5-6-80; Army document, summary of plan dated 9-26-63, Califano Papers, Record Number 198-10004-10001, declassified 10-7-97.
69. Haig and McCarry, *Inner Circles, op. cit.*, 116.
70. Phone interviews with Naval Intelligence surveillance source, 10-27-91 and 12-9-91; 4-2-64 FBI memo by T. N. Goble, cited in *Echoes of a Conspiracy* 7-22-88.
71. Memo of August 21 conversation with investigative journalist, on file at Assassinations Archives and Records Center in Washington, DC; Summers, *Conspiracy, op. cit.*, 61.
72. Allen, Deane J., DIA Historian. "Overview of the Origins of DIA." 11-95.
73. JCS 202-10002-10180; James P. Hosty, Jr., *Assignment: Oswald* (New York: Arcade Publishing, 1996), 219; *U.S. News & World Report*, 3-15-93.
74. Summers, *Conspiracy, op. cit.*, 409.
75. Hancock, *Would Have Talked, op. cit.*, 289; John Simkin citing Henry Wade testimony to the Warren Commission June 8, 1964 at www.spartacus.schoolnet.co.uk.

CHAPTER 17

1. Michael R. Beschloss, *Taking Charge* (New York: Simon & Schuster, 1997), 22; call between LBJ and Hoover, 11-23-63, 10:01 a.m.
2. Peter Noyes, *Legacy of Doubt* (New York: Pinnacle Books, 1973), 116–118; Interview with Dave Powers 6-5-91 at the John F. Kennedy Presidential Library; William Novak, *Man of the House: The Life and Political Memoirs of Speaker Tip O'Neil* (New York: Random House, 1987), 178.
3. Rather, Dan, and Mickey Herskowitz, *The Camera Never Blinks* (New York: Ballantine Books, 1978), many passages.
4. Rather and Herskowitz, *Camera Never Blinks, op. cit.*, many passages; Bob Schieffer in "JFK: Breaking the News," PBS, 11-20-03.
5. "Threats on Kennedy Made Here," *Tampa Tribune*, 11-23-63.
6. Church vol. V, 62.
7. "Threats on Kennedy Made Here," *Tampa Tribune*, 11-23-63; Skip Johnson and Tony Durr, "Ex-Tampan in JFK Plot?" *Tampa Tribune*, 9-5-76; CIA 104-10075-10006.
8. Phone interview with J. P. Mullins 12-10-96; phone interview with high Florida law-enforcement source 12-10-96.
9. "Man Held in Threats to JFK," *Miami Herald*, 11-24-63: It is bylined, "Tampa (UPI)," so it may well have appeared in other newspapers.
10. Author's phone interview with JP Mullins 12-10-96.
11. Kurtz, *JFK Assassination Debates*, *op. cit.*, 162, 240.
12. Kurtz, *JFK Assassination Debates*, *op. cit.*, 162, 240.
13. *Ibid.*
14. Anthony Summers, *Not In Your Lifetime* (New York: Marlowe & Co., 1998), 233; *People and The Pursuit of Truth*, vol. 1, No. 1, 5-75.
15. Thomas, *Very Best Men, op. cit.*, 307.
16. Thomas, *Very Best Men, op. cit.*, 307.
17. CIA 104-10295-10152.
18. Radosh, Ronald, "Conspiracies Of Dunces" *New York Sun*, 2-14-06.

19. Newman, *Oswald & CIA, op. cit.*, 356.
20. Benson, *Who's Who, op. cit.*, 119; Newman, *Oswald & CIA, op. cit.*, 412; Scott, Peter Dale, *Deep Politics III* (online excerpt available at maryferrell.org), citing TX-1915 of 11-23-63; NARA #104-10015-10055 PS#64-33. Cf. MEXI 7029 232048Z; NARA #104-10015-10091 PS#78-94.
21. CIA 104-10169-10458; Scott, *Deep Politics III*, his note 48; and *Ibid*, citing XAAZ-17958 10 Dec 63; Summary of Oswald case prepared for briefing purposes; NARA #104-10018-10040 PS#62-142.
22. FBI memo, Brennan to Sullivan, 11-27-63.
23. Anson, "They've Killed the President!" *op. cit.*, 256; Newman, *Oswald & CIA, op. cit.*, many passages; Summers, *Conspiracy, op. cit.*, 415–419, 518; Warren Commission Document #1084.
24. HSCA 180-10142-10340.
25. Fonzi, *Last Investigation, op. cit.*, many passages.
26. CIA F82-0272/1,82-165 (4); CIA F82-0272/2; 1-64 CIA cable to Director from (censored); CIA F82-0278 (might be 02781); Trento, *Secret History of CIA, op. cit.*, 226, 227.
27. Letters from Souetre and other information provided by French journalist Stephane Risset to the author in 1998; Fensterwald affidavit for the Justice Department, 7-7-82; Hilaire du Berrier, Fensterwald files at the AARC.
28. CIA F82-0272/1,82-165 (4); CIA F82-0272/2; 1-64 CIA cable to Director from (censored); CIA F82-0278 (might be 02781); Fensterwald affidavit for the Justice Department, 7-7-82; Hilaire du Berrier, Fensterwald files at the AARC; Letters from Souetre and other information provided by French journalist Stephane Risset to the author in 1998.
29. Benson, *Who's Who, op. cit.*, 72; Blakey and Billings, *Plot to Kill Prez, op. cit.*, 324; Davis, *Mafia Kingfish, op. cit.*, 603; Summers, *Conspiracy, op. cit.*, 483; *Legacy* 238–240.
30. Phone interviews with Naval Intelligence source, 10-27-91 and 12-91; HSCA vol. XI, 542–551.
31. Phone interviews with Naval Intelligence source, 10-27-91 and 12-91.
32. Phone interviews with Naval Intelligence source, 10-27-91 and 12-91; HSCA vol. XI, 542-551.
33. Phone interviews with Naval Intelligence source, 10-27-91 and 12-91; HSCA vol. XI, 542-551.
34. *Foreign Relations of the United States*, vol. XI, Department of State, #384, 12-3-63.
35. FBI memo, DeLoach to Mohr, 6-4-64, 23; "Touched," *Time* magazine, 4-15-66; Dick Russell, *The Man Who Knew Too Much* (New York: Carroll & Graf, 2003), 195–201, the German newspaper report was noted by the Warren Commission; Warren Commission, Document #1015; Joachim Joesten, *Oswald: Assassin or Fall Guy?* (New York: Marzani & Munsell, 1964), 150, 151; Anthony Summers, *Conspiracy* (New York: Paragon House, 1989), 205–217.
36. Kaiser, *Road to Dallas, op. cit.*, 391–394; Mahoney, *Sons & Brothers, op. cit.*, 271–273.
37. FBI 12490033-10074.
38. John Martino, article in *Human Events*, 12-21-63. Note: Any ghostwriter involved in the article would have only been using the information given to him by Martino, and that writer would have had no knowledge of Martino's criminal activities.
39. Harold Weisberg interview with Colonel Castorr, on file at the Assassinations Archives and Records Center; FBI memo to J. Edgar Hoover, 7-31-59; Warren Commission Document #1553D, 1, 3.
40. Warren Commission Document #657.
41. Warren Commission Document #657.
42. Fensterwald and Ewing, *Coincidence, op. cit.*, 506–509; Summers, *Conspiracy* (New York: Paragon House, 1989), 423.
43. Hedegaard, Erik, "The Last Confessions of E. Howard Hunt," *Rolling Stone* posted 3-23-07; The arrest reports and identities of the real tramps were finally released by the Dallas Police Department in the early 1990s.
44. Fonzi, Gaeton, *The Last Investigation* (New York: Thunder's Mouth Press, 1993), many passages; Morley, Jefferson. "What Jane Roman said." Accessed at mcadams.posc.mu.edu/morley1.htm 12-2-02.
45. Benson, *Who's Who, op. cit.*, 77.
46. CIA 104-10075-10256.
47. CIA cable to Director, 12-10-63, CIA 104-10076-10252, declassified 8-95; Corn, David, *Blond Ghost: Ted Shackley and the CIA's Crusades* (New York: Simon & Schuster, 1994), 110.
48. Castaneda, Jorge G. *Compañero: The Life and Death of Che Guevara*. (New York: Vintage, 1998), 250–254.
49. Memorandum to National Security Council Staff, 11-63; Memorandum from William Attwood to Gordon Chase, in Foreign Relations of the United States #379.
50. CIA 104-1040010200, declassified 10-31-98, 39, citing information from 12-3-63.
51. CIA report of their monitoring of Cuban news media, report dated 12-9-63.
52. Newman, "Oswald, CIA,& Mexico City," *op. cit.*, at pbs.org.
53. Author's interviews with confidential Kennedy aide source, 3-17-92; Blakey and Billings, *Plot to Kill Prez, op. cit.*, 76, 77.
54. Anthony and Robbyn Summers, "The Ghosts of November," *Vanity Fair*, 12-94.
55. Davis, *Mafia Kingfish, op. cit.*, 344; Summers, *Not in Your Lifetime, op. cit.*, 31.
56. "A Sad and Solemn Duty," *Time* Magazine, 12-13-63; HSCA Chronology 180-10142-10036; Mary Ferrell Foundation website at maryferrell.org; Kurtz, *JFK Assassination Debates, op. cit.*, 21.

CHAPTER 18

1. Ambrose, *Vol. 2, op. cit.*, 33.
2. *Ibid.*, 38, 39.
3. John Martino, article in *Human Events*, 12-21-63.
4. *Ibid.*
5. Ambrose, *Vol. 2, op. cit.*, 38, 39.
6. Mahoney, *Sons & Brothers, op. cit.*, 271–273. Marcello's territory was also linked to "Operation Tilt," since the FBI memo said that "Subsequent to the above raid, he was instructed to pick up $15,000.00 at Miami, which was to be used for the purchase of guns from the New Orleans, Louisiana area."
7. Morley, Jefferson. *Washington Monthly*, 12-03.
8. Morley, Jefferson. *Washington Monthly*, 12-03.

Trento, *Secret History, op. cit*, 266–268; Author's phone interview with Lopez's wife 3-2-96.

9. HSCA 180-10142-10036, Church Report, Book V, 58–59; Kurtz, *JFK Assassination Debates, op. cit.*, 173.
10. CIA 10410419-10021.
11. Author's interviews with Harry Williams 2-24-92, 4-92, 2-21-95 (some via Thom Hartmann).
12. *Ibid.*, interview on 2-24-92.
13. Thomas, *RFK: His Life, op. cit.*, many passages; Oliva, Erneido. "The End of Kennedy's Final Plan to Overthrow the Castro Regime." Accessed at camcocuba.org; Author's interviews with Harry Williams 2-24-92, 4-92, 2-21-95 (some via Thom Hartmann).
14. Oliva, "End of Kennedy's Plan." *op. cit.*
15. Oliva, "End of Kennedy's Plan." *op. cit.*
16. *Ibid.*
17. Thomas Powers, *The Man Who Kept the Secrets: Richard Helms & the CIA* (New York: Knopf, 1979), 179; Alexander M. Haig, Jr., *Inner Circles: How America Changed the World: A Memoir* (New York: Warner Books, 1992), 116.
18. Anthony and Robbyn Summers, "The Ghosts of November," *Vanity Fair*, 12-94; Staff of the *New York Times*, *The Watergate Hearings: Break-In and Cover-Up* (Bantam: New York 1973), 817–819.
19. Califano, *Inside: op. cit.*, 125; Russo, *Live by Sword, op. cit.*, 174, citing *Orlando Sentinel-Star* 6-12-77.
20. Hancock, *Would Have Talked, op. cit.*, 337; Kaiser, *Road to Dallas, op. cit.*, 402, 403.
21. Hancock, *Would Have Talked, op. cit.*, 141; CIA104-10215-190316.
22. Declassified CIA files on QJWIN.
23. Hancock, *Would Have Talked, op. cit.*, 337; Rappleye and Becker, *All American Mafioso, op. cit.*, 250 & other passages
24. Hinckle and Turner, *Fish Is Red, op. cit.*, 153; Shackley, Ted, *Spymaster: My Life in the CIA* (Washington, DC: Potomac Books, 2006), 92, 93; see mccordfamilyassn.com. The McCord family website says when McCord was a "Senior CIA Security Officer in Europe he headed a team which secretly whisked out of Europe and across national borders one of the most significant and controversial KGB officers ever to defect. This was [after] the assassination of President John F. Kennedy and the defector was highly wanted by the Warren Commission because of the vital information he possessed." McCord declined to speak about Harry Williams when called by the author; McCord had no connection to the harsh treatment Nosenko received in America.
25. Ambrose, *Vol. 2, op. cit.*, 39.
26. *Ibid.*, 39, 40.
27. *Ibid.*, 40–45.
28. *Ibid.*, 46–51.
29. *Ibid.*, 46–51.
30. *Ibid.*, 46–51.
31. Ambrose, *Vol. 2, op. cit.*, 46–51, 68, 75; Demaris, Ovid, and Reid, Ed, *The Green Felt Jungle* (New York: Pocket Books, 1964), many passages.
32. Ambrose, *Vol. 2, op. cit.*, 52, 60, 61.
33. Moldea, *Hoffa Wars, op. cit.*, many passages.
34. Davis, John H., *Mafia Kingfish: Carlos Marcello and the Assassination of John F. Kennedy* (New York: Signet Books (pb), 1989), many passages.
35. Ambrose, *Vol. 2, op. cit.*, 54, 55, 61.
36. Ambrose, *Vol. 2, op. cit.*, 68, Summers and Swan, *Nixon, op. cit.*, 261.
37. Hurt, *Reasonable Doubt, op. cit.*, 61–67; Lifton, *Best Evidence, op. cit.*, several passages.
38. Associated Press article by Mike Feinsilber, 7-2-1997.
39. Many passages in: Kaiser, David, *The Road to Dallas: The Assassination of John F. Kennedy* (Cambridge, Massachusetts: Belknap Press of Harvard University Press, 2008); Kurtz, Michael L., *The JFK Assassination Debate* (Lawrence, Kansas: University of Kansas Press, 2006); Newman, John, *Oswald and the CIA* (New York: Carroll & Graf, 1995); McKnight, Gerald D., *Breach of Trust* (University Press of Kansas, 2005).
40. Warren Commission Document #657 (years later, the HSCA tried to find out why the Warren Commission didn't investigate Martino).
41. John H. Davis, *Mafia Kingfish, op. cit.*, 344; Summers, *Not in Your Lifetime, op. cit.*, 31; Summers and Summers, "Ghosts of November," *op. cit.*; Fensterwald and Ewing, *Coincidence, op. cit.*, 134.
42. HSCA Chronology 180-10142-10036; Mary Ferrell Foundation website at maryferrell.org.
43. CIA IG Report, 1967, *op. cit.*
44. Ambrose, *Vol. 2, op. cit.*, 57, 59.
45. Szulc, *Compulsive Spy, op. cit.*, 77, 78, 96, 97.
46. A review of Barker's released CIA files shows that he remained friends with both Fiorini and Artime at this time.
47. CIA IG Report, 1967, *op. cit.*, 103.
48. Burt, Al "Cuban Exiles: The Mirage of Havana," *The Nation* 1-25-65.
49. Author's interviews with Harry Williams, 7-24-93, 2-21-95 (some via Thom Hartmann).
50. *Ibid.*, 7-24-93, 2-21-95.
51. HSCA#157-10014-10046; Thomas, Evan, *Robert Kennedy: His Life* (New York: Simon & Schuster, 2000), 238.
52. When other CIA exile agents were downsized out of the Agency, they were reportedly allowed to keep their equipment and supplies, but that was on a far smaller scale than the multi-million dollar AMWORLD operation the CIA had funded for Artime.
53. CIA document: 4-25-77, Record Number 104-10400-10123, Russ Holmes Work File, Subject: AMTRUNK Operation, declassified 12-26-98; Hinckle and Turner, *Deadly Secrets, op. cit.*, 289; Russo, *Live by Sword, op. cit.*, 247; *The New York Times* and several Cuban-sponsored publications printed accounts of the trial.
54. JFK 1994.05.16.14:12:04:280005.
55. CIA MFR 4-14-66 cited by A. J. Weberman.
56. Hinckle and Turner, *Deadly Secrets, op. cit.*, 289; Scott, Hoch, and Stetler, *Assassinations, op. cit.*, 363, citing the *New York Times*, 3-6-66.
57. Author's interview with Dean Rusk 1-5-90; Summers and Summers, "Ghosts of November," 105.
58. Bernard Fensterwald, Jr., and Michael Ewing, *Coincidence or Conspiracy* (New York: Zebra Books, 1977), 512; HSCACIA180-10144-10219.
59. Hancock, *Would Have Talked, op. cit.*, many passages.

60. Author's interview with Harry Williams 7-24-93; Johnson, *Sleepwalking, op. cit.*, 271.
61. Ambrose, *Vol. 2, op. cit.*, many passages.
62. Ambrose, *Vol. 2, op. cit.*, 60, 75.

CHAPTER 19

1. Summers and Swan, *Nixon, op. cit.*, 267.
2. *Ibid.*, 17, 18.
3. Summers and Swan, *Nixon, op. cit.*, many passages.
4. *Ibid.*, 112.
5. *Ibid.*, 108.
6. *Ibid.*, 114, 115.
7. *Ibid.*, 108, 112.
8. *Ibid.*, 108.
9. *Ibid.*, 431.
10. *Ibid.*, 112, 113.
11. *Ibid.*, 496.
12. Kohn, Howard. "Strange Bedfellows: The Hughes-Nixon-Lansky Connection." *Rolling Stone*, 5-20-76; Summers and Swan, *Nixon, op. cit.*, 496; HSCA CIA180-10144-10219.
13. FBI 124-10221-10200.
14. Rappleye and Becker, *All American Mafioso, op. cit.*, 259–264.
15. *Ibid.*, 261–263; CIA #104-10133-10005.
16. Reid, *Grim Reapers, op. cit.*, 292; Brashler, *The Don, op. cit.*, 304.
17. Blakey and Billings, *Plot to Kill President, op. cit.*, 152.
18. Reid, *Grim Reapers, op. cit.*, 160; Thomas, *RFK: His Life, op. cit.*, 329.
19. Rappleye, Charles, and Becker, Ed, *All American Mafioso: The Johnny Roselli Story* (New York: Doubleday, 1991), 273, 274.
20. CIA IG Report, 1967, *op. cit.*
21. FBI 124-10221-10200.
22. Goodwin, Richard, *Remembering America: A Voice from the Sixties* (Boston: Little, Brown, 1988), 462–465.
23. *Ibid.*
24. Newfield, Jack, "I want Kennedy killed." *Penthouse*, 5-92.
25. Talbot, *Brothers, op. cit.*, 325–326.
26. Davis, *The Kennedy Contract* (New York: Harper Paperbacks, 1993), 154; Talbot, *Ibid.*, 325-326; Thomas, *RFK: His Life, op. cit.*, 338.
27. Schlesinger, Arthur Jr. *Robert Kennedy and His Times.* (New York: Ballantine, 1979), p. 664.
28. "New documents reveal first JFK casket dumped at sea," CNN, 6-1-99; Lifton, *Best Evidence, op. cit.*, many passages.
29. Hunt and Aunapu, *American Spy, op. cit.*, 157.
30. Hunt and Aunapu, *American Spy, op. cit.*, 157; Szulc, *Compulsive Spy, op. cit.*, 100, 103.
31. Rappleye and Becker, *All American Mafioso, op. cit.*, 281–283; Evica, George Michael, *And We Are All Mortal: New Evidence and Analysis in the John F. Kennedy Assassination* (West Hartford, CT: Evica, 1978), several passages.
32. Hunt and Aunapu, *American Spy, op. cit.*, 157.
33. U.S. Information and Educational Exchange Act of 1948, commonly known as the Smith Mundt Act; Thomas, *RFK: His Life, op. cit.*, 330, 408.
34. Church Committee Vol. I, part 10, 198; Hunt and Aunapu, *American Spy, op. cit.*, 149, 157; Author's phone discussion with former New York Times bureau chief 4-11-2012.
35. Hunt and Aunapu, *American Spy, op. cit.*, 148.
36. Church Committee Vol. I, part 10, 193.
37. Hunt, E. Howard, *Give Us This Day* (New Rochelle New York: Arlington House, 1973; original date 1968); Hunt and Aunapu, *American Spy, op. cit.*, 158; memo titled "Everette Howard Hunt, Jr." in CIA file at the National Archives declassified as part of the 1994 CIA Historical Review Program.
38. Hunt, *Undercover, op. cit.*, 133; Lesar, "Valenti/Helms Plan for CIA Television Show"; CIA memo quoted by A.J. Weberman. Some accounts say there were only five novels.
39. FBI 124-10204-10205.
40. Davis, *Mafia Kingfish, op. cit.*, 356–559; see "Lucchese Crime Family Epic, Part II" at www.crimelibrary.com.
41. Davis, *Mafia Kingfish, op. cit.*, 356–559.
42. Blakey and Billings, *Plot to Kill President, op. cit.*, 324; Rappleye and Becker, *All American Mafioso, op. cit.*, 276.
43. Davis, *Mafia Kingfish, op. cit.*, 367; CIA IG Report, 1967, *op. cit.*; FBI 124-10333-10036.
44. Rappleye and Becker, *All American Mafioso, op. cit.*, 279–282, 281–283.
45. Blakey, G. Robert, and Richard N. Billings, *Fatal Hour* (New York: Berkley Books, 1992), xxii ; Garrison, Jim, *A Heritage of Stone* (New York: Berkley Medallion, 1975), 110, 111; Martin Waldron letter to the New Orleans Police Department, *New York Times*, 11-21-66.
46. 12-15-66 David Ferrie interview summary, Garrison files.
47. 1993.07.01.11:26:17:340800.
48. *Ibid.*
49. 1993.07.01.11:26:17:340800.
50. Reid, *Grim Reapers, op. cit.*, 292.
51. Rappleye and Becker, *All American Mafioso, op. cit.*, 280.
52. Kantor, *Ruby Cover-Up, op. cit.*
53. Ambrose, *Vol. 2, op. cit.*, 100.

CHAPTER 20

1. CIA 104-10404-10376; CIA104-10009-10024; David Phillips memo to Chief, CI/R & A: CIA OGC 67-2061, CIA MFR 2.14.68; See also CIA #104-10406-10022; CIA #104-10435-10007.
2. *Ibid.* all above.
3. CIA 104-10404-10376; CIA104-10009-10024
4. Blakey and Billings, *Plot to Kill President, op. cit.*, 384.
5. Holland, *Assassination Tapes, op. cit.*, 392.
6. Evica, *All Mortal, op. cit.*, 230.
7. Treasury Department/Secret Service memo to J. Edgar Hoover, 2-13-67.
8. Holland, *Assassination Tapes, op. cit.*, 396.
9. Holland, *Assassination Tapes, op. cit.*, 389, 390, 416; Treasury Department/Secret Service memo to J. Edgar Hoover, 2-13-67.
10. FBI 124-1020910451; Ragano and Raab, *Mob Lawyer, op. cit.*, 226-228; Russell, *Man Who Knew, op. cit.*, 544.
11. Holland, *Assassination Tapes, op. cit.*, 389, 398
12. R. Beschloss, *Taking Charge* (New York: Simon & Schuster, 1997), 561–563.
13. Summers, Anthony, *Not In Your Lifetime* (New York: Marlowe & Co., 1998), 233; *People and the Pursuit of Truth*, vol. 1, No. 1, 5-75.
14. CIA card 100-300-017, 4-9-68, for Oswald 201-289248.

15. Garrison, *Heritage of Stone, op. cit.*, 111; "Facts Don't Jibe in Ferrie Death," UPI, 2-23-67; Kirkwood, James, *American Grotesque* (New York, NY: Harper Perennial, 1992), 142.
16. Talbot, *Brothers, op. cit.*, 314, 322, 323.
17. *Ibid.*, 312, 313.
18. Davis, *The Kennedy Contract* (New York: Harper Paperbacks, 1993), 154; interview with business associate of Frank Grimsley, 1-30-08; Talbot, *Brothers*, 325-326; Thomas, *RFK: His Life, op. cit.*, 338.
19. 1994.05.09.10:43:33:160005.
20. Ragano and Raab, *Mob Lawyer, op. cit.*, 193, 194.
21. Ambrose, *Vol. 2, op. cit.*, 103; Summers and Swan, *Nixon, op. cit.*, 292.
22. Thomas, *RFK: His Life, op. cit.*, 334, 335; Holland, *Assassination Tapes, op. cit.*, 409; Summers and Swan, *Nixon, op. cit.*, 292.
23. Harold Weisberg, *Oswald in New Orleans: Case of Conspiracy with the C.I.A.* (New York: Canyon Books, 1967), 256, 257.
24. *Ibid.*
25. Beschloss, *Taking Charge, op. cit.*, 565–566; Holland, *Assassination Tapes, op. cit.*, 404–409.
26. Beschloss, *Taking Charge, op. cit.*, 565–566; Holland, *Assassination Tapes, op. cit.*, 404–409.
27. Beschloss, *Taking Charge, op. cit.*, 565–566; Holland, *Assassination Tapes, op. cit.*, 404–409.
28. Holland, *Assassination Tapes, op. cit.*, 414, 415.
29. *Ibid.*
30. CIA IG Report, 1967, 112.
31. CIA 104-10438-10.
32. Davis, *Katherine, op. cit.*, many passages; Thomas, *RFK: His Life, op. cit.*, 334, others.
33. CIA 104-10438-10.
34. *New Orleans States-Item* 3-3-67, 25. It's essential to note that the most important analysis of Jack Anderson's 3-3-67 and 3-7-67 columns was first done by Peter Dale Scott, in his *Crime and Cover-Up* in the 1970s, and the later *Deep Politics II* in the 1990s. As with all of his work, both are highly recommended.
35. *New Orleans States-Item*, 3-3-67, 25.
36. *Ibid.*
37. *Ibid.*
38. Mahoney, *Sons & Brothers, op. cit.*, 333; Schlesinger, *RFK & His Times, op. cit.*, 532.
39. CIA IG Report, 1967, *op. cit.*, 66.
40. Thomas, Evan, *Robert Kennedy: His Life* (New York: Simon & Schuster, 2000).
41. See the so-called CIA "Family Jewels," 21, 27, available in the National Security Archive's Electronic Briefing Book No. 222.
42. Hoover to Attorney General memo, 3-3-67.
43. *Ibid.*
44. FBI 124-10183-10239; Hoover to Attorney General memo, 3-3-67.
45. Holland, *Assassination Tapes, op. cit.*, 416.
46. Sheridan, *Rise of Hoffa, op. cit.*, several passages.
47. Martin, David C. *Wilderness of Mirrors.* (New York: Harper & Row, 1980), 188, 189.
48. CIA 104-10122-10306; CIA 104-10133-10005; Russo, *Live by Sword, op. cit.*, 446.
49. Kelly, William E, "The Exhumation and Reinterment of JFK," *Dateline: Dallas*, Spring/Summer 1993.
50. *Ibid.*
51. Kelly, "Reinterment," *op. cit.*; Russo, *Live by Sword, op. cit.*, 405.
52. Kelly, "Reinterment," *op. cit.*; Russo, *Live by Sword, op. cit.*, 328, 389, 390, 404–406.
53. *The New York Times*, 3-18-67 cited in Holland's *Kennedy Assassination Tapes, op. cit.*, 421, 422.
54. Holland, *Assassination Tapes, op. cit.*, 415.
55. FBI 124-10183-10239.
56. *Ibid.*
57. *Ibid.*
58. *Ibid.*
59. *Ibid.*

CHAPTER 21

1. CIA IG Report, 1967, *op. cit.* For example, among the material Helms withheld from LBJ was the involvement of Manuel Artime in the CIA-Mafia plots, and the Mafia's payoff of $200,000 to Tony Varona in the summer of 1963.
2. Russell, *Man Who Knew, op. cit.*, 414.
3. Powers, *Helms, op. cit.*, 136.
4. Peter Dale Scott, *Deep Politics II* (Ipswich, MA: Mary Ferrell Foundation Press, 2003), 66–67.
5. Thomas, *RFK, op. cit.*, 336.
6. SSCIA 157-10011-10019.
7. CIA files about Manolo Ray are available at maryferrell.org, including those under his CIA code-name of AMBANG (sometimes given as AMBANG-1); online interview with Manolo Ray, 2-9-06, arranged by John Simkin, www.spartacus.schoolnet.co.uk.
8. Holland, Max, *The Kennedy Assassination Tapes* (New York: Knopf, 2004), 416.
9. Church, *Plots, op. cit.*, 164.
10. CIA IG Report, 1967, *op. cit.*, 6.
11. Thomas Powers, *The Man Who Kept the Secrets: Richard Helms & the CIA* (New York: Knopf, 1979), 319, 320.
12. FBI 124-10280-10110.
13. CIA IG Report, 1967, *op. cit.*, many passages.
14. CIA IG Report, 1967, *op. cit.*, 128.
15. Powers, *Helms, op. cit.*, 179; Richard Helms Church Committee testimony, 1975.
16. Powers, *Helms, op. cit.*, 179.
17. *Ibid.*, 180.
18. Church Committee vol. X, 106; Powers, *Helms, op. cit.*, 180.
19. CIA IG Report, 1967, *op. cit.*, 132.
20. Blakey and Billings, *Plot to Kill President, op. cit.*, 385; Rappleye and Becker, *All American, op. cit.*, 287.
21. Rappleye and Becker, *All American, op. cit.*, 286–289; Reid, *Grim Reapers, op. cit.*, 188–190; Scheim, *Mafia Killed op. cit.*, 359, 360.
22. CIA 104-10122-10293; CIA 104-10122-10306.
23. CIA 104-10133-10078.
24. Summers and Swan, *Nixon, op. cit.*, 196, 197; Mahoney, *Sons & Brothers, op. cit.*, 170, 171, 400; Kaiser, *Road to Dallas, op. cit.*, 160–165; CIA document, JMWAVE to Director, 12-5-63, from "Carlos Prio Socarras [soft file]."
25. Ambrose, *Vol. 2, op. cit.*
26. Nixon, Richard Milhous, *The Memoirs of Richard Nixon* (New York: Simon & Schuster, 1990), 292; Summers and Swan, *Nixon, op. cit.*, 106.
27. Summers and Swan, *Nixon, op. cit.*, 496; Thomas, *RFK, op. cit.*, 334.
28. FBI Los Angeles Field File 58-156, 331–337; Moldea, *Hoffa Wars, op. cit.*, 64, 87, 110, 186, 187; Reid, *Reapers, op. cit.*, 291.

29. FBI Los Angeles Field File 58-156, *op. cit.*, 331–337.
30. Thomas, *Very Best Men*, *op. cit.*, 333; Fonzi, *Last Investigation*, *op. cit.*, 425.
31. David Atlee Phillips, *The Night Watch* (New York: Atheneum, 1977), 185–187
32. HSCA vol. X, pp. 44, 54.
33. HSCA 180-101432-10215.
34. Bardach, Ann Louise, *Cuba Confidential* (New York: Random House, 2002), 183; CIA104-10068-10010; HSCA180-10143-10215.
35. Joseph J. Trento, *Prelude to Terror: The Rogue CIA, and the Legacy of America's Private Intelligence Network* (New York: Carroll & Graf, 2005), 44–45; CIA104-10408-10029, 8-25-76, CIA memo.
36. Tripodi, Tom, *Crusade: Undercover Against the Mafia and KGB* (Washington, DC: Brassey's, 1993), 146–148.
37. William Colby was the other future CIA Director who told another Agency official Fiorini had been a CIA contract agent, Kaiser, *Road to Dallas*, *op. cit.*, 430; Richard Helms deposition 1984 Hunt vs. Spotlight trial, *Miami Herald* 1-31-85 cited by A.J. Weberman.
38. 1993.07.02.11:49:06:400800.
39. Hunt and Risch, *Warrior*, *op. cit.*, 107; *Miami Herald*, 9-2-73.
40. Scott, Peter Dale. *Deep Politics II*. (Ipswich, MA: Mary Ferrell Foundation Press, 2003), 117, 118, 135.
41. Castaneda, *Compañero*, *op. cit.*, many passages; Rodriguez and Weisman, *Shadow Warrior*, *op. cit.*, 171.
42. Fonzi, *Last Investigation*, *op. cit.*, 309, 373, 376, 387, 389; Larry Hancock, *Would Have Talked*, *op. cit.*, 418; Twyman, Noel. *Bloody Treason*. (Rancho Sante Fe, CA: Laurel Publishing, 1997), 466.
43. McCoy, Alfred W., *The Politics of Heroin* (Brooklyn: Lawrence Hill Books, 1991), many passages; McGovern, Ray, "CIA Officer on the Agency's Days of Shame," *CounterPunch*, 2-13-03.
44. Fonzi, *Last Investigation*, *op. cit.*, 426; Lyon, Verne, "Domestic Surveillance: The History of Operation CHAOS," *Covert Action Information Bulletin*, Summer 1990.
45. Dickerson, James, *Dixie's Dirty Secret*, (Armonk, NY: M. E. Sharp, 1998), 16–33, 39, 119–120, 134–137; Hancock, Larry, and Stuart Wexler, *Seeking Armageddon: Religious Terrorism in the 1960s and the Effort to Kill Martin Luther King* (advance manuscript, 2008).
46. Tampa FBI 6-30-65 memo re: JURE; Raziq, David, and Mark Greenblatt, "Inside the FBI's Secret Files on Coretta Scott King," 8-30-07, KHOU-TV, Houston; FBI file #62-108052-12; Hancock and Wexler, *Seeking Armageddon*, *op. cit.*
47. McGovern, Ray, "CIA Officer on the Agency's Days of Shame," *CounterPunch*, 2-13-03.
48. 4-12-2011 Pentagon Papers Project, NARA blogs.archives.gov/ndc; Wells, *Wild Man*, *op. cit.*, many passages.

CHAPTER 22

1. Branch, Taylor, *At Canaan's Edge: America in the King Years 1965–68* (New York: Simon & Schuster, 2006), 680.
2. Branch, *Canaan's Edge*, *op. cit.*, 680–682; Thomas, *RFK: His Life*, *op. cit.*, 356, 357.
3. Daniel and Kirshon, eds., *Chronicle of America*, *op. cit.*, 819; Branch, *Canaan's Edge*, *op. cit.*, 710.
4. Branch, *Canaan's Edge*, *op. cit.*, 713–715; Thomas, *RFK: His Life*, *op. cit.*, 360.
5. Branch, *Canaan's Edge*, *op. cit.*, 727, 736; Kotz, Nick, *Judgment Days* (New York: Houghton Mifflin, 2005), 398.
6. Branch, *Canaan's Edge*, *op. cit.*, 727, 728.
7. Branch, *Canaan's Edge*, *op. cit.*, 750, 751.
8. Ambrose, *Vol. 2*, *op. cit.*, 103, 141, 163–165, 177–194, 204–206.
9. Ayton, Mel, *A Racial Crime* (Las Vegas: ArcheBooks, 2005), 5; Kotz, *Judgment Days*, *op. cit.*, 422; Martin Luther King Justice Department Task Force Report, 1977, 60–62; Posner, Gerald, *Killing the Dream* (New York: Random House, 1998), 248, 249, 250; Thomas, *RFK: His Life*, *op. cit.*, 366, 367.
10. Ambrose, *Vol. 2*, *op. cit.*, 150, 151, photo section.
11. Ambrose, *Vol. 2*, *op. cit.*, 163, 174; Summers and Swan, *Nixon*, *op. cit.*, 275.
12. Ambrose, *Vol. 2*, *op. cit.*, 103; Branch, *Canaan's Edge*, *op. cit.*, 622; Daniel and Kirshon, eds., *Chronicle of America*, *op. cit.*, 815.
13. Ambrose, *Vol. 2*, *op. cit.*, 83, 89, 95.
14. Ambrose, *Vol. 2*, *op. cit.*, 186–188, 197.
15. Davis, *Mafia Kingfish*, *op. cit.*, 322.
16. CIA 104-10133-10071.
17. Rappleye and Becker, *All American*, *op. cit.*, 289.
18. *Ibid.*, 288, 289.
19. Thomas, *RFK: His Life*, *op. cit.*, 374, 375.
20. Davis, *Mafia Kingfish*, *op. cit.*, 384; FBI Memo, 7-23-68.
21. Thomas, *RFK: His Life*, *op. cit.*, 384.
22. Clarke, Thurston. *The Last Campaign: Robert F. Kennedy and 82 Days That Inspired America*. (New York: Henry Holt and Company, 2008); Sullivan, William, and Bill Brown, *The Bureau* (New York: Pinnacle Books, 1982).
23. Moldea, Dan E., *The Killing of Robert F. Kennedy* (New York: W. W. Norton & Company, 1995), 25. For a detailed analysis of the controversies that still surround RFK's murder, see the author's *Legacy of Secrecy* (2009).
24. Moldea, *Killing of RFK*, *op. cit.*, 59.
25. Melanson, Philip H., *The Robert F. Kennedy Assassination* (New York: Shapolsky, 1991), several passages; Moldea, Dan E., *The Killing of Robert F. Kennedy* (New York: W. W. Norton & Company, 1995), several passages.
26. Turner, William, and Christian, Jonn, *The Assassination of Robert F. Kennedy* (New York: Carroll & Graf, 2006), xxxii, xxxiii.
27. Talbot, *Brothers*, *op. cit.*, 312; Thomas, *RFK: His Life*, *op. cit.*, 392.
28. Scheim, *Mafia Killed*, *op. cit.*, 349.
29. Hancock, Larry, *Incomplete Justice*. Article series on the Mary Ferrell Foundation website, maryferrell.org, citing Robert Blair Kaiser, *RFK Must Die* (Nw York: Grove Press, 1970), 471; Melanson, Philip H., *The Robert F. Kennedy Assassination* (New York: Shapolsky, 1991), 108, 160; Scheim, *Mafia Killed*, *op. cit.*, 349, 350; Sirhan notebooks, California State Archives.
30. LAPD Special Unit Senator (SUS) Report, 343.
31. Demaris, Ovid. *The Last Mafioso*. (New York: Bantam, 1981), 251–254; Pease, Lisa, "Sirhan and the RFK Assassination," *Probe Magazine*, March-April and May-June, 1998; Rappleye and Ed

Becker, *All American*, *op. cit.*, 289; Scheim, *Mafia Killed*, *op. cit.*, 359.
32. Moldea, *Killing of RFK*, *op. cit.*, 301.
33. *Ibid.*, 116.
34. Moldea, *Killing of RFK*, *op. cit.*, 116. Regarding the drug contacts of some of Sirhan's brothers, one of several examples is LAPD SUS Report, 1019.
35. FBI Los Angeles Field File 58-156, 331-337 (RFK Assassination: L.A.F.O. #56-156: Sub File X-5, vol. 18); FBI Airtel from New York to Director, 10-15-68.
36. Ambrose, *Vol. 2*, *op. cit.*, 185.
37. Ambrose, *Vol. 2*, *op. cit.*, 177, 193, 199, 205, 206; Summers and Swan, *Nixon*, *op. cit.*, 517.
38. Ambrose, *Vol. 2*, *op. cit.*, 178, 140.
39. Dickinson, Tom, "How Roger Ailes Built the Fox News Fear Factory," *Rolling Stone* 6-9-2011; Author unknown, "Fox News Ailes Gets Auletta-Treatment," Drudge Report 5-18-2005; Summers and Swan, *Nixon*, *op. cit.*, 94.
40. Ambrose, *Vol. 2*, *op. cit.*, 202.
41. Lukas, *Nightmare*, *op. cit.*, 154; Scott, *Crime and Cover-Up*, *op. cit.*, 64.
42. Hinckle and Turner, *Deadly Secrets*, *op. cit.*, 338. Summers and Swan, *Nixon*, *op. cit.*, 278–287.
43. Scott, *Crime and Cover-Up*, *op. cit.*, 26; Summers and Swan, *Nixon*, *op. cit.*, 279–282.
44. Summers and Swan, *Nixon*, *op. cit.*, 278, other passages.
45. Scheim, *Mafia Killed*, *op. cit.*, 364, 365; Summers and Swan, *Nixon*, *op. cit.*, 278–287.
46. Summers and Swan, *Nixon*, *op. cit.*, 278–287.
47. Summers and Swan, *Nixon*, *op. cit.*, 273.
48. Fulsom, Don, "The Mob's President: Richard Nixon's Secret Ties to the Mafia," *Crime Magazine* 2-5-2006.
49. Summers and Swan, *Nixon*, *op. cit.*, 51, 52.
50. Ambrose, *Vol. 2*, *op. cit.*, 491.
51. Hinckle and Turner, *Deadly Secrets*, *op. cit.*, 354, 355.
52. Summers and Swan, *Nixon*, *op. cit.*, 113, 114.
53. *Ibid.*
54. Scheim, *Mafia Killed*, *op. cit.*, 364, citing *New York Times* 1-21-74; *Life* magazine 2-3-67.
55. Summers and Swan, *Nixon*, *op. cit.*, 240–245, 251, 252.
56. FBI 124-10284-10086; Buttari's connection with "Cubans for Nixon-Agnew" cited by A. J. Weberman; Hinckle and Turner, *Deadly Secrets*, *op. cit.*, 338, 339, 352, 353; Summers and Swan, *Nixon*, *op. cit.*, 496.
57. Ambrose, *Vol. 2*, *op. cit.*, 174–176; Summers and Swan, *Nixon*, *op. cit.*, 275.
58. Ambrose, *Vol. 2*, *op. cit.*, 230.
59. Ambrose, *Vol. 2*, *op. cit.*, 200–206; Summers and Swan, *Nixon*, *op. cit.*, 277.
60. Ambrose, *Vol. 2*, *op. cit.*, 186.
61. Ambrose, *Vol. 2*, *op. cit.*, 177, 193, 199, 205, 206; Summers and Swan, *Nixon*, *op. cit.*, 517.
62. Ambrose, *Vol. 2*, *op. cit.*, 196.
63. *Ibid.*, 206, 207.
64. Ambrose, *Vol. 2*, *op. cit.*, 207, 208; Summers and Swan, *Nixon*, *op. cit.*, 298.
65. Ambrose, *Vol. 2*, *op. cit.*, 208; Summers and Swan, *Nixon*, *op. cit.*, 299.
66. Ambrose, *Vol. 2*, *op. cit.*, 210–212.
67. Ambrose, *Vol. 2*, *op. cit.*, 212; Summers and Swan, *Nixon*, *op. cit.*, 302–304.
68. Ambrose, *Vol. 2*, *op. cit.*, 213, 214.
69. *Ibid.*, 214.
70. Ambrose, *Vol. 2*, *op. cit.*, 231; Summers and Swan, *Nixon*, *op. cit.*, 288, 307, 515.
71. Ambrose, *Vol. 2*, *op. cit.*, 206.
72. Summers and Swan, *Nixon*, *op. cit.*, 273, 278.

CHAPTER 23

1. *Ibid.*, 101.
2. *Ibid.*, 101.
3. Ambrose, *Vol. 2*, *op. cit.*, 228, Summers and Swan, *Nixon*, *op. cit.*, 312.
4. Ambrose, *Vol. 2*, *op. cit.*, 246, 261.
5. *Ibid.*, 232, 238.
6. *Ibid.*, 232, 238.
7. Ambrose, *Vol. 2*, *op. cit.*, 250 and other passages.
8. Ambrose, *Vol. 2*, *op. cit.*, 229, 244, 298; Summers and Swan, *Nixon*, *op. cit.*, 312.
9. Summers and Swan, *Nixon*, *op. cit.*, 312.
10. Califano, *Inside*, *op. cit.*, 216-219.
11. Colodny and Gettlin, *Silent Coup*, *op. cit.*, 330, 331; Hougan, *Agenda*, *op. cit.*, 59.
12. Colodny and Gettlin, *Silent Coup*, *op. cit.*, 330–333; Hougan, *Agenda*, *op. cit.*, 59.
13. Colodny and Gettlin, *Silent Coup*, *op. cit.*, 330; Hougan, *Agenda*, *op. cit.*, 59; Morris, Roger, *Haig: General's Progress* 97, 98; Haig, Alexander M. Jr., *Inner Circles: How America Changed the World* (New York: Warner Books, 1992), 189, 190.
14. Califano, *Inside*, *op. cit.*, several passages; Colodny and Gettlin, *Silent Coup*, *op. cit.*, 330–333; Haig, *Inner Circles*, *op. cit.*, several passages.
15. Summers and Swan, *Nixon*, *op. cit.*, 53, 54.
16. *Ibid.*, 53, 54.
17. Ambrose, *Vol. 2*, *op. cit.*, 235, 236.
18. Ambrose, *Vol. 2*, *op. cit.*, 231
19. Ambrose, *Vol. 2*, *op. cit.*, 253, 254; Powers, *Helms*, *op. cit.*, 283.
20. Nixon, *Memoirs*, *op. cit.*, 515; Haldeman and DiMona, *Ends*, *op. cit.*, 53, 54.
21. Scott, *Crime and Cover-Up*, *op. cit.*, 59, note 93; Haldeman and DiMona, *Ends*, *op. cit.*, 53, 54.
22. Summers and Swan, *Nixon*, *op. cit.*, 176, 177; Haldeman and DiMona, *Ends*, *op. cit.*, 53, 54.
23. Haldeman and DiMona, *Ends*, *op. cit.*, 54.
24. Ambrose, *Vol. 2*, *op. cit.*, 491.
25. Ambrose, *Vol. 2*, *op. cit.*, 272.
26. Ambrose, *Vol. 2*, *op. cit.*, 250, 272–274.
27. Ambrose, *Vol. 2*, *op. cit.*, 272, 273.
28. Ambrose, *Vol. 2*, *op. cit.*, 272, 273; Fensterwald and Ewing, *Coincidence*, *op. cit.*, 519–521.
29. Ambrose, *Vol. 2*, *op. cit.*, 272, 273; Fensterwald and Ewing, *Coincidence*, *op. cit.*, 519–521.
30. Summers and Swan, *Nixon*, *op. cit.*, 101.
31. Note that accounts vary as to Nixon's net worth, since it changed rapidly in the late 1960s, after he doubled his money on his Fisher's Island investment and began buying his new homes at Key Biscayne and San Clemente with the help of Rebozo; Binder, David, "Charles (Bebe) Rebozo, 85; longtime Nixon confidant." *New York Times* 5-9-98.
32. Binder, David, "Charles (Bebe) Rebozo, 85; longtime Nixon confidant." *New York Times* 5-9-98. Rebozo's last payment to Nixon might have been his $19 million gift to the Nixon library in his will: Sterngold, James "Nixon Daughters Battle Over $19 Million Library Bequest," *New York Times*, 3-16-02.

33. Summers and Swan, *Nixon*, *op. cit.*, 258, 250.
34. *Ibid.*, 258, 250.
35. *Ibid.*, 106, 280, 281; 6-22-72 FBI memo from Bebe Rebozo files (Part 6, p. 1) online at fbi.gov.
36. Summers and Swan, *Nixon*, *op. cit.*, 106, 280–282.
37. *Ibid.*, 106, 280–282.
38. Feldstein, *Poisoning*, *op. cit.*, 223.
39. Feldstein, *Poisoning*, *op. cit.*, 223; Summers and Swan, *Nixon*, *op. cit.*, 496; 223–224.
40. Summers and Swan, *Nixon*, *op. cit.*, 496.
41. Hinckle and Turner, *Deadly Secrets*, *op. cit.*, 338, 339, 352, 353; Lukas, *Nightmare*, *op. cit.*, 264, 265; Summers and Swan, *Nixon*, *op. cit.*, 496.
42. FBI 124-10284-10086.
43. *Ibid.*
44. FBI 124-10284-10086; Lernoux, Penney. "The Miami Connection: Golden Gateway for Drugs." *The Nation*, 2-18-84.
45. FBI 124-10284-10085.
46. FBI 124-10284-10086.
47. 6-22-72 FBI memo from Bebe Rebozo files (Part 6, p. 1) online at fbi.gov.
48. Ambrose, *Vol. 2*, *op. cit.*, 379; Summers and Swan, *Nixon*, *op. cit.*, 508, 509.

CHAPTER 24

1. Ambrose, *Vol. 2*, *op. cit.*, 299–302.
2. *Ibid.*, several passages.
3. *Ibid.*, 300, 303, 304, 308–310.
4. *Ibid.*, 300, 303, 304.
5. *Ibid.*, 308–311.
6. *Ibid.*, 308–312.
7. *Ibid.*, 324.
8. Ambrose, *Vol. 2*, *op. cit.*, 338, 339; McCord, *Piece of Tape*, *op. cit.*, 282.
9. Ambrose, *Vol. 2*, *op. cit.*, 338, 339.
10. *Ibid.*, 335–337, 347–355, 359.
11. Staff of *Newsday*, *The Heroin Trail* (New York: New American Library, 1992), many passages.
12. Trento, Joseph J., *Prelude to Terror: The Rogue CIA, and the Legacy of America's Private Intelligence Network* (New York: Carroll & Graf, 2005), 45.
13. *Ibid.*, 45–47.
14. O'Leary, Jeremiah, "Haig Probe: Did Nixon get Cash from Asia?" *Washington Star*, 12-5-76.
15. Moldea, *Hoffa Wars*, *op. cit.*, 352.
16. *Ibid.*, 350, 351.
17. Moldea, *Hoffa Wars*, *op. cit.*, 350; O'Leary, "Haig Probe," *Washington Star*, *op. cit.*
18. Moldea, *Hoffa Wars*, *op. cit.*, 350; O'Leary, "Haig Probe," *Washington Star*, *op. cit.*; Dean, John, *Lost Honor: The Rest of the Story* (Los Angeles: Stratford Press, 1982).
19. McCoy, Alfred W., *The Politics of Heroin* (Chicago: Lawrence Hill Books, 1991), several passages; O'Leary, "Haig Probe," *Washington Star*, *op. cit.*
20. 6-22-72 FBI memo from Bebe Rebozo files (Part 6, p. 1) online at fbi.gov.
21. Morris, *op. cit.*, 139.
22. Dave Eberhart, "Haig: Moorer a 'Great Patriot'," Newsmax, 2-6-04.
23. Woodward, *Secret Man*, *op. cit.*, 15-26; Bob Woodward, "How Mark Felt Became 'Deep Throat'," *Washington Post*, 6-2-05.
24. *Ibid.*
25. *Ibid.*
26. *Ibid.*
27. *Ibid.*
28. *Ibid.*
29. Colodny and Gettlin, *Silent Coup*, *op. cit.*, 81–88; audio files of the Woodward interview segments with Laird and the others are at watergate.com.
30. *Ibid.*, 288–292.
31. *Ibid.*, 288–292.
32. Weiner, Tim, *Enemies: A History of the FBI* (New York: Random House, 2012), 288–292.
33. Ambrose, *Vol. 2*, *op. cit.*, 367–369.
34. Weiner, *Enemies*, *op. cit.*, 288–292; Ambrose, *Vol. 2*, *op. cit.*, 367–369.
35. *Ibid.*, 288–292.
36. Riebling, Mark, *Wedge: From Pearl Harbor to 9/11: How the Secret War between the FBI and the CIA Has Endangered National Security* (New York: Simon & Schuster, 2002), many passages; Powers, *Helms*, *op. cit.*, several passages.
37. CIA 104-10103-10042; Hunt and Aunapu, *American Spy*, *op. cit.*, 157. In 1970, Hunt apparently observed a few more formalities, like interviewing with a couple of other firms before being hired by The Mullen Company. But the CIA investigators later found that in those interviews, Hunt appeared to be going through the motions and hadn't really tried to "sell himself." At the same time, they found that Richard Helms himself "was listed as a character reference on Mr. Hunt's resume and that Mr. Helms signed a letter of recommendation . . . on Mr. Hunt's behalf." In 1970, Hunt would have welcomed the potentially lucrative private sector assignment, because one of his daughters had developed a medical condition that had drained the family's finances. See Tad Szulc, *Compulsive Spy*, 100, 103, other passages.
38. CIA104-10119-10320; CIA104-10119-10317.
39. CIA104-10119-10320; CIA104-10119-10317. See Peter Dale Scott's new introduction to *Deep Politics and the Death of JFK* (Berkeley: University of California Press, 1996).
40. CIA 104-10103-10042; See also Senate Watergate Hearings, Book 8, 3383–89.
41. CIA104-10103-10042.
42. Haldeman and DiMona, *Ends*, *op. cit.*, 190–196.
43. Epstein, *Fear*, *op. cit.*, 236; McCord, *Piece of Tape*, *op. cit.*, many passages; Author's call to McCord, who declined to speak, 3-6-95; Summers and Summers, "Ghosts of November," *op. cit.*
44. Chase and Lerman, *Kennedy & Press*, *op. cit.*, 333–339; John F. Kennedy address at Rice University 9-12-62, from Public Papers of the Presidents of the United States, v. 1, 1962, 669–670; Chang and Kornbluh, eds., *The Cuban Missile Crisis 1962*, *op. cit.*, 396.
45. Ambrose, *Vol. 2*, *op. cit.*, 378, 379.
46. *Ibid.*, 378, 379.
47. Ambrose, *Vol. 2*, *op. cit.*, 396; David Corn, *Blond Ghost* (New York: Simon & Schuster, 1994), many passages.
48. Ambrose, *Vol. 2*, *op. cit.*, 396; Corn, *Blond Ghost*, *op. cit.*, several passages.
49. Ambrose, *Vol. 2*, *op. cit.*, 396; Parry, Robert, *Secrecy and Privilege: The Rise of the Bush Dynasty from Watergate to Iraq* (Arlington, Virginia: Media Consortium, 2004), 25, 26.
50. Campbell, Karl E., *Sam Ervin and the Army Spy Scandal* (New York: Simon & Schuster, 1991).
51. *Ibid.*

52. *Ibid.*
53. Ambrose, *Vol. 2*, *op. cit.*, 421.
54. *Ibid.*, 421, 422.

CHAPTER 25

1. Rappleye and Becker, *All American*, *op. cit.*, 294, 295.
2. CIA memo 8-9-76, subject: Johnny Rosselli.
3. Sheridan, Walter, *The Fall and Rise of Jimmy Hoffa* (New York: Saturday Review Press, 1972), many passages; Michael Dorman, *Pay-Off* (New York: Berkley Medallion, 1973), 114; John H. Davis, *Mafia Kingfish* (New York: Signet, 1989), 398, 399.
4. Feldstein, *Poisoning*, *op. cit.*, 111–113
5. Rappleye and Becker, *All American*, *op. cit.*, 294–296; Scott, *Crime and Cover-Up*, *op. cit.*, 26, 27; Scott, *Deep Politics II*, *op. cit.*, 68; Scott, Hoch, and Stetler, eds., *The Assassinations*, *op. cit.*, 375–380.
6. Rappleye and Becker, *All American*, *op. cit.*, 294–296; Scott, *Crime and Cover-Up*, *op. cit.*, 26, 27; Scott, *Deep Politics II*, *op. cit.*, 68; Scott, Hoch, and Stetler, eds., *The Assassinations*, *op. cit.*, 375–380.
7. Summers and Swan, *Nixon*, *op. cit.*, 197–199.
8. *Ibid.*, 196, 197.
9. Summers and Swan, *Nixon*, *op. cit.*, 197–199. Some Nixon aides hoped to prove that JFK and Bobby "had tried to kill Castro," and use that to harm Edward Kennedy's chances of running for president. However, that may have just been a cover story for the aides, since Summers points out that "Maheu's information about the CIA-Mafia plots [actually] posed a threat as much to [President] Nixon as to the Kennedys." It was really a greater threat to Nixon, since he'd been the one who originally pressed for the CIA-Mafia plots with Maheu and Rosselli, so no attempt was made to use any information like that against Edward Kennedy.
10. Summers and Swan, *Nixon*, *op. cit.*, 279–282.
11. CIA 104-10119-10163. An HSCA file notes that Virgilio Gonzalez, "the professional locksmith" used on the main Watergate break-in, was "an old friend of former Cuban President Carlos Prio." Prio himself worked with Barker and Hunt on some of their projects, and both men would visit Prio shortly before the first Watergate break-in.
12. Rosselli memo to Senator Ervin by Lenzner and Lackritz, February 1974—Senate Select Committee on Presidential Campaign Activities (Ervin Committee), staff files; Lenzner to Muse Rosselli Watergate Committee memo, February 1974—Senate Select Committee on Presidential Campaign Activities (Ervin Committee), staff files; Scott, *Crime and Cover-Up*, *op. cit.*, 26. Summers and Swan, *Nixon*, *op. cit.*, 197–199.
13. Lukas, *Nightmare*, *op. cit.*, 154; see Senate Watergate Hearings, Book 8, pp. 3369–71.
14. Hougan, *Agenda*, *op. cit.*, 58; Lukas, *Nightmare*, *op. cit.*, 105–110; Russell, "Charles Colson," *Argosy*, *op. cit*.
15. CIA memo 8-9-76, subject: Johnny Rosselli; Davis, Mafia Kingfish, op. cit., 399.
16. Church, *Plots*, *op. cit.*, 85.
17. Church, *Plots*, *op. cit.*, 85; Rappleye and Becker, *All American*, *op. cit.*, 300, 301.
18. Lukas, *Nightmare*, *op. cit.*, 157–173.
19. Summers and Swan, *Nixon*, *op. cit.*, 353–356.
20. Many articles noting the 40th anniversary of Watergate will likely follow this conventional scenario.
21. Hougan, *Agenda*, *op. cit.*, 58; Lukas, *Nightmare*, *op. cit.*, 105-110; Russell, "Charles Colson." *Argosy*, *op. cit*.
22. Lukas, *Nightmare*, *op. cit.*, 105–110; Russell, "Charles Colson." *Argosy*, *op. cit*.
23. For example, in Hunt, E. Howard, *Undercover: A Memoir of an American Secret Agent* (New York: Berkley Publishing Corp., 1974), 144; "A Man Called Macho" by Marcelo Fernandez-Zayas, *Guaracabuya*, www.amigospais-guaracabuya.org; and in Eugenio Martinez's article in *Harper's* 10-74.
24. Lukas, *Nightmare*, *op. cit.*, 105–110.
25. Hinckle, Warren and Turner, William, *Deadly Secrets* (New York: Thunder's Mouth, 1992), 338, 339, 352, 353; Anthony Summers with Robbyn Swan, *The Arrogance of Power: The Secret World of Richard Nixon* (New York: Viking, 2000), 496; Bebe Rebozo FBI files (Part 6); Eugenio Martinez's article in *Harper's* 10-74.
26. Hinckle, Warren and Turner, William, *Deadly Secrets* (New York: Thunder's Mouth, 1992), 352; "A Man Called Macho" by Marcelo Fernandez-Zayas, *Guaracabuya*, www.amigospais-guaracabuya.org.
27. Bernard Barker Senate Watergate Committee Testimony, 5-24-73; Lukas, *Nightmare*, *op. cit.*, 105–110.
28. HSCA 124-10289-10440.
29. Deposition of G. Gordon Liddy: Hunt vs. A. J. Weberman.
30. FBI 124-10280-10440; Helms's Senate testimony about Barker's firing from the Agency cited in Bernard Fensterwald, Jr., and Michael Ewing, *Coincidence or Conspiracy* (New York: Zebra Books, 1977), 512.
31. J. Anthony Lukas, *Nightmare: The Underside of the Nixon Years* (New York: Bantam Books, 1977), 265.
32. Michael Ewing and Peter Kross, HSCA 11210419, cited by Gary Buell.
33. Dick Cheney memo #1781000410114, 1-3-75.
34. Rosen, James, *The Strong Man: John Mitchell and the Secrets of Watergate* (New York: Doubleday, 2008), 109, 110; Research by Dan Froomkin; Wells, Tom, *Wild Man: The Life and Times of Daniel Ellsberg* (New York: Palgrove, 2001).
35. Wells, Tom, *Wild Man*, *op. cit.*, 247, 248.
36. *Ibid.*
37. Rosen, *Strong Man*, *op. cit.*, 154–163.
38. Rosen, *Strong Man*, *op. cit.*, 154–163.
39. Ambrose, *Vol. 2*, *op. cit.*, 447; Rosen, *Strong Man*, *op. cit.*, 154–163.
40. Rosen, *Strong Man*, *op. cit.*, 154–163.
41. Califano, *Inside*, *op. cit.*, 225, 226.
42. *Ibid.*, 216–219, 225, 226.
43. *Ibid.*, 225, 226.
44. Rosen, *Strong Man*, *op. cit.*, 154–163.
45. Ambrose, *Vol. 2*, *op. cit.*, 446–448; Rosen, *Strong Man*, *op. cit.*, 154–163.
46. Kutler, *Tapes*, *op. cit.*, 3.
47. Kutler, *Tapes*, *op. cit.*, 6. SSCIA 157-10011-10071.
48. *Ibid.*, 8.
49. Dean, John W., *Blind Ambition: Updated Edition—*

The Rest of the Story (Palm Springs, CA: Polimedia Publishers, 2009), 390.

50. Kutler, *Tapes, op. cit.*, 5.
51. Lukas, *Nightmare, op. cit.*, 107, 108.
52. Kutler, *Tapes, op. cit.*, 13.
53. *Ibid.*, 13.
54. Kutler, *Tapes, op. cit.*, 19.
55. Lukas, *Nightmare, op. cit.*, 108.
56. *Ibid.*, 108.
57. Epstein, *Fear, op. cit.*, 205; Lukas, *Nightmare, op. cit.*, 108.
58. Lukas, *Nightmare, op. cit.*, 107, 108; *NYT, Watergate Hearings, op. cit.*, 68.
59. Kutler, *Tapes, op. cit.*, 26.
60. Lukas, *Nightmare, op. cit.*, 109.
61. Lukas, *Nightmare, op. cit.*, 109.
62. *Ibid.*, 110.
63. Lukas, *Nightmare, op. cit.*, 100–104, 117–120, 125–144.
64. Lukas, *Nightmare, op. cit.*, 117–119.
65. Dean, *Blind, op. cit.*, 392; Lukas, *Nightmare, op. cit.*, 120.

CHAPTER 26

1. Kutler, Stanley I, *The Wars of Watergate: The Last Crisis of Richard Nixon* (New York: Alfred A. Knopf, 1990), 115; Lukas, *Nightmare, op. cit.*, 138.
2. Lukas, *Nightmare, op. cit.*, 119, 124.
3. *Ibid.*, 126, 127.
4. *Ibid.*, 124, 125.
5. Epstein, *Fear, op. cit.*, 204.
6. Kutler, *Tapes, op. cit.*, 27, 28; Summers and Swan, *Nixon, op. cit.*, 389, 390.
7. Lukas, *Nightmare, op. cit.*, 128; Summers and Swan, *Nixon, op. cit.*, 390, 391, 524.
8. Hougan, *Agenda, op. cit.*, 44.
9. Kutler, *Wars of Watergate, op. cit.*, 5, 6; Lukas, *Nightmare, op. cit.*, 132; Martinez, Eugenio, article, *Harper's*, 10-74.
10. Lukas, *Nightmare, op. cit.*, 134.
11. Hougan, *Agenda, op. cit.*, 42, 43; Lukas, *Nightmare, op. cit.*, 133.
12. Hougan, *Agenda, op. cit.*, 44, 45.
13. *Ibid.*, 46.
14. Hunt and Aunapu, *op. cit.*, 185–189; Lukas, *Nightmare, op. cit.*, 136.
15. Hunt and Aunapu, *op. cit.*, 185–189; Lukas, *Nightmare, op. cit.*, 136.
16. Martinez, Eugenio, article, *Harper's, op. cit.*
17. Hougan, *Agenda, op. cit.*, 47; Russell, *Man Who Knew, op. cit.*, 728; Johnson, Loch K., *A Season of Inquiry: Congress and Intelligence* (Chicago: The Dorsey Press, 1988), 278.
18. Epstein, *Fear, op. cit.*, 206; Hunt and Aunapu, *op. cit.*, 188–189.
19. Hougan, *Agenda, op. cit.*, 49, 50, 328, 329.
20. *Ibid.*, 51.
21. *Ibid.*, 48, 49.
22. *Ibid.*, 48, 49.
23. *Ibid.*, 48, 49.
24. Wells, *Wild Man, op. cit.*, 247, 248.
25. It's now known that Desmond and Frances didn't really have such a close relationship, but there was no way for the CIA to know that in 1971, since Fitzgerald had died in 1967.
26. Kutler, *Wars of Watergate, op. cit.*, 115, Summers and Swan, *Nixon, op. cit.*, 390.
27. Dean, *Blind, op. cit.*, 393.
28. Kutler, *Wars of Watergate, op. cit.*, 28.
29. Lukas, *Nightmare, op. cit.*, 138, 139, 140.
30. Epstein, *Fear, op. cit.*, 236; *NYT, Watergate Hearings, op. cit.*, 69, 70.
31. Kutler, *Wars of Watergate, op. cit.*, 28.
32. *Ibid.*, 28, 29.
33. *Ibid.*, 28, 29.
34. Kutler, *Wars of Watergate, op. cit.*, 36; Summers and Swan, *Nixon, op. cit.*, 177.
35. Summers and Swan, *Nixon, op. cit.*, 176, 177.
36. Nixon, *Memoirs, op. cit.*, 515.
37. Nixon, *Memoirs, op. cit.*, 515; Russo, *Live by Sword, op. cit.*, 423; Scott, *Deep Politics II, op. cit.*, 58.
38. Nixon, *Memoirs, op. cit.*, 515; Kutler, *Wars of Watergate, op. cit.*, many passages.
39. Fonzi, *Last Investigation, op. cit.*, 70, 71; Kutler, *Wars of Watergate, op. cit.*, 35; Lukas, *Nightmare, op. cit.*, 113; *NYT, Watergate Hearings, op. cit.*, 69–70.
40. Lukas, *Nightmare, op. cit.*, 113–117.
41. Epstein, *Fear, op. cit.*, 145; Haldeman and DiMona, *Ends, op. cit.*, 190–196; Lukas, *Nightmare, op. cit.*, 113–117; Summers and Swan, *Nixon, op. cit.*, 516, 517.
42. Hinckle and Turner, *Deadly Secrets, op. cit.*, 338; Lukas, *Nightmare, op. cit.*, 154; Scott, *Crime and Cover-Up, op. cit.*, 64; Bebe Rebozo FBI files (parts 5 and 6) at fbi.gov.
43. Lukas, *Nightmare, op. cit.*, 23, 24; Nixon tape about Schorr at www.whitehousetapes.net/transcript/nixon/going-after-dan-schorr
44. Summers and Swan, *Nixon, op. cit.*, 107, 115; Voorhis, *Strange Case, op. cit.*, 247, 248.
45. Summers and Swan, *Nixon, op. cit.*, 115; Binder, David, "Charles (Bebe) Rebozo, 85; longtime Nixon confidant," *New York Times* 5-9-98.
46. Gerth, Jeff, "Richard M. Nixon and Organized Crime," reprinted in Blumenthal, Sid, and Harvey Yazijian, *Government by Gunplay* (New York: Signet, 1976), 104; 130–151.
47. *Ramparts* magazine, 5-72; Richard Nixon White House tape, 1-3-72.
48. Epstein, *Fear, op. cit.*, 85; McCoy, *Politics of Heroin, op. cit*
49. Epstein, *Fear, op. cit.*, 201–207.
50. Epstein, *Fear, op. cit.*, 205–207; Author's phone interview with Carl Shoffler 12-14-93; Fonzi, *Last Investigation, op. cit.*, 70, 71.
51. Epstein, *Fear, op. cit.*, 200–210, 218, 219; Dean, *Blind, op. cit.*, 142; Summers and Swan, *Nixon, op. cit.*, 509; Tripodi, Tom, *Crusade: Undercover Against the Mafia and KGB* (Washington, DC, Brassey's, 1993), 4, 129–132, 169; Anthony Summers with Robbyn Swan, *The Arrogance of Power: The Secret World of Richard Nixon* (New York: Viking, 2000), 509.
52. Epstein, *Fear, op. cit.*, 144–145.
53. Epstein, Fear, *op. cit.*, many passages ; Krüger, Henrik, *The Great Heroin Coup: Drugs, Intelligence, and International Fascism* (Boston: South End Press, 1980); Staff of *Newsday, The Heroin Trail*, (New York: New American Library, 1992).
54. Reid, *Grim Reapers, op. cit.*, 115; Summers and Swan, *Nixon, op. cit.*, many passages, especially the criminal ties of many of Nixon's associates, including his best friend, Bebe Rebozo; Trento, *Prelude to Terror, op. cit.*, 451; Staff of *Newsday, The Heroin Trail*, (New York: New American Library, 1992), many passages.

55. Epstein, *Fear*, *op. cit.*, 146, 218, 219; Fonzi, *Last Investigation*, *op. cit.*, 71.
56. Dean, *Blind*, *op. cit.*, 142.
57. Jack Anderson column, *Atlanta Journal-Constitution*, 12-16-77; A.J. Weberman at www.ajweberman.com.
58. *New York Times*, 6-18-72 p. 11, 6-27-72 p. 43, 7-13-72 p. 9, cited by A. J. Weberman; Krüger, *Heroin Coup*, *op. cit.*, 161.
59. Lukas, *Nightmare*, *op. cit.*, 139.
60. HSCA Ewing JFK-Hunt report.
61. HSCA Ewing JFK-Hunt report; Russo, Gus. *Live by Sword*, *op. cit.*, 580.

CHAPTER 27

1. Rosen, *Strong Man*, *op. cit.*, 74; Fulsom, Don, "The Mob's President: Richard Nixon's Secret Ties to the Mafia," *Crime Magazine*, 2-5-06.
2. Rosen, *Strong Man*, *op. cit.*, 74; Kaiser, *Road to Dallas*, *op. cit.*, 410
3. Rosen, *Strong Man*, *op. cit.*, 491.
4. Davis, John H., *Mafia Kingfish: Carlos Marcello and the Assassination of John F. Kennedy* (New York: McGraw-Hill (pb), 1989), 465, 566, 567; Scheim, *Mafia Killed*, *op. cit.*, 367.
5. Moldea, *Hoffa Wars*, *op. cit.*, 316; Scheim, *Mafia Killed*, *op. cit.*, 362.
6. Fensterwald and Ewing, *Coincidence*, *op. cit.*, 132, 133; Kutler, *Tapes*, *op. cit.*, 3, 6; A.J. Weberman at www.ajweberman.com.
7. Holland, *Assassination Tapes*, *op. cit.*, 409; Russo, Gus, *Supermob: How Sidney Korshak and His Criminal Associates Became America's Hidden Power Brokers* (New York: Bloomsbury Press, 200), 375; Thomas, *RFK: His Life*, *op. cit.*, 334, 335; Weberman at www.ajweberman.com.
8. Summers and Swan, *Nixon*, *op. cit.*, 356.
9. Ambrose, *Vol. 2*, *op. cit.*, 491; Moldea, *Hoffa Wars*, *op. cit.*, 260–262; Summers and Swan, *Nixon*, *op. cit.*, 525.
10. Moldea, *Hoffa Wars*, *op. cit.*, 260–262.
11. Ambrose, *Vol. 2*, *op. cit.*, 491; Moldea, *Hoffa Wars*, *op. cit.*, 260–262; Summers and Swan, *Nixon*, *op. cit.*, 398.
12. Summers and Swan, *Nixon*, *op. cit.*, 398
13. Ragano and Raab, *Mob Lawyer*, *op. cit.*, 257–266.
14. *Ibid.*, 257–266.
15. Ambrose, *Vol. 2*, *op. cit.*, 491, 492; Ragano and Raab, *Mob Lawyer*, *op. cit.*, 257–266.
16. Ambrose, *Vol. 2*, *op. cit.*, 491, 492; Moldea, *Hoffa Wars*, *op. cit.*, 292.
17. Moldea, *Hoffa Wars*, *op. cit.*, 263, 264, 292–295, 319–322.
18. Davis, *Kingfish*, *op. cit.*, 398; Summers and Swan, *Nixon*, *op. cit.*, 54, 399.
19. Scheim, *Mafia Killed*, *op. cit.*, 368; Summers and Swan, *Nixon*, *op. cit.*, 525.
20. Summers and Swan, *Nixon*, *op. cit.*, 525; A.J. Weberman at www.ajweberman.com.
21. Moldea, *Hoffa Wars*, *op. cit.*, 321, 322.
22. *Ibid.*, 314, 319, 320.
23. Haldeman, *Diaries*, *op. cit.*, 382; Summers and Swan, *Nixon*, *op. cit.*, 398.
24. Moldea, *Hoffa Wars*, *op. cit.*, 293–295.
25. *Ibid.*, 294.
26. *Ibid.*, 294.
27. Moldea, *Hoffa Wars*, *op. cit.*, 294; Ragano and Raab, *Mob Lawyer*, *op. cit.*, 257–266.
28. *Ibid.*
29. *Ibid.*
30. Moldea, *Hoffa Wars*, *op. cit.*, 321.
31. Gerth, Jeff, "Richard M. Nixon and Organized Crime," reprinted in Blumenthal and Yazijian, *Gunplay*, *op. cit.*, 130–151; Moldea, *Hoffa Wars*, *op. cit.*, 263–265; 292–296; 316–322.
32. Gerth, Jeff, "Richard M. Nixon and Organized Crime," reprinted in Blumenthal and Yazijian, *Gunplay*, *op. cit.*, 130–151; Moldea, *Hoffa Wars*, *op. cit.*, 316.
33. Moldea, *Hoffa Wars*, *op. cit.*, 263, 264, 292–295, 319–322.
34. Moldea, *Hoffa Wars*, *op. cit.*, 263, 264, 292–295, 319–322.
35. Corn, *Blond Ghost*, *op. cit.*, many passages.
36. Corn, *Blond Ghost*, *op. cit.*, many passages; Twyman, Noel, *Bloody Treason* (Rancho Sante Fe, CA: Laurel Publishing, 1997), 467 and others; HSCA vol. X Veciana summary.
37. CIA #104-10098-10093, 10-31-63 AMWORLD Dispatch, declassified 6-20-96; CIA 104-10061-10115, 89–91; CIA 104-10072-102341; HSCA 180-10110-10016, 10–12, 81, 82; Fonzi, *Last Investigation*, *op. cit*, many passages; Hunt and Aunapu, *American Spy*, *op. cit.*, 135; Interview with Antonio Veciana, 6-2-93; HSCA vol. X Veciana summary.
38. Fonzi, *Last Investigation*, *op. cit*, 137; HSCA: 180-10090-10232, *op. cit.*; Hunt and Aunapu, *American Spy*, *op. cit.*, 135; interview with Antonio Veciana, 6-2-93.
39. Church, Senator Frank, *Church Committee: Supplementary Detailed Staff Reports on Foreign and Military Intelligence*, Book IV, (Washington, DC: US Government Printing Office, 1976), 66; Powers, *Helms*, *op. cit.*, 380.
40. Trento, Joseph J., *Secret History*, *op. cit.*, 366–368, 381–392.
41. Author interviews with Harry Williams 4-92, 7-24-93, and others (some via Thom Hartmann).
42. Fonzi, *Last Investigation*, *op. cit.*, 136–138, 272, 273.
43. *Ibid.*, 136–138, 272, 273.
44. Interview with Antonio Veciana, 6-2-93. Veciana had no direct mob ties, but three of Veciana's associates—Eloy Menoyo, Jose Aleman, and Eladio del Valle—had dealings with Santo Trafficante.
45. Fonzi, *Last Investigation*, *op. cit.*, 136–138, 272, 273, 344.
46. *Ibid.*, 136–138, 272, 273.
47. Fonzi, *Last Investigation*, *op. cit*, 136–138, 272, 273; HSCA: 180-10090-10232, *op. cit.*
48. Fonzi, *Last Investigation*, 136–138, 272, 273. Landau, Saul, "Reciprocity!" Progreso-weekly 3-10-10.
49. Landau, Saul, "Reciprocity!" Progreso-weekly 3-10-10; Fonzi 136–138, 272, 273.
50. *Ibid.*
51. Landau, Saul, "Reciprocity!" Progreso-weekly 3-10-10; Fonzi 136–138, 272, 273; interview with Antonio Veciana, 6-2-93.
52. *Ibid.*
53. Ambrose, *Vol. 2*, *op. cit.*, 379; Hersh, Seymour M., *The Price of Power: Kissinger in the Nixon White House* (Summit Books, 1983); Summers and Swan, *Nixon*, *op. cit.*, 508, 509.
54. Ambrose, *Vol. 2*, *op. cit.*, 379; Hersh, *Kissinger*, *op. cit.* The National Security Archive has a huge

amount of documents available online about the efforts of Nixon and the CIA to oust Allende.
55. Summers and Swan, *Nixon*, *op. cit.*, 509.
56. Epstein, *Fear*, *op. cit.*, 177; "Edward Korry, 81, is dead, falsely tied to Chile coup," *New York Times*, 1-30-03.

CHAPTER 28

1. Summers and Swan, *Nixon*, *op. cit.*, 44, 45.
2. Lukas, *Nightmare*, *op. cit.*, many passages; Scott, *Deep Politics II*, *op. cit.*, 68, citing Liddy's *Will*, 407–408; Summers and Swan, *Nixon*, *op. cit.*, many passages.
3. Rosselli memo to Senator Ervin by Lenzner and Lackritz, February 1974—Senate Select Committee on Presidential Campaign Activities (Ervin Committee), staff files; Lenzner to Muse Rosselli Watergate Committee memo, February 1974—Senate Select Committee on Presidential Campaign Activities (Ervin Committee), staff files.
4. Feldstein, *Poisoning*, *op. cit.*, 225; Lukas, *Nightmare*, *op. cit.*, 169, 170, 171; Summers and Swan, *Nixon*, *op. cit.*, 396.
5. Lukas, *Nightmare*, *op. cit.*, 171, 172; Summers and Swan, *Nixon*, *op. cit.*, 396.
6. Summers and Swan, *Nixon*, *op. cit.*, 397.
7. *Ibid.*, 396.
8. Feldstein, *Poisoning*, *op. cit.*, 225; Johnson, Loch, *Season of Inquiry*, *op. cit.*, 162, 179–185; Summers and Swan, *Nixon*, *op. cit.*, 283, 296.
9. Summers and Swan, *Nixon*, *op. cit.*, 395.
10. Lukas, *Nightmare*, *op. cit.*, 141–144.
11. *Ibid.*, 141–144.
12. Hougan, Jim, "Deep Throat, Bob Woodward and the CIA: Strange Bedfellows," Counterpunch magazine, 6-8-05.
13. "2-6-04 Haig on Moorer's death," Morris, *op. cit.*, 196; Haig, *Inner Circles* , *op. cit.*, 256, 257.
14. Califano, *Inside*, *op. cit.*, 109, 226.
15. Lukas, *Nightmare*, *op. cit.*, 210–212; Interview with Tim Gratz 6-06; additional research by Gratz, John Simkin, Pat Speer; also material from the memoirs of Anthony Ulasewicz, 240.
16. Lukas, *Nightmare*, *op. cit.*, 207–216; Keith Olbermann on MSNBC, cited in "Author of *Bush's Brain*," by David Edwards and Muriel Kane, Raw Story website; "Nixon's Revenge" by Joe Canoson, *Salon*, 6-3-05.
17. *NYT*, *Watergate Hearings*, *op. cit.*, 69–71.
18. *NYT*, *Watergate Hearings*, *op. cit.*, 69–71; Summers and Swan, *Nixon*, *op. cit.*, 399, 400.
19. Summers and Swan, *Nixon*, *op. cit.*, 400, 401.
20. *NYT*, *Watergate Hearings*, *op. cit.*, 69–71; Summers and Swan, *Nixon*, *op. cit.*, 400, 401.
21. Lukas, *Nightmare*, *op. cit.*, 187.
22. Common Cause; Dean, *Blind*, *op. cit.*, 39, 40; Hinckle and Turner, *Deadly Secrets*, *op. cit.*, 360.
23. Feldstein, *Poisoning*, *op. cit.*, 226–262.
24. *Ibid.*, 226–262.
25. *Ibid.*, 226–262.
26. Feldstein, *Poisoning*, *op. cit.*, 226–262; Lukas, *Nightmare*, *op. cit.*, 147, 248, 249
27. Feldstein, *Poisoning*, *op. cit.*, 226–262; Lukas, *Nightmare*, *op. cit.*, 248, 249, *NYT*, *Watergate Hearings*, *op. cit.*, 70.
28. *Ibid.*
29. Feldstein, *Poisoning*, *op. cit.*, 268–281.
30. *Ibid.*, 268–281.
31. *Ibid.*, 268–281.
32. *Ibid.*, 268–281.
33. Feldstein, *Poisoning*, *op. cit.*, 268–281.
34. See the so-called CIA "Family Jewels," 21, 27, available in the National Security Archive's Electronic Briefing Book No. 222.
35. Feldstein, *Poisoning*, *op. cit.*, 282–290
36. *Ibid.*, 282–290
37. *Ibid.*, 282–290
38. Feldstein, *Poisoning*, *op. cit.*, 282–290
39. Lukas, *Nightmare*, *op. cit.*, 235–243; *NYT*, *Watergate Hearings*, *op. cit.*, 171–172.
40. *Ibid.*
41. *Ibid.*
42. *Ibid.*
43. *Ibid.*
44. *Ibid.*
45. *Ibid.*
46. *Ibid.*
47. Campbell, Duncan, "Nixon Ordered Watergate, Jailed Former Aide Says," *The Guardian* [UK] 7-28-03; Collins, Dan, "Aide Says Nixon Ordered Watergate," Associated Press 7-27-03, at cbsnews.com; Ifill, Gwen, PBS, Interviews with Jeb Magruder, 7-28-03, and also Ifill, PBS special, *Watergate Plus 30: Shadow of History*, 7-30-03; Lukas, *Nightmare*, *op. cit.*, 251–257; *NYT*, *Watergate Hearings*, *op. cit.*, 246–265.
48. Campbell, *op. cit.*, *Guardian* [UK] 7-28-03; Collins, *op. cit.*, Associated Press 7-27-03; Ifill, PBS, Magruder, *op. cit.*, 7-28-03, and also Ifill, PBS, *Watergate*, *op. cit.*, 7-30-03; Lukas, *Nightmare*, *op. cit.*, 251–257; *NYT*, *Watergate Hearings*, *op. cit.*, 246–265.
49. Campbell, *op. cit.*, *Guardian* [UK] 7-28-03; Collins, *op. cit.*, Associated Press 7-27-03; Ifill, PBS, Magruder, *op. cit.*, 7-28-03, and also Ifill, PBS, *Watergate*, *op. cit.*, 7-30-03; Lukas, *Nightmare*, *op. cit.*, 251–257; *NYT*, *Watergate Hearings*, *op. cit.*, 246–265.
50. Campbell, *op. cit.*, *Guardian* [UK] 7-28-03; Collins, *op. cit.*, Associated Press 7-27-03; Ifill, PBS, Magruder, *op. cit.*, 7-28-03, and also Ifill, PBS, *Watergate*, *op. cit.*, 7-30-03; Lukas, *Nightmare*, *op. cit.*, 251–257; *NYT*, *Watergate Hearings*, *op. cit.*, 246–265.
51. Campbell, *op. cit.*, *Guardian* [UK] 7-28-03; Collins, *op. cit.*, Associated Press 7-27-03; Ifill, PBS, Magruder, *op. cit.*, 7-28-03, and also Ifill, PBS, *Watergate*, *op. cit.*, 7-30-03; Lukas, *Nightmare*, *op. cit.*, 251–257; *NYT*, *Watergate Hearings*, *op. cit.*, 246–265.
52. Campbell, *op. cit.*, *Guardian* [UK] 7-28-03; Collins, *op. cit.*, Associated Press 7-27-03; Ifill, PBS, Magruder, *op. cit.*, 7-28-03, and also Ifill, PBS, *Watergate*, *op. cit.*, 7-30-03; Lukas, *Nightmare*, *op. cit.*, 251–257; *NYT*, *Watergate Hearings*, *op. cit.*, 246–265.
53. Lukas, *Nightmare*, *op. cit.*, 256, 257; Summers and Swan, *Nixon*, *op. cit.*, 402.
54. Lukas, *Nightmare*, *op. cit.*, 256, 257; Summers and Swan, *Nixon*, *op. cit.*, 402.
55. With lawyerly caution, Dean also added, ". . . I have never seen a scintilla of evidence that Nixon knew about the plans for the Watergate break-in," Campbell, *op. cit.*, *Guardian* [UK] 7-28-03; Collins, *op. cit.*, Associated Press 7-27-03; Ifill, PBS Magruder, *op. cit.*, 7-28-03, and also Ifill, PBS *Watergate*, *op. cit.*, 7-30-03; Lukas, *Nightmare*, *op. cit.*, 251–257; *NYT*, *Watergate Hearings*, *op.*

cit., 69-71, 246–265; Summers and Swan, *Nixon, op. cit.*, 402.
56. Bernstein and Woodward, *All the President's Men, op. cit.*, 128, 129; Summers and Swan, *Nixon, op. cit.*, 402.
57. Bernstein and Woodward, *All the President's Men, op. cit.*, 128, 129; Feldstein, *Poisoning, op. cit.*, 282–290.
58. Summers and Swan, *Nixon, op. cit.*, 403, 448.
59. *Ibid.*
60. Rosen, *Strong Man, op. cit.*, 466, 467; Summers and Swan, *Nixon, op. cit.*, 197.
61. Campbell, *op. cit., Guardian* [UK] 7-28-03; Collins, *op. cit.*, Associated Press 7-27-03; Ifill, PBS Magruder, *op. cit.*, 7-28-03, and also Ifill, PBS *Watergate, op. cit.*, 7-30-03; Lukas, *Nightmare, op. cit.*, many passages; Senate Watergate Report, many passages; Summers and Swan, *Nixon, op. cit.*, many passages.
62. Kutler *Tapes, op. cit.*, 548, 549.
63. *Ibid.*, 548, 549.

CHAPTER 29

1. 6-22-72 FBI memo, from Bebe Rebozo files (Part 6, p. 1) online at fbi.gov. Ambrose, *Vol. 2, op. cit.*, several passages.
2. Feldstein, *Poisoning, op. cit.*, 228–275, 309, 409.
3. Bebe Rebozo FBI files, Parts 5 and 6, at fbi.gov.
4. Lukas, *Nightmare, op. cit.*, 193, 194, 258; *NYT, Watergate Hearings, op. cit.*, 71, 72.
5. Lukas, *Nightmare, op. cit.*, 216–223.
6. Bernstein and Woodward, *All the President's Men, op. cit.*, 127, 128, 129; Lukas, *Nightmare, op. cit.*, 216–223.
7. Emery, *Watergate, op. cit.*, 114; Lukas, *Nightmare, op. cit.*, 223; *NYT, Watergate Hearings, op. cit.*, 70, 71.
8. Frank Sturgis interview by Andrew St. George, *True* magazine, *op. cit.*; Hedegaard, Erik, "The Last Confessions of E. Howard Hunt," *Rolling Stone*, 3-23-07; Hunt and Risc, *Warrior, op. cit.*, 127.
9. Lukas, *Nightmare, op. cit.*, 258; Szulc, Tad, *Compulsive Spy: The Strange Career of E. Howard Hunt* (New York: Viking Press, 1974), several passages; Hinckle and Turner, *Deadly Secrets, op. cit.*, several passages; Anthony and Robbyn Summers, "The Ghosts of November," *Vanity Fair*, 12-94.
10. Rosen, *Strong Man, op. cit.*, 281–286.
11. Emery, *Watergate, op. cit.*, 112, 113, *NYT, Watergate Hearings, op. cit.*, 70; Rosen, *Strong Man, op. cit.*, 281–286.
12. Hougan, *Agenda, op. cit.*, 109, 110; Summers and Swan, *Nixon, op. cit.*, 185.
13. CIA 104-100096-10131; Hougan, *Agenda, op. cit.*, 109, 110; Summers and Swan, *Nixon, op. cit.*, 185; 6-26-72 FBI memo Miami 139-328 Hunt Artime call.
14. Lesar, James, "Valenti/Helms Plan for CIA Television Show," *op. cit.*; CIA files cited by Freedom of Information attorney James Lesar.
15. Lesar, *"Valenti," op. cit.*
16. Lesar, *"Valenti," op. cit.*
17. Powers, *Helms, op. cit.*, 282, 283.
18. *Ibid.*, 282, 283.
19. Summers, *Official: Hoover, op. cit.*, 417, 418.
20. *Ibid.*, 423, 424.
21. Emery, *Watergate, op. cit.*, 114; Official 423.
22. Summers, *Official: Hoover, op. cit.*, 424–426; Emery, *Watergate, op. cit.*, 114, 115.
23. Lukas, *Nightmare, op. cit.*, 266
24. Emery, *Watergate, op. cit.*, 115; Summers and Swan, *Nixon, op. cit.*, 404; additional research by John Simkin at www.spartacus.schoolnet.co.uk.
25. Summers and Swan, *Nixon, op. cit.*, 404, 405; Lukas, *Nightmare, op. cit.*, 265, 266.
26. Emery, *Watergate, op. cit.*, 115, 116; Lukas, *Nightmare, op. cit.*, 226–228, 265, 266; Summers and Swan, *Nixon, op. cit.*, 404, 405.
27. Emery, *Watergate, op. cit.*, 115, 116; Summers and Swan, *Nixon, op. cit.*, 277, 356, 357.
28. Ellsberg, Daniel, on MSNBC *Today* with Dylan Ratigan, 6-11-10; Wells, Tom, *Wild Man, op. cit.*, 497, 502.
29. Wells, Tom. *Wild Man, op. cit.*, 497, 502; Deposition of G. Gordon Liddy in Hunt vs. A.J. Weberman.
30. Hinckle and Turner, *Deadly Secrets, op. cit.*, 356.
31. Sheridan, *Rise of Hoffa, op. cit.*, 9.
32. Sheridan, *Rise of Hoffa, op. cit.*, many passages; Moldea, *Hoffa Wars, op. cit.*, 263, 264, 292–295, 319–322.
33. Sheridan, *Rise of Hoffa, op. cit.*, xi–xvii.
34. Moldea, *Hoffa Wars, op. cit.*, 108.
35. Sheridan, *Rise of Hoffa, op. cit.*, 5, 159.
36. Memo to FBI Director, FBI HQ 124-10292-10149; Woodward and Bernstein, *Final Days, op. cit.*, 307.
37. Weiner, Tim, "In Tapes, Nixon Muses About Break-Ins at Foreign Embassies," *The New York Times*, 2-26-99; 8-17-73.
38. Blumenthal and Yazijian, *Gunplay, op. cit.* 97-99; Lukas, *Nightmare, op. cit.*, 266; memo to FBI Director, FBI HQ 124-10292-10149.
39. Blumenthal and Yazijian, *Gunplay, op. cit.* 97-99; Lukas, *Nightmare, op. cit.*, 266; memo to FBI Director, FBI HQ 124-10292-10149; HSCA 180-10144-10219.
40. 8-17-73 memo to FBI Director, FBI HQ 124-10292-10149.
41. Blumenthal and Yazijian, *Gunplay, op. cit.* 98-99; Weiner, Tim, "In Tapes, Nixon Muses About Break-Ins at Foreign Embassies," *NYT*, 2-26-99.
42. Blumenthal and Yazijian, *Gunplay, op. cit.*, 93-100.
43. CIA IG File #18 Tab #1, cited by A. J. Weberman; Rappleye and Becker, *All American, op. cit.*, 307; Frank Sturgis interview by Andrew St. George, *True* magazine, *op. cit.*; Rosselli memo to Senator Ervin by Lenzner and Lackritz, February 1974—Senate Select Committee on Presidential Campaign Activities (Ervin Committee), staff files; Lenzner to Muse Rosselli Watergate Committee memo, February 1974—Senate Select Committee on Presidential Campaign Activities (Ervin Committee), staff files.
44. Frank Sturgis interview by Andrew St. George, *True* magazine, *op. cit.*
45. HSCA: 180-10090-10232, *op. cit.*; St. George, Andrew, Frank Sturgis (Fiorini) interview, *True* magazine, *op. cit.*
46. HSCA: 180-10090-10232, *op. cit.*; St. George, Andrew, Frank Sturgis (Fiorini) interview, *True* magazine, *op. cit.*
47. HSCA: 180-10090-10232, *op. cit.*; St. George, Andrew, Frank Sturgis (Fiorini) interview, *True* magazine, *op. cit.*

48. HSCA: 180-10090-10232, *op. cit.*
49. 8-17-73 memo to FBI Director, FBI HQ 124-10292-10149; St. George, Andrew, Frank Sturgis (Fiorini) interview, *True* magazine, *op. cit.*
50. HSCA: 180-10090-10232, HSCA Lopez Mexico City Report, many passages.
51. HSCA: 180-10090-10232.
52. Summers and Swan, *Nixon*, *op. cit.*, 197.
53. Hougan, *Agenda*, *op. cit.*, 8.
54. Kaiser, *Road to Dallas*, *op. cit.*, 53.
55. Woodward and Bernstein, *Final Days*, *op. cit.*, 307; Shudel, Matt, "Top D.C. Lawyer Secured Hoffa Conviction, Nixon's Pardon," *Washington Post* 11-19-2009; Weiner, Tim, "In Tapes, Nixon Muses About Break-Ins at Foreign Embassies," *NYT*, 2-26-99.
56. Author interviews with Harry Williams 4-92, 7-24-93, and others (some via Thom Hartmann).
57. Frank Sturgis interview by Andrew St. George, *True* magazine, *op. cit.*; Rappleye and Becker, *All American*, *op. cit.*, 307; Frank Sturgis interview by Andrew St. George, *True* magazine, *op. cit.*; Rosselli memo to Senator Ervin by Lenzner and Lackritz, February 1974—Senate Select Committee on Presidential Campaign Activities (Ervin Committee), staff files; Lenzner to Muse Rosselli Watergate Committee memo, February 1974—Senate Select Committee on Presidential Campaign Activities (Ervin Committee), staff files.
58. Church, *Book IV*, *op. cit.*, 148.
59. *NBC Nightly News* with Tom Brokaw 9-29-98; "A Presumption of Disclosure: Lessons from the John F. Kennedy Assassination Records Review Board," report by OMB Watch, 2000, at www.ombwatch.org; "'Denied in Full': Federal Judges Grill CIA Lawyers on JFK Secrets," *Huffington Post*, 10-22-07.
60. Memo to FBI Director, FBI HQ 124-10292-10149, 8-17-73.
61. Blumenthal and Yazijian, *Gunplay*, *op. cit.* 97–99.
62. Some accounts give the date for the break-in at Shriver's firm as May 15, 1972. Memo to FBI Director, FBI HQ 124-10292-10149, 8-17-73; Blumenthal and Yazijian, *Gunplay*, *op. cit.* 100, 101; Lukas, *Nightmare*, *op. cit.*, 266; Summers and Swan, *Nixon*, *op. cit.*, 527.
63. HSCA: 180-10090-10232, *op. cit.*
64. CIA IG Report, 1967, *op. cit.*; Summers and Swan, *Nixon*, *op. cit.*, 197, 888.
65. CIA IG Report, 1967, *op. cit.*; Summers and Swan, *Nixon*, *op. cit.*, 197, 888. Rosselli memo to Senator Ervin by Lenzner and Lackritz, February 1974—Senate Select Committee on Presidential Campaign Activities (Ervin Committee), staff files; Lenzner to Muse Rosselli Watergate Committee memo, February 1974—Senate Select Committee on Presidential Campaign Activities (Ervin Committee), staff files.
66. HSCA: 180-10090-10232, *op. cit.*

CHAPTER 30

1. St. George, Andrew, Frank Sturgis (Fiorini) interview, *True* magazine, *op. cit.*
2. Parker, Gretchen, "Liddy Testifies in Defamation Case," Associated Press, 7-1-02.
3. Blumenthal and Yazijian, *Gunplay*, *op. cit.* 57–67; Summers and Swan, *Nixon*, *op. cit.*, 405, 406.
4. Blumenthal and Yazijian, *Gunplay*, *op. cit.* 57–67; Summers and Swan, *Nixon*, *op. cit.*, 405, 406.
5. Blumenthal and Yazijian, *Gunplay*, *op. cit.* 57–67; Parry, *Secrecy and Privilege*, *op. cit.*, several passages; Summers and Swan, *Nixon*, *op. cit.*, 405, 406.
6. Parry, *Secrecy and Privilege*, *op. cit.*, 29.
7. Summers and Swan, *Nixon*, *op. cit.*, 408.
8. Parry, *Secrecy and Privilege*, *op. cit.*, 28–40.
9. *Ibid.*, 28–40.
10. Lesar, "*Valenti*," *op. cit.*
11. Lesar, "*Valenti*," *op. cit.*
12. For the McGovern-Castro cover story, see the Watergate testimony of all the Cuban exile burglars, such as Barker to the Senate Watergate Committee on 5-24-73.
13. Emery, *Watergate*, *op. cit.*, 112, 113; Epstein, *Fear*, *op. cit.*, 236; Hunt and Aunapu, *op. cit.*, 157; *NYT*, *Watergate Hearings*, *op. cit.*, 855; *NYT*, *Watergate Hearings*, *op. cit.*, 602–607; Kaiser, *Road to Dallas*, *op. cit.*, 430; Gonzalez has been identified in photos with John Martino, during the Rosselli-Pawley operation, though he has not acknowledged his participation.
14. Martinez, Eugenio, article, *Harper's*, *op. cit.*
15. St. George, Andrew. Frank Sturgis (Fiorini) interview, *True* magazine, *op. cit.*
16. Hunt and Aunapu, *American Spy*, *op. cit.*, 218.
17. Emery, *Watergate*, *op. cit.*, 118–122; Hougan, *Agenda*, *op. cit.*, 140–152; Summers and Swan, *Nixon*, *op. cit.*, 409; Martinez, Eugenio, article, *Harper's*, *op. cit.*
18. Emery, *Watergate*, *op. cit.*, 118–122; Hougan, *Agenda*, *op. cit.*, 140–152; Summers and Swan, *Nixon*, *op. cit.*,409; Martinez, Eugenio, article, *Harper's*, *op. cit.*
19. Hougan, *op. cit.*, 140–152.
20. Emery, *Watergate*, *op. cit.*, 118–122; Hougan, *Agenda*, *op. cit.*, 140–152; Lukas, *Nightmare*, *op. cit.*, 269, 270.
21. Emery, *Watergate*, *op. cit.*, 118–122; Hougan, *Agenda*, *op. cit.*, 140–152; Lukas, *Nightmare*, *op. cit.*, 269, 270; Martinez, Eugenio, article, *Harper's*, *op. cit.*
22. Emery, *Watergate*, *op. cit.*, 18–122; Hougan, *Agenda*, *op. cit.*, 140–152; Summers and Swan, *Nixon*, 409; Martinez, Eugenio, article, *Harper's*, *op. cit.*
23. Emery, *Watergate*, *op. cit.*, 118–122; Hougan, *Agenda*, *op. cit.*, 140–152; Lukas, *Nightmare*, *op. cit.*, 269–271; Summers and Swan, *Nixon*, *op. cit.*, 409; Martinez, Eugenio, article, *Harper's*, *op. cit.*
24. Emery, *Watergate*, *op. cit.*, 118–122; Hougan, *Agenda*, *op. cit.*, 140–152; Lukas, *Nightmare*, *op. cit.*, 269–271; Summers and Swan, *Nixon*, *op. cit.*, 409; Martinez, Eugenio, article, *Harper's*, *op. cit.*
25. Emery, *Watergate*, *op. cit.*, 118–122; Hougan, *Agenda*, *op. cit.*, 140–152; Lukas, *Nightmare*, *op. cit.*, 269–271; Summers and Swan, *Nixon*, *op. cit.*, 409; Martinez, Eugenio, article, *Harper's*, *op. cit.*
26. Emery, *Watergate*, *op. cit.*, 118–122; Hougan, *Agenda*, *op. cit.*, 140–152; Hunt and Aunapu, *American Spy*, *op. cit.*, 212–216; Martinez article; Summers and Swan, *Nixon*, *op. cit.*, 409; St. George, Frank Sturgis (Fiorini) interview, *True* magazine, *op. cit.*
27. Emery, *Watergate*, *op. cit.*, 118–122; Hougan, *Agenda*, *op. cit.*, 140–152; Hunt and Aunapu, *American Spy*, *op. cit.*, 212–216; Summers, *op. cit.*, 409; Martinez, Eugenio, article, *Harper's*, *op. cit.*

28. Hunt and Aunapu, *American Spy, op. cit.*, 219; Lukas, *Nightmare, op. cit.*, 226–228.
29. Emery, *Watergate, op. cit.*, 127, 128; Hougan, *Agenda, op. cit.*, 156, 157; Hunt and Aunapu, *American Spy, op. cit.*, 220; Lukas, *Nightmare, op. cit.*, 273; Martinez, Eugenio, article, *Harper's, op. cit.*
30. Emery, *Watergate, op. cit.*, 127, 128; Hougan, *Agenda, op. cit.*, 156, 157; Hunt and Aunapu, *American Spy, op. cit.*, 220; Lukas, *Nightmare, op. cit.*, 273; Martinez, Eugenio, article, *Harper's, op. cit.*
31. Emery, *Watergate, op. cit.*,127, 128; Hougan, *Agenda, op. cit.*, 156, 157; Hunt and Aunapu, *American Spy, op. cit.*, 220; Lukas, *Nightmare, op. cit.*, 273; Martinez, Eugenio, article, *Harper's, op. cit.*
32. Emery, *Watergate, op. cit.*, 127, 128; Hougan, *Agenda, op. cit.*, 156, 157; Hunt and Aunapu, *American Spy, op. cit.*, 220; Lukas, *Nightmare, op. cit.*, 273; Martinez, Eugenio, article, *Harper's, op. cit.*
33. FBI memo 6-26-72 about early June visit to Artime by Hunt, Miami 139–328.
34. CIA memo 10-19-72 HSCA 180-10142-10307; Haynes Johnson, *Sleepwalking Through History* (New York: W. W. Norton, 2003), 270, 271; Valentine, Douglas. *The Strength of the Pack: The Personalities, Politics, and Espionage Intrigues That Shaped the DEA* (Walterville, Oregon: Trine Day, 2009), 198, 473.
35. McCoy, Alfred W. *The Politics of Heroin* (Chicago, Illinois: Lawrence Hill Books, 1991), xvii.
36. *Ibid.*, xvii
37. Hougan, *Agenda, op. cit.*, 155.
38. Summers and Swan, *Nixon, op. cit.*, 532
39. Emery, *Watergate, op. cit.*, 122–125; Hougan, *Agenda, op. cit.*, 163–165.; Parry, *Secrecy and Privilege, op. cit.*, 30–40; Summers and Swan, *Nixon, op. cit.*, 410.
40. Emery, *Watergate, op. cit.*, 122–125; Hougan, *Agenda, op. cit.*, 163–165; Parry, *Secrecy and Privilege, op. cit.*, 30–40.
41. Emery, *Watergate, op. cit.*, 122–125; Hougan, *Agenda, op. cit.*, 163–165; Parry, *Secrecy and Privilege, op. cit.*, 30–40.
42. Califano, *Inside, op. cit.*, 246–255; Emery, *Watergate, op. cit.*, 122–125.
43. Summers and Swan, *Nixon, op. cit.*, 410, 411, 528.
44. *Ibid.*, 410, 411, 528.
45. Emery, *Watergate, op. cit.*, 125–127; Hunt and Aunapu, *American Spy, op. cit.*, 221–224.
46. Hougan, *Agenda, op. cit.*, 152.
47. Emery, *Watergate, op. cit.*, 125–127; Hunt and Aunapu, *American Spy, op. cit.*, 221–224.
48. See Emery, *Watergate, op. cit.*, several passages and Lukas, *Nightmare, op. cit.*, several passages.
49. Emery, *Watergate, op. cit.*, 125.
50. Emery, *Watergate, op. cit.*, 127, 128.

CHAPTER 31

1. Emery, *Watergate, op. cit.*, 129.
2. Martinez, Eugenio, article, *Harper's, op. cit.*
3. Feldstein, *Poisoning, op. cit.*, 293, 294.
4. *Ibid.*, 293, 294.
5. Emery, *Watergate, op. cit.*, 130; Martinez, Eugenio, article, *Harper's, op. cit.*
6. Hougan, *Agenda, op. cit.*, 188, 189.
7. Emery, *Watergate, op. cit.*, 131, 132.
8. Emery, *Watergate, op. cit.*, 130–142; Hougan, *Agenda, op. cit.*, 189–204.
9. Emery, *Watergate, op. cit.*, 130–142; Hougan, *Agenda, op. cit.*, 189–204.
10. Emery, *Watergate, op. cit.*, 130–142; Hougan, *Agenda, op. cit.*, 189–204.
11. Emery, *Watergate, op. cit.*, 130–142; Hougan, *Agenda, op. cit.*, 189–204.
12. St. George, Frank Sturgis (Fiorini) interview, *True* magazine, *op. cit.*
13. Emery, *Watergate, op. cit.*, 130–142; Hougan, *Agenda, op. cit.*, 189–204.
14. Emery, *Watergate, op. cit.*, 130–142; Hougan, *Agenda, op. cit.*, 189–204; Martinez, Eugenio, article, *Harper's, op. cit.*
15. Emery, *Watergate, op. cit.*, 194; Hougan, *Agenda, op. cit.*, 203, 204.
16. Hougan, *Agenda, op. cit.*, 203, 204, 214, 217.
17. Hougan, *Agenda, op. cit.*, 203, 204, 214, 217; Lukas, *Nightmare, op. cit.*, 287.
18. Hougan, *Agenda, op. cit.*, 203, 204, 214, 217; Summers and Swan, *Nixon, op. cit.*, 527, 528.
19. Hougan, *Agenda, op. cit.*, 203–227; Summers and Swan, *Nixon, op. cit.*, 527, 528.
20. Hougan, *Agenda, op. cit.*, 18.
21. Hougan, *Agenda, op. cit.*, 18; Final Report of the Senate Watergate Committee (Senate Select Committee on Presidential Campaign Activities), 1138, 1163
22. Hougan, *Agenda, op. cit.*, 226, 227.
23. Hougan, *Agenda, op. cit.*, 218; Weiner, Tim. "In Tapes, Nixon Muses About Break-Ins at Foreign Embassies," *NYT*, 2-26-99.
24. Hougan, *Agenda, op. cit.*, 215–220; Lukas, *Nightmare, op. cit.*, 284, 285.
25. Scott, Hoch, Stetler, eds., *The Assassinations, op. cit.*, 99; Thomas, *Man to See, op. cit.*, 269, 270.
26. Califano, *Inside, op. cit.*, 307, 308; Thomas, *Man to See, op. cit.*, 269–272.
27. Califano, *Inside, op. cit.*, 307, 308.
28. Emery, *Watergate, op. cit.*, 141; Hougan, *Agenda, op. cit.*, 214–217; Woodward, *Secret Man, op. cit.*, 53–55.
29. John Simkin, Watergate article at the British educational website www.spartacus.schoolnet.co.uk; Woodward, *Secret Man, op. cit.*, 53–55.
30. Woodward, *Secret Man, op. cit.*, 53–58.
31. *Ibid.*, 53–58.
32. *Ibid.*, 53–58.
33. Hougan, *Agenda, op. cit.*, 264, 265, 329–335.
34. Final Report of the Senate Select Committee on Presidential Campaign Activities, 1974, 1123–1128; Hougan, *Agenda, op. cit.*, 264, 265, 329–335.
35. Hougan, *Agenda, op. cit.*, 264, 265, 329–335.
36. Davis, Deborah, *Katharine, op. cit.*, 134.
37. Emery, *Watergate, op. cit.*, 139.
38. Emery, *Watergate, op. cit.*, 139–142; Hougan, *Agenda, op. cit.*, 214–217.
39. Emery, *Watergate, op. cit.*, 139–147.
40. Emery, *Watergate, op. cit.*, 148–158; Nixon, *Memoirs, op. cit.*, 625; Summers and Swan, *Nixon, op. cit.*, 427, 428.
41. Emery, *Watergate, op. cit.*, 149, 150.
42. Emery, *Watergate, op. cit.*, 152, 153; Summers and Swan, *Nixon, op. cit.*, 428.
43. Feldstein, *Poisoning, op. cit.*, 294, 295.
44. Author's phone interview with Carl Shoffler 12-14-93; Fensterwald and Ewing, *Coincidence,*

op. cit., 505, 506; Memo to FBI Director, FBI 124-10289-10440, 6-28-72.

45. "Bebe Rebozo" FBI files; Memo to FBI Director, FBI 124-10289-10440, 6-28-72; *NYT*, *Watergate Hearings*, *op. cit.*, 75.
46. Emery, *Watergate*, *op. cit.*, 158.
47. Emery, *Watergate*, *op. cit.*, 152; *NYT*, *Watergate Hearings*, *op. cit.*, 75, 76.
48. Emery, *Watergate*, *op. cit.*, 161, 162; *NYT*, *Watergate Hearings*, *op. cit.*, 75, 76.
49. Emery, *Watergate*, *op. cit.*, 162.
50. Bernstein and Woodward, "GOP Security Aide among Five Arrested in Bugging Affair," *Washington Post* 6-19-72.
51. Califano, *Inside*, *op. cit.*, 268–270.
52. Staff writer, "White House Consultant Linked to Bugging Suspects," *Washington Post*, 6-20-72, via the Post Wire Service in the 6-20-72 *Tri City Herald*. As of 4-19-12, the original article was not available in *The Washington Post's* online archive.
53. *NYT* News Service article carried by the Miami News, 6-20-72.
54. Summers and Swan, *Nixon*, *op. cit.*, 428.
55. Emery, *Watergate*, *op. cit.*, 173, 174; Summers and Swan, *Nixon*, *op. cit.*, 428, 429, 430, 531, 532.
56. Haldeman, *Diaries*, *op. cit.*, 473; Kutler, *Tapes*, *op. cit.*, 47; Moldea, *Hoffa Wars*, *op. cit.*, 315; Summers and Swan, *Nixon*, *op. cit.*, 428, 429, 430, 531, 532.
57. Kutler, *Tapes*, *op. cit.*, 47–49.
58. Emery, *Watergate*, *op. cit.*, 181; Summers and Swan, *Nixon*, *op. cit.*, 430.
59. Haldeman, H.R., and Joseph DiMona. *The Ends of Power* (New York: Dell Books, 1978), 50–53; Summers and Swan, *Nixon*, *op. cit.*, 430, 431.
60. Haldeman and DiMona, *Ends*, *op. cit.*, 50–53; Summers and Swan, *Nixon*, *op. cit.*, 430, 431.
61. Haldeman and DiMona, *Ends*, *op. cit.*, 52; Memo to Sam Ervin about Johnny Rosselli from Terry Lenzner and Marc Lackritz, 2-74.
62. Haldeman and DiMona, *Ends*, *op. cit.*, 50–53.
63. Kutler, *Tapes*, *op. cit.*, 49–55.
64. Hunt and Aunapu, *American Spy*, *op. cit.*, 97, 143, 144.
65. Feldstein, *Poisoning*, *op. cit.*, 294, 295; Kutler, *Tapes*, *op. cit.*, 64; Summers and Swan, *Nixon*, *op. cit.*, 444.
66. Feldstein, *Poisoning*, *op. cit.*, 294, 295; Kutler, *Tapes*, *op. cit.*, 64.
67. Emery, *Watergate*, *op. cit.*, 185, 186.
68. *Ibid.*, 170, 182–190.
69. *Ibid.*, 170, 182–190.
70. Emery, *Watergate*, *op. cit.*, 189–194; Kutler, *Tapes*, *op. cit.*, 67–70.
71. Emery, *Watergate*, *op. cit.*, 189–194; Kutler, *Tapes*, *op. cit.*, 67–70.
72. Emery, *Watergate*, *op. cit.*, 189–194; Kutler, *Tapes*, *op. cit.*, 67–70.
73. Emery, *Watergate*, *op. cit.*, 189–194; Kutler, *Tapes*, *op. cit.*, 67–70.
74. Emery, *Watergate*, *op. cit.*, 189–194; Kutler, *Tapes*, *op. cit.*, 67–70, 468.
75. Summers and Swan, *Nixon*, *op. cit.*, 432.
76. Ewing, Mike, Memo: "E. Howard Hunt's Missing Report on Assassination," HSCA 180-10112-10479; Kutler, *Tapes*, *op. cit.*, 529.
77. Haldeman and DiMona, *Ends*, *op. cit.*, 67–70.
78. *Ibid.*, 67, 68.
79. *Ibid.*, 67, 68.
80. Haldeman and DiMona, *Ends*, *op. cit.*; 67, 70; Powers, *Man Who Kept Secrets*, *op. cit.*, 302.
81. Haldeman and DiMona, *Ends*, *op. cit.*, 67, 68.
82. Summers and Swan, *Nixon*, *op. cit.*, 432, 533.

CHAPTER 32

1. Morley, Jefferson, "Watergate's Final Mystery," *Salon* 5-5-12 says that "the JFK Assassination Records Collection at the National Archives contains 366 pages of CIA documents on Howard Hunt that have never been made public." There could be far more, under the "Mr. Edward/Don Eduardo" cover identity Hunt used for his anti-Castro work. *NBC Nightly News* with Tom Brokaw 9-29-98; "A Presumption of Disclosure: Lessons from the John F. Kennedy Assassination Records Review Board," report by OMB Watch, 2000, at ombwatch.org; "'Denied in Full': Federal Judges Grill CIA Lawyers on JFK Secrets," *Huffington Post*, 10-22-07. Bernard Barker's 1978 HSCA testimony is still withheld in full, even though those of Helms and Hunt have been released.
2. Emery, *Watergate*, *op. cit.*, 195; *NYT*, *Watergate Hearings*, *op. cit.*, 82, 83.
3. Kutler, *Tapes*, *op. cit.*, 111
4. Kutler, *Tapes*, *op. cit.*, 79, 91, 111, 167, 255. While Ellsberg would not have referred to Frances FitzGerald as his "girlfriend," that would probably have been the view of those hearing about the friendship in Vietnam. It's also possible that Nixon's comment about Ellsberg's girlfiend could have been a reference to someone else.
5. Lukas, *Nightmare*, *op. cit.*, 377.
6. Ambrose, Stephen, *Nixon, Vol. 3: Ruin and Recovery* (New York: Simon & Schuster, 1991), 82, 83; Fensterwald and Ewing, *op. cit.*, 161, 513–519; Ifill, PBS, Magruder, *op. cit.*, 7-28-03, and also Ifill, PBS, *Watergate*, *op. cit.*, 7-30-03; Johnson, Haynes. *Sleepwalking Through History* (New York: W. W. Norton, 2003), 270, 271; Kutler, *Tapes*, *op. cit.*, 252; "Guns, Drugs, and the CIA," from PBS, air date 5-17-88.
7. Emery, *Watergate*, *op. cit.*, 200.
8. Emery, *Watergate*, *op. cit.*, 200; 201; *NYT*, *Watergate Hearings*, *op. cit.*, 82.
9. Bernstein and Woodward, *All the President's Men*, *op. cit.*, 30; Fulsom, *op. cit.*; Magruder, *op. cit.*, 253, 266; *NYT*, *Watergate Hearings*, *op. cit.*, 78.
10. Emery, *Watergate*, *op. cit.*, 196–199; Magruder, *op. cit.*, 270, 271.
11. Emery, *Watergate*, *op. cit.*, 196–199; *NYT*, *Watergate Hearings*, *op. cit.*, 82–85.
12. Summers and Swan, *Nixon*, *op. cit.*, 434, 435.
13. Blumenthal and Yazijian, *op. cit.*, 102; Summers and Swan, *Nixon*, *op. cit.*, 434, 435.
14. *NYT*, *Watergate Hearings*, *op. cit.*, 84; Summers and Swan, *Nixon*, *op. cit.*, 21, 22, 434, 435.
15. Kutler, *Tapes*, *op. cit.*, many passages; St. George, Andrew. Frank Sturgis (Fiorini) interview, *True* magazine, *op. cit.*
16. St. George, Andrew. Frank Sturgis (Fiorini) interview, *True* magazine, *op. cit.*; Simkin, John. Watergate error-analysis article at the British educational website www.spartacus.schoolnet.co.uk.
17. Kutler, *Tapes*, *op. cit.*, 76.
18. *Ibid.*, 535.

19. Kutler, *Tapes,* 184, 229.
20. Kutler, *Tapes, op. cit.,* xiii–xxiii for overview, many other passages.
21. Bernstein and Woodward, *All the President's Men, op. cit.,* 45, 133, 316; Summers and Swan, *Nixon, op. cit.,* 436.
22. Bernstein and Woodward, *All the President's Men, op. cit.,* 45, Califano, *Inside, op. cit.,* 264–266; Kutler, *Tapes, op. cit.,* 106, 107.
23. Califano, *Inside, op. cit.,* 263–266.
24. Talbot, *Brothers, op. cit.,* 312, 313.
25. Epstein, Edward Jay. "Did the Press Uncover Watergate?" *Commentary* July 1974.
26. Blumenthal and Yazijian, *Gunplay, op. cit.,* 132, 133.
27. Califano, *Inside, op. cit.,* 269–275.
28. *Ibid.,* 269–275.
29. Califano, *Inside, op. cit.,* 269–287; Kutler, *Tapes, op. cit.,* 63, 64.
30. Summers and Swan, *Nixon, op. cit.,* 436, 437.
31. *NYT, Watergate Hearings, op. cit.,* 84, 85.
32. Lukas, *Nightmare, op. cit.,* 370, 371.
33. Shepard, Alicia C. "Woodward and Bernstein Uncovered." 9-1-03; Obst, Mark. *Too Good to Be Forgotten.*
34. Emery, *Watergate, op. cit.,* 222; Shepard, *op. cit.;* Obst, *op. cit.*
35. Lukas, *Nightmare, op. cit.,* 371–374.
36. Kutler, *Tapes, op. cit.,* 170–172.
37. *Ibid.,* 170–172.
38. *Ibid.,* 170–172.
39. Kutler, *Tapes, op. cit.,* 170–172; Mann, James, "Deep Throat," *The Atlantic,* 5-92; cited by Max Holland at Washington Decoded.
40. Lukas, *Nightmare, op. cit.,* 373, 374.
41. *Ibid.,* 374–376.
42. *NYT, Watergate Hearings, op. cit.,* 91; Powers, *Helms, op. cit.,* 277.
43. Califano, *Inside, op. cit.,* 277, 278.
44. Emery, *Watergate, op. cit.,* 225.
45. Summers and Swan, *Nixon, op. cit.,* 435; Lukas, *Nightmare, op. cit.,* 374.
46. Powers, *Helms, op. cit.,* 277–281.
47. *Ibid.,* 277–281.
48. *Ibid.,* 277–281.
49. *Ibid.,* 277–281

CHAPTER 33

1. Haig, *Inner, op. cit.,* 314; *NYT, Watergate Hearings, op. cit.,* 124.
2. Emery, *Watergate, op. cit.,* 231; Haig, *Inner, op. cit.,* 315; Lukas, *Nightmare, op. cit.,* 329, 379.
3. Sheridan, *Rise of Hoffa, op. cit.*
4. "US arrests aide of Jack Anderson," *New York Post,* 1-31-73; Feldstein, Mark, *Poisoning, op. cit.,* 313–317.
5. Lukas, *Nightmare, op. cit.,* 376, 377; Moldea, *Hoffa Wars, op. cit.,* 316–320; Sheridan, *Rise of Hoffa, op. cit.,* 533.
6. Lukas, *Nightmare, op. cit.,* 376, 377; Moldea, *Hoffa Wars, op. cit.,* 316–320.
7. Lukas, *Nightmare, op. cit.,* 376, 377; Moldea, *Hoffa Wars, op. cit.,* 316–320.
8. Lukas, *Nightmare, op. cit.,* 376, 377; Moldea, *Hoffa Wars, op. cit.,* 316–320.
9. Moldea, *Hoffa Wars, op. cit.,* 316–320; Scheim, *Mafia Killed, op. cit.,* 368; Summers and Swan, *Nixon, op. cit.,* 525.
10. Moldea, *Hoffa Wars, op. cit.,* 316–320; Scheim, *Mafia Killed, op. cit.,* 368; Summers and Swan, *Nixon, op. cit.,* 525.
11. Scheim, *Mafia Killed, op. cit.,* 368.
12. Lukas, *Nightmare, op. cit.,* 353, 354; *NYT, Watergate Hearings, op. cit.,* 818; Scott, *Deep Politics, op. cit.,* 306.
13. Hougan, *Agenda, op. cit.,* 125, 126; Hunt and Aunapu, *American Spy, op. cit.,* 263–268; Lukas, *Nightmare, op. cit.,* 353, 354, 379, 504.
14. Hougan, *Agenda, op. cit.,* 125, 126; Hunt and Aunapu, *American Spy, op. cit.,* 263–268; Lukas, *Nightmare, op. cit.,* 353, 354, 379, 504.
15. Emery, *Watergate, op. cit.,* 228, 229.
16. *Ibid.,* 233, 234.
17. Emery, *Watergate, op. cit.,* 233, 234; Lukas, *Nightmare, op. cit.,* 355–358; *NYT, Watergate Hearings, op. cit.,* 1-73.
18. Emery, *Watergate, op. cit.,* 235–239; Lukas, *Nightmare, op. cit.,* 359–365.
19. Emery, *Watergate, op. cit.,* 235–239; Hougan, *Agenda, op. cit.,* 12; Lukas, *Nightmare, op. cit.,* 359–365.
20. Emery, *Watergate, op. cit.,* 235–239; Lukas, *Nightmare, op. cit.,* 359–365.
21. Emery, *Watergate, op. cit.,* 235–239; Lukas, *Nightmare, op. cit.,* 359–365.
22. Hougan, *Agenda, op. cit.,* 232; see the so-called CIA "Family Jewels," available online at the website of the National Security Archive, in their Electronic Briefing Book No. 222.
23. Hougan, *Agenda, op. cit.,* 232; Thomas, *Very Best Men, op. cit.,* 333; Fonzi, *Last Investigation, op. cit.,* 425.
24. Emery, *Watergate, op. cit.,* 231; Powers, *Helms, op. cit.,* 306, 307.
25. Powers, *Helms, op. cit.,* 351.
26. Powers, *Helms, op. cit.,* 12, 323, 324; Summers and Swan, *Nixon, op. cit.,* 176.
27. See the so-called CIA "Family Jewels," available online at the website of the National Security Archive, in their Electronic Briefing Book No. 222.
28. Szulc, Tad. "Cuba on Our Mind." *Esquire,* 2-73.
29. Haynes Johnson interview notes by Richard E. Sprague, 1-12-73, donated to the Assassination Archives and Records Center.
30. *Ibid.*
31. *Ibid.*
32. Author's interviews with Harry Williams 4-92, 7-24-93, and others (some via Thom Hartmann); Turner, William W. *Rearview Mirror* (Granite Bay, CA: Penmarin Books, 2001), 210–215.
33. Hinckle, Turner, *The Fish Is Red: The Story of the Secret War Against Castro* (New York: Harper & Row, 1981), many passages. As noted earlier, McCord has never acknowledged any 1963 work with Hunt or Williams, and he declined to speak with the authors or *Vanity Fair*'s Anthony Summers about the matter.
34. Author's interviews with Harry Williams 4-92, 7-24-93, and others (some via Thom Hartmann).
35. Lukas, *Nightmare, op. cit.,* 376.
36. *Ibid.,* 376.
37. *Ibid.,* 377.
38. Califano, *Inside, op. cit.,* 281–283.
39. Califano, *Inside, op. cit.,* 281–283, 514; *NYT, Watergate Hearings, op. cit.,* 96.
40. Califano, *Inside, op. cit.,* 308, 309.
41. Emery, *Watergate, op. cit.,* 268–273; Lukas, *Night-*

mare, op. cit., 410–413; McCord, James W. Jr. *A Piece of Tape: The Watergate Story—Fact or Fiction?* (Rockville, Maryland: Washington Media Services, Ltd., 1974), 59–63, 253.

42. Emery, *Watergate, op. cit.*, 268–273; Lukas, *Nightmare, op. cit.*, 410–413; McCord, *Piece of Tape, op. cit.*, 59–63, 253.
43. Emery, *Watergate, op. cit.*, 268–273; Lukas, *Nightmare, op. cit.*, 410–413; McCord, *Piece of Tape, op. cit.*, 59–63, 253.
44. Anthony and Robbyn Summers, "The Ghosts of November," *Vanity Fair*, 12-94; 1991 discussion with Bud Fensterwald.
45. Emery, *Watergate, op. cit.*, 268–273; Lukas, *Nightmare, op. cit.*, 410–413; McCord, *Piece of Tape, op. cit.*, 59–63.
46. Kutler, *Tapes, op. cit.*, 247–259.
47. *Ibid.*, 247–259.
48. *Ibid.*, 247–259.
49. *Ibid.*, 247–259.
50. *Ibid.*, 247–259.
51. McCord, *Piece of Tape, op. cit.*, 59–63. McCord's letter is printed in full inside on the book's front and back endpapers.
52. Hunt and Aunapu, *American Spy, op. cit.*, 310; Lukas, *Nightmare, op. cit.*, 412, 413.
53. Kutler, *Tapes, op. cit.*, 296, 297, 372.
54. Kutler, *Tapes, op. cit.*, 381; *NYT, Watergate Hearings, op. cit.*, 205–209; Powers, *Helms, op. cit.*, 322, 323; Haig, *Inner, op. cit.*, 337.
55. Summers and Swan, *Nixon, op. cit.*, 448–450.
56. *NYT, Watergate Hearings, op. cit.*, 106, 109; Spartacus Educational website www.spartacus.schoolnet.co.uk.
57. *NYT, Watergate Hearings, op. cit.*, 109–113.
58. Haig, *Inner, op. cit.*, 339–341; Rosen, *Strong Man, op. cit.*, 379.

CHAPTER 34

1. Califano, *Inside, op. cit.*, 285, 286.
2. Haig, *Inner, op. cit.*, 339–341; Kutler, *Tapes, op. cit.*, 532–539, 588–591.
3. *NYT, Watergate Hearings, op. cit.*, 112.
4. Hougan, *Agenda, op. cit.*, 204; Kutler, *Tapes, op. cit.*, 584–587; *NYT, Watergate Hearings, op. cit.*, 114–116,144–179.
5. Kutler, Tapes, *op. cit.*, 547; *NYT, Watergate Hearings, op. cit.*, 119; Woodward, Bob, and Carl Bernstein. *The Final Days* (New York: Simon and Schuster, 1976), 35.
6. Hougan, *Agenda, op. cit.*, xvii.
7. Scott, Hoch, and Stetler. *The Assassinations, op. cit.*, 361, 362.
8. Colodny and Gettlin, *Silent Coup, op. cit.*, 333; Kranish, Michael, "Not all would put a heroic sheen on Thompson's Watergate role," *Boston Globe* 7-4-2007.
9. Kranish, Michael, "Thompson," *op. cit.*, 7-4-2007.
10. *Ibid.*
11. Califano, *Inside, op. cit.*, 287–289.
12. *Ibid.*, 287–289.
13. *Ibid.*, 287–289.
14. Ambrose, *Vol. 3, op. cit.*, 202, 203, Summers and Swan, *Nixon, op. cit.*, 212.
15. Ambrose, *Vol. 3, op. cit.*, 208, 209; *Time* 5-13-74.
16. *NYT, Watergate Hearings, op. cit.*, 602–607; Powers, *Helms, op. cit.*, 20.
17. Fonzi, *Last Investigation, op. cit.*, 395; Toll, Roser, "Chile exhumes remains of late President Allende," AFP, 5-23-11.
18. Fonzi, *Last Investigation, op. cit.*, 395; Russell, Russell, Dick *On the Trail of the JFK Assassins* (New York: Skyhorse, 2008) 150; HSCA vol. X Veciana summary. The dates of the payoff and the arrest vary in the different accounts, but all agree on what happened.
19. *NYT, Watergate Hearings, op. cit.*, 651–666.
20. Hunt and Aunapu, *American Spy, op. cit.*, 310; Lukas, *Nightmare, op. cit.*, 412, 413.
21. Ambrose, *Vol. 3 op. cit.*, 163, 174, 231–239.
22. Ambrose, *Vol. 3, op. cit.*, 205, 206, 236; Summers and Swan, *Nixon, op. cit.*, 458, 459.
23. Summers and Swan, *Nixon, op. cit.*, 458, 459.
24. Emery, *Watergate, op. cit.*, 400.
25. Summers and Swan, *Nixon, op. cit.*, 458, 459.
26. Ambrose, *Vol. 3, op. cit.*, 260, 261; Emery, *Watergate, op. cit.*, 406, Fensterwald and Ewing, *Coincidence, op. cit.*, 544.
27. Kutler, *Tapes, op. cit.*, 591, 592; Summers and Swan, *Nixon, op. cit.*, 245, 496.
28. RN, *Memoirs, op. cit.*, 953; "Rebozo denies shifting funds to Swiss banks for President," *NYT* 3-21-74; Summers and Swan, *Nixon, op. cit.*, 496; Zeifman, Jerry, *Without Honor: Crimes of Camelot and the Impeachment of Richard M. Nixon* (New York: Thunder's Mouth Press, 1995).
29. Summers and Swan, *Nixon, op. cit.*, 462.
30. *Ibid.*, 429.
31. Lenzner to Muse, Rosselli Watergate Committee memo, February 1974— Senate Select Committee on Presidential Campaign Activities (Ervin Committee), staff files; Rappleye and Bender, *All American op. cit.*, 301–305.
32. Author's interview with Mike Cain, 4-30-2007; Cain, *Tangled Web, op. cit.*, 216–222.
33. Moldea, Dan. Interview with Dan Moldea. *Clandestine American*, vol. 3, #2 July–Aug/Sept–Oct 1979.
34. Rosselli memo to Senator Ervin by Lenzner and Lackritz, Rosselli Watergate Committee, February 1974—February 1974, Senate Select Committee on Presidential Campaign Activities (Ervin Committee), staff files.
35. *Ibid.*
36. *Ibid.*
37. Rosselli memo to Senator Ervin by Lenzner and Lackritz, *op. cit.*; Summers and Swan, *Nixon, op. cit.*, 197, 198.
38. Rosselli memo to Senator Ervin by Lenzner and Lackritz, *op. cit.*
39. Lenzner memo to Muse, *op. cit.*
40. *Ibid.*
41. Rappleye and Becker, *All American, op. cit.*, 307.
42. *Ibid.*, 307.
43. Lenzner to Muse, *op. cit.*; Rappleye and Becker, *All American, op. cit.*, 307.
44. Lenzner to Muse, *op. cit.*; Rappleye and Becker, *All American, op. cit.*, 307.
45. Lenzner to Muse, *op. cit.*
46. *Ibid.*
47. Stockton, *Flawed Patriot, op. cit.*, 175; Rappleye and Becker, *All American, op. cit.*, 145.
48. Summers and Swan, *Nixon, op. cit.*, 197, 198.
49. Rappleye and Becker, *All American, op. cit.*, 289; Summers and Swan, *Nixon, op. cit.*, 197, 198; Watergate Hearings, Volume 21.
50. Woodward and Bernstein, *Final Days, op. cit.*

51. CIA 104-10256-10287
52. Emery, *Watergate, op. cit.*, 428–433.
53. Woodward and Bernstein, *Final Days, op. cit.*, 135.
54. *Time* magazine 5-13-74; Brock, David *The Seduction of Hillary Rodham* (New York: Free Press, 1996) 47–52.
55. Brock, *Hillary, op. cit.*, 47–52.
56. Brock, *Hillary, op. cit.*, 47–52.
57. Woodward and Bernstein, *Final Days, op. cit.*, 134, 266.
58. Moldea, *Hoffa Wars, op. cit.*, 350; Valentine, *The Pack, op. cit.*, 203, 204; Woodward and Bernstein, *Final Days, op. cit.*, 134, 266; O'Leary, Jeremiah, "Haig Probe: Did Nixon get Cash from Asia?" *Washington Star*, 12-5-76.
59. Max Holland, Washington Decoded article, citing John Limpert, "If It Isn't Tricia It Must Be . . . " *The Washingtonian* 6-74 and *The Wall Street Journal* 6-25-74; CIA memo "Involvement of James McCord in Cuban Operations while an Agent" 1993.07.15.20:17:15:590380.
60. Moldea, *Hoffa Wars, op. cit.*, 350.
61. Woodward and Bernstein, *Final Days, op. cit.*, 290–308.
62. Ambrose, *Vol. 3, op. cit.*, 435–443; Woodward and Bernstein, *Final Days, op. cit.*
63. Ambrose, *Vol. 3, op. cit.* 444–445.

EPILOGUE

1. *Ibid.*, 449, 450.
2. *Ibid.*, 449–451.
3. Shudel, Matt, "Top D.C. lawyer secured Hoffa conviction, Nixon's pardon," *Washington Post* 11-19-09.
4. *Ibid.*
5. Kutler, *Wars of Watergate, op. cit.*, 620; O'Leary, Jeremiah. "Haig probe: did Nixon get cash from Asia," *Washington Star*, 12-5-76; St. George, Andrew. Frank Sturgis (Fiorini) interview, *True* magazine, *op. cit.*
6. Daniel and Kirshon, eds., *Chronicle of America, op. cit.*, 844; Haig, *Inner, op. cit.*, 516.
7. Hersh, Sy, Domestic surveillance article, *New York Times*, 12-22-74.
8. Rosen, *Strong Man, op. cit.*, 421–438; Schorr, *Clearing the Air, op. cit.*, 143, 144.
9. Church, *Plots, op. cit.*, many passages.
10. Johnson, Loch K., *Season of Inquiry, op. cit.*, 278; Russell, *Man Who Knew, op. cit.*, 728.
11. Schorr, *Clearing the Air, op. cit.*, 147.
12. See Richard Helms, Rockefeller and Church Committee testimony.
13. Johnson, Loch K., *Season of Inquiry, op. cit.*, 47, 55.
14. *Ibid.*
15. Deitche, Scott, *The Silent Don* (Fort Lee: Barricade, 2009), 207.
16. Kidner, *Crimaldi: Contract Killer, op. cit.*, 341–350.
17. Rappleye and Becker, *All American, op. cit.*, 311; Kidner, *Crimaldi: Contract Killer, op. cit.*, 217–220.
18. Dan Moldea, article in *Clandestine American, op. cit.*, 9; Moldea, *Hoffa Wars, op. cit.*, many passages.
19. HSCA: 180-10090-10232; "Castro charges CIA tried 24 death plots." *Miami Herald* 7-31-75; CIA Memo, Latin American Division, 1993.08.11.10:16:34:650060, 8-11-75.
20. "Castro charges," July 31, 1975, *op. cit.*; CIA memo, 8-11-75, *op. cit.*; HSCA: 180-10090-10232.
21. HSCA: 180-10090-10232.
22. Church, *Plots, op. cit.*; Summers and Swan, *Nixon, op. cit.*, 189, 190.
23. Richard Nixon Grand Jury Transcript 6-23-75 and 6-24-75, courtesy of George DiCaprio.
24. Nixon Grand Jury Transcript *op. cit.*
25. Nixon Grand Jury Transcript *op. cit.*
26. Binder, David. "Charles (Bebe) Rebozo, 85; longtime Nixon confidant." *New York Times* 5-9-98; Summers and Swan, *Nixon, op. cit.*, many passages.
27. Ambrose, *Vol. 3, op. cit.*, 487; CIA IG Report, 1967, *op. cit.*,
28. *Ibid.*, 487.
29. Moldea, *Hoffa Wars, op. cit.*, 350.
30. Ambrose, *Vol. 3, op. cit.*, 487.
31. Rappleye and Becker, *All American, op. cit.*, 8, 9, 321, 325–327.
32. Benson, *Who's Who, op. cit.*, 313; Corn, *Blond Ghost, op. cit.*, 118; Fonzi, *Last Investigation, op. cit.*, 40, 41, 192, 193, 443; HSCA vol. X, 37, 48; *Miami Herald*, 4-1-77.
33. Powers, *Helms, op. cit.*, 349; see HSCA testimony of Helms and Hunt; Barker's is still withheld, apparently for reasons of national security.
34. Powers, *Helms, op. cit.*, 349.
35. Between the various federal agencies, thousands of classified documents about Watergate-related matters are still being withheld, including almost all of the AMWORLD files, 366 pages of Howard Hunt's CIA files, much about Barker, and almost all of the Harry Williams CIA and FBI files. To stay on top of newly released documents, regularly visit the author's website watergatethehiddenhistory.com starting June 17, 2012.

INDEX